90 Years of Excelle

The British Antique Dealers' Association
Members' Selling Exhibitions
throughout 2008

Rowlandson. 1799

For further information:
Tel: 020 7589 4128 • Fax: 020 7581 9083
email: info@bada.org • www.bada.org

guide to the
ANTIQUE
SHOPS
of BRITAIN
2008-2009

© Copyright 2008 Antique Collectors' Club Ltd.
World Copyright reserved ISBN 978-1-85149-554-2

British Library CIP Data.
A catalogue record for this book is available from the British Library.

While every reasonable care has been exercised in compilation of information contained in this Guide,
neither the editors nor The Antique Collectors' Club Ltd., or any servants of the company accept any
liability for loss, damage or expense incurred by reliance placed on the book or through omissions or
incorrect entries howsoever incurred.

Origination by Antique Collectors' Club Ltd., England. Printed and bound in China.

U.K. OFFICE
Sandy Lane, Old Martlesham, Woodbridge,
Suffolk, IP12 4SD.
Tel: 01394 389950 Fax: 01394 389999
Email: info@antique-acc.com
Website: www.antiquecollectorsclub.com

U.S. OFFICE
Eastworks, 116 Pleasant Street - Suite 18,
Easthampton, MA 01027.
Tel: (413) 529 0861   Fax: (413) 529 0862
Email: sales@antiquecc.com
Website: www.antiquecollectorsclub.com

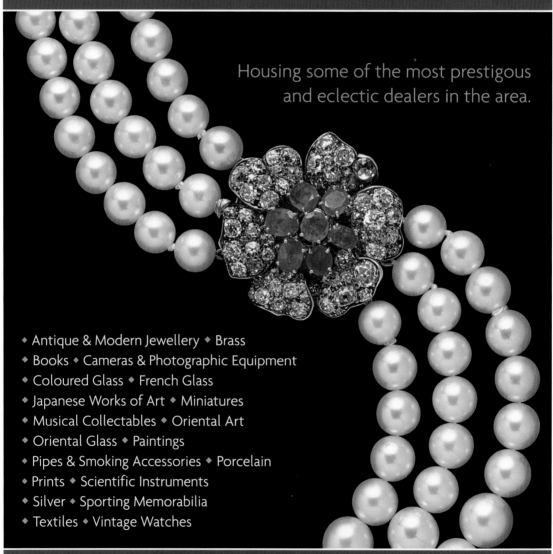

CONTENTS

INTRODUCTION

This is the 35th edition of the **Guide to the Antique Shops of Britain**, which is now universally accepted as *the* guide for anybody who wishes to buy antiques in Britain.

All the entries listed have been confirmed before reprinting. We appreciate, however, that quantity without quality is meaningless and therefore the range of information we provide is more detailed and up-to-date than in any other publication. We state the obvious facts - name of proprietor, address, telephone number, opening hours and stock and also size of showroom and price range (where supplied). Additional information gives details of major trade association members, the date the business was established, the location and also the parking situation. Whilst none of these points are decisive in themselves, we feel they build up to a useful picture of the sort of establishment likely to be found and may well influence a prospective buyer's decision whether or not to visit a particular shop.

We start preparing the next edition in early 2009. Please let us know of any changes in your area, such as openings and closures. We do not print information about other dealers without first contacting them, but obviously the more shops in a particular town or village, the more attractive it is to prospective buyers on trips around the country. We would also be grateful for your comments on the Guide and, if you find any information given in the Guide to be incorrect, please let us know. We have occasionally had prospective customers telephoning to say that the stock listed is not what they found when visiting a particular establishment but then refuse to tell us the name of the shop - which means we can do nothing about the complaint. Constructive criticism is welcomed and we look forward to your comments.

ACKNOWLEDGEMENTS

Our main sources of information are still the trade magazines but we would like to thank those dealers who provide information about new shops and closures in their area. Without their assistance our job would be far more difficult.

We would also like to thank those dealers who have supported us with advertising. It is because of their valued patronage that we can continue to produce such a high-quality, informative volume at such a low retail price. Each year we include a form at the end of the Guide which dealers can use to up-date details about their own business, or you could email your corrections to gasb@antique-acc.com

HOW TO USE THIS GUIDE

The Guide is set out under six main headings: London, Counties, Channel Islands, Northern Ireland, Scotland and Wales. Counties are listed alphabetically; within counties the towns are listed alphabetically and within towns the shops are listed, again, alphabetically. London is divided into postal districts.

To make route planning easier there is a map at the beginning of each county, and a list showing the number of shops in any one town or village. The roads indicated on the map are only a broad intimation of the routes available and it is advisable to use an up-to-date map showing the latest improvements in the road system.

Apart from the six main headings above, there are further helpful lists - an alphabetical list of towns, showing the counties in which they will be found for those not familiar with the location of towns within counties, e.g. Woodbridge is shown in the county of Suffolk. One therefore turns to the Suffolk section to look up Woodbridge. This listing is a valuable aid to the overseas visitor. The second is particularly important to British dealers and collectors - giving an alphabetical list of the name of every shop, proprietor and company director known to be connected with a shop or gallery. Thus, if A. Bloggs and B. Brown own an antique shop called Castle Antiques, there will be entries under Bloggs, A., Brown, B., and Castle Antiques. Listings of specialist dealers, auctioneers, shippers and packers and services are also included.

We strongly suggest making a prior telephone call to confirm opening hours before setting off on a long journey. In the main, dealers are factual and accurate in describing their stock to us but there are probably a few who list what they would like to stock rather than as it is! We would appreciate you letting us know of any such anomalies. Please telephone (01394) 389968 or drop us a postcard and help us to ensure that the Guide remains Britain's premier listing of antique shops and galleries.

ABBREVIATIONS IN ENTRIES

BADA:	British Antique Dealers' Association
BAFRA:	British Antique Furniture Restorers' Association
CADA:	Cotswold Art and Antique Dealers' Association
EADA:	Essex Antique Dealers' Association
KCSADA:	Kensington Church Street Antique Dealers' Association
LAPADA:	London and Provincial Antique Dealers' Association
PAADA:	Petworth Art & Antique Dealers' Association
TADA:	Tetbury Antique Dealers' Association
TVADA:	Thames Valley Antique Dealers' Association
WEADA:	West of England Antique Dealers' Association
CL:	When the business is normally closed in addition to Sunday
SIZE:	Showroom size. Small - under 60 sq. metres; medium - between 60 and 150 sq. metres; large over 150 sq. metres
LOC:	Location of shop
SER:	Additional services which the dealer offers

W1

Didier Aaron (London) Ltd   BADA
Clifford House, 15 Clifford St. W1S 4JY (Didier Leblanc and Marc Fecker)
Open by appointment. STOCK: *Mainly French 18th-19th C furniture and objets d'art; 17th-19th C paintings and drawings.* LOC: **third floor.** SIZE: **Large.** PARK: **Meters nearby.** FAIRS: **Paris Biennale, Maastricht (TEFAF); Salon du Dessin, Paris; International Fine Art, New York; Master Drawings, London.**
TEL: **020 7534 9100;** FAX: **020 7494 9437**
E-MAIL: **contact@didieraaronltd.com**

David Aaron Ancient Arts & Rare Carpets LAPADA
22 Berkeley Sq., Mayfair. W1J 6EH.
EST. **1910. Open Mon-Fri 9-6, Sat. by appointment.** STOCK: *Islamic and ancient art; antique carpets.* SER: **Valuations; restorations.** SIZE: **Large.** PARK: **Easy.** VAT: **Stan/Spec.**
TEL: **020 7491 9588;** FAX: **020 7491 9522**
E-MAIL: **david_aaron@hotmail.com**

Aaron Gallery
125 Mount St. W1K 3NS. (Manouchehr and Simon Aaron)
EST. 1910. Open 10-6, Sat. by appointment. STOCK: *Ancient art; Greek, Roman, Egyptian, Near Eastern and Islamic antiquities.*
TEL: 020 7499 9434; FAX: 020 7499 0072
E-MAIL: simon@aarongallery.com
WEBSITE: www.aarongallery.com

Adam Gallery Ltd
24 Cork St. W1S 3NJ. (Paul and Philip Dye)
STOCK: *20th C British and international paintings and prints especially St. Ives, Bacon, Nicholson, Francis, Piper, Debuffet, Kandinsky, Lanyon, Moore, Picasso, Delaunay, Hitchens, Hilton, Heron and Scott; British contemporary, £500-£50,000.*
TEL: 020 7439 6633; FAX: same
E-MAIL: info@adamgallery.com
WEBSITE: www.adamgallery.com

Agnew's   BADA
43 Old Bond St. W1S 4BA.
EST. **1817. SLAD. Open Mon-Fri 9.30-5.30** STOCK: *Paintings, drawings, watercolours, engravings of all schools; contemporary art.* LOC: **Nearest tube Green Park.** SIZE: **Large.** VAT: **Spec.**
TEL: **020 7290 9250;** FAX: **020 7629 4359**
E-MAIL: **agnews@agnewsgallery.co.uk**
WEBSITE: **www.agnewsgallery.co.uk.**

Adrian Alan Ltd   BADA LAPADA
66-67 South Audley St. W1K 2QX.
EST. **1963. Open 10-6. CL: Sat.** STOCK: *English and Continental furniture, especially fine 19th C; sculpture and works of art.* SER: **Transport, storage and shipping;** insurance and finance. SIZE: **Large.** VAT: **Stan/Spec.**
TEL: **020 7495 2324;** FAX: **020 7495 0204**
E-MAIL: **enquiries@adrianalan.com**
WEBSITE: **www.adrianalan.com.**

Altea Gallery
35 St. George St. W1S 2FN. (Massimo De Martini)
EST. 1993. PBFA. ABA. ILAB. IMCOS. Open Mon.-Fri. 10-6, Sat. 11-4. STOCK: *Antiquarian maps, 15th-19th C, £50-£5,000; travel books, atlases, 16th-19th C, £200-£20,000; globes, 17th-20th C, £200-£20,000.* LOC: 200 yards from Oxford Circus. SER: Valuations; restorations (paper, cleaning, colouring and book binding). SIZE: Medium. PARK: NCP nearby. VAT: Stan. FAIRS: London Map, Olympia (June); ABA Olympia (June).
TEL: 020 7491 0010; FAX: 010 7491 0015
E-MAIL: info@alteagallery.com
WEBSITE: www.alteagallery.com

The Antique Enamel Co.   LAPADA
23 Burlington Arcade W1J 0PR (Mr J. Jaffa)
Open 10-5. STOCK: *Objects of virtue, English enamels, golden enamel boxes.*
TEL: **020 7499 0767**
E-MAIL: **sales@antique-enamels.co.uk**
WEBSITE: **www.antique-enamels.co.uk**

Armour-Winston Ltd
43 Burlington Arcade. W1J 0QQ.
EST. 1952. Open Mon-Fri 10-5.30. Sat. 10-3 STOCK: *Jewellery, especially Victorian; gentlemen's cufflinks, vintage and contemporary watches.* LOC: Off Piccadilly. Between Green Park and Piccadilly underground stations. SER: Valuations; restorations. SIZE: Small. PARK: Savile Row. VAT: Stan/Spec.
TEL: 020 7493 8937
WEBSITE: www.armourwinston.co.uk

Victor Arwas Gallery - Editions Graphiques Gallery Ltd
3 Clifford St. W1S 2LF. (V. Arwas)
EST. 1966. Open Mon-Fri 11-6, Sat. 11-2. STOCK: *Art Nouveau and Art Deco, glass, ceramics, bronzes, sculpture, furniture, jewellery, silver, pewter, books and posters 1880-1980, £25-£50,000; paintings, watercolours and drawings, 1880 to date, £100-£50,000; original lithographs, etchings, woodcuts, 1890 to date, £5-£30,000.* LOC: Between New Bond St. and Savile Row. SER: Valuations; buys at auction. SIZE: Large. VAT: Stan/Spec.
TEL: 020 7734 3944; FAX: 020 7437 1859
E-MAIL: art@victorarwas.com
WEBSITE: www.victorarwas.com

Barakat Gallery
58 Brook St. W1K 5DT.
Open 10-6 or by appointment.
TEL: 020 7493 7778; FAX: 020 7493 9593
E-MAIL: info@barakatgallery.com
WEBSITE: www.barakatgallery.com

J. & A. Beare Ltd   BADA
30 Queen Anne St. W1G 8HX.
EST. 1892. Open 10-5. STOCK: *Violins, violas, cellos and bows.* SER: Valuations. VAT: Stan/Spec.
TEL: 020 7307 9666; FAX: 020 7307 9651
E-MAIL: violins@beares.com
WEBSITE: www.beares.com

Jan van Beers Oriental Art   BADA
34 Davies St. W1Y 1LG.
EST. 1978. Open 10-6. CL: Sat. STOCK: *Chinese and Japanese ceramics and works of art, 200BC to 1800AD.* LOC: Between Berkeley Sq. and Oxford St. SER: Valuations. SIZE: Medium. PARK: Easy. VAT: Spec.
TEL: 020 7408 0434
E-MAIL: jan@vanbeers.demon.co.uk
WEBSITE: www.janvanbeers.com

Paul Bennett   LAPADA
48A George St. W1U 7DY. (M.J. Dubiner)
EST. 1970. CINOA. Open 10-6. CL: Sat. STOCK: *Silver, 17th-20th C, £10-£10,000; Sheffield plate.* SIZE: Large. PARK: Meters. VAT: Stan/Spec. FAIRS: Olympia; LAPADA.
TEL: 020 7935 1555 or 020 7486 8836; FAX: 020 7224 4858
E-MAIL: info@paulbennettonline.com
WEBSITE: www.paulbennettonline.com

Bentley & Skinner   BADA LAPADA
8 New Bond St. W1S 3SL. (Mark Evans)
Open 10-5.30. STOCK: *Jewellery, Fabergé, objets d'art, silver.* SER: Valuations; repairs; tiara and jewellery hire.
PARK: Meters. VAT: Stan/Spec.
TEL: 020 7629 0651; FAX: 020 7491 1030
E-MAIL: info@bentley-skinner.co.uk
WEBSITE: www.bentley-skinner.co.uk

Daniel Bexfield Antiques   BADA LAPADA
26 Burlington Arcade, Mayfair. W1J 0PU.
EST. 1980. CINOA. Open 9-6. STOCK: *Silver and objects of virtu, 17th-20th C, £200-£25,000.* LOC: Next to Royal Academy, Piccadilly. SER: Valuations; restorations (repairs and polishing silver, blue glass liners). SIZE: Large. PARK: Nearby. VAT: Spec. FAIRS: BADA.
TEL: 020 7491 1720; FAX: 020 7491 1730
E-MAIL: antiques@bexfield.co.uk
WEBSITE: www.bexfield.co.uk

Peter Biddulph Ltd
99 Mortimer St. W1W 7SX.
Open 10-6. CL: Sat. STOCK: *Violins, violas, cellos and bows.* SER: Valuations; restorations.
TEL: 020 7636 1733; FAX: 020 7495 1428
WEBSITE: www.peterbiddulph.com

H. Blairman and Sons Ltd.   BADA
119 Mount St. W1K 3NL. (M.P. and P.A. Levy and P.A. Hannen)
EST. 1884. Open daily. CL: Sat. STOCK: *English and*

Continental furniture and works of art, 1800-1900. SIZE: Medium. VAT: Spec. FAIRS: TEFAF, Maastricht; Grosvenor House; Fine Art & Antique Dealers, New York.
TEL: 020 7493 0444; FAX: 020 7495 0766
E-MAIL: blairman@atlas.co.uk
WEBSITE: www.blairman.co.uk

Blunderbuss Antiques
29 Thayer St. W1U 2QW. (C. and P. Greenaway)
EST. 1968. Open 9.30-4.30. CL: Mon. STOCK: *Arms and armour, militaria.* PARK: On street. VAT: Global/Spec.
TEL: 020 7486 2444; FAX: 020 7935 1645
E-MAIL: mail@blunderbuss-antiques.co.uk
WEBSITE: www.blunderbuss-antiques.co.uk.

Browse and Darby Ltd
19 Cork St. W1S 3LP.
EST. 1977. SLAD. Open 10-5.30. Sat. 11-2 (during exhibitions). STOCK: *19th-20th C French and British paintings, drawings and sculpture, contemporary British artists.* VAT: Spec. FAIRS: Art London; Art Chicago; Fine Art & Antique Dealers Show, New York.
TEL: 020 7734 7984; FAX: 020 7851 6650
E-MAIL: art@browseanddarby.co.uk
WEBSITE: www.browseanddarby.co.uk

Bruford & Heming Ltd   LAPADA
Rear Ground Floor, Renoir House, 136 New Bond St. W1S 2TH. (Alan Kinsey)
EST. 1858. Open 9.30-5. STOCK: *Jewellery, domestic silverware and cutlery.* SER: Valuations; restorations (jewellery and silver). SIZE: Small. VAT: Stan.
TEL: 020 7499 7644; 020 7629 4289; FAX: 020 7493 5879
E-MAIL: sales@bruford-heming.co.uk

Burlington Paintings Ltd   BADA
10 and 12 Burlington Gardens. W1S 3EY. (A. Lloyd, M. Day and A. Hardy)
EST. 1981. Open 9.30-5.30, Sat. 10-5. STOCK: *British and European oil paintings, 19th-20th C, from £1,000.* LOC: Between Old Bond St. and Regent St., facing Savile Row. SER: Valuations; restorations (lining, cleaning, reframing oils and watercolours); buys at auction (pictures). SIZE: Medium. PARK: APCOA, Old Burlington St. VAT: Stan/Spec.
TEL: 020 7734 9984; FAX: 020 7494 3770
E-MAIL: pictures@burlington.co.uk
WEBSITE: www.burlington.co.uk

C. & L. Burman
Flat 5, 9 Old Pye Street. SW1P 2LD. (Charles Truman)
Open by appointment. STOCK: *18th-19th works of art including silver, glass, furniture, ceramics and sculpture.* SER: Valuations; restorations; buys at auction. VAT: Spec.
TEL: 020 7222 6776
E-MAIL: charles-truman@lineone.net

The Button Queen Ltd.
19 Marylebone Lane. W1U 2NF. (I. and M. Frith)
EST. 1953. GMC. Open 10-5, Thurs. and Fri. 10-6, Sat.
10-4. STOCK: *Antique, old and modern buttons.* LOC: Off
Wigmore St. SIZE: Large. VAT: Stan.
TEL: 020 7935 1505
E-MAIL: information@thebuttonqueen.co.uk
WEBSITE: www.thebuttonqueen.co.uk

Antoine Cheneviere Fine Arts BADA
38 Dover St. (2nd floor) W1J 6QN.
EST. 1987. Open 9.30-6. CL: Sat. STOCK: *18th-19th C*
furniture and paintings, objets d'art from Russia, Italy,
Austria, Sweden and Germany.
TEL: **020 7491 1007**
E-MAIL: **finearts@antoinecheneviere.com**
WEBSITE: **www.antoinecheneviere.com**

Andrew Clayton-Payne Ltd
2nd Floor, 14 Old Bond St. W1S 4PP.
Open by appointment. STOCK: *British paintings and*
watercolours, 1700-1850, £2,000-£500,000. SER: Valuations;
buys at auction (pictures). SIZE: Small. PARK: Easy. VAT: Spec.
TEL: 020 7493 6980; FAX: 020 7629 9151; MOBILE:
07771 563850
E-MAIL: claytonpayne@aol.com

Sibyl Colefax & John Fowler LAPADA
39 Brook St. W1K 4JE.
EST. 1933. Open 9.30-5.30. CL: Sat. STOCK: *Decorative*
furniture, pictures, lamps and carpets, 18th-19th C. LOC:
Mayfair. SIZE: Large. PARK: Meters. VAT: Spec. FAIRS:
Olympia (June).
TEL: **020 7493 2231 or 020 7355 4037; FAX: 020 7499 9721**
E-MAIL: **antiques@sibylcolefax.com**
WEBSITE: **www.colefaxantiques.com**

P. and D. Colnaghi & Co Ltd BADA
15 Old Bond St. W1S 4AX.
EST. 1760. SLAD. Open Mon.-Fri. 10-6. STOCK: *Old*
Master paintings and drawings, 14th-19th C. SER:
Experts and appraisers. SIZE: Large. VAT: Spec. FAIRS:
TEFAF, Maastricht; IFAF, New York; Grosvenor
House, London; Biennale des Antiquaires, Paris; Palm
Beach Classic; Salon du Dessin, Paris; Les
Antiquaires, Brussels.
TEL: **020 7491 7408; FAX: 020 7491 8851**
E-MAIL: **contact@colnaghi.co.uk**

Connaught Brown plc
2 Albemarle St. W1S 4HD. (A. Brown)
EST. 1985. SLAD. Open Mon-Fri 10-6, Sat. 10-12.30.
STOCK: *Post Impressionist, Scandinavian and modern*
works, from £5,000+; contemporary, from £500+. LOC: Off
Piccadilly and parallel to Bond St. SER: Valuations;
restorations (paintings, drawings, watercolours and
sculpture). SIZE: Medium. PARK: Yes, meters. VAT:
Stan/Spec. FAIRS: Int'l Fine Art Fair NY (May).
TEL: 020 7408 0362

E-MAIL: art@connaughtbrown.co.uk
WEBSITE: www.connaughtbrown.co.uk

Sandra Cronan Ltd BADA
18 Burlington Arcade. W1J 0PN.
EST. 1975. Open 10-5. STOCK: *Fine and unusual jewels,*
18th to early 20th C, £500-£150,000. SER: Valuations;
design commissions. VAT: Stan/Spec. FAIRS: Fine Art &
Antiques; BADA (March); Grosvenor House (June).
TEL: **020 7491 4851; FAX: 020 7493 2758**
E-MAIL: **enquiries@sandracronan.com**

A. B. Davis Ltd
18 Brook St., (Corner of New Bond St). W1S 1BF.
EST. 1920. NAG. Open 10-5. CL: Sat. STOCK: *Antique*
and secondhand jewellery, small silver items, objets d'art and
gold coins. SER: Valuations; repairs (jewellery and silver).
VAT: Stan/Spec.
TEL: 020 7629 1053; 020 7483 1666 or 020 7629 3611;
FAX AND ANSWERPHONE: 020 7499 6454

Day & Faber
173 New Bond St. W1S 4RF. (Richard Day and James
Faber)
EST. 1970. SLAD. Open Mon-Fri 10-5 by appointment.
STOCK: *Old Master drawings.* VAT: Stan.
TEL: 020 7629 2991; FAX: 020 7493 7569
E-MAIL: jf@dayfaber.com
WEBSITE: www.dayfaber.com

Marc Antoine du Ry Medieval Art LAPADA
13 New Burlington St. W1S 3BG.
By appointment. STOCK: *Medieval art 500-1500AD.*
FAIRS: **Royal Academy.**
TEL: **020 7287 9055; FAX: 020 7287 9056; MOBILE:**
07770 888116
E-MAIL: **info@marcdury.co.uk**
WEBSITE: **www.earlyart.net**

David Duggan Watches LAPADA
63 Burlington Arcade and Unit 1A, 1B Bond st.
Antiques Centre, 124 New Bond St. W1J 0QS.
(David and Denise Duggan)
EST. 1976. MBHI. Open 10-5.30. STOCK: *Old and*
current wristwatches - Patek Phillipe, Rolex, Cartier,
Panerai, Roger Dubuis, Lange & Sohne, Franck Muller,
Audemars Piguet, Vacheron Constantin, Breguet. LOC:
West End. SER: Valuations; restorations
(comprehensive repairs on site, Swiss-trained
technician) SIZE: Small. PARK: Meters nearby.
TEL: **020 7491 1362 / 020 7491 1675; FAX: 020 7491 2714**
E-MAIL: **enquiries@daviddugganwatches.co.uk**
WEBSITE: **www.daviddugganwatches.co.uk**

Charles Ede Ltd BADA
20 Brook St. W1K 5DE.
EST. 1970. Open 12.30-4.30 or by appointment. CL:
Mon and Sat. STOCK: *Greek, Roman and Egyptian*
antiquities, £250-£5100,000. SER: Valuations; buys at

auction. PARK: Meters. VAT: Spec.
TEL: 020 7493 4944; FAX: 020 7491 2548
E-MAIL: info@charlesede.com
WEBSITE: www.charlesede.com

Andrew Edmunds
44 Lexington St. W1F 0LW.
Open Mon.-Fri. 10-6, appointment advisable. *STOCK: 18th to early 19th C caricature and decorative prints and drawings.* SIZE: Small. VAT: Stan/Spec. FAIRS: London Original Print; Grosvenor House.
TEL: 020 7437 8594; FAX: 020 7439 2551
E-MAIL: prints@andrewedmunds.com

Emanouel Corporation (UK) Ltd
64 & 64a South Audley St. W1K 2QT. (E. Naghi)
EST. 1974. Open 10-6, Sat. by appointment. *STOCK: Important antiques and fine works of art, 18th-19th C; Islamic works of art.* VAT: Stan/Spec.
TEL: 020 7493 4350 or 020 7499 0996; FAX: 020 7629 3125; MOBILE: 07831 241899
E-MAIL: emanouelnaghi@aol.com
WEBSITE: www.emanouel.net.

Eskenazi Ltd   BADA
10 Clifford St. W1S 2LJ. (J.E. Eskenazi, P.S. Constantinidi and D.M. Eskenazi)
EST. 1960. Open 9.30-5.30, Sat. by appointment. *STOCK: Early Chinese ceramics; bronzes, sculpture, works of art; Japanese screens.* SIZE: Large. VAT: Spec.
TEL: 020 7493 5464; FAX: 020 7499 3136
E-MAIL: gallery@eskenazi.co.uk
WEBSITE: www.eskenazi.co.uk

Essie Carpets
62 Piccadilly. W1J 0DZ. (E. Sakhai)
EST. 1766. Open Mon-Fri 9.30-6.30, Sun. 10.30-6. *STOCK: Persian and Oriental carpets and rugs.* LOC: Opposite St. James St. and Ritz Hotel. SER: Valuations; restorations; commissions undertaken; exchange. SIZE: Large. PARK: Easy. VAT: Stan/Spec.
TEL: 020 7493 7766
E-MAIL: essiecarpets@aol.com
WEBSITE: www.essiecarpets.com

Simon Finch Rare Books
53 Maddox St. W1S 2PN
EST. 1976. Open 10-6; CL: Sat. *STOCK: Rare books, photography and art; antique to contemporary.* LOC: Round the corner from Sotheby's. PARK: Meters.
TEL: 020 7499 0974
E-MAIL: rarebooks@simonfinch.com
WEBSITE: www.simonfinch.com

The Fine Art Society Plc
148 New Bond St. W1S 2JT.
EST. 1876. SLAD. IFPDA. Open Mon-Fri 10-6, Sat. 10-1. *STOCK: British fine and decorative arts, 19th-20th C & contemporary art.* LOC: Bond St. or Green Park

underground stations. SER: Buys at auction. SIZE: Large. PARK: 300yds. VAT: Stan/Spec. FAIRS: London Original Print; Winter Show and IFPDA Print, New York.
TEL: 020 7629 5116; fax 020 7491 9454
E-MAIL: art@faslondon.com
WEBSITE: www.faslondon.com.

Fluss & Charlesworth Ltd   BADA
19 Fitzroy Sq. W1T 6EQ. (J. Charlesworth)
EST. 1970. Open by appointment. *STOCK: 18th to early 19th C furniture and works of art.* SER: Interior decor. FAIRS: Olympia (June/Nov); BADA; Palm Beach.
TEL: 01526 352513; MOBILE: 07831 830323

Sam Fogg   BADA
15d Clifford St. W1S 4JZ.
EST. 1971. ABA. Open Mon.-Fri. 9.30-5.30 or by appointment. *STOCK: Manuscripts - Western medieval, Islamic and Oriental and works of art; Indian paintings.* LOC: Off New Bond St. SER: Valuations; buys at auction. PARK: NCP Burlington Gardens. VAT: Margin. FAIRS: Asian Art, New York; Biennale, Paris.
TEL: 020 7534 2100; FAX: 020 7534 2122
E-MAIL: info@samfogg.com
WEBSITE: www.samfogg.com

Matthew Foster Ltd   LAPADA
27 Burlington Arcade. W1J 0PS.
Open 10-5.30. *STOCK: Period jewellery, diamond, gem set jewellery mounted in platinum and yellow gold. Victorian, Art Nouveau, Edwardian and Retro period jewellery. Art Deco rings, earrings, necklaces, pendants, bracelets and bangles.*
TEL: 020 7629 4977; FAX: same; MOBILE: 07885 964103
E-MAIL: info@matthew-foster.co.uk
WEBSITE: www.matthew-foster.co.uk

Deborah Gage (Works of Art) Ltd
38 Old Bond St. W1S 4QW. (Deborah Gage)
EST. 1982. Open 9.30-5.30. CL: Sat. *STOCK: European decorative arts, British and European paintings, Renaissance to 1940, from £5,000.* SER: Valuations; cataloguing; buys at auction; consultancy; research. VAT: Stan/Spec.
TEL: 020 7493 3249; FAX: 020 7495 1352
E-MAIL: art@deborahgage.com

Thomas Goode and Co (London) Ltd
19 South Audley St., Mayfair. W1K 2BN.
EST. 1827. Open 10-6. *STOCK: China, glass, silver, tableware, ornamental, lamps, mirrors and furniture.* SER: Restorations. SIZE: Large. VAT: Spec.
TEL: 020 7499 2823; FAX: 020 7629 4230
E-MAIL: info@thomasgoode.co.uk
WEBSITE: www.thomasgoode.com.

Grays Antique Markets
58 Davies St. and 1-7 Davies Mews. W1K 5LP.
EST. 1970. Open 10-6. CL: Sat. SER: Engraving and jewellery repair.
TEL: 020 7629 7034; FAX: 020 7493 9344

E-MAIL: charlotte@grays.biz (for all dealers).
WEBSITE: www.graysantiques.com

Below are listed the dealers at this market, who can also all be contacted via the website.

A & T Jewellers
Stand G104. *Jewellery repair.*
TEL: 020 7495 7068

Emmy Abe
Stand G324. *Jewellery.*
TEL: 020 7629 1826

Anthea A.G. Antiques   LAPADA
Stand G154-5. *Jewellery.*
TEL: 020 7493 7564

Arca
Stand G351-353. *Objets d'art and miniatures.*
TEL: 020 7629 2729

Elias Assad
Stand MJ28 & K13. *Islamic and antiquities.*
TEL: 020 7499 4778

Aurum Antiques
Stand G310-11. *Jewellery.*
TEL: 020 7409 0215

B & T Engraving
Stand G109.
TEL: 020 7408 1880

Colin Baddiel
Stand MB24-25. *Toys.*
TEL: 020 7408 1239

Bags of Glamour
Stand V0014. *Vintage accessories.*
TEL: 020 7629 7034
EMAIL: bagsofglamour@btinternet.com
WEBSITE: www.bagsofglamour.co.uk

Bakhtar Art
Stand MC12. *Ancient beads and jewellery.*
TEL: 020 7629 6484

Iris Bangerter
Stand G103.
TEL: 07824 339292
EMAIL: journeybeads@msn.com

Don Bayney
Stand MA20-21. *Militaria.*
TEL: 020 7491 7200
EMAIL: donbayney@aol.com

Karen Beagle
Stand MFS010. *Asian.*
TEL: 020 7629 7034
EMAIL: karenbeagle@aol.com

Beaut
Stand MM13. *Jewellery.*
TEL: 020 7629 0688

Linda Bee
Stand ML18-21. *Vintage fashion and accessories.*
TEL: 020 7629 5921
EMAIL: lindabeeretro@yahoo.co.uk

Barbara Berg
Stand G333-4. *Jewellery.*
TEL: 020 7499 0560

Beverley R
Stand G343-4. *Jewellery.*
TEL: 020 7408 1129

Biblion
Rare and antiquarian books.
TEL: 020 7629 1374; FAX: 020 7493 7158
EMAIL: info@biblion.co.uk
WEBSITE: www.biblion.co.uk

Lola Boggi
Stand C10-11. *Costume jewellery.*
TEL: 020 7499 8121.

David Bowden   LAPADA
Stand G126. CINOA. *Asian.*
TEL: 020 7495 1773

Patrick Boyd-Carpenter
Stand G127. *Prints and paintings.*
TEL: 020 7491 7623
EMAIL: patrickboyd_carpenter@hotmail.com

Britannia
Stand G325-6. *Ceramics.*
TEL: 020 7629 6772

Sue Brown   BADA LAPADA
Stand MM12. SJH CINOA. *Quirky antique jewellery.*
TEL: 020 7491 4287
EMAIL: sue@antique-rings.co.uk
WEBSITE: www.antique-rings.co.uk

Chris Cavey & Associates
Stand G178. *Gems and precious stones.*
TEL: 020 7495 1743
EMAIL: ccavey@btinternet.com

Cekay
Stand G172. *Small antiques.*
TEL: 020 7629 5130

Collected
Stand G384. *Watches, clocks and timepieces.*
TEL: 020 7495 1536

Collection Antiques
Stand G329-30. *Jewellery.*
TEL: 020 7493 2654

Devonshire Antiques
Stand MB027. *19th C ceramics and glass.*
TEL: 020 7629 7034

Anthony Douch Antiques
Stand ML16. *Jewellery.*
TEL: 020 7493 9413
EMAIL: vivianedouch@fsmail.net

Eastern Satrapy
Stand MM10-11. *Coins.*
TEL: 07956 597075

Evonne Antiques
Stand G301. *Silver.*
TEL: 020 7491 0143
EMAIL: evonneantiques@aol.com

Faisal's Antiques
Stand MA22. *Antiquities and Islamic jewellery.*
TEL: 020 7629 8033.

Sandra Fellner
Stand MA18-19. *Dolls and teddy bears.*
TEL: 020 7629 7034
EMAIL: sandrafellner@blueyonder.co.uk

Finishing Touch
Stand G176. *Jewellery.*
TEL: 020 7495 0592
EMAIL: ftouch@netcomuk.co.uk

Gallery Diem
Stand G171. *Jewellery.*
TEL: 020 7493 0224
EMAIL: diem@fsmail.net

Ghazi Ghafoori
Stand MC27. *Islamic items, antiquities and jewellery.*
TEL: 020 7629 7212
EMAIL: ghazighafoori2004@yahoo.co.uk

K.K. Ghafoori Antique Craft
Stand L12-13. *Ancient beads.*
TEL: 020 7491 4001

Gilded Lily   LAPADA
Stand G145-6. *Jewellery.*
TEL: 020 7499 6260; FAX: same; MOBILE: 07740 428358
EMAIL: **jewellery@gilded-lily.co.uk**

Gordon's Medals
Stand MG14-15. *Militaria.*
TEL: 020 7495 0900
EMAIL: malcolm@cocollector.co.uk

R.G. Grahame
Stand G129-30. *Prints and paintings.*
TEL: 07969 444239

Solveig & Anita Gray   LAPADA
Stand G307-309. *Asian.*
TEL: 020 7408 1638
EMAIL: **info@chinese-porcelain.com**
WEBSITE: **www.chinese-porcelain.com**

Saul Greenstein
Stand G304-306. *Jewellery.*
TEL: 020 7629 9282
EMAIL: saul_5@hotmail.com

Guest & Gray
Stand MH25-28. *Asian.*
TEL: 020 7408 1252
EMAIL: info@chinese-porcelain-art.com
WEBSITE: www.chinese-porcelain-art.com

Alice Gulesserian
Stand MK33. *Jewellery and small antiques.*
TEL: 020 7629 7034

Habibi Oriental Antiques
Stand MC20. *Oriental antiques.*
TEL: 07930 482716
EMAIL: yasin.habibi@btinternet.com

Hallmark Antiques
Stand G319. *Jewellery.*

TEL: 020 7629 8757

Diane Harby
Stand G148. *Textiles.*
TEL: 020 7629 5130

Satoe Hatrell
Stand G156-166. *Jewellery.*
TEL: 020 7629 4296

Jan Havlik
Stand MK36-38. *Jewellery.*
TEL: 020 7629 7034

Gillian Horsup
Stand MC10-11. *Jewellery.*
TEL: 020 7499 8121
EMAIL: gillian@horsup.globalnet.co.uk

J.L.A.
Stand G364-76. *Jewellery.*
TEL: 020 7499 1681

The Jewellery Exchange   LAPADA
Stand 225-360.
TEL: 020 7629 7234
EMAIL: **rowanandrowan@aol.com**
WEBSITE: **www.rowanandrowan.com**

John Joseph   LAPADA
Stand G345-7. *Jewellery.*
TEL: 020 7629 1140
EMAIL: **jewellery@john-joseph.co.uk**

Joseph's Antiques & Works of Art
Stand MK28. *19th C Continental works of art.*
TEL: 020 7495 3336

JUS Watches
Stand G108. *Clocks and watches.*
TEL: 020 7495 7404

K & M Antiques
Stand G369-70. *Ceramics.*
TEL: 020 7491 4310
EMAIL: kandmantiques@aol.com

K. & Y. Oriental Art
Stand MK24-7. *Asian.*
TEL: 020 7491 0264
EMAIL: yusui@freeuk.com

Minoo & Andre Kaae   LAPADA
Stand MG22-23. *Jewellery.*
TEL: 020 7629 1200
EMAIL: **andrekaae@aol.com**

Kikuchi Trading Co Ltd   LAPADA
Stand G357-359. *Jewellery and watches.*
TEL: 020 7629 6808
EMAIL: **kikuchi@grays.clara.net**

Lazarel
Stand G302-3. *Objets d'art.*
TEL: 020 7408 0154
EMAIL: pgszuhay@aol.com

Elliot Lee   LAPADA
Stand G328. *Silver.*
TEL: 020 7629 7034

Monty Lo
Stand G369-70. *Ceramics.*
TEL: 020 7493 7457

Michael Longmore   LAPADA
Stand G378-379. *Jewellery.*
TEL: **020 7491 2764**
EMAIL: **michaellongmore@aol.com**

Marco Polo Antiques Ltd
Stand MA16-17. *Islamic.*
TEL: 020 7629 3788

Michael Marks
Stand G385. *Jewellery.*
TEL: 020 7491 0332

Allison Massey
Stand MB32-33. *Jewellery.*
TEL: 020 7629 7034
EMAIL: allisonjet@aol.com

Mazar Antiques
Stand MA28-29. *Islamic.*
TEL: 020 7491 3001

Michaeloriental
Stand MM20-21. *Asian ceramics and works of art.*
TEL: 020 7629 8898

Michael's Boxes
Stand ML14-15. *Objets d'art and miniatures.*
TEL: 020 7629 5716
EMAIL: info@michaelsboxes.com
WEBSITE: www.michaelsboxes.com

Eva Michelson-Nonesuch Antiques
Stand 367. *Antique jewellery and objets d'art.*
TEL: 020 7629 6783

A. Mirecki
Stand MV011. *Jewellery.*
TEL: 020 7629 7034

Brian Moore
Stand V0015. *Ceramics.*
TEL: 020 7629 7034

Mousavi
Stand D4. *Jewellery, cufflinks and jade.*

Mulberry Jones
Stand MMB023. *Ceramics.*
TEL: 020 7629 7034

Susie Nelson
Stand D13-14. *Vintage accessories.*
TEL: 020 7629 7034

Howard Neville
Stand G127. *Objets d'art and miniatures.*
TEL: 020 7491 7623

Marie Niemis
Stand MV006. *Jewellery.*
TEL: 020 629 7034

A. Noori
Stand MA12. *Islamic and antiquities.*
TEL: 020 7629 6484

Nigel Norman
Stand G335. *Jewellery.*
TEL: 020 7495 3066
EMAIL: jewels@nigelnorman.co.uk
WEBSITE: www.nigelnorman.co.uk

Glenda O'Connor
Stand MA18-19. *Dolls and teddy bears.*
TEL: 020 8367 2441
EMAIL: glenda@glenda-antiquedolls.com
WEBSITE: www.glenda-antiquedolls.com

Pavlos Pavlou
Stand ML17. *Coins and medals.*
TEL: 020 7629 9449
EMAIL: pspavlou@hotmail.com

Michelle Payne
Stand ML14-15. *Jewellery.*
TEL: 07802 180940
EMAIL: michelle_payne@hotmail.com

The Pearl Gallery
Stand M14-16. *Jewellery.*
TEL: 020 7409 2743
EMAIL: pearlgallery@freenetname.co.uk

Maria Perez
Stand V23. *Antique jewellery, cufflinks, pearls and vintage costume jewellery.*
EMAIL: m.perez@btconnect.com

Persepolis Gallery
Stand MK10-12. *Islamic.*
TEL: 020 7629 7388
EMAIL: persepolisgall@aol.com

Pieces of Time   BADA
Stand MM17-19. *Watches and timepieces.*
TEL: **020 7629 3272**
EMAIL: **info@antique-watch.com**
WEBSITE: **www.antique-watch.com**

Jack Podlewski
Stand G320. *Silver.*
TEL: 020 7409 1468

Andrew Prince
Stand MG10-11. *Costume jewellery.*
TEL: 020 7493 8763
EMAIL: info@andrewprince.co.uk
WEBSITE: www.andrewprince.co.uk

Lucinda Prince
Stand MMB023-24. *Dolls and teddy bears.*
TEL: 020 7629 7034

Pushkin Antiques
Stand G371. *Jewellery.*
TEL: 07900 000562

RBR Grp
Stand G158. *Jewellery.*
TEL: 020 7629 4769

Regal Watches
Stand G128-140. *Watches and timepieces.*
TEL: 020 7491 7722

Ian Roper
Stand MK10-12. *Ancient and medieval arms and armour.*
TEL: 020 7491 4009
EMAIL: ropecoin@aol.com

Michelle Rowan
Stand G313-315. *Jewellery.*
TEL: 020 7499 5478
EMAIL: rowanandrowan@aol.com

Charlotte Sayers   LAPADA
Stand G313-315. *Jewellery.*
TEL: 020 7499 5478
EMAIL: rowanandrowan@aol.com

Walter Schaetzke
Stand MV013. *Ceramics.*
TEL: 020 7629 7034

Second Time Around
Stand G316-318. *Watches and timepieces.*
TEL: 020 7499 7442
EMAIL: k.waite@secondtimeround.com
WEBSITE: www.secondtimeround.com

Chris Seidler
Stand MG12-13. *Militaria.*
TEL: 020 7629 2851
EMAIL: chris@antique-militaria.co.uk
WEBSITE: www.antique-militaria.co.uk

Sarah Sellers
Stand MA25-B14. *Dolls and teddy bears.*
TEL: 020 7629 7034
EMAIL: sarah@allyoucanbear.com
WEBSITE: www.allyoucanbear.com

Shapiro & Co   LAPADA
Stand G380. *Jewellery.*
TEL: 020 7491 2710

Mousa Shavolian
Stand MB19-21. *Glass and perfume bottles.*
TEL: 020 7499 8273
EMAIL: mousaantiques@yahoo.com

Shiraz Antiques
Stand MH10-11. *Islamic and antiquities.*
TEL: 020 7495 0635
EMAIL: rezkia7@hotmail.com

Peter Sloane
Stand ME12-13. *Asian.*
TEL: 020 7408 1043

Solaimani Gallery
Stand ME16-17. *Islamic and antiquities.*
TEL: 020 7491 2562

Shabbir Solanki Antiques
Stand G323. *Fountain pens and lighters.*
TEL: 07789 693626

Boris Sosna
Stand G374-5. *Jewellery.*
TEL: 020 7629 2371

Spectrum
Stand G372-3. *Jewellery.*
TEL: 020 7629 3501

Jane Stewart
Stand ML25. *Pewter and medieval items.*
TEL: 020 7355 3333

Sultani Antiques
Stand E18-20. *Islamic and antiquities.*
TEL: 020 7491 3847

Timespec
Stand G366. *Clocks and timepieces.*
TEL: 020 7499 9814

Times Remembered
Stand MV007. *Jewellery and small antiques.*
TEL: 020 7629 7034
EMAIL: k.stratton-collins@virgin.net

Ting's Jewellery Box
Stand MC21. *Jewellery, ceramics and glass.*
TEL: 020 7629 7034

Michael Ventura-Pauly
Stand G354-355. *Jewellery.*
TEL: 020 7495 6868

June Victor
Stand MC10-11. *Vintage fashion.*
TEL: 020 7409 0400

Mary Wellard
Stand G165. *Small antiques.*
TEL: 020 7629 7034

Westleigh Antiques
Stand G341. *Jewellery.*
TEL: 020 7493 0123

Westminster Group   LAPADA
Stand G322. *Jewellery, watches and clocks.*
TEL: 020 7493 8672

Wheatley Antiques   LAPADA
Stand G106. *Asian.*
TEL: 020 7629 1352
EMAIL: wheatley.antiques@btinternet.com

Wheels of Steel
Stand MB10-11. *Toys.*
TEL: 020 7629 2813

David Whightman
Stand MA30. *Vintage fashion.*
TEL: 020 7409 0400
EMAIL: davidandpatrick2000@yahoo.co.uk
WEBSITE: www.vintagemodes.co.uk

Alan Wilson
Stand MFS008. *Asian.*
TEL: 020 7629 7034

Wimpole Antiques   LAPADA
Stand G338-349. *Jewellery.*
TEL: 020 7499 2889
EMAIL: lynn@wimpoleantiques.plus.com
WEBSITE: www.wimpoleantiques.plus.com

ZMS Antiques
Stand G125. *Silver.*
TEL: 020 7491 1144

HALCYON DAYS

Creators of hand-painted enamels,
specialists in antiques and *objets d' art*

14 Brook Street, London W1S 1BD
Tel: 020 7629 8811
www.halcyondays.co.uk

Richard Green   **BADA**
147 New Bond St., 33 New Bond St. and 39 Dover St.
W1S 2TS.
SLAD. Open 9.30-6, Sat. by appointment. *STOCK:*
Paintings - British, sporting and marine, French
Impressionist and Modern British, Victorian and
European, fine Old Masters. PARK: Meters. VAT:
Stan/Spec. FAIRS: Grosvenor House; 20-21 British Art
Fair; London Art Fair.
TEL: 020 7493 3939; FAX: 020 74993278
E-MAIL: **paintings@richard-green.com**
WEBSITE: **www.richard-green.com.**

Simon Griffin Antiques Ltd
3 Royal Arcade, 28 Old Bond St. W1S 4SB. (S.J.
Griffin)
EST. 1979. Open 10.30-6, Sat. 10.30-5. *STOCK: Silver, old*
Sheffield plate. SER: Repairs, restorations. VAT:
Stan/Spec.
TEL: 020 7491 7367; FAX: same

Halcyon Days   **BADA**
14 Brook St. W1S 1BD.
EST. 1950. Open 9.30-6. *STOCK: 18th to early 19th C*
enamels, fans, treen, objets de vertu, Georgian and
Victorian scent bottles. LOC: Hanover Sq. end of Brook
St. PARK: Meters and Hanover Sq. VAT: Stan/Spec.
TEL: 020 7629 8811; FAX: 020 7409 0280

E-MAIL: **info@halcyondays.co.uk**
WEBSITE: **www.halcyondays.co.uk**

Hancocks & Co (Jewellers) Ltd   **BADA**
52-53 Burlington Arcade. W1J 0HH.
EST. 1849. Open 9.30-5.30, CL: Mon. *STOCK: Fine*
estate jewellery and silver. SER: Valuations; re-
modelling. SIZE: Medium. PARK: Car park Old
Burlington St. VAT: Stan/Spec. FAIRS: Grosvenor
House; Miami Beach; Palm Beach; Maastricht
(TEFAF); IFAAD, New York.
TEL: 020 7493 8904; FAX: 020 7493 8905
E-MAIL: **info@hancocks-london.com**
WEBSITE: **www.hancocks-london.com.**

G. Heywood Hill Ltd
10 Curzon St. W1J 5HH.
Open 9-5.30, Sat. 9-12.30. *STOCK: Books, new and old,*
architecture, history, literature, children's, natural history and
illustrated.
TEL: 020 7629 0647; FAX: 020 7408 0286
E-MAIL: **books@heywoodhill.com**
WEBSITE: **www.heywoodhill.com**

Holland & Holland
31 and 33 Bruton St. W1X 8JS.
EST. 1835. Open 9.30-5.30, Sat. 10-4. *STOCK: Modern*
and antique guns, rifles, associated items; sporting prints,
pictures and antiquarian books; antique sporting objects.
SIZE: Medium. PARK: Meters.
TEL: 020 7499 4411; FAX: 020 7499 4544
E-MAIL: **gunroomuk@hollandandholland.com**
WEBSITE: **www.hollandandholland.com**

JB Silverware & John Bull (Antiques) Ltd   LAPADA
139a New Bond St. W1S 2TN. (Kenneth and Elliot
Bull)
EST. 1953. Open 9-5, CL: Sat. *STOCK: Antique silver*
and reproduction giftware, photo frames, cutlery. SER:
Valuations; repairs including antique jewellery. PARK:
NCP Grosvenor Hill or meters. VAT: Global/Margin.
FAIRS: Antiques For Everyone, NEC.
TEL: 020 7629 1251; FAX: 020 7495 3001
E-MAIL: **sales@jbsilverware.co.uk**
WEBSITE: **www.jbsilverware.co.uk** and **www.antique-**
silver.co.uk

C. John (Rare Rugs) Ltd   **BADA**
70 South Audley St., Mayfair. W1K 2RA.
EST. 1947. Open 9-5, CL: Sat. *STOCK: Rugs, carpets,*
tapestries, textiles and embroideries, 16th - 19th C. SER:
Restorations, cleaning. VAT: Stan/Spec. FAIRS:
Grosvenor House.
TEL: 020 7493 5288; FAX: 020 7409 7030
E-MAIL: **cjohn@dircon.co.uk**
WEBSITE: **www.cjohn.com.**

Johnson Walker & Tolhurst Ltd   BADA
64 Burlington Arcade. W1J 0QT. (Miss R. Gill)
EST. 1849. **Open 9.30-5.30.** STOCK: *Antique and secondhand jewellery, objets d'art, silver.* SER: **Restorations (jewellery, pearl-stringing).** VAT: **Stan/Spec.**
TEL: **020 7629 2615**

Daniel Katz Ltd
13 Old Bond St. W1S 4SX. (Daniel Katz and Stuart Lochhead)
EST. 1970. SLAD. **Open 9-6.** CL: Sat. STOCK: *European sculpture, early medieval to 19th C, from £5,000.* LOC: Near Green Park underground station. SIZE: Large. VAT: Spec.
TEL: 020 7493 0688; FAX: 020 7499 7493
E-MAIL: info@katz.co.uk
WEBSITE: www.katz.co.uk

Roger Keverne   BADA
2nd Floor, 16 Clifford St. W1S 3RG.
EST. **1996. Open Mon.-Fri. 9.30-5.30.** STOCK: *Chinese ceramics and works of art including jade, lacquer, bronzes, ivories and enamels, from 2500 BC to 1916.* SER: **Valuations; restorations; buys at auction; two exhibitions a year; catalogues available.** SIZE: **Large.** PARK: **Meters.** VAT: **Stan/Spec.** FAIRS: **New York (Winter).**
TEL: **020 7434 9100;** FAX: **020 7434 9101**
E-MAIL: **enquiries@keverne.co.uk**
WEBSITE: **www.keverne.co.uk**

D.S. Lavender (Antiques) Ltd   BADA
139a New Bond St., entrance on Bloomfield Place, W1S 2TN.
EST. **1945. Open 9.30-5.** CL: **Sat.** STOCK: *Jewels, miniatures, works of art.* SER: **Valuations.** PARK: **Meters.** VAT: **Stan/Spec.**
TEL: **020 7629 1782;** FAX: **020 7629 3106**
E-MAIL: **dslavender@clara.net**

Liberty
Regent St. W1R 6AH.
EST. 1875. Open 10-6.30, Thurs. 10-8, Fri. and Sat. 10-7. STOCK: *British furniture, ceramics, glass and metalware, 1860-1930, Gothic Revival, Aesthetic Movement and Arts & Crafts.* LOC: Regent St. joins Piccadilly and Oxford Circus. SIZE: Large. PARK: Meters and underground station in Cavendish Sq. VAT: Stan.
TEL: 020 7734 1234
E-MAIL: antiques@liberty.co.uk
WEBSITE: www.liberty.co.uk

Michael Lipitch Ltd
Mayfair. W1K 2TX.
EST. 1959. Open by appointment. STOCK: *18th to early 19th C English furniture, decoration and works of art.* SER: Specialist advice. PARK: Meters. VAT: Spec. FAIRS: Grosvenor House.
TEL: 020 8441 4340; MOBILE: 07730 954347
E-MAIL: michaellipitch@hotmail.com
WEBSITE: www.michaellipitch.com

Maas Gallery
15a Clifford St. W1S 4JZ. (R.N. Maas)
EST. 1960. SLAD. Open Mon.-Fri. 10-5.30. STOCK: *Victorian and Pre-Raphaelite paintings, drawings, watercolours and illustrations.* LOC: Between New Bond St. and Cork St. SER: Valuations; buys at auction. SIZE: Medium. PARK: Easy. VAT: Spec. FAIRS: Watercolours & Drawings Fair, Grosvenor House.
TEL: 020 7734 2302; FAX: 020 7287 4836
E-MAIL: mail@maasgallery.com
WEBSITE: www.maasgallery.com

Maggs Bros Ltd   BADA
50 Berkeley Sq. W1J 5BA. (J.F., B.D. and E.F. Maggs, P. Harcourt, R. Harding and H. Bett, J. Collins, T. Boeder, J. Reilly.)
EST. **1853.** ABA. **Open 9.30-5.** CL: **Sat.** STOCK: *Rare books, manuscripts, autograph letters and medieval miniatures.* SIZE: **Large.** PARK: **Meters.** VAT: **Stan/Spec.**
TEL: **020 7493 7160 (6 lines);** FAX: **020 7499 2007**
E-MAIL: **ed@maggs.com**
WEBSITE: **www.maggs.com.**

Mahboubian Gallery
65 Grosvenor St. W1K 3JJ. (H. Mahboubian)
Open 10-6. CL: Sat.
TEL: 020 7493 9112
E-MAIL: kmahboubian@aol.com

Mallett and Son (Antiques) Ltd   BADA
141 New Bond St. W1S 2BS. (Richard Cave)
EST. **1865.** CINOA, SLAD, NAADA. **Open 9.15-6, Sat. 10-5.** STOCK: *English furniture, 1690-1835; clocks, 17th-18th C; china, needlework, paintings and watercolours, objects and glass.* SIZE: **Large.** PARK: **Meters in Berkeley Sq.** FAIRS: **Grosvenor House; Maastricht; IFAAD New York; Winter Show, New York; Palm Beach; San Francisco (Fall).**
TEL: **020 7499 7411;** FAX: **020 7495 3179**
E-MAIL: **info@mallettantiques.com**

Mallett Fine Art   BADA
141 New Bond St. W1S 2BS.
SLAD. **Open 9.15-6, Sat. 10-4.** STOCK: *18th to early 20th C paintings, watercolours and drawings.* PARK: **Meters nearby.** VAT: **Spec.** FAIRS: **Olympia; Grosvenor House; IFAAD, New York; Maastricht; Palm Beach.**
TEL: **020 7499 7411;** FAX: **020 7495 3179**
E-MAIL: **info@mallettantiques.com**
WEBSITE: **www.mallettantiques.com.**

Mansour Gallery   BADA
46-48 Davies St. W1K 5JB. (M. Mokhtarzadeh)
Open 9.30-5.30, Sat. by appointment. STOCK: *Islamic works of art, miniatures; ancient glass and glazed wares; Greek, Roman and Egyptian antiquities.* VAT: **Stan.**
TEL: **020 7491 7444 or 020 7499 0510**
E-MAIL: **masil@mansourgallery.com**

Map World   LAPADA
25 Burlington Arcade, Piccadilly. W1J 0PT. (J. T. Sharpe)
EST. 1982. Open 10-5.30. *STOCK: Maps, worldwide,
1480-1850, £50–£150,000; antique prints, book and maps of
London.* SER: Valuations; buys at auction. SIZE: Small.
TEL: 020 7495 5377; FAX: same
E-MAIL: info@map-world.com
WEBSITE: www.map-world.com

Marks Antiques   BADA LAPADA
W1K 3NU. (Anthony Marks)
EST. 1935. Open 9.30-6, Sat. by appointment. *STOCK:
Fine 17th-19th C silver and Fabergé.* SER: Valuations;
buys at auction. SIZE: Large. PARK: Meters. VAT:
Stan/Spec. FAIRS: Grosvenor House; Maastricht
(TEFAF).
TEL: 020 7499 1788; FAX: 020 7409 3183
E-MAIL: marks@marksantiques.com
WEBSITE: www.marksantiques.com

Marlborough Fine Art (London) Ltd
6 Albemarle St. W1S 4BY.
EST. 1946. SLAD. Open 10-5.30, Sat. 10-12.30. *STOCK:
Exhibitions by leading contemporary artists.* PARK: Meters
or near Cork St. FAIRS: London; Madrid; Maastricht;
Miami; Moscow; Basel; Paris.
TEL: 020 7629 5161; FAX: 020 7629 6338
E-MAIL: mfa@marlboroughfineart.com
WEBSITE: www.marlboroughfineart.com

Marlborough Rare Books Ltd
144-146 New Bond St. W1S 2TR. (Jonathan Gestetner)
EST. 1946. ABA. Open 9.30-5.30. CL: Sat. *STOCK:
Illustrated books of all periods; rare books on fine and applied
arts and architecture; English literature.* SER: Buys at auction;
valuations; catalogues available. SIZE: Medium. PARK:
Meters. FAIRS: Olympia; Chelsea; California; New York.
TEL: 020 7493 6993; FAX: 020 7499 2479
E-MAIL: sales@mrb-books.co.uk

Jeremy Mason
Gray's Mews, Davies St. W1.
EST. 1974. Open 11-5 by appointment. *STOCK: Period
Oriental works of art, bronzes, lacquer, porcelain, glass and
pictures.* VAT: Spec.
TEL: 07939 240884

Mayfair Gallery Ltd   LAPADA
39 South Audley St. W1K 2PP. (M. Sinai)
Open 9.30-6, Sat. by appointment. *STOCK: 19th C antiques
and decorative art, Continental furniture, clocks, chandeliers,
Meissen, ivories, chandeliers, objets d'art and Russian works
of art.* LOC: Mayfair. SER: Valuations; restorations;
shipping. FAIRS: Miami Beach; Olympia (June).
TEL: 020 7491 3435 or 020 7491 3436; FAX: 020 7491
3437; MOBILE: 07768 980572
E-MAIL: mayfairgallery@mayfairgallery.com

Melton's
27 Bruton Place. W1J 6NQ. (Cecilia Neal)
EST. 1990. IIDA. BIDA. Open Mon.-Fri. 9.30-5.30.
*STOCK: Small antiques and decorative accessories: lamps,
prints, porcelain, textiles, English and Continental.* LOC:
Mayfair, near Bond St. SER: Interior design and
decoration. PARK: Meters Berkeley Sq.
TEL: 020 7629 3612; FAX: 020 7495 3196
E-MAIL: sales@meltons.co.uk
WEBSITE: www.meltons.co.uk.

Messum's   BADA LAPADA
8 Cork St. W1S 3LJ.
SLAD. SOFAA. Open 10-6, Sat. 10-4, other times by
appointment. *STOCK: British Impressionist and
contemporary paintings and sculpture.* SER: Valuations;
restorations; framing. VAT: Stan/Spec.
TEL: 020 7437 5545; FAX: 020 7734 7018
E-MAIL: info@messums.com
WEBSITE: www.messums.com

John Mitchell and Son
44 Old Bond St. W1S 4GB.
EST. 1931. SLAD. Open 9-5.30, Sat. by appointment.
*STOCK: Old Master paintings, 17th C Dutch, 18th C
English and 19th C European; Alpine paintings. Also
representing James Hart-Dyke.* SER: Valuations;
restorations (pictures); buying at auction. SIZE: Medium.
PARK: Meters. FAIRS: TEFAF; Palm Beach; IFAAD
New York; SeaFair.
TEL: 020 7493 7567; FAX: 020 7493 5537
E-MAIL: enquiries@johnmitchell.net
WEBSITE: www.johnmitchell.net

Paul Mitchell Ltd   BADA
17 Avery Row, Brook St. W1K 4BF.
Open Mon-Fri 9.30-5.30. *STOCK: Picture frames.* SIZE:
Large. PARK: Meters. VAT: Stan.
TEL: 020 7493 8732 or 020 7493 0860
E-MAIL: admin@paulmitchell.co.uk
WEBSITE: www.paulmitchell.co.uk

Moira of New Bond Street   LAPADA
11 New Bond St. W1S 3SR. (Mrs M. Cohen)
Open 10-5. *STOCK: Fine antique and Art Deco jewellery.*
SER: Valuations; repairs.
TEL: 020 7629 0160
E-MAIL: simon@moira-jewels.com
WEBSITE: www.moira-jewels.com

Morelle Davidson Ltd   LAPADA
45-46 New Bond St. W1S 2SF
EST. 1984. Open by appointment. *STOCK: Jewellery,
silver, and objets d'art.* SER: Sales, valuations, designs
and repairs. FAIRS: Miami Beach, Las Vegas and New
York Antique Jewellery & Watch shows.
TEL: 020 7408 0066; FAX: 020 7495 8885
E-MAIL: info@morelle.co.uk
WEBSITE: www.morelle.co.uk

Sydney L. Moss Ltd   BADA
51 Brook St. W1K 4HP. (P.G. Moss)
EST. 1910. Open Mon.-Fri. 10-5.30. *STOCK: Chinese and Japanese paintings and works of art; Japanese netsuke and lacquer, 17th-20th C; reference books (as stock).* LOC: From Grosvenor Sq., up Brook St. to Claridges. SER: Valuations and advice; buys at auction. SIZE: Large. PARK: Meters. VAT: Spec. FAIRS: Asian Art, New York (March).
TEL: 020 7629 4670 or 020 7493 7374; FAX: 020 7491 9278
E-MAIL: pasi@slmoss.com
WEBSITE: www.slmoss.com.

Richard Ogden Ltd   BADA
28-29 Burlington Arcade, Piccadilly. W1J 0NX.
EST. 1948. Open 9.30-5.30, Sat. 9.30-5. *STOCK: Antique and traditional fine jewellery.* SER: Bespoke designs; repairs and remodelling; engraving; valuations for insurance and probate; estimates for insurance claims. SIZE: Medium. PARK: Meters and NCP. VAT: Spec.
TEL: 020 7493 9136; (Design and repairs) 020 7499 9783; FAX: 020 7355 1508
E-MAIL: jewels@richardogden.com
WEBSITE: www.richardogden.com

Partridge Fine Art Ltd   BADA
144-146 New Bond St. W1S 2PF. (Chairman Marl Law)
EST. 1905. SLAD. CINOA. Open 9-60, Sat. 10.30-6, other times by appointment. *STOCK: 18th-19th C English, French and Continental furniture; works of art; paintings, clocks, chandeliers, tapestries, lamps, needlework, carpets, sculpture. English & Continental porcelain and jewellery.* LOC: North of Bruton St./Conduit St. crossing. SER: Valuations; buys at auction; upholstery; restorations; carving and gilding; annual exhibitions. SIZE: Very large - 4 floors. PARK: Meters and NCP nearby. VAT: Spec.
TEL: 020 7629 0834; FAX: 020 7495 6266
E-MAIL: enquiries@partridgefineart.com
WEBSITE: www.partridgefineart.com.

A. Pash & Sons
37 South Audley St. W1K 2PN. (Arnold and Robert Pash)
EST. 1926. Open 9-6, Sat by appointment. *STOCK: Fine antique silver.* SER: Restorations (silver). SIZE: Large. PARK: NCP nearby.
TEL: 020 7493 5176; FAX: 020 7355 3676
E-MAIL: info@pashantiques.com
WEBSITE: www.pashantiques.com

W.H. Patterson Ltd   BADA LAPADA
19 Albemarle St. W1S 4BB. (Cory, Anthony and Glenn Fuller and Wayne Thornton)
SLAD. Open 9.30-6. *STOCK: 19th C and regular exhibitions for contemporary artists, the New English Art Club, Paul Brown, Peter Brown, Willem and Walter Dolphyn, Clive McCartney, Lionel Aggett.* LOC: Near

Green Park underground station. SER: Valuations; restorations. SIZE: Large. PARK: Meters. VAT: Spec. FAIRS: New York Armoury; Affordable Art, Battersea; Watercolours and Drawings, Royal Academy.
TEL: 020 7629 4119; FAX: 020 7499 0119
E-MAIL: info@whpatterson.com
WEBSITE: www.whpatterson.com

Pelham   BADA
23 Berkeley Sq. W1J 6HE. (Alan and L.J. Rubin)
EST. 1928. SNA. *STOCK: Furniture, English and Continental; tapestries, decorative works of art and musical instruments. Also at 42 Rue de Varenne, 75007 Paris.* SER: Valuations. VAT: Spec. FAIRS: Maastricht; Olympia; Biennale Paris; New York.
TEL: 020 7629 0905; FAX: 020 7495 4511 (office only)
E-MAIL: antiques@pelhamgalleries.com

Pendulum of Mayfair Ltd
King House, 51 Maddox St. W1S 2PJ. (K.R. Clements and Dr H. Specht)
Open 10-6, Sat. 10-5, other times by appointment. *STOCK: Clocks, mainly longcase, also bracket, mantel and wall; Georgian mahogany furniture.* SER: Valuations; repairs. VAT: Spec.
TEL: 020 7629 6606; FAX: 020 7629 6616
E-MAIL: pendulumclocks@aol.com
WEBSITE: www.pendulumofmayfair.co.uk.

Ronald Phillips Ltd   BADA
26 Bruton St. W1J 6QL. (Simon Phillips)
EST. 1952. Open 9-6, Sat. 10-4. STOCK: *English 18th C*
furniture, objets d'art, glass, clocks and barometers. LOC:
Mayfair. VAT: Mainly Spec. FAIRS: **Grosvenor House**
(June); IAAF, New York (Oct).
TEL: **020 7493 2341**; FAX: **020 7495 0843**
E-MAIL: **advice@ronaldphillips.co.uk**
WEBSITE: **www.ronaldphillips.co.uk**

Pickering & Chatto
4th Floor, 144-146 New Bond St. W1S 2TR.
EST. 1820. ABA. PBFA. Open Mon.-Fri. 9.30-5.30 or
by appointment. STOCK: *Literature, economics, politics,*
philosophy, science, medicine, general antiquarian. SIZE:
Medium. PARK: Meters. FAIRS: Chelsea, Olympia, New
York, California.
TEL: 020 7491 2656; FAX: 020 449 2479
E-MAIL: rarebooks@pickering-chatto.com
WEBSITE: www.pickering-chatto.com

Jonathan Potter Ltd   BADA LAPADA
125 New Bond St. W1S 1DY.
EST. 1975. ABA. Open 10-6, Sat. by appointment.
STOCK: *Maps, charts and plans - worldwide including*
Britain, atlases and travel books, 16th-19th C, £50-
£10,000. LOC: **1st floor.** SER: **Valuations; restorations;**
colouring; framing; buys at auction (maps and prints);
catalogue available. SIZE: **Medium.** PARK: **Meters**
nearby. VAT: **Stan.** FAIRS: **ABA Book Fair.**
TEL: **020 7491 3520**; FAX: **020 7491 9754**
E-MAIL: **jpmaps@attglobal.net**
WEBSITE: **www.jpmaps.co.uk.**

Pullman Gallery
116 Mount St., Mayfair. W1K 3NH. (Simon
Khachadourian)
EST. 1980. Open 10-6, Sat. by appointment. STOCK:
Objets de luxe, 19th-20th C, £200-£20,000; automobile art,
pre-1950, £1,000-£20,000; cocktail shakers, bar accessories,
cigar memorabilia, 1880-1950, £250-£25,000; René
Lalique glass, 1900-1940, from £3,000. SIZE: Medium.
VAT: Stan.
TEL: 020 7499 8080; FAX: 020 7499 9090; MOBILE:
07973 141606
E-MAIL: sk@pullmangallery.com
WEBSITE: www.pullmangallery.com

Bernard Quaritch Ltd (Booksellers)   BADA
8 Lower John St., Golden Sq. W1F 9AU. (John Koh)
EST. 1847. ABA. ILAB. VDA. SLAM. AILA. Open 9-
6. CL: Sat. STOCK: *Rare antiquarian books, manuscripts*
and photographs. LOC: **5 mins. from Piccadilly Circus**
tube exit 1. Walk down Glasshouse St. and turn right
on to Air St. SER: **Buys at auction; valuations.** SIZE:
Large - 2 floors. VAT: **Stan.** FAIRS: **Various London and**
international.
TEL: **020 7734 2983**; FAX: **020 7437 0967**

E-MAIL: **rarebooks@quaritch.com**
WEBSITE: **www.quaritch.com**

Rare Jewellery Collections Ltd   LAPADA
Extraordinary Vintage Jewels, 45-46 New Bond St.
W1S 2SF.
Open by appointment. STOCK: *Jewellery and watches.*
SER: **Restorations; valuations; collection building**
service.
TEL: **020 7499 5414**; FAX: **020 7499 6906**; MOBILE:
07771 788189
E-MAIL: **info@rarejewellerycollections.net**
WEBSITE: **www.rarejewellerycollections.net**

Steven Rich & Michael Rich
111 Mount St. Mayfair. W1K 2TT.
SLAD. Open daily, Sat. by appointment. STOCK: *Master*
paintings, 16th-20th C; natural history; works of art.
LOC: Just off Berkeley Sq. SER: Valuations. SIZE:
Medium. PARK: St. James's Sq. VAT: Spec.
TEL: 020 7499 4881; FAX: 020 7499 4882
E-MAIL: art@richonline.com

David Richards and Sons
10 New Cavendish St. W1G 8UL. (M. and E. Richards)
EST. 1970. Open 9.30-6, Sat. 10-5. STOCK: *Antique and*
reproduction silver and plate. LOC: Off Harley St., at
corner of Marylebone High St. SER: Valuations;
restorations. SIZE: Large. PARK: Nearby. VAT: Stan/Spec.
TEL: 020 7935 3206 or 020 7935 0322; FAX: 020 7224
4423
E-MAIL: richards@the-silvershop.co.uk
WEBSITE: www.the-silvershop.co.uk

Michael Rose
3 Burlington Arcade, Piccadilly. W1V 9AB.
EST. 1980. NAG. Open 9.30-5.30. STOCK: *Victorian,*
antique and period diamonds; jewellery.
TEL: 020 7493 0714
E-MAIL: michael@rosejewels.com
WEBSITE: www.rosejewels.co.uk

Rose Fine Jewels
15 Burlington Arcade, Piccadilly. W1J 0PJ. (Michael Rose)
EST. 1980. NAG. Open 9.30-5.30. STOCK: *Victorian,*
antique and period diamonds, jewellery. Contemporary
Fabergé and period Russian eggs.
TEL: 020 7493 4466
E-MAIL: michael@rosejewels.com
WEBSITE: www.rosejewels.co.uk

Roses
44 Burlington Arcade, Piccadilly. W1J 0QY. (Michael
Rose)
EST. 1980. NAG. Open 9.30-5.30. STOCK: *Victorian,*
antique and period diamonds, jewellery, watches and cufflinks.
TEL: 020 7493 4941
E-MAIL: michael@rosejewels.com
WEBSITE: www.rosejewels.co.uk

Rossi & Rossi Ltd
16 Clifford Street. W1S 3RG. (Anna Maria Rossi and Fabio Rossi)
EST. 1984. SLAD. Open 10-5, Sat. and Sun. by appointment. STOCK: *Himalayan art, 12th-18th C, to £150,000; early Chinese textiles.* LOC: Off Piccadilly. SER: Valuations; buys at auction. SIZE: Large. PARK: Meters. VAT: Spec. FAIRS: Dubai
TEL: 020 77346487; FAX: 020 77346051
E-MAIL: info@rossirossi.com
WEBSITE: www.rossirossi.com

The Royal Arcade Watch Shop
4 Royal Arcade at 28 Old Bond St. W1S 4SD. (Frank H. Lord and Daniel Pizzigoni)
EST. 1995. Open 10.30-5.30. STOCK: *Modern and vintage Rolex, Cartier, Patek Philippe.* SIZE: Small. PARK: Easy.
TEL: 020 7495 4882
WEBSITE: www.royalarcadewatches.com

Sampson & Horne   BADA
120 Mount St. W1K 3NN. (Jonathan Horne)
EST. 1968. CINOA. Open 9.30-5.30, Sat. and Sun. by appointment. STOCK: *English pottery; oak and country furniture; metalwork; needlework; primitive pictures; decorative and interesting items, 17th-18th C.* SER: Valuations. SIZE: Medium. PARK: Meters. VAT: Stan/Spec. FAIRS: BADA; Olympia (June); Grosvenor House; International Ceramics.
TEL: 020 7409 1789; FAX: 020 7409 7717
E-MAIL: info@sampsonhorne.com
WEBSITE: www.sampsonhorne.com

Robert G. Sawers Ltd
PO Box 4QA. W1A 4QA.
EST. 1970. ABA. Open by appointment. STOCK: *Books on the Orient, Japanese prints, screens, paintings.* LOC: West Hampstead.
TEL: 020 7794 9618; FAX: 020 7794 9571
E-MAIL: bobsawers@clara.net
WEBSITE: www.bobsawers.clara.net

Seaby Antiquities
14 Old Bond St. W1S 4PP. (Dr. J.M. Eisenberg)
EST. 1980 ADA. Open 10-5. CL: Sat. STOCK: *Antiquities.* LOC: Just off Piccadilly, nearest underground station Green Park. SER: Valuations, expertise, identification. SIZE: Medium. PARK: Meters. FAIRS: All major European & US antiquities fairs.
TEL: 020 7495 2590; FAX: 020 7491 1595
E-MAIL: minerva@minervamagazine.com
WEBSITE: www.royalathena.com

Bernard J. Shapero Rare Books and   BADA
The Shapero Gallery
32 St George St. W1S 2EA. (Bernard J. Shapero)
EST. 1979. ABA. ILAB. IMCoS. Open 9.30-6.30, Sat. 11-5. STOCK: *Rare maps and atlases, fine prints and travel photography, 16th-20th C; 19th C photographs; all £50-£50,000; antiquarian books - travel, natural history, modern first edition, colour plate.* LOC: Near Hanover Sq. and Bond St. SER: Valuations; restorations; framing. SIZE: Large. PARK: Easy. FAIRS: Miami Map Fair; Los Angeles; Dubai; Tokyo; Milan; Maastricht TEFAF; New York; Moscow; ABA Olympia; Chelsea (Nov).
TEL: 020 7493 0876; FAX: 020 7495 5010
E-MAIL: rarebooks@shapero.com
gallery@shapero.com
WEBSITE: www.shapero.com

Sinai and Sons   LAPADA
60 South Audley St. W1K 2QW. (Raphael and Joshua Sinai)
Open 9.30-5.30, Sat. and Sun. by appointment. STOCK: *19th and 20th C decorative arts.*
TEL: 020 7495 5557; FAX: 020 7495 5558
E-MAIL: raphael@sinaiandsons.com
joshua@sinaiandsons.com
WEBSITE: www.sinaiandsons.com

W. Sitch and Co. Ltd.
48 Berwick St. W1V 4JD. (R. Sitch)
EST. 1776. Open 8-5; Sat. 9.30-1. STOCK: *Edwardian and Victorian lighting fixtures and floor standards.* LOC: Off Oxford St. SER: Valuations; restorations; repairs & rewiring service. SIZE: Large. VAT: Stan.
TEL: 020 7437 3776; FAX: 020 7437 5707
E-MAIL: wsitch_co@hotmail.com
WEBSITE: www.wsitch.co.uk.

The Sladmore Gallery of Sculpture   BADA
32 Bruton Place, Berkeley Sq. W1J 6NW. (E.F. and N. Horswell and G. Farrell)
EST. 1962 SLAD. Open Mon.-Fri. 10-5. STOCK: *Contemporary sculpture.* SER: Valuations; restorations. SIZE: Large. VAT: Stan/Spec. FAIRS: Grosvenor House.
TEL: 020 7499 0365; FAX: 020 7409 1381
E-MAIL: sculpture@sladmore.com
WEBSITE: www.sladmore.com

Henry Sotheran Ltd
2-5 Sackville St., Piccadilly. W1S 3DP.
EST. 1761. ABA. PBFA. ILAB. Open 9.30-6, Sat. 10-4. STOCK: *Antiquarian books and prints.* SER: Restorations and binding (books, prints); buys at auction. VAT: Stan.
TEL: 020 7439 6151; FAX: 020 7434 2019
E-MAIL: sotherans@sotherans.co.uk
WEBSITE: www.sotherans.co.uk

A. & J. Speelman Ltd   BADA
129 Mount St. W1K 3NX.
EST. 1931. Open Mon.-Fri. 9.30-6. STOCK: *Rare Chinese, Japanese and Himalayan works of art including Tang pottery and Chinese export ceramics, Buddhist images and ritual objects.* LOC: Mayfair. SER: Valuations. SIZE: Large. VAT: Spec.
TEL: 020 7499 5126; FAX: 020 7355 3391
E-MAIL: enquiries@ajspeelman.com
WEBSITE: www.ajspeelman.com

Stoppenbach & Delestre Ltd
25 Cork St. W1S 3NB.
SLAD. Open 10-5.30, Sat. 10-1. *Stock: French paintings, drawings and sculpture, 19th-20th C.* FAIRS: TEFAF, Maastricht; Biennale, Paris; TIFAF, New York.
TEL: 020 7734 3534
E-MAIL: contact@artfrancais.com
WEBSITE: www.artfrancais.com

Tessiers Ltd   BADA LAPADA
EST. 1851. **Open by appointment only.** *Stock: Jewellery, silver, objets d'art.* LOC: **Mayfair.** SER: **Valuations; restorations.** VAT: **Spec.**
TEL: **020 7629 0458;** FAX: **020 7629 1857**
E-MAIL: **jewellery@tessiers.co.uk**
WEBSITE: **www.tessier.co.uk**

William Thuillier   BADA
14 Old Bond St. W1S 4PP.
EST. **1982. Open by appointment.** *Stock: European and British paintings, 1600-1850.* SER: **Valuations; research.** VAT: **Margin.** FAIRS: **Olympia (Feb., June and Nov.).**
TEL: **020 7499 0106**
E-MAIL: **thuillart@aol.com**
WEBSITE: **www.thuillart.com**

Rupert Wace Ancient Art Ltd   BADA
14 Old Bond St. W1S 4PP.
EST. **1984. IADAA. ADA. CINOA. Open Mon.-Fri. 10-5 or by appointment.** *Stock: Ancient Egyptian, Classical, Near Eastern and Celtic antiquities.* LOC: **West End.** SER: **Valuations.** FAIRS: **Ancient Art, Basel; Winter Antiques Show, New York; Grosvenor House; TEFAF, Maastricht.**
TEL: **020 7495 1623;** FAX: **020 7495 8495**
E-MAIL: **info@rupertwace.co.uk**
WEBSITE: **www.rupertwace.co.uk**

Wartski Ltd   BADA
14 Grafton St. W1S 4DE.
EST. 1865. Open 9.30-5. CL: Sat. *Stock: Jewellery, 18th C gold boxes, Fabergé, Russian works of art, silver.* SER: Restorations. SIZE: Medium. PARK: Meters. VAT: Stan/Spec. FAIRS: IFAAD, New York; European Fine Art; Maastricht (TEFAF); Grosvenor House.
TEL: 020 7493 1141
E-MAIL: wartski@wartski.com
WEBSITE: www.wartski.com

Waterhouse & Dodd
26 Cork St. W1S 3ND. (R. Waterhouse and J. Dodd)
EST. 1987. SLAD. Open 9.30-6, Sat. by appointment. *Stock: British and European oil paintings, watercolours and drawings, 1850-1950, £5,000-£500,000.* SER: Complete art advisory service with offices in London, Paris and New York. SIZE: Medium. VAT: Spec. FAIRS: London Art Fair; Palm Beach; Dubai; TEFAF (Maastricht).
TEL: 020 7734 7800; FAX: 0207 734 7805

E-MAIL: jonathan@european-paintings.com
WEBSITE: www.european-paintings.com

William Weston Gallery
7 Royal Arcade, Albemarle St. W1S 4SG.
EST. 1964. SLAD. IFPDA. Open Mon-Fri 9.30-5.30, Sat. 11-4.30. *Stock: Lithographs and etchings, 1890-2000.* LOC: Off Piccadilly. SIZE: Small. VAT: Spec. FAIRS: Grosvenor House; 20th/21st C British Art; Royal Academy Print Fair; IFPDA New York; Maastricht; Winter Antiques & Fine Art Fair, Olympia.
TEL: 020 7493 0722; FAX: 020 7491 9240
E-MAIL: ww@williamweston.co.uk
WEBSITE: www.williamweston.co.uk

Wilkinson plc
1 Grafton St. W1S 4EA.
EST. 1947. Open 9.30-5. CL: Sat. *Stock: Glass, especially chandeliers, 18th C and reproduction; art metal work.* LOC: Nearest underground station - Green Park. SER: Restorations and repairs (glass and metalwork).
TEL: 020 7495 2477; FAX: 020 7491 1737
E-MAIL: enquiries@wilkinson-plc.com
WEBSITE: www.wilkinson-plc.com

Thomas Williams (Fine Art) Ltd
22 Old Bond St. W1S 4PY.
Open Mon.-Fri. 10-6. *Stock: Old Master drawings, £300-£1,000,000.* SER: Valuations; buys at auction (paintings and drawings).
TEL: 020 7491 1485; FAX: 020 7408 0197
E-MAIL: thomas.williams@thomaswilliamsfineart.com
WEBSITE: www.thomaswilliamsfineart.com

Linda Wrigglesworth Ltd   LAPADA
34 Brook St. W1K 5DN.
EST. **1978. Open by appointment.** *Stock: Chinese, Korean and Tibetan costume and textiles, 14th-19th C.* LOC: **Nr Baker St. & York St.** SER: **Valuations; restorations; mounting, framing; buys on commission (Oriental).** PARK: **Baker St.** FAIRS: **Maastricht; Asian Art, London and New York; San Francisco.**
TEL: **020 7486 8990;** FAX: **020 7935 1511**
E-MAIL: **info@lindawrigglesworth.com**
WEBSITE: **www.lindawrigglesworth.com**

A. Zadah
4 Marylebone Street W1G 8JH.
EST. 1976. Open Mon-Fri 10-6. *Stock: Oriental and European carpets, rugs, tapestries and textiles.*
TEL: 020 7935 7125; fax 020 7486 7990
E-MAIL: mail@carltone.biz
WEBSITE: www.zadah.com

Zelli Porcelain
55-57 Chiltern St.,
Marylebone. W1U 6ND. (Mrs Penelope Higham)
Open 9.30-6, Sat. 10-4. *Stock: Fine modern ornamental and figurative porcelain including Hochst, KPM,*

Ludwigsburg, Meissen and Nymphenburg. SER: Restorations. SIZE: Medium.
TEL: 020 7224 2114; FAX: 020 7486 7086; MOBILE: 07831 282732
E-MAIL: info@zelli.co.uk
WEBSITE: www.zelli.co.uk

W2

Manya Igel Fine Arts Ltd   LAPADA
21-22 Peters Court, Porchester Rd. W2 5DR. (M. Igel and B.S. Prydal)
EST. 1977. Open by appointment only. STOCK: *Traditional Modern British Art, £250-£25,000.* LOC: Off Queensway. SIZE: Large. PARK: Nearby. VAT: Spec. FAIRS: 20th/21st C British Art; Olympia (Spring); Chelsea (Spring); Claridges.
TEL: 020 7229 1669 or 020 7229 8429; FAX: 020 7229 6770
E-MAIL: paintings@manyaigelfinearts.com
WEBSITE: www.manyaigelfinearts.com

The Mark Gallery   BADA
9 Porchester Place, Marble Arch. W2 2BS. (H. Mark)
EST. 1969. CINOA. Open by appointment. STOCK: *Russian icons, 16th-19th C; modern graphics - French school.* LOC: Near Marble Arch. SER: Valuations; restorations; buys at auction. SIZE: Medium. VAT: Spec. FAIRS: Olympia (June and Nov); BADA.
TEL: 020 7262 4906; FAX: 020 7224 9416
WEBSITE: www.markgallery.co.uk

Richard Morant and David Black Carpets
27 Chepstow Corner, Chepstow Place. W2 4XE. (David Black and Richard Morant)
EST. 1966. Open 10-6, Sat 11-5. STOCK: *Custom made and outsize carpets, rugs, kilims, dhurries and silk embroideries, some antique, £500-£25,000.* LOC: Nearest tube Notting Hill. SER: Valuations; restorations; cleaning, underfelts. Bespoke design service. SIZE: Large. PARK: Meters.
TEL: 020 7727 2566; FAX: 020 7229 4599
E-MAIL: info@richardmorant.com
WEBSITE: www.richardmorant.com

Richard Nagy Ltd
EST. 1978. SLAD. Open by appointment. STOCK: *German Expressionists including Gustav Klimt and Egon Schiele; Modern British from Sickert to Auerbach. Classic Modernism; Picasso, Matisse, Giacometti.* SER: Valuations; buys at auction. SIZE: Large. VAT: Spec. FAIRS: Maastricht (TEFAF); Art Basel.
TEL: 020 7262 6400; FAX: 020 7262 6464
E-MAIL: info@richardnagy.com
WEBSITE: www.richardnagy.com

W4

The Chiswick Fireplace Co.
68 Southfield Rd., Chiswick. W4 1BD.
EST. 1992. Open 9.30-5. STOCK: *Original cast iron fireplaces, late Victorian to early 1900's, £200-£1,000; marble, wood and limestone surrounds.* LOC: 8 mins. walk from Turnham Green underground station. SER: Restorations; installation. SIZE: Medium. PARK: Pay and display. VAT: Stan.
TEL: 020 8995 4011; FAX: 020 8995 4012
WEBSITE: www.thechiswickfireplace.co.uk

David Edmonds
4 Prince of Wales Terrace, Chiswick. W4 2EY.
EST. 1985. Open 10-5, Sun. by appointment. STOCK: *Antiques and architecture from the Indian subcontinent, £10-£10,000.* LOC: Off Devonshire Rd. SER: Valuations; restorations; buys at auction (as stock). SIZE: Large. PARK: Easy. VAT: Stan.
TEL: 020 8742 1920; FAX: 020 8742 3030; MOBILE: 07831 666436
E-MAIL: dareindia@aol.com
WEBSITE: www.davidedmonds.com

Marshall Phillips
38 Chiswick Lane, Chiswick. W4 2JQ. (John Phillips)
EST. 1985. Open 10-6, Sat. 10-5. STOCK: *Decorative and unusual objects, furniture, bronzes and chandeliers, £100-£50,000; garden statuary and furniture, to £30,000.* LOC: Off A4/M4 at the Hogarth roundabout or Chiswick High Rd. SER: Valuations; restorations (oil and water gilding; metal patination and non-ferrous casting). SIZE: Medium. PARK: Easy. VAT: Spec.
TEL: 020 8742 8089; FAX: same
E-MAIL: john@marshallphillips.com
WEBSITE: www.marshallphillips.com

The Old Cinema Antique Department Store
160 Chiswick High Rd. W4 1PR. (Martin Hanness)
EST. 1977. Open 10-6, Sun. 12-5. STOCK: *Antiques, vintage, retro; decorative and architectural items, 1660-1960, £100-£6,000.* SER: Restorations; delivery. SIZE: Large. PARK: Easy. VAT: Stan/Spec.
TEL: 020 8995 4166; FAX: 020 8995 4167
E-MAIL: sales@theoldcinema.co.uk
WEBSITE: www.theoldcinema.co.uk

Strand Antiques
46 Devonshire Rd., Chiswick. W4 2HD.
EST. 1977. Open Tues.-Sat. 10.30-5.30. STOCK: *English and French brocante, furniture, glass, lighting, ceramics, jewellery and silver, garden and kitchenware, books and prints, textiles and collectables, £1-£500.* LOC: Off Chiswick High Rd. 5 mins. Turnham Green underground station. SIZE: Medium. PARK: Meters.
TEL: 020 8994 1912

W6

Architectural Antiques
351 King St. W6 9NH. (G.P.A. Duc)
EST. 1985. *Trade Only.* Open Mon.-Fri. 8.30-4.30.

STOCK: *Marble/stone chimneypieces, 18th-19th C, £500-£15,000; gilt/painted overmantels, 19th C, £300-£1,500; antique French doors, £200-£1,000; bathroom fixtures, basins, £200-£800.* SER: Valuations; restorations and installations of marble. SIZE: Medium. PARK: Easy and Black Lion Lane. VAT: Stan.
TEL: 020 8741 7883; FAX: 020 8741 1109; MOBILE: 07831 127541
WEBSITE: www.aa-fireplaces.co.uk

Paravent
Flat 10, Ranelagh Gardens, Stamford Brook Ave. W6 0YE. (M. Aldbrook)
EST. 1989. Open by appointment. STOCK: *Screens, 17th-20th C, £500-£10,000 - on view at Parsons Table Company, 362 Fulham Rd., London SW10 9UU. Tel. 020 7352 7444.* SER: Restorations; finder (screens); lectures worldwide. VAT: Stan/Spec.
TEL: 020 8748 6323; FAX: 020 8563 2912
E-MAIL: aldbrook@paravent.freeserve.co.uk
WEBSITE: www.paravent.co.uk

Richard Philp   BADA
7 Ravenscourt Sq. W6 0TW.
EST. 1961. Open by appointment. STOCK: *Old Master drawings, 16th-17th C English portraiture and Old Master paintings, medieval sculpture, early furniture and 20th C drawings, £50-£40,000.* PARK: Easy. VAT: Spec.
FAIRS: Grosvenor House.
TEL: 020 8748 5678
E-MAIL: rphilp@richardphilp.com
WEBSITE: www.richardphilp.com

H.W. Poulter and Son
42A Raynham Rd., Brackenbury Village, Hammersmith W6 0HY.
EST. 1946. Open 10-5.30. Evenings and weekends by appointment. STOCK: *English and French marble chimney pieces, grates, fenders, fire irons, brass, chandeliers.* SER: Restorations (marble work). SIZE: Large. PARK: Meters. VAT: Stan/Spec.
TEL: 020 8741 4400; FAX: 020 8741 4433
E-MAIL: info@hwpoulterandson.co.uk
WEBSITE: www.hwpoulterandson.co.uk

W8

Valerie Arieta
97b Kensington Church St. W8 7LN.
EST. 1972. Open 10.30-5, appointment advisable. STOCK: *American Indian, Eskimo and Folk art; English and Continental decorative antiques.* FAIRS: Santa Fe Ethnographic Art.
TEL: 020 7243 1074 or 020 7794 7613

Artemis Decorative Arts   LAPADA
36 Kensington Church St. W8 4BX (Mr M.E. Jones)
Open 10-5.30, Sat 11-5; CL: Mon. STOCK: *Furniture, wall decorations, bronzes and sculptures, art glass; 1940s-1970s.*
TEL: 020 7376 0377; MOBILE: 07887 734420
E-MAIL: artemis.w8@btinternet.com
WEBSITE: www.artemisdecorativearts.com

Gregg Baker Asian Art   BADA LAPADA
142 Kensington Church St. W8 4BN.
EST. 1985. KCSADA. Open Tues.-Fri. 10-6, Sat. 11-4 or by appointment. STOCK: *Japanese and Chinese works of art and screens, mainly 18th-19th C, £500-£250,000.* SER: Valuations. SIZE: Medium. PARK: Meters. VAT: Stan/Spec. FAIRS: Grosvenor House (June).
TEL: 020 7221 3533; FAX: 020 7221 4410
E-MAIL: info@japanesescreens.com
WEBSITE: www.japanesescreens.com

Eddy Bardawil   BADA
106 Kensington Church St. W8 4BH.
EST. 1981. Open 10-1 and 2-5.30, Sat. 10-1.30. STOCK: *English furniture - mahogany, satinwood, walnut; mirrors, brassware, tea caddies, all pre-1830, £500-£50,000; reverse glass paintings.* LOC: Corner premises, Berkeley Gardens/Church St. SER: Valuations; restorations (furniture); polishing. SIZE: Medium. PARK: Easy. VAT: Stan/Spec.
TEL: 020 7221 3967; FAX: 020 7221 5124
E-MAIL: e.bardawil@btinternet.com
WEBSITE: www.eddybardawil.com

David Brower Antiques   LAPADA
113 Kensington Church St. W8 7LN.
EST. 1970. KCSADA. Open 11-6, Sat. by appointment. STOCK: *Specialist in Meissen, KPM, European and Oriental porcelain, French bronzes and Japanese works of art.* SER: Buys at auction. SIZE: Large. PARK: Meters nearby. VAT: Stan/Spec. FAIRS: Olympia (June).
TEL: 020 7221 4155; FAX: 020 7221 6211; MOBILE: 07831 234343
E-MAIL: david@davidbrower-antiques.com
WEBSITE: www.davidbrower-antiques.com

Butchoff Antiques   BADA LAPADA
154 Kensington Church St. W8 4BN. (Ian Butchoff)
EST. 1964. KCSADA. Open 9.30-6, Sat. 9.30-4. STOCK: *Fine 18th-19th C English and Continental furniture, mirrors, lighting, objets d'art and paintings.* SER: Restorations (furniture). SIZE: Large. PARK: Easy. FAIRS: Olympia (Summer and Winter); BADA; Harrogate (October).
TEL: 020 7221 8174; FAX: 020 7792 8923
E-MAIL: enquiries@butchoff.com
WEBSITE: www.butchoff.com

Mrs. M.E. Crick Chandeliers
166 Kensington Church St. W8 4BN. (M.T. and E.R. Denton)
EST. 1897. KCSADA. Open Mon.-Fri. 9.30-5.30. STOCK: *English and Continental crystal, glass and ormulu chandeliers, 18th-19th C.* SIZE: Large. PARK: Meters.

TEL: 020 7229 1338; FAX: 020 7792 1073
E-MAIL: info@denton-antiques.co.uk
WEBSITE: www.crick-chandeliers.co.uk

Denton Antiques
156 Kensington Church St. W8 4BN. (M.T., E.R., and
A.C. Denton)
EST. 1897. Open Mon.-Fri. 9.30-5.30. *STOCK: Glass and
metal chandeliers, wall lights and candelabra, 18th-19th C.*
SIZE: Large. PARK: Meters.
TEL: 020 7229 5866; FAX: 020 7792 1073
E-MAIL: info@denton-antiques.co.uk
WEBSITE: www.denton-antiques.co.uk

H. and W. Deutsch Antiques
111 Kensington Church St. W8 7LN.
EST. 1897. Open 10-5. CL: Wed. and Sat. *STOCK: 18th-
19th C Continental and English porcelain and glassware;
silver, plate and enamel ware, miniature portraits; Oriental
porcelain, cloisonné, bronzes, £300-£5,000.* SIZE: Large.
VAT: Stan/Spec.
TEL: 020 7727 5984

FCR Gallery Ltd   LAPADA
58 Kensington Church St. W8 4DB. (P.C. Robinson)
EST. 1994. Open by appointment. *STOCK: Modernist
metalware, glass and ceramics including Archibald Knox,
Liberty & Co, Christopher Dresser, WMF, Wiener
Werkstatte and Hagenauer.*
TEL: 07966 188819
E-MAIL: sales@fcrgallery.com
WEBSITE: www.fcrgallery.com

C. Fredericks and Son   BADA
(R.F. Fredericks)
EST. 1947. Open by appointment. *STOCK: Furniture,
18th C, £500-£15,000.* LOC: **Near Notting Hill Gate
underground station.** SER: Restorations. SIZE:
Medium. VAT: Stan/Spec. FAIRS: **BADA; Olympia
(Winter).**
TEL: **020 7727 2240;** FAX: **same;** MOBILE: **07831
336937**
E-MAIL: **richard.fredericks@cfredericksandson.com**
WEBSITE: **www.cfredericksandson.com**

Michael German Antiques Ltd   BADA LAPADA
38B Kensington Church St. W8 4BX.
EST. **1954.** KCSADA. Open **10-5, Sat. 10-12.30.**
*STOCK: Antique walking stick specialist; European and
Oriental arms and armour.*
TEL: **020 7937 2771;** FAX: **020 7937 8566**
E-MAIL: **info@antiquecanes.com**
WEBSITE: **www.antiquecanes.com**
www.antiqueweapons.com

Adrian Harrington
64a Kensington Church St. W8 4DB.
EST. 1970. ABA. ILAB. PBFA. KCSADA. Open 10-6
or by appointment. *STOCK: Fine and rare antiquarian

books, first editions, literature, children's, fore edge paintings,
library sets, Winston Churchill.* LOC: 5 mins. from
Kensington High St. and Notting Hill Gate
underground stations. SER: Bookbinding; restoration,
valuation. SIZE: Large. PARK: Meters. VAT: Stan. FAIRS:
Olympia Book (June); Chelsea Book (Nov).
TEL: 020 7937 1465; FAX: 020 7368 0912
E-MAIL: rare@harringtonbooks.co.uk
WEBSITE: www.harringtonbooks.co.uk

Haslam and Whiteway
105 Kensington Church St. W8 7LN. (T.M.
Whiteway)
EST. 1972. KCSADA. Open Mon.-Fri. 10-6, Sat. 10-4.
*STOCK: British furniture, £300-£50,000; British decorative
arts, £200-£50,000; Continental and American decorative
arts, £200-£10,000; all 1850-1930.* LOC: From Notting
Hill Gate underground station, into Kensington Church
St., premises approx. 300yds. on right. SER: Valuations;
buys at auction. SIZE: Small. PARK: Meters. VAT: Stan.
TEL: 020 7229 1145; FAX: 020 7221 7065
E-MAIL: info@haslamandwhiteway.com
WEBSITE: www.haslamandwhiteway.com

Jeanette Hayhurst Fine Glass   BADA
32a Kensington Church St. W8 4BX.
EST. 1980. Open 10-5, Sat. 12-5. *STOCK: Glass - 18th C
English drinking, fine 19th C engraved, table glass and
decanters, contemporary art, scent bottles, Roman and
Continental.* VAT: Spec. FAIRS: BADA; Antiques For
Everyone (Birmingham); Harrogate Fine Art &
Antiques Fair.*
TEL: **020 7938 1539**
E-MAIL: **jeanettehayhurstantiqueglass@btinternet.com**
WEBSITE: **www.antiqueglasslondon.com**

**Hope and Glory Commemorative Ceramics
Specialists**
131a Kensington Church St. W8 7LP. (R.R. Lower)
EST. 1982. KCSADA. Open 10-5. *STOCK:
Commemorative china.* LOC: Entrance in Peel St. SER:
Mail order (no catalogue).
TEL: 020 7727 8424
E-MAIL: john.hopeandglory@yahoo.co.uk

Howard-Jones - The Silver Shop
43 Kensington Church St. W8 4BA. (H. Howard-Jones)
EST. 1971. Open 10-5.30. *STOCK: Silver, antique and
modern, £10-£3,000.* SIZE: Small. PARK: Nearby. VAT:
Stan.
TEL: 020 7937 4359; FAX: same
E-MAIL: hjsilvershop@aol.com

J.A.N. Fine Art   BADA
**132-134 Kensington Church St. W8 4BH. (Mrs F.K.
Shimizu)**
EST. 1976. KCSADA. Open 10-6, Sat. by appointment.
*STOCK: Japanese and Chinese porcelain, 1st to 20th C, from
£150; Japanese bronzes and works of art, 15th-20th C, from*

£150; *Japanese paintings and screens, 16th-20th C, from*
£250; Tibetan thankas and ritual objects, 12th-18th C, from
£250. SIZE: **Large.** PARK: Meters. VAT: Spec.
TEL: **020 7792 0736;** FAX: **020 7221 1380**
E-MAIL: **info@jan-fineart-london.com**
WEBSITE: **www.jan-fineart-london.com**

Japanese Gallery
66d Kensington Church St. W8 4BY. (Mr and Mrs
C.D. Wertheim)
EST. 1977. Ukiyoe Dealers' Assn. of Japan. Open 10-6.
STOCK: *Japanese woodcut prints; books, kimonos, scrolls,*
netsuke, inro and tsuba. SER: Free authentification; on-
the-spot framing for Japanese prints; sales exhibitions.
TEL: 020 7229 2934; FAX: same
E-MAIL: info@japanesegallery.co.uk
WEBSITE: www.japanesegallery.co.uk

Peter Kemp
The Antiques Centre 58-60 Kensington Church St.
W8 4BD.
EST. 1975. KCSADA. Open Mon.-Fri. 10-5. STOCK:
Porcelain - 10th-19th C Chinese, 17th-19th C Japanese,
Oriental works of art and porcelain, 18th-19th C. LOC:
200yds. from Notting Hill underground station. SER:
Valuations; restorations (porcelain). SIZE: Medium.
PARK: Meters nearby. VAT: Spec.
TEL: 020 7939 4433; MOBILE: 07836 282285
E-MAIL: peterkemp42@btconnect.com

Kensington Church Street Antiques Centre
58-60 Kensington Church St. W8 4DB.
KCSADA. Open 10-6. STOCK: *14 dealers with individual*
shops.
TEL: 020 7937 4600; FAX: 020 7937 3400

Below are listed some of the dealers at this centre.

Abstract
20th C decorative arts and design.
TEL: **020 7376 2652;** FAX: same
EMAIL: **glabstract@aol.com**
WEBSITE: **www.abstract-antiques.com**

Auction Atrium
Online auction house.
TEL: 020 7937 3259

Cartalia.com Ltd
Bespoke stationary and prints.
TEL: 020 7937 8493; FAX: 020 7937 8516

Didier Antiques
Jewellery and silver, objets d'art, 1860-1960.
TEL: 020 7938 2537; FAX: same

Colin D. Monk
Oriental porcelain.
TEL: 020 7229 3727; FAX: 020 7376 1501
EMAIL: colindmonk@yahoo.co.uk

Omar Nabi Ozbek
Eastern works of art.

Christopher Sheppard
Ancient and antique glass.
TEL: 020 7937 3450

Sandy Stanley
20th C jewellery and metalware.
TEL: 07973 147072
EMAIL: info@net-jewels.co.uk
WEBSITE: www.net-jewels.co.uk

Mary Wise & Grosvenor Antiques   BADA
(Elisabeth Lorie)
English porcelain, bronzes and Oriental works of art.
TEL: 020 7937 8649
EMAIL: info@wiseantiques.com
WEBSITE: www.wiseantiuqes.com

The Lacquer Chest

71 and 75 Kensington Church St. W8 4BG. (G. and V.
Andersen)
EST. 1959. Open 9.30-5.30, Sat. 10.30-4.30. *STOCK:
Furniture - painted, oak, mahogany; blue and white,
Staffordshire, lamps, candlesticks, samplers, prints, paintings,
brass, mirrors, garden furniture, unusual items.* LOC: Half-
way up left-hand side from High St. SIZE: Large. PARK:
Meters. VAT: Stan/Spec.
TEL: 020 7937 1306; FAX: 020 7376 0223

Lev (Antiques) Ltd

97a & b Kensington Church St. W8 7LN. (Mrs Lev)
EST. 1882. Open 10.30-5.30. *STOCK: Jewellery, silver,
plate, curios and pictures.* SER: Restorations (pictures).
SIZE: Medium. PARK: Meters.
TEL: 020 7727 9248

London Antique Gallery

66e Kensington Church St. W8 4BY. (Mr and Mrs
C.D. Wertheim)
Open Mon.-Fri. 10-6. *STOCK: Japanese earthenware, porcelain,
swords and other Japanese 3D works.* SER: Restorations.
TEL: 020 7229 2934; FAX: same

E. and H. Manners   BADA

**66a Kensington Church St. W8 4BY. (Errol and
Henriette Manners)**
EST. **1986 KCSADA. Open Mon.-Fri. 10-5.30**
appointment advisable. *STOCK: European ceramics, pre-
19th C.* VAT: Spec. FAIRS: International Ceramic.
TEL: 020 7229 5516; FAX: same; HOME: 020 8741 7084
E-MAIL: manners@europeanporcelain.com
WEBSITE: www.europeanporcelain.com

S. Marchant & Son   BADA

**120 Kensington Church St. W8 4BH. (R.P. and S.J.
Marchant)**
EST. **1925. KCSADA. Open 9.30-5.30. CL: Sat.** *STOCK:
Chinese and Japanese pottery and porcelain, jades,
cloisonné, Chinese furniture and paintings; blanc de
Chine; Ming and Qing porcelain.* SER: Valuations;
advisory service. PARK: Meters. VAT: Stan/Spec.

FAIRS: Grosvenor House; New York (March).
TEL: **020 7229 5319 or 020 7229 3770**; FAX: **020 7792 8979**
E-MAIL: **gallery@marchantasianart.com**
WEBSITE: **www.marchantique.com**

R. and G. McPherson Antiques   BADA

**40 Kensington Church St. W8 4BX. (Robert and
Georgina McPherson)**
EST. **1985. KCSADA. Open 10-5.30.** *STOCK: Chinese,
Japanese and other southeast Asian ceramics, including
Song monochromes, Chinese export ware, shipwreck
ceramics, blue and white and blanc de Chine; some
Continental ceramics.* LOC: **Kensington High St.
underground station.** SER: **Valuations (verbal);
identification.** SIZE: **Large.** PARK: **Meters.** VAT: **Spec.**
FAIRS: **Olympia (June). Asian Art, London (Nov).**
TEL: **020 7937 0812;** FAX: **020 7938 2032;** MOBILE:
07768 432630
E-MAIL: **rmcpherson@orientalceramics.com**
WEBSITE: **www.orientalceramics.com**

Michael Coins

6 Hillgate St., (off Notting Hill Gate). W8 7SR. (M. Gouby)
EST. 1966. Open 10-5. CL: Mon. and Sat. *STOCK: Coins,
English and foreign, 1066 A.D. to date; stamps, banknotes
and general items.* LOC: From Marble Arch to Notting
Hill Gate, turn left at corner of Coronet Cinema. SER:
Valuations; buys at auction. SIZE: Small. PARK: Easy.
VAT: Stan/Spec.
TEL: 020 7727 1518; FAX: 020 7727 1518
WEBSITE: www.michael-coins.co.uk

Millner Manolatos

2 Campden St. W8 7EP. (Arthur Millner and Alex
Manolatos)
EST. 1996. KCSADA. Open Tues.-Fri. 12-6, Sat. 12-4.30.
*STOCK: Indian objects, 10th-19th C, up to £8,000; Indian
paintings, 17th-19th C, £200-£4,000; Islamic art, 15th-19th
C, £500-£8,000.* LOC: Off Kensington Church St.,
Notting Hill Gate underground station. SER: Valuations;
interior design. SIZE: Small. PARK: Meters. VAT: Spec.
FAIRS: Olympia.
TEL: 020 7229 3268
E-MAIL: info@millnermanolatos.com
WEBSITE: www.millnermanolatos.com

Amir Mohtashemi Ltd

131 Kensington Church St. W8 7LP. (Amir
Mohtashemi and Farah Hakemi)
EST. 1989. KCSADA. Open 10.30-6.30, Sat. 10.30-4.30.
*STOCK: Indian and Islamic works of art especially colonial
items (boxes, ivory and furniture); Islamic tiles, ceramics and
Ottoman furniture; arms and armour.* SER: Valuations. SIZE:
Small. PARK: Nearby. FAIRS: Olympia (Summer).
TEL: 020 7727 2628; FAX: 020 7727 5734
E-MAIL: info@amirmohtashemi.com
WEBSITE: www.amirmohtashemi.com

Pruskin Gallery
73 Kensington Church St. W8 4BG.
KCSADA. Open 10-6, Sat. 11-5. STOCK: *Fine Art Nouveau and Art Deco glass, bronzes, silver, furniture, ceramics, paintings, posters and prints.*
TEL: 020 7937 1994

Raffety & Walwyn Ltd   BADA LAPADA
79 Kensington Church St. W8 4BG.
CINOA. KCSADA. Open 10-6, Sat. 10-5. STOCK: *Fine English longcase and bracket clocks, 17th-18th C; barometers and period furniture.* SER: Valuations; buys at auction. VAT: Stan/Spec. FAIRS: BADA, Olympia (June); Grosvenor House.
TEL: 020 7938 1100; FAX: 020 7938 2519; MOBILE: 07768 096869
E-MAIL: raffety@globalnet.co.uk
WEBSITE: www.raffetyantiqueclocks.com

Paul Reeves
32B Kensington Church St. W8 4HA.
EST. 1976. Open 10-5.30; CL: Tue./Thu./Sat. STOCK: *Architect designed furniture and artefacts, 1860-1960.* VAT: Spec.
TEL: 020 7937 1594; FAX: 020 7938 2163
E-MAIL: paul@paulreeveslondon.com
WEBSITE: www.paulreeveslondon.com

Reindeer Antiques Ltd   BADA LAPADA
81 Kensington Church St. W8 4BG. (Peter Alexander)
KCSADA. Open 9.30-6, Sat. 10.30-5.30. STOCK: *Period English and Continental furniture and works of art.* PARK: Meters. VAT: Stan/Spec. FAIRS: BADA; Olympia (Summer).
TEL: 020 7937 3754; FAX: 020 7937 7199; MOBILE: 07733 323543
E-MAIL: london@reindeerantiques.co.uk
WEBSITE: www.reindeerantiques.co.uk

Roderick Antique Clocks   LAPADA
23 Vicarage Gate, Kensington. W8 4AA. (Roderick Mee)
EST. 1975. Open 10-5.15, Sat. 10-4. STOCK: *Clocks – French decorative and carriage, 19th C, £250-£3,500; English longcase and bracket, 18th-19th C, £2,000-£12,000.* LOC: At junction of Kensington Church St. SER: Valuations; restorations (English and French movements and cases). PARK: Easy. VAT: Spec.
TEL: 020 7937 8517
E-MAIL: rick@roderickantiqueclocks.com
WEBSITE: www.roderickantiqueclocks.com

Brian Rolleston Antiques Ltd   BADA
104A Kensington Church St. W8 4BU.
EST. 1950. KCSADA. Open 10-1 and 2-5.30, Sat. by appointment. STOCK: *English furniture, 18th C.* SIZE: Large. FAIRS: BADA; Grosvenor House.
TEL: 020 7229 5892; FAX: same
E-MAIL: info@brianrolleston.com
WEBSITE: www.brianrolleston.com

Patrick Sandberg Antiques Ltd   BADA LAPADA
150-152 Kensington Church St. W8 4BN. (P.C.F. Sandberg)
EST. 1983. KCSADA. Open 10-6, Sat. 10-4. *STOCK: 18th to early 19th C English furniture and accessories - candlesticks, tea caddies, clocks and prints.* SIZE: **Large.** VAT: Spec. FAIRS: Olympia (June and Nov); BADA.
TEL: **020 7229 0373**; FAX: **020 7792 3467**
E-MAIL: **psand@antiquefurniture.net**
WEBSITE: **www.antiquefurniture.net**

B. Silverman   BADA LAPADA
4 Campden St., Off Kensington Church St. W8 7EP. (Robin Silverman and Bill Brackenbury)
Open 10-6, Sat. 10-4. *STOCK: Fine antique silver including flatware.* SER: Valuations; restorations. SIZE: Large. VAT: Stan/Spec. FAIRS: Olympia; BADA.
TEL: **020 7985 0555/6**
E-MAIL: **silver@silverman-london.com**
WEBSITE: **www.silverman-london.com**

Sinai Antiques Ltd
219-221 Kensington Church St. W8 7LX. (E. Sinai Ltd) EST. 1973 KCSADA. Open 10-6, Sat. and Sun. by appointment. *STOCK: Fine 19th C Continental furniture, clocks, porcelain, chandeliers and objets d'art; Oriental and Islamic decorative arts and antiques.*
TEL: 020 7229 6190; FAX: 020 7221 0543
E-MAIL: sinaiantiquesltd@aol.com

Simon Spero
3A Campden St., Off Kensington Church St. W8 4EP. EST. 1964. KCSADA. Author of *The Price Guide to 18th C English Porcelain* and four other standard reference books. Open 10-5, Sat. by appointment. *STOCK: 18th C English ceramics and enamels.* SER: Valuations; buys at auction; lecturer. SIZE: Medium. PARK: Meters. VAT: Spec.
TEL: 020 7727 7413; FAX: 020 7727 7414

Stockspring Antiques   BADA
114 Kensington Church St. W8 4BH. (Antonia Agnew and Felicity Marno)
EST. **1979.** KCSADA. Open 10-5.30, Sat. 10-1. *STOCK: English, European and Oriental pottery and porcelain.*

LOC: **Notting Hill Gate tube station.** SER: **Packing and shipping;** valuations. SIZE: **2 floors.** PARK: **Meters nearby.** VAT: **Spec.** FAIRS: **Grosvenor House Art & Antiques Fair (June).**
TEL: **020 7727 7995**; FAX: **same**
E-MAIL: **stockspring@antique-porcelain.co.uk**
WEBSITE: **www.antique-porcelain.co.uk**

Through the Looking Glass Ltd
137 Kensington Church St. W8 7LP. (J.J.A. and D.A. Pulton)
EST. 1958. KCSADA. Open 10-5.30. *STOCK: English, French and Continental mirrors, 19th C, £500–£10,000.* LOC: 200yds. from Notting Hill Gate. SIZE: Medium. PARK: Side roads. VAT: Spec.
TEL: 020 7221 4026; FAX: same
E-MAIL: ttlg@btconnect.com
WEBSITE: www.throughthelookingglass.co.uk

Jorge Welsh Oriental Porcelain   BADA
& Works of Art
116 Kensington Church St. W8 4BH.
EST. 1987. KCSADA. Open 9.30-5.30. *STOCK: Chinese export porcelain and Oriental works of art.* LOC: **Off Kensington High St.** SER: Valuations; restorations; buys at auction. SIZE: Medium. PARK: NCP Bayswater Rd. VAT: Spec. FAIRS: International Ceramic.
TEL: **020 7229 2140**; FAX: **020 7792 3535**
E-MAIL: **uk@jorgewelsh.com**
WEBSITE: **www.jorgewelsh.com**

Simon Westman   BADA
66b Kensington Church St. W8 4BY.
Open 9.30-5.30, Sat. by appointment. *STOCK: Early English pottery; creamware, English Delftware.*
TEL: **020 7221 8302**; MOBILE: **07976 821 869**
E-MAIL: **info@simonwestman.com**
WEBSITE: **www.simonwestman.com**

W9

Cox Interiors Ltd
5 Formosa St., Little Venice. W9 1EE. (Kaley Cox) EST. 1994. Open 10-6. *STOCK: French and Italian*

furniture, 18th-20th C; lighting, including chandeliers and lanterns, mirrors; painted, decorative, fruitwood and walnut furniture. SER: Restorations; upholstery; interior design service. SIZE: Medium. PARK: Easy.
TEL: 020 7266 2620; FAX: 020 7266 2622
E-MAIL: info@coxinteriors.com
WEBSITE: www.coxinteriors.com

Robert Hall
PO Box 55608. W9 1SW.
EST. 1976. Open by appointment. *STOCK: Chinese snuff bottles, Qing dynasty; Oriental works of art, 17th-19th C; all £300-£20,000; contemporary Chinese paintings.* SER: Buys at auction. VAT: Stan/Spec. FAIRS: Maastricht (TEFAF); Asian Art, New York; Olympia (June).
TEL: 020 7624 9300 FAX: 020 7624 9301
E-MAIL: roberthall@snuffbottle.com
WEBSITE: www.snuffbottle.com

The Studio
(John Beer)
Open by appointment. *STOCK: Arts and Crafts, Gothic and Art Deco, especially furniture, 1830-1960s.* SER: Valuations; buys at auction.
TEL: 07976 704306 or 07828 930050
WEBSITE: www.osbornandmercer.com

Vale Antiques
245 Elgin Ave., Maida Vale. W9 1NJ. (P. Gooley)
Open 10.30-6. *STOCK: General antiques and eclectic curiosities.*
TEL: 020 7328 4796

W10

Crawley and Asquith Ltd   BADA
Lichfield Studios, 123 Oxford Gardens. W10 6NE.
Open by appointment. *STOCK: 18th-19th C paintings; 18th-19th C prints (natural history and topography).*
TEL: 020 8969 6161; FAX: 020 8960 6494
E-MAIL: azasquith@crawleyandasquith.com

W11

Admiral Vernon Antiques Market
141-149 Portobello Rd. W11 2DY. (Portobello Group)
EST. 1995. PADA. Open Sat. 5-5. *STOCK: Wide range of general antiques and collectables.* SER: Valuations; repairs (pens, jewellery, watches, and lighters). SIZE: 200+ dealers.
TEL: 020 7727 5240; MOBILE: 07956 851283
E-MAIL: leeclifford@portobellogroup.com
WEBSITE: www.portobellogroup.com

Alexandra Alfandary   LAPADA
Gallery 85, 85 Portobello Rd. W11 2QB
EST. 1976. CINOA. Open Weds.-Fri. 10.30-4, Sat 8-5, or any day by appointment. *STOCK: Meissen and other fine European porcelain.* SER: Help to build collections; shipping quotes; porcelain restoration. VAT: Spec.
FAIRS: Olympia (Summer and Winter).

TEL: 07956 993233; FAX: 020 7727 4352
E-MAIL: alex@alfandaryantiques.co.uk
WEBSITE: www.finemeissen.com

Alice's
86 Portobello Rd. W11 2QD. (D. Carter)
EST. 1960. Open Tues.-Fri. 9-5, Sat. 7-4. *STOCK: General antiques and decorative items.* SIZE: Large.
TEL: 020 7229 8187; FAX: 020 7792 2456

Arbras Gallery
292 Westbourne Grove. W11 2PS.
EST. 1972. Open Fri. 10-4, Sat. 7-5. *STOCK: General antiques – silver, cutlery, jewellery, glass, porcelain, decorative arts and antiquities.* LOC: 50 yards from Portobello Road. SIZE: 2 floors. VAT: Stan/Spec.
TEL: 020 7229 6772; FAX: same
E-MAIL: info@arbrasgallery.co.uk
WEBSITE: www.arbrasgallery.co.uk

Atlam Silver & Watches   LAPADA
111 Portobello Rd. W11 2QB (Geoffrey Knowles and Bettina Skogland-Kirk)
Open 10-4, Sat 7-5. *STOCK: Silver, antique pocket watches.*
TEL: 020 7602 7573; FAX: 020 7602 2997; MOBILE: 07860 519600
E-MAIL: info@atlam-watches.co.uk
WEBSITE: www.atlam-watches.co.uk
www.atlamsilver.co.uk

Axia Art Consultants Ltd
121 Ledbury Rd. W11 2AQ. (Yanni Petsopoulos)
EST. 1974. Open Mon.-Fri. 10-6. *STOCK: Works of art, icons, textiles, metalwork, woodwork and ceramics, Islamic and Byzantine.*
TEL: 020 7727 9724; FAX: 020 7229 1272
E-MAIL: axia@axia-art.com

B&T Antiques   LAPADA
47 Ledbury Rd. W11 2AA. (Mrs Bernadette Lewis)
EST. 1984. Open 10-6. *STOCK: Furniture especially mirrored, silver, lighting, objets d'art, Art Deco.* LOC: Notting Hill. SER: Restorations. SIZE: 2 floors. PARK: Easy. VAT: Stan/Spec.
TEL: 020 7229 7001
E-MAIL: email@bntantiques.co.uk
WEBSITE: www.bntantiques.co.uk

Sebastiano Barbagallo
15 Pembridge Rd., Notting Hill Gate. W11 3HG.
EST. 1975. Open 10.30-6 including Sun., Sat. 9-7. *STOCK: Chinese furniture; antiques and handicrafts from India, Tibet, SE Asia and China.* LOC: Just before Portobello Road. SIZE: Medium. VAT: Stan.
TEL: 020 7792 3320; FAX: same
E-MAIL: sebastianobarbagallo@hotmail.com

Barham Antiques
83 Portobello Rd. W11 2QB. (M.J. Barham and R.P. Barham)

EST. 1954. PADA. Open 10.30-5, Sat. 7.30-5. *STOCK: Victorian and Georgian writing boxes, tea caddies, inkwells and inkstands, glass epergnes, silver plate, clocks, paintings, Victorian furniture, tantalus and jewellery boxes.* SER: Valuations; buys at auction. SIZE: Large.
TEL: 020 7727 3845; FAX: same
E-MAIL: mchlbarham@aol.com
WEBSITE: www.barhamantiques.co.uk

Caira Mandaglio LAPADA
Arch 18, Kingsdown Close, Bartle Rd. W11 1RF. (Sharon Moore-Daniel)
Open by appointment. *STOCK: 20th C decorative arts.*
TEL: 020 7243 6035; MOBILE: 07836 354632
E-MAIL: caira_mandaglio@btopenworld.com
WEBSITE: www.cairamandaglio.co.uk

Central Gallery (Portobello)
125 Portobello Rd. W11 2DY. (C. Hickey)
EST. 1996. Open Sat. 6-3. *STOCK: Jewellery - 18th C to 1960s, including cameos, hardstone, shell, lava, coral, amber, ivory, jet, tortoiseshell, piqué, micro-mosaics, pietra-dura, Art Nouveau, plique à jour, horn pendants, Art Deco, enamels, Austro-Hungarian, cut-steel, Berlin iron, Scottish, Victorian silver and gold, Alberts, Albertines, longuards, curbs, gates, fobs, seals, intaglios, pocket watches, vintage wristwatches, cufflinks, fine diamonds, rare gemstones, signed pieces, pearls, platinum jewellery; from £50-£5,000+.* LOC: Notting Hill. SIZE: 25+ dealers. PARK: Pay and Display. VAT: Stan/Spec/Global. FAIRS: Olympia; Park Lane Hotel; NEC.
TEL: 020 7243 8027; FAX: same
WEBSITE: www.centralgallery.com

Chelsea Clocks & Antiques
73 Portobello Rd., Notting Hill. W11 2QB. (Peter Dixon)
EST. 1978. Open 10-5. *STOCK: English, French and German clocks, especially dial, 1800-1930, £150-£10,000; brass, fireplace tools, stationery items, globes, boxes, scales, barometers.* SIZE: Small. PARK: Easy.
TEL: 020 7229 7762; FAX: 020 7274 5198
E-MAIL: info@chelseaclocks.co.uk
WEBSITE: www.chelseaclocks.co.uk

Garrick D. Coleman
75 Portobello Rd. W11 2QB.
EST. 1944. Open 10.30-4.30, Sat. 8.30-3.30. *STOCK: Chess sets, 1750-1880, £300-£15,000; works of art £50-£3,000; glass paperweights, £200-£3,000; also conjuring and magic items.* VAT: Stan/Spec.
TEL: 020 7937 5524; FAX: 020 7937 5530
WEBSITE: www.antiquechess.co.uk

Sheila Cook Textiles
105-107 Portobello Rd. W11 2QB.
EST. 1970. Open by appointment only. *STOCK: Textiles, costume and accessories, 1750-1980, £15-£3,000.* SER: Valuations. SIZE: Small. PARK: Meters. VAT: Global.
TEL: 020 7792 8001; FAX: 020 7243 1744
E-MAIL: sheilacook@sheilacook.co.uk
WEBSITE: www.sheilacook.co.uk

Crown Arcade
119 Portobello Rd. W11 2DY. (Angelo Soteriades)
EST. 1986. PADA. Open Sat. 5.30-5. *STOCK: 18th-19th C glass, bronzes, sculpture, silver, jewellery, Arts & Crafts, Art Nouveau, Art Deco, treen, boxes, humidors, tortoishell, ivory, Austrian glass, pewter, decorative prints, Italian glass, decanters, decorative objects.* LOC: Near Westbourne Grove Corner. SER: Valuations. SIZE: Medium, 25 stalls.
TEL: 020 7436 9416; 020 7792 3619 (Sat. only);
MOBILE: 07956 277077
WEBSITE: www.portobelloroad.co.uk

Cur· Antiques
1st Floor, 34 Ledbury Rd. W11 2AB. (G. and M. Antichi)
Open 11-6, Sat. 10.30-1. *STOCK: Continental furniture, sculptures, majolica and paintings.*
TEL: 020 7229 6880
E-MAIL: mail@cura-antiques.com
WEBSITE: www.cura-antiques.com

Daggett Gallery LAPADA
1st and 2nd Floors, 153 Portobello Rd. W11 2DY. (Caroline Daggett)
EST. 1992. Open 10-5 (prior telephone call advisable). *STOCK: Frames, 18th-20th C, from £1.* LOC: **200 yards from Westbourne Grove towards Elgin Crescent.** SER: **Restorations (frames); gilding; framing.** SIZE: **Medium.** PARK: **Meters.** VAT: **Stan/Spec.**
TEL: 020 7229 2248

Delehar
146 Portobello Rd. W11 2DZ.
EST. 1919. Open Sat. 9-4. *STOCK: General antiques, works of art. NOT STOCKED: Furniture.* SIZE: Medium. VAT: Spec.
TEL: 020 7727 9860
E-MAIL: peter@peterdelehar.co.uk
WEBSITE: www.peterdelehar.co.uk

Gavin Douglas Fine Antiques Ltd LAPADA
75 Portobello Rd. W11 2QB. (G.A. Douglas)
EST. 1993. PADA. CINOA. Open 10.30-4.30, Sat. 7.30-5. *STOCK: Neo-classical clocks, 18th-19th C, to £100,000; bronzes, sculpture, porcelain and objects, to £50,000.* SER: Valuations; restorations; buys at auction. SIZE: Medium. PARK: Easy. VAT: Stan/Spec. FAIRS: Olympia (Winter); LAPADA.
TEL: 020 7221 1121; 01825 723441; FAX: 01825 724418; MOBILE: 07860 680521
E-MAIL: gavin@antique-clocks.co.uk
WEBSITE: www.antique-clocks.co.uk

Judy Fox LAPADA
81 Portobello Rd. W11 2QB.
EST. 1970. Open 10-5. *STOCK: Furniture and decorative items, 18th-20th C; inlaid furniture, mainly 19th C; pottery and porcelain.* SIZE: Large. VAT: Stan.

TEL: 020 7229 8130; FAX: 020 7229 6998
E-MAIL: judy@judy-fox.com
WEBSITE: www.judy-fox.com

David Glick Antique Glass
300 Westbourne Grove. W11 2PS.
Sat. or by appointment. STOCK: Specialist in English and
European glass 1700-1870
TEL: 07850 615867; FAX: 020 8365 2069
WEBSITE: www.davidglickantiqueglass.com

Good Fairy Antiques Market
100 Portobello Rd. W11 2QD.
Open Sat. 4am-5pm. STOCK: Antiques and bric-a-brac.
SIZE: 50 covered stalls.
TEL: (dealer/stall enquiries) 020 7385 2525; MOBILE:
07770 432169
WEBSITE: www.goodfairyantiques.co.uk

Henry Gregory
82 Portobello Rd. W11 2QD. (H. and C. Gregory)
EST. 1969. Open 10-4, Sat. 8-5. STOCK: Antique silver
and decorative objects, vintage sports items and luggage.
Custom vintage leather trunks. LOC: Between Westbourne
Grove and Chepstow Villas. SER: Export packing and
shipping. SIZE: Medium. PARK: Easy. VAT: Stan/Spec.
TEL: 020 7792 9221; FAX: same
E-MAIL: shop@henrygregoryantiques.com
WEBSITE: www.henrygregoryantiques.com

The Harris's Arcade
161-163 Portobello Rd. W11 2DY. (Angelo Soteriades)
EST. 1951. PADA. Open Fri.and Sat. and by
appointment. STOCK: General antiques including ethnic
antiquities, bronzes, ivory statues, jade, precious metals, silver
and plate, drinking vessels, costumes, Oriental and Western
porcelain, furniture, collectables, prints, lace, linen, books,
manuscripts, paintings, etchings, sporting memorabilia,
Tibetan, East and South East Asian antiquities, decorative
arts and designer objects, jewellery - gold, silver, pearls, semi-
precious stones. SER: Valuations; shipping. SIZE: 40 dealers.
TEL: 020 7727 5242; FAX: same; MOBILE: 07956 277077
WEBSITE: www.portobelloroad.co.uk

Hickmet Fine Arts   LAPADA
75 Portobello Rd. W11 2QB. (David Hickmet)
EST. 1936. CINOA. PADA. Open Wed.-Fri.10-4, Sat.
8-4. STOCK: Art Deco sculpture, £500-£50,000; Art glass,
£200-£20,000. SER: Valuations; commission purchases.
SIZE: Medium. PARK: Easy. VAT: Spec. FAIRS:
Olympia; LAPADA; NEC; Harrogate.
TEL: 01342 841508; MOBILE: 07050 123450; FAX:
01342 841879
E-MAIL: david@hickmet.com
WEBSITE: www.hickmet.com

Hirst Antiques
59 Pembridge Rd. W11 3HG.
EST. 1963. Open 10-6. STOCK: Four poster and half-tester

beds; decorative furniture and articles; bronze and marble
sculpture; vintage costume jewellery. LOC: Start of
Portobello Rd., near Notting Hill Gate underground
station. SER: Valuations; repairs (jewellery). SIZE:
Medium.
TEL: 020 7727 9364
E-MAIL: amandatomlinson@yahoo.com
WEBSITE: www.hirstantiques.co.uk

Humbleyard Fine Art
141-149 Portobello Rd. W11 2DY. (James Layte)
EST. 1973. PADA. Open Sat. 6-2. STOCK: Scientific,
medical and marine items, sailors' woolworks, shell
valentines, primitive pictures, needleworks, boxes, pottery
and curiosities, 18th-19th C, £50-£5,000. SER: Valuations.
SIZE: Small. PARK: Easy. VAT: Spec. FAIRS: Olympia
(June, Nov); Decorative (Jan., Sept); Little Chelsea
(April, Oct); Scientific Instrument (April, Oct).
TEL: 01362 637793; FAX: same; MOBILE: 07836
349416

Jones Antique Lighting
194 Westbourne Grove. W11 2RH. (Judy Jones)
EST. 1978. Open 9.30-6 or by appointment. STOCK:
Original decorative lighting, 1860-1960. SER: Valuations;
repairs; prop hire. SIZE: Large. PARK: Meters. VAT: Stan.
TEL: 020 7229 6866; FAX: 020 7243 3547
E-MAIL: judy@jonesantiquelighting.com
WEBSITE: www.jonesantiquelighting.com

Kleanthous Antiques Ltd   LAPADA
**144 Portobello Rd. W11 2DZ. (Chris Kleanthous and
Costas Kleanthous)**
EST. 1969. Open Sat. 8.30-4. STOCK: Vintage watches,
clocks, jewellery, silver, 19th & 20th C furniture, works of
art. VAT: Stan. FAIRS: Olympia (June and Nov.),
LAPADA (May).
TEL: 020 7727 3649; FAX: 020 7243 2488; MOBILE:
07850 375501
E-MAIL: antiques@kleanthous.com
WEBSITE: www.kleanthous.com

Lacy Gallery
203 Westbourne Grove. W11 2SB. (Colin and David
Lacy)
EST. 1960. Open Wed.-Fri. 10-5, Sat. 10-4. STOCK:
Period frames, 1700 to secondhand modern; decorative
paintings and art, posters; 20th C paintings from St.
Petersburg. LOC: Two roads east of Portobello Rd. SIZE:
Large. PARK: Meters. VAT: Stan/Spec.
TEL: 020 7229 6340; FAX: 020 7229 9105

M. and D. Lewis
1 Lonsdale Rd. W11 2BY.
EST. 1960. Open 9.30-5.30, Sat. 9.30-4. STOCK:
Continental and Victorian furniture, porcelain, bronzes.
VAT: Stan.
TEL: 020 7727 3908
E-MAIL: mdlewisantiques@hotmail.com

B. Lipka & Son Arcade
282-290 Westbourne Grove. W11 2PS.
Open Sat. 6.30-5. *STOCK: General miniature antiques, silver and jewellery.* SER: Valuations; restorations. SIZE: 150 dealers.
TEL: (dealer/stall enquiries) 020 7727 5240
WEBSITE: www.portobelloroad.co.uk

M.C.N. Antiques   LAPADA
183 Westbourne Grove. W11 2SB.
EST. 1971. Open 10-6, Sat. 11-3 or by appointment.
STOCK: Japanese porcelain, cloisonné, Satsuma, bronze, lacquer, ivory. **LOC: Near Portobello Rd. market. PARK: Easy. VAT: Stan.**
TEL: 020 7727 3796; FAX: 020 7229 8839; MOBILE: 07769 652432
E-MAIL: makotoumezawa@hotmail.com

Robin Martin Antiques
44 Ledbury Rd. W11 2AB. (Paul Martin)
EST. 1972. Open 10-6. *STOCK: English and Continental furniture and works of art, 17th-19th C.* LOC: Westbourne Grove area. SIZE: Medium. VAT: Spec. FAIRS: Olympia (June and Nov).
TEL: 020 7727 1301; FAX: same; MOBILE: 07831 544055
E-MAIL: paul.martin11@btconnect.com

David Martin-Taylor Antiques   LAPADA
Geoffrey Van Arcade 105 Portobello Rd. W11 2QB.
(Mr Christian Cavet)
Open Sat., or by appointment in Chelsea.
TEL: 020 7842 8200; FAX: 020 7824 8202; MOBILE: 07889 437306
E-MAIL: dmt@davidmartintaylor.com
WEBSITE: www.davidmartintaylor.com

Mercury Antiques   BADA
1 Ladbroke Rd. W11 3PA. (L. Richards)
EST. 1963. Open 10-5.30, CL: Sat. *STOCK: English porcelain, 1745-1840; English pottery and Delft, 1700-1820. NOT STOCKED: Jewellery, silver, plate, Art Nouveau.* **LOC: From Notting Hill Gate underground station, turn into Pembridge Rd., bear left. SIZE: Medium. VAT: Spec.**
TEL: 020 7727 5106; FAX: 020 7229 3738
E-MAIL: richards@mercuryantiques.com
WEBSITE: www.mercuryantiques.com

Mimi Fifi
27 Pembridge Rd., Notting Hill Gate. W11 3HG. (Mrs Rita Delaforge)
EST. 1990. Open 11-6.30, Sat. 10-7, Sun. 11-4. *STOCK: Vintage and collectable toys, especially Snoopy, Smurfs, Betty Boop, Simpsons, and memorabilia, 20th C, £5-£500; perfume miniatures and related collectables, 19th-20th C, £5-£1,000; perfume bottles by appointment.* LOC: 200 yards from Notting Hill underground station. SER: Shipping overseas. SIZE: Medium. PARK: Nearby.
TEL: 020 7243 3154; FAX: 01932 225272
WEBSITE: www.mimififi.com

Myriad Antiques
131 Portland Rd., Holland Park Ave. W11 4LW. (S. Nickerson)
EST. 1970. Open Tues.-Sat. 11-6. CL: Aug. *STOCK: Decorative and unusual furniture (including garden) and objects, mainly Continental, 19th 20th C, £20-£2,500.* LOC: Between Notting Hill Gate and Shepherds Bush roundabout. Nr Clarendon Cross. SIZE: Large PARK: Meters. VAT: Stan.
TEL: 020 7229 1709; FAX: 020 7221 3882
E-MAIL: myriadantiques@gmail.com

The Nanking Porcelain Co. Ltd
20L-26L, Admiral Vernon Arcade, 141-149 Portobello Rd. W11 2DY. (Maurice Hyams and Elizabeth Porter)
EST. 1986. Open Sat. 8.30-3.30. *STOCK: Chinese export porcelain, Oriental ivories, Chinese taste porcelain and works of art.* SER: Valuations. SIZE: Large. VAT: Spec. FAIRS: Hong Kong Arts of Asia (May).
TEL: 020 7924 2349; FAX: 020 7924 2352; MOBILE: 07836 594885
E-MAIL: nankingporcelain@aol.com

Piano Nobile Fine Paintings
129 Portland Rd., Holland Park. W11 4LW. (Dr Robert A. Travers)
EST. 1986. SLAD. Open 10.30-5.30; CL: Mon. *STOCK: Fine 19th C Impressionist and 20th C Post-Impressionist and Modern British and Continental oil paintings and sculpture, Les Petit Maitres of the Paris Schools; modern & contemporary painters; exclusively represent Adam Birtwistle, Peter Coker RA, Jean Cooke RA, Dora Holzhandler, Leslie Marr & Greg Trickler. £100-£250,000.* SER: Valuations; restorations (paintings and sculptures); framing; buys at auction (19th-20th C oil paintings). SIZE: Medium. PARK: Easy. FAIRS: Grosvenor; 20th C British Art; Olympia; BADA; Art London.
TEL: 020 7229 1099; FAX: same
E-MAIL: info@piano-nobile.com
WEBSITE: www.piano-nobile.com

Portobello Antique Store
79 Portobello Rd. W11 2QB. (T.J. Evans)
EST. 1971. Open Tues.-Fri. 10-4, Sat. 8.15-4. *STOCK: Silver and plate, £2-£3,000.* LOC: Notting Hill end of Portobello Rd. SER: Export. SIZE: Large. PARK: Easy weekdays. VAT: Stan.
TEL: 020 7221 1994.
E-MAIL: info@tjevansantiques.com
WEBSITE: www.tjevansantiques.com

Principia Fine Art
9-10 Lipka Arcade, 328 Westbourne Grove. W11 2PS. (Michael Forrer)
EST. 1970. Open Sat. 7-1 *STOCK: Collectors' items, scientific instruments, maritime, country furniture, treen, pictures, Oriental china, porcelain, books and clocks.* SER: Valuations. Also at Marlborough and Hungerford antiques centres. SIZE: Small. FAIRS: Scientific Instrument; NEC.
FAX: 0118 934 1989; MOBILE: 07899 926020

Pruskin Gallery
96 Portland Road. W11 4LQ.
Open 10-6, Sat. 11-5. STOCK: *Furniture, paintings, lighting and mirrors.*
TEL: 020 7243 1568

Quadrille at Delehar
146 Portobello Rd. W11 2DZ. (Valerie Jackson-Harris)
Open Sat. 9-4. STOCK: *Ephemera, especially Royal and rare commemoratives, performing arts, Valentines, children's toys, games and unusual items appertaining to the history of London.* FAIRS: Ephemera Society; ABA.
TEL: 01923 829079; FAX: 01923 825207

The Red Lion Antiques Arcade
165-169 Portobello Rd. W11 2DY. (Angelo Soteriades)
EST. 1951. PADA. Open Sat. 5.30-5.30. STOCK: *General antiques including ethnic antiquities, bronzes, ivory statues, jade, precious metals, dolls, silver and plate, drinking vessels, costumes, Oriental and Western porcelain, furniture, collectables, prints, lace, linen, books, manuscripts, stamps, coins, banknotes, paintings, etchings, sporting memorabilia, Tibetan, East and South East Asian antiquities, decorative arts and designer objects, jewellery - gold, silver, pearls, semi-precious stones.* SER: Valuations; shipping. SIZE: 60 dealers.
TEL: 020 7727 5242; FAX: same; MOBILE: 07956 277077
WEBSITE: www.portobelloroad.co.uk

Rezai Persian Carpets
123 Portobello Rd. W11 2DY. (A. Rezai)
EST. 1966. Open 10-5. STOCK: *Oriental carpets, kilims, tribal rugs, tapestries, runners, Aubussons and silk embroideries.* LOC: Notting Hill. SER: Valuations; cleaning and restorations. PARK: Offstreet. VAT: Stan.
TEL: 020 7221 5012
E-MAIL: rezaimail@aol.com
WEBSITE: www.rezaipersiancarpets.co.uk

Rogers Antiques Gallery
65 Portobello Rd. W11 2QB. (Bath Antiques Market Ltd)
EST. 1965. Open Sat. 7-4. STOCK: *First and longest market in Portobello Rd, provides the eclectic mix for which the road is famous. Below are listed the dealers found at this market.*
SER: Valuations. SIZE: 40+ dealers.
TEL: 020 7267 3417 (M-F); 020 7727 1262 (Sat. only); 07887 527523 (management)

Schredds of Portobello   LAPADA
107 Portobello Rd. W11 2QB. (H.J. and G.R. Schrager)
EST. 1969. Open Sat. 7.30-3. STOCK: *Silver, 17th-19th C, £10-£5,000; Wedgwood, 18th-19th C.* LOC: Portobello Market. SER: Valuations; buys at auction; worldwide shipping. SIZE: Small. PARK: Free after 1.30 pm. VAT: Stan/Spec. FAIRS: Antiques for Everyone, Birmingham.
TEL: 020 8348 3314; HOME: same; FAX: 020 8341 5971
E-MAIL: silver@shredds.com
WEBSITE: www.schredds.com

The Silver Fox Gallery (Portobello)
121 Portobello Rd. W11 2DY. (C. Hickey)
EST. 1993. Open Sat. 6-3. STOCK: *Jewellery - 18th C to 1960s including Victorian, Art Nouveau, Arts & Crafts, Art Deco, rings (diamond and gem-set), earrings, brooches, pendants, gold and silver, Alberts, Albertines, chains longuards, bracelets, curbs, gates, fobs, seals, intaglios, pocket watches, vintage wristwatches, cufflinks, fine diamonds, rare gemstones, cameos, coral, amber, ivory, jet tortoiseshell, piqué, micro-mosaics, pietra-dura, lava, horn pendants, enamels, pearls, Austro-Hungarian cut steel, Berlin iron, Scottish, niello, £50-£5,000+.* LOC: Notting Hill.
SIZE: 25+ dealers. PARK: Pay and Display. VAT: Stan/Spec/Global. FAIRS: Olympia; Park Lane Hotel; NEC.
TEL: 020 7243 8027; FAX: same
WEBSITE: www.silverfoxgallery.com

Justin F. Skrebowski Prints
Ground Floor, 177 Portobello Rd. W11 2DY.
EST. 1985. Open Sat. 9-4, other times by appointment. STOCK: *Prints, engravings and lithographs, 1700-1850, £50-£500; oil paintings, 1700-1900, £200-£1,500; watercolours, drawings including Old Masters, 1600-1900, £50-£1,000; modern folio stands and easels; frames - gilt, rosewood, maple, carved, 18th-19th C.* SER: Valuations. SIZE: Small. PARK: Meters. VAT: Stan/Spec. FAIRS: PBFA; Hotel Russell (Monthly).
TEL: 020 7792 9742; MOBILE: 07774 612474
E-MAIL: justin@skreb.co.uk
WEBSITE: www.skreb.co.uk

Colin Smith & Gerald Robinson Antiques   LAPADA
The Van Arcade, 105 Portobello Rd. W11 2QB.
EST. 1979. Open Sat. 9-3.30; Fri. by appointment.
STOCK: *Rare and wonderful objects.* SIZE: Large. VAT: Stan. FAIRS: Olympia.
TEL: 020 8994 3783 or 020 7225 1163
E-MAIL: cwsmith@ukonline.co.uk
WEBSITE: www.smithandrobinson.com

Stern Pissarro Gallery
46 Ledbury Rd. W11 2AB. (David Stern)
EST. 1963. SLAD. Open 10-6. STOCK: *Camille Pissaro and his descendants together with British and European 19th C painting.* LOC: Off Westbourne Grove near Portobello. SER: Valuations; restorations. SIZE: Medium. PARK: Easy. VAT: Stan.
TEL: 020 7229 6187; FAX: 020 7229 7016
E-MAIL: stern@pissarro.com
WEBSITE: www.stern-art.com

Temple Gallery   BADA
6 Clarendon Cross. W11 4AP. (R.C.C. Temple)
EST. 1959. Open 10-6, weekends and evenings by appointment. STOCK: *Icons, Russian and Greek, 12th-16th C, £1,000-£50,000.* SER: Valuations; restorations; buys at auction (icons); illustrated catalogues published. SIZE: Large. PARK: Easy. VAT: Spec.
TEL: 020 7727 3809; FAX: 020 7727 1546
E-MAIL: info@templegallery.com
WEBSITE: www.templegallery.com

The Red Teapot Arcade
101-103 Portobello Rd. W11 2BQ.
Open Sat. 6-4. STOCK: *Clocks, fountain pens, silver, Scottish jewellery, wristwatches etc.*
TEL: 020 7727 5240; FAX: same; MOBILE: 07956 277077

Themes and Variations
231 Westbourne Grove. W11 2SE. (L. Fawcett)
Open 10-1 and 2-6, Sat 10-6. STOCK: *Post-war and contemporary decorative arts, furniture, glass, ceramics, carpets, lamps, jewellery.*
TEL: 020 7727 5531; FAX: 020 7221 6378
E-MAIL: go@themesandvariations.com
WEBSITE: www.themesandvariations.com

Christina Truscott
Geoffrey Van Arcade, 105-107 Portobello Rd. W11 2QB.
EST. 1967. PADA. Open Sat. 6.45-3.30. STOCK: *Chinese export lacquer, papier-mâché, tortoiseshell, fans.*
TEL: 01403 730554; (Sat. only) 020 7229 5577
E-MAIL: christinatruscott@btinternet.com
WEBSITE: www.vanarcade.com

Victoriana Dolls
101 Portobello Rd. W11 2BQ. (Mrs H. Bond)
Open Sat. 8-3 or by appointment. STOCK: *Dolls, toys and accessories.* FAIRS: The London International Antique and Artist Dolls, Toys, Miniatures and Teddy Bear Fair.
TEL: (home) 01737 249525
E-MAIL: heatherbond@homecall.co.uk

Virginia
98 Portland Rd., Holland Park. W11 4LQ. (V. Bates)
EST. 1971. Open 11-6, Sat. by appointment. STOCK: *Clothes and lace, 1880-1940, from £100.* LOC: Holland Park Ave. SIZE: Medium. PARK: Easy. VAT: Stan.
TEL: 020 7727 9908; FAX: 020 7229 2198

Johnny Von Pflugh Antiques
286 Westbourne Grove. W11 2PS.
EST. 1985. Open Sat. 8-5 at Portobello Market or by appointment. STOCK: *European works of art, Italian oil paintings, gouaches, 17th-19th C, £300-£1,500; fine ironware, 17th-18th C, £300-£800; medical and scientific instruments, 18th-19th C, £200-£1,000.* SER: Valuations; buys at auction (keys, caskets, medical instruments, Italian oil paintings and gouaches). SIZE: Small. PARK: Easy. VAT: Spec. FAIRS: Olympia (June); Parma, Italy (Sept. & March).
TEL: 020 8740 5306; FAX: 020 8749 2868; MOBILE: 07949 086243
E-MAIL: jvpantiques@london.com

Walpoles BADA. LAPADA
Geoffrey Van Arcade, 107 Portobello Rd. W11 2QB. (Graham Walpole)
EST. 1974. PADA. Open Sat. 7-4. STOCK: *British Army and Navy, campaign and colonial furniture, Chinese export trade and English country house, mid-18th to mid-20th C; fine and folk art.* FAIRS: Olympia (Summer).

TEL: 07831 561042
E-MAIL: info@walpoleantiques.com
WEBSITE: www.walpoleantiques.com

Trude Weaver (Antiques) LAPADA
71 Portobello Rd. W11 2QB.
EST. 1968. Open Fri. 10-6, Sat. 9-6 or by appointment. STOCK: *18th-19th C furniture together with a fine selection if interesting objects and works of art from around the world.* SER: Valuations. SIZE: Medium. PARK: Easy.
TEL: 020 7229 8738; FAX: same; MOBILE: 07788 587635
E-MAIL: trudeweaver@yahoo.co.uk

World Famous Portobello Market
177 Portobello Rd. W11 2DY. (Angelo Soteriades)
EST. 1951. PADA. Open Sat. 5.30-5.30. STOCK: *Stamps, coins, Art Deco, amber, jewellery, oils, watercolours, engravings, prints, maps, books, photographs, objects, teddy bears, toys, dolls, wood, soapstone, Africana, picture frames, ephemera, auction catalogues.* SER: Valuations; framing. SIZE: 60 dealers.
TEL: 020 7727 5242; MOBILE: 07956 277077
WEBSITE: www.portobelloroad.co.uk

W13

W13 Antiques
10 The Avenue, Ealing. W13 8PH.
EST. 1977. Open Sat. 10-5 or by appointment. STOCK: *Furniture, china and general antiques, 18th-20th C.* LOC: Off Uxbridge Rd., West Ealing. SER: Valuations. SIZE: Medium. PARK: Easy. VAT: Stan.
TEL: 020 8998 0390; MOBILE: 07778 177102

W14

Marshall Gallery
67 Masbro Rd. W14 0LS. (D.A. and J. Marshall)
EST. 1978. Resident. Open Wed.-Sat. 10:30-6 STOCK: *French and decorative furniture, £500-£20,000; objects and lighting, £200-£12,000; pictures, from £100; all 18th-20th C.* LOC: Just behind Olympia, off Hammersmith Rd. SER: Restorations (furniture, re-gilding, re-wiring). SIZE: Medium. PARK: Easy. VAT: Spec.
TEL: 020 7602 3317

D. Parikian
3 Caithness Rd. W14 0JB.
EST. 1960. ABA. Open by appointment. STOCK: *Antiquarian books, mythology, iconography, emblemata, Continental books, pre-1800.*
TEL: 020 7603 8375; FAX: 020 7602 1178
E-MAIL: dparikian@mac.com
WEBSITE: www.bibliopoly.com/parikian

J. Roger (Antiques) Ltd BADA
(C. Bayley)
Open by appointment. STOCK: *Late 18th to early 19th C small elegant pieces, furniture, mirrors, prints, porcelain and boxes.*
TEL: 020 7603 7627

SW1

Ackermann & Johnson   BADA
27 Lowndes St. SW1X 9HY. (Peter Johnson)
EST. 1783. Open 9-5.30, Sat. by appointment. *STOCK:
British paintings and watercolours, especially sporting,
marine and landscapes including the Norwich School,
18th-20th C.* LOC: **Opposite Carlton Tower Hotel.**
SER: **Valuations; restorations; framing.** SIZE: **Medium.**
PARK: **Meters.** VAT: **Spec.**
TEL: **020 7235 6464; FAX: 020 7823 1057**
E-MAIL: **ackermannjohnson@btconnect.com**
WEBSITE: **www.artnet.com/ackermann.johnson**

John Adams Fine Art Ltd
Ebury Galleries, 200 Ebury St. SW1W 8UN.
EST. 1980. Open 10-6, Sat. 10-4. *STOCK: Antique and
modern paintings, drawings and watercolours, £1,000-
£25,000.* SER: Valuations; restorations. SIZE: Medium.
PARK: Easy. FAIRS: BADA; Art London.
TEL: 020 7730 8999; FAX: 020 7259 9015
E-MAIL: info@johnadamsfineart.com
WEBSITE: www.johnadamsfineart.com

Verner Åmell Ltd
4 Ryder St., St. James's. SW1Y 6QB. (Verner Åmell.)
EST. 1988. SLAD. Open 10-5.30. CL: Sat. *STOCK: Dutch
and Flemish Old Masters, 16th-17th C; 18th C French and
19th C Scandinavian paintings.* VAT: Spec. FAIRS: TEFAF;
Grosvenor House; Biennale, Paris; Biennale, Florence.
TEL: 020 7925 2759
E-MAIL: leopold.deliss@amells.com
WEBSITE: www.amells.com

Albert Amor Ltd
37 Bury St., St. James's. SW1Y 6AU.
EST. 1903. Open Tues.-Thurs. 9.30-5. *STOCK: 18th to
early 19th C English ceramics, especially first period
Worcester.* SER: Valuations. SIZE: Small. PARK: Meters.
VAT: Spec.
TEL: 020 7930 2444; FAX: 020 7930 9067
E-MAIL: info@albertamor.co.uk
WEBSITE: www.albertamor.co.uk

Anno Domini Antiques   BADA
**66 Pimlico Rd. SW1W 8LS. (F. Bartman and D.
Cohen)**
EST. 1960. Open 10-1 and 2.15-5.30, Sat. 10-3. *STOCK:
Furniture, 17th to early 19th C, £500-£20,000; mirrors,
17th-19th C, £300-£3,000; glass, screens, decorative items
and tapestries, £15-£10,000. NOT STOCKED: Silver,
jewellery, arms, coins.* LOC: **From Sloane Sq. go down
Lower Sloane St., turn left at traffic lights.** SER: **Buys
at auction.** SIZE: **Large.** PARK: **Easy.** VAT: **Stan/Spec.**
TEL: **020 7730 5496; HOME: 020 7352 3084**

Appley Hoare Antiques
22 Pimlico Rd. SW1W 8LJ.
EST. 1980. Open 10.30-6, Sat. 11-5. *STOCK: House and
garden furniture, French 18th-19th C, with original paint
and patination; decorative items; English 18th-19th C stone
ornaments and statuary.* LOC: Corner of Pimlico Green.
SER: Shipping. SIZE: Medium. PARK: Easy. VAT: Spec.
TEL: 020 7730 7070
E-MAIL: appley@appleyhoare.com
WEBSITE: www.appleyhoare.com

Argyll Etkin Gallery
27 Regent St. SW1Y 4UA. (Argyll Etkin Ltd)
EST. 1954. PTS. MS. UACC. Open 9-5.30. CL: Sat.
*STOCK: Classic postage stamps, postal history and covers,
Royal autographs, signed photographs, historical documents
and antique letters, 1400-1950, £50-£25,000; stamp boxes
and associated writing equipment, 1700-1930, £50-£500.*
SER: Valuations; collections purchased. SIZE: Medium.
VAT: Stan. FAIRS: Major stamp exhibitions worldwide.
TEL: 020 7437 7800 (6 lines); FAX: 020 7434 1060
E-MAIL: philatelists@argyll-etkin.com
WEBSITE: www.argyll-etkin.com

The Armoury of St. James's Military Antiquarians
17 Piccadilly Arcade, Piccadilly. SW1Y 6NH.
EST. 1965. GMC. Open 10-6, Sat. 12-4. *STOCK: British
and foreign Orders of Chivalry, 18th C to date, £50-
£50,000; military antiques, including regimental brooches,
drums, bronzes and silver.* LOC: Between Piccadilly and
Jermyn St. SER: Valuations. SIZE: Small. VAT: Stan/Spec.
TEL: 020 7493 5082
E-MAIL: welcome@armoury.co.uk
WEBSITE: www.armoury.co.uk

Hilary Batstone Antiques inc. Rose   LAPADA
Uniacke Design
8 Holbein Place. SW1W 8NL.
EST. 1983. Open 10.30-5.30, Sat. by appointment.
*STOCK: 19th-20th C decorative furniture, mirrors and
lighting.* SER: Interior design. SIZE: Medium. VAT: Spec.
TEL: **020 7730 5335**
E-MAIL: **hilary@hilarybatstone.com**

Chris Beetles Ltd
10 Ryder St., St. James's. SW1Y 6QB.
EST. 1976. Open 10-5.30. *STOCK: English watercolours,
paintings and illustrations, 18th-20th C, £500-£50,000.*
LOC: 100yds. from Royal Academy. SER: Valuations;
framing. SIZE: Large. PARK: Meters. VAT: Spec.
TEL: 020 7839 7551;
E-MAIL: gallery@chrisbeetles.com
WEBSITE: www.chrisbeetles.com

Blanchard Ltd   LAPADA
86-88 Pimlico Rd. SW1W 8PL.
EST. 1990. Open 10-6, Sat. 10-3. *STOCK: English and
Continental furniture, lighting and objets d'art, 1700-
1950.* LOC: Near Sloane Sq. underground station. SER:
Valuations; restorations; buys at auction. SIZE:
Medium. VAT: **Stan/Spec.** FAIRS: **Olympia.**
TEL: **020 7823 6310; FAX: 020 7823 6303**

Anno Domini Antiques

66 Pimlico Road, London S.W.1
020-7730 5496

Fine small Regency rosewood brass inlaid sofa table,
c.1820. 30in. x 12in. x 28½in. (high)

E-MAIL: piers@jwblanchard.com
WEBSITE: www.blanchardcollective.com

John Bly BADA
27 Bury St., St. James's. SW1Y 6AL. (J. and V. Bly)
EST. 1891. CINOA. Open by appointment. STOCK:
*Fine English furniture, silver, glass, porcelain and fine
paintings, 18th-19th C.* SER: Restorations; valuations;
consultancy. FAIRS: BADA; Grosvenor House; W.
Palm Beach.
TEL: 020 7930 1292; FAX: 020 7839 4775
E-MAIL: john@johnbly.com
WEBSITE: www.johnbly.com

J.H. Bourdon-Smith Ltd BADA
24 Mason's Yard, Duke St., St. James's. SW1Y 6BU.
EST. 1954. CINOA. Open 9.30-6. CL: Sat. STOCK:
*Main stock: 1500-1700 £1000-50,000; 1700-1900 £100-
50,000; 1900-present £50-£5000* SER: Valuations;
restorations (silver); buys at auction. SIZE: Medium.
PARK: Meters. VAT: Stan/Spec. FAIRS: Olympia (Nov);
Harrogate; Grosvenor House; BADA; New York.
TEL: 020 7839 4714; FAX: 020 7838 3951
E-MAIL: enquiries@bourdonsmith.co.uk
WEBSITE: www.bourdonsmith.co.uk

Robert Bowman
8 Duke St., St. James's. SW1Y 6BN.
EST. 1992. SLAD. Open Mon.-Fri. 10-6. STOCK:
*European sculpture in bronze, marble and terracotta, 19th C
to date, £3,000-£500,000. Specialists in original sculpture
by Rodin.* SER: Valuations; restorations (bronze, marble
and terracotta). SIZE: Medium. PARK: Meters. VAT:
Spec. FAIRS: Maastricht; Palm Beach; New York;
Chicago.
TEL: 020 7839 3100; FAX: 020 7839 3223
E-MAIL: info@robertbowman.com
WEBSITE: www.robertbowman.com

Brandt Oriental Art
20 Georgian House, 10 Bury St. SW1Y 6AA (R.
Brandt)
EST. 1981. Open by appointment. STOCK: *Oriental works
of art, £500-£10,000.* VAT: Spec.
TEL: 020 7930 9368; FAX: 020 7390 9370; MOBILE:
07774 989661
E-MAIL: brandt@nildram.co.uk

Brisigotti Antiques Ltd
44 Duke St., St. James's. SW1Y 6DD.
Open 9.30-1 and 2-6. STOCK: *European works of art, Old
Master paintings.*
TEL: 020 7839 4441; FAX: 020 7976 1663

John Carlton-Smith BADA
19 Ryder St., St. James's. SW1Y 6PX (John and
Michelle Carlton-Smith)
EST. 1970. Open Mon.-Thurs. 9.30-5.30. Fri. & Sat.
by appointment STOCK: *Clocks, barometers,*
chronometers, 17th-19th C. SER: Valuations. VAT: Spec.
FAIRS: Grosvenor House; BADA (Chelsea)
TEL: 020 7930 6622; FAX: 020 7930 1370; MOBILE:
07967 180682
E-MAIL: jcarltonsm@aol.com
WEBSITE: www.fineantiqueclocks.com

Cavendish Fine Arts BADA
EST. 1972. Open by appointment. STOCK: *Fine Queen
Anne and English Georgian furniture, glass & porcelain.*
FAIRS: Olympia; Chelsea; BADA.
TEL: 020 7823 4722; MOBILE: 07831 295575
E-MAIL: janet@cavendishfinearts.com
WEBSITE: www.cavendishfinearts.com

Chelsea Antique Mirrors
72 Pimlico Rd. SW1W 8LS. (A. Koll)
EST. 1976. Open 10-6, Sat. 10-2. STOCK: *Antique mirrors,
£1,000-£25,000.* SER: Valuations; restorations (gilding).
SIZE: Medium. PARK: Easy.
TEL: 020 7824 8024; FAX: 020 7824 8233

Ciancimino Ltd
85 Pimlico Rd. SW1W 8PH.
Open 10-6, Sat. 11-5. STOCK: *Art Deco furniture, Oriental
art and ethnography.*
TEL: 020 7730 9950 or 020 7730 9959; FAX: 020 7730
5365
E-MAIL: info@ciancimino.com
WEBSITE: www.ciancimino.com

Classic Bindings Ltd
61 Cambridge St. SW1V 4PS. (Sasha Poklewski-
Koziell)
EST. 1989. Open Mon.-Fri. 9.30-5.30 and by appointment.
STOCK: *English and French literature, history and politics, first
editions, travel, illustrated, fine bindings, architecture and
furniture, biographies, natural history and sciences, art and sport.*
LOC: Off Warwick Way, Pimlico. PARK: Easy. FAIRS: ABA,
Olympia and Chelsea; PBFA London.
TEL: 020 7834 5554; FAX: 020 7630 6632
E-MAIL: info@classicbindings.net
WEBSITE: www.classicbindings.net

Cobra and Bellamy
149 Sloane St. SW1X 9BZ. (V. Manussis and T.
Hunter)
EST. 1976. Open 10.30-6. STOCK: *20th C and modern
jewellery, £50-£5,000.* SIZE: Medium. PARK: Meters.
VAT: Stan/Margin.
TEL: 020 7730 9993
E-MAIL: cobrabellamy@hotmail.com
WEBSITE: www.cobrabellamy.co.uk

Kenneth Davis (Works of Art) Ltd
15 King St., St. James's. SW1Y 6QU.
Open 9-5. CL: Sat. STOCK: *Antique silver and works of
art.*
TEL: 020 7930 0313; FAX: 020 7976 1306

Alastair Dickenson Ltd   BADA
**90 Jermyn St. SW1Y 6JD. (Alastair Dickenson and
Melanie Cuchet)**
EST. 2002. CINOA. Open 9.30-5.30, CL: Sat. *STOCK:
Fine English, Irish and Scottish silver, 16th to early 19th
C; unusual silver - vinaigrettes, wine labels, card cases,
caddy spoons, snuff boxes; Arts and Crafts silver including
Omar Ramsden.* LOC: Off Duke St. SER: Valuations;
restorations (repairs, gilding, re-plating), replacement
cruet and ink bottles; buys at auction. SIZE: Small.
PARK: Meters. VAT: Spec.
TEL: 020 7839 2808; FAX: 020 7839 2809; MOBILE:
07976 283530
E-MAIL: adickensonsilver@btconnect.com

Simon C. Dickinson Ltd
58 Jermyn St. SW1Y 6LX. (Simon Dickinson, David
Ker and James Roundell)
EST. 1993 SLAD. Open 10-5.30, Fri. 10-4.30. CL: Sat.
*STOCK: Important Old, Modern and contemporary Master
paintings.* LOC: 2 mins. from Piccadilly. SER: Valuations;
restorations; buys at auction. SIZE: Large. VAT: Spec.
FAIRS: Maastricht.
TEL: 020 7493 0340; FAX: 020 7493 0796
WEBSITE: www.simondickinson.com

Douwes Fine Art Ltd
Apartment 1B, 37 Duke St., St. James's. SW1Y 6DF.
EST. 1805. SLAD. By appointment only. *STOCK: 16th-
20th C paintings, drawings and watercolours, Dutch,
Flemish, French and Russian schools.* SER: Valuations;
restorations. SIZE: Medium. PARK: Meters. VAT: Spec.
FAIRS: TEFAF (Maastricht); PAN (Amsterdam).
TEL: 020 7839 5795
E-MAIL: info@douwesfineart.com
WEBSITE: www.douwesfineart.com

Peter Finer   LAPADA
38-39 Duke St., St. James's. SW1Y 6DF. (Peter Finer)
Open 10-5.30 or by appointment. *STOCK: Fine antique
arms and armour and related objects.* FAIRS: New York
(Oct/Jan); Palm Beach; Maastricht (TEFAF).
TEL: 020 7839 5666; FAX: 020 7839 5777
E-MAIL: gallery@peterfiner.com
WEBSITE: www.peterfiner.com

N. and I. Franklin   BADA
11 Bury St., St. James's. SW1Y 6AB.
EST. 1984. Open 9.30-5.30. CL: Sat. *STOCK: Fine silver
and works of art.* FAIRS: Grosvenor House; New York.
TEL: 020 7839 3131; FAX: 020 7839 3132
E-MAIL: neil@franklinsilver.com
WEBSITE: www.franklinsilver.com

S. Franses Ltd
80 Jermyn St. at Duke St., St. James's. SW1Y 6JD.
EST. 1909. SLAD. Open 9-5. CL: Sat. *STOCK: Historic and
decorative tapestries, important carpets, needlework and textiles.
New York office at 132 East 61 St.* SER: Valuations;

restorations; cleaning. SIZE: Large. VAT: Spec. FAIRS:
Biennale des Antiquaires, Paris; Grosvenor House, London.
TEL: 020 7976 1234; FAX: 020 7930 8451
E-MAIL: gallery@franses.com
WEBSITE: www.franses.com

Charles Frodsham & Co Ltd
32 Bury St., St. James's. SW1Y 6AU. (Richard
Stenning and Philip Whyte)
EST. 1834. Open by appointment. *STOCK: Clocks, watches,
marine chronometers and other horological items.* LOC:
Between Jermyn St. and St. James's St. SIZE: Medium.
PARK: Meters. VAT: Stan/Spec.
TEL: 020 7839 1234; FAX: 020 7839 2000
WEBSITE: www.frodsham.com

Frost & Reed Ltd (Est. 1808)   BADA
2-4 King St., St James's. SW1Y 6QP.
Open Mon.-Fri. 10-6. *STOCK: Fine 19th & 20th C
British and European paintings. Post-Impressionist
drawings and watercolours specialising in Sir Alfred
Munnings, Montague Dawson, Marcel Dyf.* LOC: Tube
stations Green Park or Piccadilly
TEL: 020 7839 4645; FAX: 020 7839 1166
E-MAIL: info@frostandreed.cm
WEBSITE: www.frostandreed.com

Gallery 25
26 Pimlico Rd. SW1W 8LJ. (D. Iglesis)
EST. 1969. Open 10.30-5.30, Sat. 10.30-5. *STOCK: Art
glass, £100-£5,000; signed furniture, £1,000-£10,000;
decorative fine art, £500-£5,000; all 1900-1960s.* SER:
Valuations; buys at auction (as stock). SIZE: Medium.
VAT: Stan/Spec. FAIRS: Park Lane; Olympia.
TEL: 020 7730 7516; fax 020 7730 8645
E-MAIL: david@gallery25.co.uk
WEBSITE: www.gallery25.co.uk

Nicholas Gifford-Mead   BADA LAPADA
68 Pimlico Rd. SW1W 8LS.
EST. 1972. Open 9.30-5.30, CL: Sat. *STOCK: Chimney
pieces and sculpture, 18th-19th C, from £1,000.* LOC: 3
mins. from Sloane Sq. SER: Valuations. SIZE: Medium.
VAT: Stan/Spec.
TEL: 020 7730 6233; FAX: 020 7730 6239
E-MAIL: nicholas@gifford-mead.co.uk
WEBSITE: www.nicholasgiffordmead.co.uk

Joss Graham Oriental Textiles
10 Eccleston St. SW1W 9LT.
EST. 1980. BTA. Open 10-6, other times by
appointment. *STOCK: World textiles including rugs, kilims,
embroideries, tribal costume and shawls; jewellery,
metalwork, furniture, masks and primitive art - Indian,
Middle Eastern, Central Asian and African.* LOC: 5 mins.
walk from Victoria station. SER: Valuations, conservation
and repairs. SIZE: 2 floors. PARK: Meters. FAIRS:
Olympia (Summer).
TEL: 020 7730 4370; FAX: same

E-MAIL: jossgrahamgallery@btopenworld.com
WEBSITE: www.jossgraham.com

Martyn Gregory   BADA
34 Bury St., St. James's. SW1Y 6AU.
EST. 1966. SLAD. Open 10-6, CL: Sat. STOCK: China
Trade paintings, pictures relating to China and the Far
East; early English watercolours, 18th-20th C; British
paintings, £500-£200,000. SER: Valuations. SIZE:
Medium. PARK: Meters. VAT: Spec. FAIRS: Grosvenor
House; Maastricht (TEFAF); New York Winter;
Boston (Ellis Memorial); Philadelphia; London
(Watercolours & Drawings).
TEL: 020 7839 3731; FAX: 020 7930 0812
E-MAIL: mgregory@dircon.co.uk
WEBSITE: www.martyngregory.com

Ross Hamilton Ltd   LAPADA
95 Pimlico Rd. SW1W 8PH. (Mark Boyce and John
Underwood)
EST. 1971. CINOA. Open 9-6, Sat. 11-1 and 2.30-5.
STOCK: English and Continental furniture, 17th-19th C,
£1,000-£100,000; porcelain and objects, 18th-19th C,
£1,000-£8,000; paintings, 17th-19th C, £1,000-
£10,000+. LOC: 2 mins. walk from Sloane Square. SER:
Worldwide delivery. SIZE: Large. PARK: Side streets.
VAT: Stan/Spec.
TEL: 020 7730 3015; FAX: same
WEBSITE: www.lapada.co.uk/rosshamilton
www.thepimlicoroad.com

Brian Harkins Oriental Art
3 Bury St., St. James's. SW1Y 6AB.
EST. 1978. Open Mon.-Fri. 10-6. STOCK: Japanese art,
19th-20th C, £2,000-£60,000; Japanese Art Deco, £500-
£12,000; Chinese lacquer and works of art from the Song
(960-1279) to the Qing (1643-1912), £1,000-£200,000.
LOC: Near Green Park underground station. SIZE:
Small. FAIRS: Asian Art, New York.
TEL: 020 7839 3338; FAX: 0207 839 9339
E-MAIL: info@brianharkins.co.uk
WEBSITE: www.brianharkins.co.uk

Harris Lindsay   BADA
67 Jermyn St. SW1Y 6NY. (Marieke Macmahon and
Bruce Lindsay)
CINOA. Open 9.30-6. CL: Sat. STOCK: English,
Continental and Oriental furniture and works of art. VAT:
Spec. FAIRS: IFAADS New York; TEFAF Maastricht.
TEL: 020 7839 5767; FAX: 020 7839 5768;
E-MAIL: info@harrislindsay.com
WEBSITE: www.harrislindsay.com

Harrods Ltd
Brompton Rd., Knightsbridge. SW1X 7XL.
Open 10-8, Sun. 12-6. STOCK: Fine Victorian, Edwardian
and period furniture and clocks (English and French). SIZE:
Large. PARK: Own.
TEL: 020 7225 5940

Harvey & Gore   BADA
Duke Street Gallery, 41 Duke St. SW1Y 6DF. (A.J.
Norman)
EST. 1723. CINOA. Open 10-5, Sat. 10-3. STOCK:
Jewellery, £150-£50,000; silver, £50-£15,000; old
Sheffield plate, £125-£15,000; antique paste. LOC: St.
James's. SER: Valuations; restorations (jewellery and
silver); buys at auction. SIZE: Medium. VAT:
Stan/Spec. FAIRS: BADA.
TEL: 020 7839 4033
E-MAIL: info@harveyandgore.co.uk
WEBSITE: www.harveyandgore.co.uk

Brian Haughton Antiques
15 Duke St., St James's. SW1Y 6DB.
EST. 1965. Open 10-5.30. STOCK: British and European
ceramics, porcelain and pottery, 18th-19th C, £100-
£100,000. SER: Buys at auction (porcelain and pottery).
SIZE: Large. PARK: Next door: Cavendish Hotel Garage.
VAT: Spec. FAIRS: Organiser - International Ceramics
Fair & Seminar, Park Lane Hotel; IFAAD; International
Fine Art; International Asian Art; International Art &
Design; New York.
TEL: 020 7389 6550; FAX: 020 7389 6556
E-MAIL: gallery@haughton.com
WEBSITE: www.haughton.com.

Gerard Hawthorn Ltd
Flat 20, 10 Bury St. SW1Y 6AA.
Open 11-6 Mon.-Fri. STOCK: Asian art. LOC: In
Christies' block. SER: Valuations; restorations; buys at
auction; exhibitions twice yearly (illustrated catalogues).
PARK: Easy. VAT: Spec.
TEL: 020 7839 8885; FAX: 020 7839 8882
E-MAIL: mail@gerardhawthorn.com
WEBSITE: www.gerardhawthorn.com

Hazlitt, Gooden and Fox Ltd
38 Bury St., St. James's. SW1Y 6BB.
SLAD. Open 9.30-5.30. CL: Sat. STOCK: Paintings,
drawings and sculpture. SER: Valuations; restorations.
SIZE: Large. PARK: Meters. VAT: Spec.
TEL: 020 7930 6422; FAX: 020 7839 5984
E-MAIL: info@hazlittgoodenandfox.com
WEBSITE: www.hazlittgoodenandfox.com

Thomas Heneage Art Books   LAPADA
42 Duke St., St. James's. SW1Y 6DJ.
EST. 1975. Open 9.30-6 or by appointment. CL: Sat.
STOCK: Art reference books. FAIRS: Maastricht.
TEL: 020 7930 9223; FAX: 020 7839 9223
E-MAIL: artbooks@heneage.com
WEBSITE: www.heneage.com

Christopher Hodsoll Ltd inc. Bennison   BADA
50-52 Pimlico Rd. SW1W 8LP.
EST. 1991. Open 10-6 or by appointment. STOCK:
Furniture, sculpture, pictures and objects. Further

showrooms at Core 1, The Gasworks, Michael Rd, SW6 2AD. SER: Search; interior design. SIZE: 2 shops, 6 showrooms. PARK: Meters. VAT: Stan/Spec.
TEL: 020 7730 3370; FAX: 020 7730 6405
E-MAIL: h@hodsoll.com
WEBSITE: www.hodsoll.com

Hotspur Ltd BADA
14 Lowndes St. SW1X 9EX. (R.A.B. Kern)
EST. 1924. Open 8.30-6. *STOCK: Fine English furniture, 1680-1800.* LOC: Between Belgrave Sq. and Lowndes Sq. SIZE: Large. PARK: Underground within 100yds. VAT: Spec. FAIRS: Grosvenor House.
TEL: 020 7235 1918; FAX: 020 7235 4371
E-MAIL: hotspur@hotspurantiques.com
WEBSITE: www.hotspurantiques.com

Christopher Howe
93 Pimlico Rd. SW1W 8PH.
EST. 1982. Open 9-6, Sat. 10.30-4.30. *STOCK: British and European furniture, 16th-20th C, £100-£250,000; works of art, decorative objects and lighting.* LOC: Near Sloane Square. SER: Sourcing. SIZE: Large. PARK: Meters nearby. VAT: Stan/Spec.
TEL: 020 7730 7987; FAX: 020 7730 0157
E-MAIL: antiques@howelondon.com

Humphrey-Carrasco Ltd
43 Pimlico Rd. SW1W 8NE. (David Humphrey and Marylise Carrasco)
EST. 1987. Open 10-6, Sat. by appointment. *STOCK: English furniture and lighting, architectural objects, 18th-19th C.* LOC: 10 mins. walk from Sloane Sq. PARK: Easy. VAT: Stan/Spec FAIRS: Olympia.
TEL: 020 7730 9911; FAX: 020 7730 9944
E-MAIL: hc@humphreycarrasco.demon.co.uk

Iconastas
5 Piccadilly Arcade. SW1Y 6NH. (John Gaze and Christopher Martin-Zakheim)
EST. 1968. Open 10-6, Sat. 2-5. *STOCK: Russian and Byzantine fine art and antiques, 10th C to 20th C; Soviet & Communist art; lacquer, silver, brass icons, crosses, cigarette cases; Russian porcelain.* SER: Valuations. SIZE: Small. PARK: Meters.
TEL: 020 7629 1433; FAX: 020 7408 2015
E-MAIL: info@iconastas.com
WEBSITE: www.iconastas.com

Isaac and Ede BADA
1 Duke of York St. St. James's. SW1Y 6JP. (David Isaac)
EST. 2004. Open Mon.-Fri. 10-5.30. *STOCK: 18th-19th C decorative prints, £100-£5,000.* SER: Valuations; framing; restorations. SIZE: Small. VAT: Stan/Spec. FAIRS: Olympia (June); BADA (March); San Francisco (Fall).
TEL: 020 7925 1177; FAX: 020 7925 0606
E-MAIL: info@isaacandede.com
WEBSITE: www.isaacandede.com

Jeremy Ltd BADA
29 Lowndes St. SW1X 9HX. (M. and J. Hill)
EST. 1946. Open 8.30-6, Sat. by appointment. *STOCK: English, French and Russian furniture, objets d'art, glass chandeliers, 18th to early 19th C.* SIZE: Large. PARK: Nearby. VAT: Spec. FAIRS: Grosvenor House; New York Armory Show.
TEL: 020 7823 2923; FAX: 020 7245 6197
E-MAIL: jeremy@jeremique.co.uk
WEBSITE: www.jeremy.ltd.uk

Derek Johns Ltd
12 Duke St., St. James's. SW1Y 6BN.
EST. 1980. SLAD. Open 9-6. *STOCK: Old Master paintings.* SER: Valuations; consignments; private treaty sales. FAIRS: TEFAF Maastricht; IFAAD New York; Paris & Florence Biennale; Palm Beach.
TEL: 020 7839 7671; FAX: 020 7930 0986
E-MAIL: fineart@derekjohns.co.uk
WEBSITE: www.derekjohns.co.uk

Peter Jones LAPADA
Sloane Sqare. SW1W 8EL. (John Lewis Partnership)
EST. 1915. CINOA. Open 9.30-7, Sun. 11-5. *STOCK: 18th-19th C furniture, mirrors, pictures, some glass.* LOC: Sloane Sq, Chelsea. SIZE: Large.
TEL: 020 7808 4068; FAX: 020 7808 4016
E-MAIL: peter_jones@johnlewis.co.uk
WEBSITE: www.peterjones.co.uk

Keshishian BADA
73 Pimlico Rd. SW1W 8NE.
EST. 1978. Open 9.30-6, Sat. 10-4. *STOCK: European and Oriental carpets, to late 19th C; Aubussons, mid 19th C; European tapestries, 16th-18th C; Arts and Crafts and Art Deco carpet specialists.* LOC: Off Lower Sloane St. SER: Valuations; restorations. SIZE: Large. PARK: Easy. VAT: Stan/Spec. FAIRS: Grosvenor House; Winter Show, New York; Fall Show, San Francisco.
TEL: 020 7730 8810; FAX: 020 7730 8803;
E-MAIL: info@keshishiancarpets.com
WEBSITE: www.keshishiancarpets.com

John King BADA
74 Pimlico Rd. SW1W 8LS.
EST. 1970. Open 10-6, Sat. by appointment. *STOCK: Fine and unusual antiques, £500-£150,000.* SIZE: Medium. PARK: Easy. VAT: Spec.
TEL: 020 7730 0427; FAX: 020 7730 2515
E-MAIL: kingj896@aol.com

Knapton Rasti Asian Art
1 Princes Place, Duke St., St. James's. SW1Y 6DE. (Christopher Knapton, Nader Rasti and Rachel Zamet)
STOCK: Works of art; Ming and Qing ceramics.
TEL: 020 7839 3888; FAX: 020 7839 8833
E-MAIL: knaptonrasti@btconnect.com
WEBSITE: www.knaptonandrasti.com

Knightsbridge Coins
43 Duke St., St. James's. SW1Y 6DD.
Open Mon.-Fri. 10.30-5.30. STOCK: Coins - British,
American and South African. Medals bought.
TEL: 020 7930 7597; 020 7930 8215 or 020 7930 7888.
E-MAIL: kcoins@hotmail.co.uk

Bob Lawrence Gallery
84 Pimlico Rd. SW1W 8PL.
EST. 1972. Open 10-6. STOCK: Decorative arts to 1970s -
furniture, paintings, objects and furnishings, £50-£10,000.
LOC: 2 mins. Sloane Sq., adjacent to Pimlico Rd. SER:
Valuations; restorations; buys at auction. SIZE: Medium.
PARK: Easy. VAT: Stan/Spec.
TEL: 020 7730 5900; FAX: 020 7730 5902
E-MAIL: bob@blgallery.co.uk
WEBSITE: www.blgallery.co.uk

Longmire Ltd (Three Royal Warrants)
12 Bury St., St. James's. SW1Y 6AB.
Open 9.30-5, Sat. in Nov. and Dec. only. STOCK: Individual
cufflink and dress sets: antique and contemporary, signed,
platinum, gold, gem-set, hardstone, pearl, carved crystal or
enamel - four vices, fishing, polo, golfing, shooting, big game,
ladybird and pigs. LOC: Coming from Piccadilly, down
Duke St., right into King St. past Christie's, first right into
Bury St. SER: Custom hand engraving or enamelling in
colour - any corporate logo, initials, crest, coats of arms or
tartan, any animal (cat, dog etc.), racing silks, sailing
burgees, favourite hobbies or own automobiles.
TEL: 020 7930 8720; FAX: 020 7930 1898
E-MAIL: websales@longmire.co.uk

MacConnal-Mason Gallery   BADA
14 and 17 Duke St., St. James's. SW1Y 6DB.
EST. 1893. TEFAF. Open 9-6, Sat. by appointment.
STOCK: Pictures and sculpture, 19th-20th C. SER:
Valuations; restorations. SIZE: Large. PARK: Meters.
VAT: Spec. FAIRS: TEFAF, Maastricht; International,
New York; Palm Beach; Grosvenor House, Harrogate.
TEL: 020 7839 7693; FAX: 020 7839 6797
E-MAIL: fineart@macconnal-mason.com
WEBSITE: www.macconnal-mason.com

The Mall Galleries
The Mall. SW1Y 5BD. (British Federation of Artists)
EST. 1971. Open 10-5 seven days during exhibitions.
STOCK: Paintings, sculpture, prints and drawings. LOC:
Near Trafalgar Sq. SER: Contemporary art exhibitions;
commissioning; gallery hire; workshops; education.
PARK: Nearby.
TEL: 020 7930 6844; FAX: 020 7839 7830
E-MAIL: info@mallgalleries.com
WEBSITE: www.mallgalleries.org.uk

Mathaf Gallery Ltd   LAPADA
**24 Motcomb St. SW1X 8JU. (Brian and Gina
MacDermot)**
EST. 1975. SLAD. Open 9.30-5.30, Sat. by appointment.

STOCK: Paintings, Middle East subjects, 19th C. LOC:
Knightsbridge. SER: Valuations. VAT: Spec.
TEL: 020 7235 0010; FAX: 020 7823 1378
E-MAIL: art@mathafgallery.demon.co.uk
WEBSITE: www.mathafgallery.com

Matthiesen Fine Art Ltd.
7-8 Mason's Yard, Duke St., St. James's. SW1Y 6BU.
EST. 1978. Open by appointment. STOCK: Fine Italian
Old Master paintings, 1300-1800; French and Spanish Old
Master paintings. SER: Valuations; buys at auction.
TEL: 020 7930 2437; FAX: 020 7930 1387
E-MAIL: gallery@matthiesengallery.com
WEBSITE: www.matthiesengallery.com

Duncan R. Miller Fine Arts   BADA LAPADA
4-6 Bury St., St. James's. SW1Y 6AB.
EST. 1975. Open 10-6. STOCK: Modern British and
European paintings, drawings and sculpture, especially
Scottish Colourist paintings. LOC: Green Park
underground station. SER: Valuations; conservation
and restoration (oils, works on paper and Oriental
rugs); buys at auction. SIZE: Small. VAT: Spec. FAIRS:
Grosvenor House; BADA; Olympia.
TEL: 020 7839 8806; FAX: same
E-MAIL: art@duncanmiller.com
WEBSITE: www.duncanmiller.com

Nigel Milne Ltd
38 Jermyn St. SW1Y 6DN. (Nigel and Cherry Milne)
EST. 1979. Open 9.30-5.30. STOCK: Jewellery, silver
frames and objects. SER: Valuations. SIZE: Small. VAT:
Stan/Spec.
TEL: 020 7434 9343
E-MAIL: jewels@nigelmilne.co.uk
WEBSITE: www.nigelmilne.co.uk

Peter Nahum At The Leicester Galleries   BADA
5 Ryder St. SW1Y 6PY.
EST. 1983. SLAD. CINOA. Open 9.30-6, Sat. and
Sun. by appointment. STOCK: British and European
paintings, works on paper and bronzes, including
Victorian, the Pre-Raphaelites, Symbolists and Modern
British, 19th-20th C, £1,000-£100,000+. LOC: 100yds
from Royal Academy. SER: Valuations; restorations;
framing. SIZE: Large. PARK: Meters. VAT: Spec.
TEL: 020 7930 6059; FAX: 020 7930 4678
E-MAIL: peternahum@leicestergalleries.com
WEBSITE: www.leicestergalleries.com

Odyssey Fine Arts Ltd   LAPADA
**24 Holbein Place. SW1W 8NL. (Andrew Korom-
Vokis)**
EST. 1992. Trade Only. Open 10-6. STOCK: 18th to early
19th C Italian and French provincial furniture; 18th C
engravings. SIZE: Small. FAIRS: Olympia.
TEL: 020 7730 9942; FAX: 020 7259 9941
E-MAIL: odysseyfinearts@aol.com
WEBSITE: www.odysseyfinearts.com

Old Maps and Prints
2nd Floor, Harrods, Knightsbridge. SW1X 7XL.
EST. 1976. Open 10-8. STOCK: *Maps, 16th to 20th C; engravings (all subjects); watercolours. Vintage adverts; movie posters. Antiquarian books.* LOC: Knightsbridge tube. SIZE: Large.
TEL: 020 7730 1234, ext. 2124; FAX: 020 7893 8346
E-MAIL: oldmapsandprints@btconnect.com

Ossowski BADA
83 Pimlico Rd. SW1W 8PH.
EST. **1960. Open 10-6. CL: Sat. pm.** STOCK: *Carved gilt, 18th C; mirrors, consoles, wood carvings.* SER: **Restorations (gilt furniture).** SIZE: **Medium.** VAT: **Stan/Spec.** FAIRS: **New York International (Oct).**
TEL: **020 7730 3256**

Anthony Outred BADA
72 Pimlico Rd. SW1W 8LS. (Anthony and Anne Outred)
EST. **1974. Open 10-6.** STOCK: *Exceptional English and Continental furniture and works of art especially the unusual and amusing, £1,000-£100,000.* SER: **Sourcing and advice.** SIZE: **Large - several locations.** VAT: **Stan/Spec.** FAIRS: **Olympia.**
TEL: **020 7730 7948;** FAX: **020 7834 8233;** MOBILE: **07767 848132**
E-MAIL: **antiques@outred.co.uk**
WEBSITE: **www.outred.co.uk**

Paisnel Gallery
9 Bury St., St James's. SW1Y 6AB. (Stephen and Sylvia Paisnel)
EST. 1977. SLAD. Open 10-6. CL: Sat. STOCK: *20th C British paintings, £5,000-£250,000.* LOC: Bury St. runs from Jermyn St. to King St., 1 min from Christie's. SIZE: Large. PARK: St. James Sq. VAT: Spec.
TEL: 020 7930 9293; FAX: 020 7930 7282
E-MAIL: info@paisnelgallery.co.uk
WEBSITE: www.paisnelgallery.co.uk

Trevor Philip & Sons Ltd BADA
75a Jermyn St., St. James's. SW1Y 6NP. (T. and S. Waterman)
EST. **1972. Open 9.30-6, Sat. by appointment.** STOCK: *Early scientific instruments, globes, barometers and ships models; silver and vertu.* SER: **Valuations; restorations (clocks and scientific instruments); buys at auction.** SIZE: **Medium.** PARK: **At rear.** VAT: **Stan/Spec.** FAIRS: **Maastricht.**
TEL: **020 7930 2954;** FAX: **020 7321 0212**
E-MAIL: **globe@trevorphilip.com**
WEBSITE: **www.trevorphilip.com**

Pullman Gallery
14 King St., St. James's. SW1Y 6QU. (Simon Khachadourian)
EST. 1980. Open 10-6, Sat. by appointment. STOCK: *Objets de luxe, 19th-20th C, £200-£20,000; automobile art,* pre-1950, £1,000-£20,000; cocktail shakers, bar accessories, cigar memorabilia, 1880-1950, £250-£25,000; René Lalique glass, 1900-1940, from £3,000. LOC: Corner of Bury St., adjacent Christie's. SIZE: Medium. PARK: Easy. VAT: Stan.
TEL: 020 7930 9595; FAX: 020 7930 9494; MOBILE: 07973 141606
E-MAIL: sk@pullmangallery.com
WEBSITE: www.pullmangallery.com

Mark Ransom Ltd
62, 64 and 105 Pimlico Rd. SW1W 8LS.
EST. 1989. Open 10-6. STOCK: *Furniture - French Empire and Russian, early 19th C; Continental, decorative, from late 18th C, all to £1,000+; sculpture and prints, contemporary art and furniture.* LOC: Close to Sloane Sq. underground station - turn left left, 5 mins. walk. SIZE: Large. PARK: Side streets. VAT: Stan/Spec.
TEL: 020 7259 0220; FAX: 020 7259 0323.
E-MAIL: contact@markransom.co.uk
WEBSITE: www.markransom.co.uk

Rogier et Rogier
20A Pimlico Rd. SW1W 8LJ. (Miss Lauriance Rogier)
EST. 1980. Open 10-6, Sat. 11-4. STOCK: *French and Continental lamps and wall sconces, 19th C* LOC: 5 mins. walk from Sloane Sq. SIZE: Small. PARK: Meters. VAT: Spec.
TEL: 020 7823 4780
E-MAIL: lamps@lauriancerogier.com
WEBSITE: www.lauriancerogier.com

The Silver Fund BADA LAPADA
1 Duke of York St. SW1Y 6JP. (Alastair Crawford and Michael James)
Open daily, Sat. and Sun. by appointment. STOCK: *Old Georg Jensen silver, £500-£100,000.* LOC: **Opposite Christie's (King St/Bury St).** SER: **Valuations; restorations.** SIZE: **Large.** PARK: **NCP Mayfair.** VAT: **Stan/Spec.**
TEL: **020 7839 7664;** FAX: **020 7839 8935;**
E-MAIL: **michael@thesilverfund.com**
WEBSITE: **www.thesilverfund.com**

Julian Simon Fine Art Ltd BADA
70 Pimlico Rd. SW1W 8LS. (M. and J. Brookstone)
Open 10-6, Sat. 10-4 or by appointment. STOCK: *Fine English and Continental pictures, 18th-20th C.* LOC: **Near Sloane Sq.** FAIRS: **Olympia.**
TEL: **020 7730 8673;** FAX: **020 7823 6116**
E-MAIL: **juliansimon@compuserve.com**
WEBSITE: **www.19thcenturypaintings.com**

Sims Reed Ltd
43a Duke St., St James's. SW1Y 6DD.
EST. 1977. ABA. Open 10-6 or by appointment. STOCK: *Illustrated, rare and in-print books on the fine and applied arts; antiquarian books; leather-bound literary sets; contemporary books.* FAIRS: London ABA.

TEL: 020 7930 5566; FAX: 020 7925 0825
E-MAIL: info@simsreed.com
WEBSITE: www.simsreed.com

Sims Reed Gallery
The Economist Building, 23a St James's. SW1A 1HA.
EST. 1977. Open 10-6 or by appointment. *STOCK: Modern and contemporary prints by artists including Picasso, Miro, Warhol, Chagall, Hockney; rare books.*
TEL: 020 7930 5111; FAX: 020 7930 1555;
E-MAIL: gallery@simsreed.com
WEBSITE: www.simsreed.com

Peta Smyth - Antique Textiles   LAPADA
42 Moreton St., Pimlico. SW1V 2PB.
EST. 1977. Open 9.30-5.30, CL: Sat. *STOCK: European textiles, 16th-19th C - needlework, silks and velvets, hangings and curtains, tapestries and cushions, £50-£20,000.* **PARK: Easy. VAT: Spec. FAIRS: Olympia.**
TEL: 020 7630 9898; FAX: 020 7630 5398
E-MAIL: petasmyth@ukonline.co.uk

Somlo Antiques   BADA
35-36 Burlington Arcade. SW1Y.
EST. 1972. Open 10-5.30, Sat. 10.30-5.30. *STOCK: Vintage wrist and antique pocket watches, from £1,000.* **SER: Restorations. SIZE: Medium. PARK: Meters.**
TEL: 020 7499 6526
E-MAIL: mail@somlo.com
WEBSITE: www.somloantiques.com

Bill Thomson - Albany Gallery
1 Bury St., St. James's. SW1Y 6AB. (W.B. Thomson)
EST. 1964. Open Tues.-Fri. 10-5 by appointment only. *STOCK: British drawings, watercolours and paintings, 1700-1850 and some 20th C.*
TEL: 020 7839 6119; FAX: 020 7839 6614

Kate Thurlow   LAPADA
Gallery FortyOne, 41 Moreton St. SW1V 2NY.
EST. 1970 CINOA. Open Tues.-Sat. 10-6, other times by appointment. *STOCK: European furniture, including English, and accessories, 16th-18th C, £500-£20,000.* **LOC: Lupus St. end of Moreton St., Pimlico underground station. SER: Valuations; restorations (furniture); sourcing; buys at auction. SIZE: Medium. PARK: Meters. VAT: Spec. FAIRS: Olympia.**
TEL: 020 7932 0033; FAX: same; MOBILE: 07836 588776
E-MAIL: katethurlow@galleryfortyone.co.uk
WEBSITE: www.galleryfortyone.co.uk

Trafalgar Galleries   BADA
35 Bury St., St. James's. SW1Y 6AY.
Open Mon-Fri 9.30-6. *STOCK: Old Master paintings.* **LOC: Just south of Piccadilly.**
TEL: 020 7839 6466

The Tryon Galleries
7 Bury St., St James's. SW1Y 6AL. (Oliver Swann)
EST. 1955. SLAD. Open Mon.-Thurs. 10-6, Fri. 10-5. *STOCK: Sporting, wildlife and natural history subjects; Scottish landscapes; paintings, bronzes, marine. £150-£50,000.* SER: Valuations; framing; restoration; advice; commission buying. SIZE: Large. VAT: Spec. FAIRS: Game.
TEL: 020 7839 8083; FAX: 020 7839 8085
E-MAIL: infotryon.co.uk
WEBSITE: www.tryon.co.uk

Rafael Valls Ltd   BADA
11 Duke St., St. James's. SW1Y 6BN.
EST. 1976. SLAD. Open Mon.-Fri. 9.30-5.30. *STOCK: Old Master paintings.* **VAT: Spec. FAIRS: Maastricht: Grosvenor House: BADA.**
TEL: 020 7930 1144; FAX: 020 7976 1596
E-MAIL: info@rafaelvalls.co.uk
WEBSITE: www.rafaelvalls.co.uk

Rafael Valls Ltd   BADA
6 Ryder St., St. James's. SW1Y 6QB.
EST. 1976. SLAD. Open Mon.-Fri. 9.30-6. *STOCK: Fine European paintings. Contemporary exhibitions.* **VAT: Spec.**
TEL: 020 7930 0029; FAX: 020 7976 1596
E-MAIL: info@rafaelvalls.co.uk
WEBSITE: www.rafaelvalls.co.uk

Johnny Van Haeften Ltd   BADA
13 Duke St., St. James's. SW1Y 6DB. (J. and S. Van Haeften)
EST. 1978. SLAD. TEFAF. Open 10-6, Sat. and Sun. by appointment. *STOCK: Dutch and Flemish Old Master paintings, 16th-17th C, £5,000-£5m.* **LOC: Middle of Duke St. SER: Valuations; restorations (Old Masters); buys at auction (paintings including Old Masters). SIZE: Medium. VAT: Spec. FAIRS: Grosvenor House; Maastricht.**
TEL: 020 7930 3062/3; FAX: 020 7839 6303
E-MAIL: paintings@johnnyvanhaeften.com
WEBSITE: www.johnnyvanhaeften.com

Waterman Fine Art Ltd
75A Jermyn St., St. James's. SW1Y 6NP. (Mrs. R. Waterman)
Open 9-6, Sat. 10-4. *STOCK: 20th C paintings and watercolours.* SIZE: Medium. PARK: At rear.
TEL: 020 7839 5203; FAX: 020 7321 0212

The Weiss Gallery
59 Jermyn St. SW1Y 6LX. (Mark Weiss)
SLAD. Open 10-6. *STOCK: Early English, Dutch, Flemish and French portraits.* SER: Valuations; restorations. FAIRS: TEFAF, Maastricht.
TEL: 020 7409 0035; FAX: 020 7491 9604
E-MAIL: info@weissgallery.com
WEBSITE: www.weissgallery.com

Westenholz Antiques Ltd
76-78 Pimlico Rd. SW1W 8PL.
Open Mon-Fri 10-6, Sat 11-4. *Stock: 18th-19th C furniture, pictures, objects, lamps, mirrors.* Loc: Nr Sloane Sq. tube. Park: Meters.
Tel: 020 7824 8090
E-mail: shop@westenholz.co.uk
Website: www.westenholz.co.uk

Rollo Whately Ltd
41 St. James's Place, St. James's. SW1A 1NS.
Est. 1995. Open 9-6. CL: Sat. *Stock: Picture frames, 16th-19th C, £500-£2,000.* Ser: Valuations; picture framing; frame restoration; specialised searches; buys at auction. Size: Small. Vat: Stan.
Tel: 020 7629 7861
Website: www.rollowhately.com

Whitford Fine Art
6 Duke St., St. James's. SW1Y 6BN. (Adrian Mibus)
Est. 1973. SLAD. Open 10-6. CL: Sat. *Stock: Oil paintings and sculpture, late 19th to 20th C; Modernism, post-war abstract and pop art.* Size: Medium. Vat: Spec.
Tel: 020 7930 9332; Fax: 020 7930 5577
E-mail: info@whitfordfineart.com
Website: www.whitfordfineart.com

Arnold Wiggins and Sons Ltd   BADA
4 Bury St., St. James's. SW1Y 6AB. (Michael Gregory)
Open Mon.-Fri. 9-5.30. *Stock: Picture frames, 16th-19th C.* **Ser: Restorations; adaptations. Park: Meters.**
Fairs: Grosvenor House.
Tel: 020 7925 0195
E-mail: info@arnoldwiggins.com
Website: www.arnoldwiggins.com

Wildenstein and Co Ltd
46 St. James's Place. SW1A 1NS.
Est. 1934. SLAD. Open by appointment. *Stock: Impressionist and Old Master paintings and drawings.*
Tel: 020 7629 0602; Fax: 020 7493 3924
E-mail: ebt@wildenstein.com
Website: www.wildenstein.com

Willow Gallery
40 Duke St. St James's. SW1Y 6DF.
Stock: British and European fine oil paintings, 19th-20th C, £10,000+ Fairs: Harrogate; London and internationally, contact for tickets.
Tel: 020 7968 1830
E-mail: enquiries@willowgallery.com
Website: www.willowgallery.com

Miles Wynn Cato
60 Lower Sloane St. SW1W 8BP.
Est. 1995. Open Mon.-Fri. 9.30-5.30 and by appointment. *Stock: English and Welsh pictures and works of art, 1550-1950.* Loc: 100 yds. south of Sloane Sq. Ser: Valuations; restorations; framing; appraisals. Size:

Medium. Park: Easy - meters. Vat: Spec.
Tel: 020 7259 0306; Fax: 020 7259 0305
E-mail: wynncato@welshart.co.uk
Website: www.welshart.co.uk

SW2

Chris Baron Interiors
87 Streatham Hill. SW2 4UB.
Est. 1976. Open 9.30-5.30, Thurs. until 6.30, Sat. 9.30-5. *Stock: Desks, from Victorian, £250-£1,250; bureaux, from Georgian, £200-£2,000; chests of drawers, from Georgian, £300-£1,000; all mainly mahogany, oak and walnut. Lighting and interesting items.* Loc: Opposite Megabowl. Ser: Valuations; restorations and repairs. Size: Small. Park: Easy.
Tel: 020 8671 8732; Fax: 020 8671 1984
E-mail: baronsx3@aol.com
Website: www.chrisbaroninteriors.co.uk

SW3

Norman Adams Ltd   BADA
8-10 Hans Rd., Knightsbridge. SW3 1RX.
Est. 1923. Open 10-5.30, Sat. and Sun. by appointment. *Stock: English furniture, 18th C, £650-£250,000; objets d'art (English and French) £500-£50,000; mirrors, glass pictures, 18th C; clocks and barometers.* **Loc: 30yds. off the Brompton Rd., opposite the west side entrance to Harrods. Size: Large. Vat: Spec. Fairs: Grosvenor House; BADA.**
Tel: 020 7589 5266; Fax: 020 7589 1968
E-mail: antiques@normanadams.com
Website: www.normanadams.com

After Noah
261 King's Rd. Chelsea. SW3 5EL. (M. Crawford and Z. Candlin)
Est. 1990. Open 10-6, Sun. 12-5. *Stock: Arts and Craft oak and similar furniture, leather sofas and chairs, 1880s to 1970s, £1-£5,000; iron, iron and brass beds; decorative items, bric-a-brac including candlesticks, mirrors, lighting, kitchenalia and jewellery.* Ser: Restorations. Size: Large. Vat: Stan.
Tel: 020 7351 2610; Fax: same
E-mail: enquiries@afternoah.com
Website: www.afternoah.com

The Andipa Gallery   LAPADA
162 Walton St. SW3 2JL. (Acoris Andipa and Mrs Maria Andipa)
Est. 1969. Open 9.30-6, Sat. 11-6. *Stock: Modern and contemporary prints, drawings, paintings and sculpture; icons from Byzantium, Greece, Russia, Eastern Europe, Asia Minor and North Africa.* **Loc: Knightsbridge. Ser: Valuations; restorations; research; collections.**
Tel: 020 7589 2371; Fax: 020 7225 0305
E-mail: art@andipa.com
Website: www.andipamodern.com

Antiquarius
131-141 King's Rd. SW3 4PW. (Atlantic Antiques
Centres Ltd)
EST. 1970. Open 10-6. LOC: On the corner of King's Rd.
and Flood St., next to Chelsea Town Hall. PARK:
Meters.
TEL: 020 7823 3900
E-MAIL: info@antiquarius.co.uk
WEBSITE: www.antiquarius.co.uk

Below are listed some of the many specialist dealers at
this market.

Jaki Abbott
Stand M12. *Jewellery.*

Aesthetics   LAPADA
Stand V1. *Silver, ceramics, japonisme and decorative arts.*

AM-PM
Stand V11. *Vintage watches and carriage clocks.*
TEL: 020 7351 5654
EMAIL: ampmwatches@aol.com
WEBSITE: www.ampmwatches.co.uk

Alexia Amato Antiques
Stand V8. *Decorative antiques, Bohemian and other
glassware.*
TEL: 020 7352 3666; FAX: same
EMAIL: alexia@amato.freeserve.co.uk
WEBSITE: www.amato.freeserve.co.uk

Antiques Rug Gallery
Stand V19. *Oriental carpets, Persian rugs and hangings.*

Beauty & The Beast
Stand Q9. (J. Rothman) *Costume and semi-precious
jewellery, handbags, miniatures, boxes and other decorative
arts.*

Bellum Antiques
Stand V12. *Fine jewellery, watches, bronzes, scent bottles and
objets d'art.*
TEL: 020 7352 1444

Billing
Stand M5. *Art Deco, Art Nouveau, Georgian, Victorian and
other jewellery, and silver items.*
TEL: 020 7376 8252

Alexandra Bolla
Stand J1. *Jewellery.*

Brown & Kingston
Stand V5. *Furniture, porcelain, mirrors, chandeliers, lamps
clocks painting and other decorative objects.*

Teresa Buchinger
Stand Q2. *Jewellery, match strikers, ivory, cufflinks, silver
frames, Victorian and semi-precious stone jewellery.*
TEL: 020 7352 8734

Jasmin Cameron
Stand M1. *18th and 19th C English and Irish glass, wine
glasses, candlesticks, decanters, scent bottles and vases.*

Chelsea Military Antiques
Stands R3-6. *Military antiques, jackets and militaria.*
EMAIL: richard@chelseamilitaria.com

Adrian Cohen
Stand A18. *Silver boxes, candelabra, frames, table ware and
other items.*
TEL: 020 7352 7155
EMAIL: silver@adrian-cohen.co.uk
WEBSITE: www.adrian-cohen.co.uk

The Cufflink Shop
Stand G2. *Antique cufflinks and jewellery, money clips, dress
studs, tie pins and cigar cutters.*
TEL: 020 7352 8201
EMAIL: john-szwarc@yahoo.co.uk

Glen Dewart
Stands P7-8. *Prints and paintings, decorative items, bronzes,
sculpture and jewellery.*
TEL: 020 7352 4777

M Desmond
Stands Q7, R7. *English and European Contemporary and
period art.*

Eclectic Antiques and Interiors
Stands T3-5. *Furniture, lighting, boxes, bronzes, ceramics,
sculpture, clocks, mirrors and objets d'art.*
EMAIL: eclecticantiques@waitrose.com

Ferguson Fine Art
Stand V13. *Sporting collectables, equestrian antiques,
paintings, and metalware.*
TEL: 020 7352 5272

Gallison
Stand L9. *Jewellery, ceramics and glass and decorative
accessories.*

Angelo Gibson
Stand M10. *Antique silver and silver plate boxes, candelabra,
tableware and other items.*
TEL: 020 7352 4690
EMAIL: quicksilverangelo@zoom.co.uk

Brian Gordon   LAPADA
Stand G1. *Antique silver and silver plate boxes, candelabra,
tableware and other items.*
TEL: 020 7351 5808

Robin Haydock - Rare Antiques   LAPADA
 & Textiles
Stands V21,V36. *Antique textiles, jewellery, bags, period
costumes, bronzes and decorative items.*
EMAIL: robinhaydock@talk21.com
WEBSITE: www.robinhaydock.com

Hayman & Hayman
Stands D5-6. *Photo frames and Limoges boxes.*
TEL: 020 7351 6568
EMAIL: gerogina@haymanframes.com
WEBSITE: www.haymanframes.co.uk

P. Homden
Stands N2-3. *Clocks, metalware, furniture, lighting, silver,
glassware and decorative items.*

Albert Homes
Stand H3. *Furniture, porcelain, glassware, silver, toys,
decorative objects and garden antiques.*
TEL: 020 7352 8734

Islamic Art
Stand V14. *Islamic art, oil paintings, bronzes, carpets, hangings and rugs.*

Sophie Ketley
Stands J9-10. *Over 100 mirrors, decanters, drinking glasses, giltwood and decorative furniture and objects, 1750-1900, £30-£30,000.* VAT: Spec.
TEL: 020 7351 0005; FAX: same; MOBILE: 07798 613041
EMAIL: sophieketley@aol.com

Carol Ketley Antiques
See Sophie Ketley, above.

Emmanuel Kra
Stand V37. *Antique and fine jewellery, cufflinks and objets d'art.*
EMAIL: emmanuelkra@hotmail.com

Latreville
Stand V16. *Fine silver and jewellery, bronze, sculpture, ceramics and objets d'art.*

Lana Silver
Stand R7. *Hand crafted silver jewellery.*
EMAIL: lunlana615@btinternet.com

Little River Oriental Antiques   LAPADA
Stand V15. *Neolithic - 16th C Oriental antiques and art, Buddhist and contemporary Chinese art.*
EMAIL: littleriveroa@aol.com

Mariad Antiques
Stand V38. *Vienna and other bronzes and jewellery.*

Noele McDonald-Hobley
Stand L7. *Antique jewellery, ceramics, glassware, scent bottles, silver, carriage clocks and watches.*
TEL: 020 7351 0154

M. Miller
Stand E2. *Old Master and other oil paintings.*

C. Negrillo Antiques & Jewellery
Stand P1. *Jewellery, porcelain, glass, paintings, watches, wall clocks, and objets de vertu.*
TEL: 020 7349 0038
EMAIL: negrilloc@aol.com

Sue Norman
Stand L3. *19th C blue and white transferware, English porcelain, plates, tea and coffee sets.*
TEL: 020 7352 7217; FAX: 020 8870 4677
EMAIL: sue@sue-norman.demon.co.uk
WEBSITE: www.sue-norman.demon.co.uk

P and M Jewellery
Stand V20. *Handmade gemstone and pearl jewellery.*
TEL: 020 7351 7930
EMAIL: pmjewellery@lycos.com

N. Pourshahidi
Stands N2-5. *English, European, American and modern art.*

Rabi
Stand P4. *Antique jewellery and vintage costume jewellery.* Jewellery and watch repairs and engraving.

Reilly
Stands L1-10. *Art Nouveau and Art Deco glass and ceramics and other decorative items.*

D. M. Simpson
Stand E1. *Antique ivory.*

Ouji Sormeh
Stand D1. *Art Deco and Art Nouveau, precious and semi-precious stone jewellery.*
EMAIL: sormehouji@onetel.co.uk

Miwa Thorpe
Stands M8-9. *Silver and jewellery and small objets d'art.*
EMAIL: miwathorpe@waitrose.com

Tribal Tent
Stand M14. *Middle Eastern and other jewellery, semi-precious stones and silverware.*

Rhona Valentine Textiles
Stands K1-6. *European and Islamic 17th - 20th C textiles, period clothing, decorative textile items, velvets and costumes by Mariano Fortuny.*

William Wain
Stand J6. *Vintage costume jewellery, bags and accessories.*
EMAIL: williamwain@btopenworld.com

Irene & Adrian Williams
Stands E3-5 & F1-6. *Decorative antiques, furniture, candelabra, mirrors, chandeliers and clocks.*

XS Baggage
Stands A1 & B1-6. *Antique luggage and travel requisites and range of antique decorative objects.*
TEL: 020 7376 8781
EMAIL: xsbaggage@postmaster.co.uk
WEBSITE: www.xsbaggage.co.uk

Apter Fredericks Ltd   BADA
265-267 Fulham Rd. SW3 6HY. (Harry Apter and Guy Apter)
EST. 1946. Open 9.30-5.30, Sat. and evenings by appointment. STOCK: *English furniture, late 17th to early 19th C.* FAIRS: Grosvenor House; IFAAD, New York.
TEL: 020 7352 2188; FAX: 020 7376 5619
E-MAIL: antiques@apter-fredericks.com
WEBSITE: www.apter-fredericks.com

Bentleys   LAPADA
204 Walton St. SW3 2JL. (T. Bent)
Open 10-6. STOCK: *British vintage luggage and luxury accessories; vintage Louis Vuitton trunks, cigar-related antiques from 1920s, campaign furniture 19th C.*
TEL: 020 7584 7770; FAX: 020 7584 8182
E-MAIL: shop@bentleyslondon.com
WEBSITE: www.bentleyslondon.com

Joanna Booth   BADA
247 King's Rd., Chelsea. SW3 5EL.
EST. 1963. Open 10-6. STOCK: *Sculpture, 12th-17th C; tapestries, textiles, 16th-18th C; Old Master drawings, £50-£50,000; early furniture, works of art.* SER: Buys at auction. SIZE: Medium. PARK: Meters. VAT: Spec. FAIRS: Olympia.
TEL: 020 7352 8998; FAX: 020 7376 7350
E-MAIL: joanna@joannabooth.co.uk
WEBSITE: www.joannabooth.co.uk

Bourbon-Hanby Antiques Centre
151 Sydney St. Chelsea. SW3 6NT.
EST. 1976. Open 10-6, Sun. 11-5. STOCK: *Jewellery, silver, furniture, paintings, ivory and general antiques.* LOC: Just off Kings Road, opposite town hall. SER: Jewellery repairs, design and manufacturing. PARK: NCP next door. VAT: Margin.
TEL: 020 7352 2106
WEBSITE: www.bourbonhanby.co.uk

Butler and Wilson
189 Fulham Rd. SW3 6JN.
Open daily 10-6, Wed. 10-7, Sun. 12-6. STOCK: *Jewellery, Art Deco, vintage bags and clothes, 1950s jewellery, objects and accessories.*
TEL: 020 7352 3045; FAX: 020 7376 5981
E-MAIL: enquiries@butlerandwilson.co.uk
WEBSITE: www.butlerandwilson.co.uk

Robert Dickson and Lesley Rendall Antiques BADA
263 Fulham Rd. SW3 6HY.
EST. 1969. Open 9.30-5.30, Sat. 10-5 or by appointment. STOCK: *20th C furniture, lighting and mirrors.* SER: Restorations; valuations. SIZE: Medium. PARK: Easy. VAT: Spec. FAIRS: Olympia.
TEL: 020 7351 0330
E-MAIL: info@dicksonrendall-antiques.co.uk
WEBSITE: www.dicksonrendall-antiques.co.uk

Drummonds Architectural Antiques Ltd
78 Royal Hospital Rd., Chelsea. SW3 4HN.
EST. 1988. SALVO. Open 10-6, Sat. by appointment. STOCK: *Reproduction architectural materials including wood and stone flooring, bathrooms, door furniture, garden ornaments. Also a branch on the A3 at Hindhead, Surrey stocking period antique pieces - 01428 609 444.* SER: Manufacturer of cast-iron baths, iron conservatories and brassware; restorations (stonework and gates); vitreous re-enamelling of baths. SIZE: Large. PARK: Easy.
TEL: 020 7376 4499; FAX: 020 7376 4488
E-MAIL: info@drummonds-arch.co.uk
WEBSITE: www.drummonds-arch.co.uk

Gallery Yacou BADA LAPADA
127 Fulham Rd. SW3 6RT. (Y. and R. Yacoubian)
EST. 1920. Open 10.30-6, Sat. 11.30-5. STOCK: *Decorative and antique Oriental and European carpets (room-size and over-size).* SER: Consultation, repairs and cleaning. FAIRS: Olympia: LAPADA.
TEL: 020 7584 2929; FAX: 020 7584 3535
E-MAIL: galleryyacou@aol.com

General Trading Co Ltd
2 Symons St. SW3 2TJ.
EST. 1920. Open 10-6.30. STOCK: *English and Continental furniture, £100-£10,000; objects, both 18th-20th C.* LOC: Near Sloane Sq. SIZE: Medium. VAT: Stan/Spec.
TEL: 020 7730 0411, 020 7823 5426

E-MAIL: enquiries@general-trading.co.uk
WEBSITE: www.general-trading.co.uk

Godson & Coles BADA
92 Fulham Rd. SW3 6HR. (Richard Coles)
EST. 1978. Open 9.30-5.30, Sat. by appointment. STOCK: *Fine 17th to early 19th C English furniture and works of art; modern British art.* FAIRS: Grosvenor House, Olympia (November).
TEL: 020 7584 2200; FAX: 020 7584 2223
E-MAIL: godsonandcoles@aol.com
WEBSITE: www.godsonandcoles.co.uk

Green and Stone
259 Kings Rd. SW3 5EL. (R.J.S. Baldwin)
EST. 1927 FATG. Open 9-6, Sat. 9.30-6, Sun. 12-5. STOCK: *18th-19th C writing and artists' materials, glass and china.* LOC: At junction with Old Church St. SER: Restorations (pictures and frames). PARK: Meters. VAT: Stan.
TEL: 020 7352 0837; FAX: 020 7351 1098
E-MAIL: sales@greenandstone.com
WEBSITE: www.greenandstone.com

James Hardy and Co
235 Brompton Rd. SW3 2EP.
EST. 1853. Open 10-5.30. STOCK: *Silver including tableware, and jewellery.* SER: Valuations; repairs. PARK: Meters.
TEL: 020 7589 5050; FAX: 020 7589 9009

Peter Harrington Antiquarian Bookseller
100 Fulham Rd., Chelsea. SW3 6HS. (Peter and Mati Harrington)
EST. 1969. ABA. ILAB. PBFA. *Trade Only.* Open 10-6. STOCK: *Antiquarian and collectable books, 1500-2000, £20-£50,000+.* SER: Valuations; restorations (full bookbinding); buys at auction. SIZE: Large. FAIRS: Olympia Books & Antiques, Chelsea, New York, Boston, California.
TEL: 020 7591 0220; FAX: 020 7225 7054
E-MAIL: mail@peterharringtonbooks.com
WEBSITE: www.peter-harrington-books.com

Michael Hughes BADA
88 Fulham Rd., Chelsea. SW3 6HR.
EST. 1992. Open 9.30-5.30, Sat. by appointment. STOCK: *18th to early 19th C English furniture and objects.* SIZE: Large. PARK: Meters. VAT: Spec. FAIRS: Grosvenor House.
TEL: 020 7589 0660; FAX: 020 7823 7618; MOBILE: 07880 505123
E-MAIL: info@michaelhughesantiques.co.uk
WEBSITE: www.michaelhughesantiques.co.uk

Anthony James & Son Ltd BADA
88 Fulham Rd. SW3 6HR.
EST. 1949. CINOA. Open 9.30-5.30, Sat. by appointment. STOCK: *Furniture, 1700-1880, £200-*

£50,000; mirrors, bronzes, ormolu and decorative items, £200-£20,000. SER: Valuations; buys at auction. SIZE: Large. PARK: Easy. VAT: Spec. FAIRS: Olympia (June).
TEL: 020 7584 1120; FAX: 020 7823 7618
E-MAIL: info@anthony-james.com
WEBSITE: www.anthony-james.com

John Keil Ltd BADA
1st Floor, 154 Brompton Rd. SW3 1HX.
EST. 1959. Open 9.30-5.30, Sat. by appointment. *STOCK: Fine English furniture, 18th to early 19th C.* LOC: Near Knightsbridge underground station. PARK: 200 yds. VAT: Spec.
TEL: 020 7589 6454; FAX: 020 7823 8235
E-MAIL: antiques@johnkeil.com
WEBSITE: www.johnkeil.com

Limelight Movie Art
135 Kings Rd., Chelsea. SW3 4PW
STOCK: Vintage film posters and lobby cards. SER: Sale, rental. PARK: On street.
TEL: 020 7751 5584
E-MAIL: info@limelightmovieart.com
WEBSITE: www.limelightmovieart.com

Peter Lipitch Ltd BADA
120 Fulham Rd. SW3 6HU.
EST. 1954. Open 9.30-5.30. *STOCK: Fine English furniture and mirrors.* SIZE: Large. VAT: Spec. FAIRS: BADA; Grosvenor House.
TEL: 020 7373 3328; FAX: 020 7373 8888
E-MAIL: antiques@peterlipitch.com
WEBSITE: www.peterlipitch.com

The Map House BADA
54 Beauchamp Place. SW3 1NY. (P. Curtis and P. Stuchlik)
EST. 1907. ABA. IMCOS. Open 10-6, Sat. 10.30-5 or by appointment. *STOCK: Antique and rare maps, atlases, engravings and globes.* LOC: Knightsbridge, near Harrods. SIZE: Large. VAT: Stan. FAIRS: Grosvenor House, Miami Map Fair.
TEL: 020 7589 4325 or 020 7584 8559; FAX: 020 7589 1041
E-MAIL: maps@themaphouse.com
WEBSITE: www.themaphouse.com

McKenna and Co LAPADA
28 Beauchamp Place. SW3 1NJ. (C. and M. McKenna)
EST. 1982. CINOA. NAG. Open 10-6. *STOCK: Fine jewellery, Georgian to post-war, £250-£200,000; some silver and objects.* LOC: Off Brompton Rd., near Harrods. SER: Valuations; restorations. SIZE: Medium. PARK: Meters. VAT: Stan/Margin.
TEL: 020 7584 1966; FAX: 020 7225 2893
E-MAIL: info@mckennajewels.com
WEBSITE: www.mckennajewels.com

Old Church Galleries
98 Fulham Rd., Chelsea. SW3 6HS. (Mrs Matty Harrington)
FATG. ABA. Open 10-6. *STOCK: Maps and views of London and all parts of the world; natural history, sporting and decorative prints, botanical and architectural engravings.* SER: Framing. SIZE: Large.
TEL: 020 7591 8790; FAX: 020 7591 8791
E-MAIL: sales@old-church-galleries.com
WEBSITE: www.old-church-galleries.com

Orientalist LAPADA
152-154 Walton St. SW3 2JJ. (Michael Sakhai)
EST. 1985. Open 10.30-5.15, appointment advisable. *STOCK: Oriental, European, antique and reproduction rugs - classic and tribal Persian, Caucasian, Indian and Turkish, especially over-sized; Aubusson, tapestries, cushions and contemporary rugs. New fine art division stocking post-war original masterpieces on paper - Picasso, Miro, Chagall.* SER: Valuations; restorations (cleaning and repairing rugs, carpets and tapestries). Custom-made facility. SIZE: Large. PARK: Easy. FAIRS: Olympia.
TEL: 020 7581 2332
E-MAIL: rugs@orientalist.demon.co.uk
WEBSITE: www.orientalistrugs.com
www.waltonfinearts.com

ASIAN ART

Lark E. Mason

Lark E. Mason offers a clear and concise guide to understanding the fine and decorative arts of Asia including the arts of the Islamic world. He addresses this complex subject in an easy-to-follow format beginning with an overview of the tumultuous history of the continent, leading into chapters on ceramics, metalwork, the arts of the craftsman, furniture and lacquer, textiles, prints and paintings. Each chapter includes a summary of the minor and major art forms with expert advice for judging quality and identifying fakes and over-restored objects. A valuable dictionary of terms and tables with reign dates and marks is included.

Specifications: 336pp., 336 col. illus., 11 x 9in./280 x 233mm. **£35.00 (hardback)**

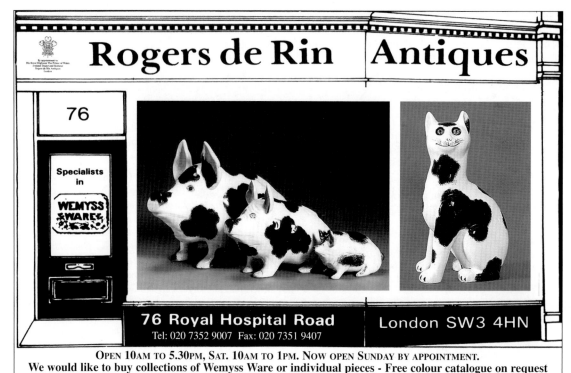
Prides of London
15 Paultons House, Paultons Sq. SW3 5DU.
Open by appointment. STOCK: *Fine 18th-19th C English and Continental furniture; objets d'art.* SER: Interior design. TEL: 020 7586 1227

Rogers de Rin   BADA
76 Royal Hospital Rd., Chelsea. SW3 4HN. (V. de Rin)
EST. 1950. **Open 10-5.30, Sat. 10-1, Sun. by appointment,** STOCK: *Wemyss pottery, objets d'art, decorative furnishings (Regency taste), collectors' specialities, Vienna bronzes, treen, sewing items and needleworks, 18th-19th C, £50-£10,000.* LOC: **Just beyond Royal Hospital, corner of Paradise Walk.** SIZE: **Small.** PARK: **Easy.** VAT: **Spec.** FAIRS: **Olympia (June and Nov); BADA (March).**
TEL: **020 7352 9007;** FAX: **020 7351 9407**
E-MAIL: **rogersderin@rogersderin.co.uk**
WEBSITE: **www.rogersderin.co.uk**

Charles Saunders Antiques
255 Fulham Rd. SW3 6HY.
EST. 1987. Open Mon.-Fri.10-6; Sat. 10-4. STOCK: *Unusual and interesting Continental and English furniture, decorations and lighting from all periods.* SIZE: Large. VAT: Spec. FAIRS: Olympia (June).
TEL: 020 7351 5242; FAX: 020 7352 8142
E-MAIL: info@charlessaundersantiques.com
WEBSITE: www.charlessaundersantiques.com

Robert Stephenson
1 Elystan St. Chelsea Green. SW3 3NT.
EST. 1984. Open 9.30-5.30, Sat. 10.30-2. STOCK: *Antique and decorative room-sized carpets and kilims; antique Oriental rugs, European tapestries and Aubussons, textiles, needlepoints and cushions; modern Bessarabian kilims; traditional and own contemporary designs.* SER: Cleaning; restorations; valuations.
TEL: 020 7225 2343; FAX: same
E-MAIL: stephensoncarpets@tiscali.co.uk
WEBSITE: www.robertstephenson.co.uk

O.F. Wilson Ltd   BADA LAPADA
3-6 Queen's Elm Parade, Old Church St. SW3 6EJ. (P. and V.E. Jackson and K.E. Simmonds)
EST. 1935. **Open 9.30-5.30, Sat. 10-2, or by appointment.** STOCK: *English and French furniture, mirrors, mantelpieces, objets d'art.* LOC: **Corner Fulham Rd.** SER: Valuations. SIZE: 6 showrooms. VAT: Spec.
TEL: **020 7352 9554;** FAX: **020 7351 0765**
E-MAIL: **ofw@email.msn.com**

SW5

Beaver Coin Room
Beaver Hotel, 57 Philbeach Gdns. SW5 9ED. (Jan Lis)
EST. 1971. BNTA, BAMS. Open by appointment. STOCK: *European coins, 10th-18th C; commemorative medals, 15th-20th C; all £5-£5,000.* LOC: 2 mins. walk

O.F. WILSON LTD.

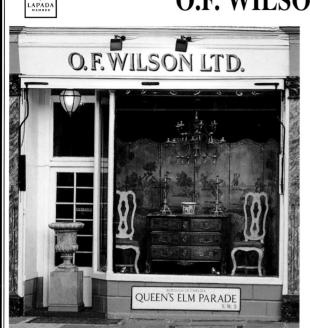

QUEEN'S ELM PARADE
OLD CHURCH STREET
LONDON, SW3 6EJ

Tel: 020 7352 9554
Fax: 020 7351 0765
Email: ofw@email.msn.com

English and Continental period
decorative furniture, mirrors,
objets d'art; period English & French
mantelpieces

Mon.–Fri. 9.30–5.30
Sat. 10.00–2.00
Other times by arrangement
Valuations given

---

from Earls Court Rd. SER: Valuations; buys at auction (coins and medals). SIZE: Small. PARK: On site. VAT: Stan. FAIRS: London Coin and Coinex.
TEL: 020 7373 4553; FAX: 020 7373 4555
E-MAIL: janjlis@yahoo.com

SW6

20th Century Gallery
821 Fulham Rd. SW6 5HG. (E. Brandl)
Open 10-6, Sat. 10-1. STOCK: *Post-Impressionist and modern British oils and watercolours; original prints.* LOC: Near Munster Rd. junction. SER: Restorations and framing. SIZE: Small. PARK: Easy. VAT: Spec.
TEL: 020 7731 5888
E-MAIL: info@20thcenturygallery.co.uk
WEBSITE: www.20thcenturygallery.co.uk

(55) For Decorative Living
55 New King's Rd., Chelsea. SW6 4SE. (Mrs J. Rhodes)
EST. 1987. BFS. Open 10.30-5.30. STOCK: *Furniture, lighting and decorative items, European, Colonial and garden.* SER: Design, interiors and furniture. SIZE: Large. PARK: Pay & Display.
TEL: 020 7736 5623
E-MAIL: info@decorativeliving.co.uk
WEBSITE: www.decorativeliving.co.uk

A&L Antiques
284 Lillie Rd., Fulham. SW6 7PX. (Andrew Harley and Loraine Plummer)
EST. 1991. Open 10-5.30. STOCK: *British and Continental furniture, paintings and objets d'art from various periods.* SER: Valuations; restorations. SIZE: Medium. PARK: Easy. VAT: Spec.
TEL: 020 7610 2694; FAX: 020 7610 2694
E-MAIL: maharley@btconnect.com
WEBSITE: www.aandlantiques.co.uk

Christopher Bangs Ltd   BADA LAPADA
PO Box 6077. SW6 7XS. (Christopher Bangs and Judy Wentworth)
EST. 1971. CINOA. Open by appointment. STOCK: *Domestic metalwork and metalware, works of art, decorative objects, 18th-19th C textiles.* SER: Research; commission buys at auction; finder. VAT: Stan/Spec.
TEL: 020 7381 3532 (24 hrs); FAX: 020 7381 2192 (24 hrs).

Sebastiano Barbagallo
661 Fulham Rd. SW6 5PZ.
EST. 1975. Open 10-6 including Sun. STOCK: *Chinese furniture; antiques and handicrafts from India, Tibet, SE Asia and China.* LOC: Near Fulham Broadway tube station.
TEL: 020 7751 0691

Barclay Samson Ltd
61 Finlay St. SW6 6HF. (Richard Barclay)
IVPDA. Open by appointment. STOCK: Pre-1950 original lithographic posters, French, German, Swiss, American, British and Russian Constructivist schools. VAT: Spec. FAIRS: Olympia (June); USA.
TEL: 020 7731 8012 or 0033 2975 88104 (France)
E-MAIL: richard@barclaysamson.com
WEBSITE: www.barclaysamson.com

Julia Boston   LAPADA
588 King's Rd. SW6 2DX.
EST. 1976. CINOA. Open 10-6 or by appointment.
STOCK: 18th-19th C furniture, lighting, tapestry cartoons, antiquarian prints and decoration. SIZE: Large. PARK: Pay and Display. VAT: Spec.
TEL: 020 7610 6783; FAX: 020 7610 6784
E-MAIL: julia@juliaboston.com
WEBSITE: www.juliaboston.com

I. and J.L. Brown Ltd
634-636 King's Rd. SW6 2DU.
Open 9-6. STOCK: English and French provincial furniture including tables, country chairs, dressers, armoires, side tables and servers; decorative items. SER: Restorations; chair re-rushing. SIZE: Large.
TEL: 020 7736 4141; FAX: 020 7736 9164
E-MAIL: sales@brownantiqueslondon.com
WEBSITE: www.brownantiques.con

Aurea Carter   LAPADA
PO Box 44134. SW6 3YX.
CINOA. STOCK: Mainly 18th and early 19th C English ceramics. FAIRS: Olympia (June).
TEL: 020 7731 3486
E-MAIL: aureacarter@englishceramics.co.uk
WEBSITE: www.englishceramics.co.uk

Rupert Cavendish Antiques
610 King's Rd. SW6 2DX. (Rupert Cavendish and Hakan Groth)
EST. 1980. Open 10-6. STOCK: Biedermeier, Art Deco and Empire furniture, 20th C French and Scandinavian paintings and alabaster lamps. LOC: Just before New King's Rd. SER: Valuations; restorations (furniture). SIZE: Large. PARK: Easy. VAT: Spec.
TEL: 020 7731 7041; FAX: 020 7731 8302
E-MAIL: rcavendish@aol.com
WEBSITE: www.rupertcavendish.co.uk

Hilary Chapman Fine Prints
20th Century Gallery, 821 Fulham Rd. SW6 5HG. (Hilary Chapman)
EST. 1984. Open 10-6, Sat. 10-1. STOCK: Early 20th C British prints, original etchings, engravings, woodcuts, wood engravings and lithographs; specialising in colour woodcuts and linocuts of the 1920s and 30s, £100-£4,000. LOC: Central Fulham. SER: Valuations. SIZE: Small. PARK: Side roads. FAIRS: Royal Academy, Modern Works on

Paper; Royal College, 20/21 International Art Fair; Chelsea Art Fair.
TEL: 020 7384 1334; FAX: 020 7384 1334; MOBILE: 07808 415048
E-MAIL: chapmanprints@aol.com
WEBSITE: www.hilarychapmanfineprints.co.uk

John Clay
263 New King's Rd., Fulham. SW6 4RB.
EST. 1974. Open 10-6. STOCK: Furniture, £50-£10,000; objets d'art and animal objects, silver and clocks, £10-£5,000; all 18th-19th C. NOT STOCKED: Pine. LOC: Close to Parsons Green, A3. SER: Restorations (furniture, objets d'art). SIZE: Medium. PARK: Easy. VAT: Stan/Spec.
TEL: 020 7731 5677
E-MAIL: johnclayantiques@btconnect.com

Charles Edwards   BADA
19a Rumbold Rd. SW6 2HX.
EST. 1972. Open 9.30-6, Sat. 10-6. STOCK: Antique light fixtures; furniture, 18th-19th C; decorative items. LOC: Just off King's Rd. SIZE: Medium. PARK: Meters. VAT: Stan/Spec.
TEL: 020 7736 7172; FAX: 020 7371 7388
E-MAIL: charles@charlesedwards.com

Hector Finch Lighting
90 Wandsworth Bridge Rd. SW6 2TF. (Mr and Mrs H. Finch)
EST. 1988. Open 10-5.30. STOCK: Antiques and period lighting, early 20th C, contemporary and reproduction. SER: Restorations (period lighting). SIZE: Medium. PARK: Side streets or Pay and Display. VAT: Global.
TEL: 020 7731 8886; FAX: 020 7731 7408
E-MAIL: hector@hectorfinch.com
WEBSITE: www.hectorfinch.com

Fiona McDonald Antiques & Interiors   LAPADA
97 Munster Rd. SW6 5RG (Fiona McDonald)
EST. 1997 CINOA. Open 10-5.30. STOCK: 20th C lighting, mid 20th C decorative furniture and 18th-20th C mirrors. PARK: Meters VAT: Margin. FAIRS: Decorative Antiques, Battersea.
TEL: 020 7731 3234; MOBILE: 07788 746778
E-MAIL: email@fionamcdonald.com
WEBSITE: www.fionamcdonald.com

The French House (Antiques) Ltd
41-43 Parsons Green Lane. SW6 4HH. (S.B. and M.J. Hazell)
EST. 1995. Open 10-6. STOCK: Wooden beds, 18th-19th C, £900-£2,500; gilt mirrors, 19th C, £300-£2,000; lighting, 19th-20th C, £200-£1,000; sofas £1,200 - £2,800; all pieces sourced from France and restored in the UK. SER: Restorations; cabinet making; upholstery; French polishing; painting. SIZE: Medium. VAT: Margin.
TEL: 020 7371 7573
E-MAIL: marcus@thefrenchhouse.co.uk
WEBSITE: www.thefrenchhouse.co.uk

Robin Greer
434 Fulham Palace Rd. SW6 6HX.
EST. 1965. ABA. PBFA. Open by appointment. STOCK:
Children's and illustrated books, original illustrations. SER:
Catalogues issued. PARK: Easy, metre
TEL: 020 7381 9113
E-MAIL: rarities@rarerobin.com
WEBSITE: www.rarerobin.com

Gregory, Bottley and Lloyd
13 Seagrave Rd. SW6 1RP.
EST. 1858. Open 9.30-5, CL: Sat. Appointment
advisable. STOCK: *Mineral specimens, £3-£4,000; fossils,
£3-£4,000; geological antiques, £20-£2,000.* LOC: Nearest
underground station West Brompton. SIZE: Medium.
PARK: Easy. VAT: Stan.
TEL: 020 7381 5522; FAX: 020 7381 5512
E-MAIL: brianlloyd@bottley.co.uk
WEBSITE: www.bottley.co.uk

Guinevere Antiques
574-580 King's Rd. SW6 2DY.
Open 9.30-6, Sat. 10-5.30 (warehouse by appointment
only). STOCK: *Period decorative antiques and accessories.*
SIZE: Large + trade warehouse.
TEL: 020 7736 2917; FAX: 020 7736 8267
E-MAIL: sales@guinevere.co.uk
WEBSITE: www.guinevere.co.uk

Gutlin Clocks and Antiques   LAPADA
606 King's Rd. SW6 2DX. (J. & M. Coxhead)
EST. 1990. Open 10-6. STOCK: *Longcase clocks, £2,000-
£8,000; mantel clocks, £300-£6,000; furniture and
lighting, £500-£3,000; all 18th-19th C.* LOC: **200 yards
from beginning of New King's Rd.** SER: **Valuations;
restorations (clocks and clock cases); buys at auction
(clocks).** SIZE: **Large - two floors.** PARK: **Maxwell Rd.**
TEL: **020 7384 2804;** FAX: **020 7384 2439;** HOME: **020
8740 6830**
E-MAIL: **mark@gutlin.com**
WEBSITE: **www.gutlin.com**

House of Mirrors
597 King's Rd. SW6 2EL. (G. Witek)
EST. 1960. Open 10-6. STOCK: *Mirrors.* SER:
Restorations.
TEL: 020 7736 5885; FAX: 020 7610 9188
E-MAIL: info@houseofmirrors.co.uk
WEBSITE: www.houseofmirrors.co.uk

HRW Antiques (London) Ltd   LAPADA
26 Sulivan Rd. SW6 3DT.
EST. **1988. Open 9-5. CL: Sat.** STOCK: *18th-19th C
English and Continental furniture.* LOC: **Within easy
reach of the King's Rd. and Chelsea Harbour.** SIZE:
Large. PARK: **Off street.** VAT: **Spec.**
TEL: **020 7371 7995;** FAX: **020 7371 9522**
E-MAIL: **iain@hrw-antiques.com**
WEBSITE: **www.hrw-antiques.com**

Indigo
275 New King's Rd., Parsons Green. SW6 4RD.
(Richard Lightbown and Marion Bender)
EST. 1983. Open 10-6. STOCK: *Chinese, Indian, Japanese
and Tibetan furniture, accessories and garden statuary,
Chinese porcelain, from early 19th C; £10-£5,000.* LOC:
Near Parsons Green underground. SIZE: Medium. PARK:
Nearby.
TEL: 020 7384 3101
E-MAIL: antiques@indigo-uk.com
WEBSITE: www.indigo-uk.com

Christopher Jones Antiques
618-620 King's Rd. SW6 2DU.
EST. 1977. Open 10-5.30. STOCK: *Continental and British
decorative objects and furniture, screens and mirrors, 18th-
19th C, £500-£10,000.* VAT: Spec. FAIRS: Olympia.
TEL: 020 7731 4655; FAX: 020 7371 8682
E-MAIL: florehouse@msn.com
WEBSITE: www.christopherjonesantiques.co.uk

King's Court Galleries
949-953 Fulham Rd. SW6 5HY. (Mrs J. Joel)
EST. 1983. ABA. FATG. Open 10-5.30. STOCK: *Antique
maps, engravings, decorative and sporting prints.* LOC:
Close to Putney Bridge. SER: Framing (on site). SIZE:
Large. PARK: Easy. VAT: Stan.
TEL: 020 7610 6939;
E-MAIL: kcgsales@kingscourtgalleries.co.uk
WEBSITE: www.kingscourtgalleries.co.uk

L. and E. Kreckovic
559 King's Rd. SW6 2EB. (John Kreckovic)
EST. 1975. Open 10-6. STOCK: *18th-19th C furniture.*
LOC: Nr. Lots Rd. SER: Restorations; bespoke furniture
manufacture.
TEL: 020 7736 0753; FAX: 020 7731 5904
E-MAIL: jk@u-k.ru

Lunn Antiques Ltd
86 New Kings Rd., Parsons Green. SW6 4LU.
(Stephen and Juliet Lunn)
EST. 1976. Open 10-6. STOCK: *Antique lace, antique and
modern bed linen, nightdresses, christening robes, period
clothing, antique textiles.* SER: Laundry and restoration
(antique linen and lace). VAT: Margin.
TEL: 020 7736 4638; FAX: 020 7371 7113
E-MAIL: lunnantiques@aol.com
WEBSITE: www.lunnantiques.com

Mark Maynard Antiques
651 Fulham Rd. SW6 5PU.
EST. 1977. Open 10-5, Sun by appointment. STOCK:
Decorative items, £10-£700. LOC: Near Fulham
Broadway underground station. SIZE: Medium, two
floors. PARK: Easy. VAT: Stan/Spec.
TEL: 020 7731 3533
E-MAIL: info@markmaynard.co.uk
WEBSITE: www.markmaynard.co.uk

Mora & Upham Antiques

584 King's Rd. SW6 2DX. (Matthew Upham)
EST. 1996. Open 9.30-6. *STOCK: Chandeliers, English and Continental furniture, decorative items, garden statuary.* LOC: Corner premises. SER: Valuations; restorations (lighting); design advice; chandelier hanging. SIZE: Medium. PARK: Meters. VAT: Spec.
TEL: 020 7731 4444; FAX: 020 7736 0440
E-MAIL: mora.upham@talk21.com
WEBSITE: www.moraandupham.com

Nimmo & Spooner

277 Lillie Rd., Fulham. SW6 7LL. (Catherine Nimmo and Myra Spooner)
EST. 1996. Open 10.30-5.30. *STOCK: Objects and furniture including painted dressers and chests of drawers, tables, mirrors, 18th-20th C, to £3,500.* LOC: Between Fulham Broadway and Hammersmith. SIZE: Medium. PARK: Nearby. FAIRS: The Decorative Antiques and Textiles Fair.
TEL: 020 7385 2724; FAX: same
E-MAIL: info@nimmoandspooner.co.uk

Old World Trading Co

565 King's Rd. SW6 2EB. (R.J. Campion)
EST. 1970. Open 9.30-6. *STOCK: Fireplaces, chimney pieces and accessories, chandeliers, mirrors, furniture including decorative, works of art, antiquities.* VAT: Spec.
TEL: 020 7731 4708; FAX: 020 7731 1291
E-MAIL: bobcampion@oldworldtrading.co.uk

Ossowski   BADA
595 King's Rd. SW6 2EL.
EST. 1960. Open 9.30-5.30. *STOCK: English 18th C gilt wood mirrors and decorative wood carvings.* SER: Valuations; restorations. SIZE: Large. VAT: Spec. FAIRS: IFAAD, New York (Oct).
TEL: 020 7731 0334.
E-MAIL: markossowski @hotmail.com

The Pine Mine (Crewe-Read Antiques)

100 Wandsworth Bridge Rd., Fulham. SW6 2TF. (D. and Caspian Crewe-Read)
EST. 1971. Open 9.45-5.45, Sat. 9.45-4.30. *STOCK: Georgian and Victorian pine, Welsh dressers, farmhouse tables, chests of drawers, boxes and some architectural items.* LOC: From Sloane Sq., down King's Rd., into New King's Rd., left into Wandsworth Bridge Rd. SER: Furniture made from old wood; stripping and restoration; export. Furniture made to order to customer's specification. SIZE: Large. PARK: Outside. VAT: Stan.
TEL: 020 7736 1092; FAX: 020 7736 5283

Daphne Rankin and Ian Conn

608 King's Rd. SW6 2DX.
EST. 1979. Open 10-5.30. *STOCK: Oriental porcelain including Chinese, Japanese, Imari, Cantonese, Satsuma, Nanking, Famille Rose, £500-£25,000; Dutch Delft; tortoiseshell tea caddies.* SER: Valuations; buys at auction

(as stock). SIZE: Medium. PARK: Maxwell Rd. adjacent to shop. VAT: Stan/Spec. FAIRS: Hong Kong (May).
TEL: 020 7384 1847; FAX: same; MOBILE: 07774 487713
E-MAIL: info@rankin-conn-chinatrade.com
WEBSITE: www.rankin-conn-chinatrade.com

Rogers & Co

604 Fulham Rd. SW6 5RP. (Sebastian Rogers)
EST. 1971. Open Mon.-Fri. 9.30-6. *STOCK: Furniture, 18th-19th C, £100-£3,000; upholstery.* LOC: Near Fulham library, Parsons Green Lane. SER: Valuations. Interior design SIZE: Large. PARK: Side streets. VAT: Stan/Spec.
TEL: 020 7731 8504; FAX: 020 7610 6040
E-MAIL: design@rogersandcodesign.com
WEBSITE: www.rogersandcodesign.com

Soo San

598A King's Rd. SW6 2DX.
EST. 1996. Open 10-6. *STOCK: Chinese furniture and accessories – cabinets, coffee tables, chairs, consol tables, desks, stools, beds, leather trunks, wedding baskets, wooden food containers, birdcages, porcelain, 18th-19th C; lacquer ware and Burmese buddhas; all £50-£18,000.* SER: Valuations; restorations (re-lacquering, gilding and wood). SIZE: Large.
TEL: 020 7731 2063; FAX: 020 7731 1566
E-MAIL: enquiries@soosan.co.uk
WEBSITE: www.soosan.co.uk

Talisman

79-91 New Kings Rd. SW6 4SQ. (Kenneth Bolam)
EST. 1980. Open 10-6. *STOCK: 20thC, 18th C Swedish and French garden statuary.* SIZE: Large. VAT: Stan/Spec.
TEL: 020 7731 4686; FAX: 020 7731 0444
E-MAIL: shop@talismanlondon.com
WEBSITE: www.talismanlondon.com

Trowbridge Gallery

555 King's Rd. SW6 2EB. (M. Trowbridge)
EST. 1980. Open 9.30-6, Sat. 10-5.30, Sun 11-5. *STOCK: Decorative prints, 17th-19th C, £50-£10,000; photography, textiles.* SER: Buys at auction (antiquarian books and prints); hand-made frames; decorative mounting. SIZE: Large. PARK: Easy. VAT: Stan.
TEL: 020 7371 8733
E-MAIL: nanette@trowbridge.co.uk
WEBSITE: www.trowbridgegallery.com

York Gallery Ltd   LAPADA
569 King's Rd. SW6 2EB. (Jane and Gerd Beyer)
EST. 1984. Open 10.30-5.30. *STOCK: Antique prints.* SER: Bespoke framing. SIZE: Medium. VAT: Stan.
TEL: 020 7736 2260; FAX: same; MOBILE: 07802 452380
E-MAIL: prints@yorkgallery.co.uk
WEBSITE: www.yorkgallery.co.uk

SW7

Campbells of London

33 Thurloe Place. SW7 4HQ. (Wendel Clement and Richard Quamina)
EST. 1967. Guild of Master Craftsmen. Open 10-6, Sat. 10-5. STOCK: *20th C Impressionist and modern British oils and watercolours; frames.* LOC: 2 mins. walk from South Kensington tube, just off Exhibition Rd. SER: Master framing, frame matching, carving, gilding; restorations. PARK: Pay and display bays outside.
TEL: 020 7584 9268
E-MAIL: info@campbellsart.co.uk
WEBSITE: www.campbellsoflondon.co.uk; www.campbellsart.co.uk

Robert Frew Ltd

8 Thurloe Place. SW7 2RX
EST. 1978. ABA. PBFA. Open 10-6, Sat. 11-5. STOCK: *Books, 15th-20th C, £50-£50,000; maps and prints, 15th-19th C, £5-£5,000.* PARK: Easy. VAT: Stan. FAIRS: ABA Olympia; Chelsea; PBFA; California; New York; Boston.
TEL: 020 7590 6650; FAX: 020 7590 6651
E-MAIL: shop@robertfrew.com
WEBSITE: www.robertfrew.com

The Gloucester Road Bookshop

123 Gloucester Rd., South Kensington. SW7 4TE. (Nicholas Dennys)
EST. 1983. Open 9.30am-10.30pm, Sat. and Sun. 10.30-6.30. STOCK: *Secondhand hardback and paperback books, all genres, mainly 19th-20th C, £1-£50; modern first editions, mainly 20th C, £5-£10,000; rare books, 17th-20th C, £70-£5,000.* LOC: 150 yards Gloucester Road underground station. Come out of station, cross the road and turn right. SER: Valuations; book search. SIZE: Medium. PARK: Loading; easy at weekends. Meters nearby.
TEL: 020 7370 3503; FAX: 020 7373 0610
E-MAIL: manager@gloucesterbooks.co.uk

M.P. Levene Ltd   BADA

5 Thurloe Place. SW7 2RR.
EST. **1889. Open 9.30-6. CL: Sat. pm.** STOCK: *English and Irish silver, silver flatware services, old Sheffield plate, scale silver models and cufflinks, antique to 20th C.* LOC: **Few mins. past Harrods, near South Kensington underground station.** SER: **Valuations.** PARK: **Easy.** VAT: **Stan/Spec.**
TEL: **020 7589 3755; FAX: 020 7589 9908**
E-MAIL: **silver@mplevene.co.uk**
WEBSITE: **www.mplevene.co.uk**

A. & H. Page (Est. 1840)

66 Gloucester Rd. SW7 4QT.
NAG. Open 9-5.45, Sat. 10-2. STOCK: *Silver, jewellery, watches.* SER: Valuations; repairs; silversmith; goldsmith.
TEL: 020 7584 7349; FAX: same
E-MAIL: rmz26@hotmail.com
WEBSITE: www.gonumber.com/75847349

The Taylor Gallery Ltd   BADA

1 Bolney Gate, Ennismore Gardens. SW7 1QW. (Jeremy Taylor)
EST. **1986. Open by appointment.** STOCK: *Irish, British, China Trade and marine paintings 19th-20th C, especially Edward Seago, Sir William Russell Flint, Montague Dawson and Norman Wilkinson.* VAT: **Stan.** FAIRS: **Olympia (June and November), BADA (March).**
TEL: **020 7581 0253; FAX: 020 7589 4495**
E-MAIL: **jeremy@taylorgallery.co.uk**
WEBSITE: **www.taylorgallery.com**

The Wyllie Gallery

44 Elvaston Place. SW7 5NP. (J.G. Wyllie)
EST. 1980. Open by appointment. STOCK: *19th-20th C marine paintings and etchings, especially works by the Wyllie family.* LOC: Short walk from Gloucester Rd. underground. PARK: Easy.
TEL: 020 7584 6024

SW8

Davies Antiques   LAPADA

c/o Cadogan Tate 6-12 Ponton Rd. SW8 5BA. (Hugh Davies)
EST. **1976. Open by appointment only.** STOCK: *Continental porcelain especially Meissen, 1710-1930.* PARK: **Own.**
TEL: **020 8947 1902; FAX: same; MOBILE: 07753 739689**
E-MAIL: hdavies@antique-meissen.com
WEBSITE: www.antique-meissen.com

LASSCO   LAPADA

Brunswick House,
30 Wandsworth Rd. SW8 2LG. (Ferrous Auger)
Open 10-5. STOCK: *Architectural reclamations, architectural antiques, fireplaces, garden ornaments, decorative stonework, flooring, doors etc.* LOC: **Corner of Wandsworth Road and Nine Elms Lane, opposite the Vauxhall Bus Depot.**
TEL: **020 7394 2100; FAX: 020 7501 7797**
E-MAIL: **brunswick@lassco.co.uk**
WEBSITE: **www.lassco.co.uk**

Paul Orssich

2 St. Stephen's Terrace, South Lambeth. SW8 1DH.
Open by appointment. STOCK: *Old, rare and out-of-print books on Spain and Hispanic studies; from £20.* LOC: Near Stockwell underground. PARK: Meters. FAIRS: Madrid Book (Nov).
TEL: 020 7787 0030; FAX: 020 7735 9612
E-MAIL: paulo@orssich.com
WEBSITE: www.orssich.com

SW9

Rodney Franklin Antiques

EST. 1968. Open by appointment. STOCK: *French and English mirrors and beds, furniture, lighting, architectural and garden items.* VAT: Stan/Spec.
TEL: 020 7274 0729; MOBILE: 07789 880057

SW10

Orientation Antiques
2 Park Walk. SW10 0AD. (Evelyne Soler)
EST. 1990. Open 10-5.30, Sat. by appointment. STOCK:
*Continental furniture, 18th-19th C; Chinese porcelain,
ceramics, works of art, China trade items, to £20,000.* LOC:
Off Fulham Rd. SIZE: Medium. VAT: Spec.
TEL: 020 7351 0234; FAX: 020 7351 7535
E-MAIL: evelynesoler@aol.com
WEBSITE: www.orientationantiques.com

Jonathan Clark & Co
18 Park Walk, Chelsea. SW10 0AQ.
SLAD. Open 10-6.30, Sat. by appointment. STOCK:
Modern British paintings and sculpture. VAT: Margin
FAIRS: Islington; Art London; 20/21 British Art Fair
TEL: 020 7351 3555; FAX: 020 7823 3187
E-MAIL: info@jonathanclarkfineart.com
WEBSITE: www.jonathanclarkfineart.com

Carlton Davidson Antiques
507 King's Rd. SW10 0TX.
EST. 1981. Open 10-6, Sat. 10-5. STOCK: *Lamps,
chandeliers, mirrors and decorative items, £1,000-£5,000.*
LOC: Near The Furniture Cave. SIZE: Medium. PARK:
Meters. VAT: Stan.
TEL: 020 7795 0905; FAX: 020 7795 0904
E-MAIL: natalie@carltondavidson.co.uk

The Furniture Cave
533 King's Rd. SW10 0TZ.
EST. 1967. Open 10-6, Sun. 11-5. LOC: Corner of Lots
Rd. SER: Shipping; forwarding. SIZE: Large. PARK:
Meters; outside the congestion charge zone.
TEL: 020 7352 2046
WEBSITE: www.thecave.co.uk

Below are listed some of the dealers at The Furniture
Cave.

Stuart Duggan
First Floor. *Georgian and Victorian furniture, especially
19th-20th C pianos.*
TEL: 020 7352 2046; FAX: 020 7352 3654

Harpur Dearden
First Floor.
TEL: 020 7352 3111; FAX: 020 7352 583

Robert Grothier
TEL: 020 7352 2045; FAX: 020 7352 6803

Kenneth Harvey Antiques   LAPADA
Ground Floor. *Decorative furniture, mirrors, chandeliers,
light fittings.*
TEL: **020 7352 3775**; FAX: **020 7352 3759**
EMAIL: **mail@kennethharvey.com**

Simon Hatchwell Antiques
Ground Floor. EST. 1961. *English and Continental
decorative furniture and objets d'art.*
TEL: 020 7351 2344; FAX: 020 7351 3520

Heritage and Heritage Ltd
First Floor. *Furniture, from William IV to modern Danish.*
Restorations.
TEL: 020 7352 6116; FAX: 020 7352 3654
EMAIL: info@heritageandheritage.co.uk
WEBSITE: www.heritageandheritage.co.uk

Hill Farm Antiques
General antiques including large tables.
TEL: 020 7352 2046; FAX: 020 7352 3654

David Loveday
First Floor. *18th - 20th C furniture.* VAT: Marg/Stan/Spec.
TEL: 020 7352 1100; FAX: 020 7351 5833

John Nicholas Antiques
TEL: 020 7352 2046; FAX: 020 7352 3654

Phoenix Trading Company
Furniture including Indian, porcelain, bronzes.
TEL: 020 7351 6543; FAX: 020 7352 9803

Christopher Preston Antiques   LAPADA
Ground Floor. *Early 19th C and Regency furniture.*
TEL: **020 7352 8587**; FAX: **020 7376 3627**
EMAIL: **christopherprestonltd@yahoo.co.uk**

Anthony Redmile
Basement. *Marble resin neo-classical Grand Tour objects.*
TEL: 020 7351 3813; FAX: 020 7352 8131

Hollywood Road Gallery
12 Hollywood Rd. SW10 9HY. (Patrick Kennaugh)
EST. 1981. Open 10.30-7, Sat. 10-4. STOCK: *Oils,
watercolours, 20th C and contemporary £300-£3,000.* LOC:
Chelsea. SER: Framing; restorations. VAT: Spec. FAIRS:
Affordable Art; Decorative Art, Chelsea.
TEL: 020 7351 1973
E-MAIL: hollywoodgallery@btconnect.com
WEBSITE: hollywoodroadgallery.com

Hünersdorff Rare Books
P.O. Box 582. SW10 9RP. (J.R. von Hünersdorff)
EST. 1969. ABA. ILAB. Open by appointment. STOCK:
*Continental books in rare editions, early printing, science and
medicine, military, Latin America, natural history.* LOC:
Chelsea. FAIRS: Olympia (June).
TEL: 020 7373 3899; FAX: 020 7370 1244
E-MAIL: huner.rarebooks@dial.pipex.com
WEBSITE: www.abebooks.com/home/hunersdorff

Lucy Johnson   BADA LAPADA
10 Billing Place. SW10 9UW.
EST. 1982. CINOA. Open by appointment. STOCK:
**Early English and Continental furniture and works of art;
modern British pictures.** SER: **Restorations.** SIZE:
Showrooms in London, Burford and Snape. PARK:
Easy. VAT: **Margin.** FAIRS: **Olympia.**
TEL: **020 7352 0114**; MOBILE: **07974 149912**
E-MAIL: **lucy-johnson@lucy-johnson.com**
WEBSITE: **www.lucy-johnson.com**

Lane Fine Art Ltd
8 Drayton Gardens. SW10 9SA. (Christopher Foley)
EST. 1958. Open by appointment. STOCK: *Oil paintings, 1500-1850, principally English, major works by the main artists of the period, £10,000-£1 million+.* SER: Valuations. VAT: Stan/Spec.
TEL: 020 7373 3130; FAX: 020 7373 2277
E-MAIL: cf@lanefineart.co.uk
WEBSITE: www.lanefineart.com

Stephen Long
348 Fulham Rd. SW10 9UH.
EST. 1966. Open 9.30-1 and 2.15-5. CL: Mon. morning and Sat. afternoon. STOCK: *English pottery, 18th-19th C, to £400; English painted furniture, 18th to early 19th C; toys and games, household and kitchen items, chintz, materials and patchwork, to £1,000.* LOC: From South Kensington along road on right between Ifield Rd. and Billing Rd. SIZE: Small. PARK: Easy. VAT: Spec.
TEL: 020 7352 8226

McVeigh & Charpentier
498 King's Rd. SW10 0LE. (Maggie Charpentier)
EST. 1979. Open 10.30-5, weekends by appointment only. STOCK: *Continental furniture, mirrors, garden ironwork and stone, 17th-19th C.* LOC: Two blocks down from Earls Court. SIZE: Medium - 2 floors and garden. PARK: In cul de sac adjacent. VAT: Spec. FAIRS: Olympia (June); Harvey (Sept., Jan. and March).
TEL: 020 7351 1442; HOME: 020 7937 6459; MOBILE: 07801 480167
WEBSITE: www.charpentierantiques.com

McWhirter
22 Park Walk, Chelsea. SW10 0AQ. (James McWhirter)
EST. 1988. Open 9.30-5.30 or by appointment. STOCK: *Decorative and unusual furniture, works of art & objects, 17th-20th C.* LOC: Near Chelsea & Westminster Hospital. SER: Consultancy (art and interior design). SIZE: Medium. PARK: Meters. VAT: Spec.
TEL: 020 7351 5399; FAX: 020 7352 9821
E-MAIL: mail@jamesmcwhirter.com
WEBSITE: www.jamesmcwhirter.com

Mrs Monro Ltd
320 Plaza, 535 Kings Rd. SW10 0SZ. (John Lusk)
EST. 1926. BIDA. Open 9.30-5.30, Fri. 9.30-5. CL: Sat. STOCK: *Small decorative furniture, £500-£1,000+; china, £50-£500+; rugs, prints, lamps, pictures and general decorative items, from £50; all 18th-19th C.* LOC: Between Sloane Sq. and Cadogan Place. SER: Interior design consultancy; restorations (furniture and china). SIZE: Medium. PARK: Garage nearby. VAT: Stan/Spec.
TEL: 08449 841524; FAX: 08449 841525
E-MAIL: design@mrsmonro.co.uk
WEBSITE: www.mrsmonro.co.uk

Opium
414 King's Rd., Chelsea. SW10 0LJ. (Tracy Kitching)
EST. 1999. Open 10-6.30, Sun. 12-5. STOCK: *Indian -*

mainly *from Rajasthan, Gujarat and Kerala - furniture including dowry chests and day beds, marble and stone jalis, stone and teak columns, mainly 18th to early 20th C, to 2,500.* SER: Kashmiri screenwork to order. SIZE: Large. PARK: Pay & Display nearby. VAT: Stan.
TEL: 020 7795 0700; FAX: 020 7795 0800
E-MAIL: shop@opium.force9.co.uk
WEBSITE: www.opiumshop.co.uk

Park Walk Gallery
20 Park Walk, Chelsea. SW10 0AQ. (J. Cooper)
EST. 1988. SLAD. Open 10-6.30, Sat. 11-4. STOCK: *Paintings, £450-£80,000; watercolours, £250-£30,000; drawings, £200-£15,000; all contemporary.* LOC: Off Fulham Rd. SER: Valuations; restorations. SIZE: Medium. PARK: Easy. VAT: Spec. FAIRS: Olympia; Art London.
TEL: 020 7351 0410; FAX: same
WEBSITE: www.jonathancooper.co.uk

Toynbee-Clarke Interiors Ltd
18 Cresswell Place. SW10 9RB. (D. Toynbee-Clarke)
EST. 1953. Open by appointment. STOCK: *Decorative English and Continental furniture and objects, 17th-18th C; Chinese hand painted wallpapers, 18th C; French scenic wallpapers, early 19th C; Chinese and Japanese paintings and screens, 17th-19th C.* SER: Buys at auction. SIZE: Medium. PARK: Meters. VAT: Stan/Spec.
TEL: 020 7373 6889

SW11

Braemar Antiques
113 Northcote Rd., Battersea. SW11 6PW. (Maria Elisabeth Ramos-de-Deus)
EST. 1995. Open 10-6. STOCK: *Painted furniture including armoires, chests of drawers, mirrors and lamps, china and glass.* LOC: Near Clapham junction. SIZE: Small. PARK: Easy. FAIRS: Brocante, Chelsea.
TEL: 020 7924 5628
E-MAIL: ramos-de-deus@msn.com
WEBSITE: www.braemar-antiques.com

Chesney's Antique Fireplace Warehouse
194-200 Battersea Park Rd. SW11 4ND.
EST. 1983. BIDA. Open 9-5.30, Sat. 10-5. STOCK: *18th-19th C marble, stone and timber chimney pieces, £1,000-£150,000; reproduction chimney pieces, £250-£7,500.* LOC: 5 min. taxi journey from Sloane Square tube. SER: Valuations. SIZE: Large. PARK: Parking bays outside. VAT: Stan/Spec.
TEL: 020 7627 1410; FAX: 020 7622 1078
E-MAIL: sales@chesneys.co.uk
WEBSITE: www.chesneys.co.uk

Eccles Road Antiques
60 Eccles Rd., Battersea. SW11 1LX. (H. Rix)
Open 10-5. STOCK: *General antiques, pine and painted furniture and smalls.* LOC: Off Clapham Common.
TEL: 020 7228 1638

Christopher Edwards
Core One The Gasworks, 2 Michael Road. SW11 6AH.
EST. 1982. Mon-Fri 10-6. Other times by appointment.
STOCK: *Furniture and distinctive design* SER: Valuations;
buys at auction. VAT: Stan/Spec.
TEL: 07831 707043
E-MAIL: christophe.ed@btconnect.com
WEBSITE: www.christopheedwards.com

Gideon Hatch Rugs
Unit M, The Old Imperial Laundry, 71-73 Warriner
Gardens, Battersea. SW11 4XW.
EST. 1998. Open by appointment. STOCK: *Oriental and
European rugs, 19th to early 20th C, £500-£25,000.* LOC:
Very close to Battersea Park. SER: Valuations;
restorations; cleaning; buys at auction (rare rugs). SIZE:
Medium. PARK: Easy. VAT: Stan/Spec. FAIRS: Olympia;
Battersea.
TEL: 020 7720 7543
E-MAIL: info@gideonhatch.co.uk
WEBSITE: www.gideonhatch.co.uk

Northcote Road Antiques Market
155A Northcote Rd., Battersea. SW11 6QB.
EST. 1986. Open 10-6, Sun. 12-5. STOCK: *Traditional and
painted furniture, lighting and mirrors, precious and costume
jewellery, silver, cutlery and flatware, prints, ceramics and
glass, Art Deco, Post War design, studio pottery.* SIZE: 30
dealers.
TEL: 020 7228 6850;
WEBSITE: www.spectrumsoft.net/nam

Overmantels
66 Battersea Bridge Rd. SW11 3AG. (Seth Taylor)
EST. 1980 BCFA. Open 9.30-5.30. STOCK: *English
giltwood mirrors, £400-£5,000; French giltwood mirrors,
£700-£6,000; both 18th-19th C.* LOC: 200m south of
Battersea Bridge. SER: Bespoke service for reproduction
range. SIZE: Medium. PARK: Outside shop. VAT:
Stan/Spec.
TEL: 020 7223 8151; FAX: 020 7924 2283
E-MAIL: brochures@overmantels.co.uk
WEBSITE: www.mirrors.co.uk

Regent House Gallery
223 St John's Hill. SW11 1TH. (Nick & Jayne
Underwood Thompson)
EST. 1988. Open 10-6, Thurs. 10-7.30. CL: Mon. STOCK:
*Watercolours and paintings, 19th-20th C, £50-£1,000; prints,
drawings, cartoons, 18th-20th C, £10-£400; small antiques,
books, 19th to early 20th C, £2-£200.* LOC: Top of St John's
Hill, mid-way between Clapham Junction and
Wandsworth Town. SER: Framing. SIZE: Small. PARK: Pay
and display (free Sat. and after 4.30 pm).
TEL: 020 7228 9344 or 020 7228 3973; HOME & FAX:
same
E-MAIL: nick@regenthousegallery.com
WEBSITE: www.regenthousegallery.com

Sieff
Studio C1, The Old Imperial Laundry, 71 Warriner
Gardens. SW11 4XW.
EST. 1994. Open by appointment. STOCK: *English &
French 18th-20th C furniture and objets, £100-£10,000.*
LOC: Bottom of Battersea Park. SER: Valuations; buys at
auction. SIZE: Large PARK: Meters, easy. FAIRS:
Battersea; Olympia; Art London.
TEL: 020 7978 2422; FAX: 020 7978 2423
E-MAIL: sieff@sieff.co.uk
WEBSITE: www.sieff.co.uk

Robert Young Antiques   **BADA**
**68 Battersea Bridge Rd. SW11 3AG. (Robert and
Josyane Young)**
**EST. 1974. CINOA. BIDA Corporate. Open 10-5, Sat.
10-4.30.** STOCK: *Fine country furniture, 17th-18th C,
£500-£50,000; folk art and naive paintings, £100-
£25,000; English and European treen, £100-£25,000;
English and European provincial pottery and metalwork,
£100-£10,000.* LOC: **Turn off King's Rd. or Chelsea
Embankment into Beaufort St., cross over Battersea
Bridge Rd., 9th shop on right.** SER: **Valuations; buys at
auction (folk art, country furniture, treen).** SIZE:
Medium. PARK: **Opposite in side street, and in front of
shop 10-4.** VAT: **Stan/Spec.** FAIRS: **Olympia; Winter
(New York); Fall (San Francisco).**
TEL: **020 7228 7847;** FAX: **020 7585 0489**
E-MAIL: **office@robertyoungantiques.com**
WEBSITE: **www.robertyoungantiques.com**

SW13

Christine Bridge   **BADA** LAPADA
78 Castelnau, Barnes. SW13 9EX.
EST. 1972. CINOA. Open any time by appointment.
STOCK: *Glass - 18th C collectors' and 19th C coloured,
engraved and decorative, £50-£15,000; small decorative
items - papier mâché, bronzes, needlework, ceramics.* LOC:
**Main road from Hammersmith Bridge, 5 mins. from
Olympia.** SER: **Valuations; restorations (glass - cutting,
polishing, declouding); buys at auction; shipping.**
SIZE: **Medium.** PARK: **Easy.** VAT: **Stan/Spec.** FAIRS:
**Olympia (June and Nov); BADA; Brussels; Tokyo;
Melbourne; Sydney; Singapore; Santa Monica;
Cleveland; Chicago.**
TEL: **020 8741 5501;** MOBILE: **07831 126668**
E-MAIL: **christine@bridge-antiques.com**
WEBSITE: **www.bridge-antiques.com and
www.antiqueglass.co.uk**

The Dining Room Shop
62-64 White Hart Lane, Barnes. SW13 0PZ. (K. Dyson)
EST. 1985. Open 10-5.30, Sun. by appointment. STOCK:
*Formal and country dining room furniture, 18th-19th C;
glasses, china, pottery, cutlery, damask and lace table linen,
19th C; associated small and decorative items.* LOC: Near
Barnes rail bridge, turning opposite White Hart public

house. SER: Valuations; restorations; bespoke furniture; finder; interior decorating. SIZE: Medium. PARK: Easy. VAT: Stan/Spec.
TEL: 020 8878 1020; FAX: 020 8876 2367
E-MAIL: enquiries@thediningroomshop.co.uk
WEBSITE: www.thediningroomshop.co.uk

Joy McDonald Antiques
50 Station Rd., Barnes. SW13 0LP. (Angela McDonald)
EST. 1966. Resident. Open 10.30-5.30, prior telephone call advisable. CL: Mon. STOCK: *19th-21st C mirrors, chandeliers and lighting; decorative items and upholstered chairs.* SIZE: Small.
TEL: 020 8876 6184; FAX: same; MOBILE: 07764 612420

New Grafton Gallery
49 Church Rd., Barnes. SW13 9HH. (Claudia Wolfers)
EST. 1968. Open Tues.-Sat. 10-6. Other times by appointment. STOCK: *Modern British and contemporary paintings, drawings and sculpture, from £150.* LOC: Off Castelnau, which runs from Hammersmith Bridge. SER: Valuations; restorations. SIZE: Medium. PARK: Easy. VAT: Stan/Spec.
TEL: 020 8748 8850; FAX: 020 8748 9818
E-MAIL: art@newgrafton.com
WEBSITE: www.newgrafton.com

John Spink Fine Watercolours   BADA
9 Richard Burbidge Mansions, 1 Brasenose Drive, Barnes. SW13 8RB.
EST. 1972. Open by appointment. STOCK: *Fine English watercolours and selected oils, 1720-1920.* FAIRS: World of Watercolours; Olympia (Summer and Winter); BADA (March).
TEL: 020 8741 6152; 07808 614168
E-MAIL: john@johnspink.com
WEBSITE: johnspink.com

Tobias and The Angel
68 White Hart Lane, Barnes. SW13 0PZ. (A. Hughes)
EST. 1985. Open 10-6. STOCK: *Quilts, textiles, furniture, country and painted beds, decorative objects, from 1800.* LOC: Parallel to Barnes High St. SER: Interior design; bespoke furniture; decorative vintage textiles. SIZE: Large. PARK: Easy. VAT: Stan/Spec.
TEL: 020 8878 8902; HOME: same
E-MAIL: enquiries@tobiasandtheangel.com
WEBSITE: www.tobiasandtheangel.com

SW14

Mary Cooke Antiques Ltd   BADA
12 The Old Power Station, 121 Mortlake High St. SW14 8SN. (Mary Cooke and Neil Shepperson)
EST. 1968. Open by appointment. STOCK: *Silver.* SER: Valuations; restorations. VAT: Stan/Spec. FAIRS: Chelsea

(Autumn); BADA; Olympia; Harrogate; NEC.
TEL: 020 8876 5777; FAX: 020 8876 1652; MOBILE:
07769 645559
E-MAIL: silver@marycooke.co.uk
WEBSITE: www.marycooke.co.uk

Paul Foster Books
49 Clifford Ave. East Sheen. SW14 7BW.
EST. 1983 ABA. PBFA. By appointment. STOCK: *Books - antiquarian, 17th-19th C, £100-£1,000; out of print, 19th-20th C, £1-£500; general, 50p-£100.* LOC: 20 yards from South Circular. SIZE: Medium. PARK: Easy.
TEL: 020 8876 7424; FAX: same
E-MAIL: paulfosterbooks@btinternet.com
WEBSITE: www.paulfosterbooks.com

SW15

The Clock Clinic Ltd   BADA LAPADA
85 Lower Richmond Rd., Putney. SW15 1EU. (R.S. Pedler)
EST. 1971 FBHI. Open 9-6, Sat. 9-1. CL: Mon. STOCK: *Clocks and barometers.* SER: Valuations; restorations (as stock); buys at auction. PARK: Meters. VAT: Stan/Spec.
FAIRS: Olympia (June and Nov).
TEL: 020 8788 1407; FAX: 020 8780 2838
E-MAIL: clockclinic@btconnect.com
WEBSITE: www.clockclinic.co.uk

Hanshan Tang Books
Unit 3 Ashburton Centre, 276 Cortis Rd. SW15 3AY.
(John Constable, John Cayley and Myrna Chua)
ABA. Open by appointment. STOCK: *Secondhand, antiquarian and new books and periodicals on Chinese, Japanese, Korean and Central Asian art and culture.* SER: Regular and special catalogues; wants lists welcome.
TEL: 020 8788 4464; FAX: 020 8780 1565;
E-MAIL: hst@hanshan.com
WEBSITE: www.hanshan.com

SW16

A. and J. Fowle
542 Streatham High Rd. SW16 3QF.
EST. 1962. Open 9.30-7. STOCK: *General antiques, Victorian and Edwardian furniture.* LOC: A23 towards Brighton from London. SIZE: Large. PARK: Easy. FAIRS: Ardingly; Newark.
TEL: 020 8764 2896; MOBILE: 07968 058790

SW17

Ash Rare Books
43 Huron Rd. SW17 8RE. (L. Worms)
EST. 1946 ABA, ILAB. Open by appointment only.
STOCK: *Books, 1800-2000, £20-£2,500; prints, 1750-1900, £20-£500.* SER: Buys at auction (books and maps).
SIZE: Small. VAT: Stan.
TEL: 020 8672 2263

E-MAIL: books@ashrare.com
WEBSITE: www.ashrare.com

Ted Few
97 Drakefield Rd. SW17 8RS.
EST. 1975. Resident. Open by appointment. STOCK: *Paintings and sculpture, 1700-1940, £500-£5,000.* LOC: 5 mins. walk from Tooting Bec underground station. SER: Valuations; buys at auction. SIZE: Medium. VAT: Spec.
FAIRS: Olympia.
TEL: 020 8767 2314

Roger Lascelles
Wimbledon Stadium Business Centre, Riverside Rd. SW17 0BA.
EST. 1978. Open Mon.-Fri. 10-5. STOCK: *Longcase painted dial clocks, from £1,500; wall, retro and modern clocks, decorative antiques.* LOC: Warehouse on industrial estate off Garratt Lane. SER: Buys at auction. Prop hire.
SIZE: Medium. PARK: On premises.
TEL: 020 8879 6011; FAX: 020 8879 1818
E-MAIL: info@rogerlascelles.com
WEBSITE: www.rogerlascelles.com www.clockprops.com

SW18

Bellows
202 Garratt Lane, Wandsworth. SW18 4ED. (S. Zoil)
Open Mon-Sat 9-5.30. STOCK: *Victorian and Edwardian fireplaces and surrounds especially cast iron.* SER: Shot-blasting.
TEL: 020 8870 5873

Earlsfield Bookshop
513 Garratt Lane, Wandsworth. SW18 4SW. (Charles Dixon)
EST. 1985. Open 4-6; Sat. 10-5. STOCK: *Books, £1-£50.* LOC: Next to Earlsfield station. SIZE: Small. PARK: Limited.
TEL: 020 8946 3744

Just a Second
284 Merton Rd., Wandsworth. SW18 5JN. (James Ferguson)
EST. 1980. Open 9.30-5.30. CL: Mon. STOCK: *Victorian, Edwardian, pre-1920s and reproduction furniture and bric-a-brac.* LOC: 5 mins. from Southfields underground station.
SER: Valuations; restorations. SIZE: Medium. PARK: Easy.
TEL: 020 8874 2520
E-MAIL: jamesferguson@beeb.net

Thornhill Galleries
SW18 1NL. (Graham and Anthony Wakefield)
EST. 1880. Open Mon-Fri 9-5.30, other times by appointment. STOCK: *Antique chimneypieces/fireplaces in marble, stone and wood. Firegrates, firedogs, fenders, firetools, firescreens and other accessories. 18th, 19th and 20th century. Several hundred pieces in stock.* LOC: Off Putney

WINE LABELS
1730-2003
A WORLDWIDE HISTORY
John Salter

Silver wine labels first made their appearance in the 1730s to identify the contents of unmarked opaque glass wine bottles. Later they adorned clear glass decanters. This book reflects the lively interest of collectors in many countries and of a group of long-standing active members of the Wine Label Circle who have contributed to the text in accordance with their own specialist expertise.

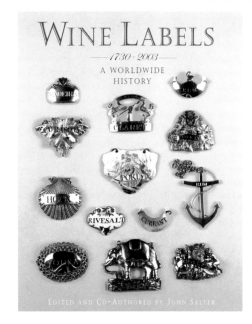

Specifications:
448pp., col. and b.&w.,
11 x 8¹/₂in./279 x 216mm.
£85.00 (hardback)

For full details of all ACC publications, log on to our website:
www.antiquecollectorsclub.com
or telephone 01394 389950 for a free catalogue

Bridge Rd. SER: Valuations; restorations (architectural items); buys at auction (architectural items). SIZE: Large. PARK: Easy, free parking outside showroom. VAT: Stan/Spec.
TEL: 020 8874 2101; FAX: 020 8877 0313
E-MAIL: sales@thornhillgalleries.co.uk
WEBSITE: www.thornhillgalleries.co.uk

SW19

Corfield Potashnick LAPADA
33 The Loft, Church Rd, SW19 5DQ. (Jonathan Corfield Fry and Simon Potashnick)
EST. 1997. Open by appointment or visit the Furniture Cave. STOCK: *Fine antique furniture.* SER: Restorations; valuations. FAIRS: Harrogate (Spring).
TEL: 020 8944 902; MOBILE: 07974 565659
E-MAIL: jonfry@btopenworld.com
WEBSITE: www.corfieldpotashnick.co.uk

Langford's Marine Antiques BADA LAPADA
(L.L. Langford)
EST. 1941. Open by appointment only. STOCK: *Ships models, marine instruments, globes, steam engine models.* VAT: Stan/Spec.
TEL: Mobile - 07768 942633 and 07771 881641
E-MAIL: langford@dircon.co.uk
WEBSITE: www.langfords.co.uk

Shaikh and Son (Oriental Rugs) Ltd
139 Arthur Rd. SW19 8AB. (M. Shaikh)
Open 10-6. CL: Sat. pm. STOCK: *Persian carpets, rugs, £100-£10,000.* SER: Repairing and cleaning.
TEL: 020 8947 9232

SW20

W.G.T. Burne (Antique Glass) Ltd BADA
PO Box 9465. (Formerly of Chelsea) SW20 9ZD.
(Mrs G. and A.T. Burne)
EST. 1936. Open by appointment. STOCK: *English and Irish glassware, Georgian and Victorian decanters, chandeliers, candelabra and lustres.* SER: Valuations; restorations. VAT: Stan/Spec.
TEL: 020 8543 6319; FAX: same; MOBILE: 07774 725834
E-MAIL: antiqueglass@burne.plus.com

W. F. Turk Antique Clocks BADA LAPADA
355 Kingston Rd., Wimbledon Chase. SW20 8JX.
EST. 1970. CINOA. Please telephone for opening hours. STOCK: *Clocks, including longcase, 17th-19th C, £4,000-£150,000; bracket, 17th-19th C, £2,000-£100,000; mantel and carriage, 19th C, £450-£25,000.* LOC: Off A3. SER: Valuations; restorations. SIZE: Large. PARK: Easy. VAT: Stan/Spec. FAIRS: Olympia.
TEL: 020 8543 3231; FAX: same; MOBILE: 07785 583500
E-MAIL: sales@wfturk.com
WEBSITE: www.wfturk.com

SE1

Europa House Antiques
160-164 Tower Bridge Rd. SE1 3LS. (G. Viventi)
EST. 1976. Open 9.30-5.15, Sat. 10-5.15. STOCK:
Furniture and general antiques. SIZE: Large.
TEL: 020 7403 0022; FAX: 020 7277 5777
E-MAIL: antiques@viventi.co.uk

Mayfair Carpet Gallery Ltd
301 Borough High St. SE1 1JH.
EST. 1975. Open 11-6. STOCK: *Persian, Oriental rugs and carpets.* SER: Repairs; cleaning.
TEL: 020 7403 8228; FAX: 020 7407 1649

Robert Bush at Tower Bridge Antiques
71 Tanner St. SE1 3PL
Open 9-5; Sat. 10-6; Sun 11-5. SER: Shipping arranged.
SIZE: Large.
TEL: 07836 236911
E-MAIL: bush.antiques@virgin.net
WEBSITE: www.robertbushantiques.co.uk

Tower Bridge Antiques
71 Tanner St. SE1 3PL.
Open 9-5; Sat 10-6; Sun 11-5. STOCK: *Victorian, Georgian and Edwardian, Art Deco and retro furniture; shipping goods.* LOC: Few mins. walk from Tower Bridge.
SIZE: Large - 8 dealers. PARK: Free parking at weekends.
VAT: Stan.
TEL: 020 7403 3660
WEBSITE: www.towerbridgeantiques.co.uk

SE3

Michael Silverman
PO Box 350. SE3 0LZ.
EST. 1989 ABA. ILAB. *Postal Only.* Open by
appointment. STOCK: *Manuscripts, autograph letters, historical documents.* LOC: London SE3. SER: Catalogue
available. PARK: Free. VAT: Stan. FAIRS: ABA - Olympia
(June); ABAA, New York (April).
TEL: 020 8319 4452; FAX: 020 8856 6006
E-MAIL: ms@michael-silverman.com
WEBSITE: www.michael-silverman.com

SE4

Rogers Turner Books
87 Breakspears Rd. SE4 1TX. (P. J. Rogers and A.J.
Turner)
EST. 1975. ABA. PBFA. Open Thurs.-Fri. 10-6 or by
appointment. STOCK: *Antiquarian books especially on clocks and scientific instruments.* SER: Buys at auction (British
and European); catalogues available.
TEL: 020 8692 2472; FAX: same; Paris: +33 139121191
E-MAIL: rogersturner@compuserve.com
WEBSITE: www.rogersturner@abebooks.com.

SE5

Robert E. Hirschhorn   BADA LAPADA
EST. 1979. CINOA. Visitors welcome by appointment.
STOCK: *Distinctive English, Welsh and Continental
country furniture, mainly oak, elm, walnut and fruitwood,
and interesting objects, 18th C and earlier; ceramics,
especially delftware; textiles, metalwork and treen.* PARK:
Easy. VAT: Spec. FAIRS: BADA (March); Olympia
(March, June and Nov).
TEL: 020 7703 7443; MOBILE: 07831 405937
E-MAIL: info@hirschhornantiques.com
WEBSITE: www.hirschhornantiques.com

SE6

Wilkinson plc
5 Catford Hill. SE6 4NU.
EST. 1947. Open 9-5. CL: Sat. STOCK: *Glass especially
chandeliers, 18th C and reproduction, art metal work.* LOC:
Opposite Catford Bridge station. Entrance through
Wickes DIY car park. SER: Restorations and repairs
(glass, metalwork). SIZE: Medium. PARK: Easy.
TEL: 020 8314 1080; FAX: 020 8690 1524
E-MAIL: enquiries@wilkinson-plc.com
WEBSITE: www.wilkinson-plc.com

SE7

Ward Antique Fireplaces Ltd
267 Woolwich Rd., Charlton. SE7 7RB. (T. and M.
Ward)
EST. 1981. Open 10-5, Sun. 11-2. STOCK: *Victorian
fireplaces, Victorian and Edwardian furniture, £50-£1,000.*
LOC: From A102(M) take Woolwich/Woolwich ferry
turn, 100yds. from roundabout immediately under rail
bridge across the road. SIZE: Medium. PARK: Easy.
TEL: 020 8305 0963; HOME: 020 8698 0771

SE9

The Fireplace
257 High St., Eltham. SE9 1TY. (A. Clark)
EST. 1978. Open daily. STOCK: *Fireplaces, 19th-20th C,
£100-£1,000.* SER: Restorations (fireplaces). SIZE:
Medium. PARK: Adjacent side streets. VAT: Stan.
TEL: 020 8850 4887

SE10

Greenwich Antiques Market
Greenwich Church St. SE10.
Open Thurs. and Fri. 7.30-5.30. STOCK: *General antiques and
collectables.* LOC: Greenwich main line station; Cutty Sark
DLR. SIZE: 50 stalls. PARK: Burney St., Cutty Sark Gdns.
TEL: 020 8293 3110; HEAD OFFICE: 020 7515 7153
(Mon-Fri)
WEBSITE: www.greenwichmarket.net

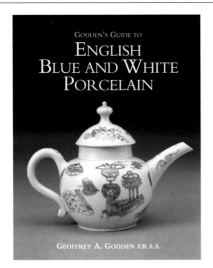

GODDEN'S GUIDE TO
ENGLISH BLUE AND WHITE PORCELAIN

GEOFFREY A. GODDEN F.R.S.A.

This is the first major book on English blue and white porcelain since the early 1970s. Not only is it the latest and most up-to-date work, but it includes types not previously studied and extends the range of wares into the early years of the nineteenth-century. It is a unique overall study.

Spec: 592pp., 153 col. illus., 711 b.&w. illus., 11 x 8½in./279 x 216mm. **£65.00 (hardback)**

The Junk Shop and Spread Eagle
9 Greenwich South St. SE10 8NW. (Toby Moy)
EST. 1965. Open 10.30-6, inc. Sun. STOCK: *Furniture, antiquarian books, maps, postcards, collectables; 20th C design up to 1970s.* LOC: Opposite Greenwich DLR. SER: Restorations (furniture). SIZE: Large - 4 rooms. VAT: Spec.
TEL: 020 8305 1666
E-MAIL: junk@spreadeagle.org
WEBSITE: www.spreadeagle.org

Lamont Antiques Ltd   LAPADA
Tunnel Avenue Antique Warehouse, Tunnel Avenue Trading Estate, Greenwich. SE10 0QH. (N. Lamont and F. Llewellyn)
Open 10-5.30; CL: Sat. STOCK: *Architectural fixtures and fittings, bars, stained glass, pub mirrors and signs, shipping furniture, £5-£25,000.* **SER: Container packing. SIZE: Large. PARK: Own.**
TEL: 020 8305 2230; FAX: 020 8305 1805
E-MAIL: lamontantiques@aol.com
WEBSITE: www.lamontantiques.com

Minerva Antiques
90 Royal Hill, Greenwich. SE10 8RT. (Jonathan Atkins)
EST. 1986. Open 10-6, Sun 11-5. STOCK: *English and French 18th-19th C gilded mirrors and wall mirrors, re-gilded as necessary. Furniture 17th-19th C.* SER: Restorations (repairs, caning, gilding and upholstery).

SIZE: Medium. PARK: Easy. VAT: Spec.
TEL: 020 8691 2221; MOBILE: 07973 833441
E-MAIL: sales@minerva-antiques.co.uk
WEBSITE: www.minerva-antiques.co.uk

The Warwick Leadlay Gallery
5 Nelson Rd., Greenwich. SE10 9JB. (Warwick Leadlay and Anthony Cross)
EST. 1974. Open 9.30-5.30, Sun. and public holidays 11-5.30. STOCK: *Antique maps, prints, fine arts, Nelson specialists, 17th-20th C.* LOC: Nelson Arcade. SER: Framing; restoration; valuations. SIZE: Medium. PARK: Nearby. VAT: Stan.
TEL: 020 8858 0317; FAX: 020 8853 1773
E-MAIL: info@warwickleadlay.com
WEBSITE: www.warwickleadlay.com

Robert Whitfield Antiques   LAPADA
Tunnel Avenue Antique Warehouse, Tunnel Avenue Trading Estate, Greenwich. SE10 0QH.
Open 10-5.30; CL: Sat. STOCK: *Edwardian, Victorian and secondhand furniture, especially bentwood chairs.* **SER: Container packing. PARK: Easy.**
TEL: 020 8305 2230; FAX: 020 8305 1805
E-MAIL: robertwhitfield@btinternet.com

SE13

Robert Morley & Co Ltd   BADA
34 Engate St. SE13 7HA.
EST. 1881. Open 9.30-5. STOCK: *Pianos, harpsichords, clavichords, spinets, virginals, harps; stools, music cabinets and stands.* **LOC: Lewisham. SER: Restorations (musical instruments). PARK: Own. VAT: Stan. FAIRS: Early Music Show, Greenwich.**
TEL: 020 8318 5838
E-MAIL: sales@morleypianos.co.uk
WEBSITE: www.morleypianos.com.

Ward Antique Fireplaces Ltd
417 Hither Green Lane. SE13 6TR (Michael and Terry Ward)
EST. 1979. Open 10-5, Sun. 11-2. STOCK: *Victorian and Edwardian fireplaces.* SER: Restorations (fireplaces).
TEL: 020 8697 6003; HOME: 020 8698 0771

SE15

CASA
159 Bellenden Rd., Peckham. SE15 4DH. (M. Tree)
EST. 1993. Open Tues.-Sat. 10-5. STOCK: *Architectural salvage including doors, floorboards, radiators, baths, sinks and taps, 19th-20th C, £15-£600; furniture, 19th-20th C; fireplaces.* LOC: Peckham Rye. SER: Fireplace fitting, shotblasting, plumbing, consultancy and project management. SIZE: Medium. PARK: Easy.
TEL: 020 7732 3911
E-MAIL: matthew.tree@yahoo.co.uk
WEBSITE: www.casaonline.co.uk

SE19

Crystal Palace Antiques
Imperial House, Jasper Rd. SE19 1SJ. (D. Roper)
EST. 1994. Open 7 days, 10-6. STOCK: *Furniture, £50-£3,000.* SER: Restoration, gilding, upholstery. PARK: Easy. FAIRS: Ardingly, Newark, Kempton.
TEL: 020 8480 7042; MOBILE: 07988 516459

SE21

Acorn Antiques
111 Rosendale Rd., West Dulwich. SE21 8EZ. (Mr P Snowdon)
EST. 1976. Open 10-6, Sat. 10-5.30. STOCK: *Furniture, sterling silver, jewellery, ceramics, glassware and fireplace accessories.* VAT: Stan.
TEL: 020 8761 3349

SE25

Engine 'n' Tender
19 Spring Lane, Woodside Green. SE25 4SP. (Mrs Joyce M. Buttigieg)
EST. 1957. Open Thurs. and Fri. 12-5.30, Sat. 10-5.30. STOCK: *Model railways, mainly pre-1939; Dinky toys, to 1968; old toys, mainly tinplate.* LOC: Near Croydon tramlink. SIZE: Small. PARK: Easy. FAIRS: Local toy.
TEL: 020 8654 0386

North London Clock Shop Ltd
Rear of 60 Saxon Rd. SE25 5EH. (D.S. Tomlin)
EST. 1960. Open 9-6, CL: Sat. STOCK: *Clocks, longcase, bracket, carriage, skeleton, 18th-19th C.* SER: Restorations (clocks and barometers); wheel cutting; hand engraving; dial painting; clock reconversions. SIZE: Medium. PARK: Easy. VAT: Stan. FAIRS: Olympia.
TEL: 020 8664 8089
E-MAIL: derek@croftse.co.uk

SE26

Behind the Boxes - Art Deco
98 Kirkdale, Sydenham. SE26 4BG. (Ray Owen)
EST. 1987. Open 10.30-5, Sun. and Mon. by appointment. STOCK: *Furniture, lighting and costume jewellery, 1930s, from £25.* LOC: 1 mile from Crystal Palace. BR station Forest Hill. SER: Valuations; buys at auction. SIZE: Large. PARK: Loading, otherwise Fransfield Rd. FAIRS: Decorama and Deco.
TEL: 020 8291 6116

E1

John Jackson at Town House
5 Fournier St., Spitafields. E1 6QE. (Fiona Atkins)
EST. **1984. Open Thurs. and Fri. 11.30-6, Sat. 11.30-5.**
STOCK: *18th to early 19th C English furniture; portrait
and still life paintings, prints, treen and curiosities.* LOC:
Near Liverpool St. station. SIZE: **Small.** PARK:
Commercial St. VAT: **Spec.**
TEL: **020 7247 4745;** MOBILE: **07711 319237**
E-MAIL: **fiona@townhousewindow.com**
WEBSITE: **www.townhousewindow.com**

La Maison
107-108 Shoreditch High St. E1 6JN. (Guillaume and
Louise Bacou)
Open 10-6. STOCK: *Beds, wardrobes; Italian and French
furniture.* SER: Restorations. SIZE: Large. VAT: Margin.
TEL: 020 7729 9646; FAX: 020 7729 6399
E-MAIL: info@lamaisonlondon.com
WEBSITE: www.lamaisonlondon.com

E2

George Rankin Coin Co. Ltd
325 Bethnal Green Rd. E2 6AH.
EST. 1965 STOCK: *Coins, medals, medallions and jewellery.*
TEL: 020 7739 1840 or 020 7729 1280; FAX: 020 7729
5023

E3

Le Style 25
Unit 1 Autumn Yard, 39 Autumn St., Bow. E3 2TT.
(Philip Varma)
EST. 1988. Open by appointment. STOCK: *British and
European Art Deco furniture, from coffee tables to dining,
lounge and bedroom suites, lighting and decorative items.*

SIZE: Medium. PARK: Easy. FAIRS: Battersea Art Deco;
Battersea Park Decorative Antiques & Textiles.
TEL: 020 8983 4285; MOBILE: 07778 310293
E-MAIL: info@lestyle25.com
WEBSITE: www.lestyle25.com

E4

Record Detector
3 & 4 Station Approach, Station Rd., North
Chingford. E4 6AL. (N. Salter)
EST. 1992. Open 10-6. CL: Thurs. STOCK: *Secondhand
and collectable records, LPs, EPs, singles and CDs.* LOC: In
forecourt of North Chingford station. SIZE: Small (2
shops). PARK: Easy.
TEL: 020 8529 6361 or 020 8529 2938
WEBSITE: www.salter.co.uk

Nicholas Salter Antiques
8 Station Approach, Station Rd., North Chingford. E4
6AL. (Sherley Salter)
EST. 1971. Open Tues. and Wed. 10-5, Fri. and Sat. 10-6.
STOCK: *Furniture, 1850-1970, £150-£1,500; china and linen,
1870-1950, £30-£150; antiquarian and secondhand books;
vintage clothes and accessories, 1860s-1970s, £5-£500.* LOC:
Next to North Chingford station. SIZE: Large. PARK: Easy.
TEL: 020 8529 2938; 020 8524 3101
E-MAIL: sherley@salter.co.uk
WEBSITE: www.salter.co.uk

E8

Boxes and Musical Instruments
2 Middleton Rd., Hackney. E8 4BL. (A. and J.
O'Kelly)
EST. 1974. Open any time by appointment. STOCK: *Boxes
– caddies, sewing, writing, snuff, vanity, jewellery and desk,
£300-£5,000; musical instruments, plucked string, £1,000-*

£3,000; all 18th-19th C. LOC: Off Kingsland Rd., continuation of Bishopsgate. SER: Valuations; restorations (exceptional instruments only). Registered with the Conservation Unit of the Museums and Galleries Commission. SIZE: Medium. PARK: Easy.
TEL: 020 7254 7074; HOME: same
E-MAIL: boxes@hygra.com
WEBSITE: www.hygra.com

E11

Brian Hawkins   LAPADA
8 High St., Wanstead E11 2AJ. (Brian Hawkins)
STOCK: *Decorative items, 18th - 20th C furniture.* SER: **Restoration.**
TEL: **020 8989 2317; FAX: same; MOBILE: 07831 888736**

Old Cottage Antiques   LAPADA
8 High St., Wanstead. E11 2AJ. (P. Blake and B. Hawkins)
EST. 1920. Open Fri. and Sat. 10-5 or by appointment. STOCK: *Furniture, clocks, paintings, 19th-20th C.* LOC: **Near Wanstead and Snaresbrook Central Line underground stations. SER: Buys at auction. SIZE: Medium plus warehouse. PARK: Easy. VAT: Stan/Spec.**
TEL: **020 8989 2317; MOBILE: 07710 031079 and 07831 888736**
E-MAIL: **brianhawkinsantiques@hotmail.com**

E14

Frontispiece Ltd
Promenade Level, Cabot Place East, Canary Wharf. E14 4QS. (Reginald and Jennifer Beer)
EST. 1989. EPSOC. Open 9-7, Sat. 10-6, Sun. 12-6. STOCK: *Over 5,000 antiquarian maps, prints and ephemera items.* LOC: Below Canary Wharf tower. SER: Framing; picture & map search. SIZE: Medium. PARK: Easy.
TEL: 020 7363 6336; FAX: 020 7515 1424
E-MAIL: sales@frontispiece.co.uk
WEBSITE: www.frontispiece.co.uk

E17

Collectors Centre - Antique City
98 Wood St., Walthamstow. E17 3HX. (Woodstow Antiques Developments Ltd.)
EST. 1978. *Trade Only.* Open 10.15-5.30. CL: Thurs. STOCK: *Antiques, collectables, 40s, 50s, 60s, £1-£500; speciallises in music and film memorabilia.* SIZE: Large. PARK: Opposite.
TEL: 020 8520 4032

E18

Victoria Antiques
The Galleria, No. 3, 180 George Lane, South Woodford. E18 2AY. (M. A. Holman)
EST. 1998. Open 11-5. CL: Tues. and Thurs. STOCK:

Clocks and carved chairs, 18th-19th C, £100-£1,000; pictures, 19th C, £50-£500; silver, £20-£500; bronze figures, £100-£1,000. LOC: 2 mins. walk from South Woodford station. SER: Valuations. SIZE: Small. PARK: George Lane. VAT: Stan.
TEL: 020 8989 1002

EC1

Jonathan Harris (Jewellery) Ltd
63-66 Hatton Garden (office). EC1N 8LE. (E.C., D. I. and J. Harris)
EST. 1958. *Trade Only.* Open by appointment. STOCK: *Antique and secondhand rings, brooches, pendants, bracelets and other jewellery, from £100.* SER: Valuations; export. PARK: Nearby. VAT: Stan/Spec.
TEL: 020 7242 9115 or 020 7242 1558; FAX: 020 7831 4417

The Heart of Hatton Garden
32 Hatton Garden. EC1N 8DL.
Open 9-6, Sun. 10-4, CL: Sat. STOCK: *Fine jewellery, watches; gemstones, loose and set in jewellery.*
TEL: 020 7362 1818; MOBILE: 07956 487132
E-MAIL: info@theheartof.co.uk
WEBSITE: www.theheartof.co.uk

Hirsh Ltd
10 Hatton Garden. EC1N 8AH. (A. Hirsh)
Open 10-5.30. STOCK: *Fine jewellery and objets d'art.* SER: Valuations; jewellery designed and re-modelled.
TEL: 020 7405 6080; FAX: 020 7430 0107
E-MAIL: enquiries@hirsh.co.uk
WEBSITE: www.hirsh.co.uk

R. Holt and Co. Ltd
98 Hatton Garden. EC1N 8NX. (R. and J. Holt)
EST. 1948. GMC. BJA. London Diamond Bourse. NAG. Open 9.30-5.30. CL: Sat. STOCK: *Gemstone specialists.* SER: Valuations; restorations (gem stone cutting and testing, bead stringing and inlaid work).
TEL: 020 7405 5286; FAX: 020 7430 1279
E-MAIL: info@rholt.co.uk
WEBSITE: www.rholt.co.uk

Joseph and Pearce Ltd   LAPADA
63-66 Hatton Garden. EC1N 8LE. (Brian Joseph, Harry Loes and David Dannece)
EST. 1896. *Trade Only.* Open by appointment. STOCK: **Jewellery 1800-1960, £100-£5,000. LOC: 6th floor. PARK: Meters VAT: Stan/Spec. FAIRS: Earls Court, NEC, New York.**
TEL: **020 7405 4604/7; FAX: 020 7242 1902**
E-MAIL: **info@josephpearce.co.uk**
WEBSITE: **www.josephpearce.co.uk**

Landsberg and Son (Antiques) Ltd.
26-27 Hatton Garden. EC1N 8BR.
Open by appointment. STOCK: *Fine jewellery, silver and objets d'art from throughout the ages.*

TEL: 020 7404 4945; fax: 020 7430 1853
E-MAIL: info@landsbergandson.co.uk
WEBSITE: www.landsbergandson.com

Andrew R. Ullmann Ltd
36 Greville St. EC1N 8TB. (J.S. Ullmann)
EST. 1939. Open 9-5, Sat. 9.30-5. STOCK: *Jewellery, gold, silver and diamond; silver and objets d'art.* LOC: Close to Farringdon and Chancery Lane underground stations. SER: Valuations; restorations. SIZE: Small. PARK: Multistorey in St. Cross St. VAT: Stan/Spec.
TEL: 020 7405 1877; FAX: 020 7404 7071
E-MAIL: enquiries@arullmann.com
WEBSITE: www.arullmann.com

EC2

Westland London
St. Michael's Church, Leonard St. EC2A 4QX.
(Geoffrey Westland)
EST. 1969. SALVO. Open 9-6, Sat. 10-5, Sun. by appt. STOCK: *Period and prestigious chimneypieces, architectural elements, panelled rooms, light fittings, statuary, paintings and furniture, £100-£100,000.* LOC: Off Gt. Eastern St., near Old St. underground. SER: Restorations; installations; shipping. SIZE: Large + warehouse. PARK: Easy but in congestion zone. VAT: Stan/Spec.
TEL: 020 7739 8094; FAX: 020 7729 3620
E-MAIL: westland@westlandlondon.com
WEBSITE: www.westlandlondon.com

EC3

Searle and Co Ltd
1 Royal Exchange, Cornhill. EC3V 3LL.
EST. 1893. NAG. Open 9-5.30. STOCK: *Georgian, Victorian, Art Nouveau, Art Deco and secondhand silver and jewellery; novelty pieces and collectables.* LOC: Near Bank underground station - exits 3 & 4. SER: Commissions; valuations; restorations; repairs; engraving. SIZE: Medium. PARK: Meters. VAT: Stan/Spec.
TEL: 020 7626 2456; FAX: 020 7283 6384
E-MAIL: mail@searleandco.ltd.uk
WEBSITE: www.searleandco.ltd.uk

EC4

Gladwell & Co. LAPADA
68 Queen Victoria St. EC4N 4SJ. (Anthony Fuller)
SLAD. Open 9-5.30, Sat. and Sun. by appointment.
STOCK: *Oil paintings, watercolours, drawings, etchings and bronzes, £50-£50,000.* LOC: **Near St Paul's Cathedral and Bank of England.** SER: Valuations; restorations; consultant. SIZE: Small. PARK: Easy.
FAIRS: LAPADA; NEC; Boston; Glasgow; New York; Chicago.
TEL: 020 7248 3824; FAX: 020 7248 6899
WEBSITE: www.gladwells.co.uk

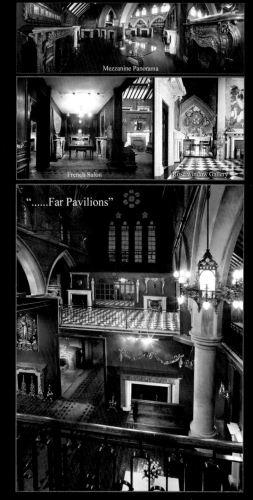

N1

After Noah

121 Upper St., Islington. N1 1QP. (M. Crawford and
Z. Candlin)
EST. 1990. Open 10-6, Sun. 12-5. STOCK: *Arts and Craft
oak and similar furniture, leather sofas and chairs, 1880s to
1950s, £1–£5,000; iron, iron and brass beds; decorative
items, bric-a-brac including candlesticks, mirrors, lighting,
kitchenalia and jewellery.* SER: Restorations. SIZE:
Medium. PARK: Side streets. VAT: Stan.
TEL: 020 7359 4281; FAX: same
E-MAIL: enquiries@afternoah.com
WEBSITE: www.afternoah.com.

Meg Andrews

EST. 1982. Open by appointment STOCK: *Worldwide
collectable, hangable and wearable antique costume and
textiles including Chinese embroideries and woven fabrics,
robes, shoes, hats, large hangings; Morris and Arts and Crafts
embroideries and woven cloths, Paisley shawls, samplers,
silkwork pictures; European costumes and textiles.* SER:
Valuations; advice. FAIRS: Antique Textiles and
Costumes, Manchester; Organisers - Textile Society
(March); Antique Textiles, Costumes and Tribal Art,
Hilton Hotel, Olympia (June and November).
TEL: 020 7359 7678
E-MAIL: meg@meg-andrews.com
WEBSITE: www.meg-andrews.com

The Angel Arcade

116 Islington High St., Camden Passage. N1 8EG.
(Bushe Developments UK Ltd)
EST. 1970. Camden Passage Dealers' Assn. Open Wed.
and Sat. 7.30-4.30. STOCK: *Decorative and interior design
items, glass, silverware, jewellery and general antiques.* SIZE:
Arcade with 14 shops. PARK: Business Design Centre.
WEBSITE: www.camdenpassageislington.co.uk

Below are listed some of the dealers in this arcade.

Ron Albert

Shop 10. *Personalites & events: royal, military, wars, sporting,
naval, aviation, theatre, political; Churchill items a speciality.*
TEL: 01255 421266; 020 7354 1873; FAX: 01255 220331
EMAIL: ronalbert@tinyonline.co.uk

Griffin Antiques

Shop 7. *Metalware, brass, candlesticks, scales, weights, pot
lids, clocks, pewter.*
TEL: 020 8366 5959
EMAIL: griffincamden.p@aol.com

Judd's Jewels

Shop 2. *Faux jewellery; art glass, silver and commemoratives;
Whitefriars; snuffboxes and spoons.*
TEL: 020 7630 8516

Tony O'Loughlin

Shop 1. *Drinking glasses, chandeliers, silver-plated cake
stands, glass candlesticks, flatware*
TEL: 020 7628 0849; MOBILE: 07944 746855

Zany

Shop F. (Marianne Landau) *Unusual, original jewellery,
handbags and collectables from 1920 to the present day.*
TEL: 020 7435 1500; MOBILE: 07769 704500
EMAIL: mariannelle@aol.com

Annie's Vintage Costume & Textiles

12 Camden Passage, Islington. N1 8ED. (A. Moss)
Open 11-6 including Sun. STOCK: *Vintage costume and
textiles.* PARK: Nearby and meters.
TEL: 020 7359 0796
E-MAIL: annie@anniesvintageclothing.co.uk
WEBSITE: www.anniesvintageclothing.co.uk

The Antique Trader

The Millinery Works, 85-87 Southgate Rd. N1 3JS. (B.
Thompson and D. Rothera)
EST. 1968. Open 11-6 Tues.-Sat., 12-5 Sun. or by
appointment. STOCK: *Arts & Crafts, Art furniture and effects;
£100–£30,000.* LOC: Close to Camden Passage Antiques
Centre. SIZE: Large. PARK: Meters. VAT: Stan/Spec.
TEL: 020 7359 2019; FAX: 020 7359 5792
E-MAIL: antiquetrader@millineryworks.co.uk
WEBSITE: www.millineryworks.co.uk

Banbury Fayre

6 Pierrepont Row Arcade, Camden Passage, Islington.
N1 8EF. (Lynette Gray and Gregory Hackett trading as
Dreamtime.)
EST. 1984. CPTA. Open Wed. and Sat., Sun. by
appointment. STOCK: *Collectables, antique jewellery and
clothing 1900-1970.* SIZE: Small. PARK: 200yds.
TEL: (home) 020 8880 6695; FAX: same; MOBILE:
07804 261082
WEBSITE: www.camdenpassageislington.co.uk

Camden Passage Antiques Market and Pierrepont Arcade Antiques Centre

Pierrepont Arcade, Islington. N1 8EF.
EST. 1960. Camden Passage Assn. Market days: Wed.
and Sat. 7am-3.30 or by appointment. Thurs. - book
market. STOCK: *Wide range of general antiques and many
specialists.* SER: Shipping. SIZE: Over 400 dealers. PARK:
Multi-storey and meters.
TEL: 020 7359 0190; MOBILE: 07960 877035
E-MAIL: murdochkdr@aol.com
WEBSITE: www.camdenpassageantiques.com

Peter Chapman Antiques and Restoration   LAPADA

10 Theberton St., Islington. N1 0QX. (P.J. and Z.A.
Chapman)
EST. 1971. CPTA. CINOA. Open 9.30-6, Sun. and
public holidays by appointment. STOCK: *Furniture and
decorative objects, 1700-1900; paintings, drawings and
prints, 17th to early 20th C; stained glass, hall lanterns;
Grand Tour items.* LOC: 5 mins. walk from Camden
Passage down Upper St. SER: Valuations; restorations
(furniture and period objects); buys at auction. SIZE:
Medium. PARK: Fairly easy. VAT: Stan/Spec.

TEL: 020 7226 5565; FAX: 020 8348 4846; MOBILE: 07831 093662
E-MAIL: pchapmanantiques@btinternet.com
WEBSITE: www.antiques-peterchapman.co.uk

Chapter One
2 Pierrepont Row Arcade, Camden Passage. N1 9EG. (Yvonne Gill)
EST. 1993. Open Wed. 9-3, Sat. 9-5 or by appointment. STOCK: *Handbags, costume jewellery, vintage accessories, fabrics, unusual collectors items, 1880-1960, £1-£300.* SER: Jewellery repairs; search. SIZE: Small.
TEL: 020 7359 1185
E-MAIL: yg@platinum.demon.co.uk

Chest of Drawers
281 Upper St., Islington. N1 2TZ. (J. Delf and K. Corbett)
Open 10-6 including Sun. STOCK: *Chinese and eastern European antiques in elm, oak, camphor and pine.*
TEL: 020 7359 5909; FAX: 020 7704 6236
WEBSITE: www.chestofdrawers.co.uk

Vincent Freeman   LAPADA
1 Camden Passage, Islington. N1 8EA.
EST. 1966. Open Wed. and Sat. 10-5. STOCK: *Music boxes, furniture and decorative items, from £100.* SIZE: Large. PARK: Nearby. VAT: Stan/Spec.
TEL: 020 7226 6178; FAX: 020 7226 7231;
E-MAIL: info@vincentfreemanantiques.com
WEBSITE: www.vincentfreemanantiques.com

Get Stuffed
105 Essex Rd., Islington. N1 2SL.
EST. 1975. Telephone mobile for appointment. STOCK: *Stuffed birds, fish, animals, trophy heads; rugs; butterflies, insects.* SER: Restorations; taxidermy; glass domes and cases supplied.
TEL: 020 7226 1364; FAX: 020 7359 8253; MOBILE: 07831 260062
E-MAIL: taxidermy@thegetstuffed.co.uk
WEBSITE: www.thegetstuffed.co.uk

David Griffiths Antiques
17 Camden Passage, Islington. N1 8EA.
Open Wed., Fri. and Sat. 10-4 or by appointment. STOCK: *Decorative antiques including library and campaign furniture, leather chairs, pub accessories, club fenders and other fittings from hotels and gentlemen's clubs; quality vintage luggage.*
TEL: 020 7226 1991; FAX: 020 7226 1126; MOBILE: 07976 800062
E-MAIL: dgantiques17@aol.com

Japanese Gallery
23 Camden Passage, Islington. N1 8EA.
Ukiyoe Dealers' Assn. of Japan. Open 10-6 inc. Sun. STOCK: *Japanese woodcut prints; books, kimonos, scrolls, netsuke, inro and Tsuba.* LOC: opp SER: Framing; free authentification.

TEL: 020 7226 3347; FAX: 020 7229 2934
E-MAIL: info@japanesegallery.co.uk
WEBSITE: www.japanesegallery.co.uk

Carol Ketley   LAPADA
PO Box 16199. N1 7WD.
EST. 1978. Open by appointment. STOCK: *Decorative antiques, specialising in mirrors and glassware 1750-1900.* LOC: See Sophie Ketley at Antiquarius. VAT: Spec. FAIRS: Olympia (Jun/Nov).
TEL: 020 7359 5529; FAX: 020 7226 4589; MOBILE: 07831 827284

John Laurie (Antiques) Ltd   LAPADA
351-352 Upper St., Islington. N1 0PD. (R. Gewirtz)
EST. 1962. Open 9.30-5. STOCK: *Silver, Sheffield plate.* SER: Restorations; packing and shipping. SIZE: Large. VAT: Stan.
TEL: 020 7226 0913 or 020 7226 6969;
FAX: 020 7226 4599
E-MAIL: rdgewirtz@aol.com

David Loveday at the Furniture Vault
50 Camden Passage, Islington. N1 8AE.
EST. 1969. Open Tues.-Sat. 9.30-4.30. STOCK: *Furniture, 18th-20th C.* LOC: 50 yds from the Camden Head pub with stairs leading down to showroom. SER: Restoration (furniture). SIZE: Large. VAT: Marg./Stan./Spec.
TEL: 020 7354 1047
E-MAIL: davidloveday1@aol.com

The Mall Antiques Arcade
359 Upper St., Islington. N1 0PD. (Atlantic Antiques Centres Ltd)
EST. 1979. Open Tues., Thurs. & Fri. 10-5, Wed. 7.30-6, Sat. 9-6, Sun 11-4. CL: Mon. STOCK: *See dealers listed below.* LOC: 5 mins. from Angel underground station. PARK: Meters.
TEL: 020 7823 3900
E-MAIL: info@themallantiques.co.uk

R. Arantes
Stand G27. *Lalique glass and other decorative glassware.*
TEL: 020 7226 6367; FAX: 020 7253 5303
EMAIL: rlaliqueglass@btinternet.com

Argosy Antiques
Stand G10. *Door furniture, lighting, silver and metalware.*
TEL: 020 7359 2517
EMAIL: buttigiegp@aol.com

Patricia Baxter
Stand B3. *Furniture and lighting.*
TEL: 020 7345 0886; FAX: 020 8368 3290
EMAIL: baxantique@aol.com

Deidre Beresford
Stand G14. *Jewellery and antiques.*
TEL: 07983 333890

Chancery Antiques
Stand G2. *Oriental and Continental porcelain and works of art.*
TEL: 020 7359 9035; FAX: same

CIRCA 1900
Stand G28. *Art Deco and Art Nouveau jewellery, bakelite and cufflinks.*
TEL: 020 7354 9227
EMAIL: info@circa1900.org
WEBSITE: www.circa1900.org

Esme
Stand G18. *Jewellery, porcelain, silver, specialist collectables and decorative items.*
TEL: 020 7704 9617
EMAIL: kezdab@yahoo.co.uk

French Touch
Stand G11. *Vintage handbags and accessories and European art.*
TEL: 020 7240 2680
WEBSITE: www.frenchtouchshop.com

Himiko
Stand G1. *Oriental antiques, art and objets d'art.*
TEL: 07904 058513
EMAIL: himikoantique@aol.com

June and Heather Antiques
Stand G22. *Lighting, furniture and glassware.*
FAX: 020 8653 7631; MOBILE: 07986 950049

Leon's Militaria
Stand G21. *Militaria, tribal art, marine and sporting collectables and silver.*
TEL: 020 7288 1070; FAX: 020 7288 1070
EMAIL: leonsmilitaria@yahoo.co.uk

Rachel Lieberman
Stand B6. *Silver tableware, frames and decorative items.*
TEL: 07956 265140

Out of the Attic and Ivan Savage Furniture
Stand G4. *Furniture, lighting, glassware, silver and metalware, clocks.*
TEL: 020 7359 1213
EMAIL: serraattic@aol.com

Rumours
Stand G26. *Art Nouveau, Art Deco china and objets d'art.*
TEL: 020 7704 6549
EMAIL: rumdec@aol.com

S & P Centre
Stand G19. *Silver, art, glassware, jewellery, clocks and watches.*
TEL: 020 7359 9588; FAX: 020 8802 7144

Chris St. James
Stand G7. *Vintage jewellery, bakelite, Art Deco decorative arts, decanters and scent bottles.*
TEL: 020 7704 0127;
EMAIL: gizzy5@yahoo.co.uk

Christina Tattum
Stand G15. *Antique boxes and inkwells.*
TEL: 020 8560 3077
EMAIL: christinatattum@btinternet.com

Agnes Wilton
Stand G23. *Jewellery, silver, watches, and glassware.*
TEL: 020 7226 5679

A.M. Woodage Antiques
Stand B8. *Furniture, oil paintings, Art Deco and Art Nouveau decorative arts.*
TEL: 020 7226 4173
EMAIL: gwoodage@btopenworld.com

Van Den Bosch
Stand G24. *Arts and Crafts and Art Nouveau silver and jewellery and decorative arts.*
TEL: 020 7226 4550
EMAIL: info@vandenbosch.co.uk
WEBSITE: www.vandenbosch.co.uk

Kevin Page Oriental Art   LAPADA
2, 4 and 6 Camden Passage, Islington. N1 8ED.
EST. 1968. Open 10.30-4. CL: Mon. and Thurs. *STOCK: Oriental porcelain and furniture, fine Japanese works of art from the Meiji period.* LOC: 1 min. from Angel underground station. SER: Valuations. SIZE: Large. PARK: Easy. VAT: Stan.
TEL: **020 7226 8558**; FAX: **020 7354 9145**
E-MAIL: **kevin@kevinpage.co.uk**
WEBSITE: **www.kevinpage.co.uk**

Piers Rankin
14 Camden Passage, Islington. N1 8ED.
EST. 1983. Open Tues.-Sat. 9.30-5.30, Mon. by appointment only. *STOCK: Silver and plate, old Sheffield plate, 1700-1930.* SER: Packing and shipping arranged. SIZE: Medium. PARK: NCP.
TEL: 020 7354 3349; FAX: 020 7359 8138
E-MAIL: piersrankin925@aol.com

Keith Skeel Antiques & Eccentricities   LAPADA
The Merchants Hall, 46 Essex Rd. N1 8LN. (Keith Skeel)
Open 10-7; Sun 10-6. *STOCK: Restored furniture and other items especially curiosities and eccentricities.* SIZE: **Very large.** PARK: **Meters.**
TEL: **020 7359 5633**; FAX: **020 7226 3780**
E-MAIL: **info@keithskeel.com**
WEBSITE: **www.keithskeel.com**

Style Gallery
10 Camden Passage, Islington. N1 8ED. (M. Webb and P. Coakley-Webb)
EST. 1980. Open Wed. and Sat. 9.30-4 or by appointment. *STOCK: Art Nouveau, WMF and Liberty pewter; Art Deco bronzes including Preiss and Chiparus; ceramics and glass.*
TEL: 020 7359 7867; HOME: 020 8361 2357; FAX: same; MOBILE: 07831 229640
E-MAIL: coakleywebb@btinternet.com
WEBSITE: www.styleantiques.co.uk

Sugar Antiques
8-9 Pierrepont Arcade, Camden Passage, Islington. N1 8EF. (Ted Kitagawa)
EST. 1990. Open Wed. and Sat. 7.30-4. *STOCK: Wrist and pocket watches, 19th-20th C, £25-£4,000; fountain pens and lighters, early 20th C to 1960s, £15-£1,000; costume jewellery and collectables, 19th-20th C, £5-£500.* LOC: 5

mins. walk from the Angel underground station (Northern Line). SER: Repairs (as stock); buys at auction (as stock). SIZE: Medium. PARK: Meters. VAT: Stan. TEL: 020 7354 9896; FAX: 01784 477460; MOBILE: 07779 636407
E-MAIL: info@sugarantiques.com
WEBSITE: www.sugarantiques.com

Swan Fine Art
12b Camden Passage, Islington. N1 8ED. (P. Child)
Open 10-5, Wed. and Sat. 9-5 or by appointment. *STOCK: Paintings, fine and decorative sporting and animal, portraits, 17th-19th C, £500-£25,000+.* SIZE: Medium. PARK: Easy, except Wed. and Sat. VAT: Spec.
TEL: 020 7226 5335; FAX: 020 7359 2225; MOBILE: 07860 795336

Tadema Gallery   BADA LAPADA
10 Charlton Place, Camden Passage, Islington. N1 8AJ. (S. and D. Newell-Smith)
EST. 1978. CINOA. Open Wed. and Sat. 10-5 or by appointment. *STOCK: Jewellery - Art Nouveau, Art & Crafts, Art Deco to 1960s artist-designed jewels; 20th C abstract art.* **SIZE: Medium. PARK: Reasonable. VAT: Spec. FAIRS: Grosvenor House**
TEL: 020 7359 1055; FAX: same; MOBILE: 07710 082395
E-MAIL: info@tademagallery.com
WEBSITE: www.tademagallery.com; www.tademagalleryart.com

C. Tapsell
16 Pierrepont Row, Camden Passage, Islington. N1 8EA.
EST. 1970. CPTA. Open Wed. 9-2.30, Sat. 9-5, other times by appointment. *STOCK: English mahogany and walnut furniture, 18th-19th C, £300-£15,000; Oriental china and works of art, 17th-19th C, £20-£5,000.* LOC: Near Angel underground station. SIZE: Small. VAT: Stan/Spec/Global.
TEL: 020 7354 3603

Turn On Lighting
11 Camden Passage. N1 8EA. (J. Holdstock)
EST. 1976. CPTA. Open Tues.-Fri. 10.30-6, Sat. 9.30-5.30. *STOCK: Lighting, 1840-1940.* LOC: Angel underground station (Northern line). SER: Interior design; museum commissions. PARK: Business Design Centre.
TEL: 020 7359 7616; FAX: same
WEBSITE: www.camdenpassageislington.co.uk

Van Den Bosch   LAPADA
24-25 The Mall, Camden Passage, Islington. N1 0PD (Jan Van Den Bosch and Carole Van Den Bosch)
Weds. 9-5 and Sat. 10-5 or by appointment. *STOCK: Silver and jewellery from Arts and Crafts, Art Nouveau, Jugendstil and Skonvirka periods.* **SIZE: Medium - 2 units. PARK: Meters or car park opposite the Business Centre. FAIRS: Olympia, June & Nov.**
TEL: 020 7226 4550

E-MAIL: **info@vandenbosch.co.uk**
WEBSITE: **www.vandenbosch.co.uk**

Vane House Antiques
15 Camden Passage, Islington. N1 8EA. (Michael J. Till)
EST. 1950. Open 10-4. CL: Mon/Tue/Thurs. *STOCK: 18th to early 19th C furniture.* SIZE: Medium - 3 floors. VAT: Spec.
TEL: 020 7359 1343; FAX: same.
E-MAIL: mcht625@aol.com

Mike Weedon   LAPADA
7 Camden Passage, Islington. N1 8EA. (Mike and Hisako Weedon)
EST. 1977. Open Wed. 9-5, Sat. 10-5. *STOCK: Large selection Art Nouveau glass - Gallé, Daum, Lötz; antique glass by artists and designers, from 1880 to 1939; Art Deco sculpture - bronze, bronze and ivory including Chiparus, Preiss, Lorenzl; lighting.*
TEL: Wed and Sat. only - 020 7226 5319; FAX: 020 7700 6387; HOME: 020 7609 6826
E-MAIL: info@mikeweedonantiques.com
WEBSITE: www.mikeweedonantiques.com www.galleglass.com

N2

Amazing Grates - Fireplaces Ltd
61-63 High Rd., East Finchley. N2 8AB (T. Tew)
EST. 1971 Resident. Open 10-5.30. *STOCK: Mantelpieces, grates and fireside items, £200-£5,000; Victorian tiling, £2-£20; specialises in marble and stone.* LOC: 100yds. north of East Finchley underground station. SER: Valuations; reproduction mantelpieces in stone and marble; installations. SIZE: Large. PARK: Own. VAT: Stan.
TEL: 020 8883 9590 or 020 8883 6017

Martin Henham (Antiques)
218 High Rd., East Finchley. N2 9AY.
EST. 1967. Open 10-6. *STOCK: Furniture and porcelain, 1710-1920, £5-£3,500; paintings, 1650-1940, £10-£4,000.* SER: Valuations; restorations (furniture); buys at auction. SIZE: Medium. PARK: Easy.
TEL: 020 8444 5274

Barrie Marks Ltd
24 Church Vale, Fortis Green. N2 9PA.
ABA. PBFA. Open by appointment. *STOCK: Antiquarian books - illustrated, private press, colourplate, colour printing;*
TEL: 020 8883 1919

Lauri Stewart - Fine Art
36 Church Lane. N2 8DT.
Open Tues. and Wed. 10.30-4.30. *STOCK: Modern British oils and watercolours.*
TEL: 020 8883 7719; FAX: 020 8883 7323
E-MAIL: lste181072@aol.com
WEBSITE: www.artonlineltd.com

N3

Intercol London
43 Templars Crecent. N3 3QR. (Yasha Beresiner)
EST. 1977. IBNS. IPCS. ANA. Open by appointment
only. STOCK: *Playing cards, maps, banknotes, freemasonry
and related literature, £5-£1,000+.* LOC: Finchley. SER:
Valuations; restorations (maps including colouring); buys
at auction (playing cards, maps, banknotes and books).
PARK: Easy. VAT: Stan. FAIRS: Major specialist
European, U.S.A. and Far Eastern.
TEL: 020 8349 2207; FAX: 020 8346 9539
E-MAIL: yasha@intercol.co uk
WEBSITE: www.intercol.co.uk

N4

Alexander Juran & Co   BADA
at Nathan Azizollahoff, OCC, Top Floor & Lift,
Building 'A', 105 Eade Rd. N4 1TJ.
EST. 1951. Open by appointment. STOCK: *Caucasian*
rugs, nomadic and tribal; carpets, rugs, tapestries. SER:
Valuations; repairs. VAT: Stan/Spec.
TEL: 020 7435 0280; FAX: same; 020 8809 5505

Kennedy Carpets
OCC Building 'D', 1st Floor, 105 Eade Rd. N4 1TJ.
(M. Kennedy and V. Eder)
EST. 1974. Open 9.30-6. STOCK: *Decorative carpets,
collectable rugs and kelims, mid-19th C to new, £500-
£50,000.* LOC: Off Seven Sisters Road. SER: Valuations;
restorations and cleaning; making to order. SIZE: Large.
PARK: Free. VAT: Stan.
TEL: 020 8800 4455; FAX: 020 8800 4466
E-MAIL: kennedycarpets@btconnect.com
WEBSITE: www.kennedycarpets.co.uk

Joseph Lavian
OCC, Building 'E', Ground Floor, 105 Eade Rd. N4 1TJ.
EST. 1950. Open 9.30-5.30. STOCK: *Oriental carpets, rugs,
kelims, tapestries and needlework, Aubusson, Savonnerie and
textiles, 17th-19th C.* SER: Valuations; restorations. SIZE:
Large.
TEL: 020 8800 0707; FAX: 020 8800 0404; MOBILE:
07767 797707
E-MAIL: lavian@lavian.com
WEBSITE: www.lavian.com

Regent Antiques
Manor Warehouse, 318 Green Lanes, N4 1BX (Tino
Quaradeghini)
EST. 1983. *Trade Only.* Open 9-6. STOCK: *Furniture,
18th C to Edwardian.* LOC: Next door to Manor House
underground station SER: Restorations (furniture) on the
premises, shipping and packing. SIZE: Large. VAT:
Stan/Spec.
TEL: 020 8802 3900; FAX: 020 8809 9605; MOBILE:
07836 294074
E-MAIL: regentantiques@aol.com

Teger Trading
318 Green Lanes. N4 1BX.
EST. 1968 *Trade Only.* Open 9-6. CL: Sat. STOCK:
*Reproduction bronzes, furniture, marble figures, paintings,
mirrors, porcelain and unusual items.* SER: Restorations;
film hire. SIZE: Large. PARK: Own.
TEL: 020 8802 0156; FAX: 020 8802 4110
E-MAIL: tegertrading@tiscali.co.uk

The Waterloo Trading Co.
Unit 'H', OCC Estate, 105 Eade Rd. N4 1TJ (Robert
Boys)
EST. 1989. Open 9-5. CL: Sat. STOCK: *Victorian and
Edwardian furniture.* SER: Robert Boys Shipping.
Worldwide shipping and packing services. SIZE: Large.
VAT: Stan.
TEL: 020 8800 3500; FAX: 020 8800 3501
E-MAIL: info@robertboysshipping.co.uk

N5

Nicholas Goodyer
8 Framfield Rd., Highbury Fields. N5 1UU.
EST. 1951. ABA. ILAB. PBFA. Open by appointment or
chance with prior phonecall. STOCK: *Antiquarian books
especially illustrated.* LOC: Highbury & Islington tube.
SER: Sale & purchase of antiquarian books with specialist
fields. Valuations. See webiste. SIZE: Small. PARK:
Nearby. FAIRS: International ILAB (London, Boston,
San Francisco); monthly PBFA, London.
TEL: 020 7226 5682; FAX: 020 7354 4716
E-MAIL: email@nicholasgoodyer.com
WEBSITE: www.nicholasgoodyer.com

Strike One   BADA
48a Highbury Hill. N5 1AP (John Mighell)
EST. 1968. Open by appointment. STOCK: *Clocks and
barometers.* SER: **Valuations and repairs.** SIZE: **Small.**
PARK: **Easy.** VAT: **Spec.**
TEL: 020 7354 2790;
E-MAIL: milo@strikeone.co.uk

N6

Fisher and Sperr
46 Highgate High St. N6 5JB. (J.R. Sperr)
EST. 1945. Open daily 10.30-5. STOCK: *Books, 15th C to
date.* LOC: From centre of Highgate Village, nearest
underground stations Archway (Highgate), Highgate.
SER: Valuations; restorations (books). SIZE: Large. PARK:
Easy. VAT: Stan.
TEL: 020 8340 7244; FAX: 020 8348 4293

N7

Dome Antiques (Exports) Ltd   LAPADA
Unit 1, Hanover Trading Estate North Rd. N7 9HD.
(Adam and Louise Woolf)
EST. 1961. Open Mon.-Fri. STOCK: *19th C furniture,*

£250-£10,000. LOC: Near junction of York Way & Caledonian Road. SER: Valuations; restorations (furniture). SIZE: Large. PARK: Easy. VAT: Stan/Spec. FAIRS: LAPADA (NEC, April; Olympia, Feb. and June; Commonwealth Institute, Oct). TEL: 020 7700 6266; FAX: 020 7609 1692; MOBILE: 07831 805888
WEBSITE: www.domeantiques.com

N8

Solomon 20th Century Design
49 Park Rd., Crouch End. N8 8SY.
EST. 1982. Open 9-6. *STOCK: Retro furniture, £200-£4,000; decorative items, £40-£500; all Retro 20th C.* LOC: 20 mins. off North Circular at Muswell Hill turn-off. SER: Valuations; restorations (furniture including upholstery). SIZE: Medium. PARK: Easy. VAT: Spec.
TEL: 020 8341 1817
E-MAIL: solomon@solomon20thcentury.com
WEBSITE: www.solomon20thcentury.com

N9

Anything Goes
83 Bounces Rd. N9 8LD. (C.J. Bednarz)
EST. 1977. Open 10-5. CL: Mon. *STOCK: General antiques including 18th-19th C furniture and bric-a-brac.* SER: Valuations. SIZE: Medium. PARK: Easy. FAIRS: Newark.
TEL: 020 8807 9399

N10

Crafts Nouveau
112 Alexandra Park Rd., Muswell Hill. N10 2AE. (Laurie Strange)
EST. 2003. Open Wed.-Sat. 10.30-6.30, Tues. and Sun. by appointment. CL: Mon. *STOCK: Arts and Crafts, Art Nouveau furniture and decorative art - desks and writing accessories, ceramics including Doulton, Moorcroft; glassware including Loetz; copper and pewter (Hugh Wallis, Archibald Knox, Liberty, Newlyn and Keswick schools); postcards, stamps, ephemera; Gallé and Daum reproduction lamps and glass.* LOC: Parade of shops, off Colney Hatch Lane. SER: Restorations (furniture including upholstery, metalware). SIZE: Large. PARK: Easy and nearby.
TEL: 020 8444 3300; MOBILE: 07958 448380
WEBSITE: www.craftsnouveau.co.uk

N12

Finchley Fine Art Galleries
983 High Rd., North Finchley. N12 8QR. (Sam Greenman)
EST. 1972. Open 1-6, Sun. by appointment. *STOCK: 18th-20th C watercolours, paintings, etchings, prints, mostly English, £25-£10,000; Georgian, Victorian, Edwardian furniture, £50-£10,000; china and porcelain - Moorcroft, Doulton, Worcester, Clarice Cliff, £5-£2,000; musical and scientific instruments, bronzes, early photographic apparatus, firearms, shotguns.* LOC: Off M25, junction 23, take Barnet road. Gallery on right 3 miles south of Barnet church, opposite Britannia Road. SER: Valuations; restorations; picture re-lining, cleaning; framing. SIZE: Large. PARK: Yellow line - call in and collect display card for 15 minutes' free parking. Meters 20 yds.
TEL: 020 8446 4848; FAX: 020 8445 2381; MOBILE: 07712 629282
E-MAIL: finchleyfineart@onetel.com

N13

Palmers Green Antiques Centre
472 Green Lanes, Palmers Green. N13 5PA. (Michael Webb)
EST. 1976. Open 10-5.30, Sun. 11-5. CL: Tues. *STOCK:*

Furniture, general antiques and collectables. SER:
Valuations, probate, house clearances. SIZE: Large. PARK:
Nearby. FAIRS: Alexandra Palace.
TEL: 020 8350 0878; MOBILE: 07986 730155

N14

C.J. Martin (Coins) Ltd   LAPADA
85 The Vale, Southgate. N14 6AT.
EST. 1974. Open by appointment. STOCK: *Ancient and
medieval coins and ancient artefacts.* FAIRS: **BNTA,
COINEX.**
TEL: **020 8882 1509 or 020 8882 4359**
E-MAIL: **ancient.art@btinternet.com**
WEBSITE: **www.ancientart.co.uk;
www.antiquities.co.uk**

N16

The Cobbled Yard
1 Bouverie Rd., Stoke Newington. N16 0AB. (C.
Lucas)
EST. 2000. Open Wed.-Sun. 11-5.30. STOCK: *Victorian
pine furniture, £50-£750; iron and brass beds, 19th C,
£200-£500; Edwardian and some period furniture, from
£100; general antiques, collectors and decorative items,
ceramics, bric-a-brac, £5-£500.* LOC: Off Church St.,
behind Daniel Defoe public house. SER: Valuations;
furniture restoration and polishing; upholstery and
carpentry. SIZE: Medium. PARK: Easy.
TEL: 020 8809 5286
E-MAIL: info@cobbled-yard.co.uk
WEBSITE: www.cobbled-yard.co.uk

N19

Chesney's Antique Fireplace Warehouse
734-736 Holloway Rd. N19 3JF.
EST. 1983. BIDA. Open 9-5.30, Sat. 10-5. STOCK: *18th-
19th C marble, stone, chimney pieces, £1,000-£150,000;
reproduction chimney pieces, £250-£7,500.* LOC: South of
Archway roundabout on A1. SER: Valuations. SIZE:
Large. PARK: Side streets adjacent. VAT: Stan/Spec.
TEL: 020 7561 8280; FAX: 020 7561 8288
E-MAIL: sales@chesneys.co.uk
WEBSITE: www.chesneys.co.uk

N21

Dolly Land
864 Green Lanes, Winchmore Hill. N21 2RS.
EST. 1987. Open 9.30-4.30. CL: Mon. and Wed. STOCK:
Dolls, teddies, trains, die-cast limited editions. SER:
Restorations; part exchange; dolls' hospital. PARK: Easy.
FAIRS: Doll and Bear.
TEL: 020 8360 1053; FAX: 020 8364 1370
WEBSITE: www.dolly-land.co.uk

NW1

Benjamin Jewellery   LAPADA
**PO Box 12656. NW1 4WJ. (Mr & Mrs Ronald
Benjamin)**
EST. 1948. Open by appointment. STOCK: *18th & 19th
C jewellery.* SER: Valuations FAIRS: In the USA only.
TEL: **020 7486 5382**

Madeline Crispin Antiques
95 Lisson Grove. NW1 6UP.
EST. 1971. Open 10-5.30. STOCK: *General antiques.* LOC:
Near Church St. and Alfie's Market.
TEL: 020 7402 6845

The Facade
99 Lisson Grove. NW1 6UP. (Mrs Gay Brown)
EST. 1973. Open Wed.-Sat. 10.30-5. STOCK: *French and
Italian decorative items and lighting, 1900-1940.* PARK:
Easy. VAT: Stan.
TEL: 020 7258 2017

Stables Market (Camden) Ltd
Chalk Farm Rd., Camden Town. NW1 8AH
EST. 1854 Every day. STOCK: *Good mix of clothing, music
and antiques.* LOC: Between Camden Town and Chalk
Farm tube.
TEL: 020 7485 5511; FAX: 020 7284 0188
WEBSITE: www.stablesmarket.com

NW2

Soviet Carpet & Art Galleries
303-305 Cricklewood Broadway. NW2 6PG. (R.
Rabilizirov)
EST. 1983. Open 10.30-5, Sun. 10.30-5.30. CL: Sat.
STOCK: *Hand-made rugs, £100-£1,500; Russian art, £50-
£5,000; all 19th-20th C.* LOC: A5. SER: Valuations;
restorations (hand-made rugs). SIZE: Large. PARK: Side
road. VAT: Stan.
TEL: 020 8452 2445
E-MAIL: rr@soviet-world.fsnet.co.uk
WEBSITE: www.russian-art.co.uk

NW3

Antiques 4 Ltd   LAPADA
**116-118 Finchley Rd. NW3 5HT. (Andrew Harding
and Simon Chaudhry)**
EST. 1994. Open 10-5.30 or by appointment. STOCK:
*Clocks, including longcase and bracket, from 1650, £400-
£60,000; furniture, from 1750; Victorian music boxes.*
SER: Valuations; restorations. SIZE: Small. PARK: Own
by arrangement.
TEL: **020 7794 6043; FAX: 020 7794 7368; MOBILE:
07712 009230**
E-MAIL: **antiques4@btconnect.com**
WEBSITE: **www.antiques4.com**

Patricia Beckman Antiques LAPADA
NW3 7SN. (Patricia and Peter Beckman)
EST. 1968. Open by appointment. STOCK: *Furniture,*
18th-19th C. LOC: Hampstead. VAT: Spec.
TEL: **020 7435 5050 or 020 7435 0500**

Tony Bingham LAPADA
11 Pond St. NW3 2PN.
EST. 1964. Open Mon.-Fri. 10-6.30. STOCK: *Musical*
instruments, books, music, oil paintings, engravings of
musical interest. VAT: Stan/Spec.
TEL: **020 7794 1596; FAX: 020 7433 3662**
E-MAIL: **tony@oldmusicalinstruments.co.uk**
WEBSITE: **www.oldmusicalinstruments.co.uk**

Keith Fawkes
1-3 Flask Walk, Hampstead. NW3 1HJ.
EST. 1970. Open 10-5.30, Sun. 1-6. STOCK: *Antiquarian and*
general books. LOC: Near Hampstead underground station.
SER: Help with searches. SIZE: 2 shops. PARK: Meters.
TEL: 020 7435 0614

Otto Haas
49 Belsize Park Gardens. NW3 4JL. (Maud and Julia
Rosenthal)
EST. 1866. Open by appointment. CL: Sat. STOCK:
Manuscripts, printed music, autographs, rare books on music.
SER: Auction representation; catalogues. PARK: Outside.
FAIRS: Occasional international.
TEL: 020 7722 1488; FAX: 020 7722 2364
E-MAIL: contact@ottohaas-music.com
WEBSITE: www.ottohaas-music.com

Hampstead Antique and Craft Emporium
12 Heath St., Hampstead. NW3 6TE.
EST. 1967. Open 10.30-5, Sat. 10-6, Sun. 11.30-5.30.
CL: Mon. STOCK: *General antiques, craft work and gifts.*
LOC: 2 mins. walk from Hampstead underground
station. On bus routes 46 and 268. SIZE: 24 units.
TEL: 020 7794 3297
WEBSITE: www.hampsteadantiqueemporium.co.uk

Duncan R. Miller Fine Arts BADA LAPADA
17 Flask Walk, Hampstead. NW3 1HJ.
EST. 1975. CINOA. Open by appointment. STOCK: *Modern*
British and European paintings, drawings and sculpture,
especially Scottish Colourist paintings. LOC: **Off Hampstead**
High St., near underground station. SER: Valuations;
conservation; restorations (oils, works on paper and
Oriental rugs); buys at auction. SIZE: Small. PARK: Nearby.
VAT: Spec. FAIRS: Grosvenor House; BADA; Olympia.
TEL: **020 7435 5462**
E-MAIL: **art@duncanmiller.com**
WEBSITE: **www.duncanmiller.com**

Recollections Antiques Ltd
The Courtyard, Hampstead Antiques Emporium, 12
Heath St., Hampstead. NW3 6TE. (June Gilbert)
EST. 1987. Open Tues.-Sat. 10.30-5. STOCK: *19th C*
English blue and white transfer print pottery; 18th C and
19th C country and decorative furniture; children's furniture
and toys; unusual decorative items - glass and kitchenalia.
SIZE: Small. PARK: Nearby.
TEL: 020 7431 9907; FAX: 020 7794 9743; MOBILE:
07930 394014
E-MAIL: junalantiques@aol.com

Malcolm Rushton - Early Oriental Art
13 Belsize Grove. NW3 4UX. (Dr Malcolm Rushton)
EST. 1997. Open by appointment, mainly evenings and
weekends. STOCK: *Fine 6th-8th C Buddhist stone sculpture*
- China Northern Wei to Tang dynasties; fine bronze items -
Shang to Han dynasties, with animal or human motif, to
£50,000. LOC: Near Belsize Park underground station, off
Haverstock Hill. SIZE: Small. PARK: Offstreet. VAT: Stan.
TEL: 020 7722 1989
E-MAIL: malcolm.rushton1@ntlworld.com

NW4

Talking Machine
30 Watford Way, Hendon. NW4 3AL.
Open 10-4, Sat. 9.30-1.30, prior telephone call advisable.
STOCK: *Mechanical music, old gramophones, phonographs,*
vintage records and 78s, needles and spare parts, early radios
and televisions, typewriters, sewing machines, juke boxes,
early telephones. LOC: 1 min. from Hendon Central
underground station. SER: Buys at auction. VAT: Spec.
TEL: 020 8202 3473; MOBILE: 07774 103139
WEBSITE: www.gramophones.ndirect.co.uk

NW5

Acquisitions (Fireplaces) Ltd
24-26 Holmes Rd., Kentish Town. NW5 3AB. (K.
Kennedy)
EST. 1974. NFA. GMC. Open 9-5. STOCK: *Fireplaces in*
marble, wood, cast-iron and stone, Georgian, Victorian,
Edwardian reproduction, fire-side accessories, £195-£5,000.
Also contemporary designs. LOC: 3 mins. walk from
Kentish Town underground station. SER: Bespoke
manufacture of chimney pieces. SIZE: Large. PARK:
Forecourt. VAT: Stan.
TEL: 020 7485 4955; FAX: 020 7276 4361
E-MAIL: sales@acquisitions.co.uk
WEBSITE: www.acquisitions.co.uk

Orientalist
74-78 Highgate Rd. NW5 1PB. (E. and H. Sakhai)
EST. 1885. Open 10-6. STOCK: *Rugs, carpets, needlepoints,*
tapestries and Aubussons, including reproduction. SER:
Valuations; restorations (cleaning and repairing rugs,
carpets and tapestries); buys at auction (Oriental carpets,
rugs and textiles). SIZE: Large. PARK: Easy and nearby.
VAT: Stan/Spec.
TEL: 020 7482 0555; FAX: 020 7267 9603
E-MAIL: orientalist80@aol.com

NW6

Gallery Kaleidoscope incorporating Scope Antiques
64-66 Willesden Lane. NW6 7SX. (K. Barrie)
EST. 1965. Open Tues.-Sat. 10-6, Thurs. 1-7.30. *STOCK: Oils, watercolours, prints, ceramics and sculpture, 19th-21st. C.* LOC: 10 mins. from Marble Arch. SER: Restorations; framing. SIZE: Large. PARK: Easy. VAT: Stan/Spec. FAIRS: Affordable Art (Spring).
TEL: 020 7328 5833; FAX: 020 7624 2913
E-MAIL: info@gallerykaleidoscope.com
WEBSITE: www.gallerykaleidoscope.com

NW8

Alfies Antique Market
13-25 Church St., Marylebone. NW8 8DT.
EST. 1976. Open Tues.-Sat. 10-6. LOC: Marylebone or Edgware Road Tube. SER: Framing, upholstery, jewellery and watch repairs; rooftop restaurant SIZE: 200 stands with 75+ dealers on 5 floors.
TEL: 020 7723 6066; FAX: 020 7724 0999;
E-MAIL: info@alfiesantiques.com
WEBSITE: www.alfiesantiques.com

Below are listed some of the dealers at this market.

Tycho Andrews
Stand S003-5. *Antique and modern design furniture.*
TEL: 07914 808159
EMAIL: tychoandrews@hotmail.com

Antiquarius Imports (UK) Ltd
Stand G058. *Georgian - 1970s jewellery.*
TEL: 07748 903378
EMAIL: gareth.brooks:virgin.net

Antique Clocks and Watches
Stand S055. *Clocks, watches and automata.*
TEL: 020 7723 5106

Bent Ply
Stand F041-42. *Avant-garde furniture.*
TEL: 020 8346 1387
EMAIL: bruna@bentply.com

Beth
Stand G028-30. *Glass and ceramics.*
TEL: 07776 136003

Beverley
Stand G023-25. *Glass and ceramics including Shelley, Claraice Cliff and Wileman.*
TEL: 020 7262 1576

Bibliopola
Stand F017-18. *Books, maps and atlases.*
TEL: 020 7724 7231.

Manley J. Black Antiques
Stand F059-60. *Art Nouveau and Art Deco, glass, ceramics, boxes, snuff boxes and collectables.*
TEL: 020 7723 0678

Paolo Bonino
Stand F019-22 & F057. *20th C decorative furniture, lighting and objets d'art.*
TEL: 07767 498766
EMAIL: boninouk@yahoo.co.uk

Peter and Neneen Brooks
Stand G139-140. *Jewellery and precious objects, paintings, glass, ceramics; Asian, Oriental and Islamic art.*
TEL: 020 7258 7784
EMAIL: nanb1@talktalk.net

Vincenzo Caffarella
Stand G033-34. *20th C decorative arts and antiques, including lighting, furniture and objets d'art.*
TEL: 020 7724 3701
EMAIL: monica@vinca.co.uk

Sheila Cameron
Stand G069. *Vintage clothing and accessories, period jewellery.*
TEL: 020 7286 8417

William Campbell
Stand G005-8. *17th-20th C antique frames and bespoke framing service.*
TEL: 020 7723 7730
EMAIL: enquiries@williamcampbellframes.com

Victor Caplin
Stand G075-6. *Coral, antique beads and hand-made jewellery, Moroccan fabrics and boxes made from Thuya wood.*
TEL: 07947 511592
EMAIL: victorcaplin@aol.com

Castaside
Stand F013-24. *Theatre-related collectables, memorabilia and ephemera.*
TEL: 020 7723 7686
EMAIL: theatrerelateditems@yahoo.co.uk

Linda Chan
Stand G073-74. *Jewellery, including jade and jet and precious objects, cameos, clocks and watches.*
TEL: 020 7724 0362

Duncan Clarke
Stand F021. *Traditional hand-woven textiles from West Africa, African studio photography and metal sculpture.*
TEL: 07710 791497
EMAIL: adire@btinternet.com

Da Silva Interiors
Stand G095. *20th C designer furniture especially Brazilian, Danish and English, chrome, glass and lighting.*
TEL: 020 7723 0564
EMAIL: dasilvainteriors@hotmail.com

Decoratum
Basement. *Original 20th C vintage furniture.*
TEL: 020 7724 6969
EMAIL: info@decoratum.com

Dimech
Stand F46-49. *Paintings, ceramics, perfume bottles and 20th C collectables.*
TEL: 020 7723 0678

Dodo
Stand F071-72. *Paintings and prints, posters, advertising and packaging.*
TEL: 020 7706 1545
EMAIL: liz@dodoposters.co.uk

Gill Drey
Stand F021. *Modern British paintings, watercolours and drawings.*
TEL: 020 7627 2355

Tony Durante
Stand G66-68. *Costume jewellery, handbags, perfume bottles, lighters, watches,1920s-1940s decorative objects, mirrored frames and boxes.*
TEL: 020 7723 0449
EMAIL: durantetony@hotmail.com

East West Antiques and Books
Stand S054-56. *Books, maps, atlases and ephemera.*
TEL: 07708 863760
EMAIL: ewa_thomson@hotmail.com

Goldsmith & Perris   LAPADA
Stand G059-G062. *Silver and silver plate tableware, cutlery, wine related items and candlesticks.*
TEL: 020 7724 7051
EMAIL: info@goldsmithandperris.com
WEBSITE: www.goldsmithandperris.com

Janes Antiques
Stand F44-45. *18th, 19th & 20th C ceramics, paintings, rare and old cameras.*
TEL: 020 7723 0678
EMAIL: chrisjanes1942@aol.com

Linetta Greco
Stand G026-G027. *Silver and gold, china glass, jewellery and handbags..*
TEL: 020 7262 0766

Christopher Hall
Stand F077-78. *19th and 20th C furniture and decorative objects.*
TEL: 020 7258 0662
EMAIL: christopher-hall@thebays.fslife.co.uk

Heaven of Gowns
Stand G081-84. *18th C clothing and textiles to vintage haute couture.*
TEL: 020 7258 3366
EMAIL: info@heavenofgowns.com

Barry Landsman
Stand G009-10-11. *British 18th - 19th C watercolours.*
TEL: 020 7723 0564
EMAIL: w.bl@virgin.net

Sarah Lewis and June Victor
Stand S040 & 41-43. *Textiles, fabrics, vintage and fashion clothing & accessories, scent bottles, embroidery .*
TEL: 020 7723 6105

MADE
The Quad. *20th C European furniture, collectables, glassware and ceramics.*
TEL: 020 7723 0564
EMAIL: lorna_lee_leslie@yahoo.co.uk

Magna Carta Antiques
Stand F051. *Inkwells and indstands.*
TEL: 07887 697168
EMAIL: alreadyink@aol.com

Manic Attic
Stand S046-49. *Bakelite, 1930s-1960s kitsch, record players, games and lighting.*
TEL: 020 7723 6105
EMAIL: ianbroughton@hotmail.com

Marie Antiques
Stand G66-69. *Period jewellery, especially garnet, precious objects and gold.*
TEL: 020 7706 3727
EMAIL: marie136@globalnet.co.uk

Francesca Martire
Stand F131-137. *20th C furniture, lighting, glass, ceramics and jewellery; Italian designer interior items.*
TEL: 020 7724 4802
EMAIL: info@francescamartire.com

Robert McKoys Fine Art
Stand F020. *Paintings and prints in watercolour and oil from 1700.*
TEL: 020 7723 0678

N & S Watches
Stand G013. *Old and designer watches, clocks and prints.*
TEL: 020 7723 1513
EMAIL: mo_heidarieh@yahoo.co.uk

Kenneth Norton Grant
Stand F052-53. *Boxes, silver candlesticks, brass and pewter.*
TEL: 020 7723 1370

The Originals
Stand S050-51 & 57-58. *Bakelite, Murano glass, Mdina glass, handbags, custome jewellery.*
TEL: 07751 084135
EMAIL: paola_iaia_london@yahoo.co.uk

Pari's Jewellery
Stand G043-45. *Art Nouveau and Art Deco watches aand clocks, gem set jewellery, pearls and pocket watches.*
TEL: 020 7723 6222
EMAIL: ellisfahimian@aol.com

Pars
Stand G031. *Antique jewellery, silver and old watches.*
TEL: 020 7535 8585
EMAIL: parsjewellery@aol.com

Persiflage
Stand S006-S008. *Textiles, fabrics, vintage clothing and accessories.*
TEL: 020 7724 7366

Johanna Pinder-Wilson
Stand S010. *20th C interior decorative furniture and objects.*
TEL: 07799 737980
EMAIL: email@johannapinder_wilson.com

Renato
Stand G064-65. *Chandeliers, lighting, 1930s glass, bakelite, photo frames, small furniture, Deco and tiles.*
TEL: 020 7723 0449
EMAIL: Engital@aol.com

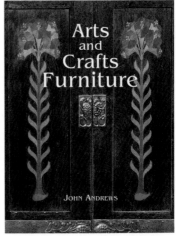
Geoffrey Robinson
Stand G077-78 & 91-92. *Glass, pottery, chrome and stainless steel, Arts and Crafts, Art Deco, 1950s-1970s.*
TEL: 020 7723 0449

Sambataro
Stand G085-86 & S050-51. *20th C decorative arts.*
TEL: 07813 842188
EMAIL: annasambataro@fsmail.net

Andreas Schmid
The Quad. *Furniture, jewellery, lighting, art, glass and pottery.*
TEL: 020 7723 0564
EMAIL: andreas.schmid@btinternet.com

Gloria Sinclair
Stand F023. *Jewellery and precious objects, glass and ceramics, porcelain, English china.*
TEL: 020 7724 7118

Connie Speight
Stand G070-71. *1920s-30s jewellery, bags, china, perfume bottles and pictures.*
TEL: 020 7724 9295
EMAIL: cbspeight@aol.com

The Girl Can't Help It
Stand G014-22. *Vintage and fashion clothing, textiles and accessories, costume jewellery, collectables and memorabilia.*
TEL: 020 7724 8984
EMAIL: cad@thegirlcanthelpit.com

Thirteen
Stand G001-G005 & G050-51. *20th C collectables, lighting and furniture.*
TEL: 07811 008114
EMAIL: thirteenchurchstreet@hotmail.com

Tin Tin Collectables
Stand G38-42. *1900s vintage clothing and accessories, costume jewellery, handbags and cufflinks.*
TEL: 020 7258 1305

Travers Antiques
Stand F080-82. *Furniture, decorative lighting, desks, chests and side furniture.*
TEL: 020 7258 0662
EMAIL: spkluth@aol.com

The Upholstery Workshop
Stand G002-4. *Work undertaken on a wide range of styles and materials with designs for a particular period a speciality.*
TEL: 07811 008144
EMAIL: theupholsteryworkshop@hotmail.co.uk
emiliaporto@hotmail.com

Louise Verber Antiques
Stand F070. *Decorative antiques and accessories.*
TEL: 020 7723 0429
EMAIL: bernardbarkoff@lineone.net

June Victor
Stand S041-43. *Textiles, fabrics, vintage clothing and accessories, scent bottles and embroidery.*
TEL: 020 7723 6105

W and L Antiques
Stand G060. *20th C collectable ceramics including Carlton Ware, Wedgwood and Royal Paragon.*
TEL: 020 7724 7051
EMAIL: teddylove@blueyonder.co.uk

Fletcher Wallis
Stand F015. *Scientific and medical instruments; corkscrews.*
fletcherwallis@btinternet.com
TEL: 020 7402 1038

Beverley
30 Church St., Marylebone. NW8 8EP.
Open 10-6 or by appointment. STOCK: *Art Nouveau, Art Deco, decorative objects.* FAIRS: NEC.
TEL: 020 7262 1576

Bizarre
24 Church St., Marylebone. NW8 8EP. (A. Taramasco and V. Conti)
Open 10-5. STOCK: *Art Deco, Modernist decorative arts 1950s-60s.*
TEL: 020 7724 1305; FAX: 020 7724 1316

Church Street Antiques
8 Church St. NW8 8ED. (Stuart Shuster)
EST. 1975. Open Mon-Sat 11-5.30. STOCK: *English brown furniture, 18th to early 20th C, £500-£2,000.* LOC: Between Edgware Rd and Lisson Grove. SER: Restorations (polishing). SIZE: Medium. PARK: Meters. VAT: Stan.
TEL: 020 7723 7415; Mobile 0797 3541308
E-MAIL: stuart@churchstreetantiques.net
WEBSITE: www.churchstreetantiques.net

Patricia Harvey Antiques and Decoration
42 Church St., Marylebone. NW8 8EP.
EST. 1961. Open 10-5.30. STOCK: *Decorative furniture, objets, accessories and paintings, £100-£20,000.* LOC: Between Lisson Grove and Edgware Rd., near Alfies Antique Market. SER: Valuations; buys at auction; interior decoration. SIZE: Medium. PARK: Pay and Display. VAT: Spec. FAIRS: Decorative Antiques and Textiles.
TEL: 020 7262 8989; FAX: same; HOME: 020 7624 1787
WEBSITE: www.patriciaharveyantiques.co.uk

Leask Ward
NW8 9LP.
EST. 1973. Open by appointment. STOCK: *Oriental and European antiques and paintings.* LOC: St John's Wood.
SER: Consultancy.
TEL: 020 7289 2429; FAX: same
E-MAIL: wardl5@aol.com

Andrew Nebbett Antiques
35-37 Church St., Marylebone. NW8 8ES.
EST. 1986. Open Tues.-Sat. 10-5.30. STOCK: *Refectory tables, leather sofas and chairs, light oak furniture, Heals, garden furniture, lamps, decorative items, military and ships furniture, 1760-1960.* LOC: 50m from Alfie's Antique Market. SIZE: Large. VAT: Stan/Spec. FAIRS: Olympia (Feb).
TEL: 020 7723 2303; MOBILE: 07768 741595
E-MAIL: anebbett@aol.com
WEBSITE: www.andrewnebbett.com

Townsends
81 Abbey Rd., St. John's Wood. NW8 0AE. (M. Townsend)
EST. 1972. Open 10-6. STOCK: *Fireplaces, £250-£6,000; stained glass, £80-£1,000; architectural and garden antiques,*

£50-£2,000; all mainly 18th-19th C. LOC: Corner of Abbey Rd. and Boundary Rd. SER: Valuations; site surveys; free delivery. SIZE: Large PARK: Easy. VAT: Stan.
TEL: 020 7624 4756; warehouse - 020 7372 4327; FAX: 020 7372 3005

Young & Son   LAPADA
12 Church St. NW8 8EP. (L. and S. Young)
EST. 1990. CINOA. Open Tues-Sat. 10-6. *STOCK: Furniture, paintings, £100-£20,000; lighting and mirrors, £80-£5,000; decorative items, £100-£5,000; all 18th-20th C. European sculpture. LOC: Off Lisson Grove and Edgware Rd. SER: Valuations; restorations (framing, French polishing, paintings lined, cleaned and restored). SIZE: Medium. PARK: Easy. VAT: Stan/Spec.*
TEL: 020 7723 5910; FAX: 020 8458 3852; MOBILE: 07958 437043
E-MAIL: leon@youngandson.com
WEBSITE: www.youngandson.com

NW9

B.C. Metalcrafts
69 Tewkesbury Gardens. NW9 0QU. (F. Burnell)
EST. 1946. Lighting Association. *Trade Only.* Open by appointment. STOCK: *Lighting, ormolu and marble lamps; Oriental and European vases; clocks, pre-1900, £5-£500.* SER: Restorations; conversions; buys at auction. PARK: Own.
TEL: 020 8204 2446; FAX: 020 8206 2871

NW10

David Malik and Son Ltd
5 Metro Centre, Britannia Way, Park Royal. NW10 7PA.
Open 9-5. CL: Sat. STOCK: *Chandeliers, wall lights.* SER: Manufactures and restores chandeliers and wall lights. PARK: Easy. VAT: Stan.
TEL: 020 8965 4232; FAX: 020 8965 2401

Willesden Green Architectural Salvage
189 High Rd., Willesden. NW10 2SD. (D. Harkin)
EST. 1996. Open 9-6. STOCK: *Architectural items.*
TEL: 020 8459 2947; FAX: 020 8415 1515; MOBILE: 07971 176547

NW11

Christopher Eimer
P.O. Box 352. NW11 7RF.
EST. 1970. BNTA. IAPN. Open 9-5 by appointment. STOCK: *Commemorative and historical medals and related art.* VAT: Global/Margin.
TEL: 020 8458 9933; FAX: 020 8455 3535
E-MAIL: art@christophereimer.co.uk
WEBSITE: www.christophereimer.co.uk

WC1

Abbott & Holder Ltd   BADA
30 Museum St. WC1A 1LH. (Philip Athill)
EST. 1936. Open 9.30-6, Thurs. till 7. *STOCK: English watercolours, drawings, oils and prints, 1760-2000.* LOC: Opposite British Museum. SER: Conservation; framing and mounting; valuations. SIZE: 3 floors. PARK: Bloomsbury Sq. VAT: Spec FAIRS: Watercolours and Drawings; BADA.
TEL: 020 7637 3981; FAX: 020 7631 0575
E-MAIL: abbott.holder@virgin.net
WEBSITE: www.abbottandholder.co.uk

Atlantis Bookshop
49a Museum St. WC1A 1LY. (Geraldine Beskin and Bali Beskin)
EST. 1922. Open 10.30-6. *STOCK: Antiquarian books on the occult and esoteric sciences; occasional related artefacts and paintings, especially Austin Osman Spare and Aleister Crowley.* LOC: Tottenham Court Rd. or Holborn underground stations.
TEL: 020 7405 2120
E-MAIL: info@theatlantisbookshop.com
WEBSITE: www.theatlantisbookshop.com

Austin/Desmond Fine Art
Pied Bull Yard, 68-69 Great Russell St. WC1B 3BN. (J. Austin)
EST. 1982. SLAD. Open 10.30-5.30, Sat. 11-2.30 during exhibitions. *STOCK: Modern and contemporary British paintings and prints; ceramics.* LOC: Near Bloomsbury. Holborn and Tottenham Court Rd. underground stations. PARK: Bloomsbury Sq. or Bury Place. VAT: Spec. FAIRS: London Art; Olympia; London Original Print; 20th/21st British Art.
TEL: 020 7242 4443; FAX: 020 7404 4480
E-MAIL: gallery@austindesmond.com
WEBSITE: www.austindesmond.com

George and Peter Cohn
Unit 21, 21 Wren St. WC1X 0HF.
EST. 1947. Open 9-5, Sat. and Fri. pm. by appointment. *STOCK: Decorative lights.* SER: Restorations (chandeliers and wall-lights). PARK: Forecourt.
TEL: 020 7278 3749

Fine Books Oriental
38 Museum St. WC1A 1LP. (Jeffrey Somers)
EST. 1970. PBFA. Open 9.30-6, Sat. 11-6. *STOCK: Books.* LOC: Near British Museum. SIZE: Medium. PARK: Meters.
TEL: 020 7242 5288; FAX: 020 7242 5344
E-MAIL: oriental@finebooks.demon.co.uk
WEBSITE: www.finebooks.demon.co.uk

HEBECO (Silver and Glass)   LAPADA
WC1N (Mr & Mrs H. Bruce)
STOCK: 17th - 20th C silver and glass.

TEL: 07710 019790
E-MAIL: hebeco.two@virgin.net
WEBSITE: www.hebeco.co.uk

Spink & Son Ltd   BADA
69 Southampton Row. WC1B 4ET.
EST. 1666. BNTA. IAPN. Open 9.30-5.30. CL: Sat. *STOCK: Coins, medals, stamps, bank notes and related books.* SER: Valuations. VAT: Stan/Spec.
TEL: 020 7563 4000; FAX: 020 7563 4066
E-MAIL: info@spink.com
WEBSITE: www.spink.com

WC2

Anchor Antiques Ltd
Suite 31, 26 Charing Cross Rd. WC2H 0DG. (K.B. Embden and H. Samne)
EST. 1964. *Trade Only.* Open by appointment. *STOCK: Continental and Oriental ceramics, European works of art and objets de vertu.* VAT: Spec.
TEL: 020 7836 5686

Apple Market Stalls
Covent Garden Market. WC2E 8RF.
EST. 1980. Open every Monday 10-6.30. *STOCK: Antiques and quality collectables.* LOC: North Hall. SIZE: 48 stalls.
TEL: 020 7836 9136
E-MAIL: theapplemarket@coventgardenmarket.co.uk
WEBSITE: www.coventgardenmarket.co.uk

A.H. Baldwin & Sons Ltd   BADA
11 Adelphi Terrace. WC2N 6BJ. (Edward Baldwin and Ian Goldbart)
EST. 1872. IAPN. BNTA. Open 9-5. CL: Sat. *STOCK: Coins, 600 BC to present; commemorative medals, 16th C to present, numismatic literature.* LOC: Off Robert St., near Charing Cross. SER: Valuations; auctioneers and auction agents for selling and purchasing. SIZE: Medium. VAT: Stan/Spec. FAIRS: Coinex; Numismata, (Germany); HICC, (Hong Kong).
TEL: 020 7930 6879; FAX: 020 7930 9450
E-MAIL: coins@baldwin.sh
WEBSITE: www.baldwin.sh

M. Bord (Gold Coin Exchange)
16 Charing Cross Rd. WC2H 0HR.
EST. 1969. Open 10.30-5.30. *STOCK: Gold, silver and copper coins, Roman to Elizabeth II, all prices; banknotes and medals, foreign coins.* LOC: Near Leicester Sq. underground station. SER: Valuations; buys at auction. SIZE: Small. VAT: Stan/Spec. FAIRS: All major coin.
TEL: 020 7836 0631 or 020 7240 0479;
FAX: 020 7240 1920

Tim Bryars Ltd
8 Cecil Court. WC2N 4HE.
EST. 2004. ABA. ILAB. IAMA. IMCoS. Open 11-6,

Sat. 12-5. *STOCK: Early printed books, classical texts and translations, atlases and maps of all regions, mainly pre 1800; topographical and natural history prints, all £10-£20,000.* LOC: From Leicester Sq. underground, south down Charing Cross Rd.(towards Trafalgar Sq.), second left. SIZE: Medium. PARK: Shelton St. or meters. VAT: Stan. FAIRS: London Map.
TEL: 020 7836 1901; FAX: 020 7836 1910
E-MAIL: tim@timbryars.co.uk
WEBSITE: www.timbryars.co.uk

Philip Cohen Numismatics
20 Cecil Court. WC2N 4HE.
EST. 1977. BNTA. Open 11-5.15, Sat. 12-5. *STOCK: English coins, 16th-20th C, £1-£1,000.* LOC: Off Charing Cross Road, near Leicester Sq. underground station. SER: Valuations. SIZE: Medium. VAT: Stan.
TEL: 020 7379 0615
E-MAIL: coinheritage@aol.com

Covent Garden Flea Market
Jubilee Market, Covent Garden. WC2E 8RB.
(Sherman and Waterman Associates Ltd)
EST. 1975. Open every Mon. from 6 am. *STOCK: General antiques.* LOC: South side of piazza, just off The Strand, via Southampton St. SIZE: 150 stalls. PARK: Easy, NCP Drury Lane.
TEL: 020 7836 2139 or 020 7240 7405

David Drummond at Pleasures of Past Times
11 Cecil Court, Charing Cross Rd. WC2N 4EZ.
EST. 1962. Open 11-2.30 and 3.30-5.45 and usually 1st Sat. monthly, other times by appointment. *STOCK: Scarce and out-of-print books of the performing arts; early juvenile and illustrated books; vintage postcards, valentines, entertainment ephemera and miscellaneous bygones. NOT STOCKED: Coins, stamps, medals, jewellery, maps, cigarette cards.* LOC: In pedestrian court between Charing Cross Rd. and St. Martin's Lane. SIZE: Medium. VAT: Stan.
TEL: 020 7836 1142; FAX: same
E-MAIL: pan.drumm@virgin.net

Elms-Lesters Tribal Art   LAPADA
1-5 Flitcroft St. WC2H 8DH. (Paul Jones and Fiona McKinnon)
EST. 1972. Open 11-6 during exhibitions, other times by appointment. *STOCK: Tribal art from Africa, Oceania and south-east Asia - sculptures, masks, ethnographic objects, furniture and textiles, 19th to mid-20th C.* **LOC: Between Soho, Covent Garden and Bloomsbury. SER: Valuations. SIZE: Medium. PARK: Meters and NCP nearby. FAIRS: LAPADA.**
TEL: 020 7836 6747; FAX: 020 7379 0789
E-MAIL: info@elmslesters.co.uk
WEBSITE: www.elmslesters.co.uk

Stanley Gibbons
399 Strand. WC2R 0LX. (Richard Purkis)
EST. 1856. PTS. Open 9-5.30, Sat. 9.30-5.30. *STOCK: Over 3 million stamps from all world countries; GB and Commonwealth specialist stamps and postal history; catalogues, albums, magazines, books, accessories, autographs and memorabilia.* LOC: Opposite Savoy Hotel. SER: Valuations; buys at auction; auctioneering. SIZE: Large. PARK: NCP. VAT: Margin/Global. FAIRS: Various.
TEL: 020 7836 8444; FAX: 020 7836 7342
E-MAIL: shop@stanleygibbons.co.uk
WEBSITE: www.stanleygibbons.com

Gillian Gould at Ocean Leisure
Embankment Place, 11-14 Northumberland Avenue. WC2N 5AQ.
EST. 1988. Open 9.30-7, Thurs. 9.30-7, Sat. 9.30-6.30 or by appointment. *STOCK: Marine antiques and collectables, scientific instruments, £30-£1,000.* LOC: Embankment underground station. SER: Valuations; restorations; hire; sources gifts for personal and corporate presentation; buys at auction. SIZE: Small. PARK: Meters. VAT: Stan.
TEL: 020 7419 0500; MOBILE: 07831 150060
E-MAIL: gillgould@dealwith.com

Grosvenor Prints
19 Shelton St., Covent Garden. WC2H 9JN.
EST. 1975. Open 10-6, Sat. 11-4. *STOCK: 18th-19th C topographical and decorative prints, specialising in portraits, dogs and British field sports.* LOC: One street north of Covent Garden underground station. SER: Valuations; restorations; buys at auction. SIZE: Large. PARK: Easy. VAT: Stan/Spec. FAIRS: ABA.
TEL: 020 7836 1979; FAX: 020 7379 6695
E-MAIL: grosvenorprints@btinternet.com
WEBSITE: www.grosvenorprints.com

P. J. Hilton (Books)
12 Cecil Court. WC2N 4HE. (Paul Hilton)
EST. 1980. Open 11-6, Sat. 11-5. *STOCK: Antiquarian books, 16th-20th C, £75-£500; secondhand books; leather cloth bindings by the yard.* LOC: Off Charing Cross Rd. SER: Valuations. SIZE: Medium.
TEL: 020 7379 9825
E-MAIL: pjhbks@tiscali.co.uk

Raymond D Holdich International Medals & Militaria
7 Whitcomb St. WC2H 7HA. (D.C. Pratchett and R.D. Holdich)
EST. 1979. OMRS. Open 9.30-3.30. CL: Sat. *STOCK: Coins and military medals, bonds, banknotes, badges and militaria, 18th-20th C, £5-£10,000.* LOC: Next to National Gallery. SER: Valuations; buys at auction (coins and military medals). PARK: NCP. VAT: Stan/Spec.
TEL: 020 7930 1979; FAX: 020 7930 1152
E-MAIL: rdhmedals@aol.com
WEBSITE: www.rdhmedals.com

Koopman Rare Art   BADA
Entrance to London Silver Vaults, Ground Floor, 53-64 Chancery Lane. WC2A 1QS. (Timo Koopman and Lewis Smith)
Open 9-5.30, Sat. 10-1. STOCK: *Fine quality English Georgian and Continental silverware.* FAIRS: Milan; Olympia; Grosvenor House; New York; Maastricht (TEFAF); Gotha, Parma.
TEL: 020 7242 7624; FAX: 020 7831 0221
E-MAIL: enquiries@rareartlondon.com
WEBSITE: www.rareartlondon.com

The London Silver Vaults
Chancery House, 53-64 Chancery Lane. WC2A 1QS. EST. 1892. Open 9-5.30, Sat. 9-1. STOCK: *Antique and modern silver, plate, jewellery, objets d'art, clocks, watches, general items.* SER: Valuations; restorations. SIZE: 34 shops. PARK: Meters. VAT: Stan/Global/Export.
TEL: 020 7242 3844.
WEBSITE: www.thesilvervaults.com

The following are some of the dealers at these vaults.

Argenteus Ltd   LAPADA
VAULT 2. VAT: Stan/Spec.
TEL: 020 7831 3637; FAX: 020 7430 0126
EMAIL: argenteus@silver-vault.com

Belmonts
EMAIL: belmont@londonsilvervaults.wanadoo.co.uk

Luigi Brian Antiques
Vault 17. *Fine English and European silver, objets d'art and icons.*
TEL: 020 7405 2484; FAX: same

B.L. Collins
Vault 20. (Barry Collins)
TEL: 020 7404 0628; FAX: 020 7404 1451
EMAIL: barrycollins259@btinternet.com
WEBSITE: www.blcollins.co.uk

Crown Silver
Vault 30.
TEL: 020 7242 4704
EMAIL: silver@silstar.co.uk

P. Daniels
Vault 51.
TEL: 020 7430 1327
EMAIL: paweldaniel@aol.com
WEBSITE: www.paweldaniel.com

Bryan Douglas   LAPADA
Vault 12-14. (Ian Bryan) *Antique, old and modern silverware.*
TEL: 020 7242 7073; FAX: 020 7405 8862
EMAIL: info@bryandouglas.co.uk
WEBSITE: www.bryandouglas.co.uk

R. Feldman Ltd   LAPADA
Vault 6. *Unusual and rare items, old Sheffield and Victorian plate, silver centrepieces, candelabra, epergnes combined with argenteus, all patterns of flatware.*
TEL: 020 7405 6111; FAX: 020 7430 0126

EMAIL: rfeldman@rfeldman.co.uk
WEBSITE: www.rfeldman.co.uk

I. Franks   LAPADA
Vault 9-11. EST. 1926. *Old and antique English silver and plate especially tableware, teasets, cutlery, epergnes, candlesticks and candelabra.*
TEL: 020 7242 4035; FAX: same
EMAIL: sales@ifranks.com
WEBSITE: www.ifranks.com

Anthony Green Antiques
Vault 54. *Vintage wrist watches.*
TEL: 020 7430 0038
EMAIL: vintagewatches@hotmail.com

M. & J. Hamilton
Vault 25. *17th -20th C silver including cutlery.*
TEL: 020 7831 7030; FAX: 020 7831 5483
EMAIL: hamiltonsilver@hotmail.com

Gary Hyams
Vault 48-50. *Silver and Sheffield Plate.*
TEL: 020 7831 4330
EMAIL: hyamssilverware@onetel.com

Stephen Kalms   LAPADA
Vault 13, 15, 31, 32.
TEL: 020 7430 1254; FAX: 020 7405 6206; MOBILE: 07831 604001
EMAIL: stephen@kalmsantiques.com
WEBSITE: www.kalmsantiques.com

Langfords   LAPADA
Vault 8-10. (Adam and Joel Langford) EST. 1940. *Silver and plate, especially cutlery.* Valuations. VAT: Stan/Spec.
TEL: 020 7242 5506; FAX: 020 7242 6656; MOBILE: 07880 706644
EMAIL: adam@langfords.com
WEBSITE: www.langfords.com

Leon Antiques
Vault 57.

Nat Leslie Ltd
Vault 21-23. (Mark Hyams) EST. 1940. *Victorian and 20th C silverware, flatware and contemporary designers, especially Stuart Devlin.* VAT: Stan/Spec.
TEL: 020 7242 4787; FAX: 020 7242 4504
EMAIL: natleslie@onetel.com
WEBSITE: www.natleslie.co.uk

Linden and Co. (Antiques) Ltd
Vault 7. (H.M. and S. C. Linden) *Silver and plate, specialising in gift items for weddings, christenings, silver weddings and retirements, £100-£750.* VAT: Stan/Spec.
TEL: 020 7242 4863; FAX: 020 7405 9946
EMAIL: lindenandco@aol.com
WEBSITE: www.lindenantiquesilver.com

C. and T. Mammon
Vault 55-64. (Claude Mammon) *Victorian and old Sheffield plate, Continental and English silver and cutlery, mirror plateaux and centrepieces.*
TEL: 020 7405 2397; FAX: 020 7405 4900
EMAIL: claudemammon@btinternet.com
WEBSITE: www.candtmammon.com

THE ENGLISH REGIONAL CHAIR

Bernard D. Cotton

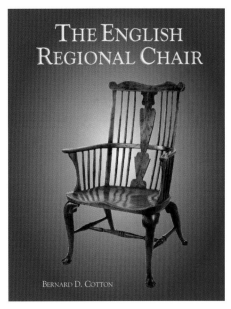

This is arguably the most detailed study ever made of any branch of British furniture. Its unique scope embraces the work of hundreds of craftsmen throughout the country, working within the general tradition of their area, yet superimposing their individual design 'signatures'.

Employing a remarkable combination of talents, the author has examined thousands of regional chairs, researched local archives, conducted field studies and collated anecdotal evidence to relate the evolution of known types and makes. The result, far from being a dry research document, is a fascinating living account of the development of hundreds of chair types from all over England and the lives of the craftsmen who produced them.

This book has revolutionised collecting and the study of vernacular furniture. It continues to be studied avidly by collectors as hundreds of new makers' names emerge from the anonymity of generalised terms such as 'Windsor', 'ladder back' and 'spindle back'. This reprint is most welcome.

Specifications: 512pp., 69 col. illus.,
over 1,400 b.&w. illus., 11 x 8½in./279 x 216mm.
£49.50 (hardback)

Windsor Chairs

Michael Harding-Hill

Specifications: 160pp., 183 col. illus.,
196 b.&w. illus., 9½ x 7½in./240 x 195mm.
£25.00 (hardback)

Windsor Chairs
Michael Harding-Hill

The Windsor chair, whether simple or complicated in construction, plain or ornate in appearance, has always served its purpose – to be utilitarian, durable, comfortable and even handsome.

Many excellent academic works have been written on the subject, but this book does not attempt to improve on their expertise. The intention rather is to complement them by showing the finest designs in greater detail. The form and construction of the chairs speak for themselves. All the chairs illustrated, although made in different centuries, are in use today. Is there another example of utilitarian furniture made in such numbers that still survives and is in everyday use?

More than 150 colour plates illustrate the very best Windsor chairs from the earliest stick-backs – literally stools with a few sticks added to the back – of the eighteenth century to those mass-produced for offices, schools, public institutions and the armed forces in the nineteenth century. There is a special section on American Windsors and the story of the Windsor chair continues through the twentieth century and concludes by illustrating a 2002 Golden Jubilee chair. This book is a celebration of the beautiful Windsor chair.

For full details of all ACC publications, log on to our website:
www.antiquecollectorsclub.com
or telephone 01394 389950 for a free catalogue

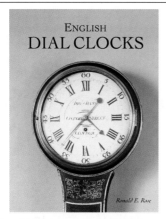

ENGLISH DIAL CLOCKS

Ronald E. Rose

The heyday of the dial clock was the Victorian period when it was to be found in every office, factory, school and railway station. The Bank of England alone had 400! While the dial clock is occasionally to be found still performing its function accurately, increasingly it is the serious collector who appreciates the simple, elegant dials and the very fine workmanship of the movements. The author is an experienced horologist who has acquired a specialised knowledge in the best possible way, by handling hundreds of examples and repairing a large number himself. Various types are carefully documented and beautifully photographed.

Specifications: 256pp., 42 col. illus., 253 b.&w. illus., 430 line drawings, 12 x 9¼in./305 x 234mm.
£39.50 (hardback)

Percy's (Silver Ltd).   LAPADA
Vault 16. (David and Paul Simons) *Fine decorative silver especially claret jugs, candelabra, candlesticks, flatware and collectables.*
TEL: 020 7242 3618; FAX: 020 7831 6541; MOBILE: 07887 716797
EMAIL: sales@percys-silver.com
WEBSITE: www.percys-silver.com

Terry Shaverin
Vault 143.
TEL: 020 8368 5869; FAX: 020 8361 7659
EMAIL: terryshaverin@silverflatware.co.uk
WEBSITE: www.silverflatware.co.uk

David S. Shure and Co
Vault 1. (Lynn Bulka) EST. 1900. Author. *Antique and modern silverware, old Sheffield plate, cutlery and jewellery.* Valuations. VAT: Stan.
TEL: 020 7405 0011; FAX: same
EMAIL: sales@davidshure.com
WEBSITE: www.davidshure.com

Silstar (Antiques Ltd)
Vault 29. (B. Stern) EST. 1955. VAT: Stan/Spec.
TEL: 020 7242 6740; FAX: 020 7430 1745
EMAIL: silver@silstar.co.uk

S. and J. Stodel   BADA.
Vault 24. (Jeremy Stodel) *Chinese export to English Art Deco silver including flatware.*

TEL: 020 7405 7009; FAX: 020 7242 6366
EMAIL: stodel@msn.com
WEBSITE: www.chinesesilver.com

J. Surtees
Vault 65. *Silver.*
TEL: 020 7242 0749

William Walter Antiques Ltd   BADA LAPADA
Vault 3-5. (Elizabeth Simpson) EST. 1927. *Georgian silver, old Sheffield plate; also modern silver.* Valuations; restorations (silver, plate).
TEL: 020 7242 3284; FAX: 020 7404 1280
EMAIL: enq@wwantiques.prestel.co.uk
WEBSITE: www.williamwalter.co.uk

Peter K. Weiss
Vault 18. EST. 1955. *Watches, clocks.* VAT: Stan.
TEL: 020 7242 8100; FAX: 020 7242 7310

Wolfe (Jewellery)
Vault 41. (John Petrook) VAT: Stan/Spec.
TEL: 020 7405 2101; FAX: same
EMAIL: dennypetrook@waitrose.com

Marchpane
16 Cecil Court, Charing Cross Rd. WC2N 4HE. (Kenneth Fuller)
EST. 1989. ABA. PBFA. ILAB. Open 10.30-6. *STOCK: Antiquarian children's and illustrated books, from 18th C to date.* LOC: Alley off Charing Cross Road. SIZE: Medium. VAT: Stan
TEL: 020 7836 8661
E-MAIL: kenneth@marchpane.com
WEBSITE: www.marchpane.com

Henry Pordes Books Ltd
58-60 Charing Cross Rd. WC2H 0BB. (Gino Della-Ragione and Nicole Pordes)
EST. 1983. Open 10-7. *STOCK: Secondhand, antiquarian and remainder books on most subjects including antiques.*
TEL: 020 7836 9031; FAX: 020 7240 4232
E-MAIL: info@henrypordesbooks.com
WEBSITE: www.henrypordesbooks.com

Bertram Rota Ltd
1st Floor, 31 Long Acre. WC2E 9LT.
EST. 1923. Open 9.30-5.30; CL: Sat. *STOCK: Antiquarian and secondhand books, especially first editions, private presses, English literature, literary autographs.*
TEL: 020 7836 0723 or 020 7497 9058
E-MAIL: bertramrota@compuserve.com

The Silver Mouse Trap
56 Carey St. WC2A 2JB. (A. Woodhouse)
EST. 1690. Open 10-5. CL: Sat. *STOCK: Jewellery, silver.* LOC: South of Lincoln's Inn Fields. SER: Valuations; restorations. SIZE: Medium. VAT: Spec.
TEL: 020 7405 2578

Storey's Ltd
3 Cecil Court, Charing Cross Rd. WC2N 4EZ. (T. Kingswood)

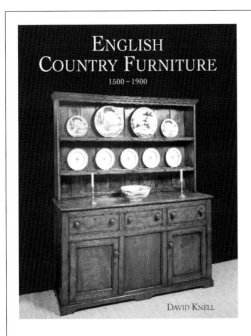
EST. 1929. Open 10-6. STOCK: *Antiquarian prints and engravings, especially naval and military; natural history and topography, including David Roberts; antiquarian maps.* LOC: Between Charing Cross Rd. and St. Martin's Lane. PARK: Trafalgar Square garage.
TEL: 020 7836 3777; FAX: 020 7836 3788
E-MAIL: storeysltd@btinternet.com
WEBSITE: www. storeysltd.co.uk

Tindley and Chapman
4 Cecil Court. WC2N 4HE.
EST. 1974. Open 10-5.30, Sat. 11-5. STOCK: *20th C first editions English and American literature including detective fiction.*
TEL: 020 7240 2161; FAX: 020 7379 1062

Travis and Emery Music Bookshop
17 Cecil Court, Charing Cross Rd. WC2N 4EZ.
EST. 1960. ABA. PBFA. Open 10.15-6.30; Sun. 11.30-4. STOCK: *Musical literature, sheet music and prints.* LOC: Between Charing Cross Rd. and St. Martin's Lane. SER: Valuations. SIZE: Medium. PARK: Meters.
TEL: 020 7240 2129; FAX: 020 7497 0790
E-MAIL: enqasb@travis-and-emery.com

Watkins Books Ltd
19-21 Cecil Court, Charing Cross Rd. WC2N 4EZ.
EST. 1880. Open 11-7. STOCK: *Mysticism, occultism, Oriental religions, astrology, psychology, complementary medicine and a wide selection of books in the field of mind, body and spirit - both new and secondhand.* LOC: Near Leicester Sq. underground station.
TEL: 020 7836 2182; FAX: 020 7836 6700
E-MAIL: service@watkinsbooks.com
WEBSITE: www.watkinsbooks.com

Nigel Williams Rare Books
25 Cecil Court, Charing Cross Rd. WC2N 4EZ.
EST. 1988. ABA. Open 10-6. STOCK: *Books - literature first editions, 18th-20th C; children's and illustrated, original artwork and prints, detective fiction.* LOC: Near Leicester Sq. underground station. SIZE: Medium. FAIRS: ABA, Olympia.
TEL: 020 7836 7757; FAX: 020 7379 5918
E-MAIL: sales@nigelwilliams.com
WEBSITE: www.nigelwilliams.com

The Witch Ball
2 Cecil Court, Charing Cross Rd. WC2N 4HE. (R. Glassman)
EST. 1969. Resident. Open 11-7. STOCK: *Prints relating to the performing arts, from 17th C, 20th C posters.* LOC: 2 mins. from Leicester Square underground station. SIZE: Small. PARK: NCP nearby. VAT: Stan.
TEL: 020 7836 2922
E-MAIL: thewitchball@btinternet.com

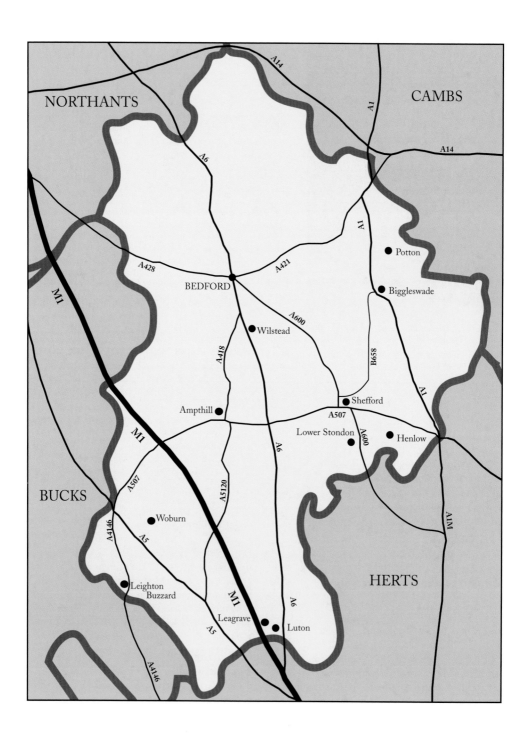

AMPTHILL ANTIQUES EMPORIUM

Experience shopping as it was over a century ago at this
unique Antiques Centre, housed in a purpose built
Victorian department store virtually unchanged since 1898.

Three floors offering a variety of town, country
and decorative antiques to suit all tastes.

Visit our rear yard for Architectural & Garden Antiques

IN-HOUSE SERVICES

• Traditional Upholsterer • Furniture Restorer
• Metal Polisher – *and* the most comprehensive range
of restoration materials in the area

Open six days 10am-5pm *Closed Tuesday*
6 Bedford Street, Ampthill, Beds.

Telephone: 01525 402131
www.ampthillantiquesemporium.co.uk
email: info@ampthillantiquesemporium.co.uk

AMPTHILL

Ampthill Antiques Emporium
6 Bedford St. MK45 2NB. (Marc Legg)
EST. 1979. Open 10-5 including Sun. CL: Tues. STOCK:
*Antique furniture, fireplaces, architectural items, smalls,
ceramics, glass and jewellery.* LOC: 5 mins. from junction
13, M1. SER: Restorations (furniture); upholstery; caning
and metal polishing. SIZE: Large - 50 dealers. PARK: Easy.
TEL: 01525 402131 FAX: 01767 640156
E-MAIL: info@ampthillantiquesemporium.co.uk
WEBSITE: www.ampthillantiquesemporium.co.uk

Antiquarius of Ampthill
107 Dunstable St. MK45 2NG. (Carmel Caldwell)
EST. 1997. Open 10.30-5, Sun. 1-5. STOCK: *Sitting and
dining room furniture, 1800-1900, to £3,000.* LOC: Town
centre. SER: Restorations; re-upholstery. SIZE: Medium.
PARK: Nearby.
TEL: 01525 841799
E-MAIL: carmel.cusack@clara.co.uk
WEBSITE: www.antiquariusofampthill.com

David Litt Antiques
8, Claridges Lane. MK45 2NG. (David and Helen Litt)
EST. 1967. Open 7.30-5, Sat. and Sun. by appointment.
STOCK: *French country items, commodes, farmhouse tables,
sets of chairs, chandeliers and mirrors.* LOC: 2B Woburn St.
SIZE: Small. FAIRS: Decorative Antiques & Textile,

Battersea; House & Garden; Olympia.
TEL: 01525 404825 MOBILE: 07802 449027 HOME -
01525 403828
E-MAIL: litt.antiques@btconnect.com
WEBSITE: www.davidlittantiques.co.uk

Paris Antiques
97b Dunstable St. MK45 2NG. (Paul and Elizabeth
Northwood)
EST. 1985. Open 9.30-5. CL: Mon. STOCK: *Furniture,
18th to early 20th C, £250-£4,000; brass and copper, silver
and plate, pictures and smalls.* LOC: Off junction 12, M1.
SER: Valuations; restorations (mainly furniture, some
metal); buys at auction. SIZE: Medium. PARK: Opposite.
TEL: 01525 840488 HOME: 01525 861420 MOBILE:
07802 535059

S. and S. Timms Antiques Ltd   LAPADA
P O Box 813. MK45 9AW. (Sue, Steve and Robbie
Timms)
EST. 1976. Open by appointment. Also trading at The
Swan and Woburn Abbey Antiques Centres. STOCK:
18th-19th C town and country furniture. VAT:
Stan/Spec. FAIRS: Olympia x 2; Battersea x 3.
TEL: 07860 482995
E-MAIL: info@timmsantiques.com
WEBSITE: www.timmsantiques.com

BEDFORD

Architectural Antiques
70 Pembroke St. MK40 3RQ. (Paul and Linda Hoare)
EST. 1989. Open 12-5, Sat. 9-5. STOCK: *Early Georgian to
early 20th C fireplaces, £500-£1,000; sanitary ware, from
late Victorian, £100-£500; doors, panelling, pews, chimney
pots and other architectural items, Georgian and Victorian,
£50-£100.* LOC: Follow signs to town centre, turn on
The Embankment or Castle Rd., shop is off Castle Rd.,
near Post Office. SER: Valuations; restorations;
installations (period fireplaces). SIZE: Medium. PARK:
Easy.
TEL: 01234 213131/308003 FAX: 01234 309858

BIGGLESWADE

Shortmead Antiques
46 Shortmead St. SG18 0AP. (S.E. Sinfield)
EST. 1989. Open 10.30-5. CL: Mon. and Thurs. STOCK:
*Furniture, £50-£1,000; boxes, porcelain, silver, bronzes,
copper and brass.* LOC: ½ mile from A1. SIZE: Small.
PARK: On street.
TEL: 01767 601780 (ansaphone)
E-MAIL: shortmead@lineone.net

Simply Oak
Potton Rd. SG18 0EP. (R. Sturman and A . Kilgarriff)
EST. 1992. Open 10-5, Sun. 11-4. STOCK: *Restored oak
furniture, 1860-1950, large range of antique clocks and
collectable bric a brac.* LOC: Off A1 towards Biggleswade,

right turn onto B1040 - 2 miles towards Potton. SER: Valuations; furniture restoration; house clearance; tours and talks of furniture. SIZE: Large. PARK: Own.
TEL: 01767 601559 FAX: 01767 310927
E-MAIL: enquiries@simplyoak.co.uk
WEBSITE: www.simplyoak.co.uk

HENLOW

Hanworth House Antiques & Interiors
Hanworth House, 92 High St. SG16 6AB. (Rosemarie Jarvis)
EST. 2001. Open 10.30-6, Sun. 12-5.30. CL: Mon. STOCK: *English furniture, £250-£5,500; glass and ceramics, 1880-1950, £50-£300; silver, 1890-1940, £50-£400; jewellery, 1900-1960, £40-£150; general small antiques including mirrors, lighting, watercolours, prints and etchings.* SER: Chinoiserie hand-painted furniture and contemporary Nomadic rug finding service. SIZE: Small. PARK: Own.
TEL: 01462 814361 HOME/FAX: same
E-MAIL: hanworthhouse@aol.com
WEBSITE: www.hanworthhouse.co.uk

LEAGRAVE

Tomkinson Stained Glass
2 Neville Rd. LU3 2JQ. (S. Tomkinson)
Open by appointment. STOCK: *Antique stained glass windows, from early Victorian to late Edwardian, Art Nouveau, Art Deco; religious church windows, French 1900; stained glass roundels.* LOC: 5 mins. from Luton station amd junction 11, M1. SER: Valuations; restorations.
PARK: Easy. VAT: Stan.
TEL: 01582 527866 MOBILE: 07831 861641
E-MAIL: sales@vitraux.co.uk
WEBSITE: www.vitraux.co.uk

LEIGHTON BUZZARD

Buffalohouse Pottery
Buffalo House, Mill Rd., Slapton. LU7 9BT. (Emma and Nick Griffin)
EST. 1992. Open by appointment. STOCK: *Pottery - South Devon including Torquay, £1-£2,000; North Devon including Brannam and Baron, £1-£1,000; Wesuma, £20-£400; Martin Brothers, £200-£5,000; modern Moorcroft, £30-£4,000; Cobridgeware, £20-£1,000; Muggins Stoneware, £5-£200.* LOC: Just south of Leighton Buzzard. SER: Valuations, items bought. SIZE: Small. PARK: Easy.
TEL: 01525 220256 HOME: same FAX: 01525 229138
E-MAIL: sales@buffalohouse.co.uk
WEBSITE: www.buffalogold.com

POTTON

W. J. West Antiques
58 King St. SG19 2QZ. (Alan, Richard and Wesley West)
EST. 1930. Open by appointment. STOCK: *Furniture,*

mainly Victorian, including upholstered, to £4,000. LOC: Town centre. SER: Valuations; restorations (furniture including upholstery). SIZE: Small. PARK: Easy.
TEL: 01767 260589 FAX: 01767 261513 MOBILE: 07758 312328

WOBURN

Christopher Sykes Antiques
The Old Parsonage, Bedford St. MK17 9QL. (Christopher and Margaret Sykes and Sally Lloyd)
EST. 1949. Open 9-4 or by appointment. STOCK: *Collectors' items - attractive, early brass, copper and pewter; scientific and medical instruments; specialist in rare corkscrews, £10-£800; silver decanter labels, taste-vins and funnels, pottery barrels and bin labels, glass decanters and tantalus.* LOC: On A50, in main street next to Heritage Centre. SER: 100 page illustrated mail order catalogue on corkscrews and wine related antiques available £7 each. Restoration and valuation of corkscrews. SIZE: Large. PARK: Easy.
TEL: 01525 290259/290467 FAX: 01525 290061
E-MAIL: sykes.corkscrews@sykes-corkscrews.co.uk
WEBSITE: www.sykes-corkscrews.co.uk

Town Hall Antiques
Market Place. MK17 9PZ. (Elfyn and Elaine Groves)
EST. 1993. Open 10-5.30, Sun. 11-5.30. STOCK: *Furniture, £50-£5,000; clocks, ceramics, glass, silver and plate, £10-£4,000; prints and pictures, £10-£2,000; all 18th to early 20th C; mirrors, domestic metalware; some antiquities; cigarette cards, tools, medals and militaria.* LOC: Off A5 and off junction 12 or 13, M1. SER: Valuations. SIZE: Medium. PARK: Easy. VAT: Global. FAIRS: Kempton Park.
TEL: 01525 290950 FAX: 01525 292501
E-MAIL: elfyn@townhallantiques.co.uk
WEBSITE: www.townhallantiques.co.uk

The Woburn Abbey Antiques Centre
Woburn Abbey MK17 9WA. (Woburn Enterprises Ltd)
EST. 1967. Open every day (including Bank Holidays) 10-5.30. CL: Christmas holidays. STOCK: *English and Continental furniture, porcelain, glass, paintings, silver and decorative items.* NOT STOCKED: *Reproduction.* LOC: From M1 junction 13, signposted Woburn Abbey, centre is in South Courtyard. SER: Carriage for large items; worldwide shipping. SIZE: Over 75 shops and showcases on two floors. PARK: Easy.
TEL: 01525 290350 FAX: 01525 292102
E-MAIL: antiques@woburnabbey.co.uk
WEBSITE: www.discoverwoburnabbey.co.uk

Woburn Fine Arts
12 Market Place. MK17 9PZ. (Z. Bieganski)
EST. 1983. Open Tues.-Sun. 2.30-5.30. STOCK: *Post-impressionist paintings, 1880-1940; European paintings, 17th-18th C; British paintings, 20th C.* SER: Restorations (oils and watercolours). SIZE: Medium. PARK: Easy.
TEL: 01525 290624 FAX: 01525 290733

JACKSON'S
SILVER & GOLD MARKS
of England, Scotland & Ireland
edited by Ian Pickford

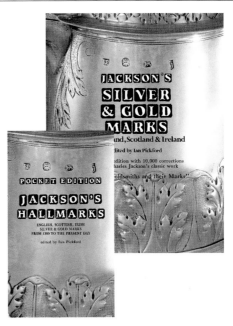

Sir Charles Jackson's *English Goldsmiths and their Marks* is the classic reference work on British antique silver hallmarks. First written in 1905 and last revised in 1921, it is a mammoth endeavour which has remained in print ever since. It is still considered indispensable by silver collectors and dealers, despite shortcomings due to its age. This major new edition has been compiled by a team of distinguished experts to take account of the vast store of information which has been unearthed as a result of much detailed and wide ranging research over the last seventy years. The text has been extensively updated with over 10,000 corrections and an enormous amount of entirely new material. For example, there are over 1,000 corrections to London eighteenth century makers' marks alone. Many ideas and attributions have changed since Jackson assembled his work and some of the makers he overlooked are now known to be of major significance. There are not many standard reference works which survive for eighty years without being displaced. This revised edition reconfirms Jackson's status as the bible for all antique silver enthusiasts and a key reference for dealers, scholars and collectors.

Specifications: 766pp., 400 b.&w. and approx. 15,000 marks, 11 x 8½in./279 x 216mm. £49.50 (hardback)
Pocket Edition: 172pp., over 1,000 marks, 8½ x 4½in./215 x 120mm. £12.50 (hardback) £6.95 (paperback)

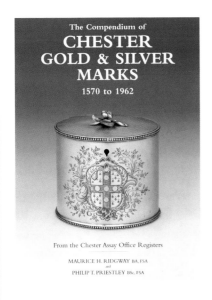

The Compendium of
CHESTER GOLD & SILVER MARKS
1570 to 1962
From the Chester Assay Office Registers
MAURICE RIDGWAY AND PHILIP PRIESTLEY

This is the first publication in a single work of all known Chester punch marks, and continues the tradition of the standard volumes of Jackson, Grimwade, Culme and Pickford. It is also the first time that the twentieth-century Chester marks have been published. It is produced in dictionary format, in alphabetical order from 1570, the date of the earliest known mark, to 1962 at which time the Chester assay office was closed. The authors, both members of the silver society, were given unlimited access to the Chester assay office records covering 1686 to 1962, and to the Chester Goldsmith's Company records dating from the 16th century. The compendium has four sections. The preface provides an historical background and details of all extant records and copper plates. Part 1 is devoted to assay office marks, with a full set of date letter tables to assist the reader in dating wares. Part 2 covers nearly 10,000 entries for makers' marks, including pictograms and monograms. Finally, the appendices include items on assay volumes and charges, thimble makers, and Liverpool watchcase makers. Since over 2,000 of the entries have Birmingham addresses, the new work will also enhance available information on jewellers and silversmiths working in this important trade center. The format of the marks' tables and the extensive index will also allow future research into the relationships between companies and agents.

Specifications:
520pp., approx. 10,000 marks recorded,
11 x 8½in./279 x 216mm.
£65.00 (hardback)

For full details of all ACC publications, log on to our website:
www.antiquecollectorsclub.com
or telephone 01394 389950 for a free catalogue

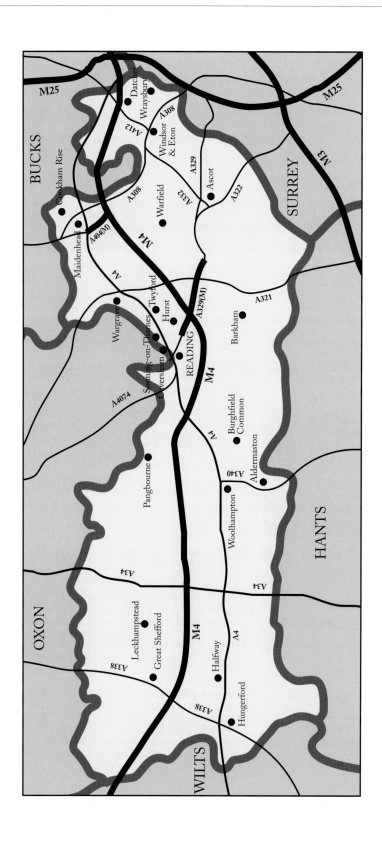

ALDERMASTON

Aldermaston Antiques
The Old Dispensary. RG7 4LW. (Vivian and Roger Green)
EST. 1994. Open 10-5.30. CL: Mon. *STOCK: Longcase clocks, furniture, lamps, silver, desks, mainly 19th C; architectural and garden stone and iron items.* LOC: A340, village centre. SIZE: Medium + yard. PARK: Easy and at rear.
TEL: 01189 712370 HOME: same
WEBSITE: www.aldermastonantiques.co.uk

ASCOT

Omell Galleries
The Corner House, Course Rd. SL5 7HL. (Omell Galleries (Windsor) Ltd.)
EST. 1947. Open 9.30-1 and 2-5 or by appointment. *STOCK: Fine paintings, £400-£6,000.* LOC: Off High St., opposite garage. SER: Valuations; restorations; cleaning; repairs (oils, watercolours and frames). SIZE: Medium.
PARK: Easy. VAT: Spec.
TEL: 01344 873443 FAX: 01344 873467
E-MAIL: aomell@aol.com
WEBSITE: www.omellgalleries.co.uk

BARKHAM

Barkham Antique Centre
Barkham St. RG40 4PJ. (Len and Mary Collins)
Open 10.30-5 including Sun. *STOCK: General antiques including furniture, china, kitchenalia, coins, Dinky toys, paintings, glassware, scientific instruments and brass; collectables including Beswick, Moorcroft, Royal Doulton, Wade.* LOC: Off M4, junction 10, A329M to Wokingham, over station crossing to Barkham (B3349), left at Bull public house, centre 300 yards on left. SER: Valuations; restorations (china, French polishing, upholstery, cabinet making). SIZE: Large - 50+ dealers. PARK: Easy.
TEL: 01189 761355

BURGHFIELD COMMON

Graham Gallery
Highwoods. RG7 3BG. (J. Steeds)
EST. 1976. Open by appointment at any time. *STOCK: English watercolours, £50-£1,500; English oil paintings, £200-£8,000; English prints, £25-£200; mainly 19th to early 20th C.* LOC: 4 miles west of Reading on Burghfield road. SER: Valuations; restorations; cleaning; framing. SIZE: Medium. PARK: Easy. VAT: Stan.
TEL: 01189 832320 FAX: 01189 831070
E-MAIL: john.steeds@btinternet.com
WEBSITE: www.grahamgallery.org.uk

CAVERSHAM

The Clock Workshop   LAPADA
17 Prospect St. RG4 8JB. (J.M. Yealland FBHI)
EST. 1980. TVADA. CINOA. Open 9.30-5.30, Sat. 10-1.

STOCK: Clocks, late 17th to late 19th C, £350-£80,000; barometers, 18th-19th C, £500-£35,000. LOC: Prospect St. is the beginning of main Reading to Henley road. SER: Valuations; restorations (clocks, barometers, chronometers, barographs); buys at auction. SIZE: Small. PARK: Behind shop in North St. VAT: Stan/Spec. FAIRS: TVADA; LAPADA; Olympia.
TEL: 01189 470741 MOBILE: 07788 410493
E-MAIL: theclockworkshop@hotmail.com

DATCHET

The Studio Gallery
The Old Bank, The Green, SL3 9JH. (Julian Bettney)
EST. 1990. Open 1.30-6.30 including Sun. Prior telephone call advisable. *STOCK: Antique trunks, drawers, pine, collectables, garden items, paintings, mosaic mirrors, objets d'art and recycled furniture.* LOC: Off junction 5, M4, opposite Manor Hotel. SER: Paintings in oils and mosaic mirrors to commission; bespoke framing (hand built, coloured, gilded and veneered). SIZE: Small. PARK: Outside or in Horton Rd. or railway station.
TEL: 01753 544100 FAX: same MOBILE: 07770 762468
E-MAIL: sales@julianbettney.me.uk
WEBSITE: www.julianbettney.me.uk

HALFWAY

Alan Walker   BADA
Halfway Manor. RG20 8NR.
EST. 1987. TVADA. Open by appointment. *STOCK: Fine barometers and weather instruments.* LOC: 4 miles west of Newbury on A4. SER: Restorations. SIZE: Large. PARK: Easy. FAIRS: Major London; some regional.
TEL: 01488 657670 MOBILE: 07770 728397
E-MAIL: walkerbarometers@aol.com
WEBSITE: www.alanwalker-barometers.com

HORTON

John A. Pearson Antiques   BADA
Horton Lodge, Horton Rd. SL3 9NU. (Mrs J.C. Sinclair Hill)
EST. 1902. Open by appointment. *STOCK: English and Continental furniture, 1700-1850; oil paintings, 17th-19th C, all £50-£50,000; decorative objects. NOT STOCKED: Items after 19th C.* LOC: From London turn off M4, exit 5, past London Airport; from M25 take exit 14. 10 mins from Heathrow. SER: Valuations; probate. SIZE: Large. PARK: Easy.
TEL: 01753 682136 FAX: 01753 687151

HUNGERFORD

Beedham Antiques Ltd   BADA
Charnham Close. RG17 0EJ. (W.H. and N. Beedham)
EST. 1980. Open 10-5 or by appointment. *STOCK: English oak furniture, 16th-18th C; objects and works of*

art. SIZE: Mediium. PARK: On street. VAT: Spec. FAIRS: Olympia (June and Nov.)
TEL: **01488 684141** FAX: **01488 684050**

Below Stairs of Hungerford
103 High St. RG17 0NB. (Stewart. L. Hofgartner)
EST. 1974. Open 10-6, including Sun. and Bank Holidays. *STOCK: Kitchen and decorative garden items, lighting, collectables, sporting items, interior fittings, ironmongery, taxidermy, advertising items, mainly 19th C English, £20-£2,500. NOT STOCKED: Reproductions.* LOC: Main street. SER: Valuations; on-line catalogue. SIZE: Large. PARK: Easy. VAT: Stan.
TEL: 01488 682317
E-MAIL: hofgartner@belowstairs.co.uk
WEBSITE: www.belowstairs.co.uk

Bow House
3-4 Faulkner Sq., Charnham St. RG17 0EP. (Jo Preston)
Open 10-5.30, Sundays by appointment. *STOCK: 18th-19th C furniture and decoratives; interiors, contemporary accessories and gifts.* LOC: First shop in Hungerford from Newbury A4. SIZE: 2 floors. PARK: Own. VAT: Spec.
TEL: 01488 680826
E-MAIL: bowhouseantiques@aol.com

Lynda Franklin Antiques
Oakridge House, 25 Charnham St. RG17 0EJ. (Lynda Franklin)
EST. 1973. Open by appointment. *STOCK: 18th-19th C French and English furniture and decorative items.* LOC: A4. SER: Valuations; restorations. SIZE: Large. PARK: Easy.
TEL: 01488 684072 MOBILE: 07831 200834
E-MAIL: antiques@lyndafranklin.com
WEBSITE: www.lyndafranklin.com

Garden Art
Barrs Yard, 1 Bath Rd. RG17 0HE. (Susan and Arnie Knowles)
EST. 1980. Open 9-5, Sun. 10-4. *STOCK: Period garden items; also some contemporary pieces.* SIZE: Large. PARK: Easy. VAT: Stan/Spec.
TEL: 01488 686811 HOME: 01488 681882
E-MAIL: sales@gardenartplus.com
WEBSITE: www.gardenartplus.com

Great Grooms of Hungerford
Riverside House, 1 Charnham St. RG17 0EP. (J. Podger)
EST. 1991. Open 9.30-5.30, Sun. and Bank Holidays 10-4. *STOCK: Wide variety of fine Continental and English furniture, glass, ceramics, pictures including Old Masters, collectors' items, lighting.* LOC: From M4 junction 14 on to A338. SER: Valuations; restorations (furniture including upholstery, pictures, silver, jewellery, ceramics). SIZE: Large - 100+ dealers. PARK: Free at rear of premises. VAT: Spec.
TEL: 01488 682314 FAX: 01488 686677
E-MAIL: hungerford@greatgrooms.co.uk
WEBSITE: www.greatgrooms.co.uk

Hungerford Arcade
26 High St. RG17 0NF. (Wynsave Investments Ltd)
EST. 1972. Open 9.30-5.30, Sun. 11-5. *STOCK: General antiques and period furniture, decorative items and books.* SIZE: 105 stallholders. PARK: Easy.
TEL: 01488 683701
E-MAIL: hungerfordarcade@btconnect.com

Roger King Antiques
111 High St. RG17 0NB. (Roger, Annabel and Simon King)
EST. 1974. Open 9.30-5 and most Sun. 11-5. *STOCK: Furniture, 1750-1910; 19th C oil paintings. NOT STOCKED: Silver, jewellery.* LOC: Opposite Hungerford Arcade. SIZE: Large. PARK: Easy. VAT: Spec.
TEL: 01488 682256
WEBSITE: www.kingantiques.co.uk

The Old Malthouse   BADA
15 Bridge St. RG17 0EG. (P.F. Hunwick)
EST. 1963. CINOA. TVADA. Open 10.30-6. *STOCK: 18th to early 19th C walnut and mahogany furniture - dining tables, sets of chairs, mirrors, chests of drawers; clocks, barometers, decorative items, boxes and tea caddies. NOT STOCKED: Orientalia.* **LOC: A338, left at Bear Hotel, shop is approx. 120 yards on left, just before bridge. SER: Valuations. SIZE: Large. PARK: Front of premises. VAT: Spec. FAIRS: Blue Coats - TVADA.**
TEL: 01488 682209 FAX: same
E-MAIL: foylehunwick@tiscali.co.uk

Phoenix Antique Arms
13 Bridge St. RG17 0EH. (Peter Reason and Tony Cribb)
EST. 1997. Open by appointment. STOCK: *Fine guns and swords, 1700-1900, £300-£15,000.* LOC: Town centre. SER: Valuations. SIZE: Small. PARK: Easy. FAIRS: London Arms; International Arms; Park Lane Arms; Bisley Arms.
TEL: 01488 684905 FAX 01787 319043
E-MAIL: sales@oldguns.co.uk
WEBSITE: www.oldguns.co.uk

Styles Silver   LAPADA
12 Bridge St. RG17 0EH. (P. and D. Styles)
EST. 1974. Open 9.30-5.30, other times by appointment. STOCK: *Antique, Victorian and secondhand silver including cutlery and 20th C design.* SER: **Repairs; finder.** SIZE: **Medium.** PARK: **Easy.**
TEL: **01488 683922;** HOME: **same** FAX: **01488 683488**
MOBILE: **07778 769559**
WEBSITE: **www.styles-silver.co.uk**

Turpin's Antiques   BADA
17 Bridge St. RG17 0EG. (Jane Sumner)
CINOA. Open Wed. - Sat. or by appointment. STOCK: *17th-18th C walnut, oak and mahogany furniture and metalware.* SIZE: **Small.** VAT: **Spec.** FAIRS: **Olympia.**
TEL: **01488 681886** HOME: **01672 870727**

Youll's Antiques
28 Charnham St. RG17 0EJ. (B. Youll)
EST. 1935. Open 10.30-5.30, Sun. 11-5. STOCK: *French and English furniture and decorative items.* FAIRS: Newark.
TEL: 01488 682046
E-MAIL: bruce.youll@virgin.net
WEBSITE: www.youllantiques.co.uk

LECKHAMPSTEAD

Hill Farm Antiques
Hill Farm, Shop Lane. RG20 8QG. (Mike Beesley)
Open 9-5, Sun. by appointment. STOCK: *19th C dining tables, chairs and library furniture.* LOC: Off B4494 between Stag public house and church. SER: Restorations; shipping arranged; buys at auction. PARK: Own at rear.
TEL: 01488 638541/638361
WEBSITE: www.hillfarmantiques.co.uk

MAIDENHEAD

Widmerpool House Antiques
7 Lower Cookham Rd., Boulters Lock. SL6 8JN. (M.L. Coleman)
Open by appointment. STOCK: *English furniture, oil paintings, watercolours, prints, porcelain and Swansea pottery, glass, silver, 18th-19th C.* PARK: Nearby.
TEL: 01628 623752

READING

Fanny's Antiques
1 Lynmouth Rd. RG1 8DE. (Julia Lyons)
EST. 1988. Open 10.30-4, Sun. 12-4. STOCK: *Wide range of decorative, period and new furniture, smalls; good stock of vintage clothing.* LOC: At the rear of Reading station. SER: Valuations; restorations. SIZE: 25 dealers. PARK: Easy. FAIRS: House & Gardens; Battersea Decorative; Chelsea Flower Show; Hampton Court; Country Living; Spirit of Christmas.
TEL: 01189 508261

Rupert Landen Antiques
Church Farm, Reading Rd., Woodcote. RG8 0QX. TVADA. Open 9-5 Mon-Fri. CL Sat. STOCK: *Late 18th to early 19th C furniture.*
TEL: 01491 682396 MOBILE: 07974 732472
WEBSITE: www.rupertsantiques.com

TWYFORD

Bell Antiques
2B High St. RG10 9AE. (Nigel, Chris and Russell Timms)
EST. 1989. Open 10-5.30 inc. Sun. STOCK: *General antiques including china and glass, silver and plate, small furniture, 18th-20th C, £10-£300.* LOC: Village centre on crossroads. SIZE: Small. PARK: 2 hours free nearby. VAT: Spec.
TEL: 01189 342501

WARGRAVE

Wargrave Antiques
66 High St. RG10 8BY. (John Connell)
EST. 1979. Open Wed.-Sun. other times by appointment. STOCK: *Furniture, Georgian-Edwardian; small items, china, glass, metal.* SER: Restorations (furniture); silver plating; metal polishing. SIZE: Large - several dealers. PARK: Nearby.
TEL: 01189 402914

WINDSOR

The Antique Wardrobe Company
89 Grove Rd. SL4 1HT. (Dee Johnson)
EST. 1975 FSB. Open Wed.-Sat. 10-6, Sun. 11-3, other times by appointment. STOCK: *18th, 19th and early 20th C wardrobes, bedsides and chests of drawers.* LOC: 5 min. stroll from town centre; map on WEBSITE. SER: Free local delivery, free storage and free installation. SIZE: Medium. PARK: Easy.
TEL: 01753 865627
E-MAIL: info@theantiquewardrobecompany.co.uk
WEBSITE: www.theantiquewardrobecompany.co.uk

Art & Antiques and Bridge Miniatures
69 High St., Eton. SL4 6AA. (Vivien and Eddie Rand)
EST. 1982. Open 10.30-5.30, Sat. 10.30-6, Sun. 2.30-6. STOCK: *Collectors' items, jewellery, furniture, doll's house miniatures, from Victorian, £1-£600.* LOC: 1st shop over Thames from Windsor at Eton. SER: Restorations (furniture, doll's houses, jewellery). SIZE: Medium. PARK: Nearby.
TEL: 01753 855727 HOME: 01628 527127

Berkshire Antiques Co Ltd
42 Thames St., SL4 1PR. (Bruce D. Sutton)
EST. 1980. Open 10.30-5.30 including Sun. (Jan. to April - Sun. by appointment). STOCK: *Antique and modern designer jewellery; general antiques, china, porcelain and glass, silver and plate, Royal commemoratives, toys and dolls, £10-£25,000.* LOC: Opposite George V memorial fountain. SER: Valuations; repairs. SIZE: Large. PARK: Nearby.
TEL: 01753 830100
E-MAIL: sales@jewels2go.co.uk
WEBSITE: www.jewels2go.co.uk

Eton Antique Bookshop
88 High St., Eton. SL4 6AF. (Maurice Bastians)
EST. 1975. Open Mon. and Wed. 11.30-6.30, Tues., Thurs.-Sun. 10.30-6. STOCK: *Secondhand and antiquarian books; antiquarian prints and maps.* SER: Book search, book binding and repairs. SIZE: Medium. PARK: Easy and at rear.
TEL: 01753 855534

Eton Antiques Partnership
80 High St., Eton. SL4 6AF. (Mark Procter)
EST. 1967. Open 10-5, Sun. 2-5.30. STOCK: *Mahogany*

and rosewood furniture, 18th-19th C. LOC: Slough East exit from M4 westbound. SER: Exporting; interior design consultants. SIZE: Large. PARK: Nearby. VAT: Stan/Spec.
TEL: 01753 860752 HOME: same

Marcelline Herald Antiques   LAPADA
41 High St., Eton. SL4 6BD.
EST. 1993. TVADA. Open Tues., Thurs., Fri. and Sat. 10-5, other days by appointment. STOCK: *Furniture, £500-£15,000; mirrors, pelmets and screens, £200-£2,500; ceramics, lamps and prints, £50-£1,000; all 18th to early 19th C.* SIZE: **Medium.** PARK: **Loading and nearby.** VAT: **Spec.** FAIRS: **TVADA; Decorative Antiques & Textile.**
TEL: 01753 833924 FAX: 01264 730376 MOBILE: 07774 607443
E-MAIL: mail@marcellineherald.com
WEBSITE: www.marcellineherald.com

J. Manley Restoration
27 High St., Eton. SL4 6AX. (Malcolm Leach)
EST. 1891. BAPCR. ICON. Open 10-5. STOCK: *19th C watercolours and engravings.* SER: Restoration (oils, watercolours, prints, frames); bespoke framing; mounting. SIZE: 800 sq. ft.
TEL: 01753 865647
E-MAIL: sales@manleygallery.com

ANTIQUE COLLECTORS' CLUB

STARTING TO COLLECT ANTIQUE
FURNITURE
JOHN ANDREWS

This concise yet wide-ranging survey of collectable antique furniture, illustrated throughout in full colour, guides the new collector through almost three centuries of Western Furniture with clarity and authority. Invaluable as a reference tool, it offers collectors the means to identify key features of a wide variety of pieces, ranging from the Gothic and Renaissance period to Art Nouveau, and the beginning of the twentieth century. The book is structured chronologically by century and, within each time period, by country. Existing collectors will find all titles in the series act as a handy and portable reference, and beginners will welcome a reliable, accessible starting point from which their interests can develop.

Specifications: 192pp., Colour throughout 9½ x 7¼in./240 x 195mm. **£12.50 (hardback)**

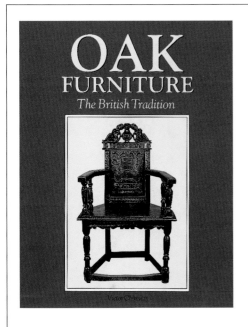
Peter J. Martin   LAPADA
40 High St., Eton. SL4 6BD. (Peter J. Martin & Son)
EST. 1963. TVADA. Open 9-1 and 2-5. *STOCK: Period,*
Victorian and decorative furniture and furnishings, £50-
£20,000; metalware, £10-£500, all from 1800. **SER:**
Restorations; shipping arranged; buys at auction. SIZE:
Large and warehouse. PARK: 50yds. opposite. VAT:
Stan/Spec.
TEL: 01753 864901 HOME: 01753 863987
E-MAIL: pjmartin.antiques@btopenworld.com
WEBSITE: www.pjmartin-antiques.co.uk

Mostly Boxes
93 High St., Eton. SL4 6AF. (G.S. Munday)
EST. 1977. Open 10-6.30. *STOCK: Wooden, mother-of-pearl and tortoiseshell boxes; nautical instruments; snuff boxes; ivory.* SER: Restorations (boxes). PARK: 100 yds. VAT: Spec. FAIRS: Newark; K&M Fairs; London weekly Park Lane Hotel and Rembrandt Hotel, Knightsbridge.
TEL: 01753 858470

Rules Antiques
39 St Leonard's Rd. SL4 3BP. (Sue Rule and Kathryn Cale)
Open 10.30-6. *STOCK: Lighting, door furniture, period fixtures and fittings; unusual small furniture.* PARK: Meters.
TEL: 01753 833210
WEBSITE: www.rulesantiques.co.uk

Times Past
59 High St., Eton. SL4 6BL. (P. Jackson)
EST. 1970. MBHI. Open 10-6, Sun. 12-5. *STOCK: Clocks, £100-£5,000.* SER: Valuations; restorations (clocks). SIZE: Medium. PARK: Reasonable.
TEL: 01753 857018
E-MAIL: philliptimespast@aol.com
WEBSITE: www.timespast.me.uk

Turks Head Antiques
98 High St., Eton. SL4 6AF. (Andrew Reeve and Anthea Baillie)
EST. 1983. Open 10-5. *STOCK: Silver and plate, porcelain, glass and interesting collectables.* PARK: Nearby.
TEL: 01753 863939

WRAYSBURY

Wyrardisbury Antiques
23 High St. TW19 5DA. (C. Tuffs)
EST. 1978. Open 10-5. CL: Mon. except by appointment. *STOCK: Clocks, £100-£6,000; barometers, small furniture, £100-£1,500.* LOC: A376 from Staines by-pass (A30) or from junction 5 M4/A4 via B470, then B376. SER: Restorations (clocks). SIZE: Small. PARK: Easy.
TEL: 01784 483225

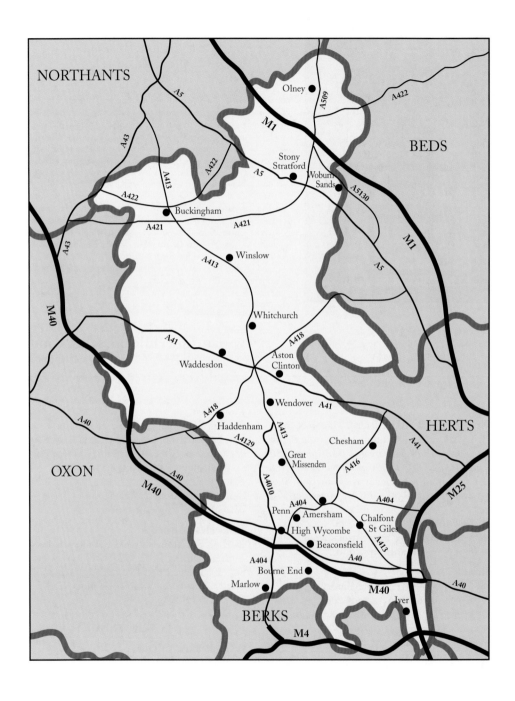

AMERSHAM

Carlton Clocks LAPADA
Station Rd., Little Chalfont. HP7 9PP. (Ian Cherkas)
EST. 1981. BWCG. Open 9-5.30, Sat. 9-4. STOCK:
Longcase, mantel, wall and carriage clocks, barometers and
pocket watches, from 1700s to reproduction, £200-
£15,000. SER: Valuations; restorations (clocks, watches
and barometers). SIZE: Large. PARK: Easy.
TEL: 01494 763793; FAX: 01494 764989
E-MAIL: info@ukclocks.com
WEBSITE: www.ukclocks.com

The Cupboard Antiques LAPADA
80 High St., Old Amersham. HP7 0DS. (N. and C.
Lucas)
EST. 1965. Open 10-5. CL: Fri. STOCK: *Georgian,*
Regency and early Victorian furniture and decorative
items. SIZE: 3 showrooms. PARK: Easy. FAIRS: Olympia
(June).
TEL: 01494 722882

Michael and Jackie Quilter
38 High St. HP7 0DJ.
EST. 1970. Open 10-5. STOCK: *General antiques, stripped*
pine, copper, brass, unusual objects. SER: Free local delivery.
SIZE: 3 floors. PARK: Easy. VAT: Stan.
TEL: 01494 433723

Sundial Antiques
19 Whielden St. HP7 0HU. (A. and Mrs M.
Macdonald)
EST. 1970. Open 10-5.30. CL: Thurs. STOCK: *English*
and European brass, copper, metalware, fireplace equipment,
18th-19th C, £5-£500; small period furniture, 1670-1910,
£25-£1,500; horse brasses, £10-£300; decorative items,
1750-1920, £5-£500; pottery, porcelain, curios, pre-1930,
£10-£750. NOT STOCKED: Jewellery, clocks, coins, oil
paintings, stamps, books, silver, firegrates. LOC: On A404,
in Old Town 200yds. from High St. on right; from High
Wycombe, 500yds. from hospital on left. SIZE: Small.
PARK: Easy.
TEL: 01494 727955

ASTON CLINTON

Pattisons Architectural Antiques - Dismantle and
Deal Direct
108 London Rd. HP22 5HS. (Tony Pattison)
EST. 1992. Open by appointment or Sat. 9-1. STOCK:
Doors, glass, 18th C to 1930; fireplaces, marble and stone,
18th C to 1920; garden ornaments, 19th C to 1950. LOC:
Off M25 junction 20, take A41. SIZE: Large. PARK:
Easy. VAT: Stan/Spec.
TEL: 01296 632300; FAX: 01296 631329
E-MAIL: tony@pattant.com
WEBSITE: www.ddd-uk.com

BEACONSFIELD

Buck House Antiques
47 Wycombe End, Old Town. HP9 1LZ. (C. and B.
Whitby)
EST. 1979. Open 10-5, Sun. 12-4. CL: Wed. STOCK:
General antiques including English and Oriental porcelain,
clocks, barometers, oak and mahogany furniture, boxes and
beds, to 1930s, £5-£5,000. LOC: A40. SER: Valuations.
SIZE: Medium. PARK: Easy.
TEL: 01494 670714

Ellison Fine Art BADA
(Claudia Hill)
EST. 2000. Open by appointment. STOCK: *16th-19th C*
portrait miniatures, enamels and silhouettes, English and
Continental, £250-£20,000+. SER: Valuations;
restorations (framing, glazing and conservation).
PARK: Easy. VAT: Margin. FAIRS: BADA; Olympia.
TEL: 01494 678880; MOBILE: 07720 317899
E-MAIL: claudia.hill@ellisonfineart.co.uk
WEBSITE: www.ellisonfineart.com

Grosvenor House Interiors
51 Wycombe End, Old Town. HP9 1LX. (T.I.
Marriott)
EST. 1970. Open 10-1 and 2-5. CL: Wed. STOCK: *Furniture*
(especially walnut) and oils, 18th-19th C. LOC: Centre of old
town. SIZE: Large. PARK: Easy. VAT: Stan/Spec.
TEL: 01494 677498
E-MAIL: terrymarriott@btconnect.com
WEBSITE: www.grosvenorhouseinteriors.co.uk

Period Furniture Showrooms
49 London End. HP9 2HW. (R.E.W. Hearne and N.J.
Hearne)
EST. 1965. TVADA. Open Mon.-Sat. 9-5.30. STOCK:
Furniture, 1700-1900, £50-£5,000. LOC: A40
Beaconsfield Old Town. SER: Restorations (furniture).
SIZE: Large. PARK: Own. VAT: Stan/Spec.
TEL: 01494 674112; FAX: 01494 681046
E-MAIL: sales@periodfurniture.net
WEBSITE: www.periodfurniture.net

BOURNE END

Bourne End Antiques Centre
67 The Parade. SL8 5SB. (S. Shepheard)
EST. 1995. Open 10-5.30, Sun. 12-4. STOCK: *Furniture -*
pine, £100-£900, darkwood, £100-£800; both from 19th C;
china and glass, £1-£250. LOC: A4155, 2 miles from
Marlow. SIZE: Large. PARK: Easy. VAT: Stan.
TEL: 01628 533298; HOME: 01300 320125

La Maison
The Crossings, Cores End Rd. SL8 5AL. (Jeremy D.
Pratt)
EST. 1995. TVADA. Open 10-5.30, Mon. 1-5.30, Sun.
11-4. STOCK: *French antiques including armoires, mirrors,*

beds, clocks and chandeliers, 19th C, to £2,000; Victorian pine, £295-£795; antique and reproduction garden furniture, some mahogany furniture. LOC: Take Marlow by-pass from junction 3, M40. SER: Valuations; restorations including re-upholstery and repairs. SIZE: Medium. PARK: Easy and opposite. VAT: Stan/Spec. TEL: 01628 525858; HOME: same; FAX: 01628 522930 WEBSITE: www.la-maison.co.uk

BURNHAM

Burnham Antiques Emporium
46-48a High St. SL1 7JP. (Alan J. Smith)
Burnham High St. Assn. Open 10-5 Mon.-Sat., 11-4 Sun. STOCK: *Antique furniture, bronzes, silverware, porcelain and china, glassware, lamps, architectural door furniture and tools, clocks, watches, vintage linen, vintage fashion and jewellery, interior design, collectables and toys, prints, paintings and original artwork, gifts, books, etc.* LOC: Village centre.
TEL: 01628 665142/01932 344744; MOBILE 07932 325360
E-MAIL: sylvie@surreyandbucksantiques.co.uk
WEBSITE: www.surreyandbucksantiques.co.uk

CHESHAM

Chess Antiques and Restorations   LAPADA
85 Broad St. HP5 3EF. (M.P. Wilder)
EST. 1966. Open 9-5, Sat. 10-5. STOCK: *Furniture and clocks.* SER: Valuations; restorations (furniture). SIZE: Small. PARK: Easy. VAT: Stan/Spec.
TEL: 01494 783043
E-MAIL: chessrest@aol.com
WEBSITE: www.chessantiquerestorations.co.uk

HADDENHAM

H.S. Wellby Ltd
The Malt House, Church End. HP17 8AH. (C.S. Wellby)
EST. 1820. BAPCR. Open by appointment 9-6. STOCK: *18th-19th C paintings.* SER: Restoration and conservation of oil paintings. VAT: Spec.
TEL: 01844 290036

HIGH WYCOMBE

Browns' of West Wycombe
Church Lane, West Wycombe. HP14 3AH.
EST. Pre-1900. BFM. Open 8-5.30. CL: Sat. STOCK: *Furniture.* LOC: On A40 approximately 3 miles west of High Wycombe on Oxford Road. SER: Restorations; hand-made copies of period chairs and furniture. PARK: Easy.
TEL: 01494 524537; FAX: 01494 439548
E-MAIL: enquiries@brownsofwestwycombe.com
WEBSITE: www.brownsofwestwycombe.com

Glade Antiques   BADA
PO Box 873. HP14 3ZQ. (Sonia Vaughan)
CINOA. Four gallery exhibitions each year, otherwise open by appointment. STOCK: *Fine Oriental ceramics, bronzes and jades: Chinese items from Han, Tang, Song, Ming and Quing periods; Japanese items - mainly Kakiemon, Nabeshima, Kutani, Satsuma and Imari; also Korean Koryo, Yi and Choson periods.* SIZE: Large.
FAIRS: Olympia.
TEL: 01494 882818; FAX: 01494 882818; MOBILE: 07771 552328
E-MAIL: sonia@gladeantiques.com

Windmill Fine Art
2 Windmill Drive, Widmer End. HP15 6BD. (Ray White)
Open by appointment. STOCK: *Fine Victorian and early 20th C watercolours and oils.* SER: Valuations; commission search. FAIRS: Most major.
TEL: 01494 713757

IVER

Yester-year
12 High St. SL0 9NG. (P.J. Frost)
EST. 1969. Resident. Open 10-6. STOCK: *Furniture, porcelain, pottery, glass, metalwork, 18th to early 20th C.* SER: Valuations; restorations (furniture and pictures); framing; buys at auction. SIZE: Small. PARK: Easy.
TEL: 01753 652072

MARLOW

Angela Hone Watercolours   BADA
EST. 1970. CINOA. Open by appointment. STOCK: *English and French watercolours and pastels, 1850-1930.* SER: Probate valuations etc. FAIRS: Olympia; BADA; Harrogate.
TEL: 01628 484170; FAX: same
E-MAIL: honewatercolours@aol.com

OLNEY

The Antiques Centre at Olney
13 Osborns Court, Off High St. South. MK46 4LA. (Robert Sklar)
Open 10-5, Sun. 12-5. CL: Mon. STOCK: *General antiques, furniture, porcelain.* LOC: Town centre. SIZE: Large, 80 dealers. PARK: Easy.
TEL: 01234 710942; FAX: 01234 710947
WEBSITE: www.antiques-of-britain.co.uk

Leo Antiques & Collectables Ltd
19 Market Place. MK46 4BA. (Mrs G. Behari)
EST. 2003. Open 10-5, Sun. and Bank Holidays 11-4. CL: Mon. STOCK: *Georgian to Edwardian furniture, to £5,000; silver, from 19th C; oils and watercolours, 19th-20th C, to £2,000; Doulton, Beswick, Royal Crown Derby and Worcester; glass, clocks, country furniture, mirrors,*

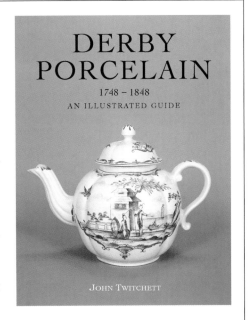
silverware and plate. SER: Search service. SIZE: Large. PARK: Easy.
TEL: 01234 240003; FAX: 01908 211112
E-MAIL: gillbehari@btinternet.com
WEBSITE: www.leoantiques.co.uk

WENDOVER

Antiques at . . .Wendover Antiques Centre
The Old Post Office, 25 High St. HP22 6DU. (N. Gregory)
EST. 1987. Open 10-5.30, Sun. and Bank Holidays 11-5. *STOCK: General antiques dateline 1940/50 - town and country furniture, kitchenalia, gardenalia, pottery and porcelain, jewellery, Art Deco, watches, silver, lamps and lighting, clocks and barometers, telescopes, games, decorative items, glass, metalware, lace and linen, garden statuary, arms, paintings and prints, tools, rugs, period clothing.* LOC: A413. SER: Restorations (china and furniture); metal polishing, gilding and re-upholstery. SIZE: Large - 30 dealers. PARK: Own.
TEL: 01296 625335
E-MAIL: antiques@antiquesatwendover.co.uk
WEBSITE: www.antiquesatwendover.co.uk

Sally Turner Antiques   LAPADA
Hogarth House, High St. HP22 6DU. (Sally A. Major)
EST. 1979. TVADA. CINOA. Open 10-5. CL: Wed. and Sun. except Dec. *STOCK: Decorative and period furniture, paintings, jewellery and general antiques.* LOC: Town centre. SER: Repairs; restorations; probate and insurance valuations. SIZE: 7 showrooms + barn. PARK: Own. VAT: Stan./Spec.
TEL: 01296 624402; MOBILE: 07860 201718
E-MAIL: enquiries@sallyturnerantiques.com
WEBSITE: www.sallyturnerantiques.com

WHITCHURCH

Deerstalker Antiques
28 High St. HP22 4JT. (R.J. and L.L. Eichler)
EST. 1980. Open 10-5.30. CL: Fri. *STOCK: General antiques, including period oak furniture.* LOC: 5 miles north of Aylesbury. SER: Restorations (furniture pre-1880); hand-made replicas. SIZE: Large. PARK: Easy.
FAIRS: Brill.
TEL: 01296 641505

WINSLOW

Winslow Antiques Centre
15 Market Sq. MK18 3AB.
EST. 1992. Open 10-5, Sun. 1-5. CL: Wed. *STOCK: Furniture, English pottery, silver and jewellery, general antiques.* LOC: A413. SIZE: 20 dealers.
TEL: 01296 714540; FAX: 01296 714556

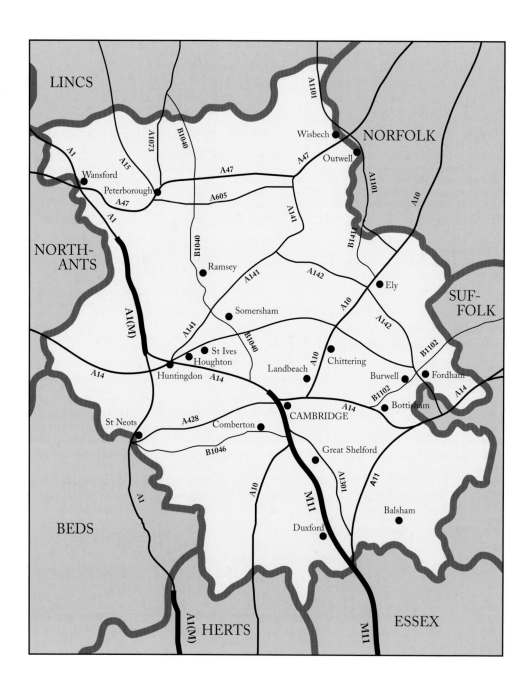

BALSHAM

Ward Thomas Antiques Ltd
7 High St. CB1 6DJ. (Christian Ward Thomas)
EST. 1997. Open 9-5, Sat. 10-5, Sun. by appointment.
STOCK: Pine furniture, £210-£950. LOC: Village centre,
opposite primary school. SER: Valuations; restorations
(Continental pine, oak flooring); bespoke kitchens.
TEL: 01223 892431; FAX: 01223 892367; MOBILE:
07887 986566
E-MAIL: wtantiques@onetel.com

BURWELL

Peter Norman Antiques and Restorations
Sefton House, 55 North St. CB25 0BA. (P. Norman
and A. Marpole)
EST. 1977. Open 9-12.30 and 2-5.30. *STOCK: Furniture,
clocks, arms and Oriental rugs, 17th-19th C, £250-£10,000.*
SER: Valuations; restorations (furniture, oil paintings,
clocks and arms). SIZE: Medium. PARK: Easy.
TEL: 01638 614744
E-MAIL: pnorman80@ntlworld.com

CAMBRIDGE

Jess Applin Antiques   BADA
8 Lensfield Rd. CB2 1EG.
EST. 1968. Open 10-5. *STOCK: Furniture, 17th-19th C;*
works of art. LOC: At junction with Hills Rd. opposite
church. PARK: Pay and display nearby. VAT: Spec.
TEL: 01223 315168
E-MAIL: jessapplin@btconnect.com

John Beazor and Sons Ltd   BADA
78-80 Regent St. CB2 1DP. (Martin Beazor)
EST. 1875. Open 9.15-5, Sat. 10.30-4 and by appointment. *STOCK: English furniture, late 17th to early 19th C;*
clocks, barometers and period accessories. SER: Valuations;
sourcing. SIZE: Medium. PARK: Pay & Display and
multi-storey. FAIRS: Open days in May and November.
TEL: 01223 355178; FAX: 01223 355183
E-MAIL: martin@johnbeazorantiques.co.uk
WEBSITE: www.johnbeazorantiques.co.uk

Cambridge Fine Art Ltd   LAPADA
Priesthouse, 33 Church St., Little Shelford. CB2
5HG. (R. and J. Lury)
EST. 1972. Resident. Open by appointment. *STOCK:*
British and European paintings, 1780-1900; modern
British paintings, 1880-1940; British prints by J.M.
Kronheim to the Baxter Process. LOC: Next to church.
SER: Valuations; restorations; buys at auction. SIZE:
Large. PARK: Easy. VAT: Stan/Spec.
TEL: 01223 842866/843537

Gabor Cossa Antiques
34 Trumpington St. CB2 1QY. (D. Theobald)
EST. 1948. Open 11-6. *STOCK: English and Chinese*
ceramics, glass, bijouterie. LOC: Opposite Fitzwilliam
Museum. SER: Valuations. SIZE: Small. PARK: 100yds.
VAT: Global. FAIRS: Horticultural Hall.
TEL: 01223 356049
E-MAIL: gaborcossa@yahoo.co.uk
WEBSITE: www.gaborcossa.com

Peter Crabbe Antiques
3 Pembroke St. CB2 3QY.
Open 10-4.30. *STOCK: Furniture, Oriental porcelain, works*
of art. VAT: Spec.
TEL: 01223 357117

G. David
16 St. Edward's Passage. CB2 3PJ. (D.C. Asplin, N.T.
Adams and B.L. Collings)
EST. 1896. ABA. PBFA. Open 9.30-5. *STOCK:*
Antiquarian books, fine bindings, secondhand and out of
print books, selected publishers' remainders. LOC: 100 yards
from Market Sq. PARK: Lion Yard.
TEL: 01223 354619

The Hive
Unit 3, Dales Brewery, Gwydir St. CB1 2LG. (B.
Blakemore and A. Morgan)
EST. 1990. Open 10-5, Sun. 11-5. *STOCK: Victorian and*
Edwardian furniture, antique pine, kitchenalia, period
lighting, ceramics, tiles, jewellery, vintage clothing and
Oriental rugs. LOC: Off Mill Rd. SIZE: 11 dealers. PARK:
Opposite.
TEL: 01223 300269
WEBSITE: www.hiveantiques.co.uk

Sarah Key
The Haunted Bookshop, 9 St. Edward's Passage. CB2
3PJ. (Sarah Key and Phil Salin)
EST. 1987. PBFA. Open 10-5. *STOCK: Children's and*
illustrated books, literature and antiquarian. LOC: City
centre. SER: Shipping. PARK: Lion Yard multi-storey.
FAIRS: Major UK.
TEL: 01223 312913
E-MAIL: info@sarahkeybooks.co.uk

The Lawson Gallery
7-8 King's Parade. CB2 1SJ. (Leslie and Lucinda
Lawson)
EST. 1967. FATG. Open 9.30-5.30. *STOCK: Posters,*
prints, limited editions, original artwork, specialists in
antiquarian and modern prints of Cambridge. LOC:
Opposite King's College. SIZE: Medium. PARK: Lion
Yard. VAT: Stan.
TEL: 01223 313970
E-MAIL: info@lawsongallery.demon.co.uk

Old Chemist Shop Antique Centre
206 Mill Rd. CB1 3NF. (Ray Warwick)
STOCK: Victorian antiques and collectables.
TEL: 01223 247324
E-MAIL: ray.warwick@btinternet.com

Solopark Plc
Station Rd., Nr. Pampisford. CB2 4HB. (R.J. Bird)
EST. 1976. SALVO. Open 8-5, Fri. and Sat. 8-4, Sun.
10-2. *STOCK: Traditional building materials and supplies,
timber and period architectural items.* SIZE: 6 acre site.
PARK: Easy.
TEL: 01223 834663; FAX: 01223 834780
E-MAIL: info@solopark.co.uk
WEBSITE: www.solopark.co.uk

Trinity St. Jewellers
31 Trinity St. CB2 1TB. (Graham Whitehead)
EST. 1972. NAG. GMC. Open 9.45-5. CL: Mon. *STOCK:
Jewellery, silver, objets d'art.* SER: Restorations; repairs. SIZE:
Medium. PARK: Multi-storey nearby. VAT: Stan/Spec.
TEL: 01223 357910; FAX: 01223 357920

Williams Art & Antqiues
5 Dale's Brewery Gwydir St. CB1 2LJ. (R & C
Williams)
Open 10-5; Sun 11-5. *STOCK: Victorian pine furniture,
fireplaces, lighting.* LOC: near Mill Rd. SIZE: Large PARK:
outside shop.
TEL: 01223 311687
WEBSITE: www.williamsart.co.uk

CHITTERING

Simon and Penny Rumble Antiques
Causeway End Farmhouse. CB5 9PW.
Open by appointment. *STOCK: Early oak, country
furniture, woodcarving and works of art.* LOC: 6 miles
north of Cambridge, off A10.
TEL: 01223 861831

DUXFORD

R. Mooney
Mill Lane CB22 4PT.
EST. 1946. Open 10-5. *STOCK: General antique furniture,
1780-1970s.* LOC: 1 mile from M11. SER: Restorations
(furniture). SIZE: Medium. PARK: Easy. VAT: Stan/Spec.
TEL: 01223 832252
WEBSITE: www.riromooney-antiques.com

ELY

Cloisters Antiques
1-1B Lynn Rd. CB7 4EG. (Barry Lonsdale)
EST. 1999. PBFA. Open 9.30-4.30, Sun. 11-4. CL: Tues.
*STOCK: Small antiques and collectables, paintings, clocks,
antiquarian and secondhand books, postcards, prints, vinyl
records, picture framing.* LOC: Opposite Lamb Inn, close
to cathedral. SER: Picture framing; portrait photography.
SIZE: Medium - 3 floors. PARK: St Mary's St.
TEL: 01353 668558; MOBILE: 07767 881677

Mrs Mills Antiques
1a St. Mary's St. CB7 4ER. (M.R. Mills)
EST. 1968. Open 10-5. CL: Tues. *STOCK: China,*
jewellery, silver. NOT STOCKED: *Furniture.* LOC: Near
cathedral. SIZE: Small. PARK: Nearby.
TEL: 01353 664268

Waterside Antiques Centre
The Wharf. CB7 4AU.
EST. 1986. Open 9.30-5.30 including Bank Holidays,
Sun. 10-4. *STOCK: General antiques and collectables.* LOC:
Waterside area. SIZE: Large. PARK: Easy.
TEL: 01353 667066

FORDHAM

Phoenix Antiques
1 Carter St. CB7 5NG.
EST. 1966. Open by appointment. *STOCK: Early European
furniture, domestic metalwork, pottery and delft, carpets,
scientific instruments, treen and bygones.* LOC: Centre of
village. SER: Valuations. SIZE: Medium. PARK: Own.
TEL: 01638 720363

GREAT SHELFORD

Storm Fine Arts Ltd
Church Street Barns. CB2 5EL. (Bill and Sue Mason)
EST. 1998. Resident. Open by appointment. *STOCK:
Paintings and pictures, 1500 to date, £500-£100,000;
porcelain, pottery and glass, 1800-1900, £150-£1,500;
decorative arts, 1700 to date, £100-£15,000; textiles, 1700-
1900, £1,000-£30,000.* SER: Valuations; restorations;
buys at auction. SIZE: Medium. PARK: Easy. VAT: Stan.
TEL: 01223 844786; FAX: 01223 847871
E-MAIL: info@stormfinearts.com
WEBSITE: www.stormfinearts.com

HOUGHTON

Houghton Antiques
Thicket Rd. PE28 2BQ. (Jean Stevens)
EST. 2001. Open 1-5.30 every day except Tuesday or by
appointment. *STOCK: Ceramics and glass, silver and plate
including cutlery, Victorian to 1930s; collectables, costume
jewellery, small items of furniture.* LOC: Village square.
SIZE: Small. PARK: Easy.
TEL: 01480 461887; HOME: 01487 813316;
MOBILE: 07803 716842
E-MAIL: jeanmstevens@btinternet.com

HUNTINGDON

Huntingdon Antiques
1 St Mary's St. PE29 3PE. (Trevor Smith)
EST. 1980. Open 9.30-5.30; Sun 10-4. *STOCK: Wide range of
general antiques, to £10,000.* SIZE: 40+ dealers. PARK: Easy.
TEL: 01480 431142

LANDBEACH

J.V. Pianos and Cambridge Pianola Company
The Limes, 85 High St. CB25 9FR. (F.T. Poole)

EST. 1972. Open Mon.-Fri., evenings and weekends by appointment. STOCK: *Pianos, pianolas and pianola rolls.* LOC: First building on right in Landbeach from A10. SER: Valuations; restorations. SIZE: Medium. PARK: Easy. VAT: Stan.
TEL: 01223 861 348/408/507; HOME: same; FAX: 01223 441276
E-MAIL: ftpoole@talk21.com
WEBSITE: www.cambridgepianolacompany.co.uk

OUTWELL

A.P. and M.A. Haylett
Glen-Royd, 393 Wisbech Rd. PE14 8PG.
Open 9-6 including Sun. STOCK: *Country furniture, pottery, treen and metalware, 1750-1900, £5-£500.* NOT STOCKED: *Firearms.* LOC: A1101. SER: Buys at auction. PARK: Easy.
TEL: 01945 772427; HOME: same.
E-MAIL: mark@haylett1366.fsnet.co.uk

PETERBOROUGH

Francis Bowers Chess Suppliers
62 Penine Way, Gunthorpe, PE4 7TE.
EST. 1991. Resident. Open by appointment. STOCK: *Chess books, boards, sets and timers; clocks.* SIZE: Small. PARK: Easy.
TEL: 01733 579569
E-MAIL: chessbower@aol.com

Ivor and Patricia Lewis Antique and Fine Art Dealers   LAPADA
Westfield, 28 Westwood Park Rd. PE3 6JL.
Open by appointment. STOCK: *Decorative English and French furniture, 19th to early 20th C.* LOC: **Off the A1.** SIZE: **6,000 sq feet.**
TEL: **01733 344567;** FAX: **01733 896088;** MOBILE: **07860 553388**

Vaughan Antiques   LAPADA
PO Box 103, PE6 6AE. (Barry and Lindy Vaughan)
EST. **1993.** STOCK: *18th-19th C furniture, decorative items, clocks, paintings, mirrors, jewellery.* LOC: **No 1 Castlegate, Newark, NG24 1AZ and Debden Antiques, Saffron Walden CB11 3JY.** SER: **Trades at antiques fairs and offers search services.** VAT: **Spec.** FAIRS: **Harrogate; NEC; Boxton.**
TEL: **Mobile: 07712 657414**
E-MAIL: **vaughanantiques@aol.com**
WEBSITE: **www.vaughanantiques.com**

RAMSEY

Abbey Antiques
63 Great Whyte. PE26 1HL. (R. and J. Smith)
EST. 1977. Open Tues.-Sat. 10-5. STOCK: *Furniture including pine, 1850-1930, £50-£500; porcelain, glass, Goss and crested china, 1830-1950, £3-£500; Beswick, Fen pottery, small collectables, Mabel Lucie Attwell, Memories*

UK *(Enesco Memories of Yesterday figurines), Attwellagy.* SER: Mabel Lucie Attwell Museum and Collectors' Club. SIZE: Medium. PARK: Easy.
TEL: 01487 814753
WEBSITE: www.mabellucieattwellclub.com

ST. IVES

Hyperion Antique Centre
Station Rd. PE27 5BH. (Rod Best and Lester Day)
EST. 1995. STOCK: *Antique furniture, jewellery & collectables.* SER: Valuations. SIZE: 30 dealers. PARK: Loading and unloading; 200+ parking spaces locally.
TEL: 01480 464140; FAX 01480 497552;
E-MAIL: enquiries@hyperionauctions.co.uk
WEBSITE: www.hyperionauctions.co.uk

B.R. Knight and Sons
Quay Court, Bull Lane, Bridge St. PE17 4AU.
(Michael Knight)
EST. 1972. Open Mon., Wed., Fri. 11-3, Sat. 11.30-4.30 or by appointment. STOCK: *Porcelain, pottery, jewellery, paintings, watercolours, prints, decorative arts.* LOC: Off Bridge St. SIZE: Medium. PARK: Nearby.
TEL: 01480 468295/300042
E-MAIL: michaelknight9@yahoo.co.uk

ST. NEOTS

Tavistock Antiques Ltd
Cross Hall Manor, Eaton Ford. PE19 7GB.
Trade Only. Open by appointment. STOCK: *Period English furniture.*
TEL: 01480 472082

WISBECH

Peter A. Crofts
117 High Rd., Elm. PE14 0DN. (Mrs Pat L. Crofts)
EST. 1949. Open by appointment. STOCK: *General antiques, furniture, porcelain, silver, jewellery.* LOC: A1101. VAT: Stan/Spec.
TEL: 01945 584614

Granny's Cupboard
34 Old Market. PE13 1NF. (R.J. Robbs)
EST. 1982. Open Tues. and Thurs. 10.30-4, Sat. 10.30-3. STOCK: *China, glass, small furniture, Victorian to 1950s, £5-£500.* SIZE: Medium. PARK: Easy. FAIRS: The Maltings, Ely.
TEL: 01945 589606; HOME: 01945 870730

R. Wilding
Lanes End, Gadds Lane, Leverington. PE13 5BJ.
EST. 1966. Resident. *Trade Only.* Open 9-6. STOCK: *Antique furniture and mirrors including reproduction.* SER: Veneering; polishing; compo carving; gilding; conversions. PARK: Easy.
TEL: 01945 588204; FAX: 01945 475712

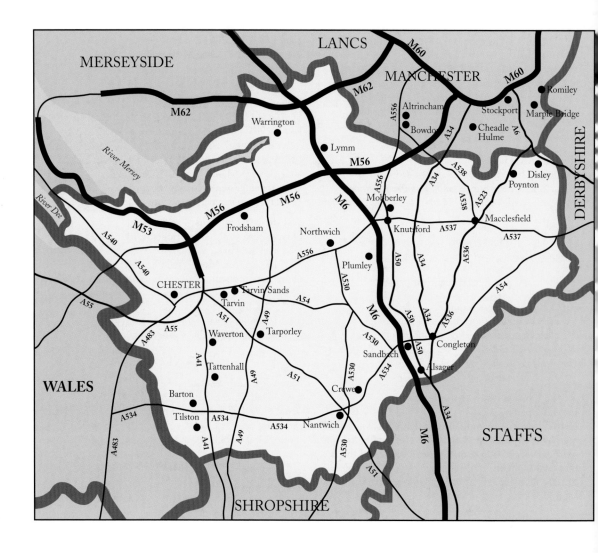

ALSAGER

Trash 'n' Treasure
(G. and D. Ogden)
EST. 1979. Open by appointment. *STOCK: Late Georgian to 1930s furniture, pictures, ceramics, £5-£10,000.* LOC: 10 mins. junction 16, M6. SER: Valuations; lectures. PARK: Nearby.
TEL: 01270 873246

ALTRINCHAM

Church Street Antiques   LAPADA
4/4a Old Market Place. WA14 4NP. (Alec Smalley and Nick Stanley)
EST. 1991. Open 10-5. CL: Tues. Sun. and Tues. by appointment. *STOCK: Furniture, 18th-19th C, £100-£20,000; 20th C design furniture, £100-£10,000; paintings, 19th C to contemporary, £100-£10,000.* LOC: A56. SER: Valuations; restorations. SIZE: Large. PARK: Easy. VAT: Spec. FAIRS: Tatton; Chester; Arley; Harrogate.
TEL: 0161 929 5196; FAX: same; MOBILE: 07768 318661
E-MAIL: sales@churchstreetantiques.com
WEBSITE: www.churchstreetantiques.com

Robert Redford Antiques & Interiors
48 New St. WA14 2QS. (S. and R. Redford)
EST. 1989. Open by appointment. *STOCK: General antiques, furniture, small silver, porcelain, glass.* LOC: Town centre. PARK: Easy.
TEL: HOME: 0161 929 1219
E-MAIL: rgredford@hotmail.com

Squires Antiques
25 Regent Rd. WA14 1RX. (V. Phillips)
EST. 1977. Open 10-5. CL: Mon., Wed. and Thurs. *STOCK: Small furniture, 1800-1930, £60-£1,500; small silver, 1850-1970, £20-£400; brass, copper and bric-a-brac, 1850-1940, £10-£400; jewellery, porcelain, fire accessories, light fittings and interior design items. NOT STOCKED: Large furniture, coins and badges.* LOC: Adjacent hospital and large car park. SER: Valuations. SIZE: Medium. PARK: Easy.
TEL: 0161 928 0749

BARNTON

Mid Cheshire Antiques & Art Centre
Runcorn Rd. CW8 4EL.
Open 10-5 Wed.-Sun. CL Mon. & Tues. except Bank Holiday Mondays. *STOCK: Fine period furniture, silverware, fine art pictures, dazzling jewellery, pine, vintage clothing, china, books, clocks, light fittings, fireplaces and Art Deco.* PARK: Own.
TEL: 01606 782288
E-MAIL: midcheshireantiques@btconnect.com
WEBSITE: www.midcheshireantiquesandart.co.uk

BARTON

Derek and Tina Rayment Antiques   BADA
Orchard House, Barton Rd. SY14 7HT. (D.J. and K.M. Rayment)
EST. 1960. Open by appointment every day. *STOCK: Barometers, 18th-20th C, from £100.* LOC: A534. SER: Valuations; restorations (barometers only); buys at auction (barometers). PARK: Easy. VAT: Stan/Spec. FAIRS: Olympia (June); USA fairs - see WEBSITE.
TEL: 01829 270429; HOME: same
E-MAIL: raymentantiques@aol.com
WEBSITE: www.antique-barometers.com

CHEADLE HULME

Andrew Foott Antiques
4 Claremont Rd. SK8 6EG.
EST. 1985. Open by appointment. *STOCK: Barometers, 18th-20th C, £200-£2,500; small furniture, 18th-20th C, £500-£3,000.* LOC: 5 mins. from new A34 by-pass. SER: Restorations (barometers and furniture). SIZE: Small. PARK: Easy. FAIRS: NEC.
TEL: 0161 485 3559
E-MAIL: andrew.foott@tesco.net

CHESTER

Aldersey Hall Ltd
Town Hall Sq., 47 Northgate St. CH1 2HQ. (Kim Wilding-Welton)
EST. 1990. Open 8.30-5.30. *STOCK: Art Deco and general British ceramics, £5-£500; small furniture, £50-£200; all 1880-1940.* LOC: Between library and Odeon cinema. SER: Valuations; buys at auction (Art Deco ceramics). SIZE: Medium. PARK: Own 100 yards. VAT: Stan/Spec. FAIRS: Ardingly, Newark, Birmingham.
TEL: 01244 324885

Antique Exporters of Chester
CH3 7RZ. (Michael Kilgannon)
EST. 1970. Open 8-8 including Sun. *STOCK: Furniture, 18th-19th C and shipping.* LOC: Waverton SER: Full packing and shipping; cabinet making and polishing. SIZE: Large warehouse. PARK: Easy. VAT: Stan/Spec.
TEL: 01829 741001; HOME: 01244 570069

Bank Gallery Antiques
Eastgate St. (Mr and Mrs M. O'Donnell)
EST. 1990. Open 10-5. *STOCK: Victorian and Edwardian furniture, £50-£1,000.* SER: French polishing. SIZE: Large. VAT: Spec.
TEL: MOBILE: 07876 633111

Baron Fine Art   LAPADA
68 Watergate St. CH1 2LA. (S. and R. Baron)
EST. 1984. Open 9.30-5.30. *STOCK: Watercolours and oils, some etchings, late 19th to early 20th C, some contemporary, £50-£60,000.* SER: **Restorations;**

framing. SIZE: Medium. PARK: Easy. VAT: Stan/Spec.
FAIRS: Tatton Park; LAPADA; NEC (Jan., April, Aug.
and Nov); Watercolours & Drawings (Jan/Feb).
TEL: 01244 342520
E-MAIL: info@baronfineart.com
WEBSITE: www.baronfineart.com

Cameo Antiques
19 Watergate St. CH1 2LB.
EST. 1994. Open 9-5, Sat. 9-5.30. STOCK: *Jewellery and
English silver, 1800-1990, £20-£4,000; English pottery
including Moorcroft and Sally Tuffin, Continental porcelain,
1750-1960; small furniture.* LOC: Off Bridge St. SER:
Valuations. SIZE: Small. PARK: Easy. VAT: Stan/Spec.
TEL: 01244 311467; FAX: same

Sandra Harris Interiors and Antiques
61 Watergate Row South. CH1 2LE.
EST. 1978. Open 10-5.30. STOCK: *English and
Continental furniture, 17th-19th C, £500-£10,000.* SIZE:
Medium. PARK: Easy. VAT: Spec.
TEL: 01244 409009
E-MAIL: sandra@sandraharris.co.uk

J. Alan Hulme
Antique Maps & Old Prints, 52 Mount Way,
Waverton. CH3 7QF.
EST. 1965. Open Mon.-Sat. by appointment. STOCK:
Maps, 16th-19th C; prints, 18th-19th C.
TEL: 01244 336472
E-MAIL: alanhulme@pssa.freeserve.co.uk

Jamandic Ltd
22 Bridge St. Row. CH1 1NN.
EST. 1975. Open 9.30-5.30, Sat. 9.30-1. STOCK:
Decorative furniture, mirrors, lighting, pictures and prints.
SER: Interior design and decoration; export. SIZE:
Medium. VAT: Stan/Spec.
TEL: 01244 312822

K D Antiques
11 City Walls. CH1 1LD. (Dorothea Gillett)
EST. 1990. Open 10-5. STOCK: *Staffordshire figures, 18th-
19th C, £50-£500; wooden boxes, 18th-19th C, £20-£300;
collectables, £5-£50; pottery, porcelain and glass, 19th C,
£50-£150; pictures and prints, small furniture.* LOC: City
centre, next to Eastgate Clock, wall level. SIZE: Medium.
TEL: 01244 314208

Kayes of Chester   LAPADA
9 St. Michaels Row. CH1 1EF. (A.M. Austin-Kaye
and N.J. Kaye)
EST. 1948. NAG. Open 10-5. STOCK: **Diamond rings
and jewellery, 1850-1950, £20-£20,000; silver and plate,
1700-1930, £20-£8,000; small objects and ceramics, 19th
to early 20th C, £50-£1,000.** SER: **Valuations;
restorations (silver, jewellery and plate); buys at
auction.** SIZE: **Medium.** PARK: **Nearby.** VAT:
Stan/Spec. FAIRS: **PBFA and north western.**

TEL: 01244 327149/343638; FAX: 01244 318404
E-MAIL: kayesgem@btopenworld.com
WEBSITE: www.kayesjewellers.com

Lowe & Sons
11 Bridge St. Row. CH1 1PD.
EST. 1770. Open 9-5.30. STOCK: *Jewellery and silver,
Georgian, Victorian and Edwardian; unusual collectors'
items.* VAT: Stan/Spec.
TEL: 01244 325850
E-MAIL: mail@waltonsofchester.co.uk
WEBSITE: www.waltonsofchester.co.uk

Melody's Antiques   LAPADA
**The Old School House, Kinnerton Rd., Lower
Kinnerton. CH4 9AE. (M. and M. Melody)**
EST. 1977. Open 10-5.30 by appointment. STOCK: *17th-
19th C oak, mahogany and walnut furniture. Antique
metalwork; porcelain; lighting; decorative items.* LOC: 3
miles from Chester. SER: Courier; container packing.
SIZE: Large. PARK: Easy VAT: Stan/Spec. FAIRS: NEC,
Harrogate, Snape, Chester, Buxton, Tatton Park.
TEL: 01244 660204
E-MAIL: m.melody@btconnect.com

Moor Hall Antiques
27 Watergate Row. CH1 2LE. (John Murphy)
EST. 1992. Resident. Open 10-5.30. STOCK: *Furniture,
18th-19th C, £500-£10,000; prints, 19th C, £50-£200;
modern decorative items, £2- £1,500.* LOC: City centre.
SER: Restorations (oils, watercolours and furniture).
SIZE: Large. PARK: Easy. VAT: Stan/Spec. FAIRS:
Buxton.
TEL: 01244 340095

Stothert Old Books
4 Nicholas St. CH1 2NX. (Alan and Marjory
Checkley)
EST. 1977. PBFA. Open 10-5. STOCK: *Books, 17th-20th
C, £2-£1,000.* LOC: At junction with Watergate St. SER:
Valuations. SIZE: Medium. PARK: Nearby. FAIRS: PBFA.
TEL: 01244 340756
E-MAIL: alancheckley@yahoo.com

DISLEY

Michael Allcroft Antiques
203 Buxton Rd., Newmills. SK12 2RA.
EST. 1984. Open Tues., Thurs. and Sat. 11-5, other times
by appointment. STOCK: *Antique, Edwardian and 1930s
furniture.* LOC: A6, 20 minutes south of Stockport. SER:
Container packing. SIZE: Large, trade warehouse.
TEL: MOBILE: 07798 781642; FAX: 01663 744014;
E-MAIL: allcrom@aol.com

Mill Farm Antiques
50 Market St. SK12 2DT. (F.E. Berry)
EST. 1968. Open every day. STOCK: *Pianos, clocks especially
longcase, mechanical music, shipping goods, general antiques,*

£50-£10,000. Loc: A6, 7 miles south of Stockport. Ser: Valuations; restorations (clocks, watches, barometers and music boxes). Size: Medium. Park: Outside premises. Vat: Stan/Spec.
Tel: 01663 764045
E-mail: enquiries@millfarmantiques.co.uk

FRODSHAM

Lady Heyes
Kingsley Rd. WA6 6SU.
Open 10-5, Sun. 11-5. *Stock: Antiques and collectables, furniture, textiles, jewellery, books, pictures, original works of art, clothing and accessories.* Size: Large.
Tel: 01928 787919
Website: www.ladyheyes.co.uk

HOYLAKE

Heritage Antiques and Interiors
16 Birkenhead Rd. CH47 3BN
Open Thurs.-Sat. 10.30-5.30; other times by appointment. *Stock: Furniture, ceramics, silver and collectables; barometers, pictures, mirrors and light fittings.* Loc: Main road. Ser: Advice on furnishing, restoration. Size: Medium. Park: Easy.
Tel: 0151 632 2224

Mansell Antiques and Collectables
Mulberry House, 128-130 Market St. CH47 3BH. (Gary Mansell and David Williamson)
Est. 1979. Open 9-5.30, Sun. and other times by appointment. CL: Wed. *Stock: Furniture, pine, china, decorative arts, architectural items and gardenalia; art nouveau, interiors.* Loc: A540 in town centre. Ser: Free local deliveries, national and international transport arranged. Size: Large plus courtyard. Park: Own. Vat: Margin. Fairs: Chester Art Deco; Birmingham Bull Ring.
Tel: 0151 632 0892; Mobile: 07944 883021; Fax: 0151 632 6137
E-mail: mansell.antiques@btconnect.com
Website: www.mansellantiques.co.uk

Now and Then
4, Albert Rd. CH47 2AB
Open 10-5. CL: Wed. *Stock: Antique furniture, decorative items, collectables, paintings.*
Tel: 0151 632 0071

Vertu
7 The Quadrant, CH47 2EE. (Angela Duffy)
Est. 1977. Open Mon./Tues./Thurs. 10.30-4.30, Sat. 10.30-2; other times by appointment. *Stock: General antiques, decorative and French furniture; mid-century and retro furniture; vintage clothes and textiles.* Loc: Central Hoylake. Park: Free parking in street. Fairs: Manchester Antique Textile Fair.
Tel: 0151 632 2711; Mobile: 07967 431184

E-mail: angeladuffy@ntlworld.com
Website: www.antiqueatatlas.com

KELSALL

Yolanda Gray Antiques   LAPADA
Unit 2, Organsdale Farm, Tarporley, CW6 0SR.
Est. 1977. Open by appointment. *Stock: Period oak furniture, 19th C furniture; specialises in antique colonial four-poster beds.* Loc: On the A54. Park: Own car park.
Tel: 01630 685273; Mobile: 07889 168252
E-mail: sales@yolagray.com
Website: www.yolagray.com

KNUTSFORD

B.R.M. Coins
3 Minshull St. WA16 6HG. (Brian Butterworth)
Est. 1968. Open 11-3, Sat. 11-1 or by appointment. *Stock: Coins, medals and banknotes, worldwide, BC to date, from 5p; money boxes, coin scales and weights.* Loc: A50. Ser: Valuations; buys at auction (as stock). Size: Small. Park: Nearby.
Tel: 01565 651480; Home: 01606 74522

Knutsford Antiques Centre
113 King St. WA16 6EH. (David and Patricia McLeod)
Est. 1995. Open 10-5, Sun. 12-5. CL: Mon. *Stock: Furniture, 18th C, £100-£2,000; pine, £200-£600; early British porcelain, ceramics and collectables, £10-£2,000; British silver, £10-£1,000; books, £1-£50; glass, £10-£500; jewellery, £25-£500.* Loc: Main street, 5 mins. from junction 19, M6. Ser: Valuations. Size: 20+ dealers. Park: Easy.
Tel: 01565 654092
Website: www.knutsfordantiques.com

Lion Gallery and Bookshop
15a Minshull St. WA16 6HG. (R.P. Hepner and V. M. Hepner)
Est. 1964. Open Fri. 10.30-4.30, Sat. 10-4.30 or by appointment. *Stock: Large stock of antiquarian maps including John Speed, Blaeu, Jansson and Ogilby; prints and books, watercolours and oils, 16th-20th C; O.S. maps and early directories.* Loc: King St. 3 mins. M6. Ser: Restorations; binding; cleaning; framing; mounting. Park: Nearby. Vat: Stan.
Tel: 01565 652915; Fax: 01565 750142; Mobile: 07850 270796
E-mail: info@liongalleries.com
Website: www.liongalleries.com

LYMM

Willow Pool Garden Centre
Burford Lane. WA13 0SH. (S. Brunsveld)
Open 9-6, including Sun. *Stock: Architectural and*

general antiques; reproductions and fine art. SIZE: Large.
FAIRS: Newark.
TEL: 01925 757827; FAX: 01925 758101
E-MAIL: sales@willowpool.co.uk
WEBSITE: www.willowpool.co.uk

MACCLESFIELD

Gatehouse Antiques
5/7 Chester Rd. SK11 8DG. (W.H. Livesley)
EST. 1973. Open 9-5. CL: Sun. except by appointment
and Wed. pm. *STOCK: Small furniture, silver and plate,
glass, brass, copper, pewter, jewellery, 1650-1880 and
collectables.* SER: Valuations; repairs; insurance estimates.
SIZE: Large. PARK: Opposite.
TEL: 01625 426476; HOME: 01625 612841
E-MAIL: bill_livesley@yahoo.co.uk
WEBSITE: www.gatehouse.com

Hills Antiques
Indoor Market, Grosvenor Centre. SK11 6SY. (D. Hill)
EST. 1968. Open 9.30-5.30. *STOCK: Small furniture,
jewellery, collectors' items, stamps, coins, postcards.* LOC:
Town centre. PARK: Easy.
TEL: 01625 420777/420467
E-MAIL: hillsantiques@tinyworld.co.uk

D.J. Massey and Son
47 Chestergate. SK11 6DG.
EST. 1900. Open 9.30-5.15. *STOCK: Jewellery, gold and
diamonds, all periods; antique silver.* SER: Valuations,
jewellery workshop, pearl re-stringing.
TEL: 01625 616133

Mereside Books
75 Chestergate. SK11 6DG. (Miss S. Laithwaite and
Mr K. S. Kowalski)
EST. 1996. Open 10.30-4, Mon. and Tues. by
appointment. *STOCK: Books - secondhand, 20th C, £2-
£100; antiquarian, 19th C, £10-£300; illustrated, 20th C,
£10-£1,000.* SER: Valuations; restorations (books
including re-binding). SIZE: Small.
TEL: 01625 425352; HOME: 01625 431160

MOBBERLEY

David Bedale
WA16 7HR.
EST. 1977. Open by appointment. *STOCK: 18th-19th C
furniture, unusual and decorative items.* SIZE: Medium.
VAT: Stan/Spec. FAIRS: Olympia (June and Nov).
TEL: 01565 872270; MOBILE: 07836 623021.

Limited Editions
The Barn, Oak Tree Farm, Knutsford Rd. WA16 7PU.
(C.W. Fogg)
EST. 1978. Open Thurs., Fri. and Sat. 10-5.30, Sun. 12-
4. STOCK: *Furniture, 19th C, especially dining tables and
chairs, £100-£5,000; armchairs and couches for re-
upholstery.* LOC: Main road between Knutsford and
Wilmslow. SER: Valuations; restorations (furniture).
SIZE: Large. PARK: Own. VAT: Stan/Spec.
TEL: 01565 874075
E-MAIL: info@ltd-editions.co.uk
WEBSITE: www.antique-co.com

NANTWICH

Adams Antiques   BADA LAPADA
**Churche's Mansion, Hospital St. CW5 5RY. (Sandy
Summers)**
**EST. 1975. Resident. Open 10-5 Mon-Sat, or by
appointment.** STOCK: *Mainly oak, walnut and fruitwood
country furniture; Welsh dressers; dresser bases; Windsor
chairs and other chairs; tables; cupboards; chests of drawers
and longcase clocks.* **LOC: A500 towards town centre,
shop on left on main roundabout. SER: Valuations;
restorations (furniture). SIZE: Large, 5 showrooms.
PARK: Own large. VAT: Stan/Spec.
TEL: 01270 625643; FAX: 01270 625609
E-MAIL: sandy@adams-antiques.net
WEBSITE: www.adams-antiques.net**

Barn Antiques
8 The Cocoa Yard, Pillory St. CW5 5BL. (J.B. Lee)
EST. 1993. CL: Wed. STOCK: *Royal Doulton figures,
Beswick animals, Royal Doulton, Wedgwood and Shelley
china, Carltonware and small furniture.* LOC: Town centre.
SER: Insurance replacement quotations; matching service
for tea and dinnerware. SIZE: Small. PARK: Town centre
car parks. VAT: Margin.
TEL: 01270 627770
E-MAIL: j.lee2@btinternet.com

Chapel Antiques
47 Hospital St. CW5 5RL. (Miss D.J. Atkin)
EST. 1983. Open 9.30-5.30, Wed. 9.30-1 or by
appointment. CL: Mon. STOCK: *Oak, mahogany and pine
furniture, Georgian and Victorian, £100-£3,000; longcase
clocks, pre-1830, £1,000-£3,000; copper, brass, silver, glass,
porcelain, pottery and small items, 19th C, £10-£500.* LOC:
Enter town via Pillory St., turn right into Hospital St.
SER: Valuations; restorations (furniture and clocks). SIZE:
Medium. PARK: Easy.
TEL: 01270 629508; HOME: same

Love Lane Antiques
Love Lane. CW5 5BH. (M. Simon)
EST. 1982. Open 10-5. CL: Wed. STOCK: *General
antiques, 19th-20th C, £5-£1,000.* LOC: 2 mins. walk

from town square. SIZE: Small. PARK: Nearby.
TEL: 01270 626239

NORTHWICH

Northwich Antiques Centre
132 Witton St. CW9 5NP. (F.J. Cockburn)
EST. 1990. Open 10-5 including Sun. STOCK: *Georgian,
Victorian and Edwardian furniture, £50-£1,000+; china,
clocks and barometers; Royal Doulton, Beswick, Moorcroft;
prints, paintings, books, jewellery.* LOC: Town centre. SER:
Valuations; French polishing; framing. SIZE: Large.
PARK: Easy.
TEL: 01606 47540; FAX: same; MOBILE: 07980 645738
E-MAIL: ron2@cockburn2686.fsnet.co.uk
WEBSITE: www.northwichantiquescentre.com

PLUMLEY

Coppelia Antiques
Holford Lodge, Plumley Moor Rd. WA16 9RS. (V. and
R. Clements)
EST. 1970. Resident. Open 10-6 including Sun. by
appointment. STOCK: *Over 500 clocks (mainly longcase and
wall), £1,000-£50,000; tables - Georgian mahogany, wine,
oak gateleg and side; bureaux, desks, chests of drawers,
lowboys, coffers - all stock guaranteed.* LOC: 4 miles junction
19, M6. SER: Restorations. SIZE: Large. PARK: Own.
VAT: Spec.
TEL: 01565 722197/020 7629 6606; FAX: 01565
722744
WEBSITE: www.pendulumofmayfair.co.uk

POYNTON

The Attic
96 London Rd. South. SK12 1LQ. (Jonathan and
Hazel Hodgson)
EST. 1998. Open 10.30-4.30 or by appointment. STOCK:
*Pine antique furniture and kitchenalia from around the
world, mainly post 1900.* LOC: A523 just outside village.
SER: Pine stripping, repair, preservation treatment, sand
and wax. SIZE: Medium. PARK: Easy.
TEL: 01625 873229; MOBILE: 07791 190931
E-MAIL: enquiries@theatticonline.co.uk
WEBSITE: www.theatticonline.co.uk

Recollections
69 Park Lane. SK12 1RD. (Angela Smith)
EST. 1985. Open 10-5. STOCK: *Secondhand furniture, con-
temporary and traditional; jewellery and decorative collectables.*
SER: House clearance; "clear and clean" service available.
SIZE: Medium. PARK: Own at rear and Civic Centre.
TEL: 01625 859373
E-MAIL: recollections.antiques@ntlworld.com

ROMILEY

Romiley Antiques & Jewellery
42 Stockport Rd. SK6 3AA. (P. Green)
EST. 1983. Open Thurs., Fri. and Sat. 9-5. STOCK:
Furniture, 18th-19th C, £100-£3,000; ceramics, 18th-19th
C, £5-£1,000; jewellery, 19th C, £5-£1,000. LOC: 5 miles
from Stockport. SER: Valuations. SIZE: Medium. PARK:
Nearby. VAT: Stan/Spec.
TEL: 0161 494 6920; HOME: same

SANDBACH

Saxon Cross Antiques Emporium
Town Mill, High St. CW11 1AH. (John and Christine
Jones)
EST. 1972. Open 10-5. STOCK: Furniture, 16th to early
20th C, £50-£10,000; glass, silver, china and porcelain,
19th-20th C, £50-£1,000; investment antiques £10,000-
£50,000. LOC: 1 mile off junction 17, M6. SER:
Valuations; restorations; buys at auction. SIZE: Large - 4
storey Georgian mill. PARK: Easy and nearby. VAT:
Stan/Spec. FAIRS: Cheshire Show.
TEL: 01270 753005; FAX: same
E-MAIL: saxoncrossantiques@tiscali.co.uk

STOCKPORT

Antiques Import Export
20 Buxton Rd., Hevley. SK2 6NU. (Paul and Mark
Ledger)
EST. 1968. Open 9-5.30. STOCK: American, Italian and
pre-1930 English furniture, to £5,000. LOC: A6 opposite
cemetery. SER: Valuations; restorations; transport from
airport or rail station. SIZE: Large. PARK: Own. FAIRS:
Newark.
TEL: 0161 476 4013; FAX: 0161 285 2860
E-MAIL: paul@antiquesimportexport.freeserve.co.uk

Flintlock Antiques
28 and 30 Bramhall Lane. SK2 6HR. (F. Tomlinson &
Son)
EST. 1968. Open 9-5. STOCK: Furniture, clocks, pictures,
scientific instruments. SIZE: Large. PARK: Easy. VAT:
Stan/Spec.
TEL: 0161 480 9973

Imperial Antiques   LAPADA
295 Buxton Rd., Great Moor. SK2 7NR. (A. Todd)
EST. 1972. Open 10-5, Sun. by appointment. STOCK:
Decorative French and English antiques; silver and plate,
19th-20th C; porcelain especially Japanese and Chinese,
18th-19th C; all £100-£10,000. LOC: A6 Buxton Rd.,
1.5 miles south of town centre. SER: Buys at auction (as
stock). SIZE: Large. PARK: Easy. VAT: Stan/Spec.
TEL: 0161 483 3322; FAX: 0161 483 3376
E-MAIL: contactus@imperialantiques.com
WEBSITE: www.imperialantiques.com

Manchester Antique Company
MAC House, St Thomas's Place. SK1 3TZ.
EST. 1967. Open 9.30-4.30. STOCK: Antique furniture,
English, Continental and shipping goods, mainly walnut
and mahogany. LOC: Town centre. SER: Containers
packed worldwide. SIZE: Very large. PARK: Own. VAT:
Stan/Spec. FAIRS: Newark.
TEL: 0161 355 5566/5577; FAX: 0161 355 5588
E-MAIL: sales@manchester-antique.co.uk
WEBSITE: www.manchester-antique.co.uk

Nostalgia Architectural Antiques   LAPADA
**Holland's Mill, Shaw Heath. SK3 8BH. (D. and E.
Durrant)**
EST. 1975. Open Tues.-Fri. 10-6, Sat. 10-5. STOCK:
Fireplaces, £200-£50,000; bathroom fittings and
architectural items, £50-£2,000; all 18th-19th C. LOC: 5
mins. from junction 1, M60. SER: Valuations. SIZE:
Large. PARK: At rear. VAT: Stan/Spec.
TEL: 0161 477 7706; FAX: 0161 477 2267
E-MAIL: sales@nostalgia-uk.com
WEBSITE: www.nostalgia-uk.com

The Old Curiosity Shop
123 Stockport Rd. West, Bredbury. SK6 2AN. (Sandra
Crook)
EST. 1984. Open 10-6, Sun. 12-5. CL: Wed. STOCK:
1920s, 1930s oak furniture, especially barley twist; brass coal
buckets, fire tools. LOC: 2 miles from M60. SER:
Restorations (furniture - hand stripping). SIZE: Medium.
PARK: Forecourt or opposite.
TEL: 0161 494 9469

TARPORLEY

Tarporley Antique Centre
76 High St. CW6 0DP.
EST. 1992. Open 10-5, Sun. 11-4. STOCK: Furniture,
ceramics, commemoratives, treen, glass, oils, watercolours,
prints, silver and plate, books, linen. LOC: Main road, near
Crown public house. SIZE: 9 dealers on two floors. PARK:
In front of premises and opposite.
TEL: 01829 733919

TARVIN

Antique Fireplaces
The Manor House, Church St. CH3 8EB. (Mrs G.
O'Toole)
EST. 1979. Open Fri., Sat. and Sun. 10-5 or by
appointment. STOCK: Fireplaces and ranges, 18th-19th C,
£150-£3,000. LOC: At junction of A556 and A51. SER:
Valuations; restorations; installations (fireplaces and ranges);
new tiles and fenders ordered from suppliers on request.
SIZE: Medium. PARK: Easy. FAIRS: Tatton Park, Knutsford.
TEL: 01829 740936; HOME: 01606 46717
E-MAIL: info@antiquefireplacesandranges.co.uk
WEBSITE: www.antiquefireplacesandranges.co.uk

TARVIN SANDS

Cheshire Brick and Slate Co.
Brook House Farm, Salters Bridge. CH3 8NR.
(Malcolm and Jason Youde)
EST. 1978. Open 7.30-5, Sat. 8-4.30. STOCK: *Reclaimed conservation building materials and timber, 16th-20th C; architectural antiques – garden statuary, stonework, lamp posts, gates, fireplaces, bathroom suites, chimney pots and ironwork, 18th-20th C, £50-£1,000; furniture, pews, leaded lights, pottery, 18th-20th C, £5-£1,000.* LOC: Directly off A54 just outside Tarvin. SER: Valuations; restorations (fireplaces, timber treatment); building/construction and demolition; renovations; manufactured doors, units and beams etc. cut to customer's specification on site. SIZE: Large. PARK: Own. VAT: Stan/Global.
TEL: 01829 740883; FAX: 01829 740481
E-MAIL: enquiries@cheshirebrickandslate.co.uk
WEBSITE: www.cheshirebrickandslate.co.uk

TATTENHALL

The Great Northern Architectural Antique Company Ltd
New Russia Hall, Chester Rd. CH3 9AH. (Jean Devoy)
Open 9.30-5, Sun. 10-4. STOCK: *Pub, shop and church interiors; period doors, fire surrounds, stained glass, garden statuary, furniture and curios.* LOC: Off A41, 6 miles south of Chester. SER: Stripping; sand blasting; cast iron repair & restoration; wood/metal polishing; joinery; bespoke stained and leaded glass; stone masonry; specialist fitting service. SIZE: Large. PARK: Easy. VAT: Stan.
TEL: 01829 770796; FAX: 01829 770971
E-MAIL: gnaacoltd@enterprise.net
WEBSITE: www.gnaa.co.uk

TILSTON

Well House Antiques
The Well House. SY14 7DP. (S. French-Greenslade)
EST. 1968. Open by appointment. STOCK: *Collectors' items, china, glass, silver.* SIZE: Small. PARK: Easy.
TEL: 01829 250332

WALGHERTON

Dagfield Crafts & Antiques Centre
Dagfields Farm CW5 7LG.
Open 10-5 inc. Sun. STOCK: *Antiques, collectables and bric-a-brac.* SIZE: Over 200 dealers.
TEL: 01270 841336; FAX: 01270 842 604
E-MAIL: ibennion@dagfields.co.uk
WEBSITE: www.dagfields.co.uk

WARRINGTON

The Rocking Chair Antiques
Unit 3, St. Peter's Way. WA2 7BL. (Mike Barratt and Keith Morris)

EST. 1976. Open 8.30-5, Sat. 10-4. STOCK: *Furniture and bric-a-brac.* LOC: Off Orford Lane. SER: Valuations; packing and shipping. SIZE: Large. PARK: Easy. VAT: Stan.
TEL: 01925 652409; FAX: same; MOBILE: 07774 492891
E-MAIL: rockingmick@aol.com

WAVERTON

The White House
Whitchurch Rd. CH3 7PB. (Mrs Elizabeth Rideal)
EST. 1979. Open 10-5. STOCK: *Stripped pine furniture, 19th-20th C, £50-£2,000; Victorian china, 19th C, £5-£100; bric-a-brac.* LOC: A41, 2.5 miles south of Sainsbury's roundabout on Whitchurch Rd. SIZE: Medium. PARK: Easy. VAT: Margin.
TEL: 01244 335063; HOME: same; FAX: 01244 335098.

WEST KIRBY

Helen Horswill Antiques and Decorative Arts
62 Grange Rd. CH48 4EG.
EST. 1977. Open 10-5.30. CL: Mon. and Wed. STOCK: *Furniture, 17th-19th C; decorative items, paintings.* LOC: A540. SER: Restoration, upholstery, valuations. SIZE: Medium. PARK: Easy.
TEL: 0151 625 2803; MOBILE: 07879 456244

Trevor Kelly Antique Clocks and Barometers
76 Banks Rd. CH48 0RE.
EST. 1986. Open 10-2. CL: Mon., Wed. & Fri. STOCK: *Antique clocks, barometer restoration and repair specialist. Quality antiques bought and sold, repaired and repolished.* SER: Valuation for insurance and probate.
TEL: 0151 625 7992; MOBILE: 07831 852776

WETTENHALL

The Chase Antiques Barn
The Chase, Long Lane. CW7 4DN. (Alison Harding)
EST. 2001. Open 10-6 inc. Sun. STOCK: *Georgian, Victorian and later furniture, brass, glassware, porcelain, pottery, prints, pictures and works of art.* SER: Arts, crafts and giftshop on site. SIZE: 15 dealers. PARK: Own.
TEL: 01270 528449528092

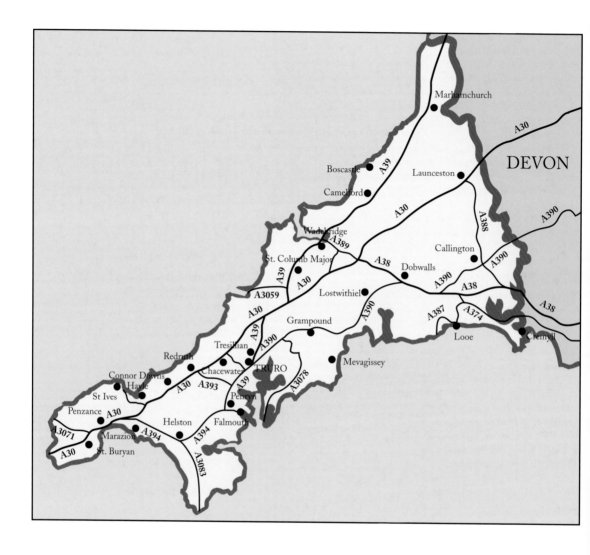

BOSCASTLE

Newlyfe Antiques
The Old Mill. PL35 0AQ. (Harry Ruddy)
Open seven days a week May-Sept., prior telephone call advisable at other times. STOCK: *Collectables, 18th-19th C furniture, French beds.* LOC: Village centre. PARK: Nearby.
TEL: 01840 250230;
WEBSITE: www.boscastle-oldmill.co.uk

Pickwick Antiques
The Old Mill, Old Rd. PL35 0AQ. (David Lamond)
EST. 1970. Open 11-5, 11-4 in winter, Sun 1-4; CL:Wed. STOCK: *General small antiques including silver and plate, jewellery, glass, pre-1950, £5-£500+.* SER: Valuations (silver, glass, jewellery). SIZE: Small. PARK: Easy.
TEL: 01840 250770; HOME/FAX: 01566 880085;
MOBILE: 07971 648107
E-MAIL: david-peter@craigmoor.freeserve.co.uk
WEBSITE: www.boscastle-oldmill.co.uk

CALLINGTON

Country Living Antiques
Weston House, Haye Rd. PL17 7JJ. (Ian Baxter CBE)
EST. 1990. Resident. Open 10-6. STOCK: *19th C oak and pine country furniture, general antiques, £1-£2,000.* LOC: Town centre. SER: Valuations; buys at auction. SIZE: Large - including barn. PARK: Own.
TEL: 01579 382245; FAX: same.

CONNOR DOWNS

Julie Strachey
Trevaskis Barn, Gwinear Rd. TR27 5JQ.
EST. 1975. Open by appointment. STOCK: *Decorative 18th-19th C farm and country furniture, especially tables, dressers, chests, wrought iron and unusual garden items.* SER: Packing and shipping. SIZE: Medium. PARK: Own. VAT: Stan. FAIRS: NEC.
TEL: 01209 613750; MOBILE: 07711 249939

DOBWALLS

Olden Days
Five Lanes. PL14 6JD. (G.M. and Mrs. H.K. Young)
EST. 1980. Open 9.30-5.30, Sun. 11-4. STOCK: *Period furniture, £50-£1,500; reclaimed and new pine furniture; bric-a-brac and collectables.* LOC: A38 between Liskeard and Bodmin. SER: Restorations; furniture made to order. SIZE: Medium. PARK: Easy and private behind shop. VAT: Stan/Spec.
TEL: 01579 321577; HOME: same
E-MAIL: glenyoung@aol.com
WEBSITE: www.oldendays.info

FALMOUTH

John Maggs
54b Church St. TR11 3DS. (Colin Nunn)
EST. 1900. Open 10-5. CL: Wed. STOCK: *Antiquarian prints and maps; topography - south of London to Bristol line; books on ships and sailing.* LOC: Facing on to central car park. SER: Restorations; framing. SIZE: Medium. PARK: At rear of shop.
TEL: 01326 313153; FAX: same
E-MAIL: colin@johnmaggs.co.uk
WEBSITE: www.johnmaggs.co.uk

Old Town Hall Antiques
3 High St. TR11 2AB. (Mary P. Sheppard and Terence J. Brandreth)
EST. 1986. Open 10-5.30. STOCK: *Furniture including French, beds and mirrors, 19th-20th C, £100-£2,000; country smalls, china and collectables, 19th-20th C, £10-£60.* LOC: From edge of Falmouth follow signs towards marina, shop situated on right under road arch (one-way street). SER: Storage and delivery. SIZE: Large + trade store. PARK: Easy. VAT: Global.
TEL: 01326 319437; HOME: 01326 377489
E-MAIL: marysheppard@btopenworld.com
WEBSITE: www.oldtownhallantiques.co.uk

FOWEY

Odds and Ends
49 Fore St. PL23 1AH. (Mrs Sandra howard)
EST. 1987. Open Mon.-Sun. 10-5.30; (Winter: Mon.-Sun. 10.30-4). STOCK: *Antiques and collectables.* SER: Jewellery repairs. SIZE: Small. PARK: Nearby.
TEL: 01726 832095

GRAMPOUND

Radnor House
Fore St. TR2 4QT. (P. and G. Hodgson)
EST. 1972. Open 10-5. STOCK: *Furniture and accessories, pre-1900. NOT STOCKED: Jewellery, coins and weapons.* LOC: A390. SER: Valuations; buys at auction. SIZE: Medium. PARK: Easy.
TEL: 01726 882921; HOME: same.
E-MAIL: radnorantiques@aol.com

HAYLE

Foundry Gallery
Unit 12, Pratt's Market, Chapel Terrace. TR27 4AB. (A.P. Dyer)
EST. 1900. Open 9-5. STOCK: *Watercolours and oils, including Newlyn and St. Ives schools; small antiques, Art Deco and studio pottery.* LOC: Off Foundry Square. SER: Framing. SIZE: Large. PARK: Easy.
TEL: 01736 752787; HOME: 01736 752960

LAUNCESTON

Antique Chairs and Museum
Colhay Farm, Polson. PL15 9QS. (Tom and Alice Brown)
EST. 1988. Open seven days. STOCK: Chairs, 18th to early
20th C. LOC: Signed from A30. SER: Restorations; buys
at auction. SIZE: Large. PARK: Easy.
TEL: 01566 777485; HOME: same.
E-MAIL: info@antiquechairs.biz
WEBSITE: www.antiquechairs.co.uk

LOOE

Tony Martin
Fore St. PL13 1AE.
EST. 1965. Open 10.30-1 and 2-5, appointment
advisable. STOCK: Porcelain, 18th C; silver, 18th-19th C,
both £20-£200; glass, furniture, oils and watercolours. LOC:
Main street. SIZE: Medium.
TEL: 01503 262734; HOME: 01503 262228

LOSTWITHIEL

The Higgins Press
South St. PL22 0BZ. (Mrs Doris Roberts)
EST. 1982. Open 10-4, Wed. and Sat. 10-1. STOCK:
Porcelain, Victorian and collectables, £5-£1,000; clocks and
glass, Victorian to Art Deco, £5-£750; furniture, Georgian to
1930s, £10-£3,000. LOC: Just off A390. SIZE: Medium.
PARK: Easy and nearby.
TEL: 01208 872755; HOME: same; MOBILE: 07748 165041

Old Palace Antiques
Old Palace, Quay St. PL22 0BS. (Jeremy and Melanie
Askew)
EST. 2003. Open 9.30-5. STOCK: Oak, country pine and
painted furniture, T. G. Green Cornishware, kitchenalia,
vintage linen, bears and dolls. LOC: In the old Duchy
Palace, by the river. SER: Free local delivery, competitive
rates for rest of UK. PARK: Nearby.
TEL: 01208 872909
E-MAIL: melaniej.askew@virgin.net
WEBSITE: www.old-palace-antiuqes.com

Uzella Court Antiques and Fine Art
2 Fore St. PL22 0BP. (Mark and Mandy Royle)
EST. 2003. WEADA. Open 10-5 STOCK: English period oak
and country furniture £300-£10,000; gold and silver jewellery
£30-£2,000; fine paintings; silver; English engraved and cut
glass. LOC: Central. SIZE: Medium. PARK: 50 metres.
TEL: 01208 872255; MOBILE: 07976 522597
E-MAIL: mark@markroyle.orangehome.co.uk
WEBSITE: www.uzellacourtantiques.co.uk

MARAZION

Antiques
The Shambles, Market Place. TR17 0AR. (Andrew S. Wood)
EST. 1988. Open Mon.-Fri. 10.30-5, also Sats. 1st Nov.-

31st March. STOCK: General antiques and collectors' items
including 19th-20th C pottery and porcelain; Victorian to
20th C glass including pressed; blue and white china, Art
Deco ceramics, Devon pottery, commemorative ware, Goss
and crested china, '50s-'60s pottery and glass, bottles. LOC:
Main street. SIZE: Small. PARK: Easy.
TEL: 01736 711381; HOME: same.

MARHAMCHURCH

Marhamchurch Antiques
Blackthorne, Endsleigh Park. EX23 0HL. (Paul
Fitzsimmons)
EST. 1991. Open 9-5 by appointment only. STOCK:
Early oak, 16th-17th C, Gothic and Renaissance furniture.
SIZE: Medium. PARK: Easy. VAT: Stan.
TEL: MOBILE: 07779 038891
E-MAIL: earlyoak@btopenworld.com
WEBSITE: www.marhamchurchantiques.co.uk

PENRYN

Old School Antiques
Church Rd. TR10 8DA. (J.M. Gavan)
EST. 1988. Open 8.30-5.30. STOCK: General antiques.
SER: Free delivery within Cornwall. PARK: Easy.
TEL: 01326 375092

Neil Willcox & Mark Nightingale
Jobswater, Mabe. TR10 9BT.
Open by appointment. STOCK: Sealed wine and other bottles,
British and Continental 1650-1850, and related items. SER:
Valuations; mail order - catalogue and photos supplied.
TEL: 01326 340533
E-MAIL: nightdes@aol.com
WEBSITE: www.earlyglass.com

PENZANCE

Antiques & Fine Art
1-3 Queens Buildings, The Promenade. TR18 4HH.
(Elinor Davies and Geoffrey Mills)
EST. 1985. Open 10-4. STOCK: Furniture, 17th C to
Edwardian, to £10,000; some decorative pieces, to £250.
LOC: Next to Queen's Hotel. SER: Valuations;
restorations (furniture including upholstery). SIZE:
Medium. PARK: Nearby.
TEL: 01736 350509; HOME: 01736 350677
E-MAIL: antiques.p3@btconnect.com
WEBSITE: www.antiquesfineart.co.uk

Chapel Street Antiques Arcade
61/62 Chapel St. TR18 4AE.
EST. 1985. Open 9.30-5. STOCK: Furniture, pottery,
porcelain, glass, silver, metalware, kitchenalia, pictures,
books, clocks, jewellery, decorative and collectors' items;
contemporary art. LOC: Opposite Newlyn Exchange Art
Gallery. SIZE: Two floors, 20 dealers.
TEL: MOBILE: 07890 542708

Daphne's Antiques

17 Chapel St. TR18 4AW. (Daphne Davies)
EST. 1976. Open 10-5. STOCK: *Early country furniture, Georgian glass, Delft, pottery and decorative objects.* SIZE: Medium.
TEL: 01736 361719

Peter Johnson

62 Chapel St. TR18 4AE. (Peter Chatfield-Johnson)
EST. 1961. Open 9.30-4, Mon. by appointment. STOCK: *Lighting, 19th-20th C, £25-£500; Oriental ceramics and furniture, 18th-19th C, £25-£2,000; handmade silk lampshades, 20th C, £25-£250, furnishing fabrics.* LOC: Left at top of Market Jew St. SER: Valuations; restorations (soft furnishings). SIZE: Small. PARK: Easy.
TEL: 01736 363267; HOME: 01736 368088

Little Jem's

41 Market Place. TR18 2JG. (J. Lagden)
Open 9.30-5. STOCK: *Antique and modern jewellery (specialising in opal and amber), gem stones, objets d'art, paintings, clocks and watches.* SER: Repairs; commissions. SIZE: Small. VAT: Stan.
TEL: 01736 351400
E-MAIL: littlejemscornwall@yahoo.co.uk

Penzance Rare Books

43 Causewayhead. TR18 2SS. (Patricia Johnstone)
EST. 1990. Open 10-5. STOCK: *Antiquarian and secondhand books.* LOC: Top of Causewayhead. SER: Valuations; search. SIZE: Medium. PARK: Nearby.
TEL: 01736 362140; HOME: 01736 367506
E-MAIL: patricia.johnstone@blue-earth.co.uk

Tony Sanders Penzance Gallery and Antiques

14 Chapel St. TR18 4AW.
EST. 1972. Open 9-5.30. STOCK: *Oils and watercolours, 19th-20th C, £50-£5,000; glass, silver, china and small furniture; specialist in Newlyn and J F Pool of Hayle copper; contemporary art, paintings and bronzes.* SIZE: 3 floors. VAT: Stan.
TEL: 01736 366620/368461

REDRUTH

The Old Steam Bakery

60A Fore St. TR14 7NU. (Stephen J. Phillips)
EST. 1986. Open 10.30-5. STOCK: *Furniture including oak, 19th to early 20th C, £50-£100+; china and glass, early 20th C.* LOC: Next to main Post Office. SER: Valuations; restorations (furniture). SIZE: Large. PARK: Easy. VAT: Stan.
TEL: 01209 315099; HOME: 01209 710650
E-MAIL: myph.162@yahoo.co.uk

Redruth Indoor Market

3 Higher Fore St. TR15 2AJ.
Open 9.30-4 Mon.-Sat. STOCK: *Furniture, glass, pictures, postcards and collectables.*
TEL: 01209 216186

ST. BURYAN

Boathouse Antiques

Churchtown. TR19 6BX. (M.A. and P.A. Cleaver)
EST. 1994. Resident. Open in summer Tues.-Sat. 10-5, other times ring or knock at Belmont House; winter - prior telephone advisable. STOCK: *Wide range of general antiques including nautical items, furniture, rugs, jewellery, pictures and ceramics.* LOC: Opposite pub in village centre. SIZE: Medium. PARK: Easy. FAIRS: DCAF.
TEL: 01736 810025; HOME: same.
E-MAIL: martin@cleaver65.freeserve.co.uk

ST. COLUMB MAJOR

Stiltskin & Walrus Antiques

61 Fore St. TR9 6RH. (Mrs Janet Prescott)
EST. 2000. Open 9.15-4, Wed. 9.15-1. STOCK: *China, glass, books, pictures and prints, postcards, furniture, curios and collectables.* LOC: Central. SER: Valuations. SIZE: Medium. PARK: Loading only and nearby.
TEL: 01841 520182; HOME: same.
E-MAIL: janet92@talktalk.net

ST. IVES

Mike Read Antique Sciences

1 Abbey Meadow, Lelant. TR26 3LL.
EST. 1974. Open by appointment. STOCK: *Scientific instruments - navigational, surveying, mining, barometers, telescopes and microscopes, medical, 18th-19th C, £10-£5,000; maritime works of art and nautical artefacts.* LOC: Turn left on hill in village, heading towards St. Ives. SER: Valuations; restorations. SIZE: Small. PARK: Easy. FAIRS: Scientific & Medical Instrument.
TEL: 01736 757237

Tremayne Applied Arts

Street-an-Pol. TR26 2DS. (Roger Tonkinson)
EST. 1998. Summer - Open 10.30-4.30, Sat. 10-1.30. CL: Mon. and Tues. Winter - open Fri. and Sat. mornings. STOCK: *Furniture, china, glass, paintings and prints, late 19th to late 20th C, £50-£7,000.* LOC: Central, close to tourist information office. PARK: Station.
TEL: 01736 797779; FAX: 01736 793222; HOME: 01736 753537
E-MAIL: tonkinson@btinternet.com

TRURO

Blackwater Pine Antiques

Blackwater. TR4 8ET. (P. Day and L.M. Cropper)
EST. 2000. Open 10-5.30; CL: Weds. STOCK: *Pine and country furniture.* LOC: On main road through village. SER: Restorations; stripping; furniture made to order. SIZE: Medium. PARK: Nearby.
TEL: 01872 560919

Bonython Bookshop
16 Kenwyn St. TR1 3BU. (Rosemary Carpenter)
EST. 1996. Open 10.30-4.30. STOCK: *Books especially Cornish, £5-£1,000; topography and art, £5-£1,000.* SER: Valuations; book search. SIZE: Small.
TEL: 01872 262886
E-MAIL: bonythonbooks@btconnect.com

Bowden-Smith Antiques
7d New Bridge St. TR1 2AA. (Craig Bowden-Smith)
Open 9.30-5. STOCK: *Furniture, silver, porcelain, works of art.* LOC: Eastern side of cathedral. SER: Restoration (furniture, porcelain). PARK: 100 yds. from shop.
TEL: 01872 273296; MOBILE: 07968 184402
E-MAIL: bencraigsmith@aol.com

Collector's Corner
45-46 Pannier Market, Back Quay. TR1 2LL. (Alan McLoughlin and John Lethbridge)
EST. 1980. Open 10-4. STOCK: *Stamps, coins, postcards, medals, postal history, militaria, £5-£1,500.* LOC: City centre. SER: Valuations. SIZE: Small. PARK: Nearby.
TEL: 01872 272729; HOME: 01326 573509; MOBILE: 07815 668551
WEBSITE: www.militarycollectables.co.uk

Once Upon A Time
The Coinage Hall, 1 Boscawen St. TR1 2QU. (Paul Booth)

EST. 1994. Open 11-4.30. STOCK: *Fine art, furniture, paintings, sculpture, lighting, architectural items, collectables including postcards.* LOC: City centre. SER: Restorations (furniture, French polishing, cabinet making, upholstery). SIZE: Medium. PARK: Easy.
TEL: 01872 262520
E-MAIL: pboothantiques@btconnect.com

Reg and Philip Remington
Belvedere, Newbridge, TR3 6BN.
EST. 1979. Open by appointment only. STOCK: *Books on voyages and travels, 17th-20th C, £5-£1,000.* SER: Buys at auction. SIZE: Medium. VAT: Stan. FAIRS: London Book; Olympia.
TEL: 01872 279820
E-MAIL: philip@remingtonbooks.com
WEBSITE: www.remingtonbooks.com

WADEBRIDGE

Victoria Antiques
21 Molesworth St. PL27 7DQ. (M. and S. Daly)
Open Mon.-Sat. STOCK: *Furniture, 17th-19th C, £25-£10,000.* LOC: On A39 between Bude and Newquay. SER: Valuations; restorations. SIZE: Large plus trade warehouse. PARK: Nearby. VAT: Stan/Spec/Global.
TEL: 01208 814160
E-MAIL: victorianantiques@macace.net

François Linke
1855-1946
The Belle Epoque of French Furniture

Christopher Payne

François Linke (1855-1946), born in Pankraz, Bohemia, is considered by many as the greatest Parisian cabinetmaker of his day, at a time when the worldwide influence of French fashion was at its height. His exquisitely finished, richly made furniture was produced for potentates and industrial magnates from Paris to New York, London to Buenos Aires, the Far East and the Cameroons. The son of a subsistence gardener, Linke trained under the strict disciplines of the Austro-Hungarian Empire and as a young man, travelled penniless, on foot, via Vienna to Paris in 1876. There he married the daughter of a local innkeeper and started a business in the days before electricity and the motor car, a business that continued, despite the loss of his two sons, through two world wars and the invention of atomic power. The *ancien régime* has always been the greatest source of inspiration for artistic design in France and, influenced amongst others by the de Goncourt brothers, the Louis XV and Louis XVI styles were revived to wide popular appeal. During the Second Empire these styles were so eclectic that they became debased. Linke wanted to create a fresh new style and his association with the enigmatic sculptor Léon Messagé resulted in a highly original series of designs, based on the rococo style fused with the latest fashion in Paris, l'art nouveau. The book, with 140,000 words of text and over 700 unique photographs, many previously unpublished and drawn from Linke's own archive and private collections, has ten chapters showing the development of this exacting and prolific man's life work.

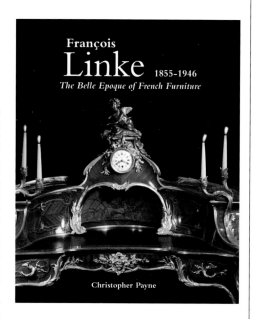

Specifications:
528pp., 200 col. illus., 500 b.&w. illus.,
11¼ x 9¼in./285 x 238mm.
£75.00 (hardback)

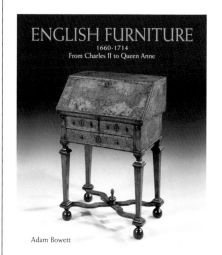

Adam Bowett

ENGLISH FURNITURE
1660-1714
from Charles II to Queen Anne

Adam Bowett

English Furniture describes the development of fashionable English furniture between the restoration of Charles II in 1660 and the death of Queen Anne in 1714. Based largely on contemporary documents and on original and firmly documented furniture, together with the latest modern scholarship, it provides a closely-reasoned analysis of changing furniture styles, together with much technical information on materials and processes. The author's radical new approach to the stylistic and structural analysis of furniture will change perceptions of English furniture and establish a new chronology for late seventeenth and early eighteenth century English furniture. This extensively illustrated book is the first comprehensive review of the subject for nearly one hundred years. Part one focuses on Charles II and James II, 1660-1688 with chapters on The Restoration, Case Furniture, Seat Furniture, Tables, Stands and Mirrors and Lacquer, Japanning and Varnish. The second part focuses on William III and Queen Anne, 1689-1714 and includes chapters on Furnishing the Williamite Court, Case Furniture, Seat Furniture, Tables, Stands and Looking Glasses. A full bibliography is included.

Specifications: 328pp., 465 col. illus.,
59 b.&w. illus., 11¼ x 9¼in./310 x 234mm.
£45.00 (hardback)

For full details of all ACC publications, log on to our website:
www.antiquecollectorsclub.com
or telephone 01394 389950 for a free catalogue

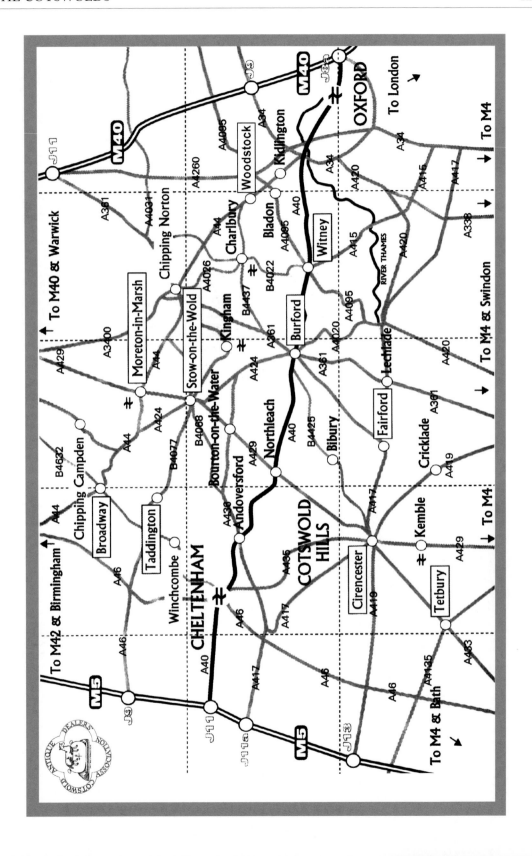

THE COTSWOLD ANTIQUE DEALERS' ASSOCIATION

Buy Fine Antiques and Works of Art at provincial prices in England's lovely and historic countryside

The Cotswolds, one of the finest areas of unspoilt countryside in the land, have been called "the essence and the heart of England." The region has a distinctive character created by the use of honey-coloured stone in its buildings and dry stone walls. Within the locality the towns and villages are admirably compact and close to each other and the area is well supplied with good hotels and reasonably priced inns. The Cotswolds are within easy reach of London (1½ hours by road or rail) and several major airports.

Cotswold sheep – which inspired the logo for the Cotswold Antique Dealers' Association – a quatrefoil device with a sheep in its centre – have played an important part in the region's history with much of its wealth created by the woollen industry. As for antiques, shops and Galleries of the CADA offer a selection of period furniture, pictures, porcelain, metalwork and collectables unrivalled outside London.

With the use of the CADA directory on the following pages, which lists the names of its members, their specialities and opening times, visitors from all over the world can plan their buying visit to the Cotswolds. CADA members will assist all visiting collectors and dealers in locating antiques and works of art. They will give you advice on where to stay in the area, assistance with packing, shipping and insurance and the exchange of foreign currencies. They can advise private customers on what can realistically be bought on their available budgets, and if the first dealer does not have the piece which you are selecting he will know of several other members who will. The CADA welcomes home and overseas buyers in the certain knowledge that there are at least forty dealers with a good and varied stock and a reputation for fair trading.

www.cotswolds-antiques-art.com

BROADWAY

Stephen Cook Antiques   BADA
58 High Street. WR12 7DT. (Stephen Cook)
CADA. Open 10-5. *Stock: 17th - 19th century oak,*
walnut, mahogany furniture and 18th century English
Delft. Loc: Opp. H.W. Keil. Size: 800 sq. ft. Park: At
front but time limited. Vat: Spec.
Tel: 01386 854716
E-mail: stephen@scookantiques.com
Website: www.scookantiques.com

Haynes Fine Art of Broadway   BADA LAPADA
Picton House Galleries, 42 High St. WR12 7DT.
(A.C. Haynes)
Est. 1971. CADA. Open 9-6. *Stock: Over 2000*
British and European 16th-21st C oil paintings and
watercolours. Loc: From Lygon Arms, 100 yards up
High St. on left. Ser: Valuations; restorations;
framing; catalogue available (£10). Size: Large - 12
showrooms. Park: Easy. Vat: Spec. Fairs: Olympia
(Summer & Winter), BADA, Harrogate (Spring &
Autumn).
Tel: 01386 852649; Fax: 01386 858187;
Mobile: 07831 893465 or 07710 108891
E-mail: email@haynesfineart.com
Website: www.haynesfineart.com

H.W. Keil Ltd   BADA
Tudor House, High St. WR12 7DP. (John Keil)
Est. 1925. CADA. Open 9.30-12.45 and 2.15-5.30,
Sat. by appointment. *Stock: Walnut, oak, mahogany*
and rosewood furniture; early pewter, brass and copper,
tapestry and works of art, 16th to early 19th C. Loc: By
village clock. Ser: Restorations. Size: Large - 12
showrooms. Park: Private by arrangement. Vat:
Spec.
Tel: 01386 852408; Fax: 01386 852069
E-mail: info@hwkeil.co.uk

John Noott Galleries   BADA LAPADA
20 High St., 14 Cotswold Court, WR12 7AA. (John,
Pamela and Amanda Noott)
Est. 1972. CADA. Open 9.30-5; 11-5 Sun. *Stock:*
Paintings, watercolours and bronzes, 19th C to
contemporary. Ser: Valuations; restorations; framing.
Size: Large. Park: Easy. Vat: Stan/Spec.
Tel: 01386 854868/858969; Fax: 01386 854919
E-mail: info@john-noott.com
Website: www.john-noott.com

BURFORD

Jonathan Fyson Antiques
50 High St. OX18 4QF. (J.R. Fyson)
Est. 1970. CADA. Open 9.30-1 and 2-5.30, Sat. from
10. *Stock: English and Continental furniture, decorative*
brass and steel including lighting and fireplace accessories;
mirrors, porcelain, table glass, jewellery. Loc: At junction

of A40/A361 between Oxford and Cheltenham. Ser:
Valuations. Size: Medium. Park: Easy. Vat: Spec.
Tel: 01993 823204; Fax: same; Home: 01367 860223
E-mail: j@fyson.co.uk

Gateway Antiques
Cheltenham Rd., Burford Roundabout. OX18 4JA.
(M.C. Ford and P. Brown)
Est. 1986. CADA. Open 10-5.30 and Sun. 1-4 *Stock:*
English and Continental furniture, 18th to early 20th C;
decorative accessories. Loc: On roundabout (A40)
Oxford/Cheltenham road, adjacent to the Cotswold
Gateway Hotel. Size: Large. Park: Easy. Vat:
Stan/Spec.
Tel: 01993 823678/822624; Fax: 01993 823857
E-mail: enquiries@gatewayantiques.co.uk
Website: www.gatewayantiques.co.uk

David Pickup   BADA
115 High St. OX18 4RG.
Est. 1977. CADA. Open 9.30-1 and 2-5.30, Sat. 10-1
and 2-4. *Stock: Fine furniture, works of art, from £500+;*
decorative objects, from £100+; all late 17th to mid 20th C,
specialising in Arts and Crafts. Size: Medium. Park:
Easy. Vat: Spec. Fairs: Olympia.
Tel: 01993 822555

Manfred Schotten Antiques
109 High St. OX18 4RG.
Est. 1974. CADA. Open 9.30-5.30 or by appointment.
Stock: Sporting antiques and library furniture. Ser:
Restorations; trophies. Size: 3 floors and trade warehouse
by appointment. Park: Easy. Vat: Stan/Margin. Fairs:
Olympia (Summer & Winter).
Tel: 01993 822302; Fax: 01993 822055
E-mail: antiques@schotten.com
Website: www.schotten.com

CIRENCESTER

William H. Stokes   BADA
The Cloisters, 6/8 Dollar St. GL7 2AJ. (W.H. Stokes
and P.W. Bontoft)
Est. 1968. CADA. Open 9.30-5.30, Sat. 9.30-4.30.
Stock: Early oak furniture, £1,000-£50,000; brassware,
£150-£5,000; all 16th-17th C. Loc: West of parish
church out of Market Place. Vat: Spec.
Tel: 01285 653907; Fax: 01285 640533
E-mail: post@williamhstokes.co.uk
Website: www.williamhstokes.co.uk

Patrick Waldron Antiques
18 Dollar St. GL7 2AN.
Est. 1965. Resident. CADA. Open 9.30-1 and 2-6, Sun.
by appointment. *Stock: Town and country furniture, 17th*
to early 19th C. Loc: In street behind church. Ser:
Restorations (furniture); buys at auction. Size: Medium.
Park: Easy and public behind shop. Vat: Stan/Spec.
Tel: 01285 652880; Workshop: 01285 643479

FAIRFORD

Blenheim Antiques
Market Place. GL7 4AB. (N. Hurdle)
EST. 1972. CADA. Resident. Open 9.30-6. *STOCK: 18th-19th C furniture and accessories.* SIZE: Medium. PARK: Easy. VAT: Stan/Spec.
TEL: 01285 712094

MORETON-IN-MARSH

Astley House - Contemporary
Astley House, London Rd. GL56 0LE. (David, Nanette and Caradoc Glaisyer)
EST. 1973. CADA. Open 10-1 and 2-5 and by appointment. CL: Wed. *STOCK: Oil paintings, 19th-21st C; large decorative oils and portraits, jewellery, ceramics, glass.* LOC: Town centre. SER: Restorations (oils and watercolours); framing (porcelain). SIZE: Large. PARK: Easy. VAT: Spec.
TEL: 01608 650608; FAX: 01608 651777
E-MAIL: astart333@aol.com
WEBSITE: www.contemporaryart-uk.com

Astley House - Fine Art
Astley House, High St. GL56 0LL. (David, Nanette and Caradoc Glaisyer)
EST. 1973. CADA. Open 9-5.30 and by appointment. *STOCK: Oil paintings, 19th-21st C, £800-£20,000.* LOC: Main street. SER: Restorations (oils and watercolours); framing. SIZE: Medium. PARK: Easy. VAT: Spec.
TEL: 01608 650601; FAX: 01608 651777
E-MAIL: astart333@aol.com
WEBSITE: www.art-uk.com;
www.contemporaryart-uk.com

The John Davies Gallery
6 Fosseway Business Park. GL56 9NQ.
EST. 1977. CADA. Open 9-1, 2-5.30. *STOCK: Contemporary and period paintings; limited edition bronzes.* LOC: A429 Fosseway. Own gate access to M.-in-M. train station. SER: Restorations and conservation to museum standard. SIZE: Large. VAT: Spec/Margin.
TEL: 01608 652255
WEBSITE: www.johndaviesgallery.com

Jon Fox Antiques
High St. GL56 0AD.
EST. 1983. CADA. Open 9.30-5.30, Tues. by appointment. *STOCK: 19th C garden items including urns, seats, troughs and tools, £50-£5,000+; 18th -19th C country furniture £300-£3,000; treen, bygones, metalware, fireplace and medical items.* SIZE: Large - 2 adjacent shops. PARK: Easy. VAT: Spec.
TEL: 01608 650325
E-MAIL: jonfoxantiques@tiscali.co.uk
WEBSITE: www.jonfoxantiques.com

STOW-ON-THE-WOLD

Duncan J. Baggott   LAPADA
Woolcomber House, Sheep St. GL54 1AA. (D.J. and C.M. Baggott)
EST. 1967. CADA. Open 9-5.30 or by appointment. CL: BH. *STOCK: 17th-20th C English oak, mahogany and walnut furniture, paintings, domestic metalwork and decorative items; garden statuary and ornaments.* SER: Worldwide shipping; UK delivery. SIZE: Large. PARK: Sheep St. or Market Sq. FAIRS: Exhibition Oct. annually (CADA).
TEL: 01451 830662; FAX: 01451 832174
E-MAIL: info@baggottantiques.com
WEBSITE: www.baggottantiques.com

Baggott Church Street Ltd   BADA
Church St. GL54 1BB. (D.J. and C.M. Baggott)
EST. 1978. CADA. Open 9.30-5.30 or by appointment. CL: BH. *STOCK: 17th-19th C English oak, mahogany and walnut furniture, portrait paintings, metalwork, pottery, treen and decorative items.* LOC: South-west corner of market square. SER: Annual exhibition - Oct. (CADA). SIZE: Large. PARK: Market Square/Sheep Street.
TEL: 01451 830370; FAX: 01451 832174
E-MAIL: info@baggottantiques.com
WEBSITE: www.baggottantiques.com

Black Ink   LAPADA
7A Talbot Court. GL54 1BQ. (David Stoddart)
EST. 1990. CADA. CINOA. Open 10-4, Sat. 10-5. CL: Tues. *STOCK: Artists' original etchings, lithographs, woodcuts and aquatints, especially 1860-1930, with emphasis on the Impressionists - Renoir, Pisarro, Gauguin, Manet, Cézanne; also works by modern artists such as Terry Frost, Mary Fedden, Ben Nicholson, etc.* SIZE: Medium. PARK: Free - town square. FAIRS: LAPADA; Cheltenham; National Fine Arts & Antiques Fair, NEC.
TEL: 01451 870022; MOBILE: 07721 454840
E-MAIL: art@blackinkprints.com
WEBSITE: www.blackinkprints.com

Christopher Clarke Antiques Ltd   LAPADA
The Fosseway. GL54 1JS. (Simon and Sean Clarke)
EST. 1961. CADA. Open 9.30-5.30 or by appointment. *STOCK: Specialists in campaign furniture and travel items.* LOC: Corner of The Fosseway and Sheep St. SIZE: Large. PARK: Easy. FAIRS: Olympia (June, Nov); CADA Exhibition.
TEL: 01451 830476; FAX: 01451 830300
E-MAIL: clarkeltd@btconnect.com
WEBSITE: www.campaignfurniture.com

Cotswold Galleries
The Square. GL54 1AB. (Richard and Cherry Glaisyer)
EST. 1961. CADA. FATG. Open 9-5.30 or by appointment. *STOCK: Oil paintings especially 19th-20th C*

landscape. SIZE: Large. PARK: Easy.
TEL: 01451 870567; FAX: 01451 870678
WEBSITE: www.cotswoldgalleries.com

Keith Hockin Antiques   BADA
The Square. GL54 1AF.
EST. 1968. CADA. **Open Thurs., Fri. and Sat. 10-5,
other times by appointment or ring the bell.** *STOCK:
Oak furniture, 1600-1750; country furniture in oak,
fruitwoods, yew, 1700-1850; pewter, copper, brass,
ironwork, all periods. NOT STOCKED: Mahogany.* SER:
Buys at auction (oak, pewter, metalwork). SIZE:
Medium. PARK: **Easy.** VAT: **Stan/Spec.**
TEL: **01451 831058**
E-MAIL: **keithhockin@ruralsat_net**
WEBSITE: **www.keithhockin.com**

Huntington Antiques Ltd   LAPADA
Church St. GL54 1BE. (M.F. and S.P. Golding)
EST. 1974. CADA. CINOA. **Resident. Open 9.30-5.30
or by appointment.** *STOCK: Early period and fine country
furniture, metalware, tapestries and works of art.* LOC:
Opposite main gates to church. SER: **Valuations; buys
at auction.** SIZE: **Large.** PARK: **Own.** VAT: **Spec.**
TEL: **01451 830842; FAX: 01451 832211**
E-MAIL: **info@huntington-antiques.com**
WEBSITE: **www.huntington-antiques.com**

Roger Lamb Antiques & Works of Art   LAPADA
The Square. GL54 1AB.
EST. 1993. CADA. **Open 10-5 or by appointment.**
*STOCK: Fine 18th to early 19th C furniture especially
small items, lighting, decorative accessories, oils and
watercolours.* LOC: **Next to town hall.** SER: **Search.**
SIZE: **3 main showrooms.** PARK: **Easy.** FAIRS: **Olympia
(June and November).**
TEL: **01451 831371; MOBILE: 07860 391959**
E-MAIL: **rl@rogerlamb.com**
WEBSITE: **www.rogerlambantiques.com**

Antony Preston Antiques Ltd   BADA
The Square. GL54 1AB.
EST. 1965. CADA. CINOA. **Open 9.30-5.30 or by
appointment.** *STOCK: 18th-19th C English and
Continental furniture and objects; barometers and period
lighting.* LOC: **Town centre.** SIZE: **Large.** PARK: **Easy.**
VAT: **Stan/Spec.** FAIRS: **BADA.**
TEL: **01451 831586; FAX: 01451 831596;**
MOBILE: **07785 975599**
E-MAIL: **antony@antonypreston.com**
WEBSITE: **www.antonypreston.com**

Queens Parade Antiques Ltd   BADA
The Square. GL54 1AB. (Sally and Antony Preston)
EST. 1985. CADA. CINOA. **Open 9.30-5.30.** *STOCK:
18th to early 19th C furniture, decorative objects,
needlework, tole and period lighting.* LOC: **Town centre.**
SIZE: **Large.** PARK: **Easy.** VAT: **Stan/Spec.** FAIRS:
BADA.

TEL: **01451 831586; FAX: 01451 831596**
E-MAIL: **antony@antonypreston.com**
WEBSITE: **www.antonypreston.com**

Ruskin Decorative Arts
5 Talbot Court. GL54 1DP. (Anne and William Morris)
EST. 1990. CADA. **Open 10-1 and 2-5.30.** *STOCK:
Interesting and unusual decorative objects, Arts and Crafts
furniture, Art Nouveau, Art Deco, glass and pottery,
metalwork, 1880-1960.* LOC: Between The Square and
Sheep St. SER: Valuations. SIZE: Small. PARK: Nearby.
TEL: 01451 832254; HOME: 01993 831880
E-MAIL: william.anne@ruskindecarts.co.uk
WEBSITE: www.ruskindecarts.co.uk

The Titian Gallery   BADA LAPADA
Sheep St. GL54 1JS. (Ilona Johnson Gibbs)
EST. 1978. CADA. CINOA. **Open 10-5 and by
appointment. CL: Mon.** *STOCK: Fine 18th-19th C
British and European oil paintings and watercolours,
£1,000-£40,000.* LOC: **Opposite the Unicorn Hotel,
near The Fosseway.** SER: **Valuations; commissions (oils
and watercolours); advice on collections.** SIZE:
Medium. PARK: **Adjacent and nearby.** VAT: **Spec.**
FAIRS: **CADA exhibition.**
TEL: **01451 830004; FAX: 01451 830126**
E-MAIL: **ilona@titiangallery.co.uk**
WEBSITE: **www.titiangallery.co.uk**

STRETTON-ON-FOSSE

Astley House - Fine Art
The Old School. GL56 9SA. (David, Nanette and
Caradoc Glaisyer)
EST. 1973. CADA. **Open by appointment.** *STOCK: Large
decorative oil paintings, 19th-21st C.* LOC: Village centre.
SER: Exhibitions; mailing list. SIZE: Large. PARK: Easy.
VAT: Spec.
TEL: 01608 650601; FAX: 01608 651777
E-MAIL: astart333@aol.com
WEBSITE: www.art-uk.com

TADDINGTON

Architectural Heritage
Taddington Manor. GL54 5RY. (Adrian, Suzy, and
Alex Puddy)
EST. 1978. CADA. **Open 9.30-5.30, Sat. 10.30-4.30.**
*STOCK: Oak and pine period panelled rooms; stone and
marble chimney pieces; stone, marble, bronze and terracotta
statuary; garden ornaments, fountains, temples, well-heads,
seats, urns, cisterns, sundials and summer houses.* SER:
**Worldwide delivery; shipping; bespoke ornaments,
chimneypieces and panelled rooms.** SIZE: **Large.** PARK:
Easy. VAT: **Stan.** FAIRS: **Chelsea Flower Show.**
TEL: 01386 584414 FAX: 01386 584236
E-MAIL: puddy@architectural-heritage.co.uk
WEBSITE: www.architectural-heritage.co.uk

TETBURY

Philip Adler Antiques
32 Long Street. GL8 8AQ.
CADA. Open 10-6 and by appointment. *STOCK: Decorative furniture and objects from the 17th and 18th centuries.*
TEL: 01666 505759; FAX: 01452 770525
E-MAIL: philipadlerantiques@hotmail.com
WEBSITE: www.philipadlerantiques.com

Alderson
61 Long St. GL8 8AA. (C.J.R. Alderson)
EST. 1977. CADA. Open 10-5. *STOCK: British 18th-19th C furniture and works of art; British colonial furniture.* SER: Valuations. SIZE: Medium. PARK: Easy. FAIRS: Olympia.
TEL: 01666 500888; MOBILE: 07836 594498
E-MAIL: kit.alderson@btopenworld.com

Breakspeare Antiques
36 and 57 Long St. GL8 8AQ. (M. and S.E. Breakspeare)
EST. 1962. CADA. Resident. Open 10-5 or by appointment. CL: Thurs. *STOCK: English period furniture - early walnut, 1690-1740, mahogany, 1750-1835.* LOC: Main street - four gables building. SIZE: Medium. PARK: Own. VAT: Spec.
TEL: 01666 503122; FAX: same.

Day Antiques   BADA
5 New Church St. GL8 8DS.
EST. **1975.** CADA. Open 10-5. *STOCK: Early oak furniture and related items.* SIZE: **Medium.** PARK: **Easy.** VAT: **Spec.**
TEL: **01666 502413**
E-MAIL: dayantiques@lineone.net
WEBSITE: www.dayantiques.com

WITNEY

Colin Greenway Antiques
90 Corn St. OX28 6BU.
EST. 1975. CADA. Resident. Open 9.30-5, Sat. 10-4, Sun. by appointment. *STOCK: Furniture, 17th-20th C; fireplace implements and baskets, metalware, decorative and unusual items; garden furniture, rocking horses.* SIZE: Large. PARK: Easy. VAT: Stan/Spec. FAIRS: Newark.
TEL: 01993 705026; FAX: same; MOBILE: 07831 585014
E-MAIL: jean_greenway@hotmail.com

W.R. Harvey & Co (Antiques) Ltd   LAPADA
86 Corn St. OX28 6BU.
EST. 1950. CADA. GMC. CINOA. Open 9.30-5.30 and by appointment. *STOCK: Fine English furniture, £500-£150,000; clocks, mirrors, objets d'art, pictures, £250-£50,000; all 1680-1830.* LOC: 300 yards from Market Place. SER: Valuations; restorations; consultancy. SIZE: Large. PARK: Easy. VAT: Stan/Spec. FAIRS: Chelsea (Sept.); Olympia (June and Nov.); NEC (Jan.); Lapada (May).
TEL: 01993 706501; FAX: 01993 706601

Witney Antiques

LSA & CJ JARRETT AND RR SCOTT
96-100 CORN STREET, WITNEY,
OXON OX28 6BU, ENGLAND.
TEL: 01993 703902. FAX: 01993 779852.
E-mail: witneyantiques@community.co.uk
Website: www.witneyantiques.com

A fine bracket clock by Haley & Son, London. English. Circa 1830.

ANTIQUE FURNITURE,
TEXTILES & CLOCKS.

E-MAIL: antiques@wrharvey.co.uk
WEBSITE: www.wrharvey.co.uk

Witney Antiques   BADA LAPADA
96/100 Corn St. OX28 6BU. (L.S.A. and C.J. Jarrett and R.R. Scott)
EST. 1962. CADA. Open 10-5, Mon. and Tues. by appointment. *STOCK: English furniture, 17th-18th C; bracket and longcase clocks, mahogany, oak and walnut; early needlework and samplers.* LOC: From Oxford on old A40 through Witney via High St., turn right at T-junction, 400yds. on right. SER: Restorations. SIZE: Large. PARK: Easy. VAT: Spec. FAIRS: BADA; Grosvenor House.
TEL: 01993 703902/703887; FAX: 01993 779852
E-MAIL: witneyantiques@community.co.uk
WEBSITE: www.witneyantiques.com

WOODSTOCK

John Howard   BADA
Heritage, 6 Market Place. OX20 1TA.
CADA. Open 10-5.30. *STOCK: 18th-19th C British pottery especially rare Staffordshire animal figures, bocage figures, lustre, 18th C creamware and unusual items.* SER: Packing; insurance service to USA. SIZE: Medium. PARK: Easy. VAT: Spec. FAIRS: Olympia; NEC.
TEL: 01993 812580; FAX: same; MOBILE: 07831 850544
E-MAIL: john@johnhoward.co.uk
WEBSITE: www.antiquepottery.co.uk

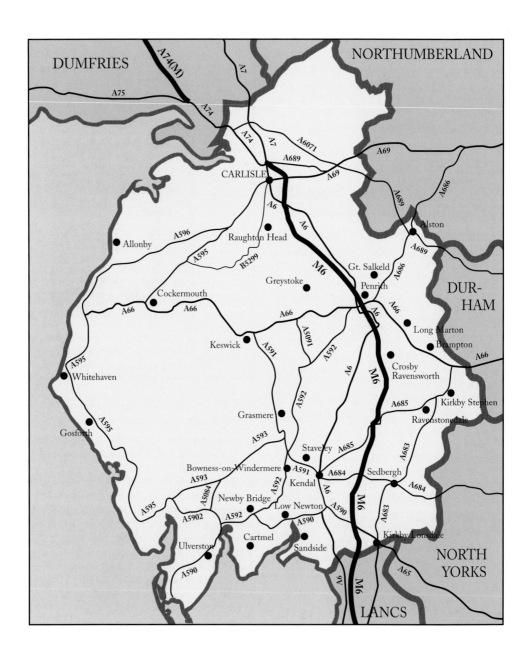

ALLONBY

Cottage Curios
Main St. CA15 6PX. (B. Pickering)
EST. 1965. Open Sat. and Sun. 2-5.

ALSTON

Alston Antiques
Front St. CA9 3HU. (Mrs J. Bell)
EST. 1976. Open 10-5, Sun. 12.30-5. CL: Tues. *STOCK:
General antiques.* SIZE: Medium. PARK: Easy.
TEL: 01434 382129; MOBILE: 07876 501929

Just Glass
Cross House, Market Place. CA9 3HS. (M.J. Graham)
EST. 1987. Open Wed., Thurs., Sat. 11-4, Sun. 12-4 or
by appointment. *STOCK: Glass, 1700-1930s, to £800.*
LOC: Town centre. PARK: Easy. FAIRS: Naworth Castle.
TEL: 01434 381263; MOBILE: 07833 994948

APPLEBY-IN-WESTMORLAND

David Hill
Town End, Gt. Ashby. CA16 6EX.
EST. 1965. Open Sat. by appointment. *STOCK: Country
clocks and furniture, 18th-19th C, £10-£1,000; glassware,
£5-£75; curios, £5-£50; shipping goods, kitchenalia, iron and
brassware.* SIZE: Medium. PARK: Easy.
TEL: 01768 352039

BRAMPTON

The Cumbrian Antiques Centre
St Martin's Hall, Front St. CA8 1NT. (S.T.
Summerson-Wright)
EST. 1976. Open 10-5, Sun. 12-5. *STOCK: Wide range of
general antiques from silver and china to longcase clocks and
furniture.* LOC: A69 Carlisle to Newcastle road into town
centre, premises on right as road forks. SER: Valuations;
restorations. SIZE: Large - 2 floors. PARK: Easy.
TEL: 01697 742741 or 01697 742515; FAX: same;
MOBILE: 07889 924843
E-MAIL: cumbrianantiques@hotmail.com
WEBSITE: www.cumbrianantiques.co.uk

BROUGH

The Book House
Grand Prix Buildings. CA17 4AY. (Brigid Irwin)
EST. 1963. PBFA. Open 10-4.30. CL: Mon. Prior
telephone call advisable if travelling any distance. *STOCK:
Books, mainly 19th-20th C, £1-£1,000.* LOC: Off A66.
North end of village main street. PARK: Easy. VAT: Stan.
FAIRS: Northern PBFA.
TEL: 01768 342748
E-MAIL: mail@thebookhouse.co.uk
WEBSITE: www.thebookhouse.co.uk

The Antique Shop
*Fine English antique furniture,
also decorative items*

Open 10.00am – 5.00pm
every day including Sunday

CARTMEL
NEAR GRANGE-OVER-SANDS
CUMBRIA
TELEPHONE 015395-36295
MOBILE TELEPHONE 07768 443757
Email: anthemioncartmel@aol.com
www.anthemionantiques.co.uk

CARLISLE

Carlisle Antiques Centre
Cecil Hall, Cecil St. CA1 1NT. (Wendy Mitton)
Open 9-4. *STOCK: Fine period furniture, porcelain,
jewellery, textiles glass and silver.* LOC: M6 junction 43.
SER: Repairs (clocks). PARK: Easy. FAIRS: Naworth
Castle, Brampton (March and Aug).
TEL: 01228 536910; FAX: same.
E-MAIL: wendymitton@aol.com
WEBSITE: www.carlisle-antiques.co.uk

Saint Nicholas Galleries Ltd. (Antiques and Jewellery)
39 Bank St. CA3 8HJ. (C.J. Carruthers)
Open 10-5. CL: Mon. *STOCK: Jewellery, diamond rings,
silver, plate, Rolex and pocket watches, clocks; collectables;
Royal Doulton; Dux, Oriental vases; pottery, porcelain;
watercolours, oil paintings; brass and copper.* LOC: City
centre. SIZE: Medium. PARK: Nearby.
TEL: 01228 544459

Souvenir Antiques
Long Lane, Castle St. CA3 8TA. (J. Higham)
EST. 1985. Open Wed., Fri. and Sat. 11-3 or later. *STOCK:
Ceramics and collectables, crested china, local prints, maps,
postcards, Roman and medieval coins, antiquities and jewellery,
fossils and minerals. NOT STOCKED: Textiles.* LOC: City centre,
off Castle St. SIZE: Small. PARK: Castle St.
TEL: 01228 401281; MOBILE: 07803 107429

WEBSITE: www.souvenirantiques.co.uk and www.cumbriamaps.co.uk

CARTMEL

Anthemion - The Antique Shop   BADA LAPADA
LA11 6QD. (J. Wood)
EST. 1982. Open 10-5 including Sun. STOCK: *English period furniture, mainly walnut and mahogany, 17th to early 19th C, £500-£50,000; decorative items, 17th-19th C, £100-£5,000; paintings and prints, 19th-20th C, £400-£8,000. NOT STOCKED: Victoriana, bric-a-brac.* LOC: Village centre. SIZE: Large. PARK: Easy. VAT: Stan/Spec. FAIRS: Olympia (Nov/June); Harrogate (April/Sept). TEL: **01539 536295**; MOBILE: **07768 443757**
E-MAIL: **anthemioncartmel@aol.com**
WEBSITE: **www.anthemionantiques.co.uk**

Norman Kerr - Gatehouse Bookshop
The Square. LA11 6PX. (H. and J.M. Kerr)
EST. 1933. PBFA. Open Wed. - Sat. afternoons or by appointment. STOCK: *Antiquarian and secondhand books.* SER: Valuations; book search; antiquarian books bought. TEL: 01539 536247
E-MAIL: enquiries@kerrbooks.co.uk

Simon Starkie Antiques
Gatehouse Cottage, Cavendish St. LA11 6QA.
EST. 1980. Open Wed., Fri. and Sat. 10.30-4.30, Sun. 11.30-4.30 and by appointment. STOCK: *Oak furniture, 17th-19th C, £100-£8,000; painted country furniture and clocks, 18th-19th C, £50-£2,500; Delftware and pewter, 18th-19th C, £30-£1,000.* LOC: 10 miles from junction 36 M6, follow signs for Cartmel priory. SER: Valuations; buys at auction (furniture and earthenware). SIZE: Medium. PARK: Ample. VAT: Stan/Spec.
TEL: 015395 36453; HOME: 01229 861222

COCKERMOUTH

CG's Curiosity Shop
43 Market Place. CA13 9LT. (Colin Graham)
EST. 1985. Open 10-12.30 and 1.30-5. STOCK: *China, glass, collectables, militaria, books, linen, furniture, advertising, radios and unusual items, from 1800, £5-£1,000+.* LOC: End of main street, over the bridge, first shop in Market Place. SER: Valuations; restorations; buys at auction; internet search. SIZE: Medium. PARK: Nearby. FAIRS: Newark.
TEL: 01900 824418; HOME: 01697 321108;
MOBILE: 07712 206786
E-MAIL: cgcuriosity@hotmail.com
WEBSITE: www.cgcuriosityshop.fws1.com

Cockermouth Antiques
5 Station St. CA13 9QW. (E. Bell and G. Davies)
EST. 1983. Open 10-5. STOCK: *General antiques especially jewellery, silver, ceramics, furniture, pictures, glass, books, metalware, quilts.* LOC: Just off A66, in town centre. SIZE: Large. PARK: Easy.

TEL: 01900 826746
E-MAIL: elainebell54@aol.com

Cockermouth Antiques Market
Courthouse, Main St. CA13 9LU.
EST. 1979. Open 10-5. STOCK: *Victorian, Edwardian and Art Deco items, furniture, printed collectables, postcards, books, linen, china, glass, textiles, jewellery and pictures.* LOC: Town centre, just off A66. SER: Restorations (furniture); stripping (pine). SIZE: Large - 4 stallholders. PARK: 50 yds. VAT: Stan/Spec.
TEL: 01900 824346

CROSBY RAVENSWORTH

Jennywell Hall Antiques
CA10 3JP. (Mrs M. Macadie)
EST. 1975. Resident. Open most days, but telephone call advisable. STOCK: *Oak and mahogany furniture, paintings, interesting objects.* LOC: 5 miles from junction 39, M6. SIZE: Medium. PARK: Easy.
TEL: 01931 715288; HOME: same

GRASMERE

Lakes Crafts & Antiques Gallery
3 Oak Bank, Broadgate. LA22 9TA. (Joe and Sandra Arthy)
EST. 1990. Open 15th Mar.-31st Oct. 9.30-6 including Sun., other times 10-4.30. STOCK: *Books, 18th-20th C, £1-£500; collectables and postcards, £1-£100; general antiques, 17th-20th C, £5-£250, crafts and gifts.* LOC: North side of village, off A591 on Ambleside to Keswick road. SIZE: Medium. PARK: Easy. VAT: Stan.
TEL: 01539 435037; HOME: 01539 444234
E-MAIL: joea@dsl.pipex.com

GREAT SALKELD

G.K. Hadfield
Old Post Office. CA11 9LW. (G.K. and J.V. Hadfield (Hon. FBHI) and N.R. Hadfield-Tilly)
EST. 1966. MBHI. MBWCG. Open by appointment only. STOCK: *Clocks - longcase, dial, Act of Parliament, skeleton and carriage; secondhand, new and out of print horological books.* LOC: From M6, junction 40 take A686 towards Alston for 3 miles, left on B6412 signed Great Salkeld, about 1.5 miles, turn left at sign for Salkeld Dykes, 1st house on right. SER: Valuations (clocks and horological books). SIZE: Medium. VAT: Stan/Spec. FAIRS: BHI; Haydock Clock and Watch.
TEL: 01768 870111
E-MAIL: gkhadfield@dial.pipex.com
WEBSITE: www.gkhadfield-tilly.co.uk

GREYSTOKE

Roadside Antiques
Watsons Farm, Greystoke Gill. CA11 0UQ. (K. and R. Sealby)

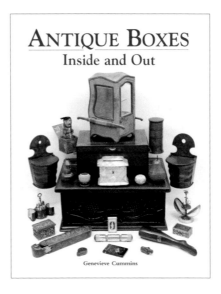
EST. 1988. Resident. Open 10-6 including Sun. *STOCK: Ceramics, longcase clocks, glass, Staffordshire figures, pot-lids, paintings, furniture, small collectables, jewellery, mainly 19th C, £5-£2,000.* LOC: B5288 Penrith/Keswick road to Greystoke, through village, first left then left again, premises second on right. SIZE: Medium. PARK: Easy.
TEL: 01768 483279

KENDAL

Architectural Antiques
146 Highgate. LA9 4HW. (G. Fairclough)
EST. 1984. Open 9.30-5. *STOCK: Fireplaces, hobs, grates, marble and wooden chimney pieces, cast-iron inserts; Victorian tiles and kitchen ranges, unusual architectural items, Flemish brass chandeliers, longcase clocks 1700-1840.* SER: Valuations; restorations. SIZE: Medium. PARK: Easy.
TEL: 01539 737147; FAX: same; MOBILE: 07801 440031
E-MAIL: gordonfairclough@aol.com

Dower House Antiques
(Mrs Blakemore)
Open by appointment. *STOCK: Pottery, porcelain, paintings, furniture, glass, Oriental, decorative.*
TEL: 01539 722778

The Silver Thimble
39 All Hallows Lane. LA9 4JH. (V. Ritchie)
EST. 1980. Open 10-4. *STOCK: Jewellery, silver, glass, linen and lace, porcelain, copper and brass.* LOC: Turn left at second set of traffic lights on main road into Kendal from south, shop 200yds. on right. SIZE: Large. PARK: Easy.

VAT: Spec.
TEL: 01539 731456
E-MAIL: gmvritchie@aol.com

Sleddall Hall Antiques Centre inc. Kendal Studios Antiques
Wildman St. LA9 6EN. (Robert and Andrew Aindow and Sleddall Hall Antiques Centre)
EST. 1950. Open 10.30-4. CL: Wed. Prior telephone call advisable. *STOCK: Ceramics, maps and prints, paintings, oak furniture, art pottery and clocks, coins and banknotes, antiquities.* LOC: Leave M6 at junction 37, follow one-way system, shop on left. SER: Finder; shipping. SIZE: Medium. PARK: Nearby. FAIRS: Rivington Barn; Colin Caggill Events; Reebok, Bolton.
TEL: 01539 723291 (24 hrs. answering service)
E-MAIL: robert@aindow.wanadoo.co.uk

Westmorland Clocks
Gillinggate. LA9 4HW. (G. and I. Fairclough)
EST. 2002. Open 9.30-5. *STOCK: Clocks, especially Lancashire and Lake District longcase.* SER: Valuations; restorations. SIZE: Small. PARK: Easy.
TEL: 01539 737147
WEBSITE: www.westmorlandclocks.com

KESWICK

The Country Bedroom and En-Suite
Lake Rd. CA12 5BZ. (W.I. Raw)
EST. 1981. Open 9.30-5. *STOCK: Brass beds, iron and brass beds, mattress and base sets for antique beds, mirrors, linen,*

quilts, £150-£2,000; traditional and contemporary bathroom accessories. LOC: *Top of Main St.* VAT: *Stan.*
TEL: 01768 774881; FAX: 01768 771424

Keswick Bookshop
4 Station St. CA12 5HT. (Jane and John Kinnaird)
EST. 1994. PBFA. Open April to end Oct. 10.30-5, and by appointment in winter. CL: Wed. STOCK: *Books, 18th-20th C; prints and maps, 18th-20th C.* LOC: Town centre. SIZE: Medium. PARK: Nearby. VAT: Stan/Spec.
TEL: 01768 775535; FAX: 01228 528567

John Young and Son (Antiques)   LAPADA
12-14 Main St. CA12 5JD. (J. W. Young)
EST. 1890. Open 9-5. STOCK: *17th-20th C furniture, clocks and decorative items.* LOC: *Town centre.* SIZE: Large. PARK: At rear. VAT: Stan/Spec.
TEL: **01768 773434**; FAX: **01768 773306**
E-MAIL: **antiques@johnyoungkeswick.co.uk**
WEBSITE: **www.johnyoungkeswick.co.uk**

KIRKBY LONSDALE

Architus Antiques
14 Main St. LA6 2AE. (J. Pearson)
EST. 1990. Open 10-4.30, Sat. 10-5.30. STOCK: *Victorian oil lamps, £100-£250; china and glass, jewellery and silver, Victorian to early 20th C.* LOC: First antique shop on left in village from A65 towards Kendal. SER: Valuations. SIZE: Medium.
TEL: 015242 72409; HOME: 015242 71517

Johnson & Johnson
New Rd. LA6 2AB. (D.J. Johnson)
EST. 1989. Open 11-4.30. CL: Mon. STOCK: *Period oak and walnut furniture, portraits, lamps and candlesticks; pewter, 17th-18th C.* LOC: Town centre. SIZE: Medium. PARK: Easy.
TEL: 01524 272916; HOME/FAX: 01539 552126;
MOBILE: 07714 146197
E-MAIL: contact@johnsonandpark.co.uk
WEBSITE: www.johnsonandpark.co.uk

KIRKBY STEPHEN

Haughey Antiques Ltd.   LAPADA
28/30 Market St. CA17 4QW. (D.M. Haughey)
EST. 1969. Open 10-5 or by appointment. STOCK: *17th-19th C oak, walnut and mahogany furniture, longcase clocks.* LOC: M6, junction 38, 10 mins. to east. SER: Valuations. SIZE: Large. PARK: Own. VAT: Stan/Spec.
FAIRS: Olympia (Summer and Winter).
TEL: **01768 371302**; FAX: **01768 372423**
E-MAIL: **info@haugheyantiques.co.uk**
WEBSITE: **www.haugheyantiques.co.uk**

LONG MARTON

Ben Eggleston Antiques Ltd
The Dovecote. CA16 6BJ. (Ben and Kay Eggleston)
EST. 1976. Open by appointment. STOCK: *Pine furniture, £5-£2,500.* LOC: 2 miles east of A66 between Appleby and Penrith. SIZE: Large. PARK: Easy.
TEL: 01768 361849
E-MAIL: ben@benegglestonantiques.co.uk

LOW NEWTON

W.R.S. Architectural Antiques Ltd
Yew Tree Barn. LA11 7RH. (Clive Wilson)
EST. 1986. SALVO. Open 10-5, Sun. 10.30-4.30. STOCK: *Architectural antiques and reclamation including fireplaces, period furniture, garden furniture and statuary.* LOC: Just off A590 on High Newton bypass. SER: Restorations (furniture); bespoke furniture/kitchens; picture framing. SIZE: Large barn. PARK: Free. VAT: Stan.
TEL: 01539 531498
E-MAIL: wrs@yewtreebarn.co.uk
WEBSITE: www.yewtreebarn.co.uk

NEWBIGGIN-ON-LUNE

Leigh Haworth Ltd.
Causeway End. CA17 4NY. (Peter and Brenda Haworth)
EST. 1965. Open by appointment. STOCK: *Scottish and Staithes Group paintings and watercolours, 1850-1950, £500-£60,000.* LOC: 6 miles from Junction 38 of the M6 on the road to Kirkby Stephen. SER: Valuations; restorations; commissions. PARK: Easy. VAT: Spec.
TEL: 01539 623236

E-MAIL: pvhaworth@yahoo.com
WEBSITE: www.peterhaworth.co.uk

NEWBY BRIDGE

Townhead Antiques   LAPADA
LA12 8NP. (C.P. Townley)
EST. **1960. Open 10-5. CL: Mon., Sun. by appointment.**
STOCK: *18th-19th C furniture, silver, porcelain, glass,
decorative pieces; clocks, pictures.* LOC: **A592. 1 mile from
Newby Bridge on the Windermere road.** SER:
Valuations. SIZE: **Large.** PARK: **Easy.** VAT: **Stan/Spec.**
TEL: **01539 531321;** FAX: **01539 530019**
E-MAIL: **townhead@aol.com**
WEBSITE: **www.townhead-antiques.com
www.townhead.com**

PENRITH

Antiques of Penrith
4 Corney Sq. CA11 7PX. (Sylvia Tiffin and Lilian
Cripps)
EST. 1964. Open 10-12 and 1.30-5, Sat. 10-1. CL: Wed.
STOCK: *Early oak and mahogany furniture, clocks, brass, copper,
glass, china, silver plate, metal, Staffordshire figures, curios,
paintings and collectables.* NOT STOCKED: *Jewellery, books, rugs.*
LOC: Near Town Hall. SIZE: Large. PARK: Easy.
TEL: 01768 862801

Brunswick Antiques
8 Brunswick Rd. CA11 7LU. (M. and L. Hodgson)
EST. 1985. Open 10-5. STOCK: *Furniture, clocks, pottery,
glass, metalware, 19th-20th C.* LOC: Town centre. SIZE:
Small. PARK: Easy. VAT: Spec.
TEL: 01768 899338; HOME: 01768 867164
E-MAIL: brunswickantiques@msn.com

Joseph James Antiques
Corney Sq. CA11 7PX. (G.R. Walker)
EST. 1970. Open 9-5. CL: Wed. STOCK: *Furniture and
upholstery, 18th C and Victorian, £10-£3,000; porcelain and
pottery, £5-£1,000; silver and plate, pictures, £2-£800; all
18th-19th C.* LOC: On the one-way system in the town,
100 yds. from the main shopping area (Middlegate), 50
yds. from the town hall. SER: Re-upholstery; soft
furnishings. SIZE: Medium. PARK: Easy and 100yds. VAT:
Stan.
TEL: 01768 862065

Penrith Coin and Stamp Centre
37 King St. CA11 7AY. (Mr and Mrs A. Gray)
EST. 1974. Resident. Open 9.30-5.15. CL: Wed. Sept.-
May. STOCK: *Coins, B.C. to date, 1p-£500; jewellery,
secondhand, £5-£500; Great Britain and Commonwealth
stamps.* LOC: Just off town centre. SER: Valuations; repairs
(jewellery). SIZE: Medium. PARK: Behind shop. VAT:
Stan.
TEL: 01768 864185; FAX: same

RAUGHTON HEAD

Cumbria Architectural Salvage
Birkshill. CA5 7DH. (K. Temple)
EST. 1988. SALVO. Open 9-5, Sat. 9-12. STOCK:
*Fireplaces, 1700-1930, £150-£2,000; kitchen ranges, cast
iron radiators, bathroom fittings, doors, church pews, bricks
and granite setts, building materials, sandstone, flags, oak
joists and beams, balusters and staircase parts.* LOC: 9 miles
SW of Carlisle. SER: Valuations; restorations (fireplaces
and ranges). SIZE: Medium. PARK: Easy.
TEL: 01697 476420; HOME/FAX: same
E-MAIL: khtemple@pentalk.org

SEDBERGH

R.F.G. Hollett and Son
6 Finkle St. LA10 5BZ. (R. F. G. and C. G. Hollett)
EST. 1951. ABA. Open by appointment only. STOCK:
*Antiquarian books, 15th-20th C, £20-£60,000+; maps, prints
and paintings, 17th-19th C, £20-£10,000+.* LOC: Town centre.
SER: Valuations. SIZE: Large. PARK: Free nearby. VAT: Stan.
TEL: 015396 20298; FAX: 015396 21396
E-MAIL: hollett@sedbergh.demon.co.uk
WEBSITE: www.holletts-rarebooks.co.uk

Westwood Books
Long Lane. LA10 5AH.
EST. 1976. ABA. PBFA. Open 10.30-5.30 including
Sun. STOCK: *Antiquarian and secondhand books on most
subjects, £2-£1,000.* SER: Valuations; buys at auction
(antiquarian books). VAT: Stan.
TEL: 01539 621233
E-MAIL: westwood.books@zen.co.uk

STAVELEY

Staveley Antiques
27-29 Main St. LA8 9LU. (P. John Corry)
EST. 1991. Open 10-5, Sun. by appointment. STOCK: *Brass
and iron bedsteads, 1830-1930, £200-£1,200; French walnut
bedsteads, from 1880, £500-£2,000; lighting, 1880-1935,
from £50.* LOC: Between Kendal and Windermere on
A591 (now bypassed). SER: Valuations; restorations (brass
and iron bedsteads, metalware). SIZE: Large. PARK: Easy.
TEL: 01539 821393; HOME: 01539 821123
E-MAIL: john@staveleyantiques.co.uk
WEBSITE: www.staveleyantiques.co.uk

WHITEHAVEN

Michael Moon - Antiquarian Booksellers
19 Lowther St. CA28 7AL. (M. Moon)
EST. 1970. SBA. PBFA. Open 9.30-5. STOCK:
Antiquarian books including Cumbrian topography. LOC:
Opposite Clydesdale Bank. SIZE: Large. PARK: Nearby.
VAT: Stan. FAIRS: PBFA Northern.
TEL: 01946 599010

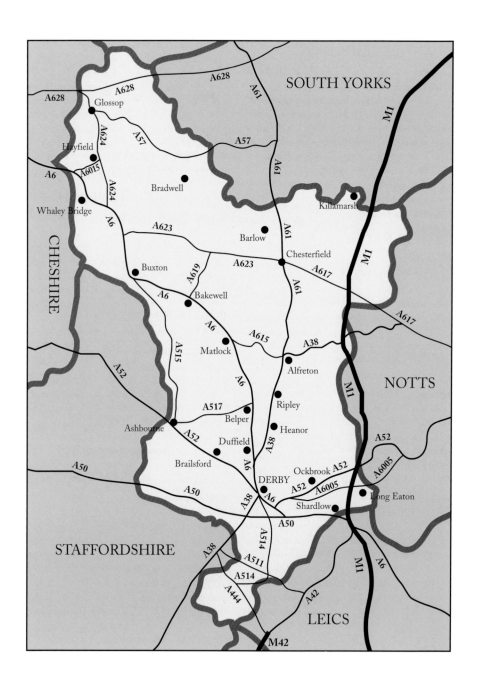

ALFRETON

Alfreton Antiques Centre
11 King St. DE55 7AF. (Helen Dixon)
EST. 1996. Open 10-4.30, Sun. 11-4.30. STOCK: *Wide range of furniture, ceramics, books, lighting, metalware, clocks, watches, glass, collectables, Deco, jewellery, pictures, militaria, silver, Denby pottery.* LOC: Off junction 28, M1, A38 to Alfreton, King St. is main street up to traffic lights, shop on right before the lights. SER: Valuations; Denby replacement service; restorations (ceramics); house clearance; watch and clock repairs. SIZE: Large - 40 dealers. PARK: Own at rear. FAIRS: Kedleston.
TEL: 01773 520781; HOME: 01773 852695; MOBILE: 07970 786968
E-MAIL: sales@alfretonantiquescentre.com
WEBSITE: www.alfretonantiquescentre.com

Steam-models.uk.com
31-32 South St., Riddings. DE55 4EJ. (Richard Evison)
EST. 1990. Open 9-5, Sat. by appointment. STOCK: *Steam models and advertising figures, 20th C.* LOC: A610 from junction 26, M1 to Codnor. Right at traffic lights, right again to Riddings. SER: Valuations; restorations (steam models); buys at auction (steam models). SIZE: Small. PARK: Easy. VAT: Stan.
TEL: 01773 541527;
E-MAIL: raevison@aol.com
WEBSITE: www.steam-models.net

ASHBOURNE

Ashbourne Antiques Ltd
Warehouse, Blake House, Shirley. DE6 3AS. (Robert Allsebrook)
EST. 1977. Open by appointment. STOCK: *English furniture, 17th-20th C and hand-made copies.* LOC: A52 Ashbourne/Derby. SER: Restorations; cabinet making; removals; packing and shipping. SIZE: Small. PARK: Easy. VAT: Stan.
TEL: 01335 361236; MOBILE: 07970 094883

J H S Antiques Ltd   LAPADA
47 Church St. DE6 1AJ. (Julian Howard Snodin)
EST. 1972. CINOA. Open 10-5. CL: Mon. and Wed. STOCK: *17th C oak, £1,000-£20,000; metalware, 17th to early 19th C, £50-£3,000; carvings, 17th to early 18th C, £300-£3,000.* LOC: A52 from junction 25, M1. SIZE: Medium. PARK: Easy. VAT: Spec.
TEL: 01335 347733; MOBILE: 07810 122248
E-MAIL: jh.snodin@hotmail.co.uk

Manion Antiques
23 Church St. DE6 1AE. (Mrs V.J. Manion)
EST. 1984. Open 10-5.30 or by appointment. STOCK: *Jewellery, silver, porcelain, paintings and small furniture.* LOC: Central. SER: Valuations. SIZE: Small. PARK: Outside.

TEL: 01335 343207; HOME: same; MOBILE: 07968 067316

Pine and Decorative Items
38 Church St. DE6 1AJ. (M. and G. Bassett)
EST. 1980. Open 10-5. CL: Wed. and Sun. except by appointment; warehouse open 9-5. CL: Sat. STOCK: *English and French pine and country furniture; garden furniture, ironwork, kitchenalia, 18th C to 1950s, from £10.* SIZE: Small + warehouse. VAT: Stan.
TEL: 01335 300061; FAX: same
E-MAIL: mgbassett@sky.com
WEBSITE: www.antiques-atlas.com

Rose Antiques
37 Church St. DE6 1AJ.
EST. 1982. Open 10-5. STOCK: *Furniture including pine, silver, porcelain, jewellery, copper and brass.* LOC: A52. SIZE: Medium. PARK: Easy.
TEL: 01335 343822; HOME: 01335 324333

Spurrier-Smith Antiques   LAPADA
28, 30 and 39 Church St. DE6 1AJ. (I. Spurrier-Smith)
EST. 1973. Open 10-5, Wed. and Sun. by appointment. STOCK: *Furniture, oils, watercolours, porcelain, pottery, metalware, instruments, Oriental bronzes, collectables, pine, decorative items. Warehouse - pine and American export goods.* SER: Valuations; restorations (furniture). SIZE: Large (5 showrooms). PARK: Easy. VAT: Stan/Spec.
TEL: 01335 342198; HOME: 01629 822502; FAX: 01335 342198; MOBILE: 07970 720130
E-MAIL: ivan@spurrier-smith.fsnet.co.uk
WEBSITE: www.spurrier-smith.co.uk

BAKEWELL

Bakewell Antiques and Works of Art
Ground Floor, 1-4 King St. DE45 1DZ. (Brian Hills)
EST. 1979. Open 9-5; Sun. 12-5 or by appointment STOCK: *17th-19th C English oak and country furniture. Sculpture, works of art, clocks, silver.* LOC: Up the side of the Rutland Hotel. SIZE: Large VAT: Spec./Global.
TEL: 01629 812496; MOBILE: 07860 453940

Peter Bunting Antiques   BADA LAPADA
Harthill Hall, Alport. DE45 1LH.
EST. 1970. Open by appointment. STOCK: *Early oak, country furniture, portraits and period decoration.* LOC: On B5056. SIZE: Medium. PARK: Own. VAT: Stan/Spec.
TEL: 01629 636203; MOBILE: 07860 540870
E-MAIL: peter@peterbunting.com
WEBSITE: www.peterbunting.com

G.W. Ford & Son Ltd.   LAPADA
Bakewell Antiques and Works of Art 1-4 King Street DE45 1DZ. (Ian Thomson)
EST. 1890. CINOA. Open 9-5; Sun 12 - 5 or by

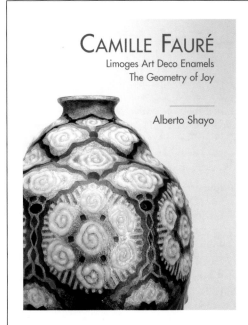
appointment. *STOCK: Period furniture, 17th-19th C, mahogany, oak and country. Works of art, sculpture. Treen.* LOC: **Up the side of the Rutland Hotel.** SIZE: **Large** VAT: **Margin/Global/Stan.**
TEL: **01629 812496**
E-MAIL: **ian@gwfordantiques.co.uk**
WEBSITE: **www.gwfordantiques.co.uk**

Martin and Dorothy Harper Antiques   LAPADA
King St. DE45 1DZ.
EST. **1973. Open 10-5, Sun. and other times by appointment.** CL: **Mon. and Thurs.** STOCK: *Furniture, £75-£7,500; metalware, £30-£500; glass, £15-£150; all 17th to early 20th C.* SER: Valuations; restorations; buys at auction. SIZE: Medium. PARK: Easy. VAT: Spec.
TEL: **01629 814757;** MOBILE: **07885 347134 and 07753 819854**

Michael Pembery Antiques
The Stables, Peppercorn House, King St. DE45 1FD. (M. and L. Pembery)
EST. 1967. Open 10-5. STOCK: *Furniture, £500-£4,000; metalware, £100-£1,000; objets d'art, £100-£1,500; all 18th-19th C.* SER: Valuations; restorations. SIZE: Medium. PARK: Nearby. VAT: Stan/Spec.
TEL: 01629 814161

BELPER

Derwentside Antiques
Derwent St. DE56 1WN. (Machall Investments)
EST. 1995. Open 8.30-5.30, Sun. 8.30-5. STOCK: *General antiques mainly furniture and collectables.* LOC: Just off A6. SER: Restorations; sourcing of period furniture. SIZE: Large - four storey mill - 20+ dealers. PARK: Own.
TEL: 01773 828008; FAX: 01773 828983
E-MAIL: enquiries@derwentsideHOMEcentre.co.uk
WEBSITE: www.derwentsidehomecentre.co.uk

Neil Wayne "The Razor Man"
The Cedars (rear of 55 Field Lane), DE56 1DD.
EST. 1969. Resident. Open every day 9.30-6 by appointment. STOCK: *Razors and shaving items, 18th to early 19th C, £20-£300.* SIZE: Medium. PARK: Easy.
TEL: 01773 824157; FAX: 01773 825573
E-MAIL: neil.wayne@derbyshire-holidays.com

BRAILSFORD

Heldreich Antiques & French Polishers
Home Farm, Ednaston. DE6 3AY. (Neil Heldreich)
EST. 1986. Open daily, Sat. by appointment. STOCK: *Furniture, late 17th C to mid 19th C, £250-£10,000; clocks, 18th-19th C, £300-£6,000; smalls, 18th-19th C, £10-£1,000.* LOC: A52 between Derby and Ashbourne,

approximately 2 miles out of Brailsford on left towards Ashbourne. SER: Valuations; restorations; conservation and French polishing. SIZE: Medium.
TEL: 01335 361676; HOME: 01283 733617
E-MAIL: neil@heldreich.com
WEBSITE: www.heldreich.com

BUXTON

The Antiques Warehouse
25 Lightwood Rd. SK17 7BJ. (N.F. Thompson)
EST. 1983. Open 10.30-4 or by appointment. STOCK: British furniture, mainly mahogany, rosewood and walnut, 17th-20th C; paintings, silver, metalware, smalls, clocks including longcase, Victorian brass and iron bedsteads. LOC: Off A6. SER: Valuations; restorations; buys at auction. SIZE: Large. PARK: Own at rear.
TEL: 01298 72967; HOME/FAX: 01298 22603; MOBILE: 07947 050552

Maggie Mays
11-12 Grove Parade. SK17 6AJ. (Mrs J. Wild)
EST. 1993. Open 10.30-5. CL: Mon. STOCK: Victorian furniture and effects, £35-£800; Art Deco glassware, mirrors, pottery, £20-£500; Edwardian furniture, £100-£800, lighting and chandeliers. LOC: Opposite Turners Memorial. SER: Valuations; buys at auction. PARK: Easy.
TEL: MOBILE: 07831 606003; HOME: 01663 733935

The Penny Post Antiques
9 Cavendish Circus. SK17 6AT. (D. and R. Hammond)
EST. 1978. Open 10-5. STOCK: Pictures, commemoratives, crested china, shaving mugs and other collectables; furniture; general antiques. LOC: Town centre, opposite Palace Hotel. SIZE: Small. PARK: Easy.
TEL: HOME: 01298 25965

What Now Antiques
Cavendish Arcade, The Crescent. SK17 6BQ.
(L. Carruthers)
EST. 1987. Open 10-5, Sun. 12-4. Prior telephone call advisable. STOCK: General antiques and collectables including Moorcroft pottery, small silver items, silver and gold jewellery, clocks, Victorian and Edwardian furniture, £1-£1,000. LOC: Central. SER: Valuations; export; foreign trade; house clearances. SIZE: Small. PARK: Easy.
TEL: 01298 27178; MOBILE: 07790 047278

CHESTERFIELD

Anthony D. Goodlad
26 Fairfield Rd., Brockwell. S40 4TP.
EST. 1974. Open by appointment. STOCK: General militaria, WWI and WWII. LOC: Close to town centre. SIZE: Small. PARK: Easy. FAIRS: Major UK Arms.
TEL: 01246 204004
E-MAIL: goodladfirst@aol.com

Ian Morris
479 Chatsworth Rd. S40 3AD.
EST. 1970. Open by chance or appointment. STOCK: Furniture, 18th-20th C, £50-£2,000; pictures, small items. LOC: A619 to Baslow and Chatsworth House. SIZE: Small. PARK: Easy.
TEL: 01246 235120

Marlene Rutherford Antiques
401 Sheffield Rd., Whittington Moor. S41 8LS.
EST. 1985. Open Thu 10-4, Tue./Fri./Sat. 1-4; CL: Mon/Wed. STOCK: Furniture, pottery, jewellery, clocks and lamps, £5-£2,000, 18th-20th C. SER: Valuations. PARK: Easy. FAIRS: Stafford; Jaguar.
TEL: 01246 450209; MOBILE: 07885 665440
WEBSITE: www.marlenerutherford.co.uk

DERBY

Finishing Touches
224 Uttoxeter Old Rd., The Rowditch. DE1 1NF.
(Lynne Robinson)
EST. 1994. Open 10.30-5.30 Thurs., Fri. and Sat. or by appointment. STOCK: Fire surrounds, £200-£800; pine furniture, £50-£500; kitchenalia and pottery, £1-£25; all late 19th to early 20th C. LOC: Off A38 at junction with A52. SER: Fireplace restoration. SIZE: Small. PARK: Rear of church.
TEL: 01332 721717
WEBSITE: www.derbyantiques.co.uk

DUFFIELD

Wayside Antiques
62 Town St. DE56 4GG. (B. and Mrs J. Harding)
EST. 1975. Open 10-6 or by appointment. STOCK: Furniture, 18th-19th C, £50-£5,000; porcelain, pictures, boxes and silver. SER: Restorations (furniture). SIZE: Medium. PARK: Forecourt. VAT: Stan/Spec.
TEL: 01332 840346

GLOSSOP

Derbyshire Clocks
104 High St. West. SK13 8BB. (J.A. and T.P. Lees)
EST. 1975. Open Thurs., Fri., Sat. and Sun. or by appointment. STOCK: Clocks. SER: Restorations (clocks and barometers). PARK: Easy. VAT: Spec.
TEL: 01457 862677

HAYFIELD

Michael Allcroft Antiques
1 Church St. SK22 2JE.
EST. 1984. Open Sat. 2-5, Sun. 1-5, other times by appointment. STOCK: Period English furniture and decorative items. SIZE: Small.
TEL: 01663 742684; MOBILE: 07798 781642; FAX: 01663 744014
E-MAIL: allcrom@aol.com

Paul Pickford Antiques

Top of the Town, Church St. SK22 2JE.
EST. 1975. Open Tues., Thurs. and Sat. 10-4, Sun. 12-5.
STOCK: *19th C furniture, stripped pine, jewellery, ceramics, glass, lighting and general antiques, £50-£1,000.* LOC: Off A6 at Newtown, near Disley, take A6015. SIZE: Medium. PARK: Easy.
TEL: 01663 747276; HOME: 01663 743356
E-MAIL: paul@pickfordantiques.co.uk
WEBSITE: www.pickfordantiques.co.uk

HEANOR

Heanor Antiques Centre

1-3 Ilkeston Rd. DE75 7AG. (Jane Richards)
EST. 1998. Open 10.30-4.30. STOCK: *Wide range of general antiques and collectables.* LOC: Off M1, junction 26 or A38. SER: Valuations; restorations. SIZE: Large. PARK: Easy.
TEL: 01773 531181; FAX: 01773 762783
E-MAIL: sales@heanorantiquecentre.co.uk

KILLAMARSH

Havenplan's Architectural Emporium

The Old Station, Station Rd. S21 1EN.
EST. 1972. Open 10-2.30. CL: Mon. and Fri. STOCK: *Architectural fittings and decorative items, church interiors and furnishings, fireplaces, doors, decorative cast ironwork, masonry, bygones, garden ornaments, 18th to early 20th C.* SER: Hire. LOC: M1, exit 30. Take A616 towards Sheffield, turn right on to B6053, turn right on to B6058 towards Killamarsh, turn right between two railway bridges. SIZE: Large. PARK: Easy.
Tel: 01142 489972; HOME 01246 433315

LONG EATON

Miss Elany

2 Salisbury St. NG10 1BA. (D. and Mrs Mottershead)
EST. 1977. Open 9-5. STOCK: *Pianos, 1900 to date, £150-£1,000; general antiques, Victorian and Edwardian, £180-£500.* SIZE: Medium. PARK: Easy. VAT: Stan.
TEL: 0115 9734835

MATLOCK

Antiques Loft

Market Place, Cromford. DE4 3QE. (Brendan Rogerson)
Open 10-5 inc. Sun. STOCK: *Furniture.*
TEL: 01629 826565

Matlock Antiques and Collectables Centre

7 Dale Rd. DE4 3LT. (W. Shirley)
EST. 1995. Open 10-5, Sun. 11-5. STOCK: *Wide range of general antiques including mahogany, oak and pine furniture, pictures and books, kitchenalia, china, clocks, linen, clothing and textiles.* LOC: Town centre. SIZE: Large - 70+

dealers. PARK: Easy. FAIRS: Chatsworth Country Show; Crufts.
TEL: 01629 760808
E-MAIL: duncanbradbury@btinternet.com
WEBSITE: www.matlock-antiques-collectables.cwc.net

RIPLEY

A.A. Ambergate Antiques

c/o Upstairs & Downstairs, 8 Derby Rd. DE5 3HR. (C.V. Lawrence)
EST. 1972. Open 10-4. STOCK: *Oak and mahogany Victorian and Edwardian furniture including bedroom, sideboards, tables and chairs, display cabinets; pottery, clocks and pictures.* LOC: Town centre. SER: Valuations; restorations. SIZE: Medium. PARK: Easy.
TEL: 01773 745201; MOBILE: 07885 327753
WEBSITE: www.upstairsdownstairsantiques.co.uk

Memory Lane Antiques Centre

28 Nottingham Rd. DE5 3DJ. (James Cullen)
EST. 1994. Open 10-4, CL: Wed. and BH. Or by appointment. STOCK: *Victoriana and 20th C collectables, pine furniture, specialist in Denby, Bourne and Langley, lighting.* LOC: Town centre, at junction with Grosvenor Rd. SER: Valuations; old Denby replacement service; Steiff agency. SIZE: Large. PARK: Easy. FAIRS: Derby University; Newark; Abacus; Kedleston Hall; Swinderby.
TEL: 01773 570184; MOBILE: 07775 940085
E-MAIL: jamesgc1@aol.com

WHALEY BRIDGE

Nimbus Antiques

14 Chapel Rd. SK23 7JZ. (L.M. and H.C. Brobbin)
EST. 1979. Open 9-5.30, Sun. 2-5.30. STOCK: *Showroom condition Georgian, Victorian and Edwardian furniture, including desks, dining tables, chests and clocks. 18th - 20th C.* LOC: A6, 20 mins. from Stockport. SIZE: Large. PARK: Own. VAT: Stan/Spec.
TEL: 01663 734248
E-MAIL: sales@nimbusantiques.co.uk
WEBSITE: www.nimbusantiques.co.uk

Richard Glass

Hockerley Old Hall, Hockerley Lane. SK23 7AS.
EST. 1985. Resident. Open by appointment. STOCK: *Oak furniture, 17th-18th C, £1,000-£5,000; paintings, drawings, metal and stoneware, 17th-19th C, £200-£2,000.* LOC: From town centre towards Stockport, turn left at station car park, up hill and 2nd right into Hockerley Lane, up farm track at the end of the lane, house on left. SER: Valuations. SIZE: Small. PARK: Easy.
TEL: 0161 236 1520; FAX: 0161 237 5174; MOBILE: 07802 860787
E-MAIL: richardathockerley@dsl.pipex.com

Late 18th & 19th Century Textiles

Francesca Galloway and Sue Kerry

Late 18th & 19th Century Textiles presents a selection of pieces chosen for their beauty, their elegance and their relevance to the history of textile design. The focus is on furnishing textiles that illustrate the tremendous shift in taste from the restrained Neo-Classical style of the late 18th century to the imperialistic, utterly luxurious fashions of the Napoleonic era and beyond.

Europe and America experienced rapid changes in interior decoration throughout the 19th century, due in part to the radical social changes wrought by the Industrial Revolution. Flamboyant *nouveau riche* taste flourished throughout the western world, encompassing spirited revivals of Medieval, Renaissance, Baroque, Rococo and Islamic styles and designs by talented figures such as Owen Jones, Eugène Viollet-le-Duc, Christopher Dresser and William Morris.

One of the earliest textiles featured is the *Verdures du Vatican*, designed by Jean-Demosthene Dugourc for King Carlos IV of Spain in 1799. Elsewhere there is a brocaded silk and metal satin rosette and medallion chair seat cover by Grand Frères for Cartier et Fils, 1808-15, the design of which was re-woven for Jacqueline Kennedy's 1962 refurbishment of the White House. The book features many more pieces of great beauty and extremely high quality.

Two British designs relate to the Aesthetic movement: the first, *Hatton*, is silk tissue with a beautiful design depicting prunus blossom and small insects, designed by Bruce Talbert, a central figure of the Aesthetic movement; the second is a hand block printed wallpaper designed by Christopher Dresser, with stylised flowers and trailing plants, inspired by Japanese decorative artwork. Also featured is *Vineyard*, a cotton and wool weave designed by Edmund Hunter, which was displayed at the 1903 Arts & Crafts Exhibition. Along with its companion volume *Twentieth Century Textiles*, this landmark publication offers an extraordinary opportunity to appreciate the evolution of textile design and technique across almost 200 years through a stunning selection of pieces rarely on public view.

310 x 250mm 176pp 173col
£35.00 hardback

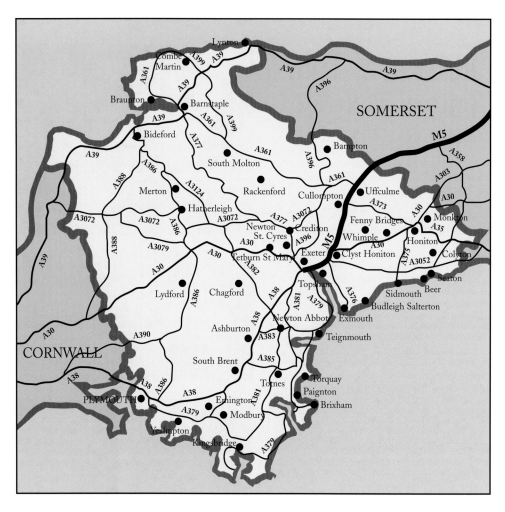

ASHBURTON

Adrian Ager Ltd
Ashburton Marbles TQ13 7QD.
EST. 1976. Open 8-5, Sat. 10-4. *STOCK: Marble and wooden fire-surrounds, decorative cast iron inserts; scuttles, fenders, overmantels, 1790-1910; architectural decorative antiques, garden statuary and related items, chandeliers, soft furnishings and furniture; mid-Victorian dining tables and bedroom furniture.* SIZE: Warehouse and showrooms. PARK: Easy.
TEL: 01364 653189; FAX: same
E-MAIL: sales@adrianager.com
WEBSITE: www.adrianager.com

Antiques Ad Hoc
17 North St. TQ13 7QH. (Helen Harvey)
EST. 1994. Open 10-5, Sat. 11-5. CL: Wed. and Mon. *STOCK: Period furniture and decorative items, mirrors and lamps, pottery and porcelain, woolwork pictures, line and stipple engravings, copper and brass, English and French, 1770-1910.* LOC: North end of North St. SIZE: Small. PARK: Loading and nearby.

TEL: 01364 654667; MOBILE: 07778 764424; HOME: 01752 402130
E-MAIL: helen@antiquesadhoc.co.uk
WEBSITE: www.antiquesadhoc.co.uk

Apollo Antiques
9 North St. TQ13 7QJ. (Mark Davis)
Open 10-5. *STOCK: 16th - 20th C, furniture, porcelain, silver.* LOC: Main street. PARK: Easy.
TEL: 01364 653922
E-MAIL: mark@apollo.uk.net
WEBSITE: www.apollo.uk.net

Dartmoor Bookshop
2 Kingsbridge Lane. TQ13 7DX. (Andy Collins and Brenda Greysmith)
EST. 1982. Open Wed.-Sat. 10-5.30. *STOCK: Books - secondhand and antiquarian.* LOC: On lane facing car park. SER: Valuations. SIZE: Large. PARK: Easy.
TEL: 01364 653356
E-MAIL: books@thedartmoorbookshop.co.uk
WEBSITE: www.thedartmoorbookshop.co.uk

Mo Logan Antiques
11 North St. TQ13 7AG. (Martin & Mo Logan)
EST. 1972. Open 10-4.30. CL: Mon. and Wed. STOCK:
*Textiles, early 20th C; rugs, gilt furniture and mirrors,
lamps, small period furniture, decorative items.* LOC: Town
centre. SIZE: Small.
TEL: 01364 654179; MOBILE: 07967 234129

The Shambles
24 North St. TQ13 7QD.
EST. 1982. Open 10-5. STOCK: *Country and general
antiques and decorative items, £5-£2,000.* LOC: Town
centre. SER: Valuations. SIZE: 5 dealers. PARK: Opposite.
VAT: Stan/Spec. FAIRS: Sandown Park; Westpoint,
Exeter; Shepton Mallet.
TEL: 01364 653848

BAMPTON

Bampton Gallery
2-4 Brook St. EX16 9LY. (Gerald Chidwick FRICS)
EST. 1997. WEADA. Open Mon., Tues. and Wed. 9.30-
3, Thurs. 9.30-5.30, Sat. 9-12, other times by
appointment or chance. STOCK: *Porcelain (especially
English hard-paste), pottery and glass, 1750-1900, £10-
£2,000; pictures and prints, furniture including upholstered,
£20-£10,000* LOC: Main street. SER: Restorations
(furniture including traditional upholstery, ceramics);
buys at auction (porcelain and furniture). SIZE: Medium.
PARK: Outside. FAIRS: Burford Ceramic; Wilton
Ceramic; Powderham and Stanway (Coopers); Naworth
(Galloways); Shepton Mallet; Westpoint, Exeter.
TEL: 01398 331354
E-MAIL: gerald@bamptongallery.co.uk
WEBSITE: www.bamptongallery.co.uk

Robert Byles Antiques and Optimum Brasses.
7 Castle St. EX16 9NS. (Robert and Rachel Byles)
EST. 1966. Open Mon.-Fri. 9-1 and 2-5 or by appoint-
ment. STOCK: *Furniture, 16th-18th C; local farmhouse
tables and settles, metalwork, pottery, unstripped period pine,
architectural items.* LOC: On Wiveliscombe road. SER:
Restoration materials; replica brass handles for antique
furniture by Optimum Brasses on the same premises.
SIZE: Medium. PARK: Nearby. VAT: Stan/Spec.
TEL: 01398 331515; FAX: 01398 331164
E-MAIL: brass@optimumbrasses.co.uk
WEBSITE: www.obida.com

BARNSTAPLE

Barn Antiques
73 Newport Rd. EX32 9BG. (T. Cusack)
Open 9.30-5, Wed. 9.30-1. STOCK: *General antiques.*
LOC: Off the link road. SIZE: Large. PARK: Free.
TEL: 01271 323131

Barnstaple Antique & Collectors' Centre
The Old Church, 18 Cross St. EX31 1BD. (P. Broome)

EST. 1985. Open 9.30-5. STOCK: *Furniture, china, 18th C
to 1960s, £5-£2,500; glass.* LOC: 40 yards off High St.
SIZE: Large. PARK: Nearby. FAIRS: Newark, Shepton
Mallet, Exeter Westpoint.
TEL: 01271 375788

Medina Gallery
80 Boutport St. EX31 1SR. (R. and C.F. Jennings)
EST. 1972. Open 9.30-5. STOCK: *Maps, prints,
photographs, oils and watercolours, £1-£500.* LOC: Town
centre. SER: Picture framing, mounting. SIZE: Medium.
PARK: Easy. VAT: Stan.
TEL: 01271 371025

Mark Parkhouse Antiques and Jewellery
106 High St. EX31 1HP.
EST. 1976. Open 10-1, 2-4.30. STOCK: *Jewellery, furniture,
silver, paintings, clocks, glass, porcelain, small collectors' items,
18th-19th C, £100-£10,000.* SER: Valuations; buys at
auction. PARK: Nearby. VAT: Stan/Spec.
TEL: 01271 374504
E-MAIL: mark@markparkhousejewellers.co.uk

BEER

Dolphin Antiques
Dolphin Courtyard. EX12 3EQ. (Ken Dolan)
EST. 1985. Open 10-5 including Sun; CL: Thur. STOCK:
*Antique fishing tackle, from £25; jewellery, £50-£2,000;
china and smalls, £2-£50; original framed cigarette cards;
dinky toys, Corgis, Matchbox; fossils; tools.* SER: Valuations;
buys at auction. SIZE: Medium. PARK: Easy.
TEL: 01297 24362; HOME: 01460 65294

BIDEFORD

J. Collins & Son   LAPADA
98 Charles Ave. EX39 2PH. (Jonathan Biggs)
EST. 1953. CINOA. Open by appointment. STOCK:
*Georgian and Regency furniture; general antiques
including framed and restored 19th-20th C oils and
watercolours, £100-£50,000.* SER: Furniture restoration.
SIZE: Medium. PARK: Opposite. VAT: Spec. FAIRS:
Olympia (November).
TEL: 01237 473103; FAX: 01237 475658
E-MAIL: biggs@collinsantiques.co.uk
WEBSITE: www.collinsantiques.co.uk

J. Collins & Son Fine Art   BADA LAPADA
PO Box 119. EX39 1WX. (J. & P. Biggs)
EST. 1953. CINOA. Open by appointment. STOCK:
19th-20th C oils and watercolours, £100-£100,000. SER:
Valuations; cleaning and framing. SIZE: Medium.
PARK: Opposite. VAT: Spec. FAIRS: BADA (March),
Olympia (November).
TEL: 01237 473103; FAX: 01237 475658; HOME: 01237
476485
E-MAIL: biggs@collinsantiques.co.uk
WEBSITE: www.collinsantiques.co.uk

Cooper Gallery

47 Mill St. EX39 2JR. (Mrs J. Bruce)
EST. 1975. Open 10-5, Wed. 10-2. *STOCK: Watercolours, mainly West Country views, late 19th to early 20th C, £200-£5,000; antique jewellery.* SER: Valuations; restorations (watercolours); cleaning; framing. SIZE: Small. VAT: Spec.
TEL: 01237 477370; FAX: same; HOME: 01237 423415
E-MAIL: coopergallery@freecall-uk.co.uk
WEBSITE: www.cooper-gallery.com

Harbour Antiques

17 Market Place. EX39 2DR. (Elaine Tucker)
Open 9.30-5.30 Mon.-Sat. or by appointment. *STOCK: Period antique furniture 18th-20th C.* PARK: 1 hr free outside shop. VAT: Margin.
TEL: 01237 425545
E-MAIL: sales@harbourantiques.com
WEBSITE: www.harbourantiques.com

BOVEY TRACEY

Courtenay House Antique Centre

Fore St. TQ13 9AE. (Tina Richardson)
EST. 1991. Open 9-7 Mon.-Fri., 9-5.30 Sat. and Sun. *STOCK: 1920s and 1930s china, Victorian furniture, jewellery and collectables.* PARK: Car park nearby.
TEL: 01626 835363
E-MAIL: info@courtenayhouse.co.uk
WEBSITE: www.courtenayhouse.co.uk

BRAUNTON

Caen Antiques

19 Caen St. EX33 1AA. (J. and C. Owen)
EST. 1992. Open 9.30-5. CL: Wed. pm. *STOCK: Clocks including longcase and bracket; barometers, Art Nouveau, Victorian oil lamps and spares, small furniture.* LOC: Village centre. SER: Longcase clock, oil lamp and barometer repairs. SIZE: Small. PARK: At rear.
TEL: 01271 817808; HOME: same; MOBILE: 07890 133820
E-MAIL: jcoa@devon942.fsnet.co.uk
WEBSITE: www.caenantiques.co.uk

BRIXHAM

Antique, Electrical & Turret Clocks

Ye Olde Coffin House, King St. TQ5 9TF. (Dr. Paul Strickland)
EST. 1999. NAWCC. Telephone for opening times. *STOCK: Antique, early electric and turret clocks.* SER: Valuations; restorations; buys and sells. SIZE: Small. PARK: Loading only and nearby. FAIRS: Shepton Mallet.
TEL: 01803 856307
E-MAIL: wer@onamission.org.uk
WEBSITE: www.clocktrust.com

BUCKFASTLEIGH

The Pennsylvania Pine Co

Units 18-20 Dart Mills, Old Totnes Rd. TQ11 0AF. (S. F. Robinson and C. A. Tolchard)
EST. 1967. Open Tues.-Sun. 10-5.30. *STOCK: Unusual English pine furniture, 18th-20th C, £50-£5,000.* SER: Valuations; restorations (pine). SIZE: Large. PARK: Easy.
TEL: 01364 644677; FAX: same; MOBILE: 07941 891640; HOME: 01364 644640
WEBSITE: www.pennsylvaniapine.co.uk

BUDLEIGH SALTERTON

Days of Grace

15 Fore St. EX9 6NH. (L. Duriez)
Open 10.30-5 *STOCK: Antique lace, vintage textiles and costume, china, jewellery, furniture, interesting decorative items.*
TEL: 01395 443730
E-MAIL: lduriez@onetel.com
WEBSITE: www.pirouettethecollection.co.uk

David J. Thorn

2a High St. EX9 6LQ.
EST. 1950. Open by appointment *STOCK: English, Continental and Oriental pottery and porcelain, 1620-1850, £100-£25,000.* SER: Valuations; commissions; inventories. SIZE: Small. PARK: Easy. VAT: Stan/Spec.
TEL: 01395 442448

CHAGFORD

Rex Antiques

The Old Rex Cinema. TQ13 8AB. (John Meredith)
EST. 1979. *Trade only.* Open by appointment. *STOCK: Country oak, 16th-19th C, £5-£2,000; Oriental brass and copper, weapons, large unusual items, granite, architectural items, old iron work.* SER: Buys at auction. SIZE: Large. PARK: Easy.
TEL: 01647 433405

CLYST HONITON

Penny's Home Farm Antiques

EX5 2LX. (Michael and Penelope Clark)
EST. 1975. Open 10-5. *STOCK: Antiques and collectables; secondhand furniture,* LOC: Off A30 Exeter Airport exit. SER: Restorations; delivery. SIZE: Large. PARK: Easy.
TEL: 01392 444491
E-MAIL: penelope.clark@btconnect.com
WEBSITE: www.pennysantiques.co.uk

COLYTON

Colyton Antiques Centre

Old Station Yard, Station Rd. EX24 6HA (R.C. Hunt and M.J. Conway)
EST. 2000. Open 10-5, Sun. 11-4. *STOCK: General antiques.* LOC: V. close to Colyton tram station. SIZE:

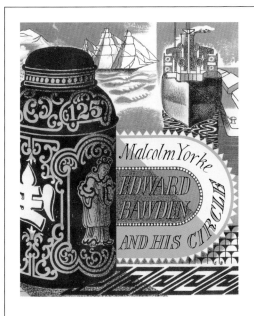
Large. PARK: Easy.
TEL: 01297 552339; FAX: same
E-MAIL: rod.hunt@tiscali.co.uk

COMBE MARTIN

Sherbrook Selectables
1A Hangman Path. EX34 0DE. (Trevor and Lesley Pickard)
EST. 1997. Open 10-5.30. CL: Wed.-Fri. STOCK: *General antiques and collectables.* LOC: 300 yards from sea front. SIZE: Medium. PARK: Easy.
TEL: 01271 889060; MOBILE: 07887 806493
E-MAIL: trevor@sherbrook1.fsbusiness.co.uk
WEBSITE: www.sherbrookselectables.com

CREDITON

Musgrave Bickford Antiques
15 East St. EX17 3AT. (Mr and Mrs D.M. Bickford)
EST. 1983. Open by appointment. STOCK: *Clocks and barometers, mainly 19th C, from £400.* LOC: From Exeter on A377 on right entering one-way system, towards Tiverton. SER: Restorations (longcase, mantel, wall clock and barometer movements, dials, cases). SIZE: Small. PARK: Easy and at rear by arrangement. VAT: Stan/Spec.
TEL: 01363 775042

CULLOMPTON

Cobweb Antiques
The Old Tannery, Exeter Rd. EX15 1DT. (R. Holmes)
EST. 1980. WEADA. Open 10-5. STOCK: *English oak, pine and country furniture, decorative and general items, 16th-19th C.* LOC: Half a mile from junction 28, M5. SER: Stripping; restorations; courier. SIZE: Large. PARK: Easy.
TEL: 01884 855748

Cullompton Antiques
The Old Tannery, Exeter Rd. EX15 1DT.
EST. 1989. WEADA. Open 10-5, Sun. by appointment. STOCK: *Pine, oak, mahogany and fruitwood country furniture - wardrobes, cupboards, tables and chairs, beds, dressers, coffers, desks, mirrors and decorative items, 17th to early 19th C, £50-£5,000.* LOC: Off M5, junction 28, through town centre, premises on right, approximately 1 mile. SIZE: Large. PARK: Easy.
TEL: 01884 38476
E-MAIL: tannery@cullompton-antiques.co.uk
WEBSITE: www.cullompton-antiques.co.uk

Miller Antiques
The Old Tannery, Exeter Rd. EX15 1DT. (Nick Miller)
Open 10-5, Sun. by appointment. STOCK: *Furniture, 18th-19th C, £25-£2,000, country, 17th-19th C, £25-£3,000; decorative accessories, £5-£2,000.* LOC: M5 junction 28,

bottom of the High St. opposite Somerfield. SER: Valuations; buys at auction. SIZE: Large. PARK: Easy. TEL: 01884 38476; FAX: same

Mills Antiques
The Old Tannery, Exeter Rd. EX15 1DT. EST. 1979. Open 10-5. STOCK: *17th C to Edwardian furniture including oak, mahogany and pine - coffers, desks, wardrobes, cupboards, tables and chairs, £50-£3,000.* PARK: Easy. TEL: 01392 860945

DARTMOUTH

Pennyfarthing Antiques
11 Lower St. TQ6 9AN. (Jill Williams) EST. 1999. Open 10-4.45, Sun. 11-4. STOCK: *Period furniture and interesting antique items.* LOC: In the old Forresters Hall, near the lower ferry. SER: Free local delivery. PARK: On street. TEL: 01803 839411 E-MAIL: jillwilliams1@btinternet.com

ERMINGTON

Mill Gallery
PL21 9NT. (Christopher Trant) EST. 1984. Resident. Open by appointment. STOCK: *Oils and watercolours, 18th-20th C, £300-£1,000.* LOC: From A38 take Ivybridge exit, follows signs, 1st premises in village. SER: Valuations; restorations (oils). SIZE: Small. PARK: Easy. VAT: Spec. TEL: 01548 830172 MOBILE 07886 687685 E-MAIL: chris@millgallery.com WEBSITE: www.millgallery.com

EXETER

The Antiques Complex   LAPADA
Exeter Airport Industrial Estate, Westcott Lane. EX5 2BA.
EST. 1975. WEADA. Open 9-5.30, Sat. 10-1. CL: Bank Holiday weekends. STOCK: *Over 1,000 items of antique, decorative, Victorian and Edwardian, Arts and Crafts and collectable furniture.* **LOC: 3 miles from junction 29, M5. After airport, turn left and follow sign to Westcott for 1 mile. SER: Container packing and shipping; courier. SIZE: 4 large warehouses. PARK: Easy. VAT: Spec/Global/Export. FAIRS: Newark. TEL: 01392 366261; FAX: 01392 365572**

Opposite are listed the dealers trading from this address.

Acorn Antiques
Writing tables and desks.

Artemis
(Bob Golding)

Ashburton Antiques
(Mark Dunscombe) *Furniture.*

M. Burbidge Antiques
Furniture.

Paul Hodgeson
Painted decorative furniture, gilt mirrors.

McBain Antique Exports
EST. 1963. *English, French and Belgian furniture suitable for export worldwide; architectural garden items.* TEL: 01392 446304; MOBILE: 07831 389236; FAX: 01392 447304 E-MAIL: mcbain.exports@zetnet.co.uk

Miscellany Antiques
Furniture, Georgian to Edwardian. TEL: 01684 566671

P & A
Arts & Crafts and decorative furniture.

Portobello Antiques
Furniture.

P. Reynolds Antiques
Mirrors, armchairs and tables.

Leon Robertson Antiques
Chests, desks and pine furniture. MOBILE: 07971 171909

Jane Strickland & Daughter
Upholstery, beds.

Tredantiques
Fine quality period furniture and decorative items. TEL: 01392 447082; MOBILE: 07967 447082 WEBSITE: www.tredantiques.com

Victoria Antiques
(Mike Daley) *Furniture.*

Ivor Doble Ltd
24 Sidwell St. EX4 1AS. (I. Doble) EST. 1950. Open 9-5.30. STOCK: *Silver and jewellery, £5-£5,000; clocks, including Georgian and Victorian, £25-£3,000.* SER: Valuations; restorations (silver and jewellery); buys at auction. SIZE: Small. PARK: Easy. VAT: Stan. TEL: 01392 272228; FAX: 01392 498128

Domani Antique & Contemporary
1 Deanery Place Palace Gate. EX1 1HU. (Jonathan Cull and Caro Brewster) EST. 2003. WEADA. Open Tues.-Sat. 10-5.30 or by appointment. STOCK: *English and Continental town and country furniture, 18th-19th C; contemporary arts.* LOC: Near Cathedral. SER: Free local delivery. SIZE: Medium. PARK: Magdalen Street & Cathedral/Quay car parks. TEL: 01392 252550; MOBILE: 07771 657522 E-MAIL: shop@domani-devon.com WEBSITE: www.domani-devon.com

Eclectique
Cellars 18 & 23, The Quay. EX2 4AP. (E.J. Henson and C. Frank) EST. 1992. Open 11-5 seven days. STOCK: *Mainly*

Victorian and Edwardian furniture including pine and oak; dining tables, chests of drawers, chairs and pictures. LOC: Town centre. SIZE: Medium. PARK: Nearby.
TEL: 01392 250799
WEBSITE: www.eclectique.co.uk

Exeter Rare Books
Guildhall Shopping Centre. EX4 3HG. (R.C. Parry)
EST. 1975. ABA. PBFA. Open 10-1 and 2-5. *STOCK: Books, antiquarian, secondhand, out-of-print, 17th-20th C; Devon and West Country topography.* £5-£500. LOC: City centre. SER: Valuations; buys at auction. SIZE: Small. PARK: Easy. FAIRS: ABA Chelsea, Bath.
TEL: 01392 436021

Exeter's Antique Centre on the Quay
The Quay. EX2 4AP. (Exeter Traders in Collectables Ltd)
EST. 1983. Open winter 10-5, Sat. and Sun. 10-5.30; summer 10-6 including Sun. *STOCK: General antiques - small furniture, clocks, ceramics, glass, jewellery, collectables, books, pictures, coins, postcards, records, tools and toys.* LOC: Quayside. SIZE: 20+ dealers. PARK: Nearby.
TEL: 01392 493501
WEBSITE: www.exeterquayantiques.co.uk

Fagins Antiques
The Old Whiteways Cider Factory, Hele. EX5 4PW. (C.J. Strong)
Open 9.15-5, Sat. 11-5. *STOCK: Furniture, decorative items, pictures, porcelain, garden furniture, architectural and shipping items.* LOC: 10 mins. from junction 28, M5 on the B3181 Cullompton - Exeter road. SER: Stripping (pine); pine furniture made to order. SIZE: Large. PARK: Easy.
TEL: 01392 882062; FAX: 01392 882194
E-MAIL: info@faginsantiques.com
WEBSITE: www.faginsantiques.com

Funkles
Unit 1-2, MacClaines Warehouse, Piazza Terracina, Haven Rd. EX2 8GT. (Simon Kielstra)
EST. 2005. Open 10-5 inc. Sun.; CL: Tues. *STOCK: Antique and Retro furniture, large items, collectables.* SIZE: Large. PARK: Nearby.
TEL: 01392 495888
E-MAIL: simon@funkels.co.uk
WEBSITE: www.funkels.co.uk

Funkles Loft
47 The Quay. EX2 4AN. (Helen Kielstra)
EST. 2005. Open 10-3, Sat./Sun. 11-5; CL: Tues, *STOCK: Antique and Retro furniture; vintage jewellery and bags; ceramics and collectables; £1-£500.* SIZE: Small. PARK: Nearby.
TEL: 01392 498995
E-MAIL: helen@funkels.co.uk
WEBSITE: www.funkels.co.uk

Mortimers
87 Queen St. EX4 3RP. (Ian Watson)
EST. 1970. Open 9-5. *STOCK: Jewellery, silver, watches and objets d'art.* LOC: City centre. SER: Valuations; repairs; probate. SIZE: Small. PARK: Easy. VAT: Margin/Global.
TEL: 01392 279994
E-MAIL: ian.watson@mortimersjewellers.co.uk
WEBSITE: www.mortimers.co.uk

Pirouette
The House That Moved, 24 West St. EX1 1BA. (L. Duriez)
EST. 1980. Open 10-5. *STOCK: Vintage wedding gown specialist; lace, shawls, babywear, linen, 1920s costume, Victorian and Edwardian bridal dresses.* LOC: West Quarter. SIZE: 3 floors and courtyard. PARK: Easy.
TEL: 01392 432643
E-MAIL: lduriez@onetel.com
WEBSITE: www.pirouettethecollection.co.uk

Steptoes Emporium
43 The Quay. EX2 4AN. (Paul Nye)
Open 10-5 seven days. *STOCK: Fine English 18th-20th C oak and mahogany furniture, marine items, porcelain, silver, plate, glass, paintings, prints, antiquities, carpets and decorative items.* LOC: Next to Old Customs House. SIZE: Medium. PARK: Easy. VAT: Spec.
TEL: 01392 213283

Toby's Architectural Antiques
Station Road, Exminster EX6 8DZ (Paul Norrish)
EST. 1985. SALVO. Open 8.30-5; 9.30-5, Sat; 10.30-4 Sun. *STOCK: Furniture, £15-£3,000; pianos, fireplaces, lighting, collectables, 19th-20th C, £5-£2,000.* SER: Valuations; delivery (UK). Bespoke kitchens and cabinets. SIZE: Large. PARK: Easy. VAT: Spec.
TEL: 01392 833499
E-MAIL: tobysreclamation@gmail.com
WEBSITE: www.tobysreclamation.co.uk

Peter Wadham Antiques
EST. 1967. Open by appointment. *STOCK: Small furniture, 1780-1880, £100-£1,000; glass, metalwork, topographical prints and local views, 1750-1870, £10-£500.* **SER: Valuations; restorations (small furniture and picture frames). SIZE: Small. PARK: Easy. VAT: Spec.**
TEL: 01392 255801

EXMOUTH

Treasures
34 Exeter Rd. EX8 1PS. (L. Treasure)
Open 9-1. *STOCK: General antiques.* SIZE: Small.
TEL: 01395 279512

FENNY BRIDGES

Alexander Paul Antiques
Unit 2. EX14 3BG. (David Steele and Mathew Yates)
EST. 1998. WEADA. Open 8.30-5.30, Sat. 10-4. *STOCK: Specialist in farmhouse tables, also dresser bases, serving, coffee and side tables, chairs, French buffets, chests of drawers and bedside cabinets; decorative mirrors, all mainly 1760-1900, £500-£6,000.* LOC: 3 miles west of Honiton on A30. SER: Restorations (inlay and veneer, re-leathering, turning, French polishing). SIZE: Medium. PARK: Easy.
TEL: 01404 850881/851298
E-MAIL: sales@alexanderpaulantiques.com
WEBSITE: www.alexanderpaulantiques.com

HATHERLEIGH

Shaw Edwards   BADA
43 Market St. EX20 3JP.
EST. 1997. WEADA. CINOA. Open by appointment. *STOCK: Early furniture and carvings, pre-1700 and related items. Stock split between Devon and premises in Berkshire.* SIZE: Small. PARK: On street. VAT: Spec.
FAIRS: BADA; Olympia (Nov); Harrogate (Sep/Oct); Powderham (Nov/Feb).
TEL: 01837 811101 or 01189 410847
E-MAIL: info@shawedwardsantiques.co.uk
WEBSITE: www.shawedwardsantiques.co.uk

Hatherleigh Antiques
15 Bridge St. EX20 3HU. (M. Dann)
Open by appointment. *STOCK: Collectors' furniture and works of art, pre-1700.* SIZE: Medium. PARK: Easy. VAT: Spec.
TEL: 01837 810159

HONITON

Jane Barnes Antiques & Interiors
Avalon, Upottery. EX14 9PQ. (J.A.C. and S.J. Barnes)
EST. 1982. Open by appointment only. *STOCK: General antiques and country pine.* LOC: Off A30. SER: Furniture copies made to order. SIZE: Medium. PARK: Easy.
TEL: 01404 861300
E-MAIL: jane@janebarnesantiques.co.uk

Roderick Butler   BADA
Marwood House. EX14 1PY. (Roderick Butler FSA and Valentine Butler)
EST. 1948. Open 9.30-5 (during August by appointment only). *STOCK: 17th-18th C and Regency furniture, curiosities, unusual items, early metalwork.* LOC: Adjacent to roundabout at eastern end of High St. SIZE: Large. PARK: In courtyard. VAT: Spec.
TEL: 01404 42169
E-MAIL: vfbutler@yahoo.co.uk

Collectables
134B High St. EX14 1JP. (Chris Guthrie)
EST. 1995. Open 10-4.30. CL: Mon. and Thurs. *STOCK: Railwayana, Wade, cigarette and 'phone cards, toys and games, breweriana, commemoratives, militaria.* SIZE: Small. PARK: Nearby.
TEL: 01404 47024
E-MAIL: chris@collectableshoniton.co.uk
WEBSITE: www.collectableshoniton.co.uk

Evans Emporium
140 High St. EX14 1JP. (Bob Evans)
EST. 1992. Open 10-5. *STOCK: General antiques and collectables, sheet music and musical instruments, silver and jewellery, furniture and furnishings, 19th-20th C, £1-£500.* SIZE: Medium. PARK: Nearby.
TEL: 01404 47869; MOBILE: 07790 546495

Leigh Extence Antique Clocks   LAPADA
The Grove, 55 High St. EX14 1PW.
EST. 1981. WEADA. Open 10-5. *STOCK: Clocks and barometers, 1710-1880.* SIZE: Medium. PARK: Outside shop. VAT: Spec.
TEL: 07967 802160
E-MAIL: leigh@extence.co.uk
WEBSITE: www.extence.co.uk

Fountain Antiques
132 High St. EX14 1JP. (A. and P. Barton and C. Bushell)
EST. 1980. Open 9.30-5.30. *STOCK: General antiques*

including pictures, furniture and textiles. SIZE: Large. PARK: Nearby.
TEL: 01404 42074
E-MAIL: fountain_antiques@yahoo.co.uk

The Grove Antiques Centre Ltd
55 High St. EX14 1PW. (Lesley V. Phillips)
EST. 1998. WEADA. Open 10-5. *STOCK: Fine period and country furniture; antique beds; glass, porcelain, Staffordshire, silver and jewellery, pictures, carpets and rugs; early longcase, bracket and carriage clocks, objets d'art; 20th C decorative design.* SER: Shipping; delivery. SIZE: Large. PARK: Easy.
TEL: 01404 43377; FAX: 01404 43390
E-MAIL: info@groveantiquescentre.com
WEBSITE: www.groveantiquescentre.com

Hermitage Antiques
37 High St. EX14 1PW. (N.R. Kirk)
EST. 1993. Open 10-5, Sun. 11-3.30 (June-Jan), Bank Holidays 11-3.30, otherwise by appointment. *STOCK: English and French furniture, 18th-20th C, £50-£10,000+; Arts and Crafts furniture, metalware, tiles, art pottery, £5-£7,500+; clocks, barometers, glass, lighting, china and collectables, 18th-20th C, £1-£5,000+.* LOC: M5 junction 28 or A30. SER: Shipping. SIZE: Large.
TEL: 01404 44406; HOME/FAX: 01884 820944;
MOBILE: 07768 553172
E-MAIL: raykirk04@aol.com

High Street Books
150 High St. EX14 8JB. (G. Tyson)
EST. 1978. PBFA. ABA. ILAB. Open 10-5. *STOCK: Books, prints and maps, 18th-20th C, £1-£1,000.* LOC: Opposite police station. SER: Valuations. SIZE: Medium. PARK: Easy. FAIRS: Major London Book.
TEL: 01404 45570; FAX: same; HOME: 01404 41771
E-MAIL: tysonbooks@hotmail.com

Honiton Antique Centre
Abingdon House, 136 High St. EX14 8JP. (N.D.A. and E.K. Thompson)
EST. 1985. Open 9.30-5.30, Sun. 10.30-4.30. *STOCK: 17th-19th C furniture, metalwork, copper, brass, pottery, porcelain, oils and watercolours, engravings and aquatints, period maps.* LOC: Exeter end of High St. SER: Valuations; restoration; delivery. SIZE: Large. PARK: Nearby.
TEL: 01404 42108
E-MAIL: tbumble84@aol.com

Honiton Antique Toys
38 High St. EX14 1PJ. (L. and S. Saunders)
EST. 1986. Open Wed., Fri. and Sat. 10.30-5. *STOCK: Diecast and tinplate toys, dolls, teddies, lead soldiers.* PARK: Easy.
TEL: 01404 41194
E-MAIL: hattoys@hotmail.com

Honiton Clock Clinic
16 New St. EX14 1EY. (David P. Newton)
EST. 1992. MBHI. MBWCG. Open 9-5, Sat. 9-3. CL: Thurs. *STOCK: Clocks - mantel, bracket, carriage and longcase, fully restored, 30 hour and 8 day, painted and brass dial, 1-year guarantee; aneriod and mercurial barometers; clock and watch keys, clock and barometer spares.* LOC: Near town centre. SER: Valuations; restorations (clocks and barometers); collection and delivery; home calls. SIZE: Small. PARK: Nearby.
TEL: 01404 47466; FAX: same

Lombard Antiques
14 High St. EX14 8PU. (B. and T. Sabine)
EST. 1974. Open 10-5.30. *STOCK: 18th-19th C English furniture, porcelain, Clarice Cliff (300+ pieces) and decorative items.* SIZE: Medium - joined to No.12 High St. PARK: Easy.
TEL: 01404 42140

Merchant House Antiques
19 High St. EX14 1PR. (Mr C. Giltsoff)
WEADA. Open 10-5, Sun. by appointment. *STOCK: English and French fine and provincial furniture, 17th-19th C; works of art, ironstone and later china, collectables and decorative items, upholstery and furnishings, £10-£20,000+.* SER: Valuations. SIZE: Large. PARK: Easy. VAT: Stan/Spec.
TEL: 01404 42694; MOBILE: 07768 960144
E-MAIL: merchant-house@btconnect.com
WEBSITE: www.merchanthouseantiques.co.uk

Otter Antiques
69 High St. EX14 1PW. (Kate Spencer)
EST. 1978. Open 9.30-4.30. CL: Mon. *STOCK: Fine antique silver, jewellery and plate including flatware; modern silver.* SER: Silverplating; restorations and repairs (glass, metal, jewellery).
TEL: 01404 42627
E-MAIL: kateotter@tiscali.co.uk

Pilgrim Antiques LAPADA
145 High St. EX14 8LJ. (Jill Mills)
EST. 1970. WEADA. Open 9-5.30. *STOCK: Period English and Continental, oak and country furniture.* SER: Packing and shipping. SIZE: Large - trade warehouse. PARK: Easy. VAT: Spec.
TEL: 01404 41219/45316; FAX: 01404 45317
E-MAIL: pilgrim1@btconnect.com
WEBSITE: www.pilgrimantiques.co.uk

Jane Strickland & Daughters LAPADA
Godford Mill, Awliscombe, EX14 1PN.
EST. 1977. WEADA. Open 10-5. *STOCK: 18th-19th C furniture especially 19th C upholstered English and French furniture; 19th C English and French mirrors; lighting, decorative items.* LOC: 10 miles from M5. SER: Restorations (upholstery). SIZE: Medium. PARK: Easy.

VAT: Stan/Spec. FAIRS: Decorative Antique Textile, Battersea.
TEL: 01404 44221
E-MAIL: jsanddaughtersuk@aol.com
WEBSITE: www.janestricklandanddaughters.co.uk

Upstairs, Downstairs
12 High St. EX14 8PU. (T. and B. Sabine)
EST. 1975. Open 10-5.30. *STOCK: 17th-19th C furniture, porcelain, metalware, pictures and clocks, Clarice Cliff.* SIZE: Large - 5 rooms. Joined to No. 14 High St. PARK: Easy.
TEL: 01404 42140

Yarrow
155/157 High St. EX14 1LJ. (James Yarrow and Sarah Wolfe)
WEADA. Open 10-5. *STOCK: Decorative antiques, painted and country furniture.* LOC: Off A303. SER: Export and packing. SIZE: Large. PARK: Own.
TEL: 01404 44399
E-MAIL: info@yarrow155.com
WEBSITE: www.yarrow155.com

Graham York Rare Books
225 High St. EX14 1LB.
EST. 1982. ABA. ILAB. PBFA. Open 9.30-5. *STOCK: Travel - especially Spain and South Africa; art - fine and applied, especially lace, costume and textiles; literature, natural history, history, biography, children's, British topography especially West Country, gypsies, George Borrow; maps and prints.* LOC: Last shop at west end of High St. SIZE: Medium. PARK: Nearby. FAIRS: Monthly (Hotel Russell, Bloomsbury); ABA Chelsea; International Book, Olympia (June); PBFA Bath (April).
TEL: 01404 41727; FAX: 01404 44993;
MOBILE: 07831 138011
E-MAIL: books@gyork.co.uk
WEBSITE: www.gyork.co.uk

LYDFORD

Skeaping Gallery
Townend House. EX20 4AR.
EST. 1972. Open by appointment. *STOCK: Oils and watercolours.* LOC: In village. PARK: On street. VAT: Spec
TEL: 01822 820383; FAX: same
E-MAIL: nicholas@skeaping.com
WEBSITE: www.skeapinggallery.com

LYNTON

Farthings of Exmoor
Churchill. EX35 6HY. (Ms Kate Pearson)
EST. 1996. Open Mon.-Sun. 10-4.30 (summer); Mon.-Sun 11-4. CL: Wed. (winter). *STOCK: Pictures, 19th-21st C; collectables, 19th-20th C; Vienna bronzes; reconditioned and novelty telephones (all converted to modern-day use); Dennis pottery; gift and local crafts.* LOC: Opposite church. SIZE: Small. PARK: Easy.

TEL: 01598 753744
E-MAIL: kate@farthingsofexmoor.co.uk
WEBSITE: www.farthingsantiques.com

Wood's Antiques
29A Lee Rd. EX35 6BS. (Pat and Brian Wood)
EST. 1994. Open 9-5.30 including Sun. (Sun. 9-2 in winter). CL: Tues. *STOCK: General antiques including small furniture, mainly Victorian, £10-£8,000.* PARK: Easy.
TEL: 01598 752722
E-MAIL: bwood.lynton@hotmail.com

MERTON

Barometer World Ltd
Quicksilver Barn. EX20 3DS.
EST. 1979. Open 9-5; CL: Mon., 2nd & 4th Saturdays. *STOCK: Mercurial wheel and stick barometers, 1780-1900, £650-£12,500; aneroid barometers, 1850-1930, £100-£1,500.* LOC: Between Hatherleigh and Torrington on A386. SER: Valuations; restorations (barometers). SIZE: Medium. PARK: Easy. VAT: Stan/Spec.
TEL: 01805 603443; FAX: 01805 603344
E-MAIL: barometers@barometerworld.co.uk
WEBSITE: www.barometerworld.co.uk

MODBURY

Devonshire Fine Art
9 Church St. PL21 0QW. (David and Karen Smith)
EST. 1991. Open 10-1 and 2-5.30. CL: Wed. pm. *STOCK: Paintings, drawings and watercolours, 18th-19th C, £75-£3,500; maps and charts, 16th-19th C, £20-£1,500; prints, 16th-19th C, £15-£1,000.* LOC: Central. SER: Restorations (frames). SIZE: Small. PARK: Easy.
TEL: 01548 830872
E-MAIL: info@devonshire-fine-art.co.uk
WEBSITE: www.antique-fine-art.com
antique-maps-online.co.uk

Wild Goose Antiques
34 Church St. PL21 0QR. (Mr and Mrs T.C. Freeman)
Open 10-5.30. *STOCK: Old pine, country furniture, decorative items.* LOC: A379 between Plymouth and Kingsbridge. SER: Delivery. PARK: Nearby. VAT: Stan.
TEL: 01548 830715
E-MAIL: wildgooseantiques@tiscali.co.uk

NEWTON ABBOT

The Attic
9 Union St. TQ12 2JX. (G.W. Gillman)
EST. 1976. CL: Mon. and Thurs., prior telephone call advisable. *STOCK: General antiques, to £1,000.* LOC: Town centre. SER: Valuations. SIZE: Medium. PARK: Easy.
TEL: 01626 355124

St Leonards Antiques & Craft Centre
Wolborough St. TQ12 1JQ. (Derick Wilson)
EST. 1970. Open 10-4.30 including Sun., Tues. 9.30-4.30. STOCK: *General antiques, 19th C, £5-£1,000+.* LOC: At start of main road to Totnes. SER: Valuations; restorations; buys at auction (furniture, decorative items); house clearance. SIZE: Large. PARK: Adjacent and opposite. FAIRS: All major.
TEL: 01626 335666; FAX: same
E-MAIL: derick@derick8.orangehome.co.uk

Toby's Architectural Antiques
Brunel Road Industrial Estate, TQ12 4PB
EST. 1985. SALVO Open 8.30-5; Sat. 9.30- 4.30. STOCK: *Furniture, £15-£3,000; pianos, fireplaces, lighting, collectables, 19th-20th C, £5-£2,000.* SER: Valuations; delivery (UK). Bespoke kitchens and cabinets. SIZE: Large. PARK: Easy. VAT: Spec.
TEL: 01626 351767
E-MAIL: tobysreclamation@gmail.com
WEBSITE: www.tobysreclamation.co.uk

PAIGNTON

The Pocket Bookshop
159 Winner St. TQ3 3BP. (L. and A.R. Corrall)
EST. 1985. Open Tues.-Sat. 10.30-5.30. STOCK: *Books, secondhand and out of print.* LOC: Outskirts. SIZE: Small. PARK: Nearby.
TEL: 01803 529804.

PLYMOUTH

Annterior Antiques
22 Molesworth Rd., Millbridge. PL1 5LZ.
(A. Tregenza and R. Mascaro)
EST. 1987. Open 9.30-5.30, Sat. 10-5 or by appointment. CL: Tues. STOCK: *Stripped pine, 18th-19th C, £50-£3,000; some painted, mahogany and decorative furniture; brass and iron beds, 19th C, £50-£3,000; decorative small items, Victorian and 20th C chairs.* LOC: Follow signs to Torpoint Ferry from North Cross roundabout, turn left at the junction of Wilton Street and Molesworth Road. SER: Buys at auction; finder; restorations. SIZE: Small. PARK: Easy. VAT: Stan/Spec.
TEL: 01752 558277; FAX: 01752 564471
E-MAIL: info@annterior.co.uk
WEBSITE: www.annterior.co.uk

Carnegie Paintings & Clocks
(Chris Carnegie)
Open by appointment. STOCK: *Clocks, barometers, paintings and small furniture.* SER: Restorations (paintings, clocks and barometers). PARK: Easy.
TEL: MOBILE: 07970 968337
WEBSITE: www.paintingsandclocks.com

New Street Antique Centre
27 New St., The Barbican. PL1 2LS. (Turner Properties)
EST. 1980. Open 10-5. STOCK: *Clocks, silver, jewellery, weapons and general antiques.* SIZE: Medium - 10 dealers and 10 cabinets. PARK: Nearby. VAT: Stan/Spec.
TEL: 01752 661165

Parade Antiques Market
27 New St., The Barbican. PL1 2NB. (John Cabello)
EST. 1982. Open 10-5 including Sun. STOCK: *Collectables, 19th-20th C, £1-£1,000; militaria, 18th-20th C, £1-£7,000.* SIZE: Medium. PARK: Easy.
TEL: 01752 221443; MOBILE: 07765 408063
E-MAIL: paradeantiques@hotmail.com

Michael Wood Fine Art
The Gallery, 17 The Parade, The Barbican, PL1 2JW.
EST. 1967. Open Tues.-Sat. 10-5, other times by appointment. STOCK: *Oils, watercolours, original prints, sculptures, ceramics, art glass and books, contemporary, RA exhibitors, modern British, Newlyn, St Ives and Victorian, £50-£250,000.* LOC: Harbour front. SER: Valuations; conservation, presentation and security advice. SIZE: Medium. PARK: Nearby. VAT: Stan/Spec.
TEL: 01752 225533; MOBILE: 07764 377899
E-MAIL: michael@michaelwoodfineart.com

SEATON

Etcetera Antiques
12 Beer Rd. EX12 2PA. (Michael and Deborah Rymer)
EST. 1969. *Trade Only.* STOCK: *General antique furniture and shipping goods.* SIZE: Medium. PARK: Own. VAT: Margin/Global.
TEL: 01297 21965; MOBILE: 07780 840507
E-MAIL: etceteraantiques@tiscali.co.uk
WEBSITE: www.etceteraantiques.co.uk

Green Dragon Antiques Centre
4 Marine Crescent. EX12 2QN.
10-5 seven days; Nov-Feb 10-4, prior telephone call advisable. STOCK: *General antiques, memorabilia, Victorian lace and baby clothes, jewellery, collectables.* SIZE: 20+ dealers.
TEL: 01297 22039
E-MAIL: denningmumsy@aol.com

SIDMOUTH

Sidmouth Antique Centre
All Saints Rd. EX10 8ES. (S. Nicholls and Mrs. S. Nicholls)
EST. 2007. Open 9-5, Sun. 10-4 (end May - end October). STOCK: *Wide range of antiques and collectables, militaria, stamps, limited edition plates, pictures and prints, linen, antique furniture, clocks, glass, copper and brass.* LOC: Near main Post Office. SIZE: 20 dealers. PARK: Nearby.
TEL: 01395 512588
E-MAIL: samnu@tiscali.co.uk
WEBSITE: www.sidmouthantiquecentre.co.uk

The Vintage Toy and Train Shop
Sidmouth Antiques Centre All Saints Rd. EX10 8ES.
(R.D.N. and J.W. Salisbury)
EST. 1982. Open 10-5. STOCK: *Hornby Gauge 0 and Dublo trains, Dinky toys, Meccano and other die-cast and tinplate toys, wooden jig-saw puzzles.* LOC: Near main Post Office. SER: Wishlists welcome. PARK: Limited and opposite.
TEL: 01395 512588; HOME: 01395 513399

SOUTH BRENT

P.M. Pollak
Moorview, Plymouth Rd. TQ10 9HT. (Dr Patrick Pollak and Mrs Jeanne Pollak)
EST. 1973. ABA. Open by appointment. STOCK: *Antiquarian books especially medicine and science; prints, some instruments, £50-£5,000.* LOC: On edge of village, near London Inn. SER: Valuations; buys at auction; catalogues issued, computer searches. SIZE: Small. PARK: Own.
TEL: 01364 73457; FAX: 01364 649126
E-MAIL: patrick@rarevols.co.uk
WEBSITE: www.rarevols.co.uk

SOUTH MOLTON

Snap Dragon
80 South St. EX36 3AG. (Mrs J.E. Aker and
G. Harris)
EST. 1994. Open 9-5. STOCK: *Pine and country furniture, kitchenalia and tools, architectural and garden artefacts.* LOC: Near town centre. SER: Restorations (furniture). SIZE: Small. PARK: Opposite.
TEL: 01769 572374; MOBILE: 07712 079818
E-MAIL: snapdragonantiques@hotmail.com
WEBSITE: www.snapdragondevon.co.uk

TAVISTOCK

Elford Fine Art   LAPADA
The Gallery, 3 Drake Rd. PL19 0AU. (Rosemary Jones)
EST. 2004. CINOA. WEADA. For exhibitions and by appointment, call for current brochure and dates. STOCK: *Oil paintings, watercolours and drawings by distinguished artists from 19th C to the present day.* **LOC: Town centre, next to Lloyds TSB. PARK: Several car parks in the town.**
TEL: 01822 612123; FAX: 01822 855715
E-MAIL: rosemary@elfordfineart.co.uk
WEBSITE: www.elfordfineart.co.uk

TEDBURN ST MARY

A. E. Wakeman & Sons Ltd
Newhouse Farm. EX6 6AL. (A.P., G.M. and A.A. Wakeman)
EST. 1967. WEADA. *Trade Only.* Open Mon.-Fri. 9-

5.30 or by appointment. STOCK: *Mahogany, walnut and rosewood furniture, mainly 19th C, £200-£5,000; some 18th C mahogany and oak, £300-£5,000.* LOC: 6 miles from Exeter. SIZE: Large. PARK: Easy. VAT: Stan/Spec. FAIRS: Newark; Ardingly.
TEL: 01647 61254; HOME/FAX: same; MOBILE: 07836 284765
E-MAIL: aewakeman@btconnect.com

TEIGNMOUTH

Extence Antiques
2 Wellington St. TQ14 8HH. (T.E. and L.E. Extence)
EST. 1928. Open Tues.-Sat. 10-5. STOCK: *Jewellery, silver, objets d'art.* SIZE: Medium. PARK: Limited. VAT: Stan/Spec.
TEL: 01626 773353

TIVERTON

Guy Dennler Antiques & Interiors
Unit 19A, Lowman Units, Tiverton Business Park. EX16 6SR.
WEADA. Open Mon.-Fri. 10-4, other times by appointment. Prior telephone call advisable. STOCK: *Fine 18th to early 19th C English furniture and decorative objects.* PARK: Easy.
TEL: 01884 243747; FAX: 01884 243758
E-MAIL: guydennler@btconnect.com

This comprehensive study of needlework tools from the 17th century to the Edwardian era starts with the heavy silver needlework tools of the 17th century related to the raised and padded embroidery of that era now known as stumpwork. The more delicate embroidery tools of the Georgian era are grouped together with fine embroideries. Palais Royal sewing boxes and their superb mother-of-pearl contents, considered by collectors to be the ultimate sewing box, are illustrated as are the glorious carved ivory needlework tools that originated from the Dieppe region of France. The Victorian lady chose her sewing box, work table or sewing set from the extensive range available, this was also the era of the sewing circle and hand-made needlework tools were created in abundant numbers, many surviving for today's collectors' market.

280 x 215 mm. 216 pp 230 col., 20 b.&w.
£25.00 Hardback

TOPSHAM

Mere Antiques   LAPADA
13 Fore St. EX3 0HF. (Marilyn Reed)
Est. **1986. WEADA. Resident. Open 9.30-5.30, Sat.
10-5.30, Sun. by appointment.** Stock: *English
porcelain, 18th-19th C, £50-£10,000; furniture, 17th-
20th C, £200-£5,000; decorative items and silver; 19th C
and contemporary paintings.* Size: **3 rooms.** Park: **Easy
and nearby.** Vat: **Spec.** Fairs: **NEC; LAPADA.**
Tel: **01392 874224**
E-mail: **info@mereantiques.com**
Website: **www.mereantiques.com**

Topsham Quay Antiques Centre
The Quay. EX3 0JA. (Stonewall Ltd)
Est. 1993. Open seven days 10-5. Stock: *Furniture,
18th-19th C, £100-£3,000+; ceramics and tools, 18th-20th
C, £5-£1,000+; collectables, 20th C, £5-£200; silver and
plate, 18th-20th C, £10-£1,500+; textiles, 18th-20th C,
£5-£500.* Loc: 4 miles from Exeter, M5 junction 30.
Ser: Valuations. Size: Large. Park: Easy. Fairs: Local.
Tel: 01392 874006; Fax: same
E-mail: office@quayantiques.com
Website: www.quayantiques.com

TORQUAY

The Schuster Gallery
PO Box 139. TQ1 2XX. (T.E. Schuster)
Est. 1973. ABA. PBFA. Open by appointment. Stock:
*Antique prints, maps, medieval manuscripts, fine and rare
colour plate books, atlases; children's illustrated books
including Beatrix Potter, Kate Greenaway and Alice in
Wonderland and related items.* Vat: Stan.
Tel: 01803 211422; Fax: 01803 211290
E-mail: tschuster@easynet.co.uk

TOTNES

The Antique Dining Room
93 High St. TQ9 5PB. (P. Gillo)
Est. 1983. Open Tues.-Sat. 10-5. Stock: *Victorian and
Edwardian furniture especially Victorian wind-out tables.*
Ser: Restorations. Size: Small. Park: Nearby.
Tel: 01803 847800

Bogan House Antiques
43-45 High St. TQ9 5NP. (Chris Mitchell)
Est. 1977. Open Fri. 10-1 and 2-4, Sat. 10.30-1 and 2-
4.30, some Tues., otherwise by appointment. Stock:
*Silver flatware, £5-£200; metalware, Victorian and Delft
tiles, £5-£40; Japanese woodblock prints, £20-£400, glass
£5-£60.* Loc: Above arch, under Butterwalk on right.
Size: Small. Park: Nearby.
Tel: 01803 862075; Home: 01803 865386; Mobile:
07989 416518

Collards Books
4 Castle St. TQ9 5NU. (B. Collard)
Est. 1970. Open 10.30-5, restricted opening in winter.
Stock: *Antiquarian and secondhand books.* Loc: Opposite
castle. Park: Nearby.
Tel: Home: 01548 550246

Fine Pine Antiques
Woodland Rd., Harbertonford. TQ9 7SX. (Nick and
Linda Gildersleve)
Est. 1973. Open 10-5, Sun. 11-4. Stock: *Stripped pine
and country furniture.* Loc: A381. Ser: Restorations.
Size: Large. Park: Easy.
Tel: 01803 732465; Home: 01548 821360
E-mail: info@fine-pine-antiques.co.uk
Website: www.fine-pine-antiques.co.uk

TYTHERLEIGH

Trading Post Antiques Centre
EX13 7BE.
Open 10-4.30; 10-4 Sun. and Bank Hols. Size: 30
dealers.
Tel: 01460 221330

UFFCULME

English Country Antiques
The Old Brewery, High St. EX15 3AB. (M.C. Mead)
Est. 1984. WEADA. Open 9-5 by appointment or
telephone call. Stock: *Country and decorating antiques -
furniture - pine including painted, fruitwoods, oak and
mahogany, bamboo, bentwood, leather and upholstered;
metalware including lighting, brass, copper and iron,
gardenalia, architectural; china and glass, mainly 19th-20th
C; textiles, leatherwork, bric-a-brac, basketware, wooden
items, model yachts, pictures and paintings, mirrors.* Loc:
Village centre. Ser: Delivery and export by arrangement.
Size: Large. Park: Own. Fairs: NEC.
Tel: 01884 841770; Fax: same; Mobile: 07768 328433
E-mail: mike@englishcountryantiques.co.uk
Website: www.englishcountryantiques.co.uk

WESTON

The Honiton Lace Shop
c/o The Barn, Elmsfield Farm, EX14 3PF. (Jonathan Page)
Est. 1983. Open by appointment only. Stock: *Lace
including wedding veils, specialist and collectors; quilts,
shawls and other textiles, bobbins and lace making
equipment.* Ser: Valuations; repairs. Size: Medium.
Park: Easy. Vat: Stan.
Tel: 01404 42416; Fax: 01404 47797
E-mail: shop@honitonlace.com
Website: www.honitonlace.com

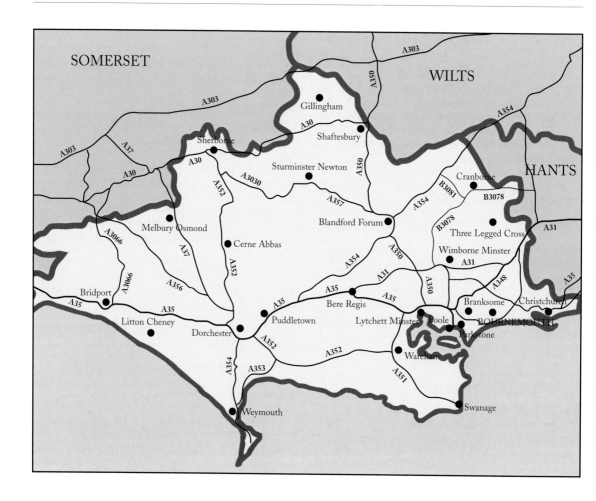

BERE REGIS

Dorset Reclamation

Cow Drove. BH20 7JZ. (Tessa Pearce)

SALVO. Open 8-5, Sat. 9-4. *STOCK: Decorative architectural and garden antiques, hard landscaping materials, fireplaces and bathrooms.* SER: Delivery; restorations. SIZE: Large.

TEL: 01929 472200; FAX: 01929 472292

E-MAIL: info@dorsetreclamation.co.uk

WEBSITE: www.dorsetreclamation.co.uk

Legg of Dorchester

The Old Mill Antiques, West St. BH20 7HS. (W. and H. Legg & Sons)

EST. 1930. Open 9-5 or by appointment. *STOCK: General antiques, Regency and decorative furniture, stripped pine.* LOC: On Bournemouth road. SER: Restorations (furniture). SIZE: Large. PARK: Easy. VAT: Spec.

TEL: 01929 472051

WEBSITE: www.leggofdorchester.co.uk

BLANDFORD FORUM

Milton Antiques

Market Place. DT11 7DX.

EST. 1993. Open 9-5, Sat. 9-4. *STOCK: Furniture, 18th-19th C, £50-£5,000; decorative items, 18th-20th C, £5-£200.* LOC: Opposite church, adjacent to town museum. SER: Valuations; restorations including polishing. SIZE: Medium. PARK: Easy.

TEL: 01258 450100

BOURNEMOUTH

Antiques and Furnishings

339 Charminster Rd. BH8 9QR. (P. Neath)

Open 9-5.30. *STOCK: Furniture, brass, copper, china, textiles and decorative objects.* PARK: 1 hr free outside.

TEL: 01202 527976

E-MAIL: aandf@btconnect.com

Boscombe Models and Collectors' Shop
802c Christchurch Rd., Boscombe. BH7 6DD. (Mr A. Hall)
Open 10-5. CL: Wed. STOCK: *Collectors' toys, 19th-20th C, £1-£1,000.*
TEL: 01202 398884

Chorley-Burdett Antiques
828-830 Christchurch Rd., Pokesdown. BH7 6DF. (Raymond Burdett)
Open 9-5.30. STOCK: *Furniture, pine furniture including reclaimed, late 19th to early 20th C, £50-£1,000.* LOC: Corner of Warwick Rd. SIZE: Large. PARK: Easy. VAT: Stan/Spec.
TEL: 01202 423363; FAX: same

Lionel Geneen Ltd   LAPADA
811 Christchurch Rd., Boscombe. BH7 6AP. (Robert Geneen)
EST. 1902. Open 9-5, Sat. 9-12, (closed lunchtimes), other times by appointment. STOCK: *English, Continental and Oriental furniture, china and works of art including some bronzes, enamels, ivories, jades, all mainly 19th C, Art Nouveau and Art Deco; specialising in tea, dinner and dessert services.* **LOC: Main road through Boscombe. SER: Valuations. SIZE: Large. PARK: Own. VAT: Stan/Spec.**
TEL: 01202 422961; HOME: 01202 520417; MOBILE: 07770 596781
E-MAIL: robert.geneen@btinternet.com

H.L.B. Antiques
139 Barrack Rd. BH23 2AW. (H.L. Blechman)
EST. 1969. STOCK: *Collectable items.* SIZE: Large. PARK: Easy.
TEL: 01202 429252

Hampshire Gallery
18 Lansdowne Rd. BH1 1SD. (Simon Keen)
EST. 1971. Open by appointment. STOCK: *Paintings and watercolours, 17th to early 20th C.* SER: Valuations. PARK: Easy. VAT: Spec.
TEL: 01202 551211

Walter James Antiques
847 Christchurch Rd., Pokesdown. BH7 6AR.
EST. 1997. Open 10-5; prior telephone call advisable. STOCK: *Antique furniture.* SIZE: Medium. PARK: Free on street.
TEL: 01202 430170

G.B. Mussenden and Son Antiques, Jewellery and Silver
24 Seamoor Rd., Westbourne. BH4 9AR.
EST. 1948. BJA. Open 9-4.30. CL: Wed. STOCK: *Antiques, jewellery, silver.* LOC: Central Westbourne, corner of R.L. Stevenson Ave. SER: Valuations. SIZE: Medium. PARK: Easy. VAT: Stan/Global/Spec.
TEL: 01202 764462.

R.E. Porter
2-6 Post Office Rd. BH1 1BA. (G.R. Broadway)
EST. 1934. Open 9.30-5. STOCK: *Silver including early*

antique spoons, Georgian, £20-£5,000; jewellery, pot lids, Baxter and Le Blond prints, clocks including second-hand. NOT STOCKED: *Furniture, arms, armour, carpets.* LOC: Walking from the square, take the Old Christchurch Rd., then the first turning on the left. SER: Valuations. SIZE: Medium. PARK: Opposite Post Office Rd. VAT: Stan/Spec.
TEL: 01202 554289
WEBSITE: www.richmondsilver.co.uk

Sainsburys Antiques Ltd
Rear of 23-25 Abbott Rd. BH9 1EU.
EST. 1918. Open by appointment. STOCK: *Furniture, fine replicas in mahogany and giltwood.* SER: Custom-made furniture. PARK: On road nearby. VAT: Stan/Spec.
TEL: 01202 529271; HOME: 01202 763616; FAX: 01202 510028
E-MAIL: sales@sainsburys-antiques.com
WEBSITE: www.sainsburys-antiques.com

Sandy's Antiques
790-792 Christchurch Rd., Boscombe. BH7 6DD.
BDADA. Open 10-5.30. STOCK: *Victorian, Edwardian and shipping goods.* SIZE: 2 large shops + warehouse. VAT: Stan/Spec/Export.
TEL: 01202 301190; FAX: same; evenings - 01202 304955; MOBILE: 07836 367384
E-MAIL: sandysantiques@btconnect.com

Sterling Coins and Medals
2 Somerset Rd., Boscombe. BH7 6JH. (W.V. Henstridge)
EST. 1969. Open 9.30-3. CL: Wed. pm. STOCK: *Coins, medals, militaria, World War II German items.* LOC: Next to 806 Christchurch Rd. SER: Valuations. SIZE: Small. VAT: Stan.
TEL: 01202 423881

M.C. Taylor
995 Christchurch Rd., Boscombe East. BH7 6BB. (Mark Taylor)
EST. 1982. MAPH. CMBHI. Open Mon.-Fri. 9-5. STOCK: *Clocks, barometers and turret clocks, £500-£20,000.* LOC: Opposite St. James' School and Kings Park entrance. SER: Valuations; restorations. SIZE: Small. PARK: Easy. VAT: Stan/Spec.
TEL: 01202 429718
E-MAIL: info@bournemouthclocks.co.uk
WEBSITE: www.bournemouthclocks.co.uk

Vintage Clobber
920 Christchurch Rd., Boscombe. BH7 6DL. (R.A. Mason)
EST. 1995. Open 10-5. STOCK: *Clothing and fabrics, from Victorian.* SIZE: Medium.
TEL: 01202 433330
E-MAIL: mail@vintageclobber.com
WEBSITE: www.vintageclobber.com

BRANKSOME

Allen's (Branksome) Ltd
447-449 Poole Rd. BH12 1DH. (P.J. D'Ardenne)
EST. 1948. Open 9-5.30. STOCK: *Furniture.* SIZE: Large.
VAT: Stan.
TEL: 01202 763724; FAX: 01202 763724;
E-MAIL: sales@allensofbranksome.co.uk
WEBSITE: www.allensofbranksome.co.uk

Branksome Antiques
370 Poole Rd. BH12 1AW. (B.A. Neal)
EST. 1971. Open 10-5. CL: Wed. STOCK: *Scientific and marine items, furniture and general small items.* SER: Buys at auction (as stock). SIZE: Medium. PARK: Easy. VAT: Stan/Spec.
TEL: 01202 763324; HOME: 01202 679932
E-MAIL: b.neal@ntlbusiness.com

Derek J. Burgess - Horologist
368 Poole Rd. BH12 1AW.
EST. 1980. Open 9.30-3; CL: Sat. STOCK: *Clocks, watches, furniture and smalls.* LOC: Opposite Tesco's, near Westbourne. SER: Restorations (clocks and watches of all periods); parts made. PARK: Street and forecourt.
TEL: 01202 751111

BRIDPORT

Battens Jewellers and Batten & Case Clock Repairs
26 South St. DT6 3NQ. (R. Batten and G. Case)
EST. 1974. BWCG. Open 9-4.30, Thurs. 9-1, Sat. 9-2
STOCK: *Jewellery, silver, clocks and watches.* LOC: Town centre. SER: Valuations; repairs. PARK: Easy and nearby.
TEL: 01308 456910
E-MAIL: battensbridport@hotmail.com
WEBSITE: www.battensbridport.com

Benchmark Antiques
Chancery Lane, DT6 3PZ. (Megan Standage)
EST. 1992. BAFRA. Open by appointment. STOCK: *English furniture and related items, 1700-1880, £100-£15,000.* LOC: Off East St. SER: Valuations; restorations; buys at auction. SIZE: Small. PARK: Easy. FAIRS: NEC.
TEL: 01308 420941; HOME: 01308 428200
E-MAIL: hohobird@netscape.net

Bridport Old Bookshop
11 South St. DT6 3NR.
EST. 1998. PBFA. Open 10-5. STOCK: *Antiquarian and secondhand books and prints.* LOC: Town centre. SIZE: Small. PARK: Nearby. FAIRS: PBFA; Bath; Lyme Regis; H&D, Royal National, London.
TEL: 01308 425689

CHRISTCHURCH

J.L. Arditti
20 Twynham Ave. BH23 1QU.
EST. 1964. Open by appointment. STOCK: *Oriental carpets and rugs, 18th to early 20th C, £500-£20,000.* LOC: From town centre take road towards Hurn airport, left turn. SER: Valuations; restorations; cleaning (Persian rugs). SIZE: Medium. PARK: Twynham Avenue. VAT: Stan/Spec.
TEL: 01202 485414/481500;
WEBSITE: www.arditti.freeserve.co.uk

Christchurch Carpets
55/57 Bargates. BH23 1QE. (J. Sheppard)
EST. 1963. Open 9-5.30. STOCK: *Persian carpets and rugs, 19th-20th C, £100-£5,000.* LOC: Main road. SER: Valuations; repairs; cleaning. SIZE: Large. PARK: Adjacent. VAT: Stan/Spec.
TEL: 01202 482712.

Hamptons
12 Purewell. BH23 1EP. (G. Hampton)
Open 10-6. CL: Sat. am. STOCK: *Furniture, 18th-19th C; general antiques, clocks, china, instruments, metalware, oil paintings, Chinese and Persian carpets and rugs.* SIZE: Large. PARK: Easy.
TEL: 01202 484000

Tudor House Antiques   LAPADA
420 Lymington Rd., Highcliffe. BH23 5HE.
(D. Burton)
EST. 1940. Open 10-5. CL: Mon. and Wed. STOCK: *General antiques.* LOC: Main road, A337. SIZE: Medium. PARK: Easy. VAT: Stan/Spec.
TEL: 01425 280440

DORCHESTER

Box of Porcelain Ltd
51d Icen Way. DT1 1EW. (R.J. and Mrs. S.Y. Lunn)
EST. 1984. Open 10-5. CL: Thurs. STOCK: *Porcelain including Worcester, Doulton, Spode, Moorcroft, Coalport, Beswick, Lladro, Crown Derby.* LOC: Close town centre, near Dinosaur Museum. PARK: Public car park in Durngate St. - 150 yds.
TEL: 01305 267110; FAX: 01305 263201
E-MAIL: rlunn@boxofporcelain.com
WEBSITE: www.boxofporcelain.com

Colliton Antique Centre
Colliton St. DT1 1XH.
EST. 1983. Open 9-4, Sun. by appointment. STOCK: *18th-20th C furniture, £25-£5,000; brass, bric-a-brac, pictures, china, pine, clocks, jewellery and silver, toys.* LOC: Rear of County Museum. SER: Restorations (metalware). SIZE: 14 dealers. PARK: Easy.
TEL: 01305 269398

De Danann Antique Centre
27 London Rd. DT1 1NF. (J. Burton)
EST. 1993. Open 9.30-5, Sun. 10-4. STOCK: *17th-20th C furniture, bedsteads, ceramics, rugs, clocks, pine, kitchenalia, brass and copper, collectables.* SER: Restorations (furniture

including French polishing, cabinet making). SIZE: Large - 20 dealers. PARK: Easy.
TEL: 01305 250066; FAX: 01305 250113

Finesse Fine Art
Empool Cottage, West Knighton. DT2 8PE. (Tony Wraight)
EST. 1982. Open strictly by appointment. STOCK: Pre-war motoring accessories - metal mascots and Lalique glassware, including mascots, fine bronzes, automobilia, picnic hampers, £1,000-£50,000.
TEL: 01305 854286; FAX: 01305 852888; MOBILE: 07973 886937
WEBSITE: www.finesse-fine-art.com

Michael Legg Antiques
8 Church St. DT1 1JN. (E.M.J. Legg)
Open 9-5.30 or any time by appointment. STOCK: 17th-19th C furniture, clocks, porcelain, pictures, silver, glass. SER: Lectures on the Arts. SIZE: Medium. VAT: Stan/Spec.
TEL: 01305 264596

Legg of Dorchester
Regency House, 51 High East St. DT1 1HU. (W. and H. Legg & Sons)
EST. 1930. Open 10.15-4.30. STOCK: General antiques, Regency and decorative furniture, stripped pine. SER: Restorations (furniture). VAT: Stan/Spec.
TEL: 01305 264964
WEBSITE: www.leggofdorchester.com

Words Etcetera
2 Cornhill. DT1 1BA. (Simon Rushbrook)
EST. 1974. PBFA. Open 10-5. STOCK: Antiquarian and quality second-hand books and prints; remainders on all subjects. LOC: Close to museum. SER: Buys at auction (books). SIZE: Medium.
TEL: 01305 251919
E-MAIL: info@wordsetcetera.co.uk
WEBSITE: www.wordsetcetera.co.uk

LITTON CHENEY

F. Whillock
Court Farm. DT2 9AU.
EST. 1979. Open by appointment. STOCK: Maps and prints. LOC: Village centre. SER: Framing. PARK: Easy.
TEL: 01308 482457.

LYTCHETT MINSTER

Old Button Shop Antiques
Dorchester Rd. BH16 6JF. (Thelma Johns)
EST. 1970. Open Tues.-Fri. 2-5, Sat 11-1. STOCK: Small antiques, curios, glass, lace, antique and Dorset buttons. LOC: 3 miles north-west of Poole. PARK: Adjacent.
TEL: 01202 622169
E-MAIL: buttonshop@btinternet.com

MELBURY OSMOND

Hardy Country
Meadow View. DT2 0NA. (Steven and Caroline Groves)
EST. 1980. Open by appointment. STOCK: Georgian, Victorian, Edwardian pine and country furniture, £40-£2,500. LOC: Off A37. SIZE: Large. PARK: Easy.
TEL: 01935 83440
WEBSITE: www.hardycountry.com

PARKSTONE

Dorset Coin Company
193 Ashley Rd. BH14 9DL. (E.J. and C.P. Parsons)
EST. 1977. BNTA. IBNS. Open by appointment. STOCK: Coins, 19th-20th C, £1-£50; banknotes, 20th C, £3-£50. LOC: Main road through Upper Parkstone. SER: Valuations. PARK: Easy. VAT: Stan/Global/Exempt FAIRS: BNTA London.
TEL: 01202 739606; FAX: 01202 739230

POOLE

Stocks and Chairs
10-11 Bank Chambers, Penn Hill Ave. BH14 9NB. (Mrs C.E. Holding-Parsons)
EST. 1992. Open Tues.-Sat. 10.30-5 and by appointment. STOCK: Furniture, 18th to early 20th C, mainly £500-£5,000; specialist in hand-dyed leather chairs and settees. SER: Restorations (including cabinet work, polishing and upholstery). SIZE: Large and trade warehouse. PARK: Easy.
TEL: 01202 718618; MOBILE: 07970 010512
E-MAIL: hp@stocksandchairsantiques.com
WEBSITE: www.stocksandchairsantiques.com

PUDDLETOWN

Antique Map and Bookshop
32 High St. DT2 8RU. (C.D. and H.M. Proctor)
EST. 1976. ABA. PBFA. Open 9-5. STOCK: Antiquarian and secondhand books, maps, prints and engravings. SER: Postal; catalogues. PARK: Easy.
TEL: 01305 848633
WEBSITE: www.puddletownbookshop.co.uk

SHAFTESBURY

Mr. Punch's Antique Market
33 Bell St. SP7 8AE.
EST. 1994. Open 10-5.30. CL: Mon. STOCK: Wide variety of general antiques, fine art and collectables. Also Punch and Judy collection. LOC: On corner with Muston's Lane. SER: Valuations; restorations; repairs (ceramics); delivery. SIZE: Large. PARK: Easy 100 yards.
TEL: 01747 855775; FAX: same
WEBSITE: www.mrpunches.co.uk

Shaston Antiques
14 Bell St. SP7 8AE. (J. D. Hine)
EST. 1996. Resident. Open 9-5. CL: Mon. STOCK:
Furniture, 18th-19th C, £300-£5,000. LOC: From town
centre, turn right opposite Grosvenor Hotel into Bell St.
SER: Restorations (furniture). SIZE: Medium.
TEL: 01747 850405; HOME: same
WEBSITE: www.shaston-antiques.com

SHERBORNE

Chapter House Books
Trendle St. DT9 3NT. (Claire Porter and Tudor Books
Ltd)
EST. 1988. PBFA. Open 10-5. STOCK: *Out-of-print,
secondhand and antiquarian books, to £400.* LOC: Next to
Almshouse and Abbey. SER: Valuations; search. SIZE:
Large.
TEL: 01935 816262
E-MAIL: chapterhousebooks@tiscali.co.uk
WEBSITE: www.chapterhouse-books.co.uk

Dodge & Son
28-33 Cheap St. DT9 3PU. (S. Dodge)
EST. 1918. Open 9-5.30, Sun. by appointment. STOCK:
*Antique and reproduction furniture, specialising in dining;
all periods.* SER: Restorations; furniture makers;
worldwide delivery. SIZE: Large. PARK: At rear. VAT:
Stan/Spec.
TEL: 01935 815151

Greystoke Antiques
Swan Yard, Off Cheap St. DT9 3AX. (F.L. and N.E.
Butcher)
EST. 1970. WEADA. Open 10-4.30. STOCK: *Silver,
Georgian, Victorian and later; early 19th C English blue
transfer printed pottery.* LOC: Off main street. PARK:
Adjacent to Swan Yard or outside shop. VAT:
Stan/Margin/Global.
TEL: 01935 812833

Nadin & Macintosh   LAPADA
**c/o Macintosh Antiques, The Courtyard, Newland.
DT9 3JG. (Patrick Macintosh and R. Nadin)**
EST. 1985. WEADA. Open 10-5. STOCK: *17th-20th C
country house furniture and accessories including Arts &
Craft movement, £100-£10,000.* LOC: Opposite
Somerfield. SER: Valuations; restorations. SIZE: Large.
PARK: Own. VAT: Spec. FAIRS: Olympia (Feb., June,
Nov); Little Chelsea; Bath; Decorative Arts, Battersea.
TEL: 01935 815827; HOME: 01935 873667; MOBILE:
07768 606811
E-MAIL: patrick@macintoshantiques.fsnet.co.uk
WEBSITE: www.macintoshantiques.co.uk

Phoenix Antiques
21 Cheap St. DT9 3PU. (Sally and Neil Brent Jones)
EST. 1998. Open 9.30-5.30, CL: Wed. STOCK: *Furniture,
17th-20th C; lighting, mirrors, furnishings, decorative and*
unusual items. LOC: Town centre. SER: Valuations;
restorations. SIZE: Medium. PARK: Easy.
TEL: 01935 812788
E-MAIL: phoenixantique@aol.com

Piers Pisani Antiques Ltd
The Court Yard, Newland. DT9 3JG.
EST. 1987. Open 10-5. STOCK: *Furniture including sofas
and armchairs, dining tables and sets of chairs, English and
French country house and reproduction; decorative items.*
LOC: Next to Sherborne House. SER: Valuations;
restorations (upholstery, chairs copied, cabinet-making).
SIZE: Medium. PARK: Own. VAT: Spec.
TEL: 01935 815209; FAX: same; MOBILE: 07973 373753
E-MAIL: pp@pierspisani.com
WEBSITE: www.pierspisani.com

Renaissance
South St. DT9 3NG. (Malcolm Heygate Browne)
Open 10-5. STOCK: *18th-19th C furniture, pottery and
porcelain.* LOC: Off Cheap St. towards station. SER:
Valuations; restorations. SIZE: Large. PARK: Easy. VAT:
Stan/Spec.
TEL: 01935 815487
E-MAIL: antiquemalcolm@aol.com

The Swan Gallery   LAPADA
51 Cheap St. DT9 3AX. (S. and Mrs K. Lamb)
EST. 1977. WEADA. Open 9.30-5. STOCK:
*Watercolours, 18th to early 20th C; oil paintings,
antiquarian maps and prints.* **SER: Valuations;
restorations (paintings, watercolours and prints);
framing. SIZE: Large. PARK: Easy, at rear. VAT:
Stan/Spec. FAIRS: Watercolours and Drawings,
Burlington Gardens, London.**
**TEL: 01935 814465; FAX: 01308 868195; MOBILE:
07785 757034**
E-MAIL: swangallery@aol.com
WEBSITE: www.swangallery.co.uk

Timecraft Clocks
Unit 2, 24 Cheap St. DT9 3PX. (Gordon M. Smith)
EST. 1993. MBHI. Open Tues.-Sat. by appointment or
chance. STOCK: *Clocks, 18th-20th C, £200-£5,000;
barometers, 18th-20th C, £80-£2,000; telephones, 20th C,
£80-£250.* SER: Restorations (clock and barometer
movements, cases and dials). SIZE: Small. PARK: Easy.
TEL: 01935 817771

Wessex Antiques
6 Cheap St. DT9 3PX. (Mrs Frances Bryant)
EST. 1986. WEADA. Open Tues.-Sat. 10-5 or by
appointment. STOCK: *Staffordshire figures, 1800-1900,
£100-£3,000; English drinking glasses, 1680-1820, £50-
£2,000; small English furniture, 1500-1850, £300-£6,000;
Oriental rugs, 1800-1950, £400-£6,000.* LOC: Town
centre. SER: Valuations; restorations (ceramics). SIZE:
Small. PARK: Loading and nearby.
TEL: 01935 816816; FAX: same

Henry Willis (Antique Silver)
38 Cheap St. DT9 3PX.
EST. 1974. WEADA. Open 10-5. STOCK: Silver, 16th-
20th C, £15-£15,000. LOC: Town centre, just off A30.
SER: Valuations; restorations (silver); buys at auction
(silver). SIZE: Small. PARK: Nearby. VAT: Stan/Spec.
FAIRS: Olympia (June).
TEL: 01935 816828
E-MAIL: hwillis.silver@tiscali.co.uk

SWANAGE

Georgian Gems Antique Jewellers
28 High St. BH19 2NU. (Brian Barker)
EST. 1971. NAG. BGA. SJH. Open 9.30-1 and 2.30-5 or
by appointment. STOCK: Jewellery, £5-£3,500; silver, £5-
£500; both from 1700. LOC: Town centre. SER: Valuations;
repairs; gem testing; special search. SIZE: Small. PARK:
Nearby. Special arrangements by prior telephone call.
TEL: 01929 424697; FREEPHONE - 0800 4710 242; FAX:
01929 426830
E-MAIL: info@georgiangems.co.uk
WEBSITE: www.georgiangems.co.uk

Reference Works Ltd.
at The Last Resort, 9 Commercial Rd. BH19 1DF.
(B. and J.E. Lamb)
EST. 1984. Open 10-4, Sat. 10-1. STOCK: Reference books
and catalogues on ceramics, all subjects, new and out-of-
print; small range of ceramics, 18th-20th C. SER: Monthly
list of books available; ceramic research and consultancy.
TEL: 01929 424423; FAX: 01929 422597
E-MAIL: sales@referenceworks.co.uk
WEBSITE: www.referenceworks.co.uk

WAREHAM

Heirlooms Antique Jewellers and Silversmiths
21 South St. BH20 4LR. (M. and Mrs G. Young)
EST. 1986. FGA. DGA. RJDip. FNAG. Open 9.30-5.
CL: Wed. STOCK: Jewellery, £30-£1,000; silver, £20-
£500; both Georgian to Edwardian. LOC: On main
thoroughfare. SER: Valuations; restorations; repairs; gem
testing; watch and clock repairs. SIZE: Medium. PARK:
At rear.
TEL: 01929 554207
E-MAIL: heirloomsofwareham@btopenworld.com

Yesterdays
13A North St. BH20 4AB.
EST. 1995. Open 9.30-4.30, Wed. 9.30-1.30. STOCK:
Pottery and porcelain - Dennis, Poole, blue and white,
Beswick, Isle of Wight, Wade, Carlton and Spode, Jonathan
Harris; okra glass. LOC: Town centre opposite Post
Office. SER: Valuations; buys at auction. PARK: Nearby.
VAT: Stan. FAIRS: Shepton Mallet, Exeter; Winchester.
TEL: 01929 550505; HOME: 01929 556381

WEYMOUTH

Books Afloat
66 Park St. DT4 7DE. (J. Ritchie)
EST. 1983. Open 9.30-5.30 (10-5 in winter). STOCK:
Rare and secondhand books especially nautical; maritime
ephemera, liner and naval memorabilia, ship models,
paintings, prints. LOC: Near rail station. SIZE: 2 floors.
PARK: Easy.
TEL: 01305 779774

The Nautical Antiques Centre
3 Cove Passage, off Hope Sq. DT4 8TR. (D.C.
Warwick)
EST. 1989. Open 10-1 and 2-5 prior telephone call
advisable, Sat., Sun. and Mon. by appointment. STOCK:
Exclusively original nautical items including sextants, logs,
ships' clocks, flags, oil lights, navigation lights, pulley blocks,
bells, ship models, telescopes, WW2 binoculars, ships' and HMS
badges and souvenirs and memorabilia, portholes, old charts,
compasses, wheels, barometers etc. 19th-20th C, £10-£2,000.
LOC: Opposite Brewers Quay, adjacent harbour. SER: Buys
at auction (nautical items). SIZE: Medium. PARK: Nearby.
TEL: 01305 777838; HOME: 01305 783180; MOBILE:
07833 707247
E-MAIL: info@nauticalantiques.org
WEBSITE: www.nauticalantiques.org

The Treasure Chest
29 East St. DT4 8BN. (P. Barrett)
Open 10-1 and 2.30-5. CL: Wed. pm. STOCK: Maps,
prints, coins, medals; army, RN and RAF badges. SER: Lost
medals replaced; medal mounting - full size or miniature,
brooches and new ribbons. PARK: Next door.
TEL: 01305 772757

WIMBORNE MINSTER

J.B. Antiques
10A West Row. BH21 1LA. (J. Beckett)
EST. 1978. Open 10-4, Fri. and Sat. 9.30-4. STOCK:
Copper, £5-£360; brass, £1-£350; furniture, £30-£1,200;
all 18th-20th C. LOC: 2 mins. from Sq. SER: Valuations;
restorations (metalware). SIZE: Small. PARK: Nearby.
FAIRS: Hinchingbrooke House, Huntingdon.
TEL: HOME: 01202 520118; MOBILE: 07786 593279

Portique
42 East St. BH21 1DX. (N. and E. Harkness)
EST. 1968. NAG. Open 9.30-4.30, Sat. 9.30-4. CL:
Mon. STOCK: Silver and jewellery; Comitti reproduction
clocks. LOC: A31 westbound, Leigh Rd., turn right at
small roundabout, take 1st left into Park Lane, over
bridge, premises on left. SER: Repairs; restorations (silver
and jewellery); valuations. VAT: Stan/Spec.
TEL: 01202 884282
E-MAIL: portiquethejewellers@hotmail.com

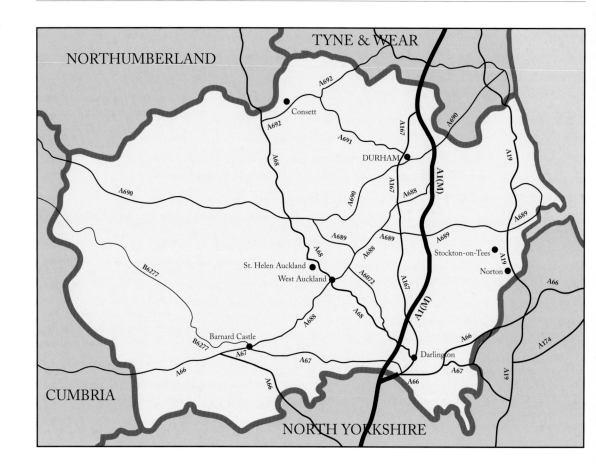

BARNARD CASTLE

The Collector
Douglas House, The Bank. DL12 8PH. (Robert A. Jordan)
EST. 1970. Open Sat. 10-5 or by appointment. *STOCK: Early oak, walnut and country furniture with complementary objects, decorative interior fittings and Eastern rugs.* SER: Restorations (especially metalwork, early furniture and interiors). SIZE: Medium. PARK: Own.
TEL: 01833 637783 FAX: same
E-MAIL: TheCollector@onetel.com
WEBSITE: www.barnard-castle.co.uk/antiques
www.thecollectorantiques.com

Robson's Antiques
36 The Bank. DL12 8PN. (Anne, David and Dale Robson)
EST. 1977. Open 10-5.30. *STOCK: Smalls including cutlery and canteens; silver, perfume bottles, cruets, photograph frames; Victorian and north east glass; pottery including Maling, Carltonware and Losol; Durham and patchwork quilts; Georgian, Victorian and Edwardian fireplaces, ranges, marble and wooden surrounds, inserts.* LOC: Below Market Cross. SER: Valuations; restorations. SIZE: Medium. PARK: Easy. VAT: Global. FAIRS: Newark; Manchester Armitage Centre Textile.
TEL: 01833 690157 MOBILE: 07977 146584
E-MAIL: dale.hunter.robson@virgin.net
WEBSITE: www.robsonsantiques.co.uk

Joan, David and Richard White Antiques
Neville House, 10 The Bank. DL12 8PQ.
EST. 1975. Open 11-5. CL: Mon. and Wed. *STOCK: Georgian, Victorian, export and pine furniture, decorative items.* LOC: 100yds. from Market Cross. SER: Delivery of large items. SIZE: Medium. PARK: Front of shop. VAT: Stan/Spec.
TEL: 01833 638329 HOME: 01325 374303
WEBSITE: www.whitesantiques.co.uk

CONSETT

Harry Raine Antiques
Kelvinside House, Villa Real Rd. DH8 6BL.
Appointment advisable. *STOCK: General antiques.*
TEL: 01207 503935

DARLINGTON

Darlington Antiques Centre
9a Northumberland St. DL3 7HJ. (Mark Evans)
EST. 2006. Open 10-4. CL: Thurs. and Sun. STOCK:
*Pottery and porcelain - Moorcroft, Royal Worcester, Royal
Doulton, Sylvac etc.* LOC: 2 mins from Darlington Market
Place - just off Grange Road. SIZE: 37 cabinets, 16
dealers. PARK: Outside, pay and display. VAT: Global.
FAIRS: NEC; Harrogate; Newark.
TEL: 01325 486724
E-MAIL: dacentre@evanscollectables.co.uk
WEBSITE: www.dacentre.co.uk

Robin Finnegan (Jeweller)
27 Post House Wynd. DL3 7LP.
EST. 1974. NAG. Open 10-5, CL: Wed. STOCK:
*Jewellery, military antiques, coins, medals, military blazer
badges and ties, £1-£10,000.* LOC: Town centre. SER:
Valuations; repairs (jewellery); mounting (medals). SIZE:
Medium. PARK: Easy. VAT: Stan.
TEL: 01325 489820
E-MAIL: diamondmerchants@btopenworld.com
WEBSITE: www.militarybadges.co.uk

NORTON

Paraphernalia
12 Harland Place, High St. TS20 1AA. (Rena Thomas)
EST. 1982. Open 9.30-5. STOCK: *Mainly 19th C
mahogany furniture, to £1,000.* LOC: Next to Red Lion
public house. SIZE: Large. PARK: Easy. VAT: Stan/Spec.
TEL: 01642 535940

ST. HELEN AUCKLAND

Something Different
34a Maude Terrace. DL14 9BD. (P. Reeves)
EST. 1968. Open 9.30-5.30, Sun. 11-4. STOCK: *Furniture,
clocks, decorative items, 19th-20th C; English &
Continental chandeliers.* SER: Delivery to UK and Europe.
SIZE: Large. PARK: Easy.
TEL: 01388 664366
E-MAIL: y.reeves@btinternet.com

STOCKTON-ON-TEES

T.B. and R. Jordan (Fine Paintings)   LAPADA
**Aslak, Eaglescliffe. TS16 0QN. (Tom and Rosamund
Jordan)**
EST. 1974. Open by appointment. STOCK: *Oil paintings
and watercolours especially Staithes group and mining art,
19th-20th C, £200-£25,000.* LOC: Village centre. SER:
Commissions. PARK: Easy. VAT: Spec. FAIRS:
Harrogate.
TEL: **01642 782599** MOBILE: **07970 503134**
E-MAIL: **info@tbrj.co.uk**
WEBSITE: **www.tbrj.co.uk**

WEST AUCKLAND

Eden House Antiques
10 Staindrop Rd. DL14 9JX. (C.W. Metcalfe)
EST. 1978. Open daily including Sun. STOCK: *Clocks,
furniture, 18th-20th C; collectables, bric-a-brac, oak and
mahogany reproductions, Continental furniture.* LOC: A68,
approx. 7 miles west of A1M. SER: Valuations;
restorations; clock repairs. SIZE: Small. PARK: Easy.
TEL: 01388 833013
E-MAIL: cchrismetcalfe@aol.com
WEBSITE: www.edenantiques.com

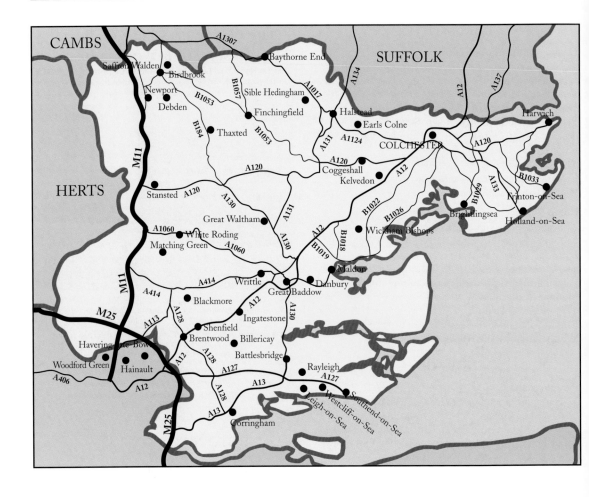

BATTLESBRIDGE

Battlesbridge Antique Centre
SS11 7RF. (Jim Gallie and Joseph Pettitt)
EST. 1967. Open 7 days 10-5. *STOCK: Wide range from large furniture to jewellery, all periods with specialist dealers for most items.* LOC: A130, mid-way between Chelmsford and Southend. Junction 29, M25, east on A127 to A130, then north for 3 miles. By rail: Liverpool St.-Southend-on-Sea, change at Wickford for Battlesbridge. SER: Restorations (furniture); container facilities; delivery (UK and overseas). SIZE: Over 80 units within adjacent premises (see below). PARK: Own.
TEL/FAX: 01268 762140
E-MAIL: info@battlesbridge.com
WEBSITE: www.battlesbridge.com

Cromwell House Antique Centre
TEL: (Management) Valerie Gallie: 01268 762612; ground floor dealers: 01268 762612; first floor dealers: 01268 734030

Haybarn and Bridgebarn Antique Centres
(J.P. Pettitt) TEL: 01268 763500/735884

Muggeridge Farm Buildings
(John Bedford) TEL: 01268 769000

The Old Granary Antique and Craft Centre
(Jim Gallie) TEL: (Management) Valerie Dyas: 01268 769000; showrooms: 01268 764197

BLACKMORE

Megarry's
Jericho Cottage, The Duckpond Green. CM4 0RR. (Judi Wood)
EST. 1986. EADA. Open Wed.-Sun. 11-5 or by appointment. *STOCK: Furniture, mainly 18th-19th C, some 20th C, £60-£3,500; ceramics, glass, treen and metalware, 19th-20th C, £5-£200; small silver and plate, jewellery and collectables, 19th-20th C, £5-£200; pine, 19th to early 20th C, £75-£1,000.* LOC: From A12, A414 or A128 into Blackmore, turn at war memorial, premises behind Bull garden on the village green. SER: Valuations. Teashop facility and open garden. SIZE: Medium. PARK: In front of shop, in drive and parking bay.
TEL: 01277 821031
E-MAIL: megarrys@yahoo.co.uk

BRENTWOOD

Brandler Galleries
1 Coptfold Rd. CM14 4BN. (J. Brandler)
Est. 1973. FATG. Open 10-5.30, Sun. by appointment.
CL: Mon. *Stock: British pictures, 20th C, £100-£100,000; original artwork for books and comics.* Loc: Near
Post Office. Ser: Valuations (photographs); restorations
(watercolour and oil cleaning, relining); framing; buys at
auction (pictures); 2-3 free catalogues annually. Size:
Medium. Park: Own at rear. Vat: Spec.
Tel: 01277 222269 (24 hrs)
E-mail: john@brandler-galleries.com
Website: www.brandler-galleries.com

Neil Graham Gallery
11 Ingrave Rd. CM15 8AP. (Mr and Mrs Neil Graham
Firkins)
Est. 1977. FATG. Open 9.30-5.30, CL: Mon., open
Sun. in December. *Stock: 19th to early 20th C
watercolours, oils and prints, £50-£1,000; Victorian and
Edwardian occasional furniture, £100-£1,500; silver,
pottery and porcelain, 19th-20th C, £25-£500.* Loc: Near
junction of Wilson's Corner, town centre. Ser:
Valuations; restorations (paintings); buys at auction.
Size: Large. Park: Easy and High St. Vat: Stan/Spec.
Tel: 01277 215383 Fax: same
E-mail: info@neilgrahamgallery.com
Website: www.neilgrahamgallery.com

Sherwin Gallery   LAPADA
4b Mascalls Lane. CM14 5LR. (Mr W.S. Sherwin)
**Open 10-5. *Stock: Late 18th-20th C watercolours and
oils.* Ser: Framing, restoration and picture cleaning.**
Size: Medium. Fairs: NEC Birmingham.
Tel: 01277 889527
E-mail: wsherwin@sherwingallery.co.uk
Website: www.sherwingallery.com

BURNHAM-ON-CROUCH

Harbour Antiques
7 High St. CH0 8AG. (R.J. Farrell)
EADA. Open 10.30-5 Mon.-Tues., 10.30-6 Sat.-Sun.
CL:Wed., Thurs. Fri. - telephone in advance. *Stock:
18th and 19th C furniture, English and Continental
ceramics, 19th C silver and plate.*
Tel: 01621 786412 Mobile: 07765 661905

COGGESHALL

English Rose Antiques
7 Church St. CO6 1TU. (Mark and Iryna Barrett)
Est. 1983. Open 10-5.30, Sun. 10.30-5.30. CL: Wed.
*Stock: English and Continental pine including dressers,
chests, tables and wardrobes, 18th-19th C, £50-£2,000;
fruitwood, ash and elm country furniture and kitchenalia,
gardenalia.* Loc: Town centre. Ser: Valuations;
restorations; stripping; repairs; finishing. Size: Medium.

Park: Loading or 50 yds. Fairs: Newark, Swinderby,
Ardingly.
Tel: 01376 562683; Home: same; Fax: same;
Mobile: 07770 880790
E-mail: englishroseantiques@yahoo.co.uk
Website: www.englishroseantiques.co.uk

Partners in Pine
63/65 West St. CO6 1NS. (W.T. and P.A. Newton)
Est. 1982. Resident. Open 10-5. CL: Wed. *Stock:
Victorian stripped pine.* Ser: Restorations; bespoke
furniture from reclaimed timber. Size: Small. Park: Easy.
Tel: 01376 561972; Fax: same
E-mail: will@newton6365.orangeHOME.co.uk

COLCHESTER

S. Bond and Son
Olivers Orchard, Olivers Lane. CO2 0HH. (R. Bond)
Trade only. Open by appointment. *Stock: Furniture and
pictures.* Ser: Valuations; restorations. Size: Large. Vat:
Stan/Spec.
Tel: 01206 331175; Mobile: 07710 823800

Elizabeth Cannon Antiques
85 Crouch St. CO3 3EZ. (Elizabeth and Brian
Cooksey)
Est. 1978. Open 10-5. *Stock: General antiques including
jewellery, silver, glass, porcelain and furniture.* Park: Easy.
Vat: Spec.
Tel: 01206 575817
E-mail: info@elizabethcannon.co.uk
Website: www.elizabethcannon.co.uk

Castle Bookshop
40 Osborne St. CO2 7DB. (J.R. Green)
Est. 1947. PBFA. Open 9-5. *Stock: Antiquarian and
secondhand books, maps & prints.* Ser: Book search. Size:
2 floors. Park: Private - telephone for instructions.
Fairs: Some PBFA.
Tel: 01206 577520; Fax: same
E-mail: castle40@gotadsl.co.uk

E. J. Markham & Son Ltd
122/3 Priory St. CO1 2PX. (Mrs S. Campbell)
Est. 1836. NAG. NPA. Open 8.30-5.30. *Stock:
Jewellery, 19th-20th C, £25-£8,000; porcelain, 18th-20th
C, £25-£2,000; furniture, 19th-20th C, £100-£1,500.*
Loc: Opposite St Botolph's priory ruins. Ser:
Valuations; restorations (porcelain). Size: Medium.
Park: NCP Priory St. Vat: Stan.
Tel: 01206 572646

DANBURY

Danbury Antiques
Eves Corner (by the Village Green). CM3 4QF. (Mrs
Pam Southgate)
Est. 1983. EADA. Open 10-5; CL: Mon. & Wed.

STOCK: *Jewellery and silver, ceramics, metalware, furniture, 18th to early 20th C, £5–£3,000.* LOC: M25, A12, A414, Maldon exit, on left after 3 miles. SER: Valuations; restorations (jewellery, upholstery, furniture). SIZE: Medium. PARK: Easy. VAT: Stan/Spec. TEL: 01245 223035

DEBDEN

Debden Antiques
Elder St. CB11 3JY. (Robert Tetlow)
EST. 1995. EADA. Open 10-5.30, Sun. and Bank Holidays 11-4, CL: Mon. STOCK: *Furniture including early oak, Victorian pine, Chinese and European painted, 17th-19th C, £100–£10,000; pictures, £50–£5,000, jewellery, silver, glass, porcelain, £5–£500, garden furniture, architectural, £50–£1,000; all 19th C.* LOC: Follow signs to Carver Barracks. SER: Valuations; restorations. SIZE: Large. PARK: Own. VAT: Stan/Spec.
TEL: 01799 543007; FAX: 01799 542482
E-MAIL: info@debden-antiques.co.uk
WEBSITE: www.debden-antiques.co.uk

EARLS COLNE

Totteridge Gallery
74 High St. CO6 2QX. (Janet Clarke)
EST. 1985. Open 10.30-5, CL: Wed. and Thurs. STOCK: *Oil paintings, £1,000–£25,000; watercolours, £300–£10,000; both 18th-20th C. Limited edition Russell Flint prints, 20th C, £500–£3,000.* SER: Valuations; restorations; free advice. SIZE: Medium. PARK: Easy. VAT: Stan/Spec.
TEL: 01787 220075
WEBSITE: www.totteridgegallery.com

FINCHINGFIELD

Finchingfield Antiques Centre
The Green. CM7 4JX. (Peter Curry)
EST. 1992. EADA BHI BWCG FSB Open 10-5 including Sun. CL: Mon. STOCK: *Vast and everchanging selection of antiques from 17th C oak to Art Deco, specialising in longcase, mantel, dial and other antique clocks.* LOC: From M11, A120 to Gt. Dunmow, then B1057. SER: Shipping arranged; clock repairs and restoration. SIZE: Large. PARK: Easy. VAT: Margin.
TEL: 01371 810258
E-MAIL: peter@antiqueclockandwatchrepairs.co.uk
WEBSITE: www.antiqueclockandwatchrepairs.co.uk

FRINTON-ON-SEA

Dickens Curios
151 Connaught Ave. CO13 9AH. (Miss M. Wilsher)
EST. 1970. Open 10-1 and 2-5.30, Sat. 10-1 and 2-5. CL: Wed. pm. STOCK: *Postcards and ephemera, Victorian and later items, £5–£200.* LOC: From Frinton Station quarter

of mile down Connaught Ave. SIZE: Small. PARK: Easy.
TEL: 01255 674134

Number 24 of Frinton
24 Connaught Ave. CO13 9PR. (Chris Pereira)
EST. 1993. Open 10-5, Sun. 2-4. CL: Wed. STOCK: *Art Deco and Victorian prints, general antiques, furniture and collectables.* SIZE: Medium. PARK: Easy.
TEL: 01255 670505
WEBSITE: www.artdecoclassics.co.uk

GREAT BADDOW

Baddow Antique Centre
The Bringey, Church St. CM2 7JW.
EST. 1969. EADA. Open 10-5, Sun. 11-5. STOCK: *18th-20th C furniture, porcelain, silver, paintings, Victorian brass bedsteads, shipping goods.* LOC: Near A12/A130 interchange. SER: Restorations; upholstery; framing; stripping (pine). SIZE: 22 dealers. PARK: Easy.
TEL: 01245 476159
WEBSITE: www.baddowantiques.co.uk

GREAT WALTHAM

The Stores
CM3 1DE. (E. Saunders)
EST. 1974. EADA. Open Thurs.-Sat. 10-5, Sun. 11-4. STOCK: *Period pine and country furniture.* LOC: Village

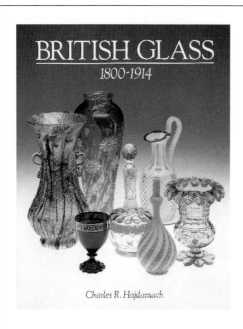
centre. SIZE: Large. PARK: At rear.
TEL: 01245 360277; HOME: 01245 360260

HALSTEAD

Antique Bed Shop
Napier House, Head St. CO9 2BT. (Veronica McGregor)
EST. 1977. Open Thurs.-Sat., other times by appointment. STOCK: *Antique wooden bedsteads - 19th C mahogany, rosewood, chestnut, oak, bergère and painted, £1,295-£3,500. NOT STOCKED: Brass, iron or pine beds.* LOC: On A131 to Sudbury. SER: Free UK delivery. SIZE: Large. PARK: Own. VAT: Spec.
TEL: 01787 477346 FAX: 01787 478757

Townsford Mill Antiques Centre
The Causeway. CO9 1ET. (I. Newman)
Open 10-5, Sun. and Bank Holidays 11-5. STOCK: *General antiques and collectables.* LOC: On A131 Braintree/Sudbury road. SIZE: 70 dealers.
TEL: 01787 474451

HARWICH

Peter J. Hadley Bookseller
21 Market St. CO12 3DX.
EST. 1982. ABA. ILAB. Open Fri. and Sat. 10-5, Sun. 1-4, other times by chance or appointment. STOCK: *Books -*

architecture, literature, art reference and illustrated. SIZE: Small. PARK: Easy.
TEL: 01255 551667
E-MAIL: books@hadley.co.uk
WEBSITE: www.hadley.co.uk

Harwich Antiques Centre
19 Kings Quay St. CO12 3ER. (Hans Scholz)
EST. 1997. Open 10-4.30, Sun. and Bank Holidays 1-4.30. CL: Mon. STOCK: *Furniture, porcelain, china, glass, silverware, jewellery, 19th C, £5-£2,000; collectables, 19th-20th C; decorative items, pictures, sports items and books.* LOC: Between the Pier and Electric Palace Cinema. SIZE: Medium. PARK: Nearby.
TEL: 01255 554719
E-MAIL: hac@antiques-access-agency.com
WEBSITE: www.antiques-access-agency.com

HOLLAND-ON-SEA

Bookworm
100 King's Ave. CO15 5EP. (Hazel Addison)
EST. 1995. Open 9-2.30, Sat. 9-4. STOCK: *Modern fiction, first editions, 1930-2001, £10-£500; rare and out-of-print, military history, motor and general sport, transport, nautical, £5-£100.* LOC: On junction with Holland Rd. SER: Valuations. SIZE: Small. PARK: Easy.
TEL: 01255 815984; FAX: same
E-MAIL: addisonbookworm@btconnect.com

KELVEDON

Colton Antiques
Station Rd. CO5 9NP. (Gary Colton)
EST. 1993. Open 8-5, Sun. by appointment. STOCK:
*Furniture, 17th to early 20th C, £300-£15,000; decorative
items, colonial furniture.* SER: Restorations (furniture).
SIZE: Medium. PARK: Own. VAT: Stan/Spec.
TEL: 01376 571504 MOBILE: 07973 797098

Chris L. Papworth MBHI
2 High St. CO5 9AG. (Kelvedon Clocks Ltd)
EST. 1970. MBHI. MBWCG. EADA. Open 9-5, Sat
10-5. CL: Fri. STOCK: *Clocks, watches (including pocket)
and barometers.* LOC: Near mainline rail station. SER:
Repairs, dial restoration, case restoration, valuations.
SIZE: Medium. PARK: Own. FAIRS: Brunel, Uxbridge,
Essex Watch & Clock, Colchester.
TEL: 01376 573434; HOME: same; MOBILE: 07802
615461
E-MAIL: info@kelvedonclocks.co.uk
WEBSITE: www.kelvedonclocks.co.uk

LEIGH-ON-SEA

Collectors' Paradise
993 London Rd. SS9 3LB. (H.W. and P.E. Smith)
EST. 1967. Open 10-5. CL: Fri. STOCK: *Clocks, 1830-1930,
from £85; bric-a-brac; postcards, 1900-1930s; cigarette cards,
1889-1939.* LOC: On A13. SIZE: Small. PARK: Easy.
TEL: 01702 473077

Deja Vu Antiques
876 London Rd. SS9 3NQ. (Stuart D. Lewis)
EST. 1990. Open 9.30-5.30, Sun. by appointment. STOCK:
*French furniture, late 18th to 19th C; antique bedsteads,
lighting and gilt mirrors.* SER: Valuations; restorations.
SIZE: Large. PARK: Easy. FAIRS: Newark; Ardingly.
TEL: 01702 470829
E-MAIL: info@deja-vu-antiques.co.uk
WEBSITE: www.deja-vu-antiques.co.uk

J. Streamer Antiques
86 Broadway and 212 Leigh Rd. SS9 1AE.
EST. 1965. Open 9.30-5.30. CL: Wed. STOCK: *Jewellery,
silver, bric-a-brac, small furniture.*
TEL: 01702 472895

MALDON

Clive Beardall Restorations Ltd
104B High St. CM9 5ET.
EST. 1982. BAFRA. EADA. Open 8-5.30, Sat 8-2.
STOCK: *Furniture, 18th-19th C, £100-£5,000.* LOC: Off
High St. up alleyway between Just Fabrics and Foulkes
Electrical. SER: Restorations (furniture). SIZE: Medium.
PARK: Easy. VAT: Stan/Spec.
TEL: 01621 857890; FAX: 01621 850753
WEBSITE: www.clivebeardall.co.uk

NEW ENGLAND

I. Westrope
Sturmer Rd. CO9 4BB.
EST. 1958. Open by appointment. STOCK: *Furniture,
china, doll's house furniture, garden ornaments including
birdbaths, fountains, statues, animals.* LOC: A1017.
TEL: 01440 780034; MOBILE: 07711 644817

NEWPORT

Omega
High St. CB11 3PF. (Tony Phillips and Sybil Hooper)
EST. 1985. Open 10-6, Sat. 10-5.30. CL: Thurs. STOCK:
*Furniture and lighting, 1880-1960, £20-£1,000; jewellery,
objects, 1900-1960, £20-£300.* LOC: B1383. SER:
Valuations; restorations (furniture including French
polishing, repairs and re-veneering). SIZE: Small. PARK:
Easy. FAIRS: Art Deco - Brighton; Chilford Hall, Cambs.
TEL: 01799 540720; HOME: same
WEBSITE: www.omegadecorativearts.co.uk

RAYLEIGH

F.G. Bruschweiler (Antiques) Ltd   LAPADA
41-67 Lower Lambricks. SS6 8DA.
EST. 1963. Open 9-5, Sat. by appointment. STOCK:
Furniture, 18th-19th C. LOC: A127 to Weir roundabout
through Rayleigh High St. and Hockley Rd., first left
past cemetery, then second left, warehouse round corner
on left. SIZE: Warehouses. PARK: Easy. VAT: Stan.
TEL: 01268 773761/773932; HOME: 01621 828152;
FAX: 01268 773318
E-MAIL: info@fgbantiques.com
WEBSITE: www.fgbantiques.com

RETTENDON

Ian F. Vince Antiques
Rawlings Farm Buildings, Main Road (old A130).
CM3 8DY.
EADA. Open 10-5 Mon.-Fri. STOCK: *18th - 20th C
furniture, 19th C paintings, Arts and Crafts movement.*
TEL: 07970 840390

SAFFRON WALDEN

Arts Decoratifs
The Cockpit, off Market Hill. CB10 1HQ. (Ann
Miller and Laurence Lattimore)
EADA. Open Tues.-Thurs. 10-4, Fri.-Sat. 10-5. CL:
Mon. STOCK: *Vintage jewellery, 19th and 20th C furniture
and glass, English and Continental ceramics, collectables, Art
Deco and decorative arts.*
TEL: 01799 513666

Ickleton Antiques
4A Gold St. CB10 1EJ. (B. Arbery)
EST. 1983. Open 10-4, Mon. 10-3, Sat. 10-5. STOCK:

Militaria including badges, medals and weapons; advertising and packaging, postcards. LOC: Just off centre of town. SER: Valuations. SIZE: Small. PARK: Nearby.
TEL: 01799 513114 HOME: 01799 527474

Lankester Antiques and Books
Old Sun Inn, Church St., and Market Hill. CB10 1JW. (P. Lankester)
EST. 1965. Open 10-5. *STOCK: Furniture, porcelain, pottery, metalwork, general antiques, books, prints and maps.* SIZE: Large. VAT: Stan.
TEL: 01799 522685

Littlebury Antiques - Littlebury Restorations Ltd
58/60 Fairycroft Rd. CB10 1LZ. (N.H. D'Oyly)
EST. 1962. Open 9-5. CL: Sat. and Sun. except by appointment. *STOCK: Barometers, marine antiques, chess sets, walking sticks and curios.* SER: Valuations; restorations; buys at auction. SIZE: Medium. PARK: Easy. VAT: Stan/Spec.
TEL: 01799 527961; FAX: same; HOME: 01279 813292
E-MAIL: ndoyly@btinternet.com

SHALFORD

Robin Butler
EST. 1963. Open by appointment. *STOCK: Wine associated antiques; decanters, coasters, corkscrews; 17th-20th C, £50-£20,000.* SER: Valuations. SIZE: 10,000 sq.ft. VAT: Spec.
FAIRS: Olympia (June/Nov); Chester; Chelsea.
TEL: 07831 194997
E-MAIL: info@butlersantiques.com
WEBSITE: www.butlersantiques.com

SHENFIELD

The Chart House
33 Spurgate, Hutton Mount. CM13 2JS. (C.C. Crouchman)
EST. 1974. Open by appointment. *STOCK: Nautical items.* LOC: Near Brentwood. SER: Buys at auction. SIZE: Small. PARK: Easy.
TEL: 01277 225012; FAX/HOME: same
E-MAIL: cccrouchman@aol.com

SIBLE HEDINGHAM

Hedingham Antiques
100 Swan St. CO9 3HP. (Patricia Patterson)
EST. 1978. Open by appointment. *STOCK: Mainly silver, some plate, china and glass, small furniture.* LOC: On A1017, village centre. SER: Repairs and restorations (small furniture). SIZE: Small. PARK: Forecourt. VAT: Spec/Global/Stan./Export.
TEL: 01787 460360; HOME: same; FAX: 01787 469109
E-MAIL: patricia@patriciapatterson.wanadoo.co.uk

Lennard Antiques   LAPADA
c/o W.A. Pinn & Sons, 124 Swan St. CO9 3HP.
(Gill Meddings)
EST. 1978. Open 9.30-6, Sun. by appointment. Prior

telephone call advisable. *STOCK: Oak and country furniture, 17th to early 19th C; English Delftware and interesting accessories.* LOC: On A1017 opposite Shell garage in village centre. SIZE: Medium. PARK: Easy. VAT: Spec. FAIRS: Olympia (June and Nov.); Harrogate.
TEL: 01787 461127 MOBILE: 07778 161301

W.A. Pinn and Sons   BADA LAPADA
124 Swan St. CO9 3HP. (K.H. and W.J. Pinn)
EST. 1943. Open 9.30-6. CL: Sun. except by appointment. Prior telephone call advisable. *STOCK: Furniture, 17th to early 19th C, £250-£5,000; brassware, lighting and interesting items, prior to 1830, £25-£2,500.* LOC: On A1017 opposite Shell Garage. SIZE: Medium. PARK: Easy. VAT: Stan/Spec. FAIRS: Olympia (June and Nov); Harrogate; Petersfield.
TEL: 01787 461127

SOUTH BENFLEET

Classique Antiques
356 High Rd., Hopes Green. SS7 5HP. (Chris Elliott)
EST. 1999. EADA. Open 9-3.30. Prior telephone call advisable. *STOCK: 18th - 20th C small furniture, ceramics, glass, paintings and prints; traditional and decorative arts.* LOC: Main road, 1.5 miles south of A13 (Tarpots). SER: Antique item searches through the EADA Members' Network. SIZE: Small, access limited. PARK: Small forecourt or adjoining roads within 50m.
TEL: 01268 566695

STANSTED

Valmar Antiques
The Barn, High Lane. CM24 8LQ. (Marina Orpin)
EST. 1960. Resident. Open by appointment. *STOCK: Furniture and decorative items including Arts and Crafts.* LOC: 2 miles from airport. SER: Upholstery; restoration. SIZE: Large.
TEL: 01279 813201; FAX: 08701 236114;
MOBILE: 07831 093701
E-MAIL: valmar-antiques@btconnect.com
WEBSITE: www.valmar-antiques.com

STEEPLE BUMPSTEAD

Bumpstead Arts & Antiques
Blois Road Business Centre, Blois Rd. CB9 7BN. (Christine Simpkin)
EADA. Open 10-5, Sat. 10-4. CL: Fri. Other times by appointment. *STOCK: 17th-20th C antique and decorative furniture, collectables and works of art.*
TEL: 01440 731888/730038 MOBILE: 07710 282329

Bumpstead Antiques & Interiors
Blois Meadow Business Centre, Blois Rd. CB9 7BN. (Graham Hessell)
EST. 1995. EADA. Open 10-5. Sat. 10-4. CL: Fri. or by appointment. *STOCK: Fine quality antique furniture, sofas*

and chairs, art, lighting and collectables from 17th C onwards. SER: Items bought; restorations; re-upholstery; valuations; free local delivery; UK and overseas deliveries arranged. SIZE: Large. PARK: Ample. Easy access.
TEL: 01440 731888 MOBILE 07710 282329

THAXTED

Harris Antiques
24 Town Street. CM6 2LA. (Fred, Maureen, Brian & Jo Harris)
EST. 1956. Resident. BAFRA. EADA. MBWCG. Open 9-6, Sun. by appointment. STOCK: *Quality period clocks, barometers and furniture, 16th-19th C, £50-£20,000+.* LOC: Near M11 and Stansted Airport. SER: Valuations; restorations. SIZE: Medium. PARK: Easy. VAT: Spec.
FAIRS: Snape Maltings, Southwold, Loddon.
TEL: 01371 832832 HOME: same
E-MAIL: harrisantiques@btconnect.com
WEBSITE: www.harrisantiques.co.uk

WESTCLIFF-ON-SEA

David Fairbanks Pens
Elderton House, 16, Elderton Rd. SS0 8AQ.
EADA. Open by appointment. STOCK: *Original fountain pens, dip pens and inkwells.* SER: Service and repairs to fountain pens.
TEL: 01702 391148

It's About Time   LAPADA
863 London Rd. SS0 9SZ. (P. Williams)
EST. 1979. EADA. Open Tues.-Sat. 9-5.30. STOCK: *Clocks, 18th-19th C, £200-£11,000; barometers, Victorian and Edwardian furniture.* LOC: **A13.** SER: **Repairs and restorations (clocks).** SIZE: **Large.** PARK: **Easy.**
TEL: **01702 472574**
E-MAIL: **shop@antiqueclock.co.uk**
WEBSITE: **www.antiqueclock.co.uk**

Ridgeway Antiques
58 The Ridgeway. SS0 8NU. (Trevor Cornforth)
EST. 1987. EADA. Open 10-5. STOCK: *General antiques and Oriental, £5-£1,000.* LOC: A13 London road, right at Chalkwell Ave., right to The Ridgeway. SER: Valuations for insurance and probate. SIZE: Large. PARK: Easy. FAIRS: Ridgeway; Hallmark.
TEL: 01702 710383

WHITE RODING

White Roding Antiques
'Ivydene', Chelmsford Rd. CM6 1RG. (F. and J. Neill)
EST. 1971. Open by appointment. STOCK: *Furniture and shipping goods, 18th-19th C, £10-£1,500.* LOC: A1060 between Bishops Stortford and Chelmsford. SIZE: Medium. PARK: Easy. VAT: Stan/Spec.
TEL: 01279 876376; HOME: same

BRIAN HARRIS

Complete Fine Quality Restoration/Conservation of all period Clocks, Barometers, Furniture etc.

24 Town Street, Thaxted
Essex   CM6 2LA
Tel: 01371 832832

Established 1956

WICKFORD

Cottage Antiques
Unit 1, The Elms Industrial Park, Cranfield Park Rd. SS12 9EP. (Robert Jarman)
EADA Open 9-6 by appointment. STOCK: *17th - 19th C Furniture, English and Continental ceramics, 19th C silver and plate, glass, 19th C and earlier paintings, Art Deco wrist-watches and clocks.*
TEL: 01268 764138; MOBILE: 07958 618629

WOODFORD GREEN

Mill Lane Antiques
29 Mill Lane. IG8 0NG. (Niki Wood and Bonnita Read)
Open Tues.-Sun. STOCK: *French lighting, furniture and Venetian mirrors.* SER: Valuations; restorations. SIZE: Medium. FAIRS: Kempton Park.
TEL: 020 8502 9930; FAX: same

WRITTLE

Whichcraft Jewellery
54-56 The Green. CM1 3DU. (A. Turner)
EST. 1978. EADA. Open 9.30-5.30. CL: Mon. STOCK: *Jewellery, silver and watches, 19th C, £30-£5,000, small silver items.* SER: Valuations; restorations (jewellery). SIZE: Small. PARK: Easy. VAT: Stan/Spec.
TEL: 01245 420183

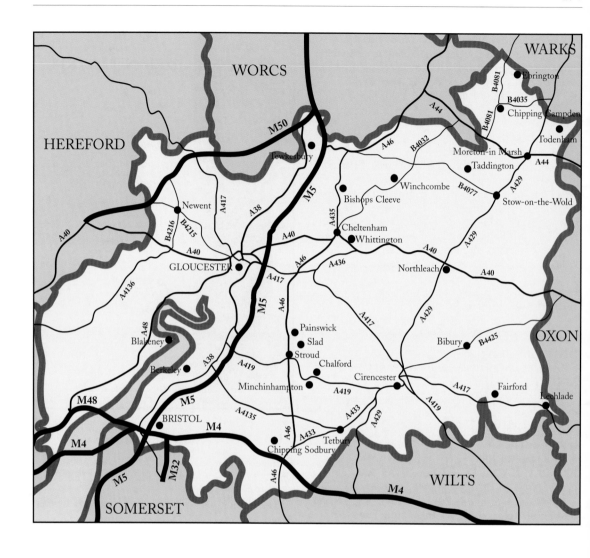

BERKELEY

Peter and Penny Proudfoot
16-18 High St. GL13 9BJ.
Est. 1956. Open 9-6, Sun. by appointment. *Stock: Furniture, 1600-1900, £100-£3,000; silver, 1700 to date, £5-£1,000; pictures, 1800 to date, £20-£3,000; jewellery, 1800 to date, £1-£1,000.* Loc: Town centre. Ser: Valuations; restorations (furniture and oil paintings); framing. Size: Small. Park: Easy.
Tel: 01453 811513; Home: same; Fax: 01453 511616
E-mail: pennyproudfoot@hotmail.co.uk

BISHOPS CLEEVE

Cleeve Picture Framing
Church Rd. GL52 8RL. (J. Gardner)
Est. 1974. FATG. Open 9-1 and 2-5.30, Sat. 9-1.

Stock: Prints, pictures (oils and watercolours), maps Ser: Framing; cleaning; restorations (oils, watercolours and prints).
Tel: 01242 672785.
Website: www.cleevepictureframing.co.uk

BLAKENEY

Lion, Witch and Lampshade
Birmingham House, High St. GL15 4EB. (Mr. and Mrs N. Dixon)
Open by appointment. *Stock: Unusual decorative objects, 18th to early 20th C, £5-£150; lamps, wall brackets, chandeliers and candlesticks, £50-£1,000.* Loc: Opposite Soudley Rd. Ser: Restorations (porcelain and glass). Park: Opposite in side road.
Tel: 01594 516422/020 7730 1774; Fax: 01594 516422

TOP BANANA ANTIQUES MALLS

GOOD TRADE CALL!

FOUR GROUP SHOPS OF DECORATIVE ANTIQUES AND INTERIOR INSPIRATION

1 New Church Street, Tetbury, Gloucestershire GL8 8DS
Tel: 0871 2881102   Fax: 0871 2881103

32 Long Street, Tetbury, Gloucestershire GL8 8AQ
Tel: 0871 2881110   Fax: 0871 2881103

48 Long Street, Tetbury, Gloucestershire, GL8 8AQ
Tel: 0871 2883058   Fax: 0871 2881103

46 Long Street, Tetbury, Gloucestershire, GL8 8AQ
Tel: 0871 2883058   Fax: 0871 2881103

Email: info@topbananaantiques.com
Website: www.topbananaantiques.com

From outside UK call: 00441666 504499
or Fax: 00441666 505599

BOURTON-ON-THE-WATER

The Looking Glass
Portland House, Victoria St. GL54 2BX. (Norman Jones)
Open 10-5 seven days. *STOCK: Glass, silver, collectables, mirrors, furniture and fittings, studio pottery.*
TEL: 01451 810818
E-MAIL: patsilooking@virgin.net

BRISTOL

Alexander Gallery
122 Whiteladies Rd. BS8 2RP. (P.J. Slade and H.S. Evans)
EST. 1971. Open 9-5.30. *STOCK: 19th-20th C paintings, watercolours and prints.*
TEL: 01179 734692; FAX: 01179 466991
WEBSITE: www.alexander-gallery.co.uk

Antique Corner with A & C Antique Clocks
86 Bryants Hill, Hanham. BS5 8QT. (D.A. and J.P. Andrews)
EST. 1985. MBWCG. Open 10-4 Tues., Thurs. and Fri. *STOCK: Clocks including longcase, wall and mantel, £5-£5,000; aneroid and mercurial barometers.* LOC: Next to The Trooper public house, A431 Bristol to Bath road. SER: Repairs (clocks and barometers). SIZE: 1 floor. PARK: Easy.
TEL: 01179 476141
E-MAIL: info@antiquecorner.org.uk
WEBSITE: www.antiquecorner.org.uk

Arcadia Antiques & Interiors
4 Boyces Ave., Clifton. BS8 4AA.
EST. 1993. Open 10-5.30. *STOCK: General antiques including sofas and chairs, lighting including chandeliers, jewellery and decorative items, £5-£2,500.* LOC: Near The Mall. SIZE: Small.
TEL: 01179 144479; FAX: 01179 239308

Au Temps Perdu
28-30 Midland Rd., St. Philips. BS2 0JY.
Open 10-5 Tues.-Sat. *STOCK: Architectural salvage, fireplaces, chandeliers, doors, antique garden ornament and related items.* SER: Repairs inc. chandeliers.
TEL: 0117 929 9143
E-MAIL: p.mcgrane@sky.com
WEBSITE: www.autempsperdu.co.uk

Bristol Brocante
123 St. Georges Rd., College Green, Hotwells. BS1 5UW. (David and Elizabeth Durant)
EST. 1966. Open 12-6, Sun. by appointment. *STOCK: 19th-20th C French decorative antiques - small furniture, crystal and brass, hanging and wall lights and unusual items, £80-£1,000.* LOC: Junction of Anchor Rd. and Hotwells Rd., 3 mins. walk from library and city centre. SIZE: Small. PARK: Meters. FAIRS: Chelsea Brocante, Newark,

Sandown Park, Ardingly, Shepton Mallet.
TEL: 01179 096688; MOBILE: 07986 612056
E-MAIL: daviddurant580@yahoo.co.uk

Caledonian Antiques
6 The Mall, Clifton. BS8 4DR.
EST. 1981. Open 9-5.30. *STOCK: Antique and secondhand jewellery, silver and plate; modern classic diamond jewellery.* LOC: Central. SER: Valuations; restorations (jewellery); engraving. SIZE: Small. PARK: Nearby. VAT: Global and Spec.
TEL: 01179 743582; FAX: 01179 667997
E-MAIL: mariateresa70@btinternet.com

Clifton Ceramics and Fine Jewellery
58 The Mall, Clifton. BS8 4JG. (Susan Courtellas)
EST. 1978. Open 10-5.30. *STOCK: Moorcroft pottery and enamels, Elliot Hall enamels, Dennis chinaworks, diamond jewellery, £250-£10,000.* LOC: Clifton village. SIZE: Small. PARK: Easy.
TEL: 01173 730256
E-MAIL: jewellery@cliftonceramics.co.uk
WEBSITE: www.cliftonceramics.co.uk

Cotham Antiques
1c Pitville Place, 39 Cotham Hill. BS6 6JZ. (Susan Miller and Cornelius Cummins)
EST. 1983. Open Tues.-Sat.10.30-5.30. *STOCK: Jewellery, 1800 to designer modern, £50-£800; ceramics, 19th C to Art Deco, £100-£500; engravings and original paintings, gramophones, vintage doll's houses, selection of fossils and crystals.* LOC: Off Whiteladies Rd from Clifton - turn left at Whiteladies shopping centre. SER: Valuations. SIZE: Small. PARK: Limited.
TEL: 01179 733326

Focus on the Past
25 Waterloo St., Clifton. BS8 4BT. (C. Hague and A. Roylance)
EST. 1976. Open 9.30-5.30, Sat. 9.30-6, Sun. 11-5. *STOCK: 19th-20th C furniture including mahogany, country, pine, French, English; beds; ceramics, kitchenalia, glass, silver, plate, jewellery, advertising and packaging, to £1,000+.* LOC: Off Princess Victoria St. SIZE: Large. PARK: Nearby.
TEL: 01179 738080

Grey-Harris and Co
12 Princess Victoria St., Clifton. BS8 4BP.
EST. 1963. Open 10-5. *STOCK: Jewellery, Victorian; silver, old Sheffield plate.* SER: Valuations; cleaning. PARK: Nearby. VAT: Stan/Spec.
TEL: 01179 737365.

Chris Grimes Militaria
13 Lower Park Row. BS1 5BN. (Chris and Hazel Grimes)
EST. 1968. Open 11-5.30. *STOCK: Militaria, scientific instruments, nautical items.* LOC: Off city centre. SIZE:

Medium. PARK: Meters or multi-storey nearby. FAIRS: Shepton Mallet; Malvern.
TEL: 01179 298205

Kemps
9 Carlton Court, Westbury-on-Trym. BS9 3DF.
Open Mon.-Fri. 9-5.15, Sat. 9-1; December Sat. 9-5.15.
STOCK: Jewellery. PARK: Free.
TEL: 01179 505090
WEBSITE: www.kempsjewellers.co.uk

Robert Mills Architectural Antiques Ltd   LAPADA
Narroways Rd., Eastville. BS2 9XB.
EST. 1969. SALVO. Open 9-5, Sat. 10-4. *STOCK: Architectural items, panelled rooms, shop interiors, Gothic Revival, stained glass, church woodwork, bar and restaurant fittings, 1600-1950s, £50-£30,000.* LOC: **Half mile from junction 2, M32.** SER: **Restoration, adaptation, sourcing.** SIZE: **Large.** PARK: **Easy.** VAT: **Stan.**
TEL: **01179 556542; FAX: 01179 558146**
E-MAIL: **info@rmills.co.uk**
WEBSITE: **www.rmills.co.uk**

Jan Morrison
3 Victorian Arcade, Boyce's Avenue, Clifton. BS8 4AA.
EST. 1982. Open Tues.-Sat. 10-5.30. *STOCK: Silver, 1750 to date; glass, 18th C to Victorian.* SIZE: Small. PARK: Victoria Square.
TEL: 01179 706822; FAX: same; HOME: 01179 247995; MOBILE: 07789 094428

Oldwoods
4 Colston Yard. BS1 5BD. (S. Duck)
Open 11-5.30, Sat. 11-4. *STOCK: Victorian and Edwardian furniture, pine and other woods.* SER: Restorations.
TEL: 01179 299023

Pastimes
22 Lower Park Row. BS1 5BN. (A.H. Stevens)
EST. 1970. Open 10.30-1.45 and 2.45-5. *STOCK: Militaria and military books, £1-£1,000.* LOC: Opposite Christmas Steps, off Colston St. SIZE: Medium. PARK: Meters.
TEL: 01179 299330.

Period Fireplaces
The Old Station, Station Rd., Montpelier. BS6 5EE.
(John and Rhian Ashton and Martyn Roberts)
EST. 1987. Open Mon.-Fri. 9-1, 2-5; Sat 10-4. *STOCK: Fireplaces, original and reproduction, £250-£1,000.* LOC: Just off Gloucester Rd. SER: Restorations; fitting. SIZE: Medium. PARK: Easy. VAT: Stan.
TEL: 01179 444449
WEBSITE: www.periodfireplaces.co.uk

Potter's Antiques and Coins
60 Colston St. BS1 5AZ. (B.C. Potter)
EST. 1965. Open 11-4.30, CL: Thurs. *STOCK: Antiquities,* 500 B.C. to 1600 A.D., £5-£500; commemoratives, 1770-1953, £4-£300; coins, 500 B.C. to 1967, £1-£100; drinking glasses, 1770-1953, £3-£200; small furniture, from 1837, £10-£200.* LOC: Near top of Christmas Steps, close to city centre. SER: Valuations; buys at auction. SIZE: Small. PARK: NCP Park Row.
TEL: 01179 262551

St. Nicholas Markets
The Exchange Hall, Corn St. BS1 1JQ. (Steve Morris)
EST. 1975. Open 9.30-5. *STOCK: Wide range of general antiques and collectors' items.* LOC: City centre. SIZE: Large; 60+ general traders, incl. 10 antique dealers.
TEL: 01179 224014
E-MAIL: markets@bristol.gov.uk

The Antiques Warehouse Ltd
430 Gloucester Rd., Horfield. BS7 8TX. (Chris Winsor)
EST. 1994. Resident. Open Tues.-Sat. 10-6, Sun. 12-4.
STOCK: Furniture, especially dining tables, wardrobes, chests, desks and chairs, 18th to early 20th C, £200-£2,500; mirrors, from 19th C, £60-£1,000; rugs, from 19th C, £150-£600; lighting £100-£1,000. LOC: A38 4 miles from M4/M5 interchange, 2 miles from city centre. SER: Valuations; restorations (furniture, upholstery and lighting). SIZE: Large warehouse. PARK: Easy. VAT: Stan/Spec.
TEL: 01179 424500; MOBILE: 07785 532173
WEBSITE: www.theantiqueswarehouseltd.co.uk

CHELTENHAM

Antique and Modern Fireplaces
43 Great Norwood St. GL50 2BQ.
Open 9-5. *STOCK: Original and reproduction fireplaces in marble, wood and cast iron. Stoves and gas fires.* SER: Design and installation (stoves and fireplaces). PARK: Nearby.
TEL: 01242 255235
E-MAIL: antfires@btconnect.com

David Bannister FRGS
26 Kings Rd. GL52 6BG.
EST. 1963. PBFA. Open by appointment only. *STOCK: Early maps and prints, 1480-1870; decorative and topographical prints; atlases and colour plate books.* SER: Valuations; restorations; lectures; buys at auction. VAT: Stan.
TEL: 01476 405013; MOBILE: 07954 400939
E-MAIL: db@antiquemaps.co.uk
WEBSITE: www.antiquemaps.co.uk

Bicks Jewellers and Antiques
5 Montpellier Walk. GL50 1SD. (Stuart Bradley)
EST. 1895. Open 10-5 or by appointment. *STOCK: Fine classical and antique jewellery.* SER: In-house workshop, bespoke items, batteries, repairs, sizings, valuations.
TEL: 01242 524738; FAX: 01242 254436
E-MAIL: bicksmontpellier@btconnect.com

Cheltenham Antique Market

54 Suffolk Rd. GL50 2AQ. (K.J. Shave)
EST. 1970. Open 10-5. STOCK: *General antiques including chandeliers.* SIZE: 6 dealers.
TEL: 01242 529812

Cocoa

9 Clarence Parade. GL50 3NY. (Cara Wagstaff)
EST. 1970. Open 10-5. CL: Wed. STOCK: *Lace, antique wedding dresses and accessories, 19th-20th C.* LOC: Town centre. SER: Wedding dress re-creations; restorations (period textiles). SIZE: Small. VAT: Stan.
TEL: 01242 233588
WEBSITE: www.cocoa-designs.co.uk

Greens of Cheltenham Ltd

15 Montpellier Walk. GL50 1SD.
EST. 1946. Open 9-5. STOCK: *Jewels, objets, porcelain and silver.* LOC: Conjunction of Promenade and main shopping centre. SER: Buys at auction. SIZE: Large. PARK: Easy. VAT: Stan/Spec.
TEL: 01242 512088
E-MAIL: steve@greensofcheltenham.co.uk

James Fine Art

14 Prestbury Rd. GL52 2PW. (Ric James)
STOCK: *Oil paintings, sculpture and bronze.*
TEL: 01242 220555; MOBILE: 07768 753627
E-MAIL: ric@jamesfineart.co.uk
WEBSITE: www.jamesfineart.co.uk

The Loquens Gallery

3 Montpellier Avenue. GL50 1SA. (Stephen and Mrs Jean Loquens)
EST. 1992. Open 10.15-5. STOCK: *18th-20th C watercolours and some oils.* LOC: Adjacent to The Queens Hotel. SER: Valuations: framing; restorations. SIZE: Small. PARK: Nearby.
TEL: 01242 254313
E-MAIL: info@loquensgallery.co.uk
WEBSITE: www.loquensgallery.co.uk

Martin and Co. Ltd

19 The Promenade. GL50 1LP. (I.M. and N.C.S. Dimmer)
EST. 1890. Open 9-5.30. STOCK: *Silver, Sheffield plate, jewellery, objets d'art.* LOC: Central SER: Valuations; cleaning. SIZE: Medium VAT: Stan/Spec.
TEL: 01242 522821; FAX: 01242 570430

Montpellier Clocks   BADA

13 Rotunda Terrace, Montpellier. GL50 1SW. (Tobias Birch)
EST. 1958. Open Tues. - Sat. 9.30-5. STOCK: *English clocks, 17th-19th C; barometers.* LOC: Close to Queens Hotel. SER: Restoration by West Dean/BADA Dip. conservator. SIZE: Medium. PARK: Easy. VAT: Spec.
TEL: 01242 242178

E-MAIL: info@montpellierclocks.com
WEBSITE: www.montpellierclocks.com

Patrick Oliver   LAPADA

4 Tivoli St. GL50 2UW.
EST. 1896. Open 9-1, or by appointment. STOCK: *General antiques, incl. furniture.* SER: Valuations VAT: Stan/Spec.
TEL: 01242 519538. MOBILE: 07970 052808

Promenade Antiques

18-20 The Promenade. GL50 1LR.
EST. 1980. Open 9-5.30 Mon.-Sat., 11-4 Sun. STOCK: *Antiques and second-hand jewellery, gold and silver, clocks, watches and barometers, rare items. Precious stone set jewellery.* SER: Valuation for replacement, insurance and probate.
TEL: 01242 524519
E-MAIL: info@promenadeantiques.co.uk
WEBSITE: www.promenadeantiques.co.uk

Q & C Militaria

22 Suffolk Rd. GL50 2AQ. (J.F. Wright)
EST. 1970. OMRS, MCCOFI, BACSEA. Open 10-5. CL: Mon. STOCK: *Military memorabilia - British orders, decorations and medals; military drums, edged weapons, cap badges.* LOC: A40 ring road. SER: Valuations; restorations (drums and military equipment); framing and mounting (medals); buys at auction. SIZE: Medium. PARK: At rear, off Old Bath Rd. FAIRS: OMRS Convention, Aldershot, Yate, Stratford-upon-Avon; Aldershot Collectors (Farnham); Britannia Medal, London.
TEL: 01242 519815; FAX: same; MOBILE: 07778 613977
E-MAIL: qcmilitaria@btconnect.com
WEBSITE: www.qcmilitaria.com

Catherine Shinn Decorative Textiles

5/6 Well Walk. GL50 3JX.
Open 10-5. STOCK: *Antique tapestry cushions, hangings, bell pulls; passementerie and upholstery pieces, old curtains and table covers, toile.* SER: Valuations; restorations; buys at auction (European textiles). SIZE: 3 floors. PARK: Rear of library. VAT: Stan.
TEL: 01242 574546; FAX: 01242 578495
WEBSITE: www.catherineshinn.com

Julian Tatham-Losh Ltd

Crescent House, 19 Eldorado Crescent. GL50 2PY. (Julian Tatham-Losh (Top Banana Antiques Mall))
EST. 1980. Resident. TADA. *Trade & Export Only.* Open any time by appointment. STOCK: *19th C decorative smalls, bamboo and interesting furniture, majolica, flow blue, Staffordshire figures and animals, boxes and caddies, candlesticks, decorative glass, primitive and folk art items, kitchenalia, mirrors, desk-related items, brass and copper, luggage, £2-£10,000.* LOC: Town centre near railway station. SER: Antique and decorative items supplied to

order, especially repeat bulk shipping items; courier (air-conditioned transport); free storage. SIZE: Medium. PARK: Own.
TEL: 0871 2881100; FAX: 0871 2881101; MOBILE: 07850 574924
E-MAIL: julian@topbananaantiques.com

Telephone Lines
304 High St. GL50 3JF.
EST. 1992. Open 9-5.30 Mon.-Sat. and by appointment. STOCK: Comprehensive range of antique, designer and fun telephones. SER: Spares, repairs, restoration, export and hire services. SIZE: Medium. PARK: Nearby. VAT: Stan.
TEL: 01242 583699
E-MAIL: enquiries@telephonelines.net
WEBSITE: www.telephonelines.net

John P. Townsend
Ullenwood Park Farm, Ullenwood. GL53 9QX. (J.P., Mrs. A. and S. Townsend)
EST. 1969. Open 9-5. CL: Sat. STOCK: Country and shipping furniture, to 1940s; books and bric-a-brac. LOC: 4 miles from Cheltenham. SIZE: Medium. PARK: Easy.
TEL: 01242 870169; HOME: 01242 870223

Triton Gallery
27 Suffolk Parade. GL50 2AE. (L. Bianco)
EST. 1984. Resident. Open 9-5.30, other times by appointment. STOCK: Period furniture, 18th C paintings, mirrors and lighting. PARK: Easy. VAT: Spec.
TEL: 01242 510477
E-MAIL: lorenzo.bianco@btconnect.com

Peter Ward Fine Paintings
Nothill Cowley. GL53 9NJ.
EST. 1972. Open 9-5. STOCK: 17th-19th C paintings. SER: Valuations; restorations; framing. PARK: Own. VAT: Spec.
TEL: 01242 870178; MOBILE: 07979 857347
WEBSITE: www.coriniumfinepaintings.co.uk

Woodward Antique Clocks   LAPADA
21 Suffolk Parade. GL50 2AE. (Patricia Woodward and Christopher Daines)
EST. 1989. Open Tues.-Sat. 10.30-5.30. STOCK: Clocks - longcase, 18th-19th C, £200-£10,000; decorative mantel especially French, 18th-19th C; wall, carriage and bracket. **SER: Valuations; restorations. SIZE: Medium. PARK: Easy. FAIRS: LAPADA, NEC.**
TEL: 01242 245667; MOBILE: 07745 101081
E-MAIL: enquiries@woodwardclocks.co.uk
WEBSITE: www.woodwardclocks.com

CHIPPING CAMPDEN

Cottage Farm Antiques
Cottage Farm, Aston sub Edge. GL55 6PZ. (A.E. and E.A. Willmore)
EST. 1986. Open 9-5 including Sun. STOCK: Furniture including 19th C wardrobes, 18th-19th C dressers and tables, to £3,000. LOC: Follow brown tourist signs. SER: Delivery. SIZE: Large. PARK: Easy. VAT: Spec.
TEL: 01386 438263; FAX and HOME: same
E-MAIL: info@cottagefarmantiques.co.uk
WEBSITE: www.cottagefarmantiques.co.uk

School House Antiques
School House, High St. GL55 6HB. (G. and M. Hammond)
EST. 1895. Open 9.30-5 including Sun. (June-Sept.). CL: Thurs. STOCK: Clocks, silver and jewellery, 18th-19th C; Georgian and Victorian furniture; works of art, oils and watercolours. SER: Valuations. SIZE: Large. PARK: At rear.
TEL: 01386 841474
E-MAIL: hamatschoolhouse@aol.com
WEBSITE: www.schoolhouseantiques.co.uk

Stuart House Antiques
High St. GL55 6HB. (J. Collett)
EST. 1985. Open 10-1 and 2-5.30 including Sun. STOCK: China, 19th C; general antiques, from 18th C; all £1-£1,000. LOC: Opposite market hall. SER: Valuations; china search; restorations (ceramics). SIZE: Large. PARK: Easy.
TEL: 01386 840995

CIRENCESTER

Walter Bull and Son (Cirencester) Ltd
10 Dyer St. GL7 2PF.
EST. 1815. NAG. Open 9-5. STOCK: Silver, from 1700, £50-£3,000; objets d'art. LOC: Lower end of Market Place. SER: Valuations; restorations. SIZE: Small. PARK: Nearby. VAT: Stan/Spec.
TEL: 01285 653875; FAX: 01285 641751
E-MAIL: info@walterbull.co.uk
WEBSITE: www.walterbull.co.uk

Cirencester Arcade
25 Market Place. GL7 2NX. (M.J. and P.J. Bird)
EST. 1995. Open 9.30-5, Sun. 11-5. STOCK: General antiques, incl. jewellery, silver, cards, tins, country furniture, racing and sports memorabilia, books. SER: Shipping. SIZE: 70+ dealers. PARK: Opposite.
TEL: 01285 644214; FAX: 01285 651267
WEBSITE: www.cirencester-arcade.co.uk

Corner Cupboard Curios
2 Church St. GL7 1LE. (P. Larner)
EST. 1972. Usually open but prior telephone call advisable. STOCK: Collectables including gramophones, radios, records. LOC: Swindon side of town. SIZE: Small. PARK: Easy.
TEL: 01285 655476; HOME: same

Fossil Decor
Unit 15 Cirencester Business Estate, Elliott Rd. GL7 1YS. (Paul Nash)
EST. 1961 Open by appointment. STOCK: Decorative fossils

William H. Stokes
EARLY OAK FURNITURE

THE CLOISTERS, 6/8 DOLLAR STREET, CIRENCESTER, GLOUCESTERSHIRE, GL7 2AJ

W.H. Stokes
P.W. Bontoft
post@williamhstokes.co.uk
www.williamhstokes.co.uk

Telephone
(01285) 653907

Fax
(01285) 640533

Private
(01285) 657101

A collected set of ten William and Mary oak dining chairs, c.1690.

and minerals. LOC: Phone for directions. SIZE: Large. PARK: Easy. VAT: Spec. FAIRS: Olympia (Summer). TEL: 01285 644515; MOBILE: 07785 570701
E-MAIL: info@fossil-decor.com
WEBSITE: www.fossil-decor.com

Hares Antiques Ltd.   LAPADA
The Old Bear, Perrotts Brook. GL7 7BP. (Allan G. Hare)
EST. 1972. **Open 10-5.30, Sun. by appointment.** STOCK: *Furniture, especially dining tables and long sets of chairs, 18th to early 19th C, £100-£100,000; Old Howard and other upholstery, pictures, carpets and decorative objects.* LOC: On A435 Cirencester to Cheltenham Road. SER: Restorations; traditional upholstery. SIZE: Medium. PARK: Own. VAT: Spec. FAIRS: Olympia; Chicago.
TEL: **01285 831311;** FAX: **01285 831344;** MOBILE: **07860 350097/07860 350096**
E-MAIL: **hares@hares-antiques.com**
WEBSITE: **www.hares-antiques.com**

William H. Stokes   BADA
The Cloisters, 6/8 Dollar St. GL7 2AJ. (W.H. Stokes and P.W. Bontoft)
EST. 1968. CADA. **Open 9.30-5.30, Sat. 9.30-4.30.** STOCK: *Early oak furniture, £1,000-£50,000; brassware,*

£150-£5,000; all 16th-17th C. LOC: **West of parish church out of Market Place.** VAT: Spec.
TEL: **01285 653907;** FAX: **01285 640533**
E-MAIL: **post@williamhstokes.co.uk**
WEBSITE: **www.williamhstokes.co.uk**

Patrick Waldron Antiques
18 Dollar St. GL7 2AN.
EST. 1965. Resident. CADA. Open 9.30-1 and 2-6, Sun. by appointment. STOCK: *Town and country furniture, 17th to early 19th C.* LOC: In street behind church. SER: Restorations (furniture); buys at auction. SIZE: Medium. PARK: Easy and public behind shop. VAT: Stan/Spec.
TEL: 01285 652880; HOME: same; WORKSHOP: 01285 643479

EASTLEACH

Mark Carter Antiques
5 Macaroni Wood. GL7 3NF. (Mark Carter)
By prior appointment. STOCK: *Furniture 17th-19th C, mahogany, oak, fruitwood, country.*
MOBILE: 07836 260567
E-MAIL: markjcarter@btinternet.com

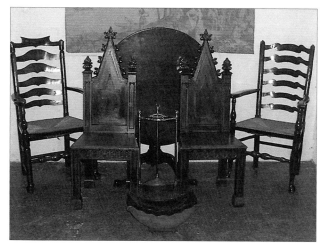
EBRINGTON

John Burton Natural Craft Taxidermy
21 Main St. GL55 6NL.
EST. 1973. Open by appointment. STOCK: Taxidermy –
Victorian and Edwardian cased fish, birds and mammals,
heads, from £65–£2,500; glass domes, sporting trophies.
LOC: Village centre. SER: Valuations; restorations
(taxidermy); buys at auction (taxidermy and natural
history items). SIZE: Medium. PARK: Easy.
TEL: 01386 593231

FAIRFORD

Blenheim Antiques
Market Place. GL7 4AB. (N. Hurdle)
EST. 1972. CADA. Resident. Open 9.30-6. STOCK: 18th–
19th C furniture and accessories. SIZE: Medium. PARK:
Easy. VAT: Stan/Spec.
TEL: 01285 712094

Anthony Hazledine
Antique Oriental Carpets, High St. GL7 4AD.
EST. 1976. Open 9.30-5. STOCK: Oriental carpets and
textiles, 18th–19th C, £150–£4,000. SER: Restorations;
cleaning; valuations; appraisals. SIZE: Small. PARK: Easy.
VAT: Stan/Spec.
TEL: 01285 713400; HOME and FAX: same
WEBSITE: www.anthonyhazledine.com

GLOUCESTER

Gloucester Antiques Centre Ltd
1 Severn Rd. GL1 2LE.
EST. 1979 Open 10-5, Sun. 11.30-4.30 STOCK: _General
antiques – furniture and furnishings, jewellery, silver, clocks,
ceramics, collectables._ LOC: Within Gloucester Docks area.
SIZE: 100+ dealers. PARK: Ample within docks.
TEL: 01452 529716; FAX: 01452 508263
WEBSITE: www.gacl.co.uk

Arthur S. Lewis
EST. 1969. Open by appointment. STOCK: _Mechanical
music, automata, clocks._ FAIRS: Antiques for Everyone,
NEC.
TEL: 01452 780258
WEBSITE: www.arthurlewisantiques.com

Upstairs Downstairs
2 Severn Rd. GL1 2LE. (Vic and Shirley Foster)
Open 10-4.30, Sat/Sun 10-5. STOCK: _Clocks, furniture,
lighting, jewellery, china._ SIZE: Large - 2 floors.
TEL: 01452 421170
E-MAIL: vfoster@btconnect.com

LECHLADE

Jubilee Hall Antiques Centre
Oak St. GL7 3AY.
EST. 1997. Open 10-5, Sun. 11-5 or by appointment.
STOCK: _18th-19th C furniture, metalwork, prints, pictures,
mirrors, pottery and porcelain, rugs, lighting, 19th C and
earlier collectables, glass, silver, arts and crafts, textiles,
jewellery, treen, Staffordshire, rugs._ NOT STOCKED:
Reproductions. LOC: On left 350 yards from town centre
going north towards Burford. SER: Shipping; valuations;
restorations. SIZE: Large. PARK: Own, free.
TEL: 01367 253777
WEBSITE: www.jubileehall.co.uk

Listed below are the dealers at this centre.

Mandy Barnes
_Georgian and Victorian furniture, decorative objects, some
textiles, prints, jewellery._

Keith and Lin Bawden
_18th-19th C English furniture, boxes, mirrors, barometers,
objects and cabinet of small items._

John Calgie
_18th-19th C period furniture, mirrors, copper, brass, Staffordshire,
collectables, Arts & Crafts, lighting, rugs and pictures._

Steve Clure
Boxes, lamps, prints, papier mâché, boxes and decorative items.

Andrew Crawforth
_Antique metalwork, treen, Arts and Crafts, musical
instruments, keys, pewter, scientific, tribal and unusual items,
sewing accessories, objets d'art and furniture._

Francoise Daniel
_Small silver, ivory, shibayama, tortoiseshell, art objects,
Tunbridge ware, jewellery and glass._

Paul Eisler
_18th-19th C ceramics, metalware, treen, small furniture,
samplers, prints and maps._

Michael Grey
Dolls, pictures, glass, pistols, metalware and unusual items.

Anita Harris
_Porcelain, decorative objects, toleware, papier mâché, jewellery,
interesting and unusual smalls._

Colin and Mary Lee
_Glass, porcelain, silver, silhouettes, pottery and objects, blue and
white, lustreware._

Colin Morris
_Oak and country furniture, early metalware, pewter, carvings,
Delft and Staffordshire pottery, horse brasses, garden items in
spring and summer._

Mark Newsome
Country and folk art related items.

Oak Antiques
(David and Vicky Wilson) _Small country items, metalware,
treen and ancient items._

Mary Pennel
Porcelain, small silver and jewellery.

Simon Rayner Art
_Oil paintings, watercolours, prints, inc. landscapes, portraits
and genre scenes by British and Continental painters._

Red Lane Antiques
(Terry Sparks) *Early oak and country furniture; 17th-19th C metalware, treen, Delft, needlework.*

LindseyRichardson
19th C ceramics including Staffordshire, blue and white and majolica; glass and small decorative items.

Liz Stabler
Prints, boxes, pottery, treen, papier mâché and interesting small items.

Jackie & Richard Stent
18th-19th C furniture, prints, pottery, porcelain, chrystoleums, Belleek and small items.

Lechlade Arcade
5, 6 and 7 High St. GL7 3AD. (Tim Lloyd)
EST. 1990. Open 9-5 including Sun. STOCK: *Bric-a-brac, books, furniture (original and reclaimed pine), collectables, militaria, carpets and rugs.* LOC: Central. SER: Made-to-order furniture. SIZE: 20+ dealers. PARK: Riverside pub car park.
TEL: 01367 252832; MOBILE: 07949 130875

The Old Ironmongers Antiques Centre
Burford St. GL7 3AP. (Mark A. Serle and Geoff Allen)
EST. 1999. Open 10-5 including Sun. STOCK: *Old ironmongery, £5-£200; furniture including country, £40-£2,000; textiles, £10-£200; Georgian glass, £20-£250; decorative china, £10-£500; treen, £50-£200; militaria including medals, £5-£300; tools and rural implements, £5-£300; Victorian bottles, £5-£150; gramophones, £80-£500.* LOC: A361. PARK: Easy.
TEL: 01367 252397

MICKLETON

The Mickleton Shed Antiques
Prospect Gardens, Stratford Rd. GL55 6SR. (Jenny and Geoff Cox)
EST. 2005. Open 10-5 seven days. STOCK: *General antiques, inc. crockery, glass, furniture, jewellery, clocks and watches, silver, books.* SIZE: 30 dealers.
TEL: 01386 438387

MINCHINHAMPTON

Mick and Fanny Wright
The Trumpet. GL6 9JA.
EST. 1979. Open Wed.-Sat. 10.30-5.30. STOCK: *General antiques, decorative items, clocks, furniture, china, silver, quirky items and books, £1-£2,000.* LOC: 200 yards west of crossroads at bottom of High St. SER: House clearance; probate valuations. SIZE: Medium. PARK: Nearby. VAT: Margin. FAIRS: Kempton Park.
TEL: 01453 883027

MORETON-IN-MARSH

Astley House - Contemporary
Astley House, London Rd. GL56 0LE. (David, Nanette and Caradoc Glaisyer)
EST. 1973. CADA. Open 10-1 and 2-5 and by appointment. CL: Wed. STOCK: *Oil paintings, 19th-21st C; large decorative oils and portraits, jewellery, ceramics, glass.* LOC: Town centre. SER: Restorations (oils and watercolours); framing (porcelain). SIZE: Large. PARK: Easy. VAT: Spec.
TEL: 01608 650608; FAX: 01608 651777
E-MAIL: astart333@aol.com
WEBSITE: www.contemporaryart-uk.com

Astley House - Fine Art
Astley House, High St. GL56 0LL. (David, Nanette and Caradoc Glaisyer)
EST. 1973. CADA. Open 9-5.30 and by appointment. STOCK: *Oil paintings, 19th-21st C, £800-£20,000.* LOC: Main street. SER: Restorations (oils and watercolours); framing. SIZE: Medium. PARK: Easy. VAT: Spec.
TEL: 01608 650601; FAX: 01608 651777
E-MAIL: astart333@aol.com
WEBSITE: www.art-uk.com;
www.contemporaryart-uk.com

Benton Fine Art   LAPADA
Regent House, High St. GL56 0AX. (J.G. Benton)
EST. 1972. CINOA. Open 10-5.30, Sun. 11-5.30, Tues. by appointment. STOCK: *Paintings, furniture, 18th to early 20th C, £500-£30,000.* SIZE: Large. PARK: Easy. FAIRS: LAPADA; Antiques for Everyone; Olympia.
TEL: 01608 652153; FAX: same; MOBILE: 07710 540549
E-MAIL: bentonfineart@excite.com
WEBSITE: www.bentonfineart.com

Cox's Architectural Reclamation Yard
Unit 10, Fosseway Industrial Estate. GL56 9NQ. (P. Watson)
EST. 1991. SALVO. Open 9-5, Sun. by appointment. STOCK: *Architectural antiques, fire surrounds and fireplaces, £250-£25,000; doors, £50-£3,500; all 19th C; stained glass, £50-£1,000.* LOC: Just off Fosseway, northern end of Moreton-in-Marsh. SER: Valuations. SIZE: Large. PARK: Easy. VAT: Stan.
TEL: 01608 652505; FAX: 01608 652881
E-MAIL: info@coxsarchitectural.co.uk
WEBSITE: www.coxsarchitectural.co.uk

Dale House Antiques
High St. GL56 0AD. (N. and A. Allen)
EST. 1977. Open 10-5.30, Sun. 11-5. STOCK: *17th-19th C town and country furniture, clocks, barometers, pictures, porcelain and pottery, metalwork, objets.* LOC: Main street. SER: Export. SIZE: Large. PARK: Easy. VAT: Spec.
TEL: 01608 652950; FAX: 01608 652424
WEBSITE: www.dalehouseantiques.com

The John Davies Gallery
6 Fosseway Business Park. GL56 9NQ.
EST. 1977. CADA. Open 9-1, 2-5.30. STOCK: *Contemporary and period paintings; limited edition bronzes.* LOC: A429 Fosseway. Own gate access to M.-in-M. train station. SER: Restorations and conservation to museum standard. SIZE: Large. VAT: Spec/Margin.

TEL: 01608 652255
WEBSITE: www.johndaviesgallery.com

Jeffrey Formby Antiques BADA
Orchard Cottage, East St. GL56 0LQ.
EST. 1994. Resident. Open by appointment. STOCK: *Fine English clocks, pre 1850, £2,000–£15,000; horological books, old and new, £5–£500.* LOC: 100 yards from High St. SIZE: Small. PARK: Easy. VAT: Spec. FAIRS: Olympia.
TEL: **01608 650558**
E-MAIL: **jeff@formby-clocks.co.uk**
WEBSITE: **www.formby-clocks.co.uk**

Jon Fox Antiques
High St. GL56 0AD.
EST. 1983. CADA. Open 9.30-5.30, Tues. by appointment. STOCK: *19th C garden items including urns, seats, troughs and tools, £50–£5,000+; 18th -19th C country furniture £300–£3,000; treen, bygones, metalware, fireplace and medical items.* SIZE: Large - 2 adjacent shops. PARK: Easy. VAT: Spec.
TEL: 01608 650325
E-MAIL: jonfoxantiques@tiscali.co.uk
WEBSITE: www.jonfoxantiques.com

Grimes House Antiques & Fine Art
High St. GL56 0AT. (S. and V. Farnsworth)
EST. 1978. FATG. Open 9.30-1 and 2-5, other times by appointment. STOCK: *Old cranberry and antique coloured glass, fine paintings.* LOC: Town centre. SER: Picture framing and restoration. PARK: Free nearby. VAT: Spec/Stan.
TEL: 01608 651029
E-MAIL: grimes_house@cix.co.uk
WEBSITE: www.grimeshouse.co.uk and www.cranberryglass.co.uk

Howards of Moreton
1 Old Market Way, High St. GL56 0AX. (Robert Light)
EST. 1989. Open 9.30-4.45. STOCK: *Jewellery, 1750 to modern; silver, 1700 to modern, both £20–£5,000; objects of virtu, 1700-1900, £50–£500.* SER: Valuations; restorations. SIZE: Small. PARK: Easy and nearby. VAT: Stan/Spec.
TEL: 01608 650583; FAX: 01608 652540
E-MAIL: robert.light@talk21.com

London House Antique Centre
London House, High St. GL56 0AH.
EST. 1979. Open 10-5 including Sun. STOCK: *Quality furniture, paintings, watercolours, prints, Doulton Lambeth, Royal Doulton, potlids, porcelain, domestic artefacts, clocks, silver, jewellery and plate, mainly 17th-19th C, £5–£3,000.* LOC: Centre of High St. (A429). SIZE: Large. PARK: Easy. VAT: Stan/Spec.
TEL: 01608 651084
E-MAIL: londonhouseantiques@msn.com
WEBSITE: www.london-house-antiques.co.uk

Simply Antiques
at Windsor House Antiques Centre, High St. GL56 0AD. (G. Ellis)

Open 10-5, Tues. and Sun. 12-5. STOCK: *Visiting card cases and small period furniture, mainly 18th to early 19th C.* LOC: In large 17th C premises, adjacent town hall. SER: Finder. PARK: Easy. VAT: Spec. FAIRS: NEC; Cooper; Penman, Harrogate; Olympia.
MOBILE: 07710 470877
E-MAIL: info@callingcardcases.com
WEBSITE: www.callingcardcases.com

Windsor House Antiques Centre
High St. GL56 0AD.
EST. 1992. Open 10-5; Sun. 11-4. STOCK: *Comprehensive selection of mid-range furniture, from 1650-1914; silver, portrait miniatures, ivory, visiting card cases, French decorative items, English and European porcelain, pottery and glass, objets de vertu, caddies and boxes, brass, copper and pewter.* LOC: Large 17th C premises, adjacent town hall. SIZE: 40 dealers. PARK: Ample, free.
TEL: 01608 650993
E-MAIL: windsorhouse@btinternet.com
WEBSITE: www.windsorhouse.co.uk

Gary Wright Antiques
Unit 5, Fosseway Business Park, Stratford Rd. GL56 9NQ.
EST. 1983. Open 9.30-5.30, Sun. by appointment. STOCK: *English and Continental furniture, 18th-19th C, £500–£50,000; unusual and decorative objects, 17th-20th C, £200–£6,000.* LOC: Entrance on A429 Fosseway next to railway bridge on north side of Moreton. SER: Valuations; restorations; buys at auction (furniture). SIZE: Large. PARK: Easy. VAT: Stan/Spec.
TEL: 01608 652007; FAX: same; MOBILE: 07831 653843
E-MAIL: gary@garywrightantiques.co.uk
WEBSITE: www.garywrightantiques.co.uk

NEWENT

Jillings Antiques - Distinctive BADA LAPADA
Antique Clocks
Croft House, 17 Church St. GL18 1PU. (Doro and John Jillings)
EST. 1986. CINOA. Open Thurs., Fri. and Sat. 10-6, other times by appointment. STOCK: *18th to early 19th C English and Continental clocks including bronze, ormolu, marble, boulle and small longcases.* SER: Clock and barometer repair and restoration; shipping worldwide. PARK: Easy. VAT: Margin. FAIRS: BADA (March); Olympia (June).
TEL: **01531 822100**; MOBILE: **07973 830110**
E-MAIL: **clocks@jillings.com**
WEBSITE: **www.jillings.com**

NORTHLEACH

The Doll's House
Market Place. GL54 3EJ. (Miss Michal Morse)

EST. 1971. Open Thurs., Fri. and Sat. 10-5, prior telephone call advisable. STOCK: *Handmade doll's houses and miniature furniture in one twelfth scale.* LOC: A40. SER: Replica houses and special designs to order. SIZE: Small. PARK: Easy.
TEL: 01451 860431; HOME and FAX: same

Keith Harding's World of Mechanical Music
The Oak House, High St. GL54 3ET. (K. Harding, FBHI and C.A. Burnett, CMBHI)
EST. 1961. Open 10-6 including Sun. STOCK: *Clocks, musical boxes and automata.* SER: Guided tours, demonstrations and written articles; valuations; restorations (musical boxes and clocks); buys at auction. SIZE: Large. PARK: Easy. VAT: Stan/Spec.
TEL: 01451 860181; FAX: 01451 861133
E-MAIL: keith@mechanicalmusic.co.uk
WEBSITE: www.mechanicalmusic.co.uk

Robson Antiques
New Barn Farm, London Rd. GL54 3LX.
EST. 1982. Open daily till late. STOCK: *Furniture, from 18th C, £50-£5,000; garden artefacts - reclaimed and stone; reclaimed flagstones, staddle stones, troughs, Cotswold stone tiles.* PARK: Easy.
TEL: 01451 861071 or 01451 861006;
MOBILE: 07737 708183
E-MAIL: robsonantiques@aol.com

PRESTON

Original Architectural Antiques
Ermin Farm, Cricklade Rd. GL7 5PN.
(John Rawlinson and Andy Hayward)
EST. 1983. Open 9-5. STOCK: *Oak beams; oak flooring; fireplaces.* SIZE: Large. PARK: Yes.
TEL: 01285 869222; FAX: 01285 862221;
MOBILE: 07774 979735
E-MAIL: john@originaluk.com
WEBSITE: www.originaluk.com

SLAD

Ian Hodgkins and Co. Ltd
Upper Vatch Mill, The Vatch. GL6 7JY. (G.A. Yablon)
EST. 1973. ABA. Open by appointment. STOCK: *Antiquarian books including pre-Raphaelites and associates, the Brontës, Jane Austen; 19th C illustrated, children's art and literature books.* FAIRS: Novotel, London (June); Chelsea (Nov.)
TEL: 01453 764270; FAX: 01453 755233
E-MAIL: i.hodgkins@dial.pipex.com
WEBSITE: www.ianhodgkins.com

STOW-ON-THE-WOLD

Yvonne Adams Antiques   BADA
The Coffee House, 3-4 Church St. GL54 1BB.
EST. 1955. Open 9.30-5 including Sun. STOCK: *18th C*

Meissen porcelain. LOC: Town centre. SER: Valuations. SIZE: Small. PARK: In square. VAT: Margin. FAIRS: Olympia (June and Nov.).
TEL: 01451 832015; MOBILE: 07971 961101
E-MAIL: antiques@adames.demon.co.uk
WEBSITE: www.antiquemeissen.co.uk

Duncan J. Baggott   LAPADA
Woolcomber House, Sheep St. GL54 1AA. (D.J. and C.M. Baggott)
EST. 1967. CADA. Open 9-5.30 or by appointment, CL: BH. STOCK: *17th-20th C English oak, mahogany and walnut furniture, paintings, domestic metalwork and decorative items; garden statuary and ornaments.* SER: worldwide shipping; UK delivery. SIZE: Large. PARK: Sheep St. or Market Sq. FAIRS: Exhibition Oct. annually (CADA).
TEL: 01451 830662; FAX: 01451 832174
E-MAIL: info@baggottantiques.com
WEBSITE: www.baggottantiques.com

Baggott Church Street Ltd   BADA
Church St. GL54 1BB. (D.J. and C.M. Baggott)
EST. 1978. CADA. Open 9.30-5.30 or by appointment, CL: BH. STOCK: *17th-19th C English oak, mahogany and walnut furniture, portrait paintings, metalwork, pottery, treen and decorative items.* LOC: South-west corner of market square. SER: Annual exhibition - Oct. (CADA). SIZE: Large. PARK: Market square/Sheep Street.
TEL: 01451 830370; FAX: 01451 832174
E-MAIL: info@baggottantiques.com
WEBSITE: www.baggottantiques.com

Black Ink   LAPADA
7A Talbot Court. GL54 1BQ. (David Stoddart)
EST. 1990. CADA, CINOA. Open 10-4, Sat. 10-5. CL: Tues. STOCK: *Artists' original etchings, lithographs, woodcuts and aquatints, especially 1860-1930, with emphasis on the Impressionists - Renoir, Pisarro, Gauguin, Manet, Cézanne; also works by modern artists such as Terry Frost, Mary Fedden, Ben Nicholson, etc.* SIZE: Medium. PARK: Free - town square. FAIRS: LAPADA; Cheltenham; National Fine Arts & Antiques Fair, NEC.
TEL: 01451 870022; MOBILE: 07721 454840
E-MAIL: art@blackinkprints.com
WEBSITE: www.blackinkprints.com

Christopher Clarke Antiques Ltd   LAPADA
The Fosseway. GL54 1JS. (Simon and Sean Clarke)
EST. 1961. CADA. Open 9.30-5.30 or by appointment. STOCK: *Specialists in campaign furniture and travel items.* LOC: Corner of The Fosseway and Sheep St. SIZE: Large. PARK: Easy. FAIRS: Olympia (June, Nov); CADA Exhibition.
TEL: 01451 830476; FAX: 01451 830300
E-MAIL: clarkeltd@btconnect.com
WEBSITE: www.campaignfurniture.com

Cotswold Galleries

The Square, GL54 1AB. (Richard and Cherry Glaisyer) EST. 1961. CADA. FATG. Open 9-5.30 or by appointment. *STOCK: Oil paintings especially 19th-20th C landscape.* SIZE: Large. PARK: Easy.
TEL: 01451 870567; FAX: 01451 870678
WEBSITE: www.cotswoldgalleries.com

Durham House Antiques Centre

Sheep St. GL54 1AA. (Alan Smith).
Open 10-5, Sun. 11-5. SIZE: 30+ dealers. PARK: Easy. SER: Buys at auction. FAIRS: NEC (Aug); Newark; Ardingly.
TEL: 01451 870404; FAX: same;
E-MAIL: DurhamHouseGB@aol.com
WEBSITE: www.durhamhouseGB.com

Below are listed the dealers at this centre.

Acorn Antiques
(Derek Howe and Stanley Taylor) EST. 1987 *19th C Staffordshire figures and animals; English pottery.*

Aldus Antiques
(Carrie and David Tarplett) *Steiff and other soft toys, dolls, doll's furnishings; samplers and other needlework.*

Michael Armson Antiques
Quality 18th-19th C mahogany and oak furniture, Staffordshire and metalware.

Paula Biggs Antiques
Quality and unusual silver including cutlery; table items.

Judi Bland Antiques
Toby jugs, Staffordshire, pot lids, Prattware, bargeware, country furniture and decorative items.

Church Lane Antiques
Silver and flatware, photograph frames, fine quality oak and mahogany furniture, mirrors, decorative items.

Simon Clarke Antiques
Oak and mahogany furniture, pictures, prints, metalware and leather items, ceramics, glass and door furniture.

Crockwell Antiques
(Philip Dawes) *18th-19th C oak and mahogany furniture, longcase clocks, silver, brass and copper, ironstone china and fireplace accessories.*

Sarah Crump
Fine and quality antique and estate jewellery, silver and piqué boxes, vintage designer handbags.

Early Worm Antiques
Unusual and interesting furniture with a French flair. Tapestries, ceramics, paintings, metalware, glass and decorative items.

Lee Elliott Antiques
Oak and mahogany furniture; lighting; 19th-20th C prints and pictures, specialising in rural pastimes.

Tony and Jane Finegan
Traditional English and French furniture, mirrors, lighting, decorative accessories including papier mâché and toile.

Beryl and Brian Harrison
Quality linen and lace accessories; table and bed linen.

Christine Hatton Antiques
Antique silver, perfume bottles, objets de vertu, jewellery, fine quality Worcester.

Dorothy Hyatt
Early English porcelain and pottery (Worcester, creamware, blue and white); 18th-19th C drinking glasses, decanters and table objects.

Ian Kellam
English and Continental porcelain; silver and jewellery; religious objects; cabinet pieces; bronzes.

Rupert Landen
Georgian and Regency furniture; mirrors, pictures, caddies; cabinets and accessories to suit period interiors.

Little Nells
(Helen Middleton) *Coronation commemoratives, automobilia, Staffordshire and majolica, collectables and small interesting items.*

Audrey McConnell
Silver and jewellery, picture frames, ceramics, ivory and micromosaics; glassware, miniatures and sewing accessories.

Vicki Mills Antiques
Beadwork and needlework pictures, quilts and bedcovers, Paisleys; blue and white; chintz pottery; bamboo and painted furniture; decorative items.

Colin Morris
Early oak furniture and carvings, pewter, copper and brass, ceramics, religious imagery and interesting vernacular objects.

Paper Moon Books
Fine 19th-20th C bindings including poetry, prose and history; prayer books and bibles.

Edith Prosser Antiques
18th-20th C furniture, mirrors, prints and lighting; decorative items including glass and ceramics; cabinet pieces.

Red Lane Antiques
Early oak and country furniture; metalware and treen a speciality. Decorative items, folk art, carvings, tapestries and needlework.

Lindsey Richardson Antiques
19th C ceramics inc. Staffordshire, blue and white, majolica and creamware; unusual selection of glass; decorative items - carvings, boxes, engravings, metalware.

The Fosse Gallery

The Square. GL54 1AF.
EST. 1979. Open Tues.-Sat. 10-5.30, prior telephone call advisable. *STOCK: British contemporary painting, specialising in figurative and narrative works; exhibiting many members of the Royal Academy.* LOC: Off Fosseway, A429. SER: Valuations. SIZE: Large. PARK: Easy.
TEL: 01451 831319; FAX: 01451 870309
E-MAIL: mail@fossegallery.com
WEBSITE: www.fossegallery.com

Fox Cottage Antiques

Digbeth St. GL54 1BN. (Sue London)
EST. 1995. Open 10-5. *STOCK: Wide variety of general*

antiques including pottery and porcelain, silver and plate, metalware, prints, small furniture, country and decorative items, mainly pre-1900, £5-£1,000. LOC: Left hand side at bottom of narrow street, running down from the square. SIZE: 10 dealers. PARK: Nearby.
TEL: 01451 870307
WEBSITE: www.foxcottageantiques.co.uk

Keith Hockin Antiques   BADA
The Square. GL54 1AF.
EST. 1968. CADA. Open Thurs., Fri. and Sat. 10-5, other times by appointment or ring the bell. *STOCK: Oak furniture, 1600-1750; country furniture in oak, fruitwoods, yew, 1700-1850; pewter, copper, brass, ironwork, all periods. NOT STOCKED: Mahogany.* SER: Buys at auction (oak, pewter, metalwork). SIZE: Medium. PARK: Easy. VAT: Stan/Spec.
TEL: 01451 831058
E-MAIL: keithhockin@ruralsat_net
WEBSITE: www.keithhockin.com

Huntington Antiques Ltd   LAPADA
Church St. GL54 1BE. (M.F. and S.P. Golding)
EST. 1974. CADA. CINOA. Resident. Open 9.30-5.30 or by appointment. *STOCK: Early period and fine country furniture, metalware, tapestries and works of art.* LOC: Opposite main gates to church. SER: Valuations; buys at auction. SIZE: Large. PARK: Own. VAT: Spec.
TEL: 01451 830842; FAX: 01451 832211
E-MAIL: info@huntington-antiques.com
WEBSITE: www.huntington-antiques.com

Kenulf Fine Arts Ltd.   LAPADA
Digbeth St. GL54 1BN. (E. and J. Ford)
EST. 1978. Open 10-5, Sun. 12-5. *STOCK: 19th to early 20th C oils, watercolours and prints; decorative items, fine period walnut and mahogany furniture; bronzes and contemporary paintings.* LOC: Near Barclays Bank. SER: Valuations; restorations (oils and watercolours, period framing). SIZE: 7 rooms. PARK: Easy. VAT: Spec. FAIRS: NEC; LAPADA; Northern; Belgian.
TEL: 01451 870878; MOBILE: 07774 107269
E-MAIL: kenulf.finearts@virgin.net
WEBSITE: www.kenulf-fine-arts.com

T.M. King-Smith & Simon W. Nutter
Wraggs Row, Fosseway. GL54 1JT.
EST. 1975. Open 9.30-5.30. *STOCK: 18th-19th C mahogany and oak furniture, £500-£10,000; brass, copper and pictures.* LOC: Near traffic lights opposite the Unicorn Hotel. SER: Buys at auction. VAT: Spec.
TEL: 01451 830658

La Chaise Antique
Beauport, Sheep St. GL54 1AA. (Roger Clark)
EST. 1968. GMC. Open 9.30-5.30, Sun. 11-4 (prior
telephone call advisable). *STOCK: Chairs, pre-1860; furniture,
18th-19th C; general antiques, decorators' items, upholstered library
and Victorian arm chairs (leather/fabric), sofas. NOT STOCKED:
Silver, porcelain and glass.* LOC: Next to Brewery Yard. SER:
Valuations; restorations; upholstery (leather and fabrics); table
top liners. SIZE: Large. PARK: Ample. VAT: Spec.
TEL: 01451 830582; MOBILE: 07831 205002
E-MAIL: lachaise@tiscali.co.uk

Roger Lamb Antiques & Works of Art   LAPADA
The Square. GL54 1AB.
EST. 1993. CADA. Open 10-5 or by appointment.
*STOCK: Fine 18th to early 19th C furniture especially
small items, lighting, decorative accessories, oils and
watercolours.* LOC: Next to town hall. SER: Search.
SIZE: 3 main showrooms. PARK: Easy. FAIRS: Olympia
(June and November).
TEL: 01451 831371; MOBILE: 07860 391959
E-MAIL: rl@rogerlamb.com
WEBSITE: www.rogerlambantiques.com

Laurie Leigh Antiques   LAPADA
Church St. GL54 1BB. (L. and D. Leigh)
EST. 1963. Open 10.30-5.30. CL: Thurs. *STOCK: Glass;
antique keyboard musical instruments.* LOC: Between
The Square and Sheep Street. SER: Restoration (glass
and antique keyboard musical instruments). SIZE:
Small. PARK: Nearby. VAT: Stan/Spec.
TEL: 01451 833693
E-MAIL: laurie@laurieleighantiques.com
david@laurieleighantiques.com
WEBSITE: www.laurieleighantiques.com
www.davidleigh.com

Park House Antiques
8 Park St. GL54 1AQ. (G. and B. Sutton)
EST. 1986. Open 10-1 and 2-4.30, or by appointment.
CL: Mon. & Tues. *STOCK: Early dolls, teddy bears, toys,
Victorian linen and lace, porcelain, collectables, small
furniture and pictures.* SER: Museum of dolls, teddies,

toys, textiles and collectables; teddy bears repaired;
antique dolls dressed. SIZE: Large. PARK: Easy.
TEL: 01451 830159
E-MAIL: info@thetoymuseum.co.uk
WEBSITE: www.thetoymuseum.co.uk

Antony Preston Antiques Ltd   BADA
The Square. GL54 1AB.
**EST. 1965. CADA. CINOA. Open 9.30-5.30 or by
appointment.** *STOCK: 18th-19th C English and
Continental furniture and objects; barometers and period
lighting.* LOC: Town centre. SIZE: Large. PARK: Easy.
VAT: Stan/Spec. FAIRS: BADA.
TEL: 01451 831586; FAX: 01451 831596;
MOBILE: 07785 975599
E-MAIL: antony@antonypreston.com
WEBSITE: www.antonypreston.com

Queens Parade Antiques Ltd   BADA
The Square. GL54 1AB. (Sally and Antony Preston)
EST. 1985. CADA. CINOA. Open 9.30-5.30. *STOCK: 18th
to early 19th C furniture, decorative objects, needlework, tole
and period lighting.* LOC: Town centre. SIZE: Large. PARK:
Easy. VAT: Stan/Spec. FAIRS: BADA.
TEL: 01451 831586; FAX: 01451 831596
E-MAIL: antony@antonypreston.com
WEBSITE: www.antonypreston.com

Ruskin Decorative Arts
5 Talbot Court. GL54 1DP. (Anne and William Morris)
EST. 1990. CADA. Open 10-1 and 2-5.30. *STOCK:
Interesting and unusual decorative objects, Arts and Crafts
furniture, Art Nouveau, Art Deco, glass and pottery,
metalwork, 1880-1960.* LOC: Between The Square and
Sheep St. SER: Valuations. SIZE: Small. PARK: Nearby.
TEL: 01451 832254; HOME: 01993 831880
E-MAIL: william.anne@ruskindecarts.co.uk
WEBSITE: www.ruskindecarts.co.uk

Samarkand Rugs   LAPADA
**7 & 8 Brewery Yard, Sheep St. GL54 1AA. (Hadi
Sarbaz)**
EST. 1982. Open 10-5.30. STOCK: Rugs and tapestries;

antique Persian carpets. SER: **Valuations; hand cleaning; repairs/restorations; free design advice.** SIZE: **Large.** PARK: **Free.**
TEL: **01451 832322**; MOBILE: **07803 896161**
WEBSITE: **www.samarkandrugs.com**

Arthur Seager Antiques
Bryden House, Sheep St. GL54 1JS.
EST. 1977. Open Tues.-Sat. 10.30-4. *STOCK: Period oak, carvings and sculpture, £500-£20,000.*
TEL: 01451 831605
E-MAIL: arthur.seager@btconnect.com
WEBSITE: www.arthurseager.co.uk

Styles of Stow
The Little House, Sheep St. GL54 1JS. (Mr W.J. Styles)
EST. 1981. Open 10-4.30, or by appointment. *STOCK: Longcase (100+) and bracket clocks, barometers, 18th-19th C, £400-£30,000; fine furniture, 18th-19th C, £250-£15,000; oils and watercolours, 19th-20th C, £25-£20,000.* LOC: Opposite post office. SER: Valuations; restorations; buys at auction (longcase and bracket clocks). SIZE: Medium. PARK: Easy. VAT: Margin.
TEL: 01451 830455
WEBSITE: www.stylesofstow.co.uk

Talbot Court Galleries
Talbot Court. GL54 1BQ. (J.P. Trevers)
EST. 1987. IMCOS. Open 9.30-1 and 1.30-5.30. *STOCK: Antiquarian prints and maps, 1580-1880, £10-£10,000.* LOC: Behind Talbot Hotel in precinct between the square and Sheep St. SER: Valuations; restorations; cleaning; colouring; framing; buys at auction (engravings, maps and atlases). SIZE: Medium. PARK: Nearby. VAT: Stan. FAIRS: London Map Fair, Olympia.
TEL: 01451 832169
WEBSITE: www.talbotgalleries.co.uk

The Titian Gallery   BADA LAPADA
Sheep St. GL54 1JS. (Ilona Johnson Gibbs)
EST. **1978.** CADA. CINOA. **Open 10-5 and by appointment.** CL: **Mon.** STOCK: *Fine 18th-19th C British and European oil paintings and watercolours, £1,000-£40,000.* LOC: **Opposite the Unicorn Hotel, near The Fosseway.** SER: **Valuations; commissions (oils and watercolours); advice on collections.** SIZE: **Medium.** PARK: **Adjacent and nearby.** VAT: **Spec.** FAIRS: **CADA exhibition.**
TEL: **01451 830004**; FAX: **01451 830126**
E-MAIL: **ilona@titiangallery.co.uk**
WEBSITE: **www.titiangallery.co.uk**

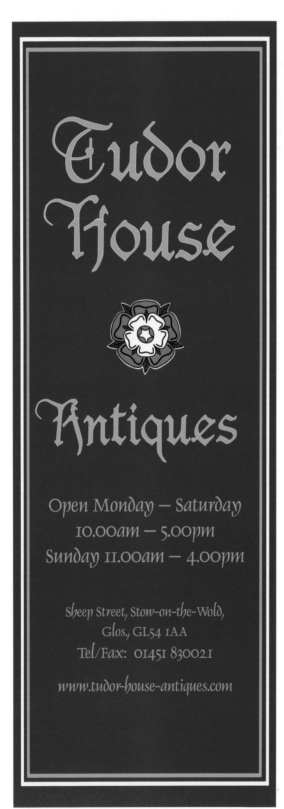

Tudor House

Sheep St. GL54 1AA. (Peter Collingridge and Roy Hooper) EST. 2001. Open 10-5, Sun. 11-4. *STOCK: Furniture, £500-£10,000; metalware, £50-£2,500; both 1700-1900, porcelain, 1720-1920, £50-£2,500; pottery 1700-1900, samplers and needlework, treen and lighting.* LOC: Turn at traffic lights from A429. SER: Valuations. SIZE: 7 showrooms. PARK: At rear. VAT: Spec.
TEL: 01451 830021; FAX: same; MOBILE: 07860 581858 WEBSITE: www.tudor-house-antiques.com

Below are listed the dealers trading from this address.

Ashley Antiques
Curios.

Jim Ball
18th - 19th C ceramics and metalware, curios.

Kate Bannister
Decorative antiques, tramp art, bamboo, lighting, papier-mâché and tôle.

Colin Brand
Clocks, porcelain, decorative furniture, militaria.

Peter Collingridge
Metalware, mirrors, lighting, furniture 1700-1900.

Bryan Collyer
English pottery and Staffordshire figures, corkscrews.

Val Cooper
Bamboo furniture, Majolica, papier-mâché, brass frames, Black Forest carvings.

NormaCordery
19th C brass including fireplace items.

David Cridland and Vivienne King
Lighting, fireside items, porcelain, objets de vertu, glass, collectables and furniture.

Dorothy and Philip Lipman
Mainly country furniture and Mason's Ironstone

Vienneta Edwards
18th-19th C pottery, metalware, decorative and collectable items.

Erna Hiscock and John Shepherd
Samplers and needlework, early carvings, ceramics, country furniture and decorative items.

Roy Hooper
Metalware, Arts & Crafts, Art Nouveau.

Maureen Lyons
Chandeliers, mirrors, french decorative furniture and accessories.

Atalanti Meyer
Decorative items including pewter, silver, glass and porcelain.

Oakdale Antiques
17th - 19th C oak and country furniture, longcase clocks.

Tim Olney
18th to early 19th C English porcelain, especially Worcester and New Hall.

Times Past
(Judy Pollitt) Needlework tools, chatelaines, small silver and objets de vertu.

Wooden Bygones
Treen.

Vanbrugh House Antiques
Park St. GL54 1AQ. (J. and M.M. Sands)
EST. 1972. Resident. Open 10-5.30 or by appointment.
STOCK: *Furniture and decorative items, 17th to early 19th
C; early maps, music boxes, clocks and barometers.* LOC:
Opposite the Bell Inn. SER: Valuations. PARK: Easy. VAT:
Stan/Spec.
TEL: 01451 830797; FAX: 01451 832509
E-MAIL: johnsands@vanbrughhouse.co.uk
WEBSITE: www.vanbrughhouse.co.uk

Wychwood Books
Sheep St. GL54 1AA. (Lucy and Henry Baggott)
EST. 2001. PBFA. Open 9.30-5.30. STOCK: *Secondhand
and antiquarian books especially architectural, art, field
sports, first editions, antiques & collectables, literature,
bindings and other general items. £1-£4,000.* LOC: Near
Post Office. SER: Restoration and rebinding (books).,
valuations, book searches, house clearances. SIZE:
Medium.
TEL: 01451 831880; FAX: 01451 870631
E-MAIL: info@wychwoodbooks.com
WEBSITE: www.wychwoodbooks.com

Wyndhams   LAPADA
**1 Brewery Yard, Sheep St. GL54 1AA. (Philip Brown
and Kevin Quin)**
EST. 1988. Open 10-5 or by appointment. STOCK: *Fine
mid-18th to early 19th C English exotic wood furniture,*
works of art including boxes and caddies; prints, lighting.
SER: Valuations. SIZE: Large - 2 showrooms. PARK:
Nearby. VAT: Spec.
TEL: 01451 870067; FAX: same; MOBILE: 07790
995536 or 07799 415586
E-MAIL: **antiques@wyndhams.com**
WEBSITE: **www.wyndhams.com**

STROUD

The Antiques Emporium
Unit 3, Griffin Mill, London Rd. GL5 2AZ.
Open 10-5, Sun 11-3. STOCK: *General antiques, French
furniture, upholstery, linen, carpets.* SIZE: 17 dealers.
TEL: 01453 889002; MOBILE: 07970 601624
WEBSITE: www.antiquesgriffinmill.co.uk

Minchinhampton Architectural
Cirencester Rd., Aston Down. GL6 8PE. (S. Tomlin
and D. Kedge)
EST. 1978. SALVO. Open 9-5, Sat. 9-3, Sun. 11-2.
STOCK: *Architectural items, chimney-pieces, garden
ornaments, stone and wood flooring, landscape and building
materials, columns and balustrading, doors and windows,
door hardware and accessories.* SER: Valuations. SIZE:
Large. PARK: Easy.
TEL: 01285 760886; FAX: 01285 760838
E-MAIL: masco@catbrain.com
WEBSITE: www.catbrain.com

TADDINGTON

Architectural Heritage

Taddington Manor. GL54 5RY. (Adrian, Suzy, and Alex Puddy)
EST. 1978. CADA. Open Mon.-Fri. 9.30-5.30, Sat. 10.30-4.30. STOCK: Oak and pine period panelled rooms; stone and marble chimney-pieces; stone, marble, bronze and terracotta statuary; garden ornaments, fountains, temples, well-heads, seats, urns, cisterns, sundials and summer-houses. SER: worldwide delivery; shipping; bespoke ornaments, chimney-pieces and panelled rooms. SIZE: Large. PARK: Easy. VAT: Stan. FAIRS: Chelsea Flower Show.
TEL: 01386 584414; FAX: 01386 584236
E-MAIL: puddy@architectural-heritage.co.uk
WEBSITE: www.architectural-heritage.co.uk

TETBURY

Alderson

61 Long St. GL8 8AA. (C.J.R. Alderson)
EST. 1977. CADA. Open 10-5. STOCK: British 18th-19th C furniture and works of art; British colonial furniture. SER: Valuations. SIZE: Medium. PARK: Easy. FAIRS: Olympia.
TEL: 01666 500888; MOBILE: 07836 594498
E-MAIL: kit.alderson@btopenworld.com

Artique

Talboys House, Church St. GL8 8JG. (George Bristow)
EST. 1982. TADA. Open 10-6, Sun. 12-4. STOCK: Interiors, textiles, carpets and kelims and objets d'art from the Orient. SIZE: Large + warehouse.
TEL: 01666 503597; FAX: same
E-MAIL: george@artique.uk.com
WEBSITE: www.artique.uk.com

Ball and Claw Antiques

45 Long St. GL8 8AA. (Chris Kirkland)
EST. 1994. TADA. Open 10-5. STOCK: Antique kitchen and farmhouse tables, chairs, etc. LOC: Town centre. SER: Finder. SIZE: Medium. PARK: Easy.
TEL: 01666 502440; MOBILE: 07957 870423
E-MAIL: chris@antiquekitchentables.co.uk
WEBSITE: www.antiquekitchentables.co.uk

Breakspeare Antiques

36 and 57 Long St. GL8 8AQ. (M. and S.E. Breakspeare)
EST. 1962. CADA. Resident. Open 10-5 or by appointment. CL: Thurs. STOCK: English period furniture - early walnut, 1690-1740, mahogany, 1750-1835. LOC: Main street - four gables building. SIZE: Medium. PARK: Own. VAT: Spec.
TEL: 01666 503122; FAX: same

Day Antiques   BADA
5 New Church St. GL8 8DS.
EST. 1975 CADA. Open 10-5. STOCK: Early oak furniture and related items. SIZE: Medium. PARK: Easy. VAT: Spec.
TEL: 01666 502413

E-MAIL: dayantiques@lineone.net
WEBSITE: www.dayantiques.com

The Decorator Source

39a Long St. GL8 8AA. (Colin Gee)
TADA, WEADA. Open 10-5 or by appointment. STOCK: French provincial furniture - armoires, farm tables, buffets; decorative and interior design items. Specialist in antler and driftwood furniture. SIZE: Large. PARK: Easy. VAT: Stan/Spec.
TEL: 01666 505358

Green and Pleasant

Shop 1, 51 Long St. GL8 8AA. (M. Matheou)
TADA. Open 10-5. STOCK: Period and contemporary sporting pictures, engravings, watercolours, oils and associated sporting items, furniture. SIZE: Medium. PARK: Easy.
TEL: 01666 500234
WEBSITE: www.greenandpleasantinteriors.co.uk

Jester Antiques

10 Church St. GL8 8JG. (Lorna Coles and Peter Bairsto)
EST. 1995. TADA. Open 10-5 including Sun. STOCK: Longcase and wall clocks, also oil portraits and pictures, Oriental objects, lamps, furniture, decorative items, outside statuary and architectural. SER: Shipping; delivery. SIZE: Large. PARK: Easy. VAT: Margin.
TEL: 01666 505125
E-MAIL: sales@jesterantiques.co.uk
WEBSITE: www.jesterantiques.co.uk

Long Street Antiques

Stamford House, 14 Long St. GL8 8AQ. (Ray and Samantha White)
EST. 2004. WEADA. Open 10-5. STOCK: Fine and country furniture, mirrors, works of art, textiles, silver, kitchenalia, barometers, clocks, glass, collectables, objets d'art, brass and leather goods. SIZE: Large - 45+ dealers. PARK: Easy.
TEL: 01666 500850
E-MAIL: longstantiques@aol.com
WEBSITE: www.longstreetantiques.co.uk

Lorfords Antiques

30 Long St. GL8 8AQ. (Toby Lorford and Lesley Ferguson)
Open 10-5.30. STOCK: Decorative antiques, painted furniture (Swedish and Italian). PARK: Own.
TEL: 01666 505111
E-MAIL: info@lorfordantiques.co.uk
WEBSITE: www.lorfordantiques.co.uk

Merlin Antiques

Shops 4 & 5 Chipping Court Shopping Mall. GL8 8ES. (Brian Smith)
EST. 1990. Open 9.30-5. STOCK: Furniture, Georgian to date, £50-£2,000; collectables, glass, pictures, china, jewellery - gold, silver and costume, £2-£500; books. SER: Valuations; restorations; house clearance. SIZE: Medium. PARK: Nearby.
TEL: 01666 505008

Porch House Antiques

40/42 Long St. GL8 8AQ. (Anne and Mervyn

Woodburn)
EST. 1977. Open 10-5. STOCK: *17th-20th C furniture and decorative items.* LOC: Town centre. SIZE: Large. VAT: Spec.
TEL: 01666 502687

Sharland & Lewis
52 Long St. GL8 8AQ. (Ali Sharland)
TADA. Open 10.30-5, or by appointment. STOCK: *Painted furniture, textiles and decorative objects.* SER: Interior design. SIZE: Medium. PARK: Easy.
TEL: 01666 500354
WEBSITE: www.sharland&lewis.com

Tetbury Old Books
21 Long St. GL8 8AA. (Philip Gibbons)
EST. 1992. TADA. Open 9.30-6, Sun 12-5. STOCK: *Antiquarian and secondhand books, prints, maps.* LOC: Main shopping street.
TEL: 01666 504330
E-MAIL: oldbooks@tetbury.co.uk

Top Banana Antiques Mall 1
1 New Church St. GL8 8DS. (Julian Tatham-Losh)
EST. 2002. TADA. Open 10-5.30, Sun. 11-5. STOCK: *Decorative antiques and interior design items, £1-£10,000.* LOC: Beginning of Long St. SER: Packing and shipping. SIZE: Large - approx. 40 dealers. PARK: Free. VAT: Stan/Spec.
TEL: 08712 881102; FAX: 08712 881103
E-MAIL: info@topbananaantiques.com
WEBSITE: www.topbananaantiques.com

Below are listed the dealers.

Gill Adams
Baths, basins and toilets.

Stuart Badcock
Garden statuary, pots and related items, small collectables.

Tim Bailey
Doulton character jugs.

Bananarama
Country furniture and kitchen items.

Mark Barton
Pictures and an eclectic mix of small items.

Sue Blacker, Thamesbrook Antiques
Glass and decorative smalls.

Sheila Briggs
Decorative quirky country antiques.

Terry Cleverly
Silver and desk related antiques.

Malcolm Cooper
Antique door furniture and decorative metalware.

Hillary Crocker
Silver, costume jewellery and small collectables.

Hedley Cullimore
Victoriana.

Terry Cusack
Decorative furniture and accessories.

Rhys Davies
Quality brown furniture, brass, lighting and mirrors.

W & B Dee
Black Forest and decorative items.

M. Ellis-Jones
Top hats, antique books and accessories.

Ezhar
Quality period brass, glass and treen.

Matthew Ford
Fine period country furniture, fine art and interesting objects pre-1820.

Keith Gormley
Tribal art and Arts and Crafts furniture and the unusual.

Jenny Horrocks
Art Nouveau lighting.

Ben Hubert
Decorative mirrors and painted furniture.

JoHuckman
Small collectables, silver and jewellery.

Kevin Jenkinson
Original painted English furniture.

Chris and Anne Kemp, Lansdown Antiques
Original painted furniture and brass and country furniture.

Mike Loveday
Sewing requisites, button hooks and small collectables.

Hillary Medcalf
Prints, oil paintings and general pictures.

Brian Moses
Victoriana.

Jenny Owen
Period oddities and children's antiques.

Mike Rawlings
Period tools and agricultural implements.

Heather Ross
Decorative small furniture, lighting and soft furnishings.

Chris Scott-Moody
Gentlemen's antiques, period china and glass.

AndrewTaylor
Fine period French fruitwood provincial tables.

JennyTurner
Sewing items, mauchline and tartan ware.

John Ward
Antique country furniture and related items.

Jan Wookey
Jewellery and accessories.

Alec and Christine Yirrell
Small silver items and collectables.

Top Banana Antiques Mall 2
32 Long St. GL8 8AQ. (Julian Tatham-Losh)

EST. 2004. TADA. Open 10-5.30, Sun. 11-5. *STOCK:
Decorative antiques and interior design, £5-£5,000.* LOC:
Halfway along Long St. SER: Packing and shipping.
SIZE: 13 dealers. PARK: Easy. VAT: Stan/Spec.
TEL: 08712 881110; FAX: 08712 881103
E-MAIL: info@topbananaantiques.com
WEBSITE: www.topbananaantiques.com

Below are listed the dealers.

Elizabeth Bradwin
Animalier bronzes.
e-mail: elizabeth@elizabethbradwin.com
website: www.elizabethbradwin.com

Clifford Butler
Early 19th C traditional furniture and decorative smalls.

Roger Emery and Jean Guillou
Painted furniture and decorative antiques mainly French.

Graham Fowler
19th C wooden boxes and caddies.

Gwyrdd
Quality collectables, furniture and jewellery.

Barbara Hale
Fine art, portraits and animal pictures; lighting.

I. and J. Howard
Silver objects and jewellery.

Melitta
French furniture, objects and textiles.

Lawrence Oliver Lighting
Antique lighting and chandeliers.

Alan Pezaro
Antique writing boxes, sporting goods and memorabilia.

Rebecca Shelton-Agar
*Decorative textiles and artefacts, linens and soft furnishings,
painted furniture.*

Trudi and SandraSpratling
*Victorian and Edwardian furniture, painted pine and
collectables.*

Ashley Wade Antiques
Early metalwork and glass.

Top Banana Antiques Malls 3 & 4

46-48 Long St. GL8 8AQ. (Julian Tatham-Losh)
EST. 2004. TADA. Open 10-5.30, Sun. 11-5. *STOCK:
Decorative antiques and interior design including jewellery,
kitchenalia, luggage, paintings, decorative and painted
furniture, Art Deco, £5-£5,000.* SER: Packing and
shipping. SIZE: 18 dealers. PARK: Free. VAT: Stan/Spec.
TEL: 08712 883058; FAX: 08712 881103
E-MAIL: info@topbananaantiques.com
WEBSITE: www.topbananaantiques.com

Below are listed the dealers.

Maite Alegre
Painted antique furniture and decorative items.

Brocante Exchange
French, and European furniture and decorative household items.

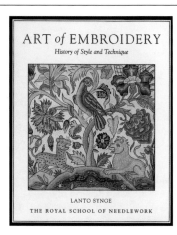

ART *of* EMBROIDERY

History of Style and Technique

LANTO SYNGE
THE ROYAL SCHOOL OF NEEDLEWORK

The story of embroidery and needlework is discussed within
the fascinating context of the history of fabrics, of decorative
costume, of interior decoration, of church and state
ceremonial, of girls' education, of furniture and pastimes.
Silk, cotton, linen, the significance of colours and dyes and
the worldwide fascination with the influence of Chinese
embroidery and Indian textiles are also considered. This
book is a broad account of the artistic achievements of every
facet of decorative needlework.

280 x 230 mm. 352 pp 320 col., 30 b.&w.
£45.00 Paperback

Ursula Burr
Swedish furniture and decorative items.

Chaney and Brandt
Antique furniture.

Jen Colley
Vintage, classic and retro clothing.

Garry Edwards
Ancient antiquities, roman and medieval items.

Richard Elder
Antique furniture and decorative items.

Ezhar
Antique furniture and collectable items.

H. Antiques
Antique furniture and smalls.

Barbara Hale
Doll's house items, teddies and sewing items.

Mike Loveday
Sewing and knitting collectables.

Magpie
*Beswick, Coalport etc., specialising in hunting, shooting and
fishing.*

Bill Matthews
Fishing related items, cameras and collectables.

Lawrence Oliver
Antique chandeliers and lighting.

R. C. Antiques
Small items of antique treen, tools, instruments etc.

Severnside
Porcelain, silver plate, glass, antiques and collectables.

Carol Walker
Antique and collectable Wedgwood, Royal Doulton etc. and silver jewellery.

Michelle Young
Contemporary and antique furniture and interesting useful items.

Westwood House Antiques
29 Long St. GL8 8AA. (Richard Griffiths)
EST. 1993. TADA, WEADA. Resident. Open 10-5 or by appointment. STOCK: *Oak, elm and ash country furniture - dressers, dresser bases and tables (especially French farmhouse), 17th-19th C; decorative country pottery.* SIZE: Large. VAT: Spec.
TEL: 01666 502328; FAX: same; MOBILE: 07774 952909
E-MAIL: westwoodhouse1@btconnect.com
WEBSITE: www.westwoodhouseantiques.com

TEWKESBURY

Gainsborough House Antiques
81 Church St. GL20 5RX. (A. and B. Hilson)
Open 9.30-5; CL: Thu. STOCK: *Furniture, 18th to early 19th C; glass, porcelain.*
TEL: 01684 293072

Tewkesbury Antiques & Collectables Centre
Tolsey Lane (by The Cross). GL20 5AE.
Open 10-5, Sun. 11-5. STOCK: *Furniture, rugs, porcelain, glass, cameras, books, records, textiles, pictures, kitchenalia and jewellery.* LOC: Town centre. SIZE: 20 dealers.
TEL: 01684 294091

TODENHAM

Geoffrey Stead   BADA
Wyatts Farm. GL56 9NY.
EST. 1963. Open by appointment. STOCK: *English and Continental furniture, decorative works of art and sculpture.* LOC: 3 miles from Moreton-in-Marsh. SER: Valuations. PARK: Easy. VAT: Spec. FAIRS: Olympia.
TEL: **01608 650997**; FAX: **01608 650597**; MOBILE: **07768 460450**
E-MAIL: **geoffreystead@geoffreystead.com**

WINCHCOMBE

Berkeley Antiques
3 Hailes St. GL54 5HU. (P.S. and S.M. Dennis)
EST. 1974. Open 10-5.30. STOCK: *Mahogany, oak, walnut, 17th-19th C, £50-£2,000; brass, copper, silver, lighting, china and glass.* SER: Valuations; restorations. SIZE: Medium. PARK: Easy. VAT: Stan./Spec.
TEL: 01242 609074
WEBSITE: www.berkeleyantiques.com

Prichard Antiques
16 High St. GL54 5LJ. (K.H. and D.Y. Prichard)
EST. 1979. Open 9-5.30, Sun. by appointment. STOCK: *Period and decorative furniture, £10-£20,000; treen and metalwork, £5-£5,000; interesting and decorative accessories.* LOC: On B4632 Broadway to Cheltenham road. SIZE: Large - six showrooms. PARK: Easy. VAT: Spec.
TEL: 01242 603566
E-MAIL: kanddprichard@msn.com
WEBSITE: www.prichardantiques.co.uk

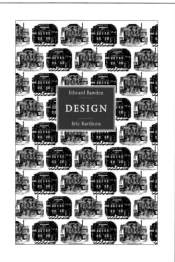

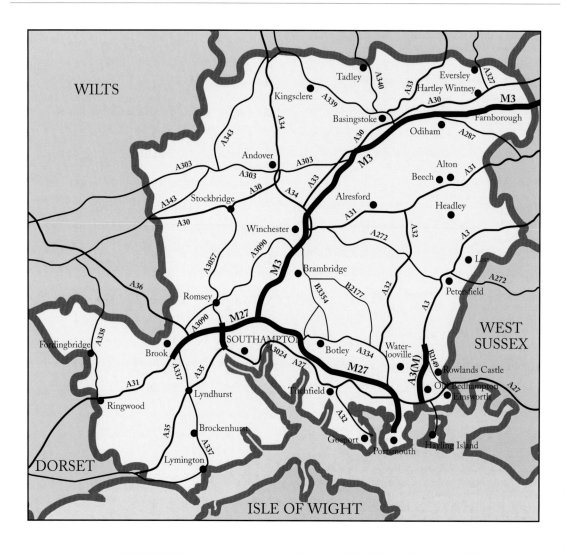

ALRESFORD

Artemesia
16 West St. SO24 9AT. (D.T.L. Wright)
EST. 1972. Open 9.30-5. *STOCK: English and Continental furniture, English, Continental and Oriental porcelain and works of art, £20-£6,000.* LOC: A31. SER: Valuations. SIZE: Medium. PARK: Nearby.
TEL: 01962 732277

Laurence Oxley Ltd
Studio Bookshop and Gallery, 17 Broad St. SO24 9AW. (Anthony Oxley)
EST. 1951. ABA. FATG. Open 9-5. *STOCK: Antiquarian books, £5-£2,500; topographical prints, £2-£250; maps, £5-£800; watercolours, (specialising in M. Birket Foster, RWS 1825-1899), £100-£30,000.* LOC: B3046. SER: Valuations; restorations (oil paintings, watercolours, prints and books); framing; book-binding. SIZE: Large. PARK: Easy. VAT: Stan. FAIRS: London ABA (Chelsea).

TEL: 01962 732188 (books), 01962 732998 (pictures)
E-MAIL: aoxley@freenet.co.uk

Pineapple House Antiques
49 Broad St. SO24 9AS. (Peter Radford)
EST. 1979. Open Thurs. and Fri. 11-4, Sat. 11-6, Sun. by appointment (Please telephone first). *STOCK: Furniture, especially dining tables, chairs, sideboards, chests of drawers and smaller items, 18th-20th C.* SER: Valuations; restorations; repairs; cabinet making. SIZE: Small. PARK: Easy.
TEL: 01962 736575; FAX: same; MOBILE: 07973 254749
E-MAIL: amanda@o2m.co.uk
WEBSITE: www.pineapplehouseantiques.com

Max Rollitt BADA
The Old Telephone Exchange, Station Rd. SO24 9JG. (M. Rollitt)
EST. 1971. Open by appointment. *STOCK: English furniture, mirrors, period decorative items, 1680-1840; reproduction sofas and chairs; interior decor.* LOC: Town

centre. SER: Interior design. SIZE: Large. PARK: Outside. VAT: Stan/Spec. FAIRS: Olympia (June, Nov).
TEL: 01962 853779/738800; FAX: 01962 735777;
MOBILE: 07771 960393
E-MAIL: sales@maxrollitt.com
WEBSITE: www.maxrollitt.com

BASINGSTOKE

Squirrel Collectors Centre
9A New St. RG21 1DF. (A.H. Stone)
EST. 1981. Open 10-5.30. STOCK: *Jewellery and silver, Victorian and Edwardian, £5–£4,500; books, postcards, watches, collectors' items, smalls, china, toys and large furniture showroom.* LOC: Near traffic lights at junction with Winchester St. SER: Valuations. SIZE: Small. PARK: Nearby. VAT: Stan.
TEL: 01256 464885
E-MAIL: ahs@squirrelsuk.fsnet.co.uk
WEBSITE: www.squirrels-antiques.com

BEECH

Jardinique
Old Park Farm, Abbey Rd. GU34 4AP. (Edward and Sarah Neish)
EST. 1994. Resident. Open 10-5. CL: Sun. and Mon. and Jan. and Feb. except by appointment. STOCK: *Garden ornaments, urns, statuary and furniture, from 17th C, £10–£5,000.* LOC: From Alton on the A339 Basingstoke road, take first left signed Beech, after 1.5 miles premises on left opposite Alton Abbey. SER: Valuations; buys at auction (as stock). SIZE: Very large. PARK: Easy. VAT: Stan/Spec.
TEL: 01420 560055
E-MAIL: enquiries@Jardinique.co.uk
WEBSITE: www.Jardinique.co.uk

BRAMBRIDGE

Brambridge Antiques
The Barn, Bugle Farm, Highbridge Rd. SO50 6HS. (Desmond and Ann May)
EST. 1982. Open 10-5. STOCK: *Furniture, including oak and pine, late Georgian to Edwardian.* SER: Valuations; restorations (furniture including upholstery and re-leathering). SIZE: Medium. PARK: Easy.
TEL: 01962 714386; HOME: 02380 269205

BROCKENHURST

Antiquiteas
37 Brookley Rd. SO42 7RB. (R. Wolstenholme)
EST. 1996. Resident. Open 10-5, Sun. 10.30-3. STOCK: *Furniture including pine, £50–£350; china and glass, copper and brass, £10–£100; all 19th-20th C.* LOC: Near watersplash and village post office. SIZE: Medium. PARK: Easy. VAT: Stan.
TEL: 01590 622120

Squirrels
Lyndhurst Rd. SO42 7RL. (Sue Crocket)
EST. 1990. Open 10-5 including Sun. - until dusk in winter. CL: Tues. STOCK: *Furniture including stripped pine, china especially blue and white, Victoriana, Art Deco, Art Nouveau, retro and gardenalia, 19th-20th C, to £1,000.* LOC: Opposite Rose and Crown. PARK: Easy.
TEL: 01590 622433

BROOK

F.E.A. Briggs Ltd
Birchenwood Farm. SO43 7JA. (Frank Briggs)
EST. 1968. Open by appointment. STOCK: *Antique and Victorian furniture.* LOC: M27 exit 1. SER: Restorations; valuations. SIZE: Large warehouse. PARK: Easy. VAT: Stan/Spec. FAIRS: Newark.
TEL: 02380 812595
E-MAIL: feabriggs@aol.com

EMSWORTH

Bookends
7 High St. PO10 7AQ. (Mrs Carol Waldron)
EST. 1982. Open 9.30-5, Sun. 10-3. STOCK: *Books, some antiquarian; music scores, £2–£200.* SER: Valuations; book search. SIZE: Medium. PARK: Nearby.
TEL: 01243 372154
E-MAIL: cawaldron@tinyworld.co.uk
WEBSITE: www.bookends.me.uk

Clockwise
10 South St. PO10 7EH. (D. Judge)
EST. 1976. AHS. GMC. Open Wed.-Sat. 10-5. STOCK: *Longcase, wall, mantel, bracket and carriage clocks, 18th-19th C, £300–£5,000.* LOC: A259 off A27, head for harbour. SER: Valuations; restorations. SIZE: Small. PARK: Easy.
TEL: 01243 377558
E-MAIL: c.537@btinternet.com

Dolphin Quay Antique Centre
Queen St. PO10 7BU. (C. and L. Creamer)
EST. 1996. Open 10-5, Sun. and Bank Holidays 10-4. STOCK: *Fine English, French and country furniture, 18th C to 1939; marine antiques; clocks - bracket, mantel, longcase; wristwatches, fobs, dress watches, vintage pens, conservatory and garden antiques, decorative arts, silver, jewellery, china including Clarice Cliff and Troika, Whitefriars glass, paintings, watercolours, prints.* SER: Resorations & repairs (clock, watch, fountain pen, gramophone); framing. SIZE: Large - 40+ dealers. PARK: Own and in square.
TEL: 01243 379994
E-MAIL: chrisdqantiques@aol.com

Tiffins Antiques
12 Queen St. PO10 7BL. (Phyl Hudson)
EST. 1987. Open 9.30-5. CL: Mon. and Tues. STOCK: *General antiques, oil lamps and silver.* LOC: 1 min. from high st. SIZE: Small. PARK: On the road.
TEL: 01243 372497; HOME: same

EVERSLEY

Eversley Barn Antiques
Church Lane. RG27 0PX. (H. Craven)
EST. 1988. Open 7 days 10-5. STOCK: *Regency, Victorian
and Edwardian furniture; glass, ceramics, pictures, mirrors,
books, rugs, silver, chandeliers, clocks, collectables and vintage
clothes.* LOC: From M3, junction 4A, A327 to Reading,
1.5 miles from Blackbush airport and Hartley Wintney.
SIZE: Large. PARK: Easy.
TEL: 01189 328518
E-MAIL: eversleybarn@hotmail.com
WEBSITE: www.eversleybarnantiques.co.uk

FORDINGBRIDGE

Quatrefoil
Burgate. SP6 1LX. (C.D. and Mrs I. Aston)
EST. 1972. Resident. Always open. STOCK: *Early oak
furniture, 16th-18th C, £50-£15,000; carvings and
sculpture, 13th-17th C, £20-£20,000; antiquities and coins,
£50-£10,000.* LOC: On A338, adjacent Tudor Rose Inn.
SIZE: Large. PARK: Easy. VAT: Stan/Spec.
TEL: 01425 653309

GOSPORT

Former Glory
49 Whitworth Rd. PO12 3AH. (Les Brannon)

EST. 1987. Open 9.30-5. STOCK: *Victorian and Edwardian
furniture, £120-£400.* LOC: Near town centre. SER:
Valuations; restorations (furniture repairs, refinishing,
repolishing, traditional upholstery) SIZE: Small. PARK: Easy.
TEL: 02392 504869

Peter Pan's Bazaar
87 Forton Rd. PO12 4TG. (S.V. Panormo and J. McClaren)
EST. 1960. Open Thurs.-Sat. 10-1, 2.30-5. STOCK:
*Vintage cameras and ephemera, £5-£1,000; glass, china,
collectable items.* LOC: Main road into town. PARK: Easy.
TEL: 02392 524254

HARTLEY WINTNEY

Nicholas Abbott   LAPADA
High St. RG27 8NY. (C.N. Abbott)
EST. 1962. Open 10.30-4.30 or by appointment. STOCK:
Walnut and mahogany English furniture, 18th to early 19th
C. LOC: Village centre. SER: Restorations; valuations.
SIZE: Medium. PARK: Easy. VAT: Stan/Spec.
TEL: 01252 842365; FAX: same.
E-MAIL: antiques@nicholasabbott.com
WEBSITE: www.nicholasabbott.com

Anvil Antiques
The White Lion, London Rd. RG27 8AE. (Andrew Pitter)
Open 10-5. STOCK: *General antiques.* LOC: Hartford
Bridge just off the A30. SER: Restorations (ceramics).
PARK: Easy.
TEL: MOBILE: 07778 934938
E-MAIL: anvilantiques@hotmail.co.uk

Cedar Antiques Limited
RG27 8NT. (Derek and Sally Green)
EST. 1964. Open by appointment only. STOCK: *English
country furniture, 17th – 18th C and accessories.* SER:
Valuations; restorations (period pieces); interior design;
fabrication of copies. SIZE: Large. VAT: Stan/Spec.
TEL: 01252 842653
E-MAIL: sg@cedar-antiques.com
WEBSITE: www.cedar-antiques.com

Bryan Clisby Antique Clocks
at Cedar Antiques Centre Ltd., High St. RG27 8NY.
(Bryan and Christine Clisby)
EST. 1976. Open 10-5.30. STOCK: *Longcase clocks, 1700-
1830, £2,000-£8,000; barometers, 1770-1850, £500-
£3,000; bracket, wall and mantel clocks.* LOC: A30 village
centre. SER: Valuations; restorations (clocks and
barometers). SIZE: Medium. PARK: Opposite.
TEL: 01252 716436
E-MAIL: bryanclisby@boltblue.com
WEBSITE: www.bryanclisby-antiqueclocks.co.uk

Deva Antiques   LAPADA
High St. RG27 8NY. (A. Gratwick)
EST. 1987. Open 9-5.30. STOCK: *18th-19th C English
mahogany and walnut furniture. LOC: Next to church.

SIZE: Large. PARK: Own. VAT: Stan/Spec.
TEL: 01252 843538; FAX: 01252 842946
E-MAIL: devaants@aol.com
WEBSITE: www.devaantiques.com

The Farthingale Centre
63 High St. RG27 8NY. (Richard Popplewell)
EST. 1998. Open 10-5.30, Sun. and Bank Holidays 11-4.
STOCK: *Quality furniture, glass, porcelain and pottery, paintings, rugs, silver, collectables from teddy bears to treen.* LOC: A30 village centre. SER: Restorations (furniture). SIZE: Large - 40+ dealers. PARK: Opposite. VAT: Stan/Spec.
TEL: 01252 843222; FAX: 01252 842111

David Lazarus Antiques   BADA
High St. RG27 8NS.
EST. 1973. Resident. Open 9.30-5.30; some Sundays, other times by appointment. STOCK: *17th to early 19th C English and Continental furniture; objets d'art.* LOC: Main street. SIZE: Medium. PARK: Own. VAT: Stan/Spec.
TEL: 01252 842272; FAX: same

A.W. Porter and Son
High St. RG27 8NY. (M.A. and S.J. Porter)
EST. 1844. Open 9.30-5, Wed. 9.30-4. CL: Mon. STOCK: *Clocks, silver, jewellery, glass.* LOC: Opposite Lloyds Bank. SER: Restorations (clocks). VAT: Stan/Spec.
TEL: 01252 842676; FAX: 01252 842064
E-MAIL: markaporter@gmail.com
WEBSITE: www.awporter.com

The White Lion Antiques & Collectables Centre
London Rd. RG27 8AE.
Open 10-5. STOCK: *General antiques.* LOC: Hartford Bridge just off the A30. SIZE: Large - individual dealers. PARK: Easy.
TEL: 01252 844000

HAYLING ISLAND

J. Morton Lee   BADA
Cedar House, Bacon Lane. PO11 0DN. (Commander and Mrs J. Morton Lee)
EST. 1984. Open by appointment. Also at the Edenbridge Galleries. STOCK: *Watercolours, 18th-21st C, £50-£10,000.* SER: Valuations; buys at auction; exhibition in Dec. PARK: Easy. VAT: Stan/Spec. FAIRS: Petersfield (Feb., Sept); Harrogate (Oct).
TEL: 02392 464444; MOBILE: 07860 810938
E-MAIL: j.mortonlee@btinternet.com

HEADLEY

Victorian Dreams
The Old Holme School, Village Green, Crabtree Lane. GU35 8QH. (S. Kay)
EST. 1990. Open 9-5.30, Sun. 10-4. STOCK: *Bedsteads including wooden, brass and iron, brass, caned and upholstered.* LOC: next to Village Green. SER: Valuations; restorations

(metalwork and woodwork). SIZE: Large. PARK: Easy.
TEL: 01428 717000; FAX: 01428 717111
E-MAIL: sales@victorian-dreams.co.uk
WEBSITE: www.victorian-dreams.co.uk

KINGSCLERE

Kingsclere Old Bookshop (Wyseby House Books)
2A George St. RG20 5NQ. (Dr. Tim and Mrs Anne Oldham)
EST. 1978. PBFA. Open 9-5. STOCK: *Old, unusual and out-of-print books on fine art, art history, architecture, decorative arts, design, photography, biology, natural history, science, horticulture and gardening; prints: all 19th-20th C, £5-£500.* SER: Valuations. SIZE: Medium. PARK: Nearby. VAT: Stan. FAIRS: PBFA London.
TEL: 01635 297995; FAX: 01635 297677
E-MAIL: info@wyseby.co.uk
WEBSITE: www.wyseby.co.uk

LISS

Plestor Barn Antiques
Farnham Rd. GU33 6JQ. (T.P. and C.A. McCarthy)
EST. 1982. Open 10-4. CL: Sat. STOCK: *Furniture including upholstered, Victorian and Edwardian, shipping goods, pine; china and glass, copper and brass, pictures, mirrors, silver and cutlery.* LOC: A325, 2 mins from A3 roundabout, near Spread Eagle public house. SIZE: Large. PARK: Easy.
TEL: 01730 893922; MOBILE: 07850 539998
E-MAIL: plestor_barn@btopenworld.com.

LYMINGTON

Barry Papworth Jewellers
28 St. Thomas St. SO41 9NE.
EST. 1960. Open 9-5.30. STOCK: *Diamond jewellery, £50-£20,000; silver, £25-£1,500 both 18th-19th C. Watches and clocks, 19th C, £50-£10,000.* LOC: A337 into town, bay window on left. SER: Valuations (NAG registered); restorations. SIZE: Small. PARK: Easy. VAT: Stan/Spec.
TEL: 01590 676422

Robert Perera Fine Art
19 St. Thomas St. SO41 9NB. (R.J.D. Perera)
Open 10-1 and 2-5, Wed. 10-1, lunch times and Sun. by appointment. STOCK: *British paintings, 19th-20th C, £100-£25,000; occasional ceramics and sculpture, 19th-20th C, £50-£1,500; paintings and etchings by W.L. Wyllie.* LOC: Top (west) end of main shopping area. SER: Framing. SIZE: Small. PARK: Easy. VAT: Margin.
TEL: 01590 678230; FAX: same
E-MAIL: sales@art-gallery.co.uk
WEBSITE: www.art-gallery.co.uk

Wick Antiques Ltd   LAPADA
Fairlea House, 110-112 Marsh Lane. SO41 9EE.
(R.W. and Mrs. C. Wallrock)

EST. 1977 CINOA. Open 9-5, Sat. by appointment. STOCK: *French and English furniture, 18th-19th C, £1,000-£15,000; small items, 19th to early 20th C, £100-£20,000.* LOC: Town outskirts. SER: Valuations; restorations; furniture polishing; repairs; upholstery; re-gilding; buys at auction. SIZE: Medium. PARK: Own. VAT: Spec. FAIRS: Olympia (June/Nov). TEL: 01590 677558; FAX: same; HOME: 01590 672515; MOBILE: 07768 877069 E-MAIL: charles@wickantiques.co.uk WEBSITE: www.wickantiques.co.uk

LYNDHURST

Acorn Antiques
13 High St. SO43 7BB. (Sharon & Jack Brown)
Open: 10-5. *STOCK: Antiques and collectables.* SIZE: 3 rooms. PARK: Public nearby.
TEL: 02380 282700

Lyndhurst Antiques Centre
19-21 High St. SO43 7BB. (Robert Sparks)
EST. 1997. Open 10-5 including Sun. *STOCK: Furniture and clocks, 18th to early 20th C, £50-£5,000; ceramics, 18th to mid 20th C, £5-£1,000; collectables, 20th C, £2-£200, pictures, jewellery, silver.* LOC: Main High Street by traffic lights. SER: Delivery; postal service, valuations. SIZE: Medium on 2 floors. PARK: Public nearby.
TEL: 02380 284000

E-MAIL: info@lyndhurstantiques.com
WEBSITE: www.lyndhurstantiques.com

MORESTEAD

The Pine Cellars
Burgess Farm Jackmans Hill. SO21 1LZ. (N. Spencer-Brayn)
EST. 1970. Open 9.30-5 (except Sun and Bank holidays), please ring first. *STOCK: Pine and country furniture, 18th-19th C, £10-£5,000; painted furniture, architectural items, lighting, eccentricities and paraphernalia.* LOC: Into Morestead, turn into Jackmans Hill on sharp bend. First gate on right. SER: Stripping, restoration and export. SIZE: Large and warehouses - 15,000sq. f.t PARK: Easy - on premises. VAT: Stan/Spec.
TEL: 01962 777546
E-MAIL: pine.cellars@virgin.net

ODIHAM

The Odiham Gallery
78 High St. RG29 1LN. (I. Walker)
Open 9.30-5.30, Sat. 10-4. *STOCK: Decorative and Oriental rugs and carpets.* SER: Repairs, restoration and cleaning. SIZE: Medium. PARK: Easy. VAT: Stan.
TEL: 01256 703415
E-MAIL: showroom@designwalker.co.uk

OLD BEDHAMPTON

J F F Fire Brigade & Military Collectables
Ye Olde Coach House, Mill Lane. PO9 3JH. (Johnny Franklin)
EST. 1982. Resident. Open by appointment. STOCK: *Brass firemen's helmets and fire related memorabilia; military, police and ambulance items including helmets, cap and collar badges, buttons, uniforms, caps, weapons, equipment, medals and brooches.* SER: Valuations; buys at auction. PARK: Easy. FAIRS: 999 Memorabilia.
TEL: 02392 486485

PETERSFIELD

The Barn
North Rd. GU31 4AH. (Victoria Hawkins and Jill Gadsden)
EST. 1956. Open 10-5. STOCK: *Victoriana, bric-a-brac; also large store of trade and shipping goods.* LOC: Just off one-way system. SIZE: Medium. PARK: Nearby.
TEL: 01730 262958

The Folly Antiques Centre
Folly Market, College St. GU31 4AD. (Red Goblet Ltd)
EST. 1980. Open 9.30-5. STOCK: *Furniture, 19th-20th C, £25-£1,000; ceramics and silver, 18th-20th C, £5-£100; jewellery, 19th-20th C; pictures, general antiques and collectables.* LOC: Behind Folly Wine Bar. SIZE: Small. PARK: Opposite - Festival Hall, Heath Rd.
TEL: 07789 902855

The Petersfield Bookshop
16a Chapel St. GU32 3DS. (A. Westwood)
EST. 1918. ABA. PBFA. Open 9-5.30. STOCK: *Books, old and modern, £1-£1,000+; maps and prints, 1600-1859, £1-£1,000+; oils and watercolours, 19th C, £20-£1,000+.* LOC: Chapel St. runs from the square to Station Rd. SER: Restorations and rebinding of old leather books; picture-framing and mount-cutting. SIZE: Large. PARK: Opposite. VAT: Stan. FAIRS: London ABA.
TEL: 01730 263438; FAX: 01730 269426
E-MAIL: sales@petersfieldbookshop.com
WEBSITE: www.petersfieldbookshop.com

PORTSMOUTH

A. Fleming (Southsea) Ltd
The Clock Tower, Castle Rd., Southsea. PO5 3DE. (A.J. and Mrs C. E. Fleming)
EST. 1908. Open Wed., Thurs. and Fri. 9.30-5.30 or by appointment. STOCK: *Furniture, silver, barometers, boxes and general antiques.* LOC: Near seafront and Royal Naval dockyard. SER: Restorations. SIZE: Medium. PARK: Easy. VAT: Stan/Spec. FAIRS: Local vetted.
TEL: 02392 822934; FAX: 02392 293501
E-MAIL: mail@flemingsantiques.fsnet.co.uk
WEBSITE: www.flemingsantiques.co.uk

Gray's Antiques
250 Havant Rd., Drayton. PO6 1PA. (Alexandra J. Gray)
EST. 1968. Open 10-5. STOCK: *English and French furniture, £200-£5,000; china, collectables, decorative items, £25-£3,000; all 19th-20th C.* LOC: On the main road. SER: Restorations (furniture and upholstery). PARK: Easy.
TEL: 02392 376379

RINGWOOD

Millers of Chelsea Antiques Ltd   LAPADA
Netherbrook House, 86 Christchurch Rd. BH24 1DR. (Alan & Carole Miller)
EST. 1897. WEADA. Open Mon. 9.30-1.30, Tues.-Fri. 9.30-5, Sat. 10-3, other times by appointment. STOCK: *Furniture - English and Continental country, mahogany, gilt and military; decorative items, treen, majolica and faience, 18th-19th C, £25-£5,000.* LOC: On B3347 towards Christchurch. SER: Restorations. SIZE: Large. PARK: Own. VAT: Stan/Spec. FAIRS: Decorative Antiques, Battersea; Wilton.
TEL: 01425 472062; FAX: 01425 472727
E-MAIL: mail@millers-antiques.co.uk
WEBSITE: www.millers-antiques.co.uk

New Forest Antiques
90 Christchurch Rd. BH24 1DR.
EST. 1984. Open Tues.-Sat. 10-5. STOCK: *Militaria and postcards.* LOC: Off A31 into Ringwood, straight over 1st roundabout, left at next roundabout, shop 150yds. on right. SER: Valuations; restorations. SIZE: Small. PARK: Easy and at rear. VAT: Stan/Spec. FAIRS: Yeovil; Woking Postcard.
TEL: 01425 474620
E-MAIL: cliveking@fsmail.net

Lorraine Tarrant Antiques
23 Market Place. BH24 1AN.
EST. 1991. Open 10-5. CL: Mon. STOCK: *Victorian furniture, to £1,000; china, glass, collectors' items, £5-£100.* LOC: Opposite church. SIZE: Medium. PARK: Easy.
TEL: 01425 461123
E-MAIL: lorraine@lorrainetarrantantiques.com

ROMSEY

Bell Antiques
8 Bell St. SO51 8GA. (M. and B.M. Gay)
EST. 1979. FGA. Open usually 9.30-5.30. CL: Wed. (winter). Prior telephone call advisable. STOCK: *Jewellery and silver, glass, pottery, porcelain, small furniture, prints and maps, mainly 19th-20th C.* LOC: Near market place. SIZE: Large. PARK: Town centre. VAT: Global/Stan/Spec.
TEL: 01794 514719

ROWLANDS CASTLE

Good Day Antiques and Decor
22 The Green. PO9 6AB. (Gillian Day)
EST. 1980. Open 11-5, Sun. 12-4.30. CL: Tues. and
Wed. STOCK: *20th C prints; porcelain and pottery, 1800-1950, £25-£500; jewellery and silver, 1840-1970, £25-£1,000; collectables, 19th-20th C, £5-£50.* LOC: Off
junction 2, A3(M). SER: Restorations (silver plating,
gilding). PARK: Easy.
TEL: 02392 413221
E-MAIL: gooddayantiques@aol.com

SOUTHAMPTON

**Mr. Alfred's "Old Curiosity Shop" and The Morris &
Shirley Galleries**
280 Shirley Rd., Shirley. SO15 3HL.
EST. 1952. Open 9-6 including Sun. STOCK: *Furniture, 18th-20th C; paintings, porcelain, bronzes, brass, glass, books, silver, jewellery and general antiques.* LOC: On left of main
Shirley road, ¾ mile from Southampton central station.
SER: Fine art dealer; valuations; auctions; curator;
restorations; framing. SIZE: Very large. PARK: Own.
TEL: 02380 774772

Amber Antiques
115 Portswood Rd., Portswood. SO17 2FX. (R. Boyle)
EST. 1985. Open 10-5, Sat. 9-5, Sun. 11-3. STOCK: *Furniture, late Victorian to 1930s, £100-£1,500.* SER:
Restorations; repairs; French polishing. SIZE: Large.
PARK: Easy. VAT: Stan/Spec.
TEL: 02380 583645; FAX: same

Cobwebs
78 Northam Rd. SO14 0PB. (P.R. and J.M. Boyd-Smith)
EST. 1975. Open 10.30-4. CL: Wed. STOCK: *Ocean liner memorabilia; china, silverplate, ephemera, paintings, furniture, ship fittings, 1840-present day, £5-£5,000.* LOC:
20 mins from M27. Main road into city centre from the
east (A334) SER: Valuations. Shipping worldwide. SIZE:
Medium. PARK: 20yds. FAIRS: Beaulieu Boat & Auto;
Ship Show, London; Southampton Transportation.
TEL: 02380 227458; FAX: same
WEBSITE: www.cobwebs.uk.com

STOCKBRIDGE

The Bakhtiyar Gallery
High St. SO20 6HF. (Masoud Mazaheri-Asadi)
Open 10-5. STOCK: *Hand-made Persian carpets, runners, kelims, new, old and antique, nomadic, village and fine city pieces; fine English and European furniture, decorative antiques and mirrors.* SER: Valuations; restorations
(furniture and carpets). SIZE: 2 floors. PARK: Front of
shop. FAIRS: Annual exhibitions, Salisbury
TEL: 01264 811033; FAX: 01264 811077; MOBILE:
07740 333333

E-MAIL: bakhtiyar@bakhtiyar.com
WEBSITE: www.bakhtiyar.com

Lane Antiques
High St. SO20 6EU. (Mrs E.K. Lane)
EST. 1981. Open 10-5. CL: Mon. STOCK: *English and Continental porcelain, 18th-20th C; silver and plate, decorative items, glass, chandeliers, lighting, small furniture, oils and watercolours; boxes, 18th-19th C.* SIZE: Small.
PARK: Easy.
TEL: 01264 810435
WEBSITE: www.stockbridge.org.uk

TADLEY

Gasson Antiques and Interiors
P O Box 7225. RG26 5IY. (Patricia and Terry Gasson)
Open by appointment. STOCK: *Georgian, Victorian and Edwardian furniture, clocks, porcelain and decorative items.*
SER: Valuation; restoration (furniture).   FAIRS:
Harrogate.
TEL: 01189 813636; MOBILE: 07860 827651
E-MAIL: tgasson@btinternet.com

TITCHFIELD

Gaylords
75 West St. PO14 4DG. (Ian & Linda Hebbard)
EST. 1970. Open 9-5. CL: Tues & Sun. STOCK: *Furniture, from 18th C; clocks, £50-£10,000.* LOC: off
Jct.9, M27. SER: Valuations. SIZE: Large. PARK: Easy.
VAT: Stan/Spec.
TEL: 01329 843402; HOME: 01329 847134
WEBSITE: www.gaylords.co.uk

WATERLOOVILLE

Goss and Crested China Centre and Goss Museum
62 Murray Rd., Horndean. PO8 9JL. (L.J. Pine)
EST. 1968. Open 9-4 Mon. - Thurs. STOCK: *Goss, 1860-1930, £2-£1,000; other heraldic china, Art Deco pottery including Carlton ware, Charlotte Rhead, Chamelion, 1890-1930, £1-£1,000.* LOC: Just off A3(M), junction 2,
on to B2149. SER: Valuations; collections purchased; mail
order catalogue; relevant books. SIZE: Medium. PARK:
Easy. VAT: Stan.
TEL: 02392 597440; FAX: 02392 591975
E-MAIL: info@gosschinaclub.co.uk
WEBSITE: www.gosschinaclub.co.uk

WINCHESTER

Bell Fine Art   LAPADA
67b Parchment St. SO23 8AT. (L.E. Bell)
EST. 1977. FATG. Open 9.30-5.30, Mon. 10-4. STOCK:
Watercolours, oils and prints, 1750-1950, £5-£10,000.
SER: Valuations; restorations (oils and watercolours);
buys at auction. SIZE: Large. PARK: 2 spaces. VAT:
Spec. FAIRS: Surrey.

TEL: **01962 860439**; FAX: **same**; HOME: **01962 862947**
E-MAIL: **bellfineart@btclick.com**
WEBSITE: **www.bellfineart.co.uk**

Burgess Farm Antiques

39 Jewry St. S023 8RY. (N. Spencer-Brayn)
EST. 1970. Open 9-5. *STOCK: Furniture, especially pine
and country, 18th-19th C, £25-£5,000; architectural items –
doors, panelling, fireplaces.* LOC: One way street, right turn
from top of High St. or St. George, shop 100 yards on
right. SER: Stripping; export. SIZE: Large. PARK: Easy.
VAT: Stan/Spec.
TEL: 01962 777546

The Clock-Work-Shop (Winchester)

6a Parchment St. SO23 8AT. (P. Ponsford-Jones and
K.J. Hurd)
EST. 1997. MBHI. AHS. Open 9-5. *STOCK: Restored
longcase, wall, dial, mantel, bracket and carriage clocks,
especially English, 18th-19th C, £300-£40,000; barometers,
books and tools.* LOC: Central, off main pedestrian
precinct, near W.H.Smith. SER: Valuations; restorations
(clocks and barometers). SIZE: Large. PARK: Easy. VAT:
Margin.
TEL: 01962 842331; FAX: 01962 878775; MOBILES:
07885 954302 and 07973 736155
WEBSITE: www.clock-work-shop.co.uk

Lacewing Fine Art Gallery   LAPADA

28 St Thomas St. SO23 9HJ. (N. James)
EST. 1979. Open 10-5. CL: Mon. *STOCK: Paintings,
watercolours, sculpture, Old Master drawings, 17th-21st C.*
LOC: Just off High St., alongside Lloyds TSB. SER: Fine
art restoration; bespoke framing; valuations and advice.
TEL: **01962 878700/01962 870583**;
MOBILE: **07710 735712**
E-MAIL: **noeljames@lacewing.co.uk**
WEBSITE: **www.lacewing.co.uk**

G.E. Marsh Antique Clocks Ltd   BADA

32a The Square. SO23 9EX.
EST. 1947. MBHI. AHS. Open 9.30-5, Sat. 9.30-1 and
2-5. *STOCK: Clocks including longcase, bracket, English,
French and Continental, watches and barometers, 1680-
1880.* LOC: Near cathedral. SER: Valuations;
restorations; commissions. PARK: Easy.
TEL: **01962 844443**; FAX: same
E-MAIL: **gem@marshclocks.co.uk**
WEBSITE: **www.marshclocks.co.uk**

Samuel Spencer's Antiques and Decorative Arts Emporium

39 Jewry St. SO23 8RY. (N. Spencer-Brayn)
Open 9.30-5. *STOCK: General antiques.* LOC: One way
street, right turn from top of High St. or St. George St.,
shop 100yds. on right. SIZE: 31 dealers. PARK: Nearby.
TEL: 01962 867014/777546

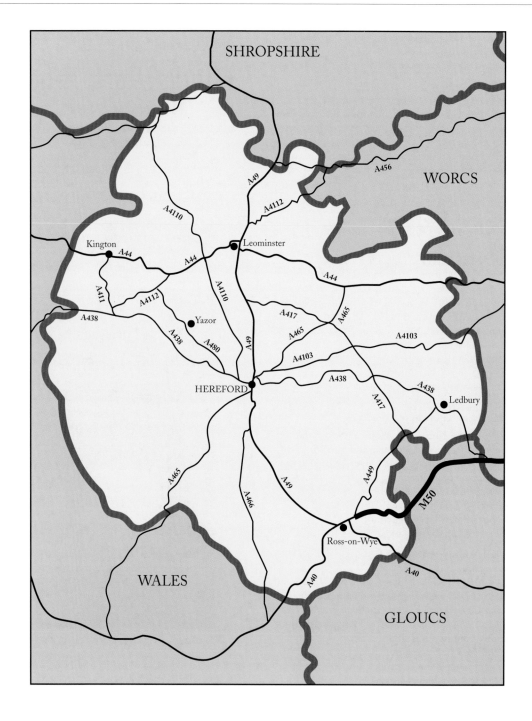

BROMYARD

Norman Blackburn
Old Print Shop, 46 Broad St. HR7 4BS. (Norman Blackburn and Maggie Houghton)
EST. 1974. Open 10-5, Tues. by appointment; CL: Mon. STOCK: *Prints in period frames - decorative, stipple and mezzotints, botanical, sporting, marine, portraits and views, pre-1860.* LOC: Market square. SER: Valuations. SIZE: Large. PARK: Off Sherford St.
TEL: 01885 488877; FAX: same; MOBILE: 07714 721846
E-MAIL: oldprints@normanblackburn.com
WEBSITE: www.normanblackburn.com

HEREFORD

I. and J.L. Brown Ltd
Whitestone Park, Whitestone. HR1 3SE.
Open 9-5.30, Sun. 11-4. STOCK: *Matched sets of period country chairs, English country, French provincial and reproduction furniture, decorative items.* LOC: A4103, 4 miles from Hereford towards Worcester. SER: Restorations; re-rushing chairs; bespoke furniture made to individual designs. SIZE: Large. PARK: Easy. VAT: Stan.
TEL: 01432 851991; FAX: 01432 851994
E-MAIL: enquiries@brownantiques.com
WEBSITE: www.brownantiques.com

Hereford Antique Centre
128 Widemarsh St. HR4 9HN. (G.P. Smith)
EST. 1991. Open 10-5, Sun. 11-4. STOCK: *General antiques and collectables.* SER: Restorations; shipping. SIZE: 30 dealers - 3 floors. PARK: Own.
TEL: 01432 266242

Wolseley Fine Arts Ltd
Middle Hunt House, Walterstone. HR2 0DY. (Rupert Otten and Hanneke van der Werf)
TEFAF. Open by appointment only. STOCK: *British and European 20th C works on paper and sculpture, works by David Jones, Eric Gill, John Buckland Wright, Pierre Bonnard, Edouard Vuillard, Ker Xavier Roussel and Eugeen van Mieghem; contemporary still life paintings, art, sculpture and carved lettering.* SER: Valuations. FAIRS: Works on Paper; New York; TEFAF; Art London; London Original Print Fair.
TEL: 01873 860525
E-MAIL: www.wolseleyfinearts.com
WEBSITE: info@wolseleyfinearts.com

KINGTON

Castle Hill Books
12 Church St. HR5 3AZ. (Peter Newman)
EST. 1988. Open 10.30-1, Sat. 10.30-1 and 2-5. STOCK: *Books - out of print, secondhand and antiquarian especially British topography, Herefordshire, Radnorshire, Wales,* archaeology and stock of all subjects. LOC: Off High St. PARK: Easy.
TEL: 01544 231195; FAX: 01544 231161
E-MAIL: sales@castlehillbooks.co.uk
WEBSITE: www.castlehillbooks.co.uk

LEDBURY

John Nash Antiques and Interiors
Tudor House, 18 High St. HR8 1DS. (J. Nash and L. Calleja)
EST. 1972. Open 10-5.30, Sun. by appointment. STOCK: *Mahogany, oak and walnut furniture, 18th-20th C, £300-£10,000; decorative items, fabrics and wallpapers.* SER: Valuations; restorations; buys at auction (furniture and silver). SIZE: Medium. PARK: Public nearby. VAT: Stan/Spec.
TEL: 01531 635714; FAX: 01531 635050
E-MAIL: enquiries@johnnash.co.uk
WEBSITE: www.johnnash.co.uk

Serendipity
The Tythings, Preston Court. HR8 2LL. (Rosemary Ford)
EST. 1967. Open 9-5 or by appointment. STOCK: *18th-19th C period furniture specialising in extending dining tables, sets of chairs and four-poster beds; general antiques.* LOC: Take A449 for 3 miles from Ledbury, at roundabout turn left on B4215, premises 800yds. on left behind half-timbered house. SER: Restorations (furniture); buys at auction. SIZE: Large. PARK: Large car park. VAT: Spec. FAIRS: Olympia.
TEL: 01531 660245; FAX: 01531 660689
E-MAIL: sales@serendipity-antiques.co.uk
WEBSITE: www.serendipity-antiques.co.uk

Keith Smith Books
78B The Homend. HR8 1BX.
EST. 1986. Open 10-5, CL: Mon. STOCK: *Secondhand and old books.* LOC: Main road. SER: Valuations. SIZE: Small. PARK: Easy. FAIRS: Churchdown Book, Gloucester; Ludlow Books and Craft.
TEL: 01531 635336
E-MAIL: keith@ksbooks.demon.co.uk

LEOMINSTER

The Barometer Shop Ltd
New St. HR6 8DP. (C.F. and V.J. Jones)
BWCG. Open 9-5, Sat. 10-4 or by appointment. STOCK: *Barometers, barographs, clocks, period furniture.* SER: Clock, barometer and fine antique repairs and restorations. PARK: Own at side of shop.
TEL: 01568 613652/610200; FAX: 01568 610200
E-MAIL: thebarometershop@btconnect.com
WEBSITE: www.thebarometershop.co.uk

Coltsfoot Gallery
Hatfield. HR6 0SF. (Edwin Collins)

EST. 1971 Open by appointment. STOCK: *Sporting and wildlife watercolours and prints, £20–£2,000.* SER: Restoration and conservation of works of art on paper; mounting. SIZE: Medium. PARK: Easy.
TEL: 01568 760277

Courts Miscellany
48A Bridge St. HR6 6DZ. (George Court)
EST. 1983. Open 10-5 or by appointment. STOCK: *General curios including corkscrews, social and political history, police, fire brigade and sporting items; tools, horse brasses, enamel signs - advertising, military, brewery; studio pottery and commemoratives.*
TEL: 01568 612995

Leominster Antique Centre
34 Broad St. HR6 8BS. (M&J Markets)
EST. 1995. Open 10-5 inc. Sun. STOCK: *Mahogany, oak, pine, kitchenalia, collectables, toys, glass, textiles, silver, postcards, Gaudy Welsh, fine china, pictures, jewellery, tools.* SER: Deliveries arranged. SIZE: 40 traders on 4 floors. PARK: Nearby. FAIRS: Ludlow 1st & 3rd Sunday each month.
TEL: 01568 615505; HOME: 01584 890013; MOBILE: 07976 628115

Leominster Antiques Market
14 Broad St. HR6 8BS. (M. & B. Cramp)
EST. 1975. Open 10-5 inc. Sun. STOCK: *Mahogany, oak, pine, kitchenalia, collectables, toys, glass, textiles, silver, postcards, Gaudy Welsh, fine china, pictures, jewellery, tools.* SER: Deliveries arranged. SIZE: 18 units - 3 floors. PARK: Nearby. FAIRS: Ludlow market 1st & 3rd Sunday each month.
TEL: 01568 612189; HOME: 01584 890013; MOBILE: 07976 628115.

The Old Shoe Box
2 Church St. HR6 8NE.
Open 10-5. STOCK: *Furniture, china, prints, watercolours and smalls.* LOC: Opposite Barclays Bank. SER: Mount cutting; framing. PARK: Loading only.
TEL: 01568 611414

Phoenix Presents Linden House Antiques
14 Broad St. HR6 8BS. (C. Scott-Mayfield)
EST. 1999. Open 10-1 and 2-5. CL: Mon. & Tues. STOCK: *Furniture 17th C to 1970s, £100–£15,000; pictures 17th C to contemporary, £100–£15,000; maps 15th C to 19th C, silver, porcelain, pottery, carvings, objets d'art, textiles 18th C to 20th C, £20–£5,000. Jewellery by appointment only - not held on premises.* LOC: Town centre. SER: Valuations; upholstery; furniture restoration. SIZE: Large. PARK: Easy. FAIRS: NEC; DMG Antiques Fairs.
TEL: 01568 611022; MOBILE: 07737 611048
E-MAIL: carolinescott-mayfield@hotmail.com

Pugh's Antiques
Portley House, Old Ludlow Rd. HR6 0AA. (G. Garner and C. Cherry)
EST. 1974. Open 9-5.30. STOCK: *French furniture, armoires, farm tables, country furniture, neo-rustique, French and Italian wooden beds; Victorian and Edwardian furniture.* LOC: B4361 Leominster to Ludlow at Old Richards Castle, opp. Leominster Reclamation Yard. SER: Importers and exporters. SIZE: Large. PARK: Easy. VAT: Stan.
TEL: 01568 616646; HOME: same; FAX: 01568 616144
E-MAIL: sales@pughsantiques.com
WEBSITE: www.pughsantiques.com

Teagowns & Textiles
30 Broad St. HR6 8AB. (Annie Townsend)
Open 10-1 and 2-5. STOCK: *Vintage costume, textiles, shoes and handbags, accessories, Victorian to 1960s.* LOC: Main street. SER: Valuations; restorations. SIZE: Large. PARK: Nearby.
TEL: 01568 612999; HOME: 01982 560422
E-MAIL: annietownsend@lineone.net
WEBSITE: www.vintage-fabrics.co.uk

ROSS-ON-WYE

Baileys Home & Garden
Whitecross Farm, Bridstow. HR9 6JU. (M. and S. Bailey)
EST. 1978. Open 9-5. STOCK: *Garden furniture, tools, orchard ladders, kitchenware, quilts, Welsh blankets, French and English lighting, bathrooms (including copper baths, metal washstands), fireplaces, industrial lamps, factory trolleys, machinists' stools, shoe lasts, baskets, bobbins.* LOC: A49 1 mile from Ross-on-Wye on Hereford Rd. SIZE: Medium. PARK: Easy. VAT: Stan.
TEL: 01989 563015; FAX: 01989 768172
E-MAIL: sales@baileys-home-garden.co.uk
WEBSITE: www.baileyshomeandgarden.com

Fritz Fryer Antique Lighting
23 Station St. HR9 7AG. (K. and S. Wallis-Smith)
EST. 1981. Open 10-5.30. STOCK: *Decorative lighting, chandeliers, lamps, gas brackets and sconces, original shades, Georgian to Art Deco.* SER: Restorations; lighting scheme design. SIZE: Large. PARK: Easy. VAT: Margin.
TEL: 01989 567416; FAX: 01989 566742
E-MAIL: enquiries@fritzfryer.co.uk
WEBSITE: www.fritzfryer.co.uk

Robin Lloyd Antiques
The Elizabethan House, Brookend St. HR9 7EE.
EST. 1970. Open 9.30-5, CL: Tues. and Wed. STOCK: *Oak, country and traditional furniture including dining tables and Windsor chairs; longcase clocks.* LOC: Ledbury end of town. SER: Export delivery to shipper; sourcing; imaging service to all buyers; picture restoration; re-polishing. SIZE: Large - 5 showrooms. PARK: Outside shop. VAT: Global/Spec/Exp.
TEL: 01989 562123

Pugh's Antiques

Portley House, Old Ludlow Road,
Leominster, HR6 0AA

**5,000 sq ft full of English and
Continental furniture.
New range of replica white French
Furniture and Antique looking
range of Leather armchairs.**

*Beds and Country
Furniture
imported monthly
from France*

Open: 9:00 – 5:30 Monday to Friday
Tel: (01568) 616646
Mobile: (07785) 225063
Email: sales@pughsantiques.com
Website: www.pughsantiques.com

E-MAIL: robjanlloyd@gmail.com
WEBSITE: www.robinlloydantiques.com

Ross Old Book and Print Shop
51-52 High St. HR9 5HH. (Phil Thredder and Sarah
Miller)
EST. 1984. PBFA. Open Wed.-Sat. 10-5. CL: Mid-Jan.
to mid-Feb. STOCK: *Antiquarian and secondhand books,
prints and maps.* SER: worldwide postal. PARK: Behind
shop.
TEL: 01989 567458
E-MAIL: enquiries@rossoldbooks.co.uk
WEBSITE: www.rossoldbooks.co.uk

Ross-on-Wye Antiques Gallery
Gloucester Rd. HR9 5BU. (Michael Aslanian)
EST. 1996. Open Fri. 11-5, other times by appointment.
STOCK: *Wide variety of general antiques, furniture and
collectables, from 17th to early 20th C.* LOC: Town centre. SER:
Valuations; buys at auction. SIZE: Large. PARK: At rear.
TEL: 01989 762290
E-MAIL: michael@rossantiquesgallery.com
WEBSITE: www.rossantiquesgallery.com

Waterfall Antiques
2 High St. HR9 5HL. (Owen McCarthy)
EST. 1991. Open 10-4. STOCK: *Country pine furniture,
Victorian and Edwardian; china and general antiques.* SER:

Valuations. SIZE: Medium. PARK: At rear.
TEL: 01989 563103; MOBILE: 07932 105542

YAZOR

M. and J. Russell
The Old Vicarage. HR4 7BA.
EST. 1969. *Mainly Trade.* Open at all times, appointment
advisable. STOCK: *English period oak and country furniture,
some garden antiques.* LOC: 7 miles west of Hereford on A480.
SER: Valuations. SIZE: Medium. PARK: Easy. VAT: Spec.
TEL: 01981 590674; MOBILE: 07889 702556

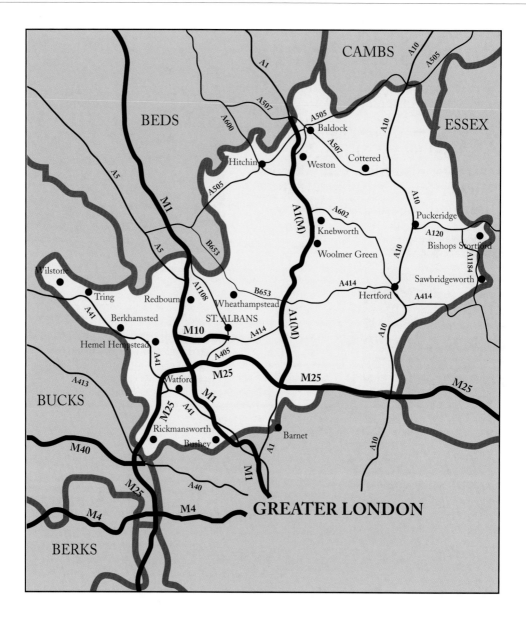

BALDOCK

The Attic
20 Whitehorse St. SG7 6QN. (P. Sheppard)
EST. 1977. CL: Thurs. *STOCK: Small furniture, china, brass and copper, dolls and teddy bears, £5–£100.* LOC: 3 mins. from A1(M). SIZE: Small. PARK: Easy.
TEL: 01462 893880

Anthony Butt Antiques
7-9 Church St. SG7 5AE.
EST. 1968. Resident. Open by appointment. *STOCK: English furniture, 17th-19th C, £500–£5,000; works of art and objects of interest. NOT STOCKED: Bric-a-brac, shipping goods.* LOC: Town centre. SER: Valuations. SIZE: Small. PARK: Easy. VAT: Spec. FAIRS: Buxton; Petersfield.
TEL: 01462 895272

Howards
33 Whitehorse St. SG7 6QF. (D.N. Howard)
EST. 1970. Open 9.30-5.00. CL: Mon. *STOCK: Clocks, 18th-19th C, £200–£5,000.* SER: Valuations; restorations; repairs. PARK: Easy. VAT: Spec.
TEL: 01462 892385

BARNET

Barnet Bygones
2 Bruce Rd. EN5 4LS.
Open Wed. 9.30-5, Fri. 11-5, Sat. 9-5. *STOCK: General antiques inc. furniture, ceramics, silver, jewellery.* SIZE: 6 dealers.
TEL: 020 8440 7304

BERKHAMSTED

Heritage Antique Centre
24 Castle St. HP4 2DW. (J. Wilshire and P. Beales)
EST. 1992. Open 10-5.30 including Sun. *STOCK: Furniture, china, glass, pictures, books, tools and clocks, 18th-20th C.* LOC: Just off High St. SIZE: Medium - 24 dealers. PARK: Nearby.
TEL: 01442 873819

Home and Colonial
134 High St. HP4 3AT. (Alison and Graeme Reid-Davies and Liz and Tony Stanton-Kipping)
EST. 1997. Open 10-5.30, Sun. 11-5. CL: Wed. *STOCK: Period, country, French fruitwood and painted furniture; Arts and Crafts, Art Deco, decorative antiques, clocks and barometers, metalware, pictures, porcelain, silver, glass, jewellery, textiles and costume, antiquarian books, radios and gramophones, toys and teddy bears, fireplaces, garden antiques and lighting, 60s and 70s design, £10-£10,000.* LOC: M25 junction 20; M1 junction 8. SER: Design; prop hire; interiors dept; antiques sourcing. SIZE: Large. PARK: Easy.
TEL: 01442 877007
E-MAIL: homeandcolonial@btinternet.com
WEBSITE: www.homeandcolonial.co.uk

BISHOP'S STORTFORD

David Penney
Grooms Cottage, Elsenham Hall, Elsenham. CM22 6DP.
EST. 1973. MBHI. *Mail Order Only.* Strictly no visitors, no stock held on premises. *STOCK: Watches, 18th-20th C, £500-£50,000; watch movements, 18th-20th C, £50-£5,000; horological books and ephemera, 18th-21st C, £5-£15,000.* SER: Valuations; restorations; specialist research; buys at auction (watches, chronometers and all technical horology). VAT: Stan/Spec.
TEL: 01279 814946
E-MAIL: info@davidpenney.co.uk
WEBSITE: www.antiquewatchstore.co.uk

HEMEL HEMPSTEAD

Cherry Antiques
101 High St. HP1 3AH. (A. and R.S. Cullen)
EST. 1981. Open 9.30-4.30. CL: Wed. pm. *STOCK: Victorian, Edwardian and some period furniture, pine, general antiques, collectors' and decorative items, bric-a-brac, needlework tools, dolls, linens, some silver, plate, jewellery, glass, pottery, porcelain, brass, copper, some shipping items.*

SIZE: Medium. PARK: Easy.
TEL: 01442 264358; MOBILE: 07720263214

Jordans Antiques Centre
63 High St., Old Town. HP1 3AF. (Michal Porter)
EST. 1999. Open 10-5 including Sun. *STOCK: General antiques, books, china, clocks, collectables, commemoratives, ephemera, furniture, glass, jewellery, kitchenalia, prints and treen, vestas and Stanhopes mainly from late 19th C, £10-£500+.* LOC: Opposite C of E church. SIZE: Medium - 12+ dealers. PARK: Nearby. FAIRS: Peterborough; Stafford.
TEL: 01442 263451; MOBILE: 07881 804840
WEBSITE: www.thecollectorscompanion.co.uk/jordans.html

Off the Wall
52 High St., Old Town. HP1 3AF. (Michelle Smith)
EST. 2001. Open 10-5.30, Sun. 11-4; prior telephone call advisable. *STOCK: Unusual and decorative items, some furniture.* LOC: Near St. Mary's Church. SER: Large item delivery. PARK: Nearby.
TEL: 01442 218300.
WEBSITE: www.off-thewall-antiques.co.uk

HERTFORD

Beckwith and Son
St. Nicholas Hall, St. Andrew St. SG14 1HZ. (G.C.M. Gray)
EST. 1904. Open 9-5.30. *STOCK: General antiques, furniture, silver, pottery, porcelain, prints, weapons, clocks, watches, glass.* LOC: A414/B158. SER: Valuations; restorations (fine porcelain, furniture, upholstery, silver and clocks). SIZE: Large. PARK: Adjacent. VAT: Spec.
TEL: 01992 582079
E-MAIL: sales@beckwithandsonantiques.co.uk
WEBSITE: www.beckwithandsonantiques.co.uk

Gillmark Gallery
25 Parliament Sq. SG14 1EX. (Mark Pretlove and Gill Woodhouse)
EST. 1997. Open 10-5, CL: Mon. and Thurs. *STOCK: Maps and prints, 16th-20th C, £10-£5000; secondhand books, 18th-20th C, £1-£5,000.* LOC: 15 yards from roundabout at junction of A414 and B158. SER: Framing, conservation, restoration, map and print colouring. SIZE: Medium. PARK: Nearby. VAT: Stan.
TEL: 01992 534444
E-MAIL: gillmark@btinternet.com
WEBSITE: www.gillmark.com

Robert Horton Antiques
13 Castle St. SG14 1ER.
EST. 1972. MBWCG. Open 9-5. *STOCK: Clocks, barometers, furniture.* SER: Restorations and repairs (clock movements, cases and dials). VAT: Stan/Spec.
TEL: 01992 587546; FAX: same

Tapestry Antiques
27 St. Andrew St. SG14 1HZ. (D.W. and P. Stokes)
EST. 1973. Open 10-1 and 2-5, Sat. 10-5, Sun. by
appointment. CL: Thurs. STOCK: *Furniture, 18th-19th C,*
£100-£1,000; porcelain, 19th to early 20th C, £25-£500;
brass and copper, 18th-19th C, £50-£300; mirrors. LOC:
Near rail station. SER: Valuations. SIZE: Medium. PARK:
Easy and behind premises.
TEL: 01992 587438
E-MAIL: tapestryantiques@yahoo.com
WEBSITE: www.geocities.com/tapestryantiques

HERTFORD HEATH

Period Style Lighting
The Barn, Fox Hole Farm, London Rd. SG13 7NT.
(Gillian and Geoff Day)
EST. 1992. Open 10-5 Thurs.-Sat. STOCK: *Lighting -*
period, Victorian and Edwardian, French and Italian
chandeliers, £150-£1,000; period style wall and centre lights,
Tiffany lamps, glass shades. Modern, traditional and
antique. LOC: North London. SER: Lighting design for
all houses; restorations; repairs. SIZE: Large. PARK: Easy.
VAT: Global.
TEL: 01992 554943
E-MAIL: sales@period-style-lighting.com
WEBSITE: www.period-style-lighting.com

HITCHIN

Michael Gander
10-11 Bridge St. SG5 2DE.
EST. 1973. Open Mon. 3-6, Wed., Thurs. and Sat. 9-6,
other times by appointment. STOCK: *Period furniture,*
metalware, ceramics, glass, pictures.
TEL: 01462 432678; MOBILE: 07885 728976

Eric T. Moore
24 Bridge St. SG5 2DF.
Open 9.30-5.30, Sun. 11-4. STOCK: *Secondhand and*
antiquarian books, maps and prints. SER: Free booksearch
and mail order. SIZE: Large. PARK: Easy.
TEL: 01462 450497
E-MAIL: booksales@erictmoore.co.uk
WEBSITE: www.erictmoore.co.uk

New England House Antiques and Rugs
New England House, London Rd., St. Ippolyts. SG4
7NG. (Jennifer and Suj Munjee)
EST. 1990. Open by appointment only. STOCK: *Fine*
Georgian and Victorian furniture, £100-£10,000; Persian
and Afghan rugs. SER: Valuations; restorations (paintings,
metalwork and furniture); searches undertaken. PARK:
Own. VAT: Stan/Spec.
TEL: 01462 432728; HOME: 01462 431914
E-MAIL: enquiries@newenglandhouseantiques.co.uk
WEBSITE: www.newenglandhouseantiques.co.uk and
www.persianandafghancarpets.co.uk

Phillips of Hitchin (Antiques) Ltd   BADA
The Manor House. SG5 1JW. (J. and B. Phillips)
EST. 1884. Open 9-5.30, Sat. by appointment. STOCK:
Mahogany furniture, 18th to early 19th C, £500-£20,000;
reference books on furniture. LOC: In Bancroft, main
street of Hitchin. SIZE: Small. PARK: Easy. VAT: Spec.
TEL: 01462 432067; FAX: 01462 441368

The Rug Studio
50a Walsworth Rd, SG4 9SU. (Gila Timur Trading Co.
Ltd.)
Open Tue-Thu 11-5, Fri & Sat 9.30-5, Sun 12-4; CL
Mon. STOCK: *Antique sales and restorers of oriental rugs,*
carpets, kilims, Aubussons and textiles. SER: Location work.
Specialist in large scale projects, workshops and
demonstrations.
TEL: 01462 435005; 020 8977 4403;
MOBILE: 07885 757796
E-MAIL: info@therugstudio.co.uk
WEBSITE: www.therugstudio.co.uk

KNEBWORTH

Hamilton Billiards & Games Co.
Park Lane. SG3 6PJ. (Hugh Hamilton)
EST. 1980. Open 8-5, Sat. 8-1; other times by
appointment. STOCK: *Victorian and Edwardian billiard*
tables, £3,000-£18,000; 19th C convertible billiard/dining
tables and accessories, £30-£5,000; indoor and outdoor
games. LOC: Near Knebworth rail station; 10 mins. off
A1(M). SER: Valuations; restorations (billiard tables and
furniture); buys at auction (as stock). SIZE: Large. PARK:
Easy. VAT: Spec. FAIRS: House & Garden
TEL: 01438 811995; FAX: 01438 814939
E-MAIL: showrooms@hamiltonbilliards.com
WEBSITE: www.hamiltonbilliards.com

LETCHWORTH

The Collector Limited
47 Willian Way SG6 2HJ. (Tom Power)
EST. 1973. Open by appointment. STOCK: *Decorative ceramics*
especially Royal Doulton, from 1900, £50-£3,000; Beswick,
from 1920, £40-£1,000. SER: Valuations; mail order. PARK:
Easy. VAT: Stan. FAIRS: Specialist Decorative Art.
TEL: 01462 678037
E-MAIL: collector@globalnet.co.uk

PUCKERIDGE

St. Ouen Antiques
Vintage Corner, Old Cambridge Rd. SG11 1SA.
(J. and S.T. Blake and Mrs P.B. Francis)
EST. 1918. Open 10.30-5. STOCK: *English and*
Continental furniture, decorative items, silver, porcelain,
pottery, glass, clocks, barometers, paintings. SER: Valuations;
restorations. SIZE: Large. PARK: Own.
TEL: 01920 821336

REDBOURN

Antique Print Shop
86 High St. AL3 7BD. (David Tilleke)
EST. 1982. AIA (Scot). Open 10-4 by appointment.
STOCK: *Prints, all categories, 1650-1930.* SER: Valuations
and auctions. SIZE: Small. PARK: Easy.
TEL: 01582 794488; MOBILE: 07801 682268; HOME:
01442 397094
E-MAIL: antiqueprintshop@btinternet.com
WEBSITE: www.antiqueprintshop.co.uk

J.N. Antiques
86 High St. AL3 7BD. (Martin and Jean Brunning)
EST. 1975. Open 9-6. STOCK: *Furniture, 18th-20th C, £5-
£2,000; brass and copper, porcelain, 19th C, £5-£100;
pictures and books, 19th-20th C.* LOC: Close to junction 8,
M1. SER: Valuations. SIZE: Medium + barn. PARK: In
High Street adjacent to shop. VAT: Spec.
TEL: 01582 793603
E-MAIL: jnantiques@btopenworld.com

Bushwood Antiques · LAPADA
Stags End Equestrian Centre, Gaddesden Lane. HP2
6HN. (Anthony Bush)
EST. 1967. CINOA. Open 8.30-4, Sat. 10-4. STOCK:
18th-19th C furniture, accessories and objects of art. LOC:
Telephone for directions. SIZE: Very large. PARK: Easy.
TEL: 01582 794700; FAX: 01582 792299
E-MAIL: antiques@bushwood.co.uk
WEBSITE: www.bushwood.co.uk

Tim Wharton Antiques · LAPADA
24 High St. AL3 7LL.
EST. 1970. Open 10-5.30, Sat. 10-4. CL: Mon. and
usually Thurs. STOCK: *Oak and country furniture, 17th-
19th C; some mahogany, 18th to early 19th C; ironware,
decorative items and general small antiques.* LOC: On left
entering village from St. Albans on A5183. PARK: Easy.
VAT: Stan/Spec.
TEL: 01582 794371; MOBILE: 07850 622880
E-MAIL: tim@timwhartonantiques.co.uk

RICKMANSWORTH

Clive A. Burden Ltd
Elmcote House, The Green, Croxley Green. WD3
3HN. (Philip D. Burden)
EST. 1966. ABA. IMCOS. Open by appointment.
STOCK: *Maps, 1500-1860, £5-£1,500; natural history,
botanical and Vanity Fair prints, 1600-1900, £1-£1,000;
antiquarian books, pre-1870, £10-£5,000.* SER: Valuations;
buys at auction (as stock). SIZE: Medium. VAT: Stan.
TEL: 01923 778097/772387; FAX: 01923 896520
E-MAIL: enquiries@caburden.com
WEBSITE: www.caburden.com

SAWBRIDGEWORTH

Charnwood Antiques and Arcane Antiques Centre
Unit E2 Ground Floor, The Maltings, Station Rd.
CM21 9JX. (Nigel and Nicola Hoy)
EST. 1997. EADA. GMC . Open 10-5, Sat. and Sun. 11-
5. CL: Mon., or by appointment. STOCK: *Furniture, 18th
C to Edwardian, £500-£8,000; Chinese and Japanese
ceramics, glass, silver and jewellery, longcase clocks, 19th C
oils and watercolours.* LOC: From Harlow on A1184, turn
right at first mini roundabout into Station Rd., over river
bridge, first right into maltings. Shop 100 yards on left.
SER: Restorations (furniture including structural and
veneer, French polishing, traditional upholstery, desk re-
leathering, brass ware supplied and fitted; clock repairs
and overhauls; glass and ceramics; jewellery including
restringing). SIZE: Large. PARK: Easy.
TEL: 01279 600562; MOBILE: 07864 676839
E-MAIL: nicola@charnwoodantiques.co.uk
WEBSITE: www.charnwoodantiques.co.uk

Cromwell Antique Centre
The Maltings, Station Rd. CM21 9JX.
EST. 2003. Open 10-5. inc. Sun. STOCK: *Quality antiques
and collectables.* LOC: Next to railway station. SIZE: Large.
TEL: 01279 722517
E-MAIL: cromwellsantiquecentre@hotmail.com

The Herts and Essex Antiques Centre
The Maltings, Station Rd. CM21 9JX.
EST. 1982. Open 10-5, Sat. and Sun. 10.30-5.30. STOCK:
General antiques and collectables, £1-£2,000. LOC: Opposite
B.R. station. SIZE: Large - over 100 dealers. PARK: Easy.
TEL: 01279 722044; FAX: 01279 725445
WEBSITE: www.antiques-of-britain.co.uk

Riverside Antiques Centre
The Maltings, Station Rd. CM21 9JX. (Shirley Rowley
and John Barrance)
EST. 1998. EADA. Open 10-5 including Sun. STOCK:
General antiques, furniture, art and collectables. LOC: Near
railway station. SER: Valuations; restorations; in house
auction room. SIZE: Large - 3 floors, 200 dealers. PARK: Easy.
TEL: 01279 600985

ST. ALBANS

By George! Antiques Centre
23 George St. AL3 4ER.
EST. 1986. Open 10-5, Thurs. 11-5, Sat. 10-5.30, Sun. 1-
5. STOCK: *A wide range of general antiques, lighting, jewellery
and collectables.* LOC: 100yds. from Clock Tower. SER:
Restorations. SIZE: 20 dealers. PARK: Internal courtyard
(loading) and Christopher Place (NCP) nearby.
TEL: 01727 853032

James of St Albans
11 George St. AL3 4ER. (S.N. and W. James)
EST. 1957. Open 10-5, Thurs. 10-4. STOCK: *Furniture*

ASIAN ART

Lark E. Mason

Featuring over 300 beautiful colour illustrations, this book offers a clear and concise guide to understanding the fine and decorative arts of Asia including the arts of the Islamic world. The easy-to-follow format begins with the tumultuous history of the continent, leading into chapters on ceramics, metalwork, the arts of the craftsman, furniture and lacquer, textiles, prints and paintings. Each chapter includes expert advice for judging quality and identifying fakes and over-restored objects. A valuable dictionary of terms and tables with reign dates and marks is included.

280 x 233 mm. 336 pp 328 col., 2 b.&w.
£35.00 Hardback

including reproduction; smalls, brass and copper; topographical maps and prints of Hertfordshire. VAT: Stan/Spec.
TEL: 01727 856996

Rug Gallery Ltd
42 Verulam Rd. AL3 4DQ. (R. Mathias and J. Blair)
BORDA. Open 9-6. STOCK: *Russian, Afghan, Turkish and Persian carpets, rugs and kelims; Oriental objets d'art.* PARK: Nearby.
TEL: 01727 841046
E-MAIL: rugs@orientalruggallery.com
WEBSITE: www.ruggallery.co.uk

TRING

Solomon Bly   BADA
The Courtyard, Church Yard. HP23 5AE. (Julian Bly)
EST. 1831. Open by appointment. STOCK: *English and American furniture.* LOC: Next to church. SER: **Restoration; valuations; consultancy and interior design.** SIZE: Large PARK: Easy. VAT: Stan. FAIRS: **Olympia (Summer and Winter); BADA.**
TEL: 01442 828011; FAX: 01442 828091
E-MAIL: jjb@solomonbly.com
WEBSITE: www.solomonbly.com

Country Clocks
3 Pendley Bridge Cottages, Tring Station. HP23 5QU.
(T. Cartmell)

EST. 1976. Resident. Prior telephone call advisable. STOCK: *Clocks, 18th-19th C.* LOC: One mile from A41 in village, cottage nearest canal bridge. SER: Restorations (clocks); valuations. SIZE: Small. PARK: Easy.
TEL: 01442 825090
E-MAIL: info@countryclockstring.co.uk
WEBSITE: www.countryclockstring.co.uk

TRINGFORD

Piggeries Pine
Tringford Piggeries, Tringford Rd. HP23 4LH. (Paul Brown)
Open 10-5 inc. Sun. STOCK: *A family business selling antique, reclaimed and new pine and oak furniture.* LOC: Nr. Tring. PARK: Own.
TEL: 01442 827961
E-MAIL: enquiries@piggeriespine.co.uk
WEBSITE: www.piggeriespine.co.uk

WATFORD

Thwaites Fine Stringed Instruments
33 Chalk Hill, WD19 4BL. (J.H. and W.J. Pamplin and C.A. Lovell)
Open 9-5, Sat. 9.30-3. STOCK: *Stringed instruments, from violins to double basses.* SER: Restorations; repairs; buys and sells instruments. PARK: Own.
TEL: 01923 232412; FAX: 01923 232463
E-MAIL: sales@thwaites.com
WEBSITE: www.thwaites.com

WESTON

Weston Antiques
Weston Barns, Hitchin Rd. SG4 7AX. (M.A. Green)
EST. 1974. BAFRA. MBHI. Open Tues.-Sat. 10.30-5, Mon. by appointment. STOCK: *Period furniture, longcase and mantel clocks, mainly 18th-19th C.* LOC: Off B197, near junction 9 A1(M). SER: Valuations; restorations (furniture and clocks). SIZE: Small. PARK: Easy. VAT: Spec.
TEL: 01462 790646; FAX: 01462 680304; MOBILE: 07802 403800
E-MAIL: gxc@freeuk.com
WEBSITE: www.greenrestorers.com

WILSTONE

Michael Armson (Antiques) Ltd
The Old Post Office, 34 Tring Rd. HP23 4PB.
EST. 1970. Prior telephone call advisable. STOCK: *Furniture, 17th-19th C.* LOC: Village centre. SIZE: Large. PARK: Easy. VAT: Spec. FAIRS: NEC and various.
TEL: 01442 890990; MOBILE: 07860 910034
E-MAIL: armsonantiques@tiscali.co.uk
WEBSITE: www.armsonantiques.com

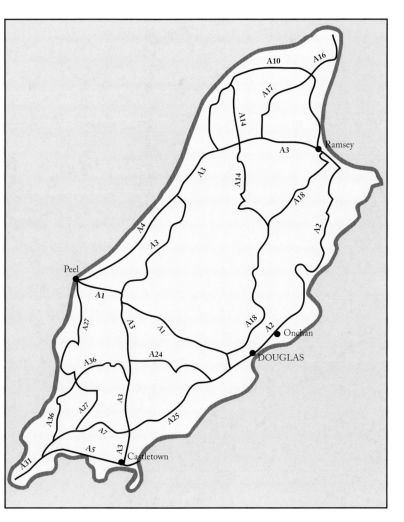

ONCHAN

Vintage Antiques & Interiors
42 Main Rd. IM3 1AN.
(Helen Robb)
EST. 2006. Open 10-4.30, Sat.
10-5. CL: Wed./Thurs./Fri.
*STOCK: General antiques inc.
jewellery, furniture, collectables,
art, ceramics and silver.* SIZE:
Medium PARK: Nearby.
TEL: 07624 486747

PEEL

**Atholl Place Antiques and
Collectables**
Atholl Place, IM5 1HE.
(Laura Lewis)
EST. 1998. Open 11-4. CL:
Mon. & Thurs. *STOCK: Silver,
collectables, jewellery, furniture &
studio glass; unusual things.*
TEL: 07624 477051
E-MAIL: lauramlewis@manx.net

Manning Collections
5 Castle St. IM5 1AN. (M.R.
Kelly)
EST.   1977.   Open   by
appointment. *STOCK: Manx
collectables specialist - coins,
medals and banknotes, maps and
prints, oils and watercolours.*
LOC: Central. SER: Valuations.
SIZE: Medium. PARK: Easy.
TEL: 01624 843897
E-MAIL: manncoll@advsys.co.uk

CASTLETOWN

J. and H. Bell Antiques
22 Arbory St. IM9 1LJ. (Jesse and Alistair Bell)
EST. 1965. Open Wed., Fri. and Sat. 10-5. *STOCK:
Jewellery, silver, china, early metalware, furniture, 18th-
20th C, £5-£5,000.* LOC: Nr. centre. SIZE: Medium.
PARK: Car parks nearby. VAT: Stan/Spec.
TEL: 01624 823132/822414.

DOUGLAS

The Bear Huggery
22 Castle St. IM1 2EZ (Carol Frazer)
EST. 2003. Open 9-5.30. *STOCK: Vintage Teddy bears.*
SER: Teddy hospital. SIZE: Medium. PARK: Easy nearby.
FAIRS: Kensington Bear Fair;
TEL: 01624 676333
E-MAIL: bearhuggery@manx.net
WEBSITE: www.thebearhuggery.co.uk

Old Bonded Warehouse
29 Castle St. IM8 1AZ (Steven Moore)
EST. 1997. Open 10.30-4.30. CL: Mon./Wed./Thurs.
*STOCK: Furniture, 18th C - 20th C; collectables, ceramics,
silver; Manx oils & watercolours.* LOC: Just off the harbour.
SIZE: Large. PARK: Harbour and nearby car park.
TEL: 01624 844565

RAMSEY

3 Collins Lane.
Isabel's Curiosity Shop IM8 1AL (Isabel Marshall)
EST. 1993. Open Tues./Thurs./Sat. 1-5, or by
appointment. *STOCK: General antiques including ceramics,
silver, furniture, 1800s-1930.* LOC: Off Parliament St.
SIZE: 2,000 sq ft. PARK: On quay.
TEL: 01624 814319; MOBILE: 07624 493139

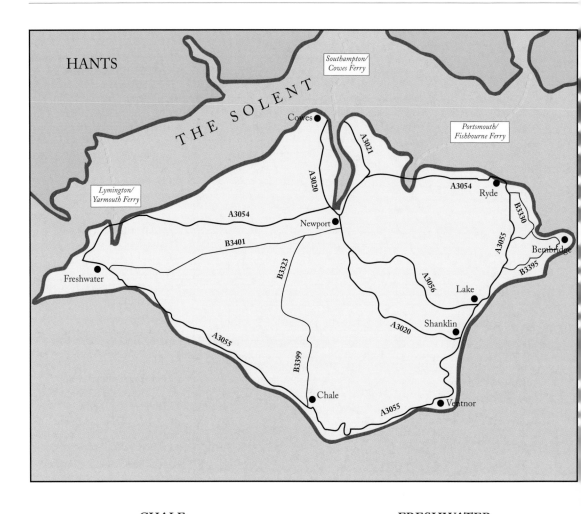

CHALE

Chale Antiques
3 Church Place. PO38 2HA. (Michael Gregory)
EST. 1983. Open 12-5 including Sun. STOCK: *Architectural items, fireplaces, £50-£500; general antiques, curios and taxidermy, £5-£500; mainly 19th C.* LOC: Off Military Rd., near Black-Gang. SER: Valuations. SIZE: Large. PARK: Easy.
TEL: 01983 730230; MOBILE: 07811 835159
E-MAIL: chaleantiques@hotmail.com

COWES

Flagstaff Antiques
Tudor House, Bath Rd. PO31 7RH. (T.A.M. Cockram)
EST. 1987. Open from 10 am. CL: Wed. STOCK: *Jewellery, 19th-20th C, £50-£2,000; porcelain, 19th C, £25-£1,000; pictures, 19th-20th C, £10-£1,000.* LOC: 100 yards from The Parade. SER: Valuations; restorations (porcelain and silver). SIZE: Small. PARK: Easy.
TEL: 01983 200138

FRESHWATER

Ye Olde Village Clock Shop
3 Moa Place. PO40 9DS. (Caroline Tayler and David Wynn)
EST. 1970. Open 10-3 Wed., Thurs. and Fri., 10-1 Sat. or by appointment. STOCK: *Clocks - longcase, Vienna, carriage, bracket, French and novelty, 17th-19th C, £200-£6,000; mechanical music.* SER: Restorations (clocks). SIZE: Small. PARK: Easy.
TEL: 01983 754930

NEWPORT

Lugley Antiques & Interiors
13 Lugley St. PO30 5HD. (S.J. Gratton)
EST. 1992. Open 10-4, Sat 10-5. CL: Thurs. STOCK: *Furniture, clocks, some china and unusual collectables, late 18th to early 20th C, £5-£5,000.* LOC: Town centre, next to rear entrance of Boots the Chemist. SER: Valuations; restorations (furniture). SIZE: Large. PARK: Meters or nearby car parks. VAT: Margin.
TEL: 01983 523348

RYDE

Nooks & Crannies
60 High St. PO33 2RJ. (David and Sally Burnett)
EST. 1984. Open 9.30-1.30 and 2.30-5. CL: Thurs.
STOCK: Lighting, clocks, old telephones, china, glass,
collectables, some furniture, gramophones and radios,
Victorian to 1950s, £1-£1,000. LOC: Near catholic
church. SIZE: Medium. PARK: Limited. FAIRS: Ardingly.
TEL: 01983 568984; HOME: 01983 868261

Victoria Antiques
Royal Victoria Arcade, Union St. PO33 2LQ.
(J. Strudwick)
EST. 2003. Open 9.30-4. STOCK: General antiques and
collectables including furniture, jewellery, porcelain and
china. SER: Restorations (furniture, porcelain). SIZE:
Small. PARK: Nearby.
TEL: 01983 564661; MOBILE: 07970 175926

SHANKLIN

The Shanklin Gallery
67 Regent St. PO37 7AE. (Jacqueline and Terry
Townsend)
EST. 1992. FATG. GCF. Open 9-5. STOCK: Oils,
watercolours, engravings, prints, maps, 17th-20th C, £10-
£2,000. LOC: Town centre near rail station. SER:
Valuations; restorations (oils, watercolours and prints);
framing. SIZE: Medium. PARK: Easy.
TEL: 01983 863113
E-MAIL: spaltown@aol.com

Taffeta Antiques
48 High St. PO37 6JN. (Carol Langham)
EST. 2001. Open 10-5, winter 10.30-4; CL: Mon.
STOCK: Porcelain, late Victorian to 1940s; glass, silver,
vintage jewellery, Victorian to 1930s. LOC: Central. SER:
Restoration and re-stringing (jewellery). SIZE: Small.
PARK: Nearby.
TEL: 07967 823434
E-MAIL: violetcloud7@hotmail.co.uk

VENTNOR

Antiques and Collectables
66 High St. PO38 1LU. (Russell Sparks)
Open 9-3.30; CL: Wed. pm. STOCK: General antiques inc.
furniture, ceramics, silver and mirrors. SER: Valuations.
SIZE: Large. PARK: Car park opposite.
TEL: 07890 982196

French Affair
66 High St. PO38 1SX. (Carol Chick)
EST. 2002. Open 10-5. STOCK: French furniture, armoires,
beds, washstands, linen. SER: Valuations. SIZE: Medium.
TEL: 01983 853856
E-MAIL: violetcloud7@hotmail.co.uk

Lake Antiques
The Old Studio, 48 High St. PO38 1LT. (P. Burfield)
EST. 1982. Open 10-5. CL: Wed. STOCK: General
antiques, Georgian and Victorian furniture, clocks. PARK:
Central car park opposite.
TEL: 01983 853996; MOBILE: 07710 067678

Ultramarine
40b High St. PO38 1LG. (Milly Stevens)
Open 10-3. CL: Mon. & Tues. STOCK: 19th-20th C
collectables including jewellery, china, studio pottery, textiles
and glass, £5-£500. LOC: Central. SIZE: Small. PARK:
Nearby.
TEL: 07845 022930

Ventnor Rare Books
32 Pier St. PO38 1SX. (Nigel and Teresa Traylen)
EST. 1989. ABA. PBFA. Open 10-5. CL: Wed. STOCK:
Antiquarian and secondhand books, prints. LOC: Town
centre. SER: Mail order, booksearch. SIZE: Large. PARK:
Nearby. FAIRS: York, London, Oxford, Wilton.
TEL: 01983 853706; FAX - 01983 854706
E-MAIL: vrb@andytron.demon.co.uk
WEBSITE: www.ukbookworld.com/
members/ventnorbooks

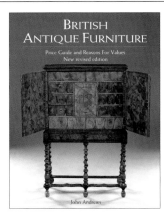

For the past thirty years this book has, in its various
editions, outsold all others on British antique furniture
simply because it is unique in explaining what to look for
when assessing the value of individual pieces. In this, the
fifth edition, the huge financial importance of patination
and colour has been explained and illustrated - something
which has become increasingly important in recent years.
This classic guide consists of over 1,600 photographs of
furniture found in shops and auction rooms throughout
the country with the author's down-to-earth comments on
important features which affect individual prices. This is,
above all, a reference book for the practising collector and
dealer, a work from which the memory may be refreshed
and points checked. This new edition contains both £
Sterling and US $ prices.

295 x 237 mm. 454 pp 500 col., 1150 b.&w.
£39.50 Hardback

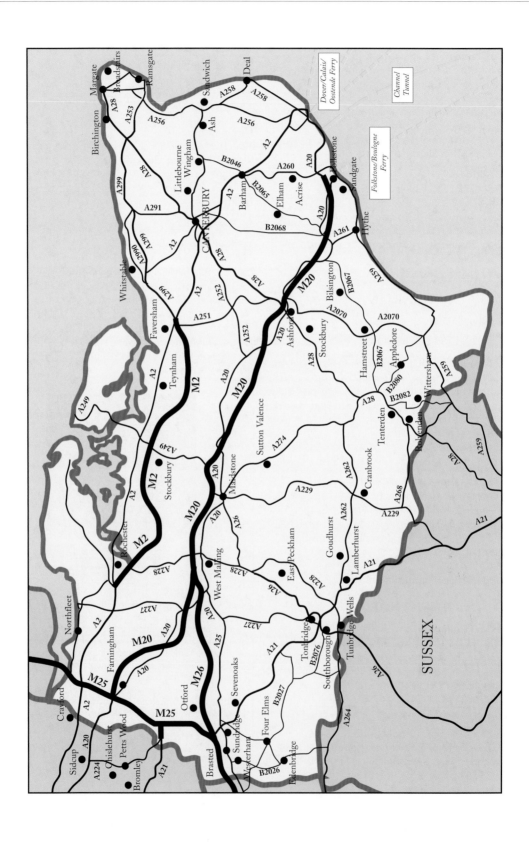

APPLEDORE

Back 2 Wood
The Old Goods Shed, Station Rd. TN26 2DF. (Steve Fowler)
EST. 1987. Open 9-5, Sun. 11-5. STOCK: *Stripped and finished pine furniture.* LOC: Adjacent to station. SIZE: Warehouse with 2 floors. PARK: Easy. VAT: Stan/Margin.
TEL: 01233 758109; MOBILE: 07971 288869
E-MAIL: pine@back2wood.com
WEBSITE: www.back2wood.com

High Class Junk
26 The Street. TN26 2BX. (Mrs Dadson)
EST. 2000. Open by appointment - just ask in The Old Forge 100 yds up road. STOCK: *Furniture, bric-a-brac, china.*
TEL: 01233 758585
WEBSITE: www.oldforgeantiques.co.uk

The Old Forge
16 The Street, TN26 2BX. (Mrs Dadson)
EST. 2000. Open 10-5, Sun. & Mon. 11-5. STOCK: *Antique pine furniture.* LOC: On the main street. SIZE: 2,000 sq ft.
PARK: Free outside or free carpark 400 yds.
TEL: 01233 758585
WEBSITE: www.oldforgeantiques.co.uk

ASH

Pine and Period Furniture
39 Guilton. CT3 2HL.
EST. 1990. Open 9-5 or by appointment. STOCK: *Antique and handmade solid wood furniture.* SER: Restoration.
TEL: 01304 812342
E-MAIL: sales@pineandperiod.com
WEBSITE: www.pineandperiod.com

ASHFORD

County Antiques
Old Mill Cottage, Kennett Lane, Stanford North. TN25 6DG. (B. Nilson)
EST. 1971. Open by appointment. STOCK: *General antiques.* VAT: Stan.
TEL: 01303 813039

BARHAM

Stablegate Antiques   LAPADA
Derringstone Hill Farm CT4 6QD. (Mr and Mrs M.J. Giuntini)
EST. 1989. CINOA. Open 10-5.30 including Sun.
STOCK: *Georgian and Victorian dining tables, chairs, sideboards, bureaux, davenports, chests of drawers; silver plate, china, clocks, jewellery, glass, objets d'art, collectables, copper, brass.* LOC: Village just off the A2 to Dover. SER: Valuations. SIZE: Large. PARK: Easy.
FAIRS: NAFAAF; Tatton Park; TVADA,

Northumberland; LAPADA.
TEL: 01227 831639; MOBILE: 07802 439777
WEBSITE: www.stablegate.co.uk

BECKENHAM

Beckenham Antiques & Collectors' Market
Public Hall, Bromley Rd. BR3 5JE.
EST. 1979. Open Wed. 8.30-2. STOCK: *General antiques and collectables.* SIZE: 16 stalls. PARK: Nearby.
TEL: 020 8660 1369

Ward Antique Fireplaces Ltd
436 Croydon Rd. BR3 4EP. (Michael and Terry Ward)
Open 10-5, Sun. 11-2. STOCK: *Fireplaces, some furniture, Victorian and Edwardian.* SER: Restorations (fireplaces).
TEL: 020 8650 9005

BILSINGTON

Gabrielle De Giles
The Barn at Bilsington Swanton Lane. TN25 7JR.
Open by appointment. STOCK: *Country furniture, mainly French, tables, mirrors, armoires, chairs, to £5,000.* LOC: 5 miles south of Ashford. PARK: Easy. VAT: Spec.
TEL: 01233 720917; FAX: 01233 720156;
MOBILE: 07721 015263
E-MAIL: gabrielle@gabrielledegiles.com
WEBSITE: www.gabrielledegiles.com

BIRCHINGTON

John Chawner
36 Station Approach. CT7 9RD.
EST. 1979. Open 10.30-12.30 and 2-5. CL: Tues. STOCK:
Clocks, barometers, smalls and bureaux. SER: Repairs
(clocks and barometers). PARK: Easy.
TEL: 01843 846943; MOBILE: 07786 902297

BRASTED

David Barrington
The Antique Shop. TN16 1JA. (James and Richard
Barrington)
EST. 1947. Open 9-6. *STOCK: Furniture, decorative items
and mirrors, 18th-19th C.* LOC: A25. SIZE: Medium.
PARK: Easy. VAT: Stan/Spec.
TEL: 01959 562479
E-MAIL: hbarringtonk@aol.com

Cooper Fine Arts Ltd
Swan House, High St. TN16 1JJ. (J. Hill-Reid)
EST. 1976. Open 10-6, Sun. 11-5. *STOCK: 17th-19th C
furniture, paintings and maritime.* SIZE: Medium. PARK:
Easy. VAT: Stan/Spec.
TEL: 01959 565818
E-MAIL: cooperfinearts@hotmail.co.uk

Courtyard Antiques
High St. TN16 1JE. (H. La Trobe)
EST. 1982. Open 10-5, Sun. and Bank Holidays 12.30-
4.30. *STOCK: Fine Georgian to Edwardian furniture, silver,
jewellery, glass, ceramics, clocks, watercolours, oils and prints.*
LOC: A25, off M25, junction 5. SER: Restorations
(furniture); French polishing; re-leathering. SIZE: Large.
PARK: Easy - at rear.
TEL: 01959 564483/563522; FAX: 01732 454726
WEBSITE: www.courtyardantiques.co.uk

Louisa Francis & S.L. Walker
High St. TN16 1JA. (Sharon Walker)
EST. 1984. Open 10.30-5. CL: Mon. *STOCK: 18th Worcester,
Caughley, Lowestoft and Bow; fine and important signed pieces
by Baldwyn, Stinton and Davis etc; 18th C drinking glasses,
jewellery and silver.* SER: Valuations. SIZE: Small. PARK: Easy.
TEL: 01959 565623
E-MAIL: sharon10@talk21.com

W. J. Gravener Antiques Ltd   LAPADA
**Courtyard Antiques, High St. TN16 1JA. (Mark
Gravener)**
Open 10-5, Sun. 12.30-4.30. *STOCK: 18th & 19th C
furniture.* LOC: On the A25. SER: Restoration. PARK:
Own free parking.
TEL: 01959 561733; FAX: same; MOBILE: 07712 651231
E-MAIL: mark@gravener-antiques.co.uk

G. A. Hill Antiques   LAPADA
5 High St. TN16 1JA.
EST. 1999. Open 10-5, Sun. and Mon. by appointment.

*STOCK: Fine Georgian period furniture of 18th and early
19th C, mirrors and works of art, £2,000-£15,000.* SIZE:
Medium. PARK: Easy. VAT: Spec.
TEL: 01959 565500; MOBILE: 07774 443455
E-MAIL: gahillantiques@btinternet.com

Keymer Son & Co. Ltd
Swaylands Place, The Green. TN16 1JY.
EST. 1977. Open 10-1 and 2.30-5. CL: Sat. *STOCK:
18th-19th C furniture, £100-£3,000.* LOC: A25. SIZE:
Small. PARK: Easy.
TEL: 01959 564203; FAX: 01959 561138
E-MAIL: keymer.london@virgin.net

Roy Massingham Antiques   LAPADA
The Coach House. High St. TN16 1JJ.
EST. 1968. Prior appointment advisable. *STOCK: 18th-
19th C furniture, pictures and decorative items.* LOC: 10
mins. from M25. PARK: Easy. VAT: Spec.
TEL: 01959 562408; MOBILE: 07860 326825
E-MAIL: roymassingham@btconnect.com

Old Bakery Antiques
High St. TN16 1JA. (P. Dyke)
EST. 1977. Open 10-5, Sun by appointment. *STOCK:
Furniture, 18th-20th C, £500-£10,000; paintings, 19th-
20th C, £500-£1,000+; decorative objects, 18th-20th C,
£150-£5,000.* SER: Valuations; buys at auction. SIZE:
Medium. VAT: Spec.
TEL: 01959 565343; MOBILE: 07776 186819

S. L. Walker Antiques
High St. TN16 1JA. (Sharon Walker)
EST. 1994. Open Tues.-Sat. 10.30-5 or by appointment.
*STOCK: Quality English and European porcelain especially
Royal Worcester, 1860-1970 including Doris Lindner, Freda
Doughty and Ruyckevelt; Royal Crown Derby, from 1890;
Royal Doulton, Sèvres and Meissen; Georgian to Victorian
furniture; oil paintings and watercolours.* SER: Valuations.
SIZE: Medium. PARK: Easy.
TEL: 01959 565623; MOBILE: 07879 626721
E-MAIL: sharon10@talk21.com

W.W. Warner (Antiques)   BADA
**The Green, High St. TN16 1JL. (C.S. Jowitt and R.J.
Russell)**
EST. 1957. Open 10-5. CL: Mon. *STOCK: 18th-19th C
English and Continental pottery, porcelain, glass, furniture.*
LOC: A25. SER: Valuations; restorations. PARK: Easy.
FAIRS: BADA, Duke of York Square, London.
TEL: 01959 563698
E-MAIL: cjowitt@btconnect.com

BROADSTAIRS

Broadstairs Antiques and Collectables
49 Belvedere Rd. CT10 1PF. (Mrs P. Law)
EST. 1980. Open 10-4.30. CL: Mon. in summer; Mon.-
Wed. in Jan. & Feb. *STOCK: General antiques, linen, china*

and small furniture. LOC: Road opposite Lloyds TSB. SIZE: Small. PARK: Easy. FAIRS: DMG.
TEL: 01843 861965

BROMLEY

Patric Capon   BADA
PO Box 581. BR1 2WX.
EST. 1979. Open by appointment. *STOCK: Unusual carriage clocks, 19th C, £2,000-£25,000; 8-day and 2-day marine chronometers, 19th C, £3,500-£18,000; clocks and barometers, 18th-19th C, £2,000-£35,000.* SER: Valuations; restorations. SIZE: Medium.
TEL: 020 8467 5722; FAX: 020 8295 1475
E-MAIL: info@caponantiqueclocks.com
WEBSITE: www.caponantiqueclocks.com

Halstead's Antiques
24a Tynley Rd. BR1 2RP. (Roger G. Halstead)
EST. 1989. Open 9.30-5.30, Sat. and Sun. by appointment. *STOCK: Dual height snooker, dining, billiard tables, 1840-1930, £1,500-£15,000.* LOC: 20 mins. from M25. SER: Restorations (snooker, dining and billiard tables). SIZE: Medium. PARK: Easy.
TEL: 020 8289 2240; FAX: 020 8289 9903
E-MAIL: halsteadrg@aol.com
WEBSITE: www.diningbilliardtable.com

Peter Morris
1 Station Concourse, Bromley North BR Station. BR1 4EQ.
EST. 1979. BNTA. OMRS. ANA. IBNS. BDOS. Open 10-1 and 2-6, Sat. 9-2. CL: Wed. *STOCK: Coins, from 1660s; medals, from 1790; antiquities, Egyptian, Greek and Roman; bank notes, from 1800; all 50p to £1,000.* LOC: Inside station. SER: Valuations; buys at auction. SIZE: Medium. PARK: Easy. VAT: Stan/Spec. FAIRS: BNTA Coinex; OMRS Convention; major UK and European Coin & Medal.
TEL: 020 8313 3410; FAX: 020 8466 8502
E-MAIL: info@petermorris.co.uk
WEBSITE: www.petermorris.co.uk

Past and Present
22 Plaistow Lane. BR1 3PA. (Mrs Jan Sibley)
EST. 1992. Open 9-5. *STOCK: General antiques and collectables including furniture and garden items.* SER: Valuations. SIZE: Small. PARK: Outside shop.
TEL: 020 8466 7056; MOBILE: 07961 995303
E-MAIL: pastandpresent_kent@hotmail.com

CANTERBURY

Burgate Antique Centre
23A Palace St. CT1 2DZ. (V. Reeves)
EST. 1986. Open 10-5. *STOCK: General antiques and collectables, militaria and British war medals; silver, jewellery and Britain's soldiers.* LOC: Just outside Cathedral precinct. SIZE: 10 dealers. PARK: Public car parks nearby. FAIRS: Military fairs.
TEL: 01227 456500

Bygones Reclamation
Nackington Rd. CT4 7BA. (Bob and Sue Thorpe)
EST. 1995. SALVO. Open 8.30-5.30, Sat. 8.30-6, Sun. 8.30-5. *STOCK: Victorian fireplaces, cast iron radiators, 19th C, £200-£1,500; garden statuary, 18th-20th C, £300-£1,500.* LOC: B2068 Hythe road, 2 miles from city centre. SER: Valuations; restorations. PARK: Own. VAT: Spec.
TEL: 01227 767453; FREEPHONE: 0800 0433012;
FAX: 01227 762153
WEBSITE: www.bygones.net

Canterbury Antiques
2 The Borough. CT1 2DR. (M.D. Patten)
EST. 1993. Open 10-5. *STOCK: Clocks and barometers, china, furniture, to Victorian, £50-£10,000.* SIZE: Medium. PARK: Loading only and nearby.
TEL: 01227 785755; FAX: 01227 766222;
MOBILE: 07711 404231.

The Canterbury Bookshop
37 Northgate. CT1 1BL. (David Miles)
EST. 1980. ABA. PBFA. Open 10-5. CL: Tues./Thurs./Sun. *STOCK: Antiquarian and secondhand books, children's books, prints.* SIZE: Medium. PARK: Easy. FAIRS: PBFA and major provincial; ABA; Olympia; Chelsea.
TEL: 01227 464773; FAX: 01227 780073
E-MAIL: canterburybookshop@btconnect.com

Chaucer Bookshop
6-7 Beer Cart Lane. CT1 2NY. (Sir Robert Sherston-Baker Bt)
EST. 1956. ABA. PBFA. Open 10-5. *STOCK: Books and prints, 18th-20th C, £5-£150; maps, 18th-19th C, £50-£1,000.* LOC: 5 mins. walk from cathedral, via Mercery Lane and St. Margaret's St. SER: Valuations; buys at auction (books, maps and prints). PARK: Castle St. VAT: Stan.
TEL: 01227 453912; FAX: 01227 451893
E-MAIL: chaucerbooks@btconnect.com
WEBSITE: www.chaucer-bookshop.co.uk

Coach House Antiques Centre
2A Duck Lane, St. Radigunds. CT1 2AE.
EST. 1975. Open 10-4. *STOCK: General antiques, small furniture, ceramics, glass, linen, books, collectors' items and bygones. NOT STOCKED: Jewellery.* SIZE: Large. PARK: Nearby in Millers Arms car park, St Radigunds.
TEL: 01227 463117

Conquest House Antiques
17 Palace St. CT1 2DZ. (C.C. Hill and D.A. Magee)
EST. 1975. Open 10-5.30. *STOCK: 18th-19th C furniture, chandeliers and decorative items.* LOC: Near cathedral, King's Mile. SER: Restorations; valuations; packing and shipping; delivery . PARK: St. Radigunds.
TEL: 01227 464587; FAX: 01227 451375
E-MAIL: caroline@empire-antiques.co.uk
WEBSITE: www.conquesthouse.com

Nan Leith's Brocanterbury

Errol House, 68 Stour St. CT1 2NZ.
EST. 1983. Resident. Open Fri. & Sat. 1-5, or by appointment. STOCK: *Art Deco, Victoriana, pressed glass and costume jewellery.* LOC: Close to Heritage Museum.
TEL: 01227 454519

Palace Street Jewellers

16 Palace St. CT1 2DZ. (Lesley Parker)
EST. 1979. Open 9.30-5. STOCK: *Silver and jewellery, 18th-19th C, £500-£10,000; handmade modern silverware, modern jewellery.* LOC: 5 mins. from cathedral, opposite The King's School. SER: Valuations; restorations; gold and silversmiths; manufacturers. SIZE: Small. PARK: Easy, St. Radigunds a 4 min. walk. VAT: Stan/Spec.
TEL: 01227 463224
WEBSITE: www.palacestreetjewellers.com

Pattinson's Galleries

25 Oaten Hill. CT1 3HZ. (Alan Pattinson)
EST. 1967. Open 9.30-5, Sat. 10-4, Sun. 11-4. STOCK: *17th-20th C fine art and antiques, furniture, porcelain, rugs.* LOC: Off the Old Dover Road. SER: Valuations; restorations (furniture); buys at auction (furniture). SIZE: Medium. PARK: Easy.
TEL: 01227 780365; HOME: same

The Saracen's Lantern

9 The Borough. CT1 2DR. (W.J. Christophers)
EST. 1970. Open at varied times as displayed on door. Prior telephone call advisable. STOCK: *General antiques, silver, clocks, watches, Victorian bottles and pot-lids, prints, porcelain and pottery, plates, Royal commemoratives, postcards, brass, copper and pewter.* LOC: Near cathedral opposite King's School. SIZE: Small. PARK: At rear, by way of Northgate and St. Radigund's St. or rear of Sainsbury's, Kingsmead Rd.
TEL: 01227 451968

Victorian Fireplace

Thanet House, 92 Broad St. CT1 2LU. (J.J. Griffith)
EST. 1980. Open 10-5.30. CL: Wed. STOCK: *Georgian to Victorian fireplaces.* LOC: Town centre. SER: Restorations; fitting. SIZE: Medium. PARK: Nearby. VAT: Stan/Spec.
TEL: 01227 767723

CHILHAM

Bagham Barn Antiques

Canterbury Rd. CT4 8DU.
Open Tues.-Sat. and Bank Holidays 10-5. STOCK: *Wide range of fine antiques, 17th to early 20th C including furniture, clocks, ceramics, silver, books and militaria.* LOC: A28 adjacent to station. SER: Restorations (clocks, furniture, ceramics, teddy bears, books and pens); exhibitions. SIZE: Large. PARK: Own large.
TEL: 01227 732522; MOBILE: 07780 675201
E-MAIL: peggyboyd@baghambarn.com
WEBSITE: www.baghambarn.com

Julian Lovegrove Fine Art

Bagham Barn Antiques, CT4 8DU. (Julian Lovegrove)
EST. 1995. GMC. Open Tues.-Sun. 10-5; STOCK: *19th - 20th C watercolours, oil paintings, prints and etchings and decorative furniture.* LOC: On the A28 Canterbury Road at Chilham, next to the railway station. SER: Restorations (furniture including French polishing and upholstery). SIZE: Medium. PARK: Free.
TEL: HOME: 01843 602526
E-MAIL: jlantiques@hotmail.com
WEBSITE: www.antiqueswestmalling.co.uk

CHISLEHURST

Chislehurst Antiques   LAPADA

7 Royal Parade. BR7 6NR. (Mrs M. Crawley)
EST. 1976. Open Sat., 10-5, Sun. 11-4. STOCK:
Furniture, 1760-1910; lighting - oil, gas, electric, 1850-1910; mirrors, 1820-1910. LOC: Half mile from A20, 3 miles from M25. SIZE: Large. PARK: Easy. VAT: Spec.
FAIRS: Olympia; NEC.
TEL: 020 8467 1530; MOBILE: 07773 345266s
E-MAIL: margaret@chislehurstantiques.co.uk
WEBSITE: www.antiquefurnishings.co.uk

Michael Sim

1 Royal Parade. BR7 5PG.
EST. 1983. Open 9-6 including Sun. STOCK: *English furniture, Georgian and Regency, £500-£50,000; clocks, barometers, globes and scientific instruments, £500-£50,000; Oriental works of art, £50-£5,000; portrait miniatures, £300-£5,000; animalier bronzes, £1,000-£10,000.* LOC: 50yds. from War Memorial at junction of Bromley Rd. and Centre Common Rd. SER: Valuations; restorations; buys at auction. SIZE: Medium. PARK: Easy. VAT: Spec.
TEL: 020 8467 7040; HOME: same; FAX: 020 8857 1313.
E-MAIL: msim@michaelsim.com
WEBSITE: www.michaelsim.com

Wrattens

51-52 High St. BR7 5AF.
Open 9.30-5 Mon.-Sat. STOCK: *Antiques and gifts.* SIZE: Over 40 dealers.
TEL: 020 8295 5933; 020 8467 7400;
MOBILE: 07773414529
E-MAIL: maureenjbrown@wrattens.co.uk
WEBSITE: www.wrattens.co.uk

CRANBROOK

Gallery Cranbrook

Scotney. TN17 3JW. (P.J. and N.A. Rodgers)
EST. 1978. Open by appointment. STOCK: *Watercolours, prints and maps, 18th-19th C.* SER: Restorations; picture search. PARK: Free nearby.
TEL: 01580 720720
E-MAIL: art@britishfineart.com
WEBSITE: www.britishfineart.com

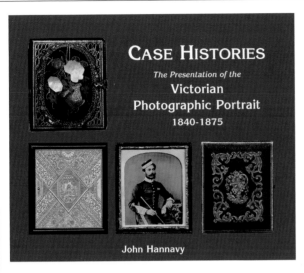
CRAYFORD

Watling Antiques
139 Crayford Rd. DA1 4AS.
Open 10-6.30. STOCK: *General antiques and shipping goods.*
TEL: 01322 523620

DEAL

McConnell Fine Books
The Golden Hind, 85 Beach St. CT14 6JB. (Nick McConnell)
EST. 1976. ABA. PBFA. Open Wed.-Sun. 11-4, other times by appointment. STOCK: *Leather-bound antiquarian books.* LOC: Seafront opposite Royal Hotel. SER: Valuations. SIZE: Medium. PARK: Nearby. FAIRS: ABA - Olympia, Chelsea Town Hall; monthly PBFA Russell Hotel.
TEL: 01304 375086; FAX: same; MOBILE: 07966 404164
E-MAIL: info@mcconnellfinebooks.com
WEBSITE: www.mcconnellfinebooks.com

Quill Antiques
12 Alfred Sq. CT14 6LR. (A.J. and A.R. Young)
Open 9-5.30. STOCK: *General antiques, porcelain, Oriental items.*
TEL: 01304 375958

Serendipity
125 High St. CT14 6BB. (M. and K. Short)
EST. 1976. Open 10-1 and 2-4.30, Sat. 9.30-4.30, or by appointment. STOCK: *Staffordshire figures, ceramics, pictures, furniture.* SER: Valuations; restorations (ceramics and oil paintings). SIZE: Medium. PARK: Easy.
TEL: 01304 369165; HOME: 01304 366536
E-MAIL: dipityantiques@aol.com; fivetake@aol.com

Toby Jug
South Toll House, Deal Pier, Beach St. CT14 6HZ. (Mrs Sandy Pettit)
EST. 1996. Open Tues.-Sat. 11-5.30. STOCK: *Toby and character jugs, 1800-2000, £10-£1,000; 20th C ceramics and collectables.* LOC: Seafront. SER: Valuations. SIZE: Small. PARK: Middle St. FAIRS: DMG, Detling.
TEL: 01304 369917; HOME: 01304 365617

EAST PECKHAM

Desmond and Amanda North
The Orchard, Hale St. TN12 5JB.
EST. 1971. Open daily, appointment advisable. STOCK: *Oriental rugs, runners, carpets and cushions, 1800-1939, mostly £100-£4,000.* LOC: On B2015, 400yds south of roundabout at northern end of Hale Street bypass (A228). SER: Valuations; restorations (reweaving, re-

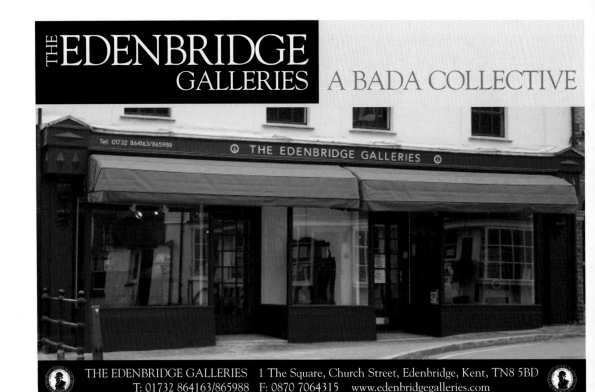

THE EDENBRIDGE GALLERIES   1 The Square, Church Street, Edenbridge, Kent, TN8 5BD
T: 01732 864163/865988   F: 0870 7064315   www.edenbridgegalleries.com

edging and patching); cleaning. SIZE: Medium. PARK: Easy.
TEL: 01622 871353; HOME: same; FAX: 01622 872998.

EDENBRIDGE

Lennox Cato   BADA LAPADA
1 The Square, Church St. TN8 5BD. (Lennox and Susan Cato)
EST. 1975. CINOA. Open 9.30-5.30, Sat. 10-12 or by appointment. *STOCK: 18th-19th C English and Continental furniture and related items, including mirrors, lamps, paintings, ceramics.* LOC: 20 mins from M25, town centre (B2026), next door to the Edenbridge Galleries. SER: Valuations; restorations. SIZE: Large. PARK: Nearby and private parking at rear of property. VAT: Stan/Spec. FAIRS: Olympia (Summer and Winter); BADA (London and Harrogate).
TEL: 01732 865988; FAX: 0870 7064315;
MOBILE: 07836 233473
E-MAIL: cato@lennoxcato.com
WEBSITE: www.lennoxcato.com

The Edenbridge Galleries
1 The Square, Church St. TN8 5BD. (Lennox and Susan Cato)
EST. 2007. CINOA. Open 9.30-5.30, Sat. 10-4.30. *STOCK:*
LOC: 20 minutes south junction 6 of M25 on the B2026,

adjacent to Lennox Cato Antiques. SER: Valuations; restoration. SIZE: Large - 10 dealers. PARK: Rear of property and free throughout the town. VAT: Stan/Spec.
TEL: 01732 864163; FAX: 01732 865988
E-MAIL: info@edenbridgegalleries.com

Below are listed the dealers trading from this address.

Amherst Antiques   BADA
Tunbridge ware.

H.C.Baxter & Son   BADA
18th C English Furniture.

Lennnox Cato   BADA
18th and 19th C furniture and related accessories.

J.Collins & Son   BADA
19th C oil paintings.

Derval   BADA
(Derek and Valerie Roberts) *18th and 19th C furniture, clocks, globes and decorative objects.* TEL:
e-mail: derval@lewins.org.uk

Mrs. Monro   BADA
Interiors and garden design

John Morton Lee   BADA
18th - 20th C watercolours.

Suffolk House Antiques   BADA
17th and 18th C period oak country furniture and related objects.

Walpoles   BADA LAPADA
(Graham Walpole) PADA *Campaign and colonial
furniture, maritime and folk art; 18th - 20th C furniture
and works of art.* TEL: **07831 561042**
e-mail: info@walpoleantiques.com
website: www.walpoleantiques.com

  Karel Weijand   BADA
  18th - 20th C rugs.

  Mark West   BADA
  18th - 20th C glass.

ELHAM

Elham Antiques
(Julian and Linda Chambers)
EST. 1990. Resident. Open by appointment. STOCK:
*Fireplaces, 18th-19th C, £500-£1,000; country furniture,
late 17th C to late 19th C, £500-£1,000; trains and models,
early 20th C, £200-£600.* SER: Valuations. SIZE: Large.
PARK: Easy. VAT: Spec.
TEL: 01303 840085; HOME: 01303 840874

FARNINGHAM

P.T. Beasley
Forge Yard, High St. DA4 0DB. (P.T. and R. Beasley)
EST. 1964. Open every day, prior telephone call advisable.
*STOCK: English furniture, pewter, brass, Delft and
woodcarvings.* LOC: Opposite Social Club. PARK: Easy.
TEL: 01322 862453

FAVERSHAM

Squires Antiques (Faversham)
3 Jacob Yard, Preston St. ME13 8NY. (A. Squires)
EST. 1985. *FTCTA* Open 10-5. CL: Wed. and Thurs.
STOCK: *General antiques.* LOC: off main road through
Faversham. SER: House clearance advice. SIZE: Large.
PARK: Nearby.
TEL: 01795 531503; FAX: 01227 750396
E-MAIL: squiresantiques@aol.com

FOLKESTONE

Marrin's Bookshop
149 Sandgate Rd. CT20 2DA. (Patrick Marrin)
EST. 1949. ABA. PBFA. ILABA. Open 10-5.30. CL:
Mon. STOCK: *Books, maps, early engravings, topographical
and sporting prints, paintings, drawings.* LOC: Town centre.
SER: Restoration; rebinding; framing. SIZE: Medium. VAT:
Stan. FAIRS: Olympia, Chelsea Town Hall.
TEL: 01303 253016; FAX: 01303 850956
E-MAIL: info@marrinbook.co.uk
WEBSITE: www.marrinbook.co.uk

Military History Bookshop
PO Box 590. CT20 2WX. (I.H. and G.M. Knight)
EST. 1975. Open by appointment. STOCK: *Military books.*

SER: Search. SIZE: Medium.
TEL: 01303 246500; FAX: 01303 245133
E-MAIL: info@militaryhistorybooks.com
WEBSITE: www.militaryhistorybooks.com.

GOUDHURST

Mill House Antiques
High St. TN17 1AL.
EST. 1968. Open 10-5. CL: Wed from 1pm. STOCK: *Oak,
pine country and painted furniture and associated items, 17th
C to Victorian, £5-£1,000.* LOC: Off A21 on to A262,
village about 3 miles. SER: Valuations. SIZE: Medium.
PARK: Easy.
TEL: 01580 212476; HOME: 01892 528223

HAMSTREET

Woodville Antiques
The Street. TN26 2HG. (A.S. MacBean)
EST. 1972. Open Tues.-Sun. 10-5.30. STOCK:
*Woodworking tools, 18th-20th C; 19th C furniture, glass
and pictures.* LOC: Village centre. SER: Valuations. SIZE:
Small. PARK: Easy.
TEL: 01233 732981; HOME: same
E-MAIL: woodvilleantique@yahoo.co.uk

HERNE BAY

Saxongate Antique and Design
Briggsy's Old Cinema, 75 High St. CT6 5LQ.
Trade Warehouse. Open Sat. or by appointment. STOCK:
*Traditional antique furniture and decorative painted &
upholstered furnishings including beds.* SER: Restoration,
french polishing & upholstery.
TEL: 01227 370621
E-MAIL: info@saxongate.com
WEBSITE: www.saxongate.com

HYTHE

Alan Lord Antiques
158 High St. CT21 5JR. (R.G. and M. Lord)
EST. 1952. Open 9.30-5. STOCK: *18th-19th C furniture;
books relating to Kent, antiques and architecture, leather
bindings, 18th and 19th C longcase and bracket clocks.* LOC:
Near Waitrose (A259). SIZE: Medium. PARK: Private
forecourt. VAT: Stan/Spec.
TEL: 01303 264239; MOBILE: 07855 547467
E-MAIL: russell@lord8829.fsnet.co.uk

Malthouse Arcade
High St. CT21 5BW. (Mr and Mrs R.M. Maxtone
Graham)
EST. 1974. Open Fri., Sat. and Bank Holiday Mon. 9.30-
5.30. STOCK: *Furniture, jewellery and collectors' items.* LOC:
West end of High St. SIZE: Large - 37 stalls. PARK: 50yds.
TEL: 01303 260103; HOME: 01304 613270

Owlets

99 High St. CT21 5JH. (Alison Maurice)
EST. 1961. NAG. NGA. Open 9-5. STOCK: *Antique and estate jewellery and silver.*
TEL: 01303 230333
E-MAIL: alison@owlets.co.uk

MAIDSTONE

Gem Antiques

10 Gabriels Hill. ME15 6JG.
EST. 1969. Open 10-5. STOCK: *Jewellery, £5-£10,000.*
SER: Restorations; repairs. SIZE: Small. VAT: Spec.
TEL: 01622 763344

Sutton Valence Antiques

Unit 4 Haslemere Estate, Sutton Rd. ME15 9NL.
(N. Mullarkey and O. Marles)
EST. 1971. Open 9-5, Sat. 9-1, CL: BH. STOCK: *Antique and shipping furniture.* LOC: Approx. 3 miles south of Maidstone, just off A274. SER: Container packing and shipping; restorations; courier; buys at auction. SIZE: Large warehouse. PARK: Easy. VAT: Margin/Global.
FAIRS: Newark.
TEL: 01622 675332; FAX: 01622 692593
E-MAIL: svantiques@surfree.co.uk
WEBSITE: www.svantiques.co.uk

MARGATE

Furniture Mart

Bath Place. CT9 2BN. (R.G. Scott)
EST. 1971. CL: Wed. STOCK: *General antiques £1-£3,000; shipping goods.* LOC: Corner of Bath Place. SER: Restorations; restoration materials supplied; container packing. SIZE: Large. VAT: Global/Stan.
TEL: 01843 220653
E-MAIL: lateron@onetel.com

NORTHFLEET

Northfleet Hill Antiques

36 The Hill. DA11 9EX. (Mrs M. Kilby)
EST. 1986. Open Mon., Tues., Fri. 10-5 and by appointment. STOCK: *Furniture, 19th to early 20th C, £50-£500; bygones and collectables, £1-£100.* LOC: A226 near junction with B261 and B2175. SIZE: Small. PARK: Easy (behind Ye Olde Coach and Horses Inn). FAIRS: Mainwaring's Chelsea Living; Whitstable Seaside Brocante.
TEL: 01474 321521

OTFORD

Otford Antiques & Collectors Centre

26-28 High St. TN14 5PQ. (Angela Scully)
EST. 1997. Open 10-5, Sun. 11-4. STOCK: *Furniture and collectables, to £800+.* SER: Restorations (upholstery). SIZE: Large. PARK: Easy.

TEL: 01959 522025; FAX: 01732 883365
E-MAIL: info@otfordantiques.co.uk
WEBSITE: www.otfordantiques.co.uk

PETTS WOOD

Beehive

22 Station Sq. BR5 1NA. (John Miller)
EST. 1994. Open 10-5, Sat. 10-4.30. STOCK: *Collectables, china, glass, jewellery and furniture, 19th-20th C, £1-£500.*
SIZE: 50 dealers. PARK: Easy. FAIRS: Detling, Ardingly.
TEL: 01689 890675

ROCHESTER

Baggins Book Bazaar - The Largest Secondhand Bookshop in England

19 High St. ME1 1PY.
EST. 1986. Open 10-6 including Sun. STOCK: *Secondhand and antiquarian books.* LOC: Next to the Guildhall Museum. SER: Book search; new book ordering. SIZE: Large. PARK: Nearby; free on Sundays.
TEL: 01634 811651
WEBSITE: www.bagginsbooks.co.uk

Cottage Style Antiques

24 Bill Street Rd. ME2 4RB. (W. Miskimmin)
EST. 1981. Open 9.30-5.30. STOCK: *General and architectural antiques.* PARK: Easy.
TEL: 01634 717623

Field Staff Antiques

93 High St. ME1 1LX. (Jim Field and Jane Staff)
EST. 1995. Open 10-5. STOCK: *Furniture silver, commemorative, crested and good quality china, ephemera and vintage clothes.* LOC: Next to visitor centre. SIZE: Large - 4 showrooms.
TEL: 01634 846144
E-MAIL: fieldstaffantiques@supanet.com
WEBSITE: www.fieldstaffantiques.com

Francis Iles

Rutland House, La Providence, High St. ME1 1LX.
(The Family Iles)
EST. 1960. Open 9.30-5.30. STOCK: *Over 700 works, all mediums including sculpture, mainly 20th C, £50-£10,000.*
SER: Restorations; cleaning; relining; framing. SIZE: Large. PARK: 40yds. VAT: Stan/Spec. FAIRS: Affordable Art (Spring), Battersea; RA Watercolour & Drawings.
TEL: 01634 843081; FAX: 01634 846681
E-MAIL: advice@artycat.com; nettie@francis-iles.com
WEBSITE: www.francis-iles.com and www.artycat.com

Kaizen International Ltd

88 High St. ME1 1JT. (Jason Hunt)
EST. 1997. Open 10-5. STOCK: *General antiques including antique and secondhand jewellery.* SER: Valuations; restorations (jewellery). SIZE: Medium. PARK: Nearby.
TEL: 01634 814132

Langley Galleries Ltd
143 High St. ME1 1EL. (K.J. Cook)
EST. 1978. Open 9-5. STOCK: *Prints, watercolours, oils, 19th-20th C.* SER: Framing.
TEL: 01634 811802

Memories
128 High St. ME1 1JT. (Mrs M. Kilby)
EST. 1985. Open 9.30-5, Sun. 11-4. STOCK: *Small furniture, £50-£500, china, glass, silver, jewellery, pictures, collectables, bric-a-brac and linen, £1-£500.* SIZE: Medium - 12 dealers PARK: Opposite. FAIRS: Chelsea; Detling.
TEL: 01634 811044

ROLVENDEN

Falstaff Antiques
63-67 High St. TN17 4LP. (C.M. Booth)
EST. 1964. Open 10-5.30, Sun. by appointment. STOCK: *English furniture, £5-£700; china, metal, glass, silver, £1-£200. NOT STOCKED: Paintings.* LOC: On A28, 3 miles from Tenterden, 1st shop on left in village. SER: Valuations. Motor Museum. SIZE: Medium. PARK: Easy.
TEL: 01580 241234
WEBSITE: www.morganmuseum.org.uk

J.D. and R.M. Walters
10 Regent St. TN17 4PE.
EST. 1977. Open 8-6, Sat. 11-4.30 or by appointment. STOCK: *Mahogany furniture, 18th-19th C.* LOC: A28 turn left in village centre onto B2086, shop on left. SER: Handmade copies of period furniture including chairs; restorations (GMC). SIZE: Small. PARK: Easy. VAT: Stan/Spec.
TEL: 01580 241563; HOME: same

SANDGATE

Christopher Buck Antiques   BADA
56-60 High St. CT20 3AP. (Christopher and Jane Buck)
EST. 1983. Open 10-5. CL: Wed. STOCK: *English furniture, 18th C, £500-£30,000; decorative items, 18th-19th C, £100-£2,000.* LOC: 5 mins. from junction 12, M20 and Channel Tunnel. SER: Valuations; restorations (furniture); buys at auction. SIZE: Medium. PARK: Easy. VAT: Stan/Spec. FAIRS: Olympia (June, Nov); BADA (March).
TEL: 01303 221229; FAX: 01303 221229
E-MAIL: cb@christopherbuck.co.uk
WEBSITE: www.gabrielledegiles.com

Michael Fitch Antiques   LAPADA
99 High St. CT20 3BY.
EST. 1980. Open 10-5.30, Sun. by appointment. STOCK: *Georgian, Victorian and Edwardian furniture and clocks.* SER: Delivery; shipping advice. SIZE: Large. PARK: Own.
TEL: 01303 249600; FAX: same
WEBSITE: www.michaelfitchantiques.co.uk

Freeman & Lloyd Antiques   BADA LAPADA
44 High St. CT20 3AP. (K. Freeman and M.R. Lloyd)
EST. 1968. CINOA. Open 10-5.30, Mon. and Wed. by appointment only. STOCK: *Fine Georgian and Regency English furniture; clocks, paintings and other period items.* LOC: On main coast road between Hythe and Folkestone (A259). SIZE: Medium. PARK: Easy. VAT: Spec.
TEL: 01303 248986; MOBILE: 07860 100073
E-MAIL: enquiries@freemanandlloyd.com
WEBSITE: www.freemanandlloyd.com

David Gilbert Antiques
30 High St. CT20 3AP.
EST. 1975. Open 9-5. STOCK: *Furniture, smalls, glass, Arts and Crafts furniture, 1790-1930, £5-£1,000.* LOC: A259 coast road. SER: Valuations. SIZE: Two floors. PARK: Easy.
TEL: 0787622230; HOME: 01304 812237

Gabrielle de Giles
Antique Country Furniture and Interiors, 40 High St. CT20 3AP.
EST. 1987. Open Thurs.-Sat. 11-5 or by appointment. STOCK: *Country furniture, mainly French, 18th-20th C, to £5,000.* LOC: A259 coast road. PARK: Behind shop. FAIRS: London.
TEL: 01303 255600; MOBILE: 07721 015263
E-MAIL: gabrielle@gabrielledegiles.com

Jonathan Greenwall Antiques   LAPADA
61-63 High St. CT20 3AH.
EST. 1964. Open 9.30-5. *STOCK: Furniture, to 19th C;
decorative items, jewellery, oils and watercolours, prints
and maps, sculpture and bronzes.* LOC: Folkestone-
Brighton road. SER: Valuations. SIZE: Large. PARK:
Easy.
TEL: **01303 248987**; MOBILE: **07799 133700**

J. Luckhurst Antiques
63 High St. CT20 3AH.
EST. 1989. Open 9.30-5 and by appointment. *STOCK:
Furniture - Georgian, Victorian, Edwardian and decorative;
gilt mirrors, carpets.* SER: Valuations; restorations (period
furniture). SIZE: Small. PARK: Nearby. FAIRS: Newark;
Ardingly.
TEL: MOBILE: 07786 983231

Old English Oak
100-102 High St. CT20 3BY. (A. Martin)
EST. 1997. Open 10-6. *STOCK: Oak furniture and white-
painted French-style furniture.* PARK: 1 hour in front of
shop and unlimited nearby.
TEL: 01303 248560.

Old English Pine
100-102 High St. CT20 3BY. (A. Martin)
EST. 1986. Open 10-6. *STOCK: Pine furniture.* SIZE: 15
showrooms. PARK: 1 hour in front of shop and unlimited
nearby.
TEL: 01303 248560

SANDWICH

All Our Yesterdays & Chris Baker Gramophones
3 Cattle Market. CT13 9AE. (Sandie and Chris Baker)
EST. 1994. CLPGS. Open 10.30-2.30, Fri. 10.30-2, Sat.
10.30-3.30, Sun. by appointment. CL: Wed. *STOCK:
General antiques, gramophones and associated items, £5-
£1,000.* LOC: Opposite Guildhall. SER: Repairs
(gramophones, phonographs, etc). SIZE: Medium. PARK:
Behind Guildhall.
TEL: 01304 614756
E-MAIL: cbgramophones@aol.com
WEBSITE: www.chrisbakergramophones.co.uk

SEVENOAKS

Antiques & Fine Furniture
18 London Rd., Dunton Green. TN13 2UE. (C.E.
West)
EST. 1977. Open 10-5. *STOCK: Clocks and watches, period
furniture, porcelain, glass, toys, bric-a-brac.* LOC: London
road into town, opposite Whitmore's Vauxhall
showroom. SER: Valuations; restorations (clocks,
furniture); re-upholstery, curtains and soft furnishings).
SIZE: Large. PARK: Easy.
TEL: 01732 464346; MOBILE: 07957 110534

Neill Robinson Blaxill   LAPADA
21 St. John's Hill. TN13 3NX.
FBHI. Open 9-6, appointment preferred. *STOCK:
Clocks, barometers, decorative items, furniture, sundials
and garden furniture, 16th-20th C.* LOC: 1 mile from
High St. SER: Restorations (fine clocks). PARK: Easy.
TEL: **01732 454179**; MOBILE: **07786 860782**
E-MAIL: **info@antiques-clocks.co.uk**
WEBSITE: **www.antiques-clocks.co.uk** and
www.hyperiondials.co.uk

Gem Antiques
122 High St. TN13 1XA.
EST. 1969. Open 10-5. *STOCK: Jewellery, 18th-20th C, £10-
£10,000.* LOC: Next door to Boots. SER: Restorations (as
stock). SIZE: Small. PARK: Nearby. VAT: Spec.
TEL: 01732 743540

SOUTHBOROUGH

Peter Hoare Antiques
14 Church Rd. TN4 0RX.
EST. 1985. Open 10-5.30. CL: Mon. *STOCK: British Arts
and Crafts furniture, Gothic revival, aesthetic movement,
19th-20th C design, £25-£5,000.* LOC: A26. SER:
Valuations. SIZE: Medium. PARK: At rear.
TEL: 01892 524623

ST NICHOLAS AT WADE, BIRCHINGTON

Farriers Antiques
The Street. CT7 0NR (Pauline Martin and Tiffany
Welch)
Open 9-5.30. CL: Mon. *STOCK: Affordable antiques and
collectables, period and country furniture, glass, china, brass,
chandeliers, stained glass, lamps, prints and paintings,
Murano glass, pendants, costume jewellery and handbags,
books and postcards.* LOC: Directly opposite the church.
TEL: 01843 840758
E-MAIL: farriersantiques@tiscali.co.uk

STOCKBURY

Steppes Hill Farm Antiques   BADA
The Hill Farm, South St. ME9 7RB. (W.F.A. Buck)
EST. 1965. Always open, appointment advisable.
*STOCK: English porcelain, pottery, pot-lids, 18th-20th C,
to £30,000; small silver; caddy spoons, wine labels, silver
boxes, furniture, 18th-19th C, to £30,000.* LOC: 5 mins.
from M2 on A249. Enquire in village for Steppes Hill
Antiques. SER: Valuations; buys at auction. SIZE:
Medium. PARK: Easy. VAT: Spec. FAIRS: BADA;
International Ceramics; Olympia (Nov).
TEL: **01795 842205**
E-MAIL: **dwabuck@btinternet.com**

SUNDRIDGE

Sundridge Gallery
9 Church Rd. TN14 6DT. (T. and M. Tyrer)
EST. 1986. Open 10-5.30. *STOCK: Watercolours and oils, 19th-20th C.* LOC: Off M25, junction 5. SER: Restorations. PARK: Easy.
TEL: 01959 564104.

SUTTON VALENCE

Sutton Valence Antiques
North St. ME17 3AP. (O. Marles and N. Mullarkey)
EST. 1971. CINOA. Open 9-5, Sat. 9-4. *STOCK: Furniture, porcelain, clocks, silver, metalware, 18th-20th C.* LOC: On A274 Maidstone to Tenterden Rd. SER: Valuations; restorations (furniture); container packing and shipping; courier; buys at auction. SIZE: Large. PARK: Side of shop. VAT: Margin/Global. FAIRS: Newark.
TEL: 01622 843333; FAX: 01622 843499
E-MAIL: svantiques@surfree.co.uk
WEBSITE: www.svantiques.co.uk

TENTERDEN

Flower House Antiques   LAPADA
90 High St. TN30 6JB. (Barry Rayner and Quentin Johnson)
Open 9.30-5.30, Sun. by appointment. *STOCK: English and Continental furniture, 16th to early 19th C; Oriental works of art, 16th-19th C; pictures, lighting, mirrors, objets d'art.* LOC: A28. SER: Valuations; restorations. SIZE: Medium. PARK: Easy and private. VAT: Spec.
TEL: 01580 763764; FAX: 01797 270386;
MOBILE: 07872 392808
E-MAIL: martensrayner@hotmail.com

Gaby's Clocks and Things
140 High St. TN30 6HT. (Gaby Gunst)
EST. 1972. Open 10.30-5. *STOCK: Clocks - longcase and grandmother, regulator wall, English dial, bracket, mantel and skeleton, restored and guaranteed.* SER: Valuations; restorations (clocks). SIZE: Small. PARK: Limited or nearby.
TEL: 01580 765818
E-MAIL: gabysclocks@tenterden140.wanadoo.co.uk
WEBSITE: www.gabysclocks.co.uk

Tenterden Antiques and Silver Vaults
66 High St. TN30 6AU. (T.J. Smith)
EST. 1991. Open 10-5, Sun. 11-4.30. *STOCK: Clocks, silver, telephones, barometers and general antiques.* PARK: Easy.
TEL: 01580 765885

TussieMussies and Cinque Ports Militaria
The Old Stables, 2b East Cross, High St. TN30 6AD (Christina and Dennis Exall)
Open 9.30-5. 10-4 Sun. (Summer only). *STOCK: Home decorations and collectables; collectors' bears. Militaria.* LOC:

Just off High St. PARK: Parking in High St.
TEL: 01580 766224
E-MAIL: tussiemussies@btinternet.com;
sales@cpmilitaria.co.uk
WEBSITE: www.tussiemussies.co.uk;
www.cpmilitaria.co.uk

Twickenham Antiques
Unit 1, Applegarth Farm, Biddenden Rd., St Michaels. TN30 1RA. (A. Clubb)
EST. 1985. Open 9-5. *STOCK: European furniture, 1700-1920, £50-£2,000.* SER: Valuations; restorations (French polishing, cabinet work, carving). SIZE: Medium. PARK: Easy. FAIRS: Swinderby; Ardingly; Kenton.
MOBILE: 07973 132847
E-MAIL: andclubb@aol.com
WEBSITE: www.twickenhamantiques.com

TEYNHAM

Jackson-Grant Antiques
The Old Chapel, 133 London Rd. ME9 9QJ. (D.M. Jackson-Grant)
EST. 1966. Open 10-5, Sun. 1-5. CL: Wed. *STOCK: General antiques, French and English furniture, bookcases, buffets, beds, smalls, 18th C to Art Deco, £5-£3,000.* LOC: A2 between Faversham and Sittingbourne. SER: Customised tester beds available. SIZE: Large. PARK: Easy.
TEL: 01795 522027; HOME: same;
MOBILE: 07831 591881
E-MAIL: david.jacksongrant@btopenworld.com

Peggottys
The Old Chapel, 133 London Rd. ME9 9QJ.
EST. 1999. Open 10-5, Sun. 1-5. CL: Wed. Prior telephone call advisable if travelling from distance. *STOCK: Beds including wooden, half-testers and four-posters, French, English and Flemish, 1800-1920; Edwardian, Victorian, Georgian, Rococo, Renaissance and Henri II, £1,150-£5,000.* LOC: A2 Village centre. SIZE: Large. PARK: Outside.
TEL: 01795 522027; HOME: same
E-MAIL: djgrant133@btopenworld.com
WEBSITE: www.peggottysbeds.co.uk

TONBRIDGE

Greta May Antiques
7 Tollgate Buildings, Hadlow Rd. TN9 1NX.
EST. 1987. Open 10-5. CL: Mon. & Wed. *STOCK: General antiques, collectables and jewellery, from Victorian; old and artist bears.* LOC: A26 off High St. SER: Valuations; restorations (teddy bears and china). SIZE: Small. PARK: Mill Lane. FAIRS: Ramada Hotel, Hollingbourne, Maidstone.
TEL: 01732 366730
E-MAIL: gretamayantiques@hotmail.com

Derek Roberts Antiques   BADA
25 Shipbourne Rd. TN10 3DN. (Paul Archard)
EST. 1968. Open 9.30-5, Sat. 9.30-1, other times by
appointment. *STOCK: Fine restored clocks, mostly*
£2,000-£100,000. LOC: From B245 to Tonbridge, left
before first lights, left again, shop 50 yards on right.
SER: Valuations; restorations (clock repairs and cabinet
making). SIZE: Large. PARK: Easy. VAT: Spec. FAIRS:
Olympia (Autumn); BADA (Spring).
TEL: 01732 358986; FAX: 01732 771842
E-MAIL: drclocks@clara.net
WEBSITE: www.qualityantiqueclocks.com.

TUNBRIDGE WELLS

Aaron Antiques
77 St. Johns Rd. TN4 9TT. (R.J. Goodman)
Open 9-5. *STOCK: Clocks and pocket watches, paintings and*
prints; period and shipping furniture; English, Continental
and Oriental porcelain; antiquarian books, postcards, coins
and medals. VAT: Stan/Spec.
TEL: 01892 517644
E-MAIL: ronald.goodman@btinternet.com
WEBSITE: www.aaronenterpriseslimited.co.uk

Amadeus Antiques
32 Mount Ephraim. TN4 8AU. (P.A. Davies)
EST. 1990. Open 11-5, Sun. by appointment. *STOCK:*

Unusual furniture, to Art Deco, £50-£5,000; china and bric-
a-brac, £25-£500; chandeliers, £100-£1,000. LOC: Near
hospital. SER: Valuations. SIZE: Medium. PARK: Easy.
TEL: 01892 544406; 01892 864884

The Architectural Stores
55 St John's Rd. TN4 9TP. (Nick Bates)
EST. 1988. SALVO. Open 10-5.30. CL: Mon. *STOCK:*
Fireplaces, garden statuary, lighting, decorative salvage,
Georgian to Edwardian. LOC: A26 towards Southborough.
SIZE: Medium. PARK: John St. VAT: Stan.
TEL: 01892 540368
E-MAIL: nic@architecturalstores.com
WEBSITE: www.architecturalstores.com

Beau Nash Antiques
29 Lower Walk, The Pantiles. TN2 5TD. (Nicola
Mason and David Wrenn)
EST. 1992. Open 11-5. CL: Mon. and Fri. *STOCK:*
Furniture, silver, copper, brass, porcelain and glass, 18th-
20th C. LOC: Behind Tourist Information Centre. SIZE:
Medium. PARK: Pantiles.
TEL: 01892 537810

Calverley Antiques
30 Crescent Rd. TN1 2LZ. (P.A. Nimmo)
EST. 1995. Open 10-5.30 including Sun. *STOCK:*
Furniture including European pine, 1920s oak, decorative
painted and garden. LOC: Near police station and

Assembly Hall. PARK: Multi-storey next door. FAIRS:
Ardingly.
TEL: 01892 538254
E-MAIL: phil@calverleyantiques.com

Chapel Place Antiques
9 Chapel Place. TN1 1YQ. (J. and A. Clare)
EST. 1984. Open 9-6. STOCK: Silver photo frames, antique
and modern jewellery, old silver plate, claret jugs, hand-painted
Limoges boxes. LOC: Near The Pantiles. SER: Jewellery
repairs and re-threading. PARK: Nearby. VAT: Stan.
TEL: 01892 546561

Down Lane Hall Antiques
Culverden Down, St John's. TN4 9SA. (Michael
Howlett)
EST. 1980. Open 9-5, Sat. 10-5. STOCK: Georgian,
Victorian and Edwardian furniture; clocks and barometers.
LOC: Half mile from town centre, on A26. SER:
Restorations; French polishing. SIZE: Large. PARK: Easy.
TEL: 01892 522440; HOME: 01892 522425
WEBSITE: www.downlanehall.co.uk

Glassdrumman Antiques
7 Union Square, The Pantiles. TN4 8HE. (Graham and
Amanda Dyson Rooke)
Open 10-5.30. CL: Mon. STOCK: Silver, jewellery,
watches, clocks, furniture, decorative items, 18th-20th C.
SER: Specialist repairs and commission work undertaken.
SIZE: Medium. PARK: Nearby. VAT: Stan/Spec.
TEL: 01892 538615; FAX: same

Hall's Bookshop
20-22 Chapel Place. TN1 1YQ. (Sabina Izzard)
EST. 1898. PBFA. Open 9.30-5. STOCK: Antiquarian and
secondhand books. LOC: Adjacent to The Pantiles.
TEL: 01892 527842
E-MAIL: info@hallsbookshop.com
WEBSITE: www.hallsbookshop.com

Kentdale Antiques
Motts Farm Estate, Forge Rd., Eridge Green. TN3
9LJ. (C. Bigwood)
EST. 1981. Trade only. Open by appointment. STOCK:
Mostly mahogany and walnut furniture. LOC: Telephone
for directions. SER: Furniture restored and sold ready to
retail. SIZE: Warehouse. PARK: Easy. VAT: Stan/Spec.
TEL: 01892 863840; FAX: same
E-MAIL: bigwoodchrsb@aol.com

Old Colonial
56 St John's Rd., St John's. TN4 9NY. (Dee Martyn
and Suzy Rees)
EST. 1982. Open Tues.-Sat. 10.30-5.30. STOCK: English
and French country and decorative furniture and associated
smalls. LOC: Approximately 1 mile outside Tunbridge
Wells. SIZE: Small. PARK: Opposite. VAT: Spec.
TEL: 01892 533993; FAX: 01892 513281
WEBSITE: www.oldcolonial.biz

The Pantiles Antiques
31 The Pantiles. TN2 5TD. (Mrs E.M. Blackburn)
EST. 1979. Open 10-5. STOCK: Georgian, Victorian and
Edwardian furniture; 19th C porcelain, silver. LOC: Lower
Walk. SER: Upholstery. SIZE: Medium. PARK: Easy.
TEL: 01892 531291

Pantiles Oriental Carpets
31A The Pantiles. TN2 5TD. (Judith Williams)
EST. 1980. Open 10-5.30. CL: Wed. STOCK: Oriental
carpets, rugs, kelims and cushions. LOC: Lower walk of The
Pantiles. SER: Restorations and cleaning (carpets, rugs,
kelims, tapestries). SIZE: Small. PARK: Nearby.
TEL: 01892 530416

Pantiles Spa Antiques
4/5/6 Union Square, The Pantiles. TN4 8HE. (Mrs.
J.A. Cowpland)
EST. 1979. Open 10-5. STOCK: Period and Victorian
furniture, specialising in dining tables and chairs, £200-
£10,000; pictures, £50-£3,000; clocks, £100-£5,000;
porcelain, £50-£2,000; silver, £50-£1,000; all 17th-19th C;
dolls, bears and toys. SER: Restorations (furniture); 30 mile
radius free delivery (large items). SIZE: Large. PARK:
Nearby. VAT: Spec.
TEL: 01892 541377; FAX: 01435 865660
E-MAIL: janettec@btconnect.com
WEBSITE: www.pantiles-spa-antiques.co.uk

Payne & Son (Silversmiths) Ltd
Clock House, 37 High St. TN1 1XL. (E.D., M.D. and
A.E. Payne)
EST. 1790. NAG. FGA. Open 9.30-5.30, Sat. 9-5.
STOCK: English jewellery, Victorian to modern; British
silver, Georgian to modern; Swiss watches, to modern; all
£50-£10,000+. LOC: Halfway along High St., marked by
projecting clock. SER: Valuations (insurance, probate,
post-loss appraisal and sale between parties); restorations
(jewellery, silver, watches and clocks). SIZE: Medium.
PARK: Street and multi-storey near station. VAT:
Stan/Spec.
TEL: 01892 525874; FAX: 01892 535447
E-MAIL: jewellers@payneandson.com
WEBSITE: www.payneandson.com

Phoenix Antiques
51-53 St. John's Rd. TN4 9TP. (Peter Janes and Robert
Pilbeam)
EST. 1982. Open 10-5.30 or by appointment. STOCK:
18th-19th C French, English, original painted and country
furniture, decorative furnishings, original gilt overmantel
mirrors, garden statuary. LOC: On A26 from A21 into
town, by St. John's Church. SIZE: Large. PARK: Easy.
VAT: Spec.
TEL: 01892 549099
E-MAIL: shop@phoenixantiques.co.uk
WEBSITE: www.phoenixantiques.co.uk

Redleaf Gallery
1 Castle St. TN1 1XJ. (Nick Hills)
Open 10.30-5. CL: Mon. *STOCK: 19th-20th C water-colours, modern British and contemporary paintings.* LOC: Off High St. PARK: Nearby. VAT: Spec.
TEL: 01892 526695
E-MAIL: info@redleafgallery.co.uk
WEBSITE: www.redleafgallery.com

Ian Relf Antiques
132-134 Camden Rd. TN1 2QZ.
Open 9.30-1.30 and 2.30-5.30. *STOCK: Mainly furniture.*
TEL: 01892 538362.

The Vintage Watch Co.
The Old Pipe House, 74 High St. TN1 1YB. (F. Lawrence)
EST. 1970. Open 10-5. CL: Mon. & Tues. *STOCK: Pre-1950's fine wrist watches, pocket watches.* SER: Restorations, repairs, casework. SIZE: Small.
TEL: 01892 616077
E-MAIL: vintagewatchco@gmail.com
WEBSITE: www.vintagewatchco.com

Yiju
27 The Pantiles. TN2 5TD.
EST. 1998. Open 10-5. *STOCK: Chinese furniture, decorative objects, lacquer ware and textiles.*
TEL: 01892 517000
E-MAIL: info@yiju.co.uk
WEBSITE: www.yiju.co.uk

WEST MALLING

The Old Clock Shop
63 High St. ME19 6NA. (S.L. Luck)
EST. 1970. Open 9-5. *STOCK: Grandfather clocks, 17th-19th C; carriage, bracket, wall clocks and barometers.* LOC: Half a mile from M20. SER: Restoration (clocks and watches). SIZE: Large. PARK: Easy. VAT: Spec.
TEL: 01732 843246
E-MAIL: theoldclockshop@tesco.net
WEBSITE: www.theoldclockshop.co.uk

WESTERHAM

Apollo Antique Galleries LAPADA
19-21 Market Sq. TN16 1AN. (S.M and R.W. Barr)
EST. 1967. Open 9.30-5.30. *STOCK: Georgian, Victorian and Edwardian furniture; 19th C oils and watercolours; bronze and marble statuary; clocks, silver.* LOC: Between junctions 5 and 6 of M25, close to Gatwick Airport. SER: Valuations; free delivery. SIZE: Large. PARK: Easy. VAT: Spec.
TEL: 01959 562200; FAX: 01959 562600
E-MAIL: apollogalleries@aol.com
WEBSITE: www.apollogalleries.com

Castle Antiques Centre
1 London Rd. TN16 1BB. (Stewart Ward Properties)
EST. 1986. Open 10-5 including Sun. *STOCK: General antiques, books, linen, collectables, costume, chandeliers, die-cast toys and theatre related items.* LOC: Just off town centre. SER: Valuations; props for stage productions; chair caning; Liberon stockist. SIZE: Small - 8 dealers in 4 rooms. PARK: Easy - nearby. FAIRS: Ardingly; Detling; Sandown Park.
TEL: 01959 562492

The Design Gallery 1850-1950 LAPADA
5 The Green. TN16 1AS. (John Masters and Chrissie Painell)
EST. 2002. Open 10-5.30, Wed. 10-4, Sun. 1-5. *STOCK: Decorative arts, 1850-1950 - Art Deco, Art Nouveau, Arts and Crafts, Aesthetic Movement, Gothic Revival furniture, ceramics, metalware, bronzes, glass, paintings, prints and etchings, jewellery, £50-£20,000.* LOC: 45 mins from London; from junction 5 or 6, M25 on A25. SIZE: Medium and large warehouse by appointment. PARK: Easy. VAT: Margin. FAIRS: Eltham Palace Art Deco Fair, London (Twice a year).
TEL: 01959 561234; FAX: same; MOBILE: 07785 503044
E-MAIL: sales@designgallery.co.uk
WEBSITE: www.designgallery.co.uk

Taylor-Smith Antiques LAPADA
4 The Grange, High St. TN16 1AH. (Ashton Taylor-Smith)
EST. 1986. Open 10-5. CL: Wed. *STOCK: Fine 18th-19th C furniture; paintings, porcelain, glass, decorative items; Churchill ephemera.* PARK: Easy.
TEL: 01959 563100; FAX: 01959 565300
E-MAIL: ashton@ts-antiques.co.uk

Taylor-Smith Books LAPADA
Owl House, Vicarage Hill. TN16 1AY.
EST. 1972. Open by appointment. *STOCK: Rare books by Sir Winston Churchill and related items.* LOC: Exactly opposite the Churchill statue on Westerham Green. PARK: Adjacent.
TEL: 01959 561561
E-MAIL: allan600taylor@btinternet.com

WHITSTABLE

Laurens Antiques
2 Harbour St. CT5 1AG. (G. A. Laurens)
EST. 1965. Open 9.30-5.30. *STOCK: Furniture, 18th-19th C, £300-£500+.* LOC: Turn off Thanet Way at Whitstable exit, straight down to one-way system in High St. SER: Valuations; restorations (cabinet work); buys at auction. SIZE: Medium. PARK: Easy.
TEL: 01227 261940; HOME: same

Tankerton Antiques
136 Tankerton Rd. CT5 2AN. (Mr & Mrs Paul Wrighton)
EST. 1985. Open Thurs., Fri. and Sat. 10.30-5. STOCK:
*Furniture, Regency to 1930s, £10-£3,000; glass, clocks and
barometers, from 1700, £30-£2,500; French, English and
German costume jewellery and contemporary bead and pearl
jewellery, £30-£300.* LOC: From A299 Thanet Way take
A290/B2205 turn off to Whitstable. Through town and
into Tankerton. Shop on right just past roundabout. SER:
Repairs (clocks and barometers). SIZE: Medium. FAIRS:
Uxbridge Clock & Watch.
TEL: 01227 266490; MOBILE: 07702 244064

WINGHAM

Esprit du Jardin
Waterlock House, Canterbury Rd. CT3 1BH. (Tina Pasco)
EST. 1993. SALVO. Open Fri., Sat. and Sun. 10-6.
STOCK: *Statues, 19th-20th C, £1,000-£60,000; garden urns
and planters, 19th-20th C, £500-£5,000; fountains and
water troughs, staddle stones; cloches and rhubarb forcers;
quality reproduction items.* SER: Restorations (stonework).
SIZE: Large. PARK: Easy. FAIRS: Battersea.
TEL: 01227 722151; HOME: same; MOBILE: 07770 922844
E-MAIL: tinapasco@tinapasco.com
WEBSITE: www.tinapasco.com; www.espritdujardin.com

WITTERSHAM

Old Corner House Antiques
6 Poplar Rd. TN30 7PG. (G. and F. Shepherd)
Open Wed.-Sat. 10-5 or by appointment. STOCK: *General
antiques, country furniture, samplers; 18th-19th C English
pottery including blue and white and creamware; watercolours,
19th to early 20th C.* SER: Local delivery. PARK: Easy.
TEL: 01797 270236

WROUTHAM

Claremont Antiques
Unit 5, Hill Park Farm Wroutham Hill Rd. TN15 7PX.
(Anthony Broad)
Open by appointment. STOCK: *British, French and
Continental original painted pine country furniture,
fruitwood farm tables, 18th-19th C; some decorative items;
all £10-£5,000. Modern art.* SER: Import and export.
SIZE: Shop and warehouse. PARK: Easy.
TEL: 07786 262843
E-MAIL: antclaremont@aol.com
WEBSITE: www.claremontantiques.com

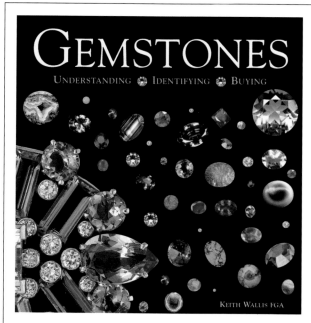

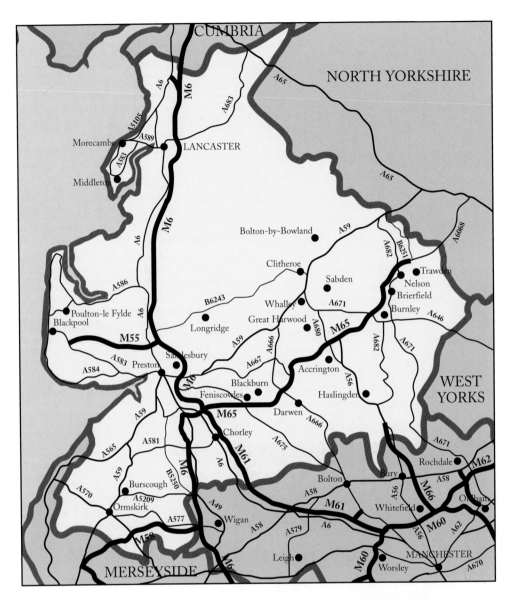

ACCRINGTON

The Coin and Jewellery Shop
129a Blackburn Rd. BB5 0AA.
EST. 1977. Open 10-5. CL: Wed. STOCK: *Coins, jewellery and small antiques.*
TEL: 01254 384757

ASHTON-UNDER-LYNE

Cathedral Jewellers
4 Market St. OL6 6BX (Jason Taylor)
EST. 1968. Open 9.30-5. STOCK: *Jewellery.* SER: Gem setting; valuations. SIZE: Medium. PARK: Meters and car park.
TEL: 0161 339 0332

BLACKBURN

Ancient and Modern
17 New Market St. BB1 7DR. (Gail and Zachary Coles)
EST. 1943. NAG. OMRS. Open 9-5.30. STOCK: *Jewellery, Georgian to date, up to £30,000; clocks, vintage and modern watches including Rolex, Cartier, Patek; militaria and silver; diamond merchants.* LOC: Town centre, opposite side entrance of Marks & Spencer. SIZE: Medium. PARK: Easy. VAT: Stan/Margin/Global. FAIRS: Bangkok; Miami; Beirut.
TEL: 01254 677866/668818; FAX: 01254 677866
E-MAIL: enquiries@ancientandmodernjewellers.co.uk
WEBSITE: www.ancientandmodernjewellers.co.uk

Mitchell's Antiques
76 Bolton Rd. BB2 3PZ. (S. Mitchell)
EST. 1972. Open 9-5. STOCK: *General antiques, gold and silver jewellery, wrist watches.* LOC: Main road. PARK: Easy.
TEL: 01254 664663
E-MAIL: slittlemitch@aol.com

BLACKPOOL

Ascot Antiques
106 Holmfield Rd. FY2 9RF. (J.C. Winwood)
EST. 1987. Open by appointment. STOCK: *Furniture and oil paintings, Georgian to Victorian.* SER: Valuations. SIZE: Small. PARK: Easy.
TEL: 01253 356383; HOME: same; MOBILE: 07816 645716

Chard Coins
521 Lytham Rd. FY4 1RJ.
EST. 1965. Open 10-5. STOCK: *Paintings and furniture, English and ancient coins, gold bullion coins, jewellery and silver,* £50-£20,000+. LOC: Between Central Promenade south and Blackpool Airport main gates, ¼ mile from airport. SER: Valuations. SIZE: Large. PARK: Easy. VAT: Stan/Spec.
TEL: 01253 343081

BOLTON

Antiques at the Swan Centre
Antique Furniture Warehouse and Salvatore Antiques. 2nd Floor, Swan Centre (Adams Selfstore), 4 Higher Swan Lane. BL3 3AQ.
Open by appointment. STOCK: *Trade warehouse. Victorian, Georgian, marquetry, inlaid and walnut antique furniture. Leather Chesterfields and antique leather.* SIZE: Large warehouse.
TEL: Antique Furniture Warehouse 07808 168964; Salvatore Antiques 07971 080372; FAX: 01204 855984
E-MAIL: info@giulianoantiques.com; info@salvatoreantiques.com
WEBSITE: www.giulianoantiques.com; www.salvatoreantiques.com

Drop Dial Antiques
Last Drop Village, Hospital Rd., Bromley Cross. BL7 9PZ. (I.W. and I.E. Roberts)
EST. 1975. Open every afternoon except Mon. and Fri. STOCK: *Clocks, mainly English and French, 18th-20th C, £100-£4,000; mercury barometers, 19th-20th C, paintings, silver, furniture and general antiques, £20-£2,000.* SER: Restorations (clocks and barometers); items bought. SIZE: Medium. PARK: Easy. VAT: Stan/Spec. FAIRS: Galloway and Bailey.
TEL: 01204 307186; HOME: 01257 480995

BOLTON-BY-BOWLAND

Harrop Fold Clocks
Harrop Fold, Lane Ends. BB7 4PJ. (Frank Robinson)

EST. 1974. Open by appointment. STOCK: *British longcase and wall clocks, barometers, 18th-19th C,* £1,000-£10,000. LOC: Through Clitheroe to Chatburn and Grindleton. Take Slaidburn road, turn left after 3 miles. (Please telephone for more details). SER: Valuations; restorations (clocks). SIZE: Medium. PARK: Own.
TEL: 01200 447665; HOME: same
E-MAIL: robinsonharrop@aol.com

BRIERFIELD

J.H. Blakey and Sons Ltd
Burnley Rd. BB9 5AD.
EST. 1905. Open 8-5.30, Sat. 8-12. STOCK: *Furniture, brass, copper, pewter, clocks, curios.* LOC: Main Burnley to Nelson road. SER: Restorations (furniture); frames made, renovated, gold-leaf gilded or bronzed. PARK: Easy. VAT: Stan.
TEL: 01282 613593
E-MAIL: sales@blakeys.fsworld.co.uk

BURNLEY

King's Mill Antique Centre
Unit 2 King's Mill, Queen St., Harle Syke. BB10 2HX. (Michael and Linda Heuer)
Open 10-5, Thurs. 10-7, Sun. 11-5. STOCK: *Furniture and bric-a-brac, Edwardian and Victorian, £5-£1,000.* LOC: From General Hospital, follow brown tourist signs for Queen's Mill. SER: Export. SIZE: Large. PARK: Easy.
TEL: 01282 431953; FAX: 01282 839470; MOBILE: 07803 153752

Lonesome Pine Antiques
19 Bank Parade. BB11 1UH (Mr Berry)
Open 9-5. STOCK: *General antiques, mainly pine and oak.* PARK: Free outside. FAIRS: Newark; Swinderby; Harrogate.
TEL: 01282 428415
E-MAIL: p.berry44@btinternet.com

BURSCOUGH

West Lancs. Antique Exports   LAPADA
Victoria Mill, Victoria St. L40 0SN. (W. and B. Griffiths)
EST. 1959. Open 9-5.30, Sat. & Sun. 10-5. STOCK: *Shipping furniture.* SER: Courier; packing and shipping. SIZE: Large. VAT: Stan.
TEL: 01704 894634; FAX: 01704 894486

BURY

Memories Antiques
37 Bridge St., Ramsbottom. BL0 9AD.
Open 10-4.30, Sat. & Sun. 10-5. STOCK: *Antiques, furniture – used, jewellery, books, collectables.*
TEL: 01706 828800

Newtons
151 The Rock. BL9 0ND. (Newtons of Bury)
EST. 1900. Open 9-5. STOCK: *General antiques, 18th-19th C, £5-£500; furniture including reproduction. NOT STOCKED: Continental furniture.* LOC: From Manchester through Bury town centre, shop is on left 200yds. before fire station. SER: Valuations; restorations. SIZE: Small. PARK: Opposite. VAT: Stan.
TEL: 0161 764 1863
E-MAIL: enquiries@tablecare.co.uk
WEBSITE: www.newtonsofbury.com

CHORLEY

Books & Bygones
8 Clifford St., PR7 1AQ. (Andrew Baxendale)
EST. 1998. Open 10-4.30. CL: Wed. & Thurs. STOCK: *Collectables, antiquarian books, glass and china; general antiques.* LOC: Next to the bus station. PARK: Local car parks.
TEL: 01257 265535
E-MAIL: andrewbaxendale1@yahoo.co.uk

Heskin Hall Antiques
Heskin Hall, Wood Lane, Heskin. PR7 5PA. (Harrison Steen Ltd)
EST. 1996. Open 10-5.30 seven days. STOCK: *Wide range of general antiques.* LOC: B5250. SER: Valuations; restorations. SIZE: Large - 60+ dealers. PARK: Easy.
TEL: 01257 452044; FAX: 01257 450690
E-MAIL: heskinhall@aol.com

CLITHEROE

Brittons - Watches and Antiques
4 King St. BB7 2EP.
EST. 1970. Open 10.30-5, Sat 10.30-4.30. STOCK: *Jewellery and collectors' watches.* LOC: Town centre opposite main Post Office. SER: Valuations. PARK: Opposite.
TEL: 01200 425555; FAX: 01200 424200
WEBSITE: www.brittons-watches.co.uk

Clitheroe Collectables and Country Furniture.
13 Duck St. BB7 1LP (John and Jean Spensley)
Open 9-5.30. STOCK: *Pottery; country furniture, oak, beech ash and pine.* LOC: Next to Tesco. SER: Furniture stripping and waxing, restoration. PARK: At Tesco.
TEL: 01200 422222; FAX: 01200 422223
E-MAIL: info@clicollect.fsnet.co.uk
WEBSITE: www.clitheroecollectables.co.uk

Driscoll Antiques Ltd   LAPADA
Unit 2, Deanfield Way, Link 59 Business Park. BB7 1QU. (Mr J.M. Driscoll)
EST. 1982. CINOA. Open 10-5. STOCK: *British antique furniture and antique collectables; all cleaned using traditional methods. New showroom stocks oak, mahogany and walnut pieces, 17th C to early 20th C.* LOC: **Situated on the A59, easily located from the M1 and M6.** SIZE:

Large. PARK: Plenty, own car park. VAT: Margin.
TEL: **0845 2415518**
E-MAIL: **driscollantiques@hotmail.com**
WEBSITE: **www.driscollantiques.co.uk**

Miles Griffiths Antiques
2/2a Shaw Bridge St. BB7 1LY.
EST. 1992. Open 10-5. STOCK: *Furniture, £30-£3,000; upholstery, mirrors and lamps, £50-£2,000; decorative items, £50-£1,000, 1760-1960.* LOC: Turn up the side of Tesco, shop opposite junction. SER: Valuations. SIZE: Medium. PARK: Easy. VAT: Spec.
TEL: 01200 443658

Past & Present
22 Whalley Rd. BB7 1AW. (Mr Hollings)
EST. 1988. Open 10.30-5 or by appointment. STOCK: *Victorian and Georgian cast-iron fireplaces and ranges, £85-£1,500; Victorian and Edwardian wooden mantels, marble fireplaces, dog grates, coal buckets, brass and cast-iron fenders; fireplace accessories, spare parts, brass and copper, small collectables.* LOC: Near town centre. SER: Restorations (repairs, refurbishing, re-tiling cast iron fireplaces). SIZE: Medium. PARK: Easy.
TEL: 01200 428678; HOME: 01200 445373; MOBILE: 07779 478716

DARWEN

Aladdin's Cave
Hampden Mill, Spring Vale Rd. BB3 2ES (Steve Hughes)
FSB. Open 9.15-5. CL: Sat. STOCK: *Furniture, architectural and garden items.* SIZE: Large, plus yard.
TEL: 01254 777144
WEBSITE: www.antique-dealeruk.com

Belgrave Antique Centre
Hampden Mill, Grimshaw St. BB3 2QJ. (Martin and Elaine Cooney)
EST. 1998. Open 9.30-5, Sun. 11-4. CL: Mon. STOCK: *Porcelain, pottery, glass, furniture, architectural, collectables.* SER: Valuations. SIZE: Large - 30 dealers. PARK: Easy. FAIRS: Newark, Ardingly, Swinderby.
TEL: 01254 777714

K.C. Antiques   LAPADA
**538 Bolton Rd. BB3 2JR. (K. and J. Anderton)
Resident. Open 9-6, Sun. 12-5. STOCK: *Oak and country furniture and decorative items.* LOC: A666. PARK: Easy. VAT: Stan/Spec.**
TEL: **01254 772252; MOBILE: 07767 340501**

G. Oakes and Son
The Courtyard, Hampden Mill, Spring Vale Rd. BB3 2ES.
EST. 1958. Open 9-5 or by appointment. STOCK: *General antiques, furniture and bric-a-brac.* LOC: Off A666 right into Watery Lane (from south); left into Grimshaw St. (from north). SER: Valuations; packing and shipping; buys at auction. SIZE: Large. PARK: Easy. VAT: Stan.

TEL: 01254 777144/776644; MOBILE: 07774 284609
E-MAIL: ycs12@dial.pipex.com
WEBSITE: www.antique-dealeruk.com

E-MAIL: john@holdenwood.co.uk
WEBSITE: www.holdenwood.co.uk

FENISCOWLES

Old Smithy
726 Preston Old Rd. BB2 5EP. (R.C. and I.R. Lynch)
EST. 1967. Open 10-4 or by appointment. STOCK: Period and Victorian fireplaces (over 1,000 in stock), pub and architectural items, violins and musical instruments, pictures and prints, furniture, shipping items, brass, copper. LOC: Opposite Fieldens Arms. SER: Valuations; restorations (wooden items); buys at auction. SIZE: Large. PARK: Own or nearby. FAIRS: Newark, Lincs.
TEL: 01254 209943
E-MAIL: lynchfires@tiscali.co.uk
WEBSITE: www.oldfires.com

GREAT HARWOOD

Benny Charlesworth's Snuff Box
51 Blackburn Rd. BB6 7DF. (N. Walsh)
EST. 1984. Open 10-5. STOCK: Furniture, china, linen, costume jewellery, teddies and limited editions. LOC: 200 yds. from town centre. SIZE: Small. PARK: Next to shop. FAIRS: Local.
TEL: 01254 888550

HASLINGDEN

P.J. Brown Antiques
8 Church St. BB4 5QU.
EST. 1979. Open 10-5, Sat. 10-4, Sun. by appointment. STOCK: Georgian, Victorian and Edwardian furniture, shipping goods, old advertising items, bottles and related items. LOC: Town centre, off Bury Rd./Regent St. SIZE: Medium. PARK: Easy. VAT: Stan/Spec.
TEL: 01706 224888; MOBILE: 07879 220263

Fieldings Antiques
176, 178 and 180 Blackburn Rd. BB1 2LG.
EST. 1956. Open 9-4.30, Fri. 9-4, Thurs. and other times by appointment. STOCK: Longcase clocks, £30-£2,000; wall clocks, sets of chairs, pine, period oak, French furniture, oil paintings, glass, shipping goods, toys, steam engines, veteran cars, vintage and veteran motor cycles. SIZE: Large. PARK: Easy.
TEL: 01706 214254; MOBILE: 07973 698961; HOME: 01254 263358
E-MAIL: andrew.fielding@btconnect.com

Holden Wood Antiques Centre
St Stephen's Church, Grane Rd. BB4 4AT. (John Ainscough)
EST. 1996. Open 10-5.30 including Sun. STOCK: Furniture, 18th-19th C, £200-£2,000; ceramics including figures, glass, 19th C, £50-£2,000. SER: Valuations; restorations. SIZE: 35 dealers. PARK: Own.
TEL: 01706 830803

LANCASTER

Anything Old & Military Collectables
55 Scotforth Rd. LA1 4SA. (Graham H. Chambers)
EST. 1985. Open 1.30-6, Sun. by appointment. CL: Mon. & Tues. STOCK: WW1 and WW11 British, Imperial German, Third Reich and Commonwealth medals, cap badges, uniforms and head dress, edged weapons and field equipment, £5-£500. LOC: 1.5 miles south of city centre on A6. SER: Valuations; full size and miniature medal mounting. SIZE: Medium. PARK: Easy.
TEL: 01524 69933; HOME: same

The Assembly Rooms Market
King St. LA1 1XD.
Open 10-4.30. CL: Mon. STOCK: General antiques, period and costume jewellery; Victorian to '70s memorabilia, costume and retro fashion, books, pop, film and general memorabilia, stamps, records, postcards. LOC: Town centre. SER: Costume hire. SIZE: Several dealers.
TEL: Market Supervisor - 01524 66627
WEBSITE: www.lancasterdistrictmarkets.co.uk

G.B. Antiques Ltd
Lancaster Leisure Park, Wyresdale Rd. LA1 3LA. (Mrs G. Blackburn)
Open 10-5 including Sun. STOCK: Porcelain, glass and silver, late 19th to early 20th C; furniture, Victorian to mid 20th C; collectables, Art Deco and retro items. LOC: Off M6, junction 33 or 34. SER: Valuations; buys at auction. SIZE: Large. 100+ dealers. PARK: Easy. VAT: Stan/Spec.
TEL: 01524 844734; FAX: 01524 844735; HOME: 01772 861593

Lancaster Leisure Park Antiques Centre
Wyresdale Rd. (on site of former Hornsea Pottery Plant). LA1 5LA.
Open 10-5 including Sun. STOCK: Wide range of general antiques and collectables. LOC: Off M6, junction 33 or 34. SIZE: 140 dealers. PARK: Easy.
TEL: 01524 844734

Lancastrian Antiques & Co
1 Spring St. LA1 1RQ. (Mr Wilkinson)
Open 10-4.30 Thurs.-Sat. STOCK: Furniture, lighting, paintings, bric-a-brac, fire surrounds. LOC: At the rear of Reeds Plc.
TEL: 01524 847004; MOBILE: 07977155939

LEIGH

Leigh Jewellery
3 Queens St. WN7 4NQ. (R. Bibby)
Open 9.30-5.30. CL: Wed. STOCK: Jewellery.
TEL: 01942 607947/722509; MOBILE: 07802 833467

MANCHESTER

A.S. Antique Galleries
26 Broad St, Salford. M6 5BY. (A. Sternshine)
Est. 1975. Open Thurs., Fri. and Sat. 10-5.30 or by appointment. STOCK: *Art Nouveau and Art Deco, bronzes, bronze and ivory figures, silver, glass, ceramics, furniture, jewellery, lighting and general antiques.* NOT STOCKED: *Weapons.* LOC: On A6, one mile north of Manchester city centre, next to Salford University College. SER: Valuations; restorations; commission purchasing. SIZE: Large. PARK: Easy.
TEL: 0161 737 5938; MOBILE: 07836 368230
E-MAIL: as@sternshine.demon.co.uk; as@artnouveau-artdeco.com
WEBSITE: www.artnouveau-artdeco.com

Antique Fireplace Warehouse
1090 Stockport Rd, Levenshulme. M19 2SU.
(D. McMullan & Son)
Open 9-6, Sun. 11-5. STOCK: *Fireplaces and architectural items.* PARK: Easy.
TEL: 0161 431 8075; FAX: 0161 431 8084

Antiques Village
The Old Town Hall, 965 Stockport Rd., Levenshulme. M19 3NP.
Est. 1978. Open 10-5, Sun. 11-4. STOCK: *Furniture and clocks, reproduction pine, fireplaces, collectables.* LOC: A6 between Manchester and Stockport. SER: Valuations; restorations; pine stripping. SIZE: 40+ dealers. PARK: Own. FAIRS: Newark.
TEL: 0161 256 4644; FAX: same; MOBILE: 07976 985982

Empire Exchange
1 Newton St., Piccadilly. M1 1HW. (David Ireland)
Est. 1975. Open every day 9-7.30 except Christmas day. STOCK: *General small antiques including silver, pottery, clocks and watches, ephemera, autographs, football memorabilia, records, books and comics, 18th-20th C, £5-£10,000.* LOC: City centre. SER: Valuations. SIZE: Large. PARK: Easy. VAT: Stan/Spec.
TEL: 0161 236 4445; FAX: 0161 273 5007;
MOBILE: 07984 203984
E-MAIL: enquiries@empire-uk.com

Fernlea Antiques SGDS
Failsworth Mill, Ashton Rd West, Failsworth. M35 0FD. (A.J. and Mrs B. McLaughlin)
Est. 1983. Open 10-5. STOCK: *General antiques and shipping goods.* SER: Container packing (worldwide). SIZE: Large. PARK: Easy.
TEL: 0161 682 0589
E-MAIL: fernlea.antiques@btinternet.com

Fulda Gallery Ltd
19 Vine St., Salford. M7 3PG. (M.J. Fulda)
Est. 1969. Open by appointment. STOCK: *Oil paintings,*

1500-1950, £500-£30,000; watercolours, 1800-1930, £350-£10,000. LOC: Near Salford police station off Bury New Rd. SER: Valuations; restorations; buys at auction.
TEL: 0161 792 1962; MOBILE: 07736 444748

In-Situ Manchester
252 Chester Road, Hulme. M15 4EX. (Laurence Green)
Est. 1983. Open irregular hours, prior telephone call advisable. STOCK: *Architectural items including fireplaces, doors, panelling, sanitary ware, radiators, flooring, glass, gardenware, staircasing.* SIZE: Large. PARK: In front of premises.
TEL: 07780 993773
E-MAIL: enquiries@insitumanchester.com
WEBSITE: www.insitumanchester.com

Eric J. Morten
6 Warburton St., Didsbury. M20 6WA.
Est. 1959. Open 10-5.30. STOCK: *Antiquarian books, 16th-20th C, £5-£5,000.* LOC: Off Wilmslow Rd., near traffic lights in Didsbury village. A34. SER: Valuations; buys at auction (antiquarian books). SIZE: Medium. PARK: Easy. FAIRS: PBFA.
TEL: 0161 445 7629 and 01265 277959;
FAX: 0161 448 1323

St. James Antiques
Open by appointment. STOCK: *Jewellery, silver and paintings.*
TEL: 0161 773 4662; MOBILE: 07808 521671

MIDDLETON VILLAGE

G. G. Antique Wholesalers Ltd
Newfield House, Middleton Rd. LA3 3PP.
(G. Goulding)
Est. 1967. *Trade Only.* Open any time by appointment. STOCK: *Shipping goods, £30-£5,000, English and European furniture.* LOC: On main road between Morecambe promenade and Middleton village. SER: Courier; packing; 40ft containers weekly worldwide. SIZE: Large. PARK: Easy. VAT: Stan. No VAT on exported goods.
TEL: 01524 850757; FAX: 01524 851565
E-MAIL: jay@ggantiques.com
WEBSITE: www.ggantique-wholesalers.com

MORECAMBE

Tyson's Antiques Ltd
Clark St. LA4 5HT. (George, Andrew and Shirley Tyson)
Est. 1952. *Trade Only.* Open Sat. 8-11.30, other times by appointment. STOCK: *Georgian, Victorian and Edwardian furniture.* SIZE: Large. PARK: Easy. VAT: Stan/Spec.
TEL: 01524 416763/425235/420098; MOBILE: 07971 836892
E-MAIL: andrew@tysons-antiques.co.uk
WEBSITE: www.tysons-antiques.freeserve.co.uk

Luigino Vescovi
135 Balmoral Rd. LA3 1HJ.
Est. 1970. Open by appointment every day. STOCK:

Georgian and Victorian furniture, inlaid Edwardian and plated ware, £50–£10,000. SIZE: Warehouse. PARK: Easy. VAT: Stan/Spec/Export.
TEL: 01524 416732; MOBILE: 07860 784856

NELSON

Colin Blakey Fireplaces
115 Manchester Rd. BB10 2LS.
EST. 1904. Open 9.30-5, Sun. 12-3.30. *STOCK: Fireplaces and hearth furniture, paintings and prints.* LOC: Exit 12, M65. SER: Manufacturers and suppliers of hand-carved marble fireplaces and hardwood mantels. SIZE: Large. PARK: Opposite. VAT: Stan.
TEL: 01282 614941; FAX: 01282 698511
E-MAIL: cbfireplaces@hotmail.com
WEBSITE: www.colinblakeyfireplaces.co.uk

OLDHAM

The Cavern Antique & Collectors Centre
Failsworth Mill, Ashton Road West. M35 0FD. (Mr. P. Stanley)
Open 10-5, CL: Sat. *STOCK: Furniture, glass, ceramics, kitchenalia, metalware, militaria, architectural* LOC: 1 mile from junc. 22 of the M60. SER: Framing. PARK: Own.
TEL: 0161 684 7802
E-MAIL: akg21353@yahoo.co.uk

Charles Howell Jeweller
2 Lord St. OL1 3EY. (N.G. Howell)
EST. 1870. NAG. Open 9.15-5.15. *STOCK: Edwardian and Victorian jewellery, £25–£2,000; silver, early to mid 20th C, £40–£1,500; watches, Victorian to mid 20th C, £50–£800.* LOC: Town centre, off High St. SER: Valuations; restorations (jewellery and watches); buys at auction. SIZE: Small. PARK: Limited or by arrangement. VAT: Stan/Spec.
FAIRS: Tatton Park; Chepstow Race Course.
TEL: 0161 624 1479

Marks Jewellers and Antique Dealers
16 Waterloo St. OL1 1SQ. (Stuart Tunney)
EST. 1969. Open 9.30-5. *STOCK: General antiques, Victorian and Edwardian jewellery, silver and watches.* LOC: Town centre, off Yorkshire St. SER: Valuations. SIZE: Medium. PARK: Nearby.
TEL: 0161 624 5975

R.J. O'Brien and Son Antiques Ltd
Ground Floor, Emerald House, Daniel St. OL1 3PL. (Ronan O'Brien)
EST. 1970. Open 8.30-4.30, CL: Sat., or by appointment. *STOCK: Furniture, 1620-1950; shipping goods, general antiques and pianos.* LOC: 2 mins. from Oldham town centre off Huddersfield Road, signs A62, if struggling phone and we will send someone to find you! SER: Container and courier service. SIZE: Very large. PARK: Own, 30 spaces. VAT: Stan./Spec./Global.
TEL: 0161 644 4414; MOBILE: 07710 455489

E-MAIL: ob.antiques@btconnect.com
WEBSITE: www.antique-exports.co.uk

H.C. Simpson & Sons Jewellers (Oldham)Ltd
37 High St. OL1 3BA.
Open 9-5.30. *STOCK: Clocks, jewellery, watches.* SER: Restorations (clocks, watches and jewellery).
TEL: 0161 624 7187
E-MAIL: grsimpson@hotmail.co.uk

ORMSKIRK

Alan Grice Antiques
106 Aughton St. L39 3BS.
EST. 1946. Open 10-6. *STOCK: Period furniture.* PARK: Easy.
TEL: 01695 572007

Malthouse Antiques
48 Southport Rd. L39 1QR.
EST. 2007. Open 10-5, prior telephone call advisable. *STOCK: Furniture - pine, mahogany and oak; longcase clocks.* SER: Restorations (longcase clocks). SIZE: Large. PARK: Easy.
TEL: 01695 580731

PRESTON

European Fine Arts and Antiques
10 Cannon St. PR1 3NR. (B. Beck)
EST. 1970. Open 9-5.30. *STOCK: Victorian paintings and furniture, to £8,000; English and Louis XV style reproduction.* LOC: City centre - Fishergate. SER: Valuations; buys at auction. SIZE: 2 floors. PARK: Loading only and nearby. VAT: Stan/Spec.
TEL: 01772 883886
E-MAIL: info@european-fine-arts.co.uk
WEBSITE: www.european-fine-arts.co.uk

Hackler's Jewellers
6b Lune St. PR1 2NL. (N.E. Oldfield)
FBHI. Open 9.30-4.30. CL: Thurs. pm. *STOCK: Silver and clocks.* VAT: Stan.
TEL: 01772 258465

Halewood & Sons
37 Friargate. PR1 2AT.
EST. 1867. ABA. PBFA. CL: Thurs pm. *STOCK: Antiquarian books and maps.*
TEL: 01772 252603
E-MAIL: halewoodandsons@aol.com

Preston Antique Centre
The Mill, New Hall Lane. PR1 5NQ.
Open 9-5, Sat. 10-4, Sun. 11-5. *STOCK: General antiques, Georgian-Edwardian; shipping furniture; shipping, Dutch, Italian and French furniture; collectables and longcase clocks.* LOC: 1 mile from exit 31 M6. SIZE: Large - 40+ dealers. PARK: Own.
TEL: 01772 794498; FAX: 01772 651694
E-MAIL: prestonantiques@talk21.com
WEBSITE: www.prestonantiquescentre.com.

BRITISH ARTISTS 1880-1940

An Antique Collectors' Club Research Project listing 41,000 Artists

Unlikely to be challenged as the standard work on the subject, *British Artists 1880-1940* includes entries for a staggering 41,000 British artists who exhibited at forty-nine of the major exhibition centres and commercial galleries throughout England, Scotland, Wales and Ireland between the years 1880-1940. The arrangement of names is alphabetical to make it as easy as possible to find the artist; where dates of birth and/or death dates are unknown, the first and last year of exhibiting has been used. The date the artist became a member of a society has been included as well as the address.

279 x 216 mm. 476 pp **£45.00 Hardback**

Preston Book Co
68 Friargate. PR1 2ED. (M. Halewood)
EST. 1950. Open 10.30-5.30. STOCK: *Large stock of antiquarian books.* LOC: Town centre. SER: Buys at auction. PARK: Easy.
TEL: 01772 252613
E-MAIL: books@mhhalewood.wanadoo.co.uk

RAMSBOTTOM

Somewhere in Time
257 Bolton Road North, Stubbins. BL0 0SA (Pauline and Steven Morgan)
EST. 2006. Open 8.30-6, Sun. 1-5. STOCK: *Furniture, Art Deco clocks and figurines, Majolica, architectural salvage items, vintage linen, lace and accessories.* LOC: Stubbins Estate. SER: House clearances; nation-wide delivery. SIZE: Medium. PARK: Outside shop.
TEL: 01706 828100
E-MAIL: stevemorgan257@btinternet.com
WEBSITE: www.somewhereintime.co.uk

RIBCHESTER

Brunswick Gallery   LAPADA
Bee Mill, Preston Rd. PR3 3XL. (Mr E Lomax)
Open by appointment. STOCK: *Fine watercolours and oil paintings.*

TEL: **01254 878086**
E-MAIL: **enquiries@brunswickgallery.co.uk**
WEBSITE: **www.brunswickgallery.co.uk**

ROCHDALE

Antiques and Bygones
100 Drake St. OL16 1PQ. (K. and E. Bonn)
EST. 1983. Open 10-2 Weds. and Fri. STOCK: *Pottery, coins and medals, jewellery, 19th-20th C, £5-£100.* SIZE: Small.
TEL: 01706 648114

SABDEN

Walter Aspinall Antiques Ltd
Pendle Antiques Centre, Union Mill, Watt St. BB7 9ED.
EST. 1964. Open 9-5, Sat. and Sun. 11-4 or by appointment. STOCK: *Furniture and bric-a-brac.* LOC: On Pendle Hill between Clitheroe and Padiham. SER: Export; packing; courier; containers; wholesale. SIZE: Large. PARK: Easy. VAT: Stan.
TEL: 01282 778642; FAX: 01282 778643
E-MAIL: beryl@a1waa.com

Pendle Antiques Centre Ltd
Union Mill, Watt St. BB7 9ED. (B. Seed and J.L. Billington)
EST. 1993. Open 10-5, Sun. 11-5 (other times by appointment for Trade). STOCK: *Furniture and bric-a-brac.* LOC: Over Pendle Hill, off the A59 between Clitheroe and Padiham. SER: Full packing and courier service. SIZE: 10 dealers. PARK: Ample. VAT: Stan./Spec.
TEL: 01282 776311; FAX: 01282 778643
E-MAIL: sales@pendleantiquescentre.co.uk
WEBSITE: www.pendleantiquescentre.co.uk

SAMLESBURY

Samlesbury Hall
(Dating from 1325). Preston New Rd. PR5 0UP.
(Samlesbury Hall Trust)
EST. 1969. Open 11-4.30. Admission - adults £3, children £1. CL: Sat. STOCK: *General collectable antiques.* LOC: Exit 31, M6 on A677 between Preston and Blackburn. SIZE: Large. PARK: Easy and free. FAIRS: Craft Exhibitions.
TEL: 01254 812010/812229
WEBSITE: www.samlesburyhall.co.uk

STANDISH

Colin de Rouffignac
234A Almond Brook Rd. WN6 0SS.
EST. 1972. BNTA. Open 10-4.30. CL: Wed. STOCK: *Furniture, jewellery, oils and watercolours.* LOC: Half a mile from Exit 27 of the M6. PARK: Easy.
TEL: 01257 425278
WEBSITE: www.standishantiques.co.uk

TRAWDEN

Jack Moore Antiques and Stained Glass
The Old Rock, Keighley Rd. BB8 8RW. (Jack Moore
and Connie Hartley)
EST. 1976. Open 10-4 or by appointment. CL: Sat.
STOCK: *Stained glass.* SER: Restoration and manufacture
of stained glass; container packing; courier. SIZE:
Medium. PARK: Easy. VAT: Stan.
TEL: 01282 869478; HOME: same; FAX: 01282 865193;
MOBILE: 07802 331594

WHALLEY

Edmund Davies & Son Antiques
32 King St. BB7 9SL. (E. and P. Davies)
EST. 1960. Open 10-5. STOCK: *Oak and country furniture,
longcase clocks, to £15,000; sets of rush seated chairs.* NOT
STOCKED: *Reproductions.* LOC: A59 (11 miles from M6).
SER: Restorations (longcase clocks). SIZE: Medium +
trade warehouse. PARK: Easy. VAT: Stan/Spec.
TEL: 01254 823764
E-MAIL: philipbryn@aol.com
WEBSITE: www.daviesantiques.com

WIGAN

John Robinson Antiques
172-176 Manchester Rd., Higher Ince. WN2 2EA.
EST. 1965. *Export and Trade Only.* Open any time.
STOCK: *General antiques.* LOC: A577 near Ince Bar. SER:
Export packing. SIZE: Large. PARK: Easy. VAT: Stan.
TEL: 01942 247773/241671; MOBILE: 07767 826393

WORSLEY

Northern Clocks LAPADA
**Boothsbank Farm, Leigh Rd. M28 1LL. (R.M. and
M.A. Love)**
EST. 1998. **Open by appointment.** STOCK: *Longcase,
bracket and wall clocks, 17th-19th C.* LOC: **Off junction
13, M60.** SER: Valuations; restorations. SIZE: **Large.**
PARK: **Easy.** VAT: **Stan.**
TEL: **0161 790 8414;** HOME: **same;**
MOBILE: **07970 820258**
E-MAIL: **info@northernclocks.co.uk**
WEBSITE: **www.northernclocks.co.uk**

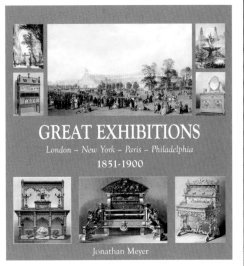

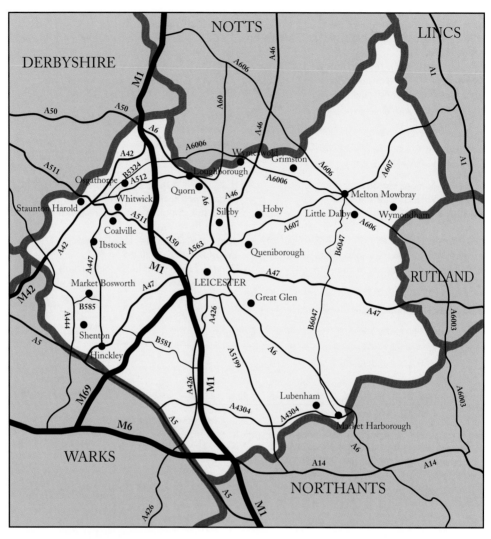

COALVILLE

Keystone Antiques
66 London Rd. LE67 3JA. (I. and H. McPherson)
EST. 1979. FGA. Open Thurs., Fri. and Sat. 10-5, Mon.
and Tues. by appointment. *STOCK: Jewellery, Victorian
and Georgian, £25-£1,500; silver, 1700-1920, £20-£500;
small collectable items, 18th-19th C, £15-£300; cranberry,
needlework tools, Victorian and Georgian table glass.* LOC:
A511 outskirts of town. SER: Valuations (jewellery); gem
testing. SIZE: Small. PARK: In front of shop.
TEL: 01530 835966
E-MAIL: keystone@heathermcpherson.co.uk

GREAT GLEN

Sitting Pretty
45a Main St. LE8 9GH. (Jennifer Jones-Fenleigh)
EST. 1979. Open Thurs., Fri. and Sat. 10-5.30, other
days by appointment. *STOCK: Upholstered furniture, 18th-
20th C, £50-£1,000.* LOC: Off A6. SER: Valuations;
restorations (re-upholstery, French polishing, caning and
rushing). PARK: Easy. VAT: Spec.
TEL: 0116 259 3711; HOME: same

GRIMSTON

Ancient & Oriental Ltd
Parkview LE14 3BZ. (A. Szolin)
ADA. Open by appointment. *STOCK: Ancient Egyptian,
Greek, Roman, Celtic, Saxon, Pre-Columbian and medieval
antiquities.* SER: Valuations; illustrated catalogues (4 per
year). SIZE: Medium. PARK: Easy.
TEL: MOBILE: 07946 385215; FAX: 01664 810087
E-MAIL: alex@antiquities.co.uk
WEBSITE: www.antiquities.co.uk

HINCKLEY

House Things Antiques
Trinity Lane, 44 Mansion St. LE10 0AU. (P.W. Robertson)
EST. 1976. Open 10-6. STOCK: *Stripped pine, satinwood, oak and walnut, mainly Victorian and Edwardian, £50-£600; small collectors' items, 1860-1960s, £5-£100; cast-iron fireplaces, brass and iron beds, 1890-1920s, £50-£1,000; garden items.* LOC: Inner ring road. SER: Valuations; restorations. SIZE: Small. PARK: Easy.
TEL: 01455 618518; HOME: 01455 212797

HOBY

Withers of Leicester
The Old Rutland, Church Lane. LE14 3DU. (S. Frings)
EST. 1860. Open 9-5.30. STOCK: *Furniture, 17th-19th C, £50-£3,000; china, 18th-19th C, £10-£300; oil paintings, 19th C, £5-£500.* NOT STOCKED: *Jewellery and coins.* SER: Valuations; restorations (furniture). SIZE: Medium. PARK: Easy. VAT: Stan/Spec.
TEL: 01664 434803

IBSTOCK

Mandrake Stevenson Antiques
103 High St. LE67 6LJ.
EST. 1979. Open 10-5. CL: Sat. STOCK: *Furniture, pre-1930s.* SER: Valuations; restorations (furniture). SIZE: Small. PARK: Easy. FAIRS: Newark.
TEL: 01530 260898/450132

LEICESTER

Britain's Heritage Ltd
Shaftesbury Hall, 3 Holy Bones. LE1 4LJ. (Mr and Mrs J. Dennis)
EST. 1980. NFA. Open 9.30-5.30, Sat. 9.30-5. STOCK: *Fireplaces, 18th-21st C, £100-£25,000.* LOC: Off Vaughan Way, 70 yards from Holiday Inn. SER: Valuations; restorations (antique fireplaces). SIZE: Large. PARK: Own. VAT: Stan/Spec.
TEL: 0116 251 9592; FAX: 0116 262 5990
E-MAIL: info@britainsheritage.co.uk
WEBSITE: www.britainsheritage.co.uk

Clarendon Books
144 Clarendon Park Rd. LE2 3AE. (Julian Smith)
EST. 1984. PBFA. Open 10-5. STOCK: *Antiquarian and second-hand books, £1-£1,000.* LOC: Between London Rd. (A6) and Welford Rd. (A50), 2 miles south of city centre. SER: Valuations; restorations; repairs; binding; buys at auction (books and maps). SIZE: Small. PARK: Easy. FAIRS: London HD; PBFA.
TEL: 0116 270 1856; HOME: 0116 270 1914;
MOBILE: 07845 211689
E-MAIL: clarendonbooks@aol.com

Corry's Antiques
24 Francis St., Stoneygate. LE2 2BD. (Mrs E.I. Corry)
EST. 1962 Open 10-5. STOCK: *Furniture, 18th-19th C, £500-£10,000; paintings, 19th C, £100-£8,000; silver, porcelain, 18th-20th C, £5-£5,000.* SER: Furniture, porcelain and glass restoration. SIZE: Medium. PARK: On street. VAT: Spec.
TEL: 0116 270 3794; MOBILE: 07989 427411
E-MAIL: timothy-warr@tiscali.co.uk
WEBSITE: www.corrys-antiques.com

Michael D. Long
86 Ireton Rd. LE4 9ET.
EST. 1970. Open by appointment. STOCK: *Arms and armour of all ages and nations.* PARK: Easy. VAT: Stan/Spec.
TEL: 08452 601910
E-MAIL: sales@michaeldlong.com
WEBSITE: www.michaeldlong.com

LITTLE DALBY

Treedale Antiques
Little Dalby Hall, Pickwell Lane. LE14 2XB. (G.K. Warren)
EST. 1972. GMC. Open 9-5, Sat. and Sun. by appointment. STOCK: *Furniture including walnut, mahogany and oak, from 1680; paintings; chandeliers. Up to £20,000.* SER: Valuations; restorations (furniture and chandeliers). Workshop at 103 Mill St., Oakham, Rutland. SIZE: Workshop, showroom and shop. PARK: Own.
TEL: 01664 454535; WORKSHOP: 01572 757521

LOUGHBOROUGH

Loughborough Antiques
5 Ashby Square LE11 5AA. (Richard Wesley)
EST. 1979. Open 10-5. CL: Mon. & Wed. STOCK: *Jewellery, silver, clocks.* SIZE: Small.
TEL: 01509 239931

Lowe of Loughborough
37-40 Church Gate. LE11 1UE.
EST. 1846. Open 9-5.30. CL: Sat. STOCK: *Furniture and period upholstery from early oak, 1600 to Edwardian; mahogany, walnut, oak, £20-£8,000; clocks, bracket and longcase, £95-£2,500; maps, copper and brass.* NOT STOCKED: *Jewellery.* LOC: Opposite parish church. SER: Upholstery; restorations; interior design. SIZE: Large - 16 showrooms. PARK: Own. VAT: Stan/Spec.
TEL: 01509 212554/217876

LUBENHAM

Oaktree Antiques
The Draper's House, Main St. LE16 9TF. (Gillian Abraham and John Wright)
Open Wed.-Sun. 10-6. STOCK: *Town and country furniture, 17th-19th C; longcase clocks and barometers,*

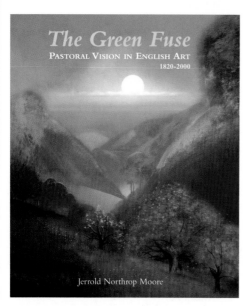
Georgian to early Victorian; works of art. Loc: A4304, 1 mile west of Market Harborough. SIZE: Medium. PARK: Opposite on village green. VAT: Spec.
TEL: 01858 410041; MOBILE: 07710 205696
E-MAIL: gillian@oaktreeantiques.co.uk
WEBSITE: www.oaktreeantiques.co.uk

Stevens and Son
61 Main St. LE16 9TF. (M.J. Stevens)
EST. 1977. Resident. Open 10-5. *STOCK: General antiques, mainly furniture.* Loc: A4304 via junction 20 M1. SER: Restorations (furniture).
TEL: 01858 463521

MARKET BOSWORTH

P. Stanworth (Fine Arts)
The Grange, 2 Barton Rd. CV13 0LQ. (Mr and Mrs G. and James Stanworth)
EST. 1965. Resident. Open by appointment. *STOCK: Oil paintings and watercolours, 18th to early 20th C.* Loc: Road just off town square. SIZE: Medium. PARK: Easy. VAT: Spec.
TEL: 01455 291023; FAX: 01455 291767
E-MAIL: james@stanworth116.freeserve.co.uk

MARKET HARBOROUGH

Coughton Galleries Ltd
The Old Manor, Arthingworth. LE16 8JT. (Lady Isabel Throckmorton)
EST. 1968. Open Wed., Thurs., Sat., Sun. and Bank Holidays 10.30-5 or by appointment. *STOCK: Modern British and Irish oil paintings and watercolours, mainly Royal Academicians.* SIZE: Medium. PARK: Easy. VAT: Spec.
TEL: 01858 525436; FAX: 01858 525535

Graftons of Market Harborough
92 St Mary's Rd. LE16 7DX. (F. Ingall)
EST. 1967. Open Mon., Tues., Fri. and Sat. 10-5.30, other times by appointment. *STOCK: Oils, watercolours, etchings and engravings, 18th-early 20th C.* PARK: Forecourt. FAIRS: Burghley Horse Trials.
TEL: 01858 433557

Walter Moores and Son   LAPADA
PO Box 5338. LE16 7WG. (Peter Moores)
EST. 1925. Open by appointment. *STOCK: Georgian furniture; complementary Victorian items.* **VAT: Spec.**
FAIRS: Most major.
TEL: 07071 226202; FAX: same; MOBILE: 07710 019045
E-MAIL: waltermoores@btinternet.com
WEBSITE: www.waltermoores.co.uk

OSGATHORPE

David E. Burrows   LAPADA
Manor House Farm. LE12 9SY.
EST. **1973. Open by appointment.** STOCK: *Pine, oak, mahogany and walnut furniture, clocks, £100–£10,000.* LOC: **Junction 23, M1, turn right off Ashby road after 4.5 miles, farm next to church or off A42.** SIZE: **Large.** PARK: **Easy.** VAT: **Stan/Spec.**
TEL: **01530 222218;** MOBILE: **07702 059030**
E-MAIL: **dburrows@btconnect.com**

QUENIBOROUGH

J. Green and Son
1 Coppice Lane. LE7 3DR. (R. Green)
EST. 1932. Resident. Appointment advisable. STOCK: *18th-19th C English and Continental furniture.* LOC: Off A607 Leicester to Melton Mowbray Rd. SER: Valuations; buys at auction. SIZE: Medium. PARK: Easy. VAT: Stan/Spec.
TEL: 0116 2606682
E-MAIL: jgreen.antiques@btinternet.com

QUORN

The Quorn Furniture Co.
The New Mills, Leicester Rd. LE12 8ES. (S. Yates)
EST. 1982. Open 9-5.30, Sat. 9.30-5.30, Sun. 2-5. STOCK: *Pine and country furniture.* SER: Stripping and restorations (pine). SIZE: Large. PARK: Own. VAT: Stan/Spec.
TEL: 01509 416031
WEBSITE: www.quornfurniture.co.uk

SHENTON

Whitemoors Antiques and Fine Art
Mill Lane. CV13 6BZ. (D. Dolby and P. McGowan)

EST. 1987. Open 11-4, (until 5 in summer), Sat. and Sun. 11-5. STOCK: *Furniture, £25–£2,000; smalls, £5–£200; prints and pictures, Victorian to early 20th C, £40–£400.* LOC: A5 onto A444 towards Burton-on-Trent, first right then second left. SIZE: Large - 20+ unit holders. PARK: Easy.
TEL: 01455 212250; 01455 212981 (ansaphone); FAX: 01455 213342

SILEBY

R. A. James Antiques
Ammonite Gallery, 25 High St. LE12 7RX.
STOCK: *Mainly stripped pine, general antiques.*
TEL: 01509 812169; MOBILE: 07713 132650

WHITWICK

Charles Antiques
Dial House, 34 Cadman St. LE67 5AE. (Brian Haydon)
EST. 1970. Open anytime by appointment. STOCK: *Clocks, 18th C, £25–£4,000; furniture, 19th C, £50–£1,000; china.* LOC: A511. SER: Buys at auction. SIZE: Small. PARK: Easy. VAT: Stan/Spec.
TEL: 01530 836932; HOME: same; MOBILE: 07831 204406
E-MAIL: charles.antiques@btopenworld.com

WYMONDHAM

Old Bakery Antiques
Main St. LE14 2AG. (Tina Bryan)
EST. 1990. Open 10-5.30, Sun. 12-5. CL: Thurs. STOCK: *Cottage, garden, architectural and reclamation items including pine furniture, kitchenalia, advertising items, chimney pots, stained glass, doors and door hardware, tiles, rural and domestic bygones.* SIZE: Medium. PARK: Easy.
TEL: 01572 787472; HOME: same

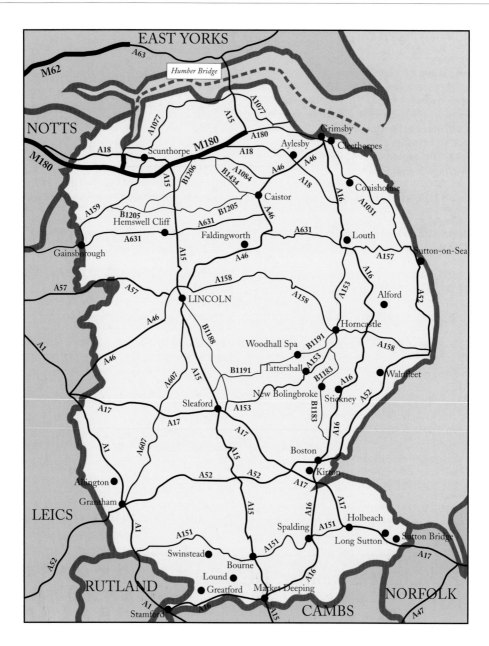

ALFORD

Town & Country Antiques Centre
7-8 West St. LN13 9DG. (Melvin Pashley)
Open 10-4.30 including Sun. STOCK: *Period furniture, rustic pine, kitchenalia, porcelain and china, garden and architectural antiques, decorative items.* LOC: *Main street.*
SER: *Valuations.* PARK: *Limited.*
TEL: 01507 466953; FAX: same;
WEBSITE: www.townandcountryantiques.biz

Trade Antiques
5 High St. LN13 9DS. (P.E. Poole)
EST. 1961. *Trade Only.* CL: Sat. STOCK: *General shipping goods, clocks and watches.* SIZE: Medium. PARK: Easy.
TEL: 01507 462854

ALLINGTON

Garth Vincent Antique Arms and Armour   LAPADA
The Old Manor House. NG32 2DH.
EST. 1979. Open by appointment. STOCK: *Militaria*

including firearms, swords, rapiers and daggers; armour, 16th-19th C, £50-£100,000. LOC: **Opposite church.** SER: **Valuations; restorations; buys at auction.** SIZE: **Medium.** PARK: **Easy.** VAT: **Spec.** FAIRS: **London and major city Arms; NEC (Aug).**
TEL: **01400 281358;** HOME: **same;** FAX: **01400 282658;**
MOBILE: **07785 352151**
E-MAIL: **garthvincent@aol.com**
WEBSITE: **www.guns.uk.com**

AYLESBY

Robin Fowler (Period Clocks)
Washing Dales, Washing Dales Lane. DN37 7LH.
(M.R. Fowler)
EST. 1968. Open by appointment. STOCK: *Clocks, barometers and scientific instruments, 17th-19th C.* SER: Restorations (clocks and barometers). SIZE: Large. PARK: Easy. VAT: Spec. FAIRS: LAPADA; Bailey; Galloway.
TEL: 01472 751335
E-MAIL: periodclocks@washingdales.fsnet.co.uk
WEBSITE: www.antiquenet.com/robinfowler

BOSTON

Portobello Row Antique & Collectors' Centre
93-95 High St. PE21 8TA.
EST. 1982. Open 10-4. STOCK: *Shipping furniture, kitchenalia, blue and white china, 1940s-1970s clothing, bric-a-brac.* SIZE: 9 dealers.
TEL: 01205 368692

BOURNE

Bourne Antiques & Art
44 West St. PE10 9NX. (R.A. and Mrs J.M. Warner)
EST. 1999. Open 10-5, Sun. 11-4. CL: Tues. and Wed.
STOCK: *Wide range of general antiques including silver, porcelain and glass, maps and prints, jewellery, clocks, £5-£1,000+.* LOC: Close to town centre. SER: Valuations.
SIZE: Medium. PARK: Own.
TEL: 01778 394725
E-MAIL: bournean@gotadsl.co.uk

A.L. Thompson, Antique Trader
The Willows, Swallow Hill, Thurlby. PE10 0JB. (A.L. Thompson)
EST. 1962. Open by appointment. STOCK: *Furniture - antique, Victorian, Edwardian, shipping, oak, reproduction, £50-£5,000.* LOC: On A15. SER: Valuations. SIZE: Large.
PARK: Own. VAT: Spec/Global. FAIRS: Newark; Ardingly.
TEL: 01778 421759; MOBILE: 07885 694299

CAISTOR

Caistor Antiques
12 High St. LN7 6TX. (Susan Rutter)
EST. 1982. Open by appointment day or night. STOCK:

Pottery, furniture, jewellery, dolls, linen, silver, 18th-20th C, and much more. LOC: Off A46 between Grimsby and Market Rasen. SER: Valuations. PARK: Own. FAIRS: Swinderby; Newark; Lincoln Show Ground.
TEL: 01472 851975; HOME: same

CLEETHORPES

Yesterday's Antiques
86 Grimsby Rd. DN35 7DP. (Jeanette and Norman Bishop)
EST. 1983. Resident. Open 9-5, Sun. by appointment.
STOCK: *Furniture, £50-£2,000; fireplaces, £500-£1,000; French beds, clocks, £300-£1,200; all 19th C; jewellery, classic motor cycles.* LOC: A180 on right entering town, opposite HTS Cars. SER: Valuations; restorations (polishing and stripping); repairs (clocks); renovations (fireplaces). SIZE: Large. PARK: Easy.
TEL: 01472 343020/504093
E-MAIL: norman.bishop8@googlemail.com

CONISHOLME

A Barn Full of Brass Beds
The Farmhouse, Ashleigh Farm, Main Rd. LN11 7LS.
(J.J. Tebbs)
EST. 1985. Open by appointment. STOCK: *Brass and iron beds, 1860-1910, from £250.* LOC: 10 miles N.E. of Louth. SER: Restorations; bespoke bases and mattresses.
SIZE: Large. PARK: Easy. VAT: Stan.
TEL: 01507 358092
E-MAIL: brassbeds@dsl.pipex.com
WEBSITE: www.brassandironbeds.co.uk;
www.princessandthepea.co.uk

GAINSBOROUGH

Stanley Hunt Jewellers Ltd
26 Marshalls Yard, Beaumont St. DN21 2NA. (R.S. Hunt)
EST. 1952. Open 9-5.30, Sat. 9-5, Sun. 11-4. STOCK: *Antique and modern jewellery.* SER: Valuations; restorations (gold, silver, clocks). SIZE: Medium.
TEL: 01427 613051
WEBSITE: www.stanleyhuntjewellers.co.uk

Pilgrims Antiques Centre
66 Church St. DN21 2JR. (Michael Wallis)
EST. 1986. CL: Mon. and Wed. STOCK: *Jewellery, miniatures, silver, silhouettes, paintings, textiles, ceramics and books, £5-£1,000; furniture, £50-£1,000.* LOC: Near Old Hall. SER: Valuations. SIZE: Large. PARK: Easy.
FAIRS: Newark; Birmingham.
TEL: 01427 810897
E-MAIL: pilgrimsdn212jr@tiscali.co.uk

GRANTHAM

Grantham Clocks
30 Lodge Way. NG31 8DD. (R. Conder)

EST. 1987 Resident. Open by appointment. *STOCK: Clocks.* PARK: Easy.
TEL: 01476 561784

Notions Antiques Centre
1 Market Place. NG31 6LQ. (Mr and Mrs L. Checkley)
EST. 1984. Open 10-5, Sat. 9.30-5, Sun. 11-4. *STOCK: Furniture, ceramics, pictures, jewellery, silver, clocks, books, toys, architectural fittings, railwayana and enamel signs.* LOC: Down from Angel and Royal Hotel. SER: Valuations. SIZE: 35+ dealers. PARK: Easy. FAIRS: Newark.
TEL: 01476 563603; MOBILE: 07736 677978
E-MAIL: scheckley@fsbdial.co.uk
WEBSITE: www.notionsantiques.com

GRIMSBY

Bell Antiques
68 Harold St. DN32 7NQ. (V. Hawkey)
EST. 1964. Open by appointment, telephone previous evening. *STOCK: Grandfather clocks, barometers and furniture. NOT STOCKED: Reproduction.* SIZE: Medium. PARK: Easy. VAT: Stan/Spec. FAIRS: Newark.
TEL: 01472 695110; HOME: same

HEMSWELL CLIFF

Astra House Antiques Centre
Old RAF Hemswell. DN21 5TL. (Barry Aucott)
EST. 1987. Open 10-5 including Sun. *STOCK: Wide variety of general antiques and shipping goods, including Victorian, Edwardian and Continental furniture and smalls.* LOC: Near Caenby Corner Roundabout A15/A631. SIZE: Large - 90 dealers. PARK: Own.
TEL: 01427 668312; FAX: same; MOBILE: 07768 626786
E-MAIL: astraantiques@hotmail.com
WEBSITE: www.astra-antiques.co.uk

Hemswell Antique Centres
Caenby Corner Estate. DN21 5TJ. (Robert and Jonathon Miller)
EST. 1986. Open 10-5 including Sun. *STOCK: Period furniture, 17th-19th C; watercolours and oils, 19th C; silver and plate, clocks, porcelain, china, jewellery, books, prints, linen and pine.* LOC: A15 from Lincoln then A631 towards Gainsborough, 1 mile from roundabout, follow signs. SER: Delivery. SIZE: 270+ dealers. PARK: Easy.
TEL: 01427 668389; FAX: 01427 668935
E-MAIL: info@hemswell-antiques.com
WEBSITE: www.hemswell-antiques.com

HORNCASTLE

G. Baker Antiques
16 South St. LN9 6DX.
EST. 1973. Open 9-5, Wed. 9-1, Sun. by appointment. STOCK: *Furniture, 18th-20th C, £10-£10,000; grandfather clocks £500-£5,000.* LOC: A153. SER: Valuations; restorations (furniture). SIZE: Small. PARK: Easy. FAIRS: Swinderby; Newark.
TEL: 01507 526553; MOBILE: 07767 216264
E-MAIL: geoffbaker100@aol.com
WEBSITE: www.gbrestorations.co.uk

Clare Boam
22-38 North St. LN9 5DX.
EST. 1977. Open 9-5, Sun. and BH 2-4.30. STOCK: *Furniture and bric-a-brac, 19th-20th C, to £1,000.* LOC: Louth/Grimsby road out of town. SIZE: Large. PARK: Easy. VAT: Global. FAIRS: Swinderby.
TEL: 01507 522381; HOME: same
E-MAIL: clareboam@btconnect.com
WEBSITE: www.greatexpectationshorncastle.co.uk

Drill Hall Antiques
The Old Drill Hall, 48 South St. LN9 6EF. (Mrs V.A. Ginn)
EST. 2004. Open 10-4.30, Sun. 1-4, Bank Holidays 11-4. STOCK: *Pre-1949 silver, jewellery and watches, furniture, paintings and prints, glass, treen and ceramics, lighting and linen, decorative items, kitchenalia and more.* LOC: 200 yards from main crossroads on A153 Sleaford. SIZE: Medium. PARK: Easy. FAIRS: Swinderby, Newark.
TEL: 01507 525370

The Horncastle Antiques Centre
26 Bridge St. LN9 5HZ. (Mrs Patricia Carlton-Sims)
EST. 1981. Open 10-5, Sun. 1-4. STOCK: *Furniture, from 18th C oak and country; ceramics, kitchenalia, French interiors and textiles, Art Nouveau, Art and Crafts and Art Deco items, Georgian to Edwardian silver, paintings, clocks, prints and mirrors, English pine, books stamps, postcards, Dinky toys and lead soldiers, militaria and ephemera, Victorian jewellery, trinkets, curios and collectables.* LOC: Town centre. SER: Restorations (clocks, furniture); upholstery and repolishing; worldwide shipping. SIZE: Large - over 70 dealers. PARK: Easy.
TEL: 01507 527777
E-MAIL: horncastleantiques@hotmail.com
WEBSITE: www.horncastleantiquescentre.com

Great Expectations
37-43 East St. LN9 6AZ. (Clare Boam)
EST. 1977. Open 9-5, Sun. and Bank Holidays 1-4.30. STOCK: *Wide variety of general antiques including pine, oak, mahogany, kitchenalia, luggage, books, china, glass, collectables, 50p to £1,000.* LOC: A158, 100 yards from traffic lights. SIZE: Large. PARK: At rear or in Trinity Centre. FAIRS: Sunderby.
TEL: 01507 524202; HOME: 01507 522381

E-MAIL: clareboam@btconnect.com
WEBSITE: www.greatexpectationshorncastle.co.uk

Seaview Antiques
Stanhope Rd. LN9 5DG. (M. Chalk and Tracey Collins)
EST. 1975. Open 9-5 most days. Prior telephone call advisable if travelling far. STOCK: *Victorian, Edwardian and decorative furniture; smalls, brassware, silver and plate, lamps, boxes.* LOC: A158. SIZE: Large + warehouse. PARK: Easy. FAIRS: Newark.
TEL: 01507 524524
WEBSITE: www.seaviewantiques.co.uk

Laurence Shaw Antiques
77 East St. LN9 6AA. (L.D. Shaw)
EST. 1971. Open 8.30-5, prior telephone call advisable. STOCK: *Furniture, china, glass, metalware, books, collectables, general antiques, 17th-20th C.* LOC: Opposite Trinity Church. SER: Consultant; valuations. SIZE: Medium. VAT: Global/Spec.
TEL: 01507 527638

The Trinity Centre
East St. LN9 5DX. (Clare Boam)
EST. 2002. Open Mon.-Fri. 9-5, Sun. and Bank Holidays 1-4.30. STOCK: *Furniture, china, glass, jewellery, linen, silver and collectables.* LOC: In the Holy Trinity Church - Skegness road out of town. SIZE: Large. PARK: Own. FAIRS: Swinderby.
TEL: 01507 525256
E-MAIL: clareboam@btconnect.com

Alan Read - Period Furniture
60 & 62 West St. LN9 5AD.
EST. 1981. Open 10-4.30. CL: Mon. and Wed. except by appointment. STOCK: *17th-19th C furniture, early oak, walnut and decorative items.* LOC: A158 Lincoln to Skegness road, at junction with B1191 Woodhall Spa road. SER: Valuations; bespoke copies; interior design; restoration. SIZE: Large. PARK: Easy. VAT: Stan/Spec.
TEL: 01507 524324; HOME: 01507 525548; MOBILE: 07778 873838
E-MAIL: tworeads@btinternet.com

KIRTON

Kirton Antiques
3 High St. PE20 1DR. (Alan Marshall)
EST. 1973. Open 8.30-5, Sat. 8.30-12 or by appointment. STOCK: *Furniture, all periods; painted pine, chairs, decorative items, glass, metal, pottery, china, picture frames.* SER: Valuations. SIZE: Large - warehouse. PARK: Own.
TEL: 01205 722595; EVENINGS 01205 722134; MOBILE: 07860 531600
E-MAIL: kirtonantiques@btconnect.com

LINCOLN

Annette Antiques & Collectables
77 Bailgate. LN1 3AR. (Mrs A. Bhalla)
EST. 1972. Open Tues.-Sat. 2-6. STOCK: *Porcelain, glass and small silver, 19th-20th C; silver flatware, watercolours, prints and drawings, 18th-20th C, £10-£500; collectables, including doll's houses, furniture and accessories.* LOC: 2 mins. from castle and cathedral. SER: Restorations (furniture). SIZE: Small. PARK: Nearby.
TEL: 07879 656332

C. and K.E. Dring
111 High St. LN5 7PY.
EST. 1977. Open 10-5.30. CL: Wed. STOCK: *Victorian and Edwardian inlaid furniture; shipping goods, porcelain, clocks, musical boxes, tin-plated toys, trains and Dinky.* PARK: Opposite.
TEL: 01522 540733/792794

Golden Goose Books and Globe Restorers, Harlequin Gallery
20-22 Steep Hill. LN2 1LT. (R. West-Skinn and Mrs A. Cockram)
EST. 1983. PBFA. Open 10-5.30. STOCK: *Antiquarian and secondhand books, maps and prints.* SER: Restorations (globes and philosophical instruments). SIZE: Large. PARK: Nearby.
TEL: 01522 522589
E-MAIL: yasanna@fsmail.net

David J. Hansord & Son   BADA
6 & 7 Castle Hill. LN1 3AA. (David, John and Anne Hansord)
EST. 1972. Open Thurs.-Sat. 10-5, other times by appointment. STOCK: *Furniture, clocks, barometers, works of art, 18th C, £50-£50,000.* LOC: **In square between cathedral and castle.** SER: **Valuations; restorations (furniture, barometers and clocks); buys at auction.** SIZE: **Large.** PARK: **Castle Hill.** VAT: **Spec.** FAIRS: **Olympia (June, Nov).**
TEL: **01522 530044;** FAX: **same;** MOBILE: **07831 183511**
E-MAIL: **info@hansord.com**
WEBSITE: **www.hansord.com**

Dorrian Lambert Antiques Centre
64, 65 Steep Hill. LN1 1YN. (R. Lambert)
EST. 1981. Open 10-5, Sun. in summer. STOCK: *Small furniture, clocks, chairs, pottery, porcelain, jewellery, books, sporting antiques, books and collectables, 18th to early 20th C.* SER: Valuations; restorations (clocks). SIZE: Medium - 15 dealers. PARK: Loading only or nearby.
TEL: 01522 545916; HOME: 01427 848686

Mansions
5a Eastgate. LN2 1QA. (J. A. Wigham)
EST. 1989. Open 10-5. STOCK: *General antiques, decorative items, period lighting.* LOC: Opposite White Hart Hotel. PARK: Limited and nearby.
TEL: 01522 513631; MOBILE: 07762 403863

Rowletts of Lincoln
338 High St. LN5 7DQ. (A.H. and P.L. Rowlett)
EST. 1965. Open 9-5. STOCK: *Antique and secondhand jewellery.* VAT: Global/Margin.
TEL: 01522 524139; FAX: 01522 523427

Timepiece Repairs
43 Steep Hill. LN2 1LU. (R. Ellis)
EST. 1978. FBHI. Open Sat. 10-4, other times by appointment. STOCK: *Clocks and watches, 18th-20th C, £10-£8,000; barometers, 19th-20th C, £100-£1,500.* LOC: Near cathedral. SER: Valuations; restorations (movements, dials and cases). SIZE: Small. PARK: 100 metres. VAT: Stan/Spec.
TEL: 01522 525831; HOME: 01522 881790
WEBSITE: www.timepiecerepairs.com

James Usher & Son Ltd
incorporating John Smith & Son, 26 & 27 Guildhall St. LN1 1TR.
EST. 1837. Open 9-5.30. STOCK: *Antique silver and jewellery.* SER: Valuations.
TEL: 01522 527547 or 01522 523120
E-MAIL: info@jamesusher.co.uk
WEBSITE: www.jamesusher.co.uk

LOUTH

Old Maltings Antique Centre
38 Aswell St. LN11 9HP. (Norman and Margaret Coffey)
EST. 1980. Open 10-4.30, Sat. 10-5. STOCK: *Furniture including Victorian and Edwardian, collectables, ceramics, glass, jewellery.* LOC: 2 mins. walk from town centre. SER: Valuations; restorations; stripping (pine). SIZE: Large - over 40 cabinets. PARK: Easy. FAIRS: Swinderby.
TEL: 01507 600366
WEBSITE: www.antiques-atlas.com

MARKET DEEPING

Portland House Antiques
23 Church St. PE6 8AN. (G.W. Cree and V.E. Bass)
EST. 1987. Open Mon.-Sat. or by appointment. STOCK: *Porcelain, glass, furniture, 18th-19th C, £100-£10,000.* SER: Buys at auction. SIZE: Medium. PARK: Easy. VAT: Stan/Spec.
TEL: 01778 347129; HOME: same

MARKET RASEN

Lindsey Court Architectural
(Lindsey White)
EST. 1989. Open by appointment. STOCK: *Architectural antiques, garden and statuary, architectural salvage.* LOC: Behind the library. SER: Container and shipping. SIZE: Medium. PARK: Own. FAIRS: Newark; Ardingley; Le Mans.
TEL: 01507 313470; MOBILE: 07768 396117
E-MAIL: lindsey.court@btinternet.com

NEW BOLINGBROKE

Junktion
The Old Railway Station. PE22 7LD. (J. Rundle)
EST. 1981. Open Wed., Thurs. and Sat. *STOCK: Early advertising, decorative and architectural items; toys, automobilia, mechanical antiques and bygones; early slot machines, wireless, telephones, bakelite, 20th C collectables. NOT STOCKED: Porcelain and jewellery.* LOC: B1183 Boston to Horncastle. SIZE: Large. PARK: Easy.
TEL: 01205 480087/480068

SCUNTHORPE

Antiques & Collectables & Gun Shop
Rear of 251 Ashby High St. DN16 2SQ. (J.A. Bowden)
EST. 1973. Open 9-5. *STOCK: Clocks, furniture, arms and collectables.* SER: Restorations and repairs to antique guns.
SIZE: Large.
TEL: 01724 865445/720606

SLEAFORD

Marcus Wilkinson
The Little Time House, 13 Southgate. NG34 7SU. (M. and P. Wilkinson)
EST. 1935. MBHI. AHS. NAWCC. Open 10-4.30. *STOCK: Jewellery, watches and silver.* LOC: High St. near River Slea. SER: Valuations; restorations (including clock and watch movements); buys at auction (rings and watches). SIZE: Small. PARK: Nearby. VAT: Stan.
TEL: 01529 413149 and 01476 560400

SPALDING

Penman Clockcare (UK) Ltd
5 Pied Calf Yard, Sheepmarket. PE11 1BE. (Michael Strutt)
EST. 1998. MBWCG. Open 9-5, Sat. 9-4. *STOCK: Clocks 18th-20th C; watches, 19th-20th C; jewellery.* LOC: In yard behind Pied Calf public house, opposite PO. SER: Valuations; restorations (clocks and watches). PARK: Nearby.
TEL: 01755 714900; 01755 840955 (ansaphone)
E-MAIL: info@penmanclockcare.co.uk
WEBSITE: www.penmanclockcare.co.uk

Spalding Antiques
1 Abbey Path, The Crescent. PE11 1AY. (John Mumford)
EST. 1980. Open 10-3. *STOCK: Clocks, furniture and smalls, 19th C, £10-£3,000.* LOC: Opposite Sessions House. SER: Valuations. SIZE: Medium. PARK: Victoria St.
TEL: 01775 713185

STAMFORD

Dawson of Stamford Ltd
6 Red Lion Sq. PE9 2AJ. (J. Dawson and S.E. Davies)
EST. 1974. Open 9-5.30. *STOCK: Fine antique furniture, jewellery and silver.* LOC: Town centre between St. John's Church and All Saint's Church. SER: Valuations; repairs. SIZE: Large. VAT: Stan/Spec.
TEL: 01780 754166; FAX: 01780 764231
E-MAIL: dawsonofstamford@hotmail.com

The Forge Antiques & Collectables
5 St. Mary's St. PE9 2DE. (Mrs Tessa Easton)
EST. 1998. Open 9.30-5. *STOCK: 19th C samplers and quilts, £95-£1,000; china and glass, from 17th C, £5-£500; brass and copper, 18th-19th C, £15-£200; jewellery, Victorian to date, £5-£1,000; collectables and memorabilia, modern sculpture; clocks and watches, £50-£6,000.* SER: Search; reference library. SIZE: Large. PARK: Nearby - The Meadows. FAIRS: Swinderby.
TEL: 07763 934703
E-MAIL: tessa@theforgeantiques.co.uk

Graham Pickett Antiques
7 High St., St Martins. PE9 2LF. (G.R. Pickett)
EST. 1990. Open 10-5.30, Sun. by appointment. *STOCK: Furniture - country, 1650-1900, French provincial, 1700-1900, both £50-£3,000; French and English beds, 1750-1900, £350-£4,000; silver, £10-£500; decorative items and mirrors, 1800-1900, £200-£2,500.* LOC: From A1 north into town, on right by 1st lights opposite George Hotel. SIZE: Medium. PARK: Easy. VAT: Stan/Spec.
TEL: 01780 481064; HOME: 01780 764502;
MOBILE: 07710 936948
E-MAIL: graham@pickettantiques.demon.co.uk
WEBSITE: www.pickettantiques.demon.co.uk

Sinclair's
11/12 St. Mary's St. PE9 2DE. (J.S. Sinclair)
EST. 1970. Open 9-5.30. *STOCK: Oak country furniture, 18th C, £200-£3,000; Victorian mahogany furniture, £100-£1,000; Edwardian furniture.* LOC: Near A1. SIZE: Large. PARK: George Hotel. VAT: Stan/Spec.
TEL: 01780 765421

St. George's Antiques
1 St. George's Sq. PE9 2BN. (G.H. Burns)
EST. 1974. Open 9-1 and 2-4.30. CL: Sat. *STOCK: Period and Victorian furniture, some small items.* SIZE: Shop + trade only warehouse. VAT: Stan/Spec.
TEL: 01780 754117; FAX: 01476 567492;
HOME: 01780 460456
E-MAIL: sga-stamford@hotmail.co.uk

St. Martins Antiques Centre
23a High St., St. Martin's. PE9 2LF. (P. B. Light)
EST. 1993. Open 10-5 including Sun. STOCK: *Georgian, Victorian and Edwardian furniture, country pine, Art Deco and Arts and Crafts furniture, porcelain, glass, copper, brass, clocks and watches, silver, jewellery, leather and willow, paintings, prints, textiles, fireplaces, surrounds and grates, 20th C lighting and other artefacts, collectables and ephemera including Roman and Chinese.* LOC: 1 mile from Carpenters Lodge roundabout on A1. SIZE: 65 dealers. PARK: At rear. FAIRS: Newark; Peterborough.
TEL: 01780 481158; FAX: 01780 764742
E-MAIL: peter@st-martins-antiques.co.uk
WEBSITE: www.st-martins-antiques.co.uk

Staniland (Booksellers)
4/5 St. George's St. PE9 2BJ. (V.A. and B.J. Valentine-Ketchum)
EST. 1973. PBFA. Open 10-5. CL: Thurs. STOCK: *Books, mainly 19th-20th C, £1-£2,000.* LOC: High St. SIZE: Large. PARK: St. Leonard's St.
TEL: 01780 755800
E-MAIL: stanilandbooksellers@btinternet.com

STICKNEY

B & B Antiques
The Beeches, Main Rd. PE22 8AD. (B.J. Whittaker)
Open by appointment. STOCK: *English oak furniture and other general pieces.* LOC: A16 north of Boston. PARK: Easy.
TEL: 01205 480204

SUTTON BRIDGE

The Antique Shop
100 Bridge Rd. PE12 9SA. (R. Gittins)
EST. 1973. Open 9-5, Sun. 11-4.30, CL: Wed. STOCK: *Victorian furniture, glass, china, oil lamps and clocks.* NOT STOCKED: *Pine.* LOC: On old A17 opposite church. SIZE: Large - 8 showrooms. PARK: Easy. VAT: Spec.

TEL: 01406 350535
E-MAIL: info@theantiqueshop.co.uk
WEBSITE: www.theantiqueshop.co.uk

Old Barn Antiques & Furnishings
48-50 Bridge Rd. PE12 9UA. (S. and Mrs T.J. Jackson)
EST. 1984. Open 9-5, Sat. 10-5, Sun. 11-4. STOCK: *19th-20th C furniture - oak, mahogany, walnut, pine and upholstered.* LOC: 200 yards from swing-bridge. SER: Shipping; storage and packing. SIZE: Large + trade warehouse. PARK: Easy. VAT: Stan./Spec.
TEL: 01406 359123; FAX: same; MOBILE: 07956 677228
E-MAIL: oldbarnants@aol.com
WEBSITE: www.oldbarnantiques.co.uk

SUTTON-ON-SEA

Knicks Knacks Emporium
41 High St. LN12 2EY. (Mr and Mrs R.A. Nicholson)
EST. 1983. Open 10.30-1 and 2-5, including Sun. CL: Mon. STOCK: *Victorian gas lights, lights and lamps, brass and iron beds, cast-iron fireplaces, bygones, curios, tools, collectables, pottery, porcelain, Art Deco, Art Nouveau, advertising items, furniture and shipping goods, £1-£1,000.* LOC: A52. SIZE: Medium + small warehouse. PARK: Easy.
TEL: 01507 441916; HOME: 01507 441657;
MOBILE: 07800 958438
E-MAIL: knicksknacks@ic24.com

SWINSTEAD

Robin Shield Antiques   LAPADA
Tyton House, 11 Park Rd. NG33 4PH. (W.R. Shield)
EST. 1974. Open by appointment any time. STOCK:
Furniture and paintings, £200-£20,000; works of art,
£100-£5,000; all 17th-19th C. LOC: Approx. 5 miles east
of Colsterworth on A1. SER: Valuations; buys at
auction. SIZE: Medium. PARK: Easy. VAT: Stan/Spec.
TEL: 01476 550905; MOBILE: 07860 520391
E-MAIL: robinshield@btinternet.com

WAINFLEET

Haven Antiques
71 High St. PE24 4BJ. (Julie Crowson MBE)
EST. 1980. Open Fri. or by appointment. STOCK: *General antiques, jewellery, porcelain and collectables.* LOC: A52. SER: Valuations. SIZE: Small. PARK: Easy and opposite. TEL: 01754 880661; HOME: same

WOODHALL SPA

Underwoodhall Antiques
5 The Broadway. LN10 6ST. (G. Underwood)
EST. 1987. Open 10-5, Sun. 1-4.30, prior telephone call advisable. STOCK: *Porcelain and china, £5-£500; general antiques, £1-£500; pictures, £5-£500, all 1750 to date.* LOC: B1191. SER: Jewellery repairs. SIZE: Medium. PARK: Easy. TEL: 01526 353815
E-MAIL: underwoodhall@tesco.net
WEBSITE: www.underwoodhall.com

V.O.C. Antiques   LAPADA
27 Witham Rd. LN10 6RW. (D.J. and C.J. Leyland)
EST. 1970. Resident. Open 9.30-5.30, Sun. 2-5. STOCK: 17th-19th C furniture, to £5,000; period brass and copper, pottery, porcelain and pictures, Lincolnshire longcase clocks, barometers. LOC: B1191. SER: Valuations. SIZE: Medium. PARK: Easy. VAT: Spec.
TEL: 01526 352753; FAX: same; HOME: same
E-MAIL: davidjleyland@tiscali.co.uk

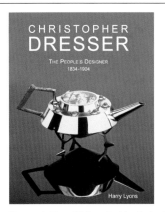
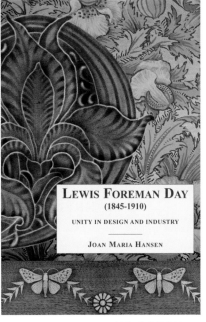

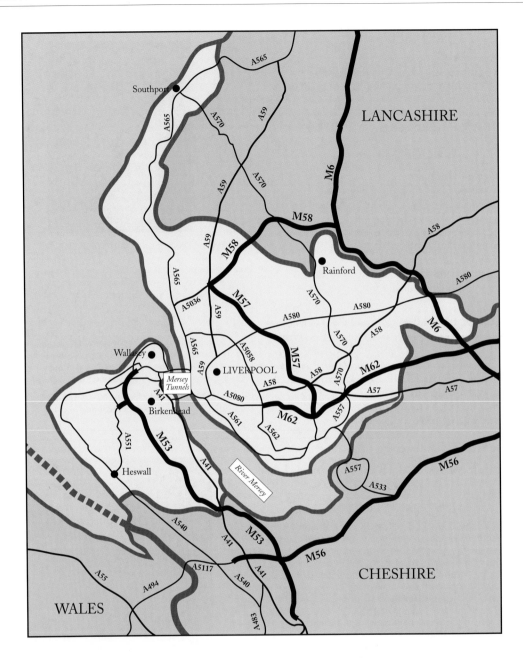

BIRKENHEAD

Bodhouse Antiques
379 New Chester Rd., Rock Ferry. CH42 1LB. (G. and
F.M. Antonini)
Open by appointment. *STOCK: Antique furniture,
paintings, prints, silver and porcelain; £50–£5,000.* SER:
Packing; courier; regular containers to Italy and Spain.
SIZE: Large. PARK: Easy. VAT: Stan/Spec. FAIRS:
Newark; Bailey.
TEL: 0151 644 9494; MOBILES: 07802 608357 and
07710 561199

E-MAIL: antonini@btinternet.com
WEBSITE: www.antiques-atlas.co.uk

HESWALL

C. Rosenberg
The Antique Shop, 120-122 Telegraph Rd. CH60 0AQ.
EST. 1960. Open Fri. and Sat. 10-5, other times by
appointment. *STOCK: Jewellery, silver, porcelain, objets
d'art.* LOC: Main road in village, next to M&S.
TEL: 0151 342 1053

LIVERPOOL

Bazooka Interiors
341 Aigburth Rd. L17 0BL. (Gary Noon)
Open 10-5.30. STOCK: *Retro furnishings, specialist in all aspects of the 50s, 60s and 70s; antiques and collectables.*
PARK: Free out front of shop.
TEL: 0151 280 9685; MOBILE: 07776 333693
E-MAIL: bazookainteriors@googlemail.com
WEBSITE: www.bazookainteriors.co.uk

Circa 1900
11-13 Holts Arcade, India Buildings, Water St. L2 0RR. (Wayne Colquhoun)
EST. 1989. Open 10-2.30 and 3.30-6, Sat. and Sun. by appointment. STOCK: *Art Nouveau, classic Art Deco, decorative and applied arts, 1860-1940, £10-£1,000+.*
LOC: 100 yards from Liver Buildings. SER: Valuations.
SIZE: Small. PARK: Easy.
TEL: 0151 236 1282
WEBSITE: www.classicartdeco.co.uk

Intandane Ltd t/a. 69A
75 Renshaw St. L1 2SJ
EST. 1976. Open 12-6, Sun. 12-5. STOCK: *20th C decorative objects, antiques, curios, African and Oriental. Vintage clothes, books and records; specialises in Chinese antiques.* LOC: Town centre. SIZE: 1,800 sq. ft.
TEL: 0151 708 8873
E-MAIL: intandane69a@yahoo.co.uk
WEBSITE: www.trocadero.com

Maggs Shipping Ltd
66-68 St Anne St. L3 3DY. (G. Webster)
EST. 1965. Open 9-5, weekends by appointment. STOCK: *General antiques, period and shipping smalls, £1-£1,000.*
LOC: By Lime Street station. SER: Restorations; container packing, courier. PARK: Meters.
TEL: 0151 207 2555; EVENINGS: 01928 564958
E-MAIL: maggsantiques@compuserve.com

Stefani Antiques
497 Smithdown Rd. L15 5AE. (T. Stefani)
EST. 1969. Open 10-5. CL: Wed. STOCK: *Furniture, to 1910, £200-£2,000; jewellery, £25-£2,000; pottery, silver, old Sheffield plate, porcelain, bronzes.* LOC: On main road, near Penny Lane. SER: Valuations; restorations (furniture including French polishing and upholstery). SIZE: Medium. PARK: Easy.
TEL: 0151 734 1933; HOME: 0151 425 4889;
MOBILE: 07946 646395
E-MAIL: info@stefaniantiques.co.uk
WEBSITE: www.stefaniantiques.co.uk

Swainbanks Ltd
50-56 Fox St. L3 3BQ. (Sue Swainbank)
Open 9-3 or by appointment. CL: Sat. STOCK: *Shipping goods and general antiques.* LOC: Half a mile from city centre. SER: Containers. SIZE: Large. PARK: Free outside.
VAT: Stan.
TEL: 0151 207 9466; Fax: 0151 284 9466
E-MAIL: sueswainbank@aol.com
WEBSITE: www.swainbanks.co.uk

MEOLS

Glass Galore and More
The Courtyard, Carr Farm Garden Centre, Birkenhead Rd. CH47 9RE
Open 11-5. STOCK: *Collectables and antique pine furniture.*
TEL: 0151 632 0637

RAINFORD

Colin Stock   BADA
8 Mossborough Rd. WA11 8QN.
EST. 1895. Open by appointment. STOCK: *Furniture, 18th-19th C.*
TEL: 0174 488 2246

SOUTHPORT

Birkdale Antiques
119a Upper Aughton Rd., Birkdale. PR8 5NH. (John Napp)
EST. 1996. CL: Tues. STOCK: *Antique chandeliers from around the world.* LOC: From Lord St. West into Lulworth Rd., first left into Aughton Rd., over railway crossing into Upper Aughton Rd. SER: Valuations; restorations; buys at auction. SIZE: Medium. PARK: Easy.
FAIRS: Stafford, Newark, Swinderby.
TEL: 01704 550117; HOME: 01704 567680;
MOBILE: 07973 303105
E-MAIL: johnnapp@tiscali.co.uk
WEBSITE: www.birkdaleantiques.co.uk

C.K. Broadhurst & Co Ltd
5-7 Market St. PR8 1HD. (Laurens R. Hardman)
EST. 1926. ABA. ILAB. PBFA. Open 9-5.30. STOCK: *18th-20th C literature, children's illustrated, private press, natural history, general and antiquarian.* LOC: Town centre, off Lord St. by Victorian bandstand. SER: Book search; valuations; restorations; rebinding. SIZE: 4 floors. PARK: Metered on street. FAIRS: Olympia; Chelsea; some provincial.
TEL: 01704 532064/534110; FAX: 01704 542009
E-MAIL: litereria@aol.com
WEBSITE: www.ckbroadhurst.co.uk

Molloy's Furnishers Ltd
6-8 St. James St. PR8 5AE. (P. Molloy)
EST. 1955. Open 9-5.30. STOCK: *Mahogany and oak, Edwardian furniture.* LOC: Off A570 Scarisbrick New Rd. SIZE: Large. PARK: Easy. VAT: Stan.
TEL: 01704 535204; FAX: 01704 548101

John Nolan - King Street Antiques
29 King St. PR8 1LH.

Est. 1972. Open Mon.-Sat. STOCK: *Furniture and decorative items.* LOC: Town centre. SER: Courier; packing and shipping. SIZE: Medium. PARK: Easy. VAT: Stan/Spec.
TEL: 01704 540808; MOBILE: 07714 322252

The Original British American Antiques
Kings House, 27 King St. PR8 1LH. (John Nolan)
Est. 1976. *Trade only.* Open 10-5, evenings by appointment. STOCK: *Export items, especially for US decorator market.* LOC: Town centre. SER: Courier; packing and shipping. SIZE: Medium + warehouse. PARK: Easy. VAT: Stan/Spec.
TEL: 01704 540808; MOBILE: 07714 322252

Osiris Antiques
3 Cambridge Arcade, PR8 1AS. (C. and P. Wood)
Est. 1983. Open 10.45-5.30, Sun. 12-5. STOCK: *Art Nouveau and Art Deco, Arts and Crafts, £10-£5,000; jewellery, 1880-1960, to £150.* LOC: Town centre. SER: Valuations; buys at auction (Art Nouveau, Art Deco); lectures given on Decorative Arts 1895-1930. SIZE: Small. PARK: Easy.
TEL: 01704 500991; MOBILE: 07802 818500;
HOME: 01704 560418

David M. Regan
25 Hoghton St. PR9 0NS.
Est. 1983. Open Mon., Wed., Fri. and Sat. 10-5. STOCK: *Roman and English coins, £2-£2,000; postcards and cigarette cards, small collectables.* SER: Valuations. SIZE: Small.
TEL: 01704 531266

Royal Arcade
129-131 Lord St. PR8 1PU. (A.M. Zachariah)
Est. 2001. Open 9.30-5.30; Sun. 11-5. SIZE: Large.
TEL: 01704 542087; FAX: 01704 542641

The Southport Antiques Centre
27-29 King St. PR8 1LH. (J. Nolan)
Open 10-5. LOC: Town centre. SIZE: Large, 11 rooms + warehouse. PARK: Easy. VAT: Stan/Spec.
TEL: 01704 540808; MOBILE: 07714 322252.

Below are listed the dealers at this centre.

The Antique Consignment Company Ltd.

Antiques and Interiors

British-American Antiques
Shipping goods.

The China Shop
China and pottery.

Collectors Corner
Collectables from 1930, including porcelain and pottery, Royal Doulton and Beswick.

Halsall Hall Antiques
Country furniture.

King St. Antiques
General antiques.

John Nolan
Period furniture.

Pine Country Antiques
Country pine furniture.

Quest
General antiques.

S.M. Collectors' Items
Doulton and pressed glass.

Tony and Anne Sutcliffe Antiques
130 Cemetery Rd., and warehouse at 37A Linaker St. PR8 6RP.
Est. 1969. Open 8.30-5 including Sun. or by appointment. STOCK: *Shipping goods, Victorian and period furniture.* LOC: Town centre. SER: Containers; courier. SIZE: Large. VAT: Stan/Spec.
TEL: 01704 537068; HOME: 01704 533465;
MOBILE: 07860 949516/480376
E-MAIL: tonysutcliffeantiques@btinternet.com

Weldons Jewellery and Antiques
567 Lord St. PR9 0BB. (N.C. Weldon)
Est. 1914. Open 9.30-5.30. STOCK: *Clocks, watches, jewellery, silver; specialist in Victorian and Art Deco jewellery.* NOT STOCKED: *Militaria.* LOC: Main street. SER: Valuations; restorations. SIZE: Medium. PARK: Easy. VAT: Stan/Spec.
TEL: 01704 532191; FAX: 01704 500091

WALLASEY

Victoria Antiques/City Strippers
155-157 Brighton St. CH44 8DU. (J.M. Colyer)
Est. 1978. Open 9.30-5.30. STOCK: *Furniture.* SER: Restorations. SIZE: Large. PARK: Easy.
TEL: 0151 639 0080
E-MAIL: steve@victoriaantiques.co.uk
WEBSITE: www.victoriaantiques.co.uk

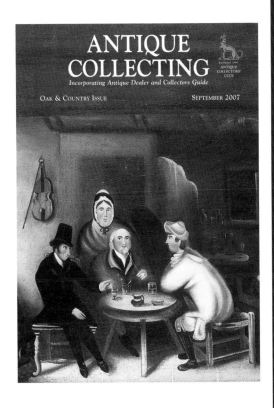

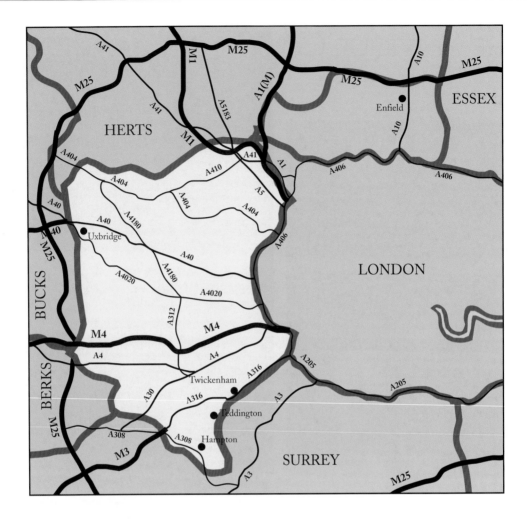

ENFIELD

East Lodge Antiques Village
East Lodge Gardens, East Lodge Lane, Botany Bay. EN2 8AS.
Open 10-5 Tues.-Sun and Bank Holidays. STOCK: *Antiques and collectables inc. furniture, silver, jewellery, Retro, pottery, vintage clothing, clocks and watches, glass, mirrors, fireplaces and architectural, radios.* SIZE: 12 shops + 60 cabinets.
TEL: 020 8363 1886; FAX: same; MOBILE: 07796 262400

Gallerie Veronique
66 Chase Side. EN2 6NJ. (Veronica Aslangul)
EST. 1993. Open 10-4, Sat. 10-5. CL: Sun (except by appointment) and Wed. STOCK: *Furniture including decorative, 1820-1970, £50-£1,000.* LOC: Near junction A10 and M25. SER: Restorations (French polishing and upholstery); chair mending and caning. SIZE: Medium. PARK: Easy.
TEL: 020 8342 1005; MOBILE: 07770 410041

E-MAIL: antiques@gallerieveronique.co.uk
WEBSITE: www.gallerieveronique.co.uk

HAMPTON

Peco
139 Station Rd. TW12 2BT. (Mrs N. Lewis)
EST. 1969. Open 9-5. STOCK: *Doors, 18th-20th C; fireplaces including French and marble, 18th-19th C; stoves.* LOC: Opposite Hampton railway station. SER: Restorations (marble, stained glass, cast-iron fireplaces, doors); stained glass made to order. SIZE: Large. PARK: Own. VAT: Stan.
TEL: 020 8979 8310
E-MAIL: pecohampton@yahoo.co.uk
WEBSITE: www.pecoofhampton.co.uk

HATCH END

AC Antiques and Collectables
266 Uxbridge Rd. HA5 4HS.
Open 10-5.30, Sun. 11.30-4. STOCK: *Furniture, silver,*

ceramics, glass, clocks and watches. SIZE: Large - 12 dealers. PARK: Free car park nearby.
TEL: 020 8421 1653

RUISLIP

Ruislip Collectables
156 High St. HA4 7AA.
EST. 1993. Open 10-5. *STOCK: General antiques - furniture, china, glass, jewellery.* SIZE: Large - 13 dealers. PARK: Ample nearby.
TEL: 01895 638216

TEDDINGTON

Chris Hollingshead Horticultural Books
10 Linden Grove. TW11 8LT.
EST. 1994. PBFA. Resident. Open 10-6 by appointment only. *STOCK: Antiquarian, scarce and out-of-print books, specialising in landscape architecture, garden history, finely illustrated, botanical and horticultural.* SIZE: Small. PARK: Easy.
TEL: 020 8977 6051
e-mail: chollingshead@btinternet.com

TWICKENHAM

Anthony C. Hall
30 Staines Rd. TW2 5AH.
EST. 1966. Open Mon., Thurs. and Fri. 10-5. *STOCK: Antiquarian books.* SIZE: Medium. PARK: Easy.
TEL: 020 8898 2638; FAX: 020 8893 8855
E-MAIL: ahall@hallbooks.co.uk
WEBSITE: www.hallbooks.co.uk

Tobias Jellinek Antiques
20 Park Rd. TW1 2PX. (Mrs D.L. and T.P. Jellinek)
EST. 1963. Open by appointment. *STOCK: Fine early furniture and objects, 16th-17th C or earlier, £500-£5,000+.* LOC: East of town centre near Richmond Bridge. SER: Valuations; buys at auction (as stock). SIZE: Small. PARK: Easy. VAT: Stan/Spec.
TEL: 020 8892 6892; FAX: 020 8744 9298;
MOBILE: 07831 523 671
E-MAIL: toby@jellinek.com

Marble Hill Gallery
70/72 Richmond Rd. TW1 3BE. (D. and L. Newson)
EST. 1974. Open 10-5.30. *STOCK: English and French marble and natural stone, pine and white Adam-style mantels.* SER: Full installation service. SIZE: Large. PARK: Easy. VAT: Stan/Spec.
TEL: 020 8892 1488
E-MAIL: sales@marblehill.co.uk
WEBSITE: www.marblehill.co.uk

UXBRIDGE

Antiques Warehouse (Uxbridge)
34-35 Rockingham Rd. UB8 2TZ. (Mike, Sue and Ben Allenby and Simon Phillips)
EST. 1977. Open 10-5. *STOCK: General antiques, shipping items, £1-£4,000.* SER: Restorations; French polishing; re-upholstery; SIZE: Large. PARK: Easy. VAT: Stan/Global.
TEL: 01895 256963; FAX: 01895 252157
E-MAIL: info@uxbridgeantiques.co.uk
WEBSITE: www.uxbridgeantiques.co.uk

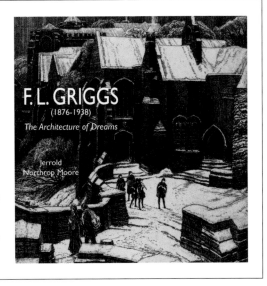

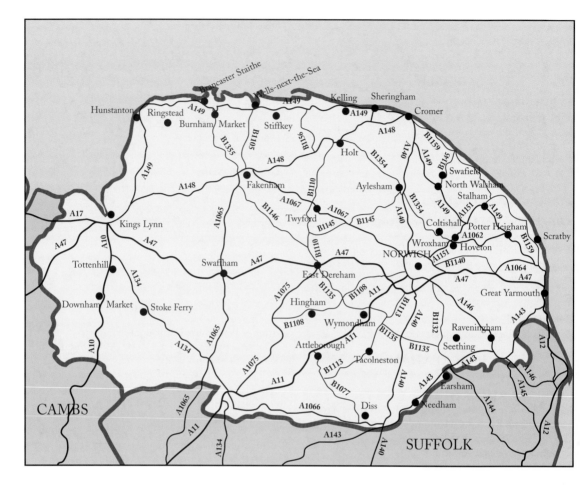

ATTLEBOROUGH

A.E. Bush and Partners
Vineyards Antiques Gallery, Leys Lane. NR17 1NE.
(A.G., M.S. and J.A. Becker)
EST. 1940. Open 9-1 and 2-5.30. *STOCK: Walnut and mahogany, 18th-19th C.* LOC: Town outskirts. SER: Restorations; wholesale antiques and export; storage; buys at auction. SIZE: Large. PARK: Easy. VAT: Stan/Spec.
TEL: 01953 454239 or 01953 452175
WEBSITE: www.fine-furniture.net

AYLSHAM

Pearse Lukies
The Old Vicarage. NR11 6HE.
EST. 1975. *Trade Only.* Open preferably by appointment. *STOCK: Period oak, sculpture, objects, 18th C furniture.*
TEL: 01263 734137

BLOFIELD

Village Clocks
High Stead, Ranworth Road NR13 4PJ. (Mike Darley)

EST. 1980. Open Tues.-Sat. by appointment. *STOCK: Clocks - 17th-19th C longcase, bracket, English wall and regulators.* SER: Valuations; restorations (cases and movements). PARK: Easy.
TEL: 07050 229758
E-MAIL: michael.darley@btinternet.com

BURNHAM MARKET

The Brazen Head Bookshop & Gallery
Market Place. PE31 8HD. (David S. Kenyon)
EST. 1997. Open 9.30-5. *STOCK: Rare, out-of-print and secondhand books; paintings, prints and ceramics.* LOC: On green, opposite PO. SER: Valuations. SIZE: Large. PARK: Easy.
TEL: 01328 730700; FAX: 01328 730929
E-MAIL: brazenheadbook@aol.com

M. and A. Cringle
The Old Black Horse. PE31 8HD.
EST. 1965. Open 10-1 and 2-5. CL: Wed. *STOCK: 18th to early 19th C furniture, £50-£2,000; china, glass, pottery, prints, maps, £10-£500; modern china and decorative items. NOT STOCKED: Large furniture.* LOC: In village centre.

SIZE: Medium. PARK: Easy.
TEL: 01328 738456
E-MAIL: pmcringle@aol.com

Hamilton Antiques
North St. PE31 8HG. (A. & W. Hudson)
EST. 1983. Open 10-1 and 2-5. STOCK: *Georgian furniture; porcelain, decorative items.* LOC: 20yds. from village green towards coast. SIZE: Medium. PARK: Easy. VAT: Stan/Spec.
TEL: 01328 738187; FAX: same
E-MAIL: wkkh@btopenworld.com

COLTISHALL

Roger Bradbury Antiques
Church St. NR12 7DJ.
EST. 1967. Open daily by appointment. STOCK: *Oriental shipwreck porcelain cargoes including Nanking, Tek Sing, Vung Tau, Diana, Ca Mau.* LOC: Close to village centre. SER: Valuations. SIZE: Medium. PARK: Easy. VAT: Stan.
TEL: 01603 737444; FAX: 01603 737018
E-MAIL: roger.bradbury@btinternet.com

CROMER

Bond Street Antiques
6 Bond St. and 38 Church St. NR27 9DA. (M.R.T., J.A. and M.L. Jones)
EST. 1970. NAG. FGA. GMC. Open 9-1 and 2-5. STOCK: *Jewellery, silver, porcelain, china, glass, 18th-20th C, £50-£15,000.* LOC: From Church St. bear right to Post Office, shop on opposite side on street further along. SER: Valuations; repairs (jewellery); gem testing. SIZE: Medium. PARK: Easy. VAT: Stan.
TEL: 01263 513134; HOME: same

Books Etc.
15a Church St. NR27 9ES. (Kevin Reynor)
EST. 1996. UACC. Open 10-5 seven days (June-Sep); Mon-Sat. 10-4 (Oct-May). STOCK: *Books, football programmes, memorabilia and autographs.* LOC: Town centre. SER: Valuations. SIZE: Large. PARK: Nearby.
TEL: 01263 515501
E-MAIL: bookskcr@aol.com

Collectors World
6 New Parade, Church St. NR27 9EP. (John and Irene Nockels)
EST. 1988. Open 10-1 and 2-4, Sat. 10-1 and 2-5, Sun. 2.30-5. CL: Mon. STOCK: *Collectables, 19th-20th C, £5-£100.* LOC: Near traffic lights on Norwich road. SIZE: Small. PARK: Limited at rear. FAIRS: Norfolk Showground; Newark.
TEL: 01263 515330; HOME: 01263 514174
E-MAIL: john.nockels@btinternet.com

DEREHAM

Paul Watson Antiques
(Paul Watson)
Open by appointment. STOCK: *General antiques, furniture.* FAIRS: Newark.
TEL: 01362 668419
E-MAIL: paulwatson10@aol.com

DERSINGHAM

Priests Antiques Ltd
Unit D, Station Road Industrial Estate. PE31 6PR.
EST. 1978. Open by appointment. STOCK: *17th-18th C oak and walnut furniture, £500-£20,000+; some 18th-19th C mahogany.* LOC: Just off High St. SER: Buys at auction. SIZE: Medium. PARK: Easy.
TEL: 07899 994304
E-MAIL: priestsantiques@freenet.co.uk

DISS

The Antiques & Collectors Centre (Diss)
3 Cobbs Yard, St Nicholas St. IP22 4LB. (Martin Moye)
EST. 1997. Open 9-4.30. STOCK: *Furniture, 18th-20th C; porcelain, Victorian to 1960s; glassware, Georgian to 1930s; silver, paintings, prints, jewellery, Georgian to modern, £10-£300; rustic bygones, £20-£200; clocks, £50-£500; wide range of militaria.* LOC: Next to Diss Ironworks, off St. Nicholas St. SIZE: Large. PARK: Easy. VAT: Spec.
TEL: 01379 644472

Diss Antiques & Interiors LAPADA
2 & 3 Market Place. IP22 4JT. (Brian Wimshurst)
EST. 1973. GMC. Open 9-5. STOCK: *Furniture, barometers, clocks, jewellery, porcelain, copper, brass.* SER: Repairs (furniture, jewellery and china). SIZE: Large. PARK: Nearby. VAT: Stan/Spec.
TEL: 01379 642213
E-MAIL: brian@dissantiques.co.uk
WEBSITE: www.dissantiques.co.uk

Patrick Marney
Baroscope House, 16 Millers Drive, Dickleburgh. IP21 4PX.
EST. 1964. Open by appointment. STOCK: *Fine barometers, 18th-19th C, £1,000-£5,000; pocket aneroids, 19th C, £150-£1,000; scientific instruments, 18th-19th C, £250-£2,000; all fully restored.* SER: Valuations; restorations (mercury barometers). SIZE: Small. PARK: Easy.
TEL: 01379 740363; MOBILE: 07773 917259
E-MAIL: patrick.marney@virgin.net
WEBSITE: www.patrickmarney.co.uk

EARSHAM

Earsham Hall Pine
Earsham Hall. NR35 2AN. (R. Derham)
EST. 1976 Open 9-5, Sun. 10.30-5. STOCK: *Pine

furniture. LOC: On Earsham to Hedenham road. SIZE: Large. PARK: Easy.
TEL: 01986 893423; FAX: 01986 895656
WEBSITE: www.earshamhallpine.co.uk

FAKENHAM

Fakenham Antique Centre
Old Congregational Church, 14 Norwich Rd. NR21 8AZ. (Julie Hunt and Mandy Allen)
EST. 1984. Open 10-4.30. STOCK: *Furniture, glass, ceramics, books, pens, oil lamps, kitchenalia, memorabilia, clocks, paintings and prints.* LOC: Turn off A148 at roundabout to town, at traffic lights turn up Queens Rd., left at second mini-roundabout, centre 50yds. on right opposite Godfrey DIY. SER: Restorations (furniture); polishing; replacement handles; cane and rush seating repairs. SIZE: 27 dealers. PARK: Easy.
TEL: 01328 862941.

Norfolk Decorative Antiques   LAPADA
Unit 7G, Millers Close, Fakenham Industrial Estate. NR21 8NW. (Jill Perry)
Open by appointment; prior telephone call advisable. STOCK: *Lighting - chandeliers from 1840-1950; pairs a speciality; large and unusual chandeliers.* SER: Cleaning, restoration and fitting - nationwide. SIZE: Warehouse and workshop. FAIRS: Battersea Decorative; NEC.
TEL: 01328 856333; FAX: same;
MOBILE: 07747 888613 or 07818 876778
E-MAIL: enquiries@norfolkdecorativeantiques.co.uk
WEBSITE: www.norfolkdecorativeantiques.co.uk

Sue Rivett Antiques and Bygones
6 Norwich Rd. NR21 8AX.
EST. 1969. Open 10-1. STOCK: *General antiques and bygones.* LOC: On Norwich Rd. into Fakenham. SER: Valuations. PARK: Easy.
TEL: 01328 862924; HOME: 01263 860462; MOBILE: 07778 819965

GREAT YARMOUTH

Barry's Antiques
35 King St. NR30 2PN.
EST. 1979. Open 9.30-4.30. STOCK: *Jewellery, porcelain, clocks, glass, pictures.* LOC: Main shopping street. SIZE: Large. PARK: Opposite. VAT: Stan/Spec.
TEL: 01493 842713

Folkes Antiques and Jewellers
74 Victoria Arcade. NR30 2NU. (Mrs J. Baldry)
EST. 1946. Open 10-4. STOCK: *General antiques especially jewellery and collectables.* LOC: From A47 into town centre, shop on right of Victoria Arcade, opposite Regent Rd. to seafront. SER: Valuations; repairs. PARK: Easy.
FAIRS: Local collectors.
TEL: 01493 851354
Gold and Silver Exchange

Theatre Plain. NR30 2BE. (C. Birch)
EST. 1981. Open 9.30-5.15. STOCK: *Coins, medals and secondhand jewellery.* LOC: Market Place.
TEL: 01493 859430

Howkins Jewellers
135 King St. NR30 2PQ. (Valerie Howkins)
EST. 1945. NAG. Open 9.30-4.45. STOCK: *Jewellery, silver, crystal, porcelain, pottery, Georgian to present day.* LOC: South of Market Place. SER: Valuations; restorations; repairs. SIZE: Medium. PARK: Limited and nearby. VAT: Spec./Margin.
TEL: 01493 844639; FAX: 01493 844857

Wheatleys
16 Northgate St., White Horse Plain and Fullers Hill. NR30 1BA.
EST. 1971. Open 9.30-5, Thurs. 9.30-1. STOCK: *Jewellery and general antiques.* LOC: 2 mins. walk from Market Place. SIZE: Large. PARK: Easy. VAT: Stan.
TEL: 01493 857219

HINGHAM

Mongers
15 Market Place. NR9 4AF. (Sam Coster)
EST. 1997. SALVO. Open 9.30-5.30. STOCK: *Fireplaces, 1700-1930, £400-£3,000; sanitaryware, 1870-1950, £250-£1,000; Victorian and Edwardian garden antiques, £50-£2,000; door furniture, from 1800 to date, £20-£100.* LOC: B1108. SER: Restorations (bath re-surfacing, fireplaces); stripping (pine). SIZE: Large. PARK: Easy. VAT: Stan/Spec.
TEL: 01953 851868; FAX: 01953 851870
E-MAIL: mongers@mongersofhingham.co.uk
WEBSITE: www.mongersofhingham.co.uk

Past & Present
16a The Fairland. NR9 4HN. (C. George)
EST. 1970. Open Tues.-Sun. 10-5. STOCK: *Furniture, £25-£1,500; smalls, 18th-19th C, £10-£500; lighting - lamps and chandeliers.* LOC: B1108. SER: Valuations. SIZE: Medium. PARK: Easy. VAT: Stan. FAIRS: Swinderby, Newark, Staffordshire.
TEL: 01953 851471; HOME: 01953 851400; FAX: 01953 851785
E-MAIL: info@past-present.co.uk
WEBSITE: www.past-present.co.uk

HOLT

Baron Art
9 & 17 Chapel Yard, Albert St. NR25 6HG. (Anthony R. Baron and Michael J. Bellis)
EST. 1992. Open 9.30-5.30. STOCK: *Paintings, 19th-20th C, £50-£5,000; prints and lithographs, 19th-20th C, £5-£500; collectables, 1830-1940, £5-£500; books and Art Deco.* SER: Valuations; buys at auction (paintings); framing. SIZE: Medium. PARK: Easy. VAT: Stan/Spec.

TEL: 01263 713906 (No. 9); 01263 713430 (No. 17);
FAX: 01263 711670
E-MAIL: baronholt@aol.com

Baskerville Bindings
3-5 Fish Hill. NR25 6BD. (Simon Finch Rare Book
Ltd.)
EST. 1982. ABA. ILAB. Open 10-5 and by appointment.
*STOCK: Antique leatherbound books for decoration and
library furnishing.* SIZE: 10 rooms.
TEL: 01263 712650; FAX: 01263 711153
E-MAIL: antique@leatherboundbooks.com
WEBSITE: www.leatherboundbooks.com

Cottage Collectables
8 Fish Hill and 3 Chapel Yard. NR25 6BD. (Philip &
Linda Morris)
EST. 1984. Open 10-5, Sun. 11-5. *STOCK: Collectables,
18th-20th C, £5-£250; furniture, 18th-20th C, £50-£300;
jewellery, from Victorian, £5-£50; linen.* SER: Valuations;
restorations (furniture and ceramics); buys at auction
(furniture and collectables). SIZE: Medium. PARK: Easy.
FAIRS: Swinderby, Peterborough, Newark and others.
TEL: 01263 711707 or 01263 712920

Anthony Fell   BADA LAPADA
**Chester House, 47 Bull St. NR25 6HP. (A.J. and C.R.
Austin-Fell)**
**EST. 1996. CINOA. Open 9.30-1 and 2-5, prior
telephone call advisable.** *STOCK: English and
Continental furniture, 16th-18th C, £1,000-£50,000;
works of art, 16th C to contemporary, £1,000-£20,000.*
LOC: Near Post Office. **SER: Valuations; restorations.**
**SIZE: Medium. PARK: Easy. VAT: Spec.   FAIRS:
Olympia (June, Nov); BADA.**
TEL: 01263 712912; FAX: same
E-MAIL: afellantiques@tiscali.co.uk
WEBSITE: www.anthonyfell.com

Simon Finch Norfolk
3-5 Fish Hill. NR25 6BD.
EST. 1976. Open 10-5. *STOCK: Antiquarian and
secondhand books; bindings.* SIZE: 10 rooms.
TEL: 01263 712650; FAX: 01263 711153
E-MAIL: simonfinch.norfolk@virgin.net
WEBSITE: www.simonfinchnorfolk.com

Hatfield Hines Gallery
3 Fish Hill. NR25 6BD. (Clare Hatfield)
Open 11-5, Thurs 11-2; CL: Mon. *STOCK: Modern
British paintings; sculptures; British prints 1900-1980.*
TEL: 01263 713000; FAX: same
E-MAIL: info@hatfieldhines.com
WEBSITE: www.hatfieldhines.com

Heathfield Antiques & Country Pine
Candlestick Lane, Thornage Rd. NR25 6SU. (S.M.
Heathfield)
EST. 1989. Open 8.30-5. *STOCK: Pine furniture, £15-*

£3,500. LOC: From Holt roundabout junction of
A148/B1149, take the Dereham/Thornage road,
business half a mile on left hand side. SER: Restorations;
painted furniture. SIZE: Large. PARK: Own. VAT:
Stan/Global.
TEL: 01263 711609
WEBSITE: www.antique-pine.net

Holt Antique Centre
Albert Hall, Albert St. NR25 6HY. (David Attfield)
EST. 1980. Open 10-4, (Sun. Easter-October). *STOCK:
Pine and country furniture, china, glass, lighting, silver
plate and kitchenalia, jewellery, clothes, soft furnishings,
18th-20th C, £1-£1,500.* LOC: Turn right from Chapel
Yard car park, 100 yards. SIZE: Large. PARK: Easy.
TEL: 01263 712097; HOME: 01263 860347.

Mews Antique Emporium
5 & 6 Manor Mews. NR25 6AW.
EST. 1998. Open 10-5. *STOCK: 18th-20th C furniture,
collectables, £1-£1,000.* LOC: Rear of 17 High St. SIZE:
Large - 12 dealers. PARK: Nearby.
TEL: 01263 713224

Past Caring Vintage Clothing
6 Chapel Yard. NR25 6HG. (L. Mossman)
EST. 1988. Open 11-5. *STOCK: Vintage clothing, linen and
textiles, Victorian to 1950, £5-£200; jewellery and
accessories, Victorian to 1960, £5-£125.* SER: Valuations;
restorations (christening gowns and some beadwork).
SIZE: Medium - on 2 floors. PARK: Easy; adjacent to
carpark.
TEL: 01263 713771; HOME: 01362 683363; FAX: 01362
680078

Richard Scott Antiques
30 High St. NR25 6BH. (Richard and Luke Scott)
EST. 1967. Open 10-5. *STOCK: Pottery, porcelain, glass,
furniture, textiles and general antiques.* LOC: On A148.
SER: Valuations; probate. SIZE: Large. PARK: Easy.
TEL: 01263 712479; MOBILE: 07979 548597
E-MAIL: luke@richardscottantiques.co.uk
WEBSITE: www.richardscottantiques.co.uk

HOVETON

Eric Bates and Sons Ltd.
Horning Road West. NR12 8QJ. (Eric, Graham and
James Bates)
EST. 1973. Open 9-5. *STOCK: Victorian and Edwardian
furniture.* LOC: Opposite rail station. SER: Restorations
(furniture); manufacturer of period-style furniture;
upholstery; container packing and shipping. SIZE: Large.
PARK: Easy. VAT: Stan/Spec.
TEL: 01603 781771; FAX: 01603 781773
E-MAIL: info@ebsfurniture.co.uk
WEBSITE: www.batesfurniture.co.uk

HUNSTANTON

Delawood Antiques
10 Westgate. PE36 5AL. (R.C. Woodhouse)
EST. 1975. Resident. Open Mon., Wed., Fri., Sat. 10-5 and most Sun. afternoons, other times by chance or appointment. STOCK: *General antiques, furniture, jewellery, collectors' items, books, £1-£1,000.* LOC: Near town centre and bus station. SER: Valuations; commission sales. SIZE: Small. PARK: Easy.
TEL: 01485 532903; home and FAX: same

Le Strange Old Barns Antiques, Arts & Craft Centre
Golf Course Rd., Old Hunstanton. PE36 6JG.
(C. Maloney and R.M. Weller)
EST. 1994. Open 10-6, (10-5 winter), including Sun. STOCK: *General antiques, collectables, arts and crafts.* LOC: Opposite Mariner Inn. SIZE: Large. PARK: Easy.
TEL: 01485 533402

R.C. Woodhouse (Antiquarian Horologist)
10 Westgate. PE36 5AL.
EST. 1975. BWCG. Resident. Open Mon., Wed., Fri, Sat. and usually Sun. afternoons, other times by chance or appointment. STOCK: *Georgian, Victorian and Edwardian longcase, dial, wall and mantel clocks; some watches and barometers.* LOC: Near town centre and bus station. SER: Restorations (longcase, bracket, chiming, carriage, French, wall clocks, dials, barometers); small locks repaired and lost keys made - postal service if required; valuations. SIZE: Small. PARK: Easy.
TEL: 01485 532903; home and FAX: same

KELLING

The Old Reading Room Gallery and Tea Room
The Street, NR25 7EL. (Brian Taylor)
EST. 1994. Open 9.30-4 seven days a week. STOCK: *Paintings and prints, Norfolk landscapes, wood carvings, books, postcards and collectables, English porcelain and pottery.* LOC: A149 coast road between Weybourne and Cley, at war memorial in village. SER: Restorations; framing. SIZE: Large. PARK: Easy. VAT: Stan/Spec.
TEL: 01263 588227; HOME: 01263 588435

KING'S LYNN

Tim Clayton Jewellery Ltd
21-23 Chapel St. PE30 1EG. (Tim and Sue Clayton)
EST. 1975. NAG. Open 9-5.30. STOCK: *Silver, jewellery, clocks, furniture and pictures.* LOC: Town centre. SER: Bespoke jewellery; repairs; picture framing. SIZE: Large. PARK: Nearby. VAT: Global/Margin.
TEL: 01553 772329; FAX: 01553 776583
WEBSITE: www.timclaytonjewellery.com

James K. Lee
Nicholson House, 29 Church St. PE30 5EB. (A.J. and J.K. Lee)

EST. 1950. Open 9-6 including Sun. STOCK: *Furniture including desks, chests of drawers and tables, 18th-19th C, £800-£10,000.* LOC: In old town, through Southgates, by mini roundabout. SER: Valuations; restorations including polishing; buys at auction (furniture). SIZE: Small. PARK: Easy and NCP opposite.
TEL: 01553 810681; FAX: 01553 760128; HOME: 01553 811522
E-MAIL: jameskleeqs@aol.com

Old Curiosity Shop
25 St. James St. PE30 5DA. (Mrs R.S. Wright)
EST. 1980. Open Mon., Thurs., Fri. and Sat. 11-5. STOCK: *General collectable smalls, glass, clothing, linen, jewellery, lighting, Art Deco and Art Nouveau, furniture, prints, stripped pine and paintings, pre-1930, £1-£500.* LOC: Off Saturday Market Place towards London Rd. SER: Restorations (teddy bears); repairs (clocks). SIZE: Small. PARK: At rear or nearby.
TEL: 01553 766591

The Old Granary Antiques and Collectors' Centre
King Staithe Lane, Off Queen St. PE30 1LZ.
(R.S. Wright)
EST. 1977. Open 10-4. STOCK: *China, coins, glass, books, stamps, silver, jewellery, brass, copper, postcards, linen, some furniture and general antiques.* LOC: Close to Customs House. SIZE: 18 dealers PARK: Easy.
TEL: 01553 775509

NORTH WALSHAM

The Angel Gallery
4 Aylsham Rd. NR28 0BH. (Mrs Susan Thorburn)
EST. 2007. Open 10-5, Sat 10-1. CL: Wed. STOCK: *Local crafts, pictures and jewellery; Victoriana; clocks.* LOC: Short walk from town centre. SIZE: Medium. PARK: Nearby.
TEL: 01692 404054

NORWICH

Albrow & Sons Family Jewellers
10 All Saints Green. NR1 3NA. (R. Albrow)
NAG Registered Valuer. Open 9.30-4.30. STOCK: *Jewellery, silver, plate, china, glass, furniture.* LOC: Opposite John Lewis. SER: Valuations; repairs. PARK: Behind John Lewis.
TEL: 01603 622569; FAX: 01603 766158
WEBSITE: www.albrowjewellers.co.uk

Liz Allport-Lomax
t/a Corner Antiques
EST. 1971. Open by appointment. STOCK: *Porcelain, glass, silver, objects of virtu, sewing accessories, small furniture and collectors' items - card cases, lace bobbins, snuff boxes, scent bottles.* FAIRS: All Lomax Antiques Fairs.
TEL: 01603 737631; MOBILE: 07747 843074
E-MAIL: lizmax@talktalk.net

Antiques & Interiors

31-35 Elm Hill. NR3 1HG. (P.S. Russell-Davis)
EST. 1976. Open 10-5. CL: Thurs. *STOCK: 19th-20th C furniture; Art Deco, Arts & Crafts and modern design; pictures, lighting, decorative objects.* PARK: Nearby.
TEL: 01603 622695; HOME: 01603 632446; FAX: same
E-MAIL: patrick.russelldavis@btopenworld.com
WEBSITE: www.englishartdeco.com

The Bank House Gallery

71 Newmarket Rd. NR2 2HW. (R.S. Mitchell)
EST. 1979. Resident. Open by appointment. *STOCK: English oil paintings especially Norwich and Suffolk schools, 19th C, £1,000-£50,000.* LOC: On A11 between City centre and ring road. SER: Valuations; restorations. PARK: Own. VAT: Stan/Spec.
TEL: 01603 633380
E-MAIL: paintings@bankart.com
WEBSITE: www.bankart.com

James Brett   BADA

42 St. Giles St. NR2 1LW.
**EST. 1870. Open 9.30-1 and 2-5, Sat. by appointment. STOCK: *Antique furniture, mahogany, walnut and oak; sculpture and metalwork.* LOC: Near City Hall. SIZE: Large. PARK: Easy. VAT: Stan/Spec. FAIRS: Olympia.
TEL: 01603 628171; FAX: 01603 630245**

Martin Causer Fine Art & Interiors

Websdale Court, Bedford St. NR2 1AR.
EST. 1993. Open 10-5, Sat. 10-3 or by appointment. *STOCK: 17th - 20th C oil paintings, bronzes and mirrors, £250-£20,000; 18th & 19th C furniture, £500-£3,000; decorative items, £250-£3,000;* LOC: Behind Jarrolds department store. SER: Valuations; restorations (pictures, frames and mirrors). SIZE: Medium. PARK: Easy VAT: Spec.
TEL: 01603 760769; home 01603 870961

Cloisters Antique & Collectors' Fair

St. Andrew's and Blackfriars Hall, St. Andrew's Plain. NR3 1AU. (Norwich City Council)
EST. 1976. Open Wed. 9-3 and the 2nd Saturday of the month. *STOCK: Wide range of antiques and collectables.* LOC: City centre. SIZE: 21 dealers. PARK: Easy.
TEL: 01603 628477; BOOKINGS: 01603 429032 (Gary Barnes)

Country and Eastern Ltd.

Old Skating Rink Gallery, 34-36 Bethel St. NR2 1NR. (J. Millward)
EST. 1978. *Lighting Assn.* Open 9.30-5. *STOCK: Oriental rugs, kelims and textiles; Indian and S.E. Asian antiques - furniture, objects, ceramics and metalwork.* LOC: Near The Forum. SER: Export. SIZE: Very large. PARK: Easy. VAT: Stan.
TEL: 01603 663890; FAX: 01603 758108
WEBSITE: www.countryandeastern.co.uk

Crome Gallery and Frame Shop

34 Elm Hill. NR3 1HG. (Ian Pusey)
EST. 1971. ICON. Open 10-5. *STOCK: Watercolours, oils and prints, mainly 20th C, some 19th C; wood carvings and sculpture.* LOC: Near cathedral. SER: Crome Gallery Conservation (oils, watercolours, prints, frames); framing. SIZE: Large. PARK: Easy.
TEL: 01603 622827
E-MAIL: info@cromegallery.co.uk
WEBSITE: www.cromegallery.co.uk

Clive Dennett Coins

66 St. Benedicts St. NR2 4AR.
EST. 1970. BNTA. CL: Thurs. and lunchtime. *STOCK: Coins and medals, ancient Greek to date, £5-£5,000; jewellery, 19th-20th C; banknotes, 20th C; both £5-£1,000.* SER: Valuations; buys at auction (as stock). SIZE: Small. PARK: Easy. FAIRS: London Coin; International Banknote, London; Maastricht.
TEL: 01603 624315

The Fairhurst Gallery

Bedford St. NR2 1AR.
EST. 1951. Open 9-5. CL: Sat. pm. *STOCK: Oil paintings, £5-£5,000; watercolours, £5-£2,000, both 19th-20th C; frames, 18th-20th C; furniture, £500-£10,000; mirrors.* LOC: Behind Travel Centre. SER: Restorations; cleaning; framemakers; gold leafing. SIZE: Medium. VAT: Spec.
TEL: 01603 614214

Nicholas Fowle Antiques   BADA

PO Box 1151. NR12 8WN.
**EST. 1965. Open by appointment. STOCK: *Furniture, £500-£20,000; works of art, £5-£1,000; both 17th-19th C.* SER: Restorations (furniture). SIZE: Medium. VAT: Stan/Spec. FAIRS: BADA.
TEL: 07831 218808; FAX: 01692 630378
E-MAIL: nicholas@nicholasfowleantiques.com
WEBSITE: www.nicholasfowleantiques.com**

Leona Levine Silver Specialist

2 Fisher's Lane. NR2 1ET. (Leona Levine and Bruce Thompson)
EST. 1865. Open Tues., Wed. and Fri. 9.15-4.30. *STOCK: Silver and Sheffield plate.* LOC: Off St Giles St., 150 yards from City Hall. SER: Valuations; engraving; restorations. PARK: Multi-storey. VAT: Stan/Spec.
TEL: 01603 628709; FAX: same
E-MAIL: leonabruce@waitrose.com

Maddermarket Antiques

18c Lower Goat Lane. NR2 1EL. (Mr and Mrs H. Tagg)
EST. 1978. NAG. Open 9-5. *STOCK: Antique, secondhand and modern jewellery and silver, £10-£10,000.* PARK: St Giles multi-storey.
TEL: 01603 620610; FAX: same
E-MAIL: maddermarketantiques@btopenworld.com

The Movie Shop
Antiquarian and Nostalgia Centre, 11 St. Gregory's
Alley. NR2 1ER. (Peter Cossey)
Open 11-5.30. STOCK: *Books, magazines and movie
ephemera; telephones, collectables and general antiques.* SIZE:
Large.
TEL: 01603 615239
E-MAIL: peter.cossey@ntlworld.com
WEBSITE: www.thenorwichmovieshop.com

Norwich Collectors Toyshop
Tombland Antiques Centre, Augustine Steward House,
14 Tombland. NR3 1HF. (S. Marshall)
EST. 1985. Open 9.30-5. STOCK: *Dinky and Corgi toys,
1940-1990, £5-£150; trains and soldiers, 1910-1980, £5-
£500; teddies and tin toys, 1920-1980, £5-£200.* SER:
Valuations. FAIRS: Sandown Park, NEC, Donington
Park, Doncaster Racecourse, Norfolk Showground.
TEL: 01603 457761

Stiffkey Bathrooms
89 Upper St. Giles St. NR2 1AB. (Brown and Hyde)
EST. 1985. RIBA Open 10-5 Tues.-Sat. Monday by
appointment. STOCK: *Victorian, Edwardian and French
bathroom fittings.* SER: Mail order period bathroom
accessories. SIZE: Small. PARK: Easy. VAT: Stan.
TEL: 01603 627850; FAX: 01603 619775
WEBSITE: www.stiffkeybathrooms.com

Tombland Antiques Centre
Augustine Steward House, 14 Tombland. NR3 1HF.
(Mrs Joan Gale)
EST. 1974. Open 10-5. STOCK: *Furniture, 18th-20th C,
£50-£2,000; china, porcelain, antiquities, dolls, Art Deco,
Art Nouveau, collectables, curios, militaria, silver, pictures,
postcards, jewellery, cranberry and other glass, toys,
kitchenalia, linen, needlework tools.* LOC: City centre,
opposite cathedral. SER: Valuations. SIZE: Large - 20
dealers. PARK: Elm Hill.
TEL: 01603 619129

The Tombland Bookshop
8 Tombland. NR3 1HF. (J.G. and A.H. Freeman)
EST. 1989. Open 9.30-5. STOCK: *Antiquarian and
secondhand books.* LOC: Opposite the Cathedral. SER:
Antiquarian and secondhand books bought and sold;
valuation, book binding and restoration. SIZE: Medium.
TEL: 01603 490000; FAX: 01603 760610
E-MAIL: sales@tomblandbookshop.co.uk

Tombland Jewellers & Silversmiths
12-13 Tombland. NR3 1HF. (Saleem Chaudhary)
EST. 1972. NAG. Open 9-5, Sat. 9-4. STOCK: *English
silver, flatware and jewellery, from 17th C; mustard pots,
collectors' items, barometers, barographs, from 18th C.* LOC:
Opposite Erpingham Gate, Norwich cathedral and
Maid's Head Hotel. SER: Valuations; restorations; export
facilities. VAT: Stan/Spec.
TEL: 01603 624914; FAX: 01603 764310

Valued History
9 Market Place. NR3 1HN. (Paul Murawski)
EST. 1995. Open 10.30-3.30. CL: Mon. STOCK:
*Antiquities, ancient to Tudor, £25-£1,000+; coins and other
artefacts, £5-£1,000.* SER: Valuations. SIZE: Small.
TEL: 01603 627413

Vintage Supplies Ltd
Crosswinds, Grubb St., Happisburgh. NR12 0RX.
Open by appointment. STOCK: *Specialist vintage motor
accessories and factors.*
TEL: 01692 650084; FAX: 01692 651451
E-MAIL: info@vintagesupplies.com
WEBSITE: www.vintagesupplies.com
www.completeautomobilist.com

POTTER HEIGHAM

Times Past Antiques
Station Rd. NR29 5AD. (P. Dellar)
Open Wed.-Sun. 10-5. STOCK: *Barometers, clocks, furniture
including reproduction, china, pictures, glass, militaria,
collectables, bric-a-brac, old fishing tackle and old guns bought
and sold.* LOC: A149 village centre. PARK: Easy.
TEL: 01692 670898

RAVENINGHAM

M.D. Cannell Antiques
Castell Farm, Beccles Rd. NR14 6NU.
EST. 1982. Resident. Open Fri., Sat., Sun. and Mon. 10-
6 or by appointment. STOCK: *Oriental rugs, carpets, kilims,
English and French furniture, metalwork and decorative
items.* LOC: On Raveningham Road. SER: Restorations
(rugs). SIZE: Large. PARK: Easy. VAT: Stan/Spec.
TEL: 01508 548441
E-MAIL: mal@norfolkrugs.co.uk
WEBSITE: www.norfolkrugs.co.uk

RINGSTEAD

The General Store & Hidden Treasures
41 High St. PE36 5JU. (Tim and Cathy Roberts)
EST. 1997. Open 8-5.30 inc. Sun; Tues., Wed. and Sat. 8-1.
STOCK: *Small furniture, porcelain, curios, kitchenalia, books
and magazines; interior and garden.* LOC: 3 miles from
Hunstanton. SIZE: 12 rooms including 2 courtyards.
PARK: Easy.
TEL: 01485 525270
E-MAIL: generalstore41@aol.com

SCRATBY

Keith Lawson Antique Clocks
Scratby Garden Centre, Beach Rd. NR29 3AJ.
EST. 1979. LBHI. Open seven days 2-6. STOCK: *Clocks
and barometers.* LOC: B1159. SER: Valuations;
restorations. SIZE: Large. PARK: Easy. VAT: Stan/Spec.
TEL: 01493 730950

SHERINGHAM

Parriss Jewellers
20 Station Rd. NR26 8RE. (H.M. Parriss)
EST. 1947. Open 9-5. STOCK: *Jewellery, £30-£5,000; silver, £40-£4,000; clocks, £100-£3,000.* LOC: A1082, in main street. SER: Valuations; restorations (jewellery, silver, clocks). SIZE: Medium. PARK: Within 150yds. VAT: Stan.
TEL: 01263 822661

The Westcliffe Gallery
2-8 Augusta St. NR26 8LA. (Richard and Sheila Parks) EST. 1979. Resident. Open 9.30-1 and 2-5.30, Sat. 9.30-5.30; (Sun. 10-4 summer only). STOCK: *Oils, watercolours and drawings, 19th-20th C, £100-£15,000; furniture.* LOC: Town centre. SER: Valuations; restorations (oils, watercolours, prints); gilding. SIZE: Medium. PARK: Easy. VAT: Stan/Spec.
TEL: 01263 824320
E-MAIL: sparks@westcliffegallery.co.uk

STALHAM

Relics
95 High St. NR12 9BB. (Nigel & Jane Hodgson)
EST. 2001. Open 9.30-4.30; CL: Wed. STOCK: *Furniture,* *country/pine, curios etc. East Anglian books and postcards.* SER: House clearance; local delivery. SIZE: Large.
TEL: 01692 582697

Stalham Antique Gallery   LAPADA
29 High St. NR12 9AH. (Mike Hicks)
EST. 1970. CINOA. Open 9-1 and 2-5, Sat. 9-1. STOCK: *Furniture, 17th C to 19th C; pictures, china, glass, brass.* **NOT STOCKED: Reproductions.** LOC: **20 mins. from Norwich.** SER: **Valuations; restorations.** SIZE: **Medium.** PARK: **Easy.** VAT: **Spec.**
TEL: **01692 580636;** FAX: **same**
E-MAIL: **mbhickslink@btinternet.com**
WEBSITE: **www.lapada.org**

STIFFKEY

Stiffkey Antiques
The Old Methodist Chapel. NR23 1AJ. (Colin Firmage)
EST. 1976. Open 10-5 including Sun. CL: Wed. and Thurs. 1st Oct. to Easter. STOCK: *Door furniture, window fittings, fireplaces and accessories, 1800-1920; bric-a-brac, bronze garden statuary and water features.* LOC: Coast road near Wells-next-the-Sea. PARK: Easy.
TEL: 01328 830690; FAX: 01328 830005

The Stiffkey Lamp Shop
Townshend Arms. NR23 1AJ. (R. Belsten and D. Mann)
EST. 1976. Open 10-5 including Sun. CL: Wed. and Thurs. 1st Oct. to Easter. STOCK: *Lamps including rare, hanging, wall and table and fittings, electric, converted gas and oil, 1800-1920, £100-£3,000.* LOC: Coast road near Wells-next-the-Sea. SIZE: Medium. PARK: Easy. VAT: Stan.
TEL: 01328 830460; FAX: 01328 830005
WEBSITE: www.stiffkeylampshop.co.uk

STOKE FERRY

Farmhouse Antiques
White's Farmhouse, Barker's Drove. PE33 9TA. (P. Philpot)
EST. 1969. Resident. Open by appointment. STOCK: *General antiques.* SER: Restorations; furniture made to order in old timber. PARK: Easy.
TEL: 01366 500588; MOBILE: 07971 859151

TACOLNESTON

Freya Antiques
St. Mary's Farm, Cheneys Lane. NR16 1DB.
EST. 1974. Usually open but appointment advisable; evenings by appointment. STOCK: *Antique furniture, especially pine and country (over 500 items in stock); secondhand and antiquarian books.* SER: Valuations; restorations. SIZE: Large. PARK: Own large. FAIRS: Own (see website for details).
TEL: 01508 489252; MOBILE: 07799 401067
E-MAIL: freyaantiques@yahoo.co.uk
WEBSITE: www.freyaantiques.co.uk; www.antiquesbarn.co.uk

TOTTENHILL

Jubilee Antiques
Coach House, Whin Common Rd. PE33 0RS. (A.J. Lee)
EST. 1953. Open daily including Sun. STOCK: *Georgian and Victorian furniture, £50-£4,000; interesting items.* LOC: Between King's Lynn and Downham Market, adjacent to A10. SER: Valuations; restorations (furniture). SIZE: Medium. PARK: Easy.
TEL: 01553 810681; HOME: same; FAX: 01553 760128.

TWYFORD

Norton Antiques
NR20 5LZ. (T. and N. Hepburn)
EST. 1966. Open by appointment. STOCK: *Furniture, 1680-1900, £25-£8,000; oils and watercolours, 19th to early 20th C, £25-£5,000; clocks, 18th-19th C, £50-£6,000; woodworking and craftsman's hand tools.* SER: Valuations. PARK: Easy.
TEL: 01362 683331

WELLS-NEXT-THE-SEA

Wells Antique Centre
The Old Mill, Maryland. NR23 1LY.
EST. 1986. Open 10-5 (10-4 winter) including Sun. STOCK: *General antiques and collectables.* SIZE: 15 dealers. PARK: Easy.
TEL: 01328 711433

WROXHAM

T.C.S. Brooke   BADA
The Grange. NR12 8RX. (S.T. Brooke)
EST. 1952. Open by appointment. STOCK: ***English porcelain, 18th C; furniture, mainly Georgian; silver, glass, works of art, Oriental rugs.*** LOC: **On main Norwich road.** SER: **Valuations.** SIZE: **2 large showrooms and gallery.** PARK: **Easy.** VAT: **Spec.**
TEL: **01603 782644**

WYMONDHAM

King
Market Place. NR18 0AX. (M. King)
EST. 1969. Open 9-4. CL: Thurs., Fri and Sat. except by appointment. STOCK: *General antiques, furniture, copper, brass, silver, jewellery, porcelain.* SIZE: 4 rooms. PARK: Easy. FAIRS: Lomax.
TEL: 01953 604758; EVENINGS: 01953 602427

Turret House
27 Middleton St. NR18 0AB. (Dr and Mrs D.H. Morgan)
EST. 1972. PBFA. Resident. STOCK: *Antiquarian books especially science and medical; occasional scientific instruments.* LOC: Corner of Vicar St., adjacent to War Memorial. SIZE: Small. VAT: Stan/Spec. FAIRS: London Scientific & Medical Instrument Fairs.
TEL: 01953 603462

Wymondham Antique and Collectors' Centre
3 Town Green. NR18 0PN. (Charles White)
EST. 1983. Open 10-5 including Sun. STOCK: *China including crested, Beswick, Moorcroft, Royal Doulton, Coalport, Victorian to 1960s; jewellery, postcards, books, glass including cranberry, toys, furniture, clocks, pine, prints, oils and watercolours.* SER: Valuations. SIZE: 2 floors, 22 dealers. PARK: Easy. FAIRS: Norwich; Swinderby; Crystal Palace; Newark; Peterborough - Easton Sports Centre.
TEL: 01953 604817; HOME: 01603 811112;
MOBILE: 07771 970112

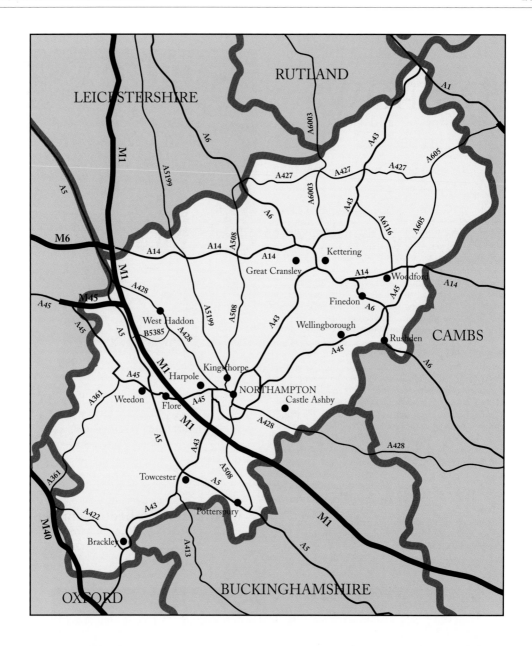

BRACKLEY

Brackley Antique Cellar
Manor Rd. NN13 6DF. (Jim Broomfield)
EST. 2000. Open 10-5 including Sun. STOCK: *Wide range
of general antiques.* LOC: Below Co-op Superstore. SIZE:
Large, over 150 dealers. PARK: Easy.
TEL: 01280 841841; FAX: 01280 841851

The Old Hall Bookshop
32 Market Place. NN13 7DP. (John and Juliet
Townsend)
EST. 1977. ABA. PBFA. ILAB BA. Open 9.30-5.30.

STOCK: *Antiquarian, secondhand and new books and maps.*
LOC: Town centre on east side of Market Place. SER:
Book search; Ordnance Survey mapping and data centre.
SIZE: Large. PARK: Easy. VAT: Stan. FAIRS: Occasional
PBFA/ABA.
TEL: 01280 704146; FAX: 01280 705131
E-MAIL: books@oldhallbooks.com
WEBSITE: www.oldhallbooks.com

Right Angle
24 Manor Rd. NN13 6AJ. (Chris and Val Pendleton)
EST. 1981. FATG. Open Tues.-Fri. 9-5, Sat. 9.30-1.
STOCK: *20th C paintings, prints and ceramics. Stock of*

antique paintings and prints at The Swan, Tetworth. SER: Framing (museum standard). PARK: Opposite.
TEL: 01280 702462
E-MAIL: chris@rightanglegallery.co.uk
WEBSITE: www.rightanglegallery.co.uk

CASTLE ASHBY

Castle Ashby Gallery
The Old Farmyard. NN7 1LF. (Geoffrey S. Wright & Son (Fine Paintings))
EST. 1987. Open 10-5 including Sun. CL: Mon. *STOCK: 19th-20th C oil paintings and watercolours, furniture and decorative furnishings.* LOC: Adjacent to Castle Ashby House. SER: Valuations; restorations (oils). PARK: Easy. VAT: Spec.
TEL: 01604 696787

EASTON NESTON

Christopher Jones Antiques
Pomfret House. NN12 7HS.
EST. 1977. Open by appointment. *STOCK: Period and decorative furniture, lighting, porcelain, glass and objects, 18th-20th C.* SER: Interior decor advice. SIZE: Large. PARK: Easy. VAT: Spec. FAIRS: Olympia.
TEL: 01327 351829; FAX: 01327 352437; MOBILE: 07775 900436
E-MAIL: pomfrethouse@msn.com

FINEDON

Affleck Bridge Antiques
7-9 High St. NN9 5JN. (Cheney Antiques & EK Antiques Robert)
EST. 1992. Open 9-5.30, Sun. 11-4. *STOCK: 18th-20th C furniture, china, silver and glass, £10-10,000.* LOC: A6. SER: Valuations; french polishing; restoration; probate valuations; light removals. SIZE: Large. PARK: Easy.
TEL: 01933 681048/681882; HOME: 01933 680085

Simon Banks Antiques
28 Church St. NN9 5NA.
EST. 1984. Open every day. *STOCK: 17th-20th C furniture, £50-£5,000; glass, silver, ceramics, prints, copper, decorative and collectable items, clocks including longcase, wall and mantel.* LOC: Near church. SER: Valuations; search; nationwide delivery. SIZE: Large. PARK: Easy. VAT: Stan/Spec.
TEL: 01933 680371; MOBILE: 07976 787539
E-MAIL: simon@banksantiques.com
WEBSITE: www.banksantiques.com

M.C. Chapman   LAPADA
EST. 1967. Open 9-5.30, Sun. 11-5 by prior appointment. *STOCK: Furniture, clocks, decorative items, 18th-20th C, £100-£4,000.* SIZE: Large. VAT: Stan/Spec/Global.
TEL: 07771 883060

Church Street Antiques
3 Church St. NN9 5NA. (Bob Harrison)
EST. 1972. Open 10-5, Sun. 11-4, CL: Mon. *STOCK: Decorative and traditional furniture, mirrors, pictures, glass, clocks, ceramics, silver and architectural items.* LOC: Junction 10, A14. SER: Delivery and shipping. SIZE: 10 dealers + warehouse. PARK: Own. VAT: Spec/Global/Export.
TEL: 01933 682515
E-MAIL: bob@bh-antiques.co.uk
WEBSITE: www.3churchstreetantiques.co.uk

FLORE

Blockheads and Granary Antiques
The Huntershields. NN7 4LZ. (Mrs C. Madeira and Richard Sear)
EST. 1968. Open 9.30-6, Sun. and other times by appointment. *STOCK: Furniture, 17th-19th C, £50-£5,000; early metalware specialist; decorative and period items, 19th C, £50-£2,000; wooden hat makers' blocks, brims and complete models.* LOC: Off M1, junction 16, into Flore, last turning on left at bollard, premises on right at bottom of lane. SIZE: Large. PARK: Easy. FAIRS: Newark.
TEL: 01327 340718; HOME: same; FAX: 01327 349263

GT. CRANSLEY

Bryan Perkins Antiques
The Old Chicken Farm. NN14 1PX. (J. Perkins)
EST. 1971. *Trade Only.* Open 9-5. CL: Sat. pm. *STOCK: Furniture and paintings, 19th C, £200-£5,000; small items.* LOC: Just off A43 south of Kettering. SER: Valuations; restorations (furniture). SIZE: Large. PARK: Easy.
TEL: Mobile - 07780 850531; HOME: 01536 790472

HARPOLE

Inglenook Antiques
23 High St. NN7 4DH. (T. and P. Havard)
EST. 1971. Open 9-7. *STOCK: General antiques, £1-£500.* LOC: Main street. SER: Restorations (longcase clocks). SIZE: Small. PARK: Easy.
TEL: 01604 830007

HIGHAM FERRERS

Cranberry House Antiques
30 High St. NN10 8BL
EST. 1963. ACG. Open 10-5, Sun 11-4. CL: BH. *STOCK: General antiques, desk collectables, dolls and bears, specialist small quality collectors' itmes.* SER: Consultation and vetting. SIZE: Small. PARK: On street outside and oppposite. VAT: Spec./Flat. FAIRS: USA and UK.
TEL: 01933 319200
E-MAIL: antiques@priority-mail.net
WEBSITE: www.sell-to.us

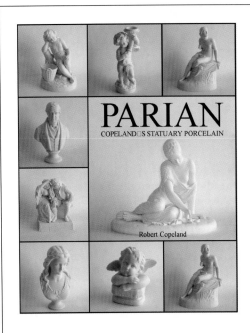

279 x 216 mm. 352 pp 84 col., 463 b.&w.
£45.00 Hardback

PARIAN

COPELAND'S STATUARY PORCELAIN

Robert Copeland

This is the first comprehensive collection of over 500 illustrations of the Parian productions by Copeland, including the making costs and selling prices over forty years and illustrations from the Copeland archives. Parian - a high-quality, unglazed porcelain - was developed in the early 1840s by Copeland & Garrett, which was the first company to exhibit it in 1845. Its purpose was to provide small sculptures for the public at a time when full size marble statues were gracing the homes of wealthy people. *Parian - Copeland's Statuary Porcelain* tells this fascinating story in detail, beginning with its origin and introduction. The book goes on to describe the manufacturing processes of mould-making and the casting of the figures. Also included is a comprehensive catalogue of Copeland's productions of statuettes, groups and portrait busts.

For full details of all ACC publications, log on to our website:
www.antiquecollectorsclub.com
or telephone 01394 389950 for a free catalogue

ISLIP

John Roe Antiques
The Furnace Site, Kettering Rd. NN14 3JW
Open 9.30-5.30. STOCK: *General antiques and shipping goods.*
TEL: 01832 732937

KETTERING

Dragon Antiques
85 Rockingham Rd. NN16 8LA. (Sandra Hunt)
EST. 1982. Open 10-4. CL: Thurs. STOCK: *Pictures, Oriental items, militaria and general antiques.* SER: Framing; restoration. PARK: Easy.
TEL: 01536 517017
E-MAIL: sandra@zen2121.orangehome.co.uk

KINGSTHORPE

Laila Gray Antiques
25 Welford Rd. NN2 8AQ.
Open 9-5.30. STOCK: *Pine.* SER: Waxing; stripping.
TEL: 01604 715277

The Old Brigade
10a Harborough Rd. NN2 7AZ. (S.C. Wilson)
EST. 1978. Open by appointment. STOCK: *Military items, especially German Third Reich, 1850s to 1945, £10-*

£10,000. LOC: Junction 15, M1. SER: Valuations. SIZE: Medium. PARK: Easy. VAT: Stan/Spec.
TEL: 01604 719389; FAX: 01604 712489
E-MAIL: theoldbrigade@btconnect.com; stewart@theoldbrigade.co.uk
WEBSITE: www.theoldbrigade.co.uk

NORTHAMPTON

Michael Jones Jeweller
1 Gold St. NN1 1SA.
EST. 1919. NAG. Open 9-5.30. STOCK: *Silver, gold and gem jewellery, silverware.* VAT: Margin.
TEL: 01604 632548; FAX: 01604 233813
E-MAIL: enquiries@michaeljonesjeweller.co.uk
WEBSITE: www.michaeljonesjeweller.co.uk

Occultique
30 St Michael's Ave. NN1 4JQ. (Michael J. Lovett)
EST. 1973. Open by appointment only. STOCK: *Books and artefacts, 50p-£500.* SER: Catalogue available. SIZE: Small. PARK: Easy. VAT: Stan.
TEL: 01604 627727
E-MAIL: enquiries@occultique.co.uk
WEBSITE: www.occultique.co.uk

POTTERSPURY

The Reindeer Antiques Centre   BADA LAPADA
43 Watling St. NN12 7QD. (John Butterworth)
**EST. 1977. Open 10-5 including Sun. and Bank
Holidays.** *STOCK: Furniture, porcelain, glass, silver,
clocks, paintings, bronzes and needlework.* SIZE: **Large.**
PARK: **Own.**
TEL: 01908 543704
E-MAIL: sales@reindeer-antiques.co.uk
WEBSITE: www.reindeerantiquescentre.co.uk

Reindeer Antiques Ltd   BADA LAPADA
43 Watling St. NN12 7QD. (John Butterworth)
EST. 1959. Open 9-6, inc. Sun. *STOCK: Fine English
furniture, 17th-19th C; caddies, clocks, small collectables,
paintings.* LOC: **A5.** SIZE: **Large.** PARK: **Own.** VAT:
Stan/Spec. FAIRS: **BADA. LAPADA.**
TEL: 01908 542407/542200; FAX: 01908 542121
E-MAIL: sales@reindeerantiques.co.uk
WEBSITE: www.reindeerantiques.co.uk

RUSHDEN

Don Sherwood Antiques
59 Little St. NN10 0LS. (Mr. & Mrs. Donald
Sherwood)
EST. 1960. Open 11-5. CL: Mon. & Thurs. *STOCK:
General antiques.* LOC: South of main shopping area.
PARK: Easy.
TEL: 01933 353265
E-MAIL: 10duckend@freeukisp.co.uk

TOWCESTER

Ron Green
227-239 Watling St. West. NN12 6DD. (Nicholas and
Christopher Green)
EST. 1952. Open 9-6, Sun. by appointment. *STOCK:
English and Continental furniture, paintings and decorative
items, £30-£30,000.* SER: Valuations; restorations. SIZE:
Large. PARK: Easy.
TEL: 01327 350387/350615; FAX: 01327 350387
E-MAIL: ron@green227.freeserve.co.uk
WEBSITE: www.rongreenantiques.com

Lorraine Spooner Antiques   LAPADA
211 Watling Street West. NN12 6BX.
**EST. 1996. Open 9.30-5.30, Sun. and Mon. by
appointment.** *STOCK: Furniture, clocks, silver, porcelain,
glass, paintings and prints, treen and metalware, linens,
books, 1790-1940, £1-£10,000.* LOC: **Main street.** SER:
Wedding lists. SIZE: **Medium.** PARK: **Nearby.**
TEL: 01327 358777; MOBILE: 07855 828962
E-MAIL: lorraine@lsantiques.com
WEBSITE: www.lsantiques.com

WEEDON

Helios & Co (Antiques)
25-27 High St. NN7 4QD. (J. Skiba and B. Walters)
EST. 1976. Open 9.30-5.30, Sat. and Sun. 10-5. CL:
Mon. *STOCK: English and Continental furniture especially
dining tables and sets of chairs; decorative accessories, longcase
clocks and pianos.* LOC: 4 miles from junction 16, M1
towards Daventry. SER: Suppliers and restorers to H. M.
Govt. SIZE: 20 showrooms. PARK: Easy. VAT: Spec.
TEL: 01327 340264; FAX: 01327 342235
E-MAIL: john@skiba.net
WEBSITE: www.heliosantiques.com

The Village Antique Market
62 High St. NN7 4QD. (E.A. and J.M. Saunders)
EST. 1967. Open 10.30-5.15 including Sun. and Bank
Holidays. *STOCK: General antiques and interesting items.*
LOC: Off junction 16, M1. SIZE: Large - 40 dealers.
PARK: In front yard.
TEL: 01327 342015

Weedon Antiques
23 High St. NN7 4QD. (N.L. Tillman)
EST. 2000. Open 10-5, Sun. and Bank Holidays 10.30-
4.30. CL: Mon. and Tues. *STOCK: Porcelain including
Royal Worcester, Coalport, Derby, Noritake, George Jones,
Clarice Cliff, Aynsley and Limoges; silver including
Georgian, all £15-£1,000; glass including cranberry,
vaseline, rummers, 17th-20th C, £15-£500; pictures, £50-
£1,000; furniture, £200-£3,000.* LOC: A45, 2 miles from
junction 16, M1. SER: Valuations. SIZE: Medium. PARK:
Easy. VAT: Global. FAIRS: NEC; Stafford (Bowman).
TEL: 01327 349777; MOBILE: 07711 570798
E-MAIL: weedonantiques@tiscali.co.uk

WELLINGBOROUGH

Antiques and Bric-a-Brac Market
Market Sq. NN8 1AF.
Open Tues. 9-4. *STOCK: General antiques and collectables.*
LOC: Town centre. SIZE: 135 stalls. PARK: Easy.
TEL: 01933 231739; MOBILE: 07786 522407

Park Gallery & Bookshop
16 Cannon St. NN8 5DJ. (Mrs J.A. Foster)
EST. 1979. Open 10-5.30. *STOCK: Books, maps and
prints, 18th-19th C, £2-£500.* LOC: Continuation of
A510 into town. SER: Framing; book search. SIZE:
Medium. PARK: Easy.
TEL: 01933 222592
E-MAIL: judy@parkbookshop.freeserve.co.uk
WEBSITE: www.ukbookworld.com/members/
parkbookshop

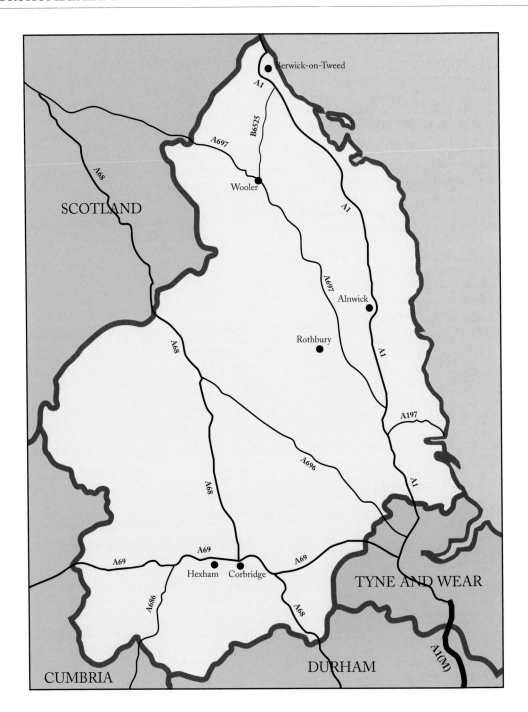

ALNWICK

G.M. Athey
Castle Corner, Narrowgate. NE66 0NP.
EST. 1980. Open 8.30-4.30. STOCK: *English oak and mahogany furniture, glass, china and brass, 18th-19th C.* LOC: Part of Alnwick Castle. SER: Restorations (furniture including upholstery). SIZE: 3 floors. PARK: Easy. FAIRS: Newark.
TEL: 01665 604229; MOBILE: 07836 718350
E-MAIL: m.athey@alncom.net

Bailiffgate Antique Pine
22 Bailiffgate. NE66 1LX. (S. Aston)
EST. 1994. Open Thurs.-Sat. 10-4.30. STOCK: *Country pine furniture.* LOC: Opposite the castle. SER: Valuations;

buys at auction. SIZE: Large. PARK: Easy.
TEL: 01665 603616
E-MAIL: saaston@msn.com

Barter Books
Alnwick Station. NE66 2NP. (Stuart & Mary Manley)
EST. 1991. IOBA. Open 9-5, inc. Sun. *STOCK: Antiquarian books, £10-£5,000.* LOC: Off A1, on left on town approach. SIZE: Large. PARK: Easy.
TEL: 01665 604888; FAX: 01665 604444
E-MAIL: webquery@barterbooks.co.uk
WEBSITE: www.barterbooks.co.uk

Tamblyn
12 Bondgate Without. NE66 1PP. (Prof. B.E. Hirst)
EST. 1981. Open 10-4.30. *STOCK: General antiques including country furniture, pottery, pictures; antiquities, Scandinavian glass, to 20th C, £5-£1,500.* LOC: Diagonally opposite war memorial at southern entrance to town. SER: Valuations. SIZE: Medium. PARK: Easy.
TEL: 01665 603024; HOME: same
E-MAIL: profbehirst@tamblynant.fsnet.co.uk

BERWICK-UPON-TWEED

Treasure Chest
53 West St. TD15 2DX. (Y. Scott and K. Russell)
EST. 1988. Open 11-4. CL: Tues. and Thurs. *STOCK: China, jewellery, glass, clothes, linen, silver plate and small furniture, from 1860, £1-£400.* LOC: Approximately 1 mile from A1. SER: Restorations (china). SIZE: Medium. PARK: Easy.
TEL: 01289 307736/305675

Woodside Reclamation (Architectural Antiques)
Woodside, Scremerston. TD15 2SY. (Keith Allan and Lynne Gray)
EST. 1990. SALVO. Open 9-5. CL: Mon. *STOCK:*

Architectural salvage 19th C including fireplaces, baths, kitchen pine, timber, beams, building materials. LOC: Adjacent A1, just south of town. SER: Restorations (stripping and finishing). SIZE: Large. PARK: Easy.
TEL: 01289 331211; HOME: 01289 302658;
E-MAIL: info@redbaths.co.uk
WEBSITE: www.redbaths.co.uk

CORBRIDGE

Hedley's of Corbridge
Bishop's Yard, Main St. NE45 5LA. (P. Torday)
Open Mon. 12-4, Tues.-Sat. 10-5. *STOCK: Furniture, specialising in Arts and Crafts, glass, china including Moorcroft and studio pottery, Limoges boxes, jewellery and silver, pictures and prints, longcase and mantel clocks.* LOC: To rear of Shell garage. SER: Valuations. SIZE: Medium. PARK: Own at rear.
TEL: 01434 634936
E-MAIL: hedleys@torday96.fsnet.co.uk

Renney Antiques
Bishops Court, Main St. NE45 5LA.
EST. 1987. Open 10-5 or by appointment. CL: Mon. *STOCK: Decorative lighting, English and French furniture, garden, architectural and decorative items, textiles, china and glass.* SIZE: Large.
TEL: 01434 633663

HEXHAM

The Finishing Touch Warehouse
26e Haugh Lane Industrial Estate. NE46 3AL. (Malcom Eglin and Patricia Eglin)
EST. 1994. Open 10-5. *STOCK: Decorative antiques and period home furnishings, 17th-19th C, ideal for interior design, specialising in country oak.* SER: Pictorial

newsletter every month. SIZE: Large PARK: Easy FAIRS: Most major UK fairs.
TEL: 01434 609609; MOBILE: 07966 398123
E-MAIL: malcolm@hexhamantiques.com
WEBSITE: www.hexhamantiques.com

Priest Popple Books
9B Priest Popple. NE46 1PF. (John B. Patterson)
EST. 1997. Open 9-5. *STOCK: Books – second-hand non-fiction, first editions, antiquarian, £5-£1,500; sheet music, LPs.* LOC: From A69 to town centre, premises top of bus station. SER: Valuations; book-binding; booksearch. SIZE: Medium. PARK: Easy.
TEL: 01434 607773
E-MAIL: priestpopple.books@tiscali.co.uk

The Violin Shop Ltd
27 Hencotes. NE46 2EQ. (D. Mann)
EST. 1970. VSA. Open 9-5 or by appointment. *STOCK: Violins, violas, cellos, basses and bows.* SER: Repairs; restorations; bow re-hairing; new instruments made.
TEL: 01434 607897
E-MAIL: davehexviolins@aol.com
WEBSITE: www.hexham-violins.co.uk

ROTHBURY

Bridgedale Antiques
Bridgedale House. Bridge St. NE65 7SE. (Peter and

Paul Leatherland)
EST. 1970. Open 10-5. *STOCK: Furniture, 18th C to 1920s; decorative china, clocks, metalware, mirrors and pictures, £5-£4,000.* LOC: Opposite Post Office. SIZE: Medium. PARK: Easy. VAT: Margin.
TEL: 01669 621117

WOOLER

Hamish Dunn Antiques
17 High St. NE71 6BU.
EST. 1986. Open 9.30-12 and 1-4.30. CL: Thurs. *STOCK: Curios and collectables, 19th-20th C, £5-£500; antiquarian and secondhand books, 18th-20th C, £1-£200; small furniture, 19th-20th C, £15-£1,000.* LOC: Off A697. SIZE: Medium. PARK: Easy.
TEL: 01668 281341; FAX: same; HOME: 01668 282013
E-MAIL: hamishoscr@aol.com

James Miller Antiques　　　　　　　　LAPADA
8 Station Rd. NE71 6SP.
EST. 1947. Open from 9am. STOCK: *18th - 20th C furniture.* LOC: A697. SIZE: Warehouse. PARK: Own. VAT: Stan/Spec. FAIRS: Newark.
TEL: 01668 281500; FAX: 01668 282383
E-MAIL: jmiller.antiques@virgin.net
WEBSITE: www.millersantiquesofwooler.com

GILLOWS
of Lancaster and London
1730-1840

Susan E. Stuart

It is hard to overstate the importance of the Gillows material in relationship to the history of both British and North American furniture. No other furniture archive covers the same period of time and in as much detail. Information on a wide variety of topics such as woods and finishes, furniture design developments, business practices, workmen, customers, family, social issues and international events which affected the Gillows firm have been extracted from the letters, sketchbooks and ledgers and pieced together to form an account of the firm's development and history from 1730-1840. Gillows was a unique firm. No other cabinetmakers were in business for as long a period, or had a showroom and workshop in eighteenth century London from which to view the fashion scene as well as another showroom and manufacturing base in the provinces. This enabled them to cover a great deal of Great Britain (to say nothing of their trans-Atlantic and European trade via the two branches) and make fashionable furniture, but cheaper than their rivals in London. The publication of this book will help owners, collectors and dealers to identify Gillows furniture and furniture made by other cabinetmakers to the firm's designs. It also has a wider application by offering a firm chronology for the development of different types of western furniture. The advice given by Gillows on furniture design and social customs, both to their customers and to their workforce, will be of interest to social as well as furniture historians and curators. This monograph also dispels some of the myths which have grown up around the firm and furniture making generally.

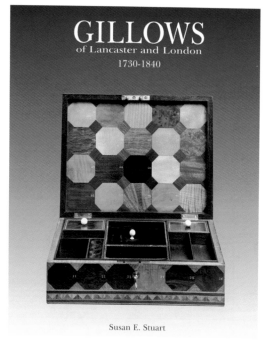

GILLOWS
of Lancaster and London
1730-1840

Susan E. Stuart

279 x 216 mm. 800 pp 600 col.
£125.00 Hardback, 2 volume slipcase

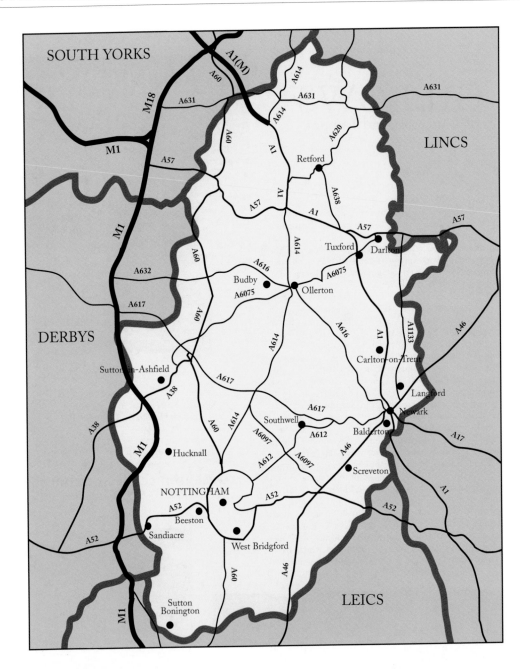

BALDERTON

Anthony W. Laywood
Kercheval House, 79 Main St. NG24 3NN.
EST. 1967. Open by appointment. STOCK: *Antiquarian books, pre-1850, £20-£8,000.* LOC: 2 miles south of Newark. SER: Valuations; buys at auction. SIZE: Medium. PARK: Easy.
TEL: 01636 659031
E-MAIL: books@anthonylaywood.co.uk

BEESTON

Turner Violins Ltd.
1-5 Lily Grove. NG9 1QL. (Steve and Liz Turner)
EST. 1987. Open 9-6, Sat. 9-5. STOCK: *18th-20th C violins, violas, cellos, basses, bows; concertinas, harps.* SER: Valuations; restorations. PARK: Easy.
TEL: 0115 943 0333; FAX: 0115 943 0444; MOBILE: 07831 265272
E-MAIL: info@turnerviolins.co.uk
WEBSITE: www.turnerviolins.co.uk

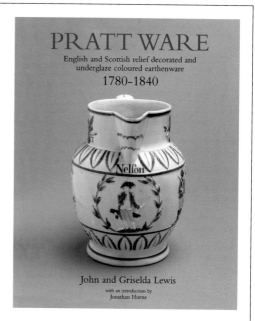
BUDBY

Dukeries Antiques Centre
Thoresby Park. NG22 9EX. (J.A. and J.E. Coupe)
EST. 1967. Open 10-5 including Sun. STOCK: *Furniture, £25-£8,000; porcelain, £10-£500; pictures, £50-£5,000; all 18th to early 20th C.* LOC: From A1 take A614 towards Nottingham to Ollerton, turn right on to A616. SER: Valuations; restorations (furniture). SIZE: Large. PARK: Easy. VAT: Stan/Spec.
TEL: 01623 822252; FAX: 01623 822209
E-MAIL: dukeriesantiques@aol.com

DARLTON

A.J. O'Sullivan Antiques   LAPADA
Whimpton House, Dunham Rd. NG22 0TA.
EST. 1977. Resident. Open 9-5, Sat. 9-1. STOCK:
Furniture, 18th-19th C, £200-£4,000: decorative items.
LOC: From A1 take A57 (Lincoln road) at Markham
Moor roundabout through Darlton, premises ¼ mile
on left. SER: Valuations; restorations (furniture). SIZE:
Medium. PARK: Easy. VAT: Stan/Spec/Global. FAIRS:
Newark.
TEL: 01777 228626; FAX: same
E-MAIL: tonyos@btconnect.com

LANGFORD

T. Baker
Langford House Farm. NG23 7RR.
EST. 1966. *Trade Only.* CL: Sun. except by appointment and Sat. STOCK: *Victoriana, period furniture and oak.* LOC: A1133. SIZE: Medium. PARK: Own.
TEL: 01636 704026

NEWARK

Castle Gate Antiques Centre
55 Castle Gate. NG24 1BE.
EST. 1985. Open 9.30-5. STOCK: *Wide variety of general antiques, dealers listed below.* LOC: A46 through town, 250yds. from castle. SER: Restorations. SIZE: Large. PARK: Easy.
TEL: 01636 700076

D.J. Green Antiques   LAPADA
Newark Antiques Warehouse, Kelham Rd. NG24 1BX. (Nick Mellors)
Open 9-5.30, Sat 10-4; Swinderby Fair Sundays 10-4;
STOCK: *17th-20th C furniture, treen, metalware, pottery, porcelain, glass, silver, samplers and textiles, clocks and collectors' items.* SIZE: Large - 50 dealers and 75 cabinets.
TEL: 01636 674869
E-MAIL: antiques@djgreen.co.uk
WEBSITE: www.newarkantiques.co.uk

M.B.G. Antiques, Fine Art & Jewellery

41B Castlegate. NG24 1BE. (Margaret Begley-Gray) EST. 1982. DGA. Open Thurs.-Sat. 10-4. STOCK: *Jewellery, paintings, miniatures, 19th to early 20th C, to £4,000.* SER: Valuations; restorations (jewellery and paintings). SIZE: Small. PARK: Nearby. FAIRS: NEC; Robert Bailey.
TEL: 01636 650790; MOBILE: 07702 209808
E-MAIL: mbegleygray@aol.com, mbgrey@gmail.com

Newark Antiques Centre

Regent House, Lombard St. NG24 1XP. (Jon Parry and Steven Jones)
EST. 1988. Open 9.30-5, Sun. and BH 11-4; Open evenings by appointment for group visits. STOCK: *Georgian, Victorian and period furniture, pottery, porcelain, glass, textiles, militaria, clocks, pictures, books, silver, antiquities, jewellery, paintings, coins, Oriental, pine, oil lamps.* LOC: Opposite bus station. SER: Upholstery; fabrics; cleaning (metal); valuations; restorations. SIZE: 55 units and 80 cabinets. PARK: Own.
TEL: 01636 643979; MOBILE: 07976 313119
E-MAIL: thephoenixexperi@btinternet.com
WEBSITE: www.newarkantiquescentre.co.uk

Newark Antiques Warehouse

Old Kelham Rd. NG24 1BX.
EST. 1984. Open 9-5.30, Sat. 10-4; Sunday prior to Swinderby Art Fair. STOCK: *Mainly 17th-20th C furniture and decorative items, smalls and collectables.* LOC: Just off A1. SER: Valuations. SIZE: 30+ dealers, 80+ cabinets. PARK: Easy. FAIRS: Swinderby; Newark.
TEL: 01636 674869; FAX: 01636 612933
E-MAIL: enquiries@newarkantiques.co.uk
WEBSITE: www.newarkantiques.co.uk

No. 1 Castlegate Antiques

1-3 Castlegate. NG24 1AZ. (Christine Kavanagh) EST. 1998. Open 9.30-5, Sat. 9.30-5.30. STOCK: *18th-19th C English mahogany furniture; 17th-19th C English oak furniture and decorative objects; all £100-£10,000.* LOC: Town centre. SER: Valuations. SIZE: Large - 8 dealers. PARK: Opposite. VAT: Stan/Spec.
TEL: 01636 701877
WEBSITE: www.castlegateantiques.com

Pearman Antiques & Interiors

9 Castle Gate. NG24 1AZ. (Jan and Stan Parnham and Sally Moulds)
EST. 1996. Open 10-4. CL: Mon. STOCK: *Chairs, single and sets, upholstered, oak, mahogany and walnut. Oak, mahogany and walnut chests of drawers. Oak mule and Lancashire chests, chiffoniers, small and side tables. English and Continental beds; decorative items.* LOC: Opposite castle. SIZE: Medium. PARK: 50 metres.
TEL: 01636 679158

NOTTINGHAM

Acanthus Antiques & Collectables incorporating Nottingham Medals

140 Derby Rd., Off Canning Circus. NG7 1LR. (Trak E. and Mrs Smith). Est. 1980. Open 10.30-2.30, Sat. 12.30-4. SIZE: Small. STOCK: *Ceramics and glass, 19th-20th C, £5-£1,000; collectors' items, mainly 20th C, £5-£800; period furniture, 18th-19th C, £200-£1,500; militaria, medals and badges.* LOC: Derby Rd. exit from Queens Medical Centre traffic island, continue for 1 mile, shop on left. PARK: Nearby. SER: Valuations; restorations (furniture and ceramics); buys at auction. FAIRS: Newark, Swinderby, Donington.
TEL: 0115 924 3226
E-MAIL: trak.e.smith22@hotmail.co.uk
WEBSITE: www.acanthusantiques-nottingham.co.uk

Castle Antiques

78 Derby Rd. NG1 5FD. (L. Adamson)
Open 9.30-5. STOCK: *General antiques, vintage lighting, maps and prints.* LOC: City centre. SIZE: 2 floors. PARK: Meters.
TEL: 0115 947 3913
E-MAIL: lezadamson@btinternet.com
WEBSITE: www.castleantiques-nottm.co.uk

Collectors World

188 Wollaton Rd., Wollaton. NG8 1HJ. (M.T. Ray) EST. 1975. Open 10.30-5. CL: Mon. STOCK: *Ancient and*

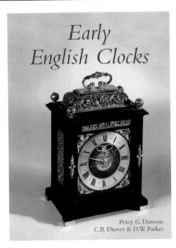

Early English Clocks

Percy G. Dawson
C.B. Drover & D.W. Parkes

A welcome reprint of the standard work of reference on English horology up to the beginning of the eighteenth century. Some 800 superb photographs, many of them details of the mechanisms, along with their careful descriptions provide an unrivalled catalogue of the work of the earlier makers, and place their work within a carefully defined chain of development.

279 x 216mm. 552pp. 36col. 800b.&w.
£45.00 Hardback

modern coins and banknotes, 20th C cigarette and postcards, 19th C medals and accessories, all £1–£100. LOC: Ring road at A609 Crown Island/Raleigh Island. SER: Valuations; buys at auction (coins and banknotes). SIZE: Small. PARK: Easy. VAT: Margin. FAIRS: Birmingham MSCF; various specialist.
TEL: 0115 928 0347; FAX: same
E-MAIL: info@collectorsworld-nottingham.com
WEBSITE: www.collectorsworld-nottingham.com

D.D. and A. Ingle
380 Carlton Hill. NG4 1JA.
EST. 1968. Open 9-5. STOCK: *Coins and medals, from Roman, £50–£100; jewellery and watches, £50–£1,000.* SER: Valuations; restorations. SIZE: Small. PARK: Nearby.
TEL: 0115 987 3325
E-MAIL: ddaingle@talk21.com

Melville Kemp Ltd   LAPADA
79-81 Derby Rd. NG1 5BA.
EST. 1900. Open 10-5, CL: Thurs. STOCK: *Jewellery, Victorian; silver, Georgian and Victorian, both £5–£10,000; ornate English and Continental porcelain, Sheffield plate.* **LOC: From Nottingham on main Derby Rd.** SER: **Valuations; restorations (silver, china, jewellery); buys at auction.** SIZE: **Small.** PARK: **Easy.** VAT: **Stan/Spec.**
TEL: **0115 941 7055;** FAX: **0115 941 3075**

Luna
139 Lower Parliament St. NG1 1EE. (Paul Rose)
EST. 1990. Open 10-6. STOCK: *Original 20th C design – glass, ceramics, furniture & telephones from £5.* SIZE: Small. PARK: Easy. VAT: Global.
TEL: 0115 924 3267
E-MAIL: info@luna-online.co.uk
WEBSITE: www.luna-online.co.uk

Nottingham Architectural Antiques & Reclamation
St. Albans Works, 181 Hartley Rd., Radford. NG7 3DW. (J. Sanders and L. Baldwin)
Open 9-6, Sun. 10-4. CL: Tues., Wed. & Thurs. STOCK: *All types of architectural salvage inc. original fireplaces and accessories in cast iron, slate, marble, stone and timber, 18th–20th C. Reclaimed doors, leaded glass, door furniture, sanitaryware. Reclaimed building materials, flooring and timber; reclaimed parquet flooring a speciality.* LOC: Close to city centre. SER: Restorations (fireplaces); repolishing; paint stripping; blasting. SIZE: Medium, with outdoor yard. PARK: Easy, free. FAIRS: SALVO Newark and Swinderby.
TEL: 0115 979 0666; FAX: 0115 979 1607
E-MAIL: nottingham.reclaims@ntlworld.com
WEBSITE: www.naar.co.uk

Vintage Wireless Shop
The Hewarths, Sandiacre. NG10 5NQ.
(Mr Dennis Yates)
EST. 1977. Open by appointment. STOCK: *Early wireless and pre-war televisions, crystal sets, horn speakers, valves, books and magazines, WW2 military radios and spy sets.* SER: Valuations; repairs; finder. PARK: Easy.
TEL: 0115 9393139; FAX: 0115 9490180;
MOBILE: 07980 912686
E-MAIL: vintagewireless@aol.com

Cynthia Walmsley   LAPADA
PO Box 337. NG7 1BF.
STOCK: **Portrait miniatures, silhouettes and portraits.**
TEL: 0115 941 7061; MOBILE: 07785 792 227; FAX: 0115 948 0785
E-MAIL: cynthia@c-walmsley.co.uk
WEBSITE: www.c-walmsley.co.uk

OLLERTON

Hamlyn Lodge
Station Rd. NG22 9BN. (N. and J.S. Barrows)
EST. 1975. Open 10-5. STOCK: *General antiques, 18th-20th C, £100-£3,000.* LOC: Off A614. SER: Restorations (furniture). SIZE: Small. PARK: Easy.
TEL: 01623 823600
E-MAIL: enquiries@hamlynlodge.co.uk
WEBSITE: www.hamlynlodge.co.uk

RETFORD

Stanley Hunt Jewellers
22 The Square. DN22 6DQ.
Open 9-5. STOCK: *Jewellery and silver including modern.*
TEL: 01777 703144

SANDIACRE

The Glory Hole
50 Station Rd. NG10 5BG. (Colin and Debbie Reid)
EST. 1984. Open 10-5.30. CL: Wed pm. STOCK: *Victorian pine, walnut, oak and mahogany furniture; bespoke kitchens; restored fireplaces and reproductions; .* SER: Restorations; stripping; polishing; repairs; reproduction cabinet fittings; fitting. SIZE: Large - 2 floors. PARK: Opposite.
TEL: 01159 394081; FAX: 01159 394085

SCREVETON

Red Lodge Antiques
Fosseway. NG13 8JJ. (Mrs L. Bradford)
EST. 1999. Resident. *Trade & Export Only.* Open by appointment. STOCK: *Shipping furniture, 1900-1930s, £25-£1,000. Large selection of stained glass windows.* LOC: A46 approx. 10 miles from Nottingham and 5 miles from Newark. SER: Container facilites available. SIZE: Large. PARK: Own.
TEL: 01949 20244; HOME: same

SHERWOOD

Treasure Chest of Sherwood
494 Mansfield Rd. NG5 2FB. (Madelaine Floyd)
Open Wed. 11-5, Thurs.-Sat. 11-6 or by appointment. STOCK: *Antique furniture, ceramics & glass, curios & collectables, arts and crafts, art nouveau, art deco & retro, 20th century fine arts, costume jewellery, reclamation etc.* LOC: On the A40 out of Nottingham, first shop on right before the Sherwood Centre. SER: Restorations (furniture); quotations; free local delivery. SIZE: Medium. PARK: On street.
TEL: 0115 960 6363; MOBILE: 07886 688042
E-MAIL: mail@sherwoodstreasurechest.co.uk
WEBSITE: www.sherwoodstreasurechest.co.uk

SOUTHWELL

Westhorpe Antiques
Old Grapes Inn, Westhorpe. NG25 0NB. (Ralph Downing)
EST. 1974. Open by appointment or take pot luck and ring bell to gain admittance. STOCK: *Furniture, mainly oak, 17th to mid 19th C, £50-£500; brass, copper and pewter, 17th to late 19th C, £10-£200; vintage fishing tackle including reels and rods, stuffed fish, sporting items, £10-£300.* LOC: 15 mins. from Newark. SER: Valuations; restorations (furniture). SIZE: Small. PARK: Easy. FAIRS: Newark.
TEL: 01636 814095; HOME: same

SUTTON BONINGTON

Goodacre Engraving
The Dial House, 120 Main St. LE12 5PF.
EST. 1948. BHI. Open Mon.-Fri. 9-5 or by appointment. STOCK: *Longcase and bracket clock movements, parts and castings.* LOC: 10 mins. from junction 24, M1. SER: Hand engraving; silvering and dial repainting; new hand-made dials. PARK: Easy. VAT: Stan.
TEL: 01509 673082; FAX: same
E-MAIL: goodacre@postmaster.co.uk
WEBSITE: www.ndirect.co.uk/~goodacre

TUXFORD

Sally Mitchell's Gallery
9 Eldon St. NG22 0LB.
EST. 1976. FATG. Open 10-5, Sun. and Mon. by appointment. STOCK: *Contemporary sporting and animal paintings, £200-£5,000; limited edition sporting and animal prints, 20th C, £20-£650.* LOC: 1 min. from A1, 14 miles north of Newark. SIZE: Medium. PARK: Easy. VAT: Stan/Spec. FAIRS: CLA Game and Burghley Horse Trials.
TEL: 01777 838 234/198
E-MAIL: info@sallymitchell.com
WEBSITE: www.sallymitchell.com

ART DECO CERAMICS IN BRITAIN

Andrew Casey

A unique approach to the subject, this important work brings together recognised experts, museum curators and specialist authors from across the world, for the first time, featuring high quality new photographs and archival material including advertising and company publicity material, and an introduction by Eric Knowles, antiques expert, author and television presenter.

Focusing on the art deco ceramics that were produced by the British pottery industry during the late twenties and early thirties, this book covers all the important aspects of the popular style from its origins in France, its breakthrough in Britain and how the style took on during the early thirties. The background of art deco is examined and how it developed in France during the early part of the twentieth century: how European designers created new shapes and patterns and how these ideas eventually made their way into British design. *Art Deco Ceramics in Britain* looks at the well-established factories such as Josiah Wedgwood and Sons Ltd and Minton who produced the top of the range wares for the upper classes and how they were forced, due to market forces, to produce art deco styled wares. At the same time the smaller factories were able to respond quickly to the art deco style, using hand painted decoration, which was an important feature of art deco patterning with the big names such as Clarice Cliff and Susie Cooper still being well known today. Also documented in the book are concise, yet comprehensive biographies of many smaller factories that are not so well known today. This listing provides an invaluable source for or ideas for new areas of collecting.

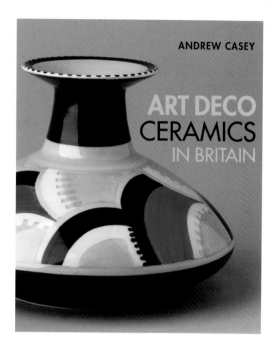

274 x 224 mm. 280 pp 300 col.
£35.00 Hardback

For full details of all ACC publications,
log on to our website:
www.antiquecollectorsclub.com
or telephone 01394 389950 for a free catalogue

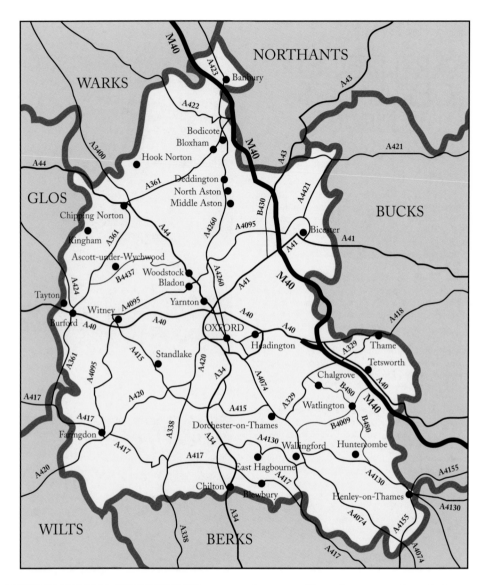

ASCOTT-UNDER-WYCHWOOD

William Antiques
Manor Farm. OX7 6AL. (Robert Gripper)
EST. 1982. Open Mon.-Fri. 9-5. *STOCK: Victorian and Georgian furniture, mainly mahogany.* LOC: Between river bridge and level crossing. SER: Valuations; restorations. SIZE: Medium. PARK: Easy. VAT: Margin.
TEL: 01993 831960; HOME: same; FAX: 01993 830395
E-MAIL: robgripper@aol.com

BICESTER

R.A. Barnes   LAPADA
PO Box 82. OX25 1RA.
Open by appointment. *STOCK: English, Oriental and Continental porcelain, antiques and collectables; Wedgwood,* *ironstone, china, glass, copper, domestic brass and other metals, 19th C; Bohemian and art glass, primitive paintings. Trades from Rogers Gallery, Portobello.* VAT: **Stan/Spec.**
TEL: **01844 237388**

BLADON

Park House Antiques Ltd
26 Park St. OX20 1RW. (H.R. & T. Thomas)
EST. 1996. Resident. Open daily including Sun. *STOCK: Furniture and decorative smalls.* LOC: On A4095 Woodstock to Witney road. SER: Valuations; restorations; buys at auction. SIZE: Medium. PARK: Own.
TEL: 01993 813888
E-MAIL: info@parkhouseantiques.co.uk
WEBSITE: www. parkhouseantiques.co.uk

BURFORD

Antiques @ The George
104 High St. OX18 4QJ. (C. Oswald and A. Palmer)
EST. 1992. Open 10-5, Sun. 12-5. STOCK: General antiques including china, furniture, textiles, silver, plate, jewellery, books, glass, pictures, early 18th C to 1930s. LOC: Main road. SER: Shipping arranged. SIZE: Large. PARK: Around corner.
TEL: 01993 823319
E-MAIL: ask@antiquesatthegeorge.com
WEBSITE: www.antiquesatthegeorge.com

Burford Antique Centre
Cheltenham Rd., At the Roundabout. OX18 4JA. (G. Viventi)
EST. 1979. Open 10-6 including Sun. STOCK: Furniture, 18th-19th C, £100-£5,000; china. LOC: A40. SER: Restorations (furniture including re-leathering). SIZE: Large. PARK: Easy.
TEL: 01993 823227

Bygones
29 High St. OX18 4RN. (C.B. Jenkins)
EST. 1986. Open 10-1 and 2-5, Sat. 10-5, Sun. 12-5. STOCK: Prints and pictures, 1900s, £5-£50; china and glass, curios, 1880-1950, £5-£250. LOC: A40, A361. SIZE: Small. PARK: Easy.
TEL: 01993 823588
E-MAIL: sales@bygones-of-burford.co.uk
WEBSITE: www.bygones-of-burford.co.uk

Jonathan Fyson Antiques
50 High St. OX18 4QF. (J.R. Fyson)
EST. 1970. CADA. Open 9.30-1 and 2-5.30, Sat. from 10. STOCK: English and Continental furniture, decorative brass and steel including lighting and fireplace accessories; mirrors, porcelain, table glass, jewellery. LOC: At junction of A40/A361 between Oxford and Cheltenham. SER: Valuations. SIZE: Medium. PARK: Easy. VAT: Spec.
TEL: 01993 823204; FAX: same; HOME: 01367 860223
E-MAIL: j@fyson.co.uk

Gateway Antiques
Cheltenham Rd., Burford Roundabout. OX18 4JA. (M.C. Ford and P. Brown)
EST. 1986. CADA. Open 10-5.30, Sun. 1-4 STOCK: English and Continental furniture, 18th to early 20th C; decorative accessories. LOC: On roundabout (A40) Oxford/Cheltenham road, adjacent to the Cotswold Gateway Hotel. SIZE: Large. PARK: Easy. VAT: Stan/Spec.
TEL: 01993 823678/822624; FAX: 01993 823857
E-MAIL: enquiries@gatewayantiques.co.uk
WEBSITE: www.gatewayantiques.co.uk

Lucy Johnson BADA LAPADA
The Stone Barn, OX18 4JS.
EST. 1983. CINOA. Open by appointment. *STOCK:*
Early English and Continental furniture and works of art;
modern British pictures. SER: Restorations. SIZE:
Large. FAIRS: Olympia.
TEL: 020 7352 0114; FAX: 020 7352 0114; MOBILE:
07974 149912
E-MAIL: lucy-johnson@lucy-johnson.com
WEBSITE: www.lucy-johnson.com

David Pickup BADA
115 High St. OX18 4RG.
EST. 1977. CADA. Open 9.30-1 and 2-5.30, Sat. 10-1
and 2-4. *STOCK: Fine furniture, works of art, from £500+;*
decorative objects, from £100+; all late 17th to mid 20th C,
specialising in Arts and Crafts. SIZE: Medium. PARK:
Easy. VAT: Spec. FAIRS: Olympia.
TEL: 01993 822555

Manfred Schotten Antiques
109 High St. OX18 4RG.
EST. 1974. CADA. Open 9.30-5.30 or by appointment.
STOCK: Sporting antiques and library furniture. SER:
Restorations; trophies. SIZE: 3 floors and trade warehouse
oppointment by appointment. PARK: Easy. VAT:
Stan/Margin. FAIRS: Olympia (Summer & Winter).
TEL: 01993 822302; FAX: 01993 822055
E-MAIL: antiques@schotten.com
WEBSITE: www.schotten.com

Brian Sinfield Gallery Ltd
150 High St. OX18 4QU.
EST. 1972. Open 10-5.30, Mon. by appointment. *STOCK:*
Mainly contemporary and late 20th C paintings and
watercolours. SER: 8 exhibitions annually; art brokers.
SIZE: Medium. PARK: Easy. VAT: Spec.

TEL: 01993 824464
E-MAIL: gallery@briansinfield.com
WEBSITE: www.briansinfield.com

The Stone Gallery
93 High St. OX18 4QA. (Mrs Phyllis M. and Simon
Marshall)
EST. 1918. Open 9.15-6. *STOCK: Pre-Raphaelite and*
modern British pictures, 1840-1980, £120-£30,000;
paperweights, from 1840, £50-£15,000; enamel boxes, from
1760, £50-£1,000; designer jewellery. LOC: Halfway down
High St. SER: Valuations (paperweights); buys at auction
(pictures and paperweights). SIZE: Medium. PARK: Easy.
VAT: Stan/Spec.
TEL: 01993 823302; fax/HOME: same
E-MAIL: mail@stonegallery.co.uk
WEBSITE: www.stonegallery.co.uk

CHALGROVE

Antique Furniture Warehouse
The Garth, Warpsgrove Lane. OX44 7RW.
(Rupert Hitchcox)
Open Tues.-Fri. 10-5; CL: Mon. & Sat. *STOCK:*
Furniture 17th-20th C; mostly trade. SIZE: Large PARK:
Easy. VAT: Spec.
TEL: 01865 890241

Rupert Hitchcox Antiques
Warpsgrove Lane. OX44 7RW. (P. and R. Hitchcox)
EST. 1957. Open Tues.-Fri. 10-5, or by appointment.
STOCK: 17th-20th C furniture. LOC: Halfway between
Oxford and Henley, just off the B480, 6 miles from junction
6, M40. SIZE: Large - 6 barns. PARK: Easy. VAT: Stan/Spec.
TEL: 01865 890241; FAX: same; MOBILE: 07710 561505
E-MAIL: rupertsantiques@aol.com
WEBSITE: www.ruperthitchcoxantiques.co.uk

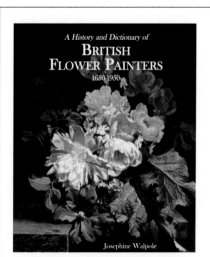

CHILTON

Country Markets Antiques and Collectables
at Country Gardens Garden Centre, Newbury Rd.
OX11 0QN. (G.W. Vaughan)
EST. 1991. Open 10-5, Mon. 10.30-5, Sun. 10.30-4.30.
STOCK: *Wide variety of general antiques including furniture,
books, jewellery, porcelain, militaria, and cased fish, £5-£5,000.*
LOC: Off A34 near Harwell, 10 mins. from junction 13,
M4, 20 mins. from Oxford. SER: Restorations (furniture and
ceramics). SIZE: Large - 30 dealers. PARK: Easy.
TEL: 01235 835125; FAX: 01235 833068
E-MAIL: country.markets.antiques@breathemail.net

CHIPPING NORTON

Georgian House Antiques   LAPADA
21 West St. OX7 5EU. (Georg and Sheila Wissinger)
**EST. 1974. Open 9-6. STOCK: *17th-19th C furniture and
paintings.* LOC: West end of town. SER: Restorations.
PARK: Easy. VAT: Stan.**
TEL: 01608 641369

Jonathan Howard
21 Market Place. OX7 5NA. (J.G. Howard)
EST. 1979. Open by appointment or ring bell. STOCK:
Clocks - longcase, wall and carriage, 18th-19th C. SER:
Valuations; restorations (movement, dials and cases).
SIZE: Small. PARK: Nearby.
TEL: 01608 643065

The Quiet Woman Antiques Centre
Southcombe. OX7 5QH. (David Belcher and Ann
Marriott)
EST. 1998. Open 10-5, Sun. 11-5. STOCK: *Wide variety of
general antiques.* SER: Arrangement of shipping. SIZE:
Large - 30 dealers. PARK: Own.
TEL: 01608 646262; FAX: same
E-MAIL: quietwomanantiq@aol.com

Station Mill Antiques Centre
Station Rd. OX7 5HX. (M.T. Langer)
EST. 1994. Open 10-5 including Sun. STOCK: *Furniture,
fine art, bric-a-brac and collectables, 17th-20th C, £2-
£2,000.* LOC: Just out of town off A44 towards Moreton-
in-Marsh. SIZE: Large. PARK: Easy.
TEL: 01608 644563
E-MAIL: info@stationmill.com
WEBSITE: www.stationmill.com

TRADA
21 High St. OX7 5AD. (Valerie Perkins)
EST. 1978. Open 9-5. CL: Mon. STOCK: *Antiquarian
maps and engravings, 1600-1900.* SER: Print renovation;
colouring; picture frame making. SIZE: Small. PARK:
Nearby.
TEL: 01608 644325

Peter Wiggins
Raffles Farm, Southcombe. OX7 5QH.

EST. 1969. Usually available. STOCK: *Barometers.* LOC: 1
mile from Chipping Norton on A34. SER: Valuations;
restorations (barometers, clocks, automata); repairs
(clocks); buys at auction.
TEL: 01608 642652; HOME: same

DEDDINGTON

Castle Antiques Ltd   LAPADA
High St., OX15 0SJ. (J. and J. Vaughan)
**EST. 1968. Open Wed.-Sat. 10-5. STOCK: *Furniture,
£25-£3,000; silver, metalware, pottery and porcelain £10-
£500.* LOC: On A4260 Oxford to Banbury road. SIZE:
Medium. PARK: Nearby. VAT: Stan/Spec.**
TEL: 01869 338688

Deddington Antiques Centre
Laurel House, Bull Ring, Market Sq. OX15 0TT. (Mrs
B. J. Haller)
EST. 1972. TVADA. Open 10-5, Sun. 11-5. STOCK:
*Furniture, Georgian to 1930s, £100-£4,000; porcelain,
glass, silver, pictures, linen, jewellery, 1700-1930, £5-
£5,000; collectables, £10-£200.* LOC: 10 mins. junction 10
M40. SER: Valuations; shipping. SIZE: 9 rooms on 4
floors. PARK: Easy and free. FAIRS: TVADA.
TEL: 01869 338968; FAX: 01869 338916

DORCHESTER-ON-THAMES

Dorchester Antiques   LAPADA
The Barn, 3 High St. OX10 7HH. (J. and S. Hearnden)
**EST. 1992. TVADA. Open Tues.-Sat. 10-5. STOCK:
*Furniture 18th-20th C, American 1970s lucite
tablelamps, consoles and coffee tables.* LOC: Opposite
Abbey. SER: Restorations; finder. SIZE: Medium.
PARK: Easy.**
TEL: 01865 341373; FAX: same
WEBSITE: www.dorchesterantiques.com

Hallidays (Fine Antiques) Ltd   LAPADA
Queen St. OX10 7HL. (E.M. and S.A. Reily Cousins)
**EST. 1950. TVADA. CINOA. Open 9-5, Sat. 10-1 and
2-4. STOCK: *English and Continental furniture, 17th-
19th C; paintings, decorative and small items, 18th-19th
C ; C pine and marble mantelpieces, firegrates, fenders,
18th-20th ; bespoke room panelling.* LOC: 8 miles south-
east of Oxford. SIZE: Large. PARK: In front of
showroom. VAT: Stan/Spec. FAIRS: LAPADA;
International Antiques, Chicago.**
TEL: 01865 340028/68; FAX: 01865 341149
E-MAIL: info@hallidays.com
WEBSITE: www.hallidays.com

EAST HAGBOURNE

Craig Barfoot
Tudor House. OX11 9LR.
EST. 1993. Open any time by appointment. STOCK:

Longcase clocks, £3,000-£20,000; bracket and lantern clocks.
LOC: Just off A34 halfway between Oxford and Newbury. SER: Restorations (clocks); buys at auction (clocks, English oak furniture). SIZE: Medium. PARK: Easy. VAT: Spec.
TEL: 01235 818968; HOME: same; MOBILE: 07710 858158
E-MAIL: craig.barfoot@tiscali.co.uk

E.M. Lawson and Co
Kingsholm. OX11 9LN. (W.J. and K.M. Lawson MBE)
EST. 1921. ABA. Usually open 10-5 but appointment preferred. CL: Sat. *STOCK: Antiquarian and rare books, 1500-1900.* PARK: Easy. VAT: Stan.
TEL: 01235 812033

FARINGDON

Aston Pine Antiques
16-18 London St. SN7 7AA. (P. O'Gara)
EST. 1982. Open Wed.-Sat. 9-5. *STOCK: Victorian and Continental pine; Victorian fireplaces, doors and bathrooms.* SER: Stripping (pine).
TEL: 01367 243840

Oxford Architectural Antiques
16-18 London St. SN7 7AA. (M. O'Gara)
Open Wed.-Sat. 9-5. *STOCK: Fireplaces, fixtures and fittings, doors.* SER: Packing and container. VAT: Margin.
TEL: 01367 242268; MOBILE: 07973 922393

HEADINGTON

Barclay Antiques
107 Windmill Rd. OX3 7BT. (C. Barclay)
EST. 1979. Open 10-5.30. CL: Wed. *STOCK: Porcelain, silver, furniture and metalware, 18th-19th C, £50-£100; period lamps, 20th C, £50-£500.* SER: Valuations. SIZE: Small. PARK: Own at rear.
TEL: 01865 769551
E-MAIL: barclay_antiques@yahoo.com

HENLEY-ON-THAMES

Friday Street Antique Centre (The Ferret)
4 Friday St. RG9 1AH. (D. Etherington and C. Fentum)
EST. 1985. Open 10-5.30, Sun. 12-5.30. *STOCK: Furniture, china, silver, books, pictures, musical instruments, unusual items.* LOC: Second left after Henley bridge, then first left, business on right. SIZE: 6 dealers. PARK: Easy.
TEL: 01491 574104

Henley Antique Centre
Rotherfield Arcade, 2-4 Reading Rd. RG9 1AG.
Open 10-5, Sun 11-4. SIZE: Large - 54 dealers.
TEL: 01491 411468

Jonkers Rare Books
24 Hart St. RG9 2AU. (Jonkers Ltd.)
EST. 1990. ABA. ILAB. PBFA. Open 10-5.30. *STOCK:*

Fine and rare books, 1800-1950, £50-£500,000. LOC: Main road. SER: Valuations; buys at auction (rare books). SIZE: Medium. PARK: Easy. FAIRS: Olympia.
TEL: 01491 576427; FAX: 01491 573805
E-MAIL: info@jonkers.co.uk
WEBSITE: www.jonkers.co.uk

The Barry Keene Gallery
12 Thameside. RG9 1BH. (B.M. and J.S. Keene)
EST. 1971. FATG. Open 9.30-5.30, CL: Mon. *STOCK: Antique, modern and contemporary art, paintings, watercolours, drawings, etchings, prints and sculpture.* LOC: Junction 8/9 M4, over Henley bridge, left along riverside, 5th building on right. SER: Restorations; conservation; framing; cleaning; relining; gilding; export. VAT: Stan/Spec.
TEL: 01491 577119
E-MAIL: barrykeene@barrykeenegallery.co.uk
WEBSITE: www.barrykeenegallery.com

Richard J. Kingston
Open by appointment. *STOCK: Furniture, 17th to early 19th C; silver, porcelain, glass, paintings, antiquarian and secondhand books.* FAIRS: Surrey.
TEL: 01491 574535

Knights Antiques
5 Friday St. RG9 1AN. (S.J. and M.L. Knight)
EST. 1988. Open 9.30-5.30. *STOCK: English country furniture, 1600-1800, £500-£10,000; pewter, 1600-1900, £10-£1,000; Persian tribal and village carpets and rugs, pre-1900 to modern, £200-£10,000; large selection of clocks, 1700-1900, £300-£10,000.* LOC: Town centre. SIZE: Medium. PARK: Easy. FAIRS: Cleaning and restorations (carpets and rugs).
TEL: 01491 414124; MOBILE: 07774 644478
E-MAIL: simon@knightsantiques.co.uk
WEBSITE: www.knightsantiques.co.uk

The Old French Mirror Co Ltd
Unit 2 Hernes Estate. RG9 4NT. (Roger and Bridget Johnson)
EST. 1999 Open by appointment. *STOCK: French mirrors, 19th to early 20th C.* LOC: 3 miles from Henley-on-Thames. SER: Shipping; "Try-at-Home" service. SIZE: Large. PARK: Easy. VAT: Margin.
TEL: 01189 482444; FAX: same
E-MAIL: info@oldfrenchmirrors.com
WEBSITE: www.oldfrenchmirrors.com

Thames Oriental Rug Co
Thames Carpet Cleaners Ltd, Newtown Rd. RG9 1HG. (B. and Mrs A. Javadi-Babreh)
EST. 1955. Resident. Open 9-5, CL: Sat. *STOCK: Oriental rugs, mid-19th C to modern.* SER: Valuations; restorations; cleaning. SIZE: Large. PARK: Easy. VAT: Stan.
TEL: 01491 574676 or 01491 577877

Tudor House Antiques
49 Duke St. RG9 1UR. (David and Linda Potter)
Open 10-5 including Sun. STOCK: *Furniture, garden ornaments, architectural items, brass, copper, tools, glass, china, silver and plate, 1750s to 1950s.* LOC: Town centre. SER: Valuations. PARK: Nearby.
TEL: 01491 573680

Richard Way Bookseller
54 Friday St. RG9 1AH. (Diana Cook and Richard Way)
EST. 1977. ABA. Open 10-5.30. STOCK: *Rare and secondhand books, £5–£1,000.* LOC: Over Henley bridge, turn immediately left behind Angel public house, follow river, turn right, shop past Anchor public house. SER: Valuations; restorations. SIZE: Small. PARK: At rear. VAT: Stan.
TEL: 01491 576663; FAX: 01491 576663

HOOK NORTON

James Holiday Ltd
Wychford Lodge Farmhouse. OX15 5BX. (James and Nicky Holiday)
EST. 1865 Open strictly by appointment only. STOCK: *Furniture, pottery, porcelain, paintings and decorative items.* LOC: Just outside village on Whichford Rd. SIZE: Medium. PARK: Easy. VAT: Spec. FAIRS: Swinderby, Ardingly, Newark.
TEL: 01608 730101; FAX: 01608 737537; MOBILE: 07771 825466

HUNTERCOMBE

The Country Seat   LAPADA
Huntercombe Manor Barn. RG9 5RY.
(Harvey Ferry and William Clegg)
EST. 1965. TVADA. CINOA. Open 9-5.30, Sat. 10-5, Sun. by appointment. STOCK: *Furniture - signed and designed, 1700-1970; garden and architectural/panelling; art pottery and metalwork, lighting and Whitefriars glass.* LOC: Signed off A4130. SER: Restorations; exhibitions. SIZE: Large. PARK: Own. VAT: Spec. FAIRS: TVADA; Radley.
TEL: 01491 641349; FAX: 01491 641533
E-MAIL: info@thecountryseat.com
WEBSITE: www.thecountryseat.com; www.whitefriarsglass.org

KINGHAM

Winson Antiques and Clive   LAPADA
Payne Restoration
Unit 11, Langston Priory Workshops. OX7 6UP.
EST. 1986 Open 9-5.30. STOCK: *Mason's ironstone china; period oak and country furniture; Georgian mahogany.* SER: Valuations; restoration (furniture). SIZE: Small. PARK: Ample, free.
TEL: 01608 658856

E-MAIL: clive.payne@virgin.net
WEBSITE: www.clivepayne.co.uk

MIDDLE ASTON

Cotswold Pine & Associates
The Old Poultry Farm. OX25 5QL. (R.J. Prancks)
EST. 1980. Open 9.30-5, Sun. 10-4. STOCK: *Furniture, 18th-20th C.* LOC: Off A4260, 15 mins. from M40. SER: Restorations; stripping; polishing; repairs. SIZE: Large. PARK: Easy. VAT: Stan/Spec.
TEL: 01869 340963

MILTON COMMON

LASSCO Three Pigeons   LAPADA
London Rd. OX9 2JN. (Anthony Reeve)
EST. 1978. Open 10-5. STOCK: *Architectural reclamations, architectural antiques, fireplaces, garden ornaments, decorative stonework, flooring, doors etc.* LOC: Off Jct. 7, M40. SIZE: Large PARK: Own carpark.
TEL: 01844 277188; FAX: 01844 277181
E-MAIL: 3pigeons@lassco.co.uk
WEBSITE: www.lassco.co.uk

NORTH ASTON

Nigel Adamson
Gate Cottage, Somerton Rd. OX25 6HX. (N.J.G. Adamson)
EST. 1863. Open by appointment. STOCK: *Furniture, 17th to early 19th C; porcelain, Chinese, English and Continental.* SER: Valuations; restorations (furniture and porcelain). PARK: Easy. VAT: Spec.
TEL: 01869 340966; MOBILE: 07957 686493
E-MAIL: nigel@nigeladamson.wanadoo.co.uk

Elizabeth Harvey-Lee
1 West Cottages, Middle Aston Lane. OX25 5QB.
EST. 1986. Open by appointment. STOCK: *Original prints, 15th-20th C; artists' etchings, engravings, lithographs, £100–£6,000.* LOC: 6 miles from junction 10, M40, 15 miles north of Oxford. SER: Illustrated catalogue available twice yearly (£16 p.a.). VAT: Spec. FAIRS: London Original Print, Royal Academy; Olympia (Nov); Le Salon de l'Estampe, Paris.
TEL: 01869 34716
E-MAIL: north.aston@btinternet.com
WEBSITE: www.elizabethharvey-lee.com

OXFORD

Antiques on High Ltd
85 High St. OX1 4BG. (Joan Lee and Tony Sloggett)
EST. 1982. TVADA. Open 10-5, Sun. and Bank Holidays 11-5. STOCK: *Small antiques and collectables including jewellery, silver and plate, ceramics, glass, antiquities, watches, books and coins, 17th-20th C.* LOC: Opposite Queen's Lane. SER: Valuations; restorations

(jewellery, silver including replating). SIZE: Large - 35 dealers. PARK: St Clements, Westgate, Seacourt/Thornhill Park and Ride. FAIRS: TVADA.
TEL: 01865 251075
E-MAIL: enquiries@antiquesonhigh.co.uk
WEBSITE: www.antiquesonhigh.co.uk

Blackwell's Rare Books
48-51 Broad St. OX1 3BQ.
EST. 1879. ABA. ILAB. PBFA. Open 9-6, Tues. 9.30-6. STOCK: *Antiquarian and rare modern books.* SER: Buys at auction; catalogues of specialist and general books issued periodically on request. SIZE: Large. PARK: Nearby. VAT: Stan/Spec. FAIRS: ABA (Olympia); PBFA (Oxford and York); ABA/ABAA (New York, Los Angeles, San Francisco).
TEL: 01865 333555; FAX: 01865 794143
E-MAIL: rarebooks@blackwell.co.uk
WEBSITE: www.rarebooks.blackwell.co.uk

Reginald Davis Ltd   BADA
34 High St. OX1 4AN.
EST. 1941. Open 9-5, Sat. 10-6. CL: Mon. STOCK: **Silver, English and Continental, 17th to early 19th C; jewellery, Sheffield plate, Georgian and Victorian.** LOC: **On A40.** SER: **Valuations; restorations (silver, jewellery).** PARK: **Nearby.** VAT: **Stan/Spec.**
TEL: 01865 248347

Christopher Legge Oriental Carpets
25 Oakthorpe Rd., Summertown. OX2 7BD. (C. & A. Legge)
EST. 1970. Open 9.30-5. STOCK: *Rugs, various sizes, 19th to early 20th C, £300-£15,000; tribal weavings; cushions.* LOC: Near shopping parade. SER: Valuations; restorations; re-weaving; handcleaning. SIZE: Medium. PARK: Easy. VAT: Stan/Margin. FAIRS: HALI, Olympia (June), Battersea Park.
TEL: 01865 557572; FAX: 01865 554877
E-MAIL: orientalcarpets@btclick.com
WEBSITE: www.leggeorientalcarpets.com

Payne and Son (Goldsmiths) Ltd   BADA
131 High St. OX1 4DH. (J.D. Payne, Joe Mitchell and A. Salmon)
EST. 1790. NAG. Open 9.30-5. STOCK: **British silver - antique, modern and secondhand; contemporary jewellery, all £50-£10,000+.** LOC: **Town centre near Carfax traffic lights.** SER: **Restorations (English silver).** SIZE: **Medium.** PARK: **800yds.** VAT: **Stan/Spec.** FAIRS: **BADA; Chelsea (Spring).**
TEL: 01865 243787; FAX: 01865 793241
E-MAIL: silver@payneandson.co.uk
WEBSITE: www.payneandson.co.uk

Sanders of Oxford Ltd
Salutation House, 104 High St. OX1 4BW.
Open 10-6. STOCK: *Prints, especially Oxford; maps; Japanese woodcuts; engraving and 20th C etchings.* SER: Restorations; framing. SIZE: Large. VAT: Margin/Global. FAIRS: PBFA (Russell Hotel London); London Original Print.
TEL: 01865 242590; FAX: 01865 721748
E-MAIL: soxinfo@btclick.com
WEBSITE: www.sandersofoxford.com

St. Clements Antiques
93 St. Clements St. OX4 1AR. (Giles Power)
EST. 1998. Open 10.30-5. STOCK: *Oak and country items, 17th-19th C, £50-£5,000; interesting curios, 17th-20th C, £5-£500.* LOC: Close to city centre, next to Magdalen Bridge. SER: Valuations. SIZE: Medium. PARK: Easy, opposite. VAT: Stan/Spec.
TEL: 01865 727010; HOME: 01865 200359

Waterfield's
52 High St. OX1 4AS.
EST. 1973. ABA. PBFA. Open 9.45-5.45. STOCK: *Antiquarian and secondhand books, all subjects, especially academic in the humanities; literature, history, philosophy, 17th-18th C English.*
TEL: 01865 721809

TETSWORTH

The Swan at Tetsworth
High St. OX9 7AB.
EST. 1995. TVADA. Open seven days 10-6. LOC: A40, 5 mins. from junctions 6 and 8a, M40. SER: Restorations (clocks); cabinet work; delivery and shipping. SIZE: 40+ rooms. PARK: Own large.
TEL: 01844 281777; FAX: 01844 281770
E-MAIL: antiques@theswan.co.uk
WEBSITE: www.theswan.co.uk

Below are listed the dealers at this centre.

Jason Abbot
Sporting guns.

Acanthus Design
Arts & Crafts and Art Nouveau furniture and accessories.

S.J. Allison
Decorative ceramics, small furniture and silver.

Aquila Fine Art
19th to early 20th C watercolours, oils and etchings.

Ray Bailey
Antique ladies' and gentlemen's watches.

Robin Barnes
Fine 19th-20th C watercolours and etchings.

Sue Barrance
Books.

Sue Barton
Silver.

Chris Bigwood
18th - 19th C English furniture, including desks, writing tables and chests of drawers.

Peter Bond
Prints, watercolours; brass and copper ware.

S. Bond & Sons
Fine period furniture.

Fred Caulfield-Kerney
Antique furniture, mirrors and collectables.

David Collins
19th C oil paintings.

Jenny Corkhill-Callin
Textiles including cushions, curtains, braids and quilts.

Janede Albuquerque
Continental and English furniture and associated decorative items.

Carol Desler Designs
Antique fans and small decorative objects.

Jacqueline Ding
Oriental antiques.

Richard and Deby Earls
Textiles, cushions, small decorative French furniture.

Elisabeth James Ltd
(Chris Millard) TVADA. *Fine furniture, 17-19th C.*

Paul Farrelly Antiques Ltd
TVADA. *Fine 18th-19th C furniture and mirrors.*

Sally Forster
Costume jewellery and antique accessories.

Mavis Foster-Abbott
20th C glass, specialising in Latticinio.

Grate Expectations
Garden items and architectural salvage.

Stephen Guth
Framed antiquarian prints and maps.

Mary-Louise Hawkins
Fine English and Continental silver.

Julian Homer
Clarice Cliff pottery.

Invogue Antiques
(Martin and Shelagh Lister) TVADA. *Georgian and 19th C furniture especially 19th C cherry, oak and pine farmhouse tables and chairs, English and French.*

Stuart James
English and Continental furniture, decorative items.

Nigel Johnston
Furniture and clocks.

Andrew Joyce
Silver, ceramics, glass and collectables.

Tricia Kent
Toys for the Boys and a wide selcetion of gentleman's accessories.

Russell Lane
Jewellery.

Susan Ling
Small furniture, brass and copper.

Rosemary Livingston
Fine silver and plate.

Graham McCartney
Frames, prints and watercolours.

Mark Milkowski
English furniture and decorative items.

Tim Millard
TVADA. 18th-19th C furniture and mirrors.

Nicholas Mitchell
Unusual period furniture and smalls.

John and Gilly Mott
Art Deco furniture and collectables.

Nazaré Antiques
Antique furniture and collectables.

Margi O'Neill
Silver.

Old Chair Company
Upholstered furniture.

Orient Carpets
Persian rugs, kelims and textiles.

Chris Pendleton
Watercolours, limited edition prints.

Peter Phillips
Ceramics, especially blue & white transferware; small period furniture.

Alistair Price
TVADA. Fine period furniture.

Andrew Priest
Period English furniture including oak.

Tim Ratcliff
Glass and Art Nouveau jewellery and objets d'art.

Sandie Roder (Solitaire)
Jewellery and antique gifts.

Guy Roe
Period furniture and decorative items.

Royal Red Robe
Chinese antiques and artefacts.

Gail Spence Antiques
English and French decorative items for the home.

Jane Smithson
Kitchenalia.

Geoffrey Sneath/Amandine Antiques
Silver and small items of furniture.

E. Stone Associates
Antique and secondhand jewellery.

Tartan Antiques
Objets d'art, pictures and toys.

Tessier
Fine quality jewellery.

THAME

Rosemary and Time
42 Park St. OX9 3HR. (Tom Fletcher)
EST. 1983. Open 9-12.30 and 1.30-5.30; CL: 12.30-1.30. STOCK: *Clocks and barometers, pre-1940s.* SER: Valuations; restorations; old spare parts. PARK: Nearby. VAT: Stan/Spec.
TEL: 01844 216923

WALLINGFORD

de Albuquerque Antiques
30 Thames St. OX10 0BH. (Michael & Jane du Albuquerque)
EST. 1982. Open by appointment. STOCK: *Furniture and objects, 18th-19th C.* SER: Framing; gilding. SIZE: Medium. PARK: At rear. VAT: Spec.
TEL: 01491 832322; FAX: same
E-MAIL: janedealb@tiscali.co.uk

Toby English
10 St Mary's St. OX10 0EL. (Toby and Chris English)
EST. 1980. PBFA. Open 9.30-5. STOCK: *Books including art and antiques reference, 19th-20th C, £5-£1,000; prints, 19th-20th C, £20-£200; maps, 18th-19th C, £30-£1,000.* LOC: Town centre. SER: Valuations; restorations; buys at auction; catalogues issued. SIZE: Medium. PARK: Cattle Market. FAIRS: PBFA London, Oxford, York.
TEL: 01491 836389; FAX: same
E-MAIL: toby@tobyenglish.com
WEBSITE: www.tobyenglish.com

The Lamb Arcade
83 High St. OX10 0BX.
EST. 1979. TVADA. Open 10-5, Sat. 10-5.30. STOCK: *See dealers listed below.* SER: Restorations (furniture). PARK: Nearby.
TEL: 01491 835166
WEBSITE: www.thelambarcade.co.uk

Below are listed the dealers at this centre.

A. Collins
China, silver, collectors' items and glassware.
TEL: 01491 833737

Anne Brewer Antiques
Furniture, china, jewellery and gifts.
TEL: 01491 838486

Circa 26
1920s china and glass, specialising in Shelley and Lalique.

Goodwood Antiques
Furniture, champagne racks and decorative items.
TEL: 07958 962272

R. Haycraft
TEL: 01491 839622
WEBSITE: www.diva-id.com and www.iasa-online.com

Pat Hayward
Furniture, light fittings and decorative items. |
TEL: 01491 824247
E-MAIL: patriciantiques@aol.com

Paula Hodge
Vintage clothes, Deco to 1960s costume jewellery and accessories.

Pemberton-Hall Collectables
Tin toys, motoring and aviation memorabilia, pictures, diecast and lead figures.
TEL: 01491 832023

Phoenix Antiques
Victorian parlour furniture in pine, mahogany, oak and walnut. Pine furniture and kitchens made to order from old wood.
TEL: 01491 833555

Dave Ruskin
Coins.

Ulla Stafford
Antique custard cups, pots à jus.

Stag Antiques & Gallery
Jewellery, porcelain, pictures, Staffordshire figures, Clarice Cliff and Belleek.
TEL: 01491 834516

Tags
(T. and A. Green) *Collectors' items, curios, doll's house furniture, jewellery, militaria, scientific instruments and furniture.*
TEL: 01491 35048

MGJ Jewellers Ltd.
1A St. Martins St. OX10 0AQ. (Dr M.R. Jane)
EST. 1971. Open 10-4.30, Sat. 10-5. STOCK: *Jewellery, Victorian and secondhand, £100-£3,500.* LOC: Town centre. SIZE: Small. PARK: Nearby. VAT: Stan/Spec.
TEL: 01491 834336

Chris and Lin O'Donnell Antiques
26 High St. OX10 0BU.
EST. 1974. Open 9.30-1 and 2-5, Sat. 9.30-5.30. STOCK: *Furniture, 18th C to Edwardian, to £3,000; rugs, to £500; unusual objects, Oriental antiques, clocks, 19th C ceramics and silver.* LOC: Into town over Wallingford Bridge, 150yds. along High St. on left-hand side. SIZE: Large. PARK: Thames St. VAT: Spec.
TEL: 01491 839332
E-MAIL: linodonnell@crowmarsh.wanadoo.co.uk

Mike Ottrey Antiques
16 High St. OX10 0BP. (M.J. Ottrey)
EST. 1980. Resident. Open 10-5. CL: Sat. STOCK: *Furniture, 17th-19th C; oil paintings, copper and brass, decorative and unusual items.* LOC: A429. SIZE: Large. PARK: Own at rear. VAT: Spec.
TEL: 01491 836429; MOBILE: 07831 538204

Summers Davis Antiques Ltd   LAPADA
**Calleva House, 6 High St. OX10 0BP. (Graham and
Pam Wells)**
EST. 1917. CINOA. TVADA. Open 9-5.30, Sat. 10-5.
STOCK: *English and Continental furniture, decorative
items and objects. NOT STOCKED: Silver, shipping goods.*
LOC: **From London, shop is on left, 50yds. from
Thames Bridge.** SER: **Restorations; interior design;
upholstery.** SIZE: **Large.** PARK: **Opposite, behind
castellated gates.** VAT: **Spec.** FAIRS: **TVADA.**
TEL: **01491 836284;** FAX: **01491 833443**
E-MAIL: **antiques@summersdavis.co.uk**
WEBSITE: **www.summersdavisantiques.co.uk**

Tooley Adams & Co
PO Box 174. OX10 0YT. (Steve Luck)
EST. 1979. ABA. IMCOS. IAMA. Open by appointment.
STOCK: *Antiquarian maps and atlases; map related reference
books.* SER: Valuations; mail order. VAT: Stan.   FAIRS:
Worldwide; London Map (June); Miami (Feb); Paris (Nov).
TEL: 01491 838298; FAX: 01491 834616
E-MAIL: steve@tooleys.co.uk
WEBSITE: www.tooleys.co.uk

WATLINGTON

Cross Antiques
37 High St. OX9 5PZ. (R.A. and I.D. Crawley)
EST. 1986. Open 10-6, Sun. and Wed. by appointment.
STOCK: *Furniture, £100-£5,000; decorative smalls, clocks
and garden items, £50-£2,000; all 1600-1900; longcase
clocks £500-£3,000.* LOC: Off B4009 in village centre.
SIZE: Small. PARK: Easy and at rear.
TEL: 01491 612324; HOME: same

WITNEY

Demetzy Books
Manor House, Ducklington. OX29 7UX. (P. and M.
Hutchinson)
EST. 1972. ABA. PBFA. STOCK: *Antiquarian leather bound
books, 18th-19th C, £5-£1,000; Dickens' first editions and
children's and illustrated books, 18-20th C, £5-£200.* SER:
Valuations; buys at auction (books). FAIRS: ABA Chelsea;
PBFA Russell Hotel, London (monthly); Oxford; York.
TEL: 01993 702209
E-MAIL: demetzybooks@tiscali.co.uk

Colin Greenway Antiques
90 Corn St. OX28 6BU.
EST. 1975. CADA. Resident. Open 9.30-5, Sat. 10-4,
Sun. by appointment. STOCK: *Furniture, 17th-20th C;
fireplace implements and baskets, metalware, decorative and
unusual items; garden furniture, rocking horses.* SIZE: Large.
PARK: Easy. VAT: Stan/Spec. FAIRS: Newark.
TEL: 01993 705026; FAX: same; MOBILE: 07831 585014
E-MAIL: jean_greenway@hotmail.com
WEBSITE: www.greenwayantiques.viewing.at

Witney Antiques
LSA & CJ JARRETT AND RR SCOTT
96-100 CORN STREET, WITNEY,
OXON OX28 6BU, ENGLAND.
TEL: 01993 703902. FAX: 01993 779852.
E-mail: witneyantiques@community.co.uk
Website: www.witneyantiques.com

*An example from our large stock of fine British
embroideries and samplers.*

ANTIQUE FURNITURE,
TEXTILES & CLOCKS.

W.R. Harvey & Co (Antiques) Ltd   LAPADA
86 Corn St. OX28 6BU.
EST. 1950. CADA. GMC. CINOA. **Open 9.30-5.30
and by appointment.** STOCK: *Fine English furniture,
£500-£150,000; clocks, mirrors, objets d'art, pictures,
£250-£50,000; all 1680-1830.* LOC: **300 yards from
Market Place.** SER: **Valuations; restorations;
consultancy.** SIZE: **Large.** PARK: **Easy.** VAT: **Stan/Spec.**
FAIRS: **Chelsea (Sept.); Olympia (June and Nov.);
NEC (Jan.); LAPADA (May).**
TEL: **01993 706501;** FAX: **01993 706601**
E-MAIL: **antiques@wrharvey.co.uk**
WEBSITE: **www.wrharvey.co.uk**

Joan Wilkins Antiques
158 Corn St. OX28 6BY.
EST. 1973. Open 10-5. STOCK: *Furniture, 18th-19th C,
£250-£3,500; 19th C glass, metalware, £10-£1,500.* LOC:
Town centre. PARK: Easy. VAT: Spec.
TEL: 01993 704749

Witney Antiques   BADA LAPADA
**96/100 Corn St. OX28 6BU. (L.S.A. and C.J. Jarrett
and R.R. Jarrett-Scott)**
EST. 1962. CADA. **Open 10-5, Mon. and Tues. by
appointment.** STOCK: *English furniture, 17th-18th C;
bracket and longcase clocks, mahogany, oak and walnut;
early needlework and samplers.* LOC: **From Oxford on**

old A40 through Witney via High St., turn right at T-junction, 400yds. on right. SER: Restorations. SIZE: Large. PARK: Easy. VAT: Spec. FAIRS: BADA; Grosvenor House.
TEL: 01993 703902/703887; FAX: 01993 779852
E-MAIL: witneyantiques@community.co.uk
WEBSITE: www.witneyantiques.com

WOODSTOCK

Antiques at Heritage
6 Market Place. OX20 1TA.
EST. 1978. TVADA. Open 10-5, Sun 1-5. STOCK: See dealers listed below. LOC: Near Town Hall. SIZE: Medium. PARK: Easy.
TEL: 01993 811332
WEBSITE: www.atheritage.co.uk

Denise Allin
Vintage luggage and assiciated accessories.

Doreen Caudwell
Textiles and porcelain.

Diana Clark
Old and interesting books.

Francoise Daniel
Boxes, porcelain and collectables.

Hall-Bakker Decorative Arts
TVADA. *Art Nouveau, Arts and Crafts metalwork, pottery, glass and jewellery.* TEL: 01993 705275; FAX: same
E-MAIL: hallbakker@fsmail.net

JohnHoward   BADA LAPADA
CADA. *18th-19th C British pottery.*
e-mail: john@johnhoward.co.uk
website: www.antiquepottery.co.uk

Barbara Johnson
Silver and decorative items.

M.V.S.
Wedgewood and porcelain.

Diana Marcovitch
Lighting and decorative items.

Rebecca Stuart-Mobey
Furniture, miniatures and glass.

Antiques of Woodstock
18-20 Market Place. OX20 1TA. (Allan James and Andrew Hennell)
EST. 1975. Open 10.30-5.30, Sun. 10.30-5. STOCK: Fine Georgian and Regency furniture especially dressers, country dining tables and country sets of chairs; Roman to medieval antiquities. LOC: Opposite The Bear Hotel. SER: Valuations; restorations; consultations; interior decor advice; buys at auction; search; commission sales. SIZE: Large. PARK: Easy. VAT: Stan/Spec.
TEL: 01993 811818; FAX: 01993 811831
E-MAIL: antiquesofwoodstock@btopenworld.com
WEBSITE: www.antiqueoakfurniture.co.uk;
www.thechairset.com

Chris Baylis Country Chairs
16 Oxford St. OX20 1TS.
EST. 1977. TVADA. Open Tues.-Sat. 10.30-5.30 or by appointment. STOCK: *English country chairs, from 1780; sets of rush-seated chairs including ladder and spindle backs, Windsors, kitchen chairs and new handmade examples.* LOC: A44. PARK: Easy. VAT: Spec.
TEL: 01993 813887; FAX: 01993 812379
E-MAIL: info@rwfco.com
WEBSITE: www.rwfco.com

The Chair Set - Antiques
18-20 Market Place. OX20 1TA. (Allan James)
EST. 1982. Open 10.30-5.30, including Sun. STOCK: *Sets of chairs, £1,000-£20,000; single and pairs of chairs, £200-£3,000; dining tables and accessories, £800-£15,000; all early 18th to late 19th C.* LOC: Opposite Bear Hotel. SER: Valuations; restorations (woodwork and upholstery); buys at auction (sets of chairs). SIZE: Large. PARK: Easy. VAT: Spec.
TEL: 01428 707301; FAX: 01428 707457
E-MAIL: allanjames@thechairset.com
WEBSITE: www.thechairset.com

John Howard   BADA
Heritage, 6 Market Place. OX20 1TA.
CADA. Open 10-5.30. STOCK: *18th-19th C British pottery especially rare Staffordshire animal figures, bocage figures, lustre, 18th C creamware and unusual items.* SER: Packing; insurance service to USA. SIZE: Medium. PARK: Easy. VAT: Spec. FAIRS: Olympia; NEC.
TEL: 01993 812580; FAX: same; MOBILE: 07831 850544
E-MAIL: john@johnhoward.co.uk
WEBSITE: www.antiquepottery.co.uk

YARNTON

Yarnton Antiques Centre
Yarnton Nurseries Garden Centre, Sandy Lane. OX5 1PA. (Michael and Sally Dunseath)
EST. 1998. Open 10-4.30 including Sun. STOCK: *Furniture, books, silver, china, brass, jewellery, lighting, decorative items and collectables.* LOC: A44 Oxford to Woodstock road. SIZE: 75 dealers. PARK: Easy.
TEL: 01865 379600

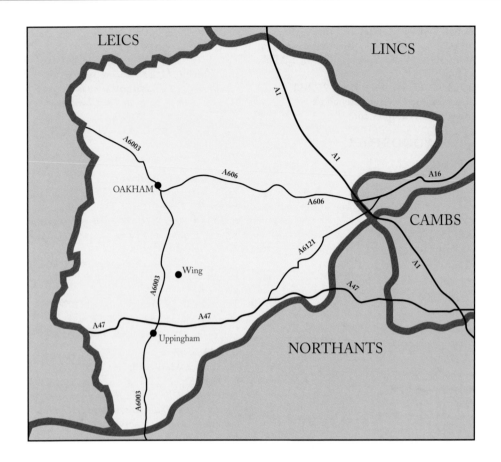

OAKHAM

The Old House Gallery
13-15 Market Place. LE15 6DT
EST. 1977. Open 10-5. *STOCK: Oil and watercolour paintings; pottery and maps; contemporary crafts.* LOC: Corner of Market Place. SER: Valuation; restoration (paintings); framing. SIZE: Small.
TEL: 01572 755538

Reynolds Antiques
The East Lodge, Burley Mansion House, Burley-on-the-Hill. LE15 7TE.
EST. 1972. Resident. Usually available but telephone call advisable. *STOCK: Early verge watches, repeater and other unusual clocks and watches.* LOC: Next to Rutland Water. SER: Verge glasses fitted; valuations. SIZE: Large. FAIRS: Birmingham Clock.
TEL: 01572 771551; MOBILE: 07836 752602
E-MAIL: eastlodge@hotmail.co.uk

Swans
17 Mill St. LE15 6EA. (Peter Jones)
EST. 1988. Open 9-5.30, Sun. and evenings by appointment. *STOCK: French and English beds and associated furniture; 18th-19th C antiques, mainly decorative and upholstered.* LOC: 150yds. from High St. SER: Manufactures new bases and mattresses; valuations; restorations; delivery (to and from France). SIZE: Large. Park: Easy. Vat: Stan/Spec.
TEL: 01572 724364; Fax: 01572 755094
E-MAIL: info@swansofoakham.co.uk
WEBSITE: www.swansofoakham.co.uk

Treedale Antiques
10b Mill St. LE15 6EA. (G.K. Warren)
EST. 1994. GMC. Open 10-5. *STOCK: Furniture including walnut, mahogany and oak, from 1680, to £3,000; portraits, paintings, tapestries, chandeliers, jewellery.* SER: Valuations; restorations (furniture).
TEL: 01572 757521; 01664 454535;
MOBILE: 07740 875230

UPPINGHAM

Aspidistra
5 Queen St. LE15 9QR. (Mike J. Sanderson)
EST. 1989. Open Tues.-Sat. 10-5. *STOCK: General antiques especially Victorian, Edwardian and painted*

furniture, decorative items, china, glass; some modern pieces.
LOC: Off High St. SIZE: Small. PARK: Easy.
TEL: 01572 822757; HOME: 01572 823105

Forest Books
7 High Street West. LE15 9QB. (David Siddons)
EST. 1986. Open 10.30-5, most Suns. 1.30-4.30. *STOCK:
Secondhand books, all periods, sheet music, postcards.* SER:
Book search. SIZE: Mediium. PARK: Easy.   FAIRS:
Farndon, Notts.; Uppingham.
TEL: 01572 821173; FAX: 08701 326314
E-MAIL: forestbooks@rutlanduk.fsnet.co.uk
WEBSITE: http://homepages.primex.co.uk/~forest

John Garner   LAPADA
51-53 High St. East. LE15 9PY.
**EST. 1966. FATG. Open 9-5.30, Sun. 2-5, prior
telephone call advisable.** *STOCK: 17th-19th C furniture,
paintings, prints, clocks, bronzes, mirrors, garden statuary,
some 20th C furniture.* LOC: **Just off A47, 80 yards from
market place.** SER: **Valuations; restorations (furniture,
paintings, prints); framing (trade); courier; export.**
SIZE: **12 showrooms + warehouse.** PARK: **Easy.** VAT:
Stan/Spec. FAIRS: **Newark; Miami.**
TEL: **01572 823607; FAX: 01572 821654; MOBILE:
07850 596556**
E-MAIL: **sales@johngarnerantiques.com**
WEBSITE: **www.johngarnerantiques.com**

M. Gilbert Antiques & Old Furniture
8 Ayston Rd. LE15 9RL.
EST. 1964. Open Mon/Tue. 12-2; Wed/Fri/Sat. 11-5.
CL: Thu. & Sun. *STOCK: General antiques; furniture; pine.*
LOC: A6003 Corby to Oakham road. SER: Pine
stripping. SIZE: Small. PARK: Easy.
TEL: 01572 821975; MOBILE: 07990 573338
E-MAIL: mgm101@hotmail.com

Marc Oxley Fine Art
EST. 1981. Resident. Open by appointment. *STOCK:
Original watercolours and drawings, 1700-1950, £5-£850;
oils, 19th-20th C, £100-£1,500; prints, mainly 19th C, £5-
£50; maps, 17th-19th C, £10-£850.* SER: Valuations;
restorations (oils).
TEL: 01572 822334; HOME: same
E-MAIL: marcoxleyfineart@aol.com
WEBSITE: www.marcoxleyfineart.com

T.J. Roberts
39/41 High St. East. LE15 9PY.
EST. 1973. Resident. Open at various times. Prior
telephone call advisable. *STOCK: Furniture, porcelain and
pottery, 18th-19th C; Staffordshire figures, general antiques.*
PARK: Easy. VAT: Stan/Spec.
TEL: 01572 821493

Rutland Antiques Centre
Crown Passage. LE15 9NB. (Wendy Foster Grindley)
EST. 2001. Open 10-5.30, Sun. 11-5. *STOCK: Wide range*

of general antiques, £5-£3,000. LOC: Behind Crown
Hotel, High St. SIZE: Large. PARK: Easy.
TEL: 01572 824011
E-MAIL: rutlandantiques@btconnect.com
WEBSITE: www.rutlandantiques.com

Uppingham Antiques Centre
17 High Street East. LE15 9PY (Nick Grindley)
EST. 2006. Open 10-5.30, Sun. 11-5. *STOCK: Wide range
of general antiques, £5-£10,000.* SIZE: Large PARK: Easy.
TEL: 01572 822155.
E-MAIL: rutlandantiques@btconnect.com
WEBSITE: www.rutlandantiques.com

WING

Robert Bingley Antiques
Wing House, 5 Church St. LE15 8RS. (Robert and
Elizabeth Bingley)
Open by appointment. *STOCK: Furniture and clocks, 17th-
19th C, £50-£5,000.* LOC: Next to church. SER:
Valuations; restorations. SIZE: Small. PARK: Own. VAT:
Spec.
TEL: 01572 737314; FAX: same; MOBILE: 07909 585285
E-MAIL: robert.bingley@tiscali.co.uk
WEBSITE: www.robertbingley.com

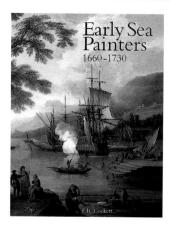

This is a unique introduction to a fascinating group of early
marine painters working in England between about 1660
and 1730, of whom relatively little is known. Marine
painting really began in England with the arrival of the Van
de Veldes (father and son) from Holland in 1673, who so
dominated the world of marine painting that work by other
competent marine artists working in England at the time
received little attention. This relatively unknown group is
the real subject of this important work. The book's wealth of
fine illustration is included to demonstrate a particular
painter's range as well as the characteristics of his technique.

279 x 216 mm. 160 pp 58 col., 47 b.&w.
£25.00 Hardback

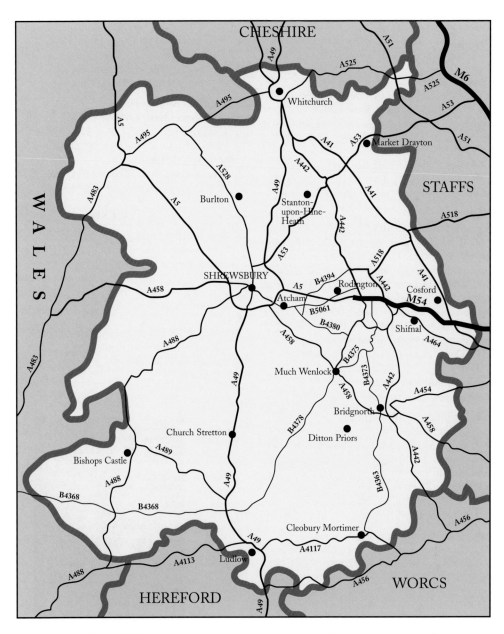

ATCHAM

Mytton Antiques
Norton Cross Roads. SY4 4UH. (M.A., E.A., J.M. and S. Nares)
Est. 1972. Open 10-5 or by appointment. *Stock: General antiques, furniture, 1700-1900, £50-£5,000; clocks, £35-£4,000; smalls, £15-£2,000.* Loc: On B5061 (the old A5) between Shrewsbury and Wellington. Ser: Buys at auction; restorations; restoration materials; shipping. Size: Medium. Park: Own. VAT: Stan/Spec. Fairs: Newark, Ardingly. Tel: 01952 740229 (24hrs.); Fax: same; Mobile: 07860 575639

E-mail: nares@myttonantiques.co.uk
Website: www.myttonantiques.co.uk

BISHOP'S CASTLE

Decorative Antiques
47 Church St. SY9 5AD. (Evelyn Bowles and Richard Moulson)
Est. 1996. Open Mon.-Sat. CL: Wed pm. *Stock: Ceramics and glass, jewellery and metalware, small furniture, 19th & 20th C, £5-£1,000.* Loc: On the main street. Ser: Valuations; advice and identification. Size: Small. Park: Easy.

TEL: 01588 638851; FAX/HOME: same
E-MAIL: enquiries@decorative-antiques.co.uk
WEBSITE: www.decorative-antiques.co.uk

BRIDGNORTH

Bridgnorth Antiques Centre
Whitburn St. WV16 4QT. (Miss G.M. Gibbons)
EST. 1992. Open 10-5, Sun. 10.30-4.30. STOCK: *Clocks, furniture, general antiques and collectables.* LOC: High Town. SER: Restorations (clocks). SIZE: Large. PARK: Easy.
TEL: 01746 768055
E-MAIL: gibbkes@aol.com
WEBSITE: www.bridgnorthantiquecentre.co.uk

English Heritage
2 Whitburn St., High Town. WV16 4QN.
(P.J. Wainwright and M. Wainwright)
EST. 1988. Open 10.30-4.30. CL: Thurs. STOCK: *Jewellery, silverware and general antiques, militaria, coins, collectibles, glassware.* LOC: Just off High St. SER: Valuations; buys jewellery, militaria, coins, collectables, giftware. SIZE: Medium. PARK: Nearby. VAT: Stan/Spec.
TEL: 01746 762097
E-MAIL: pjwainwright1988@yahoo.co.uk

Malthouse Antiques
The Old Malthouse, 6 Underhill St. WV16 4BB.
(Susan and William Mantle)
EST. 1980. Open 10-6, Sun. by appointment. CL: Wed. STOCK: *Victorian and Edwardian furniture, French beds and armoires, £100-£1,500; upholstered chairs and sofas, from 19th C, £300-£1,800; china and decorative items, 19th-20th C, £5-£150; French chandeliers.* LOC: Main road into town from Wolverhampton. SER: Valuations; restorations (furniture); upholstery. SIZE: Medium. PARK: Own (limited space) and nearby.
TEL: 01746 763054; FAX/HOME: same
E-MAIL: bill@themalthouseantiques.co.uk
WEBSITE: www.themalthouseantiques.co.uk

Micawber Antiques
64 St. Mary's St. WV16 4DR. (N. Berthoud)
EST. 1989. Open 10-5, other times by appointment. CL: Mon. and Thurs. STOCK: *English porcelain and pottery, decorative items, £5-£500; small furniture, £100-£1,000.* LOC: 100 yds. west of town hall in High St. SIZE: Medium. PARK: Easy.
TEL: 01746 763254; HOME: same

Northgate Antique & Collectables Centre
Northgate Arcade, High St. WV16 4ER.
Open 10-4; CL: Weds, Thurs. STOCK: *Coins, stamps, postcards, toys, trains, records, books, china, furniture, figurines, crested items & other collectables.* LOC: HIgh Town, under Northgate Arch. SIZE: Medium PARK: Close to town centre carparks.
TEL: 01746 764850

Old Mill Antique Centre
Mill St. WV15 5AG. (D.A. and J.A. Ridgeway)
EST. 1996. Open 10-5 including Sun. STOCK: *Wide range of general antiques including period furniture, porcelain and silver, jewellery, prints and watercolours, collectables.* LOC: Main road. SER: Valuations; restorations. SIZE: Large - 90 dealers. PARK: Own. VAT: Stan.
TEL: 01746 768778; FAX: 01746 768944
E-MAIL: denisridgway@hotmail.com

BURLTON

North Shropshire Reclamation
Wackley Lodge Farm. SY4 5TD. (S. Powell)
EST. 1997. SALVO. Open 9-5, Sat 10-4. STOCK: *Wide range of reclaimed architectural materials; chandeliers, fireplaces, beams, stone flooring.* LOC: A528. SIZE: Large. PARK: Easy.
TEL: 01939 270719; HOME/FAX: 01939 270895;
MOBILE: 07802 315038
E-MAIL: enquiries@old2new.uk.com
WEBSITE: www.old2new.uk.com

CHURCH STRETTON

Cardingmill Antiques
1 Burway Rd. SY6 6DL. (Mrs P. A. Benton)
EST. 1976. NHBS. Open Thurs., Fri. and Sat. 11-4 or by appointment. STOCK: *18th-19th C longcase and wall clocks, furniture, £250-£3,000; Measham teapots, £90-£450; original horsebrasses and martingales (NHB Soc.); Victorian oil lamps with original shades, £200-£650; 18th-19th C metalware.* LOC: A49. SIZE: Medium. PARK: Easy.
TEL: 01694 724555; HOME: 01584 877880; MOBILE: 07802 194253
E-MAIL: benton1933@aol.com
WEBSITE: www.churchstretton.co.uk

Stretton Antiques Market
36 Sandford Ave. SY6 6BH. (T. and L. Elvins)
EST. 1986. Open 9.30-5.30, Sun. and Bank Holidays 10.30-4.30. STOCK: *General antiques, shipping items and collectables.* LOC: Town centre. SIZE: Large - 55 dealers. PARK: Easy.
TEL: 01694 723718

CLEOBURY MORTIMER

M. and M. Baldwin
24 High St. DY14 8BY.
EST. 1978. Open Wed. 2-6, Fri. (Easter-Oct) and Sat. 10-1 and 2-6. STOCK: *19th-20th C books, to £500.* LOC: A4117. SER: Valuations; buys at auction (books). SIZE: Medium. PARK: Easy. VAT: Stan. FAIRS: Crick Boat Show; IWA National Festival; Wolverley Military Fair.
TEL: 01299 270110; HOME: same
E-MAIL: books@mbaldwin.free-online.co.uk

COSFORD

Martin Quick Antiques
Unit E2, Long Lane. TF11 8PJ. (C.R. Quick)
EST. 1965. *Trade Only.* Open every day by appointment
or by chance. STOCK: *English and Continental furniture
and decorative items including farmhouse tables, buffets,
armoires.* LOC: Signposted Neachley off A41. SER:
Packing and shipping. SIZE: Large. PARK: Easy. VAT:
Stan/Spec. FAIRS: Newark, Ardingly.
TEL: HOME: 01902 752908; MOBILE: 07774 124859
E-MAIL: cqantiques@aol.com

DITTON PRIORS

Priors Reclamation
Unit 65, Ditton Priors Industrial Estate. WV16 6SS.
(Vicki Bale and Martin Foley)
EST. 1996. SALVO. Open by appointment. STOCK:
*Flooring, period doors and door furniture, reclaimed and
made to order.* PARK: Easy. FAIRS: Burwarton.
TEL: 01746 712450; HOME: same
E-MAIL: vicki@priorsrec.co.uk
WEBSITE: www.priorsrec.co.uk

LUDLOW

Bayliss Antiques
22-24 Old St. SY8 1NP. (A.B., D.W. and N. Bayliss)
EST. 1966. Resident. Open 10-6 or by appointment.
STOCK: *18th-19th C furniture.* SER: Valuations. SIZE:
Medium. VAT: Spec. FAIRS: Organisers of Builth Wells
& Epsom Racecourse
TEL: 01584 873634; FAX: 01584 873763
WEBSITE: baylisantiques@aol.com

Bebb Fine Art   LAPADA
1 Church St. SY8 1AP. (Roger Bebb)
EST. 1978. CINOA. Open 10-5.30 or by appointment.
CL: Mon. STOCK: *Oils, screen prints and lithographs
including Elizabeth Frink, John Piper, Sir Terry Frost, W.
Lee-Hankey, mainly 20th C, £200-£8,000.* **LOC: Town
centre. SER: Valuations; restorations (oils). SIZE:
Medium. PARK: Nearby. VAT: Stan/spec.**
**TEL: 01584 879612; FAX/HOME: same; MOBILE: 07974
805062**
E-MAIL: bebbfineart@aol.com
WEBSITE: www.bebbfineart.co.uk

R.G. Cave and Sons Ltd   BADA LAPADA
**17 Broad St. SY8 1NG. (Mrs M.C., R.G., J.R. and
T.G. Cave)**
EST. 1962. Resident. Open 10-5.30. STOCK: *Furniture,
1630-1830; barometers, metalwork, fine art and collectors'
items.* **LOC: Old town. SER: Valuations. SIZE: Medium.
PARK: Easy. VAT: Spec.**
TEL: 01584 873568; FAX: 01584 875050

Corve Street Antiques
141a Corve St. SY8 2PG. (Mike McAvoy and David
Jones)
EST. 1990. Open 10-5. STOCK: *Oak, mahogany and pine
furniture, clocks, pocket watches, china, glass, prints and
pictures, £5-£5,000.* SER: Delivery by arrangement. SIZE:
Medium. PARK: Easy.
TEL: 01584 879100

Garrard Antiques
139a Corve St. SY8 2PG. (Caroline Garrard)
EST. 1985. Open by appointment. STOCK: *Pine and
country furniture, 18th-19th C, to £3,000.* LOC: Off the
A4. SIZE: Large. PARK: Outside warehouse.
TEL: 01584 876727; MOBILE: 07971 588063

G. & D. Ginger Antiques
5 Corve St. SY8 1DA.
EST. 1978. Resident. Open 9-5. STOCK: *17th-18th C
English and Welsh furniture, mainly oak and fruitwood,
farmhouse tables, food cupboards, presses, corner cupboards,
decorative and associated items.* SIZE: Large. VAT: Spec.
TEL: 01584 876939; MOBILE: 07970 666437
E-MAIL: gdgingerantiques@aol.com

Holloways of Ludlow
140 Corve St. SY8 2PG. (Mark Holloway)
EST. 1984. SALVO. Open 9.30-5.30. STOCK: *Bathroom
fittings, 1800-1950; fireplaces and surrounds, from 1700;*

ENGLISH FURNITURE
1660-1714
From Charles II to Queen Anne

Adam Bowett

Based largely on contemporary documents and on original and
firmly documented furniture, together with the latest modern
scholarship, this book provides a closely-reasoned analysis of
changing furniture styles, together with much technical
information on materials and processes. The author's radical
new approach to the stylistic and structural analysis of furniture
will change perceptions of English furniture and establish a
new chronology for late seventeenth and early eighteenth
century English furniture. This extensively illustrated book is
the first comprehensive review of the subject for nearly one
hundred years. A full glossary of terms is included as well as a
list of manuscript sources and a bibliography.

279 x 216 mm. 368 pp 527 col.
£45.00 Hardback

lighting and light fittings, from 1880; ranges and stoves, doors, door and window furniture, rim and box locks, leaded lights, stained glass, general fixtures and fittings. LOC: Central. SER: Restorations (lighting and fireplaces); keys cut for old locks. PARK: Easy.
TEL: 01584 876207; FAX: 020 7602 6561; MOBILE: 07786 802302
E-MAIL: mark@hollowaysofludlow.com
WEBSITE: www.hollowaysofludlow.com

Mitre House Antiques
Corve Bridge. SY8 1DY. (L. Jones)
EST. 1972. Open 9-5.30. STOCK: *Clocks, pine and general antiques. Warehouse - unstripped pine and shipping goods.* SIZE: Shop + trade warehouse. FAIRS: Newark; Ardingly.
TEL: 01584 872138; MOBILE: 07976 549013

Valentyne Dawes Gallery
Church St. SY8 1AP. (B.S. McCreddie)
Open 10-5.30. STOCK: *Paintings, 19th-21st C, £200-£40,000.* LOC: Town centre near Buttercross. SER: Valuations; restorations (oil paintings, watercolours, furniture). SIZE: Medium. PARK: Nearby. VAT: Spec.
TEL: 01584 874160; FAX: 01384 455576
E-MAIL: sales@gallery.wyenet.co.uk
WEBSITE: www.starmark.co.uk/valentyne-dawes/

Zani Lady Decorative Antiques
15 Corve St. SY8 1DA. (Susan Humphries)
Open 10.30-5.30. STOCK: *Wide range of decorative antiques, kitchenalia, mirrors, lighting, French linen, architectural items and ironwork, vintage fabrics and cushions.* LOC: Bottom of Corve St. SIZE: 3 floors - 7 dealers. PARK: Limited and private at rear.
TEL: 01584 877200; MOBILE: 07968 842219

MARKET DRAYTON

Midwinter Antiques
(Richard and Susannah Midwinter)
EST. 1983. Resident. Open any time by appointment. STOCK: *17th-19th C town and country furniture, clocks, textiles and decorative items. Specialises in personalised gift searches.* LOC: 20 minutes off the M6: jct. 14 from the south, jct. 15 from the north. SER: Restorations. SIZE: Medium. FAIRS: Olympia (June/Nov); Penman, Chester (Feb/Oct); NEC (Jan/April/Nov); Battersea Park (Jan/Apr/Oct).
TEL: 01630 673901; MOBILE: 07836 617361
E-MAIL: mail@midwinterantiques.co.uk
WEBSITE: www.midwinterantiques.co.uk

MUCH WENLOCK

Raynalds Mansion   BADA
High St. TF13 6AE. (John King)
EST. 1970. Resident. Open Mon., Tues. and Fri. 10-2, prior telephone call advisable. STOCK: *Period furniture and associated items, £500-£45,000.* SIZE: Medium. PARK: Easy. VAT: Spec.

TEL: **01952 727456**; FAX/HOME: same;
E-MAIL: **kingj896@aol.com**

Wenlock Fine Art
3 The Square. TF13 6LX. (P. Cotterill)
EST. 1990. Open Wed.-Sat. 10-5. STOCK: *Modern British paintings, mainly 20th C, some late 19th C.* SER: Valuations; restorations; cleaning; mounting; framing; buys at auction (as stock). SIZE: Medium. PARK: Nearby. VAT: Spec.
TEL: 01952 728232

RODINGTON

Brian James Antiques
Unit 9 Rodenhurst Business Park. SY4 4QU.
EST. 1985. Open 9-6, Sat. 9.30-12.30, Sun. by appointment. STOCK: *Chests of drawers, Georgian to Victorian, £50-£1,500.* LOC: Off M54, junction 6. Follow signs for Telford Hospital, Shawbirch, B5063, B5062, between Telford and Shrewsbury. SER: Restorations (inlay, veneering, polishing); conversions; linen presses, sideboards, cabinets, chests and entertainment centres made to order. PARK: Easy. VAT: Stan.
TEL: 01952 770856/243906
E-MAIL: brianjamesantiques@yahoo.co.uk
WEBSITE: www.brianjamesantiques.co.uk

SHIFNAL

Corner Farm Antiques
Weston Heath, Sheriffhales. TF11 8RY. (Tim Dams)
EST. 1994. GMC. Open 10-5 including Sun. STOCK: *Georgian to Edwardian furniture, especially dining room extending tables and sets of chairs; over 200 longcase, wall and bracket clocks and barometers; Victorian fireplaces, lighting, soft furnishings and collectables.* LOC: A41 between Tong and Newport. SER: Valuations; restorations (furniture and clocks); buys at auction. SIZE: Large. PARK: Own large. VAT: Stan.
TEL: 01952 691543
E-MAIL: cornerfarmantiques@btopenworld.com
WEBSITE: www.antiques-clocks.com

SHREWSBURY

Callaghan Fine Paintings   LAPADA
22 St Mary's St. SY1 1ED. (Daniel Callaghan)
EST. 1991. CINOA. 9.30-5 or by appointment. STOCK: *19th C British and European paintings, contemporary paintings and original bronzes.* SER: Restoration, cleaning, valuations, framing. SIZE: Large. FAIRS: Olympia; NEC; Royal Academy.
TEL: **01743 343452**; MOBILE: **07810 714545**
E-MAIL: **art@callaghan-finepaintings.com**
WEBSITE: **www.callaghan-finepaintings.com**

Candle Lane Books
28-29 Princess St. SY1 1LW. (J. Thornhill)

Est. 1974. Open 9.30-4.30. *Stock: Antiquarian and secondhand books.* Loc: Town centre. Size: Large. Park: Nearby.
Tel: 01743 365301

Collectors' Place
29a Princess St., The Square. SY1 1LW. (Keith Jones)
Est. 1996. Open 10-4, Sat. 9.30-5, Cl: Mon. *Stock: Collectables especially Prattware pot lids and bottles, 1700-1900; ceramics including Wade, Beswick, Carltonware, early 20th C; Art Deco, eyebaths.* Loc: Opposite Shrewsbury Antique Centre in town centre.
Tel: 01743 246150
E-mail: info@collectors-place.co.uk
Website: www.collectors-place.co.uk

Adrian Donnelly Antique Clocks
7 The Parade, St Mary's Place. SY1 1DL.
Est. 1985. MBHI. MBWCG. Open 10-5, Sat. 10-1. *Stock: Longcase and bracket clocks and barometers, 17th-19th C, £250-£12,000.* Loc: Town centre. Ser: Restorations (clocks and barometers). Size: Medium. Park: Easy. Vat: Stan/Spec.
Tel: 01743 361388; Fax: same
E-mail: clockshopshrewsbury@btopenworld.com

A Little Furniture Shop
1a Wyle Cop. SY1 1UT. (Heather Maskill and Mark Swain)
Est. 2000. Open by appointment. *Stock: Victorian wing and tub chairs, Edwardian armchairs, Victorian and Edwardian chaises, sofas and dining chairs, 1920s drop arm sofas.* Loc: Town centre. Ser: Restorations (upholstered furniture). Size: Small. Park: Nearby.
Tel: 01743 352102; Mobile: 07714 205660
E-mail: heather@furniture.fslife.co.uk
Website: www.alittlefurnitureshop.co.uk

Mansers Antiques
LAPADA
Coleham Head. SY3 7BJ. (Mark Manser)
Est. 1944. Open 9-5. *Stock: Furniture, 18th-20th C, £250-£50,000; silver, porcelain, glass, mirrors, decorative items, £50-£10,000; oils and watercolours. Not Stocked: Coins, books.* Loc: 150 yds. from English bridge away from town centre. Ser: Valuations; restorations. Size: Large. Park: Own. Vat: Stan/Spec.
Tel: 01743 351120; Fax: 01743 271047
E-mail: mansers@theantiquedealers.com
Website: www.theantiquedealers.com

Princess Antique Centre
14a The Square. SY1 1LH. (J. Langford)
Open 9.30-5. *Stock: General antiques and collectables.* Size: 35 dealers. Park: Nearby.
Tel: 01743 343701

Quayside Antiques
9 Frankwell. SY3 8JY. (Jean and Chris Winter)
Open Tues. and Fri. 10-4, Sat. 10-5. *Stock: Victorian and Edwardian furniture, especially dining tables and sets of* chairs, desks, bookcases, wardrobes. Loc: Near Halls Saleroom. Ser: Restorations (furniture). Size: Large. Park: Own. Fairs: NEC.
Tel: 01743 360490; Workshop: 01948 665838; Home: 01948 830363;
Website: www.quaysideantiques.co.uk

Shrewsbury Antique Centre
15 Princess House, The Square. SY1 1JZ. (J. Langford)
Est. 1978. Open 9.30-5.30. *Stock: General antiques and collectables.* Loc: Town centre just off the square. Size: Large - 50 dealers. Park: Nearby.
Tel: 01743 247704

STANTON UPON HINE HEATH

Marcus Moore Antiques
Booley House, Booley. SY4 4LY. (M.G.J. and M.P. Moore)
Est. 1980. Usually open but prior telephone call advisable. *Stock: Oak and country furniture, late 17th to 18th C; Georgian mahogany furniture, 18th to early 19th C; all £50-£7,000; some Victorian furniture; associated items.* Loc: Half a mile north of Stanton on right. Ser: Restorations (furniture); polishing; search; shipping. Size: Large. Park: Easy. Vat: Stan/Spec.
Tel: 01939 200333;
Website: www.marcusmoore-antiques.com

TELFORD

The Curio Centre Ltd
2 Waterloo St., Ironbridge. TF8 7AA.
Open 10-5 inc. Sun. *Stock: Wide range of antiques and collectables including jewellery, figurines, kitchenware, glassware and excellent gift ideas.* Size: 65 cabinets. Park: Own at front.
Tel: 01952 433844
E-mail: curiocentre@hotmail.com
Website: www.thecuriocentre.co.uk

WHITCHURCH

Age of Elegance
54 High St. SY13 1BB. (Mike and Janet Proudlove)
Est. 1988. Open Thurs., Fri., Sat. 10-4. *Stock: Collectables including china and glass; Victorian and Edwardian furniture.* Loc: Midway between Shrewsbury and Chester. Ser: Valuations. Size: Small. Park: Easy.
Tel: 01948 666145; Fax: same
E-mail: j.proudlove@btinternet.com

Dodington Antiques
7 Sherrymill Hill. SY13 1BN. (G. MacGillivray)
Est. 1978. Resident. Open by appointment. *Stock: Oak, fruitwood, walnut country and 18th to early 19th C mahogany furniture, longcase clocks, barometers, £10-£6,000.* Loc: On fringe of town centre. Ser: Buys at auction. Size: Large. Park: Easy. Vat: Stan/Spec.
Tel: 01948 663399; Mobile: 07779 724656

Twentieth Century Textiles

Francesca Galloway and Sue Kerry

310 x 245 mm 196pp 163col 7b&w
£35.00 hardback

This stunning book presents a selection of more than 100 furnishing textiles and designs that range from a spectacular printed hanging designed by the Wiener Werkstätte artist, Dagobert Peche, between 1911 and 1918, to the series of dramatic woven, silk and metal wall coverings, *Les Colombes*, designed by Henri Stephany for the 1925 Exposition Internationale des Arts Decoratifs et Industriels Modernes. The Art Deco period is well represented by the works of Raoul Dufy, Alberto Lorenzi, Robert Bonfils, Alfred Latour, Emile Alain Seguy and Paul Dumas.

Although the majority of pre-Second World War textiles are of French origin, the exhibition also includes some rare British furnishing fabrics from the 1930s, in particular the iconic and very elegant *Magnolia Leaf* by Marion Dorn, woven in off-white and silver viscut by Warner & Sons in 1936. During this period, Britain attracted talented European designers, such as Jacqueline Groag and Marian Mahler who had trained with Josef Hoffmann at the Vienna Kunstgewerbeschule. They became highly influential in creating a 'New Look' that took hold of Britain after the austerities of the Second World War. The Festival of Britain, held in 1951, was epitomised by *Calyx* which launched the career of its designer, Lucienne Day and is now considered to be a landmark of post-War design. So great was its success that several versions were produced as well as contemporary copies, all of which are reproduced here, in spectacular colour.

Two great textiles from the 1950s - *Seaweed* designed by Ashley Havinden in 1954 for Arthur Sanderson and *Grecian* by Alec Hunter in 1956 for Warner & Sons - bridge the gap between the spirit and elegance of the inter-War period and the new 'contemporary' look of the 1950s. Britain maintained its pre-eminent position in textile design throughout the 1950s, 1960s and early 1970s. This was because firms like Edinburgh Weavers, Heal & Sons and Hull Traders and museums such as the Whitworth Art Gallery in Manchester (the centre of the British textile industry) worked hard at integrating and promoting great design, often by well-known artists, with industry. Among the artists who worked with Edinburgh Weavers were Marino Marini, Victor Vasarely and Alan Reynolds. Britain was not alone in applying art to industry. An elegant example of Op Art is the work of the German artist, Wolf Bauer, whose 1969/70 designs for one of the leading American manufacturers, Knoll Textiles, is a highlight of this book.

For full details of all ACC publications,
log on to our website:
www.antiquecollectorsclub.com
or telephone 01394 389950 for a free catalogue

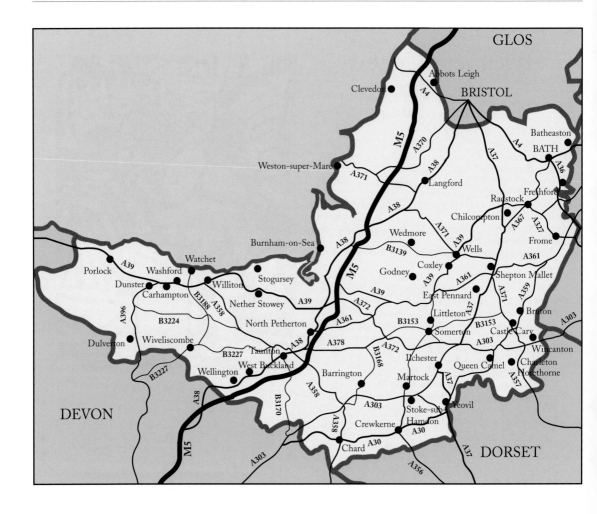

ABBOTS LEIGH

David and Sally March Antiques   LAPADA
Oak Wood Lodge, Stoke Leigh Woods. BS8 3QB.
(David and Sally March)
EST. 1981. CINOA. WEADA. Open by appointment.
STOCK: *18th to early 19th C English porcelain especially*
figures, Bristol and Plymouth. SER: Valuations; buys at
auction (as stock) or on commission. PARK: Easy. VAT:
Spec. FAIRS: NEC; LAPADA.
TEL: **01275 372422;** FAX: **same;** MOBILE: **07774**
838376
E-MAIL: **david.march@lineone.net**
WEBSITE: **www.davidandsallymarch.com**

BARRINGTON

Stuart Interiors
Barrington Court. TA19 0NG. (Peter Russell)
EST. 1977. Open 9-5, Sat. 10-5. STOCK: *Oak furniture,*
£100-£15,000; accessories, £50-£2,500; both pre-1720.

LOC: Between A303 and M5, 5 miles north-east of
Ilminster. National Trust property, signposted in area.
SER: Valuations. SIZE: Large. PARK: Easy. VAT: Spec.
TEL: 01460 240349
E-MAIL: design@stuartinteriors.com
WEBSITE: www.stuartinteriors.com

BATH

Adam Gallery Ltd
13 John St. BA1 2JL. (Paul and Philip Dye)
Open 9.30-5.30 or by appointment. STOCK: *20th C*
British and international fine art, including Ben Nicholson,
Henry Moore, John Piper, Picasso, Matisse and contemporary
paintings. SER: Contemporary exhibitions.
TEL: 01225 480406; FAX: same
E-MAIL: info@adamgallery.com
WEBSITE: www.adamgallery.com

The Antique Map Shop Ltd
9-10 Pulteney Bridge. BA2 4AY. (David Gardner)

EST. 1984. Open 10-5, Sun. and Bank Holidays 11-4. STOCK: *Antique maps.* SER: Free worldwide mailing. PARK: Nearby
TEL: 01225 446097; MOBILE: 07850 746090
E-MAIL: dave@dg-maps.com
WEBSITE: www.dg-maps.com

Antique Textiles & Lighting
34 Belvedere, Lansdown Rd. BA1 5BN. (Joanna Proops)
EST. 1980. WEADA. Open Tues.-Sat. 10-5 or by appointment. STOCK: *Chandeliers, wall lights, tapestries, paisleys, beadwork, fans, samplers, bellpulls, linen and lace, textiles from 16th - 18th C.* LOC: 5 mins. walk from city centre. SIZE: Large. PARK: Easy. FAIRS: Bath.
TEL: 01225 310795
WEBSITE: www.antiquetextilesandlighting.co.uk

Bath Galleries
33 Broad St. BA1 5LP. (J. Griffiths)
EST. 1973. Open 10-4.45. CL: Thurs. STOCK: *Clocks, furniture, paintings, porcelain, barometers, silver.* LOC: 50yds. from central Post Office. SER: Valuations; restorations; buys at auction. SIZE: Medium. PARK: Walcot St. multi-storey, 30yds. VAT: Stan/Spec.
TEL: 01225 462946

Bath Stamp and Coin Shop
Pulteney Bridge. BA2 4AY. (M.A. Swindells)
EST. 1946. Open 9.30-5.30. STOCK: *Coins - Roman, hammered, early milled, G.B. gold, silver and copper, some foreign; literature and accessories; banknotes, medals, stamps and postal history.* SER: Valuations. PARK: Laura Place; Walcot multi-storey. VAT: Stan.
TEL: 01225 463073
E-MAIL: m7swindells@hotmail.com

George Bayntun
Manvers St. BA1 1JW. (E.W.G. Bayntun-Coward)
EST. 1894. ABA. Open 9-1 and 2-5.30, Sat. 9.30-1. STOCK: *Rare books. First or fine editions of English literature, standard sets, illustrated and sporting books, poetry, biography and travel, mainly in new leather bindings; antiquarian books in original bindings.* LOC: By rail and bus stations. SER: Binding; restorations. SIZE: Large. PARK: 50 yds. by station. VAT: Stan.
TEL: 01225 466000; FAX: 01225 482122
E-MAIL: ebc@georgebayntun.com
WEBSITE: www.georgebayntun.com

Bedsteads
2 Walcot Buildings, London Rd. BA1 6AD. (Mark and Nikki Ashton)
EST. 1991. Open Tues., Wed. and Fri. 10-5.30, Sat. 10.30-6. STOCK: *Brass, iron and wooden bedsteads, 1840-1920, £500-£4,500; bedroom suites, 1880-1920, £2,000-£5,500.* LOC: 200 yards before traffic lights, end of London Road. SER: Valuations; restorations (bedsteads). PARK: Weymouth St. VAT: Stan/Spec.

TEL: 01225 339182; FAX: same; HOME: 01275 464114
E-MAIL: enquiries@bedsteads-uk.co.uk
WEBSITE: www.bedsteadsbath@btconnect.com

Lawrence Brass
Apple Studio, Ashley. BA1 3SD.
EST. 1973. Open by appointment. STOCK: *Furniture, 16th-19th C, to £50,000. NOT STOCKED: Ceramics, silver, glass.* LOC: A4 towards Chippenham. SER: Restorations (furniture, clocks and barometers). SIZE: Small. PARK: Easy. VAT: Stan/Spec.
TEL: 01225 852222; FAX: 01225 851050
E-MAIL: info@lawrencebrass.com
WEBSITE: www.lawrencebrass.com

David Bridgwater
15 Camden Crescent. BA1 5HY.
EST. 1984. Open by appointment. STOCK: *Architectural items and sculpture, including garden, decorative and practical items for the period garden.* SER: Search. PARK: Easy. VAT: Spec.
TEL: 01225 463435; MOBILE: 07710 124376
E-MAIL: david.j.bridgwater@btinternet.com

Mary Cruz   LAPADA
5 Broad St. BA1 5LJ.
EST. 1974. CINOA. WEADA. Open 10-6.30, Sun. by appointment. STOCK: *18th-19th C furniture, including country; 18th C to date paintings and sculpture; decorative items.* LOC: City centre. SER: Valuations; restorations; finder (Latin American Art). SIZE: Medium. PARK: Easy. VAT: Stan/Spec. FAIRS: LAPADA, NEC, Olympia.
TEL: 01225 334174; FAX: 01225 423300
E-MAIL: mary.cruz@btconnect.com

Frank Dux Antiques
33 Belvedere, Lansdown Rd. BA1 5HR. (F. Dux and M. Hopkins)
EST. 1988. Resident. Open Tues.-Sat. 10-2. STOCK: *18th-19th C glass - drinking, decanters, curiosities and tableware; Venetian glass; Murano, occasionally 19th C, mostly 1950s .* LOC: From Broad St. up Lansdown Hill, on right 100yds. past Guinea Lane. SER: Postal deliveries worldwide. SIZE: Medium. PARK: Easy.
TEL: 01225 312367; FAX: same
E-MAIL: m.hopkins@antique-glass.co.uk
WEBSITE: www.antique-glass.co.uk

George Street Antiques Centre
8 Edgar Buildings. BA1 2EE.
EST. 1993. Open 9.30-5. STOCK: *Clocks, barometers, pocket watches; antique and modern jewellery; paintings, silver, porcelain and Staffordshire, general antiques.* LOC: City centre. SER: Valuations; restorations (clocks, barometers and jewellery). SIZE: Small. PARK: Nearby.
TEL: 01225 422322
E-MAIL: kembery@antiquecentre.gb.com
WEBSITE: www.antiquecentre.gb.com

George Gregory
Manvers St. BA1 1JW. (C.A.W. Bayntun-Coward)
EST. 1845. Open 9-1 and 2-5.30, Sat. 9.30-1. *STOCK: Secondhand books, engraved views and portraits.* LOC: By rail station. SIZE: Large. PARK: By rail station.
TEL: 01225 466000; FAX: 01225 482122
E-MAIL: julie@georgebayntun.com
WEBSITE: www.georgebayntun.com

Haliden Oriental Rug Shop
98 Walcot St. BA1 5BG. (Andrew Lloyd and Craig Bale)
EST. 1963. Open 10-5. *STOCK: Antique and modern Caucasian, Turkish, Persian, Chinese, Afghan, Turkoman and tribal rugs and carpets, 19th C, £50-£10,000; some Oriental textiles - coats, embroideries, wall hangings, 19th C, £50-£3,000.* LOC: Off main London road, into town by Walcot Reclamation. SER: Valuations; cleaning; restorations; buys at auction. SIZE: Medium. PARK: Walcot St. or multi-storey. FAIRS: Bath Decorative.
TEL: 01225 469240
E-MAIL: enquiries@haliden.com
WEBSITE: www.haliden.com

Anthony Hepworth Fine Art Dealers
3 Margaret's Buildings, Brock St. BA1 2LP.
EST. 1989. Open during exhibitions Tues.-Sat. 11-5 other times by appointment. *STOCK: Mainly 20th C British paintings and sculpture; African tribal art and large stock of artists' monographs.* LOC: Off Brock St. between Royal Crescent and Circus. SER: Exhibitions Bath and London. PARK: Brock St./Catherine Place. FAIRS: Olympia; 20th/21st C British Art; London Art.
TEL: 01225 447480; FAX: 01225 442917; MOBILE: 07970 480650 (during fairs only)
E-MAIL: anthony.hepworth@btconnect.com

Kembery Antique Clocks Ltd
8 Edgar Buildings, George St. BA1 2EE. (P. and E. Kembery)
EST. 1993. WEADA. BWCMG. Open 10-5. *STOCK: Longcase, bracket, mantel, wall and carriage clocks and barometers, 18th-19th C, £200-£10,000.* SER: Valuations; restorations. VAT: Spec.
TEL: 01179 565281
WEBSITE: www.kdclocks.co.uk

Ann King
38 Belvedere, Lansdown Rd. BA1 5HR.
EST. 1977. Open 10-4, CL: Mon. *STOCK: Period clothes, 19th C to 1970; baby clothes, shawls, head dresses, linen, lace, curtains, cushions, quilts and textiles.* SIZE: Small. PARK: Easy.
TEL: 01225 336245

Looking Glass of Bath
94-96 Walcot St. BA1 5BG. (Anthony Reed)
EST. 1972. WEADA. Open 9-6. *STOCK: Reproduction antique mirrors. Large mirrors and picture frames, 18th-*

19th C, £50-£5,000; decorative prints, 18th-20th C. SER: Valuations; restorations (re-gilding, gesso and compo work, re-silvering and bevelling glass); manufactures arched top overmantel, pier, convex and triptych mirrors; old mirror plates supplied; simulated mercury silvered mirror glass; buys SIZE: Medium. PARK: Easy. VAT: Stan/Spec.
TEL: 01225 461969; FAX: 01225 316191; HOME: 01275 333595
E-MAIL: info@lookinglassofbath.co.uk
WEBSITE: www.lookinglassofbath.co.uk

E.P. Mallory and Son Ltd   BADA
1-5 Bridge St. BA2 4AP. (N Hall)
EST. 1898. Open 9.30-5.15, Sat 9.30-5.30. *STOCK: Antique and estate silver, jewellery, objets de vertu, £50-£10,000.* PARK: Podium carpark. VAT: Stan/Spec.
TEL: 01225 788800; FAX: 01225 442210
E-MAIL: mail@mallory-jewellers.com
WEBSITE: www.mallory-jewellers.com

Old Bank Antiques Centre
16-17 and 20 Walcot Buildings, London Rd. BA1 6AD. (A.R. Schlesinger and D.K. Moore)
EST. 1987. WEADA. Open 10-6, Sun. 11-4. *STOCK: English, Continental, pine and country furniture, glass, ceramics, rugs, metalwork, interior design items, lighting.* LOC: A4 London Road, 1/2 mile from city centre near Safeway. SER: Valuations. SIZE: 14 showrooms. PARK: Rear of premises, via Bedford St.
TEL: 01225 469282; HOME: same
E-MAIL: alexatmontague@aol.com
WEBSITE: www.oldbankantiquescentre.com

Below are listed the dealers at this centre.

> **AJ Antiques**
>
> **Richard Andrews**
>
> **Bread & Roses**
>
> **Margaret Cameron**
>
> **Robin Coleman**
>
> **Beth Cuttell**
>
> **Peter Davis**
>
> **Owen Hirst**
>
> **Simon Jackson**
>
> **Janet Kaulbach**
>
> **Norman Kemp**
>
> **Manor House Old Pine**
>
> **Trevor Matcham**
>
> **Montague Antiques**
>
> **Sarah Newsum**
>
> **Taylor Wootten**

Quiet Street Antiques
3 Quiet St. BA1 2JS. (K. Hastings-Spital)
EST. 1985. Open 10-6. STOCK: *Furniture especially English mahogany, 1750-1870, £250-£12,000; objects including bronzes, caddies, boxes, mirrors, £50-£2,000; Royal Worcester porcelain, £30-£2,000; clocks including longcase, wall, bracket and carriage, barometers, 1750-1900, £150-£8,000.* LOC: 25yds. from Milsom St. SER: Buys at auction (furniture and clocks); free delivery 100 mile radius of Bath and weekly delivery to London. Export facilities. SIZE: Large - 8 showrooms. PARK: Nearby. VAT: Spec.
TEL: 01225 315727; FAX: 01225 448300
E-MAIL: kerry@quietstreetantiques.co.uk
WEBSITE: www.quietstreetantiques.co.uk

Michael and Jo Saffell
3 Walcot Buildings, London Rd. BA1 6AD.
EST. 1975. WEADA. Open 9.30-5, Sat. and other times by appointment. STOCK: *British tins and other advertising material including showcards and enamels, 1870-1939; decorative items; all £5-£5,000.* LOC: A4 - main road into city from M4. SER: Postal. SIZE: Small. PARK: Side streets opposite. FAIRS: Newark, Winternational, Castle Donington Collectors'.
TEL: 01225 315857; FAX: same; HOME: same; MOBILE: 07941 158049
E-MAIL: michael.saffell@virgin.net

Susannah
25 Broad St. BA1 5LW. (Sue Holley)
EST. 1985. Open 10-5. STOCK: *Decorative textiles and antiques.* PARK: Opposite. FAIRS: Bath Decorative (March).
TEL: 01225 445069; FAX: 01225 339004

Vintage to Vogue
28 Milsom St. BA1 1DG. (Mrs Teresa Langton)
EST. 1995. Open Tues.-Sat. 11-5. STOCK: *Vintage clothing - women's, gentlemen's, children's - including hats, bags, shoes, gloves, scarves and formal wear, 1850-1950s; buttons, trimmings, costume jewellery, costume and antique lace, fashion and needlework books and magazines; all £1-£500.* LOC: In passage from Broad St. car park. SIZE: Medium. PARK: Public at rear of shop.
TEL: 01225 337323

Walcot Reclamation
108 Walcot St. BA1 5BG. (Mr and Mrs R. Knapp)
EST. 1977. Open 8.30-5.30, Sat. 9-5. STOCK: *Architectural items - chimney pieces, ironwork, doors, fireplaces, garden statuary, period baths and fittings and traditional building materials.* LOC: Central. SER: Valuations; restorations. SIZE: Large. PARK: Own and multi-storey nearby. VAT: Stan.
TEL: 01225 444404/448163
E-MAIL: rick@walcot.com
WEBSITE: www.walcot.com

Waterfall Antiques
57 Walcot St. BA1 5BN.
EST. 1991. WEADA. Open 10.30-5.30. STOCK: *19th C mahogany furniture, especially wardrobes; decorative objects, £20-£500.* LOC: From A4 veer left at 1st mini-roundabout. SIZE: Medium. PARK: Easy. VAT: Stan/Spec.
TEL: 01225 444201; MOBILE: 07990 690240
E-MAIL: info@waterfallantiques.com
WEBSITE: www.waterfallantiques.com

BATHEASTON

Piccadilly Antiques
280 High St. BA1 7RA.
EST. 1990. WEADA. Open 9.30-5.30 or by appointment. STOCK: *Country, some mahogany, furniture and decorative accessories, £100-£10,000.* LOC: Batheaston High St., off the M4, Jct 17. SER: Export-orientated so can offer advice on worldwide shipping; advice on restoration and delivery within the UK SIZE: Large. PARK: Easy. VAT: Stan/Spec. FAIRS: Bath Decorative.
TEL: 01225 851494; FAX: 01225 851120
E-MAIL: piccadillyantiques@ukonline.co.uk

Below are listed the dealers at this centre.

David Adams
Boxes and globes; contemporary furniture, decorative accessories. VAT: Stan.

Sandra Biss
Brass, lighting.

Robin Coleman Antiques
Interesting and decorative items, small furniture. VAT: VAT: Stan/Spec.

John Davies
18th-19th C furniture and decorative items. VAT: Stan/Spec.
TEL: Home - 01225 852103.

Paul Farnham
Decorative items.

Simon Freeman
Decorative antiques

Grierson Gower
Architectural, naive and popular art, toys, models, pub and trade signs.

BRUTON

The Antique Shop
5 High St. BA10 0AB. (D.L. Gwilliam and M.J. Wren)
EST. 1976. Open Thurs.-Sat. 10-5.30 or by appointment. STOCK: *Furniture, jewellery, silver, china, copper, brass, general collectables, decorative art and antiques, Georgian to Art Deco, £5-£4,000.* SER: Repairs (jewellery); re-stringing pearls and beads. SIZE: Medium. PARK: Easy.
TEL: 01749 813264

Michael Lewis Gallery - Antiquarian Maps & Prints
17 High St. BA10 0AB. (Leo and Mrs J. L. Lewis)
EST. 1980. Open 9.30-5.30 or by appointment. CL:
Thurs. pm. STOCK: *Prints and maps, 18th-19th C.* LOC:
A359. SER: Framing. SIZE: Large. PARK: Easy.
TEL: 01749 813557; HOME: same

M.G.R. Exports
Station Rd. BA10 0EH. (James Read)
EST. 1980. WEADA. Open Mon.-Fri. 8.30-5.30, prior
call advisable. STOCK: *Georgian, Victorian, Edwardian and
decorative items, carved oak, barley twist and shipping goods,
Continental furniture.* SER: Packing and shipping. SIZE:
Large. PARK: Easy.
TEL: 01749 812460; FAX: 01749 812882
E-MAIL: mgrexports@hotmail.co.uk
WEBSITE: www.mgrexports.com

John Prestige Antiques
MGR Exports, Station Rd. BA10 0EH. (John and
Patricia Prestige)
EST. 1971. Open 8.45-6, appointment advisable. CL:
Sat. and Sun. except by appointment. STOCK: *Period and
Victorian furniture; shipping goods; decorative smalls.* SER:
Courier (West Country). SIZE: Large + warehouse.
PARK: Own. VAT: Stan/Spec.
TEL: 01803 856141; HOME: 01803 853739; FAX: 01803
851649
WEBSITE: www.john-prestige.co.uk

BURNHAM-ON-SEA

Castle Antiques
53 Victoria St. TA8 1AW. (T.C. Germain)
EST. 1953. NAG. Open 10-5.30. CL: Wed. STOCK:
Jewellery, silver, 18th-19th C furniture, porcelain, clocks.
SER: Restorations.
TEL: 01278 785031
E-MAIL: castle.antiques@virgin.net
WEBSITE: www.castleantiques.org.uk

Heape's Antiques
39 Victoria St. TA8 1AN. (Mrs M.M. Heap)
EST. 1987. Open 10-1 and 2.30-4.30. STOCK: *Small
furniture, fine arts, porcelain, glass, memorabilia.* LOC:
Town centre. SER: Picture framing, cleaning and
restoration. PARK: Easy.
TEL: 01278 782131

CARHAMPTON

Chris's Crackers
Townsend Garage. TA24 6NH. (P. Marshall)
EST. 1995. Open 10-5.30 including Sun. STOCK: *Mainly
18th-19th C furniture, stripped pine, architectural antiques,
iron and stonework, general building reclamation materials
and country artefacts.* LOC: A39 coast road. SER: Pine
stripping. SIZE: Large warehouses. PARK: Easy.
TEL: 01643 821873

E-MAIL: info@chriscrackers.net
WEBSITE: www.chriscrackers.net

CASTEL CARY

The Clock Shop
The Pitching, Market Place, BA7 7AL.
EST. 1970. Open 10-6. CL: Mon/Wed. STOCK: *Clocks,
1685-1900, from £500; French carriage clocks, from £300.*
LOC: Next to market building on cobbles. SER:
Valuations; restorations (clocks). SIZE: Medium. PARK:
Easy. VAT: Stan/Spec.
TEL: 01963 359100
E-MAIL: theclockshop@btconnect.com
WEBSITE: www.castlecaryclockshop.co.uk

CHARD

Chard Antiques
23 High St. TA20 1QF. (A.W.E. and Mrs J. Smith)
EST. 1994. Open 10-5, other times by appointment.
STOCK: *Furniture 19th C to Edwardian specialising in pine;
decorative items, pictures and collectables.* SIZE: Medium.
PARK: Nearby.
TEL: 01460 63517
E-MAIL: info@chardantiques.co.uk
WEBSITE: www.chardantiques.co.uk

CHARLTON HORETHORNE

On-Reflection Mirrors Ltd
Bullen Farmhouse. DT9 4NL. (Alison and Alan
Roelich)
EST. 1999. WEADA. Open by appointment at any time.
STOCK: *Fine quality Continental and English gilt, silver,
painted and Venetian mirrors, mainly 19th C, £100-£7,000.*
LOC: Two miles south of A303 on B3145 between
Wincanton and Sherborne. SER: Valuations; finder. SIZE:
Large. PARK: Easy. VAT: Stan. FAIRS: Antiques for
Everyone, NEC, Birmingham; Decorative Antiques,
Battersea.
TEL: 01963 220723; home/FAX: same; MOBILE: 07971
889093
E-MAIL: info@on-reflection.co.uk
WEBSITE: www.on-reflection.co.uk

CHEDDAR

Shentonbooks
La Rochelle, Venns Gate. BS27 3BY. (Nigel Shenton,
Paul Shenton and Sue Shenton)
EST. 1973. *International postal service.* Open by
appointment. STOCK: *Books related to clocks, watches,
barometers, sundials, scientific instruments, automata and
ornamental turning, £1-£1,000.* SER: Valuations; buys at
auction (horological books); catalogues available. SIZE:
Medium. PARK: Easy. FAIRS: Birmingham, Uxbridge and
Taunton Clock and Watch.

TEL: 0845 838 5523; FAX: 0845 838 5532
E-MAIL: nps@shentonbooks.com
WEBSITE: www.shentonbooks.com

CHILCOMPTON

Billiard Room Antiques   LAPADA
The Old School, Church Lane. BA3 4HP. (Mrs J. McKeivor)
EST. 1992. **Open by appointment.** STOCK: *Billiard, snooker and pool tables and accessories, 19th C, £100-£40,000.* SER: Valuations; restorations; buys at auction; search. SIZE: Medium. PARK: Easy.
TEL: **01761 232839; home and FAX: same**
E-MAIL: **info@billiardroom.co.uk**
WEBSITE: **www.billiardroom.co.uk**

CLEVEDON

The Collector
14 The Beach. BS21 7QU. (Mrs Tina Simmonds)
EST. 1993. Open 10-5, Sun. 12-5. CL: Thurs. (Jan.-Feb. open weekends only). STOCK: *Small items and collectables, from 1880, £5-£200; postcards and ephemera, 1900-1960, £1-£30; Beatrix Potter and Bunnykins figures, from 1960, £16-£300.* LOC: On sea front, near pier. SIZE: Small. PARK: Easy.
TEL: 01275 875066; HOME: same

COXLEY

Wells Reclamation Company
BA5 1RQ. (H. Davies)
EST. 1984. Open 8.30-5.30, Sat. 9-4. STOCK: *Architectural items, 18th-19th C.* LOC: A39 towards Glastonbury from Wells. SER: Valuations. SIZE: Large including barns and grounds. PARK: Easy. VAT: Stan.
TEL: 01749 677087
WEBSITE: www.wellsreclamation.com

CREWKERNE

Julian Armytage
TA18 8QG.
EST. 1972. Open by appointment. STOCK: *Fine sporting, marine and decorative prints, 18th-19th C.* VAT: Spec.
TEL: 01460 73449; FAX: same

Crewkerne Antique Centre
16 Market St. TA18 7LA. (E. Blewden)
EST. 1987. Open 9.30-4.30. STOCK: *Furniture, £25-£3,000; collectables, £5-£1,000; pictures, £5-£2,000; all 18th-20th C, garden items.* LOC: A303 westward, A359 to Crewkerne, Chard road through town. SER: Valuations; restorations. SIZE: Large, 50 dealers. PARK: Easy.
TEL: 01460 77111
E-MAIL: crewkerneantiques@tiscali.co.uk

Gresham Books
31 Market St. TA18 7JU. (J. and A. Hine)
EST. 1972. PBFA. Open 10-5. STOCK: *Books, 50p to £1,000.* LOC: A30. SER: Valuations. SIZE: Medium. PARK: Nearby.
TEL: 01460 77726; FAX: 01460 52479
WEBSITE: www.greshambooks.co.uk

Noahs
41 Market Sq. TA18 7LP. (Mrs. Edmonds and Michael Polirer)
EST. 1967. Open Tues-Fri 10-4.30, Sat 10-1. STOCK: *General antiques and jewellery.* LOC: Town centre. SER: Valuations; restorations. SIZE: Medium. PARK: Nearby.
TEL: 01460 77786

DULVERTON

Acorn Antiques
39 High St. TA22 9DW. (P. Hounslow)
EST. 1988. Open 10-5.30. STOCK: *Decorative antique furniture, period and reproduction upholstery, sofas, fine art, textiles, country furniture.* LOC: Town centre. SER: Interior design. SIZE: Medium. PARK: Nearby.
TEL: 01398 323286; HOME: same
E-MAIL: peter@exmoorantiques.co.uk
WEBSITE: www.exmoorantiques.co.uk

Rothwell and Dunworth
2 Bridge St. TA22 9HJ. (Mrs C. Rothwell and M. Rothwell)
EST. 1975. ABA. Open 10.30-1 and 2-5.15, including Sun. STOCK: *Antiquarian and secondhand books especially on hunting, horses and military history.* LOC: 1st shop in village over River Barle. SER: Valuations. SIZE: Medium. PARK: 100yds.
TEL: 01398 323169; FAX: 01398 331161
E-MAIL: rothwellm@aol.com

Anthony Sampson Antiques
Holland House, Bridge St. TA22 9HJ.
EST. 1967. Open 9.30-5.30, Sun. by appointment. STOCK: *Town and country furniture, 17th to early 19th C, £100-£10,000+; occasional porcelain, pottery, silver, glass, pictures, garden ornaments, decorative items and militaria.* LOC: Main road, prominent position near bridge. SER: Valuations. SIZE: Medium. PARK: Nearby. VAT: Spec.
TEL: 01398 324247
E-MAIL: ant.sampson@virgin.net

DUNSTER

The Crooked Window
7 High St. TA24 6SF. (Robert Ricketts)
EST. 1984. STOCK: *Chinese ceramics and jade, 3000BC to 19th C, £50-£50,000; English furniture, 16th-18th C, £500-£50,000; maps and prints, 16th-18th C, £50-£2,000; antique jewellery, £50-£20,000.* SER: Valuations; lectures. SIZE: Small. PARK: Easy. FAIRS: Wilton House.

TEL: 01643 821606; HOME: same; MOBILE: 07787 722606
E-MAIL: bob.ricketts@tiscali.co.uk
WEBSITE: www.antiquities.uk.com

EAST KNOYLE

Edward Marnier Antiques
The Studio, Bramble Cottage. SP3 6BY.
EST. 1989. WEADA. Resident. Open by appointment any time. STOCK: *English and Continental furniture, pictures, rugs, carpets and interesting decorative objects, 17th-20th C, £5-£10,000.* LOC: Quarter mile from East Knoyle; Millbrook Lane, off the A350; 3 miles from A303. SER: Valuations; buys at auction. PARK: Easy. VAT: Spec. FAIRS: Battersea Park; Bath.
TEL: 01747 830878; MOBILE: 07785 110122
E-MAIL: emarnier@ukonline.co.uk

EAST PENNARD

Pennard House Antiques   LAPADA
BA4 6TP. (Martin Dearden)
EST. 1979. WEADA. Open 9.30-5.30 or by appointment. STOCK: French and English country furniture, £300-£5,000. LOC: From Shepton Mallet, 4 miles south off A37. One hour from Bath. SER: Valuations; restorations; export. SIZE: Large. PARK: Easy. VAT: Stan/Spec.
TEL: 01749 860731; HOME: 01749 860266; FAX: 01749 860700; MOBILE: 07802 243569
E-MAIL: pennardantiques@ukonline.co.uk

FRESHFORD

Janet Clarke
3 Woodside Cottages. BA2 7WJ.
Mail Order Only. STOCK: *Antiquarian books on gastronomy, cookery and wine.* SER: Catalogue issued.
TEL: 01225 723186; FAX: 01225 722063
E-MAIL: janetclarke@ukgateway.net
WEBSITE: www.janetclarke.com

FROME

Victor Adams
Upper Room Books, First floor, 43-44 Vallis Way, Badcox. BA11 3BA.
PBFA. Open 9.30-5.30. STOCK: *Antiquarian and out of print books.* LOC: A362 Frome to Radstock road. SIZE: Small. PARK: Free opposite. FAIRS: PBFA; DMG.
TEL: 01373 467125; FAX: same
E-MAIL: victoradams@vabooks.co.uk
WEBSITE: www.vabooks.co.uk

Antiques & Country Living
43-44 Vallis Way, Badcox. BA11 3BA. (Mrs D.M. Williams)
Open 9.30-5.30 including Sun. STOCK: *Furniture*

including country, 19th-20th C, £15-£1,000; porcelain, 18th-19th C, £5-£500; books; lighting. LOC: A362 Frome to Radstock road. SIZE: Medium. PARK: Free opposite.
TEL: 01373 463015; BOOKS: 01373 467125

Frome Reclamation
Station Approach. BA11 1RE. (S.J., K.R., R.L. and J.B. Horler)
EST. 1987. Open 8-5, Sat. 8-4.30. STOCK: *Architectural reclamation.* LOC: From A361 follow signs for rail station. SER: Valuations. SIZE: Large + yard. PARK: Easy. VAT: Stan.
TEL: 01373 463919/453122; MOBILE: 07729 263949
E-MAIL: info@fromerec.co.uk
WEBSITE: www.fromerec.co.uk

GODNEY

Country Brocante
Fir Tree Farm. BA5 1RZ. (Tim and Nicky Ovel)
EST. 1993. WEADA. *Trade Only.* Open by appointment. STOCK: *18th-19th C French farmhouse tables and early mirrors; 19th-20th C decorative lighting and chandeliers; interesting objects and furniture.* LOC: Village centre. SIZE: Medium. PARK: Easy. FAIRS: Shepton Mallet; Newark.
TEL: 01458 833052; HOME: same; FAX: 01458 835611; MOBILE: 07970 719708
E-MAIL: ovel@compuserve.com

HINTON CHARTERHOUSE

Freshfords Fine Art   LAPADA
Homewood View. BA2 7TB. (Simon Powell)
EST. 1973. CINOA. WEADA. Open by appointment. STOCK: English Regency furniture, 18th-19th C, £2,000-£50,000; Victorian oil paintings, £2,000-£12,000; decorative accessories, 18th-19th C, £2,000-£5,000. LOC: 4 miles from Bath towards Warminster, just off A36. SER: Valuations; restorations; buys at auction. SIZE: Large. PARK: Easy. VAT: Spec. FAIRS: Olympia; Armoury, New York.
TEL: 01225 722111; FAX: 01225 722991; MOBILE: 07720 838877
E-MAIL: antiques@freshfords.com
WEBSITE: www.freshfords.com.

ILCHESTER

Gilbert & Dale
The Old Chapel, Church St. BA22 8LN. (Roy Gilbert and Joan Dale)
EST. 1965 WEADA. Open 9-5.30 or by appointment. STOCK: *English and French country furniture and accessories.* LOC: Village centre on A37. SIZE: Large. PARK: Easy.
TEL: 01935 840464; FAX: 01935 841599
E-MAIL: roy@roygilbert.com

LANGFORD

Richard Essex Antiques
BS40 5BP. (B.R. and C.L. Essex)
EST. 1969. STOCK: *General antiques from mid-18th C.*
TEL: 01934 863302

LITTLETON

Westville House Antiques
TA11 6NP. (D. and M. Stacey)
EST. 1986. Open daily, Sun. by appointment. STOCK:
18th-19th C pine, mahogany and oak furniture; LOC:
B3151 approximately 1.5 miles north of Somerton. SER:
Valuations; buys at auction. SIZE: Large. PARK: Own.
VAT: Stan/Spec.
TEL: 01458 273376; FAX: same
E-MAIL: info@westville.co.uk
WEBSITE: www.westville.co.uk

MARTOCK

Castle Reclamation
Parrett Works. TA12 6AE. (T.A.B. Dance and A.J.
Wills)
EST. 1986. Open daily, Sat. 10-1. STOCK: *Architectural
antiques.* LOC: 2 miles off A303 between Martock and
South Petherton. SER: Restorations (stone). SIZE: Large.
PARK: Easy. VAT: Stan. FAIRS: Bath and West.
TEL: 01935 826483; FAX: 01935 826791
WEBSITE: www.castlereclamation.com

NETHER STOWEY

House of Antiquity
St. Mary St. TA5 1LJ. (M.S. Todd)
EST. 1967. Open 10-5 or by appointment. STOCK:
*Philatelic literature, world topographical, maps, handbooks,
postcards, ephemera, postal history.* LOC: A39. SER:
Valuations; buys at auction. SIZE: Medium. PARK: Easy.
VAT: Stan.
TEL: 01278 732426; FAX: same
E-MAIL: mstodd@lineone.net

PORLOCK

Magpie Antiques
High St. TA24 8PT. (Glenys Battams)
EST. 1980. Open Thurs., Fri. and Sat. 10-5 and some
Sun, prior telephone call advisable. STOCK: *Jewellery and
silver; Viennese bronzes; decorative objects; 18th-19th C
pottery and porcelain; objets de vertu and animalia.* LOC:
Opposite Lorna Doone Hotel. SER: Valuations for
insurance and probate; jewellery repairs; free home visits.
SIZE: Medium. PARK: Nearby. FAIRS: Shepton Mallet.
TEL: 01643 862775; FAX: same; MOBILE: 07875
914668

Rare Books and Berry
High St. TA24 8PT. (Helen and Michael Berry)
EST. 1983. Open 9.30-5. STOCK: *Secondhand and
antiquarian books.* SIZE: Medium. PARK: Nearby.
TEL: 01643 863255; FAX: 01643 863092
E-MAIL: info@rarebooksandberry.co.uk
WEBSITE: www.rarebooksandberry.co.uk

QUEEN CAMEL

Steven Ferdinando
The Old Vicarage. BA22 7NG.
EST. 1978. PBFA. Open by appointment. STOCK:
Antiquarian and secondhand books. SER: Valuations. SIZE:
Large PARK: Own. FAIRS: Shepton Mallet; PBFA.
TEL: 01935 850210
E-MAIL: stevenferdinando@onetel.com

RADSTOCK

Notts Pine
Old Redhouse Farm, Stratton-on-the-Fosse. BA3 4QE.
(Jeffery Nott)
EST. 1978. Open Mon.-Fri. 9-5.30. STOCK: *Pine furniture
including wardrobes, boxes, pot cupboards and dressers,
mainly 19th-20th C.* SER: Valuations; restorations (pine
furniture). SIZE: Medium. PARK: Easy. FAIRS: Newark.
TEL: 01761 419911; HOME: 01761 471614; MOBILE:
07968 111553

SOMERTON

John Gardiner Antiques
Monteclefe House. TA11 7NL.
EST. 1974. Appointment advisable. STOCK: *General
antiques; decorative Edwardian, Georgian and quality old
reproduction furnishings.* LOC: A303, close to M5.
TEL: 01458 272238; FAX/ANSWERPHONE: 01458
274329; MOBILE: 07831 274427

The London Cigarette Card Co. Ltd
West St. TA11 7PR. (I.A. and E.K. Laker, F.C.
Doggett and Y. Berktay)
EST. 1927. Open daily. STOCK: *Cigarette and trade cards,
1885 to date; sets from £2; other cards, from 15p; frames for
mounting cards and special albums.* SER: Publishers of
catalogues, reference books and monthly magazine; mail
order; monthly auctions. SIZE: Medium. PARK: Easy.
TEL: 01458 273452/274148
E-MAIL: cards@londoncigcard.co.uk
WEBSITE: www.londoncigcard.co.uk

Somerton Antiques Centre
1 West St. TA11 7PS.
EST. 1995. WEADA. Open 10-5. STOCK: *General
antiques, £5-£1,800.* SER: Valuations; repairs; restorations
(furniture). SIZE: Large - 25 dealers. PARK: Own. FAIRS:
Shepton Mallet.
TEL: 01458 274423

SOUTH PETHERTON

Heritage Fine Art
29 St . James St. TA13 5BN.
EST. 1988. Open 9.30-1. CL: Mon., Wed. or by appointment. STOCK: *Antique and modern art, oil paintings and watercolours £100-£2,000.* LOC: Near A303. SER: Valuations; gilding; framing; picture cleaning, re-lining and restoration - oils watercolours and acrylics; repairs to framing and gilding. SIZE: Medium. PARK: Easy.
TEL: 01460 241612/241909

STOKE-SUB-HAMDON

Wessex Antique Bedsteads
The Old Glove Works, Percombe. TA14 6RD. (Jeremy Peachell)
EST. 1991. WEADA. FSB. BSSA. Open 9-5, Sat. 10-5, Sun. and other times by appointment. STOCK: *Brass, iron and wooden bedsteads, including four-poster and half-tester, mainly Victorian and Edwardian.* LOC: Adjacent A303, north of Yeovil. SER: Restorations (wooden and metal beds); bespoke mattresses and bases; delivery and shipping. SIZE: Large. PARK: Easy.
TEL: 01935 829147; HOME: same; FAX: 01935 829148; MOBILE: 07973 884079
E-MAIL: info@wessexbeds.com
WEBSITE: www.wessexbeds.com

TAUNTON

T. J. Atkins
East Criddles Farm, Tolland, Lydeard St. Lawrence. TA4 3PW.
EST. 1958. Open by appointment. STOCK: *Porcelain and pottery including Prattware, 18th-19th C.* SIZE: Medium.
TEL: 01984 667310.

Cider Press Antiques Centre
58 Bridge St. TA1 1UD. (Norman Clarke and Mark Blake)
EST. 1998. Open 10-4; by appointment other times. STOCK: *Furniture, Georgian to Victorian, £100-£3,500; jewellery, silver and plate, ceramics, glass, collectables, stamps, postcards, records and books; reclamation items. Specialists in Doulton Lambeth and Royal Doulton Worcester.* LOC: Near town centre. SER: Valuations; restorations (furniture); probate; specialist removers (antiques). Norman Clarke can give lectures on a wide range of topics having been an antique collector for 35 years. SIZE: Medium - 10 dealers. PARK: Nearby.
TEL: 01823 283050; FAX: same; MOBILE: 07764 212520; HOME: 01823 661354

Halliday's LAPADA
35B East Reach. TA1 3ES (James Halliday)
Open by appointment. STOCK: *18th - 19th C furniture.*

SER: Upholstery.
TEL: **01823 324073**; FAX: same

Selwoods
Queen Anne Cottage, Mary St. TA1 3PE.
EST. 1927. Open 9.30-5. STOCK: *Furniture, including Victorian and Edwardian.* SIZE: Very large. PARK: Own at rear.
TEL: 01823 272780

Taunton Antiques Market - Silver Street
25/29 Silver St. TA1 3DH. (Silver Street Antiques Market)
EST. 1978. Open Mon. 9-4 including Bank Holidays. STOCK: *General antiques and collectables, including specialists in most fields.* LOC: 2 miles from M5, junction 25, to town centre, 100yds. from Sainsburys car park across lights. SER: Valuations. SIZE: 100+ dealers. PARK: Easy - Sainsburys (town centre branch).
TEL: 01823 289327; FAX: same; ENQUIRIES: 020 7351 5353.

M.G. Welch Jeweller
1 Corporation St. TA1 4AJ. (Mark and Liz Welch)
EST. 1985. NAG. Open 9.30-5. STOCK: *Antique and secondhand jewellery, £100-£10,000; antique and secondhand silver, £100-£1,000; early 20th C masters including Cartier, Tiffany, Georg Jensen, Chaumet.* LOC: Town centre, corner of High St. SER: Valuations; restorations (jewellery). SIZE: Medium. PARK: Nearby. VAT: Stan/Spec.
TEL: 01823 270456; FAX: same
E-MAIL: sales@mgwelch.com
WEBSITE: www.mgwelch.com

TEMPLE COMB

Ottery Antiques LAPADA
Bow Cottage, 17 Horsington. BA8 0EG.
EST. 1986. WEADA. Open 8-5. STOCK: *17th & 18th C English furniture and decorative items.* SER: Restoration (furniture) - see entry under Services.
TEL: 01963 371166
E-MAIL: charles@otteryantiques.co.uk
WEBSITE: www.otteryantiques.co.uk

WASHFORD

Courtyard Antiques
Rock Cottage, Torre TA23 0LA. (Nick Wass and Liz Cain)
EST. 1997. WEADA. Open 9-4 Tues.-Sun. CL: Mon. STOCK: *English vernacular furniture - oak, elm and pine, upholstered chairs, mostly 19th-20th C, £100-£2,000.* LOC: Off the A39. SER: Restoration and upholstery. SIZE: Small. PARK: Easy.
TEL: 01984 641619
E-MAIL: sales@courtyardantiques.net
WEBSITE: www.courtyardantiques.net

WATCHET

Nick Cotton Fine Art
Beachstone House, 46/47 Swain St. TA23 0AG. (Nick and Lynda Cotton)
EST. 1970. Open 10-6. STOCK: *Paintings, 1850-2000; some period furniture.* SER: Restorations; conservation; research. SIZE: Large. PARK: Adjacent. VAT: Spec.
TEL: 01984 631814
WEBSITE: www.thelyndacottongallery.co.uk

WELLINGTON

Michael and Amanda Lewis Oriental LAPADA
Carpets and Rugs
8 North St. TA21 8LT.
EST. 1982. Open 10-1 and 2-5.30, Mon. and weekends by appointment. STOCK: *Oriental carpets and rugs, mainly 19th-20th C, £25-£25,000.* LOC: 1 mile from junction 26, M5. SER: Valuations; restorations; repairs; cleaning; restoration and conservation (tapestry). SIZE: Medium. PARK: 100yds.
TEL: 01823 667430
E-MAIL: rugmike@tesco.net

WELLS

Marshalls of Wells
7 Mill St. BA5 2AS. (Trevor Marshall)
EST. 1959. Open 10-5 or by appointment. STOCK: *General antiques, antique and reproduction pine, rugs and carpets.* LOC: Town centre. SER: French polishing. SIZE: Large. PARK: Easy.
TEL: 01749 672489
E-MAIL: info@marshalls-uk.com
WEBSITE: www.marshalls-uk.com

The Sadler Street Gallery,
23 Market Place. BA5 2RF. (Jill Swale)
EST. 1993. Open 10-5. STOCK: *18th to early 20th C watercolours, oils and etchings; contemporary watercolours and oils mainly by West Country artists.* LOC: City centre. SER: Buying, restoration and cleaning. SIZE: 3 floors. PARK: Market Place or city centre car parks.
TEL: 01749 670220
E-MAIL: jillswale@thesadlerstreetgallery.co.uk
WEBSITE: www.thesadlerstreetgallery.co.uk

WESTON-SUPER-MARE

Sterling Books
43a Locking Rd. BS23 3DG.
EST. 1966. ABA. PBFA. ILAB. Open 10-5.30. CL: Mon. and Thurs. pm. STOCK: *Books, antiquarian and secondhand, some new; ephemera and prints.* SER: Bookbinding; picture framing. SIZE: Large. PARK: Easy.
TEL: 01934 625056
E-MAIL: sterling.books@talk21.com

Winters Antiques LAPADA
Truby Tor, Roman Rd., Bleadon. BS24 0AB.
Open by appointment STOCK: *Architectural and garden ornaments, decorative items, 19th & 20th C furniture, paintings in oils and watercolours.*
TEL: 01934 814610;

WILLITON

Edward Venn
Unit 3, 52 Long St. TA4 4QU.
EST. 1979. Open 10-5. STOCK: *Furniture, clocks.* SER: Restorations (furniture, barometers and clocks). PARK: Easy.
TEL: 01984 632631
WEBSITE: www.vennantiquesrestoration.co.uk

WINCANTON

Green Dragon Antiques Centre
24 High St. BA9 9JF. (Mrs Sally Denning)
EST. 1991. Open 10-5 including Sun. STOCK: *Wide variety of general antiques and collectables, £1-£1,000.* SER: Valuations. SIZE: 112 dealers. PARK: Own.
TEL: 01963 34111/34702; FAX: 01963 34111
E-MAIL: denningmumsy@aol.com

WIVELISCOMBE

J.C. Giddings
TA4 2SN.
EST. 1969. *Mainly Trade.* Open by appointment. STOCK: *Mainly 18th-19th C furniture, iron-work and reclamation timber.* SIZE: Warehouses. PARK: Easy.
TEL: 01984 623703

Heads 'n' Tails
Bournes House, 41 Church St. TA4 2LT. (D. McKinley)
Resident. Open by appointment. STOCK: *Taxidermy including Victorian cased and uncased birds, mammals and fish, £5-£2,000; decorative items, glass domes.* LOC: Opposite church. SER: Taxidermy; restorations; commissions; hire. PARK: Easy. VAT: Spec.
TEL: 01984 623097; FAX: 01984 624445
E-MAIL: mac@taxidermyuk.com
WEBSITE: www.taxidermyuk.com

YEOVIL

John Hamblin
Unit 6, 15 Oxford Rd., Penn Mill Trading Estate. BA21 5HR. (J. and M. A. Hamblin)
EST. 1980. Open 8.30-5. CL: Sat. STOCK: *Furniture, 1750-1900, £300-£3,000.* SER: Restorations (furniture); cabinet work; French polishing. SIZE: Small. PARK: Easy. VAT: Stan.
TEL: 01935 471154; HOME: 01935 476673

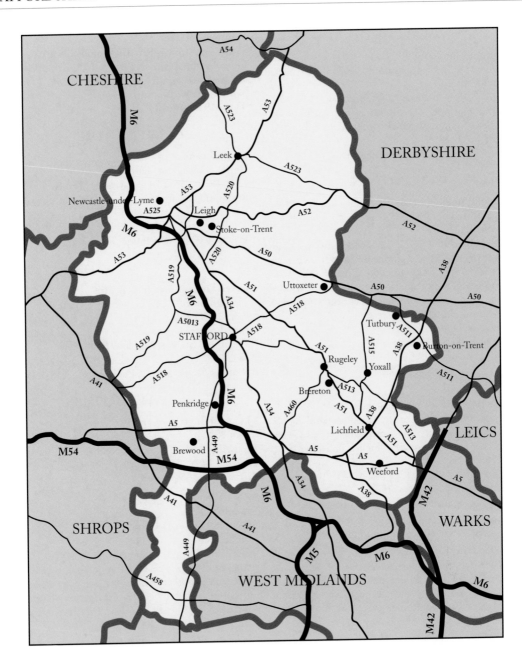

BREWOOD

Passiflora

25 Stafford St. ST19 9DX. (David and Paula Whitfield)
EST. 1988. Flexible opening - usually 10-4ish, prior
telephone call advisable. STOCK: *General antiques,
collectables, curios, copper, brass, Mabel Lucie Attwell corner,
Victorian to 1950s, £1-£300.* LOC: Off A5 and A449 near
Gailey roundabout, village on Shropshire Union canal.
SER: Valuations. SIZE: Medium. PARK: Free opposite.
FAIRS: Bowman Antique Fairs and West Midlands

Antique Fairs, Staffordshire Showground; Pat Dyer
Antique Fairs, Newport; Game Fair (August); Weston
Park Game Fair (September).
TEL: 01902 851557 (answerphone); MOBILE: 07711 682216
E-MAIL: paula.whitfield@ukonline.co.uk

BURTON-UPON-TRENT

Burton Antiques

1-2 Horninglow Rd. DE14 2PR. (M. J. Rodgers)
EST. 1977. Open 9-5, Sun. 11-3. STOCK: *Pine furniture.*

LOC: A511. SER: Valuations; stripping (pine); buys at auction. SIZE: Large. PARK: Nearby.
TEL: 01283 542331

M.A.J. Morris
Weavers Green, Needwood. DE13 9PQ.
EST. 1993. *Mainly Trade.* Open by appointment only. *STOCK: Maps, plans, charts and prints, atlases, county histories, documents and paintings, 1550-1950, £5 and upwards.* LOC: Telephone for directions. SER: Valuations. SIZE: Small. PARK: Easy. VAT: Stan.
TEL: 01283 575344
WEBSITE: www.trademaps.co.uk

LEEK

Antiques Within Ltd
Ground Floor, Compton Mill. ST13 5NJ. (R. and K. Hicks)
EST. 1992. Open 10-5.30. Sun. 1-5. *STOCK: Pine, oak and mahogany, £50-£3,000; bric-a-brac, £5-£500.* LOC: A520 towards Cheddleton, opposite Catholic church. SER: Courier, packing and shipping. PARK: Easy. VAT: Stan. FAIRS: Newark; Swinderby; Europe.
TEL: 01538 387848; FAX: same
E-MAIL: antiques.within@virgin.net
WEBSITE: www.antiques-within.com

Anvil Antiques Ltd
Antiques Trade Centre, Pretty Polly Mill, Buxton Rd. ST13 6EJ. (J.S. Spooner and N.M. Sullivan)
EST. 1975. Open 9-5, Sat. 10-5, Sun. 12-4. *STOCK: Stripped pine, old and reproduction; oak, mahogany, bric-a-brac and decorative items, architectural items.* LOC: Ashbourne Rd., from town centre roundabout, turn first left, Victorian mill on right. SIZE: Large. PARK: Easy. VAT: Stan.
TEL: 01538 384522

Compton Mill Antique Emporium
Compton. ST13 5NJ. (Kelly Butler)
Open Tues-Sat 10-5.30, Sun 1-5. CL: Mon. *STOCK: Grandfather clocks, pine old and reproduction, kitchenalia, oak and mahogany.* LOC: Opposite St Mary's Church. SIZE: Large - 10 dealers. PARK: Own.
TEL: 01538 373396; FAX: 01538 399092
E-MAIL: john.butler3@btconnect.com

England's Gallery
Ball Haye House, 1 Ball Haye Terrace. ST13 6AP. (F.J. and S.J. England)
EST. 1968. Open 2-5. CL: Mon., other times by appointment. *STOCK: Oils and watercolours, 18th-20th C, £500-£10,000; etchings, engravings, lithographs, mezzotints, £50-£4,000.* LOC: Towards Ball Haye Green from A523 turn at lights. SER: Valuations; restorations; cleaning; relining; regilding; framing; mount cutting; buys at auction (paintings). SIZE: Large. PARK: Nearby. VAT: Stan.
TEL: 01538 373451

Gilligan's Antiques
59 St. Edward St. ST13 5DN. (M.T. Gilligan)
EST. 1977. Open 9-5.30. *STOCK: Victorian and Edwardian furniture; modern pine furniture.*
TEL: 01538 384174

Roger Haynes - Antique Finder
54 Shoobridge St. ST13 5JZ.
EST. 1960. *Trade only.* Open by appointment. *STOCK: Pine, smalls and decorative items.* SIZE: 3 large buildings.
TEL: 01538 385161; FAX: same;
E-MAIL: info@rogerhaynesantiquefinder.com

Johnson's
Chorley Mill, 1 West St. ST13 8AF. (P.M. and Mrs. J.H. Johnson)
EST. 1976. Open 9-5, Sat. and Sun by appointment. *STOCK: 18th-19th C English, European and French country furniture, £50-£2,000; decorative accessories, £10-£500 plus unique objects.* LOC: Opposite pentecostal church. SIZE: Large. PARK: Own.
TEL: 01538 386745; FAX: 01538 388375
E-MAIL: johnsonsantiques@btconnect.com

The Leek Antiques Centre (Barclay House)
4-6 Brook St. ST13 5JE. (Peter Lumley)
EST. 1977. Open 10.30-5, Sun. by appointment. *STOCK: Extending dining tables, sets of chairs, chests of drawers, bedroom furniture, pottery, watercolours and oils, upholstered furniture.* SER: Valuations; restorations (furniture). SIZE: 3 floors - 17 showrooms. PARK: Easy. VAT: Stan/Spec. FAIRS: Bowman's and West Midland, Staffordshire Showground.
TEL: 01538 398475

Leek Restorations   LAPADA
2 Duke St. ST13 5LG. (Tony Williams)
EST. 1980. *Mainly Trade.* Open 9-4. STOCK: Mirrors - gilt, painted and wooden, 19th C, £350-£4,000. LOC: On A53 from Stoke-on-Trent, right at 1st traffic lights, shop 200 yards on left. SER: Restorations; export packing; special commissions. SIZE: Medium. PARK: Easy. VAT: Stan/Spec. FAIRS: NEC.
TEL: 01538 372553
E-MAIL: info@williamsantiquemirrors.co.uk
WEBSITE: www.williamsantiquemirrors.co.uk

Odeon Antiques
76-78 St. Edward St. ST13 5DL. (Steve Ford)
EST. 1990. Open 11-5. *STOCK: Lighting, beds, pine, country furniture, free-standing kitchens and decorative collectables.* LOC: Junction of St. Edward St. and Broad St. SER: Restorations (lighting); free standing kitchen design. SIZE: Large. PARK: Own.
TEL: 01538 387188; FAX: 01538 384235
E-MAIL: odeonantiques@hotmail.com
WEBSITE: www.odeanantiques.co.uk

Page Antiques

Ground Floor, Compton Mill. ST13 5NJ. (Denis and Alma Page)

Est. 1974. Open 10-5.30, Sun. 1-5. *Stock: Georgian to Edwardian furniture, stripped pine and decorative items.* Loc: Town centre. Ser: Courier. Size: Medium. Park: Easy. Vat: Stan/Spec. Fairs: Newark; Swinderby; Buxton. Tel: Mobile: 07966 154993; Home: 01663 732358.

LEIGH

John Nicholls

Open by appointment. *Stock: Oak furniture and related items, 17th-18th C.* Tel: 01538 702339; Mobile: 07836 244024

LICHFIELD

Mike Abrahams Books

14 Meadowbrook Rd. WS13 7RW.

Est. 1975. Open by appointment. *Stock: Books and ephemera especially Midlands topography, sport, transport, children's, illustrated, military and antiquarian, 17th C to date, £2-£1,000.* Loc: Off A5127 on to Eastern Ave., left at Samuel Johnson public house, immediately right into Purcell Ave., past church and right turn into Meadowbrook Rd. Ser: Valuations. Size: Large. Park: Easy. Fairs: Stafford, Bingley Hall and Pavilion; Midland Antiquarian Book (organiser). Tel: 01543 256200; Home: same

Curborough Hall Farm Antiques Centre

Watery Lane. WS13 8TS.

Est. 1995. Open 10-4.30 inc. Sun. and BH; CL: Mon. *Stock: General antiques and furniture; specialised jewellery days once a month; vintage costume jewellery and handbags.* Loc: The link road between A51 and A38. Size: Medium - 30 dealers. Park: Own. Tel: 01543 417100

The Essence of Time

Unit 2 Curborough Hall Farm Antiques & Craft Centre, Watery Lane, Off Eastern Ave. WS13 8ES. (M.T.O. Hinton)

Est. 1990. Open Wed.-Sun. 11-5. *Stock: Antique clocks - 30 hour and 8 day longcase, 1700-1900; Vienna regulator wall, English and French wall; mantel and novelty.* Loc: North of Lichfield, 1 mile from city centre. Ser: Removing and resetting of Loncase clocks. Size: Medium. Park: Own large. Tel: 01543 418239; Home: 01902 764900; Mobile: 07944 245064

James A. Jordan

7 The Corn Exchange. WS13 6JU.

CMBHI. Open 9-5. CL: Wed. *Stock: Clocks, longcase, barometers, jewellery and small furniture.* Loc: Market Sq. city centre. Ser: Restorations (clocks and chronometers). Park: Nearby. Tel: 01543 416221

Milestone Antiques

5 Main St., Whittington. WS14 9JU. (Humphrey and Elsa Crawshaw)

Est. 1988. Resident. Open Thurs.-Sat. 10-6, Sun. 11-3, other times by appointment. *Stock: Georgian and Victorian British furniture, ceramics (especially Coalport), copper and other decorative items.* Loc: A51 Lichfield/Tamworth road, turn north at Whittington Barracks, shop 50yds. past crossroads in village centre. Size: Medium. Park: Easy. Vat: Spec. Tel: 01543 432248

NEWCASTLE-UNDER-LYME

Bridge Street Antiques

31 Bridge St. ST5 2RY. (Alistair Mitchelhill)

Est. 1976. Open 10-4. *Stock: Furniture, oak, walnut, mahogany, 17th-19th C, £50-£10,000; longcase, mantel and wall clocks, £150-£4,000; paintings, £35-£3,000, both 18th-19th C; ceramics, especially Doulton Lambeth, and watercolours, 19th C, £15-£1,500; silver, £50-£2,000. Not Stocked: Pine and ephemera.* Loc: Close to Sainsburys and the Magistrates Courts. Ser: Valuations; restorations; gilding; repairs (clocks). Size: Medium. Fairs: Ardingly, Detling, Shepton, Newark; all international antiques fairs. Tel: 01782 712483; Mobile: 07825 107778

PENKRIDGE

Golden Oldies

1 and 5 Crown Bridge. ST19 5AA. (W.A. and M.A. Knowles)

Est. 1980. Open Mon. 9.30-1.30, Tues-Sat. 9.30-5.30, Sun. 12-4. *Stock: Victorian, Edwardian and later furniture; paintings, decorative items.* Loc: 2 miles south junction 13, M6. Park: Easy. Vat: Global. Fairs: Newark; Swinderby. Tel: 01785 714722.

RUGELEY

Cawarden Brick Co Ltd

Cawarden Springs Farm, Blithbury Rd. WS15 3HL. (R.G. Parrott)

Est. 1987. SALVO. Open 8-5, Sat. 8-4, Sun. 10-4. *Stock: Architectural salvage and antiques - bricks, tiles, beams, cobbles and York stone; furniture, sanitaryware, fireplaces and garden items.* Loc: 1.5 miles from town, in rural setting. Park: Easy. Tel: 01889 574066; Fax: 01889 575695; E-mail: sales@cawardenreclaim.co.uk Website: www.cawardenreclaim.co.uk

Eveline Winter

1 Wolseley Rd. WS15 2QH. (Mrs E. Winter)

Est. 1962. Open 10.30-5 appointment advisable. CL: Wed. *Stock: Staffordshire figures, pre-Victorian, from £90;*

Victorian, £30-£500; copper, brass, glass and general antiques. NOT STOCKED: Coins and weapons. LOC: Coming from Lichfield or Stafford stay on A51 and avoid town by-pass. SIZE: Small. PARK: Easy and at side of shop.
TEL: 01889 583259

STAFFORD

Windmill Antiques
9 Castle Hill, Broadeye. ST16 2QB.
EST. 1990. Open 10-5. *STOCK: General antiques and decorative items.* LOC: Opposite Sainsbury's. SER: Valuations; restorations (ceramics). SIZE: Medium - several dealers. PARK: Easy.
TEL: 01785 228505

STOKE-ON-TRENT

Ann's Antiques
26 Leek Rd., Stockton Brook. ST9 9NN. (Ann Byatte)
EST. 1980. Open Fri. and Sat. 10-5 and by appointment. *STOCK: Victorian and Edwardian glass, porcelain, furniture, brass, copper, jewellery, paintings, pottery and unusual items; toys, rocking horses, teddies, dolls and doll's houses.* LOC: A53 main road between Hanley and Leek. SER: Valuations. SIZE: Small. PARK: Opposite. VAT: Stan.
TEL: 01782 503991

Burslem Antiques & Collectables
11 Market Place, Burslem. ST6 3AA. (D. Bradbury)
EST. 1972. Open 9.30-5.30. *STOCK: Pottery and porcelain including Minton, Doulton, Wedgwood, Worcester, Goss, Spode, Copeland, S Allcock, George Jones, Carlton, MacIntyre, Moorcroft, Moor Bros., Cauldon, Shelley, Paragon, Royal Stanley, 1750's to date.* LOC: Main road. SER: Valuations; packing and shipping worldwide. SIZE: Large. PARK: At rear and town centre.
TEL: 01782 577855; FAX: 01782 577222;
MOBILE: 07801 473524; HOME: 01782 710711
E-MAIL: info@burslemantiques.co.uk
WEBSITE: www.burslemantiques.com

The Potteries Antique Centre Ltd
271 Waterloo Rd., Cobridge. ST6 3HR. (W. Buckley)
EST. 1990. Open 9-5.30. *STOCK: Pottery and porcelain including Doulton, Moorcroft, Beswick, Wedgwood, Coalport, Shelley, 19th and especially 20th C British; collectors' items, silver plate, clocks, brass, jewellery, pictures, furniture, 18th-20th C, £1-£5,000.* LOC: Off M6, junction 15 or 16 on to A500, follow signs for Festival Park or Potteries Shopping Centre. SER: Valuations; export facilities - supply and packing; buys at auction (pottery and collectors' items); pottery auctions held on site. SIZE: Large + trade and export warehouse. PARK: Easy. VAT: Stan/Spec. FAIRS: Newark; Doulton and Beswick.
TEL: 01782 201455; FAX: 01782 201518; 01782 286622 (auctions)

E-MAIL: sales@potteriesantiquecentre.com
WEBSITE: www.potteriesantiquecentre.com

The Pottery Buying Centre
535 Etruria Rd., Basford. ST4 6HT. (Paul Hume)
EST. 1989. Open 10-4. *STOCK: Pottery and porcelain, 19th-20th C; collectables, 20th C; furniture, 18th-20th C; all £10-£1,000.* SER: Valuations; restorations. SIZE: 2 floors. PARK: Easy.
TEL: 01782 635453
E-MAIL: potbuyingcentre@aol.com

TUTBURY

R.A. James - The Clock Shop
1 High St. DE13 9LP. (Rob and Alison James)
EST. 1988. MBHI. Open 8.30-4. *STOCK: Longcase, bracket and wall clocks, £500-£10,000.* LOC: 2 miles from A38/A50 junction. SER: Valuations; restorations (clocks, watches and barometers). SIZE: Medium. PARK: Easy. VAT: Stan/Spec.
TEL: 01283 814596; FAX: 01283 814594;
MOBILE: 07710 161949
E-MAIL: sales@antique-clocks-watches.co.uk
WEBSITE: www.antique-clocks-watches.co.uk

Old Chapel Antique & Collectables Centre
High St. DE13 9LP. (Peter Hill)
EST. 1996. OCS. Open 10-5 including Sun., other times by appointment. *STOCK: China, glass, furniture.* SER: Mail order. SIZE: Large. PARK: Easy. FAIRS: Swinderby.
TEL: 01283 815255; MOBILE: 07774 238775
E-MAIL: rocla@supanet.com

WEEFORD

Blackbrook Antiques Village
London Rd. WS14 0PS. (Oliver Curran)
Open seven days, 10-5.30. *STOCK: Architectural antiques including fireplaces, lighting, garden statuary, stained glass, furniture.* LOC: A38. SER: Delivery and installation. SIZE: 6 large showrooms. PARK: Large forecourt. VAT: Margin.
TEL: 01543 481450; FAX: 01543 480275
E-MAIL: info@blackbrook.co.uk
WEBSITE: www.blackbrook.co.uk

YOXALL

H.W. Heron and Son Ltd   LAPADA
The Antique Shop, 1 King St. DE13 8NF. (H.N.M. and J. Heron)
EST. 1949. Open 9-6, Sat. 9-5.30, Bank Holidays 10.30-5.30, Sun. by appoinment. *STOCK: 18th-19th C furniture, ceramics and decorative items.* LOC: A515 village centre, opposite church. SER: Valuations. SIZE: Medium. PARK: Easy. VAT: Spec.
TEL: 01543 472266; HOME: same; FAX: 01543 473800
E-MAIL: shop@hwheronantiques.com
WEBSITE: www.hwheronantiques.com

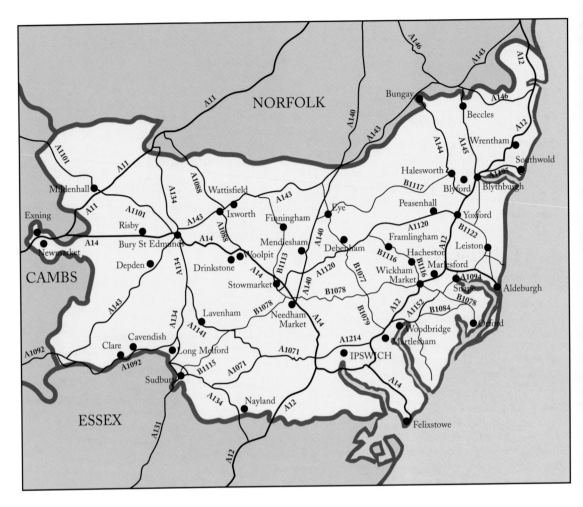

ALDEBURGH

Mole Hall Antiques
102 High St. IP15 5AB. (Peter Weaver)
Est. 1976. Open 10-4, Sun. by appointment. *Stock: Paintings, prints, unusual decorative items and country furniture.* Size: Small. Park: Easy.
Tel: 01728 452361; Home: same.

Thompson's Gallery
175 High St. IP15 5AN. (J. and S. Thompson)
Est. 1982. Open 10-5 or by appointment. *Stock: 19th-20th C paintings; contemporary paintings and sculptures.* Size: Large - 6 rooms. Park: Easy. Vat: Spec.
Tel: 01728 453743
E-mail: john@thompsonsgallery.co.uk
Website: www.thompsonsgallery.co.uk

BECCLES

Besleys Books
4 Blyburgate. NR34 9TA. (P.A. and P.F. Besley)
Est. 1978. ABA. PBFA. Open 9.30-1 and 2-5. *Stock:*
Books, 50p-£1,000; prints, £7-£50; maps, £3-£100; all 17th-20th C. Loc: Town centre. Ser: Valuations; restorations (book binding); buys at auction (books). Size: Medium. Park: Nearby. Fairs: Various ABA and PBFA.
Tel: 01502 715762; home/Fax: 01502 675649
E-mail: piers@besleysbooks.demon.co.uk
Website: www.besleysbooks.demon.co.uk

Blyburgate Antiques
27-29 Blyburgate. NR34 9TB. (Mrs K. Lee)
Est. 1997 Resident. Open 10-4.30. Cl: Mon/Wed.
Stock: 19th-20th C china, jewellery, furniture and metalware, £5-£1,000. Ser: Valuations; restorations (china). Size: Small. Park: Rainbow supermarket at rear.
Fairs: Alexandra Palace; Newmarket.
Tel: 01502 711174; fax/Home: same

Fauconberges
8 Smallgate. NR34 9AD. (Richard D. Howard and Richard J. Crozier)
Est. 1977. Open 10.30-4. Cl: Mon. am and Wed.
Stock: Furniture, 1700-1850; pictures, clocks, glass,

porcelain, silver. LOC: Town centre. SER: Valuations; delivery. SIZE: Medium. PARK: Easy. FAIRS: Lomax, Langley (Autumn and Spring); Burnham Market; Long Melford; Snape Maltings, July.
TEL: 01502 716147

One Step Back
2 Exchange Square. NR34 9HL. (Ian and Diane Wells)
EST. 1970. Open 9-5, Wed. 9-4. *STOCK: Furniture, from 17th C; porcelain and rugs, from 18th C; both £50-£3,000.* SER: Valuations; restorations. SIZE: Medium. PARK: Easy. VAT: Stan./Spec./Global/Margin.
TEL: 01502 714121; MOBILE: 07962 212968;
E-MAIL: diane@onestepback.wanadoo.co.uk

BLYTHBURGH

E.T. Webster
Westwood Lodge. IP19 9NB.
EST. 1974. Open 7.30-5. *STOCK: Ancient oak beams, oak ceilings, panelling, quality reproduction oak furniture, doors, mullioned windows, oak framed barns.* SIZE: Large.
TEL: 01502 478539; FAX: 01502 478164

BUNGAY

Black Dog Antiques
51 Earsham St. NR35 2PB. (K. Button)
EST. 1986. Open 10-5; Sun and BH 11-4.30. *STOCK: General antiques including oak, mahogany and stripped pine, china, linen and collectables, antiquities, Saxon and Roman, £1-£1000.* LOC: Opposite Post Office. SER: Valuations. PARK: Easy.
TEL: 01986 895554

Cork Brick Antiques
6 Earsham St. NR35 1AG. (G. and K. Skipper)
EST. 1990. Open 10.30-5.30. CL: Mon. *STOCK: Country and decorative antiques; contemporary art.* PARK: Easy.
TEL: 01986 894873; HOME: 01502 712646
E-MAIL: corkbrick@xlr.co.uk

BURY ST. EDMUNDS

The Enchanted Aviary
Lapwings, Rushbrooke Lane. IP33 2RS. (C.C. Frost)
EST. 1970. Open by appointment. *STOCK: Cased and uncased mounted birds, animals and fish, mostly late Victorian, £15-£800.* SER: Restorations. PARK: Easy.
TEL: 01284 725430
E-MAIL: christophercfrost@tiscali.co.uk

CAVENDISH

Cavendish Antiques & Interiors
The Old Forge Shop, The Green. CO10 8BB. (Graham Hessell and Andrew Young)
EADA. Open Fri. 11-5, Sat./Sun./Mon. 10-5; other times by appointment. *STOCK: Good quality antique*

furniture, art and collectables from the 17th C onwards. SER: Restorations; re-upholstery; valuations, advise, consultations; items bought; free local delivery; shipping and UK deliveries arranged. SIZE: Large.
TEL: 01440 731888/01799 599373; mobile 07710 282329

CLARE

20th Century Fashion
Trinders', Malting Lane. CO10 8NW. (P. and R. Trinder)
EST. 1974. PBFA. Open 10-5.30 Wed.-Sat. Other times by appointment. *STOCK: 20th C designer clothes, shoes and accessories; related books on fashion, design, jewellery.* SER: Internet sales. SIZE: Medium. PARK: Easy.
TEL: 01787 277130; HOME: sames
E-MAIL: rosemary@20thcenturyfashion.co.uk
WEBSITE: www.20thcenturyfashion.co.uk

Clare Antiques and Interiors
The Mill, Malting Lane. CO10 8NW.
EST. 1989. Open 9.30-5, Sun. 1-5. *STOCK: 17th-20th C furniture, textiles, pictures, porcelain, glass, silver, decorative items.* LOC: 100yds. from High St. Follow signs for Clare Castle, Country Park. SER: Valuations; restorations. SIZE: Large - over 80 dealers. PARK: Easy. VAT: Stan/Spec.
TEL: 01787 278449

F.D. Salter Antiques
1-2 Church St. CO10 8NN.
EST. 1959. Open 9-5. CL: Wed. pm. *STOCK: 18th to early 19th C English furniture, porcelain and glass.* LOC: A1092. SER: Valuations; restorations (furniture). SIZE: Medium. PARK: Easy. VAT: Stan/Spec. FAIRS: Petersfield; Penman fairs.
TEL: 01787 277693
E-MAIL: f.salter@clara.co.uk
WEBSITE: www.salterantiques.co.uk

DEBENHAM

Edward Bigden Fine Art Ltd.
48 High St. IP14 6QW.
EST. 2001. Open by appointment. *STOCK: Fine paintings and sculpture, 16th-21st C; early furniture.* LOC: Opposite church. SIZE: Small. PARK: Easy.
TEL: 01728 862065; HOME: same; MOBILE: 07882 319818
E-MAIL: eb@edwardbigden.com
WEBSITE: www.edwardbigden.com

Debenham Antiques Ltd.
73 High St. IP14 6QS. (Ian Collins)
EST. 1969. Open 9.15-5.30 or by appointment. *STOCK: 17th-19th C furniture and paintings, £50-£25,000.* SER: Made to order; sourcing; deliveries. SIZE: Large. PARK:

Own. VAT: Stan/Spec.
TEL: 01728 860707; FAX: 01728 860333
E-MAIL: ian@antiquefurniture.tv
WEBSITE: www.antiquefurniture.tv

Josh Antiques

2a Chancery Lane. IP14 6RN. (John W. Etheridge)
EST. 1991. Usually open seven days 9.30-3.30, some days
until 4.30. *STOCK: Oil lamps, Victorian to 1950s, £20-
£200; pictures, £5-£150; metalware, china, glass, £2-100;
cigarette and phone cards; kitchenalia, fire related items;
crested china; postcards.* LOC: Just off High St. SER:
Valuations. SIZE: Small. PARK: Easy.
TEL: 01728 861680; HOME: same
E-MAIL: shirley.etheridge@virgin.net

DEPDEN

Coblands Farm Antiques

Bury Rd. IP29 4BT. (Mrs Janet Harding)
Open 10-5.30. *STOCK: Antique pine and other furniture,
especially wing chairs and sofas, £5-£2,000.* LOC: A143
between Haverhill and Bury St. Edmunds. SER:
Restorations (upholstery). SIZE: Large. PARK: Easy.
TEL: 01440 820007; HOME: same; FAX: 01440 821165

EXNING

Exning Antiques & Interiors

14-16 Oxford St. CB8 7EW. (Geoffrey Tabbron)
EST. 1982. Open 9-5. *STOCK: Period lighting, gasoliers and
electroliers, table and standing lamps; drapes and decorative
items.* SER: Restorations, conversions, cleaning and re-
wiring. SIZE: Medium. PARK: Easy.
TEL: 01638 600015; FAX: 01638 600073; HOME: 01638
602337

EYE

Bramley Antiques

4 Broad St. 1P23 7AF. (C. Grater)
EST. 1987. Open Wed. and Sat. 9.30-5, other times by
appointment. *STOCK: Porcelain and glass, £5-£500; silver
and plate, boxes, pictures, general antiques, all 18th to early
20th C.* LOC: Town centre. SER: Valuations; restorations.
SIZE: Medium. PARK: Easy.
TEL: 01379 871386
E-MAIL: chris.grater@btinternet.com

English and Continental Antiques

1 Broad St. IP23 7AF. (Steve Harmer)
EST. 1977. Open Wed.-Sat. 11-5. *STOCK: Furniture, 17th-
19th C, £10-£20,000.* LOC: Opposite town hall. SER:
Restorations; upholstery. SIZE: Medium. PARK: Easy.
TEL: 01379 871199
E-MAIL: englishantiques@onetel.com
WEBSITE: www.englishandcontinentalantiques.com

FELIXSTOWE

John McCulloch Antiques

1a Hamilton Rd. IP11 7HN.
EST. 1984. Open 10-4.30. CL: Wed. *STOCK: Furniture,
copper, brass, pictures, clocks and bric-a-brac.* LOC: Main
street, seafront end, at top of Bent Hill. PARK: Around
corner.
TEL: 01394 283126

Tea & Antiques

109 High Rd. East. IP11 9PS. (D. George)
EST. 1999. Open Thurs.-Sun. and Bank Holidays 10-5.
*STOCK: General antiques and collectables, bygones and
furniture, £5-£500.* LOC: Main road to Felistowe ferry.
SIZE: Small + outbuildings. PARK: Easy.
TEL: 01394 277789
E-MAIL: david.george47@tesco.net

FINNINGHAM

Abington Books

Primrose Cottage, Westhorpe Rd. IP14 4TW. (J.
Haldane)
EST. 1971. Open by appointment. *STOCK: Books on
Oriental rugs, from 1877, £1-£5,000; books on classical
tapestries, from 17th-19th C, £1-£3,000.* LOC: At bottom
of private drive, about 150m. west of intersection with
B1113. SER: Valuations; book binding. SIZE: Small.
PARK: Easy.
TEL: 01449 780303; FAX: 01449 780202;
E-MAIL: abington-books@btconnect.com

FRAMLINGHAM

Bed Bazaar

The Old Station, Station Rd. IP13 9EE. (B.J.
Goodbrey)
EST. 1979. GMC. National Bed Federation. Open 10-5.
CL: Weds. *STOCK: Antique bedsteads in brass/iron;
reproductions.* LOC: 15 mins. off A12 between Lowestoft
and Woodbridge. SER: Restorations and cleaning
(antique bedsteads); SIZE: Large. PARK: Own. VAT:
Margin.
TEL: 01728 723756; FAX: 01728 724626
E-MAIL: bengoodbrey@bedbazaar.co.uk
WEBSITE: www.bedbazaar.co.uk

Dix-Sept

17 Station Rd. IP13 9EE. (S. Goodbrey and M. Cluzan)
EST. 1996. Open Sat. 10-1 and 2-5, other times by
appointment. *STOCK: French furniture and decoration,
pottery, garden furniture, mirrors and textiles.* LOC: On
approach road from A12. PARK: Easy. VAT: Global.
FAIRS: Newark.
TEL: 01728 621505; FAX: 01728 724884
E-MAIL: dix-sept@tiscali.co.uk

Goodbreys
29 Double St. IP13 9BN. (R. and M. Goodbrey)
EST. 1965. *Mainly Trade.* Open Sat. 9.30-1 and 2-5.30 or
by appointment. STOCK: *18th and 19th C decorative
furniture and accessories; painted furnishings, Antler
furnishings and unusual items; china, glass, mirrors and bric-
a-brac.* LOC: Up Church St. towards Framlingham
Castle, opposite church gates turn right into Double St.
SER: Restorations. SIZE: Large. PARK: Easy. VAT: Mainly
Spec/Global. FAIRS: Newark; Ardingly.
TEL: 01728 621191; FAX: 01728 724727

Honeycombe Antiques
8 Market Hill. IP13 9AN. (K. Honeycombe)
EST. 1997. Open 9.30-5. STOCK: *Silver, Georgian to 1950,
£10-£1,000; furniture - small tables, chairs, plant stands,
mainly Georgian to Edwardian, £30-£600; ceramics, glass
and pictures, £10-£300; jewellery, £30-£500; boxes, caddies
and writing slopes, £100-£400, clocks £100-£4,000.* LOC:
Market Sq. SER: Valuations; silver cutlery matching and
replacement. SIZE: Medium. PARK: Market Sq. and
nearby free car parks.
TEL: 01728 622011

The Theatre Antiques Centre
10 Church St. IP13 9BH. (W. Darby)
EST. 2001. Open 9.30-5.30. STOCK: *Furniture, 18th-21st
C, £30-£2,000; European 18th-20th C, £100-£1,000;
country pine, 19th C, £100-£750; objets d'art, £50-£100.*
SER: Valuations. SIZE: Large. VAT: Spec.
TEL: 01728 621069

Witchball Antiques
18 Well Close Square. IP13 9DU. (Jill and Brian Upton)
EST. 1967. Open 10-6. STOCK: *General antiques, clocks,
Chinese porcelain, dolls and toys, jewellery, English porcelain
and pottery.* SER: Restringing (dolls). SIZE: Small. PARK:
2 spaces outside.
TEL: 01728 723086
E-MAIL: brianeupton@hotmail.com

HACHESTON

Hardy's
IP13 0DS.
Resident. Open Tues-Fri. 10-5, Sat. 10-2. STOCK: *Pine -
dressers, corner cupboards, butcher's blocks, old farmhouse
tables, wardrobes, chests of drawers, pot cupboards.* LOC:
B1116, Framlingham Rd. PARK: At rear.
TEL: 01728 746485.

HALESWORTH

P & R Antiques Ltd
Fairstead Farm Buildings, Wash Lane, Spexhall. IP19 0RF.
(Pauline and Robert Lewis)
EST. 1997. Open by appointment. STOCK: *Chests of
drawers, £900-£3,000; dining and drawing room furniture,
£500-£4,000; all 18th-19th C.* LOC: From A12, take
Halesworth turning, through town, turn left into Wissett
Road, then right after half mile into Wash Lane, farm is
half mile on right. SER: Worldwide delivery. SIZE: Large.
PARK: Easy. VAT: Spec. FAIRS: Snape.
TEL: 01986 873232; HOME: same; FAX: 01986 874682
E-MAIL: pauline@prantiques.com
WEBSITE: www.prantiques.com

IPSWICH

A. Abbott Antiques Ltd
757 Woodbridge Rd. IP4 4NE. (C. Lillistone)
EST. 1965. Open Thurs., Fri. and Sat. 10.30-5. STOCK: *Small
items, especially clocks and jewellery; Victorian, Edwardian and
shipping furniture, £5-£5,000.* SIZE: Medium. PARK: Easy.
VAT: Global. FAIRS: Newark; Ardingly.
TEL: 01473 728900; MOBILE: 07771 533413
E-MAIL: abbott_antiques@hotmail.com

Claude Cox at College Gateway Bookshop
3 Silent St. IP1 1TF. (Anthony Cox)
EST. 1944. ABA. PBFA. Open Wed.-Sat. 10-5. STOCK:
Books, from 1470; some local maps and prints. LOC: Leave
inner ring road at Novotel double roundabout, turn into
St. Peters St., then second on right. SER: Valuations;

restorations (rebinding); buys at auction; catalogue available. SIZE: Medium. PARK: Cromwell Square and Buttermarket Centre. FAIRS: Oxford Fine Press.
TEL: 01473 254776; FAX: same
E-MAIL: books@claudecox.co.uk
WEBSITE: www.claudecox.co.uk

The Edwardian Shop
556 Spring Rd. IP4 4NT. (Joseph Hodgson)
EST. 1979. Open 9-5. STOCK: Victorian, Edwardian and 1920s shipping goods, £10-£400. LOC: Half a mile from the hospital. PARK: Own.
TEL: 01473 716576
E-MAIL: joehodgson556@googlemail.com

Hubbard Antiques
16-18 St. Margarets Green. IP4 2BS.
EST. 1964. Trade & Export. Open 10-5.30 and by appointment. STOCK: Furniture and decorative items, 18th-19th C. SER: Valuations; restorations; desk re-leathering; upholstery; lacquer repairs. SIZE: Large. PARK: Easy.
VAT: Stan/Spec.
TEL: 01473 226033 or 01473 233034; FAX: 01473 253639
E-MAIL: sales@hubbard-antiques.com
WEBSITE: www.hubbard-antiques.com

Maud's Attic
25 St. Peter's St. IP1 1XF. (Wendy Childs)
EST. 1996. Open Tues.-Sat. 10-5. STOCK: General

antiques, collectables and reproduction including porcelain, lamps, glass, jewellery, furniture, linen and mirrors. LOC: Town centre. SER: Valuations. SIZE: Small PARK: Easy.
TEL: 01473 221057; FAX: 01473 221056
E-MAIL: maudsattic@hotmail.com

IXWORTH

E.W. Cousins and Son   LAPADA
The Old School, Thetford Rd. IP31 2HJ.
(E.J.A., J.E. and R.W. Cousins)
EST. 1920. CL: Sat. pm. STOCK: General antiques, 18th-19th C, £50-£20,000. LOC: A143. SER: Restorations. SIZE: **Large and warehouse.** PARK: Easy. VAT: Stan/Spec.
TEL: **01359 230254**; FAX: 01359 232370
E-MAIL: **john@ewcousins.co.uk**
WEBSITE: **www.ewcousins.co.uk**

LAVENHAM

The Timbers Antique & Collectables Centre
High St. CO1 9PY. (Jeni White)
EST. 1996. Resident. Open 9.30-5 every day including Bank Holidays. STOCK: Smalls and furniture, to £5,000. SIZE: Medium. PARK: Easy.
TEL: 01787 247218
E-MAIL: white-jeni@hotmail.com
WEBSITE: www.timbersantiques.com

LEISTON

Leiston Trading Post
Frederick House, 17 High St. IP16 4EL. (L.K. Smith)
Est. 1967. Open 10-1 and 2-5, other times by
appointment. CL: Wed. Stock: Bric-a-brac, Victoriana,
Victorian and Edwardian furniture, collectables. Loc: 4
miles from Aldeburgh, Snape, and Saxmundham. Ser:
Valuations; house clearance. Size: Large. Park: Easy.
VAT: Stan.
Tel: 01728 830081; Home: 01728 831488
E-mail: lisa@renaultsuffolk.co.uk
Website: www.leistontradingpost.co.uk

Michael Lewis
5 Highbury Cottages, Waterloo Ave. IP16 4TW.
Est. 1980. Open by appointment. Stock: General
antiques. Ser: Consultations. Size: Small. Park: Easy.
Tel: 01728 833276; Mobile: 07976 307056

Warrens Antiques Warehouse
High St. IP16 4EL. (J.R. and J.J. Warren)
Est. 1980 CL: Wed. and Sat. pm. except by
appointment. Stock: Furniture, Georgian to Edwardian,
£20-£2,000. Loc: Off High St., driveway beside Geaters
Florists. Ser: Valuations; restorations (furniture). Size:
Medium. Park: Easy. Fairs: Newark; Ardingly.
Tel: 01728 831414; Home: same; Mobile: 07989
865598
E-mail: jrwantiques@aol.com
Website: www.warrenantiques.co.uk

LONG MELFORD

Sandy Cooke Antiques
Hall St. CO10 9JQ.
Est. 1982. Open Fri., Sat. and Mon. 10-5. Stock:
Furniture, 17th to early 19th C, £500-£40,000. Not
Stocked: Silver and glass. Loc: A134. Size: Large.
Park: Easy. VAT: Stan/Spec.
Tel: 01787 378265; Fax: 01284 830935; Mobile:
07860 206787
E-mail: sandycooke@englishfurniture.co.uk
Website: www.englishfurniture.co.uk

Long Melford Antiques Centre
Chapel Maltings. CO10 9HX. (Baroness V. von Dahlen)
Est. 1984. Open 9.30-5.30 or by appointment. Stock:
Furniture - oak, Georgian, Edwardian and Victorian; silver,
china, glass, clocks and decorators' items. Loc: A134,
Sudbury end of village. Ser: Packing and shipping. Size:
Large - 42 dealers. VAT: Stan/Spec.
Tel: 01787 379287

Alexander Lyall Antiques
Belmont House, Hall St. CO10 9JF. (A.J. Lyall)
Est. 1977. Open 10-5.30. Stock: Furniture, 18th-19th
C. Loc: A134 opposite Crown Hotel. Ser: Restorations
(furniture); buys at auction (English furniture). Size:

Medium. Park: Easy. VAT: Stan/Spec.
Tel: 01787 375434; Home: same
E-mail: alex@lyallantiques.com
Website: www.lyallantiques.com

Mayflower Antiques
Chapel Maltings. CO10 9HX. (J.W. Odgers)
Est. 1970. Open 10-5. Stock: Clocks, mechanical music,
scientific and marine instruments, general antiques. Size:
Medium. Park: Easy. Fairs: Newark; London
Scientific and Medical Instrument.
Tel: 07860 843569
E-mail: mayflower@johnodgers.com;
mail@johnodgers.co.uk
Website: www.oldjunk.co.uk

Melford Antique Warehouse
Hall St. CO10 9JG. (D. Edwards, J. Tanner and P.
Scholz)
Open 10-5, Sun. 1-5. Stock: 18th-20th C furniture and
decorative items. Size: 150 dealers exhibiting. Park: Easy.
Tel: 01787 379638
Website: www.antiques-access-agency.com

Noel Mercer Antiques
Aurora House, Hall St. CO10 9RJ.
Est. 1990. Open 10-5 or by appointment. Stock: Early
oak, walnut and country furniture, including refectory and
gateleg tables, sets of chairs and dressers; works of art, £500-
£30,000. Loc: Centre of Hall St. Ser: Valuations;
restorations. Size: Large. Park: Easy. VAT: Stan/Spec.
Tel: 01787 311882; Mobile: 07984 643223
E-mail: info@noelmercerantiques.com
Website: www.noelmercerantiques.com

The Persian Carpet Studio Ltd
The Old White Hart. CO10 9HX. (Sara Barber)
Est. 1990. Open 10-5.30. Stock: Antique and decorative
Oriental carpets and rugs, from 1860, from £50 - £15,000.
Loc: Sudbury end of Long Melford. Ser: Valuations;
repairs and hand-cleaning (Oriental rugs); buys at
auction (Oriental carpets, rugs and textiles). Exhibitions
held. Size: Medium. Park: Own. VAT: Stan/Margin.
Tel: 01787 882214; Fax: 01787 882213
E-mail: info@persian-carpet-studio.net
Website: www.persian-carpet-studio.net

Stable Antique Centre
Hall St. CO10 9JU.
Open 10-4.30. CL: Thurs. Stock: Antique and modern
collectables. Size: 10 units.
Tel: 01787 310754

LOUDHAM

Keith Skeel Antiques & Eccentricities   LAPADA
Loudham Hall. IP13 0NN.
**Open by appointment through the shop in Islington,
London, N1.** Stock: Chests, armoires, bookcases, seating,

desks, sideboards, tables, accessories, lighting, mirrors.
TEL: 01728 745900
E-MAIL: info@keithskeel.com
WEBSITE: www.keithskeel.com

MARLESFORD

The Antiques Warehouse
The Old Mill, Main Rd. IP13 0AG. (John M. Ball)
EST. 1989. Open 9-5, Sun. and BH 11-4.30. *STOCK:*
Furniture including fine country, 18th-20th C, £50-£5,000;
mirrors and decorative items, 18th-20th C, £10-£2,000.
LOC: A12, 7 miles north of Woodbridge. SER:
Valuations; buys at auction. SIZE: Large. PARK: Easy.
TEL: 01728 747438; FAX: 01728 747627; HOME: 01394
382426
E-MAIL: antiqueswarehouse@btinternet.com
WEBSITE: www.antiqueswarehouse.it

MARTLESHAM

Martlesham Antiques
The Thatched Roadhouse. IP12 4RJ. (R.F. Frost)
EST. 1973. Open Mon.-Sat., Sun. by appointment.
STOCK: Furniture and decorative items, 17th-20th C, £25-
£3,000. LOC: A1214 opposite Red Lion public house.
SIZE: Large. PARK: Own. VAT: Spec./Export.
TEL: 01394 386732; FAX: 01394 382959
E-MAIL: martleshamantiques@keme.co.uk

John Read Antiques
29 Lark Rise, Martlesham Heath. IP5 3SA.
EST. 1992. Open by appointment. *STOCK: Pre-1840*
Staffordshire figures, animals and English pottery, including
Delft, salt glaze, creamware and pearlware, coloured glazed,
underglazed (Pratt) and enamel decoration, 1750-1840,
£100-£8,000. LOC: A12 Ipswich bypass, opposite BT
tower. SER: Valuations; restorations (as stock). PARK:
Easy. FAIRS: Chelsea; NEC.
TEL: 01473 624897; HOME: same
E-MAIL: momokat@hotmail.co.uk

MENDLESHAM

Tower Reclaim
Tower Farm, Norwich Rd. IP14 5NE. (James Webster)
EST. 1974. SALVO. Open by appointment or chance.
STOCK: Architecural antiques, 16th C to date; garden
statuary, stone items and paving, reclaimed building
materials. PARK: Easy.
TEL: 01449 766095
WEBSITE: www.architecturalsalvage.uk.com

NEEDHAM MARKET

Roy Arnold Books
77 High St. IP6 8AN.
EST. 1974. Open 10-5, appointment advisable, Sun. by
appointment. *STOCK: Books - new, secondhand and*

antiquarian - on tools and trades, trade catalogues; all £10-
£5,000. LOC: Off A14, centre of High St. SIZE:
Medium. PARK: Easy. VAT: Stan.
TEL: 01449 720110; FAX: 01449 722498
E-MAIL: books@royarnold.com
WEBSITE: www.royarnold.com

Old Town Hall Antique & Collectors Centre
High St. IP6 8AL. (Rod Harrison)
EST. 1980. Open 10-5. Also all Bank Holiday Sun. and
Mon. and Good Friday. *STOCK: Antiques and collectables,*
bric-a-brac, gold, silver and costume jewellery, books and
ephemera. LOC: Main street. SIZE: 40+ cabinets and stalls.
PARK: Easy.
TEL: 01449 720773

The Tool Shop   LAPADA
78 High St. IP6 8AW. (Tony Murland)
EST. 1988. Open 10-5. *STOCK: Antique and usable*
woodworking tools, from 19th C. **LOC: Opposite the Post**
Office. SER: Valuations; buys at auction; tool auctions
held. SIZE: Small. PARK: Easy. VAT: Stan.
TEL: 01449 722992; FAX: 01449 722683
E-MAIL: tony@antiquetools.co.uk
WEBSITE: www.antiquetools.co.uk

NEWMARKET

R.E. and G.B. Way
Brettons, Burrough Green. CB8 9NA. (Gregory Way)
EST. 1964. ABA. PBFA. Open 8.30-5 appointment
advisable. *STOCK: Antiquarian and secondhand books on*
shooting, fishing, horses, racing and hunting and small
general section.
TEL: 01638 507217; FAX: 01638 508058
E-MAIL: greg@waybooks.demon.co.uk
WEBSITE: www.way-books.co.uk

ORFORD

Castle Antiques
Market Sq. IP12 2LH. (S. Simpkin)
EST. 1969. Open daily including Sun. 11-4. *STOCK:*
Furniture, general small antiques, bric-a-brac, glass, china,
clocks. SIZE: Medium. PARK: Easy.
TEL: 01394 450100
E-MAIL: steph@castle-antiques.co.uk
WEBSITE: www.castle-antiques.co.uk

PEASENHALL

Peasenhall Art and Antiques Gallery
The Street. IP17 2HJ. (A. and M. Wickins)
EST. 1972. Resident. Open every day. *STOCK: 19th to early*
20th C watercolours and oils; some furniture; walking sticks.
SER: Restorations (oils, watercolours). PARK: Easy.
FAIRS: Snape.
TEL: 01728 660224; HOME: same
E-MAIL: ann@peasenhallart.fsnet.co.uk

RISBY

The Risby Barn
IP28 6QU. (R. and S. Martin)
EST. 1986. Open 9-5.30, Sun. and Bank Holidays 10-5. STOCK: *Furniture, porcelain, metalware, tools, pine, Art Deco, oil lamps.* LOC: Just off A14 west of Bury St. Edmunds. SIZE: Large - 24 dealers. PARK: Own.
TEL: 01284 811126; FAX: 01284 810783
WEBSITE: www.risbybarn.co.uk

SNAPE

Snape Antiques and Collectors Centre
Snape Maltings. IP17 1SR.
EST. 1992. Open 7 days 10-5 or until dusk in winter. STOCK: *Antiques and collectables, especially smalls - pens, sewing, silver, jewellery, ceramics from 18th C, Doulton, Deco, Studio, glass, maps, prints, paintings, textiles; country, decorative and useful furniture; stamps, costume jewellery, drinking glasses, antiquities, coins, advertising, books; clothing, from Victorian to 1970s; massive selection of cutlery from antique to modern including canteens.* LOC: Next to the concert hall. SIZE: 45 dealers. PARK: Easy.
TEL: 01728 688038

SOUTHWOLD

Puritan Values at the Dome
The Dome Art and Antiques Centre, Southwold Business Centre, St. Edmunds Rd. IP18 6BZ. (A.F. Geering)
EST. 1984. Resident. Open 10-6, Sun. 11-5. STOCK: *Arts and Crafts, Gothic Revival, Aesthetic, decorative arts and Art Nouveau,* £50-£100,000. SER: Valuations; restorations. SIZE: Large. PARK: Easy. VAT: Stan/Spec. FAIRS: Earls Court; Newark; NEC; Scottish Exhibition Centre.
TEL: 01502 722211; MOBILE: 07966 371676
E-MAIL: sales@puritanvalues.com
WEBSITE: www.puritanvalues.com

T. Schotte Antiques
The Old Bakehouse, Black Mill Rd. IP18 6AQ.
(T. and J. Schotte)
Open 10-1 and 2-4. CL: Wed. STOCK: *Small furniture,* £25-£500; *decorative objects,* £5-£250; *both 18th-19th C. Unusual collectables,* £5-£500. LOC: Turn right at the King's Head, then first left. SIZE: Small. FAIRS: Long Melford monthly; Adams, Horticultural Hall, London; Lomax Fair, Langley Park (May and Oct.).
TEL: 01502 722083

Southwold Antiques Centre
Buckenham Mews, 83 High St. IP18 6DS.
(Anne Stolliday)
Open 10-4.30, Wed. 10-1, Sun. 12-4. STOCK: *General antiques and collectables; replacement china.* LOC: Off High St. SIZE: Medium. PARK: Nearby.
TEL: 01502 723060

S. J. Webster-Speakman
(F.P. and S.J. Webster-Speakman)
EST. 1970. Open by appointment. STOCK: *English furniture, clocks, Staffordshire pottery, general antiques.* SER: Valuations; restorations (clocks, furniture and ceramics). PARK: Easy. FAIRS: Various.
TEL: 01502 722252

SUDBURY

Napier House Antiques
Church St. CO10 6BJ. (Veronica McGregor)
EST. 1977. Open 10-4.30 and by appointment. STOCK: *18th-19th C mahogany furniture, especially larger items - linen presses, wardrobes, desks, bureaux, bookcases, dining tables, sideboards, wing chairs,* £350-£5,000. SER: Free UK delivery. SIZE: Large. PARK: Easy. VAT: Spec.
TEL: 01787 375280; FAX: 01787 478757

Neate Militaria & Antiques
PO Box 3794, Preston St Mary. CO10 9PX.
(Gary C. Neate)
EST. 1983. OMRS. OMSA. MMSSA. MCCofC. *Mail order and website only.* Open Mon.-Fri. 9-6. STOCK: *Orders, decorations and medals of the world,* £5-£15,000. SER: Valuations; periodic catalogues. VAT: Spec. FAIRS: Brittania Medal; Aldershot Medal & Militaria.
TEL: 01787 248168; FAX: 01787 248363
E-MAIL: gary@neatemedals.co.uk
WEBSITE: www.neatemedals.co.uk

THURSTON

Denzil Grant Antiques   BADA LAPADA
Green Farm Gallery. IP31 3SN.
EST. 1979. Open any time by appointment. STOCK: **Furniture, especially French farm tables, 16th to early 19th C.** LOC: **Off A14 between Bury St. Edmunds and Ipswich.** SIZE: **Large.** PARK: **Easy.**
TEL: **01449 736576;** FAX: **01449 737679**
E-MAIL: **denzil@fish.co.uk**
WEBSITE: **www.denzilgrant.com**

WICKHAM MARKET

Ashe Antiques Warehouse
The Old Engine Shed, Station Rd., Campsea Ashe.
IP13 0PT. (Graham Laffling)
EST. 1986. Open 10-5 including Sun. STOCK: *Furniture, 18th-20th C,* £100-£5,000; *collectables, pictures and prints, 19th-20th C,* £50-£500. LOC: 1.5 miles from A12 Wickham Market by-pass, signposted Orford and Tunstall. SER: Valuations; restorations (furniture); French polishing; upholstery; buys at auction. SIZE: Large. PARK: Easy. FAIRS: Newark.
TEL: 01728 747255; 01394 460490

Roy Webb Antiques
179 & 181 High St. IP13 0RQ.
Open Mon., Thurs. and Sat. 10-6 or by appointment.

STOCK: *17th-20th C furniture (including shipping) and
clocks.* LOC: Just off A12. SER: Shippiong arranged. SIZE:
Large warehouse. PARK: Own large. VAT: Stan/Spec.
TEL: 01728 746077; EVENINGS: 01394 382697

WOODBRIDGE

David Gibbins Antiques   **BADA**
The White House, 14 Market Hill. IP12 4LU.
EST. **1964. Open by appointment.** STOCK: *English
furniture, late 16th to early 19th C, £300-£40,000;
English pottery and porcelain, metalwork.* SER:
Valuations; buys at auction. PARK: Own in Theatre St.
VAT: Spec. FAIRS: BADA; Harrogate (Autumn).
TEL: **01394 382685; MOBILE: 07702 306914**
E-MAIL: **david@gibbinsantiques.co.uk**
WEBSITE: **www.gibbinsantiques.co.uk**

Hamilton Antiques   LAPADA
(H. Ferguson and Mrs. R. Ferguson)
EST. **1977. CINOA. Open by appointment only.**
STOCK: *18th - early 20th C furniture.* SER: Restoration;
polishing. SIZE: Small. PARK: Own.
TEL: **01394 460237; MOBILE: 07747 03343
or 07914 873247**
E-MAIL: **enquiries@hamiltonantiques.co.uk**
WEBSITE: **www.hamiltonantiques.co.uk**

Anthony Hurst Antiques
13 Church St. IP12 1DS. (Christopher Hurst)
EST. 1957. Open 10-1 and 2-5. CL: Wed. and Sat. pm
STOCK: *English furniture, oak, walnut and mahogany,
1600-1900, £100-£5,000.* SER: Valuations; restorations
(furniture); buys at auction. SIZE: Large. PARK: Easy.
VAT: Spec.
TEL: 01394 382500

R.A and S.M. Lambert & Son
The Bull Ride, 70a New St. IP12 1DX.
EST. 1963. Open 9.30-1 and 2-5. STOCK: *19th-20th C
furniture.* LOC: 2 minutes from Market Hill. SIZE: Large.
VAT: Stan/Spec.
TEL: 01394 382380
E-MAIL: mary@lambert667.fsnet.co.uk
WEBSITE: www.bullrideantiques.co.uk

Edward Manson (Clocks)
8 Market Hill. IP12 4LU.
Open by appointment. STOCK: *Clocks.* SER: Restorations
(clocks); dial painting.
TEL: 01394 380235
E-MAIL: edward.manson@virgin.net

Melton Antiques
Kingdom Hall, Melton Rd., Melton. IP12 1NZ.
(A. Harvey-Jones)
EST. 1975. Open 9.30-5. CL: Wed. STOCK: *Silver,
collectors' items, £5-£500; decorative items and furniture,
£15-£500; both 18th-19th C; Victoriana and general
antiques, 19th C, £5-£500; sewing items.* LOC: On right
hand-side coming from Woodbridge. SIZE: Small. PARK:
Outside shop. VAT: Global. FAIRS: Sandown Park.
TEL: 01394 386232

Sarah Meysey-Thompson Antiques
10 Church St. IP12 1DH.
EST. 1962. Usually open 10.30-4 or by appointment any
time. STOCK: *Small furniture, late 18th-20th C; unusual
and decorative items.* LOC: Town centre. SIZE: Medium.
PARK: Easy. VAT: Spec. FAIRS: Decorative Antiques &
Textile, London.
TEL: 01394 382144
E-MAIL: smtantiques@hotmail.com

Isobel Rhodes
10-12 Market Hill. IP12 4LU.
EST. 1964. Open 10-1, 2-5. STOCK: *Furniture, oak,
country, mahogany; brassware.* PARK: Easy. VAT: Spec.
TEL: 01394 382763

Woodbridge Antiques Centre
7 Quay St. IP12 1BX. (Natalie Smith)
EST. 2007. Open 9.30-5.30, Sun 10.30-4.3. CL: Tue.
STOCK: *Silver, porcelain, glass, fine jewellery, vintage
costume jewellery, clocks and decorative items.* SIZE:
Medium - 20 dealers' cabinets. PARK: Nearby.
TEL: 01394 387210

Suffolk House Antiques
Early oak and country furniture and works of art

Situated just off the A12 in the middle of the village of Yoxford, Suffolk House Antiques has extensive showrooms on two floors with parking available right outside the shop.

Stock usually includes a range of dressers, gateleg and refectory tables, cupboards, chests of drawers, sets of chairs and smaller pieces of furniture. In addition there are always good examples of early ceramics, especially delftware, early carvings and metalware.

Hours of business are
10 am - 1 pm - 2.15 pm - 5.15 pm
Closed Wednesdays and Sundays,
or by appointment.

Suffolk House Antiques, High Street, Yoxford,
Suffolk IP17 3EP.
Telephone/Fax: 01728 668122
E-mail: andrew.singleton@suffolk-house-antiques.co.uk
Website: www.suffolk-house-antiques.co.uk

E-MAIL: natalie@woodbridgeantiquescentre.co.uk
WEBSITE: www.woodbridgeantiquescentre.co.uk

WOOLPIT

J.C. Heather
The Old Crown. IP30 9SA.
EST. 1946. Open 9-8 including Sun. *STOCK: Furniture, 18th-19th C, £20-£1,000. NOT STOCKED: China.* LOC: Near centre of village on right. SER: Restorations. SIZE: Medium. PARK: Easy.
TEL: 01359 240297
E-MAIL: john@johnheather.co.uk

Rococo Architectural & English Vintage
The Street, IP30 9SA. (Neville Griffiths and Esther Fortisque)
Resident. Open 11-6, Sun 12-5. CL: Mon.-Weds. *STOCK: Architectural goods; country furniture; soft furnishings.* LOC: Close to Bury St. Edmunds, Long Melford, Lavenham. SER: Delivery. PARK: On road.
TEL: 07904 419222; 07939 212542
E-MAIL: englishvintage@yahoo.com
WEBSITE: www.nevillegriffiths.co.uk

YOXFORD

Garden House Antiques
High St. IP17 3ER. (Janet Hyde-Smith, Anne Gray

and Michael Lewis)
EST. 1979. Open 10-5. CL: Wed. *STOCK: Small decorative antiques including furniture, 18th-20th C, £1-£500.* LOC: Opposite church. SIZE: Medium. PARK: Easy.
TEL: 01728 668044; HOME: 01986 874685;
MOBILE: 07767 896401

Suffolk House Antiques BADA
High St. IP17 3EP. (A. Singleton)
EST. 1990. Open 10-1 and 2.15-5.15. CL: Wed. *STOCK: 17th-18th C oak and country furniture, works of art, paintings, delftware and metalware.* LOC: A1120, just off A12. SER: Advice on interiors. SIZE: Large. PARK: Easy. FAIRS: BADA; Snape.
TEL: 01728 668122; FAX: same; MOBILE: 07860 521583
E-MAIL: andrew.singleton@suffolk-house-antiques.co.uk
WEBSITE: www.suffolk-house-antiques.co.uk

Yoxford Antique Centre & Gardens
Askers Hill. IP17 3JW. (Malcolm and June Purvis)
Open 10-5, Sun. and Bank Holidays 10-4. *STOCK: Wide range of general antiques including oak, mahogany and pine furniture, longcase clocks, ceramics and smalls, 17th to early 20th C, £5-£15,000.* LOC: A1120, 1 mile from A12 towards Sibton. SIZE: Large. PARK: Own.
TEL: 01728 668844
E-MAIL: malcolm@purvis193.fsnet.co.uk
WEBSITE: www.yoxfordantiques.com

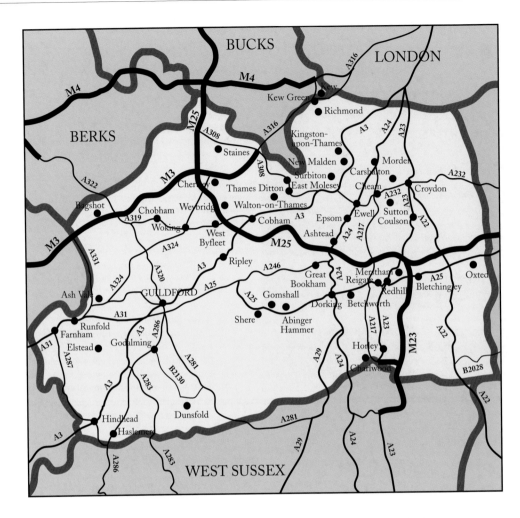

ABINGER HAMMER

Stirling Antiques
Aberdeen House. RH5 6RY. (V.S. Burrell)
EST. 1968. Open 10-6. CL: Thurs. STOCK: *Stained glass, furniture, copper, brass, jewellery, silver, curios, dolls.* PARK: Easy. VAT: Stan.
TEL: 01306 730706

ASH VALE

House of Christian
5-7 Vale Rd. GU12 5HH. (A. Bail)
EST. 1978. Open 10.30-5. CL: Sat. STOCK: *Pine, oak, mahogany and walnut furniture, 19th-21st C; small items, 18th-21st C.* LOC: On B3411 between Ash and Ash Vale railway stations. From Ash Wharf over canal bridge, shop (bright green) on left on hill. SER: Valuations; restorations (including waxing and staining); cabinet making; stockists of Briwax and Liberon products. SIZE: Small. PARK: Easy - opposite.
TEL: 01252 314478; FAX: 01252 310311

ASHTEAD

Bumbles
90 The Street. KT21 1AW. (Barbara Kay)
EST. 1992. Open 10-5. STOCK: *Cigarette cards; gifts and collectables.* SER: Restoration (furniture). PARK: Easy.
TEL: 01372 276219

BETCHWORTH

Stoneycroft Farm
Chalkpit Lane, Reigate Rd. RH3 7EY. (J.G. Elias)
EST. 1970. Open by appointment. STOCK: *Oak and country furniture, library bookcases, dining tables and chairs, special writing furniture, cupboards and wardrobes.* LOC: North of A25. 2 miles east of Dorking. SER: Search; shipping. SIZE: Medium. PARK: Own.
TEL: 01737 845215
E-MAIL: dorkingdesks@aol.com
WEBSITE: www.desk.uk.com

BLETCHINGLEY

John Anthony Antiques
71 High St. RH1 4LJ. (J.A. and N. Hart)
EST. 1973. Resident. Open by appointment. *STOCK: 18th to early 19th C furniture.* LOC: A25 between Redhill and Godstone. PARK: Easy. VAT: Spec/Margin.
TEL: 01883 743197; FAX: 01883 742108
E-MAIL: johnanthonyantiques@hotmail.com

Cider House Galleries Ltd   BADA LAPADA
Norfolk House, 80 High St. RH1 4PA.
(T. Roberts and A.H. Roberts)
EST. 1967. Open 10-5.30. CL: Sat. pm, Sun. and Mon. except by appointment. *STOCK: Paintings, 17th-20th C, from £450.* LOC: A25, behind Lawrence Auctioneers. SER: Valuations. SIZE: Large. PARK: Own. VAT: Stan/Spec. FAIRS: Olympia.
TEL: 01883 742198; FAX: 01883 744014
E-MAIL: tony@chgart.com
WEBSITE: www.ciderhousegalleries.com

CARSHALTON

Carshalton Antique Galleries
5 High St. SM5 3AP. (B.A. Gough)
EST. 1968. Open 9-4. CL: Wed. *STOCK: General antiques, furniture, clocks, glass, china, pictures and collectables.* LOC: Carshalton Ponds. SER: Probate. SIZE: Large. PARK: Nearby. VAT: Stan/Spec.
TEL: 020 8647 5664; HOME: 01306 887187

Collectors' Corner
3 The Square. SM5 3BN. (A.J. and B.M. Wilton)
EST. 1975. Open 11.30-3.30, Sat. 10-4. CL: Wed. *STOCK: Collectors' items, china, glass, 1780-1980, £50-£500; stamps, coins, medals, postcards, 19th-20th C, £5-£250.* LOC: Carshalton Ponds. SER: Valuations; restorations. SIZE: Small. PARK: Easy.
TEL: 020 8669 7377

CHEAM

Cheam Village Antiques
16 Malden Rd. SM3 8QF. (Martyn K. Reed)
EST. 1975. Open Mon., Fri. and Sat. 10-6. *STOCK: General antiques and decorative items, from 19th C.* LOC: 10 mins. off A3 towards Worcester Park. SIZE: Medium. PARK: Easy.
TEL: 020 8644 4422; MOBILE: 07949 136499
E-MAIL: mrantiques@hotmail.com

CHERTSEY

Chertsey Antiques
10 Windsor St. KT16 8AS. (Leandro Ulisse)
Open 10-5. *STOCK: Furniture, jewellery, glass, pottery and porcelain, silver, silver plate, pictures, kitchenalia,* *memorabilia, books, linen, clocks.* SER: Local free delivery. SIZE: Medium. PARK: Easy.
TEL: 01932 563313; FAX: 01753 685538
E-MAIL: antiques@ulisse.co.uk

D'Eyncourt
21 Windsor St. KT16 8AY. (Mr and Mrs Davies)
EST. 1968. Open 10-5.15, Sat. 7-5.30, Sun. 11-4. *STOCK: Furniture, Victorian to Art Deco, £50-£1,500; china, £5-£250; lighting and fireplaces, Victorian to present day, £25-£500.* LOC: Town centre. SER: Valuations; restorations. SIZE: Medium. PARK: Easy and Guildford St. VAT: Stan. FAIRS: London Photograph (Bonnington Hotel, Southampton Row).
TEL: 01932 563411

CHOBHAM

Greengrass Antiques   LAPADA
Hookstone Farm, Hookstone Lane, West End. GU24 9QP. (D. Greengrass)
EST. 1970. Open by appointment. *STOCK: Decorative items; 19th C furniture; works of art; shipping goods.* PARK: Easy. VAT: Spec/Global.
TEL: 01276 857582; FAX: 01276 855289; MOBILE: 07860 399686

Mimbridge Antiques Centre
Mimbridge Garden Centre, Station Rd. GU24 8AS. (Jo Monteath Scott)
EST. 1998. Open 10-5 including Sun. *STOCK: Collectors' items, furniture, prints, watercolours, maps, books, toys, dolls, dolls' houses and garden antiques, 18th-20th C, £5-£2,500.* LOC: Main road. SER: Consultants; fine art installation. SIZE: Medium. PARK: Easy. FAIRS: Kempton.
TEL: 01276 855736; MOBILE: 07833 504077

CLAYGATE

Fleur de Lys Gallery
16 Albany Crescent, KT10 0PF. (Henri S. Coronel and Mrs. Beatriz S. Coronel)
EST. 1967. Every day. *STOCK: 19th C paintings.* PARK: Easy.
TEL: 01372 467934; FAX: same
E-MAIL: fleurdelysgallery@yahoo.com
WEBSITE: www.fleur-de-lys.com

COMPTON

Old Barn Antique Centre
The Street. GU3 1EB.
EST. 1995. Open 10-4 Mon.-Sat. CL: Bank Holidays. *STOCK: General antiques and collectables, books and ephemera.* LOC: Opposite the church. SIZE: 8 dealers. PARK: Own. FAIRS: Maltings Market, Farnham.
TEL: 01483 810819.

COULSDON

Decodream
233 Chipstead Valley Rd. CR5 3BY.
Open by appointment. STOCK: *Pottery - Clarice Cliff, Shorter, Shelley, Foley, F. and C. Rhead and Carlton ware.* LOC: Off junction 7, M25. PARK: Free.
TEL: 020 8668 5534

D. Potashnick Antiques
7 Stoats Nest Parade, 73 Stoats Nest Rd. CR5 2JJ.
EST. 1974. Open 9-5.30, Sat. 9-12 or by appointment. STOCK: *Furniture.* LOC: Close to M23/M25. SER: Restorations (furniture). PARK: Easy.
TEL: 020 8660 8403

CROYDON

Oscar Dahling Antiques
87 Cherry Orchard Rd. CR0 6BE.
EST. 1988. Open Tues., Wed., Thurs. 10.30-6, Sat. 10.30-4.30, other times by appointment. STOCK: *Furniture, £50-£2,500; ceramics, £10-£250; jewellery and costume, £10-£1,000; all 18th-20th C.* LOC: First left after leaving East Croydon B.R. station. shop 300 yards, near The Glamorgan public house. SER: Valuations; probate services. SIZE: Medium. PARK: Easy.
TEL: 020 8681 8090; HOME: same
E-MAIL: oscar.dahling@virgin.net

DORKING

Arkell Antiques Ltd   LAPADA
64-65 West St. RH4 1BS. (Margaret Monk)
EST. 2001. CINOA. Open 10-5. STOCK: *Georgian furniture, dining tables, chairs, Edwardian satinwood, £500-£50,000.* SIZE: Large. FAIRS: Olympia; Guildford (Oct).
TEL: 01306 742152; FAX: same; MOBILE: 07973 122905
E-MAIL: info@arkellantiques.co.uk
WEBSITE: www.arkellantiques.com and www.arkellantiques.co.uk

Christique Antiques Centre
11 West St. RH4 1BL. (Christine and Roy Arnot)
EST. 2005. Open 10-5.30. STOCK: *English period and French country style furniture, linens, cushions, lamps, jewellery, silver, textiles, fine porcelain, ceramics, vintage handbags and compacts, paintings and accessories.* SER: Restoration; re-upholstery; carpet and interior design service. SIZE: Large. PARK: Opposite.
TEL: 01306 883849
E-MAIL: christique@btconnect.com
WEBSITE: www.christique.com

J. and M. Coombes
44 West St. RH4 1BU.
EST. 1965. Open 10-5. CL: Mon. STOCK: *General antiques.* VAT: Stan.
TEL: 01306 885479

The Dorking Desk Shop   LAPADA
J.G.Elias Antiques Ltd., 41 West St. RH4 1BU. (J.G. and G.B. Elias)
EST. 1969. Open 8-5.30, Sat. 10.30-5, last Sun. of month 11-4. STOCK: *Desks, dining tables, bookcases, chairs, wardrobes, oak and country furniture, 18th to late 19th C, £100-£60,000.* LOC: Western end of High Street. SER: Shipping. SIZE: Large. PARK: Nearby. VAT: Stan/Spec.
TEL: 01306 883327; FAX: 01306 875363
E-MAIL: dorkingdesks@aol.com
WEBSITE: www.desk.uk.com

Dorking House Antiques
17/18 West St. RH4 1BS. (Mrs G.D. Emburey)
EST. 1989. Open 10-5. STOCK: *Period and pine furniture, silver, porcelain, longcase, wall and table clocks, treen, jewellery, copper and brass, pictures and prints, decorative and collectors' items.* LOC: Continuation of High St. into one-way system. SER: Restorations. SIZE: 30 dealers. PARK: Opposite.
TEL: 01306 740915

Elias Antiques of Dorking
42 West St. RH4 1BU. (J.G. and G.B. Elias)
EST. 1969. Open 8-5.30 Mon.-Fri., 10.30-5 Sat., 11-4 last Sun. of month. STOCK: *Furniture, desks, dining tables, bookcases, chests, wardrobes, chairs and boxes.* LOC: Western end of High St. SER: Shipping. SIZE: Large. PARK: Nearby.
TEL: 01306 883327; FAX: 01306 875363
E-MAIL: dorkingdesks@aol.com
WEBSITE: www.desk.uk.com

Great Grooms of Dorking
50-52 West St. RH4 1BU. (J. Podger)
EST. 1971. Open 9.30-5.30, last Sun. in the month 10-4. STOCK: *Wide variety of fine English furniture, glass, ceramics, pictures, jewellery and silver, collectors' items and lighting.* SER: Export orders arranged. SIZE: 15 showrooms over 3 floors. PARK: Rear of premises. VAT: Spec.
TEL: 01306 887076; FAX: 01306 881029
E-MAIL: dorking@greatgrooms.co.uk
WEBSITE: www.greatgrooms.co.uk

Harman's
19 West St. RH4 1QH. (Paul and Nicholas Harman)
EST. 1956. Open 10-5. STOCK: *Oak refectory tables. English mahogany and walnut furniture including tables and chairs, linen presses, sideboards, bookcases, 18th-19th C, £100-£15,000; Moorcroft, mirrors and lamps.* SER: Restorations; polishing; repairs; upholstery; valuations. SIZE: Large. PARK: Nearby. VAT: Stan/Spec.
TEL: 01306 743330; HOME: same; FAX: 01306 742593
E-MAIL: shop@harmans.uk.com
WEBSITE: www.harmans.uk.com

Holmwood Antiques
Norfolk Rd., South Holmwood. RH5 4LA. (R. Dewdney)
Open 9-6.30, evenings and weekends by appointment.
STOCK: *Georgian and Victorian furniture.*
TEL: 01306 888174 or 01306 888468

The Jewel Box, Antique Jewellery & Silver
4 Old King's Head Court. RH4 1AR. (Pauline Watson)
EST. 1960 FGA, NAG. Open 9.30-5. STOCK: *Jewellery and silver especially Victorian.* LOC: Off 11 High St. at the top of West St. SER: NAG registered valuer; lecturer; photographer. SIZE: Small. PARK: Behind shop in North St. VAT: Stan/Spec.
TEL: 01306 885452

King's Court Galleries
54 West St. RH4 1BS. (Mrs J. Joel)
ABA. FATG. IMCOS. Open 9.30-5.30. STOCK: *Antique maps, engravings, decorative and sporting prints.* SER: Framing.
TEL: 01306 881757
WEBSITE: www.kingscourtgalleries.co.uk

Malthouse Antiques
49 West St. RH4 1BU. (Colin Waters)
EST. 1988. Open 10-5, Sat. 10-5.30, Sun. 11-4. STOCK: *18th-19th C mahogany, rosewood and walnut, 17th-19th C oak and country, £100-£10,000; giltwood mirrors, 18th-19th C, £300-£5,000, rocks, fossils and minerals, decor, £10-£2,000, clocks, £500-£3,000.* SER: Restoration of pictures, furniture. etc. SIZE: Large. PARK: Pay and display behind shop. VAT: Spec.
TEL: 01306 886169

Norfolk House Galleries
48 West St. RH4 1BU.
EST. 1979. Open 10-5. STOCK: *18th-19th C furniture, especially dining tables and sets of chairs.* SIZE: 5 showrooms. PARK: Public behind showrooms.
TEL: 01306 881028

Pilgrims Antique Centre
7 West St. RH4 1BL.
EST. 1974. Open 10-5. STOCK: *Furniture, 19th-20th C; china and glass, silver and plate; copper and brass; telephones and collectables.* LOC: A25 through town, just off High St. SER: Resorations (furniture). SIZE: 15 dealers. PARK: Easy.
TEL: 01306 875028

Scotts of Dorking
70 High St. RH4 1AY.
NAG. Open 9.30-5. STOCK: *Jewellery, gemstones, silver, watches.* LOC: Opposite Boots chemist. SER: Repairs (jewellery). SIZE: Medium. PARK: Behind shop.
TEL: 01306 880790
WEBSITE: www.scottsofdorking.co.uk

Surrey Hills Antique Centre
61 West St. RH4 1BS.
Open 10-5. STOCK: *Furniture, silver, jewellery.* SIZE: 20 dealers.

TEL: 01306 886336
E-MAIL: enquiries@surreyhillsantiques.co.uk

West Street Antiques
63 West St. RH4 1BS. (J.G. Spooner, R.A. Ratner and P.J. Spooner)
EST. 1986. Open 9.30-1 and 2.15-5.30. STOCK: *Arms and armour, 17th-19th C, £500-£30,000; paintings.* LOC: A25, one-way system. SER: Sales on commission; valuations. SIZE: Medium. PARK: Nearby. VAT: Spec.
FAIRS: Park Lane Arms Fair; Windsor Arms Fair.
TEL: 01306 883487; FAX: same; HOME: 01306 730182 or 01372 452877
E-MAIL: weststant@aol.com
WEBSITE: www.antiquearmsandarmour.com

The Westcott Gallery
4 Guildford Rd., Westcott. RH4 3NR. (Anthony Wakefield)
EST. 1989. Open by appointment only. STOCK: *Specialist in contemporary paintings and ceramics by Surrey artists.* LOC: Village centre, opposite the green.
TEL: 01306 734100/876261; FAX: 01306 740770
E-MAIL: info@westcottgallery.co.uk
WEBSITE: www.westcottgallery.co.uk

DUNSFOLD

Antique Buildings Ltd
GU8 4NP. (Peter Barker)
EST. 1975. Resident. Open daily, Sat. and Sun. by appointment. STOCK: *Oak timbers, 17th C, £25-£1,000; architectural items, 15th-18th C, £25-£500; barn frames, 17th C, £2,000-£50,000.* LOC: From Sun public house, 500 yards down Alfold road, row of white posts on left-hand side, premises up tarmac drive between last two. SER: Valuations; restorations (ancient oak framed buildings); buys at auction (buildings and architectural items). SIZE: Large. PARK: Easy. VAT: Stan.
TEL: 01483 200477

EAST MOLESEY

The Bothy
53 Bridge Rd., Hampton Court. KT8 9ER. (Hannah Jones)
EST. 2005. Open 10-6, Sat. 10.30-5.30, Sun. 11-5. CL: Mon. STOCK: *French antique furniture; Edwardian and Victorian furniture and decorative items, soft furnishings.* LOC: 5 mins. walk from Hampton Court rail station, 10 mins from the Palace. SIZE: Medium. PARK: Easy. VAT: Stan.
TEL: 020 8783 0595
E-MAIL: info@the-bothy.co.uk
WEBSITE: www.the-bothy.co.uk

Bridge Road Antiques Centre
77 Bridge Rd., Hampton Court. KT8 9HH.
Open 10.30-5.30, Sun. 12-5. CL: Mon. STOCK: *18th to early 20th C furniture, silver, ceramics, glass, prints,*

jewellery, decorative antiques and retro design. LOC: Turn down Creek Rd., opposite Hampton Court station, into Bridge Rd. SIZE: 8 dealers.
TEL: 020 8979 7954

Hampton Court Emporium
52-54 Bridge Rd., Hampton Court. KT8 9HA. (A.J. Smith)
EST. 1992. Bridge Road Traders. Open 10-5.30, Sun 11-5.30. *STOCK: Furniture, paintings, silver, jewellery, mirrors, books, clocks, brass and copper, objets d'art, lamps, china and porcelain, collectors' cameras, Art Deco.* LOC: Corner of Bridge Rd and Creek Rd, nr. Hampton Court Palace/Bridge and station. SER: Valuations; restorations. SIZE: Medium. PARK: Palace Rd. station.
TEL: 020 8941 8876
E-MAIL: info@surreyandbucksantiques.co.uk
WEBSITE: www.surreyandbucksantiques.co.uk

London Taxidermy
144A Bridge Rd. KT8 9HW.
EST. 1992. Open by appointment only. *STOCK: Victorian and Edwardian natural history and taxidermy and associated curiosities, pre-1945, £10-£10,000.* LOC: Near Hampton Court Palace. SIZE: Small. PARK: In road opposite. VAT: Margin.
TEL: Mobile: 07770 880960
E-MAIL: info@londontaxidermy.com
WEBSITE: www.londontaxidermy.com

ELSTEAD

Honeypot Antiques Ltd
Milford Rd. GU8 6HP.
EST. 2002. Open 10-5, Sun. 11-5. *STOCK: Furniture, books, paintings, prints, tools, jewellery, silver, boxes, lighting, china, architectural fittings, telephones and clocks.* LOC: Main road. SIZE: Medium. PARK: Easy.
TEL: 01252 703614
E-MAIL: sales@honeypotantiques.co.uk
WEBSITE: www.honeypotantiques.co.uk

EPSOM

Vandeleur Antiquarian Books
6 Seaforth Gdns., Stoneleigh. KT19 0NR. (E.H. Bryant)
EST. 1971. PBFA. Open by appointment. *STOCK: Antiquarian and secondhand books on all subjects, including Africana, big game hunting and mountaineering; prints including rowing, and maps; Indian Mogul-style paintings.* SER: Subject lists quoted on request. VAT: Stan. FAIRS: Various book.
TEL: 020 8393 7752; FAX: same

EWELL

J.W. McKenzie
12 Stoneleigh Park Rd. KT19 0QT.
EST. 1971. Appointment advisable. *STOCK: Old and new books and memorabilia on cricket.*
TEL: 020 8393 7700
E-MAIL: mckenziecricket@btconnect.com

FARNHAM

Annie's Antiques
1 Ridgway Parade, Frensham Rd. GU9 8UZ.
EST. 1982. Open 9.30-5.30, Fri. 10.30-5.30, Sun. by appointment. *STOCK: Furniture, bric-a-brac, jewellery, 19th to early 20th C, £5-£1,000; general antiques.* LOC: 1 mile out of Farnham on A287 towards Hindhead. SIZE: Medium. PARK: Easy.
TEL: 01252 713447; HOME: 01252 723217

The Antiques Warehouse
Badshot Farm, St George's Rd., Runfold. GU9 9HR. (Hilary Burroughs)
EST. 1995. Open 10-5.30, including Sun. *STOCK: Furniture, 17th C to 1940s, £75-£10,000; china, glass, silver, jewellery, paintings, prints and interesting collectables, 18th C to 1960s, £5-£2,000.* LOC: A31 from Farnham towards Guildford, 1st exit (signed Runfold), left at end of slip road towards Badshot Lea, premises 200 yards on left. SER: Restorations (furniture); shipping; gilding. SIZE: Large - 2 barns, 30 dealers. PARK: Own large.
TEL: 01252 317590
WEBSITE: www.theantiqueswarehouse.com.

Bourne Mill Antiques
39-43 Guildford Rd. GU9 9PY. (G. Evans)
EST. 1960. Open 9.30-5 including Sun. *STOCK: Antique and reproduction furniture in oak, walnut, mahogany, yew and pine; china, glass, pictures, jewellery, fireplaces, beds, kitchenalia, bespoke furniture, collectors' items, books, bric-a-brac; garden ornaments, furniture and buildings.* LOC: Eastern outskirts of Farnham. SER: Shipping. SIZE: Large - 85 dealers. PARK: Own.
TEL: 01252 716663

Casque and Gauntlet Militaria
55/59 Badshot Lea Rd., Badshot Lea. GU9 9LP. (R. and A. Colt)
EST. 1957. Open 11-5. *STOCK: Militaria, arms, armour.* LOC: A324 Aldershot to Farnham road. SER: Restorations (metals); re-gilding. SIZE: Large. PARK: Easy.
TEL: 01252 320745
E-MAIL: rayko37@msn.com

Christopher's Antiques
Penn Croft, Crondall. GU10 5PX. (Christopher and Sheila Booth)
EST. 1972. Resident. Open 8-4.30, weekends by appointment. *STOCK: French country furniture.* LOC: From Guildford on the A31, turn right at second roundabout. SER: Restorations (furniture); French polishing. SIZE: Large. PARK: Own - 20 spaces. VAT: Stan/Spec.

TEL: 01252 713794
E-MAIL: cbooth7956@aol.com
WEBSITE: www.christopherantiques.com

Heytesbury Antiques LAPADA
PO Box 222. GU10 5HN. (Ivor and Sally Ingall)
EST. 1974. Open by appointment. STOCK: 18th-19th C
Continental and English furniture, statuary, bronzes and
decorative items, £1,000-£15,000. LOC: 5 miles west of
Farnham. SIZE: Medium. VAT: Spec.
TEL: 01252 850893; FAX: 0870 0515724; MOBILE:
07836 675727
E-MAIL: ingall@heytesbury.demon.co.uk

Karel Weijand Fine BADA LAPADA
Oriental Carpets
Lion and Lamb Courtyard. GU9 7LL.
EST. 1975. BIDA. Open 9.30-5.30. STOCK: Fine antique
and contemporary Oriental rugs and carpets, from £150.
LOC: Off West St. SER: Valuations; restorations;
cleaning. SIZE: Large. PARK: Easy. VAT: Stan/Spec.
FAIRS: BADA; LAPADA; Chelsea.
TEL: 01252 726215; FAX: 01252 737379
E-MAIL: carpets@karelweijand.com
WEBSITE: www.karelweijand.com

GODALMING

Heath-Bullocks BADA
**8 Meadrow. GU7 3HN. (Roger, Mary and Charlotte
Heath-Bullock)**
EST. 1926. Open 10-4.30. STOCK: English and
Continental furniture. LOC: A3100. From Guildford on
the left side approaching Godalming. SER: Valuations;
restorations. SIZE: Large. PARK: Own.
TEL: 01483 422562
E-MAIL: heathbullocks@aol.com
WEBSITE: www.heath-bullocks.com and
www.antiquescare.com and www.sheridanwolf.com

Priory Antiques
29 Church St. GU7 1EL. (P. Rotchell)
Open 10-4. CL: Mon./Wed. STOCK: General antiques.
TEL: 01483 421804

GOMSHALL

The Coach House Antiques
60 Station Rd. GU5 9NP. (P.W. and L. Reeves)
EST. 1985. Resident. Open Weds-Sat 12-5. STOCK:
Longcase clocks, 1780 to 19th C, £4,000-£20,000; furniture,
1790 to late 19th C, £1,000-£20,000. LOC: Between
Guildford and Dorking on the Shere by-pass. SER:
Restorations (clocks and furniture). SIZE: Medium.
PARK: Easy. VAT: Spec.
TEL: 01483 203838; FAX: 01483 202999
E-MAIL: info@coachhouseantiques.com
WEBSITE: www.coachhouseantiques.com

GUILDFORD

Cry for the Moon
17 Tunsgate. GU1 3QT. (Jonathan Owen and Harry
Diamond)
EST. 1977. Open 10-5.30. STOCK: Mainly jewellery, £30-
£50,000; silver and objets d'art. LOC: Town centre. SER:
Valuations; repairs; jewellery commissions undertaken.
SIZE: Medium. PARK: On street. VAT: Stan/Margin.
TEL: 01483 306600

Horological Workshops BADA
204 Worplesdon Rd. GU2 9UY. (M.D. Tooke)
EST. 1968. BHI. Open Tues.-Fri. 8.30-5.30, Sat. 9-
12.30 or by appointment. STOCK: Clocks, watches,
barometers. LOC: On A322 two miles from centre of
Guildford. SER: Restorations; collection and delivery.
SIZE: Large. PARK: Easy.
TEL: 01483 576496; FAX: 01483 452212
E-MAIL: enquiries@horologicalworkshops.com
WEBSITE: www.horologicalworkshops.com

HASLEMERE

Surrey Clock Centre
3 Lower St. GU27 2NY. (J.P. Ingrams and S. Haw)
EST. 1962. Open 9-1 and 2-5. STOCK: Clocks and
barometers. SER: Restorations; hand-made parts; shipping
orders; clocks made to order. SIZE: Large. PARK: Easy.
VAT: Stan/Spec.
TEL: 01428 651313
WEBSITE: www.surreyclockcentre.co.uk

HINDHEAD

Albany Antiques Ltd
8-10 London Rd. GU26 6AF. (T. Winstanley)
EST. 1965. Open 9-6. CL: Sun. except by appointment.
STOCK: Furniture, 17th-18th C, £20-£400; china including
Chinese, £5-£400; metalware, £7-£50; both 18th-19th C. NOT
STOCKED: Silver. LOC: A3. PARK: Easy. VAT: Stan/Spec.
TEL: 01428 605528.

Drummonds Architectural Antiques
The Kirkpatrick Buildings, 25 London Rd. GU26 6AB.
EST. 1988. SALVO. Open 9-6, Sat. 10-5. STOCK:
Architectural and decorative antiques, garden statuary and
furniture, period bathrooms, reclaimed flooring, door
furniture, fire surrounds. LOC: West side of A3, 50 yards
north of traffic lights. SER: Restorations (stonework and
gates); handmade cast-iron baths and fittings; vitreous
re-enamelling of baths. SIZE: Large. PARK: Own. VAT:
Stan/Spec.
TEL: 01428 609444; FAX: 01428 609445
E-MAIL: sales@drummonds-arch.co.uk
WEBSITE: www.drummonds-arch.co.uk

KEW GREEN

Andrew Davis
6 Mortlake Terrace. TW9 3DT.
(Andrew and Glynis Davis)
EST. 1969. Resident. Open most days or by appointment.
STOCK: *Mainly pictures – oil, watercolours and prints, 18th–20th C; decorative and functional items including furniture, ceramics, glass, clocks, garden and architectural items, £10–£5,000.* LOC: South end of Kew Green on South Circular Rd. SER: Valuations and advice; practical assistance with administration of estates for trustees and executors, from fine art to disposal of residual effects. SIZE: Small. PARK: Easy - side road or Kew Green.
TEL: 020 8948 4911

KINGSTON-UPON-THAMES

Glencorse Antiques   LAPADA
321 Richmond Rd., Ham Parade, Ham Common. KT2 5QU. (M. Igel and B.S. Prydal)
EST. 1983. Open 10-5.30. CL: Mon. STOCK: *18th-19th C furniture; traditional modern British art, oils and watercolours, 20th-21st C.* PARK: Own. FAIRS: LAPADA Objects of Desire.
TEL: 020 8541 0871 and 020 7229 6770
E-MAIL: paintings@manyaigelfinearts.com
WEBSITE: www.manyaigelfinearts.com

Glydon & Guess Ltd
14 Apple Market. KT1 1JE.
EST. 1940. NAG. GMC. Open 9.30-5. STOCK: *Jewellery, small silver, £100-£5,000.* LOC: Town centre. SER: Valuations; restorations.
TEL: 020 8546 3758

Kingston Antique Market
29-31 Old London Rd. KT2 6ND.
EST. 1995. Open 10-6, Sat. 9.30-6, Sun. 10-5. STOCK: *General antiques including period furniture, porcelain, collectables and jewellery.* LOC: Off Clarence St. SIZE: 100 dealers. PARK: Easy. FAIRS: Newark; Ardingly; Shepton Mallet.
TEL: 020 8549 2004

NEW MALDEN

Coombe Antiques
25 Coombe Rd. KT3 4PX. (Sandra Sephton)
EST. 1985. Open 10-5.30. STOCK: *Georgian, Victorian and Edwardian furniture including chests of drawers, bookcases and wardrobes, to £1,200; cutlery, china, glass and jewellery.* SER: Restorations. SIZE: Large. PARK: Easy. FAIRS: Kempton Park Antique Market.
TEL: 020 8949 4238; MOBILE: 07970 718214
E-MAIL: sandrasephton@hotmail.co.uk

OXTED

Secondhand Bookshop
27 Station Rd. West. RH8 9EU. (David Neal)
EST. 1985. Open 10-5. STOCK: *Books, 18th C to present day, £1-£500.* LOC: Adjacent to station. SER: Valuations; buys at auction (books). SIZE: Small. VAT: Stan. FAIRS: Book - in south-east.
TEL: 01883 715755; HOME: 01883 723131.

REDHILL

F.G. Lawrence & Sons
(Rear of) 89 Brighton Rd. RH1 6PS. (Chris Lawrence)
EST. 1891. Open 9-5, Sat. 9-1. STOCK: *1920s, Edwardian, Victorian, Georgian and reproduction furniture.* LOC: A23. SER: Valuations; restorations. SIZE: Large. PARK: Own. VAT: Stan. FAIRS: Newark.
TEL: 01737 764196; FAX: 01737 240446
E-MAIL: fglawrence@btinternet.com

Mark J. West   BADA
Cobb Antiques. PO Box 595. RH1 3XB.
Open by appointment. STOCK: *Large stock of 18th-20th C table glass; selection of South East Asian pottery.* FAIRS: Olympia (Jun/Nov); BADA (March); Grosvenor House; New York; Palm Beach; Chicago; Baltimore.
TEL: 01737 643646
E-MAIL: westglass@aol.com
WEBSITE: www.markwest-glass.com
www.maitrading.co.uk

REIGATE

Bourne Gallery Ltd   BADA LAPADA
31/33 Lesbourne Rd. RH2 7JS. (John Robertson)
EST. 1970. Open 10-1 and 2-5. CL: Mon. STOCK: *19th-20th C oils and watercolours, £250-£50,000; contemporary works, £250-£5,000.* LOC: Side street. SIZE: Large. PARK: Easy. VAT: Spec. FAIRS: Olympia; Chelsea; Watercolours & Drawings.
TEL: 01737 241614; FAX: 01737 223291
E-MAIL: bournegallery@aol.com
WEBSITE: www.bournegallery.com

Cohen & Cohen   BADA
P.O. Box 366. RH2 2BB. (Ewa and Michael Cohen)
EST. 1973. TEFAF. Open by appointment only. STOCK: *Chinese export porcelain and works of art.* LOC: Betchworth, Surrey (30 mins. from London Victoria to Redhill). SER: Valuation, buys at auction. SIZE: Large. PARK: Easy. VAT: Stan/Spec. FAIRS: New York Ceramics; Palm Beach; Maastricht; Seafair.
TEL: 01737 242180; FAX: 01737 226236
E-MAIL: info@cohenandcohen.co.uk
WEBSITE: www.cohenandcohen.co.uk

Bertram Noller (Reigate)
14a London Rd. RH2 9HY. (A.M. Noller)

EST. 1970. Open Tues., Thurs., Sat. 9.30-1 and 2-5.30.
STOCK: *Collectors' items, furniture, grates, fenders, mantels, copper, brass, glass, pewter, £1-£500.* LOC: West side of one-way traffic system. Opposite Upper West St. car park. SER: Valuations; restorations (furniture, clocks, bronzes, brass and copper, marble). SIZE: Small. PARK: Opposite.
TEL: 01737 242548

RICHMOND

The Gooday Gallery
14 Richmond Hill. TW10 6QX. (Debbie Gooday)
EST. 1971. Open Thurs.-Sat. 11-5 or any time by appointment. STOCK: *Decorative and applied design, 1880-1980, Arts and Crafts, Art Nouveau, Art Deco, furniture, pictures, ceramics, metalwork, jewellery; African and Oceanic tribal artefacts; 1950s and 1960s designer items, all £100-£5,000.* LOC: 100yds. from Richmond Bridge. SER: Valuations; buys at auction. SIZE: Medium. PARK: Easy.
TEL: 020 8940 8652; MOBILE: 07710 124540
E-MAIL: goodaygallery@aol.com
WEBSITE: www.thegoodaygallery.com

Roland Goslett Gallery
139 Kew Rd. TW9 2PN.
EST. 1974. Open Thurs. and Fri. 10-6, Sat. 10-2 or by appointment. STOCK: *English watercolours and oil paintings, 19th to early 20th C, £100-£5,000.* SER: Valuations; restorations (oils, watercolours and frames); framing. SIZE: Medium. PARK: Meters. VAT: Spec.
TEL: 020 8940 4009
E-MAIL: rolandgoslett@btconnect.com
WEBSITE: www.rolandgoslettgallery.co.uk

Horton   LAPADA
2 Paved Court, The Green. TW9 1LZ. (D. Horton)
EST. 1978. FGA. Open 10-5. STOCK: *Jewellery and silver, 18th-20th C, £500-£5,000.* LOC: Off The Green, behind House of Fraser. SIZE: Small. PARK: Easy.
TEL: 020 8332 1775; FAX: 020 8332 1994
E-MAIL: richmond@hortonlondon.co.uk
WEBSITE: www.hortonlondon.co.uk

F. and T. Lawson Antiques
13 Hill Rise. TW10 6UQ.
EST. 1965. Resident. Open 10-5.30, Sat. 10-5. CL: Wed. and Sun. am. STOCK: *Furniture, 1680-1870; paintings and watercolours; both £30-£1,500; clocks, 1650-1930, £50-£2,000; bric-a-brac, £5-£300.* LOC: Near Richmond Bridge at bottom of Hill Rise on the river side, overlooking river. SER: Valuations; buys at auction. SIZE: Medium. PARK: Limited and further up Hill Rise.
TEL: 020 8940 0461

Manya Igel Fine Arts   LAPADA
Glencrose, 321 Richmond Rd., Ham Common. KT2 5QU. (M. Igel and B.S. Prydal)
Open 10-5.30 Tues.-Sat. STOCK: *Traditional Modern*

British Art, £250-£25,000. VAT: Spec. FAIRS: 20th/21st C. British Art; Olympia (Spring); Chelsea (Spring); Claridges.
TEL: 020 8541 0871
E-MAIL: paintings@manyaigelfinearts.com
WEBSITE: www.manyaigelfinearts.com

Marryat   LAPADA
88 Sheen Rd. TW9 1AJ. (Maxine Samuels)
EST. 1990. Open 10-5.30. CL: Mon. STOCK: *English and Continental furniture, watercolours and oils, £100-£5,000; porcelain, pottery, glass, silver, objets and decorative antiques, £2-£1,000; mainly 18th-19th C.* LOC: Follow M3/A316 towards Richmond, first left into Church Rd. then left again. Close to underground station and British Rail. SER: Restorations. SIZE: Large. PARK: Easy. VAT: Stan/Spec.
TEL: 020 8332 0262
E-MAIL: johnsamuels@tiscali.co.uk
WEBSITE: www.marryat-antiques.co.uk

Vellantiques
127 Kew Rd. TW9 2PN. (Saviour Vella)
EST. 1984. Open 10-6. STOCK: *Furniture, gold and silver, porcelain, paintings and curios, £50-£3,000.* SER: Valuations. SIZE: Medium. FAIRS: Ardingly.
TEL: 020 8940 5392; FAX: same; MOBILE: 07960 897075

RIPLEY

J. Hartley Antiques Ltd   LAPADA
186 High St. GU23 6BB. (Joe and John Hartley)
EST. 1949. Open 9.15-6, Sat. 9.45-4.45. STOCK: *Queen Anne, Georgian and Edwardian furniture.* LOC: Next to Talbot Hotel. SIZE: Medium. VAT: Stan.
TEL: 01483 224318.

Sage Antiques and Interiors   LAPADA
High St. GU23 6BB. (H. and C. Sage)
EST. 1971. GMC. Open 9.30-5.30. STOCK: *Furniture, mahogany, oak, walnut, 1600-1900, £150-£8,000; oil paintings, £100-£5,000; watercolours, £50-£1,000, china, £2-£500, all 18th-19th C; silver, Sheffield plate, brass, pewter, decorative items, 18th-19th C, £50-£1,000.* LOC: Village centre, on main road. SER: Restorations (furniture); interior furnishing. SIZE: Large. PARK: Easy. VAT: Stan.
TEL: 01483 224396; FAX: 01483 211996

Sweerts de Landas   BADA
Dunsborough Park, Newark Lane. GU23 6AL. (A.J.H. and A.C. Sweerts de Landas)
EST. 1979. SALVO. Open by appointment. STOCK: *Garden ornaments and statuary, 17th-20th C, £500-£250,000.* LOC: From High St. turn into Newark Lane (between estate agent and Suzuki garage), continue 400 yards, through archway on right, follow drive to gate. SER: Valuations; restorations (stone, lead, cast

iron, marble); buys at auction (as stock). SIZE: Large.
PARK: Easy. VAT: Stan/Spec.
TEL: **01483 225366**; HOME: same
E-MAIL: **info@sweerts.com**

Talbot Walk Antique Centre
The Talbot Hotel, High St. GU23 6BB. (I. and J. Picken)
EST. 1999. Open 10-5, Sun. and BH 11.30-4.30. *STOCK:
English furniture, 1750-1930, £50-£5,000+; glass and
ceramics, 1800-1940, £10-£3,000+; lighting, 1850-1940,
£50-£2,000+; general antiques including mirrors and clocks,
£10-£1,000+.* LOC: 1 mile south of A3/M25, junction
10, take the B2215 to Ripley, 400yds on left after
entering village. SIZE: Large - 40 dealers. PARK: Own at
rear. VAT: Stan/Spec.
TEL: 01483 211724; FAX: same
E-MAIL: sales@talbotwalkantiques.com
WEBSITE: www.talbotwalkantiques.com

Below are listed some of the dealers at this centre.

Jane Aspinall
*English furniture, 1800-1920; upholstery, lighting and
decorative items.*
E-MAIL: interiors@janeaspinall.com
WEBSITE: www.janeaspinall.com

Patricia Caswell
Antique furniture, mirrors and decorative items.

Claret Antiques and Interiors Ltd.
Decorative furniture and objects.
E-MAIL: portico1@btconnect.com

P. Crowder
Prints and maps.

Maura Dorrington
Victorian furniture, pictures and silver.
E-MAIL: mauradorrington@hotmail.com

Draper Antiques
(Dave and Sheena Draper) TVADA. *Victorian, Edwardian
and 1920's dining room furniture.*
TEL: 01483 211724; MOBILE: 07768 213491
WEBSITE: www.chairs4u2.com

Every Cloud
(A. Machen) *Furniture, jewellery, glass and decorative
antiques.*
E-MAIL: andrea@rietveld.freeserve.co.uk

Colleen Francis
French country copper, kitchenalia and decorative items.
E-MAIL: colleencosta@hotmail.com

Deidre Geer
Decorative French provincial antiques and mirrors.

F. Green
Victorian and Edwardian furniture and objects.

The Hayloft Antiques
(N. Thomas) *Antique furniture and mirrors 1800-1930.*

Nick Hill
19th C furniture and works of art.

Laleham Antiques
Furniture and decorative objects.

The Lamp Gallery
(Graham Jones) *Interior lighting, 1860-1940 including Arts
& Crafts and Art Deco and Art Nouveau.*
TEL: 01903 884712
E-MAIL: jacksprat.jones@virgin.net

H. Loveland
19th C European ceramics and glass.

Carol Martin
Victorian furniture and objects.

Valerie Swan
Silver, jewellery and general antiques.

Times Tables
*Late 18th - early 20th C furniture, watercolours, silver and
objects.*
E-MAIL: bernardheyes@btconnect.com

Anthony Welling Antiques   BADA
Broadway Barn, High St. GU23 6AQ.
**EST. 1970. Open 9.30-1 and 2-5. Sun. and evenings by
appointment. STOCK: English oak, 17th-18th C, £250-
£8,000; country furniture, 18th C, £200-£6,000; brass,
copper, pewter, 18th C, £100-£750. NOT STOCKED: Glass,
china, silver. LOC: Turn off A3 at Ripley, shop in village
centre on service road. SER: Restoration (furniture).
SIZE: Medium. PARK: Easy. VAT: Spec.
TEL: 01483 225384; FAX: same
E-MAIL: ant@awelling.freeserve.co.uk
WEBSITE: www.anthonywellingantiques.com**

RUNFOLD

The Packhouse
Hewetts Kilns, Tongham Rd. GU10 1PQ.
(A.J. Hougham)
EST. 1991. Open 10.30-5.30, Sat. and Sun. 10-5.30.
*STOCK: Furniture including period, 1930s, country pine,
Gustavian, French shabby chic; garden statuary, architectural
items.* LOC: Off A31 (Hogs Back). SER: UK delivery
SIZE: Large. PARK: Free on site.
TEL: 01252 781010; FAX: 01252 783876
E-MAIL: info@packhouse.com
WEBSITE: www.packhouse.com

SHERE

Helena's Collectables
Shops 1 and 2, Middle St. GU5 9HF. (Mrs K. White
and Mrs H. Lee)
EST. 1995. Open 9.30-4.30, Sat. 10-4.30. *STOCK: Royal
Doulton, from 1930s, £100-£2,500; Beswick, from 1950s,
from £50+; Walt Disney classics, Border Fine Art, Bunnykins
and Beatrix Potter, Royal Crown Derby.* LOC: A24. SER:
Valuations; restorations; search; buys at auction. SIZE:
Medium. PARK: Behind sports ground. VAT: Stan. FAIRS:
DMG.

TEL: 01483 203039; FAX: same
E-MAIL: helen@helenascollectables.com
WEBSITE: www.helenascollectables.com

Shere Antiques
(Jean Watson)
EST. 1986. Open by appointment. *STOCK: Small
decorative furniture pre-1900, decorative items and ceramics.*
VAT: Stan/Spec.
TEL: 01483 205082
E-MAIL: jeanwatson@shereantiques.com
WEBSITE: www.shereantiques.com

STAINES

K.W. Dunster Antiques
23 Church St. TW18 4EN. (Keith and Cynthia
Dunster)
EST. 1972. Open 9-4.30. CL: Thurs. *STOCK: Clocks,
furniture, general antiques, interior décor, jewellery, nautical
items.* SER: Valuations. SIZE: Medium. PARK: Easy. VAT:
Stan/Spec.
TEL: 01784 453297; FAX: 01784 483146
E-MAIL: kdunsterantiques@aol.com

Clive Rogers Oriental Rugs
PO Box 234. TW19 5PE.
EST. 1974. PADA. Open by appointment. *STOCK:
Oriental rugs, carpets, textiles; Near and Central Asian and
Islamic works of art.* LOC: On B376, 15 mins. from
Terminal Five Heathrow Airport. SER: Valuations;
restorations (as stock); historical analysis commission
agents; buys at auction. SIZE: Medium. PARK: Own.
VAT: Stan/Spec. FAIRS: ICOC; Hali; San Francisco
(Caskey Lees), ACOR.
TEL: 01784 481177/481100; FAX: 01784 481144
E-MAIL: info@orient-rug.com
WEBSITE: www.orient-rug.com

SURBITON

Cockrell Antiques
278 Ewell Rd. KT6 7AG. (Sheila and Peter Cockrell)
EST. 1982. Resident. Open most Fri., Sat., Sun. and
evenings, prior telephone call advisable. *STOCK: Furniture
including Art Deco, from 19th C, up to £5,000; decorative
items, £50-£5,000.* LOC: Off A3 at Tolworth Tower on
A240. SIZE: Medium. PARK: Easy. VAT: Stan/Spec.
TEL: 020 8390 8290; HOME: same
E-MAIL: antiques@cockrell.co.uk
WEBSITE: www.cockrell.co.uk

B. M. and E. Newlove
139-141 Ewell Rd. KT6 6AL.
EST. 1958. Open by appointment. *STOCK: Furniture
especially early oak and Georgian mahogany, 17th-19th C,
£500-£10,000; china, 18th-19th C, £75-£200; paintings,
all periods, £50-£2,000; longcase clocks, Georgian
barometers. NOT STOCKED: Pot-lids, fairings.* LOC: Down

Kingston by-pass at Tolworth underpass, turn right into
Tolworth Broadway, then into Ewell Rd., store at rear 1
mile. SER: Gilding. PARK: Easy. VAT: Stan/Spec.
TEL: 020 8399 8857; MOBILE: 07879 823502.

Laurence Tauber Antiques
131 Ewell Rd. KT6 6AL.
Open 10-5. CL: Wed. pm. *STOCK: General antiques,
especially lighting, mainly for Trade.* PARK: Easy. VAT:
Stan/Spec.
TEL: 020 8390 0020; MOBILE: 07710 443293

SUTTON

S. Warrender and Co
4 and 6 Cheam Rd. SM1 1SR. (F.R. Warrender)
EST. 1947. NAG. Open 9-5.30. *STOCK: Jewellery, 1790 to
date, £10-£10,000; silver, 1762 to date, £10-£1,000;
carriage clocks, 1860-1900, £115-£800.* SER: Valuations;
restorations (jewellery, silver, quality clocks). SIZE:
Medium. VAT: Stan.
TEL: 020 8643 4381
E-MAIL: info@warrenders.co.uk
WEBSITE: www.warrenders.co.uk

THAMES DITTON

Clifford and Roger Dade
Boldre House, Weston Green. KT7 0JP.
EST. 1937. Resident. Open 9.30-6. *STOCK: Mahogany
furniture, 18th to early 19th C, £500-£5,000.* LOC: A309
between Esher and Hampton Court, near Sandown Park
Racecourse. SIZE: Large. PARK: Outside shop. VAT:
Spec.
TEL: 020 8398 6293; FAX: same; MOBILE: 07932 158949

TWICKENHAM

Williams and Son
1c Royal Parade, Kew Gardens. TW9 3QD (John
Williams)
EST. 1931. By appointment only. *STOCK: British and
European paintings, 19th-20th C.* LOC: 3 mins. from Kew
Gardens station. SIZE: Medium. PARK: Free after 11 am.
VAT: Stan./Spec.
TEL: 020 8940 7333; FAX: same
E-MAIL: art@williamsandson.com
WEBSITE: www.williamsandson.com

WALDINGHAM

Arundel Bridge Antiques
Fairdene, High Drive. CR3 7ED.
EST. 1987. Open 10-5, 10.30-5 Sun. *STOCK: General
antiques; cameras.* LOC: Central Arundel. SIZE: Large -
34 dealers.
TEL: 01903 884164
E-MAIL: info@arundelantiques.co.uk
WEBSITE: www.arundelantiques.co.uk

WALTON-ON-THAMES

Antique Church Furnishings

Rivernook Farm, Sunnyside. KT12 2ET. (L. Skilling and S. Williams)

EST. 1989. Open 10-6. CL: Sat. STOCK: *Church chairs and pews, £10-£750; altar tables and screens, pulpits, lecterns, reredos, pine and architectural items, £20-£2,000; all late 19th C to early 20th C.* LOC: Between A3050 and River Thames. SER: Valuations; buys at auction (church fixtures and furnishings, stained glass). SIZE: Large. PARK: Easy. VAT: Stan/Spec.
TEL: 01932 252736; FAX: same
E-MAIL: info@churchantiques.com
WEBSITE: www.churchantiques.com

S. & H. Jewell

17 Wolsey Dr. KT12 3AY. (Geoffrey Boyes Korkis)

EST. 1830. Open by appointment. STOCK: *Small and decorative furniture.* SER: Valuations; restorations; finder. VAT: Stan/Spec.
TEL: 01932 222690; MOBILE: 07973 406255
E-MAIL: geoff@bkwalton.freeserve.co.uk

WEST BYFLEET

Academy Billiard Company

5 Camphill Industrial Estate. KT14 6EW. (R.W. Donnachie)

EST. 1975. Open any time by appointment. STOCK: *Period and antique billiard/snooker tables, all sizes, 1830-1920; combined billiard/dining tables, period accessories including other games-room equipment and lighting.* LOC: On A245, 2 miles from M25/A3 junction. SER: Valuations; restorations; removals; structural advice. SIZE: Large warehouse and showroom. PARK: Easy. VAT: Stan/Spec.
TEL: 01932 352067; FAX: 01932 353904; MOBILE: 07860 523757
E-MAIL: academygames@fsbdial.co.uk
WEBSITE: www.games-room.com

WEYBRIDGE

Brocante

120 Oatlands Drive, Oatlands Village. KT13 9HL. (Barry Dean and Ray Gwilliams)

EST. 1988. Open 10-4. CL: Mon. & Wed. STOCK: *Furniture, 19th C, £300-£1,500; porcelain, 19th C, £10-£250; Sheffield plate, 18th-19th C, £10-£300; silver 1750-1950.* SER: Valuations. SIZE: Small. PARK: Easy.
TEL: 01932 857807; HOME: 01932 345524
E-MAIL: raymond@raywilliams.co.uk
WEBSITE: www.brocanteantiques.co.uk

Church House Antiques

42 Church St. KT13 8DP. (M.I. Foster)

EST. 1886. Open 10-5.30. CL: Mon.-Wed. STOCK: *Furniture, 18th-19th C, £95-£7,000; jewellery, 18th-19th C, some modern, £30-£5,000; pictures, silver, plate, decorative items including modern.* NOT STOCKED: *Coins and stamps.* LOC: Main road through Weybridge. SIZE: Medium. PARK: Behind library. VAT: Stan/Spec.
TEL: 01932 842190
E-MAIL: churchhouseantiques@supanet.com

Edward Cross Fine Paintings

128 Oatlands Drive. KT13 9HL.

EST. 1973. Open Fri. 10-1, Sat. 10-12. STOCK: *Fine paintings and bronzes, 18th-20th C, £500-£20,000.* LOC: A3050. SER: Valuations; restorations (watercolours and oil paintings); buys at auction (pictures). SIZE: Medium. PARK: Opposite. VAT: Spec.
TEL: 01932 851093

Not Just Silver

16 York Rd. KT13 9DT. (Mrs S. Hughes)

EST. 1969. BJA. NAG. Open 9.30-6, Sun. by appointment. STOCK: *Silver, Georgian to modern.* LOC: Opposite car park, just off Queens Rd. SER: Valuations; repairs; silver plating. PARK: Opposite.
TEL: 01932 842468; FAX: 01932 830054;
MOBILE: 07774 298151
E-MAIL: info@not-just-silver.com
WEBSITE: www.not-just-silver.com

Willow Gallery   BADA LAPADA

75 Queens Rd. KT13 9UQ. (Andrew and Jean Stevens and Alick Forrester)

EST. 1987. Open 10-6, Sun. by appointment. STOCK: **British and European fine oil paintings, 19th C onwards, £10,000+. Also has a showroom at 40 Duke St., London.** LOC: **Near town centre.** SER: **Restorations; conservation; framing; catalogue available; purchases fine paintings.** SIZE: **Large.** PARK: **Easy and nearby.** VAT: **Spec.** FAIRS: **London, Harrogate and internationally - contact for tickets.**
TEL: **01932 846095/6**
E-MAIL: **enquiries@willowgallery.com**
WEBSITE: **www.willowgallery.com**

WOKING

Bakers of Maybury Ltd

42 Arnold Rd. GU21 5JU. (Keith Baker)

Open 9-4.30. CL: Mon. & Tues. STOCK: *General antiques.* SER: Clearances or single items purchased. PARK: Easy.
TEL: 01483 767425

DESIGN: Festival of Britain 1951
Paul Rennie

Inspired by the Great Exhibition of 1851, the Festival of Britain followed soon after the austerity of the war years. The major events were focused on the twenty-seven-acre bomb site around Waterloo Station, although events happened throughout the UK. The Festival was almost immediately unfashionable amongst commentators. It was viewed with suspicion by political conservatives and quickly dismantled. An establishment orthodoxy quickly emerged that called into question the Festival's objectives. This political ambivalence towards the Festival is confounded by the popularity of the Festival amongst collectors, social historians and anybody interested in post-war British culture and society. This book is the first to present the story of the Festival of Britain, held in 1951, through its souvenirs. These objects were produced to commemorate 'The Tonic to the Nation'. Retrospectively, they testify to the enormous popular appeal of the Festival. *Festival of Britain 1951*, the most recent addition to the popular *Design* series, places these souvenirs and objects into their historical context and explains the continuing appeal of these modest artefacts.

216 x 142 mm. 128 pp 135 col., 20 b.&w. **£14.95 Hardback**

DESIGN: Paul Nash and John Nash
Brian Webb, Peyton Skipwith

The brothers Paul and John Nash, in their very different ways, were a major influence on twentieth century British design. Paul Nash (1889-1946) is now recognised as the most significant war artist of the last century; John Nash (1893-1977) as a plantsman artist. Both worked as designers and as tutors at the Royal College of Art, Paul encouraging a generation of designer artists that included Eric Ravilious, Edward Bawden and Enid Marx. As a committee member of the Design and Industries Association and President of the newly formed Society of Industrial Artists (now the Chartered Society of Designers) Paul promoted design as no less an art form than the fine arts of painting and sculpture. His clients included London Transport, Shell and Curwen Press, and publishers the Nonesuch and Golden Cockerel Presses. John became well known for his Edward Lear influenced humorous illustrations and his superb plant drawings and wood engravings that illustrate innumerable books and publications. *Paul Nash and John Nash: Design* features over 150 illustrations, including graphic design, textile design, ceramics and glass, many not reproduced before. With descriptions by Brian Webb and an introductory essay by Peyton Skipwith.

216 x 142 mm. 96 pp 95 col., 65 b.&w. **£12.50 Hardback**

DESIGN: Lewitt & Him
Ruth Artmonsky

Jan Le Witt and George Him were a comparative rarity, a design duo. Both Polish by birth they arrived in London in 1937, sponsored by the Victoria and Albert Museum and Lund Humphries. They established their reputation for fine poster work in World War II, and for their exhibition work with their much loved Guinness Clock at the Festival of Britain. In Poland their illustrations for 'Locomotiva' helped make it a children's classic and they continued with book illustration throughout their partnership. Of very different temperaments and artistic interests the partnership lasted some twenty years, to 1954, when Le Witt left to develop his career as an artist. Him continued his commitment to graphic design - illustration, exhibitions and general commercial work - most remarkable of which were his witty illustrations marrying Stephen Potter's texts for Schweppes - 'Schweppeshire', one of the longest lasting advertisement campaigns.

216x142mm 96pp 125col **£12.50 Hardback**

For full details of all ACC publications, log on to our website:
www.antiquecollectorsclub.com
or telephone 01394 389950 for a free catalogue

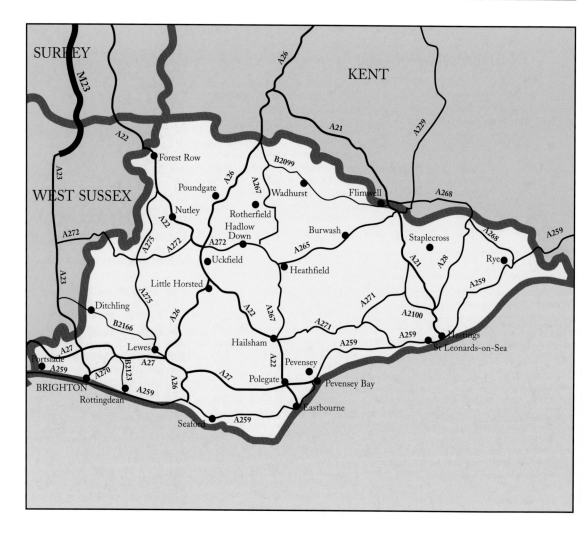

BRIGHTON

Alexandria Antiques

3 Hanover Place, Lewes Rd. BN2 2SD. (A.H. Ahmed)
Est. 1978. Open 9.30-6, Sat. by appointment. *Stock: Georgian and Victorian furniture; Oriental and European porcelain; oil and watercolour paintings; Oriental carpets, objets d'art.* Size: 3 showrooms. Park: Own. VAT: Stan. Fairs: Ardingly; Newark; Sandown.
Tel: 01273 688793; Fax: same
E-mail: alexantiques1@yahoo.co.uk

Brighton Antique Wholesalers

39 Upper Gardner St. BN1 4AN. (George McKechnie)
Open 9-5.30. *Stock: Furniture, from 17th C.* Loc: Off North Rd. Ser: Restorations. Size: Large.
Tel: 01273 695457; Fax: same

Brighton Architectural Salvage

33-34 Gloucester Rd. BN1 4AQ. (R.L. Legendre)
Open Mon.-Sat. 10-5.30 *Stock: Restored architectural items including pine furniture; fireplaces and surrounds in stone, marble, pine, mahogany, cast iron, Victorian tiled and cast inserts and over-mantels; doors, stained glass, panelling; gas coal fires, light fittings; garden seats and ornaments, reclaimed flooring.* Park: NCP 100 yds.
Tel: 01273 681656

Brighton Flea Market

31A Upper St. James's St. BN2 1JN. (A. Wilkinson)
Est. 1990. Open seven days. *Stock: Bric-a-brac, furniture and collectables, 19th-20th C, £5-£1,000.* Loc: 50 yards from coast road, Kemp Town. Size: Large.
Tel: 01273 624006; Mobile: 07884 267194
E-mail: arrw@btinternet.com
Website: www.flea-markets.co.uk

Brighton Lanes Antique Centre

12 Meeting House Lane. BN1 1HB. (Peter Brynin)
Est. 1967. Open 10-5, Sun. 12-4. *Stock: Furniture, clocks, silver, glass, jewellery, lighting, porcelain, watches and bronzes.* Loc: North entrance to The Lanes. Ser:

Valuations; shipping. SIZE: Medium. PARK: Loading bay on site.
TEL: 01273 823121; FAX: 01273 726328
E-MAIL: peter@brightonlanesantiques.co.uk
WEBSITE: www.brightonlanes.antiques.co.uk

C.A.R.S. (Classic Automobilia & Regalia Specialists)
The White Lion Garage, Clarendon Place, Kemp Town. BN2 1JA. (G.G. Weiner and A.P. Gayler)
EST. 1976. Open by appointment only. STOCK: *Collectors' car badges, motoring mascots, René Lalique crystal glass car mascots and figures, selected automobilia along with associated ephemera. Classic and modern pedal and powered children's cars/replica juvenile automobiles of many famous marques from around the world.* SER: SAE for catalogue/price list; mail order suppliers. PARK: Easy. FAIRS: NEC; Alexandra Palace; Ardingly; Brighton Classic Car.
TEL: 01273 622722; FAX: same; MOBILE: 07890 836734
E-MAIL: whiteliongarage@fsmail.net
WEBSITE: www.brmmbrmm.com/pedalcars
www.carsofbrighton.co.uk

Faques Gallery
29 Upper St James's St., BN2 1JN.
EST. 1962. Open 10-5.30. STOCK: *Reproduction oil paintings.* LOC: Kemp Town area. SIZE: Large. PARK: Side roads. VAT: Stan.
TEL: 01273 624432; FAX: 01273 683692

Paul Goble Jewellers
44 Meeting House Lane, The Lanes. BN1 1HB.
EST. 1965. NAG. Open 9-5.30, Sat. 9-6, Sun. 10-6. STOCK: *Jewellery, watches, silver, pictures and prints.* SER: Trade/export; valuations. VAT: Stan/Margin.
TEL: 01273 202801; FAX: 01273 202736
E-MAIL: paulgoble1@yahoo.co.uk

Douglas Hall Ltd
23 Meeting House Lane. BN1 1HB. (K.J. and G.J. Draper)
EST. 1968. Open 9.30-5. STOCK: *Silver, jewellery.* VAT: Stan.
TEL: 01273 325323

Hallmark Jewellers
4 Union St., The Lanes. BN1 1HA. (J. Hersheson)
EST. 1966. Open 9-5. STOCK: *Diamond and gem-set jewellery; antique and modern silver.* SIZE: Small. PARK: Churchill Square and The Lanes car parks. VAT: Stan/Spec.
TEL: 01273 725477; FAX: same

Heritage Antiques BADA LAPADA
PO Box 2974. BN1 3QG. (Anjula Daniel)
EST. 1975. CINOA. Open by appointment. STOCK: *Metalware, £50-£5,000; interesting and decorative items.* SIZE: Large. PARK: Easy. VAT: Stan/Spec. FAIRS: Olympia; BADA.

TEL: 01273 326850; FAX: same; MOBILE: 07802 473422
E-MAIL: ahd@heritage-antiques.com
WEBSITE: www.heritage-antiques.com

The Lanes Armoury
26 Meeting House Lane, The Lanes. BN1 1HB. (Mark and David Hawkins)
EST. 1972. Open 10-5.15. STOCK: *Militaria, arms, especially Japanese samurai swords, armour and books, from 500BC to WWII.* LOC: Centre of the Old Lanes area. SER: Worldwide delivery. SIZE: Medium. PARK: By arrangement. VAT: Spec.
TEL: 01273 321357
E-MAIL: mail@thelanearmoury.co.uk
WEBSITE: www.thelanesarmoury.co.uk

Leoframes
70 North Rd. BN1 1YD. (S. Round)
EST. 1985. Open 9.30-5.20. STOCK: *Prints and maps.* SER: Restorations; framing.
TEL: 01273 695862
E-MAIL: info@leoframes.com

Harry Mason
PO Box 687, Hove. BN3 6JY.
EST. 1954. Open by appointment. STOCK: *Silver and plate, 18th-20th C; jewellery, 19th-20th C.* SER: Valuations; restorations (silver and jewellery); buys at auction (as stock); buyers of scrap silver and gold. VAT: Stan/Spec. FAIRS: Sunday London Hotel.
TEL: 01273 500330; FAX: 01273 553300
E-MAIL: mason@fastnet.co.uk

Patrick Moorhead Antiques
Spring Gardens, 76 Church St. BN1 1RL. (Patrick and Heather Moorhead)
EST. 1984. Open 9.30-5.30, Sat. and other times by appointment. STOCK: *Victorian, Georgian and Continental furniture; Oriental, Continental and English porcelain, clocks, pictures, decorative objects and bronzes.* SER: Collection from local station and Gatwick airport. SIZE: Large trade warehouse. PARK: Large car park. VAT: Stam./Spec.
TEL: 01273 779696; FAX: 01273 220196
E-MAIL: info@patrickmoorhead.co.uk

Michael Norman Antiques Ltd BADA
61 Holland Rd., Hove. BN3 1JN. (Michael P. Keehan)
EST. 1965. Open 9-1 and 2-5.30, other times by appointment. STOCK: *18th-19th C English furniture.* LOC: Close to station and seafront. SER: Restorations; upholstery. PARK: Easy. VAT: Spec.
TEL: 01273 329253 or 01273 326712; FAX: 01273 206556
E-MAIL: armonando.fava@btconnect.com
WEBSITE: www.michaelnorman.com

The North Laine Antiques Market, incorporating Alan Fitchett Antiques
5-5A Upper Gardner St. BN1 4AN. (Alan and Heidi Fitchett)
EST. 1969. Open 10-5.30, Sat. 9-5.30, Sun. 10-4. STOCK:

Furniture, 18th–20th C, £50–£10,000; works of art, silver, ceramics, books, jewellery, paintings, prints, collectables, £1–£2,000. LOC: North Laine (station area). SER: Valuations; restorations. SIZE: Large. PARK: Easy.
TEL: 01273 600894; FAX: same

Odin Antiques
43 Preston St. BN1 2HP. (Audun Sjovold)
EST. 1981. Resident. Open 10.30-5.30. *STOCK: Furniture, 18th–19th C; telescopes, scientific instruments, 19th–20th C, £500–£1,500; maritime instruments, 19th–20th C, £500–£1,000.* LOC: Off Kings Rd. (seafront) near West Pier. SIZE: Medium. PARK: Regency Sq. VAT: Stan/Spec.
TEL: 01273 732738; HOME: same

Colin Page Antiquarian Books
36 Duke St. BN1 1AG. (John Loska)
EST. 1969. Open 9.30-5.30. *STOCK: Antiquarian and secondhand books, especially topography, travel, natural history, illustrated and leather bindings, 16th–20th C, £1–£30,000.* LOC: Town centre. PARK: Multi-storey nearby.
TEL: 01273 325954

Dermot and Jill Palmer Antiques   LAPADA
7-8 Union St., The Lanes. BN1 1HA.
EST. 1968. Resident. Open 9.30-5.30, Sun. by appointment. *STOCK: French and English furniture, objects, pictures, mirrors, screens, garden furniture and ornamental pieces, textiles, £50–£5,000.* **SIZE: Large + warehouse. PARK: NCP. VAT: Stan/Spec. FAIRS: Olympia; Decorative Antiques & Textile.**
TEL: 01273 328669 (2 lines); FAX: 01273 777641
E-MAIL: jillpalmer@jillpalmerantiques.co.uk
WEBSITE: www.jillpalmerantiques.co.uk

Sue Pearson
18 Brighton Square, The Lanes. BN1 1HD.
EST. 1982. Open 10-5 including Sun. *STOCK: Vintage and Steiff teddy bears; antique dolls, dolls' house miniatures.* SER: Valuations; restorations; buys at auction (dolls and bears). SIZE: Large. PARK: NCP. VAT: Stan/Spec. FAIRS: Major London Doll and Bear.
TEL: 01273 329247
WEBSITE: www.sue-pearson.co.uk

Snoopers' Paradise
7-8 Kensington Gardens. BN1 4AL.
Open 10-6, Sun. 11-4. *STOCK: General antiques and collectables.* LOC: North Laines. SIZE: 90 dealers. PARK: Loading.
TEL: 01273 602558
E-MAIL: nic@internetdropshop.co.uk
WEBSITE:
www.northlaine.co.uk/snoopersparadise/snoopers

Wardrobe
51 Upper North St. BN1 3FH. (Clive Parks and Philip Parfitt)
EST. 1984. Open Wed.-Sat. 11-5, other times by

appointment or chance. *STOCK: Vintage clothing, '20s to '50s, £150–£1,500; bakelite, especially jewellery, £20–£300.* SIZE: Small. PARK: Meters. FAIRS: Royal Horticultural Hall, Vincent Square.
TEL: 01273 202201; FAX: same

Yellow Lantern Antiques Ltd   LAPADA
34 & 34B Holland Rd., Hove. BN3 1JL. (B.R. and E.A. Higgins)
EST. 1950. Open 10-1 and 2.15-5.30, Sat. 10-4. *STOCK: Mainly English furniture, £200–£10,000; French and English clocks; both to 1850; bronzes, 19th C, £100–£5,000; Continental porcelain, 1820-1860, £50–£1,000.* **LOC: From Brighton seafront to Hove, turn right after parade of Regency houses, shop 100yds. on left past traffic lights. SER: Valuations; restorations; buys at auction. SIZE: Medium. PARK: Easy. VAT: Spec. FAIRS: Buxton; Harrogate; NEC; Olympia; Chester.**
TEL: 01273 771572; FAX: 01273 455476; MOBILE: 07860 342976
E-MAIL: brhiggins@yellowlantern.wanadoo.co.uk

BURWASH

Chateaubriand Antiques
High St. TN19 7ES. (William Vincent and Rosalind Chislett)
EST. 1985. Open 10-5, Sun. 12-5. CL: Mon. & Tues. *STOCK: Furniture, paintings, maps and engravings, porcelain, decorative items and linen.* LOC: Centre of village. SER: Valuations; local deliveries, shipping, picture framing. SIZE: 3 showrooms. PARK: Nearby.
TEL: 01435 882535
WEBSITE: www.chateaubriandantiques.co.uk

DITCHLING

Dycheling Antiques
34 High St. BN6 8TA. (E.A. Hudson)
EST. 1977. Open Sat. 10.30-5, other days by appointment. *STOCK: Georgian, Victorian and Edwardian furniture, especially dining and armchairs, £25–£5,000.* LOC: Off A23 on A273-B2112 north of Brighton. SER: Chair search service. SIZE: Mediium. PARK: Easy. VAT: Spec.
TEL: 01273 842929; HOME: same; FAX: 01273 841929; MOBILE: 07885 456341
E-MAIL: hudson@icsgroup.demon.co.uk
WEBSITE: www.antiquechairmatching.com
www.antiques-atlas.com

EASTBOURNE

Baxter & Sons   BADA LAPADA
PO Box 3010. BN21 9BY. Also at Edenbridge Galleries and showroom at Laughton by appointment. (T.J.J. and G.J. Baxter and T.J. Hunter)
EST. 1928. Open by appointment. *STOCK: English*

furniture, 1730-1830, £1,000-£35,000. SER: Restoration. SIZE: Medium. VAT: Spec. FAIRS: Grosvenor House (June); BADA (March); Olympia (Nov).
TEL: 07850 618812
E-MAIL: partners@hcbaxter.co.uk
WEBSITE: www.hcbaxter.co.uk

W. Bruford Jewellers
11-13 Cornfield Rd. BN21 3NA.
EST. 1883. Open 9.30-5. *STOCK: Jewellery, Victorian, late Georgian; some silver, clocks (bracket and carriage).* SER: Valuations; restorations (clocks and silver). SIZE: Medium. VAT: Stan/Spec.
TEL: 01323 725452

Camilla's Bookshop
57 Grove Rd. BN21 4TX. (C. Francombe and S. Broad)
EST. 1976. Open 10-5.30. *STOCK: 75,000 books including antiquarian, art, antiques and collectables, naval, military, aviation, technical, needlework, broadcasting, literature, biography, history, occult and photography.* LOC: Next to police station, 5 mins. from rail station. SER: Valuations; postal service; own book tokens; internet sales. SIZE: Large, 3 floors. PARK: Nearby.
TEL: 01323 736001
E-MAIL: camillas.books@virgin.net

John Cowderoy Antiques Ltd   LAPADA
The Clock and Musical Box Centre, 42 South St. BN21 4XB. (D.J. and R.A. Cowderoy)
EST. 1973. Open 8.30-5.30. CL: Wed. pm. *STOCK: Clocks, musical boxes, furniture, porcelain, silver and plate, jewellery, copper, brass.* LOC: 150yds. from town hall. SER: Restorations (clocks, barometers, music boxes and furniture). SIZE: Large. PARK: Easy. VAT: Stan/Margin.
TEL: 01323 720058; FAX: 01323 410163
E-MAIL: david@cowderoyantiques.co.uk
WEBSITE: www.cowderoyantiques.co.uk

John Day of Eastbourne Fine Art
9 Meads St. BN20 7QY.
EST. 1964. Open during exhibitions 11-1 and 2-5, otherwise by appointment. *STOCK: English, especially East Anglian, and Continental paintings and watercolours, 19th-20th C.* LOC: Meads village, west end of Eastbourne, near Beachy Head. SER: Restorations; framing (oils and watercolours). SIZE: Medium. PARK: Easy.
TEL: 01323 725634; MOBILE: 07960 274139

Roderick Dew
10 Furness Rd. BN21 4EZ.
EST. 1971. Open by appointment. *STOCK: Antiquarian books, especially on art and antiques.* LOC: Town centre. SER: Search; catalogues available. PARK: Easy.
TEL: 01323 720239
E-MAIL: roderick@dewroderick.wanadoo.co.uk

Eastbourne Antiques Market
80 Seaside. BN22 7QP.
EST. 1969. Open 10-5.30, Sat. 10-5. *STOCK: A wide selection of general antiques and collectables.* SIZE: Large - 30+ stalls. PARK: Easy.
TEL: 01323 642233

Enterprise Collectors' Market
The Enterprise Centre, Station Parade. BN21 1BE.
EST. 1989. Open 9.30-5. *STOCK: Wide range of general antiques and collectables.* LOC: Next to rail station. SER: Valuations. SIZE: Medium. PARK: Easy.
TEL: 01323 732690

A. & T. Gibbard
1-2 Calverley Walk. BN21 4UB.
EST. 1993. PBFA. Open 9.30-5.30. *STOCK: Secondhand and antiquarian books, 16th-20th C, £1-£1,000.* LOC: 200yds. east of Town Hall. SER: Valuations. SIZE: Medium. VAT: Stan.
TEL: 01323 734128

Timothy Partridge Antiques
Open by appointment. *STOCK: Victorian, Edwardian and 1920s furniture.* LOC: In old town, near St. Mary's Church. PARK: Easy.
TEL: 07860 864709

Seaquel Antique & Collectors' Market
37 Seaside Rd. BN21 3PP. (Mrs P. Mornington-West)
EST. 1997. Open 10-5, Sun. 11-4. *STOCK: General antiques, collectables and bric-a-brac.* LOC: Just off main shopping area. SIZE: Small. PARK: Nearby.
TEL: 01323 645032

E. Stacy-Marks   BADA LAPADA
8-9 Grand Hotel Buildings, Compton St. BN21 4EJ.
STOCK: Paintings in oils and watercolour, works of art. SER: Restoration.
TEL: 01323 647711; FAX: same
E-MAIL: paintings@estacy-marks.co.uk
WEBSITE: www.estacy-marks.co.uk

FLIMWELL

Graham Lower
Stonecrouch Farmhouse. TN5 7QB. (Graham and Penny Lower)
EST. 1972. Open by appointment. *STOCK: English and Continental 17th-18th C oak furniture.* LOC: A21. SER: Valuations. SIZE: Small. PARK: Own. VAT: Spec.
TEL: 01580 879535

FOREST ROW

Brookes-Smith Antiques
16 Hartfield Rd. RH18 5HE. (Richard and Kate Brookes-Smith)
EST. 1980. Open 9.30-5. *STOCK: Fine furniture, objects,*

works of art, silver and glass, £50-£20,000. LOC: 3 miles south of East Grinstead on A22, left at roundabout down Hartfield Rd. SER: Valuations. SIZE: 3 floors. PARK: Behind shop.
TEL: 01342 826622; FAX: 01342 826634
E-MAIL: rick@brookes-smith.com
WEBSITE: www.brookes-smith.com

Dandelion Clock Antiques Centre
Lewes Rd. RH18 5ES. (Lindi Chapman)
EST. 1994. Open 10-5. *STOCK: Old pine; antiques and collectables.* SER: Reclaimed pine furniture made to order. SIZE: 12 dealers. PARK: Easy.
TEL: 01342 822335
E-MAIL: lindi.chapman@btconnect.com
WEBSITE: www.dandelion-clock.co.uk

Jeroen Markies   LAPADA
5 Newlands Place, Hartfield Rd. RH18 5DQ.
Open 10-5.30. *STOCK: 19th-20th C decorative arts - Art Deco, Art Nouveau, Arts and Crafts.* **SER: Valuations; restorations. SIZE: Medium. PARK: Nearby.**
TEL: 01342 824980
E-MAIL: info@markies.co.uk
WEBSITE: www.jeroenmarkies.co.uk

FRAMFIELD

Chevertons Antiques Ltd.   BADA LAPADA
Unit 8, New Place, Blackboys Rd. TN22 5EQ. (Angus Adam)
EST. 1961. CINOA. Open by appointment. *STOCK: English and Continental furniture and accessories, £500-£40,000.*
TEL: 01825 891223; FAX: 01825 891224; MOBILE: 07711 234010
E-MAIL: info@chevertons.com
WEBSITE: www.chevertons.com

HADLOW DOWN

Hadlow Down Antiques
Hastingford Farm, School Lane. TN22 4DY. (Adrian Butler and Caroline Knight)
EST. 1989. Open by appointment. *STOCK: French and English country and formal furniture, 18th C to date, £25-£5,000; English and French decorative accessories.* LOC: 2 mins. down School Lane from A272 in village. SER: Courier. SIZE: Large - export showrooms. PARK: Easy. VAT: Export.
TEL: 01825 830707; HOME: same; MOBILE: 07813 050925
E-MAIL: sales@hadlowdownantiques.co.uk
WEBSITE: www.hadlowdownantiques.co.uk

HAILSHAM

Golden Cross Antiques
Fiveways House, Golden Cross. BN27 4AN. (Ian and Rhoda Buchan)

EST. 1970. Open 9.30-5.30, Sun. 10-5 or by appointment. *STOCK: Copper, brass, pewter and iron ware, especially fireside equipment and lamps, furniture including pine, 18th-20th C; silver, 19th to early 20th C; collectables and china.* LOC: A22 8 miles north of Eastbourne. SER: Valuations. SIZE: Medium. PARK: Easy.
TEL: 01825 872144; HOME: same; MOBILE: 07957 224165
E-MAIL: antiques@goldencross.fsbusiness.co.uk

HASTINGS

Coach House Antiques
42 George St. TN34 3EA. (R.J. Luck)
EST. 1972. Open 10-5 including Sun. *STOCK: Longcase clocks, 18th-19th C, £1,000+; furniture, 19th C, £100+; collectables including Dinky toys, trains, dolls' houses.* SER: Valuations; restorations (clocks and furniture); buys at auction (clocks and furniture). SIZE: Medium. PARK: Nearby. VAT: Spec.
TEL: 01424 461849

George Street Antiques Centre
47 George St. TN34 3EA. (F. Stanley-McKay and H. Stallybrass)
EST. 1969. Open 11-4 inc. Sun. CL: Mon. Oct.-Mar. *STOCK: Small items, 19th-20th C, £5-£1,000; antique jewellery.* LOC: In old town, parallel to seafront. SIZE: Medium - 10 dealers. PARK: Seafront.
TEL: 01424 429339; HOME: 01424 813526/428105

Howes Bookshop
Trinity Hall, Braybrooke Terrace. TN34 1HQ. (Miles Bartley)
EST. 1920. ABA. PBFA. Open Mon.-Fri. 9.30-1 and 2-5. *STOCK: Antiquarian and academic books in literature, history, arts, bibliography.* LOC: Near rail station. PARK: Own. FAIRS: ABA; PBFA.
TEL: 01424 423437; FAX: 01424 460620
E-MAIL: rarebooks@howes.co.uk
WEBSITE: www.howes.co.uk

Spice
Samphire House, 75 High St., Old Town. TN34 3EL. (S. Dix)
Open by appointment. *STOCK: Early furniture and decorative items.*
TEL: 07710 209556
E-MAIL: samphirehouse@btinternet.com

HEATHFIELD

Graham Price Antiques Ltd
Satinstown Farm, Broad Oak. TN21 8RU.
EST. 1979. Open by appointment. *STOCK: Furniture - country, decorative, French, Irish, painted, some formal and decorative accessories.* LOC: 1 mile east of Heathfield on A265 (Burwash Road). SER: Export; packing and shipping; courier; restorations. SIZE: Large. PARK: Ample.

TEL: 01435 866828; FAX: 01435 883761; MOBILE: 07768 330842
E-MAIL: mail@grahampriceantiques.co.uk
WEBSITE: www.grahampriceantiques.co.uk

LEWES

Bow Windows Book Shop
175 High St. BN7 1YE. (A. and J. Shelley)
EST. 1964. ABA. PBFA. Open 9.30-5. *STOCK: Books including natural history, English literature, travel, topography.* LOC: Off A27. SER: Valuations for probate and insurance. SIZE: Large. FAIRS: ABA; PBFA.
TEL: 01273 480780; FAX: 01273 486686
E-MAIL: rarebooks@bowwindows.com
WEBSITE: www.bowwindows.com

Church-Hill Antiques Centre
6 Station St. BN7 2DA. (S. Miller and S. Ramm)
EST. 1970. Open 9.30-5. *STOCK: Wide range of general antiques including furniture, china, silver, jewellery, clocks, lighting, paintings and decorative items.* LOC: From rail station, in town centre. SIZE: 60 stalls and cabinets. PARK: Easy, own. VAT: Stan.
TEL: 01273 474842; FAX: 01273 846797
E-MAIL: churchhilllewes@aol.com
WEBSITE: www.church-hill-antiques.com

Cliffe Antiques Centre
47 Cliffe High St. BN7 2AN.
EST. 1984. Open 9.30-5. *STOCK: General antiques, £5-£1,000.* LOC: Follow town centre signs, turning left 200 yards past Waitrose. SIZE: Medium - 16 dealers. PARK: Easy.
TEL: 01273 473266

A. & Y. Cumming
84 High St. BN7 1XN.
EST. 1976. ABA. Open 10-5, Sat. 10-5.30. *STOCK: Antiquarian and out-of-print books.* SER: Buys at auction; books bought - buyer will call. FAIRS: Chelsea; Olympia.
TEL: 01273 472319; FAX: 01273 486364
E-MAIL: a.y.cumming@ukgateway.net

The Emporium Antique Centre
42 Cliffe High St. BN7 2AN. (Doyle and Madigan)
EST. 1990. Open 10-5, Sat. 9.30-5.30, Sun. 12-4. *STOCK: Furniture, pictures, clocks, collectables, books, jewellery, Art Nouveau and Deco, decorative arts, collector's toys, studio ceramics, postcards, vintage clothes and accessories.* LOC: Town centre. SIZE: 60 dealers.
TEL: 01273 486866
E-MAIL: steve@smadigan.fsnet.co.uk

The Fifteenth Century Bookshop
99-100 High St. BN7 1XH. (Mrs S. Mirabaud)
EST. 1938. PBFA. Open 10-5.30. Sun. 10.30-4. *STOCK: Antiquarian and general secondhand books, especially children's and illustrated; prints, teddies and china.* LOC: At

top of cobbled lane, just beyond the castle. SER: Postal. PARK: Opposite.
TEL: 01273 474160
E-MAIL: fifteenthcenturybookshop@oldenyoungbooks.co.uk
WEBSITE: www.oldenyoungbooks.co.uk

Lewes Antique Centre
20 Cliffe High St. BN7 2AH. (Jamie Pettit)
EST. 1968. Open 9.30-5, Sun. 12-4. *STOCK: Furniture, china, copper and metalware, glass, clocks, architectural salvage, books and collectables.* LOC: A27 from Brighton, 2nd roundabout into Lewes, end of tunnel turn left, then next left, next right into Phoenix car park. 100m. walk to Cliffe High St. SER: Shipping; stripping; restorations; valuations. SIZE: Large - 125 stallholders. PARK: Easy.
TEL: 01273 476148

Lewes Clock Shop
5 North St. BN7 2PA. (W.F. Bruce)
EST. 1982. Open 10-4 Tues., Thurs. and Sat. or by appointment. *STOCK: Clocks, especially early lantern clocks.* SER: Valuations; restorations. SIZE: Medium. PARK: Nearby. VAT: Spec.
TEL: 01273 473123; FAX: same
E-MAIL: info@wfbruce.co.uk
WEBSITE: www.wfbruce.co.uk

Lewes Flea Market
14a Market St. BN7 2NB.
EST. 1995. Open daily including Sun. *STOCK: Bric-a-brac, furniture, collectables, 18th-20th C, £5-£1,000.* LOC: 50 metres north of monument. SIZE: Large. PARK: Nearby.
TEL: 01273 480328
E-MAIL: arrw@btinternet.com
WEBSITE: www.flea-markets.co.uk

Pastorale Antiques
15 Malling St. BN7 2RA. (O. Soucek)
EST. 1984. Open 10-5.30 or by appointment. *STOCK: Pine and European country furniture, Georgian and Victorian mahogany and decorative items and garden items.* SER: Delivery (Europe). SIZE: Large.
TEL: 01273 473259; HOME: 01435 863044; FAX: 01273 473259
E-MAIL: csoucek@toucansurf.com
WEBSITE: www.pastorale.cz

Southdown Antiques
48 Cliffe High St. BN7 2AN. (Miss P.I. and K.A. Foster)
EST. 1969. Open by appointment. *STOCK: Small antiques, especially 18th-19th C English, Continental and Oriental porcelain, objets d'art, works of art, glass, papier mâché trays, silver plate, £50-£350,000; reproduction and interior decor items.* LOC: A27. One-way street north. SIZE: Medium. PARK: Easy. VAT: Stan/Spec.
TEL: 01273 472439

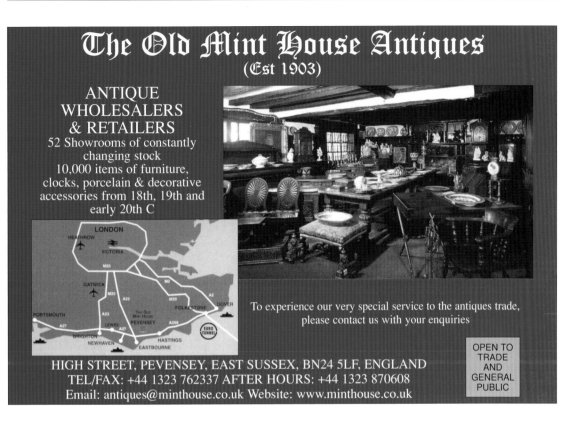
NUTLEY

Nutley Antiques
Libra House, High St. TN22 3NF. (Liza Hall)
Open 10-5, Sun. and Bank Holidays 12-3.30. STOCK: Country and cottage furniture, £10-£1,000; decorative items, £1-£400; prints, oils, watercolours, £5-£500. LOC: A22 between East Grinstead and Uckfield. SIZE: Small. PARK: Easy. VAT: Stan.
TEL: 01825 713220

PEVENSEY

The Old Mint House
High St. BN24 5LF. (J.C., A.J. and P.G. Nicholson)
EST. 1903. Open 9-5.30, Sat. 10.30-3.30, otherwise by appointment. STOCK: Furniture - Georgian, Victorian, Edwardian; porcelain, clocks, barometers and decorative items, 18th C to 1920s, £50-£10,000. LOC: A27, 1 mile from Eastbourne. SER: London trains met at local station (Polegate). SIZE: Large + export warehouse. PARK: Easy. VAT: Stan/Spec.
TEL: 01323 762337; FAX: same
E-MAIL: antiques@minthouse.co.uk
WEBSITE: www.minthouse.co.uk

POLEGATE

E. Stacy-Marks Limited   BADA LAPADA
The Flint Rooms, PO Box 808. BN26 5ST.
EST. **1889**. STOCK: *Paintings, English, Dutch and Continental schools, 18th-20th C*. SIZE: **Large**. VAT: **Stan.**
TEL: **01323 482156**; FAX: **01323 482513**
E-MAIL: **paintings@estacy-marks.co.uk**
WEBSITE: **www.estacy-marks.co.uk**

Summer Antiques
63 High St. BN26 6AH. (R. Millis)
EST. 1992. Open 9-5, Sat. 9-12. STOCK: *General antiques including silver, china, furniture, brass and copper.* LOC: 250 yards from station. SER: Valuations. SIZE: Small. PARK: Easy. FAIRS: Ardingly.
TEL: 01323 483834; MOBILE: 07762 309870

PORTSLADE

Craftsmen in Wood
524 Mile Oak Rd. BN41 2RF. (Victor Potter)
EST. 1963. STOCK: *Furniture and paintings.* SER: Restoration of period wooden furniture and architectural woodwork. PARK: Easy.
TEL: 01273 423730; MOBILE: 07768 274461
E-MAIL: cvpotter@aol.com
WEBSITE: www.craftsmen-in-wood.com

POUNDGATE

Nicholas Bowlby
Owl House, TN22 4DE.
EST. 1981. Open by appointment. *STOCK: 19th-20th C watercolours, contemporary paintings and sculpture, £200-£20,000.* SER: Valuations; restorations; buys at auction (watercolours and drawings); framing. SIZE: Medium. VAT: Stan/Spec.
TEL: 01892 667809
E-MAIL: nicholasbowlby@hotmail.com
WEBSITE: www.nicholasbowlby.co.uk

ROTHERFIELD

6A Antiques
6A High St. TN6 3LL. (Bryan Samworth)
STOCK: Antique mahogany, walnut and oak furniture, mantel and longcase clocks. LOC: 6 miles south of Tunbridge Wells. SER: Complete clock restoration service.
TEL: 01892 852008

David Hinton @ Olinda House
High St. TN6 3LN.
EST. 1987. Open 10.30-5. CL: Wed. *STOCK: Antiques and collectables.* SER: Valuations for probate and insurance; house clearance; furniture restoration. SIZE: 6 dealers. VAT: Margin/Global.
TEL: 01892 852609
E-MAIL: david.hinton@btconnect.com

David Hinton Antiques
5 High St. TN6 3LL.
EST. 1987. Open 10.30-5. CL: Wed. *STOCK: Furniture, porcelain, silver and objets d'art.* LOC: Village centre opposite the Kings Arms. SER: Valuations for probate and insurance; specialists in probate house clearance. SIZE: Medium. PARK: Village car park and off street parking. VAT: Margin/Global. FAIRS: Newark.
TEL: 01892 852609/852412
E-MAIL: david.hinton@btconnect.com

Forge Interiors
South St. TN6 3LN. (Douglas Masham)
EST. 1998. Open 10-1 and 2-5. CL: Mon. *STOCK: Asian and English antiques and decorative items, furniture, pictures and lighting; Tansu, Hibatchi and Ranma; Japanese woodblocks always available.* SER: Restorations; caning and rushing. SIZE: Medium. PARK: Easy.
TEL: 01892 853000; HOME/FAX: 01892 853122

ROTTINGDEAN

Farthings of Rottingdean
45 High St. BN2 7HR.
EST. 1997. Open 9.30-5 inc Sun. *STOCK: Antiques and collectables, quality china & glass, books (old & new), jewellery, original paintings & prints, occasional furniture.*

LOC: 3 miles north of Brighton. SIZE: 40 dealers. PARK: Own.
TEL: 01273 309113

Trade Wind
15A Little Crescent. BN2 7GF. (R. Morley Smith)
EST. 1974. Open by appointment. *STOCK: Caddy spoons, wine labels (80+ instock) and other interesting items, including coloured glass, Bristol blue, green and amethyst; early 18th-19th C white glass including folded foot and engraved items, 1710-1830.* FAIRS: Goodwood House, Chichester.
TEL: 01273 301177

RYE

Bragge and Sons
Landgate House. TN31 7LH. (J.R. Bragge)
EST. 1840. Open 9-5. CL: Tues. and Sat. pm. *STOCK: 18th C English furniture and works of art.* LOC: Entrance to town - Landgate. SER: Valuations; restorations. SIZE: Medium.
TEL: 01797 223358

Herbert Gordon Gasson
The Lion Galleries, Lion St. TN31 7LB. (T.J. Booth)
EST. 1909. Open 10-5, Tues. and Sun. by appointment. *STOCK: 17th-19th C oak, walnut and mahogany furniture; decorative items. NOT STOCKED: Silver and glass.* LOC: Town centre. SER: Restorations. SIZE: Large. PARK: Easy. VAT: Spec.
TEL: 01797 222208
E-MAIL: hggassonantiques@hotmail.com
WEBSITE: www.antiquesrye.co.uk

Needles Antique Centre
15-17 Cinque Port St. TN31 7AD.
EST. 1996. FSB. *STOCK: Jewellery, pottery, metal, brass, fireside, garden.*
TEL: 01797 225064

Strand Quay Antiques
1 & 2 The Strand. TN31 7BD. (A.M. Sutherland)
EST. 1984. Open 10-5 inc. Sun. *STOCK: Victorian, Edwardian and shipping furniture, paintings and porcelain; French furniture.* SIZE: Medium. PARK: Easy. FAIRS: Ardingly.
TEL: 01797 226790; MOBILE: 07775 602598

Wish Barn Antiques
Wish St. TN31 7DA. (Robert sWheeler)
EST. 1993. Open 10-5 inc. Sun. *STOCK: 19th C furniture including oak, mahogany and pine, £50-£5,000; silver plate.* LOC: Just off A259. SIZE: Medium. PARK: Easy.
TEL: 01797 226797; mobile 07973 819771

SEAFORD

Martin D. Johnson Antiques
15-17 High Street. BN25 1PE. (Martin D. Johnson)
EST. 1968. Open 9-5, Sat. 10-12.30 or by appointment.

STOCK: *Traditional and decorative antiques. 18th & 19th C brown, painted and country furniture. Accessories for US and other overseas buyers.* LOC: In town centre close to train station. Pick-up service from Gatwick Airport for overseas buyers. SIZE: Large PARK: Easy. VAT: Spec./Global. FAIRS: Ardingly; Newark.
TEL: 01323 897777; MOBILE: 07860 899774
E-MAIL: info@martindjohnsonantiques.com
WEBSITE: www.martindjohnsonantiques.com

The Old House
18 High St. BN25 1PG. (Mr S.M. Barrett)
EST. 1928. Open 9-5, Wed. 9-1. STOCK: *18th-20th C furniture, china and glass, £5-£5,000.* LOC: Near rail station. SER: Valuations; restorations (furniture); shippers. SIZE: Large. PARK: Opposite in Pelham Yard. VAT: Stan/Spec.
TEL: 01323 892091 or 01323 893795

ST. LEONARDS-ON-SEA

Gensing Antiques
70 Norman Rd. TN38 0EJ. (Peter Cawson)
Open normal shop hours and by appointment. STOCK: *General antiques especially early Chinese furniture and other Oriental items.*
TEL: 01424 424145/714981

The Hastings Antique Centre
59-61 Norman Rd. TN38 0EG. (R.J. Amstad)
Open 10-5.30, Sun. by appointment. SIZE: Large.
TEL: 01424 428561

Below are listed some of the dealers at this centre.

R.J. Amstad
Furniture.

Bruno Antiques
French furniture.

K. Gumbrell
Decorative items.

Jackie's Dolls
(Jacqueline Osborne) *Dolls.*

G. Mennis
Sporting, leather goods.

Monarch Antiques
371 Bexhill Rd. TN38 8AJ. (J.H. King)
EST. 1983. Open 8.30-5, or by appointment. CL: Sat. STOCK: *General furniture, especially 1930s oak furniture for the Japanese, Korean, American and European markets.* LOC: A259. SER: Packing and shipping; courier; restorations. SIZE: Warehouse. PARK: Own. FAIRS: Newark.
TEL: 01424 204141; FAX: 01424 204142; HOME: 01424 214158; MOBILES: 07802 217842/213081
E-MAIL: monarch.antiques@virgin.net
WEBSITE: www.monarch-antiques.co.uk

UCKFIELD

Ringles Cross Antiques
Ringles Cross. TN22 1HF. (J. Dunford)
EST. 1965. Resident. Open 10-5 or by appointment. STOCK: *English furniture, mainly oak and country, 17th-18th C; accessories.* LOC: 1 mile north of Uckfield. SIZE: Large. PARK: Own.
TEL: 01825 762909

WADHURST

Park View Antiques
High St., Durgates. TN5 6DE. (B. Ross)
EST. 1985. Open 10-4 Thurs.-Sat. and by appointment. STOCK: *Pine, oak and painted country furniture, 17th-19th C, £100-£1,500; decorative items, 1930s, £25-£150; iron and metalware, 17th-19th C, £25-£250.* LOC: On B2099 Frant-Hurst Green road. SER: Valuations; restorations (furniture). SIZE: Medium. PARK: Easy.
TEL: 01892 783630; FAX: 01892 740264; HOME: 01892 740264
E-MAIL: leithruss@btconnect.com
WEBSITE: www.parkviewantiques.co.uk

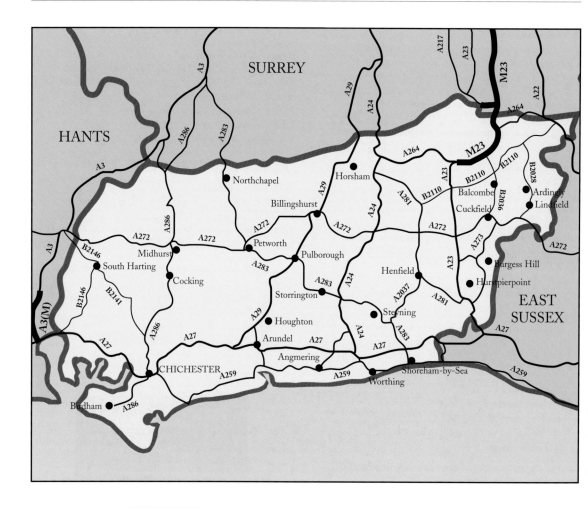

ARDINGLY

Rocking Horse Antique Market

16 High St. RH17 6TD. (Peter and Mrs Joy Livett)
EST. 1993. Open 9.30-5.30, Sun. 10-5.30 (winter until 5
every day). STOCK: General antiques. SIZE: Small. PARK:
Rear of village hall. FAIRS: Ardingly.
TEL: 01444 892205

ARUNDEL

Antiquities

5-7 Tarrant St. BN18 9DG. (Ian and Christina Fenwick)
EST. 1990. Open 10-5, other times by appointment, any
day. STOCK: Decorative and unusual - including 19th C
English and French furniture, mahogany and fruitwood,
painted items, Staffordshire, majolica, metalware, French
mirrors, pond yachts, luggage, garden, architectural items,
tole. LOC: Just off town square. SER: Shipping. SIZE:
Large + displayed warehouses. PARK: Nearby. VAT:
Stan/Spec.
TEL: 01903 884355; FAX: same
E-MAIL: antiquities@btconnect.com

Baynton-Williams

1st Floor, 37A High St. BN18 9AG. (R.H. and S.C.
Baynton-Williams)
EST. 1946. Open 10-6. STOCK: Maps, views, sporting,
marine and decorative prints. SER: Valuations; cataloguing.
SIZE: Medium. PARK: Nearby. VAT: Stan/Spec.
TEL: 01903 883588; FAX: same
E-MAIL: gallery@baynton-williams.freeserve.co.uk
WEBSITE: www.baynton-williams.com

Cleall Antiques

34 High St. BN18 9AB. (Damian Cleall)
EST. 1994. Open 10.15-5.15, Sun. by appointment.
STOCK: Eclectic and decorative items including painted
furniture, majolica; lighting including chandeliers; period
furniture including fruitwood, 1750-1950s. SER: Courier.
SIZE: Medium. PARK: Easy. FAIRS: Arundel Castle;
Battersea Decorative; Loseley Park.
TEL: 01903 882234; FAX: same; MOBILE: 07831 869955
E-MAIL: damiancleall@hotmail.com
WEBSITE: www.cleallantiques.com

Spencer Swaffer   LAPADA
30 High St. BN18 9AB.
EST. **1974. Open 9-6, other times by appointment.**
STOCK: *Quirky decorative and traditional items, English,*
French, Italian, brown and painted furniture, chandeliers,
lighting, marble tables, iron low tables, bamboo, shop
fittings, garden furniture, upholstered chairs and lamps
made from 18th and 19th C fragments. LOC: **Town**
centre. SIZE: **Large.** PARK: **Easy.** VAT: **Stan/Spec.**
TEL: **01903 882132;** FAX: **01903 884564**
E-MAIL: **spencerswaffer@btconnect.com**
WEBSITE: **www.spencerswaffer.com**

The Walking Stick Shop
8-9 The Old Printing Works, Tarrant St. BN18 9JH.
(S. Thompson)
EST. 1981. Open 8.30-5.30, Wed. 8.30-1, Sun. pm by
appointment. STOCK: *Walking sticks and canes, 1620 to*
date, £10-£2,000. LOC: Off High St. SIZE: Large. PARK:
Easy. VAT: Stan.
TEL: 01903 883796; FAX: 01903 884491
E-MAIL: stuart.walkingsticks@btinternet.com
WEBSITE: www.walkingstickshop.co.uk

BILLINGSHURST

Michael Wakelin & Helen Linfield BADA LAPADA
P.O Box 48. RH14 0YZ.
EST. **1968. CINOA. Open any time by appointment.**
STOCK: *Fine English and Continental formal and country*
furniture - walnut, fruitwoods, faded mahogany and other
exotic woods; early brass, bronze, iron and steel; wood
carvings, treen, needlework, naive pictures and lighting.
LOC: **Wisborough Green.** SER: **Shipping; valuations;**
interior and landscape design. PARK: **Easy.** VAT:
Stan/Spec. FAIRS: **Olympia; BADA; LAPADA; Chelsea.**
TEL: **01403 700004;** FAX: **01403 701173**
E-MAIL: **wakelin_linfield@btinternet.com**
WEBSITE: **www.wakelin-linfield.com**

BIRDHAM

Whitestone Farm Antiques
Whitestone Farm, Main Rd. PO20 7HU. (C.L.
Mordue)
Open 10-5.30. STOCK: *Town and country furniture,*
including pine and oak, £50-£2,000; books, £3-£200;
gardenalia, £5-£250; china, glass and collectables. SIZE:
Medium. PARK: Easy.
TEL: 01243 513706; FAX: same
E-MAIL: antiques@whitestonefarm.f9.co.uk
WEBSITE: www.whitestonefarm.f9.co.uk

BURGESS HILL

Recollect Dolls Hospital
17 Junction Rd. RH15 0HR. (P. Jago)
EST. 1970. Open 10-4. CL: Mon. and Sat. STOCK: Dolls

and supplies, doll restoration materials. SER: Restorations
(dolls); catalogues available (£3 stamps).
TEL: 01444 871052
E-MAIL: dollshopuk@aol.com
WEBSITE: www.dollshospital.co.uk

CHICHESTER

Almshouses Arcade
19 The Hornet. PO19 4JL. (Mrs Viv Barnett)
EST. 1983. Open 9.30-4.30. LOC: 200yds. from Cattle
Market at eastern end of city. On one-way system (A286)
just before traffic lights at Market Ave. PARK: Easy.
TEL: 01243 528089.

Below are listed the dealers at these premises.

> **Antics**
> (P. German) *General antiques and collectables.*

> **R .K. Barnett**
> *Antiques and collectables; furniture; toys.* TEL: 01243 528089

> **Collectors' Corner**
> *Small collectables and antiques.*

The Canon Gallery   BADA
39 East Street, PO19 1HX. (Jeremy Green and James
Fergusson)
EST. **1987. PAADA. Open by appointment.** STOCK:
Oils and watercolours, 18th-20th C. and contemporary,
£500-£100,000. SER: **Valuations; restorations; framing.**
SIZE: **Small.** VAT: **Spec.** FAIRS: **World of Watercolours.**
TEL: **01243 532927**
E-MAIL: **enquiries@canongallery.co.uk**
WEBSITE: **www.thecanongallery.co.uk**

Chichester Gallery
8 The Hornet. PO19 4JG. (Tom and Mary McHale)
EST. 1997. Open Tues., Wed. and Fri. 10-1 and 2-4.
STOCK: *Victorian oils, watercolours, etchings and engravings,*
£250-£7,000; fine prints, contemporary paintings, including
local views. SER: Cleaning; restorations; commission
sales; inventories; valuations; period frames. SIZE: 5
rooms. PARK: Cattlemarket at rear of gallery.
TEL: 01243 779821; FAX: 01243 773345

Frensham House Antiques
Hunston. PO20 1NX. (J. and M. Riley)
EST. 1966. Open 9-6. STOCK: *English furniture, 1700-*
1830, £500-£6,000; clocks, paintings, copper. LOC: One
mile south of Chichester by-pass on B2145. PARK: Easy.
TEL: 01243 782660

Furniture and Mirror Warehouse
Unit 5 & 6 Terminus Mill, Terminus Rd. Industrial
Estate. PO19 8UN. (W.D. Priddy)
EST. 1983. Open 10-5, Sun. 11-4 or by appointment.
STOCK: *Oak, mahogany, walnut and pine furniture, mid-*
19th C to pre-war and shipping, £20-£7,000. LOC: Runs
off A27 Chichester bypass. SIZE: Large. PARK: Easy on
site. VAT: Stan/Spec.

TEL: 01243 783960
E-MAIL: bill.priddy@btconnect.com
WEBSITE: www.furnitureandmorror.co.uk

Gems Antiques
39 West St. PO19 1RP. (M.L. Hancock)
EST. 1985. Open 10-1 and 2.30-5.30. CL: Mon. STOCK:
*Period furniture, Staffordshire and porcelain figures, glass
and pictures.* PARK: Easy.
TEL: 01243 786173

Peter Hancock Antiques
40-41 West St. PO19 1RP.
EST. 1950. Articles on coins. Open 10.30-1 and 2.30-
5.30. CL: Mon. STOCK: *Silver, jewellery, porcelain,
furniture, £20-£2,000; pictures, glass, clocks, books, £5-
£500; all 18th-19th C; enthnographica, Art Nouveau, Art
Deco, 19th-20th C, £5-£500.* LOC: From Chichester
Cross, 17 doors past cathedral. SER: Valuations; repairs.
SIZE: Medium. PARK: Easy. VAT: Spec.
TEL: 01243 786173

Heritage Antiques
84 St. Pancras. PO19 7NL. (D.R. Grover)
EST. 1987. Open 9.30-5. STOCK: *Furniture and decorative
items.*
TEL: 01243 783796

Rathbone Law
59 North St. PO19 1NB. (Mr and Mrs R. Law)
EST. 1902. NAG. Open 9.30-5. CL: some Mon. STOCK:
*Victorian and Edwardian fine jewellery, silver, designer
pieces in gold and silver, objets d'art, fine gems; contemporary
jewellery.* SER: Valuations. PARK: Nearby.
TEL: 01243 787881
E-MAIL: rathbonelaw@yahoo.co.uk
WEBSITE: www.rathbonelaw.com

COCKING

The Victorian Brass Bedstead Company
Hoe Copse. GU29 0HL. (David Woolley)
EST. 1970. Resident. Open by appointment. STOCK:
*Victorian and Edwardian brass and iron bedsteads, bases and
mattresses, 19th-20th C, £300-£3,500.* LOC: Right behind
village Post Office, 3/4 mile left turning to Hoe Copse.
SER: Valuations; restorations (brass and iron bedsteads).
SIZE: Large. PARK: Easy. VAT: Stan.
TEL: 01730 812287
E-MAIL: toria@hoecopse.fsnet.co.uk
WEBSITE: www.victorianbrassbeds.co.uk

CUCKFIELD

David Foord-Brown Antiques   BADA
High St. RH17 5JU.
(David Foord-Brown and Sean Barry)
EST. 1988. Open 10-5.30. STOCK: *Furniture, 1700-
1825; old Sheffield plate and period accessories. NOT*

STOCKED: *Country furniture.* LOC: A272, east of A23.
SIZE: **Medium.** PARK: **Easy.** VAT: **Spec.** FAIRS: BADA
(March); Olympia (June and Nov).
TEL: **01444 414418**
E-MAIL: **antiques@davidfoord-brown.com**
WEBSITE: **www.davidfoord-brown.com**

HAYWARDS HEATH

Donay Traditional Games & Pastimes
(Carol Goddard)
EST. 1980. Open by appointment. STOCK: *Board and
mechanical games – horse racing, cricket, golf and football;
treen, paper and metal puzzles including Journet and
mechanical Hoffman; chess, backgammon, cribbage,
dominoes; card games and scorers; tinplate including Schuco;
dice, shakers, mahjong, marbles, artists' colourboxes; animal
bronzes, Punch & Judy puppets including ephemera, 1780-
1970s, £5-£5,000.* PARK: Own.
TEL: 01444 416412
E-MAIL: donaygames@btconnect.com
WEBSITE: www.donaygames.com

HENFIELD

Ashcombe Coach House   LAPADA
PO Box 2527. BN5 9SU.
EST. 1954. CINOA. **Open by appointment only.**
STOCK: *Furniture and objects, 17th to early 19th C.* PARK:
Own. FAIRS: Olympia; LAPADA.
TEL: **01273 491630;** FAX: **01273 492681;** MOBILE:
07803 180098
E-MAIL: **rgreen@anglocontinentalplacements.com**

HORSHAM

Queen St. Antiques Centre
39 Queen St. RH13 5AA. (Jonathan Dick)
EST. 2003. Open 10-5. CL: Mon. STOCK: *General
antiques and collectables especially furniture.* LOC: A281
east of town centre. SER: Small repairs and restoration.
SIZE: Large. PARK: On street in afternoons and public
nearby.
TEL: 01403 756644

HOUGHTON

Stable Antiques at Houghton
The Old Church, Main Rd. BN18 9LW. (Ian. J. Wadey)
EST. 1993. Open 11-4, Sun. 1-4. CL: Mon. STOCK:
General antiques and furniture, £20-£1,000. LOC: B2139
between Storrington and Arundel. SIZE: Large. PARK:
Own.
TEL: 01798 839555 or 01903 740555;
FAX: 01798 839555
WEBSITE: www.stableantiques.co.uk

HURSTPIERPOINT

Julian Antiques
124 High St. BN6 9PX. (Julian and Carol Ingram)
EST. 1964. Open by appointment. STOCK: *French 19th C mirrors, fireplaces, fenders, furniture.* PARK: Easy.
TEL: 01273 832145

Samuel Orr Antique Clocks
34-36 High St. BN6 9RG.
EST. 1968. Open 9-6 including Sun., or by appointment. STOCK: *18th-19th longcase, table and wall clocks.* SER: Restorations (clocks and furniture). PARK: Easy.
TEL: 01273 832081; MOBILE: 07860 230888
E-MAIL: clocks@samorr.co.uk
WEBSITE: www.samorr.co.uk

LINDFIELD

Lindfield Galleries   BADA
62 High St. RH16 2HL. (David Adam)
EST. **1972. Open 9.30-5, Sat. 9.30-4.30. CL: Mon.**
STOCK: *Antique and contemporary Oriental carpets and rugs.* SER: **Restorations; cleaning.** SIZE: **Large.** PARK:
Easy. VAT: **Stan/Spec.**
TEL: **01444 483817;** FAX: **01444 484682**
E-MAIL: **david@lindfieldgalleries.fsnet.co.uk**
WEBSITE: **www.davidadam.co.uk**

MIDHURST

Churchill Clocks
Rumbolds Hill. GU29 9BZ. (W.P. and Dr. E. Tyrrell)
EST. 1970. Open 9-5, Wed. 9-1. STOCK: *Clocks and furniture.* LOC: *Main street.* SER: Restorations (clocks).
TEL: 01730 813891
WEBSITE: www.churchillclocks.co.uk

PETWORTH

Antiquated
10 New St. GU28 0AS. (Vicki Emery)
EST. 1989. PAADA. Open 10-5.30 or by appointment.
STOCK: *18th-19th C original painted furniture, decorative items, garden furniture; 19th C rocking horses.* VAT: Spec.
TEL: 01798 344011; FAX: same
E-MAIL: info@antiquated.co.uk
WEBSITE: www.antiquated.co.uk

Baskerville Antiques   BADA
Saddlers House, Saddlers Row. GU28 0AN. (A. and
B. Baskerville)
EST. **1978. Open 10-5.30 or by appointment.** CL:
Mon.-Tue. STOCK: *English clocks and barometers, £1,000-£40,000; decorative items and instruments, £500-£10,000; all 17th-19th C.* LOC: **Town centre.** SIZE:
Medium. PARK: **Public, adjoining shop.** VAT: **Spec.**
TEL: **01798 342067;** HOME: **same**
E-MAIL: **brianbaskerville@aol.com**

John Bird Antiques
High St. GU28 0AU.
EST. 1972. PAADA. Open 10.15-5.15. STOCK: *Decorative furniture and objects - painted, oak, mahogany, architectural, upholstered, formal, country and primitive, £100-£10,000.* SER: Sourcing. SIZE: Medium. PARK: Easy. VAT: Spec. FAIRS: Battersea.
TEL: 01798 343250; MOBILE: 07970 683949
E-MAIL: mail@johnbirdantiques.com
WEBSITE: www.johnbirdantiques.com

Bradley's Past & Present
21 High St. GU28 0AU. (M. and A. Bradley)
EST. 1975. CL: Mon. STOCK: *Furniture, 19th-20th C, £50-£500; china and decorative items, £5-£100; metalware, phonographs, gramophones and records, antique golf clubs.* SER: Restorations and repairs (gramophones); metalwork repairs. SIZE: Small. PARK: Free nearby.
TEL: 01798 343533

Brownrigg @ Home   LAPADA
1 Pound St. GU28 0DX. (George Perez Martin)
EST. **1999. PAADA. Open 10.30-5.30, Sun. by appointment.** STOCK: *General antiques including Continental furniture, 13th C to 1920s; lighting, luggage, ceramics, decorative items.* SER: Interior design. SIZE:
Large. PARK: **Easy.** FAIRS: **Battersea.**
TEL: **01798 344321;** FAX: **same;** MOBILE: **07751 542149**
E-MAIL: **brownrigg@mac.com**
WEBSITE: **www.brownrigg-interiors.com**

Ronald G. Chambers Fine Antiques   LAPADA
**Market Sq. GU28 0AH. (Ronald G. Chambers and
Jacqueline F. Tudor)**
EST. **1985. CINOA. PAADA. Open 10-5.30, Sun. 10-
4.30.** STOCK: *Fine 18th-19th C furniture and objets d'art.*
SER: **Search; valuations; shipping; storage.** SIZE: **5
showrooms.** PARK: **Free.**
TEL: **01798 342305;** FAX: **01798 342724;** MOBILE:
07932 161968
E-MAIL: **jackie@ronaldchambers.com**
WEBSITE: **www.ronaldchambers.com**

Oliver Charles Antiques   LAPADA
**The Clockhouse, Lombard St. GU28 0AG. (Allan
and Deborah Gardner)**
EST. **1987. PAADA. Open 10-5.30 (including Sun.
from April to Sept) or by appointment.** STOCK:
*Georgian, Regency and selected French furniture, 1700-
1850, £1,000-£25,000; Victorian paintings, £750-
£100,000.* LOC: **Opposite church.** SER: **Valuations.**
SIZE: **Medium.** PARK: **Easy.**
TEL: **01798 344443;** FAX: **01798 343916**
E-MAIL: **sales@olivercharles.co.uk**
WEBSITE: **www.olivercharles.co.uk**

Cosby Antiques
19-21 East St. GU28 0AB. (Peter Cosby)
EST. 1992. PAADA. Open 10-6. STOCK: *17th-18th C*

English oak country furniture, clocks, mirrors, pictures, decorative items. French farmhouse tables. SER: Valuations; restorations; fine art brokerage. SIZE: Large. PARK: Easy.
TEL: 01798 345212; FAX: same; MOBILE: 07971 757226
E-MAIL: cosbyantiques@btopenworld.com
WEBSITE: www.cosbyantiques.com

Heather Denham Antiques
6 High St. GU28 0AU.
EST. 1965. PAADA. Open 10.30-5.30, Sun. and Mon. by appointment. *STOCK: 18th-19th C English and Continental decorative furniture, mirrors and chandeliers.* LOC: Near main square. SIZE: Medium. PARK: Easy and nearby.
TEL: 01798 344622; FAX: 01798 343436

Richard Gardner Antiques   LAPADA
Swan House, Market Sq. GU28 0AN. (Richard and Janice Gardner)
EST. 1992. PAADA. Resident. Open 10-5.30. *STOCK: Fine period furniture and works of art, to £250,000; English and Continental porcelain, Victorian Staffordshire figures, bronzes, silver, paintings, 17th-19th C; associated items; globes.* **SIZE: Large. PARK: 50 yards. VAT: Spec.**
TEL: 01798 343411
E-MAIL: **rg@richardgardnerantiques.co.uk**
WEBSITE: **www.richardgardnerantiques.co.uk**

John Giles   LAPADA
High St. GU28 0AU.
EST. 1980. PAADA. Open 10-5.30. *STOCK: Furniture - formal, painted and country, £300-£5,000; lamps, mirrors and objects.* **SIZE: Medium. PARK: Easy, free nearby.**
TEL: 01798 342136; MOBILE: 07770 873689
E-MAIL: **john@johngilesantiques.co.uk**
WEBSITE: **www.johngilesantiques.co.uk**

William Hockley Antiques
East St. GU28 0AB. (D. and V. Thrower)
EST. 1974. PAADA. Open 10-5.30. *STOCK: French and country furniture; English fruitwood; early oak.* SER: Interior design. PARK: Easy. VAT: Stan/Spec.
TEL: 01403 701917

Octavia Antiques
East St. GU28 0AB. (Aline Bell)
EST. 1973. PAADA. Open 10.30-5.30. CL: Fri. *STOCK: Unusual decorative items - blue and white china, lamps, mirrors, chairs, small sofas, mainly 19th C.* SIZE: Small. PARK: Easy, outside.
TEL: 01798 342771

Period Oak of Petworth   LAPADA
Church St. GU28 0AD. (Jackie Simonini)
PAADA. Open 10-5.30 or by appointment. *STOCK: 16th, 17th & 18th century early English antique oak and country furniture, metalware and treen.* **SIZE: Large. PARK: Free. VAT: Spec.**

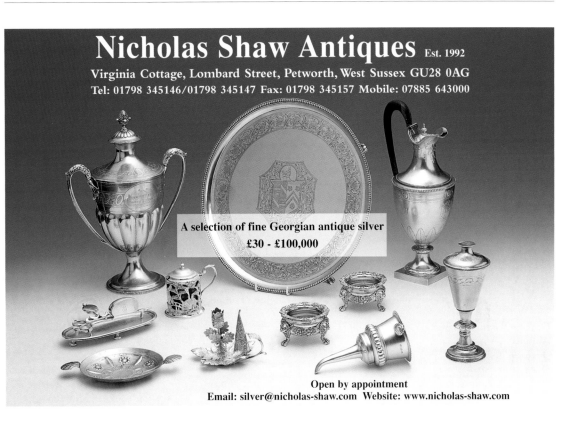

TEL: 01798 344111; MOBILE: 07917 571350
E-MAIL: sales@periodoakofpetworth.com
WEBSITE: www.periodoakofpetworth.com

Persian Carpet Gallery
Church St. GU28 0AD. (Dr. Ali Mandegaran)
EST. 1973. PAADA. Open 10-5. STOCK: *Antique and new Persian, Turkish, Indian, Pakistani and Afghan rugs and carpets. Sumac & kilim, oversized, made to measure.* LOC: On A272. SER: Valuations; restorations; hand cleaning; insurance claims. PARK: Nearby.
TEL: 01798 343344; FAX: 01798 342673
E-MAIL: pcg1973@yahoo.co.uk
WEBSITE: www.persiancarpetgallery.co.uk

Petworth Antique Centre
East St. GU28 0AB. (D.M. Rayment)
EST. 1967. PAADA. Open 10-5.30. STOCK: *General antiques, books, furniture, brass, copper, pictures, textiles.* LOC: Near church. SIZE: Large - 36 dealers. PARK: Adjoining. VAT: Stan/Spec.
TEL: 01798 342073; FAX: 01798 344566
E-MAIL: info@petworthantiquecentre.co.uk
WEBSITE: www.petworthantiquecentre.co.uk

Nicholas Shaw Antiques   BADA LAPADA
Virginia Cottage, Lombard St. GU28 0AG.
EST. 1992. CINOA. PAADA. Open 10-5. STOCK: *Fine*
and rare English, Scottish and Irish silver, 16th to mid 20th C, £30-£15,000.* LOC: Town centre. SER: Valuations; restorations. SIZE: Small. PARK: Nearby. FAIRS: BADA; Olympia; Harrogate; NEC.
TEL: 01798 345146/345147; FAX: 01798 345157;
MOBILE: 07885 643000
E-MAIL: silver@nicholas-shaw.com
WEBSITE: www.nicholas-shaw.com

David Swanson Antiques
2 Leppards, High St. GU28 0AU.
EST. 1980. Resident. Open 10-5 or by appointment. STOCK: *17th-18th C oak and walnut; decorative items.* SER: Restoration (antique and metalwork) and blacksmith workshop. SIZE: Medium. PARK: Outside and nearby. VAT: Spec.
TEL: 01798 342074; MOBILE: 07774 289543
WEBSITE: www.davidswansonantiques.com

Thakeham Furniture Ltd   LAPADA
Golden Square. GU28 0AP. (T. and B. Chavasse)
EST. 1988. PAADA. Open 10-5. STOCK: *18th-19th C English furniture, £100-£8,000; clocks.* SIZE: Large. PARK: Easy. VAT: Spec.
TEL: 01798 342333
E-MAIL: tim@thakehamfurniture.com
WEBSITE: www.thakehamfurniture.com

Giovanna Ticciati
New St. GU28 0AS.
EST. 2000. Open 10.30-5.30. *STOCK: Lighting, furniture, chairs, mirrors, etc.* SIZE: Medium PARK: Free up to 1 hr outside, or free car park. VAT: Margin.
TEL: 01798 342777; MOBILE: 07973 122417
E-MAIL: mail@giovannaticciati.com
WEBSITE: www.giovannaticciati.com

Tudor Rose Antiques
East St. GU28 0AB. (Mrs E.J. Lee)
EST. 2001. PAADA. Open 10-5.15, Sun. 11-4.15. *STOCK: General antiques; 18th-19th C furniture, pictures, lighting and chandeliers, antique mirrors, chairs, sofas, country furniture, silver, ceramics, painted and decorative furniture.* LOC: Town centre. SER: Shipping. SIZE: Medium - 13 dealers. PARK: Free nearby.
TEL: 01798 343621; MOBILE: 07980 927331
E-MAIL: info@tudor-rose-antiques.co.uk
WEBSITE: www.tudor-rose-antiques.co.uk

Jane Walton Antiques   LAPADA
The Showroom, Off Market Sq. GU28 0AH. (Jane Walton)
Open 10.30-5.30 or by appointment. CL: Mon. STOCK: Architectural and garden ornaments, decorative items, continental, painted and 20th C furniture. SIZE: Large PARK: Easy
TEL: 01798 345200; MOBILE: 07782 339699
E-MAIL: janeandpeter.walton@virgin.net
WEBSITE: www.janewalton.co.uk

T.G. Wilkinson Antiques Ltd.   BADA
Market Sq. GU28 0AH. (Tony Wilkinson)
EST. 1973. PAADA. Open 10-5.30. *STOCK: English furniture - mahogany, rosewood and walnut, 1720-1840; mirrors and pictures; all £100-£45,000.* SIZE: Medium. PARK: Nearby.
TEL: 01798 343638
E-MAIL: wilkinson.antiques@virgin.net

PULBOROUGH

Georgia Antiques
The Barn, Broomershill Farm. RH20 2HZ. (Georgia Hicks)
EST. 1979. CINOA. Open by appointment. *STOCK: English furniture, pictures and fine art, 18th-19th C; decorative lighting, 19th C.* SIZE: Medium. PARK: Easy. VAT: Spec.
TEL: 01798 872348
E-MAIL: georgia@georgia-antiques.com
WEBSITE: www.georgia-antiques.com

Elaine Saunderson Antiques   BADA
(Mr. John Saunderson)
EST. 1988. Open by appointment. *STOCK: Furniture, late 18th to early 19th C, £1,000-£25,000; decorative items.* SER: Valuations; restorations (furniture). SIZE:

Medium. VAT: Spec. FAIRS: BADA; Olympia (June).
TEL: 01798 875528; FAX: 01798 872860; MOBILE: 07836 597485
E-MAIL: elaine.saunderson@lineone.net

SHOREHAM-BY-SEA

Rodney Arthur Classics
Unit 5 Riverbank Business Centre, Old Shoreham Rd. BN43 5FL. (Rodney Oliver)
EST. 1979. Open 9.30-5, Sat. and Sun. by appointment. *STOCK: Furniture, 1800-1920, £100-£2,500.* LOC: From A27 take A283 exit near Shoreham Airport, then south towards sea, shop opposite Swiss Cottage pub. SER: Restorations; French polishing. SIZE: Large. VAT: Stan/Spec.
TEL: 01273 441606; FAX: 01273 441977

SOUTH HARTING

Julia Holmes Antique Maps and Prints
South Gardens Cottage. GU31 5QJ.
EST. 1971. FATG. Open by appointment. *STOCK: Maps, mainly British Isles, 1600-1850, £25-£2,000; prints, especially sporting, 1740 to date, to £500.* LOC: End of main street, on the Chichester road. SER: Valuations; restorations; cleaning; colouring maps and prints; framing; buys at auction. SIZE: Medium. PARK: Opposite. FAIRS: Local and major sporting events.
TEL: 01730 825040;
E-MAIL: southgardens@beeb.net
WEBSITE: www.juliamaps.co.uk

STEYNING

David R. Fileman
Squirrels, Bayards. BN44 3AA. (David, Sandra, John, Adam, Daniel and Rachael Fileman)
EST. 1972. Open daily. *STOCK: Table glass, £20-£1,000; chandeliers, candelabra, £500-£20,000; all 18th-19th C. Collectors' items, 17th-19th C, £25-£2,000; paperweights, 19th C, £50-£5,000.* LOC: A283 to north of Steyning village. SER: Valuations; restorations (chandeliers and candelabra). SIZE: Small. VAT: Stan/Spec.
TEL: 01903 813229
E-MAIL: david@filemanantiques.co.uk

STORRINGTON

Stable Antiques
46 West St. RH20 4EE. (Ian J. Wadey)
EST. 1993. Open 10-6 including Sun. *STOCK: General antiques, furniture and bric-a-brac, £1-£1,000.* LOC: A283 west of A24 towards Pulborough, just before Amberley turn. SIZE: Large. 35 stallholders. PARK: Easy.
TEL: 01903 740555; FAX: 01903 740441
WEBSITE: www.stableantiques.co.uk

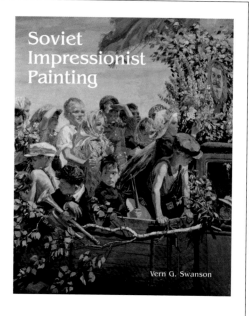
WISBOROUGH

William Hockley Antiques
Malthouse Cottage. RH14 0ES. (D. and V. Thrower) EST. 1974. Open by appointment. *STOCK: French and country furniture, English fruitwood and early oak.* SER: Interior design. PARK: Easy. VAT: Stan/Spec.
TEL: 01403 701917

WORTHING

Acorn Antiques
91 Rowlands Rd. BN11 3JX. (Henry Nicholls) EST. 1992. Open 9-5.30, Mon. and Wed. 9-4. *STOCK: Furniture, china and porcelain, silver and jewellery, 18th-20th C.* LOC: Off Heene Road near seafront. SER: House clearance, probate valuations. SIZE: Large. PARK: Easy. FAIRS: Ardingly; Kempton Park.
TEL: 01903 216926.
E-MAIL: hnic@ntlworld.com

Chloe Antiques
61 Brighton Rd. BN11 3EE. (Mrs D. Peters) EST. 1960. Chamber of Trade; Town Centre Initiative.

Open 10-4.30. CL: Wed. *STOCK: General antiques, jewellery, china, glass, bric-a-brac.* LOC: From Brighton, on main road just past Beach House Park on corner. SIZE: Small. PARK: Opposite.
TEL: 01903 202697

Wilsons Antiques   LAPADA
45-47 New Broadway, Tarring Rd. BN11 4HS. (F. and K.P. Wilson)
EST. 1936. CINOA. Open 10-4.30, other times by appointment. CL: Mon. *STOCK: Period furniture, 18th-19th C, £100-£10,000; Edwardian furniture, £50-£4,000; decorative items, 19th C, £10-£750; watercolours and oil paintings, 19th-20th C. NOT STOCKED: Pine.* LOC: Near West Worthing railway station. SER: Valuations. SIZE: Medium. PARK: Easy. VAT: Stan/Spec/Global. FAIRS: Goodwood House; Petersfield; Olympia.
TEL: 01903 202059; FAX: 01903 206300;
MOBILE: 07778 813395
E-MAIL: frank@wilsons-antiques.com
WEBSITE: www.wilsons-antiques.com

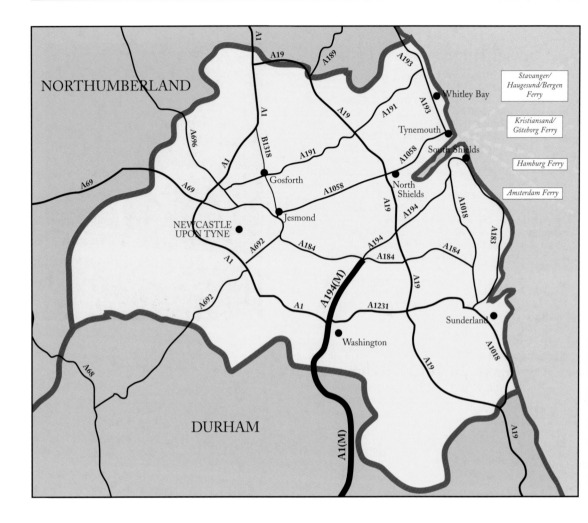

CLEADON

Cleadon Antiques and Gifts
41a Front St. SR6 7PG (Mrs. J. Brown)
EST. 2004. Open 10-4.30 Tues. and Thurs., 10-1 Weds., 10-4 Fri., 9.30-3.30 Sat. STOCK: *Affordable antiques, small pieces of furniture, quality gifts.* SER: Small items bought. SIZE: Small. FAIRS: Colin Caygill.
TEL: 0191 519 4444
E-MAIL: judybtreach@aol.com

JESMOND

@ Fern Avenue
75-79 Fern Ave. NE2 2RA. (Barbara Oliver)
EST. 2006. Open 10-5, Sun 11-2. STOCK: *Victorian and Edwardian British furniture, textiles, 17th–18th C, glass, chandeliers, mirrors.* LOC: Follow city centre motorway to Jesmond exit, north up Osborne Rd. then right into Fern Ave. SER: Framing. SIZE: Large. PARK: Own.
TEL: 0191 209 4321; MOBILE: 07951 035038

E-MAIL: boliver@fernavenue.co.uk
WEBSITE: www.fernavenue.co.uk

Shiners of Jesmond
81 Fern Avenue, NE2 2RA. (M. Nolan and B. Gibbons)
EST. 2003. SALVO. Open 10-5, Sun 11-1.30. STOCK: *Antique and period fireplaces, fires, door furniture, pine and vestibule doors, lighting, fenders.* LOC: Near city centre next to Little Theatre Antiques Centre. SER: Fireplace fitting; brass polishing. SIZE: Large. PARK: Easy. VAT: Stan.
TEL: 0191 281 6474
E-MAIL: shinersjesmond@btconnect.com

A.C. Silver LAPADA
at Graham Smith Antiques, 83 Fern Avenue. NE2 2RA. (Andrew Campbell)
EST. 1976. Open 10-5. STOCK: *Silver, 17th-20th C, £100-£10,000; silver plate, 19th-20th C, £50-£15,000; jewellery, £100-£10,000.* SER: Valuations. PARK: Easy. VAT: Stan/Spec.
TEL: 0191 281 5065; MOBILE: 07836 286218

E-MAIL: andrew.campbell@acsilver.co.uk
WEBSITE: www.acsilver.co.uk

Graham Smith Antiques   LAPADA
83 Fern Avenue. NE2 2RA. (Graham Smith)
EST. 1999. Open 10-5. STOCK: *Furniture, 18th-20th C,*
£50-£8,000; works of art, 18th-19th C, £100-£10,000;
smalls, 18th-20th C, £10-£2,000. LOC: **Follow signs to**
Fern Avenue Antiques Village off Osborne Rd. SER:
Valuations. SIZE: Large. PARK: Easy. VAT: Stan/Spec.
FAIRS: Newark; Mansion House, Newcastle.
TEL: **0191 281 5065**; MOBILE: **07836 251873**
E-MAIL: gsmithantiques@aol.com
WEBSITE: www.grahamsmithantiques.co.uk
www.lapada.org (online gallery)

NEWCASTLE-UPON-TYNE

Corbitt Stamps Ltd
5 Mosley St. NE1 1YE. (David McMonagle)
EST. 1962. PTS. BNTA. ASDA (New York). Open 9-5,
Sat. 9.30-4. STOCK: *Worldwide stamps, some coins and*
medals, post and cigarette cards, bank notes. LOC: Near Tyne
bridge. SER: Valuations; regular stamp and coin auctions.
PARK: Opposite.
TEL: 0191 232 7268; FAX: 0191 261 4130
E-MAIL: info@corbitts.com
WEBSITE: www.corbitts.com

Davidsons the Jewellers Ltd
94 and 96 Grey St. NE1 6AG. (Anthony and Helen
Davidson)
EST. 1898. NAG. Open 9-5.30. STOCK: *Jewellery, silver.*
TEL: 0191 232 2551; FAX: 0191 232 0714
WEBSITE: www.davidsonsthejewellers.co.uk

Intercoin
103 Clayton St. NE1 5PZ.
EST. 1968. Open 9-4.30. STOCK: *Coins and items of*
numismatic interest; jewellery, silver. LOC: City centre.
TEL: 0191 232 2064

Newcastle Antique Centre
2nd Floor, 142 Northumberland St. NE1 7DQ.
(L. Ingham, D. King and C. Parkin)
EST. 1972. Open 10-5. STOCK: *Art Deco, Arts & Crafts,*
Art Nouveau, Maling, militaria, stamps, coins and postcards;
railway items, tinplate, watches, Georgian and Victorian
silver, glass, gold, silver, jewellery; football memorabilia.
LOC: Opposite Haymarket Metro. SER: Valuations;
restorations (china and jewellery); repairs (watches,
clocks and jewellery). SIZE: Small. PARK: NCP nearby.
FAIRS: Newark; NEC; Swinderby; Edinburgh.
TEL: 0191 232 9832; MOBILE: 07885 060155
E-MAIL: timeantique@talktalk.net
WEBSITE: www.timeantiques.co.uk

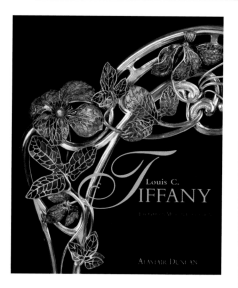

NORTH SHIELDS

Keel Row Books
11 Fenwick Terrace. NE29 0LU. (Anthony J. Smithson)
EST. 1980. PBFA. Open 10-5 including Sun. *STOCK: Books - military, cinema, theatre, local history, art, railways, children's, topography, sci-fi, crime fiction, Penguin aircraft, maritime, antiquarian, £1-£1,000.* LOC: Off Preston Rd. SER: Valuations; restorations. SIZE: Large. PARK: Nearby. FAIRS: York; Edinburgh; Durham.
TEL: 0191 296 0664; HOME: 0191 259 1331
E-MAIL: anthony.books@wildmail.com
WEBSITE: www.keelrowbookshop.co.uk

SUNDERLAND

Peter Smith Antiques   LAPADA
12-14 Borough Rd. SR1 1EP.
EST. 1968. Open 9.30-4.30, Sat. 10-1, other times by appointment. *STOCK: Georgian, Victorian, Edwardian longcase clocks, shipping goods, £5-£15,000.* **LOC: 10 miles from A1(M); towards docks/Hendon from town centre. SER: Valuations; restorations; some shipping; containers packed; buys at auction. SIZE: Warehouse. PARK: Easy. VAT: Stan/Spec.**
TEL: 0191 567 3537/567 7842; HOME: 0191 514 0008; MOBILE: 07802 273372
E-MAIL: petersmithantiques@btinternet.com
WEBSITE: www.petersmithantiques.com

TYNEMOUTH

Curio Corner
Unit 5/6 The Land of Green Ginger, Front St. NE30 4BP. (S. Welton)
EST. 1988. Open 10.30-4.30 inc. Sun. *STOCK: Reproduction and antique furniture, chandeliers, clocks, lighting.* LOC: Converted church. SIZE: Medium. PARK: Easy.
TEL: 0191 296 3316; MOBILE: 07809 504517
E-MAIL: susanwelton@msn.com
WEBSITE: www.curiocorner.co.uk

Ian Sharp Antiques Ltd.   LAPADA
23 Front St. NE30 4DX.
EST. 1988. Open 10-1 and 1.30-5. CL: Mon. or by appointment. *STOCK: Furniture, 19th to early 20th C; British pottery including northern especially Sunderland lustreware, 18th to early 20th C; paintings by north eastern artists, 19th-20th C.* **SIZE: Small. PARK: Easy. VAT: Global/Spec. FAIRS: Newark.**
TEL: 0191 296 0656; FAX: same
E-MAIL: iansharp@sharpantiques.com
WEBSITE: www.sharpantiques.com

Tynemouth Architectural Salvage
Correction House, 28 Tynemouth Rd. NE30 4AA. (Robin S. Archer)
EST. 1998. Open 9-5, Sat. 10-5. *STOCK: Antique doors and furniture, bathroom fittings, cast iron radiators (fully restored); other internal architectural features.* LOC: Short walk from Tynemouth Metro station, opposite Tanners Bank; 10 miles from Newcastle, 2 miles from Tyne Tunnel. SER: Restoration of cast iron radiators, antique plumbing fittings (electroplating). SIZE: Large. PARK: Easy.
TEL: 0191 296 6070
E-MAIL: robin@tynarcsal.demon.co.uk
WEBSITE: www.tynemoutharchitecturalsalvage.co.uk

WASHINGTON

Harold J. Carr Antiques
Field House, Rickleton. NE38 9HQ.
EST. 1970. Open by appointment. *STOCK: General antiques and furniture.* SER: Shippers.
TEL: 0191 388 6442.

WHITLEY BAY

Northumbria Pine
54 Whitley Rd. NE26 2NF. (C. and V. Dowland)
EST. 1979. Open 10-5. *STOCK: Reproduction, stripped, reclaimed and made to order pine items. Also oak, beech, ash and painted.* LOC: Cullercoats end of Whitley Rd. behind sea front. SER: Free local delivery; restorations (table tops). SIZE: Small. PARK: Easy. VAT: Stan.
TEL: 0191 252 4550
WEBSITE: www.northumbria-pine.co.uk

Olivers Bookshop
48A Whitley Rd. NE26 2NF. (J. Oliver)
EST. 1986. Open 11-5. CL: Tues. and Wed. *STOCK: Antiquarian and secondhand books, 50p to £500.* SER: Valuations. SIZE: Medium. PARK: Easy. FAIRS: Tynemouth Book.
TEL: 0191 251 3552

Treasure Chest
2 and 4 Norham Rd. NE26 2SB.
EST. 1974. Open 10.30-1 and 2-4. *STOCK: General antiques.* LOC: Just off main shopping area of Park View, leading to Monkseaton rail station. SER: Valuations. SIZE: Small. PARK: Easy.
TEL: 0191 251 2052; MOBILE: 07808 966611

The Ewers-Tyne Collection of
WORCESTER PORCELAIN
at CHEEKWOOD
John Sandon

This catalogue of the Ewers-Tyne Collection provides lovers of fine porcelain with a very special opportunity. Curiously, this is the first time that all three centuries of Worcester porcelain have been presented together in a single book. The earliest pieces at Cheekwood were made in the middle of the eighteenth century. During the Dr Wall Period, Worcester porcelain was inspired by China and Japan and yet has an English charm all of its own. Important early coloured wares copy royal productions from Dresden and Sèvres. Here are special pieces from famous services, some painted in the Giles workshop in London. Split into two separate factories during the Regency period, the Flight family ran the original Worcester works in partnership with the Barrs. Meanwhile the Chamberlain family set up a rival factory across the city. Many masterpieces from the early nineteenth century are in the Ewers-Tyne Collection, including specimens from some of the finest armorial services finished off with sumptuous gilding. The Worcester Royal Porcelain Company, known today as Royal Worcester, was established in 1862. The Victorian period is represented at Cheekwood by the incredible figures of James Hadley and Thomas Brock, while painted porcelain by senior artists show how the traditions of fine craftsmanship continued into the twentieth century. Henry and John Sandon are the leading authorities on Worcester porcelain and their informative text accompanies clear colour illustrations of every piece. The result is a beautiful as well as invaluable reference book detailing the long history of porcelain making at Worcester. This sumptuous volume provides a fitting tribute to an inspired collection housed in the gorgeous setting of Cheekwood in Nashville, Tennessee.

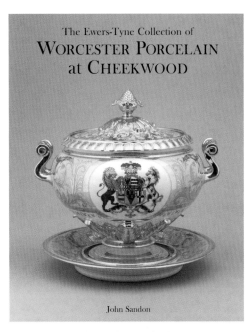

The Ewers-Tyne Collection of
WORCESTER PORCELAIN
at CHEEKWOOD

John Sandon

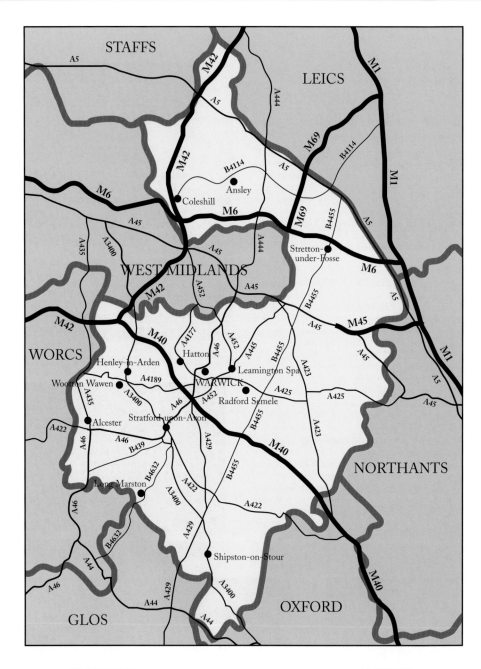

ALCESTER

High St. Antiques
11A High St. B49 5AE. (V.F.S. and J.F. Baldwin)
EST. 1979. Open Fri. 12-5 and Sat. 10-5 or by appointment. STOCK: *Glass and china, 18th-20th C, £5-£200; postcards, books, brass and copper, silver and jewellery.* LOC: On left-hand side near church coming from Stratford-on-Avon road. SIZE: Small. PARK: Rear of High St.
TEL: 01789 764009

ANSLEY

Granary Antiques
Hoar Park Craft Centre. CV10 0QU. (P.H. Cutler)
EST. 1987. Open 10-5 including Sun. CL: Mon. except Bank Holidays. STOCK: *Furniture, china, glass, jewellery, lighting, books and collectables.* SIZE: Medium. PARK: Easy. FAIRS: Newark.
TEL: 02476 395551
E-MAIL: granaryantiques@aol.com

HATTON

The Stables Antique Centre
Hatton Country World, Dark Lane. CV35 8XA. (John and Margaret Colledge)
EST. 1990. Open 10-5 including Sun. STOCK: *Furniture, 18th-19th C, £50–£3,000; china, 19th-20th C, £5–£200; clocks, 18th-19th C, £200–£4,000; linen, glass, brass and copper, paintings and prints, jewellery and telephones.* LOC: Just off A4177 Solihull-Warwick road, 5 mins. from junction 15, M40. SER: Valuations. SIZE: Large - 25 units. PARK: Own.
TEL: 01926 842405
E-MAIL: hatton@hattonworld.com
WEBSITE: www.hattonworld.com

HENLEY-IN-ARDEN

Arden Gallery
54 High St B95 5AN. (G.B. Horton)
EST. 1963. Open 2-6. CL: Thurs. and Sat. STOCK: *Victorian oil paintings, £20–£1,000; watercolours, all periods, to £1,500; portrait miniatures.* LOC: A3400. SIZE: Medium. PARK: Easy. VAT: Spec.
TEL: 01564 792520

Henley Antiques Centre
92 High St. B95 5BY. (Mrs Rosie Montague and Mrs Gill Rayson)
EST. 2001. Open 10.30-5, Sun. and BH 11-4. STOCK: *Furniture, porcelain and collectables, 19th to early 20th C, £20–£2,000.* LOC: Behind bakery at pedestrian crossing lights. SER: Valuations; restorations (furniture). SIZE: Large. PARK: Easy. FAIRS: NEC.
TEL: 01564 795979; MOBILE: 07950 324376

LEAMINGTON SPA

King's Cottage Antiques   LAPADA
4 Windsor St. CV32 5EB. (G. and A. Jackson)
EST. 1993. Open 9-4, Sat. by appointment. STOCK: *Early oak and country furniture, 16th-18th C.* SIZE: Large.
TEL: 01926 422927

LONG MARSTON

Barn Antiques Centre
Station Rd. CV37 8RP. (Bev and Graham Simpson)
EST. 1978. Open 10-5, Sun. 12-6. STOCK: *Georgian, Victorian, Edwardian and later furniture, collectables, silver, porcelain, china, kitchenalia, fireplaces, linen, pictures, 18th C to 1950, £5–£2,000.* LOC: Approx. 5 miles from Stratford. SIZE: Large - 50+ dealers. PARK: Own.
TEL: 01789 721399
WEBSITE: www.barnantique.co.uk

RADFORD SEMELE

Arcadia Antiques
Westfield Farm, Fosse Way. CV31 1XL. (Jack Harness)
EST. 1981. Open by appointment. STOCK: *French and English country furniture.* SER: Restorations; courier. VAT: Stan/Spec.
TEL: 01926 611923; FAX: 01926 611924; MOBILE: 07768 666833
E-MAIL: jackharness@aol.com
WEBSITE: www.arcadiaantiques.co.uk.

SHIPSTON-ON-STOUR

London House Antiques
17 High St. CV36 4AJ.
Open 10-5 inc. Sun. STOCK: *General antiques.*
TEL: 01608 663737

Pine and Things
Portobello Farm, Campden Rd. CV36 4PY. (Richard Wood)
EST. 1991. Open 9-5. STOCK: *Pine, 18th-19th C, £50–£2,000.* LOC: A429/B4035. SIZE: Large - 6 showrooms. PARK: Ample. VAT: Stan/Spec.
TEL: 01608 663849; HOME: same
E-MAIL: sales@pinethings.co.uk
WEBSITE: www.pinethings.co.uk

Time in Hand (Shipston) Ltd

11 Church St. CV36 4AP. (F.R. Bennett)
EST. 1979. Open 9-1 and 2-5.30, Sat. 9-5. STOCK: *Longcase, carriage, mantel and wall clocks, barometers.* LOC: Opposite church on main road. SER: Restorations (clocks, watches, barometers and mechanical instruments). SIZE: Large. PARK: Free - Banbury Road.
TEL: 01608 662578
WEBSITE: www.timeinhand.co.uk

STRATFORD-UPON-AVON

Burman Antiques

34 College St. CV37 6BW. (J. and J. Burman Holtom)
EST. 1973. Open by appointment. STOCK: *Ruskin ware, pot-lids, fishing tackle.*
TEL: 01789 295164

Thomas Crapper & Co

The Stable Yard, Alscot Park. CV37 8BL. (S.P.J. Kirby)
EST. 1861. SALVO. Open by appointment. STOCK: *Hand-made replicas of Crapper's original fittings. Antique decorated WCs.* SER: Valuations; restorations (bathroom fittings). SIZE: Medium. PARK: Easy.
TEL: 01789 450522; FAX: 01789 450523
E-MAIL: wc@thomas-crapper.com
WEBSITE: www.thomas-crapper.com

Howards Jewellers

44a Wood St. CV37 6JG.
EST. 1985. NAG. Open 9.30-5.30. STOCK: *Jewellery, silver, objets d'art, 19th C.* LOC: Town centre. SER: Valuations; restorations (as stock). PARK: Nearby. VAT: Stan/Spec.
TEL: 01789 205404

George Pragnell Ltd

5 & 6 Wood St. CV37 6JA. (Jeremy Pragnell)
EST. 1954. NAG. Open 9.30-5.30. STOCK: *Fine jewellery, silver, clocks and watches.* LOC: Town centre. SER: Valuations; repairs; remodelling. SIZE: Large. PARK: Nearby. VAT: Stan/Spec. FAIRS: NEC.
TEL: 01789 267072; FAX: 01789 415131
E-MAIL: enquiries@pragnell.co.uk
WEBSITE: www.pragnell.co.uk

Stratford Antique Centre

60 Ely St. CV37 6LN. (Sherman and Waterman)
Open 10-5 including Sun. STOCK: *General antiques.* SIZE: 30 dealers.
TEL: 01789 204180; 020 7240 7405

The Stratford Antiques and Interiors Centre Ltd

Dodwell Industrial Park, Evesham Rd. CV37 9ST. (David & Sue Wilkes)
EST. 1980. Open 10-5 including Sun. STOCK: *Georgian, Victorian, Edwardian and shipping furniture, £100-£10,000; china and smalls, 19th-20th C, £5-£2,000; reclaimed pine, £50-£10,000.* LOC: B439. SER:

Valuations; restorations. SIZE: 25+ dealers. PARK: Easy. VAT: Margin. FAIRS: Newark; Ardingly; NEC; Earls Court.
TEL: 01789 297729; FAX: 01789 297710
WEBSITE: www.stratfordantiques.org.uk

STRETTON-ON-FOSSE

Astley House - Fine Art

The Old School. GL56 9SA. (David, Nanette and Caradoc Glaisyer)
EST. 1973. CADA. Open by appointment. STOCK: *Large decorative oil paintings, 19th-21st C.* LOC: Village centre. SER: Exhibitions; mailing list. SIZE: Large. PARK: Easy. VAT: Spec.
TEL: 01608 650601; FAX: 01608 651777
E-MAIL: astart333@aol.com
WEBSITE: www.art-uk.com

WARWICK

Duncan M. Allsop

68 Smith St. CV34 4HS.
EST. 1965. ABA. Open 10-4.30. CL: Mon. STOCK: *Antiquarian and modern books.* LOC: East Gate, opposite Roebuck Inn. SER: Valuations; buying, especially antiquarian. SIZE: Medium. PARK: Nearby. VAT: Stan. FAIRS: Royal National Hotel; Pavilion Gardens, Buxton; Memorial Hall, Long Melford.
TEL: 01926 493266; FAX: same; MOBILE: 07770 895924
E-MAIL: veronica.allsop@btinternet.com
WEBSITE: www.ukbookworld.com/members/allsop

Apollo Antiques   LAPADA

1a St Johns. CV34 4NE. (J. Mynott)
EST. 1968. Usually open Mon.-Fri., prior telephone call advisable. STOCK: *English furniture, 17th-20th C; Arts and Crafts and decorative items.* SIZE: Large. PARK: Easy. VAT: Stan/Spec
TEL: 01926 494666; FAX: 01926 401477
E-MAIL: mynott@apolloantiques.com

Castle Antiques

24 Swan St. CV34 4BJ. (Julia Reynolds)
EST. 1979. Open 10-5, Sun. by appointment. STOCK: *China, linen, silver, jewellery, furniture - 19th to early 20th C, £100-£3,000.* LOC: Town centre. SER: Restorations (ceramics). SIZE: Medium. PARK: Easy - at rear.
TEL: 01926 401511; FAX: 01926 492469
E-MAIL: juliamarica@hotmail.co.uk

John Cornall Antiques

28 West St. CV34 6AN. (John Cornwall and Sarah Lovelock)
EST. 2000. Open 11-5.30. CL: Mon. STOCK: *Country and primitive furniture, painted pine, folk art, textiles, British and continental paintings.* SER: Warehouse viewing by appointment. SIZE: Large PARK: Outside. VAT: Global.

FAIRS: Newark
TEL: 01296 492029; MOBILE: 07813 975175
E-MAIL: johncornall@aol.com
WEBSITE: www.johncornallantiques.com

Cornmarket Antiques Centre
40 Brook St. CV34 4BL. (Terry Hare-Walker)
EST. 1982. Open 10-5. STOCK: *General antiques including silver, jewellery, watches, porcelain, pictures and militaria.* LOC: Opposite Post Office. SER: Repairs (silver, jewellery). SIZE: 8 dealers. PARK: Metered nearby.
TEL: 01926 419119

Russell Lane Antiques
2-4 High St. CV34 4AP. (R.G.H. Lane)
Open 9.30-5. STOCK: *Fine jewellery and silver.* SER: Valuations; repairs; redesign. PARK: Metered nearby.
TEL: 01926 494494; FAX: 01926 492972
E-MAIL: russell-lane@tiscali.co.uk

Patrick and Gillian Morley Antiques   LAPADA
62 West St. CV34 6AW.
EST. 1968. Open 10-5, or by prior appointment. CL: Mon. STOCK: *Furniture, 17th to late 19th C; unusual and decorative items, sculpture, carvings; all £250-£100,000.* SIZE: **Large.** PARK: **Easy.** VAT: **Spec.**
TEL: 01926 494464; MOBILE: 07768 835040
E-MAIL: morleyantiques@tinyworld.co.uk

James Reeve
at Quinneys of Warwick, 9 Church St. CV34 4AB.
(J.C. and D.J. Reeve)
EST. 1865. Open 9.30-5.30. CL: Sat. pm. STOCK: *Furniture, mahogany, oak, and rosewood, 17th-18th C, £80-£30,000; furniture, 19th C, £50-£10,000; glass, copper, brass, pewter, china.* LOC: Town centre. SER: Restorations; re-polishing. PARK: Easy. VAT: Stan/Spec.
TEL: 01926 498113
E-MAIL: jamesreeve@callnetuk.com
WEBSITE: www.jamesreeveantiques.co.uk

Summersons
172 Emscote Rd. CV34 5QN. (Peter Lightfoot)
EST. 1969. MBHI. Open 10-5, Sat. 10-1. STOCK: *Clocks and barometers.* LOC: A445 Rugby Rd. SER: Restorations; repairs; materials and parts. SIZE: Small. PARK: Free. VAT: Spec.
TEL: 01926 400630; FAX: same; MOBILE: 07770 300695
E-MAIL: clocks@summersons.com
WEBSITE: www.summersons.com

Vintage Antiques Centre
36 Market Place. CV34 4SH. (Peter Sellors)
EST. 1977. WADA. Open 10-5.30. STOCK: *Ceramics, glass, collectables and small furniture, 19th-20th C.* LOC: Town centre. SIZE: 20 dealers + cabinets. PARK: Easy.
FAIRS: NEC; National Glass.
TEL: 01926 491527

E-MAIL: vintage@globalnet.co.uk
WEBSITE: www.warwickchamberoftrade.co.uk

The Warwick Antique Centre
20-22 High St. CV34 4AP. (P.E. Viola)
EST. 1973. BNTA. Open 10-5. STOCK: *Porcelain, silver and plate, jewellery, coins, militaria, books, furniture, stamps, metalware, toys, collectables, postcards, glass.* SIZE: 25 dealers. PARK: Easy.
TEL: 01926 491382/495704

WOOTTON WAWEN

Le Grenier Antiques
Yew Tree Craft Centre, Stratford Rd. B95 6BY. (Joyce Ellis and Clive Evans)
EST. 1991. FSB. Open 9-5, Sat. and Sun. 10-5. CL: Mon. STOCK: *French furniture, mainly beds; bedroom furniture, tables, chairs, armoires and buffet cabinets. Made to measure bases and mattresses.* LOC: A3400. SER: Valuations; restorations. SIZE: Medium. PARK: Easy. VAT: Margin.
TEL: 01564 795401; MOBILE: 07712 126048
E-MAIL: info@legrenierantiques.co.uk
WEBSITE: www.legrenierantiques.co.uk

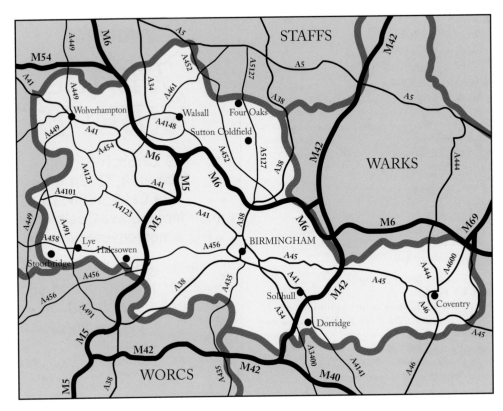

BALSALL COMMON

Antiques in a Barn
Old Lodge Farm, Kenilworth Rd. CV7 7EY. (Diane and John Wright)
EST. 1995. Open 11-4, Sat. and Sun. 10-5. STOCK: *19th and 20th C furniture, china, jewellery and collectables.* SIZE: Large. PARK: Own.
TEL: 01676 535282
E-MAIL: xoxsilversky929@aol.co.uk

BIRMINGHAM

Peter Asbury Antiques
Greenfield House Farm, 6 Hales Lane, Smethwick, Warley. B67 6RS. (Mrs Susan Asbury)
EST. 1986. Open 9.30-5. STOCK: *General antiques.* SER: Repairs (dolls, teddy bears). PARK: Limited.
TEL: 0121 558 0579

Paul Baxter
B47 6LS.
Open by appointment. STOCK: *Oriental ceramics and general antiques.* FAIRS: Newark.
TEL: 01564 824920
E-MAIL: wpaulbaxter@blueyonder.co.uk

The Birmingham Antique Centre
1403-1407 Pershore Rd., Stirchley. B30 2JR. (David Baldock and Sandra Arblaster)

EST. 1960. Open 9-5, Sun. 10-4. STOCK: *General antiques, collectables, jewellery, Clarice Cliff, Royal Doulton, Oriental art, toys, trade display cabinets.* LOC: Corner with Maryvale Rd. SIZE: 3 showrooms, 60 cabinets. PARK: Free at rear.
TEL: 0121 459 4587
E-MAIL: bhamantiquecent@aol.com
WEBSITE: www.birminghamantiquecentre.co.uk

Chesterfield Antiques
181 Gravelly Lane. B23 5SG. (Mara Cirjanic)
EST. 1977. Open 9.30-5. STOCK: *General antiques and fine art; specialising in Victorian and Edwardian items and some Art Deco.*
TEL: 0121 373 3876

R. Collyer
185 New Rd., Rubery. B45 9JP.
EST. 1947. Open 9.15-5.30. STOCK: *Secondhand jewellery.* LOC: 1 mile from junction 4, M5. SER: Valuations; restorations. PARK: Free.
TEL: 0121 453 2332

Dolly Mixtures
B68 0AU.
EST. 1979. Open by appointment. STOCK: *Dolls and teddies.* SER: Restorations.
TEL: 0121 422 6959

Format of Birmingham Ltd
Burlington Court, 2nd floor, 18 Lower Temple St. B2

4JD. (G. Charman and D. Vice)
EST. 1973. BNTA. IAPN. Open 9.30-5. CL: Sat. STOCK: *Coins, medals.* PARK: New St. station. VAT: Stan/Spec.
TEL: 0121 643 2058

A.W. Hone and Son Oriental Carpets
1486 Stratford Rd., Hall Green. B28 9ET. (Ian Hone)
EST. 1949. BORDA. Open 9.30-5.30, Sun. 11-4. STOCK: *Persian rugs and carpets, late 19th C to date.* LOC: A34 south of city on Robin Hood Island. SER: Valuations; restorations; finder. SIZE: Medium. PARK: Own forecourt. VAT: Stan.
TEL: 0121 744 1001; FAX: same
E-MAIL: honerugs@btopenworld.com
WEBSITE: www.honerugs.co.uk

Rex Johnson and Sons
8 Corporation St. B2 4RN. (D. Johnson)
Open 9.15-5.15. STOCK: *Gold, silver, jewellery, porcelain and glass.*
TEL: 0121 643 9674
E-MAIL: rexjohnsonandson@aol.com
WEBSITE: www.rexjohnson.com

F. Meeks & Co
197 Warstone Lane, Hockley. B18 6JR. (M.L. and S.R. Durham)
Open 9-5, Sat. 9-12. STOCK: *Clocks especially longcase, mantel and wall; vintage wrist watches and antique pocket watches; all £100-£10,000.* SER: Valuations; restorations (clocks); clock and watch parts supplied. VAT: Stan/Spec.
TEL: 0121 236 9058

Moseley Emporium
116 Alcester Rd., Moseley. B13 3EF. (G. Dorney)
EST. 1982. Open 10-6. STOCK: *Georgian to 1930s furniture, £75-£3,800.* SER: Restorations (stripping, polishing, finishing furniture). SIZE: Medium. PARK: Easy. FAIRS: Newark.
TEL: 0121 449 3441; MOBILE: 07973 156902
E-MAIL: gmd13@hotmail.co.uk

Piccadilly Jewellers
105 New St. B2 4HD. (R. and R. Johnson)
Open 10-5. STOCK: *Jewellery, silver and objets d'art.* SER: Valuations.
TEL: 0121 643 5791

David Temperley Fine and Antiquarian Books
19 Rotton Park Rd., Edgbaston. B16 9JH. (D. and R.A. Temperley)
EST. 1967. Resident. Open 9.30-5.30 by appointment. STOCK: *Fine antiquarian and rare books, 16th-20th C especially fine bindings, illustrated and private press; fine colour plate books - natural history, costume, travel; British topography and atlases; children's books, especially moveable and pop-up; early and rare English and European playing cards; games.* LOC: 150 yards off Hagley Rd. (A456) and under 2 miles from city centre. 4 miles junction 3, M5. SER: Valuations; restorations (book

binding and paper); buys at auction (antiquarian books). SIZE: Small. PARK: Easy.
TEL: 0121 454 0135; FAX: 0121 454 1124

S. and E.M. Turner Violins
1 Gibb St., Digbeth. B9 4AA. (Steve and Liz Turner)
EST. 1987. Open 9.30-5.30, Sat 9-5. STOCK: *18th-20th C violins, violas, cellos, basses, bows; old flutes, clarinets, concertinas, guitars, harps, oboes and saxophones.* SER: Valuations; restorations.
TEL: 0121 772 7708; FAX: 0121 772 8450; MOBILE: 07831 265272
E-MAIL: info@turnerviolins.co.uk
WEBSITE: www.turnerviolins.co.uk

COVENTRY

Antiques Adventure
Rugby Rd., Binley Woods. CV3 2AW. (J. Green)
EST. 1969. Open 10-5 including Sun. STOCK: *Georgian, Victorian, Edwardian, contemporary, 1950s and 1960s furniture and effects; French and Chinese furniture, jewellery. Also some reproduction interior furnishings.* LOC: Just off A46 eastern bypass, entrance off A428 Rugby road. SER: Delivery (UK); shipping advice. SIZE: Large - 40 dealers. PARK: Easy. VAT: Global/Spec/Stan.
TEL: 02476 453878; FAX: 02476 445847
E-MAIL: sales@antiquesadventure.co.uk
WEBSITE: www.antiquesadventure.co.uk

FOUR OAKS

M. Allen Watch and Clockmaker
76A Walsall Rd. B74 4QY. (M.A. Allen)
EST. 1969. Open 9-5.30, Sun. by appointment. STOCK:
*Vintage wristwatches - Omega, Longines, Girard, Perregaux
and Jaeger le Coultre.* LOC: By Sutton Park, close to
television mast. SER: Valuations; restorations (clocks and
watches). SIZE: Small. PARK: Easy. VAT: Stan/Spec.
TEL: 0121 308 6117
WEBSITE: www.michaelallenwatchmaker.co.uk

HALESOWEN

S.R. Furnishing and Antiques
Unit 1, Eagle Trading Estate, Stourbridge Rd. B63
3UA. (S. Willder)
EST. 1975. STOCK: *General antiques and shipping furniture.*
TEL: MOBILE: 07860 820221

LYE

Lye Antique Furnishings
206 High St. DY9 8JY. (P. Smith)
EST. 1979. Open 9-5. STOCK: *Furniture, china, glass,
metalware, jewellery and collectors' items.* SER: Valuations.
SIZE: Medium. PARK: Easy.
TEL: 01384 897513; MOBILE: 07976 765142

SOLIHULL

Renaissance
18 Marshall Lake Rd., Shirley. B90 4PL. (S.K. Macrow)
EST. 1981. GMC. Open 9-5. STOCK: *General antiques.*
LOC: Near Stratford Rd. SER: Restorations (repairs, re-
upholstery and polishing). SIZE: Small.
TEL: 0121 745 5140

Yoxall Antiques   LAPADA
68 Yoxall Rd. B90 3RP. (Paul Burrows)
**EST. 1984. Open 9.30-5. STOCK: *Georgian and Regency
furniture including mahogany, walnut and rosewood;
clocks and barometers, glass and china; desks, tea caddies,
figures.* LOC: Just outside town centre. SER: Valuations;
restorations (furniture). SIZE: Medium. PARK: Easy.
FAIRS: NEC; LAPADA.
TEL: 0121 744 1744; MOBILE: 07860 168078
E-MAIL: sales@yoxallantiques.co.uk
WEBSITE: www.yoxallantiques.co.uk**

STOURBRIDGE

Oldswinford Gallery
106 Hagley Rd., Oldswinford. DY8 1QU. (A.R.
Harris)
Open 9.30-5. CL: Mon. and Sat. p.m. STOCK: *18th-20th
C oil paintings, watercolours, antiquarian prints and maps.*
SER: Restorations; framing.
TEL: 01384 395577

Regency Antique Trading Ltd.
116 Stourbridge Rd. DY9 7BU. (D. Bevan)
Open 9.30-5. STOCK: *Architectural antiques, entranceways
and stained glass.* SER: Stripping; container shipping;
fireplaces and kitchens from reclaimed pine. SIZE: 2
floors. PARK: Free.
TEL: 01384 868778
E-MAIL: regencytradingltd@blueyonder.co.uk
WEBSITE: www.regency-antiques.co.uk

Retro
48 Worcester St. DY8 1AS. (M. McHugo)
EST. 1978. Open 10-5. STOCK: *Furniture and architectural
items.*
TEL: 01384 442065; MOBILE: 07929 082076
E-MAIL: info@retroantiques.co.uk
WEBSITE: www.retroantiques.co.uk

SUTTON COLDFIELD

Thomas Coulborn and Sons   BADA
Vesey Manor, 64 Birmingham Rd. B72 1QP.
(Jonathan and Peter Coulborn)
**EST. 1939. Open 9.30-1 and 2-5.30, or by appointment.
CL: Sat. STOCK: *General antiques, 1600-1830; fine
English and Continental furniture, 17th-18th C; paintings
and clocks.* LOC: 3 miles from Spaghetti Junction. From
Birmingham A5127 through Erdington, premises on
main road opposite cinema.** SER: Valuations;
restorations (furniture and paintings); buys on
commission. SIZE: Large. PARK: Easy. VAT: Spec.
TEL: 0121 354 3974; FAX: 0121 354 4614
E-MAIL: jc@coulborn.com
WEBSITE: www.coulborn.com

Driffold Gallery
78 Birmingham Rd. B72 1QR. (David Gilbert)
EST. 1974. Open 10-6. STOCK: *Oil paintings and
watercolours, 19th C to contemporary.* LOC: Town centre
approach. SER: Valuations; restorations. SIZE: Medium.
PARK: Own. FAIRS: NEC Antiques for Everyone.
TEL: 0121 355 5433
E-MAIL: enquiries@driffoldgallery.com
WEBSITE: www.driffoldgallery.com

WALSALL

The Doghouse (Antiques)
309 Bloxwich Rd. WS2 7BD. (John and Kate Rutter)
EST. 1971. Open 9-5.30. STOCK: *General antiques,
fireplaces, architectural items.* LOC: B4210. SIZE: Large.
PARK: At rear. VAT: Stan/Spec/Global.
TEL: 01922 630829; FAX: 01922 631236
WEBSITE: www.doghouseantiques.co.uk

L.P. Furniture Ltd.
The Old Brewery, Short Acre St. WS2 8HW.
(Pierre Farouz)
EST. 1982. Open 9-5.30, weekends by appointment.

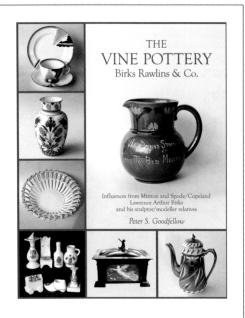
STOCK: *French, Spanish and Continental including French and Spanish decorative furniture - armoires, buffets, beds, mirrors; French style reproduction mirrors, consoles, tables, chairs and Deco furniture.* LOC: Junction 10, M6, A454 towards town centre, left on A34 towards Cannock. SIZE: Warehouse. PARK: Own. VAT: Stan. FAIRS: Swinderby.
TEL: 01922 746764; FAX: 01922 611316;
E-MAIL: pierrefarouz@btconnect.com;
lpfurniture@btconnect.com
WEBSITE: www.lpfurniture.net

WOLVERHAMPTON

No 9 Antiques
9 Upper Green, Tettenhall. WV6 8QQ.
Open 10-5.30. CL: Mon. and Tues. STOCK: *Furniture, 18th-19th C, £200-£1,000; ceramics, silver and prints, 19th C, £25-£500; works of art, £25-£1,000.* LOC: Corner of the Green. SIZE: Medium. PARK: Easy.
TEL: 01902 755333

The Red Shop
7 Hollybush Lane, Penn. WV4 4JJ. (B. Savage)
Open 9.30-5.30, Sat 9.30-4. STOCK: *Furniture including pine.* SER: Bespoke kitchens.
TEL: 01902 342915

Martin Taylor Antiques   LAPADA
140b and 323 Tettenhall Rd. WV6 0BQ.
EST. 1976. Open 8.30-5.30, Sat. 10-5, or by appointment. STOCK: *Furniture, mainly 1800-1930, for the UK, USA, Japanese and Italian markets, £50-£10,000.* **LOC: One mile from town centre on A41.** SER: **Restorations; French polishing.** SIZE: **Large + showroom.** PARK: **Easy.** VAT: **Stan/Spec.**
TEL: **01902 751166;** SHOWROOM: **01902 751122;**
MOBILE: **07836 636524;** HOME: **01785 284539;**
FAX: **01902 746502**
E-MAIL: **enquiries@mtaylor-antiques.co.uk**
WEBSITE: **www.martintaylorantiques.com**

Wolverhampton Antiques and Collectors' Market
Basement of Retail Market, Salop St. WV3 0SF.
EST. 1984. Open 9-4. CL: Mon. and Thurs. STOCK: *China, glass, jewellery, militaria, books and comics, linen, football memorabilia, 19th-20th C.* LOC: Wolverhampton ring road, exit Chapel Ash island, market signposted. SIZE: 20 units. PARK: Easy - Peel St. and Pitt St.
TEL: 01902 555212

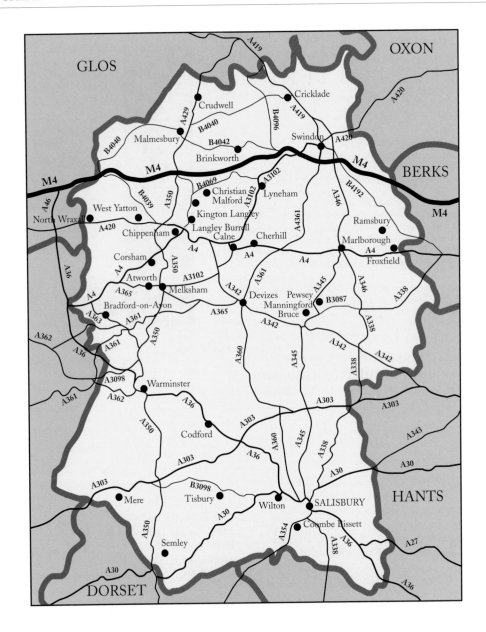

BRADFORD-ON-AVON

Avon Antiques   BADA
32 Market St. BA15 1LL. (V. and A. Jenkins BA)
EST. 1963. Open 9.45-5.30, Sun. by appointment.
STOCK: *English and some Continental furniture, 1600-*
1880; metalwork, treen, some clocks, barometers, textiles,
painted furniture; English naive pictures. LOC: A363,
main street of town. SIZE: Large. PARK: Ask at shop for
key to private parking opposite. VAT: Spec. FAIRS:
Grosvenor House; Olympia (winter).
TEL: 01225 862052; FAX: 01225 868763
E-MAIL: avonantiques@aol.com
WEBSITE: www.avon-antiques.co.uk

Andrew Dando   BADA
34 Market St. BA15 1LL. (A.P. and J.M. Dando)
EST. 1915. Open 10-5 by prior appointment. CL: Mon.
STOCK: *English (including Staffordshire), Continental and*
Oriental porcelain and pottery, 17th to mid-19th C; local
topographical and decorative antique prints. LOC: Town
centre. SER: Valuations. SIZE: Medium. PARK: Nearby.
VAT: Stan/Spec. FAIRS: Olympia (June).
TEL: 01225 865444
E-MAIL: andrew@andrewdando.co.uk
WEBSITE: www.andrewdando.co.uk

Mac Humble Antiques   BADA
7-9 Woolley St. BA15 1AD. (W. Mc. A. and B.J.
Humble)
EST. 1979. Open by appointment. STOCK: *17th-19th C*
oak, mahogany, fruitwoods, metalware, treen, samplers,
silkwork pictures, decorative objects. SER: Valuations;
restorations. SIZE: Medium. PARK: Nearby. VAT:
Stan/Spec. FAIRS: BADA (March); Olympia (Nov).
TEL: 01225 866329; FAX: same
WEBSITE: www.machumbleantiques.co.uk

Moxhams Antiques   LAPADA
17 Silver St. BA15 1JZ. (R., J. and N. Bichard)
EST. 1967. Open 9-5.30 or by appointment. STOCK:
English and Continental furniture, clocks, 1650-1850;
European and Oriental pottery and porcelain, 1700-1850;
decorative items, 1600-1900, all £50-£50,000. LOC: Near
town centre on B3107 towards Melksham. SER:
Restorations. SIZE: Large + store. PARK: Own, at rear.
VAT: Spec. FAIRS: Olympia (June, Nov).
TEL: 01225 862789; FAX: 01225 867844; HOME: 01225
783199; MOBILE: 07802 506167
E-MAIL: info@moxhams-antiques.co.uk
WEBSITE: www.moxhams-antiques.com

Trevor Waddington Antique Clocks
5 Trowbridge Rd. BA15 1EE.
EST. 1996. MBHI. WEADA. Open strictly by
appointment. STOCK: *17th-19th C clocks - longcase, £3,000-*
£30,000; wall, £1,500-£3,500; carriage, bracket and mantel,
£1,000-£9,000. LOC: Quarter mile south of town bridge
on A363. SER: Valuations; restorations (BADA/West

Dean Dip. conservator). SIZE: Small. PARK: Easy.
TEL: 01225 862351; HOME: same
E-MAIL: twclocks@aol.com
WEBSITE: www.clocks-antique.co.uk

BRINKWORTH

North Wilts Exporters
Farm Hill House. SN15 5AJ. (M.W. and C.S. Thornbury)
EST. 1972. WEADA. Open 8-5 or by appointment.
STOCK: *Pine, oak and mahogany, 18th-20th C; retro teak and elm.* LOC: 4 miles west of M4 junction 16, Malmesbury road. SER: Valuations; shipping; import and export. SIZE: Large. PARK: Own. VAT: Stan/Global.
TEL: 01666 510876; MOBILE: 07836 260730
E-MAIL: mike@northwilts.demon.co.uk
WEBSITE: www.northwiltsantiqueexporters.com

CALNE

Calne Antiques
London Rd. SN11 0AB. (M. Blackford)
EST. 1981. GMC. Open 10-5 seven days. STOCK: *Antique pine and country furniture, Victorian to 1930s; waxed and painted.* LOC: A4, next to White Hart Hotel. SER: Furniture made to order; free-standing kitchens. SIZE: Medium. PARK: Own. VAT: Stan.
TEL: 01249 816311; FAX: same

Clive Farahar and Sophie Dupre - Rare Books, Autographs and Manuscripts
Horsebrook House, 15 The Green. SN11 8DQ.
EST. 1980. ABA. ILAB. PADA. UACC. Manuscript Society. Open by appointment. STOCK: *Rare books on voyages and travels, autograph letters and manuscripts, 15th-20th C, £5-£5,000+.* LOC: Off A4 in town centre. SER: Valuations; buys at auction (as stock). SIZE: Medium. PARK: Easy. VAT: Stan. FAIRS: Universal Autograph Collectors' Club; Olympia (June).
TEL: 01249 821121; FAX: 01249 821202
E-MAIL: post@farahardupre.co.uk
WEBSITE: www.farahardupre.co.uk

Hilmarton Manor Press
Hilmarton Manor. SN11 8SB. (H. Baile de Laperriere)
EST. 1967. Open 9-6. STOCK: *New, out-of-print and antiquarian art related books including fine, applied, dictionaries and reference.* LOC: 3 miles from Calne on A3102 towards Swindon. SER: Buys at auction; publishers of 'Who's Who in Art'. SIZE: Medium. PARK: Easy.
TEL: 01249 760208; FAX: 01249 760379

CHERHILL

P.A. Oxley Antique Clocks and Barometers LAPADA
The Old Rectory, Main Rd. SN11 8UX.
EST. 1971. WEADA. Open 9.30-5, other times by appointment. CL: Wed. STOCK: *Longcase, bracket, carriage clocks and barometers, 17th-19th C, £500-*

£30,000. LOC: A4, not in village. SIZE: Large. PARK: Easy. VAT: Spec.
TEL: 01249 816227; FAX: 01249 821285
E-MAIL: info@paoxley.com
WEBSITE: www.british-antiqueclocks.com

CODFORD

Tina's Antiques
75 High St. BA12 0ND. (T.A. Alder)
EST. 1975. Open 9-6, Sat. 9-4. STOCK: *General antiques.* PARK: Ample.
TEL: 01985 850828

COOMBE BISSETT

Edward Hurst BADA
The Battery, Rockbourne Rd. SP5 4LP.
EST. 1983. Usually open. STOCK: *English furniture and associated works of art, 1650-1820.* LOC: **Just west of Salisbury.** SIZE: **Medium.** PARK: **Easy.** VAT: **Spec.**
FAIRS: **Olympia (June, November).**
TEL: **01722 718859; MOBILE: 07768 255557**

CORSHAM

Harley Antiques
23 Pickwick, SN13 0JB. (Geoffrey Harley)
EST. 1959. WEADA. Open 9-5 including Sun. or later by appointment. STOCK: *Furniture, 18th-19th C, £250-£6,000; decorative objects, £30-£8,000.* LOC: Main road from Bath to Chippenham. SIZE: Large. PARK: Own. VAT: Stan.
TEL: 01249 716662; FAX: 01249 712006
E-MAIL: info@harleyantiques.co.uk
WEBSITE: www.harleyantiques.co.uk

CRICKLADE

Edred A.F. Gwilliam
Candletree House, Bath Rd. SN6 6AX.
EST. 1976. Open by appointment. STOCK: *Arms and armour, swords, pistols, long guns, £50-£20,000+.* SER: Valuations; buys at auction. SIZE: Medium. PARK: Easy. VAT: Stan/Spec. FAIRS: Major arms.
TEL: 01793 750241; FAX: 01793 750359

DEVIZES

Cross Keys Jewellers
The Ginnel, Market Pl. SN10 1HN. (D. and D. Pullen)
EST. 1967. Open 9-5. STOCK: *Jewellery, silver and watches.* LOC: Alley adjacent to Nationwide Building Society. SER: Valuations; repairs; re-stringing (pearls). PARK: Easy. VAT: Stan.
TEL: 01380 726293

St Mary's Chapel Antiques
(Richard Sankey)
EST. 1971. Open by appointment. STOCK: *Original*

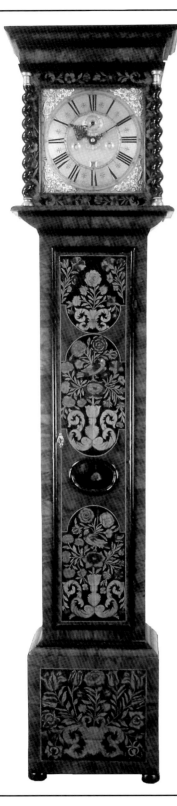

painted and Continental furniture, decorative accessories, garden items. SER: Restorations. SIZE: Large. FAIRS: Bath Decorative (Mar).
TEL: 01380 721399
E-MAIL: richard@rsankey.freeserve.co.uk

Upstairs, Downstairs Collectors' Centre
40 Market Place. SN10 1GJ. (J. Coom)
EST. 2002. Open 9.30-4.30, Thurs. 9.30-3, Sun. 9.30-3. CL: Wed. *STOCK: Oak, mahogany and pine furniture, toys, dolls and teddies, postcards, records, china, glass, prints, militaria, clocks and books.* LOC: Next to Lloyds TSB. SER: Valuations; restorations (dolls and teddies); clock repairs. SIZE: Large - 30 dealers PARK: Free, 1 hr. FAIRS: Newark; Ardingly; Kensington; Carmarthen; NEC; Sandown.
TEL: 01380 730266; FAX: same
E-MAIL: devizesantiques@btconnect.com

FROXFIELD

Blanchard   LAPADA
Bath Rd. SN8 3LD.
EST. 1940. Open 9.30-5.30. *STOCK: 18th-20th C antiques and decorative pieces including garden furniture.* LOC: A4 between Hungerford and Marlborough. SIZE: Large. PARK: Easy. VAT: Stan. FAIRS: Olympia (June).
TEL: 01488 680666; FAX: 01488 680668
E-MAIL: info@jwblanchard.com
WEBSITE: www.blanchardcollective.com

KINGTON LANGLEY

Willow UK
Church Farm, Middle Common. SN15 5NN. (Willow Bicknell)
EST. 1990. Resident. Open Fri. 10-5 and any other time by appointment. *STOCK: Furniture, objects and art for home and garden, 1770-1970; contemporary designed furniture and home wares.* LOC: 2 miles junction 17, M4. A350 to Chippenham, within mile of traffic lights, turn left. 500 metres, pass school on right, Church Farm on right, opposite church. SER: Finder; copy and design; interior and exterior design. SIZE: Medium. PARK: Easy. VAT: Spec. FAIRS: TVADA; Bath Decorative.
TEL: 01249 758333; FAX: same; MOBILE: 07770 554559
E-MAIL: willow@willowuk.com
WEBSITE: www.willowuk.com

LANGLEY BURRELL

Harriet Fairfax Fireplaces and General Antiques
Langley Green. SN15 4LL.
Open by appointment and regular sale days. *STOCK: China, glass, dolls, furniture, fabrics and needlework; architectural items and fittings, brass and iron knobs, knockers; fireplaces, pine and iron, 1780-1950.* SER: Design consultancy.
TEL: 01249 655899

LYNEHAM

Pillars Antiques
10 The Banks. SN15 4NS. (K. Clifford)
EST. 1986. Resident. Open 10-5, including Sun., CL: Wed. and Thurs. *STOCK: Victorian and Edwardian pine, shipping oak.* LOC: B4069 Chippenham road, 1 mile from village. SIZE: Large. PARK: Easy. VAT: Global.
TEL: 01249 890632; HOME: same
E-MAIL: enquiries@pillarsantiques.com
WEBSITE: www.pillarsantiques.com

MALMESBURY

Cross Hayes Antiques   LAPADA
Unit 21, White Walls, Easton Grey. SN16 0RD. (D. Brooks)
EST. 1975. Open 9-5, other times by appointment. CL: Sat. *STOCK: Furniture, 1850-1930, Victorian, Edwardian and shipping oak.* LOC: B4042 two miles west of Malmesbury. SER: Packing and shipping; courier (UK and Normandy, France). SIZE: Large warehouse. PARK: Own. VAT: Stan/Spec. FAIRS: Newark; Ardingly.
TEL: 01666 822877; FAX: same; HOME: 01666 822062
E-MAIL: david@crosshayes.co.uk
WEBSITE: www.crosshayes.co.uk

Rene Nicholls Antiques
56 High St. SN16 9AT. (Mrs R. Nicholls)
EST. 1980. Open 10-5.30, Sun. by appointment. *STOCK: English pottery and porcelain, 18th to early 19th C, £50-£900; small furniture.* SIZE: Small. PARK: Opposite.
TEL: 01666 823089; HOME: same.

MANNINGFORD BRUCE

Indigo Antiques Ltd.
Dairy Barn. SN9 6JW. (Richard Lightbown and Marion Bender)
EST. 1982. Open 10-5, Sat. 10-4. *STOCK: Furniture and architectural items, decorative accessories from India, China, Japan and Tibet, from early 19th C, £10-£5,000.* LOC: A345 2 miles from Pewsey. SER: Collection from Pewsey station by arrangement; importers; restorers. SIZE: Large. PARK: Forecourt. VAT: Stan.
TEL: 01672 564722; FAX: 01672 564733
E-MAIL: antiques@indigoantiques.com
WEBSITE: www.indigoantiques.com

MARLBOROUGH

William Cook (Marlborough)   LAPADA
High Trees House, Savernake Forest. SN8 4NE. (W.J. Cook)
EST. 1963. BAFRA. Open by appointment. *STOCK: Furniture, 18th to early 19th C; objets d'art, 18th-19th C.* LOC: 1.5 miles from Marlborough on A346 towards Burbage. SER: Valuations; restorations (furniture

including polishing and gilding); buys at auction (furniture). SIZE: Medium. PARK: Easy. VAT: Stan/Spec. FAIRS: Olympia; Harrogate; Claridges; Chester; Tatton Park.
TEL: 01672 512561; FAX: 01672 514455; MOBILE: 07885 031301
E-MAIL: billy@williamcookantiques.com
WEBSITE: www.williamcookantiques.com

Katharine House Gallery
Katharine House, The Parade. SN8 1NE. (Chris Gange)
EST. 1983. Open 10-5.30. CL: Mon. STOCK: 20th C British paintings and prints, £50-£5,000; furniture, 18th-19th C, £200-£2,000; decorative items, £100-£1,000; Chinese, Roman and Greek antiquities, 2000BC-1000AD, £100-£1,000; books, £5-£500. SIZE: Medium. PARK: Easy. VAT: Spec.
TEL: 01672 514040; HOME: same
E-MAIL: chrisgange@fsmail.net
WEBSITE: www.katherinehousegallery.co.uk

The Marlborough Parade Antique Centre
The Parade. SN8 1NE. (G. Wilkinson and P. Morgan)
EST. 1985. Open 10-5 including Sun. STOCK: Furniture, paintings, silver, porcelain, glass, clocks, jewellery, copper, brass and pewter, 5-5,000. LOC: 100 yds off the high street, down from Town Hall. SER: Upholstery; restorations (furniture, porcelain, copper, brass). SIZE: 40 dealers. PARK: 2 hrs free outside. VAT: Spec.
TEL: 01672 515331
E-MAIL: marlantiques@aol.com
WEBSITE: www.marlboroughparadeantiques.com

The Military Parade Bookshop
The Parade. SN8 1NE. (G. and P. Kent)
EST. 1988. Open 10.30-1 and 2-5. STOCK: Military history books especially regimental histories and the World Wars. LOC: Next to The Lamb.
TEL: 01672 515470; FAX: 01980 630150
E-MAIL: enquiry@militaryparadebooks.com
WEBSITE: www.militaryparadebooks.com

MARTEN

Sir William Bentley Billiards (Antique Billiard Table Specialist Company)
Dering Estates. SN8 3SJ.
EST. 1975. GMC. Open by appointment. STOCK: Billiard tables, billiard/dining tables; antique and modern accessories including panelling, brass lights, marker boards and seating. SER: Restorations; removals and storage. SIZE: Large. PARK: Own; helicopter facilities. VAT: All schemes. FAIRS: House & Garden; Ideal Home; Decorex; Grand Design; Architectural Digest, New York; Dubai.
TEL: 01264 731210; 020 8940 1152; FAX: 01264 731480
E-MAIL: sales@billiards.co.uk
WEBSITE: www.billiards.co.uk

MELKSHAM

Dann Antiques Ltd
Unit 1, Avonside Enterprise Park, New Broughton Rd. SN12 8BS. (Gary Low)
EST. 1983. Open 9-5.30, Sat. 9.30-3.30. STOCK: 18th-19th C English furniture; French and decorative pieces, lighting, fenders, mirrors, pottery, porcelain. SER: Restorations. SIZE: Large. PARK: Own. VAT: Stan/Spec.
TEL: 01225 707329; FAX: 01225 790120
E-MAIL: sales@dannantiques.com
WEBSITE: www.dannantiques.com.

Alan Jaffray
16 Market Place. SN12 6EX.
EST. 1956. WEADA. Open 9-5, or by appointment. CL: Sat. STOCK: Furniture and smalls, 18th-19th C, 50-2,000. LOC: Main Bath to Devizes Road. SER: Restoration. SIZE: Large. PARK: On premises. VAT: Stan/Spec.
TEL: 01225 702269; FAX: 01225 790413
E-MAIL: jaffrayantiques@fsmail.net

Andrew Jennings Antiques
1 Farmhouse Court, Bowerhill Park. SN12 6FG.
EST. 2003. Open by appointment. STOCK: Carvings and corkscrews, some early oak. SIZE: Small. PARK: Easy.
TEL: 01225 707400; MOBILE: 07970 651253
E-MAIL: andy@closa.co.uk
WEBSITE: www.antiquecarvings.co.uk
www.antiquecorkscrews.co.uk

King Street Curios
8 King St. SN12 6HD. (Lizzie Board)
EST. 1991. Open 10-5. CL: Wed. STOCK: Militaria, vintage phones, postcards, jewellery, furniture, discontinued Derby, vintage glass, linen, Art Deco, kitchenalia. LOC: A350. SER: Buys old and interesting items. SIZE: 20 units. PARK: Own at rear. FAIRS: Shepton Mallett, Malvern, Regal Fairs, specialist postcard and paper fairs.
TEL: 01225 790623; MOBILE: 07974 193786

MERE

Louis Stanton   BADA
Woodlands Farm, Woodlands Rd. BA12 6BY. (L.R. and S.A. Stanton)
EST. 1965. CINOA. Open by appointment. STOCK: Early English oak furniture, medieval sculpture and works of art, metalware, unusual decorative items. SER: Valuations; buys at auction. SIZE: Large. PARK: Own.
TEL: 01747 860747; FAX: same

NORTH WRAXALL

Delomosne and Son Ltd   BADA
Court Close. SN14 7AD. (T.N.M. Osborne, M.C.F. Mortimer and V.E. de C. Osborne)
EST. 1905. WEADA. Articles on chandeliers, glass and porcelain. Open 9.30-5.30, by appointment. CL: Sat.

STOCK: *English and Irish glass, pre-1830, from £20; glass chandeliers, English and European porcelain, needlework, papiermâché and treen.* LOC: **Off A420 between Bristol and Chippenham.** SER: **Valuations; buys at auction.** SIZE: **Large.** PARK: **Easy.** VAT: **Spec.** FAIRS: **Winter Olympia; Grosvenor House.**
TEL: **01225 891505; FAX: 01225 891907**
E-MAIL: **delomosne@delomosne.co.uk**
WEBSITE: **www.delomosne.co.uk**

PEWSEY

Time Restored Ltd
18-20 High St. SN9 5AQ. (J. H. Bowler-Reed and D.I. Rider)
EST. 1975. Open 10-6. STOCK: *Clocks, barometers and musical boxes.* LOC: Village centre. SER: Valuations; restorations. SIZE: Small. PARK: Free at rear of premises.
TEL: 01672 563544
E-MAIL: mail@timerestored.co.uk
WEBSITE: www.timerestored.co.uk

RAMSBURY

Heraldry Today
Parliament Piece. SN8 2QH. (Mrs Rosemary Pinches)
EST. 1954. ABA. ILAB. Open 10-4, Fri. 10-5. CL: Sat. STOCK: *Heraldic and genealogical books and manuscripts, £3-£10,000.* SER: Book search; catalogues. SIZE: Medium. PARK: Own.
TEL: 01672 520617; FAX: 01672 520183
E-MAIL: heraldry@heraldrytoday.co.uk
WEBSITE: www.heraldrytoday.co.uk

Inglenook Antiques
59 High St. SN8 2QN. (Dennis White)
EST. 1969. Open 10-1 and 2-5, prior telephone call advisable. CL: Mon. and Wed. except by appointment. STOCK: *Oil lamps, £50-£850; clocks, barometers and spare parts, £150-£4,000; some furniture.* LOC: 3 miles from A4 between Hungerford and Marlborough. SER: Restorations (longcase clock movements only). SIZE: Small. PARK: Easy.
TEL: 01672 520261; HOME: same

SALISBURY

21st Century Antics
13 Brown St. SP1 1HE. (David, Geraldine, Jonathan and Ben Scott)
EST. 1988. Open 9-5.30. STOCK: *Furniture, Georgian to date, £30-£3,000; small collectables, £2-£250.* SIZE: Large. PARK: Own.
TEL: 01722 337421; FAX: 01722 334136
E-MAIL: sales@21stcenturyantics.co.uk
WEBSITE: www.21stcenturyantics.co.uk

Antique and Collectors' Market
37 Catherine St. SP1 2DH. (Peter Beck)

EST. 1977. Open 10-5. STOCK: *Silver, plate, china, glass, toys, books, prints, pens, furniture, Art Deco, antiquities.* LOC: City centre. SER: Silver plating; repairs. SIZE: Large, 3 floors. PARK: Nearby.
TEL: 01722 326033/338487
WEBSITE: www.salisburyantiques.com

The Avonbridge Antiques and Collectors' Market
United Reformed Church Hall, Fisherton St. SP2 7RG. (D.J. Fars)
EST. 1978. Open every Tues. 8-2. STOCK: *General antiques.* LOC: Opposite old hospital. SIZE: 15 dealers. PARK: Nearby.
TEL: 01202 669061. 07736 424231

Boston Antiques
223 Wilton Rd. SP2 7JY. (Nicholas Boston)
EST. 1964. Open by appointment any time. STOCK: *Fine rare world furniture, 16th-19th C.* LOC: Main A36 at Skew Bridge, on edge of city. SIZE: Medium. PARK: Nearby. VAT: Stan/Spec.
TEL: 01722 322682; 07713 756439
E-MAIL: daboston@gotadsl.co.uk

Robert Bradley Antiques
71 Brown St. SP1 2BA.
EST. 1970. Open by appointment. STOCK: *Furniture, 17th-18th C; decorative items.* VAT: Spec.
TEL: 01722 333677; FAX: 01722 339922

Castle Galleries
81 Castle St. SP1 3SP. (John C. Lodge)
EST. 1971. Open 9-4.30, Sat. 9-1. CL: Mon. & Wed. STOCK: *Coins and medals, jewellery and objets d'art.* SER: Medal mounting and framing; miniature medals supplied and mounted. PARK: Easy.
TEL: 01722 333734; MOBILE: 07709 203745
E-MAIL: john.lodge1@tesco.net

Myriad
48-54 Milford St. SP1 2BP. (Karen Montlake and Stuart Hardy)
EST. 1982. Open 9.30-5, Sat. 10-5, other times by appointment. STOCK: *Georgian mahogany, oak and pine – chairs, corner cupboards, wardrobes, dressers, tables, chests of drawers, coffers; Victorian mahogany, pine and fruitwood – chests of drawers, wardrobes, chairs, dressing tables and dressing chests, boxes, kitchen and dining tables.* LOC: Near town centre. SER: Restorations (furniture); free collection/delivery (30 mile radius). SIZE: Large. PARK: Culver St. VAT: Spec.
TEL: 01722 413595; HOME: 01722 718203;
MOBILE: 07775 627662; FAX: 01722 416395
E-MAIL: karen@myriad-antiques.co.uk
WEBSITE: www.myriad-antiques.co.uk

Salisbury Antiques Centre   LAPADA
94 Wilton Rd. SP2 7JJ. (Mr and Mrs Chris Watts)
EST. **1964. Open 9-5.30, Sat 10-4, Sun by**

appointment. STOCK: *18th-20th C English and Continental furniture, decorative works of art and objects, clocks, oil paintings and watercolours, arms and armour. Painted furniture. Space available for professional dealers.* LOC: **A36 Warminster-Southampton road.** SER: **Valuations. Restorations can be arranged.** SIZE: **Large.** PARK: **On premises.** VAT: **Stan/Spec.**
TEL: **01722 410634;** MOBILE: **07802 635055**
E-MAIL: **info@salisburyantiquescentre.com**
WEBSITE: **www.salisburyantiquescentre.com**

Chris Wadge Clocks
83 Fisherton St. SP2 7ST. (Patrick Wadge)
Open 9-4. CL: Mon. STOCK: *Clocks and spare parts for 400 day clocks.* SER: 400 day clock specialist; repairs (antique/mechanical clocks).
TEL: 01722 334467
E-MAIL: cwclocks@aol.com

SEMLEY

Dairy House Antiques
Station Rd. SP7 9AN. (Mr A. Stevenson)
EST. 1998. WEADA. Open 9-5. STOCK: *Furniture, paintings, decorative items, 1600-1960.* LOC: Just off the A350, 2 miles north of Shaftesbury. SER: Valuations. SIZE: Large. PARK: Easy. VAT: Spec.
TEL: 01747 853317

SWINDON

Penny Farthing Antiques Arcade
Victoria Centre, 138/9 Victoria Rd., Old Town. SN1 3BU. (Ann Farthing)
EST. 1999. Open 10-5. STOCK: *Furniture, silver, porcelain, watches, clocks.* LOC: On left on hill between Old Town and college. SIZE: Large. PARK: Prospect Place. VAT: Stan.
TEL: 01793 536668

Allan Smith Antique Clocks
162 Beechcroft Rd., Upper Stratton. SN2 7QE.
EST. 1988. Open any time by appointment. STOCK: *50-60 longcase clocks including automata, moonphase, painted dial, brass dial, 30 hour, 8 day, London and provincial, £1,950-£39,500; occasionally stick and banjo barometers, mantel, wall, bracket, Vienna and lantern clocks.* LOC: Near Bakers Arms Inn. SIZE: Large. PARK: Own. VAT: Spec.
TEL: 01793 822977; FAX: same; MOBILE: 07778 834342
E-MAIL: allansmithclocks@ntlworld.com
WEBSITE: www.allansmithantiqueclocks.co.uk

TISBURY

Heatons
2-3 High St. SP3 6PS. (Ros King)
EST. 2000. WEADA. Open Mon., Fri. and Sat. 9-4 or by appointment. STOCK: *Original maps, prints, etchings and*

engravings, from 1600; furniture and decorative items, from Georgian to 1960s designer pieces; modern art glass from Daum to Liskeard. LOC: Top of hill. SER: Valuations. SIZE: Large. PARK: Limited; free nearby.
TEL: 01747 873025; FAX: 01747 870059; EVENINGS: 01747 870048
E-MAIL: rosking@freenetname.co.uk
WEBSITE: www.heatons-of-tisbury.co.uk

WARMINSTER

Annabelle's Gilt Shop
3 Silver St. BA12 8PS. (Annabelle Semke)
EST. 1983. WEADA. Open 9.30-5. *STOCK: 19th C English gilt mirrors, £25-£3,000.* LOC: Main road through town. SER: Restorations (mirrors, frames and furniture gilding; oil paintings). SIZE: Medium. PARK: Easy.
TEL: 01985 218933
E-MAIL: isabellaantiques@aol.com
WEBSITE: www.isabellaantiques.co. uk

Cassidy's Antiques
7 Silver St. BA12 8PS. (M. Cassidy)
EST. 1989. WEADA. Open 9-5, Sat. 10-5. *STOCK: Furniture, 17th-19th C, 200-5,000.* SER: Restorations (furniture and cabinet making). SIZE: Large - 2 floors. PARK: Outside shop.
TEL: 01985 213313
E-MAIL: mat_cassidy@yahoo.co.uk
WEBSITE: www.cassidyantiques.co.uk

Chloe
4 Silver St. BA12 8PS. (Chloe Cyphus)
EST. 2000. WEADA. Open Wed.-Sat. 10-5, other times by arrangement. *STOCK: Decorative painted furniture and accessories including textiles and garden items, mainly 19th C, £10-£1,000.* SER: Sewing commissions; sourcing. SIZE: Medium. PARK: Easy. FAIRS: Bath Decorative.
TEL: 01985 218924; HOME: 01985 212767; MOBILE: 07977 127862
E-MAIL: chloe@chloeantiques.co.uk
WEBSITE: www.chloeantiques.co.uk

Isabella Antiques
3 Silver St. BA12 8PS. (Barry Semke and A. Giltsoff)
EST. 1990. WEADA. Open 9.30-5. *STOCK: English furniture, late 18th C to late 19th C, £100-£5,000; English gilt mirrors, 19th C, £50-£3000.* LOC: Main road. SER: Buys at auction (furniture). SIZE: Medium. PARK: Easy. VAT: Spec.
TEL: 01985 218933
E-MAIL: isabellaantiques@aol.com
WEBSITE: www.isabellaantiques.co.uk

Maxfield House Antiques
Maxfield House, 16 Silver St. BA12 8PS. (Rosemary Reynolds)
EST. 1992. Open Wed.-Sat. 10-5, or by appointment.

STOCK: Mainly English oak and mahogany, some painted, 18th-20th C; town and country furniture; pictures and decorative objects; all £50-£2,000. LOC: Main Bath road leading into Silver St. SIZE: Small. PARK: Outside premises.
TEL: 01985 212121; MOBILE: 07747 654244

Obelisk Antiques   LAPADA
2 Silver St. BA12 8PS. (P. Tanswell)
EST. 1980. Open 10-1 and 2-5. *STOCK: English and Continental furniture, 18th-19th C; decorative items, objets d'art.* **SIZE: Large. PARK: Easy. VAT: Spec.**
TEL: 01985 846646; FAX: 01985 219901
E-MAIL: all@obeliskantiques.com
WEBSITE: www.obeliskantiques.com

Warminster Antiques Centre
6 Silver St. BA12 8PT. (Peter Walton)
EST. 1970. Open 10-5. *STOCK: Furniture, home embellishments, textiles, silver, jewellery, collectors' items.* SIZE: 15 dealers. PARK: Easy. FAIRS: Newark.
TEL: 01985 847269; MOBILE: 07860 584193
WEBSITE: www.warminsterantiques.co.uk

WEST YATTON

Heirloom & Howard Limited
Manor Farm. SN14 7EU. (A.M. Howard)
EST. 1972. Open 10-6 by prior appointment. *STOCK: Porcelain mainly Chinese armorial and export, 18th C, £100-£5,000; decorative heraldic items, 18th-19th C, £10-£1,000.* LOC: 10 miles from Bath, ¼ mile off A420 Chippenham/Bristol road. Transport from Chippenham station (4 miles) if required. SER: Valuations; buys at auction (Chinese porcelain). SIZE: Medium. PARK: Own. VAT: Spec.
TEL: 01249 783038; FAX: 01249 783039
WEBSITE: www.heirloom-howard.co.uk

WILTON

Hingstons of Wilton
36 North St. SP2 0HJ.
EST. 1976. Open 9-5, Sat. 10-4. *STOCK: 18th-20th C furniture, clocks, pictures and objects.* SIZE: Large. PARK: Easy.
TEL: 01722 742263; MOBILE: 07887 870569
E-MAIL: nick@hingstons-antiques.freeserve.co.uk
WEBSITE: www.hingstons-antiques.co.uk

A.J. Romain & Sons
The Old House, 11 and 13 North St. SP2 0HA.
EST. 1954. Open 9-5. CL: Wed. pm. *STOCK: Furniture, mainly 17th-18th C; early oak, walnut and marquetry; clocks, copper, brass and miscellanea.* PARK: Market Sq.
TEL: 01722 743350

Georgian Jewellery
1714-1830

Ginny Redington Dawes with Olivia Collings

Georgian Jewellery is a celebration of the quality and style of the eighteenth century and of the endless ingenuity in design and workmanship that produced such a wealth of fabulous and wearable pieces of jewellery. This thoroughly researched look at the jewellery of the time offers both good basic knowledge for the beginner and new and/or little-known facts for the expert about the techniques, styles and materials of the age. The only book solely on the Georgian period, and the largest ever catalogue of the diverse range of eighteenth century jewellery, it incorporates interesting portraits of characters of the period and their influence on the jewels of the time, with some contemporary gossip, outrageous cartoons and period fashion tips. Heavy academic tomes have already been written about the period, so this book illuminates the subject in a more colourful and accessible way. Much disparate information about the jewellery has been gathered together. Some might think that Georgian jewellery is the stuff of museums or safe-deposit boxes, but since many of the pieces pictured here have been on the market in the last few years, it is hoped this book will encourage people to realise this lovely jewellery is as beautiful an adornment today as it was over two hundred years ago. Information is given on how to recognise Georgian jewellery, buy it and repair it and there are tips on how to distinguish the real thing from the plethora of reproduction jewellery on the market today.

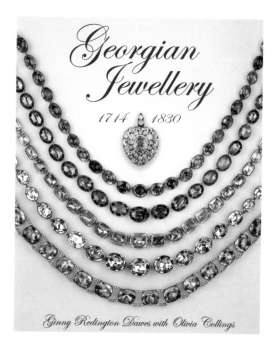

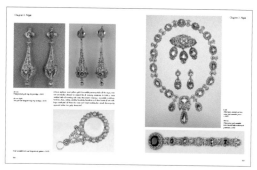

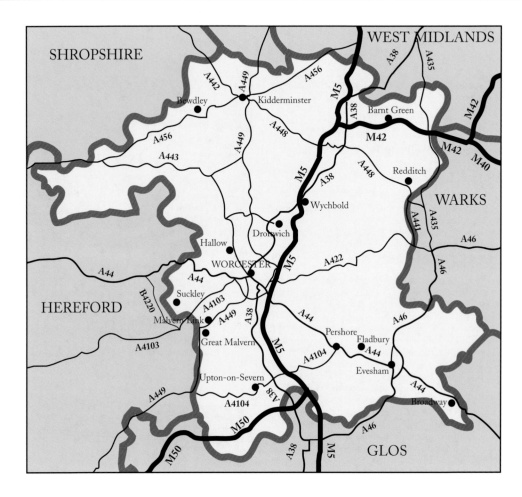

BARNT GREEN

Barnt Green Antiques
93 Hewell Rd. B45 8NL. (N. Slater)
EST. 1977. BAFRA. Open 9-5.30, Sat. 9.30-1. *STOCK: Furniture, 17th-19th C, £100-£5,000.* SER: Restorations (furniture, gilt frames, clocks and oils). SIZE: Medium. PARK: Easy. VAT: Stan/Spec.
TEL: 0121 445 4942

BEWDLEY

Bewdley Antiques
62a Load St. DY12 2AP.
EST. 1999. Open 10-5. *STOCK: 25 cabinets displaying 19th-20th C collectables and decorative furniture.* LOC: A456 town centre. SIZE: Small. PARK: Easy.
TEL: 01299 405636

BROADWAY

Stephen Cook Antiques   **BADA**
58 High St. WR12 7DP.
EST. 1987. Open 10-5. *STOCK: 17th-18th C oak, walnut*

and mahogany, treen and paintings. SER: Valuations; restorations (cabinet and polishing furniture). SIZE: Large. PARK: Easy.
TEL: **01386 854716**
E-MAIL: **stephen@scookantiques.com**
WEBSITE: **www.scookantiques.com**

Fenwick and Fenwick Antiques
88-90 High St. WR12 7AJ. (George and Jane Fenwick)
EST. 1980. Open 10-6 and by appointment. *STOCK: Furniture, oak, mahogany and walnut, 17th to early 19th C; samplers, boxes, treen, Tunbridgeware, Delft, decorative items and corkscrews.* LOC: Upper High St. SIZE: Large. PARK: Nearby. VAT: Spec.
TEL: 01386 853227; AFTER HOURS: 01386 841724; FAX: 01386 858504

Richard Hagen Gallery
Stable Lodge, 55-57 High St. WR12 7DP.
EST. 1972. Open 9.30-5, Sun. by appointment. CL: 1-2 *STOCK: 20th-21st C oils, watercolours and bronzes.* PARK: Own at rear. VAT: Spec.
TEL: 01386 853624 or 01386 858561; FAX: 01386 852172

E-MAIL: fineart@richardhagen.com
WEBSITE: www.richardhagen.com

Haynes Fine Art of Broadway   BADA LAPADA
Picton House Galleries, 42 High St. WR12 7DT.
(A.C. Haynes)
EST. 1971. CADA. Open 9-6. *STOCK: Over 2000 British*
and European 16th-21st C oil paintings and watercolours.
LOC: From Lygon Arms, 100 yards up High St. on left.
SER: Valuations; restorations; framing; catalogue
available (£10). SIZE: Large - 12 showrooms. PARK:
Easy. VAT: Spec. FAIRS: Olympia (Summer & Winter),
BADA, Harrogate (Spring & Autumn)
TEL: 01386 852649; FAX: 01386 858187; MOBILE:
07831 893465, 07710 108891
E-MAIL: **email@haynesfineart.com**
WEBSITE: **www.haynesfineart.com**

H.W. Keil Ltd   BADA
Tudor House, High St. WR12 7DP. (John Keil)
EST. 1925. CADA. Open 9.30-12.45 and 2.15-5.30,
Sat. by appointment. *STOCK: Walnut, oak, mahogany and*
rosewood furniture; early pewter, brass and copper,
tapestry and works of art, 16th to early 19th C. LOC: By
village clock. SER: Restorations. SIZE: Large - 12
showrooms. PARK: Private by arrangement. VAT: Spec.
TEL: 01386 852408; FAX: 01386 852069
E-MAIL: **info@hwkeil.co.uk**

John Noott Galleries   BADA LAPADA
20 High St., 14 Cotswold Court, WR12 7AA. (John,
Pamela and Amanda Noott)
EST. 1972. CADA. Open 9.30-5, Sun. 11-5. *STOCK:*
Paintings, watercolours and bronzes, 19th C to
contemporary. SER: Valuations; restorations; framing.
SIZE: Large. PARK: Easy. VAT: Stan/Spec.
TEL: 01386 854868/858969; FAX: 01386 854919
E-MAIL: **info@john-noott.com**
WEBSITE: **www.john-noott.com**

DROITWICH

Robert Belcher Antiques
128 Worcester Rd. WR9 8AN. (Robert & Wendy Belcher)
EST. 1986. Open 9-5.30, Sat. 10-5.30, Sun. by appointment.
CL: Mon. *STOCK: Furniture, 18th-19th C, £500-£10,000;*
ceramics, silver, glass, paintings and prints, 19th-20th C, £50-
£1,000. SER: Valuations; restorations; picture framing. SIZE:
Large. PARK: Easy. VAT: Spec. FAIRS: NEC.
TEL: 01905 772320
E-MAIL: wendy@robertbelcherantiques.com

Grant Books
The Coach House, New Rd., Cutnall Green. WR9 0PQ.
EST. 1971. PBFA. Open by prior appointment only.
STOCK: Books, prints, pictures, clubs, golfiana, £5-£1,000.
LOC: A442 Droitwich to Kidderminster road. SIZE:
Small. PARK: Easy.
TEL: 01299 851588; FAX: 01299 851446

E-MAIL: golf@grantbooks.co.uk
WEBSITE: www.golfbooks-memorabilia.com

EVESHAM

Bookworms of Evesham
81 Port St. WR11 6AF. (T.J. Sims)
EST. 1971. PBFA. Open 10-5, Mon. by appointment.
STOCK: Books - Gloucestershire and Worcestershire, 18th-
20th C, £5-£1,200; John Moore, 20th C, £5-£75; general
books, 19th-20th C, from 50p. SER: Valuations;
restorations; buys at auction. SIZE: Small. PARK: Behind
premises. VAT: Stan. FAIRS: PBFA Bath, Birmingham,
Cheltenham, Cirencester & Churchdown.
TEL: 01386 45509
E-MAIL: terry-bookworms@hotmail.com

Magpie Jewellers and Antiques and Magpie Arms &
Armour
Manchester House 1 High St. WR11 4DA. (R.J. and
E.R. Bunn)
EST. 1975. Open 9-5.30. CL: Wed. *STOCK: Silver, jewellery,*
furniture, general antiques, arms and armour, books, stamps and
coins. LOC: Town centre. SIZE: Large. PARK: Own at rear.
TEL: 01386 41631
E-MAIL: magpie2500@aol.com
WEBSITE: www.magpieantiques.co.uk

Twyford Antique Centre
86 High St. WR11 4EU. (Andy Mayhew)
EST. 1999. Open 9.30-5. *STOCK: Furniture, antiques and*
collectables. SIZE: 20 units. PARK: Outside.
TEL: 01386 446923
E-MAIL: twyfordantiques@tiscali.co.uk

GREAT MALVERN

Carlton Antiques
43 Worcester Rd. WR14 4RB. (Dave Roberts)
EST. 1985. Open 10-5. *STOCK: Collectables including*
Edwardian postcards and cigarette cards; a selection of old
and modern furniture. SER: Valuations.
TEL: 01684 573092
E-MAIL: dave@carlton-antiques.com
WEBSITE: www.carlton-antiques.com

Foley House Antiques
28 Worcester Rd. WR14 4QW. (Nigel Hicks)
Open 10-5, Sun. 11-5. *STOCK: General furnishings, 19th-*
20th C; collectables, china, £5-£100. LOC: A449. SER:
Restorations; French polishing; buys at auction. SIZE:
Large. PARK: Easy. VAT: Stan/Spec.
TEL: 01684 575750; MOBILE: 07841 643719
WEBSITE: www.foleyhouseantiques.com

Malvern Bookshop
7 Abbey Rd. WR14 3ES. (Howard and Julie Hudson)
EST. 1955. Open 10-5. CL: Thurs. *STOCK: Antiquarian,*
secondhand books and sheet music. LOC: By priory church

steps. SIZE: 5 rooms. PARK: Short stay on road above.
TEL: 01684 575915
E-MAIL: browse@malvernbookshop.co.uk

Malvern Studios
56 Cowleigh Rd. WR14 1QD. (L.M. Hall and D.D.J. Hall)
EST. 1961. BAFRA. Open 9-5.15, Fri. and Sat. 9-4.45.
CL: Wed. *STOCK: Period, Edwardian painted and inlaid furniture, general furnishings.* SER: Antique restoration; polishing. SIZE: Large. VAT: Stan/Spec.
TEL: 01684 574913; FAX: 01684 569475
E-MAIL: malvern.studios@btinternet.com
WEBSITE: www.malvernstudios.co.uk

Miscellany Antiques
20 Cowleigh Rd. WR14 1QD. (Ray and Liz Hunaban)
EST. 1974. Resident. Opening hours vary. Please telephone in advance. *STOCK: Victorian, Edwardian and Georgian furniture, including shipping goods, £300-£20,000; some porcelain, silver, bronzes and jewellery.* LOC: B4219 to Bromyard. SIZE: Medium + trade warehouse. PARK: Own. VAT: Stan/Spec.
TEL: 01684 566671; FAX: 01684 560562
E-MAIL: liz.hunaban@virgin.net

Promenade Antiques
41 Worcester Rd. WR14 4RB. (Mark Selvester)
Open 10-5.30, Sun. 12-5; often open later. *STOCK: General antiques including Victorian and Edwardian furniture, lamps, bric-a-brac and replica collectables.* PARK: Nearby.
TEL: 01684 566876
E-MAIL: promant@aol.com

Whitmore
Teynham Lodge, Chase Rd., Upper Colwall. WR13 6DT. (John and Stella Whitmore)
EST. 1965. BNTA. *Postal Only. STOCK: British and foreign coins, 1700-1950; trade tokens, 1650-1900; commemorative medallions, 1600-1950; all £1-£500.*
TEL: 01684 540651; 01684 541417
E-MAIL: teynhaml@aol.com

HALLOW

Antique Map and Print Gallery
April Cottage, Main Rd. WR2 6LS. (G.P. Nichols)
EST. 1969. Open by appointment. *STOCK: Antiquarian maps (including Speed and Blaeu) of every country; prints including Baxter and Le Blond, and books.* LOC: Approx. 4 miles from Worcester on the Tenbury Wells Rd. SER: Greetings cards reproduced from original prints. PARK: Easy.
TEL: 01905 641300
E-MAIL: antiqmap@aol.com
WEBSITE: www.ampgworcester.com

KIDDERMINSTER

The Antique Centre
5-8 Lion St. DY10 1PT. (Vivien and Robin Lapham)

EST. 1980. Open 10-5. *STOCK: Furniture, early 18th C to 1930s, £10-£2,000; collectables, to 1930s, £1-£1,000; Victorian, Edwardian and reproduction fireplaces; jewellery, silver, lighting, pictures, prints, mirrors, architectural items.* LOC: Off Bromsgrove St. SER: Valuations; restorations (furniture); door stripping; jewellery repairs and commissions. SIZE: Large. PARK: Easy.
TEL: 01562 740389; FAX: same; MOBILE: 07980 300660
E-MAIL: theantiquecentre@btconnect.com
WEBSITE: www.theantiquecentre.co.uk

B.B.M. Coins.
1st Floor, 9 & 10 Lion St. DY10 1PT. (W.V. and A. Crook)
EST. 1977. BJA. Open 10-5. CL: Mon. & Tues. *STOCK: Coins, £5-£1,000; coin and stamp accessories, jewellery including modern, £5-£10,000.* LOC: Adjacent Youth Centre, off ring road. SIZE: Medium. PARK: Easy. VAT: Stan/Spec/Global.
TEL: 01562 744118/515007
E-MAIL: williamvcrook@btconnect.com

MALVERN LINK

Kimber & Son
16 Lower Howsell Rd. WR14 1EF. (E.M. and M.E. Kimber)
EST. 1956. Open 9-5.30, Sat. 9-1. *STOCK: 18th-20th C antiques for English, Continental and American markets.* SER: Restoration. PARK: Own. VAT: Stan/Spec.
TEL: 01684 574339; HOME: 01684 572000; MOBILE: 07950 619670
WEBSITE: www.kimbersofmalvern.com

PERSHORE

Hansen Chard Antiques
126 High St. WR10 1EA. (P.W. Ridler BSc.)
EST. 1984. Open Fri. & Sat. 10-4, or by appointment. CL: April and August. *STOCK: Clocks, barometers, models, tools, books, antique and secondhand, £5-£10,000.* LOC: On B4084. SER: Valuations; restorations (as stock); buys at auction (as stock). SIZE: Large. PARK: Easy. FAIRS: Midlands; Uxbridge.
TEL: 01386 553423; HOME: same
E-MAIL: hansenclocks-shop@yahoo.co.uk
WEBSITE: www.hansenchardantiques.com

S.W. Antiques   LAPADA
Abbey Showrooms, Newlands. WR10 1BP. (A.M. Whiteside)
EST. 1978. CINOA. Open 9-5. *STOCK: 19th-20th C furniture including beds and bedroom furniture, to £4,000. NOT STOCKED: Jewellery, small items.* **LOC: 2 mins. from Abbey. SIZE: Large. PARK: Own. VAT: Stan/Spec.**
TEL: 01386 555580; FAX: 01386 556205
E-MAIL: sales@sw-antiques.co.uk
WEBSITE: www.sw-antiques.co.uk

SUCKLEY

Holloways
Lower Court. WR6 5DE. (Edward and Diana Holloway)
EST. 1989. Open 9-5, Sun. (April-August) 11-4. *STOCK: Antique and period garden ornaments and furniture.* LOC: A44 from Worcester towards Leominster, left at Knightwick, 3.5 miles on right close to village church. SER: Valuations; restorations; buys at auction. SIZE: Large. PARK: Easy. VAT: Stan/Spec. FAIRS: RHS Chelsea.
TEL: 01886 884665
WEBSITE: www.agos.co.uk

UPTON-UPON-SEVERN

The Highway Gallery
40 Old St. WR8 0HW. (J. Daniell)
EST. 1969. Open 10.30-5, appointment advisable. CL: Thurs. and Mon. *STOCK: Oils, watercolours, 19th-20th C, £100-£10,000.* LOC: 100yds. from crossroads towards Malvern. SER: Valuations; restorations; relining; cleaning; buys at auction (pictures). SIZE: Small. PARK: Easy.
TEL: 01684 592645; HOME: 01684 592909; FAX: 01684 592909

WORCESTER

Antique Warehouse
Rear of 74 Droitwich Rd, Barbourne. WR3 8BW. (D. Venn)
Open 9-5, Sat. 10-4.30. *STOCK: General antiques, shipping, restored pine and satin walnut, Victorian doors and fireplaces.* SER: Stripping (wood and metalwork). SIZE: Large. PARK: Easy.
TEL: 01905 27493
E-MAIL: davidcvenn3310@fsbuisness.co.uk

Bygones by the Cathedral   LAPADA
Deansway. WR1 2JD. (Gabrielle Doherty Bullock)
EST. 1946. FGA. DGA. Gemmological Assn of GB.
Open 9.30-5.30, Sat. 9.30-1 and 2-5.30. *STOCK: Furniture, 17th-19th C; silver, jewellery, paintings, glass; English and Continental pottery and porcelain especially Royal Worcester; 20th C collectables.* **LOC: Adjacent main entrance to cathedral. SER: Valuations. SIZE: Medium. PARK: NCP opposite cathedral. VAT: Spec.**
TEL: 01905 25388/23132
E-MAIL: bygones.antiques@tiscali.co.uk

Bygones of Worcester   LAPADA
3 College Precincts. WR1 2LG. (Gabrielle Bullock)
EST. 1946. FGA. DGA. Gemmological Assn of GB.
Open by appointment. *STOCK: 17th-20th C walnut, oak, mahogany and exotic wood furniture, brass and copper, oil paintings, porcelain, pottery and glass and decorative objects.* **LOC: Opposite East window of cathedral. SER:**

Valuations. SIZE: Medium. PARK: In the Precincts adjacent to the building. VAT: Stan/Spec.
TEL: 01905 23132/25388
E-MAIL: bygones.antiques@tiscali.co.uk

Heirlooms
46 Upper Tything. WR1 1JZ. (L. Rumford)
Open 10-4.30. *STOCK: General antiques, objets d'art, Royal Worcester porcelain, prints.*
TEL: 01905 23332

M. Lees and Sons   LAPADA
Tower House, 1 Castle Place, Severn St. WR1 2NB.
EST. 1955. Resident. Open 9.15-5.15, Sat. by appointment. CL: Thurs. pm. *STOCK: Furniture, 1780-1880; porcelain, 1750-1920; mirrors, Oriental and decorative.* **LOC: At southern end of Worcester Cathedral adjacent to Edgar Tower; near Royal Worcester Porcelain Museum and factory. SER: commissions; valuations. SIZE: Medium. PARK: Easy. VAT: Stan/Spec.**
TEL: 01905 26620; MOBILE: 07860 826218
E-MAIL: michael@leesandsons.fsnet.co.uk
WEBSITE: www.leesantiquesworcester.com

Jenny Wood Antiques
47 Upper Tything. WR1 1JZ.
Open 10-5, Mon by appointment. *STOCK: Books, furniture, glass, jewellery, prints, paintings, silver, objets d'art.* LOC: 1 mile from Worcester on the A38; M5 jct 6 or 7.
TEL: 01905 22163
E-MAIL: jennywoodantiques@btinternet.com
WEBSITE: www.jennywoodantiques.com

Worcester Antiques Centre
15 Reindeer Court, Mealcheapen St. WR1 4DF. (Stephen Zacaroli)
EST. 1992. Open 10-5. *STOCK: Pottery and porcelain, 1750-1970, £10-£5,000; silver, 1750-1940, £10-£5,000; jewellery, 1800-1940, £5-£5,000; furniture, 1650-1930, £50-£10,000.* SER: Valuations; restorations (furniture, ceramics and metalware). PARK: Loading only or 50 yards. FAIRS: East Berkshire (May and Oct).
TEL: 01905 610680/1
E-MAIL: worcsantiques@aol.com

WYCHBOLD

D & J Lines Antiques
Papermill Lane. WR9 0DE. (Derek and Jill Lines)
Open by appointment. *STOCK: Oak and country furniture, 17th-18th C, £500-£8,000; metalware, 18th-19th C, £50-£500; Persian carpets, 19th-20th C, £50-£1,000; pearls, diamond set jewellery.* SER: Valuations; restorations; desk re-leathering. SIZE: Medium.
TEL: 01527 861282

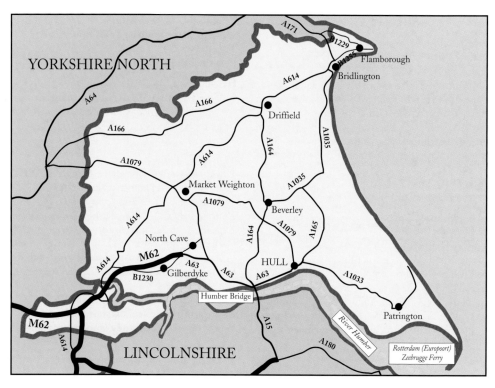

BEVERLEY

Guest & Philips
24 Saturday Market Place. HU17 8BB. (Karen and Philip Guest)
EST. 1966. NAG registered Valuer and Jeweller. HRD Dip. of Diamond Grading. Open 9.15-5. *STOCK: Jewellery and silver, 18th-20th C, £50-£20,000.* LOC: Town centre. SER: Valuations; restorations. SIZE: Medium. PARK: Easy. VAT: Stan/Spec.
TEL: 01482 882334; FAX: same
E-MAIL: guestandphilips@hotmail.co.uk
WEBSITE: www.guestandphilips.co.uk

David Hakeney Antiques
P O Box 171. HU17 7WH.
EST. 1970. Open by appointment. *STOCK: Porcelain, silver, clocks and watches, 19th C and Edwardian furniture, decorative items.* LOC: Showroom at Hemswell Antique Centre. FAIRS: NEC(April, Aug. and Dec); Newark; Harrogate.
TEL: 01482 677006; MOBILE: 07860 507774
E-MAIL: dhakeney@aol.com

St Crispin Antique Centre
11 Butcher Row. HU17 0AA. (Chris Fowler and Jill Northgraves)
EST. 1971. Open 10-5, Sun. 10.30-4.30. *STOCK: Ceramics, glass, furniture, books, jewellery, stamps, coins, medals, chandeliers, retro clothing and walking sticks.* LOC: Town centre. SER: Valuations. SIZE: 100+ dealers.
TEL: 01482 869583

James H. Starkey Galleries
49 Highgate. HU17 0DN.
EST. 1968. Open 9.30-4.30 by appointment only. CL: Sat. *STOCK: Oil paintings, 16th-19th C; drawings and watercolours, 17th-19th C.* LOC: Opposite Minster. SER: Valuations; restorations (paintings); buys at auction. SIZE: Medium. PARK: Easy. VAT: Stan/Spec.
TEL: 01482 881179; FAX: 01482 861644

Time and Motion
1 Beckside. HU17 0PB. (Peter A. Lancaster)
EST. 1977. FBHI. Open 10-5. CL: Thurs. *STOCK: English longcase clocks, 18th-19th C, £2,000-£10,000; English, German and French mantel and wall clocks, 19th C, £300-£3,500; aneroid and mercurial barometers, 18th-19th C, £150-£3,000.* LOC: 1 mile from town centre and Minster, 300 yards from Leisure Centre. SER: Valuations; restorations (clocks and barometers). SIZE: Large. PARK: Easy. VAT: Stan/Spec.
TEL: 01482 881574; HOME: same

BRIDLINGTON

C.J. and A.J. Dixon Ltd
1st Floor, 23 Prospect St. YO15 2AE. (Christopher Dixon)
EST. 1969. OMSA. OMRS. Open 9.30-5. *STOCK: British war medals, orders and decorations.* LOC: Town centre. SER: Valuations; renovations; commission agents for medal auctions. SIZE: Large. PARK: Easy. VAT: Stan/Spec. FAIRS: UK and overseas plus all major medal auctions.
TEL: 01262 676877/603348; FAX: 01262 606600

E-MAIL: chris@dixonsmedals.co.uk
WEBSITE: www.dixonsmedals.co.uk

The Georgian Rooms
56 High St., Old Town. YO16 4QA. (Andrew Davison
and Diane Davison)
EST. 1999. Open 10-5, Sun. 10-3. (CL: two weeks at
Christmas and New Year.) STOCK: *Wide range of general
antiques and collectables, Georgian to modern, £1-£13,000.*
SER: Restorations, dipping, painting. SIZE: 10
showrooms. PARK: Free nearby.
TEL: 01262 608600
E-MAIL: georgianrooms@aol.com
WEBSITE: www.thegeorgianroomsbridlington.webeden.co.uk

Sedman Antiques
106 Cardigan Rd. YO15 3LR. (R.H.S. and M.A. Sedman)
EST. 1971. Open 10-5.30, Sun. by appointment. STOCK:
*General antiques, period and shipping furniture, Oriental
porcelain, Victorian collectors' items.* PARK: Easy.
TEL: 01262 675671

DRIFFIELD

The Crested China Co
Highfield, Windmill Hill. YO25 5YP. (D. Taylor)
EST. 1978. Open by appointment. STOCK: *Goss and crested
china.* SER: Colour catalogues. PARK: Easy. FAIRS: Goss.
TEL: 01377 257042 (24 hr.)
E-MAIL: dt@thecrestedchinacompany.com
WEBSITE: www.thecrestedchinacompany.com

Guest & Phillips
80A Middle St. South. YO25 6QE.
EST. 1989. NAG. HRD Diploma of Diamond Grading.
Open 9.30-5. STOCK: *Jewellery and silver, 18th-20th C,
£50-£5,000.* SER: Valuations; restorations. SIZE: Small.
VAT: Stan/Spec.
TEL: 01377 241467
WEBSITE: www.guestandphilips.co.uk

FLAMBOROUGH

Lesley Berry Antiques
The Manor House. YO15 1PD. (Mrs L. Berry)
EST. 1972. Resident. Open 9.30-5.30, other times by
appointment. STOCK: *Furniture, silver, jewellery, amber,
Whitby jet, oils, watercolours, prints, copper, brass, textiles,
secondhand and antiquarian books on-line.* LOC: On corner
of Tower St. and Lighthouse Rd. SER: Buys at auction.
SIZE: Small. PARK: Easy.
TEL: 01262 850943
E-MAIL: lb@flamboroughmanor.co.uk
WEBSITE: www.flamboroughmanor.co.uk

GILBERDYKE

Lewis E. Hickson FBHI
Antiquarian Horologist, Sober Hill Farm. HU15 2TB.

EST. 1965. MBHI. MBWCG. Open by appointment.
STOCK: *Longcase, bracket clocks, barometers and instruments.*
SER: Restorations; repairs; valuations. SIZE: Small. PARK:
Easy.
TEL: 01430 449113

HULL

Grannie's Parlour
33 Anlaby Rd. HU1 2PG. (A. and Mrs. N. Pye)
EST. 1974. Open 11-5. CL: Thurs. STOCK: *General
antiques, ephemera, Victoriana, dolls, toys, kitchenalia.* LOC:
Near rail and bus station. SIZE: Medium. PARK: Nearby.
TEL: 01482 228258; HOME: 01482 341020

Grannie's Treasures
1st Floor, 33 Anlaby Rd. HU1 2PG. (Mrs N. Pye)
EST. 1974. Open 11-5. CL: Thurs. STOCK: *Advertising
items, dolls prams, toys, small furniture, china and pre-1940s
clothing.* LOC: Near rail and bus station. PARK: Nearby.
TEL: 01482 228258; HOME: 01482 341020

Kevin Marshall's Antiques Warehouse
17-20A Wilton St., HU8 7LG.
EST. 1981. Open 10-5. STOCK: *Bathroom ware,
architectural items, fires, lighting, furniture and
reproductions, 19th C, £5-£5,000.* LOC: 1st right off
Dansom Lane South. SER: Valuations; restorations;
boardroom tables made to order. SIZE: Large. PARK:
Easy. VAT: Stan/Spec.
TEL: 01482 326559; FAX: same
E-MAIL: kevinmarshall@antiquewarehouse.karoo.co.uk

MARKET WEIGHTON

Mount Pleasant Antiques Centre
46 Cliffe Rd. YO43 3BP. (Linda and John Sirrs)
EST. 1999. Open 9.30-5, including Sun. STOCK: *18th -
20th C furniture, inc. large dining tables, bureaux, display
cabinets, occasional furniture, clocks, silver, porcelain, jewellery.*
LOC: A1079 Market Weighton by-pass. SER: Restorations
(furniture) by J Sirrs Restoration, trade and public, est. 30
years. SIZE: Large - 20 dealers. PARK: Easy.
TEL: 01430 872872; HOME: same
E-MAIL: johnmpac@aol.com
WEBSITE: www.mountpleasantantiquescentre.co.uk

NORTH CAVE

Penny Farthing Antiques
Albion House, 18 Westgate. HU15 2NJ. (C.E. Dennett)
EST. 1987. Open by appointment only. STOCK: *19th-20th
C furniture, Victorian brass and iron bedsteads, £25-£2,000;
linen, textiles and samplers, 18th-20th C, £5-£500; general
collectables, china and glass, 19th-20th C, £5-£500.* LOC:
Main road (B1230). SER: Valuations; buys at auction.
SIZE: Medium. PARK: Easy. FAIRS: Newark.
TEL: 01430 422958; MOBILE: 07980 624583

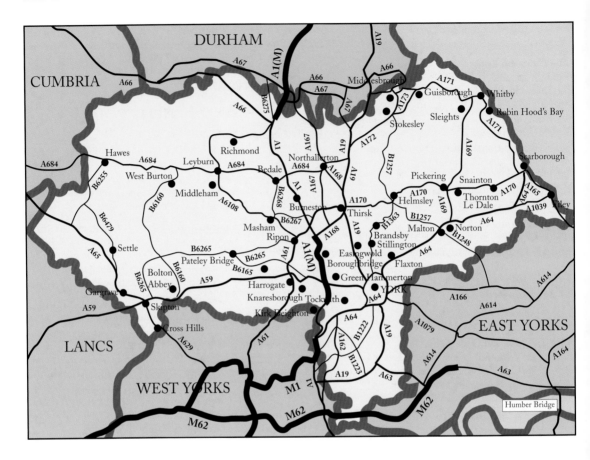

BOLTON ABBEY

Grove Rare Books
The Old Post Office. BD23 6EX. (Andrew and Janet Sharpe)
EST. 1984. ABA. PBFA. Open 10-5. CL: Mon. STOCK: *Antiquarian books and maps; topographical and sporting prints.* LOC: 1 mile from A59. SER: Valuations; restorations; buys at auction (as stock). SIZE: Medium. PARK: At rear.
TEL: 01756 710717; FAX: 01756 711098
E-MAIL: antiquarian@groverarebooks.co.uk
WEBSITE: www.groverarebooks.co.uk

BOROUGHBRIDGE

Mauleverer
Waingate Chambers, Roecliffe Business Centre. YO51 9NE. (Louise Forster)
EST. 1987. Open Sat. 11-5.30, other times by appointment; prior telephone call advisable. STOCK: *Early English oak furniture, paintings, 1660-1780. All pieces guaranteed re: authenticity, full condition reports supplied.* LOC: Off A1 at Boroughbridge, in middle of Boroughbridge take turning marked Roecliffe 1 mile. SER: Storage; restoration and conservation (furniture);

delivery worldwide. SIZE: Medium. PARK: Own - 30 spaces.
TEL: 01423 322200
E-MAIL: reception@earlyenglishoak.co.uk
WEBSITE: www.earlyenglishoak.co.uk

BRANDSBY

L.L. Ward and Son
Bar House. YO61 4RQ. (R. Ward)
EST. 1970. Open 8.30-5. STOCK: *Antique pine.* LOC: Midway between York and Helmsley. SIZE: Medium. PARK: Easy.
TEL: 01347 888651
E-MAIL: pine@brandsby1.freeserve.co.uk
WEBSITE: www.brandsbypine.co.uk

BURNESTON

W. Greenwood (Fine Art)
Oak Dene, Church Wynd. DL8 2JE.
EST. 1978. Open by appointment. STOCK: *Paintings and watercolours, 19th-20th C, £100-£5,000; frames, £20-£500; mirrors.* LOC: Take B6285 left off A1 northbound, house ¼ mile on right. SER: Valuations; restorations (paintings and frames); framing. SIZE: Small. PARK: Easy.

TEL: 01677 424830; HOME: 01677 423217; MOBILE: 07885 175279

CROSS HILLS

Heathcote Antiques
Skipton Rd. Junction. BD20 7DS. (M.H. and S.A. Webster Ltd)
EST. 1979. Resident. Open 10-5.30, Sun. 12.30-4.30. CL: Mon. and Tues. STOCK: *Furniture, clocks, barometers, unstripped English pine, pottery, porcelain, brass and metal wares.* SIZE: Very large showroom + trade warehouse. PARK: Own large.
TEL: 01535 635250; FAX: 01535 637205; MOBILE: 07836 259640

EASINGWOLD

Milestone Antiques
Farnley House, 101 Long St. YO61 3HY. (A.B. and S.J. Streetley)
EST. 1982. Open daily, Sun. by appointment. STOCK: *Mahogany and oak furniture especially dining tables, upholstered armchairs and sofas; longcase and wall clocks; all 18th to early 20th C.* LOC: Old A19, village centre. SER: Valuations. SIZE: Medium. PARK: Easy. VAT: Stan/Spec.
TEL: 01347 821608; HOME: same
E-MAIL: milestoneantiques-easingwold@fsmail.net
WEBSITE: www.milestoneantiques.co.uk

Old Flames
30 Long St. YO61 3HT. (P. Lynas and J.J. Thompson)
EST. 1988. Open 10-5. STOCK: *Fireplaces, 18th-19th C, £100-£4,000; lighting, 19th C, £100-£5,000; architectural items, 18th-19th C, £50-£2,000.* SER: Valuations. SIZE: Medium. PARK: Easy. VAT: Stan/Spec. FAIRS: Newark.
TEL: 01347 821188; FAX: same
E-MAIL: philiplynas@aol.com
WEBSITE: www.oldflames.co.uk

Vale Antiques
Mooracres, North Moor. YO61 3NB. (J.M., C.M. and D.N. Leach)
EST. 1986. GADAR. Open 9-5. STOCK: *Furniture, 18th-20th C, £20-£1,500; china, brass and copper, £5-£100; prints and paintings, £15-£100.* LOC: Outskirts, just off Thirsk Rd. SER: Restorations (furniture repair and re-polishing). SIZE: Medium. PARK: Easy.
TEL: 01347 821298; HOME/FAX: same
E-MAIL: chris.leach2@ukonline.co.uk

The White House Antiques & Architectural Reclamation
Thirsk Rd. YO61 3NF. (G. Hood)
EST. 1960. Resident. Usually open but prior telephone call advisable. STOCK: *Rural and domestic bygones, stone troughs, architectural reclamation and garden ornaments.* LOC: 1 mile north of Easingwold, 200 yards from northern junction of bypass (A19). PARK: Easy.

TEL: 01347 821479
E-MAIL: info@grahamhood.co.uk

FILEY

Cairncross and Sons
31 Bellevue St. YO14 9HU. (G. Cairncross)
EST. 1971. Open 9.30-12.45 and 2-4.30. CL: Wed. pm (Apr.-Oct.), Wed. (Nov.-Mar.). STOCK: *Medals, uniforms, insignia, cap badges, general militaria.* NOT STOCKED: *Weapons.*
TEL: 01723 513287
E-MAIL: george.cairnxson@hotmail.com

FLAXTON

Elm Tree Antiques   LAPADA
YO60 7RJ. (John Jackson)
EST. 1975. Open 9-4.30, Sat 10-4. CL: Mon. STOCK: *Furniture, 17th C to Edwardian; small items, £5-£5,000, Staffordshire figures.* LOC: 1 mile off A64. SER: Valuations; restorations (cabinet making, polishing and upholstery). SIZE: Large. PARK: Easy. FAIRS: Newark.
TEL: 01904 468462; HOME: same; MOBILE: 07831 757065
WEBSITE: www.elmtreeantiques.co.uk

Flaxton Antique Gardens
Glebe Farm. YO60 7RU. (Tim Richardson)
EST. 1992. SALVO. Open by appointment. STOCK: *Stone troughs, staddle stones, sundials, bird baths, urns, pedestals; statues – lead, stone, reconstituted stone; chimney pots, agricultural implements, cartwheels, Victorian edging tiles, old terracotta oil jars from Morocco, Portugal and Greece.* SER: Valuations. SIZE: Medium. PARK: Easy.
TEL: 01904 468468; FAX: same
WEBSITE: www.salvo.co.uk/dealers/flaxton

GARGRAVE

Antiques at Forge Cottage
22a High St. BD23 3RB. (Philip Carrol)
EST. 1979. Open Mon. & Fri. 10-5, Wed. & Thu. 1-5, Sat. 12-5. CL: Tue. STOCK: *Pottery and porcelain.* LOC: A65. SER: Restorations; valuations. SIZE: Medium. PARK: Easy. VAT: Spec. FAIRS: NEC; Harrogate.
TEL: 01756 748272; MOBILE: 07860 525579
E-MAIL: philipcarrol@yahoo.com
WEBSITE: www.philipcarrol.com

Dickinson's Antiques Ltd
The Estate Yard, West St. BD23 3RD. (Hugh Mardall and Adrian Eyles)
EST. 1958. Open 9-5.30 or by appointment. CL: Sat. STOCK: *Early English furniture.* LOC: Just off A65 Skipton to Settle road. SER: Restorations. PARK: By shop. VAT: Spec.
TEL: 01756 748257; MOBILE: 07971 958303

E-MAIL: enquiries@dickinsons-antiques.co.uk
WEBSITE: www.dickinsons-antiques.co.uk

Gargrave Gallery
48 High St. BD23 3RB. (B. Herrington)
EST. 1975. Appointment advisable. STOCK: General antiques, oak, mahogany, metal, paintings, 18th to early 20th C. LOC: A65. PARK: Easy.
TEL: 01756 749641

R.N. Myers and Son BADA
Endsleigh House, High St. BD23 3LX. (Jean M. and Simon Myers)
EST. 1890. Open 10-5.30 or by appointment. STOCK: Furniture, oak, mahogany, 17th to early 19th C; pottery, porcelain and metalware. NOT STOCKED: Victoriana, weapons, coins, jewellery. LOC: A65. Skipton-Settle road. SER: Valuations. SIZE: Medium. PARK: Behind shop and opposite. VAT: Spec.
TEL: 01756 749587; FAX: 01756 749322
E-MAIL: rnmyersson@aol.com

GREEN HAMMERTON

TMPL Ltd. The Main Furniture Company
The Green. YO26 8BQ. (C. and K.M. Main)
EST. 1976. Open 9-5, Sun. 11-4. STOCK: Pine furniture, 18th-19th C, £100-£1,500; reproductions from reclaimed pine; painted and bespoke furniture. LOC: Just off A59. SER: Export; containers packed. SIZE: Large. PARK: Easy. VAT: Stan.
TEL: 01423 330451; HOME: 01423 331078; FAX: 01423 331278
E-MAIL: info@mainfurniturecompany.com
WEBSITE: www.mainfurniturecompany.com

HARROGATE

Armstrong BADA
10-11 Montpellier Parade. HG1 2TJ. (M.A. Armstrong)
EST. 1983. Open 10.30-5.30. STOCK: Fine English furniture, 18th to early 19th C; works of art, 18th C. SIZE: Medium. PARK: Easy. VAT: Spec. FAIRS: Olympia (June, Nov).
TEL: 01423 506843
E-MAIL: armsantiques@aol.com

Bryan Bowden
Oakleigh, 1 Spacey View, Leeds Rd., Pannal. HG3 1LQ. (Bryan and Elizabeth Bowden)
EST. 1969. Open by appointment. STOCK: English pottery and porcelain, 1750-1850; small Georgian furniture. LOC: 2.5 miles south of Harrogate on Leeds road. SER: Valuations; restorations (pottery and porcelain); buys at auction (English pottery and porcelain). SIZE: Small. PARK: Easy. VAT: Spec. FAIRS: Northern.
TEL: 01423 870007; HOME: same

The Ginnel Antiques Centre
The Ginnel. HG1 2RB. (Pauline Stephenson)
EST. 1986. Open 9.30-5.30. STOCK: All date-lined and vetted - see individual entries. LOC: Off Parliament St. opposite Debenhams. SER: Courier. SIZE: Large. PARK: Nearby.
TEL: 01423 508857
WEBSITE: www.ginnel.co.uk
www.ginnel.com

Below are listed the specialist dealers at this centre.

Appleton Antiques
19th-20th pottery including Carlton, Moorcroft, Linthorpe, Poole and crested china; drinking glasses, paintings, small furniture.

Art-iques & Design
Silver especially Georg Jenson.

Fiona Aston
Objets d'art including porcelain and miniatures.

J. Bishop
General antiques.

Brackmoor Antiques
Silver, porcelain and objets d'art.

Lee Burgess
Ancient art and antiques, general antiques.

Catkins Jewellery and Antiques
Jewellery.

Elliot Chew
19th to early 20th C silver and plate.

Stuart Clark
Art Deco.

The Clock Inn
(R.K. Mayes) Clocks.

Mary Cooper
Antique costumes and textiles to 1929, including lace, fans, shawls, linen, quilts, samplers, wool and beadwork.

Elegant Era
Jewellery & personal antiques.

Eliza Antiques
Jewellery and personal antiques.

Garden House
Prints and maps.

The Gilded Lily
Jewellery and personal antiques.

Emilia Greenwood
Jewellery and personal antiques.

James Hardy (Antiques) Ltd
Decorative silver, glass and porcelain.

R. Himsworth
Silver and jewellery.

Holmedale Antiqes
Porcelain, pottery.

Keepsakes
Jewellery and personal antiques.

Claude Lee
Glass, porcelain, pottery.

Ian Legard
Silver

March Antiques
Victorian and early 20th C porcelain; mantle clocks.

Ann Morton Antiques
19th C furniture, oil paintings and watercolours.

Mulberry Fine Arts
Furniture, jewellery.

Odyssey Antiquities
Ancient artifacts and coins.

S. Ogley
19th-20th C collectables.

Parker Gallery
19th to early 20th C oils and watercolours, £100-£3,000.

Karen Peacock
Furniture.

Peartree Antiques
General antiques, paintings and prints.

Pedlars Past
Furniture, general.

Paul Raine
19th C silver.

Rb Gallery
Furniture, general, paintings and prints.

A. Rogers
Ancient art and general antiques.

Sara Jane Antiques
Jewellery and personal antiques.

Elisa Silverton
Silver, furniture and paintings.

G. Skinn
Pottery and porcelain.

Trafalgar Antiques
General antiques.

Turner Galleries
Paintings and prints.

C.E. Tweedale
Victorian and Edwardian pottery.

Watts Antiques
Jewellery and personal antiques.

Westmead Antiques
Pottery and porcelain.

Chris Wilde
Paintings and prints.

Wrangbrook Antiques
Pottery and porcelain.

Michael Green Pine & Country Antiques
Library House, Regent Parade. HG1 5AN.
EST. 1976. Open 8.30-5.30, Sat. 8.45-4, Sun. by

appointment. STOCK: *Oak, mahogany and antique pine furniture, from 17th C, £5-£3,000; treen, kitchenalia, collectors' treasures, lamps and decorative items.* LOC: Overlooking the Stray. SER: Valuations; restorations; stripping. SIZE: Medium. PARK: Easy. VAT: Stan/Spec.
TEL: 01423 560452.
WEBSITE: www.pineandcountryantiques.co.uk

Havelocks
13-17 Westmoreland St. HG1 5AY. (Philip Adam)
EST. 1989. Open 10-5. CL: Weds. STOCK: *Antique pine; general antique furniture.* LOC: A59 towards Skipton, turn left into Westmoreland St. SER: Valuations; restorations; stripping and finishing. SIZE: Large. PARK: Free.
TEL: 01423 506721.

London House Oriental Rugs and Carpets
9 Montpellier Parade. HG1 2TJ. (M.J.S Roe)
EST. 1981. Open 10-5. STOCK: *Persian, Turkish, Indian, Tibetan, Nepalese and Afghan rugs and carpets, 19th-20th C, £25-£5,000; kelims and camel bags, 19th-20th C, £25-£2,000.* LOC: Town centre, on the Stray. SER: Valuations; restorations (handmade rugs). SIZE: Medium. PARK: Easy. VAT: Stan.
TEL: 01423 567167
E-MAIL: sales@londonhouserugs.co.uk
WEBSITE: www.londonhouserugs.co.uk

David Love   BADA
10 Royal Parade. HG1 2SZ.
EST. 1969. Open 9-1 and 2-5.30, Sat. 9-1. STOCK: *Furniture, English, 17th-19th C; pottery and porcelain, English and Continental; decorative items, all periods.* LOC: Opposite Pump Room Museum. SER: Valuations; buys at auction. SIZE: Large. PARK: Easy. VAT: Stan/Spec.
TEL: 01423 565797/525567

Charles Lumb and Sons Ltd   BADA
2 Montpellier Gardens. HG1 2TF. (A.R. and Mrs C.M. Lumb)
EST. 1920. Open 10-1 and 2-6, Sat. 10-1 or by appointment. STOCK: *Furniture, 17th to early 19th C; metalware, period accessories.* LOC: Low Harrogate near Crown Hotel. SER: Advice. SIZE: Medium. PARK: 20yds. immediately opposite. VAT: Spec.
TEL: 01423 503776; HOME: 01423 863281; FAX: 01423 530074

McTague of Harrogate
17/19 Cheltenham Mount. HG1 1DW. (P. McTague)
Open 11-5. CL: Mon. STOCK: *Quality traditional art including old prints, watercolours, oil paintings, mainly 18th to early 20th C.* LOC: From Conference Centre on Kings Rd., go up Cheltenham Parade and turn first left. SIZE: Medium. PARK: Easy. VAT: Stan/Spec.
TEL: 01423 567086; MOBILE: 07885 108190
E-MAIL: paul@mctague.co.uk
WEBSITE: www.mctague.co.uk

Montpellier Mews Antique Centre
Montpellier St. HG1 2TG. (Mrs Weatherall)
Open 10-5. STOCK: *General antiques - porcelain, jewellery, furniture, paintings, interior decor, linen, glass, silver, costume jewellery and vintage clothes.* LOC: Behind Weatherells Antiques. SIZE: 8 dealers. PARK: Car park nearby
TEL: 01423 530484

Ogden Harrogate Ltd BADA
38 James St. HG1 1RQ. (G.M. Ogden)
EST. 1893. Open 9.15-5.30. STOCK: *Jewellery, English silver and plate; watches and clocks.* LOC: Town centre. SER: Repairs; restorations; valuations. SIZE: Large. VAT: Stan/Spec.
TEL: 01423 504123; FAX: 01423 522283
E-MAIL: sales@ogdenharrogate.co.uk
WEBSITE: www.ogdenharrogate.co.uk

Paraphernalia
38A Cold Bath Rd. HG2 0NA. (Peter F. Hacker)
EST. 1986. Open 10-5. STOCK: *Wallplates, crested and commemorative china, cutlery, glass including carnival, Mauchlineware, bric-a-brac, small furniture and collectables.* LOC: Adjacent Lancaster's Home Bakery. SER: Free local delivery. SIZE: Small. PARK: Free for 1 hr. with free disc from shop. FAIRS: Harrogate Showground.
TEL: (Evenings) 01423 567968; FAX: same

Paul M. Peters Fine Art Ltd. LAPADA
Unit 15, Valley House, off Hookstone Rd. HG82 8QT
EST. 1967. By appointment only. STOCK: *Chinese and Japanese ceramics and works of art, 17th-19th C; European ceramics and glass, 18th-19th C; European metalware, scientific instruments and unusual objects.* SER: Valuations. SIZE: Medium. PARK: Easy. VAT: Stan/Spec. FAIRS: Olympia (June).
TEL: 01423 870860

Elaine Phillips Antiques Ltd BADA
1 and 2 Royal Parade. HG1 2SZ. (Colin and Louise Phillips)
EST. 1968. Open 9.30-5.30, other times by appointment. STOCK: *Oak furniture, 1600-1800; country furniture, 1700-1840; some mahogany, 18th to early 19th C; period metalwork and decoration.* LOC: Opposite Crown Hotel, Montpellier Quarter. SER: Interior design. SIZE: Large. PARK: Nearby. VAT: Spec. FAIRS: Harrogate (Autumn).
TEL: 01423 569745; MOBILE: 07710 793753
E-MAIL: louise@elainephillipsantiques.wanadoo.co.uk

Smith's (The Rink) Ltd
Dragon Rd. HG1 5DR.
EST. 1906. Open 9-5.30, Sun. 11-4.30. STOCK: *General antiques, 1750-1820, £150; Victoriana, 1830-1900, £50.* LOC: From Leeds, right at Prince of Wales roundabout, left at next roundabout, 1/2 mile on Skipton Rd., left into Dragon Rd. SIZE: Large. PARK: Easy. VAT: Stan/Spec.
TEL: 01423 567890
WEBSITE: www.smithstherink.co.uk

Sutcliffe Galleries BADA
5 Royal Parade. HG1 2SZ. (G.G. & H.V. Sutcliffe)
EST. 1947. Open 10-5. STOCK: *Paintings, 19th C.* LOC: Opposite Crown Hotel. SER: Valuations; restorations; framing. VAT: Spec. FAIRS: Harrogate, Olympia (Nov).
TEL: 01423 562976; FAX: 01423 528729;
E-MAIL: enquiries@sutcliffegalleries.co.uk
WEBSITE: www.sutcliffegalleries.co.uk

Thorntons of Harrogate LAPADA
1 Montpellier Gdns. HG1 2TF. (R.H. and R.J. Thornton)
EST. 1971. Open 9.30-5.30. STOCK: *17th-19th C furniture, barometers, decorative items, clocks, paintings, porcelain, scientific instruments.* SER: Valuations and restorations. SIZE: Medium. PARK: Easy. VAT: Spec.
TEL: 01423 504118; FAX: 01423 528400
E-MAIL: info@harrogateantiques.com
WEBSITE: www.harrogateantiques.com

Walker Galleries Ltd BADA LAPADA
6 Montpellier Gdns. HG1 2TF.
EST. 1972. Open 9.30-1 and 2-5.30. STOCK: *Oil paintings and watercolours, 18th C furniture.* LOC: Lower Harrogate near the Crown Hotel. SER: Valuations; restorations; framing. SIZE: Medium. PARK: Montpellier car park nearby. VAT: Spec. FAIRS: BADA, London; Harrogate: Olympia.
TEL: 01423 567933; FAX: 01423 536664
E-MAIL: wgltd@aol.com
WEBSITE: www.walkergalleries.com and www.walkerfineart.co.uk

Paul Weatherell Antiques LAPADA
30-31 Montpellier Parade. HG1 2TG.
EST. 2004. Open 9-5.30. STOCK: *Period and fine decorative furniture; lighting, pictures, mirrors, garden items.* LOC: Opposite Crown Hotel. SER: Restorations (furniture, upholstery & gilding). SIZE: Large. PARK: Nearby. VAT: Spec.
TEL: 01423 507810; FAX: 01423 520005
E-MAIL: paul@weatherells.com
WEBSITE: www.weatherells.com

Weatherell's of Harrogate Antiques LAPADA
& Fine Arts
10-11 Montpellier Mews, Montpellier St. HG1 2TQ.
Open 10-5.30. STOCK: *Period and decorative furniture.* SIZE: Two showrooms.
TEL: 01423 525004; FAX: 01423 520005

HARTLEPOOL

Period Interiors
Unit 1, Cromwell St. Depot, Whitby St. South. TS24 7LR. (D.J. Crowther)
EST. 2005. Open 9-4.30. STOCK: *Victorian and Edwardian fireplaces, Victorian 4-panel pine doors, wide range of architectural antiques.* SIZE: Large. PARK: Easy.

TEL: 01429 265111; MOBILE: 07774 639754
E-MAIL: sales@period-interiors.com
WEBSITE: www.period-interiors.com

HAWES

Cellar Antiques
Bridge St. DL8 3QL. (Ian Milton Iveson)
EST. 1987. Open 10-5, Sun. 11-5. *STOCK: 17th-19th C oak and country furniture, longcase clocks, metalware and pottery.* LOC: Cobbled street near bridge. SER: Valuations. SIZE: Large. PARK: Rear of shop.
TEL: 01969 667224
E-MAIL: cellar.antiques@fsmail.net
WEBSITE: www.cellarantiques.co.uk

Sturman's Antiques   LAPADA
Main St. DL8 3QW. (P.J. Sturman)
EST. 1985. Open 10-5 including Sun. *STOCK: Georgian and Victorian furniture; porcelain and pottery including Moorcroft; longcase, wall and mantel clocks and barometers.* SER: Nationwide delivery. PARK: Opposite. VAT: Spec.
TEL: 01969 667742
E-MAIL: enquiries@sturmansantiques.co.uk
WEBSITE: www.sturmansantiques.co.uk

HELMSLEY

Castle Gate Antiques
14 Castle Gate. YO62 5AB. (D. Hartshorne)
EST. 1999. Open 10-5. *STOCK: Silver, from 17th C; early English glass, pottery and china; paintings, mainly sporting and Yorkshire interest; early oak furniture.* LOC: Off Market Place, down side of town hall and across beck. SER: Valuations. SIZE: Medium. PARK: Easy.
TEL: 01439 771580; FAX: same

E. Stacy-Marks Limited   LAPADA
24 High Street YO62 5AG.
EST. 1889. Open by appointment. *STOCK: Paintings, English, Dutch and Continental schools, 18th-20th C.* SER: Restorations (oils and watercolours); buys at auction; valuations; delivery.
TEL: 01439 771950; FAX: same
E-MAIL: info@esm-ltd.co.uk
WEBSITE: www.estacy-marks.co.uk

York Cottage Antiques
7 Church St. YO62 5AD. (G. and E.M. Thornley)
EST. 1976. Open 10-5. *STOCK: Early oak and country furniture.* LOC: Opposite church, within 'The Rievaulx Collection'. SIZE: Small. PARK: Adjacent.

KIRK DEIGHTON

Elden Antiques
23 Ashdale View. LS22 4DS. (E. and D. Broadley)
EST. 1970. Open 9-5, Sat. 12-5, Sun. 10-4. *STOCK: General antiques including furniture.* LOC: Main road

between Wetherby and Knaresborough. SIZE: Medium.
PARK: Easy.
TEL: 01937 584770; HOME: same

KIRKBY MALHAM

Crispian Riley-Smith
Summergill. BD23 4BS
EST. 1997. Open by appointment only. *STOCK: Old Master drawings, 1500-1900, £500-£100,000.* SER: Valuations. FAIRS: Master Drawings, London and New York.
TEL: 01729 830734; FAX: same; MOBILE: 07771 552509
E-MAIL: crispian@riley-smith.com
WEBSITE: www.riley-smith.com

KNARESBOROUGH

Robert Aagaard & Co
Frogmire House, Stockwell Rd. HG5 0JP.
EST. 1961. GMC. Open 9-5, Sat. 10-4. *STOCK: Chimney pieces, marble fire surrounds, stone and wood fireplaces, fire baskets and cast iron inserts.* LOC: Town centre. SER: Fireplace restoration and design. SIZE: Large. PARK: Own. VAT: Stan.
TEL: 01423 864805; FAX: 01423 869356
E-MAIL: robertaagaardco@btconnect.com

Omar (Harrogate) Ltd
21 Boroughbridge Rd. HG5 0LY. (P. McCormick)
EST. 1946. Open by appointment. *STOCK: Persian, Turkish, Caucasian rugs and carpets.* SER: Cleaning; restorations. PARK: Easy. VAT: Stan.
TEL: 01423 863199; FAX: same
E-MAIL: philipmccormick@hotmail.com

Starkie/Bowkett
9 Abbey Rd. HG5 8HY. (E.S. Starkie)
EST. 1919. Resident. Open 9-6. *STOCK: Chairs, small furniture, books, pottery and collectables.* LOC: By the river at the lower road bridge. SIZE: Medium. PARK: Easy.
TEL: 01423 866112

LEYBURN

Leyburn Antiques Centre
Harmby Rd. DL8 5NS. (Paul Ashford)
EST. 1984. Open 9.30-4.30 including Sun. *STOCK: Fine Georgian, Victorian and Edwardian furniture, pine, pottery and porcelain, glass, lighting, silver and jewellery, oil paintings, prints, taxidermy, books, garden reclamation items and bygones.* LOC: 300 yards from Tennants Auctioneers. SER: Valuations; restorations. SIZE: Large - 40 dealers. PARK: Easy.
TEL: 01969 625555
E-MAIL: leyburnantiques@aol.com
WEBSITE: www.leyburnantiques.com

Thirkill Antiques
Newlands, Worton. DL8 3ET. (Tomasso Bros. Fine Art)
EST. 1963. Open any time. STOCK: Musicals, pottery, porcelain, small furniture, 18th-19th C. SER: Restorations. PARK: Free.
TEL: 01969 650725

MALTON

Magpie Antiques
9-13 The Shambles. YO17 7LZ. (G.M. Warren)
EST. 1987. Open 10-4. CL: Thurs. STOCK: General antiques and collectables, 19th-20th C, £5-£50; kitchenalia, £5-£100; some furniture. LOC: Town centre, near Cattle Market. SIZE: Small. PARK: Nearby. FAIRS: Newark.
TEL: 01653 627292; MOBILE: 07969 852849

MASHAM

Aura Antiques
1-3 Silver St. HG4 4DX. (R. and R. Sutcliffe)
EST. 1985. Open 9.30-4.30, Sun. by appointment. STOCK: Furniture especially period mahogany and oak, 17th to mid-19th C, £50-£5,000; metalware - brass and copper, fenders, £5-£250; china, glass, silver and decorative objects, £5-£1,000; all 18th-19th C. LOC: Corner of Market Sq. SER: Valuations; UK delivery. SIZE: Medium. PARK: Easy. VAT: Spec.
TEL: 01765 689315; HOME: 01765 658192
E-MAIL: robert@aura-antiques.co.uk
WEBSITE: www.aura-antiques.co.uk

MELBOURNE

St. Julien's & Abacus
Common End Farm, Thornton, YO42 4RS. (H.J. White)
Open 9.30-4.30. STOCK: Antique and period fireplaces, architectural antiques, door & window furniture, period lighting and bathroom ware. SER: Restoration (fireplaces, all architectural items), fitting period fireplaces. PARK: Easy.
TEL: 01759 318575
E-MAIL: abacus03@globalnet.co.uk

MIDDLEHAM

Middleham Antiques
The Corner Shop, Kirkgate. DL8 4PF. (Angela Walton)
EST. 2004. Usually open 10-5.30 - prior telephone call advisable. STOCK: Victorian and Edwardian decorative antiques, curios, collectables, £20-£1,000. SIZE: Small. PARK: Easy. FAIRS: Local.
TEL: 01969 622982; MOBILE: 07917 571180
E-MAIL: angiwal@yahoo.com

BRIAN LOOMES

Specialist dealer in antique British clocks. Internationally recognised authority and author of numerous books on antique clocks. Large stock of lantern clocks with a number of longcase clocks.

Restoration work undertaken

Established 1966

Resident on premises. Available six days a week but strictly by prior telephone appointment.

Copies of my current books always in stock.

CALF HAUGH FARMHOUSE, PATELEY BRIDGE, NORTH YORKS. (On B6265 Pateley-Grassington road.)
Tel: (01423) 711163   www.brianloomes.com

PATELEY BRIDGE

Country Oak Antiques
Yorkshire Country Wines, The Mill, Glasshouses. HG3 5QH. (Richard Brown)
EST. 1980. Open 11.30-4.30. CL: Mon. & Tues. (reduced hours Jan. and Feb) - most times by appointment. STOCK: Oak and country furniture, 17th-19th C, £50-£5,000. LOC: 1/4 mile from crossroads of B6165. SIZE: Medium. PARK: Easy.
TEL: 01423 711947; FAX: same; HOME: 01423 711223
E-MAIL: info@countryoakantiques.co.uk
WEBSITE: www.countryoakantiques.co.uk.

Brian Loomes
Calf Haugh Farm. HG3 5HW. (Brian and Joy Loomes)
EST. 1966. (Author of clock reference books). Open by appointment. STOCK: British clocks, especially lantern clocks, £2,000-£20,000. NOT STOCKED: Foreign clocks. LOC: From Pateley Bridge, first private lane on left on Grassington Rd. (B6265). SIZE: Medium. PARK: Own. VAT: Spec.
TEL: 01423 711163
WEBSITE: www.brianloomes.com

PICKERING

Pickering Antique Centre
Southgate. YO18 8BL. (Tina and Jim Vance)
EST. 1998. Open 10-5, Sun. 11-5. STOCK: Victorian and

Edwardian furniture; pictures and prints, pottery and porcelain, books, collectables, glass, clocks, jewellery, silver and plate, postcards, lighting and metalware. LOC: Next to traffic lights on A170 Helmsley road. SER: Valuations. SIZE: Large - 45 dealers. PARK: Own at rear.
TEL: 01751 477210; MOBILE: 07899 872309
E-MAIL: sales@pickantiques.freeserve.co.uk
WEBSITE: www.pickeringantiquecentre.co.uk

C.H. Reynolds Antiques
The Old Curiosity Shop, 122 Eastgate. YO18 7DW.
(C.H. and D.M. Reynolds)
EST. 1947. Open 9.30-5.30, Sun. by arrangement. *STOCK: Furniture, glass, china.* LOC: A170. PARK: Free, outside shop.
TEL: 01751 472785

RICHMOND

York House (Antiques)
York House, 60 Market Place. DL10 4JQ. (Christina Swift)
EST. 1986. Open 9.30-5.30, Sun. 12-4. *STOCK: Furniture, mainly Victorian and Edwardian including pine, £500-£1,800; china, lamps, figures, Victorian to 1930s, £20-£500; kitchenalia, garden artifacts, French and English fires and fireplaces, Victorian and later, to £800.* SER: Interior design; 'layaway' scheme (items paid for monthly or as required). SIZE: Medium. PARK: Loading bay or nearby.
TEL: 01748 850338; FAX: same; HOME: 01748 850522;
MOBILE: 07711 307045
E-MAIL: christina.swift@tiscali.co.uk
WEBSITE: www.yorkhouseantiques.co.uk

RIPON

Milton Holgate
PO Box 77. HG4 3XX. (Milton and Brenda Holgate)
EST. 1972. Open by appointment. *STOCK: Fine English furniture and accessories, 17th-19th C.*
TEL: 01765 620225

Hornsey's of Ripon
3 Kirkgate. HG4 1PA. (Bruce, Susan and Daniel Hornsey)
EST. 1976. Open 10-6. *STOCK: Textiles, rare and secondhand books; art gallery.* SIZE: Medium. PARK: Market Square.
TEL: 01765 602878
E-MAIL: thegallery@hornseys.com
WEBSITE: www.hornseys.com

Sigma Antiques and Fine Art
The Old Opera House, Water Skellgate. HG4 1BH. (David Thomson)
EST. 1963. Open 10.30-5, other times by appointment. *STOCK: 17th-20th C furniture, furnishing items, pottery, porcelain, objets d'art, paintings, jewellery and collectors' items.* LOC: Near town centre. SER: Restorations (furniture); repairs (jewellery and silver); valuations.

SIZE: Large. PARK: Nearby. VAT: Spec.
TEL: 01765 603163; FAX: same
E-MAIL: sigmaantiques@aol.com

ROBIN HOOD'S BAY

John Gilbert Antiques
King St. YO22 4SH.
EST. 1990. Open Sat. 10-5, Sun. 11-4 most weekends. Prior telephone call advisable. *STOCK: Country furniture, 18th-19th C, £100-£1,500; oak furniture from 1650, £250-£1,500; 19th C furniture, £50-£1,000; treen, £5-£500, metalware.* LOC: At bottom of old village, between Bay and Dolphin Hotels under the coat of arms. SER: Valuations; restorations (furniture). SIZE: Small. PARK: Top of hill.
TEL: 01947 880528; MOBILE: 07969 004320

SCARBOROUGH

Antiques & Collectors' Centre
35, St. Nicholas Cliff. YO11 2ES. (C.H. Spink and Mrs. C.E. Bowne)
EST. 1965. PTA. Open 9.30-4.30. *STOCK: Collectables and accessories including postcards, coins, cigarette cards, stamps, military items and jewellery.* LOC: Next to the Grand Hotel. PARK: Outside.
TEL: 01723 365221; MOBILE: 07730 202405
E-MAIL: sales@collectors.demon.co.uk
WEBSITE: www.collectors.demon.co.uk

Hanover Antiques & Collectables
32 St Nicolas Cliff. YO11 2ES. (R.E. and P.J. Baldwin)
EST. 1976. Open 10-4. *STOCK: Small collectables, medals, badges, militaria, toys, 50p-£500.* LOC: Close to Grand Hotel. PARK: Nearby.
TEL: 01723 374175

SETTLE

Mary Milnthorpe and Daughters Antique Shop
Market Place. BD24 9DX. (Judith Milnthorpe)
EST. 1958. Open 9.30-5. CL: Wed. *STOCK: Antique and 19th C jewellery and English silver.* LOC: Opposite Town Hall. SIZE: Small. PARK: Easy. VAT: Stan/Spec.
TEL: 01729 822331

E. Thistlethwaite
The Antique Shop, Market Sq. BD24 9EF.
EST. 1972. Open 9-5. CL: Wed. *STOCK: Country furniture and metalware, 18th-19th C.* LOC: Town centre, A65. SIZE: Medium. PARK: Forecourt. VAT: Stan/Spec.
TEL: 01729 822460

SHERBURN-IN-ELMET

French and Country Living
Low Street Farm, Low St. LS25 6BB
Open by appointment. *STOCK: French, English and*

Continental furniture, mirrors, textiles, lighting and accessories.
TEL: 07999 693292
WEBSITE: www.frenchandcountryliving.com

SKIPTON

Manor Barn
Providence Mill, The Old Foundry Yard, Cross St. BD23 2AE. (John Bradford)
EST. 1972. Open 9-5. *STOCK: Pine, 17th-19th C and reproduction; oak.* LOC: Behind Christ Church. SIZE: Large. PARK: Easy. VAT: Stan/Spec.
TEL: 01756 798584; FAX: 01756 798536
E-MAIL: info@manorbarnpine.co.uk
WEBSITE: www.manorbarnpine.co.uk

Skipton Antiques Centre
The Old Foundry, Cavendish St. BD23 2AB. (Andrew Tapsell)
EST. 1994. Open 10.30-4.30, Sun. 11-4. *STOCK: Wide range of general antiques and collectables, Georgian to 1950s; clocks, jewellery, furniture and Art Deco.* LOC: West side of town off A59. SIZE: Large - 30 dealers. PARK: Loading and nearby.
TEL: 01756 797667

SLEIGHTS

Coach House Antiques
75 Coach Rd. YO22 5BT. (C.J. Rea)
EST. 1973. Resident. Open Sat. from 10 and by appointment. *STOCK: Furniture, especially oak and country; metalware, paintings, pottery, textiles, unusual and decorative items.* LOC: On A169, 3 miles south west of Whitby. SIZE: Small. PARK: Easy, opposite.
TEL: 01947 810313.

Eskdale Antiques
164 Coach Rd. YO22 4BH. (Philip Smith)
EST. 1978. Open 9-5.30 including Sun. *STOCK: Pine furniture and farm bygones, 19th-20th C, £50-£500.* LOC: Main Pickering road. SER: Valuations; buys at auction. SIZE: Medium. PARK: Easy.
TEL: 01947 810297; HOME: same

SNAINTON

Antony, David & Ann Shackleton
19 & 72 High St. YO13 9AE.
EST. 1984. Resident. CL: Fri. *STOCK: Longcase clocks, Victorian rocking horses, Georgian and Victorian furniture, collectables, £1-£3,500.* LOC: A170, equidistant Scarborough and Pickering. SER: Restorations (furniture, longcase clocks, rocking horses). SIZE: Medium. PARK: Easy.
TEL: 01723 859577/850172

STILLINGTON

Pond Cottage Antiques
Brandsby Rd. YO61 1NY. (C.M. and D. Thurstans)
EST. 1970. Resident. Open seven days 9-5. *STOCK: Pine, oak, kitchenalia, country furniture, treen, metalware, brass, copper.* LOC: B1363 York to Helmsley road. SER: Repolishing. SIZE: Medium. PARK: Own. VAT: Global.
TEL: 01347 810796
E-MAIL: info@yorkshirepine.co.uk
WEBSITE: www.yorkshirepine.co.uk
www.pondcottageantiques.co.uk

STOKESLEY

Alan Ramsey Antiques   LAPADA
7 Wainstones Court, Stokesley Industrial Park. TS9 5JY.
EST. 1973. Open by appointment. *STOCK: Victorian, Edwardian and Georgian furniture; longcase, wall and bracket clocks; interesting pine.* **SIZE: Warehouse. PARK: Easy. VAT: Stan/Spec.**
TEL: 01642 711311/713008; MOBILE: 07702 523246; 07762 049848
E-MAIL: a.ramseyantiques@btinternet.com
WEBSITE: www.alanramseyantiques.co.uk

THIRSK

Classic Rocking Horses
(B. and J. Tildesley)
EST. 1980. Open by appointment. *STOCK: Restored antique rocking horses and authentic replicas of Victorian rocking horses, £1,500-£5,000.* PARK: East.
TEL: 01845 501330; FAX: 01845 501700
E-MAIL: info@classicrockinghorses.co.uk
WEBSITE: www.classicrockinghorses.co.uk

Kirkgate Fine Art & Conservation
The Studio, 3 Gillings Yard. YO7 1SY. (Richard Bennett)
EST. 1979. BAPCR. Open by appointment. *STOCK: Oil paintings, £50-£2,000; watercolours, £50-£500; both 19th C to present.* LOC: Joins Market Place. SER: Restorations (oil paintings and framing); buys at auction. SIZE: Small. PARK: Nearby.
TEL: 01845 524085; HOME: same
E-MAIL: richard.bennett@traditionalwatercolours.co.uk
WEBSITE: www.fineartandconservation.co.uk

Millgate Pine & Antiques
Abel Grange Farm, Newsham Rd. YO7 4DB. (T.D. and M. Parvin)
EST. 1990. Open 8.30-5. *STOCK: English and European pine especially doors, 1730-1930, Victorian 4-panel, Georgian 6-panel and farmhouse board and ledge. Feature leaded glass/vestibule doors. 4-panel Victorian replicas made to measure from antique pine. Stripped wardrobes, dressers, cupboards, bookshelves, tables.* LOC: 2.5 miles north of

PERSIAN RUGS AND CARPETS
The Fabric of Life

Essie Sakhai
Edited by Ian Bennett

Persian Rugs and Carpets: The Fabric of Life presents a pictorial journey around Persia, reflecting the weaving and pattern styles of the many regions and tribes - including Esfahan, Kashan, Nain, Qum, Kerman, Tabriz, Bakhtiari, Senneh, Malayer and Qashqa'i - showing the vast range of carpets woven in Persia from about 1850 to the third quarter of the 20th century. The introductory text to each section explains the particular aspects of that region's weaving style. In addition, each caption gives an in-depth account of the carpet, not only the date and region in which it was woven, but also the motifs and patterns, the technique used, even the weaver, and, in the case of pictorial carpets, the fascinating stories being depicted. The introductory essay takes the reader through the history and geography of the Persian rug, including information on structure, weaving and knotting, the different output of the city and urban workshops compared to tribal and village weaving, flatweaves, and identification. It also features points of note for the collector, such as conservation and cleaning, as well as highlighting the difficulties in dating rugs, and the problems with fakes. Lavishly illustrated in colour throughout, *Persian Rugs and Carpets: The Fabric of Life* shows these carpets at their very best, with incredible clarity of detail, bringing together in one place the diversity of weaving styles and the great variety of patterns, allowing the reader to compare carpets at a glance. This exquisite book - an essential addition to the bookshelves of all carpet collectors and aficionados - is a testament to the rich and vibrant art form of Persian carpets.

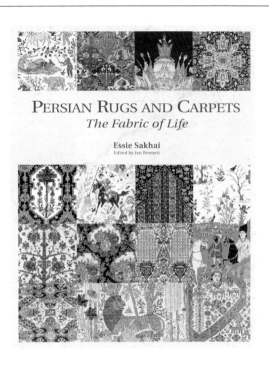

PERSIAN RUGS AND CARPETS
The Fabric of Life

Essie Sakhai
Edited by Ian Bennett

324 x 266 mm. 448 pp 300 col.
£55.00 Hardback

For full details of all ACC publications,
log on to our website:
www.antiquecollectorsclub.com
or telephone 01394 389950 for a free catalogue

Thirsk. SER: Repairs; stripping; restorations. SIZE: Large + warehouse. PARK: Easy.
TEL: 01845 523878
WEBSITE: www.millgatepine.co.uk

Potterton Books
The Old Rectory, Sessay. YO7 3LZ. (Clare Jameson)
EST. 1980. Open 9-5. STOCK: *Classic reference works on art, architecture, interior design, antiques and collecting.* SER: Book search; catalogues. SIZE: Large. PARK: Easy. FAIRS: London; Frankfurt; Paris; New York; Milan; Dubai.
TEL: 01845 501218; FAX: 01845 501439
WEBSITE: www.pottertonbooks.co.uk

THORNTON-LE-DALE

Cobweb Books
1 Pickering Rd. YO18 7LG. (Robin and Sue Buckler)
EST. 1990. Open every day June-Oct. 10-5. CL: Mon. in winter. STOCK: *Books - leather bindings, illustrated, modern first editions, literature, military, poetry, history.* SIZE: Medium. PARK: Nearby.
TEL: 01751 476638; HOME: 01751 474402
E-MAIL: sales@cobwebbooks.co.uk
WEBSITE: www.cobwebbooks.co.uk

TOCKWITH

Tomlinsons   LAPADA
Moorside. YO26 7QG.
EST. 1977. BIDA Corporate. Open Mon-Fri. 8-5, or by appointment. Club members - Sat. 9-4.30 and Sun. 10-4. STOCK: *Furniture, antique, upholstered and reproduction, £10-£20,000; clocks, porcelain, silver plate and decorative items, £10-£5,000.* LOC: A1 Wetherby take B1224 towards York. After 3 miles turn left on to Rudgate. At end of this road turn left, business 200m on left. SER: Export; restorations; container packing, delivery, desk leathering and bespoke reproductions. SIZE: Very large. PARK: Easy. VAT: Stan/Spec.
TEL: 01423 358833; FAX: 01423 358188
E-MAIL: info@antique-furniture.co.uk
WEBSITE: www.antique-furniture.co.uk

WEST BURTON

The Old Smithy
DL8 4JL. (Pete and Elaine Dobbing)
EST. 2000. *Trade Only.* Open 11.30-4.30. Prior telephone call advisable for winter opening. CL: Mon. and Fri. STOCK: *General antiques, silver and jewellery, collectables, £5-£300; clocks and country pine and oak*

TOMLINSON ANTIQUES

Antiques-Restoration-Reproduction-Cabinet Making

THE BIGGEST SELECTION
of antique furniture in the UK,
over 5,000 items in stock

UK largest
antique
furniture
trade
warehouse

Contact Tomlinson Antiques

Tel: 01423 358833
Fax: 01423 358188
Email: ffc@antique-furniture.co.uk
Address: Moorside, Tockwith, York,
            North Yorkshire, YO26 7QG

Open: *Trade*
            8am - 5.00pm   Mon - Fri

            Club Members
            8am - 5.00pm   Sat
            10am - 4pm   Sun

Visit our website at:
www.antique-furniture.co.uk

LAPADA
MEMBER

LONDON AND PROVINCIAL
ANTIQUE DEALERS ASSOCIATION

Predominantly a trade warehouse, we welcome members of the Tomlinson Fine
Furniture Club on Saturdays from 8am - 5.00pm and Sundays
from 10am - 4pm. Please call us for information on membership.
Restoration, or any other enquiries are welcome anytime.

furniture, £50-£1,000; all 18th-20th C. LOC: Between Leyburn and Hawes, take Kettlewell road B6160. SER: Valuations. SIZE: Small. PARK: Easy.
TEL: 01969 663999; HOME: 01969 663438; MOBILE: 07765 306572
E-MAIL: oldsmithyantiques@tiscali.co.uk

WHITBY

'Bobbins' Wool, Crafts, Antiques
Wesley Hall, Church St. YO22 4DE. (Dick and Pam Hoyle)
EST. 1984. Open 10-5 including Sun. *STOCK: General antiques especially oil lamps, bric-a-brac, 78 records and postcards, kitchenalia and fireplaces, 19th-20th C.* LOC: Between Market Place and steps to Abbey on cobbled East Side. SER: Repairs and spares (oil lamps). SIZE: Small. PARK: Nearby (part of Church St. is pedestrianised). VAT: Stan.
TEL: 01947 600585 (answerphone)
E-MAIL: bobbins@globalnet.co.uk

Caedmon House
14 Station Sq. YO21 1DU. (E.M. Stanforth)
EST. 1977. Open 11-4.30. *STOCK: General antiques, mainly small, including jewellery, dolls, Disney and china, especially Humme and Dresden, up to £1,200.* SER: Valuations; restorations (china); repairs (jewellery). SIZE:

Medium. PARK: Easy. VAT: Stan/Spec.
TEL: 01947 602120; HOME: 01947 603930

WHIXLEY

Michael Scott Antiques
Garden House, Stonegate. YO26 8AS (Michael Scott)
EST. 2000. Open by appointment only. *STOCK: Period furniture, clocks, barometers and fine art.* LOC: 5 mins. off A1, junction 47. SER: Furniture restoration. VAT: Stan/Spec.
TEL: 01423 331854; MOBILE: 07734 438103
E-MAIL: michaelscottantiques@btinternet.com
WEBSITE: www.michaelscottantiques.co.uk

YORK

Antiques Centre York
Allenby House, 41 Stonegate. YO1 8AW.
(David Waggott)
EST. 2003. Open 9-5.30, Sun 9-4. *STOCK: Wide range of general antiques, from £1-£7,000, ceramics, glass, vintage clothing, jewellery.* LOC: In pedestrianised thoroughfare between Minster and main shopping area, 10 mins. from station. SIZE: Large - 120 dealers. PARK: Nearby. VAT: Stan.
TEL: 01904 635888; FAX: 01904 676342
WEBSITE: www.theantiquescentreyork.co.uk

Barbican Bookshop

24 Fossgate. YO1 9TA.
EST. 1961. PBFA. Open 9.15-5.30. *STOCK: Books - antiquarian, secondhand and new.* LOC: City centre. SER: Mail order. SIZE: Large. PARK: Multi-storey nearby. VAT: Stan. FAIRS: PBFA.
TEL: 01904 653643; FAX: 01904 653643
E-MAIL: mail@barbicanbookshop.co.uk
WEBSITE: www.barbicanbookshop.co.uk

Bishopsgate Antiques

23/24 Bishopsgate St. YO2 1JH. (R. Wetherill)
EST. 1965. Open 9.15-6. *STOCK: General antiques.* VAT: Stan.
TEL: 01904 623893; FAX: 01904 626511
E-MAIL: robin-2@hotmail.co.uk

Barbara Cattle   BADA

45 Stonegate. YO1 8AW. (H.L Brown group of jewellers)
Open 9-5.30. *STOCK: Jewellery and silver, Georgian to date.* SER: Valuations; repairs; restorations.
TEL: 01904 623862; FAX: 01904 651675
E-MAIL: info@barbaracattle.co.uk
WEBSITE: www.barbaracattle.co.uk

Cavendish Antiques & Collectors' Centre

44 Stonegate. YO1 8AS. (Debbie and Mark Smith)
EST. 1996. NAG. Open seven days 9-6. *STOCK: Wide range of general antiques, £1-£7,000.* LOC: In pedestrianised thoroughfare between Minster and main shopping area. SIZE: Large. PARK: Nearby. VAT: Stan.
TEL: 01904 621666; FAX: 01904 675747
E-MAIL: info@cavendishantiques.co.uk
WEBSITE: www.cavendishantiques.co.uk

Coulter Galleries

Open by appointment. *STOCK: Watercolours and oils, pre-1900; frames.*
TEL: 07850 665144; FAX: 01904 792285
E-MAIL: robert.coulter@btinternet.com

Fossgate Books

36 Fossgate. YO1 9TF. (Alex Helstrip)
EST. 1992. Open 10-5.30. *STOCK: Out-of-print and antiquarian books.* LOC: City centre. SIZE: Large. PARK: Nearby.
TEL: 01904 641389

The French House (Antiques) Ltd

74 Micklegate. YO1 6LF (S.B. and M.J. Hazell)
EST. 1995. Open 9.30-5.30. *STOCK: Wooden beds, 18th-19th C, £900-£2,500; gilt mirrors, 19th C, £300-£2,000; lighting, 19th-20th C, £200-£1,000; sofas £1,200 - £2,800; all pieces sourced from France and restored in the UK.* SER: Restorations; cabinet making; upholstery; French polishing; painting; gilding. SIZE: Medium. PARK: Meters. VAT: Margin.
TEL: 01904 624465; FAX: 01904 624965

E-MAIL: kath@thefrenchhouse.co.uk
WEBSITE: www.thefrenchhouse.co.uk

London House Oriental Rugs at Geoffrey Benton & Son

York Rd., Green Hammerton. YO26 8DH. (M.J.S Roe)
EST. 1978. Open 10-5 *STOCK: Persian, Turkish, Indian, Tibetan, Nepalese and Afghan rugs and carpets, 19th-20th C, £25-£5,000; kelims and camel bags, 19th-20th C, £25-£2,000.* LOC: A59.
TEL: 01423 331901
E-MAIL: sales@londonhouserugs.co.uk
WEBSITE: www.londonhouserugs.co.uk

Minster Gate Bookshop

8 Minster Gates. YO1 7HL. (N. Wallace)
EST. 1970. PBFA. Open 10-5.30, Sun 11-5. *STOCK: Antiquarian and secondhand books; old maps and prints.* LOC: Opposite south door of Minster. SER: Valuations; restorations; book finding. SIZE: Large. VAT: Margin.
TEL: 01904 621812; FAX: 01904 622960
E-MAIL: rarebooks@minstergatebooks.co.uk
WEBSITE: www.minstergatebooks.co.uk

Janette Ray Rare and Out of Print Books

8 Bootham. YO30 7BL.
EST. 1987. PBFA. ABA. Open Wed. and Sat. 9.30-5.30 or by appointment. *STOCK: Out-of-print books on design, architecture and gardens.* LOC: City centre. SER: Valuations; catalogues issued; finder. SIZE: Small. PARK: Opposite. FAIRS: ABA Olympia.
TEL: 01904 623088; FAX: 01904 620814
E-MAIL: books@janetteray.co.uk
WEBSITE: www.janetteray.co.uk

The Red House Antiques Centre

Duncombe Place. YO1 7ED. (Pauline Stephenson and Ginnel Antiques Centres)
EST. 1986. Open 9.30-5.30, (June-Sept. 9.30-6), Sun. 10.30-5.30. *STOCK: Wide variety of datelined antiques from 50 specialist dealers.* LOC: 200 yards from Minster. SER: Packing and shipping; arts and antiques lectures. SIZE: 10 showrooms.
TEL: 01904 637000
E-MAIL: enquiries@redhouseyork.co.uk
WEBSITE: www.redhouseyork.co.uk

Below are listed the specialist dealers at this centre.

March Antiques
Art Nouveau silver and metalware.

P.W. Raine
Silver, pewter, metalware and ceramics.

Station Road Antiques
Silver and jewellery.

Abacus
General antiques.

Art Decoration
Art Deco furniture.

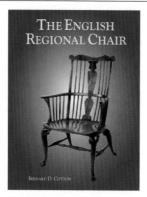

THE ENGLISH
REGIONAL CHAIR

BERNARD D. COTTON

This is arguably the most detailed study ever made of any branch of British furniture. Its unique scope embraces the work of hundreds of craftsmen throughout the country, working within the general tradition of their area, yet superimposing their individual design signatures. Employing a remarkable combination of talents, the author has examined thousands of regional chairs, researched local archives, conducted field studies and collated anecdotal evidence to relate the evolution of known types and makes. The result, far from being a dry research document, is a fascinating living account of the development of hundreds of chair types from all over England and the lives of the craftsmen who produced them.

279 x 216 mm. 512 pp 69 col., 1400 b.&w.
£49.50 Hardback

Art-Iques & Design
Art Deco.

Fiona Aston
19th C porcelain, silver and objets d'art.

Caroline Barkway
Jewellery.

J.Bishop
General antiques.

J&A Boothroyd
Metalware, general antiques.

Brackmoor Antiques
Silver, porcelain and objets d'art.

Brigantia
Ancient art and antiques, militaria.

Lee Burgess
Ancient art and antiques, decorative art and general antiques.

Bygones
Jewellery and dolls.

Elliot Chew
19th to early 20th C silver and plate.

The Clock Room
Clocks, watches.

Cornucopia
Jewellery and coins.

Curiosa
Lighting.

Nick Curry
Jewellery.

Fraser Antiques
General, pottery and porcelain.

Garden House Antiques
19th C prints and maps.

Geoffrey Gardner
Pottery, porcelain, general antiques.

The Gilded Lily
Jewellery

James Hardy (Antiques) Ltd
18th-19th C silver.

Laurel Bank Antiques
Clocks and watches.

Jean Linford
Deco chrome, clocks, jewellery and accessories.

Lycurgus Glass
19th-20th C decorative art glass and mirrors.

Mallaby Antiques
General antiques, pottery, porcelain, silver.

Stella Mar Antiques
19th C furniture and furnishings, porcelain, metalware, treen and objes d'art.

Olivia Meyler
Jewellery and Russian artefacts.

John Moor
Ancient art and antiques.

Francis O'Flynn
Antique prints, maps and books

Octavia Antiques
Art Deco, silver.

Karen Peacock
Furniture.

Anne Powell
18th-19th C ceramics, Tunbridgeware and silver.

Alan Price
17th-18th C oak furniture, brass and copper.

Pure Imagination
Scandinavian Deco furniture, metalware and ceramics.

Purr-fect Antiques
General, jewellery, pottery, porcelain, silver.

David Robinson
Militaria.

Sara Jane Antiques
Jewellery.

Janice Scanlon
Art Deco ceramics and jewellery.

Swords & Pistols
Militaria.

Topaz Antiques
Victorian and Edwardian jewellery.

C.E. Tweedale
Victorian and Edwardian pottery and porcelain.

Paul Wheeler
Glass, porcelain and pottery.

Chris Wilde
Furniture, paintings & prints.

Willow & Urn
American jewellery.

Gwen Wood
Belleek.

Jack Yarwood
18th-19th C wood, metalware and objets d'art.

York Decorative Antiques
Boxes, caddies and Oriental decoratives.

J. Smith
47 The Shambles. YO1 7LX.
EST. 1963. BNTA. Open 9.30-4. CL: Mon. STOCK: *Numismatic items, mainly English coins.* LOC: City centre. SIZE: Small. VAT: Stan/Spec.
TEL: 01904 654769; FAX: 01904 677988

Ken Spelman
70 Micklegate. YO1 6LF. (Peter Miller and Tony Fothergill)

EST. 1948. ABA. PBFA. Open 9-5.30. STOCK: *Secondhand and antiquarian books especially fine arts and literature, 50p-£20,000.* LOC: City centre. SER: Valuations; buys at auction (books); catalogues issued. SIZE: Large. PARK: Easy. VAT: Spec. FAIRS: Bath, Oxford, York, Harrogate, Cambridge, Edinburgh and London PBFA and ABA.
TEL: 01904 624414; FAX: 01904 626276
E-MAIL: ask@kenspelman.com
WEBSITE: www.kenspelman.com

St. John Antiques
26 Lord Mayor's Walk. YO31 7HA. (R. and N. Bell)
EST. 1985. Open Sat. 10-5 or any time by appointment. STOCK: *Victorian stripped pine, curios, blue and white pottery.* LOC: Near Minster. SER: Stripping and finishing. SIZE: Small. PARK: At rear.
TEL: 01904 644263

York Antiques Centre
2a Lendal. YO1 8AA. (Sherman and Waterman Ltd.)
EST. 1984. Open 10-5. STOCK: *Antiques and collectable items, 18th-20th C.* LOC: Opposite the museum gardens. SIZE: 25 dealers. PARK: Easy.
TEL: 01904 641445

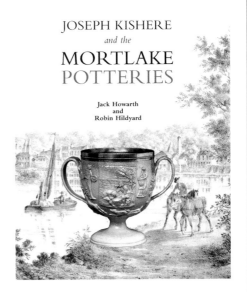

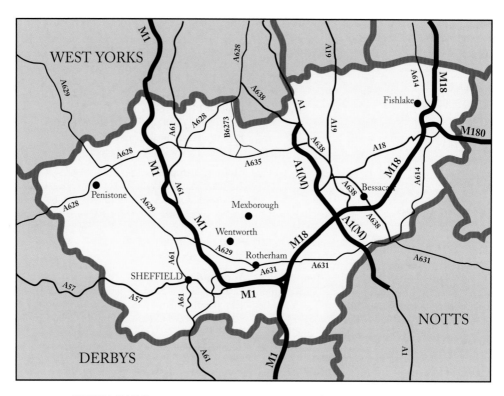

BESSACARR

Keith Stones Grandfather Clocks
5 Ellers Drive. DN4 7DL.
EST. 1988. Open by appointment. STOCK: *Grandfather clocks, especially painted dials, 30 hour and 8 day movements, Georgian to early 19th C, £1,250-£3,750.* LOC: Take A638 Bawtry road off racecourse roundabout, through traffic lights after 3/4 mile, take second right into Ellers Rd. then second left. SER: Valuations. SIZE: Small. PARK: Easy.
TEL: 01302 535258; HOME: same
E-MAIL: clocks@kstones.fsnet.co.uk
WEBSITE: www.kstones.fsnet.co.uk

FISHLAKE

Fishlake Antiques
Pinfold Lane. DN7 5LA.
EST. 1972. Resident. Open Sun. 1-5 and by appointment. STOCK: *Rural furniture especially stripped pine; clocks including longcase and wall clocks, garden and small architectural items, Victorian to mid-19th C, £30-£2,000; smalls, £3-£70.* LOC: Off A63. SIZE: Medium. PARK: Own.
TEL: 01302 841411

PENISTONE

Penistone Pine and Antiques
Units 2 and 3 Penistone Court, Sheffield Rd. S36 6HP. (Peter Lucas)
EST. 1984. Open 9-5. STOCK: *Stripped and finished pine,*

1800-1920. SER: Restorations. SIZE: Large. PARK: Easy. VAT: Stan.
TEL: 01226 370018; HOME: 01226 791330; Mobile: 07891 193828
E-MAIL: pandb@webmap.co.uk

ROTHERHAM

Foster's Antique Centre
Foster's Garden Centre, Doncaster Rd., Thrybergh. S65 4BE. (The Foster Family)
EST. 1996. Open 10-4.30, Sun. 11-5. STOCK: *Wide range of general antiques and collectables including furniture, jewellery, Rockingham china.* LOC: A630 between Rotherham and Doncaster. SIZE: 20 dealers. PARK: Own large.
TEL: 01709 850337; FAX: 01709 850402

Philip Turnor Antiques
94a Broad St., Parkgate. S62 6EG.
EST. 1980. Open 9-5, Sat. 10-4. STOCK: *Shipping furniture including oak, 1880-1940.* LOC: Main road. SER: Export (Japan and USA). SIZE: Medium. PARK: Easy. FAIRS: Swinderby.
TEL: 01709 524640
E-MAIL: philip.turnor@btinternet.com

SHEFFIELD

Acorn Antiques
298-300 Abbeydale Rd. S7 1FL. (R.C. and B.C. Priest)

EST. 1984. Open 10-5. STOCK: *Furniture, 19th-20th C,*
£20-£500; bronzes, sculptural and unusual items. LOC:
A625 to Bakewell. SIZE: Medium. PARK: Easy.
TEL: 0114 255 5348; HOME: same
E-MAIL: info@acornantique.co.uk

Barmouth Court Antiques Centre   LAPADA
Unit 2 Barmouth Rd., Off Abbeydale Rd. S7 2DH.
(NP & A Salt)
Open 10-5, Sun. 11-4. STOCK: **General antiques and**
collectables. LOC: **South of the city.** SER: **Valuations;**
packing and shipping; courier. SIZE: **50 dealers on 2**
floors. PARK: **Ample.**
TEL: 0114 255 2711; FAX: same
E-MAIL: chris@barmouth.fsnet.co.uk

Chapel Antiques Centre
99 Broadfield Rd. S8 0XH. (Mr D. Green and Mrs S.
Sleath)
Open 10-5, Sun. and Bank Holidays 11-5. STOCK:
Furniture, textiles and accessories. LOC: From city centre, 1
mile along A61 Chesterfield Rd., turn right. SER:
Upholstery and furniture stripping; paint effects; interior
design. SIZE: 20+ dealers. PARK: Easy.
TEL: 0114 258 8288; FAX: same
WEBSITE: www.antiquesinsheffield.com

Dovetail Antiques
336 Abbeydale Rd. S7 1FN. (D.W. Beedle)
EST. 1980. Open 9.30-4.30. STOCK: *Georgian, Victorian*
and Edwardian mahogany, walnut, oak and pine furniture.
SER: Restorations. SIZE: Medium. PARK: Easy.
TEL: 0114 2551554; Mobile: 07801 278257;
E-MAIL: dovetailantiques@tiscali.co.uk

Dronfield Antiques
375-377 Abbeydale Rd. S7 1FS. (H.J. Greaves)
EST. 1968. Open 11-6 or by appointment anytime. CL:
Mon. and Tues. STOCK: *Trade and shipping goods,*
Victoriana, glass, china. LOC: A621, 1 mile south of city
centre. SER: Container packing facilities. SIZE: Large.
PARK: Easy. VAT: Stan.
TEL: 0114 2550172/2581821; HOME and FAX: 0114
2556024

Kelly Lighting
679 Ecclesall Rd. S11 8TG. (Frank R. Kelly)
EST. 1982. Open Fri. 9-5, Sat. 10.30-5, other days by
appointment. STOCK: *Lighting - ceiling, wall, table and*
floor, Edwardian and Victorian, £160-£10,000. LOC: Half
mile from Sheffield Parkway End. SER: Restorations
(polishing, lacquering, re-wiring). SIZE: 2 showrooms.
PARK: Easy.
TEL: 0114 267 8500; FAX: 0114 268 3242
E-MAIL: sales@kellyantiquelighting.co.uk
WEBSITE: www.kellyantiquelighting.co.uk

Langtons Antiques & Collectables
443 London Rd./Courtyard, 100 Guernsey Rd., Heeley

Bottom. S2 4HJ. (Langton Family)
EST. 1999. Open 10-5, Sun. 10.30-4.30. STOCK:
Furniture, clothing 1940s-1970s, 1950s fun house,
porcelain, jewellery, clocks, military, Art Deco, from 1850,
£5-£3,000. LOC: M1, exit 33, A61 to city centre. SER:
Delivery. SIZE: Large, 70+ dealers. PARK: Easy. VAT:
Stan. FAIRS: Newark.
TEL: 0114 258 1791
E-MAIL: jill.mitchell@langtons-antiques.co.uk
WEBSITE: www.langtons-antiques.co.uk

The Oriental Rug Shop
763 Abbeydale Rd. S7 2BG. (Kian A. Hezaveh)
EST. 1880. Open 10-5. STOCK: *Handmade rugs and carpets*
especially large carpets. LOC: A621. SER: Restorations.
SIZE: Large.
TEL: 0114 2552240; FAX: 0114 2509088
E-MAIL: sales@orientalrugshop.co.uk
WEBSITE: www.orientalrugshop.co.uk

Paraphernalia
66/68 Abbeydale Rd. S7 1FD. (W.K. Keller)
EST. 1972. Open 9.30-5. STOCK: *General antiques,*
stripped pine, lighting, brass and iron beds. LOC: Main
road. PARK: Easy.
TEL: 0114 2550203

Tilley's Vintage Magazine Shop
281 Shoreham St. S1 4SS. (A.G.J. and A.A.J.C. Tilley)
EST. 1978. Open 9.30-4.30, other times by appointment.
CL: Mon. STOCK: *Magazines, comics, newspapers, books,*
postcards, programmes, posters, cigarette cards, prints,
ephemera. LOC: Opposite Sheffield United F.C. SER:
Mail order; valuations. SIZE: Large. PARK: Easy.
TEL: 0114 2752442; FAX: same
E-MAIL: tilleys281@aol.com
WEBSITE: www.tilleysmagazines.com

Paul Ward Antiques
Owl House, 8 Burnell Rd., Owlerton. S6 2AX.
EST. 1976. Resident. Open by appointment. STOCK:
Matched sets of Victorian dining and kitchen chairs, country
chairs, general antiques. LOC: 2 miles north of city on
A61. SER:
SIZE: Large. PARK: Easy. VAT: Stan/Global.
TEL: 0114 2335980

WENTWORTH

Wentworth Arts, Crafts and Antiques Ltd
The Old Builders Yard, Cortworth Lane. S62 7SB.
(Mrs Jan Sweeting)
EST. 1999. Open 10-5 including Sun. STOCK: *Furniture,*
to £2,500; Royal Doulton, Crown Devon and collectables.
LOC: 5 mins. from junctions 35 and 36, M1. SIZE: Large
- 50 dealers. PARK: Easy.
TEL: 01226 744333
WEBSITE: www.wentworthartscraftsandantiques.co.uk

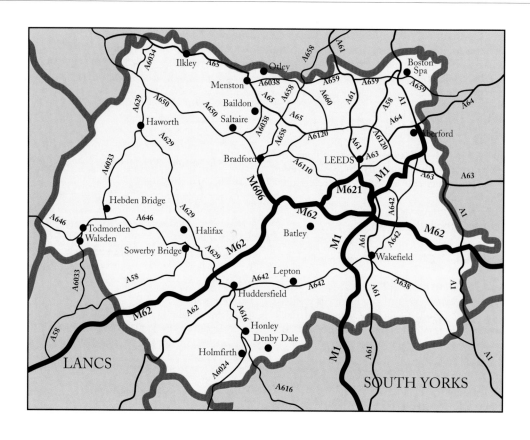

ABERFORD

Aberford Interiors
Hicklam House. LS25 3DP. (J.W.H. Long and C.A. Robinson)
EST. 1973. Open 9.30-5.30, Sun. 10.30-4.30. CL: Mon. STOCK: *French oak furniture; French painted furniture, occasional English mahogany and accessories.* LOC: Large detached property at south end of village opposite Alms Houses. SIZE: Large. PARK: Easy. VAT: Stan/Spec.
TEL: 0113 281 3209; FAX: 0113 281 3121
E-MAIL: enquiries@aberfordinteriors.co.uk
WEBSITE: www.aberfordinteriors.co.uk

BATLEY

Muir Hewitt Art Deco Originals
Redbrick Mill, 218 Bradford Rd. WF17 6JF.
EST. 1982. Open 9.30-5.30, Thurs. 9.30-8, Sat. 9-6, Sun. 10.30-5; STOCK: *20th C ceramics including Clarice Cliff, Susie Cooper, Charlotte Rhead, Shelley; furniture, metalware, lighting and mirrors; Art Deco furniture.* LOC: Town centre. SER: Valuations. PARK: Ample. VAT: Spec. FAIRS: Ann Zierold Art Deco at Leeds and Chester.
TEL: 01924 458800
E-MAIL: muirhewitt@hotmail.com
WEBSITE: www.muirhewitt.com

Tansu Oriental Antiques
Redbrick Mill, 218 Bradford Rd, Batley Carr. WF17 6JF. (Stephen P. and C.J. Battye)
EST. 1993. Open 9.30-5.30, Sat. 9-6, Sun. 11-5. STOCK: *Japanese and Chinese furniture, chests including staircase and shop display, wheeled trunks, calligraphy boxes, granite lanterns, 1850-1900, £100-£20,000; kimono, 1930-1960, £20-£200.* LOC: Close to M1 and M62. SER: Valuations; restorations (Japanese antique furniture). SIZE: Medium. PARK: Own large. VAT: Stan.
TEL: 01924 460044/459441; FAX: 01924 462844

BOSTON SPA

London House Oriental Rugs and Carpets
London House, High St. LS23 6AD. (M.J.S. Roe)
EST. 1978. Open 10-5. STOCK: *Caucasian, Turkish, Afghan and Persian rugs, runners and carpets, £50-£10,000; kelims and textiles.* LOC: Off A1, south of Wetherby. SER: Restorations (Oriental carpets and rugs); SIZE: Large. PARK: Easy. VAT: Stan.
TEL: 01937 845123; HOME: same
E-MAIL: sales@londonhouserugs.co.uk
WEBSITE: www.londonhouserugs.co.uk

BRADFORD

The Corner Shop
89 Oak Lane. BD9 4QU. (Miss Badland)
EST. 1961. Open Tues. and Thurs. 2-5.30, Sat. 11-5.30.
STOCK: *Pottery, small furniture, clocks and general items.*

Heaton Antiques
1 Hammond Place, Emm Lane, Heaton. BD9 4AL. (T.
Steward)
EST. 1991. Open 10-4. CL: Mon. & Sat. STOCK: *Silver
plate and bric-a-brac, pre 1930.* LOC: Near A650. SER:
Valuations. SIZE: Small. PARK: Easy. FAIRS: Harrogate.
TEL: 01274 480630

CULLINGWORTH

Bingley Antiques Ltd.
Cullingworth Mill, Greenside Rd. BD13 5AB. (J.B.
and J. Poole)
EST. 1965. Open Tues.-Sat. 8.45-5, or by appointment.
STOCK: *Furniture, 18th-19th C; shipping goods, porcelain,
architectural antiques, stained glass and doors.* SER: Container
packing. SIZE: Large. PARK: Easy. VAT: Stan/Spec.
TEL: 01535 270660; FAX: 01535 270500
E-MAIL: john@bingleyantiques.com
WEBSITE: www.bingleyantiques.com

HALIFAX

Collectors' Old Toy Shop and Antiques
89 Northgate. HX1 1XF. (S. Haley)
EST. 1983. Open 10.30-4.30. CL: Mon. & Thurs.
STOCK: *Collectors' toys, clocks and antiques.* SER: Valuations;
TV hire. SIZE: 2 floors. PARK: Nearby. FAIRS: Newark.
TEL: 01422 360434/822148
E-MAIL: collectorsoldtoy@aol.com
WEBSITE: www.collectorsoldtoyshop.com

Andy Thornton Architectural Antiques Ltd
Victoria Mills, Stainland Rd., Greetland. HX4 8AD.
EST. 1975. SALVO. Open 9-5. STOCK: *Architectural
antiques - doors, stained glass, fireplaces, panelling, garden
statuary, furniture, light fittings, décor items, church interiors
including pews.* LOC: Off junction 24, M62. SER:
Delivery; worldwide shipping. SIZE: Large. PARK: Easy
and free. VAT: Stan.
TEL: 01422 377314; FAX: 01422 310372
E-MAIL: antiques@andythornton.com
WEBSITE: www.andythornton.com

HAWORTH

Clock House Antiques
2 Janet St. BD22 9ET. (P.A. Langham)
Open Tues., Wed. and Thurs. 1-4, Sat. 11-4. STOCK:
Clocks, porcelain and small furniture. SER: Valuations;
repairs (clocks). SIZE: Medium. PARK: Easy.
TEL: 01535 648777; MOBILE: 07956 137298

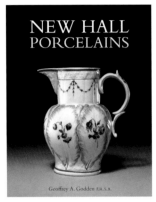

In this fascinating volume, china-ware expert Geoffrey
Godden shows how collectable and decorative New Hall
Porcelain is. The factory produced over three thousand
patterns, which served to enhance a long series of attractive
yet very functional forms, and were welcomed for their
excellence over a period of over fifty years, from 1782 to
1835. The New Hall firm in England were market-leaders
in their own time, their shapes and styles widely copied by
their several imitators. *New Hall Porcelains* presents
historical facts in a novel, helpful manner, with a broad
selection of clear illustrations.

280 x 220 mm. 480 pp 83 col., 511 b.&w.
£65.00 Hardback

HEBDEN BRIDGE

Cornucopia Antiques
9 West End. HX7 8JP. (Noel Strophair)
EST. 2004. Open Fri.-Sun. 12-5. STOCK: *Furniture inc.
French, Art Deco, lighting, mirrors, stoves, bric-a-brac,
garden furniture and accessories.* LOC: Town centre. SIZE:
Small. PARK: Easy.
TEL: 01422 845844

HOLMFIRTH

Chapel House Fireplaces
Netherfield House, St. Georges Rd., Scholes. HD9 1UH.
(J. and M. Forster)
EST. 1979. Open strictly by appointment, Mon.-Fri. 9-5,
Sat. 10-4. STOCK: *Georgian, Victorian and Edwardian
grates and mantels; French chimneypieces.* SER:
Restorations. SIZE: Large. PARK: Own.
TEL: 01484 682275
E-MAIL: info@chapelhousefireplaces.co.uk
WEBSITE: www.chapelhousefireplaces.co.uk

The Toll House Bookshop
32/34 Huddersfield Rd. HD9 2JS. (Elaine V. Beardsell)
EST. 1977. PBFA. ABA. Open 9-5. STOCK: *Books
including antiquarian.* LOC: Town centre. SER:
Valuations; commission bidding. SIZE: Large. PARK:

Nearby. FAIRS: Major PBFA.
TEL: 01484 686541/688406
E-MAIL: tollhouse.bookshop@virgin.net
WEBSITE: www.toll-house.co.uk

HONLEY

A. and Y.M. Frost Antique Clocks
Honey Head Farm, Meltham Rd. HD9 6RG. (Alan
and Yvonne Frost)
EST. 1979. Open by appointment only. STOCK: 17th-18th
C bracket, wall and longcase clocks, £5,000-£100,000. LOC:
Edge of village. SIZE: Small. PARK: Easy.
TEL: 01484 66131
WEBSITE: www.aymfrostantiqueclocks.com

ILKLEY

Coopers of Ilkley   LAPADA
46-50 Leeds Rd. LS29 8EQ. (Charles and Jane
Cooper)
EST. 1910. Open 9-1 and 2-5.30. STOCK: English and
Continental furniture, pre-1900, £100-£10,000; porcelain
and metalware. LOC: A65. SER: Valuations; furniture
restorations and repairs, upholstery and polishing.
SIZE: Large. PARK: Own. VAT: Stan/Spec.
TEL: 01943 608020; FAX: 01943 604321
E-MAIL: enquiries@coopersantiquesilkley.co.uk
WEBSITE: www.cooperantiquesilkley.co.uk

Jack Shaw and Co   LAPADA
The Old Grammar School, Skipton Rd. LS29 9EJ.
EST. 1945. Open Thurs., Fri. and Sat. 9.30-12.45 and
2-5.30. STOCK: Silver especially cutlery and 18th C
domestic. LOC: A65 towards Skipton. SIZE: Small. VAT:
Spec. FAIRS: NEC; many northern fairs.
TEL: 01943 609467; MOBILE: 07711 679836

LEEDS

Aladdin's Cave
19 Queens Arcade. LS1 6LF. (R. Spencer)
EST. 1954. STOCK: Jewellery, £15-£5,000; collectors' items.
LOC: Town centre. SER: Valuations; repairs. SIZE: Small.
PARK: 100 yards. VAT: Stan.
TEL: 0113 245 7903
E-MAIL: robertajspencer@hotmail.com

Geary Antiques
(J.A. Geary)
EST. 1933. Open by appointment. STOCK: Furniture,
Georgian, Victorian and Edwardian; copper and brass. SER:
Restorations (furniture); interior design. VAT: Stan/Spec.
TEL: 0113 256 4122; FAX: 08700 511346
E-MAIL: jag@t-nlbi.demon.co.uk;
jag@gearyantiquefurniture.co.uk
WEBSITE: www.gearyantiquefurniture.co.uk

J. Howorth Antiques/Swiss Cottage Furniture
85 Westfield Crescent, Burley. LS3 1DJ.
EST. 1986. Open 10-5.30. CL: Tues. STOCK: Collectables,
furniture, architectural items, £5-£3,000. LOC: Town hall
to Burley Rd., road opposite YTV. SER: Prop hire for
film and TV. SIZE: Warehouse. PARK: Easy. VAT:
Stan/Spec. FAIRS: Newark.
TEL: 0113 242 9994; FAX: 0113 245 0639
E-MAIL: info@swisscottageantiques.com
WEBSITE: www.swisscottageantiques.com
www.filmtvprops.com

Pairs Antiques Ltd
(Iain Brunt)
EST. 1994. STOCK: 18th-19th C furniture, decorative objects
and paintings, £500-£20,000. SER: Restorations; buys at
auction.
TEL: 0845 2602260; MOBILE: 07798 684694

The Piano Shop
39 Holbeck Lane. LS11 9UL. (B. Seals)
Open 9-5. STOCK: Pianos, especially decorated cased grand.
LOC: 5 mins. from city centre. SER: Restorations; French
polishing; hire. SIZE: 2 floors. PARK: Own.
TEL: 0113 244 3685
E-MAIL: info@thepianoshop.co.uk
WEBSITE: www.thepianoshop.co.uk

Year Dot
41 The Headrow. LS1 6PU. (A. Glithro)
EST. 1977. Open 9.30-5. STOCK: Jewellery, watches, silver,
pottery, porcelain, glass, clocks, prints, paintings, bric-a-brac.
LOC: City centre.
TEL: 0113 246 0860

MENSTON

Antiques
101 Bradford Rd. LS29 6BU. (W. and J. Hanlon)
EST. 1974. Open Thurs.-Sat. 2.30-5. STOCK:
Handworked linen, textiles, pottery, porcelain, Art Nouveau,
Art Deco, silver, plate, jewellery, small furniture, collectors
items. LOC: A65 near Harry Ramsden. SIZE: Small.
PARK: Forecourt. FAIRS: Newark.
TEL: 01943 877634; HOME: 01943 463693

Park Antiques
2 North View, Main St. LS29 6JU. (Brian O'Connell)
EST. 1975. Resident. Open 10-5. CL: Mon. STOCK:
Furniture, Georgian to Edwardian, £200-£20,000;
decorative items, £50-£1,000; porcelain and ceramics, £10-
£2,000; paintings, £100-£5,000. NOT STOCKED: Pine,
silver. LOC: Opposite the park. SER: Furniture repairs,
restorations and French polishing; porcelain restoration.
SIZE: Medium. PARK: Easy.
TEL: 01943 872392; MOBILE: 07887 812858
E-MAIL: brian@parkantiques.com
WEBSITE: www.parkantiques.com;
www.beacon-antiques.co.uk

SALTAIRE

Carlton Antiques Ltd.
Salts Mill, Victoria Rd. BD18 3LA. (Malcolm Gray)
EST. 1989. Open 10.30-5.30. CL: Mon. & Tues. *STOCK:*
Georgian, Victorian, Edwardian and Art Deco furniture;
fine oil paintings and watercolours up to 1940; objets d'art,
jewellery and collectables. LOC: In World Heritage village.
SER: Repair and restoration (furniture and oil paintings).
SIZE: Large. PARK: Easy.
TEL: 01274 592103
E-MAIL: graymalcolm@aol.com
WEBSITE: www.carlton-art-antiques.co.uk

SOWERBY BRIDGE

Memory Lane
69 Wakefield Rd. HX6 2UX. (L. Robinson)
EST. 1978. Open 10.30-5, Sun. 12-4. *STOCK: Pine, oak,*
books and collectables. SER: Renovation of country furniture.
SIZE: Warehouse + showroom. PARK: Easy. FAIRS: Local.
TEL: 01422 833223; FAX: 01422 835230
WEBSITE: www.memorylaneantiques.co.uk and
www.memorylanebears.co.uk

Talking Point Antiques
66 West St. HX6 3AP. (Paul Austwick)
EST. 1986. Usually open Thurs., Fri., Sat. 10.30-5.30, prior
telephone call advisable. *STOCK: Restored gramophones and*
phonographs, 78rpm records, gramophone accessories and
related items. LOC: From Haliax, on A58 through village,
last row of shops. SER: Restorations (gramophones). PARK:
Nearby. FAIRS: NVCF, Warks. Int. Showground; Elsecar
Heritage Centre; Reebok Stadium.
TEL: 01422 834126

E-MAIL: tpagrams@aol.com
WEBSITE: www.talkingpointgramophones.co.uk

TODMORDEN

Echoes
650a Halifax Rd., Eastwood. OL14 6DW. (P. Oldman)
EST. 1980. CL: Mon. and Tues. *STOCK: Costume,*
textiles, linen and lace, £5-£500; jewellery, £5-£150; all
19th-20th C. LOC: A646. SER: Valuations; restorations
(costume); buys at auction (as stock). SIZE: Medium.
PARK: Easy.
TEL: 01706 817505; HOME: same

WAKEFIELD

Robin Taylor Fine Arts
36 Carter St. WF1 1XJ. (Robin and Julie Taylor)
EST. 1981. Open 9.30-5.30. *STOCK: Oils and watercolours.*
LOC: Off Westgate.
TEL: 01924 381809
WEBSITE: www.picrestoration.co.uk

WALSDEN

Cottage Antiques
788 Rochdale Rd. OL14 7UA. (Angelika and Neil
Strophair)
EST. 1978. Resident. Open Thurs.-Sun. 11-5.30. CL:
Mon.-Wed. *STOCK: Pine, country and decorative painted*
furniture, kitchenalia; collectables, garden items and accessories.
LOC: A6033 Todmorden to Littleborough road. SER:
Restorations; stripping (pine); import/export of European
pine and collectables. SIZE: Medium. PARK: Easy.
TEL: 01706 813612

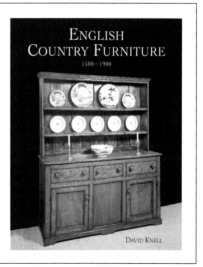

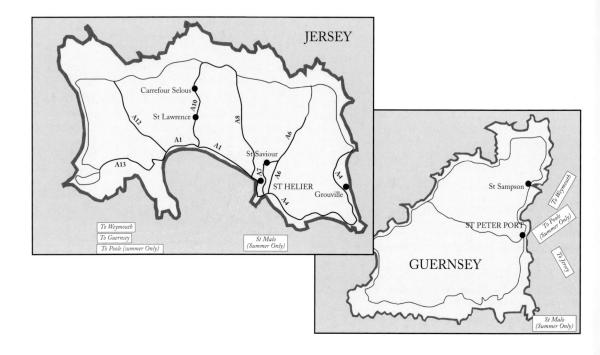

ALDERNEY

ST. ANNE'S

Beverley J. Pyke - Fine British Watercolours
22 Victoria St. GY9 3TA.
EST. 1988. Open by appointment. STOCK: *20th C watercolours, £150-£2,000.*
TEL: 01481 824092

GUERNSEY

ST. PETER PORT

Stephen Andrews Gallery
5 College Terrace, Grange. GY1 2PX. (J. Geddes and S. Wilkowski)
EST. 1984. Open 9.30-5. STOCK: *Furniture, pottery and porcelain, paintings, 19th-20th C.* LOC: Main road. SER: Buys at auction. SIZE: Medium. PARK: Adjacent. FAIRS: Local.
TEL: 01481 710380

The Collectors' Centre
1 Sausmarez St. GY1 2PT. (Andrew Rundle)
EST. 1984. Open 11-6. STOCK: *Prints, engravings, maps, coins, banknotes, stamps, postcards, books and ephemera.* SER: Valuations. SIZE: Small. PARK: Opposite.
TEL: 01481 725209

W. De la Rue Antiques
29 Mill St. GY1 1HG.
EST. 1972. Open 10-12.30 and 2-4. CL: Thurs. pm.

STOCK: *General antiques and collectors' items.* SIZE: Small. PARK: Nearby.
TEL: 01481 723177

N. St. J. Paint & Sons Ltd
26-29 The Pollet. GY1 1WQ. (Michael St John Paint)
EST. 1947. NAG. Open 9-5. STOCK: *Jewellery, silver and objets d'art, 18th-20th C, £10-£75,000.* LOC: Town centre. SER: Valuations; restorations (silver and jewellery). SIZE: Large.
TEL: 01481 721096; FAX: 01481 710241
E-MAIL: paint@guernsey.net

ST. SAMPSON

The Curiosity Shop
Commercial Rd. GY2 4QP. (Mike Vermeulen and Diana Walker)
EST. 1978. Open 10-2. CL: Thurs. STOCK: *Books, prints, postcards, ephemera, paintings, small furniture, china, glass, silver, jewellery, brass, £1-£5,000.* SER: Picture framing.
FAIRS: Organiser.
TEL: 01481 245324

Ray & Scott Ltd
The Bridge. GY2 4QN. (M. J. Search)
EST. 1962. NAG. Open 9-5.15, Sat. 9-5. STOCK: *Jewellery and watches, 19th C, £500-£20,000.* SER: Valuations; restorations (jewellery and engraving). SIZE: Medium. PARK: Easy.
TEL: 01481 244610; FAX: 01481 247843

VALE

The Pine Collection
Unit 6, La Hure Mare Industrial Estate. GY3 5UB. (P. Head)
EST. 1986. Open 10-5, Sat. 10-2. STOCK: Antique and comtemporary pine furniture. SER: Restoration, free local delivery. SIZE: Large. PARK: Easy.
TEL: 01481 240708
E-MAIL: pjh@phrooms.com

JERSEY

CARREFOUR SELOUS, ST. LAWRENCE

David Hick Interiors
Alexandra House. JE3 1GL.
(David and Rosemary Hick)
EST. 1977. Open 9.30-5, Thurs. 9.30-6.30. CL: Mon.
STOCK: Furniture and objets d'art. SER: Shipping (UK and overseas). SIZE: Large and warehouse. PARK: Own.
TEL: 01534 865965; FAX: 01534 865448
E-MAIL: info@davidhickinteriors.com
WEBSITE: www.davidhickinteriors.com

GROUVILLE

Atelier Ltd   BADA LAPADA
Le Bourg Farm, Le Grand Bourg. JE3 9UY. (Jonathan Voak)
EST. 1997. CINOA. Open by appointment only.
STOCK: 17th to early 20th C oil paintings, watercolours and drawings especially early marine paintings and views of the Channel Islands and London - the Thames in particular, £200-£25,000+. LOC: Half mile from Grouville church. SER: Valuations; period frames; conservation of oil paintings, watercolours, prints and drawings. SIZE: Small. PARK: Easy. FAIRS: BADA; LAPADA; annual exhibitions.
TEL: 01534 855728; FAX: 01534 852099; MOBILE: 07797 729231
E-MAIL: art@atelierlimited.com
WEBSITE: www.atelierlimited.com

ST. HELIER

John Blench & Son (Selective Eye Gallery)
50 Don St. JE2 4TR. (W. and J. Blench)
EST. 1972. Open 9.30-5, Thurs. and Sat. 9.30-12.30.
STOCK: Oil paintings, 19th-20th C; maps, prints and antiquarian books, 16th-20th C. LOC: Town centre. SER: Valuations; restorations. SIZE: Medium. PARK: Nearby.
TEL: 01534 725281; FAX: 01534 758789
E-MAIL: segart@jerseymail.co.uk

John Cooper Antiques
16 The Market. JE2 4WL. (John M. Cooper and Antonio de Lemos)
STOCK: General antiques.
TEL: 01534 723600

Falle Fine Art Limited   LAPADA
18 Hill St. JE2 4UA. (John Falle)
EST. 1993. Open 10-5. CL: Mon. STOCK: 20th C paintings, watercolours and bronzes. SER: Valuations; restorations; exhibitions. SIZE: Large.
TEL: 01534 887877; FAX: 01534 723459
WEBSITE: www.fallefineart.com

David Hick Antiques
45 Halkett Place. JE2 4WQ.
(David and Rosemary Hick)
Open 9.30-5. STOCK: Furniture and smalls.
TEL: 01534 721162; FAX: same
E-MAIL: info@davidhickinteriors.com
WEBSITE: www.davidhickinteriors.com

A. & R. Ritchie
7 Duhamel Place. JE2 4TP.
EST. 1973. Open 9.30-4.30. STOCK: Silver, militaria, jewellery, small items. LOC: Behind central library. SIZE: Medium. PARK: Opposite.
TEL: 01534 873805

Robert's Antiques
14 York St. JE2 3RQ. (Robert Michieli)
EST. 1975. Open 9.30-4.45. STOCK: English silver, ceramics, clocks, glass, jewellery, 19th C, £50-£10,000. LOC: Opposite town hall. SER: Valuations; buys at auction (as stock). SIZE: Medium. PARK: Easy.
TEL: 01534 509071; HOME: 01534 865005; MOBILE: 07798 876553
E-MAIL: count.roberto@jerseymail.co.uk

Thesaurus (Jersey) Ltd.
8 Burrard St. JE2 4TT. (I. Creaton)
EST. 1973. Open 9-5.30. STOCK: Antiquarian and out of print books, £1-£2,000. LOC: Town centre. SER: Buys at auction. SIZE: Small. PARK: 100yds. VAT: Spec.
TEL: 01534 737045

Thomson's
60 Kensington Place and 10 Waterloo St. JE2 3PA.
(R.N. Thomson)
EST. 1967. Open 10-5. STOCK: General antiques and collectors' items, mainly furniture. LOC: 60 Kensington Place at the side of Grand Hotel. SER: Valuations. SIZE: Large. PARK: Easy.
TEL: 01534 723673; MOBILE: 07797 826414

ST. SAVIOUR

Grange Gallery - Fine Arts Ltd.
10 Victoria Rd. JE2 7QG. (G.J. Morris)
EST. 1973. Open 9-5.30. STOCK: 19th-20th C oil paintings and watercolours, local items, £10-£10,000. LOC: 1 mile east of St Helier. SER: Valuations; restorations (paintings); framing. SIZE: Medium. PARK: Forecourt.
TEL: 01534 720077
E-MAIL: cassy@localdial.com

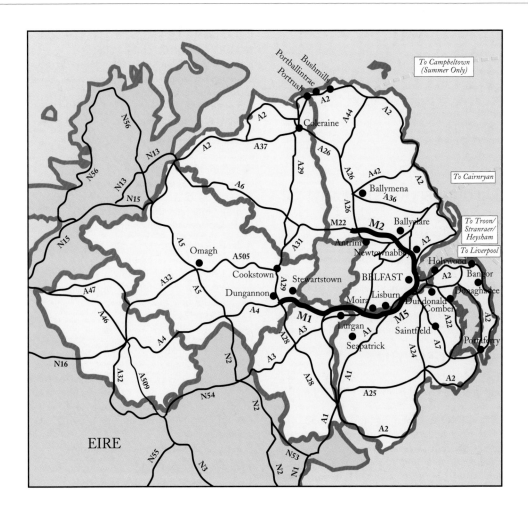

CO. ANTRIM

ANTRIM

David Wolfenden Antiques   LAPADA
219b Lisnevenagh Rd. BT41 2JT.
EST. 1984. IADA. Open 10-6 or by appointment.
STOCK: 18th-19th C furniture, £200-£10,000; porcelain,
£100-£3,000. LOC: A26 main Antrim-Ballymena line.
SER: Valuations; restorations. SIZE: Large. PARK: Easy.
VAT: Spec. FAIRS: Dublin.
TEL: 028 9442 9498
E-MAIL: antiquewolfirl@aol.com
WEBSITE: www.davidwolfendenantiques.com

BALLYMENA

Once upon a Time Antiques
The Old Mill, 2 Parkfield Rd., Ahoghill. BT42 2QS.
(Ronan McLaughlin)
EST. 1971. Open 10-5. *STOCK: Furniture, porcelain, art,*
silver and jewellery, 18th-20th C; Art Nouveau, Art Deco;
garden furniture and lighting. LOC: Edge of village. SER:
Valuations; restorations (jewellery, furniture, brass and
copper, pictures and frames). SIZE: Large. PARK: Free.
FAIRS: Tullyglass Hotel, Ballymena; Kings Hall, Belfast;
RDS, Dublin.
TEL: 028 2587 1244; FAX: 028 2587 9295; MOBILE:
07703 360447
E-MAIL: ronanarsk@aol.com
WEBSITE: onceuponatimeantiquesireland.com

BELFAST

Archives Antiques
88 Donegal Pass. BT7 1BX. (L. Johnston)
EST. 1992. Open 10.30-5.30 or by appointment. *STOCK:*
Irish silver, light fittings, porcelain, glass, coins and medals,
collectables, bottles, advertising signs, pharmacy. LOC: Close
to city centre. SER: Valuations; restorations (copper and
brass polishing and repairs, re-wiring). SIZE: Medium.
PARK: Easy. FAIRS: Kings Hall, Belfast.
TEL: 028 9023 2383; MOBILE: 07889 104719
E-MAIL: brightcut@hotmail.com

John Carroll Antiques   LAPADA
82 Donegal Pass. BT7 1BX.
Open 10.30-5. CL: Sat. *STOCK: 18th C furniture;*
mirrors.
TEL: 02890 238246; FAX: same; MOBILE: 07802 345529
E-MAIL: johncarrolluk2003@yahoo.co.uk

T.H. Kearney & Sons
Treasure House, 123 University St. BT7 1HP.
Resident. Open by appointment. *STOCK: Small antiques.*
SER: Restorations and upholstery. VAT: Stan.
TEL: 028 9023 1055

BUSHMILLS

Dunluce Antiques
33 Ballytober Rd. BT57 8UU. (Mrs C. Ross)
EST. 1978. Open 10-6 or by appointment. CL: Fri. and
Sat. morning. *STOCK: Furniture, £100-£5,000; porcelain*
and glass, £10-£2,000; silver, £10-£2,000; all Georgian to
1930s; paintings, mainly Irish, £100-£25,000. LOC: 1.5
miles off Antrim coast road, at Dunluce Castle. SER:
Restorations (porcelain). SIZE: Small. PARK: Easy.
TEL: 028 2073 1140
E-MAIL: dunluceantiques@btinternet.com
WEBSITE: www.dunlucegallery.com

LISBURN

Parvis Sigaroudinia
Mountainview House, 40 Sandy Lane, Ballyskeagh.
BT27 5TL.
EST. 1974. IADA. Open any time by appointment and 11-
8 during quarterly exhibitions. *STOCK: Oriental and*
European carpets and tapestries; cushions, lamps, furniture,
architectural items, William Yeoward crystal, bronze sculpture
by David Williams-Ellis and Anthony Scott, Irish art, hand-
crafted furniture by Richard Reade. LOC: Take Malone Road
from Belfast, then Upper Malone Road towards Lisburn,
cross Ballyskeagh bridge over M1, 1st left into Sandy
Lane. SER: Valuations; buys at auction; exhibitions held in
Belfast. PARK: Easy. VAT: Stan. FAIRS: IADA in RDS
Dublin and King's Hall, Belfast occasionally.
TEL: 02890 621824; HOME: same; FAX: 02890 623311;
MOBILE: 07801 347358
E-MAIL: parvissig@aol.com
WEBSITE: www.parvis.co.uk

NEWTOWNABBEY

MacHenry Antiques
Caragh Lodge, Glen Rd., Jordanstown. BT37 0RY.
(R. and A. MacHenry)
EST. 1964. IADA. Open Fri. and Sat. 12-6 or by
appointment. *STOCK: Georgian and Victorian furniture*
and objects. LOC: 6 miles from Belfast on M2/M5 to
Whiteabbey village, left at traffic lights at Woody's, then
left into Old Manse Rd. and continue straight into Glen
Rd. SER: Valuations. SIZE: Medium. PARK: Easy. VAT:
Stan/Spec. FAIRS: Dublin, Belfast and Irish.
TEL: 028 9086 2036; FAX: 028 9085 3281; MOBILE:
07831 135226
E-MAIL: rupert.machenry@ntlworld.com

PORTBALLINTRAE

Brian R. Bolt Antiques
88 Ballaghmore Rd. BT57 8RL. (Brian and Helen Bolt)
EST. 1977. Open 11-5.30 and by appointment. *STOCK:*
Silver - small and unusual items, objects of vertu, snuff boxes,
vesta cases, table, Scottish and Irish provincial; treen; English

and Continental glass, antique and 20th C; art and studio glass and ceramics; Arts and Crafts, Art Nouveau and Art Deco jewellery and metalwork; vintage fountain pens. LOC: 1 mile from Bushmills. SER: Search; illustrated catalogues available; worldwide postal service; valuations. SIZE: Small. PARK: Nearby. FAIRS: Local.
TEL: 028 2073 1129; FAX: same; MOBILE: 07712 579802
E-MAIL: brianbolt199@btinternet.com

PORTRUSH

Alexander Antiques
108 Dunluce Rd. BT56 8NB. (Mrs M. and D. Alexander)
EST. 1974. Open 10-5.30. CL: Sun. except by appointment. *STOCK: Furniture, silver, porcelain, fine art, 18th-20th C; oils and watercolours, 19th-20th C.* LOC: 1 mile from Portrush on A2 to Bushmills. SER: Valuations; buys at auction. SIZE: Large. PARK: Easy. VAT: Stan/Spec.
TEL: 028 7082 2783; FAX: 028 7082 2364

Kennedy Wolfenden
86 Main St. BT56 8BN. (Eleanor Wolfenden-Orr)
EST. 1977. Open 10-5.30 - later in summer. *STOCK: Furniture, porcelain, paintings, antique and modern jewellery.* SER: Valuations; restorations (silver and furniture including upholstery). SIZE: Medium.
TEL: 02870 825587 and 02870 822995; MOBILE: 07831 453038
E-MAIL: eleanor@kennedywolfenden.com
WEBSITE: www.kennedywolfenden.com

RANDALSTON

The Bell Gallery
8 Mount Shalghs Lane, BT41 3LE. (J.N. Bell)
EST. 1964. Open by appointment. *STOCK: British and Irish art, 19th-20th C.* LOC: End of the M2, turn right. SER: Valuations; buys at auction. PARK: Easy. VAT: Stan/Spec.
TEL: 028 9447 9179
E-MAIL: bellgallery@btinternet.com
WEBSITE: www.bellgallery.com

CO. ARMAGH

LURGAN

Charles Gardiner Antiques
48 High St. BT66 8AU.
EST. 1968. Open 9-1 and 2-6. CL: Wed. *STOCK: Clocks, furniture and general antiques.* PARK: Own.
TEL: 028 3832 3934

MOIRA

Fourwinds Antiques
96 Main St. BT67 0LH. (John and Tina Cairns)
EST. 1997. Open 10-5. *STOCK: Quality longcase and bracket clocks; Georgian to Edwardian furniture, porcelain*

ROBERT CHRISTIE ANTIQUES

Antique Furniture & Decorative Objects
Member of the Irish Antique Dealers Association

7 The Square, Hillsborough, Co. Down BT26 6AG
Tel: 028 9268 1066 Mobile: 07802 968 846

and paintings. LOC: Village centre. SER: Valuations. PARK: Beside premises. FAIRS: Bohill House Hotel, Coleraine; Kings Hall, Belfast.
TEL: 028 9261 2226; FAX: same; HOME: 028 3833 6352; MOBILE: 0776292369

CO. DOWN

COMBER

Jacquart Antiques
BT23 5SF. (Daniel Uprichard)
EST. 1992. Open by appointment. *STOCK: Town and country French antiques including fruitwood, walnut, oak and rosewood dining tables, chairs, beds, sideboards and occasional furniture; mirrors, chandeliers, kitchenalia and champagne memorabilia, mainly 1820-1939.* SER: Advice; interior designers and architects supplier; minor repairs. SIZE: Medium.
TEL: 02897 521109; MOBILE: 07831 548803
E-MAIL: jacquart@nireland.com

DONAGHADEE

Phyllis Arnold Gallery Antiques
4a Shore St. BT21 0DG.
EST. 1968. Open Wed.-Sat. 11-5. *STOCK: General antiques, jewellery, small furniture, Irish paintings and watercolours, portrait miniatures, maps and engravings of*

Ireland. LOC: On promenade. SER: Restorations (maps, prints, watercolours, portrait miniatures); conservation framing. PARK: Easy. FAIRS: Belfast International. TEL: 02891 888199; HOME: 02891 853322; FAX: same E-MAIL: phyllisarnold2@gmail.com WEBSITE: www.irishantiquesandart.com

DUNDONALD

Stacks Bookshop
67 Comber Rd. BT16 2AA. (Jim Tollerton)
EST. 1992. Open 10-6. STOCK: *Books - paperback fiction; military, religious, ancient and modern Irish, Arts & Crafts, travel, educational text.* LOC: Near Stormont. SER: Valuations. SIZE: Medium. PARK: Easy.
TEL: 028 9048 6880

GREYABBEY VILLAGE

Balloo Moon
Hoops Courtyard, BT22 2NE. (Marie Erwin)
EST. 2001. Open 10-5.30. STOCK: *Furniture, Victorian to 1970s; ceramics, collectables and costume jewellery.* LOC: Village centre. SIZE: Small. PARK: In village.
TEL: 028 4278 8898

HILLSBOROUGH

Robert Christie Antiques
7 The Square. BT26 6AG.
EST. 1976. IADA. Open 12-5. STOCK: *Furniture, 1750–1900, £500-£5,000; clocks, 1750-1900, £500-£4,000; decorative objects, 1800-1900, £50-£1,000.* LOC: Opposite Hillsborough Castle. SER: Valuations. SIZE: Medium. PARK: Easy. FAIRS: Kings Hall, Belfast; all RDS Dublin fairs.
TEL: 02892 681066; MOBILE: 07802 968846
E-MAIL: robertchristie@btconnect.com

SAINTFIELD

Agar Antiques
92 Main St. BT24 7AD. (Rosie Agar)
EST. 1990. Open 11-5. CL: Mon. STOCK: *Light fittings, Victorian and Edwardian, £15-£2,000; furniture, mainly Victorian, some Georgian and Edwardian, £30-£1,000; general small items, £1-£500; French beds and armoires, £100-£1,000.* SER: Valuations. SIZE: Medium. PARK: Nearby.
TEL: 028 9751 1214

Peter Francis Antiques
92 Main St. BT24 7AD.
EST. 1998. Open Tues.-Sat. 11-5. STOCK: *English, Irish and Oriental ceramics, 18th-20th C; English and Irish glass, mainly 18th-19th, some 20th C; smalls including ethnographic, Indian, European, bronzes, metalwork, treen and prints; all £5-£500.* SER: Valuations. SIZE: Medium. PARK: Nearby.
TEL: 028 9751 1214
E-MAIL: irishantiq@aol.com

Town & Country Antiques
92 Main St. BT24 7AB. (Patricia Keller)
EST. 1997. Open Wed.-Sat. 10.30-5. STOCK: *Prints, botanical, ornithological and sporting, £100-£400; 18th-19th C French tapestries, £600-£1,500; French chandeliers £300-£600; Venetian, French and Victorian mirrors, £400-£700; Georgian, Victorian and Edwardian small mahogany furniture, £500-£1,000; table lamps, rugs and equestrian items, desks.* SER: Restorations (furniture, prints and tapestries). SIZE: Medium. PARK: Easy. VAT: Stan.
TEL: 028 4461 4721; HOME: same; FAX: 028 4461 9716; MOBILE: 07710 840090
E-MAIL: l.w.k@btinternet.com

SEAPATRICK

Millcourt Antiques
99 Lurgan Rd. BT32 4NE. (Gillian Close)
EST. 1982. Open 11-5.30. CL: Thurs. STOCK: *Furniture, 18th-19th C, £30-£4,000; work and writing boxes, clocks; china, glass and collectables, to Art Deco, to £1,000; linen, quilts and textiles; jewellery, Victorian and 20th C, £20-£500.* SER: Valuations. SIZE: Small. PARK: Easy.
TEL: 028 4066 2909
E-MAIL: gillian@mill-court.demon.co.uk

CO. LONDONDERRY

COLERAINE

The Forge Antiques
24 Long Commons. BT52 1LH. (M.W. and R.G.C. Walker)
EST. 1977. Open 10-5.30. CL: Thurs. STOCK: *General antiques, silver, clocks, jewellery, porcelain, paintings.* SIZE: Medium. PARK: Easy. VAT: Stan.
TEL: 028 7035 1339

LONDONDERRY

Foyle Antiques and Whitehouse Furniture
16 Whitehouse Rd. BT48 0NE. (John Helferty)
EST. 1982. Open 9.30-5.30, Sun. 3-6. STOCK: *Victorian and Edwardian furniture, £200-£3,000; lamps, pictures, ornaments, prints, clocks and decorative items, £30-£300; reproduction furniture, four-poster beds, bedroom and dining suites, £1,000-£5,000.* LOC: Buncrana Rd., just out of Londonderry. SER: Restorations (furniture including upholstery). SIZE: Large. PARK: Own.
TEL: 02871 267626; FAX: same
E-MAIL: John@foyleantiques.com
WEBSITE: www.foyleantiques.com

Foyle Books
12 Magazine St. BT48 6HH. (A. Byrne and K. Thatcher)
EST. 1982. Open 11-5. STOCK: *Antiquarian books on Ireland, Derry, Donegal, theology, French and general.* LOC: Town

Godden's Guide to ENGLISH BLUE AND WHITE PORCELAIN
Geoffrey A Godden

This is the first major book on English blue and white porcelain since the early 1970s. It is a unique, comprehensive study. The number of instructive illustrations exceeds seven hundred, including helpful comparison photographs and details of identifying features - footrims, handle forms, manufacturing characteristics and marks. This unique coverage comprises details of over twenty distinct makes, including the relatively newly researched eighteenth century factories at Isleworth, Limehouse and Vauxhall. The inclusion of the several post-1790 factories covers new ground. The section on fakes and reproductions will also prove instructive and helpful. Guidance is given on the popularity of the various types in the market and on past and more recent prices paid for specimens in the London auction rooms. Particular attention has been directed at the three large sales of the late Dr. Bernard Watney's world renowned collection, held by Messrs. Phillips in 1999 and 2000. General estimates of market values are also offered.

279 x 216 mm. 592 pp 153 col., 711 b.&w. **£65.00 Hardback**

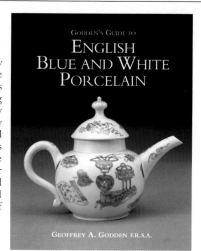

GODDEN'S GUIDE TO
ENGLISH
BLUE AND WHITE
PORCELAIN

GEOFFREY A. GODDEN F.R.S.A.

centre. SER: Valuations. SIZE: Medium. PARK: Quayside.
TEL: 028 7137 2530
E-MAIL: foylebookshopni@btconnect.com

CO. TYRONE

COOKSTOWN

Cookstown Antiques
16 Oldtown St. BT80 8EF. (G. Jebb)
EST. 1976. Open Thurs. and Fri. 2-5.30, Sat. 10.30-5.30.
STOCK: *Jewellery, silver, £10-£2,000; coins, £25-£200; pictures, ceramics and militaria, £5-£1,000; general antiques, all 19th-20th C.* LOC: Going north, through both sets of traffic lights, on left at rear of estate agency. SER: Valuations; buys at auction. SIZE: Small. PARK: Easy.
TEL: 028 8676 5279; FAX: 028 8676 2946;
HOME: 028 8676 2926

The Saddle Room Antiques
4 Coagh St. BT80 8NG. (C.J. Leitch)
EST. 1968. Open 10-5.30. CL: Mon. and Wed. STOCK: *China, silver, furniture, glass, jewellery.* SIZE: Medium.
TEL: 028 8676 4045

DUNGANNON

Moy Antiques
12 The Square, Moy. BT71 7SG. (Laurence MacNeice)
EST. 1970. Open 9.30-5.30 or by appointment. STOCK: *Georgian to pre-1940s furniture, paintings, clocks, mirrors, objets d'art and fireplaces; cast-iron, marble and bronze garden statuary; Irish pine furniture.* LOC: Village centre.
SER: Valuations; restorations. SIZE: Large. PARK: Easy.
FAIRS: IDA, Dublin.
TEL: 028 8778 4755; HOME: same; FAX: 028 8778 4895;
MOBILE: 07778 373509

E-MAIL: moyantiques@btconnect.com
WEBSITE: www.moyantiques.com

OMAGH

Kelly Antiques
Mullaghmore House, Old Mountfield Rd. BT79 7EX. (Louis Kelly)
EST. 1932. IPRCA. Board of Irish Conservators. Open 9-6. CL: Sat. STOCK: *Fireplaces, from early Adam inlaid to Edwardian slate, European chimney pieces, £80-£125,000; hardwood furniture including dining and bedroom, Georgian to early Victorian, £150-£40,000; early architectural salvage, £10-£10,000.* LOC: One mile from town centre.
SER: Valuations; restorations (Elizabethan to Edwardian furniture; fireplaces); short and full-time courses for conservation, heritage and restoration. SIZE: Large.
PARK: Easy.
TEL: 028 8224 2314; HOME: same; FAX: 028 8225 0262
E-MAIL: mullaghmorehouse@aol.com
WEBSITE: www.mullaghmorehouse.com

STEWARTSTOWN

RyanSmith Ltd. Antique Fireplaces
1 North St. BT71 5JE.
EST. 1977. Open 10.30-1 and 2-6, Thurs. until 9, Sat. 10.30-6. STOCK: *Fireplaces, from early Georgian - marble, £1,500-£60,000; metal, £250-£10,000; wooden, £950-£20,000; slate, £1,150-£5,000; brass, antique leaded and stained glass, brass and iron beds.* LOC: Town centre. SER: Valuations; restorations (fireplaces). SIZE: Large. PARK: Town square.
TEL: 028 8773 8071; FAX: 028 8773 8059
WEBSITE: www.pjsmithantiques.com

A History of
Napoleonic and American
PRISONERS OF WAR 1756-1816
Hulk, Depot and Parole

The Arts and Crafts of Napoleonic and American
PRISONERS OF WAR 1756-1816

Clive L. Lloyd

Whilst many books have been published about war, the role of the prisoner of war has been largely ignored, or paid scant attention. These two books aim to correct this imbalance, and are the result of the author's quest over thirty years into this almost-forgotten field of history.

A History of Napoleonic and American Prisoners of War 1756-1816: Hulk, Depot and Parole is almost exclusively a textual volume, divided into three parts, the first of which provides a detailed account of the historical background to the wars that saw these men become prisoners, and many personal tales of some of the individuals themselves. The rest of the book is largely devoted to the prison hulks (part two) describing the vessels, many of which would once have been warships, and the conditions on board. Part three concerns itself primarily with the depots and prisons on land and the terms and conditions of various types of parole and the punishments which could be expected should parole be broken. Written with numerous personal accounts, and drawing upon many years of painstaking and dedicated research, this important book fills a significant gap in the literature of military history.

The Arts and Crafts of Napoleonic and American Prisoners of War 1756-1816 is lavishly illustrated in colour with an extensive selection of prisoner of war artefacts from museums around the world and the author's own collection - one of the largest private collections of prisoner of war artefacts in existence - revealing the incredible skills of these imprisoned craftsmen. The items - delicate, intricate and highly detailed - include boxes, toys and automata made from bone, straw or paper, as well as paintings by artists whose work is now much in demand. It also records in great detail the fascinating accounts of the lives and occupations of the prisoners of war, and the prison markets in which they were permitted to sell their wares. It tells of the comings and goings of the highly interesting variety of characters who lived and worked alongside the prisoners, or were paroled prisoners themselves, and who would travel for many miles to trade with these, quite literally, captive audiences.

Although both books are able to stand on their own merits, neither is complete without the other. Together these books present a fascinating and detailed insight into the lives and occupations of these men, as well as setting their accounts in the wider historical context.

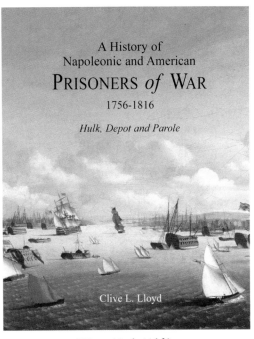

A History of
Napoleonic and American
PRISONERS *of* WAR
1756-1816

Hulk, Depot and Parole

Clive L. Lloyd

378 pp., 16 col., 16 b.&w.
£35.00 Hardback

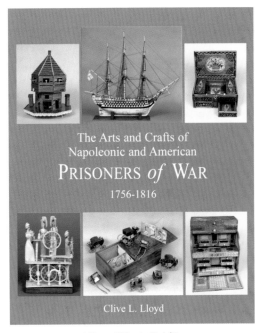

The Arts and Crafts of
Napoleonic and American
PRISONERS *of* WAR
1756-1816

Clive L. Lloyd

335 pp., 202 col., 10 b.&w.
£45.00 Hardback

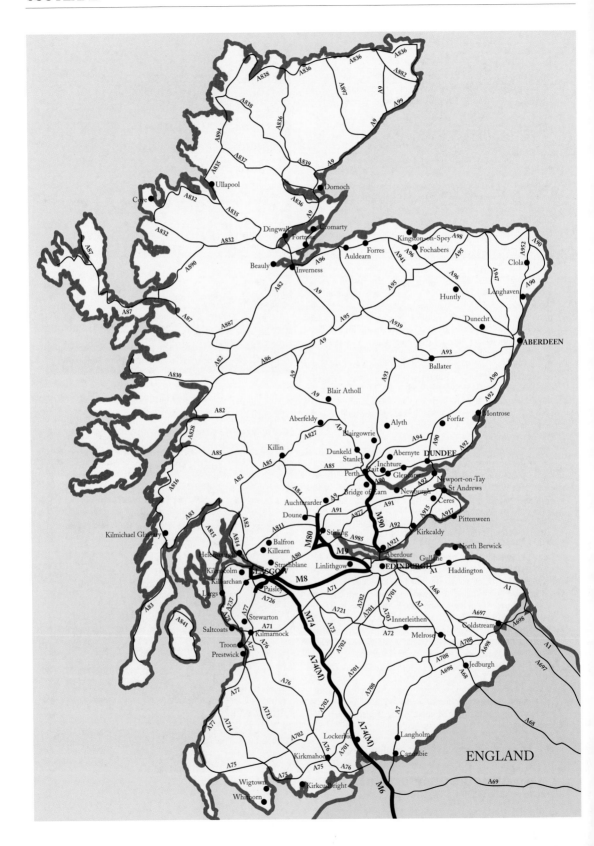

SCOTLAND
DISTRICTS

ABERDEEN

Atholl Antiques
322 Great Western Rd. AB10 6PL. (Gordon Murray)
EST. 1971. Open 10.30-1 and 2.30-6 or by appointment.
STOCK: *Scottish paintings and furniture.* LOC: Central.
SIZE: Small. PARK: Easy. VAT: Stan/Spec.
TEL: 01224 593547

Burning Embers
165-167 King St. AB2 3AE. (J. Bruce)
EST. 1988. Open 10-5. STOCK: *Fireplaces, bric-a-brac and pine.* LOC: Off Union St. SER: Installations. SIZE: Medium. PARK: Outside.
TEL: 01224 624664

Gallery
239 George St. AB25 1ED. (M. Gray)
EST. 1981. Open 9-5.30. STOCK: *Jewellery, post-1850; curios and Victoriana, paintings and prints, post-1800.* SER: Valuations; repairs (jewellery and clocks). SIZE: Large.
TEL: 01224 632522

McCalls (Aberdeen)
90 King St. AB24 5BA. (B. McCall)
EST. 1948. Open 10-5.30. STOCK: *Jewellery.* SER: Repairs (clocks, watches). PARK: Nearby.
TEL: 01224 641916

McCalls Limited
11 Bridge St. AB11 6JL. (Iain Hawthorne)
EST. 1887. Open 9.30-5.30, Thurs. 9.30-6. STOCK: *Victorian, Edwardian, Georgian, Art Deco and Scottish jewellery; small silver collection.* LOC: Town centre, just off Union St. SER: Jewellery repairs, pearl stringing, valuations. PARK: Trinity centre adjacent. VAT: Margin. FAIRS: Local.
TEL: 01224 405303; FAX: 01224 213656
E-MAIL: jewellery@mccalls.co.uk
WEBSITE: www.mccalls.co.uk

The Rendezvous Gallery
100 Forest Ave. AB15 4TL.
EST. 1973. Open 10-1 and 2.30-6. CL: Fri. STOCK: *Art Nouveau, Art Deco, glass, jewellery, bronzes, furniture, £100-£5,000; paintings, watercolours, Scottish School, £200-£10,000.* LOC: Just off Great Western Rd. to Braemar. SIZE: Medium. PARK: Easy. VAT: Stan/Spec.
TEL: 01224 323247; FAX: 01224 326029
E-MAIL: info@rendezvous-gallery.co.uk
WEBSITE: www.rendezvous-gallery.co.uk

Thistle Antiques
28 Esslemont Ave. AB25 1SN. (Paul Bursill)
EST. 1967. Open Thurs. and Fri. 10-4, Sat. 10-1. STOCK: *General antiques, Georgian and Victorian furniture, period lighting.* LOC: City centre. SER: Lighting restoration; metal repolishing. SIZE: Medium. PARK: Easy. VAT: Spec.
TEL: 01224 634692; MOBILE: 07759 429685
E-MAIL: sales@thistleantiques.co.uk

Colin Wood (Antiques) Ltd
25 Rose St. AB10 1TX.
EST. 1968. Open 10-5, Sat 10-4. STOCK: *Specialist in maps of Scotland, 16th-19th C; furniture, 17th-19th C; works of art, Scottish paintings, prints and silver;* SIZE: Medium. PARK: Multi-storey in Chapel St. VAT: Stan/Spec.
TEL: 01224 644786; FAX: same

ABERDOUR

Antiques and Gifts
26 High St. KY3 0SW.
EST. 1976. CL: Mon., Wed. pm. and Fri. am. STOCK: *China, pottery, glass and collectables.* LOC: A921. SER: Restorations (china). SIZE: Small. PARK: Nearby.
TEL: 01383 860523

ABERFELDY

Sonia Cooper
19 Bridgend. PH15 2DF.
EST. 1983. Open Thurs.-Sat. 11-4, Mon. in summer. STOCK: *China, glass, cutlery, wood and metal, from 18th C, £1-£100.* LOC: 10 miles from A9. SER: Buys at auction. SIZE: Medium. PARK: Easy.
TEL: 01887 820266

ABERNYTE

Scottish Antique & Arts Centre
PH14 9SJ. (Bob Templeman)
Open 10-5 including Sun. STOCK: *Furniture, £50-£5,000; accessories, £5-£2,000; collectables, £5-£50; all 18th-19th C.* LOC: A90 Perth-Dundee road, Inchture junction. SER: Valuations; restorations. SIZE: Very large - 220 dealers. PARK: Own. VAT: Stan/Spec/Global.
TEL: 01828 686401; FAX: 01828 686199
WEBSITE: www.scottish-antiques.com

AUCHTERARDER

Ian Burton Antique Clocks   LAPADA
at The Antique Galleries, 125 High St. PH3 1AA.
Open 9-5, Sat. 10-5. STOCK: *Clocks.*
TEL: 07785 114800
E-MAIL: ian@ianburton.com
WEBSITE: www.ianburton.com

John Whitelaw and Sons Antiques   LAPADA
125 High St. PH3 1AA.
Open 9-5. STOCK: *General antiques; furniture, 17th-19th C.* SER: Repairs (furniture). PARK: Easy. VAT: Stan/Spec.
TEL: 01764 662482; FAX: 01764 663577
E-MAIL: jwsantique@aol.com
WEBSITE: www.whitelawantiques.com

AULDEARN

Auldearn Antiques
Dalmore Manse, Lethen Rd. IV12 5HZ.
EST. 1980. Open 9.30-5.30 including Sun. STOCK: *Victorian linen and lace, kitchenalia, china, furniture, architectural items.* LOC: 1 mile from village. SIZE: Medium.
TEL: 01667 453087; HOME: same

BALLATER

The McEwan Gallery   LAPADA
Bridge of Gairn. AB35 5UB. (D., P. and R. McEwan)
EST. 1968. ABA. PBFA. Open 11-5, Sun. 2-5. CL: Mon. Prior telephone call advisable during winter. STOCK: *18th-20th C British and European paintings, specialising in Scottish; rare and elusive polar, Scottish, sporting, including large stock on golf, and natural history books.* LOC: First house on the east side of A939 after its junction with A93 outside Ballater. SER: Valuations; restorations; framing; buys at auction (paintings, watercolours, books); golf catalogues. SIZE: Medium. PARK: Easy. VAT: Spec.
TEL: 01339 755429; FAX: 01339 755995
E-MAIL: pjmm@easynet.co.uk
WEBSITE: www.mcewangallery.com

Treasures of Ballater & Rowan Antiques
1, 5 & 7 Victoria Rd. AB35 5QQ. (Mrs Nichola L. Henderson)
EST. 1982. Open 10.30-5.30. STOCK: *Victorian furniture,* *porcelain and pottery, Scottish silver and jewellery, antique, fine and estate jewellery, paintings and engravings, £10-£3,000.* LOC: Village centre. SER: Valuations; restorations (jewellery); upholstery; shipping. SIZE: 2 shops + store. PARK: Easy.
TEL: 01339 756035; HOME: 01339 755676
E-MAIL: nikki.rowan@lineone.net

BEAULY

Iain Marr Antiques   LAPADA
3 Mid St. IV4 7DP. (I. and A. Marr)
EST. 1975. HADA. Open 10.30-1 and 2-5.30. CL: Thurs. STOCK: *Silver, jewellery, clocks, porcelain, scientific instruments, arms, oils, watercolours, small furniture, Scottish regalia.* LOC: Off the square, on left going north (the only shop on Mid Street). PARK: Easy. VAT: Stan/Spec/Global.
TEL: 01463 782372
E-MAIL: info@iain-marr-antiques
WEBSITE: www.iain-marr-antiques.com

BLAIR ATHOLL

Blair Antiques
By Bruar Falls. PH18 5TW. (Duncan Huie)
EST. 1976. Open 9-5. STOCK: *Period furniture, Scottish oil paintings, silver - some provincial, curios, clocks, pottery and porcelain.* LOC: Opposite House of Bruar. SER: Valuations; buys at auction. SIZE: Medium. PARK: Easy. VAT: Stan/Spec.
TEL: 01796 483264
E-MAIL: adhuie@aol.com

BLAIRGOWRIE

Roy Sim Antiques
The Granary Warehouse, Lower Mill St. PH10 6AQ. (Roy and Ann Sim)
EST. 1977. Open 9-5, Sun. 10-5. STOCK: *Furniture, clocks, silver, EPNS, collectables, decorative and furnishing items.* LOC: Town centre. SER: Shipping. SIZE: Large. PARK: Own. VAT: Spec.
TEL: 01250 873860
E-MAIL: roy.sim@btconnect.com
WEBSITE: www.roysim.com

CANONBIE

The Clock Showrooms
DG14 0SY. (John R. Mann)
EST. 1987. MCWG. Open by appointment. STOCK: *Clocks - over 80 restored longcase, 17th-19th C, £2,500-£90,000; bracket, 17th-19th C, £3,500-£35,000; wall, 19th C, £500-£6,000; small antiques and collectables.* LOC: Leave M6, junction 44, A7 north through Longtown, follow sign to village, premises next to Cross Keys Hotel. SER: Valuations; restorations (clock movements, cases

and dials); buys at auction (clocks). SIZE: Large. PARK: Easy. VAT: Stan.
TEL: 01387 371337/71827; FAX: 01387 371337;
MOBILE: 07850 606147
E-MAIL: jmannclock@aol.com
WEBSITE: www.johnmannantiqueclocks.co.uk

CERES

Ceres Antiques
1 High St. KY15 5NF. (Mrs E. Norrie)
STOCK: General antiques, china and linen. SIZE: Medium.
PARK: Easy.
TEL: 01334 828384

CLOLA BY MINTLAW

Clola Antiques Centre
Shannas School House. AB42 5AE. (Joan and David Blackburn)
EST. 1985. Open 10-5, Sun. 11-5 or by appointment.
STOCK: Victorian and Edwardian furniture, antique and modern jewellery, collectables, china, militaria, books, vintage clothing and silver. LOC: 3 miles south of Mintlaw on the A952 and 25 miles north of Aberdeen on the A90 and A952. SIZE: Large - 10 dealers. PARK: Own. VAT: Margin.
TEL: 01771 624584

COLDSTREAM

Fraser Antiques
65 High St. TD12 4DL. (R. Fleming)
EST. 1968. Open by appointment only. STOCK: Porcelain, glass, pictures, silver, small furniture, general antiques. SER: Valuations; restorations. SIZE: Medium. PARK: Easy. VAT: Spec.
TEL: 01890 882450
E-MAIL: m13border@aol.com

Hand in Hand
Hirsel Law Schoolhouse. TD12 4HX. (Mrs Ruth Hand)
EST. 1969. Open by appointment. STOCK: Paisley shawls, period costume, fine linens, quilts, curtains and interesting textiles. SER: Restorations; valuations. SIZE: Small. PARK: Own. FAIRS: Textile (London, Manchester).
TEL: 01890 883496
E-MAIL: ruth.hand@tiscali.co.uk

CROMARTY

Cromarty Antiques
24 Church St. IV11 8XA. (Jean and Jenny Henderson)
EST. 2000. Open Tues.-Sat. 10.30-4.30 in summer, other days and winter by appointment. STOCK: Georgian, Victorian and Edwardian fine furniture; porcelain, glass, metalware, silver including Scottish provincial. LOC: On the Black Isle (just north of Inverness), follow signs for Cromarty from A9. SIZE: Large. PARK: Easy. VAT: Spec.

TEL: 01381 600404; FAX: 01381 610408; HOME: 01381 610269
E-MAIL: jean@cromartyantiques.com

DORNOCH

Castle Close Antiques
Castle Close. IV25 3SN. (Mrs J. Maclean)
EST. 1982. Open 10-1 and 2-5. CL: Thurs. pm. STOCK: General antiques including furniture, stripped pine, porcelain, jewellery and silver, paintings. SIZE: Medium. PARK: Easy. VAT: Spec.
TEL: 01862 810405; HOME: 01862 81057
E-MAIL: enquiries@castle-close-antiques.com

DOUNE

Scottish Antique and Art Centre
FK16 6HE. (Robert Templeman)
EST. 1999. Open 10-5 including Sun. STOCK: General antiques, collectables, Georgian and Victorian furniture, jewellery, glass, paintings, books. LOC: A84 Stirling to Callander road, 1 mile north of Doune. SIZE: Large - 100 dealers. PARK: Own large. VAT: Stan/Spec.
TEL: 01786 841203; FAX: 01786 842561
E-MAIL: info@scottish-antiques.com
WEBSITE: www.scottish-antiques.com

DUNDEE

Neil Livingstone   LAPADA
3 Old Hawkhill. DD2 1LS.
EST. 1976. Open any time by appointment. STOCK:
French and Italian furniture and decorative items, 17th-20th C. SER: **Shipping worldwide.** SIZE: **Small.**
TEL: **01382 907788/221751;** FAX: **01382 566332;**
MOBILE: **07775 877715**
E-MAIL: **npl88@onetel.com**

DUNKELD

Dunkeld Antiques
Tay Terrace. PH8 0AQ. (D. Dytch)
EST. 1986. Open 10-5, Sun. 12-5. Nov.-Mar. open Fri. and Sat. only. STOCK: 18th-19th C furniture, clocks, paintings, decorative items, out-of-print and antiquarian books. LOC: Converted church, overlooking River Tay. SER: Valuations. SIZE: Large. PARK: Easy. VAT: Spec.
TEL: 01350 728832; FAX: 01350 727008
E-MAIL: david@dunkeldantiques.co.uk
WEBSITE: www.dunkeldantiques.co.uk

EDINBURGH

Armchair Books
72-74 West Port. EH1 2LE. (David Govan)
EST. 1993. Open 10-6 including Sun. STOCK: Antiquarian books, 50p-£1,000. LOC: West from Grassmarket. SER: Valuations with a view to purchase. SIZE: 2 shops. PARK: Nearby.

TEL: 0131 229 5927
E-MAIL: armchairbooks@hotmail.com
WEBSITE: www.armchairbooks.co.uk

Berland's of Edinburgh
143 Gilmore Place. EH3 9PW. (R. Melvin)
GMC. Open 9-4.45. CL: Wed. STOCK: Restored antique
light fittings. SER: Lighting restorations; stockist of old
style braided flex.
TEL: 0131 228 6760
E-MAIL: melvins@btclick.com

Joseph Bonnar, Jewellers
72 Thistle St. EH2 1EN.
Open 10.30-5 or by appointment. STOCK: Antique and
period jewellery. LOC: Parallel with Princes St. SIZE:
Medium. VAT: Stan/Spec.
TEL: 0131 226 2811; FAX: 0131 225 9438
E-MAIL: enquiries@josephbonnar.com

Bourne Fine Art Ltd
6 Dundas St. EH3 6HZ. (P. Bourne)
EST. 1978. Fine Art Society. Open 10-6, Sat. 11-4.
STOCK: Scottish paintings, 1650 to date. LOC: New Town.
SER: Valuations; conservation; buys at auction; framing.
SIZE: Medium. PARK: Easy. VAT: Stan/Spec.
TEL: 0131 557 4050
E-MAIL: art@bournefineart.com
WEBSITE: www.bournefineart.com

Calton Gallery   BADA
6A Regent Terrace. EH7 5BN. (A.G. Whitfield)
EST. 1979. Open by appointment. STOCK: Paintings,
especially Scottish, marine and watercolours, £100-
£100,000; prints, £10-£1,000; sculpture, to £20,000; all
19th to early 20th C. LOC: East end of Princes St. SER:
Valuations; buys at auction (paintings). SIZE: Medium.
PARK: Pay & Display. VAT: Stan/Spec.
TEL: 0131 556 1010; HOME: same; FAX: 0131 558 1150
MOBILE: 07887 793781
E-MAIL: mail@caltongallery.com
WEBSITE: www.caltongallery.com

Castle Antiques
330 Lawnmarket. EH1 2PN. (H. Parry)
Open 10-5. CL: Sat. STOCK: Silver, porcelain, English and
Continental furniture, clocks.
TEL: 0131 225 7615

The Carson Clark Gallery - Scotland's Map Heritage Centre
181-183 Canongate, The Royal Mile. EH8 8BN. (A.
Carson Clark and Paul Scott Clark)
EST. 1969. FRGS. FBCartS. Open 10.30-5.30. STOCK:
Maps, sea charts, prints and books. SER: Collections valued
and purchased.
TEL: 0131 556 4710; FAX: same
E-MAIL: scotmap@aol.com
WEBSITE: www.carsonclarkgallery.co.uk

The Collectors Shop
49 Cockburn St. EH1 1BS. (D. Cavanagh)
EST. 1970. Open 11-5. STOCK: Coins, medals, militaria,
cigarette and postcards, small collectors' items, jewellery, silver
and plate. NOT STOCKED: Postage stamps.
TEL: 0131 226 3391

Craiglea Clocks
88 Comiston Rd. EH10 5QJ. (R.J. Rafter)
EST. 1977. Open 10-5. STOCK: Antique clocks and
barometers. LOC: On Biggar road from Morningside.
SER: Restorations (clocks and barometers). SIZE: Small.
PARK: Adjacent streets.
TEL: 0131 452 8568
WEBSITE: www.craigleaclocks.co.uk

Alan Day Antiques   LAPADA
25A Moray Place. EH3 6DA.
EST. 1973. Open by appointment. STOCK: Furniture
and paintings, 18th-19th C; general antiques. LOC: City
centre. SER: Painting restoration. PARK: Nearby.
TEL: 0131 225 2590

Duncan & Reid Books & Antiques
5 Tanfield, Inverleith. EH3 5DA. (Margaret Duncan,
Susie Reid and Pippa Scott)
EST. 1992. Open Tues.-Sat. 11-5. STOCK: 18th-19th C
English, Chinese and Continental ceramics, glass and
decorative objects; books including sets, modern and
antiquarian. LOC: Near Royal Botanic Gardens. SIZE:
Small. PARK: Meters.
TEL: 0131 556 4591

EASY - Edinburgh Architectural Salvage Yard
31 West Bowling Green St. EH6 5NX.
EST. 1985. Open 9-5, Sat. 12-5. STOCK: Fireplaces, stained
glass, roll-top baths, carriage gates, panelled doors, cast-iron
radiators. SIZE: Large.
TEL: 0131 554 7077; FAX: 0131 554 3070
E-MAIL: easy_edinburgh@hotmail.com
WEBSITE: www.easy-arch-salv.co.uk

Edinburgh Books
145-147 West Port EH3 9DP. (William Lytle)
EST. 2005. Open 10-6. STOCK: Scottish books, literature,
military, music, theology and travel; some antiquarian.
Formerly West Port Books, has been reopened under
new ownership. PARK: Loading outsdie and meters.
TEL: 0131 229 4431
E-MAIL: edinburghbooks@homtail.co.uk
WEBSITE: www.edinburghbooks.net

Edinburgh Coin Shop
11 West Crosscauseway. EH8 9JW. (T.D. Brown)
Open 10-5. STOCK: Coins, medals, badges, militaria,
postcards, cigarette cards, stamps, jewellery, clocks and
watches, general antiques; bullion dealers. SER: Valuations;
auctions. VAT: Stan.
TEL: 0131 668 2928/667 9095; FAX: 0131 668 2926

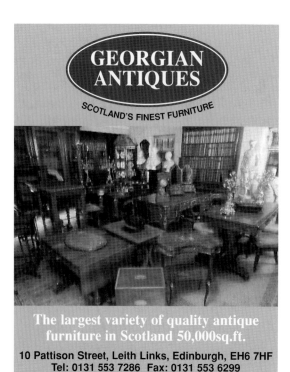

Georgian Antiques   LAPADA
10 Pattison St., Leith Links. EH6 7HF.
EST. 1976. Open 8.30-5.30, Sat. 10-2. STOCK: *Furniture, Georgian, Victorian, inlaid, Edwardian; shipping goods, smalls, £10–£10,000.* LOC: **Off Leith Links.** SER: **Valuations; restorations; buys at auction; packing and shipping; courier.** SIZE: **2 large warehouses.** PARK: **Easy.** VAT: **Stan/Spec.**
TEL: **0131 553 7286 (24 hrs.);** FAX: **0131 553 6299**
E-MAIL: **info@georgianantiques.net**
WEBSITE: **www.georgianantiques.net**

Goodwin's Antiques Ltd
15-16 Queensferry St. EH2 4QW.
EST. 1952. Open 9-5.30, Sat. 9-5. STOCK: *Antique and modern fine jewellery and silver.* SIZE: Medium. VAT: Stan/Spec.
TEL: 0131 225 4717; FAX: 0131 220 1412
E-MAIL: enquiries@goodwinsantiques.com
WEBSITE: www.goodwinsantiques.com

Harlequin Antiques
30 Bruntsfield Place. EH10 4HJ. (C. S. Harkness)
EST. 1995. Open 10-5 and Sun. (Dec. only) 12-4. STOCK: *Clocks and watches, silver, ceramics, small furniture, curios, £10–£5,000.* LOC: 2 miles south of Princes St. (west end). SER: Valuations; restorations (clocks); clocks and watches bought. SIZE: Small. PARK: Easy.
TEL: 0131 228 9446

Holyrood Architectural Salvage
Holyrood Business Park, 146 Duddingston Rd. West. EH16 4AP. (Ken Fowler)
EST. 1993. Open 9-5. STOCK: *Original and reproduction fireplaces, doors, radiators, pews, brassware, flooring.* LOC: 5 minutes drive from Holyrood Palace, 2 mins. from Duddingston village - telephone for directions. SER: Fireplace fitting. SIZE: Very large. PARK: Easy and free. VAT: Stan/Global.
TEL: 0131 661 9305; FAX: 0131 656 9404
WEBSITE: www.holyroodarchitecturalsalvage.com

Allan K. L. Jackson
67 Causewayside. EH9 1QF.
EST. 1974. Open 10-6. CL: Mon. STOCK: *General small antiques, from Victorian, £5-100.* SER: Valuations; house clearance. SIZE: Medium. PARK: Easy. FAIRS: Ingliston; Grassmarket in August and others.
TEL: 0131 668 4532; MOBILE: 07989 236443.

J. Martinez Antiques
17 Brandon Terrace. EH3 5DZ. (Joe Martinez and Mrs. Jacquie Martinez)
EST. 1975. Open 11-5, Wed. 11-2. STOCK: *Clocks, jewellery and general antiques, mainly Victorian, £50–£1,000.* SER: Valuations; clock and watch repairs; buys at auction., public and trade. SIZE: Small. PARK: Easy. FAIRS: Midland Clock & Watch, NEC; Antique Clock & Watch, Haydock Park; Freemasons Hall, Edinburgh.
TEL: 0131 558 8720; FAX: same
E-MAIL: jacquie@jandjantiquefairs.co.uk
WEBSITE: jandjantiquefairs.co.uk

McNaughtan's Bookshop
3a and 4a Haddington Place. EH7 4AE. (Elizabeth Strong)
EST. 1957. ABA. ILAB. Open 11-5 Wed.-Sat. STOCK: *Antiquarian books.* LOC: Leith Walk. SER: Book search; valuations. SIZE: Large. PARK: Limited. FAIRS: ABA; Olympia; Chelsea; Edinburgh.
TEL: 0131 556 5897
E-MAIL: mcnbooks@btconnect.com
WEBSITE: www.mcnaughtansbookshop.com

The Meadows Lamp Gallery
48 Warrender Park Rd. EH9 1HH. (Scott Robertson)
EST. 1992. Open Tues., Thurs. and Sat. 10-6. STOCK: *Old glass lampshades, table lamps, brass light fittings and accessories, especially Art Nouveau.* LOC: 10 minutes walk from city centre. SER: Restorations (cleaning, polishing, lacquering, silver plating). SIZE: Small. PARK: Easy.
TEL: 0131 221 1212; MOBILE: 07836 223311
E-MAIL: s4sarok@aol.com

The Old Town Bookshop
8 Victoria St. EH1 2HG. (Ronald Wilson)
EST. 1982. Open 10.30-5.45. STOCK: *Books, 16th-20th C; prints, from 1450s to 19th C.* LOC: Centre of old town. SER: Valuations. SIZE: Medium. PARK: Nearby. FAIRS:

Book - London, York, Oxford, Cambridge, Edinburgh and Glasgow.
TEL: 0131 225 9237; FAX: 0131 229 1503
WEBSITE: www.oldtownbookshop.com

Open Eye Gallery Ltd
34 Abercromby Place. EH3 6QE. (T. and P. Wilson)
EST. 1976. Open 10-6, Sat. 10-4. STOCK: *Early 20th C etchings, contemporary paintings, ceramics and jewellery.* LOC: Corner of Dundas St. SER: Valuations; restorations (paintings and ceramics); buys at auction. SIZE: Medium. PARK: Easy. VAT: Mainly Spec.
TEL: 0131 557 1020; FAX: same
E-MAIL: mail@openeyegallery.co.uk
WEBSITE: www.openeyegallery.co.uk

Royal Mile Curios
363 High St. EH1 1PW. (L. Bosi and R. Eprile)
EST. 1875. Open 10.30-5. STOCK: *Jewellery and silver.*
TEL: 0131 226 4050
WEBSITE: www.antique-jewelry.cc

Royal Mile Gallery
272 Canongate, Royal Mile. EH8 8AA. (J. A. Smith)
EST. 1970. Open 11.30-5. STOCK: *Maps, engravings, etchings and lithographs.* LOC: Between castle and Holyrood Palace. SER: Valuations; restorations; framing; buys at auction. SIZE: Medium. PARK: Market Street.
TEL: 0131 558 1702; HOME: 0131 668 4007
E-MAIL: james@royalmilegallery.com
WEBSITE: www.royalmilegallery.com

James Scott
43 Dundas St. EH3 6JN.
EST. 1964. Open 11-1 and 2-5.30. CL: Thurs. pm. STOCK: *Curiosities, unusual items, silver, jewellery, small furniture.* VAT: Stan.
TEL: 0131 556 8260; MOBILE: 07714 004370

The Scottish Gallery
16 Dundas St. EH3 6HZ. (Aitken Dott Ltd)
EST. 1842. Open 10-6, Sat. 10-4. STOCK: *20th C and contemporary Scottish paintings; British and international applied art.* LOC: in New Town. SER: Valuations. SIZE: Large. VAT: Stan/Spec. FAIRS: Collect; London Art Fair; Art London; 20/21 British Art Fair.
TEL: 0131 558 1200; FAX: 0131 558 3900
E-MAIL: mail@scottish-gallery.co.uk
WEBSITE: www.scottish-gallery.co.uk

Second Edition
9 Howard St. EH3 5JP. (Mr and Mrs W.A. Smith)
EST. 1978. Open 10.30-5.30, Sat. 9.30-5.30. STOCK: *Antiquarian and secondhand books, £10-£1,000; late 19th to early 20th C maps and prints, £7-£75.* LOC: 200 yards south of Royal Botanical Gardens. SER: Valuations; book-binding. SIZE: Medium. PARK: Nearby.
TEL: 0131 556 9403; HOME: 0131 552 1850
WEBSITE: www.secondeditionbookshop.com

Still Life
54 Candlemaker Row. EH1 2QE. (Ewan Lamont)
EST. 1984. Open 12-5. STOCK: *Small, portable curios, antiques and collectables.* LOC: City centre. SER: Valuations. SIZE: Small. PARK: Crichton St.
TEL: 0131 225 8524
E-MAIL: ewanlamont@mac.com

The Thrie Estaits
49 Dundas St. EH3 6RS. (Peter D.R. Powell)
EST. 1970. Open Tues.-Sat. 11-5. STOCK: *Pottery, porcelain, glass, contemporary and period paintings and prints, unusual and decorative items, some early oak and country furniture.* LOC: New Town. SIZE: Small. PARK: Meters; free Saturdays.
TEL: 0131 556 7084
E-MAIL: thethrieestaits@aol.com
WEBSITE: peter@thethrieestaits.co.uk

Trinity Curios
4-6 Stanley Rd., Trinity. EH6 4SJ. (Alan Ferguson)
EST. 1987. Resident. Open 10-5, Wed. 12-6. CL: Sat. STOCK: *Furniture, ceramics and silver, 19th C, £50-£1,000.* LOC: From Ferry Rd. turn north on to Newhaven Rd., shop 300 yards on left. SER: Restorations (furniture including upholstery). SIZE: Medium. PARK: Easy. VAT: Stan.
TEL: 0131 552 8481

Unicorn Antiques
65 Dundas St. EH3 6RS. (N. Duncan)
EST. 1967. Usually open 10.30-7. STOCK: *Architectural and domestic brassware, lights, mirrors, glass, china, cutlery and bric-a-brac. NOT STOCKED: Weapons, coins, jewellery.* LOC: From Princes St. turn into Hanover St. - Dundas St. is a continuation. SIZE: Medium. PARK: Meters.
TEL: 0131 556 7176; HOME: 0131 332 9135

John Whyte
116b Rose St. EH2 3JF.
EST. 1928. Open 9.30-5. STOCK: *Jewellery, watches, clocks and silver.* SER: Valuations, repair, cleaning, restoration. VAT: Stan.
TEL: 0131 225 2140
E-MAIL: whytejohnj@aol.com

Anthony Woodd Gallery Ltd   LAPADA
4 Dundas St. EH3 6HZ.
EST. 1981. Open 10-6, Sat. 11-4. STOCK: Scottish natural history and sporting pictures, 1750 to date. SER: Valuations; restorations; framing. SIZE: Medium. PARK: Easy. VAT: Spec. FAIRS: Lapada; Cheltenham Game Fairs; Scone and Moy.
TEL: 0131 558 9544; FAX: 0131 558 9525; MOBILE: 07717 744014
E-MAIL: sales@anthonywoodd.com
WEBSITE: www.anthonywoodd.com

Young Antiques
185 Bruntsfield Place. EH10 4DG. (T.C. Young)

EST. 1979. Open 10.30-1.30 and from 2.30. CL: Wed. pm. STOCK: *Victorian and Edwardian furniture, £50-£1,000; ceramics, £20-£2,000; oils and watercolours, £50-£1,500.* SER: Valuations. SIZE: Medium. PARK: Easy. TEL: 0131 229 1361

FORFAR

Gow Antiques & Restoration Ltd.   LAPADA
Pitscandly Farm. DD8 3NZ. (Jeremy Gow)
EST. 1994. ICON. Resident. Appointment advisable.
STOCK: *Fine Continental and British furniture, 17th-19th C, £50-£20,000. Accredited by BAFRA.* LOC: 3 miles off A90, take B9134 out of Forfar, through Lunenhead, first right at sign Myreside, premises next left, in farmyard. SER: Restorations; valuations; disaster management; 3-day antique furniture recognition courses. SIZE: Medium. PARK: Easy. FAIRS: LAPADA; NEC; LAPADA, Cheltenham.
TEL: 01307 465342; MOBILE: 07711 416786
E-MAIL: jeremy@knowyourantiques.com
WEBSITE: www.knowyourantiques.com

FORRES

Michael Low Antiques
45 High St. IV36 2PB.
EST. 1967. Open 10-1 and 2-5. STOCK: *Small antiques.*
TEL: 01309 673696

FORTROSE

Cathedral Antiques
45 High St. IV10 8SU. (Patricia MacColl)
EST. 1996. Open Fri. and Sat. March to Dec. (extra days in summer months). CL: Jan. and Feb. except by appointment. STOCK: *Fine furniture, 1780-1920, £100-£5,000; silver and plate, 1780-1940, £5-£1,000; small decorative antiques, £20-£1,000.* LOC: 20 mins. from Inverness. SER: Valuations. SIZE: Medium - 2 showrooms. PARK: Easy. VAT: Global/Margin. FAIRS: Scone Palace, Perth; Fettes College, Edinburgh.
TEL: 01381 620161; HOME: same; MOBILE: 07778 817074
E-MAIL: cathant@hotmail.com

GLASGOW

The Roger Billcliffe Fine Art
134 Blythswood St. G2 4EL.
EST. 1992. Open 9.30-5.30, Sat. 10-1. STOCK: *British paintings, watercolours, drawings, sculpture, especially Scottish, from 1850; jewellery, metalwork, glass and woodwork.* SER: Valuations, repair, restoration and cleaning (paintings). SIZE: Large. VAT: Spec.
TEL: 0141 332 4027; FAX: 0141 332 6573
E-MAIL: info@billcliffegallery.com
WEBSITE: www.billcliffegallery.com

A.D. Hamilton and Co
7 St. Vincent Place. G1 2DW. (Jeffrey Lee Fineman)
EST. 1890. Open 10-4.30. STOCK: *Jewellery and silver, 19th to early 20th C, £100-£3,000; British coins, medals and banknotes, £10-£1,000.* LOC: City centre, next to George Square. SER: Valuations; repairs (jewellery). SIZE: Small. PARK: Meters. VAT: Stan/Spec.
TEL: 0141 221 5423; FAX: 0141 248 6019
E-MAIL: jefffineman@hotmail.com
WEBSITE: www.adhamilton.co.uk

Ewan Mundy Fine Art Ltd
Lower Ground Floor, 211 West George St. G2 2LW.
EST. 1981. Open 10-5. CL: Sat. STOCK: *Fine Scottish, English and French oils and watercolours, 19th-20th C, from £250; Scottish and English etchings and lithographs, 19th-20th C, from £100; Scottish contemporary paintings, from £50.* LOC: City centre. SIZE: Medium. PARK: Nearby. VAT: Stan/Spec.
TEL: 0141 248 9755.

Pastimes Vintage Toys
126 Maryhill Rd. G20 7QS. (Gordon and Anne Brown)
EST. 1980. Open Tues.-Sat. 10-5. STOCK: *Vintage toys, die-cast, railways and dolls' houses, from 1910, £1-£300; medals and militaria.* LOC: From the west off junction 17, M8; from the east junction 16, M8. SER: Valuations. SIZE: Medium. PARK: Easy. VAT: Stan.
TEL: 0141 331 1008
WEBSITE: www.dinkydoll.com

Jeremy Sniders Antiques
158 Bath St. G2 4TB.
EST. 1983. Open 9-5. STOCK: *British decorative arts including furniture, 1850-1960; Scandinavian decorative arts including furniture, silver and jewellery, 1800 to date; silver, mainly 19th-20th C; all £30-£5,000.* SER: Will source Scandinavian articles - eg. Georg Jensen, Royal Copenhagen. SIZE: Medium. PARK: Nearby - Sauchiehall St. Centre. VAT: Spec.
TEL: 0141 332 0043; FAX: 0141 332 5505
E-MAIL: snidersantiques@aol.com
WEBSITE: www.jeremysnidersantiques.com and www.jeremysnidersantiques.co.uk

Strachan Antiques
40 Darnley St., Pollokshields. G41 2SE. (Alex and Lorna Strachan and Saranne Jenkins)
EST. 1990. Open 10-6, Sat. 10-5, Sun. 12-5. STOCK: *Furniture especially Arts and Crafts, Art Nouveau and Glasgow Style, £50-£5,000; some decorative items.* LOC: 2 mins. from M8, junction 20 westbound, junction 21 eastbound. SER: Restoration (hand-stripping, refinishing, french polishing). SIZE: Large - warehouse. PARK: Own. VAT: Stan/Spec. FAIRS: NEC Birmingham.
TEL: 0141 429 4411
E-MAIL: alex.strachan@btconnect.com
WEBSITE: www.strachanantiques.co.uk

Voltaire & Rousseau
12-14 Otago Lane. G12 8PB. (Joseph McGonigle)
EST. 1972. Open 10-6. *STOCK: Books - classic, literature, foreign, literature, Scottish, some rare and first editions; student textbooks.* SER: Valuations (books). SIZE: Medium. PARK: Gibson St.
TEL: 0141 339 1811

Tim Wright Antiques   LAPADA
147 Bath St. G2 4SQ. (T. and J. Wright)
EST. 1971. Open 9.45-5, Sat. 10.30-4 or by appointment. *STOCK: Furniture, European and Oriental ceramics and glass, decorative items, silver and plate, brass and copper, mirrors and prints, textiles, samplers, all £50-£6,000.* **LOC: On opposite corner to Christie's. SIZE: 6 showrooms. PARK: Multi-storey opposite and meters. VAT: Mainly Spec.**
TEL: 0141 221 0364; FAX: same
E-MAIL: tim@timwright-antiques.com
WEBSITE: www.timwright-antiques.com

GLENCARSE

Michael Young Antiques at Glencarse
PH2 7LX.
EST. 1887. Open 10.30-5.30 and by appointment *STOCK: 17th-19th C furniture, paintings and silver.* LOC: A90 3 miles east of Perth. SER: Valuations; restorations. SIZE: Large. PARK: Easy.
TEL: 01738 860001; FAX: same

GRANDTULLY

John Walker Antiques
PH9 0PL. (John Walker)
EST. 1971. Open Tues.-Sun. 10-5 and BH or by appointment. *STOCK: Period furniture, decorative items, 18th-19th C; garden furniture, sporting engravings.* SER: Valuations; restorations; buys at auction. SIZE: Medium. PARK: Easy. VAT: Spec.
TEL: 01887 840775; HOME: 01738 828627; MOBILE: 07710 122244
E-MAIL: johnwalkerantiques@btopenworld.com

GULLANE

Gullane Antiques
5 Rosebery Place. EH31 2AN. (E.A. Lindsey)
EST. 1981. Open Tues., Fri. and Sat. 10.30-1 and 2.30-5. *STOCK: China and glass, 1850-1930, £5-£150; prints and watercolours, early 20th C, £25-£100; metalwork, 1900s, £5-£150; jewellery, £5-£200.* LOC: 6 miles north of Haddington, off A1. SIZE: Medium. PARK: Easy.
TEL: 01620 842994

HADDINGTON

Leslie & Leslie
EH41 3JJ. (R. Skea)

EST. 1920. Open 9-1 and 2-5. CL: Sat. *STOCK: General antiques.* PARK: Nearby. VAT: Stan.
TEL: 01620 822241; FAX: same

HAWICK

Borthwick Trading Antiques
The Mill, 2 Lothian St., TD9 9HB. (Maurice Manning)
Open 9.30-5, Sat. 12-2. *STOCK: Furniture, clocks, porcelain, pottery, glass, metalware and pictures.*
TEL: 01450 363916; MOBILE: 07966 102404
E-MAIL: borthwicktrading@hotmail.com
WEBSITE: www.borthwicktrading-antiques.com

INCHTURE

Inchmartine Fine Art
Inchmartine House. PH14 9QQ. (P.M. Stephens)
EST. 1998. Open 9-5.30. *STOCK: Mainly Scottish oils and watercolours, £150-£2,500.* LOC: Take A90 Perth/Dundee road, entrance on left at Lodge. SER: Cleaning; restorations; framing. SIZE: Medium. PARK: Easy. VAT: Spec. FAIRS: Chester; Scone; Naworth; Harrogate.
TEL: 01828 686412; HOME: same; FAX: 01828 686748; MOBILE: 07702 190128
E-MAIL: fineart@inchmartine.freeserve.co.uk

C.S. Moreton (Antiques)
Inchmartine House. PH14 9QQ. (P.M. and Mrs M. Stephens)
EST. 1922. Open 9-5.30. *STOCK: Furniture, £100-£10,000; carpets and rugs, £50-£3,000; ceramics, metalware; all 16th C to 1860; old cabinet makers' tools.* LOC: Take A90 Perth/Dundee road, entrance on left at Lodge. SER: Valuations; cabinet making and repairs. SIZE: Large. PARK: Easy. VAT: Mainly Spec. FAIRS: Chester; Scone; Naworth; Harrogate.
TEL: 01828 686412; HOME: same; FAX: 01828 686748; MOBILE: 07702 190128
E-MAIL: moreton@inchmartine.freeserve.co.uk

INNERLEITHEN

Keepsakes
96 High St. EH44 6HF. (Margaret Maxwell)
EST. 1995. CL: Tues., Wed. and lunchtimes. *STOCK: Ceramics and glass, £50-£800; dolls, teddies and toys, £100-£500; books, post and cigarette cards, £5-£25; jewellery, £5-£100; some 19th C but mainly 20th C.* LOC: A72. SIZE: Small. PARK: Easy. FAIRS: Ingliston; some Border.
TEL: 01896 831369; HOME: 01896 830701
E-MAIL: maxwells@keepsakes.freeserve.so.uk
WEBSITE: www.keepsakes.freeserve.co.uk

INVERNESS

Gallery Persia
Upper Myrtlefield, Nairnside. IV2 5BX. (G. MacDonald)
EST. 1979. *STOCK: Persian, Turkoman, Afghanistan,*

Caucasus, Tibetan, Anatolian rugs and carpets, late 19th C to 1940, £500-£2,000+; quality contemporary pieces, £100+. LOC: From A9 1st left after flyover, 1st left at roundabout, then 2.25 miles on B9006, then 1st right, 1st left. SER: Valuations; restorations; cleaning; repairs. PARK: Easy. FAIRS: Game, Scone Palace, Perth (July). TEL: 01463 798500; HOME: 01463 792198; FAX: same; E-MAIL: mac@gallerypersia.co.uk
WEBSITE: www.gallerypersia.co.uk

JEDBURGH

Mainhill Gallery
Ancrum. TD8 6XA. (Diana Bruce)
EST. 1981. Open by prior telephone call. *STOCK: Oil paintings, watercolours, etchings, some sculpture and ceramics, 19th C to contemporary, £35-£7,000.* LOC: Just off A68, 3 miles north of Jedburgh, centre of Ancrum. SER: Exhibitions; valuations. SIZE: Medium. PARK: Easy. VAT: Spec. FAIRS: London; Edinburgh.
TEL: 01835 830545; FAX: same
E-MAIL: mainhillgallery@aol.com
WEBSITE: www.mainhill-gallery.co.uk

R. and M. Turner (Antiques Ltd)   LAPADA
34-36 High St. TD8 6AG. (R.J. Turner)
EST. 1965. Open 9.30-5.00, Sat. 10-5. CL: Mon. STOCK: Furniture, clocks, porcelain, paintings, silver, jewellery, 17th-20th C and fine reproductions. LOC: On A68 to Edinburgh. SER: Valuations; packing and shipping. SIZE: 6 large showrooms and warehouse. PARK: Own. VAT: Stan/Spec.
TEL: 01835 863445; FAX: 01835 863349

KILBARCHAN

Gardner's The Antique Shop   LAPADA
Wardend House, Kibbleston Rd. PA10 2PN. (G.D., R.K.F. and D.D. Gardner)
EST. 1950. Open to trade 7 days, retail 9-6, Sat. 10-5, Sun. 1-5. STOCK: Smalls, furniture, general antiques. LOC: 12 miles from Glasgow, at far end of Tandlehill Rd. 10 mins. from Glasgow Airport. SER: Valuations. SIZE: 11 showrooms. PARK: Easy. VAT: Spec.
TEL: 01505 702292
WEBSITE: www.gardnersantiques.co.uk

McQuade Antiques
7 Shuttle St. PA10 2JN. (W. G. McQuade)
EST. 1967. Open 10-5.30, Sun. 2-5.30 or by appointment. CL: Sat. *STOCK: Furniture, porcelain, clocks, brass and silver, 19th-20th C.* LOC: Next to Weavers Cottage. SER: Valuations. SIZE: Large. PARK: Easy. VAT: Spec. FAIRS: Newark.
TEL: 01505 704249
E-MAIL: billy-mcquade@tiscali.co.uk

KILLEARN

Country Antiques
G63 9AJ. (Lady J. Edmonstone)
EST. 1975. Open Mon.-Sat. *STOCK: Small antiques and decorative items. NOT STOCKED: Reproduction.* LOC: A81. In main street. SER: Interior decoration. PARK: Easy.
TEL: 01360 770215

KILLIN

Maureen H. Gauld
Craiglea, Main St. FK21 8UN.
EST. 1975. Open March-Oct. 10-5, Nov.-Feb. Thurs., Fri., Sat. *STOCK: General antiques, furniture, silver, paintings and etchings, £5-£3,500.* SIZE: Medium. PARK: Easy.
TEL: 01567 820475; HOME: 01567 820605
E-MAIL: killingallery@btopenworld.com
WEBSITE: www.killingallery.co.uk

Killin Gallery
Craiglea, Main St. FK21 8UN. (J.A. Gauld)
EST. 1992. Open 10-5, Sun. by appointment. *STOCK: Etchings and drypoints, £100-£1,000; paintings, £300-£3,000; furniture, £100-£2,000; all 1860-1960.* LOC: Village centre. SER: Valuations. SIZE: Medium. PARK: Easy.
TEL: 01567 820475; HOME: 01567 820605
E-MAIL: killingallery@btopenworld.com
WEBSITE: www.killingallery.co.uk

KILMACOLM

Kilmacolm Antiques Ltd
Stewart Place. PA13 4AF. (H. Maclean)
EST. 1973. Open 10-1 and 2.30-5.30. CL: Sun. except by appointment. *STOCK: Furniture, 18th-19th C, £100-£8,000; objets d'art, 19th C; jewellery, £5-£5,000; paintings, £100-£5,000.* LOC: First shop on right when travelling from Bridge of Weir. SER: Restorations (furniture, silver, jewellery, porcelain). SIZE: Medium. PARK: Easy. VAT: Stan/Spec/Global. FAIRS: Scone Palace.
TEL: 01505 873149

KILMARNOCK

QS Antiques and Cabinetmakers
Moorfield Industrial Estate. KA2 0DP. (J.R. Cunningham and D.A. Johnson)
EST. 1980. Open 9-5.30, Sat. 9-5. *STOCK: Furniture including stripped pine, 18th-19th C; shipping goods, architectural and collectors' items.* SER: Restorations; stripping; custom-built kitchens and furniture. SIZE: Large. PARK: Easy. VAT: Stan.
TEL: 01563 571071
WEBSITE: www.qsantiques.co.uk

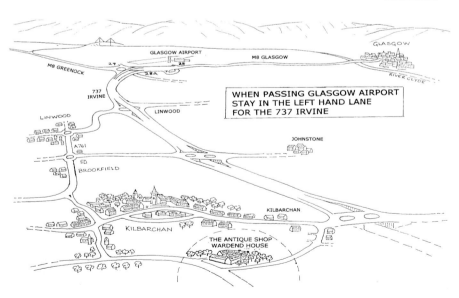

KILMICHAEL GLASSARY

Rhudle Mill
PA31 8QE. (D. Murray)
EST. 1979. Open daily, weekends by appointment. STOCK: *Furniture, 18th C to Art Deco, £30-£3,000; small items and bric-a-brac, £5-£500.* LOC: Signposted 3 miles south of Kilmartin on A816 Oban to Lochgilphead road. SER: Restorations (furniture); French polishing; buys at auction. SIZE: Medium. PARK: Easy.
TEL: 01546 605284; FAX: 01546 606173.

KIRKCALDY

A. K. Campbell & Sons
277 High St. KY1 1LA.
EST. 1977. STOCK: *Coins, medals, old banknotes, militaria, china and porcelain, pictures, small furniture, die-cast models, postcards.* SER: Valuations. SIZE: Small. PARK: Easy.
TEL: 01592 264305

KIRKCUDBRIGHT

The Antique Shop
67 St Mary St. DG6 4DU. (Paul and Marisa Mairs)
EST. 1993. Open 10-5. STOCK: *General antiques and reproductions, collectors' items, linen and lace, kichenalia, 18th-20th C, to £1,500, contemporary interiors, stockist of "Comptoir de Famille".* LOC: Near entrance of town, at junction to Gatehouse of Fleet. PARK: Easy.
TEL: 01557 332400
E-MAIL: mjmantiques@hotmail.com
WEBSITE: www.antiqueshopkirkcudbright.com

Osborne Antiques
63 High St. DG6 4JD. (David Mitchell)
EST. 1889. Open 10-12.30, 1.30-5. CL: Tue/Wed in winter. STOCK: *Georgian and Victorian furniture, smalls.* SER: Restoration (furniture). SIZE: Large. PARK: On street. VAT: Stan.
TEL: 01557 330441; FAX: 01557 331791
E-MAIL: mitch0106@hotmail.com
WEBSITE: www.osborne-scotland.co.uk

LARGS

Narducci Antiques
11 Waterside St. KA30 9LN. (G. Narducci)
Mainly Trade and Export. Open Tues., Thurs. and Sat. 2.30-5.30 or by appointment - trade any time. STOCK: *General antiques and shipping goods.* SER: Packing and shipping. SIZE: Warehouse. PARK: Own. VAT: Stan.
TEL: 01475 672612; 01294 461687; FAX: 01294 470002; MOBILE: 07771 577777;
WEBSITE: www.narducci-antiques.co.uk

LINLITHGOW

County Antiques
30 High St. EH49 7AE. (Mrs M. Flynn)
EST. 1987. Open 10-5. STOCK: *Jewellery and small antiques.* LOC: East end High St. SER: Valuations; jewellery repairs. SIZE: Small. PARK: Nearby.
TEL: 01506 671201

Town & County
20 High St. EH49 7AE. (Mrs M. Flynn)
EST. 1987. Open 10-5. STOCK: *Furniture and general antiques.* SER: Valuations. PARK: Nearby.
TEL: 01506 845509

LOCKERBIE

Cobwebs of Lockerbie Ltd
30 Townhead St. DG11 2AE.
EST. 1992. Open 9-5. STOCK: *Victorian furniture and china, collectables.* LOC: Outskirts of town. SER: Valuations. SIZE: Medium. PARK: Easy. VAT: Global.
TEL: 01576 202554

MELROSE

Michael Vee Design - Birch House Antiques
High St. TD6 9PB. (Michael Vee and Enid Cranston)
EST. 1990. Open 9.30-12.30 and 1.30-5, Sat. 9.30-4, Sun. by appointment. STOCK: *Mirrors and lighting, French, English, decorative and some garden furniture, 1850-1920, £20-£5,000.* LOC: 1.5 miles off A68. SER: Interior design; upholstery; specialist paint finishes. SIZE: Medium. PARK: Easy. VAT: Margin.
TEL: 01896 822116; HOME: 01896 822835; MOBILE: 07761 913349
E-MAIL: michael.vee@btinternet.com

The Whole Lot
Melrose Antique, Art and Gift Centre, St Dunstans, High St. TD6 9RU. (I. Purves)
EST. 2002. Open 9.30-5, Sat. 9.30-5.30, Sun. 12-5. STOCK: *Wide range of general antiques including furniture, silver, china, glass, jewellery, curios and collectables, smalls.* LOC: Edge of town centre. SER: Valuations. SIZE: Medium - 30 dealers. PARK: Easy and public behind building.
TEL: 01896 823039; FAX: 01896 823484
WEBSITE: www.thewholelot.co.uk

NEWBURGH

Henderson-Dark Antiques Ltd   LAPADA
237-241 High St. KY14 6DY.
EST. 1995. CINOA. Open 10-5. STOCK: **Staffordshire pottery, furniture, blue & white transfer ware, paintings & etchings, tea caddies, tortoiseshell, Scottish jewellery, antique copper and metalware, mirrors & lighting.** SER: **Restoration (clocks, paintings, furniture).** SIZE: **Medium.** PARK: **Own.**

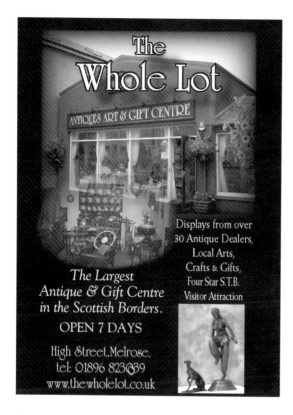

TEL: 01337 840248; FAX: same
E-MAIL: hendersondarkantiques@hotmail.com
WEBSITE: www.hendersondarkantiques.com

NEWPORT-ON-TAY

Mair Wilkes Books
3 St. Mary's Lane. DD6 8AH. (James Mair and Alan Wilkes)
EST. 1969. PBFA. Open Tues.-Fri. 10-12.30 and 2-4.30, Sat. 10-5. STOCK: *Books, all subjects, from 16th C to date, £1-£1,000.* SER: Valuations. SIZE: Medium. PARK: Nearby.
TEL: 01382 542260
E-MAIL: mairwilkes.books@zoom.co.uk

NORTH BERWICK

Kirk Ports Gallery
49A Kirk Ports. EH39 4HL. (Alan Lindsey and Stephen Alan Lindsey)
EST. 1995. Open 10.30-5. CL: Thurs. STOCK: *Oil paintings, £100-£1,000; watercolours, £50-£600; etchings and prints, £30-£100; all 19th C to 1940.* LOC: Behind main street. SER: Valuations. SIZE: Medium. PARK: Own.
TEL: 01620 894114
E-MAIL: antiques@lindsey.eclipse.co.uk
WEBSITE: www.lindseyantiques.co.uk

Lindsey Antiques
49a Kirk Ports. EH39 4HL. (Stephen Lindsey)
EST. 1995. Open 10-1 and 2-5. CL: Thurs. STOCK: *Ceramics and glass, 1800-1935, £20-£500; furniture, 1750-1910, £150-£2,000.* LOC: Behind main street. SER: Valuations. SIZE: Medium. PARK: Own.
TEL: 01620 894114
E-MAIL: antiques@lindsey.eclipse.co.uk
WEBSITE: www.lindseyantiques.co.uk

Penny Farthing
23 Quality St. EH39 4HR. (S. Tait)
EST. 1981. Open 9.30-5.30, Sun. 2.30-6.30. STOCK: *Secondhand books, collectables, 20th C, £5-£500.* LOC: On corner with High St. SER: Valuations; buys at auction. SIZE: Medium. PARK: Easy. FAIRS: Scot, Meadowbank, Edinburgh.
TEL: 01620 890114; FAX: same; MOBILE: 07817 721928
E-MAIL: pennyfarthing@amserve.net

PAISLEY

Corrigan Antiques
Woodlands, High Calside. PA2 6BY.
EST. 1938. Open by appointment. STOCK: *Furniture and accessories.* LOC: 5 mins. from Glasgow Airport. SER: Valuations. SIZE: Small. PARK: Off road. VAT: Stan./Spec.
TEL: 01418 896653; FAX: 0141 848 9700; MOBILE: 07802 631110
E-MAIL: corriganantiques@btconnect.com

PERTH

Hardie Antiques
25 St. John St. PH1 5SH. (T.G. Hardie)
EST. 1980. Open 10-4.30. STOCK: *Jewellery and silver, 18th-20th C, £30-£10,000.* SER: Valuations; specialist jewellery repairs. SIZE: Medium. PARK: Nearby. VAT: Stan/Spec.
TEL: 01738 633127; FAX: same
E-MAIL: info@timothyhardie.co.uk
WEBSITE: www.timothyhardie.co.uk

Henderson
5 North Methven St. PH1 5PN. (S.G. Henderson)
EST. 1938. Open 9.30-5. STOCK: *Silver, jewellery, £5-£2,000.* LOC: A9. SER: Valuations; repairs. SIZE: Small. PARK: Easy. VAT: Stan/Margin.
TEL: 01738 624836
E-MAIL: scott-henderson@btconnect.com
WEBSITE: www.jewellers-perth.co.uk

Yesterdays Today
37 South Methven St. PH1 5NU. (Bill and Nora MacGregor)
EST. 1996. Open 9-5. STOCK: *General collectables especially china and furniture, £25-£1,000.* SER: Valuations; buys at auction. SIZE: Medium. PARK: Nearby. VAT: Global.

TEL: 01738 587888
E-MAIL: macgregor-s@hotmail.com

PITTENWEEM

The Little Gallery
20 High St. KY10 2LA. (Dr. Ursula Ditchburn-Bosch)
EST. 1988. Open 10-5, Sun. 2-5. CL: Mon. STOCK: China,
18th C to 1950s, £5-£100; small furniture, mainly Victorian,
£30-£500; rustica, £5-£150; contemporary paintings, £40-
£2,500. LOC: From Market Sq. towards church, on right.
SER: Valuations. SIZE: Small. PARK: Easy.
TEL: 01333 311227; HOME: same

PRESTWICK

Crossroads Antiques
7 The Cross. KA9 1AJ. (Timothy O'Keeffe)
EST. 1989. Open 9-5. STOCK: Furniture, 18th-20th C, £5-
£1,000+; china and silver, 19th-20th C, £5-£500+,
paintings. SER: Valuations. SIZE: Medium. PARK: Nearby.
TEL: 01292 474004.

RAIT

Hardies   LAPADA
The Old Sawmill, Rait Antique Centre. PH2 7RT.
EST. 1991. STOCK: 19th C furniture. SER: Storage. SIZE:
Small. PARK: Plenty.
TEL: 01821 670760
WEBSITE: www.timhardie.com

A lavish review of one of this century's most important
manufacturers of classic mechanical toys, featuring
hundreds of delightful, original modern photographs mixed
with illustrations from original Schuco catalogues. This
informative and beautifully illustrated book is an absorbing
record of the history of this internationally famous
mechanical toy producer. Anyone interested in collectable
toys will be entranced by the illustrations; anyone who is
interested in the history of transport will be fascinated by
the changes that this century has seen.

230 x 230 mm. 128 pp 200 col. **£19.95 Hardback**

Neilsons Ltd
Court 1, Rait Village Antiques Centre PH2 7RT. (Mr
J. Neilson)
EST. 1932. NFA. Open 10-5, Sun. 12-4.30; we are there
on Mondays or can be contacted on 07899 995869.
STOCK: Fireplaces, 18th-20th C, £100-£20,000; interiors,
stoves, fenders, fire irons; marble (including French), wood
and stone chimney-pieces. SER: We can help obtain similar
pieces to those displayed or to find particular items. SIZE:
Large. PARK: Easy. VAT: Stan.
TEL: 01821 670549; MOBILE: 07899 995869
E-MAIL: info@chimneypiece.co.uk
WEBSITE: www.chimneypiece.co.uk

Rait Village Antiques Centre
PH2 7RT.
EST. 1985. Open 10-5, Sun. 12-4.30. STOCK: General
antiques, furniture, paintings, clocks, fireplaces and
Wemyssware. LOC: Midway between Perth and Dundee,
1 mile north of A90. SIZE: 16 showrooms. PARK: Easy.
TEL: 01821 670379
E-MAIL: lynda.templeman@yahoo.co.uk

Below are listed the dealers at this centre.

Abernethy Antiques

The Bothy Antiques & Collectables
Agricultural and farming memorabilia.

L. Christie Campbell Fine Art

Fair Finds
(Lynda Templeman) *Large stock of antique and early 20th C
country house furnishings, pictures, rugs, silver and clocks, £50-
£10,000.* TEL: 01821 670379.

Forget-me-Not

Tim Hardie Antiques

Kaeleigh International

Gordon Loraine Antiques
(Liane and Gordon Loraine) *Georgian, Victorian and
Edwardian furniture, decorative items and collectables.* TEL:
01821 670760.

The Luckenbooth

Now and Then

Old Timers

Rait Interiors

St Michael Antiques
Furniture and furnishings.

Thistle & Rose

Tickety Boo Antiques

The Undercroft
Farming memorabilia.

Whimsical Wemyss
(Lynda Templeman and Chris Comben) *Wemyssware, £50-
£3,000.* TEL: 01821 67039

SALTCOATS

Narducci Antiques
Factory Place. KA21 5LA. (G. Narducci)
EST. 1972. *Mainly Trade and Export.* Open by
appointment. STOCK: *Furniture, general antiques and
shipping goods.* SER: Packing, export, shipping and
European haulage. PARK: Easy.
TEL: 01294 461687; FAX: 01294 470002; MOBILE:
07771 577777
E-MAIL: narducci.antiques@virgin.net

ST. ANDREWS

The David Brown (St. Andrews) Gallery
9 Albany Place. KY16 9HH. (Mr and Mrs D.R. Brown)
EST. 1973. CL: 1-2 daily. STOCK: *Golf memorabilia, 19th
C, £100-£20,000; silver, jewellery especially Scottish, 18th-
20th C, £100-£20,000; general antiques, from 18th C, £50-
£5,000.* LOC: Main street. SER: Valuations; restorations
(jewellery, silver); buys at auction (golf memorabilia).
SIZE: Medium. PARK: Easy. VAT: Stan.
TEL: 01334 477840; FAX: 01334 476915

St. Andrews Fine Art
84 Market St. KY16 9PA. (J. Carruthers)
EST. 1972. FATG. Open 10-5.30. STOCK: *Scottish oils,
watercolours and drawings, 19th-20th C.* SIZE: Large.
PARK: Easy.
TEL: 01334 474080
E-MAIL: info@st-andrewsfineart.co.uk
WEBSITE: www.st-andrewsfineart.co.uk

STEWARTON

Woolfsons of James Street Ltd t/a Past & Present
3 Lainshaw St. KA3 5BY.
EST. 1983. Open 9.30-5.30, Sun. 12-5.30. STOCK:
*Furniture, £100-£500; porcelain, £25-£500; bric-a-brac,
£5-£50; all from 1800.* LOC: Stewarton Cross. SER:
Valuations; restorations (French polishing, upholstery,
wood). SIZE: Medium. PARK: Easy. VAT: Stan/Spec.
TEL: 01560 484113; FAX: same

STIRLING

Abbey Antiques
4 Friars St. FK8 1HA. (S. Campbell)
EST. 1980. Resident. Open 9-5. STOCK: *Jewellery, £10-
£5,000; silver and plate, £5-£1,000; paintings, £50-
£2,500; bric-a-brac, £1-£100; coins and medals, £1-£1,000;
all 18th-20th C; china, porcelain, collectables; antiquarian,
modern and second hand books £1-£1,000 esp. Scottish.* LOC:
Off Murray Place, part of main thoroughfare. SER:
Valuations. SIZE: Small. PARK: Nearby.
TEL: 01786 447840.
E-MAIL: stuart_campbell@btconnect.com

STRATHBLANE

Whatnots
16 Milngavie Rd. G63 9EH. (F. Bruce)
EST. 1965. STOCK: *Furniture, paintings, jewellery, silver
and plate, clocks, small items.* LOC: A81, 10 miles NW of
Glasgow. SIZE: Medium. PARK: Easy.
TEL: 01360 770310

TROON

Tantalus Antiques
79 Templehill. KA10 6BQ. (Iain D. Sutherland)
EST. 1995. MBWCG. Open 10-5. CL: Mon. or by
appointment. STOCK: *Furniture, clocks and watches, pictures
and paintings, silverware, jewellery, ceramics.* LOC: Town
centre, main road to the harbour. SER: Valuations;
restorations; jewellery restoration workshop on-site.
SIZE: Medium. PARK: Easy.
TEL: 01292 315999
E-MAIL: idsantique@aol.com
WEBSITE: www.scottishantiques.com

UPPER LARGO

D.V. & C.A. St. Clair
13 Main St. KY8 6EL.
EST. 1958. Open 10.30-5.30, Sun. by appointment.
STOCK: *Pictures, furniture, china, pottery, glass and works of
art.* LOC: Coast road from Leven to St. Andrews. SER:
Valuations. SIZE: Medium. PARK: Easy.
TEL: 01333 360437; HOME: same.

WHITHORN

Priory Antiques
29 George St. DG8 8NS. (Mary Arnott)
EST. 1988. Open most days 11-4, prior telephone call
advisable. CL: Thurs. STOCK: *Silver, ceramics and
furniture, pre 1940, £5-£500.* LOC: Town centre. SER:
Valuations. SIZE: Small. PARK: Easy.
TEL: 01988 500517; HOME: same.

WIGTOWN

Ming Books
Beechwood House, Acre Place. DG8 9DU. (Marion
and Robin Richmond)
EST. 1982. Open 10-6 in summer, by appointment in
winter. STOCK: *Books.* SER: Valuations. SIZE: Small. PARK:
Easy. FAIRS: Belfast Book, Festival of the Book, Wigton.
TEL: 01988 403241; HOME: same
E-MAIL: mingbooks@aol.com
WEBSITE: www.mingbooks.co.uk

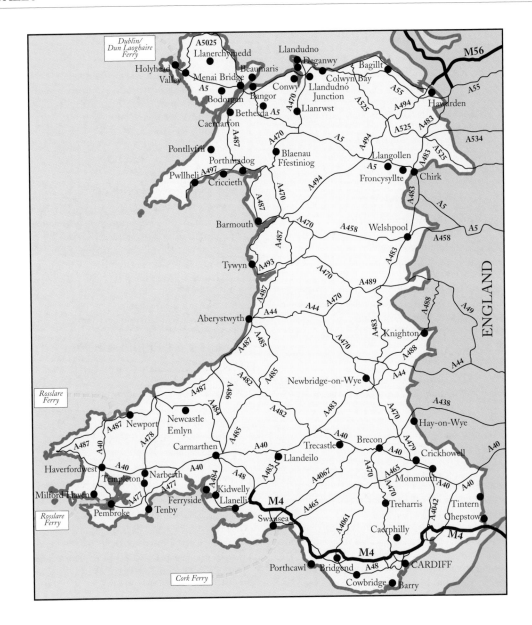

ABERYSTWYTH

The Furniture Cave
33 Cambrian St. SY23 1NZ. (P. David)
EST. 1975. Open 9-5, Sat. 10-5. *STOCK: General antiques,
Victorian and Edwardian, £30-£3,000; small items, 19th
C, £10-£500; maps.* LOC: First right off Terrace Rd., at
rail station end. SER: Restorations. PARK: Nearby. VAT:
Spec.
TEL: 01970 611234
E-MAIL: thecave@btconnect.com
WEBSITE: www.furniture-cave.co.uk

BANGOR

David Windsor Gallery
173 High St. LL57 1NU. (Mrs. E. Kendrick)
EST. 1970. FATG. Open 10-5. CL: Wed. *STOCK: Oils and
watercolours, 18th-20th C; maps, engravings, lithographs.*
SER: Restorations; framing; mounting. VAT: Stan/Spec.
TEL: 01248 364639
E-MAIL: windsorgallery@aol.com

BARMOUTH

Fronhouse Antiques
Jubilee Rd. LL42 1EE. (Jamie Howard)

EST. 1967. Open seven days 10-5. CL: Wed. and Sun. Dec to Mar. STOCK: *Nautical items, 19th C £5-£250; oil lamps, bric-a-brac and small furniture, £5-£200.* LOC: On corner of Church St. SER: Valuations; restorations (nautical items). SIZE: Small. PARK: Easy. FAIRS: Swinderby, Newark.
TEL: 01341 280649; HOME/FAX: same

BARRY

Fires 'n Fireplaces
99-100 High St. CF6 8DS. (A. Galsworthy)
Open 9-5.30. STOCK: *Antique and reproduction fireplaces and surrounds.*
TEL: 01446 744788
WEBSITE: www.firesnfireplaces.co.uk

BEAUMARIS (ANGLESEY)

Charltons Antiques
Little Lane. LL58 8DL. (R. Charlton)
EST. 2003. Open Mon.-Sat. 10-5., Sun. 11-3. STOCK: *General antiques, collectables.* SIZE: Large.
TEL: 01248 811377
E-MAIL: charltons@hotmail.com
WEBSITE: www.art4wales.com

The Clock Shop
46 Castle St. LL58 8BB.
EST. 1988. MBWCG. Open by appointment. STOCK: *Antique clock repairs, collectables, mahogany furniture.* SER: House clearances. SIZE: Small.
TEL: 01248 811482

M Jones ai fab Welsh Country Antiques
42a Castle St. LL58 8BB.
EST. 1979. Open Mon.-Sat. 10-4.30. STOCK: *Welsh country furniture, folk art and related decorative items.* LOC: On the main street. SIZE: Medium. PARK: Free outside.
TEL: 01248 810624; EVE - 01248 490009
WEBSITE: www.mjonesaifabantiques.co.uk

BETHESDA

A.E. Morris (Books)
40 High St. LL57 3AN.
EST. 1980. Open 10-5. STOCK: *Antiquarian and secondhand books.* SIZE: Medium. PARK: Easy.
TEL: 01248 602533

BODORGAN

Michael Webb Fine Art   LAPADA
Cefn-Llwyn, Llangristiolus. LL62 5DN.
EST. 1972. Open by appointment. STOCK: *Victorian oil paintings and watercolours.* SER: Valuations; restorations; framing. VAT: Spec. FAIRS: Tatton Park; Ruthim; Chester; Carmarthen; Anglesey; Arley Hall.
TEL: 01407 840336

BRECON

Brecon Antiques Centre
22a High St. LD3 7LA.
Open 10-5. STOCK: *General antiques and collectables.* SIZE: Units and cabinets. PARK: 200 yds.
TEL: 01874 623355; FAX: same
E-MAIL: pheulwen@aol.com

Hazel of Brecon & Silvertime
6 The Bulwark. LD3 7LB. (H. Hillman)
EST. 1969. Open 10-5.30. CL: Wed. STOCK: *Jewellery and silver 19th-20th C, £20-£10,000.* LOC: Main square, town centre. SER: Valuations; repairs; probate. SIZE: Medium. PARK: Easy.
TEL: 01874 625274 (24 hr. answering service)
E-MAIL: hazel@hazelofbrecon.co.uk

BRIDGEND

J. & A. Antiques
1 Prince Rd., Kenfig Hill. CF33 6ED. (Jennifer Lawson)
EST. 1990. Open 10-12.30 and 2-4.30, Sat. 10-12.30. CL: Wed. STOCK: *Furniture, china and clocks, 19th to early 20th C, £10-£800.* LOC: From A48 Pyle take B4281. SIZE: Small. PARK: Easy.
TEL: 01656 746681; HOME: 01656 744709

Nolton Antiques
66 Nolton St. CF31 3BP. (Gittins and Beynon)
EST. 1997. Open 10-4. CL: Wed. STOCK: *General antiques including Clarice Cliff, majolica, Victorian furniture, military and mining.* LOC: Off M4, junction 35. SER: Valuations; house clearance and probate valuations. SIZE: Large. PARK: Nearby.
TEL: 01656 667774; 07855 958461
WEBSITE: www.welsh-antiques.com

CAERWYS

Afonwen Craft & Antiques Centre
Afonwen. CH7 5UB. (Janet and Adrian Delolio)
Open 9.30-5.30, inc. Sun. CL Mon. STOCK: *General antiques and crafts.*
TEL: 01352 720965; FAX: 01352 720346
WEBSITE: www.afonwen.co.uk

CARDIFF

Cardiff Antiques Centre
10-12 Royal Arcade. CF10 1AE. (I. Roberts)
Open 10-5. STOCK: *General antiques, Victorian, £5-£1,000; collectables, 50s, 60s, 70s.* LOC: Nera Cardiff Castle. SER: Valuations; restorations (ceramics and furniture); buys at auction; prop. hire. SIZE: Large - 2 floors. PARK: Easy. FAIRS: Newark.
TEL: 029 20398891; MOBILE: 07891 080714
E-MAIL: info@cheapaschips.cc
WEBSITE: www.cheapaschips.cc

Cardiff Reclamation
Site 7 Tremorfa Industrial Estate, Rover Way. CF24 5SD. (Jeff and John Evans)
EST. 1990. Open 9-5, Sat. 9-1, Sun. 10-1. STOCK: *Architectural antiques, fireplaces, doors, wood flooring, stained glass, bathrooms, church fittings, flagstones, chimney pots, £10-£3,000.* SER: Restorations. SIZE: Large. PARK: Easy.
TEL: 02920 458995; FAX: same; MOBILE: 07855 038629
E-MAIL: j.evans02@btconnect.com

Jacobs Antique Centre
West Canal Wharf. CF10 5DB.
Open Thurs.-Sat. 9.30-5. STOCK: *General antiques and collectables.* LOC: 2 mins. from main rail and bus stations. SER: Valuations; restorations. SIZE: Large - 50 dealers. PARK: 100yds.
TEL: 02920 390939

Llanishen Antiques
26 Crwys Rd., Cathays. CF2 4NL. (Mrs J. Boalch)
Open 10.30-4.30. CL: Wed. except by appointment. STOCK: *Furniture, silver, china, glass, bric-a-brac.*
TEL: 02920 397244

Pumping Station Antiques
Penarth Rd. CF11 8TT.
Open 9.30-5.30. STOCK: *Victorian and decorative furniture, fireplaces and surrounds, militaria, ceramics, glass and general collectables.* SIZE: 35 dealers.
TEL: 02920 221085; FAX: 02920 232588
E-MAIL: info@the-pumpingstation.co.uk
WEBSITE: www.the-pumpingstation.co.uk

San Domenico Stringed Instruments
249 Cathedral Rd., Pontcanna. CF11 9PP. (H.W. Morgan)
EST. 1978. Open 10-4, Sat. 10-1. STOCK: *Fine violins, violas, cellos and bows, mainly 18th-19th C, £300-£20,000.* LOC: On Cathedral Rd. SER: Valuations; restorations; buys at auction. SIZE: Small. PARK: Easy. VAT: Stan/Spec. FAIRS: Mondomusica, Cremona, Italy.
TEL: 029 2023 5881; FAX: 029 2034 4510; HOME: 029 2077 7156
E-MAIL: HWM@san-domenico.co.uk
WEBSITE: www.san-domenico.co.uk

Ty-Llwyd Antiques
Lisvane Rd., Lisvane. CF14 0SF. (G.H. Rowsell)
EST. 1981. Open by appointment only. STOCK: *Longcase clocks, some period furniture.* LOC: North Cardiff, near Griffin public house. SER: Valuations; restorations (clocks). SIZE: Medium. PARK: Easy. FAIRS: Carmarthen; Motorcycle Museum.
TEL: 02920 754109; FAX: same; MOBILE: 07778 117624
E-MAIL: ghrowsell@supanet.com

CARMARTHEN

Audrey Bull
2 Jacksons Lane. SA31 1QD. (Jonathan and Jane Bull)
EST. 1945. Open 10-5. STOCK: *Period and Welsh country furniture, general antiques especially jewellery and silver, designer jewellery.* VAT: Spec.
TEL: 01267 222655; HOME: 01834 813425
E-MAIL: jonathan.bull2@btinternet.com

The Mount Antiques Centre
1 & 2 The Mount, Castle Hill. SA31 1JW. (R. Lickley)
EST. 1987. Open 10-5, Thu 10-4, Sun. 11-3 (summer only). STOCK: *Fine furniture including country, pine and oak, 18th-19th C; collectables; 19th-20th C fireplaces; blankets (Welsh); Oriental rugs; Ewenny, Claypits, Swansea and Llanelly pottery; Murano glass.* LOC: A40 near County Hall. SER: Valuations; restorations (furniture and china). International deliveries www.a2cdeliveries.com SIZE: Large. PARK: Easy. FAIRS: Towy - Cowbridge, Bristol; Cardiff.
TEL: 01267 220005; 07855 459572

CHEPSTOW

Foxgloves
20 St. Mary St. NP16 5EW. (Lesley Brain)
EST. 1994. Open 10ish-5. CL: Wed. STOCK: *Period and antique furniture; pictures, china and objets d'art.* LOC: Central. SER: Restorations. SIZE: Medium. PARK: Nearby.
TEL: 01291 622386

Intaglio
(John Harrison)
EST. 1995. CINOA. Open by appointment. STOCK: *Fine sculpture, marble and bronze 19th to early 20th C, £2,000-£20,000.* SER: Valuations; restorations; cleaning; conservation; buys at auction (bronze and marble sculpture). SIZE: Medium. PARK: Easy.
TEL: 01291 621476 / 01873 810036; FAX: 01291 621476
E-MAIL: intaglios@tiscali.co.uk

CHIRK

Seventh Heaven
Chirk Mill. LL14 5BU.
EST. 1971. Open 9-5, Sun. 10-4. STOCK: *Brass, iron and wooden beds including half-tester, four-poster and canopied, mainly 19th C.* LOC: B5070, below village, off A5 bypass. SIZE: Large. PARK: Easy. VAT: Stan.
TEL: 01691 777622; FAX: 01691 777313
E-MAIL: requests@seventh-heaven.co.uk
WEBSITE: www.seventh-heaven.co.uk

COLWYN BAY

North Wales Antiques - Colwyn Bay
58 Abergele Rd. LL29 7PP. (F. Robinson)
EST. 1958. Open 9-5. STOCK: *Shipping items, Victorian,*

early oak, mahogany and pine. LOC: On A55. SIZE: Large warehouse. PARK: Easy. VAT: Stan.
TEL: 01492 530521; EVENINGS: 01352 720253

CONWY

Lovejoy Antiques
10 Castle St. LL32 8AY.
EST. 1996. Open 8.30-4 inc. Sun. *STOCK: Antiques, collectables, jewellery, gold, silver and furniture .* LOC: Off the High St. SIZE: Small. PARK: Free outside.
TEL: 07756 484190

COWBRIDGE

Havard and Havard   LAPADA
59 Eastgate. CF71 7EL. (Philip and Christine Havard)
EST. 1992. Open 10.30-5. CL: Mon. and Wed. *STOCK: Mahogany and oak furniture especially Welsh country, £100-£10,000; metalware and samplers, £25-£1,000; all 18th-19th C.* **LOC: Main street, 500 yards after lights on right. SER: Valuations. SIZE: Small. PARK: Easy. VAT: Stan/Spec. FAIRS: Margam Park.**
TEL: 01446 775021
E-MAIL: info@havardandhavard.com
WEBSITE: www.havardandhavard.com

The Vale of Glamorgan Antiques Centre
Ebenezer Chapel, 48a Eastgate. CF71 7AB. (Malcolm Davies)
EST. 1984. Open 10-4. *STOCK: General antiques; 18th and 19th C furniture; longcase clocks; silver, antique jewellery; pottery and porcelain (English and Welsh). All pieces datelined.* LOC: Main street. SIZE: Large - 20 dealers. PARK: Nearby.
TEL: 01446 771190

CRICCIETH

Criccieth Gallery
London House, High St. LL52 0RN. (Mrs Anita Evens)
EST. 1972. Open 9-5.30. CL: Wed pm. Nov-Feb. *STOCK: General antiques, Staffordshire figures, china and porcelain, paintings and prints, clocks and watches (mainly pocket), small furniture, mainly 19th C, £5-£250+.* SER: Valuations; restorations (china, watch and clock repairs). SIZE: Small. PARK: Easy. FAIRS: Newark; Mona, Anglesey; Builth Wells.
TEL: 01766 522836

CRICKHOWELL

Gallop and Rivers Architectural Antiques
Ty-r-ash, Brecon Rd. NP8 1SF. (G. P. Gallop)
Open 9.30-5. *STOCK: Architectural items, paving, interior flooring, fireplaces, garden features.* LOC: A40 between Crickhowell and Brecon, 100 yds past the Manor Hotel. VAT: Stan.
TEL: 01873 811084; FAX: 01873 811084

E-MAIL: enquiries@gallopandrivers.co.uk
WEBSITE: www.gallopandrivers.co.uk

DEGANWY

Acorn Antiques
Castle Buildings. LL31 9EJ. (K.S. Bowers-Jones)
Open 10-5. *STOCK: Ceramics, glass, furniture, pictures, brass and copper, 19th C.* PARK: Opposite.
TEL: 01492 584083

ERBISTOCK

Simon Wingett Fine Art   LAPADA
The Garden House. LL13 0DL.
EST. 1910. Open by appointment. *STOCK: Paintings in oils and watercolours, sculpture.* LOC: 6 miles from Wrexham.
TEL: 01978 781149; FAX: 01978 781144; MOBILE: 07930 338688
E-MAIL: art@simonwingett.com
WEBSITE: www.simonwingett.com

FERRYSIDE

Tim Bowen Antiques   LAPADA
Ivy House. SA17 5SS. (Tim and Betsan Bowen)
EST. 2003. Resident. Open Fri. and Sat. or by appointment. *STOCK: Oak and country furniture, 1650-1900, £100-£20,000; spongeware and country pottery, 19th C, £20-£500; longcase clocks, 18th-19th C, £2,000-£7,000; folk art, 18th-19th C, £40-£3,000.* **LOC: Main road, near Three Rivers Hotel. SER: Valuations. SIZE: Medium. PARK: Easy. VAT: Stan/Spec. FAIRS: Carmarthen, Margam.**
TEL: 01267 267122; HOME: same; FAX: 01267 267045; MOBILE: 07967 728515
E-MAIL: info@timbowenantiques.co.uk
WEBSITE: www.timbowenantiques.co.uk

GLAN CONWY

Drew Pritchard Ltd
Llanrwst Rd. LL28 5TH. (A.T. Pritchard)
EST. 1987. SALVO. Open 9-5, Sat. 10-4. *STOCK: English decorative architectural antiques, to 1950s; antique stained glass.* SER: Valuations; restorations (stained and leaded glass, metal polishing). SIZE: Medium. PARK: Easy. FAIRS: Swinderby; Newark, SALVO; Cheshire and Staffordshire shows.
TEL: 01492 874004; FAX: 01492 874003; MOBILE: 07740 289099
E-MAIL: enquiries@drewpritchard.co.uk
WEBSITE: www.drewpritchard.co.uk

HAWARDEN

On the Air Ltd
The Vintage Technology Centre, The Highway. CH5 3DN. (Steve Harris)

EST. 1990. Open by appointment only. *STOCK: Vintage wireless, gramophones and telephones, £50-£500.* LOC: Near St. David's Park, Ewloe, opposite Crown & Liver public house. SER: Valuations; restorations (vintage wireless and gramophones). SIZE: Small. PARK: Rear of premises. FAIRS: National Vintage Communications, NEC.
TEL: 01244 530300; FAX: same
E-MAIL: info@vintageradio.co.uk
WEBSITE: www.vintageradio.co.uk

HAY-ON-WYE

Richard Booth's Bookshop Ltd
44 Lion St. HR3 5AA. (Elizabeth Haycox and Paul Greatbatch)
EST. 1974. Open 9-5.30, Sun. 11.30-5.30. *STOCK: Books, magazines, photographs, records, postcards, leather bindings.* LOC: Town centre. SIZE: Very large. PARK: Nearby.
TEL: 01497 820322; FAX: 01497 821150
WEBSITE: www.richardbooth.demon.co.uk

Hay Antique Market
6 Market St. HR3 5AF.
EST. 1990. Open 10-5, Sun. 11-5. *STOCK: Antiques and collectables.* LOC: By the Butter Market. SIZE: 17 units. PARK: Easy.
TEL: 01497 820175

Hay-on-Wye Bookbuyers
Hay Castle HR3 5AA. (Richard Booth)
EST. 1974. WBA. Open 10-5.30 inc. Sun. *STOCK: Books, magazines, photographs, prints, records, postcards, leather bindings; specialises in books on Native American culture, photography, film, art, architecture, humour and antiquarian.* LOC: Town centre. SIZE: Medium. PARK: Nearby.
TEL: 01497 820503
WEBSITE: www.richardbooth.demon.co.uk

Rose's Books
14 Broad St. HR3 5DB. (Maria Goddard)
EST. 1982. Resident. Open 7 days. *STOCK: Children's books, 1900-1960, £5-£25.* SIZE: Large.
TEL: 01497 820013; FAX: 01497 820031
E-MAIL: enquiry@rosesbooks.com
WEBSITE: www.rosesbooks.com

HOLYHEAD (ANGLESEY)

Ann Evans LAPADA
Carna Shop, Station Rd., Valley LL65 3HB.
EST. 1990. Open Thurs.-Sat. 10-4.30, other days by appointment. *STOCK: Welsh oak dressers and pottery; 18th-19th C cranberry glass, Staffordshire figures, silver and jewellery.* **LOC: Just off junction 3, A55, 100 yards from traffic lights, turn left towards Trearddur Bay.** **SER: Valuations. SIZE: Medium. PARK: Easy. VAT: Spec.**

TEL: **01407 741733; tel/FAX: 01407 740109; MOBILE: 07753 650376;**
E-MAIL: **annevans@btconnect.com**

Gwynfair Antiques
74 Market St. LL65 1UW. (Mrs A.D. McCann)
EST. 1984. Open Mon. and Fri.10-4.30, Wed. 10-1. *STOCK: Jewellery £10-£1,000, china, ornaments, £5-£250, furniture, £20-£1,000; all 1860-1950s.* SER: Valuations. SIZE: Small. PARK: Loading outside shop, parking 100 yds. FAIRS: Mona showground.
TEL: 01407 763740; HOME: same
E-MAIL: anwenholyhead@aol.com

KIDWELLY

WelshAntiques.com BADA
Castle Mill. SA17 4UU. (Richard Bebb)
EST. 1971. Open Tues.-Sat. 10-5 by appointment. *STOCK: Welsh oak furniture and folk art; Welsh dressers, cupboards, clocks, pottery and treen.* **LOC: Leave bypass (A484), into centre of village, turn opposite war memorial, turn right by Boot and Shoe public house. SER: Valuations; lectures; research; consultancy. SIZE: Large. PARK: Own. VAT: Stan/Spec.**
TEL: **01554 890534**
E-MAIL: **info@welshantiques.com**
WEBSITE: **www.welshantiques.com**

WelshFurniture.com
31 Bridge St. SA17 4UU. (Richard Bebb and S. Bebb)
EST. 1971. Open by appointment. LOC: Leave bypass (A484), into centre of village, castle side of bridge. SER: Consultancy, publishing. PARK: Opposite shop. VAT: Stan/Spec.
TEL: 01554 890328
E-MAIL: info@welshfurniture.com
WEBSITE: www.welshfurniture.com

KNIGHTON

Offa's Dyke Antique Centre
4 High St. LD7 1AT. (I. Watkins)
EST. 1985. Open 10-1 and 2-5. *STOCK: 18th - 19th C pottery and porcelain, 19th - 20th C glass, bijouterie, British paintings and drawings, small furniture, £5-£1,000.* LOC: Near town clock. SIZE: Medium - 16 dealers. PARK: Easy.
TEL: 01547 528635; EVENINGS: 01547 528940

Islwyn Watkins
4 High St. LD7 1AT.
EST. 1978. Open 10-1 and 2-5. *STOCK: Pottery including studio, 18th-20th C, £25-£1,000; country and domestic bygones, treen, 18th-20th C, £5-£200; small country furniture, 18th-19th C, £20-£600. NOT STOCKED: Jewellery, silver, militaria.* LOC: By town clock. SER: Valuations. SIZE: Small. PARK: Easy.
TEL: 01547 520145; HOME: 01547 528940

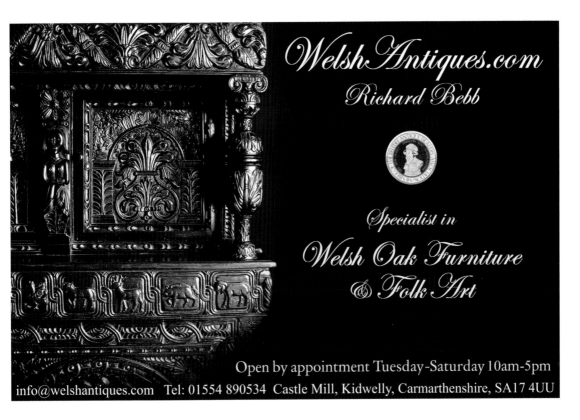
LLANDEILO

Jim and Pat Ash
The Warehouse, 5 Station Rd. SA19 6NG.
EST. 1977. Open 10.30-5, other times by appointment.
STOCK: *Victorian and antique furniture, Welsh country, oak, mahogany, walnut.* LOC: 50yds. off A40. SIZE: Large.
PARK: Easy. VAT: Stan/Margin/Export.
TEL: 01558 823726/822130; FAX: same

The Works Antiques Centre
Station Rd. SA19 6NH. (Steve Watts and Jon Storey)
EST. 2000. Open Tues.-Sat. 10-6, Sun. 10-5. STOCK: *Period furniture including country oak and Welsh country; china, treen, books, jewellery, architectural salvage, clocks, brass and copper, dolls and toys, musical instruments, lighting, textiles and clothing.* LOC: On outskirts of village, near A40 roundabout. SER: Restorations (furniture repair and renovation, picture framing and upholstery). SIZE: Large. PARK: Easy.
TEL: 01558 823964
E-MAIL: theworks@storeyj.clara.co.uk
WEBSITE: www.works-antiques.co.uk

LLANDUDNO

The Antique Shop
24 Vaughan St. LL30 1AH. (C.G. Lee)
EST. 1938. Open 10-5. STOCK: *Jewellery, silver, porcelain,*

glass, ivories, metalware, from 1700; period furniture, shipping goods. LOC: Near promenade. SIZE: Medium. PARK: Easy.
TEL: 01492 875575

LLANDUDNO JUNCTION

Collinge Antiques
Old Fyffes Warehouse, Conwy Rd. LL31 9LU. (Nicky Collinge)
EST. 1978. Open seven days. *STOCK: General antiques including Welsh dressers, dining, drawing and bedroom furniture, clocks, porcelain and pottery, silver, copper and brass, paintings, prints, glass and collectables, mainly Victorian and Edwardian.* LOC: Just off A55, Deganwy exit (A546). SER: Valuations; restorations including French polishing; buys at auction. SIZE: Large. PARK: Easy. VAT: Stan/Spec.
TEL: 01492 580022; FAX: same
E-MAIL: sales@collinge-antiques.co.uk
WEBSITE: www.collinge-antiques.co.uk

The Country Seat
29-31 Conwy Rd. LL31 9LU. (Steve and Helen Roberts)
EST. 1994. Open 11-4.30, Sat. 10-5. CL Mon. & Wed. *STOCK: Old and interesting items including paintings, pottery and porcelain, jewellery, furniture, linen, ephemera and bric-a-brac; decorative arts, 19th-20th C.* LOC: Just off A55. SIZE: Small. PARK: Easy. FAIRS: Newark; Birmingham Rag; Chester Northgate.
TEL: 01492 573256
E-MAIL: info@thecountryseat.co.uk
WEBSITE: www.thecountryseat.co.uk

LLANERCHYMEDD (ANGLESEY)

Two Dragons Oriental Antiques
8 High St. LL71 8EA. (Tony Andrew)
EST. 1976. Open by appointment. *STOCK: Chinese country furniture, signed prints by C.F. Tunnicliffe.* SIZE: Large + warehouse. PARK: Easy. FAIRS: Newark.
TEL: 01248 470204/470100; FAX: 01248 470040;
MOBILE: 07811 101290

LLANFAIRFECHAN

Alchemy Antiques
Waverley, Station Rd. LL33 0AL.
Open 10.30-4.30. CL: Weds. *STOCK: Small collectables, postcards, jewellery, handbags, ties, toy cars, teapots.* PARK: On street or in car park nearby.
TEL: 01248 680010; MOBILE: 07715 554709
WEBSITE: www.llanfairfechan-antiques.com

LLANGOLLEN

Passers Buy (Marie Evans)
Oak St/Chapel St. LL20 8NR. (Mrs M. Evans)
EST. 1970. Open 11-5 always on Tues., Fri. and Sat, often on Mon., Wed. and Thurs., prior telephone call

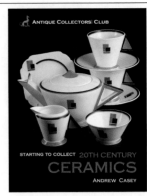

This book is for any collector interested in 20th century ceramics, whether a collector who concentrates on one factory, on a single designer, such as Clarice Cliff, or on a type of item, such as toast racks, egg cups or preserve pots. Fifty British manufacturers are included, as well as twenty-two of the most interesting and important companies from Europe, Scandinavia and the USA, as well as many factories that have never before been discussed. Written by the award-winning author Andrew Casey, an acknowledged expert on twentieth-century ceramics, this book covers the diverse range of pottery produced during the twentieth century, aiming to provide a starting point for all those collectors.

240 x 195 mm. 224 pp 295 col., 5 b.&w.
£14.95 Hardback

advisable, Sun. by appointment. *STOCK: Furniture, Staffordshire figures, Gaudy Welsh, fairings, fenders, rugs, maps and pictures.* LOC: Just off A5. Junction of Chapel St. and Oak St. SIZE: Medium. PARK: Easy.
TEL: 01978 860861/757385

LLANIDLOES

Arcadia Antiques
6, Great Oak St. SY18 6BN. (R.A. and L. P. Hallett)
EST. 2007. Open 10-5. CL: Mon. *STOCK: General antiques.* LOC: Town centre. SIZE: Medium. PARK: On street.
TEL: 01686 412628
E-MAIL: raharc@supanet.com

LLANRWST

Carrington House
26 Ancaster Sq. LL26 0LD. (Richard Newstead)
EST. 1975. Open 10-5. CL: Mon. *STOCK: 19th C pine, £200-£1,000; oak and mahogany, 20th-21st C, £100-£2,000.* LOC: From A55 take A470, 10 miles towards Betws-y-Coed. SIZE: Medium. PARK: Easy.
TEL: 01492 642500; FAX: same; HOME: 01492 641279
E-MAIL: sales@carringtonhouse.co.uk

Snowdonia Antiques
LL26 0EP. (J. Collins)
EST. 1961. Open 9-5.30, Sun. by appointment. *STOCK:*

Period furniture especially longcase clocks. LOC: Turn off A5 just before Betws-y-Coed on to A496 for 4 miles. SER: Restorations (furniture); repairs (grandfather clocks). SIZE: Medium. PARK: Easy. TEL: 01492 640789.

MENAI BRIDGE (ANGLESEY)

Peter Wain
44 High St. LL59 5EF. (Peter and Susan Wain) EST. 1980. Open by appointment. *STOCK: Chinese ceramics and works of art, over 1,000 years, £100-£10,000.* SER: Valuations. SIZE: Small. PARK: Opposite. VAT: Spec.
TEL: 01407 710077; FAX: 01407 710294; MOBILE: 07860 302945
E-MAIL: peterwain@supanet.com

MILFORD HAVEN

Milford Haven Antiques
Robert St. SA73 2JQ.
EST. 1968. Open 10-5. *STOCK: General antiques.*
TEL: 01646 692152

MONMOUTH

Frost Antiques & Pine
8 Priory St. NP25 3BR. (Nicholas Frost) EST. 1960. GMC. Resident. Open 9-5, Sun. and other times by appointment. *STOCK: Pine furniture and Staffordshire pottery, 19th C, £100-£1,500.* LOC: When entering town from east - first shop on left. SER: Valuations; restorations (furniture); buys at auction (Victorian furniture and ceramics). SIZE: Small. PARK: Easy.
TEL: 01600 716687
WEBSITE: www.frostantiques.com

NARBERTH

Malt House Antiques
Back Lane. SA67 7AR. (P. Griffiths) EST. 1995. Open 10-5.30. *STOCK: Country furniture, 18th-20th C, £5-£5,000; pine, oak, Persian carpets, prints and paintings, collectables and china.* LOC: Village centre. SIZE: Large. PARK: Easy.
TEL: 01834 860303

NEWBRIDGE-ON-WYE

Allam Antiques
Old Village Hall. LD1 6HL. (Paul Allam) EST. 1985. Open Sat. 10-5. *STOCK: Furniture, 1700-1930, £50-£3,000.* LOC: A470. SER: Valuations; restorations. SIZE: Medium. PARK: Easy.
TEL: 01597 860455

NEWPORT

The Carningli Centre
East St. SA42 0SY. (Ann Gent and Graham Coles) EST. 1994. Open 10-5.30, Sun. by appointment. *STOCK: Furniture, 17th-19th C, £50-£5,000; railwayana, nautical items, country collectables including oil lamps and tools, £1-£500; secondhand books, fine art gallery.* LOC: A487, town centre. SER: Valuations; restorations (furniture); polishing; turning; buys at auction (railwayana). SIZE: Medium. PARK: Free in Long St. VAT: Spec.
TEL: 01239 820724
WEBSITE: www.carningli.co.uk

PEMBROKE

Pembroke Antiques Centre
Wesley Chapel, Main St. SA71 4DE. (Michael Blake) EST. 1986. Open 10-5. *STOCK: Pine, oak, mahogany and shipping furniture; china, rugs, paintings, Art Deco enamel signs, kitchenalia, pottery, toys, curios, collectables, postcards, advertising and decorative items.* LOC: Opposite end of Main St. to the castle. SER: Valuations; restorations; delivery. SIZE: Large. PARK: Free.
TEL: 01646 687017

PORTHMADOG

Huw Williams Antiques
Madoc St. LL49 9LR.
EST. 1993. Open 10-5, Mon. 12-5. CL: Wed. *STOCK: Weapons, 18th-19th C, £50-£5,000; country furniture, 18th-19th C, £100-£1,000; general antiques, 19th-20th C, to £300.* LOC: Opposite entrance to main car park. SIZE: Small. PARK: Opposite. FAIRS: Stockport Arms; International Arms, Motorcycle Museum, Birmingham; Big Brum (Rag Market); London Arms, Lillie Road.
TEL: 01766 514741; MOBILE: 07785 747561
E-MAIL: huwantiques@aol.com
WEBSITE: www.antiquegunswales.co.uk

PWLLHELI

Rodney Adams Antiques
Hall Place, Old Town Hall, Penlan St. LL53 5DH. (R. and C. Adams)
EST. 1965. Resident. Open 9-5. CL: Sun. except by appointment. *STOCK: Longcase clocks, country oak and period furniture.* SER: Delivery; export. PARK: At rear. VAT: Stan/Spec.
TEL: 01758 613173; EVENINGS: 01758 614337

SWANSEA

John Carpenter Musical Instruments
671a Middle Rd., Ravenhill. SA14 7HA. (John and Caroline Carpenter)
EST. 1973. Resident. Tues. 10-5.30, Wed.-Fri. 10-5, Sat. 10-1 or by appointment. *STOCK: Musical instruments.* SER:

Repairs (musical instruments). PARK: Own. VAT: Stan.
TEL: 01792 589211
E-MAIL: sales@johncarpenterviolins.co.uk
WEBSITE: www.johncarpenterviolins.co.uk

Dylan's Bookstore
Salubrious House, 23 King Edward Rd. SA3 4LL.
(J.M. Towns)
EST. 1971. ABA. PBFA. Open 10-5, prior telephone call
advisable. STOCK: *Antiquarian books on Welsh history and
topography, Anglo/Welsh literature and general books.* FAIRS:
London; Boston; Los Angeles; San Francisco.
TEL: 01792 655255; FAX: same; MOBILE: 07850 759199
E-MAIL: jefftowns@dylans.com
WEBSITE: www.dylans.com

Magpie Antiques
57 St. Helens Rd. SA1 4BH. (H. Hallesy)
EST. 1984. Open 10-5. Tues. and Fri. Other days by
appointment. STOCK: *Ceramics including Swansea and
other Welsh potteries; oak, pine and mahogany furniture;
small antiques; registered firearms dealer, antique guns.* LOC:
Five minutes from Guildhall, Crown Court. SER:
Valuations; restorations (furniture and ceramics). PARK:
Opposite. FAIRS: Carmarthen Antiques Fair.
TEL: 01792 648722
E-MAIL: helen@hallesy.wanadoo.co.uk

TENBY

Audrey Bull
15 Upper Frog St. SA70 7DJ.
EST. 1945. Open 9.30-5. STOCK: *Period and Welsh country
furniture, paintings, general antiques especially jewellery and
silver; secondhand and designer jewellery.* VAT: Spec.
TEL: 01834 843114; WORKSHOP: 01834 871873;
HOME: 01834 813425
E-MAIL: jonathan.bull2@btinternet.com

TINTERN

Tintern Antiques
The Old Bakehouse. NP6 6SE. (Dawn Floyd)
Open 9.30-5.30. STOCK: *Antique jewellery and general
antiques.*
TEL: 01291 689705

TRECASTLE

Trecastle Antiques Centre
The Old School. LD3 8YA. (A. Perry)
EST. 1980. Open 10-5 including Sun. STOCK: *General
antiques, £5-£1,500.* LOC: A40. SER: Valuations;
restorations. SIZE: Large. PARK: Easy. FAIRS: Newark,
Shepton Mallet.
TEL: 01874 638007
WEBSITE: www.trecastleantiques.co.uk

TREHARRIS

Treharris Antiques & Collectables
18 Perrott St. CF46 5ER. (Mrs Janet Barker)
EST. 1974. Open 9.30-5. STOCK: *Local mining memorablia
– lamp checks and miners' lamps, twist boxes; tokens, English
coins, banknotes; medals, military and civil badges; local
maps, history books and artefacts; general collectors' items;
swords, bayonets and guns.* LOC: Opposite police station.
SER: Valuation and indentification (coins and
antiquities). SIZE: Medium. PARK: Easy.
TEL: 01443 413081; HOME: same

TYWYN

Welsh Art
(Miles Wynn Cato)
EST. 1989. Open by appointment (also in London).
STOCK: *Welsh paintings, 1550-1950; Welsh portraits of all
periods and historical Welsh material.* SER: Consultancy
(Welsh art).
TEL: 020 7259 0306 and 01654 711715; MOBILE:
07766 460127
E-MAIL: wynncato@welshart.co.uk
WEBSITE: www.welshart.co.uk

WELSHPOOL

F.E. Anderson and Son   LAPADA
5 High St. SY21 7JF. (I. Anderson)
EST. 1842. Open 9-5. STOCK: *Furniture, 17th-19th C;
mirrors, paintings and decorative items.* SIZE: **3 large
showrooms.** VAT: Margin. FAIRS: Olympia; LAPADA.
TEL: **01938 553340;** HOME: **01938 590509;** FAX: **01938
555998;** MOBILE: **07773 795931**
E-MAIL: **antiques@feanderson.fsnet.co.uk**

Rowles Fine Art   BADA LAPADA
**The Old Brewery, Brook St. SY21 7LF. (Mark and
Glenn Rowles)**
EST. 1978. CINOA. Open 9.30-5.30, Sat. 9.30-2, other
times by appointment. STOCK: *Victorian paintings and
watercolours, some contemporary; small furniture.* SER:
Valuations; restorations (paintings). SIZE: **Large.**
PARK: **Own.** FAIRS: **NEC; LAPADA; Olympia (June);
Chester; Harrogate.**
TEL: **01938 558811;** FAX: **01938 558822;** MOBILE:
07836 348688; 07802 303506
E-MAIL: **enquiries@rowlesfineart.co.uk**
WEBSITE: **www.rowlesfineart.co.uk**

WREXHAM

Bryn-y-grog Antiques Emporium
Marchwiel LL13 0SR. (W. Price)
Open 10-5. STOCK: *General antiques and collectables.* LOC:
A525 Wrexham to Whitchurch road. SIZE: Large - 30
dealers. PARK: Own.
TEL: 01978 355555

Index of
Packers and Shippers:
Exporters of Antiques (Containers)

LONDON

Anglo Pacific Fine Art Division LAPADA
5 Willen Field Rd., NW10 7BQ.
Specialist antique and fine art packers and shippers serving worldwide destinations by land, sea or air. Free estimates and advice. Courier services available.
TEL: **020 8838 8008**; FAX: **020 8453 0225**
E-MAIL: **antiques@anglopacific.co.uk**

Art Logistics Ltd
Unit 1, Victoria Industrial Estate, Victoria Rd. W3 6UU.
Fine art packing, freight forwarding.
TEL: 020 8993 8811; FAX: 020 8993 8833
E-MAIL: mail@artlogistics.co.uk

BBF Shipping Ltd
12 Ashmead Business Centre, North Crescent, Cody Rd. E16 4TG.
Fine art packers, worldwide shippers by sea, air and road.
TEL: 020 7511 6107; FAX: 020 7511 6109
E-MAIL: bbfshipping@aol.com

Robert Boys & AR.GS International LAPADA
Transport
Unit H, OCC Estate, 105 Eade Rd. N4 1TJ *Worldwide shipping by air, sea and road cargo. Specialists in the Far East. Road freight Italy. Fine art and antiques packers and shippers.*
TEL: 020 8800 3500/1777; FAX: 020 8800 3501
E-MAIL: info@robertboysshipping.co.uk
WEBSITE: www.robertboysshipping.com

Cadogan Tate Fine Art Logistics Ltd   LAPADA
6-12 Ponton Rd. SW8 5BA.
Specialist in packing and shipping antiques and works of art worldwide.
TEL: 020 7819 6600
E-MAIL: fineart@cadogantate.com
WEBSITE: www.cadogantate.com

Davies Turner Worldwide Movers Ltd
London Headquarters : 49 Wates Way, Mitcham.
CR4 4HR.
Fine art and antiques packers and shippers. Courier and finder service. Full container L.C.L. and groupage service worldwide.
TEL: 020 7622 4393; FAX: 020 7720 3897
E-MAIL: antiques@daviesturner.co.uk

Focus Packing Services Ltd
37-39 Peckham Rd. SE5 8UH.
Specialist packers of antiques and works of art. Premises in Portobello Rd. for on-the-spot quotations; drop-off service available.
TEL: 020 7703 4715; FAX: same
E-MAIL: focuspacking@aol.com

Gander and White Shipping Ltd   LAPADA
Unit 1 St Martin's Way, Wimbledon, London. SW17 0JH.

Specialist packers and shippers of antiques and works of art. Offices in Paris, New York and Palm Beach.
TEL: 020 8971 7171; FAX: 020 8946 8062
E-MAIL: uk.info@ganderandwhite.com
WEBSITE: www.ganderandwhite.com

Hedleys Humpers Ltd   LAPADA
3 St Leonard's Rd., North Acton. NW10 6SX.
IATA. BAR (overseas group). RMA. *Weekly collection services in Europe for consolidation and onward shipment worldwide. Offices in Paris, Avignon and New York.*
TEL: 020 8965 8733; FAX: 020 8965 0249
E-MAIL: gasb@hedleyshumpers.com
WEBSITE: www.hedleyshumpers.com

Kuwahara Ltd   LAPADA
6 McNicol Drive, NW10 7AW.
Specialist packers and shippers of antiques and works of art. Regular groupage service to Japan.
TEL: 020 8963 1100; FAX: 020 8963 0100
E-MAIL: info@kuwahara.co.uk
WEBSITE: www.kuwahara.co.uk

Lockson Services Ltd
See entry under Essex.

Stephen Morris Shipping plc   LAPADA
Unit 4, Brent Trading Estate, 390 North Circular Rd. NW10 0JF.

Specialist packers and shippers of antiques and fine art worldwide. Weekly European and Scandinavian road services.
TEL: 020 8830 1919; FAX: 020 8830 1999
E-MAIL: **enquiries@shipsms.co.uk**
WEBSITE: **www.shipsms.co.uk**

Nelson Shipping
Unit C3, Six Bridges Trading Estate, Marlborough Grove. SE1 5JT.
Fine art expert export and packing service.
TEL: 020 7394 7770; FAX: 020 7394 7707

Robinsons International   LAPADA
The Gateway, Priestley Way, Staples Corner. NW2 7AJ.
Specialist packers and shippers of antiques and fine art worldwide. Weekly consolidated container service to America. Established over 100 years.
TEL: 020 8208 8484; FAX: 020 8208 8488
WEBSITE: **www.robinsons-intl.com/antiques**

T. Rogers and Co. Ltd
PO Box No. 8, 1A Broughton St. SW8 3QL.
Specialists in storage, packing, removal, shipping and forwarding antiques and works of art. Insurance.
TEL: 020 7622 9151; FAX: 020 7627 3318
E-MAIL: trogersco@aol.com

BERKSHIRE

PODS Cargo Ltd   LAPADA
PODS House, Colndale Road, Colnbrook. Sl3 0HQ.
Packers and shippers.
TEL: 020 8797 8888/0800 731 1747; FAX: 020 8797 8787
E-MAIL: **info@cargobookers.com**
WEBSITE: **www.cargobookers.co.uk**

BUCKINGHAMSHIRE

Clark's of Amersham
Higham Mead, Chesham. HP5 2AH.
Removals and storage, domestic and commercial; export packing and shipping – worldwide door to door.
TEL: 01494 774186; FAX: 01494 774196
E-MAIL: michael@bluelorry.com
WEBSITE: www.bluelorry.com

CHESHIRE

The Rocking Chair Antiques
Unit 3, St. Peters Way, Warrington. WA2 7BT.
Exporters and packers.
TEL: 01925 652409; FAX: same; MOBILE: 07774 492891
E-MAIL: rockingmick@aol.com
WEBSITE: www.rockingchairantiques.co.uk

DERBYSHIRE

Lichfield Shipping UK Ltd.
Unit 7, Belfont Trading Estate, Mucklowsbridge
Halesowen. B62 8DR.
Specialist shippers of fine antiques; crating, transport and packing.
TEL: 01384 878589; MOBILE: 07870 592652
E-MAIL: sales@lichfieldshipping.com
WEBSITE: www.lichfieldshipping.com

DEVON

Barnstaple Removal
14/15 Meadow Way, Treebeech Rural Enterprise Park,
Gunn, Barnstaple. EX32 7NZ.
Overseas freight and shipping, full or part loads, worldwide door to door. Export packing and documentation. Regular European services. Storage facilities.
TEL: 01271 831164; FAX: 01271 831165
E-MAIL: sales@Barnstapleremovals.com
WEBSITE: www.Barnstapleremovals.co.uk

Bishop's Blatchpack
Kestrel Way, Sowton Industrial Estate, Exeter. EX2 7PA.
International fine art packers and shippers.
TEL: 01392 202040; FAX: 01392 201251
E-MAIL: blatchpack@bishopsmove.com

DORSET

Alan Franklin Transport Ltd   LAPADA
26 Blackmoor Rd., Ebblake Industrial Estate,
Verwood. BH31 6BB.
Worldwide container packing and shipping. Weekly door-to-door European service.
TEL: 01202 826539; FAX: 01202 827337;
E-MAIL: enquiries@afteurope.co.uk
WEBSITE: www.alanfranklintransport.co.uk

Belgian office: **De Klerckstraat 41, B8300, Knokke.**
TEL: **00 32 50 623 579;** FAX: **00 32 50 620 747.**
Paris office: **2 Rue Etienne Dolet, 93400 St. Ouen, Paris.**
TEL: **00 33 1 4011 5000;** FAX: **00 33 1 4011 4821.**
South of France office: **Quartier La Tour de Sabran, 84440 Robion (Vaucluse).** TEL: **00 33 4 90 76 4900;** FAX: **00 33 4 9076 4902.**

ESSEX

Geo. Copsey and Co. Ltd
178 Crow Lane, Romford. RM7 0ES.
Worldwide packers and shippers.
TEL: Romford 01708 724213,
London 020 8592 1003
E-MAIL: shipping@copsey.org.uk
WEBSITE: www.copsey.org.uk

Lockson Services Ltd   LAPADA
Unit 1, Heath Park Industrial Estate, Freshwater Rd.,
Chadwell Heath. RM8 1RX.
BIFA. *Specialist packers and shippers of fine art and
antiques by air, sea and road to the USA, Japan, Far East,
Canada and other worldwide destinations. A complete
personalised service. At Olympia, Newark and Ardingly
fairs. Shipping to all major US fairs. Secure storage.*
TEL: 020 8597 2889; FAX: 020 8597 5265
E-MAIL: **shipping@lockson.co.uk**
WEBSITE: **www.lockson.co.uk**

GLOUCESTERSHIRE

The Removal Company - Loveday & Loveday
2 Wilkinson Rd., Cirencester. GL7 1YT.
Shipping and packing.
TEL: 01285 651505
E-MAIL: cirencester@int-moving.com
WEBSITE: www.int-moving.com

Robinsons International   LAPADA
Aldermoor Way, Longwell Green, Bristol. BS30 7DA.
*Specialist packers and shippers of antiques and fine art
worldwide. Weekly consolidated container service to
America. Established over 100 years.*
TEL: **0117 980 5858**; FAX: **0117 980 5830**
WEBSITE: **www.robinsons-intl.com/antiques**

The Shipping Company Ltd
Bourton Industrial Park, Bourton-on-the-Water. GL54 2HQ.
*Export packers and shippers specialising in the antique, fine
art and interior design markets worldwide. Single,
consolidated and full container shipments by air and sea. All
risks insurance offered.*
TEL: 01451 822451; FAX: 01451 810985
WEBSITE: www.theshippingcompanyltd.com

HAMPSHIRE

Robinsons International   LAPADA
**Atlantic House Oakley Rd., Shirley, Southampton.
SO16 4LL.**
*Specialist packers and shippers of antiques and fine art
worldwide. Weekly consolidated container service to
America. Established over 100 years.*
TEL: **02380 515111**; FAX: **02380 515112**
WEBSITE: **www.robinsons-intl.com/antiques**

KENT

Sutton Valence Antiques
15-17 North St., Sutton Valence. ME17 3AP.
*Antique and furniture shipping. Container packing and
shipping. Facilities for 20ft. and 40ft. containers, all
documentation. Worldwide service.*
TEL: 01622 843333; FAX: 01622 843499
E-MAIL: svantiques@surfree.co.uk
WEBSITE: www.svantiques.co.uk

LANCASHIRE

Robinsons International   LAPADA
Unit 13, Moss Lane Industrial Estate, Whitfield,
Manchester. M45 8FJ.
*Specialist packers and shippers of antiques and fine art
worldwide. Weekly consolidated container service to
America. Established over 100 years.*
TEL: **0161 766 8414**; FAX: **0161 767 9057**
WEBSITE: **www.robinsons-intl.com/antiques**

MIDDLESEX

Air-Sea Packing Group Ltd   LAPADA
**Air-Sea House, Third Cross Rd., Twickenham. TW2
5EB.**
ASID; BIFA *Specialist Packers & Shippers of Antiques,
with our own offices and warehouses in New York; Los
Angeles and Paris.*
TEL: **020 8893 3303**; FAX: **020 8893 3068**;
E-MAIL: **Lloyd.Brammer@airseapacking.com**
WEBSITE: **www.airseapacking.com**

New York: Tel + 1 718 937 6800 / Fax +1 718 937 9646,
Los Angeles: Tel + 1 310 632 4800 / Fax +1 310 632 5800
Paris: Tel + 33 1 48468142 / Fax +33 1 48460333.

Crown Worldwide Ltd.
19 Stonefield Way, South Ruislip. HA4 0BJ.
*Offices worldwide. Corporate and household relocation; fine
art management; specialist packing, casing and storage and
warehouse facilities.*
TEL: 020 8839 8000; FAX: 020 8839 8041
E-MAIL: uk@crownfineart.com
WEBSITE: www.crownfineart.com

Nippon Express (UK) Ltd
Heathrow 360, 2 Millington Rd., Hayes. UB3 4AZ.
BIFA, RITA, UKWA, BAR. *International import, export,
relocation. Specialists in fine art, antiques, exhibitions,
logistics, scm, warehousing and transport.*
TEL: 020 8737 4240 Commercial (Export); FAX: 020 873
E-MAIL: martyns@neuk.co.uk
WEBSITE: www.express.net

PDQ-Art Move   LAPADA
Unit 4, Court 1, Challenge Rd., Ashford, TW15 1AX.
CINOA. GTA. IATA. *Fine art air freight packers and
shippers, including firearms.*
TEL: **01784 243695**; FAX: **01784 242237**
E-MAIL: **artmove@pdq.uk.com**
WEBSITE: **www.pdg.uk.com**

Seabourne Mailpack Worldwide Ltd   LAPADA
Unit 13, Saxon Way Trading Estate, Moor Lane, West
Drayton. UB7 0LW.
Packers and shippers
TEL: **020 8897 3888**; FAX: **020 8897 3898**
E-MAIL: **info@seabournemailpack.com**
WEBSITE: **www.seabourne.co.uk**

Williams & Hill Forwarding Ltd LAPADA
Westgate 2, Avia Park Staines Rd., Bedfont. TW14
8RS.
BIFA. *Exporters and shippers. Fine art packers.*
TEL: 01784 424884; FAX: 01784 424889
E-MAIL: info@williamsandhill.co.uk
WEBSITE: www.williamsandhill.co.uk

OXFORDSHIRE

Cotswold Carriers
Unit 2, The Walk, Hook Norton Rd., Chipping
Norton. OX7 5TG.
RHA, Guild of Removers. *Removals, storage, shipping,*
door-to-door Continental deliveries. Specialists to the
antique trade, UK and Continental.
TEL: 01608 730500; FAX: 01608 730600
E-MAIL: bill@cotswold-carriers.com
WEBSITE: www.cotswoldcarriers.com

Robinsons International LAPADA
Nuffield Way, Abingdon. OX14 1TN.
Specialist packers and shippers of antiques and fine art
worldwide. Weekly consolidated container service to
America. Established over 100 years.
TEL: 01235 552255; FAX: 01235 553573
WEBSITE: www.robinsons-intl.com/antiques

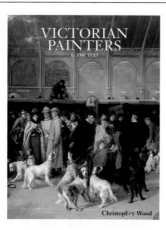

Containing over 11,000 entries, this is the only Dictionary of
English art to include comprehensive bibliographies on
individual artists. In addition to those on artists who have not
featured before, many of the existing entries have been revised
and updated. In the case of the giants of Victorian painting,
the entries take the form of short, analytical essays. Every
attempt has been made to list all artists recorded during the
period 1837-1901. An invaluable feature of this volume is the
lengthy and comprehensive general bibliography, also
extensively revised, and this, together with the individual
entries, makes the *Dictionary* an essential research tool and
the undisputed reference on the art of the Victorian era.

279 x 216 mm. 596 pp. **£35.00 Hardback**

SOMERSET

Mark Chudley Ltd
Unit 10, Ilton Business Park, Ilton. TA19 9DU.
International shipping.
TEL: 01460 55655; FAX: 01460 55770
WEBSITE: www.markchudley.com

A.J. Williams (Shipping) LAPADA
Unit 32, Fourth Avenue, Westfield Trading Estate,
Midsomer Norton, Radstack. BA3 4XE.
Packing and shipping of antiques and fine art. Courier
service.
TEL: 01761 413976; FAX: 01761 410868
E-MAIL: ajw_4@hotmail.com

STAFFORDSHIRE

Acorn G.D.S Ltd
183 Queen's Rd., Penkhull, Stoke-on-Trent. ST4 7LF.
RHA. *Container packing and export documentation.*
Freight forwarding; UK furniture transport and storage.
TEL: 01782 845051
E-MAIL: acorn@acorn-freight.co.uk
WEBSITE: www.acorn-freight.co.uk

SURREY

W. Ede's (UK) Ltd
The Ede's Business Park, Restmor Way, Wallington.
SM6 7AH.
Packing and shipping, complete documentation and removals
service, container packing.
TEL: 020 8773 6700; FAX: 020 8773 9011
E-MAIL: sales@edes-removals.co.uk
WEBSITE: www.edes.com

Traders Delivery Service
105 King's Rd., Long Ditton, Surbiton. KT6 5JE.
Removals and general carriers. Tailift service.
TEL: 020 8398 3681

SUSSEX EAST

Neil Curl Transport
Unit 2, Foords Farm, Foord Lane, Vines Cross,
Heathfield. TN21 9EX.
Containerised packing and shipping service for the antiques
trade.
TEL: 01892 852672; MOBILE: 07803 603507
E-MAIL: neilcurl-transport@freenet.co.uk

SUSSEX WEST

Gander and White Shipping Ltd LAPADA
Newpound, Wisborough Green, Billinghurst. RH14 0AZ.
Specialist packers and shippers of fine art and antiques.
Offices in London, Paris, New York and Palm Beach.
TEL: 01403 700044; FAX: 01403 700814
E-MAIL: ukinfo@ganderandwhite.com

Martells International
Units 3-4, Charlwoods Rd., East Grinstead. RH19 2HG. BAR, RHA, LACMA, SSA. *National and international removers, export packers and shippers. Fire-safe container storage; self storage; packing materials.*
TEL: 01342 321303; FAX: 01342 302145
E-MAIL: removals@martells.co.uk
WEBSITE: www.martells.co.uk

WEST MIDLANDS

The British Shop
Village Inn Works, Windmill Street, Walsall, WS1 3EE. *Specialist packers and shippers of fine art and antiques worldwide. Weekly container from Birmingam (UK) to High Point, North Carolina, USA. Pick up and pack - no minimums.*
TEL: 01922 721088; FAX: 01922 723123

Clentons Removals Ltd
13 Daw End, Rushall, Walsall. WS4 1LH. *Collections arranged in UK and Europe for clients' goods. Storage available. Packing and wrapping of all goods for container shipments. All paperwork done for containers. Packing of containers and shipment of containers.*
TEL: 01922 624431; FAX: 01922 613053
E-MAIL: clentons@yahoo.co.uk
WEBSITE: www.clentonsremovals.com

Robinsons International   LAPADA
Bartleet Rd., Washford, Redditch. B98 0DG. *Specialist packers and shippers of antiques and fine art worldwide. Weekly consolidated container service to America. Established over 100 years.*
TEL: 01527 830860; FAX: 01527 500777
WEBSITE: www.robinsons-intl.com/antiques

WILTSHIRE

Martin Bros Ltd
The Old Sawmills, The Street, Kilmington, Nr. Warminster. BA12 6RG. *Specialist carriers of fine art and furniture throughout mainland UK.*

TEL: 01985 844144; FAX: 01985 844113
WEBSITE: www.martinbrosltd.com

WORCESTERSHIRE

Simon Hall Ltd   LAPADA
Willersey Industrial Estate, Willersey, Nr. Broadway. WR12 7RR.
Specialist packers and shippers for fine art and antiques worldwide. Removals and storage.
TEL: **01386 858555**; FAX: **01386 858501**
E-MAIL: **enquiries@simonhalllimited.com**
WEBSITE: **www.simonhalllimited.com**

SCOTLAND

Crown Relocations
Cullen Square, Deans Rd. Industrial Estate, Livingstone. EH54 8SJ.
Packers and shippers.
TEL: 01506 468150; FAX: 01506 468151
E-MAIL: uk@crownfineart.com
WEBSITE: www.crownfineart.com

Forfar Removals   LAPADA
Carseview Rd., Suttieside Industrial Estate, Forfar. DD8 3BT.
Packers and Shippers.
TEL: **01307 468478**; FAX: **01307 464763**
E-MAIL: **enquiries@forfar-removals.co.uk**
WEBSITE: **www.forfar-removals.co.uk**

Martin Bros. Ltd

The Old Sawmills, The Street,
Kilmington, Nr Warminster, Wilts. BA12 6RG
Tel: 01985 844 144
Fax: 01985 844 113
Specialist Carriers of
Fine Art and Furniture
throughout mainland UK.

Index of Auctioneers

LONDON

Baldwin's Auctions Ltd.
11 Adelphi Terrace. WC2N 6BJ.
EST. 1872. *Coins: ancient, British and foreign; commemorative and military medals, orders and decorations; banknotes, books and coin cabinets.*
TEL: 020 7930 6879; FAX: 020 7930 9450
E-MAIL: auctions@baldwin.sh
WEBSITE: www.baldwin.sh

Bloomsbury Auctions
Bloomsbury House, 24 Maddox St., Mayfair. W1S 1PP.
Approximately fifty sales per annum featuring books and works on paper. Valuations. Collection service.
TEL: 020 7495 9494; FAX: 020 7495 9499
E-MAIL: info@bloomsburyauctions.com
WEBSITE: www.bloomsburyauctions.com

Bonhams Auctioneers
101 New Bond St. W1S 1SR.
EST. 1793. *Extensive network of international and UK salerooms and offices. Regular auctions of vintage motor cars, automobilia, sporting items, watercolours, Old Masters, European and modern pictures, portrait miniatures, prints, carved frames, furniture, clocks and watches, decorative arts, European porcelain and glass, Oriental and contemporary ceramics, objects of art, tribal art and antiquities, silver, jewellery, objets de vertu, books and manuscripts, antique and modern guns, musical instruments, Oriental carpets and rugs. Viewing Mon.-Fri. 9-4.30, Sun. 11-3.*
TEL: 020 7447 7447; FAX: 020 7447 7400
E-MAIL: info@bonhams.com
WEBSITE: www.bonhams.com

Christie's
8 King St., St.James'. SW1Y 6QT.
EST. 1766. *Monday-Friday 9-5, on Tues open till 8pm when there is a view and at weekends open for views 12-5.*
TEL: 020 7839 9060; FAX: 020 7839 1611
E-MAIL: info@christies.com
WEBSITE: www.christies.com

85 Old Brompton Rd., South Kensington. SW7 3LD.
Monday-Friday 9-5, on Mon. till 7.30pm when there is a view and at weekends for views and sale 10-4.
TEL: 020 7930 6074; FAX: 020 7752 3321
E-MAIL: info@christies.com
WEBSITE: www.christies.com

Criterion Auctioneers
53 Essex Rd., Islington. N1 2FF.
Sales every Mon. at 5 pm of general antiques, reproduction and contemporary furniture, glass, china, rugs and smalls. Viewing Fri. 2-7, Sat. and Sun. 10-6, Mon. prior to sale.
TEL: 020 7359 5707; FAX: 020 7354 9843
E-MAIL: info@criterion-auctioneers.co.uk
WEBSITE: www.criterion-auctioneers.co.uk

Dix Noonan Webb
16 Bolton St., Piccadilly. W1J 8BQ.
EST. 1991. BNTA. ANA. IAPN. SAAND. *Auctioneers and valuers of British and World coins; ancient coins; tokens; historical and art medals; orders; decorations and medals; militaria, and British and World paper money.*
TEL: 020 7016 1700; FAX: 020 7016 1799
E-MAIL: auctions@dnw.co.uk
WEBSITE: www.dnw.co.uk

Fraser's Autographs
399 Strand. WC2R 0LX.
EST. 1978. *Historic documents, autographs and memorabilia sales throughout the year – see website for details.*
TEL: 020 7836 8444; FAX: 020 7836 7342
E-MAIL: sales@frasersautographs.co.uk
WEBSITE: www.frasersautographs.com

Stanley Gibbons Auctions
399 Strand. WC2R 0LX.
EST. 1901. *Regular auctions throughout the year.*
TEL: 020 7836 8444; FAX: 020 7836 7342
E-MAIL: auctions@stanleygibbons.co.uk
WEBSITE: www.stanleygibbons.com

Harmers of London Stamp Auctioneers Ltd.
Unit 11, 111 Power Rd., Chiswick. W4 5PY.
EST. 1918. *Monthly auctions of Great Britain, British Commonwealth, foreign countries, airmail stamps, also postal history and literature, stamp boxes, postal scales and related ephemera. Fully illustrated catalogues. Valuations for sale, probate or insurance.*
TEL: 020 8747 6100; FAX: 020 8996 0649

E-MAIL: auctions@harmers.demon.co.uk
WEBSITE: www.harmers.com

Hornsey Auctions Ltd.
54-56 High St., Hornsey. N8 7NX.
Fortnightly sales on Wed. at 6.30. Viewing Tues and Wed. from 10 am. Open Thurs., Fri. 10-5.30 and Sat. 10-4 to take in for next auction.
TEL: 020 8340 5334

Lots Road Auctions
71-73 Lots Rd., Chelsea, SW10 0RN.
EST. 1978. *Two auctions every Sunday, 300 lots of traditional, modern and contemporary furnishings (1 pm), and 300 lots of selected antiques to include paintings, rugs and carpets, decorative items and furniture (4 pm). Viewing Wed. 6-8 pm, Thurs. 10-6, Fri. and Sat. 10-4, and Sun. from 10 am. Goods accepted Mon.-Fri. For sellers: swift payment 10 days after sale. Fully illustrated catalogue on line at www.lotsroad.com. Valuers, consultants and carriers. VAT registered.*
TEL: 020 7376 6800; FAX: 020 7376 6899
E-MAIL: info@lotsroad.com
WEBSITE: www.lotsroad.com

Lyon & Turnbull
11/12 Pall Mall. SW1Y 5LU.
EST. 1826. SOFAA. *See website for further information.*
TEL: 020 7930 9115
E-MAIL: info@lyonandturnbull.com
WEBSITE: www.lyonandturnbull.com

Morton and Eden Limited
45 Maddox St. W1S 2PE.
Auction sales of collectors' coins of all periods and types, war medals, orders and decorations, historical medals and banknotes.
TEL: 020 7493 5344; FAX: 020 7495 6325
E-MAIL: info@mortonandeden.com
WEBSITE: www.mortonandeden.com

Rosebery's
74-76 Knights Hill, West Norwood. SE27 0JD.
EST. 1987. *Quarterly selected and monthly antique and collectors' auctions on Tues. and Wed. Specialist auctions of toys and collectors' items, decorative arts, modern design, musical instruments, books and textiles held periodically.*
TEL: 020 8761 2522; FAX: 020 8761 2524
E-MAIL: auctions@roseberys.co.uk
WEBSITE: www.roseberys.co.uk

Sotheby's
34-35 New Bond St. W1A 2AA.
EST. 1744.
TEL: 020 7293 5000
WEBSITE: www.sothebys.com

Southgate Auction Rooms
55 High St., Southgate. N14 6LD.
EST. 1977. *Weekly Mon. sales at 4 pm of jewellery, silver, china, porcelain, paintings, furniture. Viewing Sat. 9-12*
noon and from 9 am on day of sale.
TEL: 020 8886 7888
WEBSITE: www.southgateauctionrooms.com

Spink & Son Ltd.
69 Southampton Row, Bloomsbury. WC1B 4ET.
Specialist sales of stamps, coins and banknotes, commemorative medals, orders, decorations, medals & militaria.
TEL: 020 7563 4000; FAX: 020 7563 4066
E-MAIL: info@spink.com
WEBSITE: www.spink.com

BEDFORDSHIRE

W. & H. Peacock
The Auction Centre, 26 Newnham St., Bedford. MK40 3JR.
EST. 1901. *Antiques sales first Fri. monthly. Viewing Fri. prior 9 am-8 pm. General sales every Sat. at 9.30 am. Specialist auctions throughout the year, see website for dates.*
TEL: 01234 266366
E-MAIL: info@peacockauction.co.uk
WEBSITE: www.peacockauction.co.uk

Charles Ross (Auctioneers)
The Old Town Hall, Woburn. MK17 9PZ.
EST. 1982. *Sales once a month on a Thursday.*
TEL: 01525 290502
E-MAIL: info@charles-ross.co.uk
WEBSITE: www.charles-ross.co.uk

BERKSHIRE

Cameo Fine Art Auctioneers
Kennet Holme Farm, Bath Rd., Midgham. RG7 5UX.
Regular Tuesday specialist sales.
TEL: 0118 971 3772
E-MAIL: office@cameo-auctioneers.co.uk
WEBSITE: www.cameo-auctioneers.co.uk

Dreweatt Neate
Donnington Priory, Donnington, Nr. Newbury. RG14 2JE.
EST. 1759. *Sales on the premises mainly on a weekly basis. Antique furniture - six annually. Paintings, books, prints, silver and jewellery, ceramics - three of each annually. Buyers' premium 19.5% inc. VAT.*
TEL: 01635 553553; FAX: 01635 553599
E-MAIL: donnington@dnfa.com
WEBSITE: www.dnfa.com

Martin and Pole
The Auction House, 10 Milton Rd., Wokingham. RG40 1DB.
Sale of antiques and collectables held usually every third week of the month.
TEL: 0118 979 0460; FAX: 0118 977 6166
E-MAIL: a@martinpole.co.uk
WEBSITE: www.martinpole.co.uk

Special Auction Services
Kennetholme, Midgham. RG7 5UX.
EST. 1991. *Regular specialist auctions of: toys for the collector (including diecast, toys, dolls, teddy bears and model railways, jewellery, silver and watches, signed & design, Staffordshire pot-lids, prattware and commemoratives.*
TEL: 0118 971 2949; FAX: 0871 7146905
E-MAIL: mail@specialauctionservices.com
WEBSITE: www.specialauctionservices.com

Thimbleby & Shorland
Market House, PO Box 175, 31 Great Knollys St., Reading. RG1 7HU.
EST. 1901. *Collective sales of antique and modern furniture held monthly at Reading Auction Market. Also sales and valuations of horse-drawn carriages and driving equipment with four sales annually in Reading.*
TEL: 0118 950 8611; FAX: 0118 950 5896
E-MAIL: info@thimbleby-shorland.co.uk
WEBSITE: www.tsauction.co.uk

BUCKINGHAMSHIRE

Amersham Auction Rooms
125 Station Rd., Amersham. HP7 0AH.
EST. 1877. RICS. CFAAS. *Weekly general and monthly selected antique sales held on Thurs. at 10.30 am.*
TEL: 08700 460606; FAX: 08700 460607
E-MAIL: info@amershamauctionrooms.co.uk
WEBSITE: www.amershamauctionrooms.co.uk

Bourne End Auction Rooms
Station Approach, Bourne End. SL8 5QH.
EST. 1992. NAVA. *Monthly antiques and collectors' sales.*
TEL: 01628 531500; fax 01628 522158
E-MAIL: be.auctions@virgin.net
WEBSITE: www.bourneendauctionrooms.com

Dickins Auctioneeers Ltd.
The Claydon Saleroom, Calvert Rd., Middle Claydon, Buckingham. MK18 2EZ.
Regular sales of specialist items and antiques and collectables.
TEL: 01296 714434; FAX: 01296 714492
E-MAIL: info@dickinsauctioneers.com
WEBSITE: www.dickinsauctoineers.com

Old Amersham Auction Rooms
2 School Lane, Amersham. HP7 0EL.
TEL: 01494 722758
E-MAIL: martinjking8@hotmail.com
WEBSITE: www.old-amersham-auctions.co.uk

CAMBRIDGESHIRE

Bonhams Auctioneers
The Golden Rose, 17 Emmanuel Rd., Cambridge. CB1 1JW.
Auctioneers and valuers.
TEL: 01223 366523; FAX: 01223 300208
WEBSITE: www.bonhams.com

Cheffins
Clifton House, 1 and 2 Clifton Rd., Cambridge. CB1 7EA.
EST. 1825. *Regular fine art and general auction sales including pictures, furniture, works of art, silver and jewellery, ceramics and collectors' items.*
TEL: 01223 213343 (10 lines)
E-MAIL: fine.art@cheffins.co.uk
WEBSITE: www.cheffins.co.uk

Hyperion Auctions Ltd.
Station Rd., St. Ives. PE27 5BH.
EST. 1995. *Regular sales of antiques and collectables.*
TEL: 01480 464140; FAX: 01480 497552
E-MAIL: enquiries@hyperionauctions.co.uk
WEBSITE: www.hyperionauctions.co.uk

W. & H. Peacock
The Auction Centre, 75 New St., St Neots. PE19 1AJ.
Two general sales every Thurs. at 11 am. including 1,000 lots of general furniture, electrical goods, plants and produce. Viewing Wed 9-8 and morning of sale.
TEL: 01480 474550
E-MAIL: info@peacockauction.co.uk
WEBSITE: www.peacockauction.co.uk

Rowley Fine Art Auctioneers & Valuers
8 Downham Rd., Ely. CB6 1AH.
Monthly general sales held on the second Saturday of the month. Regular sales of fine art and antiques at Tattersalls Sale Ring, Newmarket. Valuations.
TEL: 01353 653020; FAX: 01353 653022
E-MAIL: mail@rowleyfineart.com
WEBSITE: www.rowleyfineart.com

Willingham Auctions
25 High St., Willingham. CB24 5ES.
Sales of antique and fine furniture, silver, ceramics, paintings and clocks.
TEL: 01954 261252; fax 01954 201396
E-MAIL: info@willinghamauctions.com
WEBSITE: www.willinghamauctions.com

CHESHIRE

Andrew, Hilditch and Son Ltd.
Hanover House, 1A The Square, Sandbach. CW11 0AP.
EST. 1866. *Biannual sales of fine pictures and period furnishings. General and Edwardian furniture sales held fortnightly.*
TEL: 01270 767246/762048

Bonhams Auctioneers
New House, 150 Christleton Rd., Chester. CH3 5TD.
EST. 1793. *Auctioneers and valuers.*
TEL: 01244 313936; FAX: 01244 340028
WEBSITE: www.bonhams.com

Byrne's Auctioneers and Valuers
Pullman House, The Sidings, Chester St., Saltney Chester. CH4 8RD.

EST. 2003. RICS. *Quarterly antique sales. Fortnightly general antiques and later effects. Collectors' sales 3 times a year. Valuation day Thurs. 10-1 and 2-4. Home visits by appointment. Office open Mon.-Fri. 10-5.*
TEL: 01244 681311; FAX: 01244 681650
E-MAIL: auctions@byrnesauctioneers.co.uk
WEBSITE: www.the-saleroom.com/byrnes

Cheyne's Auctions
38 Hale Rd., Altrincham. WA14 2EX.
EST. 1983. RICS. *Bi-monthly sales held at St Peter's Assembly Rooms, Cecil Road, Hale. Viewing day prior 2-4.30 and 6-8 and sale morning 9-10.30.*
TEL: 0161 941 4879
E-MAIL: patrickcheyne@aol.com
WEBSITE: www.ukauctioneers.com

Frank R. Marshall and Co.
Marshall House, Church Hill, Knutsford. WA16 6DH.
EST. 1948. *Regular sales of antique furniture, objets d'art, silver, pewter, glass, porcelain, toys, musical instruments, pictures, brass and copper. Fortnightly general collective sales. Specialised sales at The Knutsford Auction Salerooms.*
TEL: 01565 653284; FAX: 01565 652341
E-MAIL: antiques@frankmarshall.co.uk
WEBSITE: www.frankmarshall.co.uk

Maxwells of Wilmslow
The Auction Rooms, Levens Rd., Hazel Grove. SK7 5DL.
Regular antiques & chattels auctions.
TEL: 0161 439 5182; FAX: same
E-MAIL: info@maxwells-auctioneers.co.uk
WEBSITE: www.maxwells-auctioneers.co.uk

Whittaker & Biggs
Brown Street Saleroom, Congleton. CW12 1QY.
EST. 1931. *Regular general sales and four sales of antiques and collectables.*
TEL: 01260 279858; FAX: 01260 291053
E-MAIL: allan.pickering@whittakerandbiggs.co.uk
WEBSITE: www.whittakerandbiggs.co.uk

Peter Wilson Fine Art Auctioneers Ltd.
Victoria Gallery, Market St., Nantwich. CW5 5DG.
EST. 1955. *Five catalogued (illustrated in colour) two-day sales each year. Uncatalogued auctions every Thurs., shipping goods and household effects (500+ lots).*
TEL: 01270 623878; FAX: 01270 610508
E-MAIL: auctions@peterwilson.co.uk
WEBSITE: www.peterwilson.co.uk

Wright Manley Auctioneers
Beeston Castle Salerooms, Tarporley. CW6 9NZ.
EST. 1861. *Fortnightly Victoriana and household sales and quarterly catalogued fine art and furniture sales.*
TEL: 01829 262150; FAX: 01829 261829
E-MAIL: lillianrogerson@wrightmanley.co.uk
WEBSITE: www.wrightmanley.co.uk

CORNWALL

Bonhams Auctioneers
Cornubia Hall, Eastcliffe Road Par. PL24 2AQ.
Auctioneers and valuers.
TEL: 01726 814047; FAX: 01726 817979
WEBSITE: www.bonhams.com

Jefferys
The Auction Rooms, 5 Fore St., Lostwithiel. PL22 0BP.
Fortnightly sales of antique furniture, ceramics, glass, jewellery, silver and plate, pictures, prints and collectors' items, on Wed. at 10 am. Viewing day prior 10-1, 2-5.
TEL: 01208 871947; FAX: 01208 873260
E-MAIL: enquiries@jefferysauctions.co.uk
WEBSITE: www.jefferysauctions.co.uk

W. H. Lane & Son
Jubilee House, Queen St., Penzance. TR18 4DF.
EST. 1934. FSB. FPB. *The Southwest's only specialist fine art auctioneers selling art and nothing but art. Five + major art sales per year. Specialists in the sale and valuation of paintings from the Newlyn, St. Ives & Modern British schools of paintings. Illustrated catalogues mailed worldwide and published on the internet. Live on-line bidding available for all sales. Valuations for insurance, probate & Family Division. Principal: Graham J Bazley B.A.(Hons).*
TEL: 01736 361447; FAX: 01736 350097
E-MAIL: info@whlane.co.uk
WEBSITE: www.invaluable.com/whlane;
www.antiquestradegaz

David Lay FRICS
The Penzance Auction House, Alverton, Penzance. TR18 4RE.
Regular sales of fine art, antiques, collectors' items, books and studio pottery. Three-weekly general household sales.
TEL: 01736 361414; FAX: 01736 360035
E-MAIL: david.lays@btopenworld.com
WEBSITE: www.davidlay.co.uk

Tresillian Antiques
The Elms, Tresillian, TR2 4BA.
EST. 1972. *Three-weekly auctions of jewellery, fine art and furniture. Valuations.*
TEL: 01872 520173; MOBILE: 07974 022893
E-MAIL: lulubudd@aol.com

CUMBRIA

Bonhams Auctioneers
48 Cecil Street, Carlisle. CA1 1NT.
Auctioneers and valuers.
TEL: 01228 542422; FAX: 01228 590106
WEBSITE: www.bonhams.com

Kendal Auction Rooms
Sandylands Rd., Kendal. LA9 6EU.
Special bi-monthly catalogued auctions of fine arts, antiques

and collectables mainly with a 'Lakeland' flavour.
TEL: 01539 733770
E-MAIL: info@kendalauctionrooms.co.uk
WEBSITE: www.kendalauctionrooms.co.uk

H. & H. King
The Auction Centre, Rosehill, Carlisle. CA1 2RS.
Weekly sales of antiques, Victorian and later furnishings, collectors' items and household effects. Quarterly catalogue sales of fine art, furniture and general antiques.
TEL: 01228 640927
E-MAIL: enquiries@cumbriaauctions.com
WEBSITE: www.cumbriaauctions.com

Mitchell's Auction Co.
The Furniture Hall, 47 Station Rd., Cockermouth. CA13 9PZ.
EST. 1873. SOFAA. RICS. *Weekly (Thurs.) sales of antique, reproduction and modern furniture and effects, approximately 800 lots, starting at 9.30 am. Viewing Wed. 2-7 and throughout sale. Six fine art sales per annum. Viewing: prior Sun 11-3, Mon 10-5, Tues 10-5, Wed 10-7.*
TEL: 01900 827800; FAX: 01900 828073
E-MAIL: info@mitchellsfineart.com
WEBSITE: www.mitchellsfineart.com

Penrith Farmers' and Kidds plc
Skirsgill Saleroom, Skirsgill, Penrith. CA11 0DN.
Fortnightly sales of Victoriana and later furnishings on Wed. commencing 9.30 am., view Tues. prior 10-6. Quarterly sales of antiques and collectors' items are held in Mar., June, Sept. and Dec. 10.30 am. start. Viewing 2 days prior - Mon. 10-5, Tues. 10-7.
TEL: 01768 890781; FAX: 01768 895058
E-MAIL: info@pfkauctions.co.uk
WEBSITE: www.pfkauctions.co.uk

Thomson, Roddick and Medcalf
Coleridge House, Shaddongate, Carlisle. CA2 5TU.
EST. 1880. *Regular catalogue sales of antiques and collectors' items and regular specialist sales particularly antiquarian books, coins, medals and militaria. Monthly general furniture sales at Wigton.*
TEL: 01228 528939; FAX: 01228 592128
E-MAIL: auctions@thomsonroddick.com
WEBSITE: www.thomsonroddick.com

DERBYSHIRE

Bamfords Auctioneers
The Derby Auction House, Chequers Road, off Pentagon Island, Derby. DE21 6EN.
Fine art and antiques specialists. Also at Matlock.
TEL: 01332 210000; FAX: 01332 368424
E-MAIL: info@bamfords-auctions.co.uk
WEBSITE: www.bamfords-auctions.co.uk

DEVON

Bearne's
St Edmund's Court, Okehampton St., Exeter. EX4 1DU.
EST. 1945. SOFAA. *Regular sales of antique furniture, works of art, silver, jewellery, collectors' items, books, clocks and watches, paintings, ceramics and glass, carpets and rugs.*
TEL: 01392 207000/207007
E-MAIL: enquiries@bearnes.co.uk
WEBSITE: www.bearnes.co.uk

Bonhams Auctioneers
Dowell St., Honiton. EX14 1LX.
Auctioneers and valuers.
TEL: 01404 41872; FAX: 01404 43137
WEBSITE: www.bonhams.com

Michael J. Bowman
6 Haccombe House, Netherton, Newton Abbot. TQ12 4SJ.
EST. 1986. *Regular sales of antiques and collectors items at Chudleigh Town Hall.*
TEL: 01626 872890; FAX: 01626 872890
E-MAIL: michael_bowman@btconnect.com

Chilcotts of Tiverton
The Chilcott School Saleroom, St Peter St., Tiverton. EX16 6NU.
Regular auctions of antique furniture, silver, jewellery, paintings, ceramics, clocks and collectors' items. General sales held at the Silver Street Salerooms, Honiton.
TEL: 01884 250020; FAX: 01884 250030
E-MAIL: info@chilcottsauctioneers.co.uk
WEBSITE: www.chilcottsauctioneers.co.uk

Eldreds
1 Belliver Way, Roborough, Plymouth. PL6 7BP.
Regular sales to include furniture, works of art, pictures, ceramics, collectors' items, books, silver and jewellery.
TEL: 01752 721199; FAX: 01752 786042
E-MAIL: enquiries@eldreds.net
WEBSITE: www.eldreds.net

S.J. Hales Antique & Fine Art Auctioneers & Valuers
Tracey House Salerooms, Dolphin Sq., Newton Rd., Bovey Tracey, Newton Abbot. TQ13 9AZ.
EST. 2000. *Sales held monthly on Wed. at 10am, viewing Sat. and Sun. 10-4, Mon. 9-5, Tues. 9-7 and from 8am on sale day.*
TEL: 01626 836684; FAX: 01626 836318
E-MAIL: info@sjhales.com
WEBSITE: www.sjhales.com

Hampton & Littlewood Auctioneers
The Auction Rooms, Alphinbrook Rd., Alphington, Exeter Devon. EX2 8TH.
Fortnightly antiques and collectables auctions; quarterly fine sales of selected antiques. All sales held on Wed. Viewing - fortnightly sales - Sat. morning prior 9-12, Mon. and Tues. prior 9-5.30; quarterly - Sat. prior 9-1, Sun. prior 2-4, Mon. and Tues. prior 9-5.30. Annual antiquarian book sale. Annual maritime sale and annual sporting sale.

TEL: 01392 413100; FAX: 01392 413110
E-MAIL: enquiries@hamptonandlittlewood.co.uk
WEBSITE: www.hamptonandlittlewood.co.uk

Lyme-Bay Auctions Ltd.
Harepath Rd. Seaton. EX12 2SX.
EST. 1981. *General household and antique auctions held every four to six weeks.*
TEL: 01297 22453; FAX: 01297 23386
E-MAIL: info@lymebayauction.co.uk
WEBSITE: www.lymebayauction.co.uk

Oaks and Partners
The Old Tannery, Exeter Road, Cullompton. EX15 1DT.
Sales of antiques, collectables and fine art.
TEL: 01884 35848; FAX: 01884 38000
E-MAIL: auctions@oaksandpartners.co.uk
WEBSITE: www.invaluable.com/oaksandpartners

Potbury and Sons
The Auction Rooms, Temple St., Sidmouth. EX10 8LN.
EST. 1850. NAVA. *Fortnightly sales held on Tues. Viewing Mon. prior 9-7 and Sat prior 9.30-12.30; fine art sales every two months.*
TEL: 01395 515555/517300; FAX: 01395 512608
E-MAIL: potburysauctions@btconnect.com
WEBSITE: www.potburys.co.uk

Rendells
Stone Park, Ashburton. TQ13 7RH.
Sales every four weeks (Thurs. and Fri.) of antique and reproduction furniture, ceramics, silver, jewellery, pictures, clocks and barometers, copper and brass, miscellanea, toys and collectables. 10% + buyer's premium + VAT.
TEL: 01364 653017: FAX: 01364 654251
E-MAIL: stonepark@rendells.co.uk
WEBSITE: www.rendells.co.uk

Shobrook Auctions Ltd.
20 Western Approach, Plymouth. PL1 1TG.
EST. 1920s. *Regular monthly sales of antiques and collectables.*
TEL: 01752 663341; FAX: 01752 255157
E-MAIL: info@shobrook.co.uk
WEBSITE: www.shobrook.co.uk

Martin Spencer-Thomas
The Bicton Street Auction Rooms, Bicton Street, Exmouth. EX8 2RT.
Regular auction sales of antique furniture, porcelain, china, glass, jewellery, silver, paintings & pictures, rugs, objets d'art, collectables, memorabilia, etc.
TEL: 01395 267403
E-MAIL: martin@martinspencerthomas.co.uk
WEBSITE: www.martinspencerthomas.co.uk

Stannary Gallery Auctioneers
Drake Rd., Tavistock. PL19 0AX.
Regular and specialist sales of antiques and collectables.

TEL: 01822 617800; FAX: 01822 617595
E-MAIL: sales@stannarygallery-auctioneers.co.uk

Ward and Chowen
Tavistock Auction Rooms, Market Rd., Tavistock. PL19 0BW.
EST. 1830. RICS. *General household and antiques & collectables.*
TEL: 01822 612603; FAX: 01822 617311
E-MAIL: tavistockauctionrooms@wardchowen.co.uk
WEBSITE: www.wardchowen.co.uk

Whitton and Laing
32 Okehampton St., Exeter. EX4 1DY.
EST. 1884. *Monthly auctions of antiques, silver and jewellery. Book and stamp auctions two or three times a year. Picture sales bi-monthly. General auctions weekly.*
TEL: 01392 252621; FAX: 01392 496607
E-MAIL: whitton@whittonandlaing.eclipse.co.uk
WEBSITE: www.whittonandlaing.com

DORSET

The Auction House of Bridport
St Michaels Trading Estate, Bridport. DT6 3RR.
Specialist sales and monthly sales of general antiques.
TEL: 01308 459400
E-MAIL: info@bridportauctionhouse.com
WEBSITE: www.bridportauctionhouse.com

Charterhouse
The Long Street Salerooms, Sherborne. DT9 3BS.
Regular monthly auctions of general antiques plus a specialist section including jewellery, militaria, pictures, furniture, clocks, collectors' items, books, wine and classic cars.
TEL: 01935 812277; FAX: 01935 389387
E-MAIL: enquiry@charterhouse-auctions.co.uk
WEBSITE: www.charterhouse-auctions.co.uk

Cottees
The Market, East St., Wareham. BH20 4NR.
EST. 1903. *Sales of furniture, silver and jewellery, pottery and porcelain etc. fortnightly on Tues. Viewing previous day 10-7.*
TEL: 01929 552826; FAX: 01929 554916
E-MAIL: info@cottees.co.uk
WEBSITE: www.auctionsatcottees.co.uk

Davey & Davey
The Poole Salerooms, 13 St Peters Rd., Parkestone. BH14 0NZ.
Antiques and collectors' sales throughout the year.
TEL: 01202 748567; FAX: 01202 716258
E-MAIL: adefor@daveyanddavey.com
WEBSITE: www.daveyanddavey.com

Hy. Duke and Son
Dorchester Fine Art Salerooms, Weymouth Avenue, Dorchester. DT1 1QS.
EST. 1823. *Regular sales including specialist sections of silver and jewellery, Oriental and English porcelain, English and*

Continental furniture, pictures, books and Oriental rugs. Complete valuation and advisory service including insurance, probate and forward tax planning.
TEL: 01305 265080; FAX: 01305 260101
E-MAIL: enquiries@dukes-auctions.com
WEBSITE: www.dukes-auctions.com

House and Son
11-14 Lansdowne House, Christchurch Rd., Bournemouth. BH1 3JW.
EST. 1939 *Fortnightly sales of selected furniture, pictures, books, silver, porcelain and glass. Catalogues £2.50 including postage.*
TEL: 01202 298044; FAX: 01202 292668
E-MAIL: info@houseandson.com
WEBSITE: www.houseandson.com

Onslow Auctions Ltd.
The Coach House, Manor Rd., Stourpaine. DT11 8TQ.
EST. 1984. *Sales three to four times a year including posters, railwayana, aero and motor, printed ephemera, Titanic and maritime, Louis Vuitton luggage. Viewing as published prior to sale.*
TEL: 01258 488838; MOBILE: 07831 473400
E-MAIL: bogue.onslows@btinternet.com

Semley Auctioneers
Station Rd., Semley, Shaftesbury. SP7 9AN.
Monthly sales of antique items including paintings, furniture, ceramics, jewellery. Monthly specialist sales.
TEL: 01747 855122; FAX: 01747 855222
E-MAIL: enquiries@semleyauctioneers.com
WEBSITE: www.semleyauctioneers.com

DURHAM

Addisons of Barnard Castle
The Auction Rooms, Staindrop Rd., Barnard Castle. DL12 8TD.
Quarterly fine art and antiques catalogue auctions, sixteen antiques, Victoriana and household effects sales and two specialist garden sales per annum.
TEL: 01833 690545; FAX: 01833 638567
E-MAIL: enquiries@addisons-auctioneers.co.uk
WEBSITE: www.addisons-auctioneers.co.uk

G.H. Edkins & Son
Auckland Auction Rooms, 58 Kingsway, Bishop Auckland. DL14 7JF.
EST. 1907. *General and antique sales from time to time.*
TEL: 01388 603095; FAX: 01388 661239

Vectis Auctions Ltd.
Fleck Way, Thornaby, Stockton- on-Tees. TS17 9JZ.
EST. 1988. *Sales of trains held six times a year at the Benn Hall, Rugby and at Thornaby. Viewing Fri. evening 5-7 and Sat. morning 8-10.30.*
TEL: 01642 767116; FAX: 01642 769478
E-MAIL: vicky@vectis.co.uk
WEBSITE: www.vectis.co.uk

Thomas Watson and Son
Northumberland St., Darlington. DL3 7HJ.
EST. 1840. *Regular sales of antiques and good quality house contents.*
TEL: 01325 462559; FAX: 01325 284587
E-MAIL: enquiries@thomaswatson.co.uk
WEBSITE: www.thomaswatson.com

ESSEX

Boningtons Auctioneers & Valuers
Ambrose House, Old Station Rd., Loughton. IG10 4PE.
Fortnightly antique sales on a Mon. Viewing Thurs., Fri. and Sat. of previous week.
TEL: 020 8598 4800
E-MAIL: admin@boningtons.com
WEBSITE: www.boningtons.com

Brentwood Antique Auctions
45 North Rd., Brentwood. CM14 4UZ.
Fortnightly auctions of antiques, collectables and general items.
TEL: 01277 224599; FAX: 01277 261502
E-MAIL: wendy@brentwoodantiqueauction.co.uk
WEBSITE: www.brentwoodantiqueauction.co.uk

Reeman Dansie
8 Wyncolls Rd., Severalls Business Park. Colchester. CO4 9HT.
Fortnightly Tues. sales, viewing Sat. 9-1, Mon. 9.30-5.30. Bi-monthly antique sales. Quarterly specialist collectors' sales.
TEL: 01206 754754
E-MAIL: enquiries@reemans.com
WEBSITE: www.reemans.com

Simon H. Rowland
Chelmsford Auction Rooms, 42 Mildmay Rd., Chelmsford. CM2 0DZ.
EST. 1946. *Regular sales by order of the Sheriff of Essex and private vendors.*
TEL: 01245 354251
E-MAIL: chelmauction@fsbdial.co.uk
WEBSITE: www.chelmsfordauctionrooms.co.uk

John Stacey & Sons (Leigh-on-Sea) Ltd.
959 London Rd., Leigh-on-Sea. SS9 3LB.
EADA. TED. *Monthly sales of period and other furniture, works of art and collectors' items. Specialist jewellery sale every November. Annual catalogue subscription £45.*
TEL: 01702 477051
E-MAIL: mark@staceyauction.com
WEBSITE: www.staceyauction.com

Stanfords
Colchester Cattle Market, Wyncolls Rd., Colchester. CO4 9HU.
Weekly Sat. sales at 10 along with the country market and intermittent fine art and antiques sales. Viewing Fri. prior

2-6 and sale morning from 8.30.
TEL: 01206 842156
E-MAIL: info@stanfords-colchester.co.uk
WEBSITE: www.stanfords-auctions.co.uk

G.E. Sworder and Sons
14 Cambridge Rd., Stansted Mountfitchet.
CM24 8BZ.
EST. 1782. SOFAA. *Six fine art auctions. Viewing Fri. 10-5,
Sat. 10-1, Sun 10-1, Mon. 10-5, Tues. from 9 prior to sale.
Fully illustrated catalogue available and online. Weekly Wed. at
11 am auctions of Victorian, Edwardian and later furniture and
collectables. Viewing Tues. 2-7 and Wed. from 9 prior to sale.*
TEL: 01279 817778; FAX: 01279 817779
E-MAIL: auctions@sworder.co.uk
WEBSITE: www.sworder.co.uk

GLOUCESTERSHIRE

Bonhams Auctioneers
22a Long Street, Tetbury, GL8 8AQ.
Auctioneers and valuers.
TEL: 01666 502200; FAX: 01666 505107
WEBSITE: www.bonhams.com

Simon Chorley Art & Antiques Ltd.
Prinknash Abbey Park, Prinknash. GL4 8EX.
TEL: 01452 344499; FAX: 01452 814533
E-MAIL: enquiries@simonchorley.com
WEBSITE: www.simonchorley.com

The Cotswold Auction Co.
Chapel Walk Saleroom, Chapel Walk, Cheltenham.
GL50 3DS.
EST. 1998. RICS. *Three sales monthly - specialist and
general; including furniture, clocks, paintings, silver,
jewellery, toys, books, collectables, textiles, costume.*
TEL: 01242 256363; FAX: 01242 571734
E-MAIL: info@cotswoldauction.co.uk
WEBSITE: www.cotswoldauction.co.uk

The Cotswold Auction Co.
The Coach House, Swan Yard, 9-13 West Market
Place, Cirencester. GL17 2NH.
RICS. *Monthly sales.*
TEL: 01285 642420
E-MAIL: info@cotswoldauction.co.uk
WEBSITE: www.cotswoldauction.co.uk

Dreweatt Neate
St. John's Place, Apsley Rd., Clifton, Bristol. BS8 2ST.
EST. 1759. *Occasional specialist sales, transport, jewellery,
silver, clocks, post cards and advertising art.*
TEL: 0117 973 7201; FAX: 0117 973 5671
E-MAIL: bristol@dnfa.com
WEBSITE: www.dnfa.com/bristol

Mallams Fine Art Auctioneers and Valuers
26 Grosvenor St., Cheltenham. GL52 2SG.
EST. 1788. SOFAA. *Monthly auctions of antique furniture,
clocks, paintings, silver, bronzes, rugs and works of art;
Cotswold craft furniture to include Gordon Russell, Waals,
Barnsley, Morris and Co, Gimson, 1950s-1980s designer
furniture and works of art. Specialist biannual ceramics
auctions. House sales on the premises.*
TEL: 01242 235712; FAX: 01242 241943
E-MAIL: cheltenham@mallams.co.uk
WEBSITE: www.mallams.co.uk/fineart

Moore, Allen & Innocent
The Salerooms, Norcote, Cirencester. GL7 5RH.
EST. 1852. *Fortnightly sales of over 1,000 lots of antique
and other furniture and effects. Quarterly sales of selected
antiques. Bi-annual specialist picture and sporting sales. Fri.
at 9.30 am. Viewing day prior 10.30-8. 15% buyers'
premium.*
TEL: 01285 646050; FAX: 01285 652862
E-MAIL: fineart@mooreallen.co.uk
WEBSITE: www.mooreallen.co.uk

Smiths of Newent Auctioneers
16 Broad St., Newent. GL18 1AJ.
EST. 1976. RICS. *Sales include a full range of antiques,
collectables including furniture, ceramics, glass, pictures,
clocks, silver, jewellery and decorative arts. We also include an
additional specialist section to each sale.*
TEL: 01531 820767; FAX: 01531 822648
E-MAIL: enquiries@smithsnewentauctions.co.uk
WEBSITE: www.smithsnewentauctions.co.uk

Dominic Winter Book Auctions
Mallard House, Broadway Lane, South Cerney.
GL7 5UQ.
EST. 1988. *Specialist auctioneers of antiquarian and
collectable books, manuscripts, autographs and works of art on
paper.*
TEL: 01285 860006; FAX: 01285 862461
E-MAIL: info@dominicwinter.co.uk
WEBSITE: www.dominicwinter.co.uk

Wotton Auction Rooms Ltd.
(formerly Sandoe Luce Panes) Tabernacle Rd., Wotton-
under-Edge. GL12 7EB.
EST. 1846. SOFAA. *Monthly two-day sales of antiques and
collectables, 1,500+ lots. Calendar cards on request.
Valuations.*
TEL: 01453 844733; FAX: 01453 845448
E-MAIL: info@wottonauctionrooms.co.uk
WEBSITE: www.wottonauctionrooms.co.uk

HAMPSHIRE

Bonhams Auctioneers
The Red House, Hyde Street, Winchester. SO23 7DX.
Auctioneers and valuers.
TEL: 01962 862515; FAX: 01962 865166
WEBSITE: www.bonhams.com

Hampshire Auctions

41A London Street, Andover. SP10 2NU.
Auctions held weekly of antique and modern furniture, ceramics and glass, silver, plated items, jewellery, works of art, collectables, general household chattels, gardening, other tools, etc.
TEL: 01264 364820; FAX: 01264 323402
E-MAIL: sales@hampshireauctions.com
WEBSITE: www.hampshireauctions.com

Jacobs and Hunt Fine Art Auctioneers

26 Lavant St., Petersfield. GU32 3EF.
EST. 1895. *Monthly general antique sales and five-weekly fine art sales held on Fri.*
TEL: 01730 233933; FAX: 01730 262323
E-MAIL: auctions@jacobsandhunt.com
WEBSITE: www.jacobsandhunt.com

George Kidner Auctioneers & Valuers

The Lymington saleroom Emsworth Road Lymington. SO41 9BL.
Specialist sales of furniture, works of art, silver, jewellery, paintings, ceramics, arms, armour, militaria, collectable toys, model railways, railwayana, marine items, books and maps. Also fortnightly sales of furniture and effects.
TEL: 01590 670070; FAX: 01590 675167
E-MAIL: info@georgekidner.co.uk
WEBSITE: www.georgekidner.co.uk

Nesbits

7 Clarendon Rd., Southsea, Portsmouth. PO5 2ED.
Monthly sales of antique furniture, silver, porcelain and pictures.
TEL: 023 9286 4321; FAX: 023 9229 5522
E-MAIL: auctions@nesbits.co.uk
WEBSITE: www.nesbits.co.uk

Andrew Smith & Son

The Auction Rooms, Manor Farm, Itchen Stoke, Winchester. SO24 0QT.
Regular sales of fine art, antiques, later and decorative furnishings.
TEL: 01962 735988; FAX: 01962 738879
E-MAIL: auctions@andrewsmithandson.com
WEBSITE: www.andrewsmithandson.com

HEREFORDSHIRE

Brightwells

The Fine Art Dept., Easters Court., Leominster. HR6 0DE.
EST. 1846. *Monthly sales of antiques (approximately 1,200 lots); Monthly sales of Victorian furniture and collectors items. Quarterly sales of pictures, silver and jewellery, books, wine, dolls and toys, textiles, sporting and militaria; classic cars and automobilia.*
TEL: (head office) 01568 611166; FAX: 01568 611802;
WEBSITE: www.brightwells.com

Lots of Leominster Ltd.

13 South St., Leominster. HR6 8JA.
Eight auctions per year of antiques, general furniture and effects.
TEL: 01568 612127
E-MAIL: carolinescott-mayfield@hotmail.co.uk

H. J. Pugh & Co.

Newmarket House, Market St., Ledbury. HR8 2AQ.
Regular sales to include antique furniture and effects, railwayana and military memorabilia.
TEL: 01531 631122; FAX: 01531 631818
E-MAIL: auctions@hjpugh.com
WEBSITE: www.hjpugh.com

Nigel Ward & Company

The New Salerooms, Pontrilas, Hereford. HR2 0EH.
Regular sales of antique & country furniture, effects, porcelain, objets d'art & collectables.
TEL: 01981 240140; FAX: 01981 240340
E-MAIL: office@nigel-ward.co.uk
WEBSITE: www.nigel-ward.co.uk

HERTFORDSHIRE

G. E. Sworder & Sons

42 St Andrew St., Hertford. SG14 1JA.
SOFAA. *Specialist auctions of fine art and antiques; weekly auctions of general and decorative items. Valuations for sale, insurance and inheritance tax assessment.*
TEL: 01992 583508; FAX: 01992 586074
E-MAIL: herfordofficef@sworder.co.uk
WEBSITE: sworderauctions@ic24.net

Tring Market Auctions

Brook St., Tring. HP23 5EF.
Fortnightly Sat. sales of antiques and collectables (approximately 2,000 lots) held at The Market Premises, Brook St., Tring. Fine art sales held on last Fri. of alternate months.
TEL: 01442 826446
E-MAIL: sales@tringmarketauctions.co.uk
WEBSITE: www.tringmarketauctions.co.uk

KENT

Bentley's Fine Art Auctioneers

The Old Granary, Waterloo Rd., Cranbrook. TN17 3JQ.
Monthly auctions of high quality fine art, antique furniture, fine quality porcelain, chattels, silver and jewellery.
TEL: 01580 715857; FAX: same
E-MAIL: bentleyskent@aol.com
WEBSITE: www.bentleysfineartauctioneers.co.uk

Bonhams Auctioneers

13 Lime Tree Walk, Sevenoaks. TN13 1YH.
Auctioneers and valuers.
TEL: 01732 740310; FAX: 01732 741842
WEBSITE: www.bonhams.com

The Canterbury Auction Galleries
40 Station Rd. West, Canterbury. CT2 8AN.
EST. 1911. *Fine art and antique sales held quarterly on Tues. commencing at 10 am., viewing Sun. prior 2-5, Mon. prior 10-7. Monthly auctions of Victorian and later furniture, usually first Saturday each month at 10 am. Viewing Thurs. and Fri. prior 3-8. Free valuation service held most Fri. from 10-1. Professional valuations for insurance, probate, Family Division or sale by auction.*
TEL: 01227 763337; FAX: 01227 456770
E-MAIL: auctions@thecanterburyauctiongalleries.com
WEBSITE: www.thecanterburyauctiongalleries.com

Dreweatt Neate
Fine Art Auctioneers, Auction Hall, The Pantiles, Tunbridge Wells. TN2 5QL.
EST. 1759. *Regular fine art and antique sales throughout the year, including specialist sales of Tunbridge Ware. Fortnightly sales of Victorian and later furniture and effects as part of The Fine Art Auction Group.*
TEL: 01892 544500; FAX: 01892 515191
E-MAIL: sales@dnfa.com
WEBSITE: www.dnfa.com

Gordon Day & Partners
23 Homefield Rd., Riverhead, Sevenoaks. TN13 2DU.
Sales of fine antiques, victorian furniture, Chippendale tools, Edwardian mahogany, estate sales, and general auctions. Saleroom address: Bowen's Yard, Park Corner, Knockholt, Kent. Tel/fax: 01959 533263.
TEL: 01732 454797
WEBSITE: www.gordondayauctions.com

Gorringes
15 The Pantiles, Tunbridge Wells. TN2 5TD.
Office and bookshop. Valuations undertaken for sale, probate and insurance by appointment at the office, at your home or your bank. Items can be entered for auction in our Lewes or Bexhill salerooms. Bookshop - wide range of reference books on antiques, fine art and collectables.
TEL: 01892 619670; FAX: 01892 619671
E-MAIL: tunbridge.wells@gorringes.co.uk
WEBSITE: www.gorringes.co.uk

Hobbs Parker
Romney House, Ashford Market, Orbital Park, Ashford. TN24 0HB.
EST. 1850. *Monthly general sales including household furniture; sales of antiques every six-eight weeks.*
TEL: 01233 502222; FAX: 01233 502211
E-MAIL: info@hobbsparker.co.uk
WEBSITE: www.hobbsparker.co.uk

Humberts Fine Art
The Estate Office, Stone St., Cranbrook. TN17 3HE.
Auction sales held regularly at successful venues such as Wye College and St Ronans School in Hawkhurst.
TEL: 01580 713828; FAX: 01580 712339
E-MAIL: cranbrook.auctions@humberts.co.uk
WEBSITE: www.humberts.co.uk

Ibbett Mosely
125 High St., Sevenoaks. TN13 1UT.
EST. 1900. *Antiques and objets d'art.*
TEL: 01732 456731; FAX: 01732 740910
E-MAIL: auctions@ibettmosely.co.uk
WEBSITE: www.ibettmosely.co.uk

Kent Auction Galleries Ltd.
Unit C Highfield Industrial Estate, Off Warren Rd., Folkestone. CT19 6DD.
Fine art saleroom - fortnightly sales.
TEL: 01303 240808; 01303 246810; FAX: 01303 246256
E-MAIL: admin@kentauctiongalleriesltd.co.uk
WEBSITE: www.kentauctiongalleriesltd.co.uk

Lambert & Foster Auction Sale Room
102 High St., Tenterden. TN30 6HU.
Four offices in Kent. Monthly general sales of antique and other furniture and effects.
TEL: 01580 762083; FAX: 01580 764317
E-MAIL: saleroom@lambertandfoster.co.uk
WEBSITE: www.lambertandfoster.co.uk

Pettmans
The Depository, 52 Athelstan Rd., Margate. CT9 2BH.
Monthly sales of antiques and collectables.
TEL: 01843 220234; FAX: 01843 293085
WEBSITE: www.pettmans.com

LANCASHIRE

Capes Dunn & Co Fine Art Auctioneers & Valuers
The Auction Galleries, 38 Charles St., Manchester. M1 7DB.
EST. 1826. RICS. *Catalogues of specialist sales available on request. Regional office in Lytham.*
TEL: 0161 273 1911; FAX: 0161 273 3474
WEBSITE: www.capesdunn.com

Gerrards Auction Rooms
St Georges Rd., St Annes on Sea. FY8 2AE.
Tri-weekly sales of fine art, antique and quality collectables.
TEL: 01253 725476; FAX: 01253 725596
E-MAIL: info@gerrardsauctionrooms.com
WEBSITE: www.gerrardsauctionrooms.com

Kingsway Auction Rooms Ltd.
The Galleries, Kingsway, Ansdell, Lytham St. Annes. FY8 1AB.
Sales of antique, reproduction and modern furnishings and appointments fortnightly or every three weeks on Tues. Approximately 600 lots commencing 9.30 am. Viewing Fri. 10-12, 2-4, Sat. 10-12, Mon. 9-4. Buyers' premium 15%.
TEL: 01253 735442
E-MAIL: enquiries@kingswayauctions.co.uk
WEBSITE: www.kingswayauctions.co.uk

Silverwoods of Clitheroe
Clitheroe Auction Mart, Ribblesdale Centre, Lincoln
Way, Clitheroe. BB7 1QD.
EST. 2001. *Weekly sales of general household goods.*
TEL: 01200 423322; FAX: 01200 429263
E-MAIL: info@silverwoods.co.uk
WEBSITE: www.silverwoods.co.uk

James Thompson
64 Main St., Kirkby Lonsdale. LA6 2AJ.
*Monthly auction of silver, jewellery, ceramics, glass, furniture
and frequently a selection of curios. Bi-monthly art sales
specialising in Lakeland artists.*
TEL: 01524 271555; FAX: 01524 272939
E-MAIL: sales@jthompson-auctioneers.co.uk
WEBSITE: www.jthompson-auctioneers.co.uk

Trafford Books
PO Box 152, Salford, Manchester. M17 1BP.
EST. 1980. *Tues. sales, approximately every seven weeks,
held at Unit 6, Block C, Astra Business Centre, Guiness
Rd., Trafford Park, Manchester. Eight per year all
specialising in paper collectables - postage stamps and
history, manuscripts, autographs, picture and cigarette
cards, books, prints, drawings and watercolours. Sales
commence at 2 pm. Viewing prior Mon. 10.30-6.30 and
sale morning 9-1.15.*
TEL: 0161 877 8818
E-MAIL: george@traffordbooks.fsnet.co.uk

Warren & Wignall Ltd.
The Mill, Earnshaw Bridge, Leyland Lane, Leyland.
PR5 3PH.
*Sales of general antiques every three weeks on Wed. at 10 am.
Viewing Tues. 9-7.*
TEL: 01772 451430; FAX: 01772 454516
E-MAIL: enquiries@warrenandwignall.co.uk
WEBSITE: www.warrenandwignall.co.uk

LEICESTERSHIRE

Bonhams Auctioneers
34 High Street, Market Harborough, LE16 7NL.
Auctioneers and valuers.
TEL: 01858 438900; FAX: 01858 438909
WEBSITE: www.bonhams.com

Gilding's Ltd. Auctioneers and Valuers
Roman Way, Market Harborough. LE16 7PQ.
*Quarterly fine art sales, weekly (excluding Bank Holidays)
antiques and collectors' sales. Free valuations by appointment
each Weds. and Thurs.*
TEL: 01858 410414; FAX: 01858 432956
E-MAIL: sales@gildings.co.uk
WEBSITE: www.gildings.co.uk

Shoulers
County Auction Rooms, Kings Road, Melton Mowbray.
LE13 1QF.

Regular sales of antiques and collectables.
TEL: 01664 560181; FAX 01664 410449
E-MAIL: salerooms@shoulers.co.uk
WEBSITE: www.shoulers.co.uk

LINCOLNSHIRE

Batemans Auctioneers & Valuers of Stamford
The Saleroom, Ryhall Road, Stamford. PE9 1XF.
*First Sat. monthly fine art, antiques and collectables auctions
at 10.30am. Viewing Thurs. prior 10-5, Fri. 10-7 and from
9am on sale day. All auctions catalogued and on-line.*
TEL: 01780 766466; FAX: 01780 765071
E-MAIL: info@batemans-auctions.co.uk
WEBSITE: www.batemans-auctions.co.uk

Robert Bell & Company
Old Bank Chambers, Horncastle. LN9 5HY.
*Monthly general sales and six monthly catalogued sales of
antiques and fine art.*
TEL: 01507 522222; FAX: 01507 524444
E-MAIL: auctions@robert-bell.org
WEBSITE: www.robert-bell.org

Brown & Co.
Old Court Rd., Brigg. DN20 8JD.
SLSAA. *Four sales a year of fine art & antiques. General,
household and shipping goods auctions fortnightly. Valuations
for insurance, probate and divorce - free on 'for sale' items.
Valuation clinic Thurs. 9.30-12 noon.*
TEL: 01652 650172; FAX: 01652 650085
E-MAIL: auctionrooms@brown-co.com
WEBSITE: www.brown-co.com

Eleys Auctions
Haven Business Park, Slippery Gowt Lane, Boston.
PE21 7AA.
*Auctioneers and valuers. Specialist, property, antique and
collectables auctions held throughout the year.*
TEL: 01206 316600
E-MAIL: auctions@eleys.co.uk
WEBSITE: www.eleysauctions.co.uk

Golding Young
Old Wharf Rd., Grantham. NG31 7AA.
Monthly collective and quarterly selective sales.
TEL: 01476 565118; FAX: 01476 561475
E-MAIL: enquiries@goldingyoung.com
WEBSITE: www.goldingyoung.com

Thomas Mawer & Son Ltd.
Dunston House, Portland St., Lincoln. LN5 7NN.
EST. 1864. *Sales on first Sat. every month at 10 am.
Viewing Fri. prior 12-4 and sale morning from 8.30.
Catalogue sales quarterly.*
TEL: 01522 524984; FAX: 01522 535600
E-MAIL: auctions@thosmawer.co.uk
WEBSITE: www.thosmawer.com

Richardsons

Bourne Auction Rooms, Spalding Rd., Bourne. PE10 9LE.
Antiques & collectable sales every month. Antique and modern sales every other Sat. Regular sales of books, stamps, postcards and cigarette cards.
TEL: 01778 422686; FAX: 01778 425726
E-MAIL: enquiries@richardsonsauctions.co.uk
WEBSITE: www.richardsonsauctions.co.uk

Marilyn Swain

The Old Barracks, Sandon Rd., Grantham. NG31 9AS.
EST. 1989. SOFAA. *Bi-monthly antique, fine art and collectable sales. Regular sales of Victorian and later furniture, general effects and collectables. Specialist toy and collectable sales. Valuations.*
TEL: 01476 568861; FAX: 01476 576100
E-MAIL: marilynswain@btconnect.com
WEBSITE: www.marilynswainauctions.co.uk

MANCHESTER

Bonhams Auctioneers

The Stables, 213 Ashley Road, Hale. WA15 9TB.
Auctioneers and valuers.
TEL: 0161 927 3822; FAX: 0161 927 3824
WEBSITE: www.bonhams.com

MERSEYSIDE

Bonhams Auctioneers

33 Botanic Road, Churchtown, Southport. PR9 7NE.
Auctioneers and valuers.
TEL: 01704 507875; FAX: 01704 507877
WEBSITE: www.bonhams.com

Cato Crane & Company

6 Stanhope St., Liverpool. L8 5RF.
Fine art and antiques sales first Mon. monthly. Collectors' sales weekly on Tues at 10.30. Chester and N. Wales office: 01244 680055.
TEL: 0151 709 5559; FAX: 0151 707 2454
E-MAIL: john@catocrane.co.uk
WEBSITE: www.catocrane.co.uk

Kingsley Auctions Ltd.

3/4 The Quadrant, Hoylake. CH47 2EE.
Sales every Tues. at 10 am., of antiques, fine art, general chattels. Viewing Sat. 9-12.30, Mon. 9-5 and Tues. 9-10.
TEL: 0151 632 5821

Outhwaite and Litherland

43 Hoghton St., Southport. PR9 0PG.
EST. 1907. SOFAA. *Auction sales by negotiation and in association with Thomson, Roddick & Metcalf. Specialist valuers for probate, IHT, matrimonial, insurance and sale.*
TEL: 01704 538489; FAX: same
E-MAIL: auction@lots.uk.com
WEBSITE: www.lots.uk.com

MIDDLESEX

Bainbridge's

The Auction Room, Ickenham Rd., Ruislip. HA4 7DL.
EST. 1979. *Monthly sales on Thurs. at 11 am. Viewing on sale day from 9.30 and day before 1-7.*
TEL: 01895 621991; FAX: 01895 623622
WEBSITE: www.thecollectorscompanion.co.uk

Northwood Missionary Auctions

Freepost, Northwood, HA6 1BR.
EST. 1969. *Frequency of sales: Twice a year, April and October. Specialist auctions: General. Bric-a-brac sale the morning of the auction. Christian Charitable Trust set up in 1969 with the purpose of selling items donated and the proceeds being passed on to a nominated Christian charity or outreach programme in the UK or abroad. Sells antiques, collectables and memorabilia.*
TEL: 01923 836634; FAX: 01923 829472
E-MAIL: enquiries@nmauctions.org.uk
WEBSITE: www.nmauctions.org.uk

NORFOLK

James Beck Auctions

The Cornhall, Cattle Market St., Fakenham. NR21 9AW.
EST. 1857. *Weekly sales of antique furniture and collectables every Thurs. at 11 am.*
TEL: 01328 851557
E-MAIL: jamesbeck@auctions18.fsnet.co.uk
WEBSITE: www.jamesbeckauctions.co.uk

Bonhams Auctioneers

The Market Place, Reepham. NR10 4JJ.
Auctioneers and valuers.
TEL: 01603 871443; FAX: 01603 872973
WEBSITE: www.bonhams.com

T. W. Gaze and Son

Diss Auction Rooms, Roydon Rd., Diss. IP22 4LN.
RICS. AFAF. *Weekly Fri. auctions (over 2,000 lots) including antiques and collectables, Victorian pine and country furniture. Regular specialist sales including special antiques, decorative arts, modern design, toys and nostalgia, rural bygones, architectural salvage and statuary etc. Online catalogues.*
TEL: 01379 650306; FAX: 01379 644313
E-MAIL: sales@dissauctionrooms.co.uk
WEBSITE: www.twgaze.com

Horners Auctioneers

Acle Salerooms, Norwich Rd., Acle. NR13 3BY.
EST. 1890. *Special Saturday auctions of antiques and collectables held at Acle. Viewing Fri. prior 10-8. Weekly Thurs. general sales. Details, dates and catalogue on website.*
TEL: 01493 750225; FAX: 01493 750506
E-MAIL: auction@horners.co.uk
WEBSITE: www.horners.co.uk

Keys Fine Art Auctioneers

Auctioneers & Valuers, Off Palmers Lane, Aylsham.
NR11 6JA.
Est. 1953. *Antiques: two-day auctions held every month;
section of watches, clocks, barometers and scientific
instruments bi-monthly; six picture sales a year; three selected
quality picture sales a year; three print sales a year; six two-
day book sales a year; six quality boxed books sales a year.
Country sale: weekly sale held every Monday (Tuesdays after
Bank Holidays), over 1,000 lots. Valuations for sale, probate,
Family Division or insurance.*
Tel: 01263 733195; Fax: 01263 731222
E-mail: mail@aylshamsalerooms.co.uk
Website: www.keysauctions.co.uk

Tawn Landles

Blackfriars Chambers, Blackfriars St., Kings Lynn.
PE30 1NY.
Auctions of antiques, collectables, household goods and effects.
Tel: 01553 772816; Fax: 01553 762423
E-mail: sales@tawnlandles.co.uk
Website: www.tawnlandles.co.uk

NORTHAMPTONSHIRE

Goldsmiths

15 Market Place, Oundle. PE8 4BA.
Est. 1964. *Sales approximately quarterly.*
Tel: 01832 272349
E-mail: mail@goldsmithsofoundle.com
Website: www.goldsmithsofoundle.com

J. P. Humbert Auctioneers Ltd.

The Towcester Salerooms Burcote Rd., Towcester.
NN12 6TF.
*Monthly fine art, antiques and collectables sales and regular
specialist sales.*
Tel: 01327 359595; Fax: 01327 352038
E-mail: jphumbert.auctioneersltd@virgin.net
Website: www.jphumbertauctioneers.com

Wilfords Auctioneers Ltd.

76 Midland Rd., Wellingborough. NN8 1NB.
Est. 1937. *Weekly antique and general sales on Thurs. from
9.30 am (1,200 lots).*
Tel: 01933 222760/222762; fax 01933 271796
E-mail: sales@wilfords.org
Website: www.wilfords.org

NORTHUMBERLAND

Jim Railton

Nursery House, Chatton, Alnwick. NE66 5PY.
Est. 1990. *Furniture, ceramics, pictures, jewellery, books
and collectors items at various country house venues.*
Tel: 01668 215323; Fax: 01668 215400
E-mail: office@jimrailton.com
Website: www.jimrailton.com

NOTTINGHAMSHIRE

Bonhams Auctioneers

Chancery Lane, Retford. DN22 6DF.
Auctioneers and valuers.
Tel: 01777 708633; Fax: 01777 706724
Website: www.bonhams.com

Arthur Johnson and Sons (Auctioneers)

The Nottingham Auction Centre, Meadow Lane,
Nottingham. NG2 3GY.
*Approximately 1,800 lots weekly on Sat. at 10 am. of antique
and shipping furniture, silver, gold, porcelain, metalware and
collectables.*
Tel: 0115 986 9128; Fax: 0115 986 2139
E-mail: clientservices@arthurjohnson.co.uk
Website: www.arthurjohnson.co.uk

Mellors & Kirk Fine Art Auctioneers

Gregory St., Nottingham. NG7 2NL.
Est. 1993. RICS. *Two-day selected fine art sales every six
weeks including antique furniture, clocks, pictures, ceramics,
Oriental works of art, books and ephemera, collectors' toys and
dolls, coins and medals and other specialist items. Bi-weekly
general sales of 500-800 lots on Tues. 10.30 am. Viewing
Sat. 9-12 and Mon. 9-5.*
Tel: 0115 979 0000; Fax: 0115 978 1111
E-mail: enquiries@mellorsandkirk.com
Website: www.mellorsandkirk.com

Neales

192-194 Mansfield Rd., Nottingham. NG1 3HU.
*Bi-monthly specialist sales of paintings, drawings, prints and
books; silver, jewellery, bijouterie and watches; European and
Oriental ceramics and works of art, glass; furniture and
decoration; clocks, barometers and mechanical music;
metalwork, fabrics, needlework, carpets and rugs; collectors'
toys and dolls; stamps, coins and medals, post and cigarette
cards; autographs and collectors' items. Fortnightly collective
sales (Mon.) of general antique and later furnishings,
shipping goods and reproduction furnishings. Contents sales
on the premises of town and country properties.*
Tel: 0115 962 4141; Fax: 0115 985 6890
E-mail: nottingham@dnfa.com
Website: www.dnfa.com

Northgate Auction Rooms Ltd.

17 Northgate, Newark. NG24 1EX.
*Monthly sales of antique and Victorian furniture, oil
paintings, silver etc. Weekly sales of early 20th C and general
household furniture.*
Tel: 01636 605905; Fax: 01636 612607
E-mail: auctions@northgateauctionroomsnewark.co.uk
Website: www.northgateauctionroomsnewark.co.uk

Scotarms Ltd.

The White House, Primrose Hill, Besthorpe, Newark.
NG23 7HR.
Ten sales annually, approximately every five weeks, of antique

and modern firearms, edged weapons, militaria etc. Periodic sales of specialist items - military vehicles and associated military equipment. Postal bids accepted. Illustrated catalogue available.
TEL: 01636 893946; FAX: 01636 893916
E-MAIL: auctions@scotarms.co.uk
WEBSITE: www.scotarms.co.uk

T. Vennett-Smith
11 Nottingham Rd., Gotham. NG11 0HE.
EST. 1989. *Specialist auctions of postcards, cigarette & trade cards, autographs & ephemera, sporting memorabilia.*
TEL: 0115 983 0541; FAX: 0115 983 0114
E-MAIL: info@vennett-smith.com
WEBSITE: www.vennett-smith.com

OXFORDSHIRE

Bonhams Auctioneers
39 Park End St., Oxford. OX1 1JD.
Auctioneers and valuers.
TEL: 01865 723524; FAX: 01865 791064
WEBSITE: www.bonhams.com

Holloway's Ltd.
49 Parsons St., Banbury. OX16 5NB.
SOFAA. *General or specialist sales on own premises every other week.*
TEL: 01295 817777; FAX: 01295 817701
E-MAIL: enquiries@hollowaysauctioneers.co.uk
WEBSITE: www.hollowaysauctioneers.co.uk

Jones & Jacob Ltd.
Watcombe Manor Saleroom, Ingham Lane, Watlington, OX49 5EJ.
EST. 2005. *Eight antique and eight general sales per year held at The Saleroom, Watcombe Manor, Ingham Lane, Watlington, Oxon. Sales start 10.30am. Viewing Sat. previous 9.30-12.30, Mon. prior 10-6, Tues. prior 10-6 and morning of sale.*
TEL: Tel 01491 612810, FAX: 01491 614564
E-MAIL: saleroom@jonesandjacob.com
WEBSITE: www.jonesandjacob.com

Mallams Fine Art Auctioneers
Bocardo House, 24 St. Michael's St., Oxford. OX1 2EB.
EST. 1788. SOFAA. *Frequent sales of furniture, silver & jewellery, paintings and works of art. House sales arranged on the premises.*
TEL: 01865 241358; FAX: 01865 725483
E-MAIL: oxford@mallams.co.uk
WEBSITE: www.mallams.co.uk

Soames County Auctioneers
Unit 4, 2 River Industrial Estate, Station Lane, Witney. OX28 4BH.
Sales of antiques, fine arts & other collectors' items.
TEL: 01993 775650
E-MAIL: soame@msn.com
WEBSITE: www.soamesauctioneers.co.uk

SHROPSHIRE

Brettells Antiques and Fine Art
58 High St. Newport. TF10 7AQ.
Antique and fine art sales every two months and weekly general sales.
TEL: 01952 815925
E-MAIL: auction@brettells.com
WEBSITE: www.brettells.com

Halls Fine Art
Welsh Bridge Salerooms, Shrewsbury. SY3 8LA.
EST. 1845. RICS. SOFAA. *Weekly Fri. household and Victoriana sales. Monthly catalogued antique sales.*
TEL: 01743 281682; FAX: 08451 308246
WEBSITE: www.hallsestateagents.co.uk

Mullock's Specialist Auctioneers & Valuers
The Old Shippon, Wall-under-Heywood, Church Stretton. SY6 7DS.
EST. 1997. *Specialist auctions of historical documents, sporting memorabilia and fishing tackle.*
TEL: 01694 771771
E-MAIL: auctions@mullocksauctions.co.uk
WEBSITE: www.mullocksauctions.co.uk

Perry and Phillips
Auction Rooms, Old Mill Antique Centre, Mill St., Bridgnorth. WV15 5AG.
EST. 1853. *Monthly first Tues antiques and collectables sales.*
TEL: 01746 762248
E-MAIL: denisridgway@hotmail.com

Walker Barnett and Hill
Cosford Auction Rooms, Long Lane, Cosford. TF11 8PJ.
EST. 1780. *Regular sales of Victoriana, reproduction, shipping, modern furniture and effects on Saturdays. 10.30. Fine art and antiques sales every six-eight weeks Tues and Wed.*
TEL: 01902 375555; FAX: 01902 375566
E-MAIL: wbhauctions@lineone.net
WEBSITE: www.walker-barnett-hill.co.uk

SOMERSET

Aldridges of Bath
Newark House, 26-45 Cheltenham St., Bath. BA2 3EX.
EST. 1976. *Fortnightly Tues. sales, broken down into specialist categories:- antique furniture to include clocks and Oriental carpets; silver and porcelain, glass and metalware; paintings and prints; collectors' sales; Victorian and general furniture. Viewing Sat. 9-12 and Mon. 9-6. Catalogues available upon annual subscription.*
TEL: 01225 462830; FAX: 01225 311319

Bonhams Auctioneers
1 Old King St., Bath. BA1 2JT.
Auctioneers and valuers.
TEL: 01225 788988; FAX: 01225 446675
WEBSITE: www.bonhams.com

Clevedon Salerooms
The Auction Centre, Kenn Rd., Kenn, Clevedon. BS21 6TT.
EST. 1885. *Quarterly auctions of antique furniture, fine art and collectors' items. Fortnightly sales of Victorian, Edwardian and general furniture and effects. Occasional specialist sales and sales held on vendors' property. Valuations.*
TEL: 01934 830111; FAX: 01934 832538
E-MAIL: info@clevedon-salerooms.com
WEBSITE: www.clevedon-salerooms.com

Cooper & Tanner Chartered Surveyors
The Agricultural Centre, Standerwick, Frome. BA11 2QB.
EST. 1908. *Weekly sales of antiques and general household chattels on Wed. at 10.30 am. Viewing morning of sale. Haulage service.*
TEL: 01373 831010; FAX: 01373 831103
E-MAIL: agricultural@cooperandtanner.co.uk
WEBSITE: www.cooperandtanner.co.uk

Hosegood Ford
3 Fore St., Williton, Taunton. TA4 4PX.
Sales approximately every two months.
TEL: 01984 632040; FAX: 01984 633898
E-MAIL: mail@exmoorproperties.co.uk
WEBSITE: www.exmoorproperties.co.uk

Lawrence Fine Art Auctioneers Ltd.
South St., Crewkerne. TA18 8AB.
SOFAA. RICS. ARVA. *Specialist auctioneers and valuers. Quarterly sales of antiques and fine art. General sales every Wed. (uncatalogued). Collectors' section first Wed. monthly. Bi-annual book sales (Jan. and July); bi-annual militaria sales (April and Oct). Catalogue on website.*
TEL: 01460 73041; FAX: 01460 270799
E-MAIL: enquiries@lawrences.co.uk
WEBSITE: www.lawrences.co.uk

Lawrences at Greenslade Taylor Hunt
Magdalene House, Church Square, Taunton. TA1 1SB.
Specialist fine art sales, Collectors' sales and well-established, popular bi-annual sporting sales. Weekly general sales of modern and antique furnishings and effects (every Thursday). Contact the auctioneers for details. Now merged with Lawrences in Crewkerne.
TEL: 01823 332525; FAX: 01823 353120
E-MAIL: fine.art@gth.net
WEBSITE: www.gth.net

The London Cigarette Card Co. Ltd.
Sutton Rd., Somerton. TA11 6QP.
EST. 1927. *Suppliers of thousands of different series of cigarette and trade cards and special albums. Publishers of catalogues, reference books and monthly magazine on card collecting. Regular auctions. S.A.E. for details. Shop open Mon-Sat in West St., Taunton, TA11 6AP.*
TEL: 01458 273452; FAX: 01458 273515
E-MAIL: cards@londoncigcard.co.uk
WEBSITE: www.londoncigcard.co.uk

McCubbing & Redfern
3 Court Ash, Yeovil. BA20 1HG.
Also at 66-68 Southover, Wells, BA5 1UH. Tel 01749 678099. Antique & collectable auctions every four weeks in Wells and in Yeovil. E-mail for free catalogues.
TEL: 01935 428101; MOBILE: 07870 740324
E-MAIL: admin@mccubbingandredfern.co.uk
WEBSITE: www.mccubbingandredfern.co.uk

Tamlyn & Son
Market St., Bridgwater. TA6 3BN.
Regular sales of antiques. Specialist sales of collectors items, clocks, fine art.
TEL: 01278 445251; FAX: 01278 458242
E-MAIL: saleroom@tamlynandson.co.uk
WEBSITE: www.tamlyns.co.uk

STAFFORDSHIRE

Cuttlestones Ltd.
Penkridge Auction Rooms, Pinfold Lane, Penkridge. ST19 5AP.
EST. 2007.
TEL: Tel 01785 714905; FAX: 01785 715918
E-MAIL: office@cuttlestones.co.uk
WEBSITE: www.cuttlestones.co.uk

Potteries Specialist Auctions
271 Waterloo Rd., Cobridge, Stoke-on-Trent. ST6 3HR.
EST. 1997. *Specialist auctions of 20th C British pottery monthly; Royal Doulton, Beswick, Moorcroft, Wade, Wedgwood. Usually Wed. at 11 am. Viewing Tues. prior 10-4.*
TEL: 01782 286622; FAX: 01782 201518
E-MAIL: enquiries@potteriesauctions.com
WEBSITE: www.potteriesauctions.com

Louis Taylor Fine Art Auctioneers
Britannia House, 10 Town Rd., Hanley, Stoke-on-Trent. ST1 2QG.
EST. 1877. RICS. *Quarterly fine art sales including furniture, pictures, pottery, porcelain, silver and works of art. Specialist Royal Doulton and Beswick auctions. General Victoriana auctions held every two weeks. Fine art auctions through www.auction-net.co.uk and antiquestradegazette.com.*
TEL: 01782 214111; FAX: 01782 215283
E-MAIL: louis.taylor@ukonline.co.uk
WEBSITE: www.louistaylorfineart.co.uk

Wintertons Fine Arts
8 Short Street, Uttoxeter ST14 7LH.
EST. 1864. SOFAA. RICS. *Bi-monthly sales of antiques and fine art and sales of Victorian and general furniture every two weeks. Quarterly sales jewellery and antiques at the Agricultural Business Centre, Bakewell; monthly sales of Victorian and general antiques and quarterly toy sales at Uttoxeter. Fine arts manager, Neil Grenyer MRICS.*
TEL: 01889 564385; FAX: 01889 567949
E-MAIL: enquiries@wintertons.co.uk
WEBSITE: www.wintertons.co.uk

SUFFOLK

Abbotts Auction Rooms
Campsea Ashe, Woodbridge. IP13 0PS.
*Extensive calendar of fine art and antique auctions held on Wed.
Sales calendar and catalogues available. Weekly sales of Victoriana
& household furniture held on Mon. Viewing Sat. 9-11.*
TEL: 01728 746323; FAX: 01728 748173

Bonhams Auctioneers
32 Boss Hall Rd., Ipswich. IP1 5DJ.
Auctioneers and valuers.
TEL: Tel: 01473 740494; fax 01473 741091
WEBSITE: www.bonhams.com

Diamond Mills and Co. Fine Art Auctioneers
117 Hamilton Rd., Felixstowe. IP11 7BL.
*Periodic fine art sales. Monthly general sales. Auctions at The
Orwell Hall, Orwell Rd., Felixstowe.*
TEL: 01394 282281 (3 lines)

Durrant's
The Old School House, Peddars Lane, Beccles. NR34 9UE.
EST. 1854. *Monthly sales of fine antiques, furniture and
collectables.*
TEL: 01502 713490
E-MAIL: info@durrantsauctionrooms.com
WEBSITE: www.durrants.com

Dyson & Son
The Auction Room, Church St., Clare. CO10 8PD.
EST. 1978. *Sales of antiques and chattels every three weeks
on Sat. at 11 am. Viewing Fri. 9-8, Sat. from 9 am.*
TEL: 01787 277993; FAX: 01787 277996
E-MAIL: info@dyson-auctioneers.co.uk
WEBSITE: www.dyson-auctioneers.co.uk

Lacy Scott and Knight Fine Art & Furniture
10 Risbygate St., Bury St. Edmunds. IP33 3AA.
EST. 1869. SOFAA. *Free auction advice & valuations.
Probate & insurance valuations prepared. Transport &
storage service. Extensively illustrated catalogues. Internet-
hosted catalogues. Regular e-newsletter & notifications.
Quality items always sought for auction. Local, national &
international advertising.*
TEL: Tel: 01284 748623 Fax: 01284 748620
E-MAIL: fineart@lsk.co.uk
WEBSITE: www.lsk.co.uk

Neal Sons and Fletcher
26 Church St., Woodbridge. IP12 1DP.
*Two special mixed antiques sales annually. Individual
specialised sales and complete house contents sales as required.
Household furniture sales monthly on Wed.*
TEL: 01394 382263; FAX: 01394 383030
E-MAIL: enquiries@nsf.co.uk
WEBSITE: www.nsf.co.uk

Sworders incorporating Olivers
The Saleroom, Burkitts Lane, Sudbury. CO10 1HB.

EST. 1766. SOFAA. *Specialist auctions of fine art &
antiques; srms, armour, medals & militaria. Fortnightly
auctions of general antiques & decorative items. Valuations
for sale, insurance, probate and Family Division.*
TEL: 01787 880305; FAX: 01787 883107
E-MAIL: olivers@sworder.co.uk

SURREY

Bonhams Auctioneers
Millmead Guilford GU2 4BE.
Auctioneers and valuers.
TEL: 01483 504030; FAX: 01483 450205
WEBSITE: www.bonhams.com

Cartels
2 Tanners Court, Middle St., Brockham, Dorking.
RH3 7NH.
*Contents of house sales of antique and later furniture, china,
glass, pictures and other collectables.*
TEL: 01737 844646; MOBILE: 0776 8004293
E-MAIL: info@cartels-sales.co.uk

Clarke Gammon Weller
The Sussex Barn, Loseley Park, Guildford. GU3 1HS.
EST. 1919. *Six sales a year of fine art, antiques and
collectables. Auctions can be conducted on owners' premises.
Valuations for probate, insurance and Family Division.*
TEL: 01483 207570; FAX: 01483 207579
WEBSITE: www.clarkegammonwellers.co.uk

Crow's Auction Gallery
Rear of Dorking Halls, The Car Park, Reigate Rd.,
Dorking. RH4 1SG.
Antiques and collectables and general sales.
TEL: 01306 740382; 01306 881672
E-MAIL: enquiries@crowsauctions.co.uk
WEBSITE: www.crowsauctions.co.uk

Ewbank Auctioneers
Burnt Common Auction Rooms, London Rd., Send,
Woking. GU23 7LN.
EST. 1990. SOFAA. *Quarterly antique and fine art
auctions. Regular sales of Victorian and later furnishings.*
TEL: 01483 223101; FAX: 01483 222171
E-MAIL: antiques@ewbankauctions.co.uk
WEBSITE: www.ewbankauctions.co.uk

Lawrences' Auctioneers Limited
Norfolk House, 80 High St., Bletchingley. RH1 4PA.
EST. 1964. *Six-weekly antique and reproduction furniture
and effects.*
TEL: 01883 743323; FAX: 01883 744578
E-MAIL: enquries@lawrencesbletchingley.co.uk
WEBSITE: www.lawrencesbletchingley.co.uk

John Nicholson Auctioneers
The Auction Rooms, Longfield, Midhurst Rd.,
Fernhurst, Haslemere. GU27 3HA.
Regular fine art, antiques, pictures and general sales.

TEL: 01428 653727; FAX: 01428 641509
E-MAIL: sales@johnnicholsons.com
WEBSITE: www.johnnicholsons.com

Wellers Auctioneers
The Surrey Auction House, 70 Guildford St., Chertsey.
KT16 9BB.
EST. 1866. *Monthly two-day sales of silver, objets de vertu, clocks & watches and jewellery, antiques & collectables. Occasional special auctions.*
TEL: 01932 568678; FAX: 01932 568626
E-MAIL: auctions@wellersauctions.com
WEBSITE: www.wellersauctions.com

P. F. Windibank Auctioneers
The Dorking Halls, Reigate Rd., Dorking. RH4 1SG.
EST. 1945. *Antique auctions held every 4-5 weeks on Sat. at 10.30 am. Viewing Thurs. evening prior 5-9, Fri. prior 9-5 and morning of sale 8.15-10.15. Catalogues available one week before. Fully photographed website. 10% buyers' premium.*
TEL: 01306 884556/876280; FAX: 01306 884669
E-MAIL: sjw@windibank.co.uk
WEBSITE: www.windibank.co.uk

EAST SUSSEX

Bonhams Auctioneers
19 Palmeira Square, Hove. BN3 2JN.
Auctioneers and valuers.
TEL: 01273 220000; FAX: 01273 220335
WEBSITE: www.bonhams.com

Burstow and Hewett
Abbey Auction Galleries and Granary Sale Rooms, Battle. TN33 0AT.
Monthly sales of antique furniture, silver, jewellery, porcelain, brass, rugs etc. at the Abbey Auction Galleries. Also monthly evening sales of fine oil paintings, watercolours, prints, and engravings. At the Granary Sale Rooms - monthly sales of furniture, china, silver, brass, etc.
TEL: 01424 772374
E-MAIL: auctions@burstowandhewett.co.uk
WEBSITE: www.burstowandhewett.co.uk

Eastbourne Auction Rooms
Auction House, Finmere Rd., Eastbourne. BN22 8QL.
Fine art, antiques and quality collectables sales held every six weeks on a Friday, 10am. Collectables every six weeks on a Saturday, 10am.
TEL: 01323 431444; FAX: 01323 417638
E-MAIL: enquiries@eastbourneauction.com
WEBSITE: www.eastbourneauction.com

Gorringes
Garden St., Lewes. BN7 1XE.
General sales held weekly on Mon. at 10.30 am.
TEL: 01273 478221; FAX: 01273 475762
WEBSITE: www.gorringes.co.uk

Gorringes LLP
Terminus Rd., Bexhill-on-Sea. TN39 3LR.
Quarterly antiques and collectables sales.
TEL: 01424 212994; FAX: 01424 224035
E-MAIL: bexhill@gorringes.co.uk
WEBSITE: www.gorringes.co.uk

Raymond P. Inman
The Auction Galleries, 98a Coleridge St. Hove.
BN3 5AA.
EST. 1929. *Monthly sales of antiques, furniture, china, glass, pictures, silver, jewellery, collectables, etc.*
TEL: 01273 774777; FAX: 01273 735660
E-MAIL: r.p.inman@talk21.com
WEBSITE: www.invaluable.com/raymondinman

Rosan and Co incorporating E. Reeves Auctions
Springham Farm, Springham Farm Estate, Grove Hill, Hailsham. BN27 4HF.
Monthly Sat. collective sales at 10.30 am. Viewing morning of sale 8-10.30.
TEL: 01435 810410
E-MAIL: rosans@hotmail.co.uk

Wallis and Wallis
West Street Auction Galleries, Lewes. BN7 2NJ.
EST. 1928. *Nine annual sales of arms and armour, militaria and medals. Two connoisseur collectors' sales spring and autumn. Specimen catalogue £3.50. Current catalogues £9.50. Die-cast and tin plate toys and models - catalogue £7.00. Commission bids (without charge) accepted. Valuations.*
TEL: 01273 480208; FAX: 01273 476562
E-MAIL: auctions@wallisandwallis.org
WEBSITE: www.wallisandwallis.org

Watsons
Heathfield Furniture Salerooms, The Market, Burwash Rd., Heathfield. TN21 8RA.
Sales of general furniture and effects.
TEL: 01435 862132; FAX: 01435 867167
E-MAIL: watsonsauctions@btconnect.com
WEBSITE: www.watsonsauctioneers.co.uk

WEST SUSSEX

Henry Adams Fine Art Auctioneers
Rowans House, Baffins Lane, Chichester. PO19 1UA.
EST. 2000. RICS. SOFAA. *Monthly catalogue specialist sales, usually on Thurs. at 10.30. Viewing two days preceding sale. Valuations undertaken for sales, insurance and probate.*
TEL: 01243 532223; FAX: 01243 532299
E-MAIL: enquiries@henryadamsfineart.co.uk
WEBSITE: www.henryadamsfineart.co.uk

John Bellman Ltd.
New Pound, Wisborough Green, Billingshurst.
RH14 0AZ.
Three-day sale once a month; Wed. pm ceramics and glass and

Oriental; Thurs. am furniture; Thurs. pm silver, vertu, jewellery and watches, clocks; Fri. am toys, collectors' items, works of art, paintings, textiles, carpets and rugs. Viewing Sat. 9-12, Mon. 9-4, Tues. 9-7, Wed. 9-1. Book sales three times a year.
TEL: 01403 700858; FAX: 01403 700059
E-MAIL: enquiries@bellmans.co.uk
WEBSITE: www.bellmans.co.uk

Denham's
The Auction Galleries, Warnham, Horsham. RH12 3RZ.
EST. 1884. *Monthly sales of antique furniture, clocks, scientific instruments, metalware, collectors' items, ceramics, glassware, paintings, silver and jewellery.*
TEL: 01403 255699/253837; FAX: 01403 253837
E-MAIL: enquiries@denhams.com
WEBSITE: www.denhams.com

Stride and Son
Southdown House, St. John's St., Chichester. PO19 1XQ.
EST. 1890. *Sales last Fri. monthly - antiques and general; periodic book and document sales.*
TEL: 01243 780207; FAX: 01243 786713
E-MAIL: enquiries@stridesauctions.co.uk
WEBSITE: www.stridesauctions.co.uk

Sussex Auction Galleries
Unit 2, Grange Industrial Estate, Albion St., Southwick, Brighton. BN42 4EN.
Monthly sales of fine art including antique furniture, pictures, silver, Oriental carpets and rugs and ornamental items.
TEL: 01273 870371; FAX: 01273 595706
WEBSITE: www.worthing-auctions.co.uk

Tooveys
Spring Gardens, Washington. RH20 3BS.
SOFAA. *Antiques, fine art and collectors' items.*
TEL: 01903 891955; FAX: 01903 891966
E-MAIL: auctions@tooveys.com
WEBSITE: www.tooveys.com

TYNE & WEAR

Anderson and Garland
Anderson House, Crispin Court, Newbiggin Lane, Westerhope, Newcastle-upon-Tyne. NE5 1BF.
EST. 1840. *Regular sales of paintings, prints, antique furniture, silver and collectors' items. Anderson House.*
TEL: 0191 430 3000; FAX: 0191 430 3001
E-MAIL: info@andersonandgarland.com
WEBSITE: www.andersonandgarland.com

Boldon Auction Galleries
24a Front St., East Boldon. NE36 0SJ.
EST. 1981. *Quarterly antique auctions.*
TEL: 0191 537 2630; FAX: 0191 536 3875

E-MAIL: boldon@btconnect.com
WEBSITE: www.boldonauctions.co.uk

Bonhams Auctioneers
30/32 Grey Street, Newcastle-upon-Tyne. NE1 6AE.
Auctioneers and valuers.
TEL: 0191 233 9930; FAX: 0191 233 9933
WEBSITE: www.bonhams.com

Thomas N. Miller Auctioneers
Algernon Rd., Byker, Newcastle-upon-Tyne. NE6 2UN.
EST. 1902. *China and glass auctions every Tues. at 10 am. Antique auctions every Wed. at 10 am.*
TEL: 0191 265 8080; FAX: 0191 265 5050
E-MAIL: info@millersauctioneers.co.uk
WEBSITE: www.millersauctioneers.co.uk

WARWICKSHIRE

Bigwood Fine Art Auctioneers Ltd.
The Old School, Tiddington, Stratford-upon-Avon. CV37 7AW.
EST. 1974. SOFAA. *Sales every Friday weekly of general furnishings and house contents. Monthly antiques and selected collectables. Also special interest sales - sporting items and taxidermy, toys and wine.*
TEL: 01789 269415; FAX: 01789 294168
E-MAIL: enquiries@bigwoodauctioneers.co.uk
WEBSITE: www.bigwoodauctioneers.co.uk

Henley-in-Arden Auction Sales Ltd.
The Estate Office, Warwick Rd., Henley-in-Arden. B95 5BH.
Sales of antique and modern furniture and effects fourth Sat. each month.
TEL: 01564 792154; FAX: 01564 794916
E-MAIL: henleyauctions@btconnect.com

Locke & England
18 Guy St., Leamington Spa. CV32 4RT.
EST. 1834. *Regular sales of antique furniture and effects, jewellery, 20th C design, collectors' items and general household items.*
TEL: 01926 889100; FAX: 01926 470608
E-MAIL: info@leauction.co.uk
WEBSITE: www.leauction.co.uk

Warwick and Warwick Ltd.
Chalon House, Scar Bank, Millers Rd., Warwick. CV34 5DB.
EST. 1958. PTA. ASDA. BNTA. *Auctioneers and valuers of collectables. Stamp auctions held monthly. Postcards, cigarette cards, autographs, ephemera, medals, militaria, coins, banknotes, sports memorabilia, die-cast toys and models and other collectables sold by auction quarterly.*
TEL: 01926 499031; FAX: 01926 491906
E-MAIL: colin.such@warwickandwarwick.com
WEBSITE: www.warwickandwarwick.com

Warwick Auctions of Coventry
3 Queen Victoria Rd., Coventry. CV1 3JS.
Antiques and collectables sale first Wednesday of every month.
TEL: 02476 223377; FAX: 02476 220044
E-MAIL: info@warwick-auctions.co.uk
WEBSITE: www.warwick-auctions.co.uk

WEST MIDLANDS

Biddle & Webb Ltd.
Icknield Square, Ladywood, Middleway, Birmingham.
B16 0PP.
*Antique sale first Thursday of each month, fine arts, silver &
jewellery first Friday of each month. Toys & juvenalia sale is
every two months. Antiques & militaria every two months.*
TEL: 0121 455 8042; FAX: 0121-454-9615
E-MAIL: info@biddleandwebb.com
WEBSITE: www.biddleandwebb.com

Bonhams Auctioneers
The Old House, Station Rd., Knowle, Solihull.
B93 0HT.
Auctioneers and valuers.
TEL: 01564 776151; FAX: 01564 778069
WEBSITE: www.bonhams.com

City Auctioneering Ltd.
Bristol Sales Centre, Easter Compton, Bristol.
BS35 5RE.
*Auctions throughout the year to include fine furniture, rugs &
textiles, metalware, paintings & prints, silver and fine wine.*
TEL: 01454 632332; fax 01454 633160
E-MAIL: citybidding@btconnect.com
WEBSITE: www.bid-city.net

Fellows and Sons
Augusta House, 19 Augusta St., Hockley, Birmingham.
B18 6JA.
EST. 1876. BJA. *Auctioneers and valuers of jewels, silver,
fine art.*
TEL: 0121 212 2131; FAX: 0121 212 1249
E-MAIL: info@fellows.co.uk
WEBSITE: www.fellows.co.uk

Fieldings Auctioneeers Ltd.
Mil Race Lane, Stourbridge. DY8 1JN.
Monthly sales of antiques and objets d'art.
TEL: 01384 444140; FAX: 01384 444138
E-MAIL: info@fieldingsauctioneers.co.uk
WEBSITE: www.fieldingsauctioneers.co.uk

WILTSHIRE

Henry Aldridge & Son
The Devizes Auctioneers, Unit 1, Bath Road Business
Centre, Bath Rd., Devizes. SN10 1XA.
*Specialists in Titanic and marine memorabilia, also monthly
sales of antique and collectable items.*
TEL: 01380 729199; FAX: 01380 730073

E-MAIL: andrew@henry-aldridge.co.uk
WEBSITE: www.henry-aldridge.co.uk

Gardiner Houlgate
9 Leafield Way, Corsham. SN13 9SW.
EST. 1984. *Regular sales of antique furniture, works of art,
Clarice Cliff and decorative arts. Frequent sales of Victorian
and later furnishings. Fortnightly jewellery sales, quarterly
musical instrument sales, specialist painting and clocks and
watches sales. Valuations.*
TEL: 01225 812912; FAX: 01225 811777
E-MAIL: auctions@gardinerhoulgate.co.uk
WEBSITE: www.gardinerhoulgate.com

Harrison Auctions Ltd.
Jubilee Auction Rooms, Fordbrook Business Centre,
Pewsey. SN9 5NU.
General auctions at 10.30am on a Wednesday of each month.
TEL: 01672 562012
E-MAIL: info@harrisonauctions.co.uk
WEBSITE: www.harrisonauctions.co.uk

Kidson-Trigg
Friars Estate Office & Auction Rooms, Nr Highworth,
Swindon. SN6 7PZ.
*Selected antiques, fine art, general antique and later furniture
and effects. Specialist sales held throughout the year to include
outside effects, period stoneware & architectural items, sporting
memorabilia, stamps & coins, toys & modern collectables, etc.*
TEL: 01793 861000
E-MAIL: kidsontriggauctions@btconnect.com
WEBSITE: www.kidsontrigg.co.uk

May and Son
Units 1, 3 and 4 Delta Works, Salisbury Rd., Shipton
Bellinger. SP9 7UN.
EST. 1925. *Three auctions every months; two general held on
Saturdays and one antique on a Wednesday. All sales start at
10am. Viewing two days prior to sale. Buyers' premium 15%
+ VAT.*
TEL: 01980 846000; FAX: 01980 846027
WEBSITE: www.mayauctioneers.co.uk

Wessex Auction Rooms
Westbrook Farm, Draycott Cerne, Chippenham. SN15
5LH.
*Antique & fine art, sporting memorabilia, and classic car &
automobilia auctions. Collectors and toy sales x 5 per year as
well as monthly antique and general auctions.*
TEL: 01249 720888
E-MAIL: enquiries@wessexauctionrooms.co.uk
WEBSITE: www.wessexauctionrooms.co.uk

Woolley and Wallis
Salisbury Salerooms Ltd. 51-61 Castle St., Salisbury.
SP1 3SU.
EST. 1884. SOFAA. RICS. *Specialist sales of antique
furniture, ceramics, pictures, silver, jewellery and 20th C
decorative arts. Written valuations for probate and*

insurance.
TEL: 01722 424500; FAX: 01722 424508
E-MAIL: enquiries@woolleyandwallis.co.uk
WEBSITE: www.woolleyandwallis.co.uk

WORCESTERSHIRE

Carter's Auctioneers
Dodfordd Village Hall Priory Lane, Dodford,
Nr Bromsgrove.
Five auctions per year of antiques and collectables.
TEL: 01299 271130; FAX: same; MOBILE: 07779
311792
E-MAIL: barnabys@btinternet.com
WEBSITE: www.cartersauction.co.uk

Griffiths & Charles
57 Foregate St., Worcester. WR1 1DZ.
EST. 1870. *General auctioneers.*
TEL: 01905 720160
E-MAIL: info@griffiths-charles.co.uk

Philip Serrell - Auctioneers & Valuers
The Malvern Sale Room, Barnards Green Rd.,
Malvern. WR14 3LW.
EST. 1996. *Bi-monthly catalogued antique and fine art
auctions. Fortnightly general sales. Specialist on the premises
sales. Free sales estimates.*
TEL: 01684 892314; FAX: 01684 569832
E-MAIL: serrell.auctions@virgin.net
WEBSITE: www.serrell.com

EAST YORKSHIRE

Gilbert Baitson
The Edwardian Auction Galleries, 389-395 Anlaby
Rd., Hull. HU3 6AB.
EST. 1935. *Sales of antique and modern furnishings every
sixth Wed. at 10.30 am. Viewing day prior until 7 pm.*
TEL: 01482 500500; (after hours) 01482 645241
E-MAIL: info@gilbert-baitson.co.uk
WEBSITE: www.gilbert-baitson.co.uk

Dee, Atkinson & Harrison
The Exchange Saleroom, The Exchange Driffield.
YO25 6LD.
RICS *Bi-monthly antique & fine art auctions.Fortnightly
Victorian & general auctions. Regular specialist auctions of
antiquarian books, toys & collectables, 20th C ceramics.*
TEL: 01377 253151
E-MAIL: info@sledmerehouse.com
WEBSITE: www.dahauctions.com

Haller Evans - Auctioneers and Valuers
1 Parliament St., Hull. HU1 2AR.
EST. 1889. *Regular auctions of antiques and modern
furniture and effects.*
TEL: 01482 323033; FAX: 01482 211954
E-MAIL: hallerevans@hull24.com

WEBSITE: www.hallerevans.com

Spencers Auctions
The Imperial and Repository Salerooms, Olivers Lane,
Bridlington. YO15 2AS.
EST. 1892. *General auctions every Thurs. Regular sales of
antiques and fine art.*
TEL: 01262 676724; FAX: 01262 673617
E-MAIL: johncook@spencersauctions.co.uk
WEBSITE: www.spencersauctions.co.uk

NORTH YORKSHIRE

Bonhams Auctioneers
Market Chambers, 14 Market Place, Bedale. DL8 1EQ.
Auctioneers and valuers.
TEL: 01677 424114; FAX: 01677 424115
WEBSITE: www.bonhams.com

Boulton and Cooper Ltd.
St. Michaels House, Market Place, Malton. YO17 0LR.
SOFAA. *Alternating monthly antique sales at Malton and
York. Fortnightly general sales at Pickering.*
TEL: 01653 696151
E-MAIL: antiques@boultoncooper.co.uk
WEBSITE: www.boultoncooper.co.uk

Cundalls
15 Market Place, Malton. YO17 7LP.
*Regular catalogue sales of fine art, antique furniture, glass,
china and antique bric-a-brac together with a large number
of specialist sales including up to five railwayana sales. Also a
bespoke auction service to suit all needs.*
TEL: 01653 697820; FAX: 01653 698305
E-MAIL: malton@cundalls.co.uk
WEBSITE: www.cundalls.co.uk

David Duggleby
The Paddock Salerooms, Whitby. YO21 3DB.
SOFAA. *Special picture sales, Staithes Group, marine and
Yorkshire artists. 15% buyers' premium excluding VAT.*
TEL: 01947 820033; FAX: 01947 825680
E-MAIL: auctions@davidduggleby.com

David Duggleby Ltd.
The Vine Street Salerooms, Scarborough. YO11 1XN.
SOFAA. *Special picture sales - Staithes group, marine and
Yorkshire artists. Buyers' premium 15% excluding VAT.*
TEL: 01723 507111; FAX: 01723 507222
E-MAIL: auctions@davidduggleby.com
WEBSITE: www.davidduggleby.com

Hutchinson-Scott
The Grange, Marton-le-Moor, Ripon. HG4 5AT.
EST. 1976. *Periodic general sales plus two or three catalogue
sales annually. Specialist in fine antiques and works of art.*
TEL: 01423 326236; FAX: 01423 324264
E-MAIL: sales@hutchinson-scott.co.uk
WEBSITE: www.hutchinson-scott.co.uk

Morphets of Harrogate

6 Albert St., Harrogate. HG1 1JL.
Est. 1895. *Sales of antiques and works of art, interspersed with regular sales of general furniture and effects. Catalogue subscription scheme.*
Tel: 01423 530030; Fax: 01423 500717
E-mail: enquiries@morphets.co.uk
Website: www.morphets.co.uk

Richardson & Smith

8 Victoria Square, Whitby. YO21 1EA.
Sales of modern and antique items including paintings, furniture, ceramics, jewellery, bric-a-brac, electrical goods, etc.
Tel: 01947 602298; Fax: 01947 820594
E-mail: auctions@richardsonandsmith.co.uk
Website: www.richardsonandsmith.co.uk

Summersgill Auctioneers

8 Front St., Acomb, York. YO24 3BZ.
Est. 1959. *Auctions of antiques and collectors' items.*
Tel: 01904 791131
E-mail: timsummersgill@tiscali.co.uk
Website: www.summersgills.com

Tennants

The Auction Centre, Leyburn. DL8 5SG.
16 specialist departments offering expertise in all areas of fine art, antiques & collectables. Weekly 800 lot sales of antiques and also house contents. International & specialist catalogue sales.
Tel: 01969 623780; Fax: 01969 624281
E-mail: enquiry@tennants-ltd.co.uk
Website: www.tennants.co.uk

D. Wombell & Son Ltd.

The Auction Gallery, North Minister Business Park, Northfield Lane, Upper Poppleton. YO26 6QU.
Monthly general sales of antiques and collectables first Sat.
Tel: 01904 790777; Fax: 01904 798018
E-mail: wwheritage@aol.com
Website: www.invaluable.com/wombells

SOUTH YORKSHIRE

Paul Beighton Auctioneers Ltd.

Woodhouse Green, Thurcroft, Rotherham. S66 9AQ.
Est. 1982 *General antiques and collectables sales every two weeks on Sun. from 11 am. Viewing Fri. 10-4 and sale day from 9 am. Quarterly specialist sales of antique furniture and fine art.*
Tel: 01709 700005; Fax: 01709 700244
E-mail: paul.beighton@btconnect.com
Website: www.pbauctioneers.co.uk

A. E. Dowse and Son

Cornwall Galleries, Scotland St., Sheffield. S3 7DE.
Est. 1915. NAAVA. *Monthly Sat. sales of antiques. Quarterly fine art and antique sales. Quarterly sales of diecast, tin plate and collectors' toys. Monthly sales of modern furniture and shipping goods.*
Tel: 0114 2725858; Fax: 0114 2490550
E-mail: info@aedoweandson.com
Website: www.aedoweandson.com

ELR Auctions Ltd.

The Nichols Building, Shalesmoor, Sheffield. S3 8UJ.
Est. 1840. *Extensive calendar of fortnightly antiques & collectables sales and quarterly antique & fine art auctions.*
Tel: 0114 281 6161; Fax: 0114 281 6162
E-mail: elrauctions@btconnect.com
Website: www.elrauctions.com

Wilbys

6A Eastgate, Barnsley. S70 2EP.
Regular auction sales of items of fine art and antiques.
Tel: 01226 299221
E-mail: contact@wilbys.net
Website: www.wilbys.net

Wilkinson's Auctioneers Ltd.

28 Netherhall Rd. Doncaster. DN1 2PW.
Est. 1997. *Catalogue sales every two months, alternating between fine furniture, paintings, bronzes and effects and period oak, country furniture and carvings.*
Tel: 01302 814884; Fax: 01302 814883
E-mail: sid@wilkinsons-auctioneers.co.uk
Website: www.wilkinsons-auctioneers.co.uk

WEST YORKSHIRE

Bonhams Auctioneers

30 Park Square West. Leeds. LS1 2PF.
Auctioneers and valuers.
Tel: 0113 234 5755; Fax: 0113 244 3910
Website: www.bonhams.com

Gary Don Auctioneers

The Wharf Salerooms, Curtis Buildings, Berking Avenue, Leeds. LS9 9LF.
Est. 1929. *Antiques, fine art and collectables.*
Tel: 0113 248 3333; Fax: 0113 248 3232
E-mail: garydon@ntlworld.com
Website: www.garydon.co.uk

Andrew Hartley Auctions

Victoria Hall Salerooms, Little Lane, Ilkley. LS29 8EA.
Est. 1906. *Six catalogued fine art and antique auctions. Specialist toy/collectors sales and wine sales. Weekly Victoriana and general auctions; approx 900 lots per week.*
Tel: 01943 816363; fax- 01943 817610
E-mail: info@hartleysauctions.co.uk
Website: www.hartleysauctions.co.uk

Malcolm's No 1 Auctions

Boston Spa, Wetherby. LS23 6AA.
Monthly sales of general antiques and collectables.
Tel: 01977 684971; Fax: same
E-mail: info@malcolmsno1auctions.co.uk
Website: www.malcolmsno1auctions.co.uk

CHANNEL ISLANDS

Bonhams Auctioneers
39 Don Street St. Helier JE2 4TR.
Auctioneers and valuers.
TEL: 01534 722441; FAX: 01534 759354
WEBSITE: www.bonhams.com

Martel Maides Auctions
Cornet St., St. Peter Port, Guernsey. GY1 1LF.
*Fortnightly antique and modern auction sales and quarterly
fine art catalogue sales.*
TEL: 01481 722700
E-MAIL: auctions@martelmaides.co.uk
WEBSITE: www.martelmaides.co.uk

NORTHERN IRELAND

John Ross & Company
37 Montgomery St., Belfast. BT1 4NX.
*Antique and reproduction furniture, paintings, jewellery,
porcelain etc. The last Thursday of the month is the antiques
sale. Occasional specialist sales.*
TEL: 02890 325448; FAX: 02890 333642
E-MAIL: info@rosss.ie
WEBSITE: www.rosss.ie

Viewback Antiques & Auctions
39 Erganagh Rd., Omagh, Co Tyrone. BT79 7SX.

EST. 1977. *Regular general and specialist sales. House
clearances and specialist sales of antiques. Small retail shop by
appointment.*
TEL: 02882 246271; MOBILE: 07760275247
E-MAIL: auctioneer@viewbackantiquesandauctions.com
WEBSITE: www.viewbackantiquesandauctions.com

Wilson's Auctions
22 Mallusk Rd., Newtownabbey, Co Antrim. BT36 8PP.
EST. 1936. FNAVA. *Antique, fine art & collectables sales
every two months.*
TEL: 02890 342626; FAX: 02890 342528
E-MAIL: gavincarvill@wilsonsauctions.com
WEBSITE: www.wilsonsauctions.com

SCOTLAND

Auction Rooms
Castle Laurie, Bankside Ind Est, Falkirk. FK2 7XF.
*Weekly Wed. sales at 6 pm. Mixed sale of antique, general
household and new furniture. Specialised sales are held,
details available on website. Viewing Tues. 8–8, Wed. 8–6.*
TEL: 01324 623000; FAX: 01324 630343
E-MAIL: robert@auctionroomsfalkirk.co.uk
WEBSITE: www.auctionroomsfalkirk.co.uk

Bonhams Auctioneers
65 George St., Edinburgh, EH2 2JL.
Auctioneers and valuers.
TEL: Tel: 0131 225 2266, Fax: 0131 220 2547
WEBSITE: www.bonhams.com

Thomas R. Callan
22 Smith St. Ayr. KA7 1TF.
Weekly Thursday sales of antiques and general items.
TEL: 01292 267681; FAX: 01292 261671
E-MAIL: trcallan@fsmail.net
WEBSITE: www.trcallan.com

Collins & Paterson LLP
141 West Regent St., Glasgow. G2 2SG.
TEL: 0141 229 1326; FAX: 0141 248 1591
E-MAIL: cp-enquiries@fsmail.net
WEBSITE: www.cp-auctioneers.co.uk

Curr & Dewar
Unit E, 6 North Isla Street, Dundee. DD3 7JQ.
*Regular sales on Tuesdays, commencing at 10am that include
antiques, quality furnishings, collectables and household
effects.*
TEL: 01382 833974; FAX: 01382 835740
E-MAIL: enquiries@curranddewar.com
WEBSITE: www.curranddewar.com

Frasers (Auctioneers)
8a Harbour Rd., Inverness. IV1 1SY.
Monthly sales last Wed of the month, commencing at 6 pm.
TEL: 01463 232395; FAX: 01463 233634

Leslie and Leslie

77 Market St., Haddington, East Lothian. EH41 3JJ.
EST. 1920. *Antique auctions every six weeks.*
TEL: 01620 822241; fax 01620 822251
E-MAIL: lesley.lesley@hotmail.co.uk

Lindsay Burns & Co.

6 King St., Perth. PH2 8JA.
General sales bi-weekly on Thurs. at 10.30 am., viewing day prior 9-5. Quarterly fine art sales (illustrated colour catalogues available, every item illustrated in colour on our website) held on Tues. Viewing previous Sat. 9-2, Sun 1-3, and Mon. 9-5.
TEL: 01738 633888; FAX: 01738 441322
E-MAIL: mail@lindsayburns.co.uk
WEBSITE: www.lindsayburns.co.uk

Loves Auction Rooms

Arran House, Arran Road, Perth. PH1 3DZ.
EST. 1869. SOFAA. *Regular sales of antique and decorative furniture, jewellery, silver and plate, ceramics, works of art, metalware, glass, pictures, clocks, mirrors, pianos, Eastern carpets and rugs, garden furniture, architectural items. Every 2nd Wednesday sales of Victoriana and household effects at 6pm. Specialist sales of books and collectors' items. Valuations.*
TEL: 01738 633337; FAX: 01738 629830
E-MAIL: enquiries@lovesauctions.co.uk
WEBSITE: www.lovesauctions.co.uk

Lyon & Turnbull

33 Broughton Place, Edinburgh. EH1 3RR.
EST. 1826. SOFAA. *Open Mon.-Fri. 8.30-5.30. 24 sales annually including pictures, books, decorative arts, furniture and works of art, jewellery and silver. Valuations.*
TEL: 0131 557 8844; FAX: 0131 557 8668
E-MAIL: info@lyonandturnbull.com
WEBSITE: www.lyonandturnbull.com

McTear's

31 Meiklewood Road Glasgow. G51 4EU.
EST. 1842. IAAS. *Auctions every week on Fridays & Saturdays; fine, collectors' & antiques auctions live on the internet through the-saleroom.com. Valuations for all purposes, free auction advice.*
TEL: 0141 810 2880; FAX: 0141 883 9920
E-MAIL: auction@mctears.co.uk
WEBSITE: www.mctears.co.uk

John Milne Auctioneers

9 North Silver St., Aberdeen. AB10 1RJ.
EST. 1867. *Weekly general sales, regular catalogue sales of antiques, silver, paintings, books, jewellery and collectors' items.*
TEL: 01224 639336
E-MAIL: info@johnmilne-auctioneers.com
WEBSITE: www.johnmilne-auctioneers.com

Ramsay Cornish

15/17 Jane St., Edinburgh. EH6 5HE.

Fine art and antique sales, specialist sales of silver and jewellery, porcelain and paintings. Weekly general sales of collectable and residual items.
TEL: 0131 553 7000
E-MAIL: info@ramsaycornish.com
WEBSITE: www.ramsaycornish.com

Shapes Auctioneers & Valuers

Bankhead Avenue, Sighthill, Edinburgh. EH11 4BY.
Antiques and fine art sales each month. Contacts: Paul Howard or Hamish Wilson.
TEL: 0131 453 3222; FAX: 0131 453 6444
E-MAIL: admin@shapesauctioneers.co.uk
WEBSITE: www.shapesauctioneers.co.uk

L. S. Smellie and Sons Ltd.

The Furniture Market, Lower Auchingramont Rd., Hamilton. ML10 6BE.
Fine antiques auctions on third Thurs. in Feb., May, Aug. and Nov. Weekly sales every Mon. at 9.30 am. (600 lots) household furniture, porcelain and jewellery.
TEL: 01698 282007
E-MAIL: hamiltonauction@btconnect.com
WEBSITE: www.hamiltonauctionmarket.co.uk

Taylor's Auction Rooms

11 Panmure Row, Montrose. DD10 8HH.
Antiques sales held every second Sat.
TEL: 01674 672775; FAX: 01674 672479
E-MAIL: jonathan@taylors-auctions.demon.co.uk
WEBSITE: www.scotlandstreasures.co.uk

Thomson Roddick Scottish Auctions

Irongray Rd., Dumfries. DG2 0JE.
EST. 1880. *Quarterly catalogued antique and collectors' sales including art, pottery, silver and jewellery. Fortnightly general sales.*
TEL: 01387 721635; FAX: 01387 721835
E-MAIL: dumfries@thomsonroddick.com
WEBSITE: www.thomsonroddick.com

WALES

Anthemion Auctions

15 Norwich Rd., Cardiff. CF23 9AB.
General and specialist sales.
TEL: 02920 472444
E-MAIL: valuations@anthemionauctions.com
WEBSITE: www.anthemionauctions.com

Aqueduct Auctions

Methodist Chapel, Holyhead Rd., Froncysyllte. LL20 7RA.
EST. 2007. *Valuations; house clearance; auction room.*
TEL: 01691 774567; MOBILE: 07778 279614
E-MAIL: antiquesauctions@aol.com
WEBSITE: www.aqueductauctions.co.uk

Bonhams Auctioneers

7/8 Park Place, Cardiff. CF10 3DP.

Auctioneers and valuers.
TEL: 02920 727980; FAX: 02920 727989
WEBSITE: www.bonhams.com

Dodds Auctioneers & Valuers
Victoria Auction Galleries, Mold. CH7 1EG.
EST. 1952. *Weekly Wed. auctions of general furniture and shipping goods at 10.30 am. Bi-monthly auctions of antique furniture, silver, porcelain and pictures etc. at 10.30 am on Sat. Catalogues available.*
TEL: 01352 755705; FAX: 01352 752542
E-MAIL: mail@doddsauctioneers.co.uk
WEBSITE: www.doddsauctioneers.co.uk

Peter Francis
Curiosity Salerooms, 19 King St., Carmarthen.
SA31 1BH.
Catalogued antiques and fine art sales every eight weeks. Monthly general sales.
TEL: 01267 233456; FAX: 01267 233458
E-MAIL: enquiries@peterfrancis.co.uk
WEBSITE: www.peterfrancis.co.uk

Walter Lloyd Jones Saleroom
Glan-y-Don, High St., Barmouth. LL42 1DW.
EST. 1905. *Open in summer 10-5.30, Sat. 10-4.30. Winter Mon., Thurs. and Fri. 10-5.30, Sat. 10-4.30.*
TEL: 01341 281527
E-MAIL: info@walterlloydjones-saleroom.co.uk
WEBSITE: www.walterlloydjones-saleroom.co.uk

Morgan Evans & Co Limited (Gaerwen)
The Gaerwen Auction Centre, Lon Groes, Gaerwen, Isle of Anglesey. LL60 6DF.
Sales of antiques and fine art, household goods and collectables.
TEL: 01248 421582; FAX: 01248 421908
E-MAIL: auctions@morganevans.com
WEBSITE: www.morganevans.com

Newland Rennie Wilkins
87 Monnow St., Monmouth. NP5 3EW.
TEL: 01600 712916
E-MAIL: auctioneers@nrproperty.com
WEBSITE: www.nrproperty.com

Harry Ray & Co
37 Broad St., Welshpool. SY21 7RR.
EST. 1946. *Regular sales of antiques, collectables, memorabilia, furniture and insolvency sales.*
TEL: 01938 552555
E-MAIL: info@harryray.com
WEBSITE: www.harryray.com

Rogers Jones & Co.
33 Abergele Rd., Colwyn Bay. LL29 7RU.
Antiques, collectables, fine art and Welsh paintings.
TEL: 01492 532176; FAX: 01492 533308
E-MAIL: info@rogersjones.co.uk
WEBSITE: www.rogersjones.co.uk

J. Straker, Chadwick & Sons
Market Street Chambers, Market Street, Abergavenny.
NP7 5SD.
Regular sales of antique furniture and effects are held as well as specialist and collectors' sales.
TEL: 01873 852624; FAX: 01873 857311
E-MAIL: info@strakerchadwick.co.uk
WEBSITE: www.strakerchadwick.co.uk

Wingetts
29 Holt St., Wrexham. LL13 8DH.
EST. 1950. NAVA. RICS. *General & Collectables every Monday. Antique and Fine Art every four-six weeks on a Wednesday. Valuations for insurance/probate etc.*
TEL: 01978 353553; FAX: 01978 353264
E-MAIL: auctions@wingetts.co.uk
WEBSITE: www.wingetts.co.uk

Services

This section has been included to enable us to list those businesses which do not sell antiques but are in associated trades, mainly restorations. The following categories are included: Art, Books, Carpets & Rugs, Ceramics, Clocks & Barometers, Consultancy, Courier, Enamel, Engraving, Framing, Furniture, Glass, Insurance & Finance, Ivory, Jewellery & Silver, Locks & Keys, Metalwork, Musical Instruments, Photography, Reproduction Stonework, Suppliers, Textiles, Tortoiseshell, Toys. We would point out that the majority of dealers also restore and can give advice in this field.

Below are listed the trade associations mentioned within this section.

ASFI - Assn. of Suppliers to Furniture Industry	**GADAR** - Guild of Antique Dealers & Restorers
BAFRA - British Antique Furniture Restorers' Assn	**GAI** - Guild of Architectural Ironmongers
BCFA - British Contract Furniture Assn.	**GMC** - Guild of Master Craftsmen
BFMA - British Furniture Manufacturers' Assn.	**ICON** - The Institute for Conservation
BTCM - British Traditional Cabinet Makers	**MBHI** - Member of British Horological Institute
CGCG - Ceramic & Glass Conservation Group	**MBWCG** - Member of the British Watch & Clock-
FATG - Fine Art Trade Guild	makers' Guild

ART

The Antique Restoration Studio
See entry under Furniture.

Armor Paper Conservation Ltd
Church Farm, Middle Common, Kington Langley, Wilts. SN15 5NN.
(Kate Armor) EST. 1996. *Conservation and restoration of drawings, prints, watercolour paintings, documents and archive material.*
TEL: 01249 758444; FAX: same
E-MAIL: paper@armor.co.uk
WEBSITE: www.armor.co.uk

A. Clark
Sambrook Cottage, Main St. Cosgrove, Northhants. MK19 7JL.
EST. 1963. By appointment. *Restoration of oil paintings.*
LOC: Bottom of the A5. PARK: Own - 12 spaces.
TEL: 01908 563369

Paul Congdon-Clelford
The Conservation Studio, 59 Peverells Wood Ave., Chandler's Ford, Hants. SO53 2FX.
IPC. ABPR. FATG. GADAR. EST. 1894. Open by appointment. *Conservators of oil paintings and western art on paper; home and business consultations. Collection and delivery. All areas. Conservators to museums, institutions, dealers and private owners.*
TEL: 02380 268167; FAX: same
E-MAIL: winstudio@aol.com
WEBSITE: www.conservationstudio.org

Everett Fine Art Ltd.
Budleigh Studios, Budleigh. West Buckland, Somerset. TA21 9LW.
(Tim and Karen Everett) EST. 1953. *Restoration and conservation of paintings and frames. Framemakers.* LOC: 3 miles from junction 26, M5.
TEL: 01823 421710

E-MAIL: info@everett-art.co.uk
WEBSITE: www.everett-art.co.uk

Kirkgate Fine Art & Conservation
The Studio, 3 Gillings Yard, Thirsk, Yorks. North. YO7 1SY.
(Richard Bennett) ICON. BAPCR. EST. 1979. Open by appointment. *Oil paintings cleaned and lined on the premises; gilt/gesso frames restored and repaired; framing.* LOC: 100 yards from Market Place, off Kirkgate.
TEL: 01845 524085; HOME: same
E-MAIL: richard.bennett@fineartandconservation.co.uk
WEBSITE: www.fineartandconservation.co.uk

Manor House Fine Arts
32, The Grange, Llandaff, Cardiff, CF5 2LH.
(S.K. Denley-Hill) NAVA. EST. 1979. Open by appointment. *Valuers, auctioneers and restorers of fine arts, antiques and general chattels.*
TEL: 029 20 553666
E-MAIL: valuers@manorhousefinearts.co.uk
WEBSITE: www.manorhousefinearts.co.uk

Stephen Messer Picture Restoration
Tarifa, Millstream Moorings, Mill Lane, Clewer, Windsor, Berks. SL4 5JH.
Associate member ABPR. *Restorations - paintings, mainly oils including re-lining, frames including gilding.*
TEL: 01753 622335

Claudio Moscatelli Oil Painting Restoration
46 Cambridge St., London. SW1V 4QH.
BPR. Open 10-6. *Oil paintings cleaned, relined, retouched and varnished. Trade; private; museums.*
TEL: 020 7828 8457
E-MAIL: claudio06@tiscali.co.uk
WEBSITE: www.claudiomoscatelli.co.uk

The Picture Restoration Studios
The Old Coach House, 16A Tarrant St., Arundel, West Sussex. BN18 9DJ.
(Garve Hessenberg) ICON. Open by appointment only.

Cleaning and restoration of oil paintings, watercolours, prints and old gilded frames. Antique, traditional and contemporary framing. Also in Oxford - 01865 200289; Guildford - 01483 479666; Haslemere 01428 641010; Chichester - 01243 778785. VAT: Stan.
TEL: 01903 885775; FAX: 01903 889649; MOBILE: 07971 184477

Plowden & Smith Ltd
190 St Ann's Hill, London. SW18 2RT.
(Keith Butler ACR, Valerie Kaufmann ACR and Robert Butler.) Conservation Register, 3 Accredited Conservator/ Restorers. EST. 1966. Open 9-5 and outside hours in an emergency. Conservation and restoration of fine art and antiques. Specialist departments for furniture, ceramics, paintings, metal, stone, decorative arts, mounting/display. VAT: Stan.
TEL: 020 8874 4005; FAX: 020 8874 7248
E-MAIL: Info@plowden-smith.co.uk
WEBSITE: www.plowden-smith.co.uk

Mrs. C. Reason
Tandridge Priory Lodge, Godstone Rd., Oxted, Surrey. RH8 9JU.
(Christine Reason) FATG. EST. 1980. Open by appointment. Valuations; restoration and cleaning of watercolours, prints and oils; framing including conservation. Watercolours bought and sold. LOC: 2 miles from jct. 6, M25 on A25, Oxted.
TEL: 01883 717010; MOBILE: 07711 485486
E-MAIL: chris@camr.fsnet.co.uk

Colin A. Scott
1st Floor Studio, Anthony Hurst Antiques, 13 Church St., Woodbridge, Suffolk. IP12 1DS.
Open 9-5.30, Sat. 9-1. Picture restoration and framing.
TEL: 01394 388528; HOME: 01473 622127
E-MAIL: scottstation26@aol.com

BOOKS

Brignell Bookbinders
25 Gwydir St., Cambridge, Cambs. CB1 2LG.
SOB. EST. 1982. Open 8.30-4.45, Fri. 7.30-4. CL: Sat. Book restoration, conservation including paper, leather photo albums, journal and thesis bindings, boxes and limited editions. Initialling leather goods. VAT: Stan.
TEL: 01223 321280; FAX: same
E-MAIL: brignell@ntlworld.com
WEBSITE: www.brignellbookbinders.com

The Manor Bindery Ltd
Calshot Rd., Fawley, Southampton, Hants. SO4 1BB.
EST. 1977. Manufacturers of false books, either to use as a display or for cabinet makers to apply to doors and cupboards. Also decorative objects and accessories, various decorative replica book boxes. Leather library shelf edging.
TEL: 023 8089 4488; FAX: 023 8089 9418
E-MAIL: manorbindery@btconnect.com
WEBSITE: www.manorbindery.co.uk

CARPETS AND RUGS

Barin Carpets Restoration
57a New Kings Rd., London. SW6 4SE.
GMC. Conservation Register Museums and Galleries Commission. ICON. EST. 1976. Open 9.30-6; prior telephone call advisable. Oriental carpets, rugs, European tapestries, Aubussons expertly cleaned, restored and lined. Expert advice, free estimates.
TEL: 020 7731 0546; FAX: 020 7384 1620

CERAMICS

The Antique Restoration Studio
See entry under Furniture.

China Repair by Roger Carter
Studio CF4, The Terrace (off Flaxengate) Grantham St., Lincoln, Lincs. LN2 1BD.
(Roger and Angela Carter) ICON. EST. 1990. Please ring for an appointment at the Studio. Repairs, restoration and conservation of all china and related items including ivory and papier mâché. Attendance at Peterborough, Newark and Lincoln antiques fairs for delivery and collection. VAT: Stan.
TEL: 01522 845020; MOBILE: 07918 193370
E-MAIL: rogercarter@enterprise.net
WEBSITE: www.ceramicrepair.com

Porcelain Repairs Ltd
240 Stockport Rd., Cheadle Heath, Stockport, Cheshire. SK3 0LX.
CGCG. ICON. EST. 1970. Open 9-5. CL: Sat. Highest standard restorations of European and Oriental ceramics, especially under glaze blue and white, museum repairs, carat gilding and modelling. Cracks and crazing removed without any overpainting or glazing.
TEL: 0161 428 9599; FAX: 0161 286 6702
E-MAIL: porcelain@repairs999.fsnet.co.uk

CLOCKS AND BAROMETERS

Albion Clocks
4 Grove End, Grove Hill, South Woodford, London. E18 2LE.
(C.D. Bent) CMBHI. EST. 1981. Open 9-7, Sun. by appointment. Full restoration of clocks and watches - movements, dials cases. Full cabinet work, French polishing, gold leaf and lacquer work a speciality. Clocks made on commission, copies of Georgian library globes and globe stands. Showroom of restored decorative clocks and furniture for sale; free estimates and collection, delivery and setting up service nationwide. LOC: Edge of M11, collection from South Woodford station by arrangement. PARK: Free.
TEL: 020 8530 5570; MOBILE: 07860 487830
WEBSITE: www.albionclocks.info

Gordon Caris
30 Fenkel St., Alnwick, Northumbs. NE66 1HR.
EST. 1972. Open Thurs. and Fri. 10-5. The business has

been in the family since the early 1800s and is now into its fifth generation of clock repairers. Repair and restoration of antique and valuable clocks, watches, barometers and musical boxes. Also has a branch in Hexham.
TEL: 01665 510820
E-MAIL: gordoncaris@caris-clocks.com
WEBSITE: www.caris-clocks.com

The Clock Gallery
Clarke's Rd., North Killingholme, Lincs. DN40 3JQ.
Guild of Lincolnshire Craftsmen. *Clock movements and dials, brass work. Agent for several German clock movement makers.* VAT: Stan.
TEL: 01469 540901; FAX: 01469 541512
WEBSITE: www.martinhdunn.co.uk

Clive and Lesley Cobb
3 Pembroke Crescent, Hove, East Sussex. BN3 5DH.
Listed by the Conservation Unit of the Museum and Galleries Commission. EST. 1972. *Quality, sympathetic restoration of lacquer clock cases, furniture and painted clock dials.*
TEL: 01273 772649;
E-MAIL: londinifecit@aol.com

Edmund Czajkowski and Son
See entry under Furniture.

Farbrother Furniture Restoration
See entry under Furniture.

Richard Higgins (Conservation)
See entry under Furniture.

E. Hollander   **BADA**
1 Bennetts Castle, 89 The Street, Capel, Dorking, Surrey. RH5 5JX.
(D.J. and B. Pay) MBWCG. MBHI. EST. 1886. Open 8-4. CL: Sat., or by appointment. *Conservation and restoration of all forms of clocks, mechanisms, cases, dials and barometers.*
LOC: Midway between Dorking and Horsham.
TEL: 01306 713377
E-MAIL: davidpay36@aol.com
WEBSITE: www.hollanderclocks.co.uk

Robert B. Loomes
3 St Leonard's Street, Stamford, Lincs. PE9 1HD.
MBWCG. MBHI. EST. 1966. Open 9-5. *Restoration of longcase, lantern, French and bracket clocks, specialist painted dial restoration. Home visits a pleasure in Rutland and N.London.* PARK: NCP opposite. VAT: Stan.
TEL: 01780 481319
WEBSITE: www.dialrestorer.co.uk

William Mansell
24 Connaught St., Marble Arch, London. W2 2AF.
(Will Salisbury) MBHI. MBWCG. EST. 1864. Open 9.30-5.30, Sat. 10.30-12.30. *Repair/restoration/sales of all types of clocks, watches and barometers etc., also antique jewellery and silverware. On-line catalogue of antique,*

vintage and modern watches, clocks, jewellery and silverware.
TEL: 020 7723 4154; FAX: 020 7724 2273
E-MAIL: mail@williammansell.co.uk
WEBSITE: www.williammansell.co.uk

Meadows and Passmore Ltd
1 Ellen Street, Portslade, Brighton, East Sussex. BN41 1EU.
MBWCG. NAWCC (USA). EST. 1977. Open by arrangement. *Clock and barometer parts, watch batteries, tools and materials.*
TEL: 01273 421321; FAX: 01273 421322
E-MAIL: sales@m-p.co.uk
WEBSITE: www.m-p.co.uk

Menim Restorations
Baulks Yard, Bow St., Langport, Somerset. TA10 9PJ.
GMC. EST. 1830. *Specialists in English clocks, full cabinet making and horological service; French polishing.*
TEL: 01458 252157

Repton Clocks
Acton Cottage, 48 High St., Repton, Derbys. DE65 6GF.
(P.Shrouder) MBWCG. MBHI. EST. 1980. Open by appointment 9-6. CL: Sat. *Antique and modern watch and clock restoration; musical box repairs; gear cutting; clocks made to order.*
TEL: 01283 703657

Kevin Sheehan
15 Market Place, Tetbury, Glos. GL8 8DD.
EST. 1978. Open 9-4.30, Sat. 10-12. *Specialist repairer of English and French 18th-19th C clocks. Written estimates given, all work guaranteed. Awarded Royal Warrant.*
TEL: 01666 503099

Surrey Clock Repairs
62a West St. Dorking, Surrey. RH4 1BS.
(Patrick Thomas) *House calls for minor repairs, setting up and moving clocks, valuations and advice. Collection and delivery of clocks overhauled in our workshop. Restore painted or brass dials and cases. Complicated repairs, cutting of wheels and pinions etc. All work guaranteed for one year.*
TEL: 01732 810600; MOBILE: 07976 971024
E-MAIL: patrickthomas@btconnect.com
WEBSITE: www.surreyclockrepairs.co.uk

Time Products (UK) Ltd
Alexander House, Chartwell Drive, Wigston, Leics. LE18 2EZ.
BJA. MBWCG. Jewellery Industry Distributors' Assn. *Watch and clock replacement and restoration materials; specialised tools for the horological trade.* VAT: Stan.
TEL: 0870 8508200
WEBSITE: www.timeproducts.co.uk

CONSULTANCY

Athena Antiques of Fleet
59 Elvetham Rd., Fleet, Hants. GU13 8HH.

(Richard Briant) EST. 1975. *Available seven days by appointment. Consultancy; valuations (jewellery, silver, clocks and furniture); restorations (clocks and furniture); buys at auction on commission; militaria.* LOC: Near Fleet railway station.
TEL: 01252 615526; HOME: same; MOBILE: 077990 998032

The Drawing Room
The Studio, 11 Bridge St. Pershore, Worcs.
(Janet Davie) IDS. EST. 1980. *Interior design consultant; personalised antique buying service.* PARK: Easy (in main square or opposite)
TEL: 01386 555747; FAX: 01386 555071

Geoffrey Godden   **BADA**
3 The Square, Findon, West Sussex. BN14 0TE.
Consultant, author and lecturer in ceramics. Study days and ceramics 'house parties' arranged, write for details.
TEL: **01903 873456**

Littleton & Hennessy Asian Art
1 Princes Place, Duke St., St James's, London.
SW1Y 6DE.
Art advisory and acquisition service for private collectors and museums.
TEL: 020 7930 0888; FAX: 020 7930 4988
E-MAIL: info@littletonandhennessy.com
WEBSITE: www.littletonandhennessy.com

Gerald Sattin   **BADA**
PO Box 20627, London. NW6 7GA.
CINOA. EST. 1967. Open by appointment. *Consultant and commission agent for the purchase of English and Continental porcelain, 1720-1900; English glass, 1700-1900; English collectable silver, 1680-1920.* VAT: **Stan/Spec.**
TEL: **020 8451 3295**; FAX: same
E-MAIL: **gsattin@compuserve.com**

COURIERS

Antique Tours & Conrad Chauffeur Hire
11 Farleigh Rise, Monkton Farleigh, Nr. Bradford-on-Avon, Wilts. BA15 2QP.
(John Veal) EST. 1988. *Chauffeur service for up to four persons; tours of antique shops, fairs, dealers and warehouses in and around the West Country, (other areas as requested); packing and shipping arranged; air and sea port transfers.*
TEL: 01225 858527 (answerphone);
MOBILE: 07860 489831
E-MAIL: conradveal@hotmail.com
WEBSITE: www.conradchauffeurhire.co.uk

The English Room
London. SW11 4PY.
(Mrs Val Cridland) EST. 1985. *Search and courier (trade and private), London and country - shipment of goods purchased arranged.* VAT: Stan/Spec.
TEL: 020 7720 6655; MOBILE: 07770 275414;
FAX: 020 7978 2397

ENGRAVING

Eastbourne Engraving
12 North Street, Eastbourne, East Sussex. BN21 3HG.
(D. Ricketts) EST. 1882. Open 9.15-4.45. CL: Sat. & Mon. *Engraving trophies, polishing, silver plating, repairs, hardwood plinths, etc.*
TEL: 01323 723592

FRAMING

Sebastian D'Orsai Ltd
39 Theobalds Rd., Holborn, London. WC1X 8NW.
(A. Brooks) EST. 1967. Open 9.30-4. CL: Sat. *Traditional framing to museum standard including hand-coloured finishing to suit individual pictures.* VAT: Stan.
TEL: 020 7405 6663; FAX: 020 7831 3300

Everett Fine Art Ltd.
See entry under Art.

FURNITURE

Abbey Antiques & Furnishings Ltd
Plot 1 Maldon Rd., Danes Road Industrial Estate, Off Crow Lane, Romford, Essex. RM7 0JB.
EST. 1992. Open 8-5, Fri. 8-1, Sat. and Sun. by appointment. *Copies of Victorian and Edwardian four door breakfront bookcases, bureau bookcases, wall panelling, partners and pedestal desks, walnut or mahogany, old or new timber. Furniture repairs - glazing, leathering, gilding, turnings, inlays, veneering. Any bespoke work undertaken. Any veneers obtainable.* LOC: Near New Queens Hospital. VAT: Stan.
TEL: 01708 741135; FAX: 01708 746419; HOME: 01708 343103
E-MAIL: info@abbeyantiques.net
WEBSITE: www.abbeyantiques.net

Anthony Allen Conservation and Restoration
Old Wharf Workshop, Redmoor Lane, New Mills, High Peak, Derbys. SK22 3JL.
BAFRA. ICON. Listed on the Register of Conservation Unit by the Museums and Galleries Commission. *Early oak and walnut furniture; conservation; clocks, cases, and movements; artefacts and metalwork.*
TEL: 01663 745274

Alpha Antique Restorations
Coombe Rd. Compton, Newbury, Berks. RG20 6RQ.
(Graham Childs) EST. 1972. *Fine oak, walnut and mahogany. Traditional hand finishes. Veneering and inlaying. Clock cases.*
TEL: 01635 578245

Antique Leathers
Lower Rock House, South Cheriton, Templecombe. Somerset. BA8 0BB.
(R. A. Holliday, Mrs F. Crisp and Mrs C Holliday) EST. 1968. Open 9.30-4.30. *Table lining with gold tooling; traditional upholstery, leather covered; bookshelf edging;*

leather restoration. VAT: Stan.
TEL: 01963 370126; FAX: same
WEBSITE: www.antique-leathers.co.uk

The Antique Restoration Centre
14 Suffolk Rd., Cheltenham, Glos. GL50 2AQ.
(M.H.Smith-Wood) EST. 1974. Open 9.30-5. CL: Sat.
All types of restoration - all restorers BADA qualified.
TEL: 01242 262549

The Antique Restoration Studio
The Stable Block, Milwich Rd. Stafford, Staffs. ST18 0EG.
(P. Albright) EST. 1980. Open 9-5. *Repairs and restoration (furniture, rush and cane, French polishing, leatherwork and upholstery, ceramics, glassware, paintings, clocks and watches, rare books, documents and photographs). Five-year guarantee on all work. Collection and delivery service.* LOC: 4 miles NE of Stafford.
TEL: 01889 505544; FAX: 01889 505543
E-MAIL: ars@uk-hq.demon.co.uk
WEBSITE: www.uk-hq.demon.co.uk

Michael Barrington
The Old Rectory, Warmwell, Dorchester, Dorset.
DT2 8HQ.
BAFRA. Conservation Register. BDMA. EST. 1983.
Open 9-5. *Conservator and restorer of 17th-20th C furniture, clocks, barometers, gilding, upholstery, metalwork, music boxes and barrel pianos, automatons and rocking horses, historic lighting eg. Colza Oil and Argand.*
TEL: 01305 852104; FAX: 01305 854822
E-MAIL: headoffice@bafra.org.uk

Batheaston
20 Leafield Way, Corsham, Wilts. SN13 9SW.
BFMA. BCFA. *Oak reproduction furniture made from solid kiln-dried timbers, antique hand finish. Extensive range of Windsor, ladderback and country Hepplewhite chairs; refectory, gateleg and other extendable tables, Welsh dressers, sideboards and other cabinet models.*
TEL: 01225 811295; FAX: 01225 810501
E-MAIL: sales@batheaston.co.uk
WEBSITE: www.batheaston.co.uk

David Battle
Brightley Pound, Umberleigh, Devon. EX37 9AL.
BAFRA. EST. 1984. Open by appointment. *Cabinet making, restoration and conservation work; polishing, clock cases, veneer and marquetry work, woodturning. Specialists in 17th-19th C English and Continental furniture. Collections and deliveries.*
TEL: 01769 540483
WEBSITE: www.davidbattle.co.uk

Keith Bawden - Restorer of Antiques
Romanhurst Cottage, Birdlip Hill, Witcombe, Glos.
GL3 4SN.
BAFRA. *All period furniture, plus restoration of items made from wood, metals, porcelain, pottery, fabrics, leather, ivory, papier-mâché, etc.*
TEL: 01452 862280
WEBSITE: www.bawdenantiques.co.uk

Clive Beardall Restorations Ltd
104b High St., Maldon, Essex. CM9 5ET.
BAFRA. Conservation Register. EST. 1982.
Comprehensive restoration and conservation services to all types of English and Continental period furniture.
TEL: 01621 857890; FAX: 01621 850753
E-MAIL: info@clivebeardall.co.uk
WEBSITE: www.clivebeardall.co.uk

Belvedere Reproductions
11 Dove St., Ipswich, Suffolk. IP4 1NG.
(Stuart Curtis) EST. 1984. Open 8-5. *Suppliers of traditionally constructed and hand-polished oak and fruitwood country furniture.* VAT: Stan.
TEL: 01473 214573; FAX: 01473 253229; MOBILE: 07860 782888
E-MAIL: stuartcurtis@btopenworld.com
WEBSITE: www.belvederereproductions.co.uk

Berry & Crowther
The Workshops, Nine Whitestones, Stocksmoor, Huddersfield, West Yorks. HD4 6XQ.
(Peter N. Berry and David Crowther) EST. 1979. Open 9-6.30. *Fine antique restorers and conservators; restoration with traditional methods to highest standards on fine furniture and clocks. Insurance work approved.* LOC: 10 miles junction 39,

Boulle Mantle Clock by Japy Frères.

M1; 6 miles south of Huddersfield from M62. Location map available on request. PARK: Own.
TEL: 01484 609800
E-MAIL: peternberry@aol.com

Bevan & Hely-Hutchinson
40 Fulham High St., London. SW6 3LQ.
Reproducing and restoring antique furniture. VAT: Stan.
TEL: 020 7731 1919; FAX: same
WEBSITE: www.bandhh.com

Peter Binnington
Barn Studio, Botany Farm, East Lulworth, Wareham, Dorset. BH20 5QH.
BAFRA. SOG. EST. 1979. Open 9-5.30, CL: Sat.
Restoration of verre églomisé, giltwork, decorated surfaces.
TEL: 01929 400224; FAX: 01929 400744
E-MAIL: pbinn@fmail.co.uk

Martin Body - Giltwood Restoration
7 Addington Sq., London. SE5 7JZ.
(Martin Body) EST. 1988. Open 9-5. *Specialist conservation of fine gilded furniture and frames.*
TEL: 020 7703 4351; FAX: 020 7703 1047
E-MAIL: giltwooduk@aol.com
WEBSITE: giltwoodrestoration.co.uk

A.E. Booth & Son
300 Hook Rd., Hook, Nr. Chessington, Surrey. KT9 1NY.
EST. 1934. Open 9-5 by appointment. *Furniture restorations, polishing and upholstery.* LOC: A243 towards A3. PARK: Own.
TEL: 020 8397 7675; FAX: same
E-MAIL: aebrestore@talk21.com
WEBSITE: www.aebooth.co.uk

Stuart Bradbury
The Barn, Hanham Lane, Paulton, Bristol. BS39 7PF.
(M & S Bradbury) BAFRA. EST. 1988. Open 8-5. *All aspects of antique furniture restoration.*
TEL: 01761 418910
E-MAIL: enquiries@mandsbradbury.co.uk
WEBSITE: www.mandsbradbury.co.uk

Lawrence Brass
Apple Studio, Ashley Bath, Somerset. BA1 3SD.
ICON. Approved by the Museums and Galleries Commission. *Conservation and restoration of fine antiques, metalwork, gilding and upholstery.*
TEL: 01225 852222; FAX: 01225 851050
E-MAIL: info@lawrencebrass.com
WEBSITE: www.lawrencebrass.com

A. J. Brett & Co Ltd
168c Marlborough Rd., London. N19 4NP.
GMC. EST. 1965. Open 7-3.30. *Restorers of antique furniture and upholstery; French polishing and gilding; free estimates.*
TEL: 020 7272 8462; FAX: 020 7272 5102
E-MAIL: ajbretts@aol.com
WEBSITE: www.ajbrett.co.uk

British Antique Replicas
School Close, Queen Elizabeth Avenue., Burgess Hill,
West Sussex. RH15 9RX.
EST. 1963. Open 9-5.30. *Replica and bespoke furniture.*
LOC: 3 miles west of A23. PARK: Easy. VAT: Stan.
TEL: 01444 245577
E-MAIL: office@british-antique-replicas
WEBSITE: www.british-antique-replicas.co.uk

Brushwood Antiques
29 Marlborough St. Faringdon, Oxon. SN7 7JL.
(Nathan Sherriff) TVADA. EST. 1989. *Restoration of
antique furniture including clocks; valuations.*
TEL: 01367 244269; MOBILE: 07768 360350
E-MAIL: nathan@brushwoodantiques.com
WEBSITE: www.brushwoodantiques.com

Bruton Classic Furniture Company Ltd
Unit 1 Station Road Industrial Estate, Bruton,
Somerset. BA10 0EH.
Open 8-5, Sat. and Sun. by appointment. *Quality antique
replica furniture – mahogany, teak and pine.*
TEL: 01749 813266; FAX: same; MOBILE: 07973 342047
E-MAIL: sales@brutonclassic.co.uk
WEBSITE: www.brutonclassic.co.uk

Mike Burgess
The Barn, North St., Rotherfield, Crowborough,
Sussex. TN6 3NA.
Full antique furniture restoration service.
TEL: 01892 852060

Campion Restoration Ltd
Unit 9, The Old Dairy, Rushley Lane, Winchcombe,
Glos. GL54 5JE.
(Mike Shorrock) EST. 1959. Open 9-5.30 Sat. and other
times by appointment. *Furniture restoration, conservation,
polishing, insurance work, furniture designed and made to
order.* LOC: Opposite the exit of Sudeley Castle car park.
TEL: 01242 604403; FAX: same;

Cane & Able Antiques and Affordable Pianos
The Limes, 22 The Street, Beck Row, Bury St.
Edmunds, Suffolk. IP28 8AD.
EST. 1991 *Specialists in antique and designer cane,
upholstery and rush seating, furniture and architectural
restoration and copying. Pianos reconditioned and renovated.*
TEL: 01638 515529
E-MAIL: bobcaneandable@yahoo.co.uk
WEBSITE: www.affordablepianos.co.uk

Carvers & Gilders Ltd
Unit 4, Spaces Business Centre, Ingate Place, London.
SW8 3NS.
ICON. Master Carvers' Assn. Furniture History Society.
GMC. EST. 1979. *Designs, makes, restores and conserves
fine decorative woodcarving and giltwood furniture, mirror
frames etc. Specialists in water gilding.* VAT: Stan.
TEL: 020 7498 5070; FAX: 020 7498 1221

E-MAIL: acc@carversandgilders.com
WEBSITE: www.carversandgilders.com

Peter G. Casebow
Pilgrims, Mill Lane, Worthing, West Sussex.
BN13 3DE.
BAFRA. EST. 1987. Open 9-5.30. *Restorer of antique and
modern furniture, with additional expertise in square piano
cases and metalwork.*
TEL: 01903 264045
E-MAIL: pcasebow@hotmail.com

Castle House Antique Restoration Limited
1 Bennetts Field Estate, Wincanton, Somerset. BA9 9DT.
(Michael Durkee) BAFRA. Conservation Register. EST.
1975. Open 8.30-5.30. CL: Sat. *Professional restoration
and conservation of period furniture; comprehensive service
to private clients, trade, museums and galleries.*
TEL: 01963 33884; FAX: 01963 31278
E-MAIL: m.durkee@ukonline.co.uk

Charles Perry Restorations Ltd
Praewood Farm, Hemel Hempstead Rd., St. Albans,
Herts. AL3 6AA.
(John Carr) BAFRA. Royal Warrant Holders. ICON.
EST. 1988. Open 8.30-6. *Restorations to all types of antique
furniture; cabinet/veneer repairs; polishing; carving; gilding;
upholstery; canework; marble.*
TEL: 01727 853487; FAX: 01727 846668
E-MAIL: johncarr@cperryrestorations.co.uk

Graham Childs - Alpha Antique Restorations
Danetree Compton, Newbury, Berks. RG20 6RQ.
EST. 1972. *Fine oak, walnut and mahogany restored
carefully and faithfully. Traditional hand finishes. Veneering
and inlaying. Clock cases.*
TEL: 01635 578245; MOBILE: 07860 575203

Clare Hall Company
The Barns, Clare Hall, Cavendish Rd., Clare, Nr.
Sudbury, Suffolk. CO10 8PJ.
(Michael Moore) EST. 1970. Open 8-4.30. *Replicas of
18th and 19th C floor standing and table globes. Full cabinet
making especially four poster beds; restoration of all antiques
and upholstery.* VAT: Stan/Spec.
TEL: 01787 278445; FAX: 01787 278803; (ansaphone)
01787 277510

Benedict Clegg
Rear of 20 Camden Rd., Tunbridge Wells, Kent. TN1 2PT.
BAFRA. EST. 1985.
TEL: 01892 548095.

Coltman Restorations
18 Blandford Square. Newcastle-upon-Tyne, Tyne &
Wear. NE1 4HZ
TEL: 0191 233 1430; MOBILE: 07786707539
E-MAIL: info@coltmanantiques.com
WEBSITE: www.coltmanantiques.com

Compton & Schuster Ltd
Studio A133 Riverside Business Centre, Haldane Place, London. SW18 4UQ.
(Lucinda Compton and Dominic Schuster) BAFRA. ICON. York Consortium. EST. 1990. *Conservation and restoration - lacquer, gilding, painted and japanned furniture, papier-mâché, tôle, architectural gilding and painting. Replica antique mirror place in silver or mercury.*
TEL: 020 8874 0762
E-MAIL: info@comptonandschuster.com
WEBSITE: www.comptonandschuster.com

William J. Cook & Sons Antique Restorations
High Trees, Savernake Forest, Wilts. SN8 4NE.
BAFRA. EST. 1963. *18th C and English period furniture. Also has a workshop in Battersea, London.*
TEL: 01672 513017 or 020 7736 5329
WEBSITE: www.wjcookandsons.com

Courtlands Restorations
Courtlands Park Rd., Banstead, Surrey. SM7 3EF.
(David A. Sayer) BAFRA. EST. 1985. Open 8-5, Sat. and Sun. by appointment. *Comprehensive restoration service including repairs, polishing, carving, turning, veneering, gilding. Metal parts - replacement or repair.*
TEL: 01737 352429
E-MAIL: davidsayer007@aol.com
WEBSITE: www.antiquerestorationlondon.co.uk

Crawley Studios
39 Woodvale, London. SE23 3DS.
BAFRA. EST. 1985. *Painted furniture, papier-mâché, tôle ware, lacquer and gilding.*
TEL: 020 8516 0002; FAX: same
E-MAIL: info@crawleystudios.co.uk
WEBSITE: www.crawleystudios.co.uk

Crudwell Furniture
Wilts. (Philip Ruttleigh) *Complete furniture resoration service, including stripping; bead blasting for architectural antiques.*
TEL: 07989 250077
E-MAIL: info@crudwellfurniture.co.uk
WEBSITE: www.crudwellfurniture.co.uk

Michael Czajkowski, Edmund Czajkowski and Son
96 Tor-o-Moor Rd., Woodhall Spa, Lincs. LN10 6SB.
BAFRA. ICON. EST. 1951. *Furniture, clocks (including church) and barometers restored. Veneering, marquetry, English lacquer and boulle work, carving, gilding, polishing and upholstery.*
TEL: 01526 352895
E-MAIL: michael.czajkowski@ntlworld.com

Dalbergia Ltd
23 Bridge St., Fordingbridge, Hants. SP6 1AH
(Piers Paterson.) *Restoration, upholstery and cabinet making.*
TEL: 0845 230 5123
E-MAIL: enquiries@dalbergia.co.uk
WEBSITE: www.dalbergia.co.uk

Michael Dolling
Church Farm Barns, Glandford, Holt, Norfolk. NR25 7JR. Also at White Hart St., East Harling, Norfolk.
BAFRA. EST. 1984. Open by appointment. *Furniture repairs; veneering; marquetry; French polishing.*
TEL: 01263 741115 or 01953 718658.

EFMA
4 Northgate Close, Rottingdean, Brighton, East Sussex. BN2 7DZ.
(Tony Hoole) Fed. of Sussex Industries. IDDA. Inst. of Export. BFMA. EST. 1973. *Catalogues on classical repro designs (mostly veneered) in yew/mahogany/walnut/elm plus solid country pieces, especially custom-built dining tables, in oak and cherry. Specialist sourcing service for overseas clients/importers.* VAT: Stan.
TEL: 01273 308899
E-MAIL: info@efma.co.uk
WEBSITE: www.efma.co.uk

D.S. Embling - The Cabinet Repair Shop
Woodlands Farm, Blacknest, Alton, Hants. GU34 4QB.
C&G London Inst. GMC. League of Professional Craftsmen. EST. 1977. Open 8-5. CL: Sat. *Antique and modern furniture restoration and repair including marquetry and veneering, French polishing, modern finishes. Parts made, wood turning, collection and delivery; insurance claim repairs.*
TEL: 01252 794260; FAX: 01252 793084
WEBSITE: www.dsembling.co.uk

Everitt and Rogers
Dawsnest Workshop, Grove Rd., Tiptree, Essex. CO5 0JE.
(David Rogers & Darren Burgess) GADAR. EST. 1969. *Expert antique furniture restoration.*
TEL: 01621 816508; FAX: 01621 814685
E-MAIL: everittandrogers@aol.com

John Farbrother Furniture Restoration
Ivy House, Main St., Shipton-by-Beningbrough, York, North Yorks. YO30 1AB.
GADAR. EST. 1987. *All repairs undertaken, refinishing process from complete strip to reviving existing finish. French polishing, oil, wax and lacquers. Clocks inc. movements are a speciality.*
TEL: 01904 470187; FAX: 01904 470187
E-MAIL: jb_farbrother@yahoo.co.uk
WEBSITE: www.johnfarbrother.co.uk

Fauld Town and Country Furniture
Whitestone Park, Whitestone, Hereford, Herefs. HR1 3SE.
EST. 1972. Open 8-5, appointment advisable. *Windsor chairs, extensive range of farmhouse tables, dressers and racks and many other case pieces. Bespoke work a speciality to traditional styles and methods.* VAT: Stan.
TEL: 01432 851992; FAX: 01432 851994
E-MAIL: enquiries@fauld.com
WEBSITE: www.fauld.com

Fenlan
17B Stilebrook Rd., Yardley Road Industrial Estate,
Olney, Bucks. MK46 5EA.
(Brian Harrison and Stephen Bryden) Est. 1982. Open
9-5. CL: Sat. *Furniture restoration. Restoration products
and fittings supplied; cabinet making and non-caustic
stripping.* Loc: 8 miles from junction 14, M1. VAT: Stan.
TEL: 01234 711799; FAX: same
E-MAIL: fenlan2000@aol.com

Forge Studio Workshops
Stour St., Manningtree, Essex. CO11 1BE.
(David Darton) Est. 1978. Open 8.30-5.30, Sat. 8.30-1.
*Carving, general restoration, copying and bespoke cabinet
making.*
TEL: 01206 396222

Glen Fraser-Sinclair
Hays Bridge Farm, Brickhouse Lane, South Godstone,
Surrey. RH9 8JW.
(G. and R. Fraser-Sinclair) BAFRA. Est. 1978. Open 8-
6. *18th C furniture.*
TEL: 01342 844112

Alistair J. Frayling-Cork
2 Mill Lane, Wallingford, Oxon. OX10 0DH.
BAFRA. Est. 1979. Open 10-6 or by appointment.
*Antique and period furniture, clock cases, ebonising, wood
turning, stringed instruments and brass fittings repaired.*
TEL: 01491 826221
WEBSITE: www.frayling-cork.co.uk

Furniture Revival
Autumn Lodge Loudham Lane, Ufford Woodbridge,
Suffolk. IP13 6EA.
(Paul Warner) Open 8.30-5. *Cleaning, colouring, wax
polishing, French polishing. Have your furniture brought
back to life. Antique furniture specialist.* VAT: No
TEL: 01394 460878. Mobile 07851 429617
E-MAIL: furniturerevival@aol.com

Georgian Cabinets Manufacturers Ltd
Unit 4 Fountayne House, 2-8 Fountayne Rd., London.
N15 4QL.
(Hassan Chelebi) Est. 1964. *Manufacturers, restorers and
polishers. Large stock of inlaid furniture. Container services
worldwide.* Loc: Near Seven Sisters underground,
Tottenham. PARK: Free. VAT: Stan.
TEL: 020 8885 1293; FAX: 020 8365 1114

Gow Antiques & Restoration
Pitscandly Farm, Forfar, by Lunanhead, Angus,
Scotland. DD8 3NZ.
(Jeremy Gow) ICON. Accredited by BAFRA. Est.
1993. Appointment advisable. *17th-19th C English and
Continental furniture. Specialist in marquetry, tortoiseshell
and fine furniture. Three-day courses on antique furniture
recognition.*
TEL: 01307 465342; MOBILE: 07711 416786

E-MAIL: jeremy@knowyourantiques.com
WEBSITE: www.knowyourantiques.com

Peter Hall & Son
Danes Rd., Staveley, Kendal, Cumbria. LA8 9PL.
(Jeremy Hall) ICON. Est. 1972. Open 9-5, Sat. 10-4
(closing 1 pm in winter) and by appointment. *Antique
furniture restoration and conservation, traditional
upholstery, furniture maker, interior design consultants.*
Loc: Off A591 Kendal to Windermere road.
TEL: 01539 821633; FAX: 01539 821905
E-MAIL: info@peter-hall.co.uk
WEBSITE: www.peter-hall.co.uk

Hamilton Antique Restoration
1a Orry Place. Douglas, Isle of Man. IM1 1BP.
(C. Sayle.) Est. 1988. Open by appointment. *Restoration
and conservation of antique furniture.*
TEL: 01624 662483

Hamilton Antiques   **LAPADA**
Woodbridge, Suffolk.
**(H. and Mrs. R. Ferguson) Est. 1977. Open by
appointment.** *18th - early 20th C furniture restoration
and polishing.*
**TEL: 01394 460237; MOBILE: 07747 033437 or 07914
873247**
E-MAIL: enquiries@hamiltonantiques.co.uk
WEBSITE: www.hamiltonantiques.co.uk

John Hartley
Johnson's Barns, Waterworks Rd., Sheet, Petersfield,
Hants. GU32 2BY.
BAFRA. ICON. Est. 1977. Open 8-5.30, CL: Sat.
*Comprehensive restoration and conservation service,
including carving, gilding, painted furniture, lacquer,
marquetry, boulle and architectural woodwork. Adviser to the
National Trust.*
TEL: 01730 233792; FAX: 01730 233922
E-MAIL: mail@tankerdale.co.uk
WEBSITE: www.tankerdale.co.uk

Philip Hawkins
Glebe Workshop, Semley, Shaftesbury, Dorset.
SP7 9AP.
BAFRA. Est. 1986. Open 8.30-5.30. *16th to early 18th C
oak furniture restoration. Bespoke cabinetmakers.*
TEL: 01747 830830
E-MAIL: philip@hawkinsfurniture.co.uk
WEBSITE: www.hawkinsfurniture.co.uk

Roland Haycraft
The Lamb Arcade, Wallingford, Oxon. OX10 0BX.
GADAR. LPC. Est. 1980. *All aspects of antique
restorations; one-off reproductions and copying service. Fine
furniture designed and made to traditional standards. Antique
archiving (DIVA - Digital Inventory & Visual Archive),
museum cataloguing and digital photography combined to
produce a modern inventory system designed to combat theft.*

TEL: 01491 839622
E-MAIL: roland.haycraft@fsbdial.co.uk
WEBSITE: www.diva-id.com and www.iasa-online.com

Hedgecoe and Freeland Ltd
21 Burrow Hill Green, Chobham, Surrey. GU24 8QS.
(Justin Freeland) BAFRA. EST. 1980. *General restorations, cabinet work, polishing, upholstery, chair making. Bespoke furniture, metalwork, decorative paintwork and gilding.*
TEL: 01276 858206; FAX: 01276 857352
E-MAIL: hedgecoefreeland@aol.com
WEBSITE: www.hedgecoe-freeland.com

Heritage Antiques
Unit 2 Trench Farm, Tilley Green, Wem, Shrops. SY4 5PJ.
(M.R. Nelms) GADAR. EST. 1989. Open 9-5, Sat. by appointment (24 hours' notice). *Furniture, including antique and fitted, full restoration service, antique boxes and clock cases a speciality.*
TEL: 01939 235463; FAX: 01939 235416
E-MAIL: heritageantiques@btconnect.com
WEBSITE: www.heritageantiques.co.uk

Alan Hessel
The Old Town Workshop, St. George's Close, Moreton-in-Marsh, Glos. GL56 0LP.
BAFRA. EST. 1976. Open 9-5 or by appointment, CL: Sat. *Comprehensive restoration service. English and Continental fine period furniture.*
TEL: 01608 650026; FAX: same
E-MAIL: alan.hessel@zen.co.uk

Richard Higgins (Conservation)
The Old School, Longnor, Nr. Shrewsbury, Shrops. SY5 7PP.
BAFRA. LBHI. Conservation Register of the Museums and Galleries Commission. ICON. EST. 1988. Open by appointment. *Comprehensive restoration of all fine furniture and clocks, including movements and dials; specialist work to boulle, marquetry, carving, turning, cabinet and veneer work, lacquer, ormolu, metalwork, casting, glazing, polishing, upholstery, cane and rush seating. Stocks of old timber, veneers, tortoiseshell etc. held to ensure sympathetic restoration.*
TEL: 01743 718162; FAX: 01743 718022
E-MAIL: richardhigginsco@aol.com

Stuart Hobbs Antique Furniture Restoration
Meath Paddock, Meath Green Lane, Horley, Surrey. RH6 8HZ.
GMC. BAFRA. Open by appointment. *Full restoration service for period furniture.*
TEL: 01293 782349

John Hubbard Antique Restorations
Castle Ash, Birmingham Rd., Blakedown, Worcs. DY10 3SE.
CINOA. GMC. EST. 1968. Open 9-5.30. CL: Sat. *Restorations of furniture including French polishing, desk leathers and upholstery.* LOC: A456. PARK: Outside. VAT: Stan.
TEL: 01562 701020; FAX: 01562 700001
E-MAIL: sales@johnhubbardantiques.com
WEBSITE: www.johnhubbardantiques.com

Donald Hunter
The Old School Room, Shipton Oliffe, Cheltenham, Glos. GL54 4JB.
Restoration of fine antiques, cabinet making, water gilding, lacquer work, decorative finishes.
TEL: 01242 820755

D. Hurst Restoration
4 Gleneldon Mews, London. SW16 2AZ.
(Deborah Hurst) EST. 1996. Open 9-6. *French polishing, gilding, wood carving, restoration.*
TEL: 020 8696 0315
E-MAIL: info@dhrestoration.co.uk
WEBSITE: www.dhrestoration.co.uk

Francis Jevons
London, SE19.
Interior decoration; furniture restoration and repair; sourcing items of furniture.
TEL: 020 8761 6612
WEBSITE: www.francisjevons.com

George Justice
12A Market St., Lewes, East Sussex. BN7 2HE.
(J.C., C.C. and S.M. Tompsett) GMC. EST. 1910. Open 8-1 and 2-5. CL: Sat. *Furniture restoration, upholstery, French polishing, caning and rushing, leather re-lining.* LOC: 1 minute from war memorial.
TEL: 01273 474174
E-MAIL: geo.justice@virgin.net
WEBSITE: www.georgejustice.co.uk

Kendal Furniture Restoration
5 Oakfield Corner, Works Rd., Letchworth Garden City, Herts. SG6 1FB (head office).
CINOA. Open 8-4. CL: Sat. *Restoration and upholstery; picture framing.* Branches at Cambridge: 01223 84111; Huntingdon: 01480 411811; St Albans: 01727 850500; London: 020 7435 4351; Freephone 0800 970 44 55.
TEL: (head office) 01462 682000
E-MAIL: terry@kendalrestoration.co.uk
WEBSITE: www.kendalrestoration.co.uk

Roderick Larwood
The Oaks, Station Rd., Larling, Norfolk. NR16 2QS.
BAFRA. EST. 1983. Open 8-5.30. CL: Sat. *Brass inlay, 18th to early 19th C furniture; French polishing; traditional finishes; Tunbridgeware.*
TEL: 01953 717937; FAX: same
E-MAIL: rodlar88@btinternet.com

John Lloyd
Bankside Farm, Ditchling Common, West Sussex. RH15 0SJ.
BAFRA. EST. 1990. Open 9-5. *Sympathetic restoration and conservation of English and Continental furniture; traditional hand finishing, veneering, marquetry and inlay work, carving and turning, gilding, upholstery, rush/cane work, leather lining and tooling, lock repairs and keys. Antique furniture copied, furniture designed and made to order. Regular delivery/collection service to London. Short courses in furniture restoration, cabinet making and gilding.* LOC: 12 miles north of Brighton.
TEL: 01444 480388; FAX: same; MOBILE: 07941 124772
E-MAIL: info@johnlloydfinefurniture.co.uk
WEBSITE: www.johnlloydfinefurniture.co.uk

Lomas Pigeon & Co. Ltd
37 Beehive Lane, Great Baddow, Chelmsford, Essex. CM2 9TQ.
BAFRA. AMU. BDMA EST. 1938. Open 10-4, Sat. 9-12, CL: Wed. *Antique restoration, French polishing, traditional and modern upholstery. Retailers and makers of fine furniture and rocking horses. Curtains and soft furnishings made to order. Leather table top linings.*
TEL: 01245 353708; FAX: 01245 355211
E-MAIL: wpigeon@lomas-pigeon.co.uk
WEBSITE: www.lomas-pigeon.co.uk

Timothy Long Restoration
St. John's Church, London Rd., Dunton Green, Sevenoaks, Kent. TN13 2 TE.
(Timothy Long) BAFRA. EST. 1987. Open 8-5, CL: Sat. *Cabinet restoration, French polishing, upholstery and gilding.* LOC: Sevenoaks
TEL: 01732 743368; FAX: 01732 742206
E-MAIL: info@timlong.co.uk
WEBSITE: www.timlong.co.uk

Bruce Luckhurst
The Little Surrenden Workshops, Ashford Rd., Bethersden, Kent. TN26 3BG.
BAFRA. EST. 1976 *Conservation and restoration training plus comprehensive restoration service.*
TEL: 01233 820589
E-MAIL: woodwise@tiscali.co.uk
WEBSITE: www.bruceluckhurst.co.uk

Mackenzie & Smith Fine Furniture Restoration
4 Bull Ring, Ludlow, Shrops. SY8 1AD.
(Tim Smith) ICON. Open 9-5, Sat. 10-1. Please ring to make an appointment. *Restoration of 17th, 18th & 19th C furniture and clock cases.* LOC: Town centre shopfront, nr. Feathers Hotel.
TEL: 01584 877133

Malvern Studios
56 Cowleigh Rd., Malvern, Worcs. WR14 1QD.
(L.M., D.D. and J. Hall) BAFRA. EST. 1961. Open 9-5.15, Fri. and Sat. 9-4.45. CL: Wed. *Antique furniture restoration.*
TEL: 01684 574913; FAX: 01684 569475
E-MAIL: malvern.studios@btinternet.com
WEBSITE: www.malvernstudios.co.uk

Oliver Manning Press
Underdown Yard, Chartham, Nr. Canterbury, Kent. CT4 7BX.
AF RF, Dip European Centre of Conservation, Venice. Dip Conservation Antique Furniture. Open by appointment. *Antique furniture restoration - insurance and museum work. Cabinet making; wax finishing; French polishing. Small amount of stock for sale.*
TEL: 01227 731765; MOBILE: 07808 001844
E-MAIL: olivermanningpress@tiscali.co.uk
WEBSITE: www.olivermanningpress.co.uk

Tim Morris Restorations
(Rear of) 89 Brighton Rd. Redhill, Surrey. RH1 6PS.
Prior telephone call advisable. *Antique furniture restoration, woodwork, cabinet making.*
TEL: 07877 190694

Ben Norris & Co
Unit 8, Orchard Business Park, Cottismore Farm, Kingsclere, Newbury, Berks. RG20 4SY.
BAFRA. EST. 1982. *All aspects of furniture restoration including carving, gilding, copy chair making and architectural woodwork. Excellent storage facilities.* VAT: Stan.
TEL: 01635 297950; FAX: 01635 299851
E-MAIL: colin.bell3@btconnect.com

Nigel Northeast Cabinet Makers
Furniture Workshops, Back Drove, West Winterslow, Salisbury, Wilts. SP5 1RY.
(Nigel Northeast) GADAR. EST. 1982. Open 8-5.30. *Antique restoration and French polishing. New furniture made to order, chairs made to complete sets. Cane and rush seating; fire and flood damage service.* VAT: Stan.
TEL: 01980 862051; FAX: 01980 863986
E-MAIL: nigel@nigelnortheast.co.uk
WEBSITE: www.nigelnortheast.co.uk

Ottery Antique Restorers
Bow Cottage, 17 Horsington. Temple Comb, Somerset. BA8 0EG.
(C.J. James) WEADA. EST. 1986. Open 8-5. *Marquetry, inlay and veneering repairs and cutting; carving, desk leathers and baize replacement; lead linings to cellarettes and wine coolers; handle repair, matching and replacement; lock repair and period keys cut; brass casting for mounts, castors and handles etc. Cabinet and furniture making, French polishing and wax finishing; upholstery, cane and rush seating.* LOC: A303/A357; see website for more detailed instructions. PARK: Ample.
TEL: 01963 371166
E-MAIL: charles@otteryantiques.co.uk
WEBSITE: www.otteryantiques.co.uk

Simon Paterson Fine Furniture Restoration
Whitelands, West Dean, Chichester, West Sussex.
PO18 0RL.
BAFRA. EST. 1993. Open 9-6. *Boulle, marquetry, frets, tortoiseshell and general furniture restoration.*
TEL: 01243 811900
E-MAIL: hotglue@tiscali.co.uk

Clive Payne Restorations
Unit 11 Langston Priory Workshops, Kingham, Chipping Norton, Oxon. OX7 6UR.
BAFRA. EST. 1987. Open 8-6, Sat. 9-1 or by appointment. *17th-19th furniture restoration.*
TEL: 01608 658856; FAX: same; MOBILE: 07764 476776
E-MAIL: clive.payne@virgin.net
WEBSITE: www.clive.payne.co.uk

Noel and Eva Louise Pepperall
Dairy Lane Cottage, Walberton, Arundel, West Sussex.
BN18 0PT.
Antique furniture restoration; cabinet making, polishing.
TEL: 01243 551282
E-MAIL: evalouisepepperall@hotmail.com

T. L. Phelps - Fine Furniture Restoration
15A Nidd Valley Business Park, Market Flat Lane, Scotton, Knaresborough, North Yorks. HG5 9JA
(Tim Phelps) ICON. BAFRA; listed on the Conservation Register. EST. 1984. Open 8.30-6 by appointment only. CL: Sat. *Specialist restoration (especially water damaged surfaces), and conservation services; all cabinet work, including dining tables, breakfront bookcases; all veneer work; architectural woodwork; traditional hand polishing, colouring and waxed finishes. Condition and treatment reports, reports for insurance loss adjustors;* LOC: Map available on request. PARK: Easy. VAT: Stan.
TEL: 01423 862752
E-MAIL: phelps@furniturerestoration.fsnet.co.uk

Pinewood Furniture Studio Ltd
1 Eagle Trading Estate, Stourbridge Rd., Halesowen, West Midlands. B63 3UA.
EST. 1987. *Manufacturers of furniture. Special orders undertaken in all types of timber.* VAT: Stan.
TEL: 0121 550 8228; FAX: 0121 585 5611

Plain Farm Workshop
The Old Dairy, Plain Farm, East Tisted, Alton, Hants.
GU34 3RT.
(Simon Worte) EST. 1990. Open 10-5.30. *18th to 19th C English furniture restoration.* LOC: 4 miles south of Alton and close to A32.
TEL: 01420 588362
E-MAIL: simonworte@fsmail.net

Plowden & Smith Ltd
See entry under Art.

A.J. Ponsford Antiques at Decora
Northbrook Rd., off Eastern Ave., Barnwood, Glos.
GL4 3DP.
(A.J. and R.L. Ponsford) EST. 1962. Open 8-5. CL: Sat. *Restorations (furniture); upholstery; manufacturers of period book simulations and decorative accessories.* LOC: Off junction 11A, M5. VAT: No
TEL: 01452 307700

Neil Postons Restorations
29 South St., Leominster, Herefs. HR6 8JQ.
ICON. Registered with the Museums and Galleries Commission. EST. 1988. Open 8.45-5.30, Sat. and other times by appointment. *Antique and fine furniture restorations including reconstruction, veneering, carving, turning, French and wax polishing, re-upholstery, rush and cane seating. Cabinetmaking.*
TEL: 01568 616677; FAX: same; MOBILE: 07710 297602
E-MAIL: neilpostons@btinternet.com
WEBSITE: www.neilpostonsrestorations.co.uk

Ludovic Potts Restorations
Elm Tree Farm, Parnall Rd. Guyhirn, Cambs. CB6 3XD.
BAFRA. EST. 1986. *Comprehensive restorations and conservation of furniture and effects. Ely, Cambs. office, 01353 741537; London office 020 7655 0810.*
TEL: 01733 849007; FAX: 01733 849027
E-MAIL: mail@restorers.co.uk
WEBSITE: www.restorers.co.uk

The Real Wood Furniture Company
London House, 16 Oxford St, Woodstock, Oxon.
OX20 1TS.
(Chris Baylis). Open 10.30-5.30, Sun. 11-5. CL: Mon. *Large stock of superb hand-crafted country furniture in traditional antique styles - solid oak, ash and cherry. Tables, dressers etc made to order. Large range of rush seated, Windsor and kitchen style chairs.* VAT: Stan.
TEL: 01993 813887; FAX: 01993 812379
E-MAIL: info@rwfco.co.uk
WEBSITE: www.rwfco.co.uk

Rectory Bungalow Workshop
Station Rd., Elton, Bingham, Notts. NG13 9LF.
(E.M. Mackie) EST. 1981. Open by appointment. *Restorations - cane and rush seating, painted furniture.*
TEL: 01949 850878

Restoration & Conservation Ltd
Rear of 1-9 Tennyson Rd., Wimbledon, London.
SW19 8SH.
(Harpur Dearden) EST. 2007. Open by appointment. *Restoration of antique furniture and French polishing.*
TEL: 020 8543 1118; FAX: same

Riches Upholstery Ltd
Wixamtree, 69 Wood Lane, Cottonend, Beds. MK45 3AP.
(R.J. Jennings) EST. 1980 *Re-upholstery, repairs and re-caning.*
TEL: 01234 742121

Michael Schryver Antiques Ltd
Unit 1, Book House, Glebelands Centre, Vincent Lane,
Dorking, Surrey. RH4 3HW.
EST. 1970. Open 8.30-5.30. CL Sat. *Cabinet work,
polishing, upholstery, metalwork.* VAT: Stan/Spec.
TEL: 01306 881110

Michael Slade
42 Quernmore Rd. London. N4 4QP.
(Michael Slade) EST. 1987. Open 10-6. *Valuations;
restoration of furniture, including upholstery, French
polishing and cabinet repairs.* PARK: Easy
TEL: 020 8341 3194; MOBILE: 07813 377029
WEBSITE: www.antiquesnorthlondon.co.uk

Phillip Slater
93 Hewell Rd., Barnt Green, Worcs. B45 8NL.
BAFRA. EST. 1977. Open 9-5.30, Sat. 9.30-1. *Antique
furniture restoration, conservation, sales and valuations.*
TEL: 0121 445 4942

**Eric Smith Antique Furniture Restoration &
Conservation**
The Old Church, Park Rd., Darwen, Lancs. BB3 2LD.
BAFRA. ICON. Conservation Register of the Museums &
Galleries Commission. Open 9-6. *Conservation and
restoration of fine furniture and longcase clocks; carving, French
polishing, desk leathers, fire and flood damage, marquetry
repairs, turning, cabinet making, wax polishing, specialists in
colour matching; retention of patination with all restorations.*
TEL: 01254 776222
E-MAIL: workshop@ericsmithrestorations.co.uk
WEBSITE: www.ericsmithrestorations.co.uk

Julian Stanley Woodcarving - Furniture
1 Caeflwyn, Ewyas Harold Common, Ewyas Harold,
Herefs. HR2 0JD.
MCA. EST. 1983. Open 9-5. *Carved furniture - the
classical work of the 18th C is re-created alongside
contemporary designs, figure work and architectural pieces.
Showroom on site includes contemporary paintings and
sculpture.* VAT: Stan/Spec.
TEL: 01981 241411; FAX: same
E-MAIL: julian.stanley1@virgin.net
WEBSITE: www.julianstanley-
woodcarvingfurniture.co.uk

Robert Tandy Restoration
Lake House Barn, Lake Farm, Colehouse Lane, Kenn,
Clevedon, Somerset. BS21 6TQ.
BAFRA. EST. 1987. *Furniture restoration especially 17th-
19th C longcase clock cases; French polishing and traditional
oil and wax finishing.*
TEL: 01275 875014
E-MAIL: robertptandy@hotmail.com

Thakeham Furniture Ltd
Golden Square, Petworth, West Sussex. GU28 0AP.
(Tim and Belinda Chavasse) EST. 1984. Open 10-5.
*Cabinet work, veneer repairs, wax and French polishing,
turning, marquetry, carving, etc.* LOC: In courtyard of
shops leading from large free car park. PARK: Free
parking nearby.
TEL: 01798 342333; MOBILE: 07803 086828
E-MAIL: enquiries@thakehamfurniture.com
WEBSITE: www.thakehamfurniture.com

The Restored Seat
Exmouth, Devon.
(Denise Viles). Open by appointment only. *Specialises in
the buying, selling and restoration of cane, rush and
upholstery seats.*
TEL: 01395 263985
E-MAIL: denise/viles@hotmail.com
WEBSITE: www.therestoredseat.co.uk

Titian Studio
62a Valetta Road Acton, London. W3 7TN
(Rodrigo and Rosaria Titian) BAFRA. EST. 1963. Open
8.30-5.30. *Carving, gilding, lacquer, painted furniture,
French polishing, japanning.*
TEL: 020 8222 6600; FAX: 020 8749 2220
E-MAIL: enquiries@titianstudios.co.uk
WEBSITE: www.titianstudios.co.uk

Tolpuddle Antique Restorers
The Stables, Southover Yard, Tolpuddle, Dorchester,
Dorset. DT2 7HE.
(Raymond Robertson) West Dean/BADA Award
Winner. RFS. EST. 1979. Open 9-5.30. *Furniture, clock
and barometer cases, marquetry, veneering and boulle work,
japanning and gilding, insurance work undertaken.*
TEL: 01305 848739; HOME: 01305 267799

Treen Antiques
Treen House, 72 Park Rd., Prestwich, Manchester,
M25 0FA.
(Simon J. Feingold) GADAR. RFS. FHS. ICON.
EST. 1988. Open by appointment. *Conservation and
restoration of all antique furniture (including vernacular)
and woodwork, with emphasis on preserving original finish.
Research undertaken, housekeeping advice, environmental
monitoring and all aspects of conservation. Furniture
assessment and advice on purchase and sales. Courses in
restoration work held on request. Listed in Bonham's
Directory.*
TEL: 0161 720 7244; FAX: same; MOBILE: 07973
471185
E-MAIL: simonfeingold@hotmail.com
WEBSITE: www.treenantiques.com

Tony Vernon
15 Follett Rd., Topsham, Devon. EX3 0JP.
BAFRA. EST. 1975. *Furniture, cabinet making, upholstery,
gilding, veneering, inlay and French polishing.*
TEL: 01392 874635
E-MAIL: tonyvernon@antiquewood.co.uk
WEBSITE: www.antiquewood.co.uk

Barry J. Wateridge
Padouk, Portsmouth Rd., Bramshott Chase, Hindhead,
Surrey. GU26 6DB.
French polishing and antique furniture restorations.
TEL: 01428 607235

Gerald Weir Antiques
Unit 1, Sun Wharf, Deben Road, Woodbridge, Suffolk.
IP12 1AZ.
Open 8-5.30. CL: Sat. *Suppliers of reproduction oak and
cherry country furniture, mainly for European and American
markets.* PARK: Own car park
TEL: 01394 610900; FAX: 01394 610901
E-MAIL: geraldweirantiques@btintgernet.com
WEBSITE: www.geraldweir.co.uk

Wick Antiques
Fairlea House, 110-112 Marsh Lane, Lymington,
Hants. SO41 8EE.
CINOA EST. 1980. *Furniture polishing, repairs, upholstery
and re-gilding.*
TEL: 01590 677558; FAX: same

Jonathan Wilbye
Blue Bell Farm, North Stainmore, Kirkby Stephen,
Cumbria. CA17 4DY.
(Jonathan Wilbye) EST. 1983. Open by appointment.
*Full restoration service including all carving, inlay, turning
and polishing. Longcase clock cases a speciality. Free delivery
in Cumbria, Yorkshire and Lancashire.*
TEL: 01768 341715.

GLASS

F.W. Aldridge Ltd
Unit 3 St John's Industrial Estate, Dunmow Rd.,
Takeley, Essex. CM22 6SP.
(J.L. Garwood). Open 9-5. *Antique glass restoration
including removing chips; suppliers of Bristol blue glass liners
and stoppers; makers of stems for glasses and claret jugs.*
TEL: 01279 874000/874001; FAX: 01279 874002
E-MAIL: angela@fwaldridge.abel.co.uk
WEBSITE: www.fwaldridgeglass.com

The Antique Restoration Studio
See entry under Furniture.

Facets Glass & Antique Restoration
107 Boundary Rd., Leyton, London. E17 8NQ.
By appointment. *Glass restoration including grinding and
polishing; supplier of glass liners and other bespoke items to
replace those lost or broken. Stoppers, knobs, tops.
Manufacturing clock, locket & barometer galss. Cutlery
restoration, brush re-bristling and many other services.* LOC:
Near Bakers Arms shopping area.
TEL: 020 8520 3392; MOBILE: 07778 758304
E-MAIL: repairs@facetsglass.co.uk
WEBSITE: www.facetsglass.co.uk

INSURANCE AND FINANCE

London Market Insurance Brokers Ltd
LG3A, London Underwriting Centre, 3 Minster Court,
Mincing Lane. London. EC3R 7DD.
*Specialists in all types of fine art, exhibition and memorabilia
insurance.*
TEL: 020 7617 4740; FAX: 020 7617 4754
E-MAIL: info@lmib.co.uk
WEBSITE: www.johncahill.co.uk

**Shearwater Insurance Services Ltd incorporating
Allen Flindall & Assoc.Ltd**
Shearwater House, 8 Regent Gate, High St., Waltham
Cross, Herts. EN8 7AE.
BIBA. FSA. EST. 1992. Open 9-5.30. CL: Sat. *Specialist
insurance scheme for antique and fine art dealers, collectors,
household and all risks insurance.*
TEL: 08700 718666; FAX: 08700 750043
E-MAIL: enquiries@shearwater-insurance.co.uk

Anthony Wakefield & Company Ltd
Suite C, South House, 21-37 South St., Dorking,
Surrey. RH4 2JZ.
Members IIB. Authorised and regulated by the Financial
Services Authority. EST. 1983. *Fine art and household
insurance brokers; special terms for collectors; exclusive
antique and fine art dealers policy with Axa Insurance UK
Plc; exclusive Connoisseur household policy with dealers/fairs
extension. Connoisseur online policy for collections between
£5,000 and £50,000 (see website).*
TEL: 01306 740555; FAX: 01306 740770
E-MAIL: info@anthonywakefield.com and
info@connoisseurpolicies.com
WEBSITE: www.anthonywakefield.com and
www.connoisseurpolicies.com

Windsor Partners Ltd.
International House, Trinity Business Park, Wakefield,
West Yorks. WF2 8EF.
Lloyd's Insurance Brokers. *Specialist brokers in antique
and fine art dealers, fine art galleries, contemporary art
galleries, restorers and conservators and antique centres.*
TEL: 01924 331214; FAX: 01924 383118
E-MAIL: tracy.edwards@windsor.co.uk
WEBSITE: www.windsor.co.uk

IVORY

Coromandel
The Pound House, Leysters, Leominster, Herefs. HR6 0HS.
(P. Lang & B. Leigh.) Resident. Open any time by
appointment. *Special restoration of items of ivory,
tortoiseshell, horn, mother-of-pearl etc.* See entry under
Herefs. in the dealers section.
TEL: 01568 750294; FAX: 01568 750237
E-MAIL: info@antiqueboxes.com
WEBSITE: www.antiqueboxes.com

E. and C. Royall Antiques
See entry under Metalwork.

JEWELLERY AND SILVER

Eastbourne Engraving
See entry under Engraving.

Goldcare
5 Bedford St., Middlesborough, TS1 2LL.
Open 9.30-5, CL: Weds. & Sun. *Jewellery repair, engraving, re-stringing, stone cutting. Restoration of silver and cutlery; brass, copper, pinchbeck restoration.* VAT: Stan.
TEL: 01642 231343
E-MAIL: goldcare.repairs@ntlworld.com
WEBSITE: www.goldcarerepairs.co.uk

LIGHTING

Government House
St George's House, High St. Winchcombe, Glos.
GL54 5LJ.
EST. 1979. *Restorations to antique and pre-war lighting and accessories. Spare parts stocked.* LOC: Village centre.
PARK: Own.
TEL: 07970 430684

LOCKS & KEYS

Bramah Security Centres Ltd
31 Oldbury Place, London. W1U 5PT.
MLA. EST. 1784. Open 8.30-5.30, Sat. 9-1. *Keys cut to old locks; old locks opened; repair of old locks; new locks made to an old design; original Bramah locks dated. Quotation provided. Overseas work undertaken.* LOC: Near Baker Street tube station. VAT: Stan.
TEL: 020 7935 7147; FAX: 020 7935 2779
E-MAIL: lock.sales@bramah.co.uk
WEBSITE: www.bramah.co.uk

METALWORK

Rupert Harris Conservation
Studio 5c, 1 Fawe St., London. E14 6PD.
ICON. IIC. NACE. SPAB. ICOM. EST. 1982. Open by appointment. *Conservation of fine metalwork and sculpture including bronze, lead, zinc and electrotype; chandeliers, lanterns, gold and silver, fine ironwork, arms and armour, ecclesiastical metalwork, casting, replication and gilding; consultancy and maintenance. Appointed metalwork advisors to the National Trust for England and Wales.*
TEL: 020 7987 6231 or 020 7515 2020;
FAX: 020 7987 7994
E-MAIL: enquiries@rupertharris.com
WEBSITE: www.rupertharris.com

Raymond Konyn Antique Restorations
Brass Foundry Castings Ltd, P O Box 151, Westerham,

Kent. TN16 1YF.
BAFRA. EST. 1979. Open by appointment. *Furniture fittings and mounts, brass casting.* VAT: Spec.
TEL: 01959 563863; FAX: 01959 561262;
E-MAIL: info@brasscastings.co.uk
WEBSITE: www.brasscastings.co.uk

Optimum Brasses
7 Castle St., Bampton, Devon. EX16 9NS.
(Robert and Rachel Byles) EST. 1981. Open 9-1 and 2-4, Sat. and other times by appointment. *Over 5,000 replica brass handles etc. for antique furniture. Copying service, authentic lost-wax castings.* LOC: On Wiveliscombe road. VAT: Stan.
TEL: 01398 331515; FAX: 01398 331164
E-MAIL: brass@optimumbrasses.co.uk
WEBSITE: www.optimumbrasses.co.uk

Plowden & Smith Ltd
See entry under Art.

E. and C. Royall Antiques
10 Waterfall Way, Medbourne, Leics. LE16 8EE.
EST. 1981. Open 9-5. *Restorations - English and Oriental furniture, bronzes, ivories, brass including inlay work, metalware, woodcarving, French polishing.* VAT: Stan.
TEL: 01858 565744

H.E. Savill Period Furniture Fittings
9-12 St Martin's Place, Scarborough, North Yorks.
YO11 2QH.
Open 9-5.30. *Period brass cabinet fittings.* VAT: Stan.
TEL: 01723 373032; FAX: 01723 376984.

Shawlan Antiques Metal Restorers
Croydon/South London area.
(Shawn Parmakis) BIDA. EST. 1976. Open 9-8.30. *High quality restoration of metalware, using traditional methods and materials. Over 30 years' experience.*
TEL: 020 8684 5082; FAX: same;
MOBILE: 07889 510253
E-MAIL: shawlanantiques@aol.com
WEBSITE: www.shawlanantiques.com

MUSICAL INSTRUMENTS

Cane & Able Antiques and Affordable Pianos
See entry under Furniture.

J V Pianos & Cambridge Pianola
85 High St., Landbeach, Cambridge, Cambs. CB4 8DR.
(Tom Poole) EST. 1972. Open Mon.-Fri. prior telephone call advisable, or by appointment. *Restoration and sales of period pianos, pianolas and player pianos; music rolls, repair materials, books and accessories.*
TEL: 01223 861348/861408; FAX: 01223 441276
E-MAIL: ftpoole@talk21.com
WEBSITE: www.cambridgepianolacompany.co.uk

PHOTOGRAPHY

Chris Challis Photography   LAPADA
Kenvale, High Street, Lower Brailes. Oxon.
OX15 5AQ.
Photography for antiques brochures, adverts, catalogues,
books and photographer for the LAPADA diary since 1990.
TEL: 01608 686167; MOBILE: 07866 801302
E-MAIL: chrismanx@yahoo.co.uk
WEBSITE: www.chrischallis-photographer.co.uk

Gerry Clist Photography
Unit 235 Webheath Workshops, Netherwood St.
London. NW6 2JX.
MPA. EST. 1991. Open 10-6. *Specialising in sculptures,*
antiques and works of art photography - studio and location.
TEL: 020 7691 3200; MOBILE: 07798 838839
E-MAIL: gerry@gerryclist.biz
WEBSITE: www.gerryclist.biz

REPRODUCTION STONEWORK

Hampshire Gardencraft
Rake Industries, Rake, Nr. Petersfield, Hants.
GU31 5DR.
EST. 1984. *Manufacturers of antiqued garden ornaments,*
troughs and pots in reconstituted stone in an old Cotswold
stone finish. Many designs, catalogue available.
TEL: 01730 895182; FAX: 01730 893216
E-MAIL: sales@hampshire-gardencraft.com

WEBSITE: www.hampshire-gardencraft.com

Lucas Garden Statuary
Firsland Park Estate, Henfield Road, Albourne, West
Sussex. BN6 9JJ.
EST. 1970. Open 9-5. CL: Sat. *Manufacturers of Lucas*
Stone since 1970, huge range of unusual aged reconstituted
stone statuary. Available in two unique finishes, original
classical and contempory designs. Large full colour catalogue
available.
TEL: 01273 494931; FAX: 01273 495125
E-MAIL: trade@lucasstone.com
WEBSITE: www.lucasstone.com

SUPPLIERS

Antom Ltd t/a Antiques of Tomorrow
The Glue Pot, Kyles, Stockinish, Isle of Harris,
Scotland. HS3 3EN.
(Simon Burke) EST. 2001. Open by appointment.
Wholesale and mail order of reproduction chairs, stools and
armchairs - unpolished frames. VAT: Stan.
TEL: 01859 530300; FAX: 01859 502777

Casemate Ltd.
Spella Barn, Lower Boddington. Northhants. NN11 6XX.
(Simon Moss) EST. 1986. *Display cases for organisations*
attending trade fairs; for hire and for sale.
TEL: 01327 264624; FAX: SAME; MOBILE: 07774 244559
E-MAIL: casematemoss@aol.com
WEBSITE: www.casemate.co.uk

Dauphin Museum Services Ltd
PO Box 602, Oxford, Oxon. OX44 9LU.
(John Harrison-Banfield) Royal Warrant Holders.
EST. 1985. Open 9-5, Sat. by appointment. Please
telephone for directions. *Design and manufacture of stands,*
mounts, cabinets and environmental cases. Mounting service.
Acrylic display stands - other materials utilised include glass,
wood, metal, stone, marble, brass and bronze. Free mail order
catalogue available. Conservation and restoration.
TEL: 01865 343542; FAX: 01865 343307
E-MAIL: sales@dauphin.co.uk
WEBSITE: www.dauphin.co.uk

Devon Metalcrafts & Suffolk Brass
2-3 Victoria Way, Exmouth, Devon. EX8 1EW.
(Trevor Ford and Steve Lendon) EST. 1975. Open 8.30-5.
CL: Sat. *Rine-cast replicas of period cabinet fittings; brass*
and bronze casting service. VAT: Stan.
TEL: 01395 272846; FAX: 01395 276688
E-MAIL: trevor@devonmetalcrafts.co.uk
WEBSITE: www.devonmetalcrafts.co.uk

Just Bros. and Co
Roeder House, Vale Rd., London. N4 1QA.
Member British Jewellery and Giftware Federation Ltd.
Open 9-5, Fri. 9-12.30. *Large supplier of jewellery and*
presentation cases, UK and Europe, inc. reproduction cases.

Catalogue on request.
TEL: 020 8880 2505; FAX: 020 8802 0062
E-MAIL: info@justbros.co.uk

Marshall Brass
Keeling Hall Rd., Foulsham, Norfolk. NR20 5PR.
(Andrew and Tracey Marshall) GMC. EST. 1985.
*Suppliers of quality period furniture fittings in brass and
iron. 320 page catalogue available.*
TEL: 01362 684105; FAX: 01362 684280
E-MAIL: admin@marshall-brass.com
WEBSITE: www.marshall-brass.com

Martin and Co. Ltd
160 Dollman St., Duddeston, Birmingham, West
Midlands. B17 4RS.
ASFI. EST. 1950. Open 8-5. CL: Sat. *Cabinet hardware
supplied – handles, locks, hinges, castors etc.*
TEL: 0121 359 2111; FAX: 0121 359 4698
E-MAIL: sales@martin.co.uk
WEBSITE: www.martin.co.uk

Alan Morris Wholesale
Stonecourt, Townsend, Nympsfield, Glos. GL10 3UF.
*Display stands – coated wire, plastic, acrylic and wood for
plates, cups, saucers, bowls etc; wire and disc; jewellery boxes,
polishing and cleaning cloths, pealable white labels and
strung tickets. Mail order available.* VAT: Stan.
TEL: 01453 861069
WEBSITE: www.alanmorris.co.uk

Relics of Witney Ltd
35 Bridge St., Witney, Oxon. OX28 1DA.
EST. 1987. Open 8-5. *Suppliers of furniture restoration
materials, brass castors, handles, locks, waxes and polish,
upholstery and caning requisites, Farrow & Ball and
reproduction paints, stencils etc. Mail order also. Online
catalogue.* LOC: Main road.
TEL: 01993 704611
E-MAIL: sales@tryrelics.co.uk
WEBSITE: www.tryrelics.co.uk

The Victorian Ring Box Company
Unit 1, Fleetside, Gatehouse of Fleet,
Kirkcudbrightshire, Scotland. DG7 2JY.
(The Franca Bruno Company) EST. 1990. Open by
appointment. *Manufacturers and distributors of high
quality antique style presentation boxes; also available with
sterling silver tops and in tartan.*
TEL: 01557 814466/814054; FAX: same
E-MAIL: francambruno@hotmail.com

TEXTILES

The Textile Conservancy Company Ltd
The Calf House, Halden Place, Halden Lane
Rolvenden, Kent. TN17 4JG.
(Alexandra Seth-Smith) ICON. EST. 1997 *Cleaning and
repair of historic textiles, tapestries and rugs. Professional
advice on correct storage and display. Collection surveys and
condition reports.*
TEL: 01580 241439
E-MAIL: alex@textile-conservation.co.uk
WEBSITE: www.textile-conservation.co.uk

The Textile Restoration Studio
2 Talbot Rd., Bowdon, Altrincham, Cheshire.
WA14 3JD.
(Jacqueline and Michael Hyman) Conservation Register.
ICON. EST. 1982 *Cleaning and repair of all antique
textiles including tapestries, samplers, canvas work,
beadwork, lace, costume, ecclesiastical vestments and
furnishings, dolls and fans. Mail order catalogue of specialist
textile conservation materials (free with large stamped
addressed envelope).*
TEL: 0161 928 0020; FAX: same
E-MAIL: studio@textilerestoration.co.uk
WEBSITE: www.textilerestoration.co.uk
www.conservationconsortium.com

TOYS

Robert Mullis Restoration Services Ltd
55 Berkeley Rd., Wroughton, Swindon, Wilts.
SN4 9BN.
(Robert Mullis) BTG. Strictly by appointment. *Full or
partial restorations of antique horses, some wooden toy
restoration. Traditional methods and materials used.
Collection and delivery. New rocking horses made in five
sizes, commissions undertaken.*
TEL: 01793 813583; FAX: 01793 813577
E-MAIL: robert@rockinghorses.freeserve.co.uk

Tobilane Designs
The Toyworks, Holly House, Askham, Penrith,
Cumbria. CA10 2PG.
(Paul and Elaine Commander) EST. 1985. Open 7.30-6,
inc. Sundays. *Traditional toymakers and restorers of old toys
including rocking horses and teddies. Identification and
valuation service.* LOC: Opposite Queen's Head public
house, village centre, 5 miles south of Penrith. VAT: Stan.
TEL: 01931 712077
E-MAIL: info@thetoyworks.co.uk
WEBSITE: www.thetoyworks.co.uk

ALPHABETICAL LIST OF TOWNS AND VILLAGES AND COUNTIES UNDER WHICH THEY ARE LISTED.

A
Abbots Leigh, Somerset.
Aberdeen, Scotland.
Aberdour, Scotland.
Aberfeldy, Scotland.
Aberford, Yorks. West.
Abernyte, Scotland.
Aberystwyth, Wales.
Abinger Hammer, Surrey.
Accrington, Lancs.
Alcester, Warks.
Aldeburgh, Suffolk.
Aldermaston, Berks.
Alford, Lincs.
Alfreton, Derbys.
Allington, Lincs.
Allonby, Cumbria.
Alnwick, Northumbs.
Alresford, Hants.
Alsager, Cheshire.
Alston, Cumbria.
Altrincham, Cheshire.
Amersham, Bucks.
Ampthill, Beds.
Ansley, Warks.
Antrim, Co. Antrim, Northern
  Ireland.
Appleby-in-Westmorland,
  Cumbria.
Appledore, Kent.
Ardingly, Sussex West.
Arundel, Sussex West.
Ascot, Berks.
Ascott-under-Wychwood, Oxon.
Ash, Kent.
Ash Vale, Surrey.
Ashbourne, Derbys.
Ashburton, Devon.
Ashford, Kent.
Ashtead, Surrey.
Ashton-under-Lyne, Lancs.
Aston Clinton, Bucks.
Atcham, Shrops.
Attleborough, Norfolk.
Auchterarder, Scotland.
Auldearn, Scotland.
Aylesby, Lincs.
Aylsham, Norfolk.

B
Bakewell, Derbys.
Balderton, Notts.
Baldock, Herts.
Ballater, Scotland.
Ballymena, Co. Antrim, Northern
  Ireland.
Balsall Common, West Mids.
Balsham, Cambs.
Bampton, Devon.
Bangor, Wales.
Barham, Kent.
Barkham, Berks.
Barmouth, Wales.
Barnard Castle, Durham.
Barnet, Herts.
Barnstaple, Devon.
Barnt Green, Worcs.
Barnton, Cheshire.
Barrington, Somerset.
Barry, Wales.

Barton, Cheshire.
Basingstoke, Hants.
Bath, Somerset.
Batheaston, Somerset.
Batley, Yorks. West.
Battlesbridge, Essex.
Beaconsfield, Bucks.
Beauly, Scotland.
Beaumaris, Wales.
Beccles, Suffolk.
Beckenham, Kent.
Bedford, Beds.
Beech, Hants.
Beer, Devon.
Beeston, Notts.
Belfast, Co. Antrim, Northern
  Ireland.
Belper, Derbys.
Bere Regis, Dorset.
Berkeley, Glos.
Berkhamsted, Herts.
Berwick-upon-Tweed,
  Northumbs.
Bessacarr, Yorks. South.
Betchworth, Surrey.
Bethesda, Wales.
Beverley, Yorks. East.
Bewdley, Worcs.
Bicester, Oxon.
Bideford, Devon.
Biggleswade, Beds.
Billingshurst, Sussex West.
Bilsington, Kent.
Birchington, Kent.
Birdham, Sussex West.
Birkenhead, Merseyside.
Birmingham, West Mids.
Bishop's Castle, Shrops.
Bishops Cleeve, Glos.
Bishop's Stortford, Herts.
Blackburn, Lancs.
Blackmore, Essex.
Blackpool, Lancs.
Bladon, Oxon.
Blair Atholl, Scotland.
Blairgowrie, Scotland.
Blakeney, Glos.
Blandford Forum, Dorset.
Bletchingley, Surrey.
Blofield, Norfolk.
Blythburgh, Suffolk.
Bodorgan, Wales.
Bolton, Lancs.
Bolton Abbey, Yorks. North.
Bolton-by-Bowland, Lancs.
Boroughbridge, Yorks. North.
Boscastle, Cornwall.
Boston, Lincs.
Boston Spa, Yorks. West.
Bourne, Lincs.
Bourne End, Bucks.
Bournemouth, Dorset.
Bourton-on-the-Water, Glos.
Bovey Tracey, Devon.
Brackley, Northants.
Bradford, Yorks. West.
Bradford-on-Avon, Wilts.
Brailsford, Derbys.
Brambridge, Hants.
Brampton, Cumbria.

Brandsby, Yorks. North.
Branksome, Dorset.
Brasted, Kent.
Braunton, Devon.
Brecon, Wales.
Brentwood, Essex.
Brewood, Staffs.
Bridgend, Wales.
Bridgnorth, Shrops.
Bridlington, Yorks. East.
Bridport, Dorset.
Brierfield, Lancs.
Brighton, Sussex East.
Brinkworth, Wilts.
Bristol, Glos.
Brixham, Devon.
Broadstairs, Kent.
Broadway, Worcs.
Brockenhurst, Hants.
Bromley, Kent.
Bromyard, Herefs.
Brook, Hants.
Brough, Cumbria.
Bruton, Somerset.
Buckfastleigh, Devon.
Budby, Notts.
Budleigh Salterton, Devon.
Bungay, Suffolk.
Burford, Oxon.
Burgess Hill, Sussex West.
Burghfield Common, Berks.
Burlton, Shrops.
Burneston, Yorks. North.
Burnham, Bucks.
Burnham Market, Norfolk.
Burnham-on-Crouch, Essex.
Burnham-on-Sea, Somerset.
Burnley, Lancs.
Burscough, Lancs.
Burton-upon-Trent, Staffs.
Burwash, Sussex East.
Burwell, Cambs.
Bury, Lancs.
Bury St. Edmunds, Suffolk.
Bushmills, Co. Antrim, Northern
  Ireland.
Buxton, Derbys.

C
Caerwys, Wales.
Caistor, Lincs.
Callington, Cornwall.
Calne, Wilts.
Cambridge, Cambs.
Canonbie, Scotland.
Canterbury, Kent.
Cardiff, Wales.
Carhampton, Somerset.
Carlisle, Cumbria.
Carmarthen, Wales.
Carrefour Selous, St. Lawrence,
  Jersey, Channel Islands.
Carshalton, Surrey.
Cartmel, Cumbria.
Castel Cary, Somerset.
Castle Ashby, Northants.
Castletown, Isle of Man.
Cavendish, Suffolk.
Caversham, Berks.
Ceres, Scotland.

Chagford, Devon.
Chale, Isle of Wight.
Chalgrove, Oxon.
Chard, Somerset.
Charlton Horethorne, Somerset.
Cheadle Hulme, Cheshire.
Cheam, Surrey.
Cheddar, Somerset.
Cheltenham, Glos.
Chepstow, Wales.
Cherhill, Wilts.
Chertsey, Surrey.
Chesham, Bucks.
Chester, Cheshire.
Chesterfield, Derbys.
Chichester, Sussex West.
Chilcompton, Somerset.
Chilham, Kent.
Chilton, Oxon.
Chipping Campden, Glos.
Chipping Norton, Oxon.
Chirk, Wales.
Chislehurst, Kent.
Chittering, Cambs.
Chobham, Surrey.
Chorley, Lancs.
Christchurch, Dorset.
Church Stretton, Shrops.
Cirencester, Glos.
Clare, Suffolk.
Claygate, Surrey.
Cleadon, Tyne & Wear.
Cleethorpes, Lincs.
Cleobury Mortimer, Shrops.
Clevedon, Somerset.
Clitheroe, Lancs.
Clola by Mintlaw, Scotland.
Clyst Honiton, Devon.
Coalville, Leics.
Cockermouth, Cumbria.
Cocking, Sussex West.
Codford, Wilts.
Coggeshall, Essex.
Colchester, Essex.
Coldstream, Scotland.
Coleraine, Co. Londonderry,
  Northern Ireland.
Coltishall, Norfolk.
Colwyn Bay, Wales.
Colyton, Devon.
Combe Martin, Devon.
Comber, Co. Down, Northern
  Ireland.
Compton, Surrey.
Conisholme, Lincs.
Connor Downs, Cornwall.
Consett, Durham.
Conwy, Wales.
Cookstown, Co. Tyrone,
  Northern Ireland.
Coombe Bissett, Wilts.
Corbridge, Northumbs.
Corsham, Wilts.
Cosford, Shrops.
Coulsdon, Surrey.
Coventry, West Mids.
Cowbridge, Wales.
Cowes, Isle of Wight.
Coxley, Somerset.
Cranbrook, Kent.

Crayford, Kent.
Crediton, Devon.
Crewkerne, Somerset.
Criccieth, Wales.
Crickhowell, Wales.
Cricklade, Wilts.
Cromarty, Scotland.
Cromer, Norfolk.
Crosby Ravensworth, Cumbria.
Cross Hills, Yorks. North.
Croydon, Surrey.
Cuckfield, Sussex West.
Cullingworth, Yorks. West.
Cullompton, Devon.

D
Danbury, Essex.
Darlington, Durham.
Darlton, Notts.
Dartmouth, Devon.
Darwen, Lancs.
Datchet, Berks.
Deal, Kent.
Debden, Essex.
Debenham, Suffolk.
Deddington, Oxon.
Deganwy, Wales.
Depden, Suffolk.
Derby, Derbys.
Dereham, Norfolk.
Dersingham, Norfolk.
Devizes, Wilts.
Disley, Cheshire.
Diss, Norfolk.
Ditchling, Sussex East.
Ditton Priors, Shrops.
Dobwalls, Cornwall.
Donaghadee, Co. Down,
    Northern Ireland.
Dorchester, Dorset.
Dorchester-on-Thames, Oxon.
Dorking, Surrey.
Dornoch, Scotland.
Douglas, Isle of Man.
Doune, Scotland.
Driffield, Yorks. East.
Droitwich, Worcs.
Duffield, Derbys.
Dulverton, Somerset.
Dundee, Scotland.
Dundonald, Co. Down, Northern
    Ireland.
Dungannon, Co. Tyrone,
    Northern Ireland.
Dunkeld, Scotland.
Dunsfold, Surrey.
Dunster, Somerset.
Duxford, Cambs.

E
Earls Colne, Essex.
Earsham, Norfolk.
Easingwold, Yorks. North.
East Hagbourne, Oxon.
East Knoyle, Somerset.
East Molesey, Surrey.
East Peckham, Kent.
East Pennard, Somerset.
Eastbourne, Sussex East.
Eastleach, Glos.
Easton Neston, Northants.
Ebrington, Glos.
Edenbridge, Kent.
Edinburgh, Scotland.
Elham, Kent.
Elstead, Surrey.

Ely, Cambs.
Emsworth, Hants.
Enfield, Middx.
Epsom, Surrey.
Erbistock, Wales.
Ermington, Devon.
Eversley, Hants.
Evesham, Worcs.
Ewell, Surrey.
Exeter, Devon.
Exmouth, Devon.
Exning, Suffolk.
Eye, Suffolk.

F
Fairford, Glos.
Fakenham, Norfolk.
Falmouth, Cornwall.
Faringdon, Oxon.
Farnham, Surrey.
Farningham, Kent.
Faversham, Kent.
Felixstowe, Suffolk.
Feniscowles, Lancs.
Fenny Bridges, Devon.
Ferryside, Wales.
Filey, Yorks. North.
Finchingfield, Essex.
Finedon, Northants.
Finningham, Suffolk.
Fishlake, Yorks. South.
Flamborough, Yorks. East.
Flaxton, Yorks. North.
Flimwell, Sussex East.
Flore, Northants.
Folkestone, Kent.
Fordham, Cambs.
Fordingbridge, Hants.
Forest Row, Sussex East.
Forfar, Scotland.
Forres, Scotland.
Fortrose, Scotland.
Four Oaks, West Mids.
Fowey, Cornwall.
Framfield, Sussex East.
Framlingham, Suffolk.
Freshford, Somerset.
Freshwater, Isle of Wight.
Frinton-on-Sea, Essex.
Frodsham, Cheshire.
Frome, Somerset.
Froxfield, Wilts.

G
Gainsborough, Lincs.
Gargrave, Yorks. North.
Gilberdyke, Yorks. East.
Glan Conwy, Wales.
Glasgow, Scotland.
Glencarse, Scotland.
Glossop, Derbys.
Gloucester, Glos.
Godalming, Surrey.
Godney, Somerset.
Gomshall, Surrey.
Gosport, Hants.
Goudhurst, Kent.
Grampound, Cornwall.
Grandtully, Scotland.
Grantham, Lincs.
Grasmere, Cumbria.
Great Baddow, Essex.
Great Glen, Leics.
Great Harwood, Lancs.
Great Malvern, Worcs.
Great Salkeld, Cumbria.

Great Shelford, Cambs.
Great Waltham, Essex.
Great Yarmouth, Norfolk.
Green Hammerton, Yorks. North.
Greyabbey Village, Co. Down,
    Northern Ireland.
Greystoke, Cumbria.
Grimsby, Lincs.
Grimston, Leics.
Grouville, Jersey, Channel Islands.
Gt. Cransley, Northants.
Guildford, Surrey.
Gullane, Scotland.

H
Hacheston, Suffolk.
Haddenham, Bucks.
Haddington, Scotland.
Hadlow Down, Sussex East.
Hailsham, Sussex East.
Halesowen, West Mids.
Halesworth, Suffolk.
Halfway, Berks.
Halifax, Yorks. West.
Hallow, Worcs.
Halstead, Essex.
Hampton, Middx.
Hamstreet, Kent.
Harpole, Northants.
Harrogate, Yorks. North.
Hartlepool, Yorks. North.
Hartley Wintney, Hants.
Harwich, Essex.
Haslemere, Surrey.
Haslingden, Lancs.
Hastings, Sussex East.
Hatch End, Middx.
Hatherleigh, Devon.
Hatton, Warks.
Hawarden, Wales.
Hawes, Yorks. North.
Hawick, Scotland.
Haworth, Yorks. West.
Hayfield, Derbys.
Hayle, Cornwall.
Hayling Island, Hants.
Hay-on-Wye, Wales.
Haywards Heath, Sussex West.
Headington, Oxon.
Headley, Hants.
Heanor, Derbys.
Heathfield, Sussex East.
Hebden Bridge, Yorks. West.
Helmsley, Yorks. North.
Hemel Hempstead, Herts.
Hemswell Cliff, Lincs.
Henfield, Sussex West.
Henley-in-Arden, Warks.
Henley-on-Thames, Oxon.
Henlow, Beds.
Hereford, Herefs.
Herne Bay, Kent.
Hertford, Herts.
Hertford Heath, Herts.
Heswall, Merseyside.
Hexham, Northumbs.
High Wycombe, Bucks.
Higham Ferrers, Northants.
Hillsborough, Co. Down,
    Northern Ireland.
Hinckley, Leics.
Hindhead, Surrey.
Hingham, Norfolk.
Hinton Charterhouse, Somerset.
Hitchin, Herts.
Hoby, Leics.

Holland-on-Sea, Essex.
Holmfirth, Yorks. West.
Holt, Norfolk.
Holyhead, Wales.
Honiton, Devon.
Honley, Yorks. West.
Hook Norton, Oxon.
Horncastle, Lincs.
Horsham, Sussex West.
Horton, Berks.
Houghton, Cambs.
Houghton, Sussex West.
Hoveton, Norfolk.
Hoylake, Cheshire.
Hull, Yorks. East.
Hungerford, Berks.
Hunstanton, Norfolk.
Huntercombe, Oxon.
Huntingdon, Cambs.
Hurstpierpoint, Sussex West.
Hythe, Kent.

I
Ibstock, Leics.
Ilchester, Somerset.
Ilkley, Yorks. West.
Inchture, Scotland.
Innerleithen, Scotland.
Inverness, Scotland.
Ipswich, Suffolk.
Islip, Northants.
Iver, Bucks.
Ixworth, Suffolk.

J
Jedburgh, Scotland.
Jesmond, Tyne and Wear.

K
Kelling, Norfolk.
Kelsall, Cheshire.
Kelvedon, Essex.
Kendal, Cumbria.
Keswick, Cumbria.
Kettering, Northants.
Kew Green, Surrey.
Kidderminster, Worcs.
Kidwelly, Wales.
Kilbarchan, Scotland.
Killearn, Scotland.
Killin, Scotland.
Kilmacolm, Scotland.
Kilmarnock, Scotland.
Kilmichael Glassary, Scotland.
Kingham, Oxon.
King's Lynn, Norfolk.
Kingsclere, Hants.
Kingsthorpe, Northants.
Kingston-upon-Thames, Surrey.
Kington, Herefs.
Kington Langley, Wilts.
Kirk Deighton, Yorks. North.
Kirkby Lonsdale, Cumbria.
Kirkby Malham, Yorks. North.
Kirkby Stephen, Cumbria.
Kirkcaldy, Scotland.
Kirkcudbright, Scotland.
Kirton, Lincs.
Knaresborough, Yorks. North.
Knebworth, Herts.
Knighton, Wales.
Knutsford, Cheshire.

L
Lancaster, Lancs.
Landbeach, Cambs.

Langford, Notts.
Langford, Somerset.
Langley Burrell, Wilts.
Largs, Scotland.
Launceston, Cornwall.
Lavenham, Suffolk.
Leagrave, Beds.
Leamington Spa, Warks.
Lechlade, Glos.
Leckhampstead, Berks.
Ledbury, Herefs.
Leeds, Yorks. West.
Leek, Staffs.
Leicester, Leics.
Leigh, Lancs.
Leigh, Staffs.
Leigh-on-Sea, Essex.
Leighton Buzzard, Beds.
Leiston, Suffolk.
Leominster, Herefs.
Letchworth, Herts.
Lewes, Sussex East.
Leyburn, Yorks. North.
Lichfield, Staffs.
Lincoln, Lincs.
Lindfield, Sussex West.
Linlithgow, Scotland.
Lisburn, Co. Antrim, Northern Ireland.
Liss, Hants.
Little Dalby, Leics.
Littleton, Somerset.
Litton Cheney, Dorset.
Liverpool, Merseyside.
Llandeilo, Wales.
Llandudno, Wales.
Llandudno Junction, Wales.
Llanerchymedd, Wales.
Llanfairfechan, Wales.
Llangollen, Wales.
Llanidloes, Wales.
Llanrwst, Wales.
Lockerbie, Scotland.
Londonderry, Co. Londonderry, Northern Ireland.
Long Eaton, Derbys.
Long Marston, Warks.
Long Marton, Cumbria.
Long Melford, Suffolk.
Looe, Cornwall.
Lostwithiel, Cornwall.
Loudham, Suffolk.
Loughborough, Leics.
Louth, Lincs.
Low Newton, Cumbria.
Lubenham, Leics.
Ludlow, Shrops.
Lurgan, Co. Armagh, Northern Ireland.
Lydford, Devon.
Lye, West Mids.
Lymington, Hants.
Lymm, Cheshire.
Lyndhurst, Hants.
Lyneham, Wilts.
Lynton, Devon.
Lytchett Minster, Dorset.

M
Macclesfield, Cheshire.
Maidenhead, Berks.
Maidstone, Kent.
Maldon, Essex.
Malmesbury, Wilts.
Malton, Yorks. North.
Malvern Link, Worcs.

Manchester, Lancs.
Manningford Bruce, Wilts.
Marazion, Cornwall.
Margate, Kent.
Marhamchurch, Cornwall.
Market Bosworth, Leics.
Market Deeping, Lincs.
Market Drayton, Shrops.
Market Harborough, Leics.
Market Rason, Lincs.
Market Weighton, Yorks. East.
Marlborough, Wilts.
Marlesford, Suffolk.
Marlow, Bucks.
Marten, Wilts.
Martlesham, Suffolk.
Martock, Somerset.
Masham, Yorks. North.
Matlock, Derbys.
Melbourne, Yorks N.
Melbury Osmond, Dorset.
Melksham, Wilts.
Melrose, Scotland.
Menai Bridge, Wales.
Mendlesham, Suffolk.
Menston, Yorks. West.
Meols, Merseyside.
Mere, Wilts.
Merton, Devon.
Mickleton, Glos.
Middle Aston, Oxon.
Middleham, Yorks. North.
Middleton Village, Lancs.
Midhurst, Sussex West.
Milford Haven, Wales.
Milton Common, Oxon.
Minchinhampton, Glos.
Mobberley, Cheshire.
Modbury, Devon.
Moira, Co. Armagh, Northern Ireland.
Monmouth, Wales.
Morecambe, Lancs.
Moreton-in-Marsh, Glos.
Much Wenlock, Shrops.

N
Nantwich, Cheshire.
Narberth, Wales.
Needham Market, Suffolk.
Nelson, Lancs.
Nether Stowey, Somerset.
New Bolingbroke, Lincs.
New England, Essex.
New Malden, Surrey.
Newark, Notts.
Newbiggin-on-Lune, Cumbria.
Newbridge-on-Wye, Wales.
Newburgh, Scotland.
Newby Bridge, Cumbria.
Newcastle-under-Lyme, Staffs.
Newcastle-upon-Tyne, Tyne and Wear.
Newent, Glos.
Newmarket, Suffolk.
Newport, Essex.
Newport, Isle of Wight.
Newport, Wales.
Newport-on-Tay, Scotland.
Newton Abbot, Devon.
Newtownabbey, Co. Antrim, Northern Ireland.
North Aston, Oxon.
North Berwick, Scotland.
North Cave, Yorks. East.
North Shields, Tyne and Wear.

North Walsham, Norfolk.
North Wraxall, Wilts.
Northampton, Northants.
Northfleet, Kent.
Northleach, Glos.
Northwich, Cheshire.
Norton, Durham.
Norwich, Norfolk.
Nottingham, Notts.
Nr Winchester, Hants.
Nutley, Sussex East.

O
Oakham, Rutland.
Odiham, Hants.
Old Bedhampton, Hants.
Oldham, Lancs.
Ollerton, Notts.
Olney, Bucks.
Omagh, Co. Tyrone, Northern Ireland.
Onchan, Isle of Man.
Orford, Suffolk.
Ormskirk, Lancs.
Osgathorpe, Leics.
Otford, Kent.
Outwell, Cambs.
Oxford, Oxon.
Oxted, Surrey.

P
Paignton, Devon.
Paisley, Scotland.
Parkstone, Dorset.
Pateley Bridge, Yorks. North.
Peasenhall, Suffolk.
Peel, Isle of Man.
Pembroke, Wales.
Penistone, Yorks. South.
Penkridge, Staffs.
Penrith, Cumbria.
Penryn, Cornwall.
Penzance, Cornwall.
Pershore, Worcs.
Perth, Scotland.
Peterborough, Cambs.
Peterborough, Lincs.
Petersfield, Hants.
Petts Wood, Kent.
Petworth, Sussex West.
Pevensey, Sussex East.
Pewsey, Wilts.
Pickering, Yorks. North.
Pittenweem, Scotland.
Plumley, Cheshire.
Plymouth, Devon.
Polegate, Sussex East.
Poole, Dorset.
Porlock, Somerset.
Portballintrae, Co. Antrim, Northern Ireland.
Porthmadog, Wales.
Portrush, Co. Antrim, Northern Ireland.
Portslade, Sussex East.
Portsmouth, Hants.
Potter Heigham, Norfolk.
Potterspury, Northants.
Potton, Beds.
Poundgate, Sussex East.
Poynton, Cheshire.
Preston, Lancs.
Preston, Glos.
Prestwick, Scotland.
Puckeridge, Herts.
Puddletown, Dorset.

Pulborough, Sussex West.
Pwllheli, Wales.

Q
Queen Camel, Somerset.
Queniborough, Leics.
Quorn, Leics.

R
Radford Semele, Warks.
Radstock, Somerset.
Rainford, Merseyside.
Rait, Scotland.
Ramsbottom, Lancs.
Ramsbury, Wilts.
Ramsey, Cambs.
Ramsey, Isle of Man.
Randalston, Co. Antrim, Northern Ireland.
Raughton Head, Cumbria.
Raveningham, Norfolk.
Rayleigh, Essex.
Reading, Berks.
Redbourn, Herts.
Redhill, Surrey.
Redruth, Cornwall.
Reigate, Surrey.
Retford, Notts.
Rettendon, Essex.
Ribchester, Lancs.
Richmond, Surrey.
Richmond, Yorks. North.
Rickmansworth, Herts.
Ringstead, Norfolk.
Ringwood, Hants.
Ripley, Derbys.
Ripley, Surrey.
Ripon, Yorks. North.
Risby, Suffolk.
Robin Hood's Bay, Yorks. North.
Rochdale, Lancs.
Rochester, Kent.
Rodington, Shrops.
Rolvenden, Kent.
Romiley, Cheshire.
Romsey, Hants.
Ross-on-Wye, Herefs.
Rothbury, Northumbs.
Rotherfield, Sussex East.
Rotherham, Yorks. South.
Rottingdean, Sussex East.
Rowlands Castle, Hants.
Rugeley, Staffs.
Ruislip, Middx.
Runfold, Surrey.
Rushden, Northants.
Ryde, Isle of Wight.
Rye, Sussex East.

S
Sabden, Lancs.
Saffron Walden, Essex.
Saintfield, Co. Down, Northern Ireland.
Salisbury, Wilts.
Saltaire, Yorks. West.
Saltcoats, Scotland.
Samlesbury, Lancs.
Sandbach, Cheshire.
Sandgate, Kent.
Sandiacre, Notts.
Sandwich, Kent.
Sawbridgeworth, Herts.
Scarborough, Yorks. North.
Scratby, Norfolk.
Screveton, Notts.

Scunthorpe, Lincs.
Seaford, Sussex East.
Seapatrick, Co. Down, Northern Ireland.
Seaton, Devon.
Sedbergh, Cumbria.
Semley, Wilts.
Settle, Yorks. North.
Sevenoaks, Kent.
Shaftesbury, Dorset.
Shalford, Essex.
Shanklin, Isle of Wight.
Sheffield, Yorks. South.
Shenfield, Essex.
Shenton, Leics.
Sherborne, Dorset.
Sherburn-in-Elmet, Yorks N.
Shere, Surrey.
Sheringham, Norfolk.
Sherwood, Notts.
Shifnal, Shrops.
Shipston-on-Stour, Warks.
Shoreham-by-Sea, Sussex West.
Shrewsbury, Shrops.
Sible Hedingham, Essex.
Sidmouth, Devon.
Sileby, Leics.
Skipton, Yorks. North.
Slad, Glos.
Sleaford, Lincs.
Sleights, Yorks. North.
Snainton, Yorks. North.
Snape, Suffolk.
Solihull, West Mids.
Somerton, Somerset.
South Benfleet, Essex.
South Brent, Devon.
South Harting, Sussex West.
South Molton, Devon.
South Petherton, Somerset.
Southampton, Hants.
Southborough, Kent.
Southport, Merseyside.
Southwell, Notts.
Southwold, Suffolk.
Sowerby Bridge, Yorks. West.
Spalding, Lincs.
St. Albans, Herts.
St. Andrews, Scotland.
St. Anne's, Alderney, Channel Islands.
St. Buryan, Cornwall.
St. Columb Major, Cornwall.
St. Helen Auckland, Durham.
St. Helier, Jersey, Channel Islands.
St. Ives, Cambs.
St. Ives, Cornwall.
St. Leonards-on-Sea, Sussex East.
St. Neots, Cambs.
St. Nicholas at Wade, Birchington, Kent.
St. Peter Port, Guernsey, Channel Islands.
St. Sampson, Guernsey, Channel Islands.
St. Saviour, Jersey, Channel Islands.
Stafford, Staffs.
Staines, Surrey.
Stalham, Norfolk.
Stamford, Lincs.
Standish, Lancs.
Stansted, Essex.
Stanton upon Hine Heath, Shrops.

Staveley, Cumbria.
Steeple Bumpstead, Essex.
Stewarton, Scotland.
Stewartstown, Co. Tyrone, Northern Ireland.
Steyning, Sussex West.
Stickney, Lincs.
Stiffkey, Norfolk.
Stillington, Yorks. North.
Stirling, Scotland.
Stockbridge, Hants.
Stockbury, Kent.
Stockport, Cheshire.
Stockton-on-Tees, Durham.
Stoke Ferry, Norfolk.
Stoke-on-Trent, Staffs.
Stokesley, Yorks. North.
Stoke-sub-Hamdon, Somerset.
Storrington, Sussex West.
Stourbridge, West Mids.
Stow-on-the-Wold, Glos.
Stratford-upon-Avon, Warks.
Strathblane, Scotland.
Stretton-on-Fosse, Warks.
Stroud, Glos.
Suckley, Worcs.
Sudbury, Suffolk.
Sunderland, Tyne and Wear.
Sundridge, Kent.
Surbiton, Surrey.
Sutton, Surrey.
Sutton Bonington, Notts.
Sutton Bridge, Lincs.
Sutton Coldfield, West Mids.
Sutton Valence, Kent.
Sutton-on-Sea, Lincs.
Swanage, Dorset.
Swansea, Wales.
Swindon, Wilts.
Swinstead, Lincs.

T
Tacolneston, Norfolk.
Taddington, Glos.
Tadley, Hants.
Tarporley, Cheshire.
Tarvin, Cheshire.
Tarvin Sands, Cheshire.
Tattenhall, Cheshire.
Taunton, Somerset.
Tavistock, Devon.
Tedburn St Mary, Devon.
Teddington, Middx.
Teignmouth, Devon.
Telford, Shrops.
Temple Comb, Somerset.
Tenby, Wales.
Tenterden, Kent.
Tetbury, Glos.
Tetsworth, Oxon.
Tewkesbury, Glos.
Teynham, Kent.
Thame, Oxon.
Thames Ditton, Surrey.
Thaxted, Essex.
Thirsk, Yorks. North.
Thornton-le-Dale, Yorks. North.
Thurston, Suffolk.
Tilston, Cheshire.
Tintern, Wales.
Tisbury, Wilts.
Titchfield, Hants.
Tiverton, Devon.
Tockwith, Yorks. North.
Todenham, Glos.
Todmorden, Yorks. West.

Tonbridge, Kent.
Topsham, Devon.
Torquay, Devon.
Totnes, Devon.
Tottenhill, Norfolk.
Towcester, Northants.
Trawden, Lancs.
Trecastle, Wales.
Treharris, Wales.
Tring, Herts.
Tringford, Herts.
Troon, Scotland.
Truro, Cornwall.
Tunbridge Wells, Kent.
Tutbury, Staffs.
Tuxford, Notts.
Twickenham, Middx.
Twickenham, Surrey.
Twyford, Berks.
Twyford, Norfolk.
Tynemouth, Tyne and Wear.
Tytherleigh, Devon.
Tywyn, Wales.

U
Uckfield, Sussex East.
Uffculme, Devon.
Upper Largo, Scotland.
Uppingham, Rutland.
Upton-upon-Severn, Worcs.
Uxbridge, Middx.

V
Vale, Guernsey, Channel Islands.
Valley, Wales.
Ventnor, Isle of Wight.

W
Wadebridge, Cornwall.
Wadhurst, Sussex East.
Wainfleet, Lincs.
Wakefield, Yorks. West.
Waldingham, Surrey.
Walgherton, Cheshire.
Wallasey, Merseyside.
Wallingford, Oxon.
Walsall, West Mids.
Walsden, Yorks. West.
Walton-on-Thames, Surrey.
Wareham, Dorset.
Wargrave, Berks.
Warminster, Wilts.
Warrington, Cheshire.
Warwick, Warks.
Washford, Somerset.
Washington, Tyne and Wear.
Watchet, Somerset.
Waterlooville, Hants.
Watford, Herts.
Watlington, Oxon.
Waverton, Cheshire.
Weedon, Northants.
Weeford, Staffs.
Wellingborough, Northants.
Wellington, Somerset.
Wells, Somerset.
Wells-next-the-Sea, Norfolk.
Welshpool, Wales.
Wendover, Bucks.
Wentworth, Yorks. South.
West Auckland, Durham.
West Burton, Yorks. North.
West Byfleet, Surrey.
West Kirby, Cheshire.
West Malling, Kent.
West Yatton, Wilts.

Westcliff-on-Sea, Essex.
Westerham, Kent.
Weston, Devon.
Weston, Herts.
Weston-Super-Mare, Somerset.
Wettenhall, Cheshire.
Weybridge, Surrey.
Weymouth, Dorset.
Whaley Bridge, Derbys.
Whalley, Lancs.
Whitby, Yorks. North.
Whitchurch, Bucks.
Whitchurch, Shrops.
White Roding, Essex.
Whitehaven, Cumbria.
Whithorn, Scotland.
Whitley Bay, Tyne and Wear.
Whitstable, Kent.
Whitwick, Leics.
Whixley, Yorks. North.
Wickford, Essex.
Wickham Market, Suffolk.
Wigan, Lancs.
Wigtown, Scotland.
Williton, Somerset.
Wilstone, Herts.
Wilton, Wilts.
Wimborne Minster, Dorset.
Wincanton, Somerset.
Winchcombe, Glos.
Winchester, Hants.
Windsor, Berks.
Wing, Rutland.
Wingham, Kent.
Winslow, Bucks.
Wisbech, Cambs.
Wisborough, Sussex West.
Witney, Oxon.
Wittersham, Kent.
Wiveliscombe, Somerset.
Woburn, Beds.
Woking, Surrey.
Wolverhampton, West Mids.
Woodbridge, Suffolk.
Woodford Green, Essex.
Woodhall Spa, Lincs.
Woodstock, Oxon.
Wooler, Northumbs.
Woolpit, Suffolk.
Wootton Wawen, Warks.
Worcester, Worcs.
Worsley, Lancs.
Worthing, Sussex West.
Wraysbury, Berks.
Wrexham, Wales.
Writtle, Essex.
Wroutham, Kent.
Wroxham, Norfolk.
Wychbold, Worcs.
Wymondham, Leics.
Wymondham, Norfolk.

Y
Yarnton, Oxon.
Yazor, Herefs.
Yeovil, Somerset.
York, Yorks North.
Yoxall, Staffs.
Yoxford, Suffolk.

Specialist Dealers' Index

Most antique dealers in Britain sell a wide range of goods from furniture, through porcelain and pottery, to pictures, prints and clocks. Much of the interest in visiting antiques shops comes from this diversity. However, there are a number of dealers who specialise and the following is a list of these dealers. Most of them will stock a representative selection of the items found under their classification.

The name of the business, together with the area of London or the town and county under which the detailed entry can be found are given in the listing. Again we would like to repeat the advice given in the introduction that, if readers are looking for a particular item, they are advised to telephone first, before making a long journey.

CLASSIFICATIONS

Antiques Centres and Markets
Antiquarian Books
Antiquities
Architectural Items
Arms & Armour
Art Deco & Art Nouveau
Barometers - see also Clock Dealers
Beds
Brass (see Metalwork)
Bronzes
Carpets & Rugs
Cars & Carriages
Chinese Art - see Oriental
Church Furniture & Furnishings
Clocks & Watches
Coins & Medals
Dolls & Toys
Etchings & Engravings
Fire Related Items
Frames
Furniture-
   Continental (mainly French)
   Country
   Georgian
   Oak

Pine
Victorian
Garden Furniture, Ornaments &
   Statuary
Glass - see also Glass Domes &
   Paperweights
Glass Domes
Icons - see Russian Art
Islamic Art
Japanese Art - see Oriental
Jewellery - see Silver & Jewellery
Lighting
Maps & Prints
Metalware/work
Miniatures
Mirrors
Musical Boxes, Instruments &
   Literature
Nautical Instruments - see Scientific
Needlework - see Tapestries
Netsuke - see Oriental
Oil Paintings
Oriental Items
Paperweights
Photographs & Equipment

Porcelain & Pottery
Prints - see Maps
Rugs - see Carpets
Russian/Soviet Art
Scientific Instruments
Sculpture
Shipping Goods & Period Furniture for
   the Trade
Silver and Jewellery
Sporting Items & Associated
   Memorabilia
Sporting Paintings & Prints
Stamps
Tapestries, Textiles & Needlework
Taxidermy
Tools - including Needlework &
   Sewing
Toys - see Dolls
Trade Dealers - see Shipping Goods
Treen
Vintage Cars - see Carriages & Cars
Watercolours
Wholesale Dealers - see Shipping Goods
Wine Related Items

Antique Markets & Centres
Collectors Centre - Antique City, London, E17.
The Mall Antiques Arcade, London, N1.
Camden Passage Antiques Market and Pierrepont
  Arcade Antiques Centre, London, N1.
The Angel Arcade, London, N1.
Palmers Green Antiques Centre, London, N13.
Hampstead Antique and Craft Emporium, London, NW3.
Alfies Antique Market, London, NW8.
The Junk Shop and Spread Eagle, London, SE10.
Greenwich Antiques Market, London, SE10.
Northcote Road Antiques Market, London, SW11.
Antiquarius, London, SW3.
Bourbon-Hanby Antiques Centre, London, SW3.
Admiral Vernon Antiques Market, London, W11.
Central Gallery (Portobello), London, W11.
Crown Arcade, London, W11.
The Harris's Arcade, London, W11.
The Red Lion Antiques Arcade, London, W11.
The Silver Fox Gallery (Portobello), London, W11.

World Famous Portobello Market, London, W11.
Arbras Gallery, London, W11.
B. Lipka & Son Arcade, London, W11.
Rogers Antiques Gallery, London, W11.
Grays Antique Markets, London, W1.
The Old Cinema Antique Department Store, London,
  W4.
Kensington Church Street Antiques Centre, London, W8.
The London Silver Vaults, London, WC2.
Covent Garden Flea Market, London, WC2.
Apple Market Stalls, London, WC2.
Ampthill Antiques Emporium, Ampthill, Beds.
Woburn Abbey Antiques Centre, Woburn, Beds.
Barkham Antique Centre, Barkham, Berks.
Hungerford Arcade, Hungerford, Berks.
Great Grooms of Hungerford, Hungerford, Berks.
Buck House Antiques, Beaconsfield, Bucks.
Antiques Centre at Olney, Olney, Bucks.
Antiques at . . .Wendover Antiques Centre, Wendover,
  Bucks.

Winslow Antiques Centre, Winslow, Bucks.
Hive, Cambridge, Cambs.
Waterside Antiques Centre, Ely, Cambs.
Huntingdon Antiques, Huntingdon, Cambs.
Knutsford Antiques Centre, Knutsford, Cheshire.
Northwich Antiques Centre, Northwich, Cheshire.
Tarporley Antique Centre, Tarporley, Cheshire.
Chapel Street Antiques Arcade, Penzance, Cornwall.
Once Upon A Time, Truro, Cornwall.
Cumbrian Antiques Centre, Brampton, Cumbria.
Carlisle Antiques Centre, Carlisle, Cumbria.
Cockermouth Antiques Market, Cockermouth, Cumbria.
Alfreton Antiques Centre, Alfreton, Derbys.
Heanor Antiques Centre, Heanor, Derbys.
Matlock Antiques and Collectables Centre, Matlock,
    Derbys.
Memory Lane Antiques Centre, Ripley, Derbys.
Shambles, Ashburton, Devon.
Barnstaple Antique & Collectors' Centre, Barnstaple,
    Devon.
Colyton Antiques Centre, Colyton, Devon.
Pennyfarthing Antiques, Dartmouth, Devon.
Exeter's Antique Centre on the Quay, Exeter, Devon.
Honiton Antique Centre, Honiton, Devon.
St Leonards Antiques & Craft Centre, Newton Abbot,
    Devon.
New Street Antique Centre, Plymouth, Devon.
Sidmouth Antique Centre, Sidmouth, Devon.
Topsham Quay Antiques Centre, Topsham, Devon.
Colliton Antique Centre, Dorchester, Dorset.
Punch's Antique Market, Shaftesbury, Dorset.
Battlesbridge Antique Centre, Battlesbridge, Essex.
Finchingfield Antiques Centre, Finchingfield, Essex.
Baddow Antique Centre, Great Baddow, Essex.
Townsford Mill Antiques Centre, Halstead, Essex.
Harwich Antiques Centre, Harwich, Essex.
Mickleton Shed Antiques, Mickleton, Glos.
Antiques Emporium, Stroud, Glos.
St. Nicholas Markets, Bristol, Glos.
Cheltenham Antique Market, Cheltenham, Glos.
Cirencester Arcade, Cirencester, Glos.
Gloucester Antiques Centre Ltd, Gloucester, Glos.
Jubilee Hall Antiques Centre, Lechlade, Glos.
Old Ironmongers Antiques Centre, Lechlade, Glos.
London House Antique Centre, Moreton-in-Marsh,
    Glos.
Fox Cottage Antiques, Stow-on-the-Wold, Glos.
Durham House Antiques Centre, Stow-on-the-Wold,
    Glos.
Long Street Antiques, Tetbury, Glos.
Top Banana Antiques, Tetbury, Glos.
Tewkesbury Antiques & Collectables Centre,
    Tewkesbury, Glos.
Squirrel Collectors Centre, Basingstoke, Hants.
Dolphin Quay Antique Centre, Emsworth, Hants.
Farthingale Centre, Hartley Wintney, Hants.

Acorn Antiques, Lyndhurst, Hants.
Folly Antiques Centre, Petersfield, Hants.
Samuel Spencer's Antiques and Decorative Arts
    Emporium, Winchester, Hants.
Hereford Antique Centre, Hereford, Herefs.
Leominster Antique Centre, Leominster, Herefs.
Ross-on-Wye Antiques Gallery, Ross-on-Wye, Herefs.
Heritage Antique Centre, Berkhamsted, Herts.
Jordans Antiques Centre, Hemel Hempstead, Herts.
Herts and Essex Antiques Centre, Sawbridgeworth,
    Herts.
By George! Antiques Centre, St. Albans, Herts.
Beckenham Antiques & Collectors' Market,
    Beckenham, Kent.
Burgate Antique Centre, Canterbury, Kent.
Bagham Barn Antiques, Chilham, Kent.
Malthouse Arcade, Hythe, Kent.
Beehive, Petts Wood, Kent.
Memories, Rochester, Kent.
Farriers Antiques, St Nicholas at Wade, Birchington,
    Kent.
Castle Antiques Centre, Westerham, Kent.
King's Mill Antique Centre, Burnley, Lancs.
Heskin Hall Antiques, Chorley, Lancs.
Belgrave Antique Centre, Darwen, Lancs.
Holden Wood Antiques Centre, Haslingden, Lancs.
Assembly Rooms Market, Lancaster, Lancs.
Antiques Village, Manchester, Lancs.
The Cavern Antique & Collectors Centre, Oldham, Lancs.
Preston Antique Centre, Preston, Lancs.
Aspinall Antiques Ltd, Sabden, Lancs.
Pendle Antiques Centre Ltd, Sabden, Lancs.
Whitemoors Antiques and Fine Art, Shenton, Leics.
Town & Country Antiques Centre, Alford, Lincs.
Portobello Row Antique & Collectors' Centre, Boston,
    Lincs.
Pilgrims Antiques Centre, Gainsborough, Lincs.
Notions Antiques Centre, Grantham, Lincs.
Astra House Antiques Centre, Hemswell Cliff, Lincs.
Great Expectations, Horncastle, Lincs.
Horncastle Antiques Centre, Horncastle, Lincs.
Lambert Antiques Centre, Lincoln, Lincs.
Old Maltings Antique Centre, Louth, Lincs.
St. Martins Antiques Centre, Stamford, Lincs.
Southport Antiques Centre, Southport, Merseyside.
East Lodge Antiques Village, Enfield, Middx.
AC Antiques and Collectables, Hatch End, Middx.
Ruislip Collectables, Ruislip, Middx.
Antiques & Collectors Centre (Diss), Diss, Norfolk.
Fakenham Antique Centre, Fakenham, Norfolk.
Holt Antique Centre, Holt, Norfolk.
Mews Antique Emporium, Holt, Norfolk.
Le Strange Old Barns Antiques, Arts & Craft Centre,
    Hunstanton, Norfolk.
Old Granary Antiques and Collectors' Centre, King's
    Lynn, Norfolk.

Cloisters Antique & Collectors' Fair, Norwich, Norfolk.

The General Store & Hidden Treasures, Ringstead, Norfolk.

Wells Antique Centre, Wells-next-the-Sea, Norfolk.

Wymondham Antique and Collectors' Centre, Wymondham, Norfolk.

Brackley Antique Cellar, Brackley, Northants.

Village Antique Market, Weedon, Northants.

Antiques and Bric-a-Brac Market, Wellingborough, Northants.

Castle Gate Antiques Centre, Newark, Notts.

Antiques @ The George, Burford, Oxon.

Quiet Woman Antiques Centre, Chipping Norton, Oxon.

Station Mill Antiques Centre, Chipping Norton, Oxon.

Country Markets Antiques and Collectables, Chilton, Oxon.

Deddington Antiques Centre, Deddington, Oxon.

Friday Street Antique Centre (The Ferret), Henley-on-Thames, Oxon.

Henley Antique Centre, Henley-on-Thames, Oxon.

Antiques on High Ltd, Oxford, Oxon.

Swan at Tetsworth, Tetsworth, Oxon.

Lamb Arcade, Wallingford, Oxon.

Antiques at Heritage, Woodstock, Oxon.

Yarnton Antiques Centre, Yarnton, Oxon.

Rutland Antiques Centre, Uppingham, Rutland.Old Mill Antique Centre, Bridgnorth, Shrops.

Bridgnorth Antiques Centre, Bridgnorth, Shrops.

Stretton Antiques Market, Church Stretton, Shrops.

Zani Lady Decorative Antiques, Ludlow, Shrops.

Princess Antique Centre, Shrewsbury, Shrops.

George Street Antiques Centre, Bath, Somerset.

Piccadilly Antiques, Batheaston, Somerset.

Chard Antiques, Chard, Somerset.

Crewkerne Antique Centre, Crewkerne, Somerset.

Somerton Antiques Centre, Somerton, Somerset.

Cider Press Antiques Centre, Taunton, Somerset.

Green Dragon Antiques Centre, Wincanton, Somerset.

Compton Mill Antique Emporium, Leek, Staffs.

Leek Antiques Centre (Barclay House), Leek, Staffs.

Curborough Hall Farm Antiques Centre, Lichfield, Staffs.

Windmill Antiques, Stafford, Staffs.

Old Chapel Antique & Collectables Centre, Tutbury, Staffs.

Clare Antiques and Interiors, Clare, Suffolk.

Long Melford Antiques Centre, Long Melford, Suffolk.

Old Town Hall Antique & Collectors Centre, Needham Market, Suffolk.

Risby Barn, Risby, Suffolk.

Snape Antiques and Collectors Centre, Snape, Suffolk.

Southwold Antiques Centre, Southwold, Suffolk.

Yoxford Antique Centre & Gardens, Yoxford, Suffolk.

Mimbridge Antiques Centre, Chobham, Surrey.

Old Barn Antique Centre, Compton, Surrey.

Dorking House Antiques, Dorking, Surrey.

Bridge Road Antiques Centre, East Molesey, Surrey.

The Bothy, East Molesey, Surrey.

Bourne Mill Antiques, Farnham, Surrey.

Kingston Antique Market, Kingston-upon-Thames, Surrey.

Talbot Walk Antique Centre, Ripley, Surrey.

Shere Antiques, Shere, Surrey.

Arundel Bridge Antiques, Waldingham, Surrey.

Brighton Flea Market, Brighton, Sussex East.

Snoopers' Paradise, Brighton, Sussex East.

Eastbourne Antiques Market, Eastbourne, Sussex East.

Dandelion Clock Antiques Centre, Forest Row, Sussex East.

George Street Antiques Centre, Hastings, Sussex East.

Church-Hill Antiques Centre, Lewes, Sussex East.

Lewes Flea Market, Lewes, Sussex East.

Hastings Antique Centre, St. Leonards-on-Sea, Sussex East.

Rocking Horse Antique Market, Ardingly, Sussex West.

Almshouses Arcade, Chichester, Sussex West.

Petworth Antique Centre, Petworth, Sussex West.

Stable Antiques, Storrington, Sussex West.

ewcastle Antique Centre, Newcastle-upon-Tyne, Tyne and Wear.

Stables Antique Centre, Hatton, Warks.

Barn Antiques Centre, Long Marston, Warks.

Stratford Antique Centre, Stratford-upon-Avon, Warks.

Vintage Antiques Centre, Warwick, Warks.

Birmingham Antique Centre, Birmingham, West Mids.

Antiques Adventure, Coventry, West Mids.

Wolverhampton Antiques and Collectors' Market, Wolverhampton, West Mids.

Upstairs, Downstairs Collectors' Centre, Devizes, Wilts.

Marlborough Parade Antique Centre, Marlborough, Wilts.

King Street Curios, Melksham, Wilts.

Antique and Collectors' Market, Salisbury, Wilts.

Dairy House Antiques, Semley, Wilts.

Penny Farthing Antiques Arcade, Swindon, Wilts.

Warminster Antiques Centre, Warminster, Wilts.

Bewdley Antiques, Bewdley, Worcs.

Carlton Antiques, Great Malvern, Worcs.

Worcester Antiques Centre, Worcester, Worcs.

St Crispin Antique Centre, Beverley, Yorks. East.

Georgian Rooms, Bridlington, Yorks. East.

Grannie's Treasures, Hull, Yorks. East.

Mount Pleasant Antiques Centre, Market Weighton, Yorks. East.

Ginnel Antiques Centre, Harrogate, Yorks. North.

Leyburn Antiques Centre, Leyburn, Yorks. North.

Pickering Antique Centre, Pickering, Yorks. North.

Skipton Antiques Centre, Skipton, Yorks. North.

Antiques Centre York, York, Yorks. North.

Foster's Antique Centre, Rotherham, Yorks. South.

Barmouth Court Antiques Centre, Sheffield, Yorks. South.

Langtons Antiques & Collectables, Sheffield, Yorks. South.
Wentworth Arts, Crafts and Antiques Ltd, Wentworth, Yorks. South.
Carlton Antiques Ltd., Saltaire, Yorks. West.
Scottish Antique & Arts Centre, Abernyte, Scotland.
Clola Antiques Centre, Clola by Mintlaw, Scotland.
Scottish Antique and Art Centre, Doune, Scotland.
Rait Village Antiques Centre, Rait, Scotland.
Mount Antiques Centre, Carmarthen, Wales.
Jacobs Antique Centre, Cardiff, Wales.
Vale of Glamorgan Antiques Centre, Cowbridge, Wales.
Hay Antique Market, Hay-on-Wye, Wales.
Offa's Dyke Antique Centre, Knighton, Wales.
Works Antiques Centre, Llandeilo, Wales.
Pembroke Antiques Centre, Pembroke, Wales.
Trecastle Antiques Centre, Trecastle, Wales.
Bryn-y-grog Antiques Emporium, Wrexham, Wales.

Antiquarian Books
Barrie Marks Ltd, London, N2.
Nicholas Goodyer, London, N5.
Fisher and Sperr, London, N6.
Keith Fawkes, London, NW3.
The Junk Shop and Spread Eagle, London, SE10.
Rogers Turner Books, London, SE10.
H¸nersdorff Rare Books, London, SW10.
Regent House Gallery, London, SW11.
Paul Foster Books, London, SW14.
Hanshan Tang Books, London, SW15.
Ash Rare Books, London, SW17.
Earlsfield Bookshop, London, SW18.
Classic Bindings Ltd, London, SW1.
Sims Reed Ltd, London, SW1.
Thomas Heneage Art Books, London, SW1.
Peter Harrington Antiquarian Bookseller, London, SW3.
Robin Greer, London, SW6.
Robert Frew Ltd, London, SW7.
The Gloucester Road Bookshop, London, SW7.
Paul Orssich, London, SW8.
Crawley and Asquith Ltd, London, W10.
D. Parikian, London, W14.
Robert G. Sawers Ltd, London, W1.
Bernard Quaritch Ltd (Booksellers), London, W1.
Maggs Bros Ltd, London, W1.
G. Heywood Hill Ltd, London, W1.
Jonathan Potter Ltd, London, W1.
Bernard J. Shapero Rare Books and Shapero Gallery, London, W1.
Altea Gallery, London, W1.
Pickering & Chatto, London, W1.
Marlborough Rare Books Ltd, London, W1.
Henry Sotheran Ltd, London, W1.
Holland & Holland, London, W1.
Adrian Harrington, London, W8.
Fine Books Oriental, London, WC1.
Atlantis Bookshop, London, WC1.

Bertram Rota Ltd, London, WC2.
Henry Pordes Books Ltd, London, WC2.
David Drummond at Pleasures of Past Times, London, WC2.
Tim Bryars Ltd, London, WC2.
Eton Antique Bookshop, Windsor, Berks.
G. David, Cambridge, Cambs.
Stothert Old Books, Chester, Cheshire.
Lion Gallery and Bookshop, Knutsford, Cheshire.
Mereside Books, Macclesfield, Cheshire.
John Maggs, Falmouth, Cornwall.
Penzance Rare Books, Penzance, Cornwall.
Bonython Bookshop, Truro, Cornwall.
Reg and Philip Remington, Truro, Cornwall.
The Book House, Brough, Cumbria.
Norman Kerr - Gatehouse Bookshop, Cartmel, Cumbria.
Lakes Crafts & Antiques Gallery, Grasmere, Cumbria.
G.K. Hadfield, Great Salkeld, Cumbria.
Keswick Bookshop, Keswick, Cumbria.
R. F. G. Hollett and Son, Sedbergh, Cumbria.
Westwood Books, Sedbergh, Cumbria.
Michael Moon - Antiquarian Booksellers, Whitehaven, Cumbria.
Dartmoor Bookshop, Ashburton, Devon.
Exeter Rare Books, Exeter, Devon.
High Street Books, Honiton, Devon.
The Pocket Bookshop, Paignton, Devon.
P.M. Pollak, South Brent, Devon.
The Schuster Gallery, Torquay, Devon.
Collards Books, Totnes, Devon.
Bridport Old Bookshop, Bridport, Dorset.
Words Etcetera, Dorchester, Dorset.
Antique Map and Bookshop, Puddletown, Dorset.
Chapter House Books, Sherborne, Dorset.
Reference Works Ltd., Swanage, Dorset.
Books Afloat, Weymouth, Dorset.
Castle Bookshop, Colchester, Essex.
Peter J. Hadley Bookseller, Harwich, Essex.
Bookworm, Holland-on-Sea, Essex.
Pastimes, Bristol, Glos.
David Bannister FRGS, Cheltenham, Glos.
Ian Hodgkins and Co. Ltd, Slad, Glos.
Wychwood Books, Stow-on-the-Wold, Glos.
Tetbury Old Books, Tetbury, Glos.
Laurence Oxley Ltd, Alresford, Hants.
Bookends, Emsworth, Hants.
Kingsclere Old Bookshop (Wyseby House Books), Kingsclere, Hants.
The Petersfield Bookshop, Petersfield, Hants.
Castle Hill Books, Kington, Herefs.
Keith Smith Books, Ledbury, Herefs.
Ross Old Book and Print Shop, Ross-on-Wye, Herefs.
Gillmark Gallery, Hertford, Herts.
Eric T. Moore, Hitchin, Herts.
Clive A. Burden Ltd, Rickmansworth, Herts.
Ventnor Rare Books, Ventnor, Isle of Wight.

The Canterbury Bookshop, Canterbury, Kent.
McConnell Fine Books, Deal, Kent.
Military History Bookshop, Folkestone, Kent.
Baggins Book Bazaar - The Largest Secondhand
  Bookshop in England, Rochester, Kent.
Alan Lord Antiques, Hythe, Kent.
Aaron Antiques, Tunbridge Wells, Kent.
Taylor-Smith Books, Westerham, Kent.
Eric J. Morten, Manchester, Lancs.
Halewood & Sons, Preston, Lancs.
Clarendon Books, Leicester, Leics.
Golden Goose Books and Globe Restorers, Harlequin
  Gallery, Lincoln, Lincs.
Staniland (Booksellers), Stamford, Lincs.
C.K. Broadhurst & Co Ltd, Southport, Merseyside.
Chris Hollingshead Horticultural Books, Teddington,
  Middx.
Anthony C. Hall, Twickenham, Middx.
The Brazen Head Bookshop & Gallery, Burnham
  Market, Norfolk.
Books Etc., Cromer, Norfolk.
Baskerville Bindings, Holt, Norfolk.
The Old Reading Room Gallery and Tea Room,
  Kelling, Norfolk.
The Angel Gallery, North Walsham, Norfolk.
The Tombland Bookshop, Norwich, Norfolk.
Turret House, Wymondham, Norfolk.
The Old Hall Bookshop, Brackley, Northants.
Occultique, Northampton, Northants.
Park Gallery & Bookshop, Wellingborough, Northants.
Barter Books, Alnwick, Northumbs.
Priest Popple Books, Hexham, Northumbs.
Anthony W. Laywood, Balderton, Notts.
E.M. Lawson and Co, East Hagbourne, Oxon.
Richard Way Bookseller, Henley-on-Thames, Oxon.
Jonkers Rare Books, Henley-on-Thames, Oxon.
Blackwell's Rare Books, Oxford, Oxon.
Tooley Adams & Co, Wallingford, Oxon.
Toby English, Wallingford, Oxon.
Demetzy Books, Witney, Oxon.
Forest Books, Uppingham, Rutland.
M. and M. Baldwin, Cleobury Mortimer, Shrops.
Candle Lane Books, Shrewsbury, Shrops.
George Bayntun, Bath, Somerset.
Shentonbooks, Cheddar, Somerset.
Gresham Books, Crewkerne, Somerset.
Rothwell and Dunworth, Dulverton, Somerset.
Janet Clarke, Freshford, Somerset.
Rare Books and Berry, Porlock, Somerset.
Steven Ferdinando, Queen Camel, Somerset.
Sterling Books, Weston-Super-Mare, Somerset.
M.A.J. Morris, Burton-upon-Trent, Staffs.
Mike Abrahams Books, Lichfield, Staffs.
Besleys Books, Beccles, Suffolk.
20th Century Fashion, Clare, Suffolk.
Abington Books, Finningham, Suffolk.

Claude Cox at College Gateway Bookshop, Ipswich,
  Suffolk.
R.E. and G.B. Way, Newmarket, Suffolk.
Honeypot Antiques Ltd, Elstead, Surrey.
Vandeleur Antiquarian Books, Epsom, Surrey.
J.W. McKenzie, Ewell, Surrey.
Secondhand Bookshop, Oxted, Surrey.
Colin Page Antiquarian Books, Brighton, Sussex East.
Camilla's Bookshop, Eastbourne, Sussex East.
Howes Bookshop, Hastings, Sussex East.
Bow Windows Book Shop, Lewes, Sussex East.
Keel Row Books, North Shields, Tyne and Wear.
Olivers Bookshop, Whitley Bay, Tyne and Wear.
Duncan M. Allsop, Warwick, Warks.
David Temperley Fine and Antiquarian Books,
  Birmingham, West Mids.
Clive Farahar and Sophie Dupré - Rare Books,
  Autographs and Manuscripts, Calne, Wilts.
The Military Parade Bookshop, Marlborough, Wilts.
Heraldry Today, Ramsbury, Wilts.
Bookworms of Evesham, Evesham, Worcs.
Malvern Bookshop, Great Malvern, Worcs.
Antique Map and Print Gallery, Hallow, Worcs.
Grove Rare Books, Bolton Abbey, Yorks. North.
Potterton Books, Thirsk, Yorks. North.
Cobweb Books, Thornton-le-Dale, Yorks. North.
Barbican Bookshop, York, Yorks. North.
The Toll House Bookshop, Holmfirth, Yorks. West.
John Blench & Son (Selective Eye Gallery), St. Helier,
  Jersey, Channel Islands.
Stacks Bookshop, Dundonald, Co. Down, Northern
  Ireland.
Foyle Books, Londonderry, Co. Londonderry, Northern
  Ireland.
The McEwan Gallery, Ballater, Scotland.
Armchair Books, Edinburgh, Scotland.
McNaughtan's Bookshop, Edinburgh, Scotland.
Voltaire & Rousseau, Glasgow, Scotland.
Mair Wilkes Books, Newport-on-Tay, Scotland.
Penny Farthing, North Berwick, Scotland.
Ming Books, Wigtown, Scotland.
A.E. Morris (Books), Bethesda, Wales.
Richard Booth's Bookshop Ltd, Hay-on-Wye, Wales.
Rose's Books, Hay-on-Wye, Wales.
Dylan's Bookstore, Swansea, Wales.

Antiquities
C.J. Martin (Coins) Ltd, London, N14.
Aaron Gallery, London, W1.
Charles Ede Ltd, London, W1.
Mansour Gallery, London, W1.
Seaby Antiquities, London, W1.
Potter's Antiques and Coins, Bristol, Glos.
Ancient & Oriental Ltd, Grimston, Leics.
Valued History, Norwich, Norfolk.
Katharine House Gallery, Marlborough, Wilts.

Architectural Items

Westland London, London, EC2.
Willesden Green Architectural Salvage, London, NW10.
Townsends, London, NW8.
Lamont Antiques Ltd, London, SE10.
CASA, London, SE15.
Humphrey-Carrasco Ltd, London, SW1.
Thornhill Galleries, London, SW18.
Drummonds Architectural Antiques Ltd, London, SW3.
LASSCO, London, SW8.
Rodney Franklin Antiques, London, SW9.
Architectural Antiques, London, W6.
Architectural Antiques, Bedford, Beds.
The Studio Gallery, Datchet, Berks.
Pattisons Architectural Antiques - Dismantle and Deal
   Direct, Aston Clinton, Bucks.
Solopark Plc, Cambridge, Cambs.
Willow Pool Garden Centre, Lymm, Cheshire.
Nostalgia Architectural Antiques, Stockport, Cheshire.
Cheshire Brick and Slate Co., Tarvin Sands, Cheshire.
The Great Northern Architectural Antique Company
   Ltd, Tattenhall, Cheshire.
Architectural Antiques, Kendal, Cumbria.
W.R.S. Architectural Antiques Ltd, Low Newton,
   Cumbria.
Cumbria Architectural Salvage, Raughton Head,
   Cumbria.
Adrian Ager Ltd, Ashburton, Devon.
Fagins Antiques, Exeter, Devon.
Yarrow, Honiton, Devon.
Dorset Reclamation, Bere Regis, Dorset.
Au Temps Perdu, Bristol, Glos.
Robert Mills Architectural Antiques Ltd, Bristol, Glos.
Cox's Architectural Reclamation Yard, Moreton-in-
   Marsh, Glos.
Minchinhampton Architectural, Stroud, Glos.
Architectural Heritage, Taddington, Glos.
The Pine Cellars, Nr Winchester, Hants.
Burgess Farm Antiques, Winchester, Hants.
Baileys Home & Garden, Ross-on-Wye, Herefs.
Chale Antiques, Chale, Isle of Wight.
The Architectural Stores, Tunbridge Wells, Kent.
Old Smithy, Feniscowles, Lancs.
Antique Fireplace Warehouse, Manchester, Lancs.
Old Bakery Antiques, Wymondham, Leics.
Lindsey Court Architectural, Market Rasen, Lincs.
Peco, Hampton, Middx.
Mongers, Hingham, Norfolk.
Stiffkey Antiques, Stiffkey, Norfolk.
Woodside Reclamation (Architectural Antiques),
   Berwick-upon-Tweed, Northumbs.
Nottingham Architectural Antiques & Reclamation,
   Nottingham, Notts.
Aston Pine Antiques, Faringdon, Oxon.
Oxford Architectural Antiques, Faringdon, Oxon.
The Country Seat, Huntercombe, Oxon.

North Shropshire Reclamation, Burlton, Shrops.
Priors Reclamation, Ditton Priors, Shrops.
Holloways of Ludlow, Ludlow, Shrops.
Walcot Reclamation, Bath, Somerset.
David Bridgwater, Bath, Somerset.
Chris's Crackers, Carhampton, Somerset.
Wells Reclamation Company, Coxley, Somerset.
J.C. Giddings, Wiveliscombe, Somerset.
Frome Reclamation, Frome, Somerset.
Castle Reclamation, Martock, Somerset.
Cawarden Brick Co Ltd, Rugeley, Staffs.
Blackbrook Antiques Village, Weeford, Staffs.
E.T. Webster, Blythburgh, Suffolk.
Tower Reclaim, Mendlesham, Suffolk.
Rococo Architectural & English Vintage., Woolpit,
   Suffolk.
Antique Buildings Ltd, Dunsfold, Surrey.
Drummonds Architectural Antiques, Hindhead, Surrey.
The Packhouse, Runfold, Surrey.
Antique Church Furnishings, Walton-on-Thames, Surrey.
Brighton Architectural Salvage, Brighton, Sussex East.
Shiners of Jesmond, Jesmond, Tyne and Wear.
Tynemouth Architectural Salvage, Tynemouth, Tyne
   and Wear.
Thomas Crapper & Co, Stratford-upon-Avon, Warks.
Regency Antique Trading Ltd., Stourbridge, West
   Mids.
Willow UK, Kington Langley, Wilts.
Harriet Fairfax Fireplaces and General Antiques,
   Langley Burrell, Wilts.
Kevin Marshall's Antiques Warehouse, Hull, Yorks. East.
Old Flames, Easingwold, Yorks. North.
Period Interiors, Hartlepool, Yorks. North.
Bingley Antiques Ltd., Cullingworth, Yorks. West.
Andy Thornton Architectural Antiques Ltd, Halifax,
   Yorks. West.
EASY - Edinburgh Architectural Salvage Yard,
   Edinburgh, Scotland.
QS Antiques and Cabinetmakers, Kilmarnock, Scotland.
Cardiff Reclamation, Cardiff, Wales.
Gallop and Rivers Architectural Antiques, Crickhowell,
   Wales.
Drew Pritchard Ltd, Glan Conwy, Wales.

Arms & Armour

Finchley Fine Art Galleries, London, N12.
The Armoury of St. James's Military Antiquarians,
   London, SW1.
Blunderbuss Antiques, London, W1.
Michael German Antiques Ltd, London, W8.
Raymond D Holdich International Medals & Militaria,
   London, WC2.
Phoenix Antique Arms, Hungerford, Berks.
Anthony D. Goodlad, Chesterfield, Derbys.
Sterling Coins and Medals, Bournemouth, Dorset.
Ickleton Antiques, Saffron Walden, Essex.

Chris Grimes Militaria, Bristol, Glos.
Q & C Militaria, Cheltenham, Glos.
J F F Fire Brigade & Military Collectables, Old
  Bedhampton, Hants.
New Forest Antiques, Ringwood, Hants.
Anything Old & Military Collectables, Lancaster, Lancs.
Michael D. Long, Leicester, Leics.
Garth Vincent Antique Arms and Armour, Allington,
  Lincs.
The Old Brigade, Kingsthorpe, Northants.
English Heritage, Bridgnorth, Shrops.
West Street Antiques, Dorking, Surrey.
Casque and Gauntlet Militaria, Farnham, Surrey.
The Lanes Armoury, Brighton, Sussex East.
Edred A.F. Gwilliam, Cricklade, Wilts.
Magpie Jewellers and Antiques and Magpie Arms &
  Armour, Evesham, Worcs.
Cairncross and Sons, Filey, Yorks. North.
Hanover Antiques & Collectables, Scarborough, Yorks.
  North.
Edinburgh Coin Shop, Edinburgh, Scotland.
Huw Williams Antiques, Porthmadog, Wales.

Art Deco & Art Nouveau
Le Style 25, London, E3.
After Noah, London, N1.
Crafts Nouveau, London, N10.
The Facade, London, NW1.
Beverley, London, NW8.
Behind the Boxes - Art Deco, London, SE26.
Ciancimino Ltd, London, SW1.
Butler and Wilson, London, SW3.
After Noah, London, SW3.
Rupert Cavendish Antiques, London, SW6.
Victor Arwas Gallery - Editions Graphiques Gallery
  Ltd, London, W1.
Caira Mandaglio, London, W11.
FCR Gallery Ltd, London, W8.
The Studio, London, W9.
Aldersey Hall Ltd, Chester, Cheshire.
Maggie Mays, Buxton, Derbys.
Lionel Geneen Ltd, Bournemouth, Dorset.
Ruskin Decorative Arts, Stow-on-the-Wold, Glos.
Peter Hoare Antiques, Southborough, Kent.
The Design Gallery 1850-1950, Westerham, Kent.
A.S. Antique Galleries, Manchester, Lancs.
Circa 1900, Liverpool, Merseyside.
Osiris Antiques, Southport, Merseyside.
Decorative Antiques, Bishop's Castle, Shrops.
Puritan Values at the Dome, Southwold, Suffolk.
Decodream, Coulsdon, Surrey.
The Gooday Gallery, Richmond, Surrey.
Cockrell Antiques, Surbiton, Surrey.
Jeroen Markies, Forest Row, Sussex E.
Peter Hancock Antiques, Chichester, Sussex West.
Willow UK, Kington Langley, Wilts.

Muir Hewitt Art Deco Originals, Batley, Yorks. West.
The Rendezvous Gallery, Aberdeen, Scotland.
Jeremy Sniders Antiques, Glasgow, Scotland.
Rhudle Mill, Kilmichael Glassary, Scotland.

Barometers
John Carlton-Smith, London, SW1.
The Clock Clinic Ltd, London, SW15.
Ronald Phillips Ltd, London, W1.
Raffety & Walwyn Ltd, London, W8.
The Clock Workshop, Caversham, Berks.
Alan Walker, Halfway, Berks.
The Old Malthouse, Hungerford, Berks.
Wyrardisbury Antiques, Wraysbury, Berks.
Carlton Clocks, Amersham, Bucks.
John Beazor and Sons Ltd, Cambridge, Cambs.
Derek and Tina Rayment Antiques, Barton, Cheshire.
Andrew Foott Antiques, Cheadle Hulme, Cheshire.
Mike Read Antique Sciences, St. Ives, Cornwall.
Musgrave Bickford Antiques, Crediton, Devon.
Leigh Extence Antique Clocks, Honiton, Devon.
Barometer World Ltd, Merton, Devon.
M.C. Taylor, Bournemouth, Dorset.
Timecraft Clocks, Sherborne, Dorset.
Chris L. Papworth MBHI, Kelvedon, Essex.
Littlebury Antiques - Littlebury Restorations Ltd,
  Saffron Walden, Essex.
It's About Time, Westcliff-on-Sea, Essex.
Montpellier Clocks, Cheltenham, Glos.
Antony Preston Antiques Ltd, Stow-on-the-Wold, Glos.
Bryan Clisby Antique Clocks, Hartley Wintney, Hants.
The Clock-Work-Shop (Winchester)., Winchester,
  Hants.
The Barometer Shop Ltd, Leominster, Herefs.
Robert Horton Antiques, Hertford, Herts.
John Chawner, Birchington, Kent.
Patric Capon, Bromley, Kent.
Michael Sim, Chislehurst, Kent.
Neill Robinson Blaxill, Sevenoaks, Kent.
Drop Dial Antiques, Bolton, Lancs.
Harrop Fold Clocks, Bolton-by-Bowland, Lancs.
Oaktree Antiques, Lubenham, Leics.
Robin Fowler (Period Clocks), Aylesby, Lincs.
David J. Hansord & Son, Lincoln, Lincs.
Keith Lawson Antique Clocks, Scratby, Norfolk.
Patrick Marney, Diss, Norfolk.
Peter Wiggins, Chipping Norton, Oxon.
Rosemary and Time, Thame, Oxon.
R.G. Cave and Sons Ltd, Ludlow, Shrops.
Adrian Donnelly Antique Clocks, Shrewsbury, Shrops.
Dodington Antiques, Whitchurch, Shrops.
Kembery Antique Clocks Ltd, Bath, Somerset.
James A. Jordan, Lichfield, Staffs.
Horological Workshops, Guildford, Surrey.
Surrey Clock Centre, Haslemere, Surrey.
B. M. and E. Newlove, Surbiton, Surrey.

Baskerville Antiques, Petworth, Sussex West.
Time in Hand (Shipston) Ltd, Shipston-on-Stour, Warks.
Summersons, Warwick, Warks.
P.A. Oxley Antique Clocks and Barometers, Cherhill, Wilts.
Time Restored Ltd, Pewsey, Wilts.
Inglenook Antiques, Ramsbury, Wilts.
Hansen Chard Antiques, Pershore, Worcs.
Time and Motion, Beverley, Yorks. East.
Lewis E. Hickson FBHI, Gilberdyke, Yorks. East.
Craiglea Clocks, Edinburgh, Scotland.

Beds

La Maison, London, E1.
The Cobbled Yard, London, N16.
Tobias and The Angel, London, SW13.
The French House (Antiques) Ltd, London, SW6.
Hirst Antiques, London, W11.
The Country Bedroom and En-Suite, Keswick, Cumbria.
Staveley Antiques, Staveley, Cumbria.
The Antiques Warehouse, Buxton, Derbys.
The Grove Antiques Centre Ltd, Honiton, Devon.
Annterior Antiques, Plymouth, Devon.
Antique Bed Shop, Halstead, Essex.
Deja Vu Antiques, Leigh-on-Sea, Essex.
Victorian Dreams, Headley, Hants.
Serendipity, Ledbury, Herefs.
Pugh's Antiques, Leominster, Herefs.
Peggottys, Teynham, Kent.
House Things Antiques, Hinckley, Leics.
A Barn Full of Brass Beds, Conisholme, Lincs.
Graham Pickett Antiques, Stamford, Lincs.
Pearman Antiques & Interiors, Newark, Notts.
Swans, Oakham, Rutland.
Malthouse Antiques, Bridgnorth, Shrops.
Wessex Antique Bedsteads, Stoke-sub-Hamdon, Somerset.
Bedsteads, Bath, Somerset.
Bed Bazaar, Framlingham, Suffolk.
The Victorian Brass Bedstead Company, Cocking, Sussex West.
Le Grenier Antiques, Wootton Wawen, Warks.
S.W. Antiques, Pershore, Worcs.
Penny Farthing Antiques, North Cave, Yorks. East.
Paraphernalia, Sheffield, Yorks. South.
RyanSmith Ltd. Antique Fireplaces, Stewartstown, Co. Tyrone, Northern Ireland.
Seventh Heaven, Chirk, Wales.

Brass - see Metalware

Bronzes

Style Gallery, London, N1.
Finchley Fine Art Galleries, London, N12.
Robert Bowman, London, SW1.
Christine Bridge, London, SW13.

Anthony James & Son Ltd, London, SW3.
Victor Arwas Gallery - Editions Graphiques Gallery Ltd, London, W1.
Gavin Douglas Fine Antiques Ltd, London, W11.
Artemis Decorative Arts, London, W8.
The John Davies Gallery, Moreton-in-Marsh, Glos.
Kenulf Fine Arts Ltd., Stow-on-the-Wold, Glos.
Michael Sim, Chislehurst, Kent.
Apollo Antique Galleries, Westerham, Kent.
Callaghan Fine Paintings, Shrewsbury, Shrops.
Edward Cross Fine Paintings, Weybridge, Surrey.
Richard Hagen Gallery, Broadway, Worcs.
Falle Fine Art Limited, St. Helier, Jersey, Channel Islands.

Carpets & Rugs

Alexander Juran and Co, London, N4.
Soviet Carpet & Art Galleries, London, NW2.
Orientalist, London, NW5.
Mayfair Carpet Gallery Ltd, London, SE1.
S. Franses Ltd, London, SW1.
Gideon Hatch Rugs, London, SW11.
Shaikh and Son (Oriental Rugs) Ltd, London, SW19.
Gallery Yacou, London, SW3.
David Aaron Ancient Arts & Rare Carpets, London, W1.
Rezai Persian Carpets, London, W11.
Richard Morant and David Black Carpets, London, W2.
Peter Norman Antiques and Restorations, Burwell, Cambs.
J.L. Arditti, Christchurch, Dorset.
Wessex Antiques, Sherborne, Dorset.
Anthony Hazledine, Fairford, Glos.
The Odiham Gallery, Odiham, Hants.
The Bakhtiyar Gallery, Stockbridge, Hants.
Rug Gallery Ltd, St. Albans, Herts.
Desmond and Amanda North, East Peckham, Kent.
Pantiles Oriental Carpets, Tunbridge Wells, Kent.
Country and Eastern Ltd., Norwich, Norfolk.
M.D. Cannell Antiques, Raveningham, Norfolk.
Knights Antiques, Henley-on-Thames, Oxon.
Christopher Legge Oriental Carpets, Oxford, Oxon.
Haliden Oriental Rug Shop, Bath, Somerset.
Michael and Amanda Lewis Oriental Carpets and Rugs, Wellington, Somerset.
The Persian Carpet Studio Ltd, Long Melford, Suffolk.
Karel Weijand Fine Oriental Carpets, Farnham, Surrey.
Clive Rogers Oriental Rugs, Staines, Surrey.
Lindfield Galleries, Lindfield, Sussex West.
Persian Carpet Gallery, Petworth, Sussex West.
A.W. Hone and Son Oriental Carpets, Birmingham, West Mids.
D & J Lines Antiques, Wychbold, Worcs.
London House Oriental Rugs and Carpets, Harrogate, Yorks. North.
Omar (Harrogate) Ltd, Knaresborough, Yorks. North.
The Oriental Rug Shop, Sheffield, Yorks. South.

London House Oriental Rugs and Carpets, Boston Spa, Yorks. West.

Parvis Sigaroudinia, Lisburn, Co. Antrim, Northern Ireland.

C.S. Moreton (Antiques), Inchture, Scotland.

Gallery Persia, Inverness, Scotland.

Cars & Carriages

Finesse Fine Art Dorchester, Dorset.

C.A.R.S. (Classic Automobilia & Regalia Specialists) Brighton, Sussex East.

Fieldings Antiques Haslingden, Lancs.

Chinese art - see Oriental

Church Furniture & Furnishings

Westland London, London, EC2.

LASSCO, London, SW8.

Tomkinson Stained Glass, Leagrave, Beds.

Cumbria Architectural Salvage, Raughton Head, Cumbria.

Robert Mills Architectural Antiques Ltd, Bristol, Glos.

Antique Church Furnishings, Walton-on-Thames, Surrey.

Cardiff Reclamation, Cardiff, Wales.

Clocks & Watches

Sugar Antiques, London, N1.

Antiques 4 Ltd, London, NW3.

North London Clock Shop Ltd, London, SE25.

John Carlton-Smith, London, SW1.

The Clock Clinic Ltd, London, SW15.

Roger Lascelles, London, SW17.

W. F. Turk Antique Clocks, London, SW20.

Norman Adams Ltd, London, SW3.

Gutlin Clocks and Antiques, London, SW6.

A. & H. Page (Est. 1840), London, SW7.

David Duggan Watches, London, W1.

Central Gallery (Portobello), London, W11.

Raffety & Walwyn Ltd, London, W8.

The London Silver Vaults, London, WC2.

The Clock Workshop, Caversham, Berks.

The Old Malthouse, Hungerford, Berks.

Times Past, Windsor, Berks.

Wyrardisbury Antiques, Wraysbury, Berks.

Carlton Clocks, Amersham, Bucks.

Peter Norman Antiques and Restorations, Burwell, Cambs.

John Beazor and Sons Ltd, Cambridge, Cambs.

Chapel Antiques, Nantwich, Cheshire.

Coppelia Antiques, Plumley, Cheshire.

Little Jem's, Penzance, Cornwall.

David Hill, Appleby-in-Westmorland, Cumbria.

Saint Nicholas Galleries Ltd. (Antiques and Jewellery), Carlisle, Cumbria.

G.K. Hadfield, Great Salkeld, Cumbria.

Westmorland Clocks, Kendal, Cumbria.

Haughey Antiques Ltd., Kirkby Stephen, Cumbria.

Heldreich Antiques & French Polishers, Brailsford, Derbys.

Derbyshire Clocks, Glossop, Derbys.

Antique, Electrical & Turret Clocks, Brixham, Devon.

Musgrave Bickford Antiques, Crediton, Devon.

Ivor Doble Ltd, Exeter, Devon.

Leigh Extence Antique Clocks, Honiton, Devon.

Carnegie Paintings & Clocks, Plymouth, Devon.

M.C. Taylor, Bournemouth, Dorset.

Derek J. Burgess - Horologist, Branksome, Dorset.

Battens Jewellers and Batten & Case Clock Repairs, Bridport, Dorset.

Timecraft Clocks, Sherborne, Dorset.

Eden House Antiques, West Auckland, Durham.

Chris L. Papworth MBHI, Kelvedon, Essex.

Harris Antiques, Thaxted, Essex.

It's About Time, Westcliff-on-Sea, Essex.

Antique Corner with A & C Antique Clocks, Bristol, Glos.

Montpellier Clocks, Cheltenham, Glos.

School House Antiques, Chipping Campden, Glos.

Arthur S. Lewis, Gloucester, Glos.

Jeffrey Formby Antiques, Moreton-in-Marsh, Glos.

Jillings Antiques - Distinctive Antique Clocks, Newent, Glos.

Keith Harding's World of Mechanical Music, Northleach, Glos.

Styles of Stow, Stow-on-the-Wold, Glos.

Clockwise, Emsworth, Hants.

Bryan Clisby Antique Clocks, Hartley Wintney, Hants.

Barry Papworth Jewellers, Lymington, Hants.

Gaylords, Titchfield, Hants.

The Clock-Work-Shop (Winchester)., Winchester, Hants.

Robin Lloyd Antiques, Ross-on-Wye, Herefs.

Howards, Baldock, Herts.

David Penney, Bishop's Stortford, Herts.

Robert Horton Antiques, Hertford, Herts.

Country Clocks, Tring, Herts.

Weston Antiques, Weston, Herts.

Ye Olde Village Clock Shop, Freshwater, Isle of Wight.

John Chawner, Birchington, Kent.

Patric Capon, Bromley, Kent.

Michael Sim, Chislehurst, Kent.

Neill Robinson Blaxill, Sevenoaks, Kent.

Gaby's Clocks and Things, Tenterden, Kent.

Derek Roberts Antiques, Tonbridge, Kent.

Aaron Antiques, Tunbridge Wells, Kent.

The Vintage Watch Co., Tunbridge Wells, Kent.

The Old Clock Shop, West Malling, Kent.

Ancient and Modern, Blackburn, Lancs.

Drop Dial Antiques, Bolton, Lancs.

Harrop Fold Clocks, Bolton-by-Bowland, Lancs.

Brittons - Watches and Antiques, Clitheroe, Lancs.

Fieldings Antiques, Haslingden, Lancs.
Charles Howell Jeweller, Oldham, Lancs.
Hackler's Jewellers, Preston, Lancs.
Edmund Davies & Son Antiques, Whalley, Lancs.
Northern Clocks, Worsley, Lancs.
Loughborough Antiques, Loughborough, Leics.
Lowe of Loughborough, Loughborough, Leics.
Oaktree Antiques, Lubenham, Leics.
Charles Antiques, Whitwick, Leics.
Trade Antiques, Alford, Lincs.
Robin Fowler (Period Clocks), Aylesby, Lincs.
Grantham Clocks, Grantham, Lincs.
David J. Hansord & Son, Lincoln, Lincs.
Marcus Wilkinson, Sleaford, Lincs.
Penman Clockcare (UK) Ltd, Spalding, Lincs.
Weldons Jewellery and Antiques, Southport,
  Merseyside.
Village Clocks, Blofield, Norfolk.
R.C. Woodhouse (Antiquarian Horologist),
  Hunstanton, Norfolk.
Tim Clayton Jewellery Ltd, King's Lynn, Norfolk.
Keith Lawson Antique Clocks, Scratby, Norfolk.
Parriss Jewellers, Sheringham, Norfolk.
Norton Antiques, Twyford, Norfolk.
M.C. Chapman, Finedon, Northants.
Michael Jones Jeweller, Northampton, Northants.
Goodacre Engraving, Sutton Bonington, Notts.
Jonathan Howard, Chipping Norton, Oxon.
Craig Barfoot, East Hagbourne, Oxon.
Rosemary and Time, Thame, Oxon.
Witney Antiques, Witney, Oxon.
W.R. Harvey & Co (Antiques) Ltd, Witney, Oxon.
C. Reynolds Antiques, Oakham, Rutland.
Mytton Antiques, Atcham, Shrops.
R.G. Cave and Sons Ltd, Ludlow, Shrops.
Adrian Donnelly Antique Clocks, Shrewsbury, Shrops.
Dodington Antiques, Whitchurch, Shrops.
Quiet Street Antiques, Bath, Somerset.
Kembery Antique Clocks Ltd, Bath, Somerset.
The Clock Shop, Castel Cary, Somerset.
The Essence of Time, Lichfield, Staffs.
James A. Jordan, Lichfield, Staffs.
Bridge Street Antiques, Newcastle-under-Lyme, Staffs.
R.A. James - The Clock Shop, Tutbury, Staffs.
Mayflower Antiques, Long Melford, Suffolk.
Edward Manson (Clocks), Woodbridge, Suffolk.
The Coach House Antiques, Gomshall, Surrey.
Horological Workshops, Guildford, Surrey.
Surrey Clock Centre, Haslemere, Surrey.
B. M. and E. Newlove, Surbiton, Surrey.
S. Warrender and Co, Sutton, Surrey.
Yellow Lantern Antiques Ltd, Brighton, Sussex East.
W. Bruford Jewellers, Eastbourne, Sussex East.
Coach House Antiques, Hastings, Sussex East.
Lewes Clock Shop, Lewes, Sussex East.
The Old Mint House, Pevensey, Sussex East.

Samuel Orr Antique Clocks, Hurstpierpoint, Sussex
  West.
Churchill Clocks, Midhurst, Sussex West.
Baskerville Antiques, Petworth, Sussex West.
Peter Smith Antiques, Sunderland, Tyne and Wear.
Curio Corner, Tynemouth, Tyne and Wear.
Time in Hand (Shipston) Ltd, Shipston-on-Stour,
  Warks.
George Pragnell Ltd, Stratford-upon-Avon, Warks.
Summersons, Warwick, Warks.
F. Meeks & Co, Birmingham, West Mids.
M. Allen Watch and Clockmaker, Four Oaks, West
  Mids.
Moxhams Antiques, Bradford-on-Avon, Wilts.
P.A. Oxley Antique Clocks and Barometers, Cherhill,
  Wilts.
Time Restored Ltd, Pewsey, Wilts.
Inglenook Antiques, Ramsbury, Wilts.
Chris Wadge Clocks, Salisbury, Wilts.
Allan Smith Antique Clocks, Swindon, Wilts.
Hansen Chard Antiques, Pershore, Worcs.
Time and Motion, Beverley, Yorks. East.
Lewis E. Hickson FBHI, Gilberdyke, Yorks. East.
Milestone Antiques, Easingwold, Yorks. North.
Middleham Antiques, Middleham, Yorks. North.
Brian Loomes, Pateley Bridge, Yorks. North.
Tomlinsons, Tockwith, Yorks. North.
Keith Stones Grandfather Clocks, Bessacarr, Yorks. South.
Fishlake Antiques, Fishlake, Yorks. South.
Clock House Antiques, Haworth, Yorks. West.
A. and Y.M. Frost Antique Clocks, Honley, Yorks. West.
Fourwinds Antiques, Moira, Co. Armagh, Northern
  Ireland.
Robert Christie Antiques, Hillsborough, Co. Down,
  Northern Ireland.
Ian Burton Antique Clocks, Auchterarder, Scotland.
The Clock Showrooms, Canonbie, Scotland.
Craiglea Clocks, Edinburgh, Scotland.
Ty-Llwyd Antiques, Cardiff, Wales.
Snowdonia Antiques, Llanrwst, Wales.
Rodney Adams Antiques, Pwllheli, Wales.

Coins & Medals
George Rankin Coin Co. Ltd, London, E2.
C.J. Martin (Coins) Ltd, London, N14.
Christopher Eimer, London, NW11.
The Armoury of St. James's Military Antiquarians,
  London, SW1.
Beaver Coin Room, London, SW5.
Michael Coins, London, W8.
Spink & Son Ltd, London, WC1.
A.H. Baldwin & Sons Ltd, London, WC2.
B.R.M. Coins, Knutsford, Cheshire.
Souvenir Antiques, Carlisle, Cumbria.
Penrith Coin and Stamp Centre, Penrith, Cumbria.
Sterling Coins and Medals, Bournemouth, Dorset.

Dorset Coin Company, Parkstone, Dorset.
The Treasure Chest, Weymouth, Dorset.
Robin Finnegan (Jeweller), Darlington, Durham.
Potter's Antiques and Coins, Bristol, Glos.
Peter Morris, Bromley, Kent.
Aaron Antiques, Tunbridge Wells, Kent.
The Coin and Jewellery Shop, Accrington, Lancs.
Chard Coins, Blackpool, Lancs.
David M. Regan, Southport, Merseyside.
Gold and Silver Exchange, Great Yarmouth, Norfolk.
Clive Dennett Coins, Norwich, Norfolk.
Collectors World, Nottingham, Notts.
Bath Stamp and Coin Shop, Bath, Somerset.
Neate Militaria & Antiques, Sudbury, Suffolk.
Intercoin, Newcastle-upon-Tyne, Tyne and Wear.
Format of Birmingham Ltd, Birmingham, West Mids.
Castle Galleries, Salisbury, Wilts.
Whitmore, Great Malvern, Worcs.
B.B.M. Coins., Kidderminster, Worcs.
C.J. and A.J. Dixon Ltd, Bridlington, Yorks. East.
Cookstown Antiques, Cookstown, Co. Tyrone,
    Northern Ireland.
The Collectors Shop, Edinburgh, Scotland.
A.D. Hamilton and Co, Glasgow, Scotland.
A. K. Campbell & Sons, Kirkcaldy, Scotland.
Abbey Antiques, Stirling, Scotland.

Dolls & Toys

Dolly Land, London, N21.
Engine 'n' Tender, London, SE25.
Stephen Long, London, SW10.
Mimi Fifi, London, W11.
London Antique Gallery, London, W8.
Berkshire Antiques Co Ltd, Windsor, Berks.
Honiton Antique Toys, Honiton, Devon.
The Vintage Toy and Train Shop, Sidmouth, Devon.
Boscombe Models and Collectors' Shop, Bournemouth,
    Dorset.
The Doll's House, Northleach, Glos.
Park House Antiques, Stow-on-the-Wold, Glos.
The Attic, Baldock, Herts.
C. and K.E. Dring, Lincoln, Lincs.
Norwich Collectors Toyshop, Norwich, Norfolk.
Northgate Antique & Collectables Centre, Bridgnorth,
    Shrops.
C.A.R.S. (Classic Automobilia & Regalia Specialists),
    Brighton, Sussex East.
Coach House Antiques, Hastings, Sussex East.
Recollect Dolls Hospital, Burgess Hill, Sussex West.
Antiquated, Petworth, Sussex West.
Dolly Mixtures, Birmingham, West Mids.
Grannie's Parlour, Hull, Yorks. East.
Classic Rocking Horses, Thirsk, Yorks. North.
Collectors Old Toy Shop and Antiques, Halifax, Yorks.
    West.
Memory Lane, Sowerby Bridge, Yorks. West.

Pastimes Vintage Toys, Glasgow, Scotland.

Etchings & Engravings

Gladwell & Co., London, EC4.
Old Maps and Prints, London, SW1.
Odyssey Fine Arts Ltd, London, SW1.
The Map House, London, SW3.
Hilary Chapman Fine Prints, London, SW6.
The Wyllie Gallery, London, SW7.
Agnew's, London, W1.
Justin F. Skrebowski Prints, London, W11.
Storey's Ltd, London, WC2.
Antique Map and Bookshop, Puddletown, Dorset.
Black Ink, Stow-on-the-Wold, Glos.
The Shanklin Gallery, Shanklin, Isle of Wight.
Marrin's Bookshop, Folkestone, Kent.
Graftons of Market Harborough, Market Harborough,
    Leics.
TRADA, Chipping Norton, Oxon.
The Barry Keene Gallery, Henley-on-Thames, Oxon.
Elizabeth Harvey-Lee, North Aston, Oxon.
George Gregory, Bath, Somerset.
The Sadler Street Gallery, Wells, Somerset.
England's Gallery, Leek, Staffs.
King's Court Galleries, Dorking, Surrey.
Heatons, Tisbury, Wilts.
Heirloom & Howard Limited, West Yatton, Wilts.
Open Eye Gallery Ltd, Edinburgh, Scotland.
Ewan Mundy Fine Art Ltd, Glasgow, Scotland.
Mainhill Gallery, Jedburgh, Scotland.
Killin Gallery, Killin, Scotland.
David Windsor Gallery, Bangor, Wales.

Fireplaces & related items

Westland London, London, EC2.
Chesney's Antique Fireplace Warehouse, London, N19.
Amazing Grates - Fireplaces Ltd, London, N2.
Acquisitions (Fireplaces) Ltd, London, NW5.
Townsends, London, NW8.
Ward Antique Fireplaces Ltd, London, SE13.
CASA, London, SE15.
Ward Antique Fireplaces Ltd, London, SE7.
The Fireplace, London, SE9.
Nicholas Gifford-Mead, London, SW1.
Chesney's Antique Fireplace Warehouse, London,
    SW11.
Bellows, London, SW18.
O.F. Wilson Ltd, London, SW3.
Old World Trading Co, London, SW6.
LASSCO, London, SW8.
The Chiswick Fireplace Co., London, W4.
Architectural Antiques, London, W6.
Architectural Antiques, Bedford, Beds.
Sundial Antiques, Amersham, Bucks.
Pattisons Architectural Antiques - Dismantle and Deal
    Direct, Aston Clinton, Bucks.

Nostalgia Architectural Antiques, Stockport, Cheshire.
Antique Fireplaces, Tarvin, Cheshire.
Architectural Antiques, Kendal, Cumbria.
W.R.S. Architectural Antiques Ltd, Low Newton, Cumbria.
Cumbria Architectural Salvage, Raughton Head, Cumbria.
Staveley Antiques, Staveley, Cumbria.
Finishing Touches, Derby, Derbys.
Adrian Ager Ltd, Ashburton, Devon.
Robson's Antiques, Barnard Castle, Durham.
Period Fireplaces, Bristol, Glos.
Cox's Architectural Reclamation Yard, Moreton-in-Marsh, Glos.
Minchinhampton Architectural, Stroud, Glos.
Ward Antique Fireplaces Ltd, Beckenham, Kent.
Bygones Reclamation, Canterbury, Kent.
Elham Antiques, Elham, Kent.
The Architectural Stores, Tunbridge Wells, Kent.
Past & Present, Clitheroe, Lancs.
Old Smithy, Feniscowles, Lancs.
Antique Fireplace Warehouse, Manchester, Lancs.
Colin Blakey Fireplaces, Nelson, Lancs.
House Things Antiques, Hinckley, Leics.
Britain's Heritage Ltd, Leicester, Leics.
Peco, Hampton, Middx.
Marble Hill Gallery, Twickenham, Middx.
Mongers, Hingham, Norfolk.
Woodside Reclamation (Architectural Antiques), Berwick-upon-Tweed, Northumbs.
Nottingham Architectural Antiques & Reclamation, Nottingham, Notts.
Hallidays (Fine Antiques) Ltd, Dorchester-on-Thames, Oxon.
Aston Pine Antiques, Faringdon, Oxon.
Oxford Architectural Antiques, Faringdon, Oxon.
Colin Greenway Antiques, Witney, Oxon.
Holloways of Ludlow, Ludlow, Shrops.
Walcot Reclamation, Bath, Somerset.
Cawarden Brick Co Ltd, Rugeley, Staffs.
Blackbrook Antiques Village, Weeford, Staffs.
Brighton Architectural Salvage, Brighton, Sussex East.
Golden Cross Antiques, Hailsham, Sussex East.
Shiners of Jesmond, Jesmond, Tyne and Wear.
Tynemouth Architectural Salvage, Tynemouth, Tyne and Wear.
Harriet Fairfax Fireplaces and General Antiques, Langley Burrell, Wilts.
The Antique Centre, Kidderminster, Worcs.
Old Flames, Easingwold, Yorks. North.
Period Interiors, Hartlepool, Yorks. North.
Robert Aagaard & Co, Knaresborough, Yorks. North.
Andy Thornton Architectural Antiques Ltd, Halifax, Yorks. West.
Chapel House Fireplaces, Holmfirth, Yorks. West.
Kelly Antiques, Omagh, Co. Tyrone, Northern Ireland.

RyanSmith Ltd. Antique Fireplaces, Stewartstown, Co. Tyrone, Northern Ireland.
Burning Embers, Aberdeen, Scotland.
EASY - Edinburgh Architectural Salvage Yard, Edinburgh, Scotland.
Neilsons Ltd, Rait, Scotland.
Fires 'n Fireplaces, Barry, Wales.
Cardiff Reclamation, Cardiff, Wales.
Gallop and Rivers Architectural Antiques, Crickhowell, Wales.

Frames
Rollo Whately Ltd, London, SW1.
Nigel Milne Ltd, London, SW1.
Paul Mitchell Ltd, London, W1.
Daggett Gallery, London, W11.
The Fairhurst Gallery, Norwich, Norfolk.
Looking Glass of Bath, Bath, Somerset.
Heritage Fine Art, South Petherton, Somerset.
W. Greenwood (Fine Art), Burneston, Yorks. North.
Coulter Galleries, York, Yorks North.

Furniture - Continental (mainly French)
La Maison, London, E1.
Robert E. Hirschhorn, London, SE5.
Appley Hoare Antiques, London, SW1.
Harris Lindsay, London, SW1.
Orientation Antiques, London, SW10.
Lucy Johnson, London, SW10.
Prides of London, London, SW3.
I. and J.L. Brown Ltd, London, SW6.
A&L Antiques, London, SW6.
Didier Aaron (London) Ltd, London, W1.
Barham Antiques, London, W11.
Marshall Gallery, London, W14.
Reindeer Antiques Ltd, London, W8.
Cox Interiors Ltd, London, W9.
David Litt Antiques, Ampthill, Beds.
John A. Pearson Antiques, Horton, Berks.
Lynda Franklin Antiques, Hungerford, Berks.
La Maison, Bourne End, Bucks.
Phoenix Antiques, Fordham, Cambs.
Ivor and Patricia Lewis Antique and Fine Art Dealers, Peterborough, Cambs.
Sandra Harris Interiors and Antiques, Chester, Cheshire.
Manchester Antique Company, Stockport, Cheshire.
Old Town Hall Antiques, Falmouth, Cornwall.
Pine and Decorative Items, Ashbourne, Derbys.
Hermitage Antiques, Honiton, Devon.
Merchant House Antiques, Honiton, Devon.
Lionel Geneen Ltd, Bournemouth, Dorset.
Piers Pisani Antiques Ltd, Sherborne, Dorset.
Deja Vu Antiques, Leigh-on-Sea, Essex.
Mill Lane Antiques, Woodford Green, Essex.
Gary Wright Antiques, Moreton-in-Marsh, Glos.

Antony Preston Antiques Ltd, Stow-on-the-Wold, Glos.
Westwood House Antiques, Tetbury, Glos.
The Decorator Source, Tetbury, Glos.
Geoffrey Stead, Todenham, Glos.
Artemesia, Alresford, Hants.
Cedar Antiques Limited, Hartley Wintney, Hants.
Gray's Antiques, Portsmouth, Hants.
Wick Antiques Ltd, Lymington, Hants.
Millers of Chelsea Antiques Ltd, Ringwood, Hants.
The Bakhtiyar Gallery, Stockbridge, Hants.
I. and J.L. Brown Ltd, Hereford, Herefs.
Pugh's Antiques, Leominster, Herefs.
Gabrielle De Giles, Bilsington, Kent.
Lennox Cato, Edenbridge, Kent.
Gabrielle de Giles, Sandgate, Kent.
Flower House Antiques, Tenterden, Kent.
Phoenix Antiques, Tunbridge Wells, Kent.
Claremont Antiques, Wroutham, Kent.
J. Green and Son, Queniborough, Leics.
Graham Pickett Antiques, Stamford, Lincs.
Anthony Fell, Holt, Norfolk.
Ron Green, Towcester, Northants.
Helios & Co (Antiques), Weedon, Northants.
Jonathan Fyson Antiques, Burford, Oxon.
Hallidays (Fine Antiques) Ltd, Dorchester-on-Thames, Oxon.
Summers Davis Antiques Ltd, Wallingford, Oxon.
Swans, Oakham, Rutland.
Malthouse Antiques, Bridgnorth, Shrops.
Martin Quick Antiques, Cosford, Shrops.
M.G.R. Exports, Bruton, Somerset.
Edward Marnier Antiques, East Knoyle, Somerset.
Pennard House Antiques, East Pennard, Somerset.
Country Brocante, Godney, Somerset.
Gilbert & Dale, Ilchester, Somerset.
Johnson's, Leek, Staffs.
Dix-Sept, Framlingham, Suffolk.
Heytesbury Antiques, Farnham, Surrey.
Heath-Bullocks, Godalming, Surrey.
Marryat, Richmond, Surrey.
Dermot and Jill Palmer Antiques, Brighton, Sussex East.
Graham Lower, Flimwell, Sussex East.
Graham Price Antiques Ltd, Heathfield, Sussex East.
Julian Antiques, Hurstpierpoint, Sussex West.
Brownrigg @ Home, Petworth, Sussex West.
Arcadia Antiques, Radford Semele, Warks.
Le Grenier Antiques, Wootton Wawen, Warks.
L.P. Furniture Ltd, Walsall, West Mids.
Avon Antiques, Bradford-on-Avon, Wilts.
St Mary's Chapel Antiques, Devizes, Wilts.
Obelisk Antiques, Warminster, Wilts.
Coopers of Ilkley, Ilkley, Yorks. West.
Jacquart Antiques, Comber, Co. Down, Northern Ireland.

Neil Livingstone, Dundee, Scotland.
Gow Antiques & Restoration Ltd., Forfar, Scotland.
Jeremy Sniders Antiques, Glasgow, Scotland.
Michael Vee Design - Birch House Antiques, Melrose, Scotland.

Furniture - Country
Robert E. Hirschhorn, London, SE5.
Rogier et Rogier, London, SW1.
The Furniture Cave, London, SW10.
Robert Young Antiques, London, SW11.
I. and J.L. Brown Ltd, London, SW6.
S. and S. Timms Antiques Ltd, Ampthill, Beds.
Simon and Penny Rumble Antiques, Chittering, Cambs.
A.P. and M.A. Haylett, Outwell, Cambs.
Adams Antiques, Nantwich, Cheshire.
Country Living Antiques, Callington, Cornwall.
Julie Strachey, Connor Downs, Cornwall.
Blackwater Pine Antiques, Truro, Cornwall.
David Hill, Appleby-in-Westmorland, Cumbria.
Simon Starkie Antiques, Cartmel, Cumbria.
Pine and Decorative Items, Ashbourne, Derbys.
Peter Bunting Antiques, Bakewell, Derbys.
Rex Antiques, Chagford, Devon.
Cobweb Antiques, Cullompton, Devon.
Miller Antiques, Cullompton, Devon.
The Grove Antiques Centre Ltd, Honiton, Devon.
Fine Pine Antiques, Totnes, Devon.
Nadin & Macintosh c/o Macintosh Antiques, Sherborne, Dorset.
Piers Pisani Antiques Ltd, Sherborne, Dorset.
The Collector, Barnard Castle, Durham.
English Rose Antiques, Coggeshall, Essex.
The Stores, Great Waltham, Essex.
Lennard Antiques, Sible Hedingham, Essex.
John P. Townsend, Cheltenham, Glos.
Patrick Waldron Antiques, Cirencester, Glos.
Jon Fox Antiques, Moreton-in-Marsh, Glos.
Keith Hockin Antiques, Stow-on-the-Wold, Glos.
Westwood House Antiques, Tetbury, Glos.
Cedar Antiques Limited, Hartley Wintney, Hants.
The Pine Cellars, Nr Winchester, Hants.
Millers of Chelsea Antiques Ltd, Ringwood, Hants.
Burgess Farm Antiques, Winchester, Hants.
I. and J.L. Brown Ltd, Hereford, Herefs.
Pugh's Antiques, Leominster, Herefs.
Robin Lloyd Antiques, Ross-on-Wye, Herefs.
M. and J. Russell, Yazor, Herefs.
Tim Wharton Antiques, Redbourn, Herts.
Gabrielle De Giles, Bilsington, Kent.
Elham Antiques, Elham, Kent.
Mill House Antiques, Goudhurst, Kent.
Gabrielle de Giles, Sandgate, Kent.
Phoenix Antiques, Tunbridge Wells, Kent.
Claremont Antiques, Wroutham, Kent.

Edmund Davies & Son Antiques, Whalley, Lancs.
Oaktree Antiques, Lubenham, Leics.
The Quorn Furniture Co., Quorn, Leics.
Graham Pickett Antiques, Stamford, Lincs.
Dorchester Antiques, Dorchester-on-Thames, Oxon.
Knights Antiques, Henley-on-Thames, Oxon.
Antiques of Woodstock, Woodstock, Oxon.
Garrard Antiques, Ludlow, Shrops.
Midwinter Antiques, Market Drayton, Shrops.
Marcus Moore Antiques, Stanton upon Hine Heath,
    Shrops.
Dodington Antiques, Whitchurch, Shrops.
Mary Cruz, Bath, Somerset.
Anthony Sampson Antiques, Dulverton, Somerset.
Pennard House Antiques, East Pennard, Somerset.
Gilbert & Dale, Ilchester, Somerset.
Johnson's, Leek, Staffs.
The Theatre Antiques Centre, Framlingham, Suffolk.
Michael Lewis, Leiston, Suffolk.
Noel Mercer Antiques, Long Melford, Suffolk.
The Antiques Warehouse, Marlesford, Suffolk.
Suffolk House Antiques, Yoxford, Suffolk.
Stoneycroft Farm, Betchworth, Surrey.
Christopher's Antiques, Farnham, Surrey.
Anthony Welling Antiques, Ripley, Surrey.
Hadlow Down Antiques, Hadlow Down, Sussex East.
Graham Price Antiques Ltd, Heathfield, Sussex East.
Pastorale Antiques, Lewes, Sussex East.
Ringles Cross Antiques, Uckfield, Sussex East.
Park View Antiques, Wadhurst, Sussex East.
Antiquities, Arundel, Sussex West.
Michael Wakelin & Helen Linfield, Billingshurst,
    Sussex West.
John Bird Antiques, Petworth, Sussex West.
William Hockley Antiques, Wisborough, Sussex West.
King's Cottage Antiques, Leamington Spa, Warks.
Arcadia Antiques, Radford Semele, Warks.
L.P. Furniture Ltd, Walsall, West Mids.
Calne Antiques, Calne, Wilts.
Maxfield House Antiques, Warminster, Wilts.
D & J Lines Antiques, Wychbold, Worcs.
Elaine Phillips Antiques Ltd, Harrogate, Yorks. North.
Cellar Antiques, Hawes, Yorks. North.
Middleham Antiques, Middleham, Yorks. North.
Country Oak Antiques, Pateley Bridge, Yorks. North.
John Gilbert Antiques, Robin Hood's Bay, Yorks.
    North.
E. Thistlethwaite, Settle, Yorks. North.
Coach House Antiques, Sleights, Yorks. North.
Fishlake Antiques, Fishlake, Yorks. South.
Cottage Antiques, Walsden, Yorks. West.
Audrey Bull, Carmarthen, Wales.
Havard and Havard, Cowbridge, Wales.
Tim Bowen Antiques, Ferryside, Wales.
WelshAntiques.com, Kidwelly, Wales.
Islwyn Watkins, Knighton, Wales.

Jim and Pat Ash, Llandeilo, Wales.
Collinge Antiques, Llandudno Junction, Wales.
Malt House Antiques, Narberth, Wales.
Rodney Adams Antiques, Pwllheli, Wales.
Audrey Bull, Tenby, Wales.

Furniture - Georgian
John Jackson at Town House, London, E1.
Peter Chapman Antiques and Restoration, London,
    N1.
Finchley Fine Art Galleries, London, N12.
Martin Henham (Antiques), London, N2.
Regent Antiques, London, N4.
Dome Antiques (Exports) Ltd, London, N7.
Antiques 4 Ltd, London, NW3.
Patricia Harvey Antiques and Decoration, London,
    NW8.
Tower Bridge Antiques, London, SE1.
Robert E. Hirschhorn, London, SE5.
Anno Domini Antiques, London, SW1.
The Furniture Cave, London, SW10.
Lucy Johnson, London, SW10.
The Dining Room Shop, London, SW13.
Chris Baron Interiors, London, SW2.
Norman Adams Ltd, London, SW3.
Michael Hughes, London, SW3.
John Clay, London, SW6.
H. Blairman and Sons Ltd., London, W1.
Judy Fox, London, W11.
Marshall Gallery, London, W14.
J. Roger (Antiques) Ltd, London, W14.
Michael Lipitch Ltd, London, W1K.
Eddy Bardawil, London, W8.
C. Fredericks and Son, London, W8.
Antiquarius of Ampthill, Ampthill, Beds.
Town Hall Antiques, Woburn, Beds.
John A. Pearson Antiques, Horton, Berks.
Lynda Franklin Antiques, Hungerford, Berks.
Turpin's Antiques, Hungerford, Berks.
Widmerpool House Antiques, Maidenhead, Berks.
Rupert Landen Antiques, Reading, Berks.
Wargrave Antiques, Wargrave, Berks.
Eton Antiques Partnership, Windsor, Berks.
The Cupboard Antiques, Amersham, Bucks.
Grosvenor House Interiors, Beaconsfield, Bucks.
Leo Antiques & Collectables Ltd, Olney, Bucks.
Peter Norman Antiques and Restorations, Burwell,
    Cambs.
Jess Applin Antiques, Cambridge, Cambs.
Tavistock Antiques Ltd, St. Neots, Cambs.
Trash 'n' Treasure, Alsager, Cheshire.
Church Street Antiques, Altrincham, Cheshire.
Andrew Foott Antiques, Cheadle Hulme, Cheshire.
Antique Exporters of Chester, Chester, Cheshire.
David Bedale, Mobberley, Cheshire.
Chapel Antiques, Nantwich, Cheshire.

Coppelia Antiques, Plumley, Cheshire.
Romiley Antiques & Jewellery, Romiley, Cheshire.
Saxon Cross Antiques Emporium, Sandbach, Cheshire.
Manchester Antique Company, Stockport, Cheshire.
Helen Horswill Antiques and Decorative Arts, West Kirby, Cheshire.
Antique Chairs and Museum, Launceston, Cornwall.
Antiques & Fine Art, Penzance, Cornwall.
Victoria Antiques, Wadebridge, Cornwall.
Anthemion - The Antique Shop, Cartmel, Cumbria.
Johnson & Johnson, Kirkby Lonsdale, Cumbria.
Haughey Antiques Ltd., Kirkby Stephen, Cumbria.
Ashbourne Antiques Ltd, Ashbourne, Derbys.
Heldreich Antiques & French Polishers, Brailsford, Derbys.
Martin and Dorothy Harper Antiques, Bakewell, Derbys.
The Antiques Warehouse, Buxton, Derbys.
Ian Morris, Chesterfield, Derbys.
Wayside Antiques, Duffield, Derbys.
Nimbus Antiques, Whaley Bridge, Derbys.
Bampton Gallery, Bampton, Devon.
J. Collins & Son, Bideford, Devon.
David J. Thorn, Budleigh Salterton, Devon.
Cullompton Antiques, Cullompton, Devon.
Miller Antiques, Cullompton, Devon.
Domani Antique & Contemporary, Exeter, Devon.
Alexander Paul Antiques, Fenny Bridges, Devon.
Roderick Butler, Honiton, Devon.
Merchant House Antiques, Honiton, Devon.
A. E. Wakeman & Sons Ltd, Tedburn St Mary, Devon.
Guy Dennler Antiques & Interiors, Tiverton, Devon.
Mere Antiques, Topsham, Devon.
Milton Antiques, Blandford Forum, Dorset.
Lionel Geneen Ltd, Bournemouth, Dorset.
Benchmark Antiques, Bridport, Dorset.
Hamptons, Christchurch, Dorset.
Michael Legg Antiques, Dorchester, Dorset.
Hardy Country, Melbury Osmond, Dorset.
Stocks and Chairs, Poole, Dorset.
Shaston Antiques, Shaftesbury, Dorset.
Renaissance, Sherborne, Dorset.
Joan, David and Richard White Antiques, Barnard Castle, Durham.
Eden House Antiques, West Auckland, Durham.
Colton Antiques, Kelvedon, Essex.
Clive Beardall Restorations Ltd, Maldon, Essex.
F.G. Bruschweiler (Antiques) Ltd, Rayleigh, Essex.
Robin Butler, Shalford, Essex.
W.A. Pinn and Sons, Sible Hedingham, Essex.
Harris Antiques, Thaxted, Essex.
White Roding Antiques, White Roding, Essex.
Peter and Penny Proudfoot, Berkeley, Glos.
The Antiques Warehouse Ltd, Bristol, Glos.
Triton Gallery, Cheltenham, Glos.
Cottage Farm Antiques, Chipping Campden, Glos.

Hares Antiques Ltd., Cirencester, Glos.
Blenheim Antiques, Fairford, Glos.
Benton Fine Art, Moreton-in-Marsh, Glos.
Gary Wright Antiques, Moreton-in-Marsh, Glos.
Robson Antiques, Northleach, Glos.
Duncan J. Baggott, Stow-on-the-Wold, Glos.
Alderson, Tetbury, Glos.
Gainsborough House Antiques, Tewkesbury, Glos.
Berkeley Antiques, Winchcombe, Glos.
Max Rollitt, Alresford, Hants.
Pineapple House Antiques, Alresford, Hants.
Brambridge Antiques, Brambridge, Hants.
F.E.A. Briggs Ltd, Brook, Hants.
Nicholas Abbott, Hartley Wintney, Hants.
Lita Kaye Antiques, Lymington, Hants.
Millers of Chelsea Antiques Ltd, Ringwood, Hants.
The Bakhtiyar Gallery, Stockbridge, Hants.
Gasson Antiques and Interiors, Tadley, Hants.
Gaylords, Titchfield, Hants.
John Nash Antiques and Interiors, Ledbury, Herefs.
Anthony Butt Antiques, Baldock, Herts.
Tapestry Antiques, Hertford, Herts.
Michael Gander, Hitchin, Herts.
J.N. Antiques, Redbourn, Herts.
Bushwood Antiques, Redbourn, Herts.
Charnwood Antiques and Arcane Antiques Centre, Sawbridgeworth, Herts.
Weston Antiques, Weston, Herts.
Michael Armson (Antiques) Ltd, Wilstone, Herts.
Stablegate Antiques, Barham, Kent.
David Barrington, Brasted, Kent.
Cooper Fine Arts Ltd, Brasted, Kent.
Conquest House Antiques, Canterbury, Kent.
Chislehurst Antiques, Chislehurst, Kent.
Lennox Cato, Edenbridge, Kent.
Alan Lord Antiques, Hythe, Kent.
Mill House Antiques, Goudhurst, Kent.
J.D. and R.M. Walters, Rolvenden, Kent.
Christopher Buck Antiques, Sandgate, Kent.
Freeman & Lloyd Antiques, Sandgate, Kent.
Steppes Hill Farm Antiques, Stockbury, Kent.
Sutton Valence Antiques, Sutton Valence, Kent.
Flower House Antiques, Tenterden, Kent.
Down Lane Hall Antiques, Tunbridge Wells, Kent.
Apollo Antique Galleries, Westerham, Kent.
Laurens Antiques, Whitstable, Kent.
Ascot Antiques, Blackpool, Lancs.
K.C. Antiques, Darwen, Lancs.
P.J. Brown Antiques, Haslingden, Lancs.
Luigino Vescovi, Morecambe, Lancs.
Alan Grice Antiques, Ormskirk, Lancs.
Sitting Pretty, Great Glen, Leics.
Withers of Leicester, Hoby, Leics.
Corry's Antiques, Leicester, Leics.
Treedale Antiques, Little Dalby, Leics.
Lowe of Loughborough, Loughborough, Leics.

Oaktree Antiques, Lubenham, Leics.
Walter Moores and Son, Market Harborough, Leics.
J. Green and Son, Queniborough, Leics.
G. Baker Antiques, Horncastle, Lincs.
Alan Read - Period Furniture, Horncastle, Lincs.
David J. Hansord & Son, Lincoln, Lincs.
Dawson of Stamford Ltd, Stamford, Lincs.
Robin Shield Antiques, Swinstead, Lincs.
Underwoodhall Antiques, Woodhall Spa, Lincs.
Stefani Antiques, Liverpool, Merseyside.
Colin Stock, Rainford, Merseyside.
Tony and Anne Sutcliffe Antiques, Southport, Merseyside.
Tobias Jellinek Antiques, Twickenham, Middx.
A.E. Bush and Partners, Attleborough, Norfolk.
Pearse Lukies, Aylsham, Norfolk.
M. and A. Cringle, Burnham Market, Norfolk.
Priests Antiques Ltd, Dersingham, Norfolk.
Anthony Fell, Holt, Norfolk.
James K. Lee, King's Lynn, Norfolk.
James Brett, Norwich, Norfolk.
Stalham Antique Gallery, Stalham, Norfolk.
Jubilee Antiques, Tottenhill, Norfolk.
Norton Antiques, Twyford, Norfolk.
T.C.S. Brooke, Wroxham, Norfolk.
Christopher Jones Antiques, Easton Neston, Northants.
Affleck Bridge Antiques, Finedon, Northants.
Blockheads and Granary Antiques, Flore, Northants.
Reindeer Antiques Ltd, Potterspury, Northants.
G.M. Athey, Alnwick, Northumbs.
James Miller Antiques, Wooler, Northumbs.
Dukeries Antiques Centre, Budby, Notts.
A.J. O'Sullivan Antiques, Darlton, Notts.
No. 1 Castlegate Antiques, Newark, Notts.
William Antiques, Ascott-under-Wychwood, Oxon.
Burford Antique Centre, Burford, Oxon.
Rupert Hitchcox Antiques, Chalgrove, Oxon.
Georgian House Antiques, Chipping Norton, Oxon.
Dorchester Antiques, Dorchester-on-Thames, Oxon.
Richard J. Kingston, Henley-on-Thames, Oxon.
The Country Seat, Huntercombe, Oxon.
Winston Antiques, Kingham, Oxon.
Nigel Adamson, North Aston, Oxon.
de Albuquerque Antiques, Wallingford, Oxon.
Cross Antiques, Watlington, Oxon.
Colin Greenway Antiques, Witney, Oxon.
W.R. Harvey & Co (Antiques) Ltd, Witney, Oxon.
Antiques of Woodstock, Woodstock, Oxon.
Swans, Oakham, Rutland.
Treedale Antiques, Oakham, Rutland.
John Garner, Uppingham, Rutland.
T.J. Roberts, Uppingham, Rutland.
Robert Bingley Antiques, Wing, Rutland.
Mytton Antiques, Atcham, Shrops.
Martin Quick Antiques, Cosford, Shrops.
Bayliss Antiques, Ludlow, Shrops.

Midwinter Antiques, Market Drayton, Shrops.
Raynalds Mansion, Much Wenlock, Shrops.
Brian James Antiques, Rodington, Shrops.
Corner Farm Antiques, Shifnal, Shrops.
Mansers Antiques, Shrewsbury, Shrops.
Marcus Moore Antiques, Stanton upon Hine Heath, Shrops.
Dodington Antiques, Whitchurch, Shrops.
Lawrence Brass, Bath, Somerset.
M.G.R. Exports, Bruton, Somerset.
Chris's Crackers, Carhampton, Somerset.
The Crooked Window, Dunster, Somerset.
Anthony Sampson Antiques, Dulverton, Somerset.
Edward Marnier Antiques, East Knoyle, Somerset.
Freshfords Fine Art, Hinton Charterhouse, Somerset.
Westville House Antiques, Littleton, Somerset.
J.C. Giddings, Wiveliscombe, Somerset.
John Hamblin, Yeovil, Somerset.
Page Antiques, Leek, Staffs.
Milestone Antiques, Lichfield, Staffs.
Bridge Street Antiques, Newcastle-under-Lyme, Staffs.
H.W. Heron and Son Ltd, Yoxall, Staffs.
F.D. Salter Antiques, Clare, Suffolk.
Debenham Antiques Ltd., Debenham, Suffolk.
English and Continental Antiques, Eye, Suffolk.
The Theatre Antiques Centre, Framlingham, Suffolk.
P & R Antiques Ltd, Halesworth, Suffolk.
Hubbard Antiques, Ipswich, Suffolk.
J. and J. Baker, Lavenham, Suffolk.
Warrens Antiques Warehouse, Leiston, Suffolk.
Sandy Cooke Antiques, Long Melford, Suffolk.
Martlesham Antiques, Martlesham, Suffolk.
Napier House Antiques, Sudbury, Suffolk.
Denzil Grant Antiques, Thurston, Suffolk.
David Gibbins Antiques, Woodbridge, Suffolk.
J.C. Heather, Woolpit, Suffolk.
Suffolk House Antiques, Yoxford, Suffolk.
John Anthony Antiques, Bletchingley, Surrey.
Arkell Antiques Ltd, Dorking, Surrey.
Malthouse Antiques, Dorking, Surrey.
Honeypot Antiques Ltd, Elstead, Surrey.
Christopher's Antiques, Farnham, Surrey.
Heath-Bullocks, Godalming, Surrey.
The Coach House Antiques, Gomshall, Surrey.
Glencorse Antiques, Kingston-upon-Thames, Surrey.
F.G. Lawrence & Sons, Redhill, Surrey.
Marryat, Richmond, Surrey.
J. Hartley Antiques Ltd, Ripley, Surrey.
Cockrell Antiques, Surbiton, Surrey.
Clifford and Roger Dade, Thames Ditton, Surrey.
Church House Antiques, Weybridge, Surrey.
Alexandria Antiques, Brighton, Sussex East.
Dycheling Antiques, Ditchling, Sussex East.
Hadlow Down Antiques, Hadlow Down, Sussex East.
The Old Mint House, Pevensey, Sussex East.
Bragge and Sons, Rye, Sussex East.

The Old House, Seaford, Sussex East.
Michael Wakelin & Helen Linfield, Billingshurst, Sussex West.
Frensham House Antiques, Chichester, Sussex West.
David Foord-Brown Antiques, Cuckfield, Sussex West.
Ashcombe Coach House, Henfield, Sussex West.
Antiquated, Petworth, Sussex West.
Georgia Antiques, Pulborough, Sussex West.
Wilsons Antiques, Worthing, Sussex West.
Graham Smith Antiques, Jesmond, Tyne and Wear.
Apollo Antiques, Warwick, Warks.
Moseley Emporium, Birmingham, West Mids.
Yoxall Antiques, Solihull, West Mids.
Thomas Coulborn and Sons, Sutton Coldfield, West Mids.
Avon Antiques, Bradford-on-Avon, Wilts.
Edward Hurst, Coombe Bissett, Wilts.
Harley Antiques, Corsham, Wilts.
William Cook (Marlborough), Marlborough, Wilts.
Dann Antiques Ltd, Melksham, Wilts.
21st Century Antics, Salisbury, Wilts.
Cassidy's Antiques, Warminster, Wilts.
A.J. Romain & Sons, Wilton, Wilts.
Barnt Green Antiques, Barnt Green, Worcs.
Stephen Cook Antiques, Broadway, Worcs.
Robert Belcher Antiques, Droitwich, Worcs.
Miscellany Antiques, Great Malvern, Worcs.
Bygones by the Cathedral, Worcester, Worcs.
Milestone Antiques, Easingwold, Yorks. North.
Elm Tree Antiques, Flaxton, Yorks. North.
Dickinson's Antiques Ltd, Gargrave, Yorks. North.
Armstrong, Harrogate, Yorks. North.
Sturman's Antiques, Hawes, Yorks. North.
Aura Antiques, Masham, Yorks. North.
Milton Holgate, Ripon, Yorks. North.
Antony, David & Ann Shackleton, Snainton, Yorks. North.
Alan Ramsey Antiques, Stokesley, Yorks. North.
Tomlinsons, Tockwith, Yorks. North.
Dovetail Antiques, Sheffield, Yorks. South.
Bingley Antiques Ltd., Cullingworth, Yorks. West.
Coopers of Ilkley, Ilkley, Yorks. West.
Geary Antiques, Leeds, Yorks. West.
Park Antiques, Menston, Yorks. West.
Dunluce Antiques, Bushmills, Co. Antrim, Northern Ireland.
MacHenry Antiques, Newtownabbey, Co. Antrim, Northern Ireland.
Robert Christie Antiques, Hillsborough, Co. Down, Northern Ireland.
Millcourt Antiques, Seapatrick, Co. Down, Northern Ireland.
Moy Antiques, Dungannon, Co. Tyrone, Northern Ireland.
Kelly Antiques, Omagh, Co. Tyrone, Northern Ireland.
Colin Wood (Antiques) Ltd, Aberdeen, Scotland.

Georgian Antiques, Edinburgh, Scotland.
Gow Antiques & Restoration Ltd., Forfar, Scotland.
Cathedral Antiques, Fortrose, Scotland.
Michael Young Antiques at Glencarse, Glencarse, Scotland.
John Walker Antiques, Grandtully, Scotland.
C.S. Moreton (Antiques), Inchture, Scotland.
Kilmacolm Antiques Ltd, Kilmacolm, Scotland.
QS Antiques and Cabinetmakers, Kilmarnock, Scotland.
Rhudle Mill, Kilmichael Glassary, Scotland.
Osborne Antiques, Kirkcudbright, Scotland.
Michael Vee Design - Birch House Antiques, Melrose, Scotland.
Crossroads Antiques, Prestwick, Scotland.
Havard and Havard, Cowbridge, Wales.
WelshFurniture.com, Kidwelly, Wales.
Snowdonia Antiques, Llanrwst, Wales.
Allam Antiques, Newbridge-on-Wye, Wales.
Rodney Adams Antiques, Pwllheli, Wales.
F.E. Anderson and Son, Welshpool, Wales.

Furniture - Pine
Chest of Drawers, London, N1.
The Cobbled Yard, London, N16.
The Furniture Cave, London, SW10.
The Pine Mine (Crewe-Read Antiques), London, SW6.
The Antique Wardrobe Company, Windsor, Berks.
Bourne End Antiques Centre, Bourne End, Bucks.
Ward Thomas Antiques Ltd, Balsham, Cambs.
Abbey Antiques, Ramsey, Cambs.
Melody's Antiques, Chester, Cheshire.
Chapel Antiques, Nantwich, Cheshire.
The Attic, Poynton, Cheshire.
The White House, Waverton, Cheshire.
Country Living Antiques, Callington, Cornwall.
Blackwater Pine Antiques, Truro, Cornwall.
Ben Eggleston Antiques Ltd, Long Marton, Cumbria.
Michael Allcroft Antiques, Hayfield, Derbys.
Pine and Decorative Items, Ashbourne, Derbys.
Robert Byles Antiques and Optimum Brasses, Bampton, Devon.
The Pennsylvania Pine Co, Buckfastleigh, Devon.
Cobweb Antiques, Cullompton, Devon.
Annterior Antiques, Plymouth, Devon.
Fine Pine Antiques, Totnes, Devon.
Chorley-Burdett Antiques, Bournemouth, Dorset.
Legg of Dorchester, Dorchester, Dorset.
English Rose Antiques, Coggeshall, Essex.
The Stores, Great Waltham, Essex.
Oldwoods, Bristol, Glos.
Berkeley Antiques, Winchcombe, Glos.
Brambridge Antiques, Brambridge, Hants.
Squirrels, Brockenhurst, Hants.
The Pine Cellars, Nr Winchester, Hants.

Burgess Farm Antiques, Winchester, Hants.
Waterfall Antiques, Ross-on-Wye, Herefs.
Back 2 Wood, Appledore, Kent.
Pattinson's Galleries, Canterbury, Kent.
Old English Pine, Sandgate, Kent.
Claremont Antiques, Wroutham, Kent.
House Things Antiques, Hinckley, Leics.
The Quorn Furniture Co., Quorn, Leics.
R. A. James Antiques, Sileby, Leics.
Earsham Hall Pine, Earsham, Norfolk.
Heathfield Antiques & Country Pine, Holt, Norfolk.
Laila Gray Antiques, Kingsthorpe, Northants.
Bailiffgate Antique Pine, Alnwick, Northumbs.
Aston Pine Antiques, Faringdon, Oxon.
Cotswold Pine & Associates, Middle Aston, Oxon.
Garrard Antiques, Ludlow, Shrops.
Chris's Crackers, Carhampton, Somerset.
Westville House Antiques, Littleton, Somerset.
Notts Pine, Radstock, Somerset.
Burton Antiques, Burton-upon-Trent, Staffs.
Antiques Within Ltd, Leek, Staffs.
Coblands Farm Antiques, Depden, Suffolk.
The Theatre Antiques Centre, Framlingham, Suffolk.
Hardy's, Hacheston, Suffolk.
Michael Lewis, Leiston, Suffolk.
House of Christian, Ash Vale, Surrey.
The Packhouse, Runfold, Surrey.
Antique Church Furnishings, Walton-on-Thames, Surrey.
Dandelion Clock Antiques Centre, Forest Row, Sussex East.
Hadlow Down Antiques, Hadlow Down, Sussex East.
Graham Price Antiques Ltd, Heathfield, Sussex East.
Pastorale Antiques, Lewes, Sussex East.
Park View Antiques, Wadhurst, Sussex East.
Antiquities, Arundel, Sussex West.
John Bird Antiques, Petworth, Sussex West.
Northumbria Pine, Whitley Bay, Tyne and Wear.
Arcadia Antiques, Radford Semele, Warks.
Pine and Things, Shipston-on-Stour, Warks.
The Red Shop, Wolverhampton, West Mids.
North Wilts Exporters, Brinkworth, Wilts.
Calne Antiques, Calne, Wilts.
Pillars Antiques, Lyneham, Wilts.
L.L. Ward and Son, Brandsby, Yorks. North.
TMPL Ltd. The Main Furniture Company, Green Hammerton, Yorks. North.
Michael Green Pine & Country Antiques, Harrogate, Yorks. North.
Manor Barn, Skipton, Yorks. North.
Eskdale Antiques, Sleights, Yorks. North.
Millgate Pine & Antiques, Thirsk, Yorks. North.
St. John Antiques, York, Yorks. North.
Fishlake Antiques, Fishlake, Yorks. South.
Penistone Pine and Antiques, Penistone, Yorks. South.
Dovetail Antiques, Sheffield, Yorks. South.

Aberford Interiors, Aberford, Yorks. West.
Memory Lane, Sowerby Bridge, Yorks. West.
Cottage Antiques, Walsden, Yorks. West.
The Pine Collection, Vale, Guernsey, Channel Islands.
QS Antiques and Cabinetmakers, Kilmarnock, Scotland.
Abbey Antiques, Stirling, Scotland.
The Furniture Cave, Aberystwyth, Wales.
Carrington House, Llanrwst, Wales.
Jim and Pat Ash, Llandeilo, Wales.
Frost Antiques & Pine, Monmouth, Wales.

Furniture - Victorian
John Jackson at Town House, London, E1.
Peter Chapman Antiques and Restoration, London, N1.
Finchley Fine Art Galleries, London, N12.
Martin Henham (Antiques), London, N2.
Regent Antiques, London, N4.
Dome Antiques (Exports) Ltd, London, N7.
Solomon 20th Century Design, London, N8.
Antiques 4 Ltd, London, NW3.
Church Street Antiques, London, NW8.
Tower Bridge Antiques, London, SE1.
Minerva Antiques, London, SE10.
CASA, London, SE15.
Ward Antique Fireplaces Ltd, London, SE7.
Hilary Batstone Antiques inc. Rose Uniacke Design, London, SW1.
Overmantels, London, SW11.
Christopher Edwards, London, SW11.
A. and J. Fowle, London, SW16.
Just a Second, London, SW18.
Chris Baron Interiors, London, SW2.
General Trading Co Ltd, London, SW3.
Michael Hughes, London, SW3.
John Clay, London, SW6.
Adrian Alan Ltd, London, W1.
Barham Antiques, London, W11.
Marshall Gallery, London, W14.
Butchoff Antiques, London, W8.
Antiquarius of Ampthill, Ampthill, Beds.
W. J. West Antiques, Potton, Beds.
Town Hall Antiques, Woburn, Beds.
Lynda Franklin Antiques, Hungerford, Berks.
Hill Farm Antiques, Leckhampstead, Berks.
Widmerpool House Antiques, Maidenhead, Berks.
Rupert Landen Antiques, Reading, Berks.
Wargrave Antiques, Wargrave, Berks.
Eton Antiques Partnership, Windsor, Berks.
The Cupboard Antiques, Amersham, Bucks.
Grosvenor House Interiors, Beaconsfield, Bucks.
Bourne End Antiques Centre, Bourne End, Bucks.
Leo Antiques & Collectables Ltd, Olney, Bucks.
Jess Applin Antiques, Cambridge, Cambs.
Ivor and Patricia Lewis Antique and Fine Art Dealers, Peterborough, Cambs.

Trash 'n' Treasure, Alsager, Cheshire.
Church Street Antiques, Altrincham, Cheshire.
Andrew Foott Antiques, Cheadle Hulme, Cheshire.
Antique Exporters of Chester, Chester, Cheshire.
Michael Allcroft Antiques, Disley, Cheshire.
David Bedale, Mobberley, Cheshire.
Chapel Antiques, Nantwich, Cheshire.
Romiley Antiques & Jewellery, Romiley, Cheshire.
Saxon Cross Antiques Emporium, Sandbach, Cheshire.
Helen Horswill Antiques and Decorative Arts, West
   Kirby, Cheshire.
Country Living Antiques, Callington, Cornwall.
Old Town Hall Antiques, Falmouth, Cornwall.
Antique Chairs and Museum, Launceston, Cornwall.
Antiques & Fine Art, Penzance, Cornwall.
The Old Steam Bakery, Redruth, Cornwall.
Victoria Antiques, Wadebridge, Cornwall.
Haughey Antiques Ltd., Kirkby Stephen, Cumbria.
Ashbourne Antiques Ltd, Ashbourne, Derbys.
Martin and Dorothy Harper Antiques, Bakewell,
   Derbys.
The Antiques Warehouse, Buxton, Derbys.
Maggie Mays, Buxton, Derbys.
Ian Morris, Chesterfield, Derbys.
Wayside Antiques, Duffield, Derbys.
A.A. Ambergate Antiques, Ripley, Derbys.
Nimbus Antiques, Whaley Bridge, Derbys.
Bampton Gallery, Bampton, Devon.
Miller Antiques, Cullompton, Devon.
Mills Antiques, Cullompton, Devon.
Domani Antique & Contemporary, Exeter, Devon.
Alexander Paul Antiques, Fenny Bridges, Devon.
Hermitage Antiques, Honiton, Devon.
Merchant House Antiques, Honiton, Devon.
Farthings of Exmoor, Lynton, Devon.
A. E. Wakeman & Sons Ltd, Tedburn St Mary, Devon.
Guy Dennler Antiques & Interiors, Tiverton, Devon.
Mere Antiques, Topsham, Devon.
The Antique Dining Room, Totnes, Devon.
Milton Antiques, Blandford Forum, Dorset.
Chorley-Burdett Antiques, Bournemouth, Dorset.
Benchmark Antiques, Bridport, Dorset.
Hamptons, Christchurch, Dorset.
Michael Legg Antiques, Dorchester, Dorset.
Hardy Country, Melbury Osmond, Dorset.
Stocks and Chairs, Poole, Dorset.
Shaston Antiques, Shaftesbury, Dorset.
Renaissance, Sherborne, Dorset.
Joan, David and Richard White Antiques, Barnard
   Castle, Durham.
Paraphernalia, Norton, Durham.
Eden House Antiques, West Auckland, Durham.
Colton Antiques, Kelvedon, Essex.
Clive Beardall Restorations Ltd, Maldon, Essex.
F.G. Bruschweiler (Antiques) Ltd, Rayleigh, Essex.
Robin Butler, Shalford, Essex.

Harris Antiques, Thaxted, Essex.
It's About Time, Westcliff-on-Sea, Essex.
White Roding Antiques, White Roding, Essex.
Peter and Penny Proudfoot, Berkeley, Glos.
The Antiques Warehouse Ltd, Bristol, Glos.
Oldwoods, Bristol, Glos.
Cottage Farm Antiques, Chipping Campden, Glos.
Patrick Waldron Antiques, Cirencester, Glos.
Blenheim Antiques, Fairford, Glos.
Benton Fine Art, Moreton-in-Marsh, Glos.
Gary Wright Antiques, Moreton-in-Marsh, Glos.
Robson Antiques, Northleach, Glos.
Duncan J. Baggott, Stow-on-the-Wold, Glos.
Alderson, Tetbury, Glos.
Berkeley Antiques, Winchcombe, Glos.
Pineapple House Antiques, Alresford, Hants.
Brambridge Antiques, Brambridge, Hants.
F.E.A. Briggs Ltd, Brook, Hants.
Eversley Barn Antiques, Eversley, Hants.
Former Glory, Gosport, Hants.
Deva Antiques, Hartley Wintney, Hants.
Plestor Barn Antiques, Liss, Hants.
Wick Antiques Ltd, Lymington, Hants.
Gray's Antiques, Portsmouth, Hants.
Lorraine Tarrant Antiques, Ringwood, Hants.
Amber Antiques, Southampton, Hants.
Gasson Antiques and Interiors, Tadley, Hants.
Gaylords, Titchfield, Hants.
John Nash Antiques and Interiors, Ledbury, Herefs.
Pugh's Antiques, Leominster, Herefs.
Anthony Butt Antiques, Baldock, Herts.
Tapestry Antiques, Hertford, Herts.
New England House Antiques and Rugs, Hitchin,
   Herts.
J.N. Antiques, Redbourn, Herts.
Bushwood Antiques, Redbourn, Herts.
Charnwood Antiques and Arcane Antiques Centre,
   Sawbridgeworth, Herts.
Michael Armson (Antiques) Ltd, Wilstone, Herts.
Stablegate Antiques, Barham, Kent.
David Barrington, Brasted, Kent.
Cooper Fine Arts Ltd, Brasted, Kent.
Conquest House Antiques, Canterbury, Kent.
Chislehurst Antiques, Chislehurst, Kent.
Lennox Cato, Edenbridge, Kent.
Mill House Antiques, Goudhurst, Kent.
Alan Lord Antiques, Hythe, Kent.
Northfleet Hill Antiques, Northfleet, Kent.
J.D. and R.M. Walters, Rolvenden, Kent.
Michael Fitch Antiques, Sandgate, Kent.
Steppes Hill Farm Antiques, Stockbury, Kent.
Sutton Valence Antiques, Sutton Valence, Kent.
Down Lane Hall Antiques, Tunbridge Wells, Kent.
Apollo Antique Galleries, Westerham, Kent.
Laurens Antiques, Whitstable, Kent.
Ascot Antiques, Blackpool, Lancs.

K.C. Antiques, Darwen, Lancs.
P.J. Brown Antiques, Haslingden, Lancs.
Luigino Vescovi, Morecambe, Lancs.
R.J. O'Brien and Son Antiques Ltd, Oldham, Lancs.
European Fine Arts and Antiques, Preston, Lancs.
Sitting Pretty, Great Glen, Leics.
House Things Antiques, Hinckley, Leics.
Withers of Leicester, Hoby, Leics.
Corry's Antiques, Leicester, Leics.
Lowe of Loughborough, Loughborough, Leics.
Oaktree Antiques, Lubenham, Leics.
J. Green and Son, Queniborough, Leics.
Charles Antiques, Whitwick, Leics.
A.L. Thompson, Antique Trader, Bourne, Lincs.
G. Baker Antiques, Horncastle, Lincs.
Alan Read - Period Furniture, Horncastle, Lincs.
C. and K.E. Dring, Lincoln, Lincs.
Graham Pickett Antiques, Stamford, Lincs.
The Antique Shop, Sutton Bridge, Lincs.
Robin Shield Antiques, Swinstead, Lincs.
Underwoodhall Antiques, Woodhall Spa, Lincs.
Stefani Antiques, Liverpool, Merseyside.
Colin Stock, Rainford, Merseyside.
Tony and Anne Sutcliffe Antiques, Southport,
    Merseyside.
Gallerie Veronique, Enfield, Middx.
A.E. Bush and Partners, Attleborough, Norfolk.
Eric Bates and Sons Ltd., Hoveton, Norfolk.
James K. Lee, King's Lynn, Norfolk.
Nicholas Fowle Antiques, Norwich, Norfolk.
Stalham Antique Gallery, Stalham, Norfolk.
Jubilee Antiques, Tottenhill, Norfolk.
Norton Antiques, Twyford, Norfolk.
Christopher Jones Antiques, Easton Neston, Northants.
Affleck Bridge Antiques, Finedon, Northants.
Blockheads and Granary Antiques, Flore, Northants.
Bryan Perkins Antiques, Gt. Cransley., Northants.
Reindeer Antiques Ltd, Potterspury, Northants.
G.M. Athey, Alnwick, Northumbs.
James Miller Antiques, Wooler, Northumbs.
Dukeries Antiques Centre, Budby, Notts.
A.J. O'Sullivan Antiques, Darlton, Notts.
No. 1 Castlegate Antiques, Newark, Notts.
William Antiques, Ascott-under-Wychwood, Oxon.
Burford Antique Centre, Burford, Oxon.
Rupert Hitchcox Antiques, Chalgrove, Oxon.
Georgian House Antiques, Chipping Norton, Oxon.
Hallidays (Fine Antiques) Ltd, Dorchester-on-Thames,
    Oxon.
Richard J. Kingston, Henley-on-Thames, Oxon.
The Country Seat, Huntercombe, Oxon.
Winston Antiques, Kingham, Oxon.
de Albuquerque Antiques, Wallingford, Oxon.
Cross Antiques, Watlington, Oxon.
Colin Greenway Antiques, Witney, Oxon.
Swans, Oakham, Rutland.

John Garner, Uppingham, Rutland.
T.J. Roberts, Uppingham, Rutland.
Robert Bingley Antiques, Wing, Rutland.
Mytton Antiques, Atcham, Shrops.
Malthouse Antiques, Bridgnorth, Shrops.
Martin Quick Antiques, Cosford, Shrops.
Bayliss Antiques, Ludlow, Shrops.
Brian James Antiques, Rodington, Shrops.
Corner Farm Antiques, Shifnal, Shrops.
A Little Furniture Shop, Shrewsbury, Shrops.
Quayside Antiques, Shrewsbury, Shrops.
Lawrence Brass, Bath, Somerset.
Waterfall Antiques, Bath, Somerset.
M.G.R. Exports, Bruton, Somerset.
Chris's Crackers, Carhampton, Somerset.
Edward Marnier Antiques, East Knoyle, Somerset.
Westville House Antiques, Littleton, Somerset.
Selwoods, Taunton, Somerset.
Courtyard Antiques, Washford, Somerset.
John Hamblin, Yeovil, Somerset.
Gilligan's Antiques, Leek, Staffs.
Milestone Antiques, Lichfield, Staffs.
Bridge Street Antiques, Newcastle-under-Lyme, Staffs.
H.W. Heron and Son Ltd, Yoxall, Staffs.
Debenham Antiques Ltd., Debenham, Suffolk.
English and Continental Antiques, Eye, Suffolk.
P & R Antiques Ltd, Halesworth, Suffolk.
A. Abbott Antiques Ltd, Ipswich, Suffolk.
Warrens Antiques Warehouse, Leiston, Suffolk.
Alexander Lyall Antiques, Long Melford, Suffolk.
Napier House Antiques, Sudbury, Suffolk.
Ashe Antiques Warehouse, Wickham Market, Suffolk.
Anthony Hurst Antiques, Woodbridge, Suffolk.
J.C. Heather, Woolpit, Suffolk.
House of Christian, Ash Vale, Surrey.
The Dorking Desk Shop, Dorking, Surrey.
Malthouse Antiques, Dorking, Surrey.
Honeypot Antiques Ltd, Elstead, Surrey.
Christopher's Antiques, Farnham, Surrey.
The Coach House Antiques, Gomshall, Surrey.
Glencorse Antiques, Kingston-upon-Thames, Surrey.
F.G. Lawrence & Sons, Redhill, Surrey.
Marryat, Richmond, Surrey.
Sage Antiques and Interiors, Ripley, Surrey.
Cockrell Antiques, Surbiton, Surrey.
Brocante, Weybridge, Surrey.
Alexandria Antiques, Brighton, Sussex East.
Dycheling Antiques, Ditchling, Sussex East.
Timothy Partridge Antiques, Eastbourne, Sussex East.
Hadlow Down Antiques, Hadlow Down, Sussex East.
Coach House Antiques, Hastings, Sussex East.
Graham Price Antiques Ltd, Heathfield, Sussex East.
The Old Mint House, Pevensey, Sussex East.
Wish Barn Antiques, Rye, Sussex East.
The Old House, Seaford, Sussex East.
Furniture and Mirror Warehouse, Chichester, Sussex

West.
Antiquated, Petworth, Sussex West.
Georgia Antiques, Pulborough, Sussex West.
Wilsons Antiques, Worthing, Sussex West.
Graham Smith Antiques, Jesmond, Tyne and Wear.
Ian Sharp Antiques Ltd., Tynemouth, Tyne and Wear.
Apollo Antiques, Warwick, Warks.
Moseley Emporium, Birmingham, West Mids.
Martin Taylor Antiques, Wolverhampton, West Mids.
Mac Humble Antiques, Bradford-on-Avon, Wilts.
Cross Hayes Antiques, Malmesbury, Wilts.
William Cook (Marlborough), Marlborough, Wilts.
Dann Antiques Ltd, Melksham, Wilts.
21st Century Antics, Salisbury, Wilts.
Cassidy's Antiques, Warminster, Wilts.
Hingstons of Wilton, Wilton, Wilts.
Barnt Green Antiques, Barnt Green, Worcs.
Robert Belcher Antiques, Droitwich, Worcs.
Carlton Antiques, Great Malvern, Worcs.
S.W. Antiques, Pershore, Worcs.
M. Lees and Sons, Worcester, Worcs.
Penny Farthing Antiques, North Cave, Yorks. East.
Milestone Antiques, Easingwold, Yorks. North.
Elm Tree Antiques, Flaxton, Yorks. North.
David Love, Harrogate, Yorks. North.
Sturman's Antiques, Hawes, Yorks. North.
Milton Holgate, Ripon, Yorks. North.
John Gilbert Antiques, Robin Hood's Bay, Yorks.
    North.
Antony, David & Ann Shackleton, Snainton, Yorks.
    North.
Alan Ramsey Antiques, Stokesley, Yorks. North.
Acorn Antiques, Sheffield, Yorks. South.
Aberford Interiors, Aberford, Yorks. West.
Bingley Antiques Ltd., Cullingworth, Yorks. West.
Geary Antiques, Leeds, Yorks. West.
Park Antiques, Menston, Yorks. West.
North Wales Antiques - Colwyn Bay, Colwyn Bay,
    Wales.
Havard and Havard, Cowbridge, Wales.
WelshFurniture.com, Kidwelly, Wales.
Collinge Antiques, Llandudno Junction, Wales.
Carrington House, Llanrwst, Wales.
Allam Antiques, Newbridge-on-Wye, Wales.

Garden Furniture, Ornaments & Statuary
Westland London, London, EC2.
Townsends, London, NW8.
Appley Hoare Antiques, London, SW1.
McVeigh & Charpentier, London, SW10.
Drummonds Architectural Antiques Ltd, London,
    SW3.
Mora & Upham Antiques, London, SW6.
LASSCO, London, SW8.
Rodney Franklin Antiques, London, SW9.
Myriad Antiques, London, W11.

Marshall Phillips, London, W4.
Below Stairs of Hungerford, Hungerford, Berks.
Garden Art, Hungerford, Berks.
Pattisons Architectural Antiques - Dismantle and Deal
    Direct, Aston Clinton, Bucks.
La Maison, Bourne End, Bucks.
Cheshire Brick and Slate Co., Tarvin Sands, Cheshire.
The Great Northern Architectural Antique Company
    Ltd, Tattenhall, Cheshire.
Julie Strachey, Connor Downs, Cornwall.
Pine and Decorative Items, Ashbourne, Derbys.
Dorset Reclamation, Bere Regis, Dorset.
I. Westrope, New England, Essex.
Au Temps Perdu, Bristol, Glos.
Jon Fox Antiques, Moreton-in-Marsh, Glos.
Robson Antiques, Northleach, Glos.
Duncan J. Baggott, Stow-on-the-Wold, Glos.
Minchinhampton Architectural, Stroud, Glos.
Architectural Heritage, Taddington, Glos.
Jardinique, Beech, Hants.
Baileys Home & Garden, Ross-on-Wye, Herefs.
Bygones Reclamation, Canterbury, Kent.
The Architectural Stores, Tunbridge Wells, Kent.
Esprit du Jardin, Wingham, Kent.
Lindsey Court Architectural, Market Rasen, Lincs.
Mongers, Hingham, Norfolk.
Renney Antiques, Corbridge, Northumbs.
Colin Greenway Antiques, Witney, Oxon.
Walcot Reclamation, Bath, Somerset.
David Bridgwater, Bath, Somerset.
Cawarden Brick Co Ltd, Rugeley, Staffs.
Drummonds Architectural Antiques, Hindhead, Surrey.
Sweerts de Landas, Ripley, Surrey.
The Packhouse, Runfold, Surrey.
Brighton Architectural Salvage, Brighton, Sussex East.
Antiquated, Petworth, Sussex West.
Holloways, Suckley, Worcs.
The White House Antiques & Architectural
    Reclamation, Easingwold, Yorks. North.
Flaxton Antique Gardens, Flaxton, Yorks. North.
Moy Antiques, Dungannon, Co. Tyrone, Northern
    Ireland.
John Walker Antiques, Grandtully, Scotland.

Glass - see also Glass Domes & Paperweights
Mike Weedon, London, N1.
Wilkinson plc, London, SE6.
Pullman Gallery, London, SW1.
Christine Bridge, London, SW13.
W.G.T. Burne (Antique Glass) Ltd, London, SW20.
Thomas Goode and Co (London) Ltd, London, W1.
David Glick Antique Glass, London, W11.
H. and W. Deutsch Antiques, London, W8.
Tomkinson Stained Glass, Leagrave, Beds.
Berkshire Antiques Co Ltd, Windsor, Berks.
Gabor Cossa Antiques, Cambridge, Cambs.

Antiques, Marazion, Cornwall.
Just Glass, Alston, Cumbria.
Martin and Dorothy Harper Antiques, Bakewell, Derbys.
Wessex Antiques, Sherborne, Dorset.
Robson's Antiques, Barnard Castle, Durham.
Jan Morrison, Bristol, Glos.
Laurie Leigh Antiques, Stow-on-the-Wold, Glos.
Grimes House Antiques & Fine Art, Moreton-in-Marsh, Glos.
A.W. Porter and Son, Hartley Wintney, Hants.
Louisa Francis & S.L. Walker, Brasted, Kent.
Jack Moore Antiques and Stained Glass, Trawden, Lancs.
Keystone Antiques, Coalville, Leics.
Liz Allport-Lomax, Norwich, Norfolk.
Weedon Antiques, Weedon, Northants.
Joan Wilkins Antiques, Witney, Oxon.
Frank Dux Antiques, Bath, Somerset.
Marryat, Richmond, Surrey.
David R. Fileman, Steyning, Sussex West.
Delomosne and Son Ltd, North Wraxall, Wilts.
Castle Gate Antiques, Helmsley, Yorks. North.
Dunluce Antiques, Bushmills, Co. Antrim, Northern Ireland.
Brian R. Bolt Antiques, Portballintrae, Co. Antrim, Northern Ireland.
Peter Francis Antiques, Saintfield, Co. Down, Northern Ireland.
Drew Pritchard Ltd, Glan Conwy, Wales.

Glass Domes
Get Stuffed, London, N1.
John Burton Natural Craft Taxidermy, Ebrington, Glos.
Heads 'n' Tails, Wiveliscombe, Somerset.

Icons - see Russian Art

Islamic Art
David Aaron Ancient Arts & Rare Carpets, London, W1.
Axia Art Consultants Ltd, London, W11.
Millner Manolatos, London, W8.
Clive Rogers Oriental Rugs, Staines, Surrey.

Japanese Art - see Oriental

Jewellery - see Silver

Lighting
Turn On Lighting, London, N1.
David Malik and Son Ltd, London, NW10.
Young & Son, London, NW8.
B.C. Metalcrafts, London, NW9.
Wilkinson plc, London, SE6.
Hilary Batstone Antiques inc. Rose Uniacke Design,

London, SW1.
Carlton Davidson Antiques, London, SW10.
Joy McDonald Antiques, London, SW13.
Chris Baron Interiors, London, SW2.
W.G.T. Burne (Antique Glass) Ltd, London, SW20.
Robert Dickson and Lesley Rendall Antiques, London, SW3.
Charles Edwards, London, SW6.
Partridge Fine Art Ltd, London, W1.
Jones Antique Lighting, London, W11.
Marshall Gallery, London, W14.
Marshall Phillips, London, W4.
H.W. Poulter and Son, London, W6.
Mrs. M.E. Crick Chandeliers, London, W8.
Cox Interiors Ltd, London, W9.
George and Peter Cohn, London, WC1.
David Litt Antiques, Ampthill, Beds.
Peter Johnson, Penzance, Cornwall.
Johnson & Johnson, Kirkby Lonsdale, Cumbria.
Staveley Antiques, Staveley, Cumbria.
Mill Lane Antiques, Woodford Green, Essex.
The Antiques Warehouse Ltd, Bristol, Glos.
Triton Gallery, Cheltenham, Glos.
Antony Preston Antiques Ltd, Stow-on-the-Wold, Glos.
Fritz Fryer Antique Lighting, Ross-on-Wye, Herefs.
Period Style Lighting, Hertford Heath, Herts.
Conquest House Antiques, Canterbury, Kent.
Chislehurst Antiques, Chislehurst, Kent.
The Architectural Stores, Tunbridge Wells, Kent.
Knicks Knacks Emporium, Sutton-on-Sea, Lincs.
Norfolk Decorative Antiques, Fakenham, Norfolk.
The Stiffkey Lamp Shop, Stiffkey, Norfolk.
Renney Antiques, Corbridge, Northumbs.
Holloways of Ludlow, Ludlow, Shrops.
Antique Textiles & Lighting, Bath, Somerset.
Exning Antiques & Interiors, Exning, Suffolk.
David R. Fileman, Steyning, Sussex West.
Curio Corner, Tynemouth, Tyne and Wear.
Delomosne and Son Ltd, North Wraxall, Wilts.
Old Flames, Easingwold, Yorks. North.
Kelly Lighting, Sheffield, Yorks. South.
Jacquart Antiques, Comber, Co. Down, Northern Ireland.
Agar Antiques, Saintfield, Co. Down, Northern Ireland.
Berland's of Edinburgh, Edinburgh, Scotland.
Michael Vee Design - Birch House Antiques, Melrose, Scotland.

Maps & Prints
Frontispiece Ltd, London, E14.
Gallery Kaleidoscope incorporating Scope Antiques, London, NW6.
The Warwick Leadlay Gallery, London, SE10.
Isaac and Ede, London, SW1.
Ash Rare Books, London, SW17.

The Map House, London, SW3.
20th Century Gallery, London, SW6.
Robert Frew Ltd, London, SW7.
Paul Orssich, London, SW8.
Adam Gallery Ltd, London, W1.
Crawley and Asquith Ltd, London, W10.
Justin F. Skrebowski Prints, London, W11.
Abbott & Holder Ltd, London, WC1.
Tim Bryars Ltd, London, WC2.
Graham Gallery, Burghfield Common, Berks.
The Studio Gallery, Datchet, Berks.
Eton Antique Bookshop, Windsor, Berks.
The Lawson Gallery, Cambridge, Cambs.
J. Alan Hulme, Chester, Cheshire.
Lion Gallery and Bookshop, Knutsford, Cheshire.
John Maggs, Falmouth, Cornwall.
Souvenir Antiques, Carlisle, Cumbria.
Sleddall Hall Antiques Centre inc. Kendal Studios
    Antiques, Kendal, Cumbria.
Keswick Bookshop, Keswick, Cumbria.
R. F. G. Hollett and Son, Sedbergh, Cumbria.
Medina Gallery, Barnstaple, Devon.
High Street Books, Honiton, Devon.
Devonshire Fine Art, Modbury, Devon.
The Schuster Gallery, Torquay, Devon.
Bridport Old Bookshop, Bridport, Dorset.
Words Etcetera, Dorchester, Dorset.
F. Whillock, Litton Cheney, Dorset.
Antique Map and Bookshop, Puddletown, Dorset.
The Swan Gallery, Sherborne, Dorset.
The Treasure Chest, Weymouth, Dorset.
Castle Bookshop, Colchester, Essex.
Cleeve Picture Framing, Bishops Cleeve, Glos.
Alexander Gallery, Bristol, Glos.
David Bannister FRGS, Cheltenham, Glos.
Kenulf Fine Arts Ltd., Stow-on-the-Wold, Glos.
Laurence Oxley Ltd, Alresford, Hants.
Kingsclere Old Bookshop (Wyseby House Books),
    Kingsclere, Hants.
The Petersfield Bookshop, Petersfield, Hants.
Bell Fine Art, Winchester, Hants.
Norman Blackburn, Bromyard, Herefs.
Ross Old Book and Print Shop, Ross-on-Wye, Herefs.
Gillmark Gallery, Hertford, Herts.
Eric T. Moore, Hitchin, Herts.
Antique Print Shop, Redbourn, Herts.
Clive A. Burden Ltd, Rickmansworth, Herts.
The Shanklin Gallery, Shanklin, Isle of Wight.
Ventnor Rare Books, Ventnor, Isle of Wight.
The Canterbury Bookshop, Canterbury, Kent.
Gallery Cranbrook, Cranbrook, Kent.
Marrin's Bookshop, Folkestone, Kent.
Langley Galleries Ltd, Rochester, Kent.
Halewood & Sons, Preston, Lancs.
Bourne Antiques & Art, Bourne, Lincs.
Golden Goose Books and Globe Restorers, Harlequin

Gallery, Lincoln, Lincs.
Baron Art, Holt, Norfolk.
The Old Reading Room Gallery and Tea Room,
    Kelling, Norfolk.
Crome Gallery and Frame Shop, Norwich, Norfolk.
Right Angle, Brackley, Northants.
Park Gallery & Bookshop, Wellingborough, Northants.
TRADA, Chipping Norton, Oxon.
The Barry Keene Gallery, Henley-on-Thames, Oxon.
Elizabeth Harvey-Lee, North Aston, Oxon.
Sanders of Oxford Ltd, Oxford, Oxon.
Toby English, Wallingford, Oxon.
Tooley Adams & Co, Wallingford, Oxon.
Marc Oxley Fine Art, Uppingham, Rutland.
The Antique Map Shop Ltd, Bath, Somerset.
Michael Lewis Gallery - Antiquarian Maps & Prints,
    Bruton, Somerset.
Julian Armytage, Crewkerne, Somerset.
House of Antiquity, Nether Stowey, Somerset.
M.A.J. Morris, Burton-upon-Trent, Staffs.
Besleys Books, Beccles, Suffolk.
King's Court Galleries, Dorking, Surrey.
Vandeleur Antiquarian Books, Epsom, Surrey.
Leoframes, Brighton, Sussex East.
Baynton-Williams, Arundel, Sussex West.
Julia Holmes Antique Maps and Prints, South Harting,
    Sussex West.
Andrew Dando, Bradford-on-Avon, Wilts.
Heatons, Tisbury, Wilts.
Antique Map and Print Gallery, Hallow, Worcs.
Grove Rare Books, Bolton Abbey, Yorks. North.
McTague of Harrogate, Harrogate, Yorks. North.
Minster Gate Bookshop, York, Yorks. North.
John Blench & Son (Selective Eye Gallery), St. Helier,
    Jersey, Channel Islands.
Phyllis Arnold Gallery Antiques, Donaghadee, Co.
    Down, Northern Ireland.
Colin Wood (Antiques) Ltd, Aberdeen, Scotland.
The McEwan Gallery, Ballater, Scotland.
Calton Gallery, Edinburgh, Scotland.
David Windsor Gallery, Bangor, Wales.

Metalware & Metalwork
Robert Young Antiques, London, SW11.
Christopher Bangs Ltd, London, SW6.
Johnny Von Pflugh Antiques, London, W11.
Christopher Sykes Antiques, Woburn, Beds.
Turpin's Antiques, Hungerford, Berks.
Peter J. Martin, Windsor, Berks.
Sundial Antiques, Amersham, Bucks.
Phoenix Antiques, Fordham, Cambs.
A.P. and M.A. Haylett, Outwell, Cambs.
Johnson & Johnson, Kirkby Lonsdale, Cumbria.
J H S Antiques Ltd, Ashbourne, Derbys.
Martin and Dorothy Harper Antiques, Bakewell,
    Derbys.

Roderick Butler, Honiton, Devon.
J.B. Antiques, Wimborne Minster, Dorset.
William H. Stokes, Cirencester, Glos.
Duncan J. Baggott, Stow-on-the-Wold, Glos.
Prichard Antiques, Winchcombe, Glos.
Cedar Antiques Limited, Hartley Wintney, Hants.
Michael Gander, Hitchin, Herts.
V.O.C. Antiques, Woodhall Spa, Lincs.
James Brett, Norwich, Norfolk.
M.D. Cannell Antiques, Raveningham, Norfolk.
Blockheads and Granary Antiques, Flore, Northants.
Jonathan Fyson Antiques, Burford, Oxon.
Knights Antiques, Henley-on-Thames, Oxon.
Mike Ottrey Antiques, Wallingford, Oxon.
Colin Greenway Antiques, Witney, Oxon.
R.G. Cave and Sons Ltd, Ludlow, Shrops.
Anthony Welling Antiques, Ripley, Surrey.
Heritage Antiques, Brighton, Sussex East.
Golden Cross Antiques, Hailsham, Sussex East.
Park View Antiques, Wadhurst, Sussex East.
Michael Wakelin & Helen Linfield, Billingshurst,
    Sussex West.
Avon Antiques, Bradford-on-Avon, Wilts.
Harriet Fairfax Fireplaces and General Antiques,
    Langley Burrell, Wilts.
H.W. Keil Ltd, Broadway, Worcs.
D & J Lines Antiques, Wychbold, Worcs.
Charles Lumb and Sons Ltd, Harrogate, Yorks. North.
Aura Antiques, Masham, Yorks. North.
E. Thistlethwaite, Settle, Yorks. North.
Geary Antiques, Leeds, Yorks. West.
Unicorn Antiques, Edinburgh, Scotland.
Tim Wright Antiques, Glasgow, Scotland.

Miniatures

D.S. Lavender (Antiques) Ltd, London, W1.
H. and W. Deutsch Antiques, London, W8.
Ellison Fine Art, Beaconsfield, Bucks.
Michael Sim, Chislehurst, Kent.
M B G Antiques, Fine Art & Jewellery, Newark, Notts.
Arden Gallery, Henley-in-Arden, Warks.
Phyllis Arnold Gallery Antiques, Donaghadee, Co.
    Down, Northern Ireland.

Mirrors

Young & Son, London, NW8.
Minerva Antiques, London, SE10.
Anno Domini Antiques, London, SW1.
Carlton Davidson Antiques, London, SW10.
McVeigh & Charpentier, London, SW10.
Overmantels, London, SW11.
Joy McDonald Antiques, London, SW13.
Norman Adams Ltd, London, SW3.
Fiona McDonald Antiques & Interiors, London, SW6.
Through the Looking Glass Ltd, London, W8.
Cox Interiors Ltd, London, W9.

David Litt Antiques, Ampthill, Beds.
Old Town Hall Antiques, Falmouth, Cornwall.
Peter Wadham Antiques, Exeter, Devon.
Jane Strickland & Daughters, Honiton, Devon.
Mill Lane Antiques, Woodford Green, Essex.
The Antiques Warehouse Ltd, Bristol, Glos.
Triton Gallery, Cheltenham, Glos.
Max Rollitt, Alresford, Hants.
David Barrington, Brasted, Kent.
Chislehurst Antiques, Chislehurst, Kent.
Phoenix Antiques, Tunbridge Wells, Kent.
The Old French Mirror Co Ltd, Henley-on-Thames,
    Oxon.
W.R. Harvey & Co (Antiques) Ltd, Witney, Oxon.
Looking Glass of Bath, Bath, Somerset.
On-Reflection Mirrors Ltd, Charlton Horethorne,
    Somerset.
Country Brocante, Godney, Somerset.
Leek Restorations, Leek, Staffs.
Malthouse Antiques, Dorking, Surrey.
Dermot and Jill Palmer Antiques, Brighton, Sussex
    East.
Julian Antiques, Hurstpierpoint, Sussex West.
T.G. Wilkinson Antiques Ltd., Petworth, Sussex West.
Annabelle's Gilt Shop, Warminster, Wilts.
W. Greenwood (Fine Art), Burneston, Yorks. North.
Michael Vee Design - Birch House Antiques, Melrose,
    Scotland.

Musical Boxes, Instruments & Literature

Boxes and Musical Instruments, London, E8.
Vincent Freeman, London, N1.
Tony Bingham, London, NW3.
Talking Machine, London, NW4.
Robert Morley & Co Ltd, London, SE13.
J. & A. Beare Ltd, London, W1.
Travis and Emery Music Bookshop, London, WC2.
J.V. Pianos and Cambridge Pianola Company,
    Landbeach, Cambs.
Mill Farm Antiques, Disley, Cheshire.
Miss Elany, Long Eaton, Derbys.
M.C. Taylor, Bournemouth, Dorset.
Arthur S. Lewis, Gloucester, Glos.
Keith Harding's World of Mechanical Music,
    Northleach, Glos.
Laurie Leigh Antiques, Stow-on-the-Wold, Glos.
Vanbrugh House Antiques, Stow-on-the-Wold, Glos.
Thwaites Fine Stringed Instruments, Watford, Herts.
Old Smithy, Feniscowles, Lancs.
The Violin Shop Ltd, Hexham, Northumbs.
Turner Violins Ltd., Beeston, Notts.
Mayflower Antiques, Long Melford, Suffolk.
John Cowderoy Antiques Ltd, Eastbourne, Sussex East.
S. and E.M. Turner Violins, Birmingham, W. Mids.
Time Restored Ltd, Pewsey, Wilts.
The Piano Shop, Leeds, Yorks. West.

Talking Point Antiques, Sowerby Bridge, Yorks. West.
San Domenico Stringed Instruments, Cardiff, Wales.
John Carpenter Musical Instruments, Swansea, Wales.

Nautical Related Items
Charles Frodsham & Co Ltd, London, SW1.
Langford's Marine Antiques, London, SW19.
Humbleyard Fine Art, London, W11.
Gillian Gould at Ocean Leisure, London, WC2.
Mostly Boxes, Windsor, Berks.
Boathouse Antiques, St Buryan, Cornwall.
Mike Read Antique Sciences, St. Ives, Cornwall.
Books Afloat, Weymouth, Dorset.
The Nautical Antiques Centre, Weymouth, Dorset.
Bookworm, Holland-on-Sea, Essex.
The Chart House, Shenfield, Essex.
Chris Grimes Militaria, Bristol, Glos.
Cobwebs, Southampton, Hants.
Roger Bradbury Antiques, Coltishall, Norfolk.
K.W. Dunster Antiques, Staines, Surrey.
Fronhouse Antiques, Barmouth, Wales.
The Carningli Centre, Newport, Wales.

Needlework - see Tapestries

Netsuke - see Oriental

Oil Paintings
Gladwell & Co., London, EC4.
Peter Chapman Antiques and Restoration, London,
   N1.
Finchley Fine Art Galleries, London, N12.
Martin Henham (Antiques), London, N2.
Duncan R. Miller Fine Arts, London, NW3.
Gallery Kaleidoscope incorporating Scope Antiques,
   London, NW6.
Patricia Harvey Antiques and Decoration, London,
   NW8.
Ackermann & Johnson, London, SW1.
Wildenstein and Co Ltd, London, SW1.
Jonathan Clark & Co, London, SW10.
Lane Fine Art Ltd, London, SW10.
Regent House Gallery, London, SW11.
New Grafton Gallery, London, SW13.
Ted Few, London, SW17.
The Andipa Gallery, London, SW3.
20th Century Gallery, London, SW6.
Campbells of London, London, SW7.
Didier Aaron (London) Ltd, London, W1.
Crawley and Asquith Ltd, London, W10.
Cur· Antiques, London, W11.
Piano Nobile Fine Paintings, London, W11.
Marshall Gallery, London, W14.
Manya Igel Fine Arts Ltd, London, W2.
Richard Philp, London, W6.
Butchoff Antiques, London, W8.

Abbott & Holder Ltd, London, WC1.
Woburn Fine Arts, Woburn, Beds.
Omell Galleries, Ascot, Berks.
Graham Gallery, Burghfield Common, Berks.
The Studio Gallery, Datchet, Berks.
John A. Pearson Antiques, Horton, Berks.
Roger King Antiques, Hungerford, Berks.
Grosvenor House Interiors, Beaconsfield, Bucks.
H.S. Wellby Ltd, Haddenham, Bucks.
Windmill Fine Art, High Wycombe, Bucks.
Cambridge Fine Art Ltd, Cambridge, Cambs.
Storm Fine Arts Ltd, Great Shelford, Cambs.
Baron Fine Art, Chester, Cheshire.
Lion Gallery and Bookshop, Knutsford, Cheshire.
Foundry Gallery, Hayle, Cornwall.
Tony Sanders Penzance Gallery and Antiques,
   Penzance, Cornwall.
Leigh Haworth Ltd., Newbiggin-on-Lune, Cumbria.
R. F. G. Hollett and Son, Sedbergh, Cumbria.
Medina Gallery, Barnstaple, Devon.
J. Collins & Son, Bideford, Devon.
Mill Gallery, Ermington, Devon.
Skeaping Gallery, Lydford, Devon.
Farthings of Exmoor, Lynton, Devon.
Devonshire Fine Art, Modbury, Devon.
Michael Wood Fine Art, Plymouth, Devon.
Hampshire Gallery, Bournemouth, Dorset.
The Swan Gallery, Sherborne, Dorset.
T.B. and R. Jordan (Fine Paintings), Stockton-on-Tees,
   Durham.
Brandler Galleries, Brentwood, Essex.
S. Bond and Son, Colchester, Essex.
Peter and Penny Proudfoot, Berkeley, Glos.
Cleeve Picture Framing, Bishops Cleeve, Glos.
Alexander Gallery, Bristol, Glos.
Triton Gallery, Cheltenham, Glos.
Peter Ward Fine Paintings, Cheltenham, Glos.
School House Antiques, Chipping Campden, Glos.
Astley House - Contemporary, Moreton-in-Marsh,
   Glos.
Baggott Church Street Ltd, Stow-on-the-Wold, Glos.
Robert Perera Fine Art, Lymington, Hants.
The Petersfield Bookshop, Petersfield, Hants.
Bell Fine Art, Winchester, Hants.
Lacewing Fine Art Gallery, Winchester, Hants.
The Shanklin Gallery, Shanklin, Isle of Wight.
Old Bakery Antiques, Brasted, Kent.
Michael Sim, Chislehurst, Kent.
Francis Iles, Rochester, Kent.
Sundridge Gallery, Sundridge, Kent.
Pantiles Spa Antiques, Tunbridge Wells, Kent.
Apollo Antique Galleries, Westerham, Kent.
Ascot Antiques, Blackpool, Lancs.
Fulda Gallery Ltd, Manchester, Lancs.
European Fine Arts and Antiques, Preston, Lancs.
Corry's Antiques, Leicester, Leics.

P. Stanworth (Fine Arts), Market Bosworth, Leics.
Coughton Galleries Ltd, Market Harborough, Leics.
Graftons of Market Harborough, Market Harborough, Leics.
Robin Shield Antiques, Swinstead, Lincs.
Baron Art, Holt, Norfolk.
Hatfield Hines Gallery, Holt, Norfolk.
The Old Reading Room Gallery and Tea Room, Kelling, Norfolk.
The Bank House Gallery, Norwich, Norfolk.
The Westcliffe Gallery, Sheringham, Norfolk.
Norton Antiques, Twyford, Norfolk.
Castle Ashby Gallery, Castle Ashby, Northants.
Bryan Perkins Antiques, Gt. Cransley, Northants.
Ron Green, Towcester, Northants.
Brian Sinfield Gallery Ltd, Burford, Oxon.
Georgian House Antiques, Chipping Norton, Oxon.
The Barry Keene Gallery, Henley-on-Thames, Oxon.
Mike Ottrey Antiques, Wallingford, Oxon.
Marc Oxley Fine Art, Uppingham, Rutland.
Bebb Fine Art, Ludlow, Shrops.
Wenlock Fine Art, Much Wenlock, Shrops.
Callaghan Fine Paintings, Shrewsbury, Shrops.
Adam Gallery Ltd, Bath, Somerset.
Freshfords Fine Art, Hinton Charterhouse, Somerset.
Heritage Fine Art, South Petherton, Somerset.
Nick Cotton Fine Art, Watchet, Somerset.
The Sadler Street Gallery, Wells, Somerset.
England's Gallery, Leek, Staffs.
Thompson's Gallery, Aldeburgh, Suffolk.
J. and J. Baker, Lavenham, Suffolk.
Peasenhall Art and Antiques Gallery, Peasenhall, Suffolk.
Suffolk House Antiques, Yoxford, Suffolk.
Cider House Galleries Ltd, Bletchingley, Surrey.
Glencorse Antiques, Kingston-upon-Thames, Surrey.
Bourne Gallery Ltd, Reigate, Surrey.
Roland Goslett Gallery, Richmond, Surrey.
Sage Antiques and Interiors, Ripley, Surrey.
B. M. and E. Newlove, Surbiton, Surrey.
Edward Cross Fine Paintings, Weybridge, Surrey.
John Day of Eastbourne Fine Art, Eastbourne, Sussex East.
E. Stacy-Marks Limited, Polegate, Sussex East.
Nicholas Bowlby, Poundgate, Sussex East.
The Canon Gallery, Chichester, Sussex West.
Oliver Charles Antiques, Petworth, Sussex West.
Georgia Antiques, Pulborough, Sussex West.
Wilsons Antiques, Worthing, Sussex West.
John Nicholson Fine Art, Jesmond, Tyne & Wear.
Ian Sharp Antiques Ltd., Tynemouth, Tyne and Wear.
Arden Gallery, Henley-in-Arden, Warks.
Astley House - Fine Art, Stretton-on-Fosse, Warks.
Oldswinford Gallery, Stourbridge, West Mids.
Driffold Gallery, Sutton Coldfield, West Mids.
Richard Hagen Gallery, Broadway, Worcs.

Haynes Fine Art of Broadway, Broadway, Worcs.
The Highway Gallery, Upton-upon-Severn, Worcs.
James H. Starkey Galleries, Beverley, Yorks. East.
W. Greenwood (Fine Art), Burneston, Yorks. North.
Sutcliffe Galleries, Harrogate, Yorks. North.
E. Stacy-Marks Limited, Helmsley, Yorks. North.
Kirkgate Fine Art & Conservation, Thirsk, Yorks. North.
Coulter Galleries, York, Yorks. North.
Robin Taylor Fine Arts, Wakefield, Yorks. West.
Atelier Ltd, Grouville, Jersey, Channel Islands.
Falle Fine Art Limited, St. Helier, Jersey, Channel Islands.
Grange Gallery - Fine Arts Ltd, St. Saviour, Jersey, Channel Islands.
Dunluce Antiques, Bushmills, Co. Antrim, Northern Ireland.
The Bell Gallery, Randalston, Co. Antrim, Northern Ireland.
Atholl Antiques, Aberdeen, Scotland.
Colin Wood (Antiques) Ltd, Aberdeen, Scotland.
The McEwan Gallery, Ballater, Scotland.
Bourne Fine Art Ltd, Edinburgh, Scotland.
Anthony Woodd Gallery Ltd, Edinburgh, Scotland.
The Roger Billcliffe Fine Art, Glasgow, Scotland.
Michael Young Antiques at Glencarse, Glencarse, Scotland.
Mainhill Gallery, Jedburgh, Scotland.
Killin Gallery, Killin, Scotland.
Kilmacolm Antiques Ltd, Kilmacolm, Scotland.
Inchmartine Fine Art, Inchture, Scotland.
Kirk Ports Gallery, North Berwick, Scotland.
St. Andrews Fine Art, St. Andrews, Scotland.
Abbey Antiques, Stirling, Scotland.
David Windsor Gallery, Bangor, Wales.
Michael Webb Fine Art, Bodorgan, Wales.
Welsh Art, Tywyn, Wales.
Rowles Fine Art, Welshpool, Wales.

Oriental Items
Japanese Gallery, London, N1.
Malcolm Rushton - Early Oriental Art, London, NW3.
Leask Ward, London, NW8.
B.C. Metalcrafts, London, NW9.
Brandt Oriental Art, London, SW1.
Orientation Antiques, London, SW10.
Sebastiano Barbagallo, London, SW6.
John Eskenazi Ltd, London, W1.
Sebastiano Barbagallo, London, W11.
Gregg Baker Asian Art, London, W8.
Robert Hall, London, W9.
Glade Antiques, High Wycombe, Bucks.
Peter Johnson, Penzance, Cornwall.
Rex Antiques, Chagford, Devon.
Yarrow, Honiton, Devon.
Lionel Geneen Ltd, Bournemouth, Dorset.

Artique, Tetbury, Glos.
Charnwood Antiques and Arcane Antiques Centre,
  Sawbridgeworth, Herts.
Rug Gallery Ltd, St. Albans, Herts.
Michael Sim, Chislehurst, Kent.
Flower House Antiques, Tenterden, Kent.
Aaron Antiques, Tunbridge Wells, Kent.
Roger Bradbury Antiques, Coltishall, Norfolk.
Country and Eastern Ltd., Norwich, Norfolk.
M.D. Cannell Antiques, Raveningham, Norfolk.
Haliden Oriental Rug Shop, Bath, Somerset.
The Crooked Window, Dunster, Somerset.
Clive Rogers Oriental Rugs, Staines, Surrey.
Patrick Moorhead Antiques, Brighton, Sussex East.
Gensing Antiques, St. Leonards-on-Sea, Sussex East.
Paul Baxter, Birmingham, West Mids.
Indigo Antiques Ltd., Manningford Bruce, Wilts.
Heirloom & Howard Limited, West Yatton, Wilts.
Paul M. Peters Fine Art Ltd., Harrogate, Yorks. North.
Tansu Oriental Antiques, Batley, Yorks. West.
Peter Wain, Menai Bridge, Wales.
Two Dragons Oriental Antiques, Llanerchymedd,
  Wales.

Paperweights
Garrick D. Coleman, London, W11.
The Stone Gallery, Burford, Oxon.
David R. Fileman, Steyning, Sussex West.

Photographs & Equipment
Finchley Fine Art Galleries, London, N12.
Argyll Etkin Gallery, London, SW1.
Trowbridge Gallery, London, SW6.
Simon Finch Rare Books, London, W1.
Bernard J. Shapero Rare Books and Shapero Gallery,
  London, W1.
Bernard Quaritch Ltd (Booksellers), London, W1.
Medina Gallery, Barnstaple, Devon.
Tewkesbury Antiques & Collectables Centre,
  Tewkesbury, Glos.
Peter Pan's Bazaar, Gosport, Hants.
Hampton Court Emporium, East Molesey, Surrey.
Arundel Bridge Antiques, Waldingham, Surrey.
Richard Booth's Bookshop Ltd, Hay-on-Wye, Wales.

Pottery & Porcelain
Finchley Fine Art Galleries, London, N12.
Martin Henham (Antiques), London, N2.
Albert Amor Ltd, London, SW1.
Ross Hamilton Ltd, London, SW1.
Brian Haughton Antiques, London, SW1.
Stephen Long, London, SW10.
Robert Young Antiques, London, SW11.
The Dining Room Shop, London, SW13.
Rogers de Rin, London, SW3.
Davies Antiques, London, SW8.

Thomas Goode and Co (London) Ltd, London, W1.
Sampson & Horne, London, W1.
Zelli Porcelain, London, W1.
Alexandra Alfandary, London, W11.
Alexandra Alfandary, London, W11.
Judy Fox, London, W11.
M. and D. Lewis, London, W11.
Mercury Antiques, London, W11.
Schredds of Portobello, London, W11.
David Brower Antiques, London, W8.
H. and W. Deutsch Antiques, London, W8.
Hope and Glory, London, W8.
Peter Kemp, London, W8.
London Antique Gallery, London, W8.
E. and H. Manners, London, W8.
Simon Spero, London, W8.
Stockspring Antiques, London, W8.
Anchor Antiques Ltd, London, WC2.
Buffalohouse Pottery, Leighton Buzzard, Beds.
Berkshire Antiques Co Ltd, Windsor, Berks.
Gabor Cossa Antiques, Cambridge, Cambs.
Abbey Antiques, Ramsey, Cambs.
Aldersey Hall Ltd, Chester, Cheshire.
Barn Antiques, Nantwich, Cheshire.
Romiley Antiques & Jewellery, Romiley, Cheshire.
Imperial Antiques, Stockport, Cheshire.
Antiques, Marazion, Cornwall.
Saint Nicholas Galleries Ltd. (Antiques and Jewellery),
  Carlisle, Cumbria.
Dower House Antiques, Kendal, Cumbria.
Bampton Gallery, Bampton, Devon.
David J. Thorn, Budleigh Salterton, Devon.
Lombard Antiques, Honiton, Devon.
Mere Antiques, Topsham, Devon.
Box of Porcelain Ltd, Dorchester, Dorset.
Renaissance, Sherborne, Dorset.
Reference Works Ltd., Swanage, Dorset.
Yesterdays, Wareham, Dorset.
Robson's Antiques, Barnard Castle, Durham.
E. J. Markham & Son Ltd, Colchester, Essex.
Clifton Ceramics and Fine Jewellery, Bristol, Glos.
Stuart House Antiques, Chipping Campden, Glos.
Yvonne Adams Antiques, Stow-on-the-Wold, Glos.
Artemesia, Alresford, Hants.
Lita Kaye Antiques, Lymington, Hants.
Lane Antiques, Stockbridge, Hants.
Goss and Crested China Centre and Goss Museum,
  Waterlooville, Hants.
The Collector Limited, Letchworth, Herts.
Flagstaff Antiques, Cowes, Isle of Wight.
Louisa Francis & S.L. Walker, Brasted, Kent.
Serendipity, Deal, Kent.
Steppes Hill Farm Antiques, Stockbury, Kent.
Aaron Antiques, Tunbridge Wells, Kent.
Corry's Antiques, Leicester, Leics.
Underwoodhall Antiques, Woodhall Spa, Lincs.

Howkins Jewellers, Great Yarmouth, Norfolk.
Liz Allport-Lomax, Norwich, Norfolk.
T.C.S. Brooke, Wroxham, Norfolk.
Weedon Antiques, Weedon, Northants.
Melville Kemp Ltd, Nottingham, Notts.
Winston Antiques, Kingham, Oxon.
Nigel Adamson, North Aston, Oxon.
John Howard, Woodstock, Oxon.
T.J. Roberts, Uppingham, Rutland.
Micawber Antiques, Bridgnorth, Shrops.
Collectors' Place, Shrewsbury, Shrops.
David and Sally March Antiques, Abbots Leigh,
    Somerset.
Quiet Street Antiques, Bath, Somerset.
T. J. Atkins, Taunton, Somerset.
Milestone Antiques, Lichfield, Staffs.
Eveline Winter, Rugeley, Staffs.
Burslem Antiques & Collectables, Stoke-on-Trent,
    Staffs.
The Pottery Buying Centre, Stoke-on-Trent, Staffs.
John Read Antiques, Martlesham, Suffolk.
David Gibbins Antiques, Woodbridge, Suffolk.
Decodream, Coulsdon, Surrey.
Elias Antiques of Dorking, Dorking, Surrey.
Marryat, Richmond, Surrey.
Helena's Collectables, Shere, Surrey.
Brocante, Weybridge, Surrey.
Patrick Moorhead Antiques, Brighton, Sussex East.
Southdown Antiques, Lewes, Sussex East.
Herbert Gordon Gasson, Rye, Sussex East.
Gems Antiques, Chichester, Sussex West.
Richard Gardner Antiques, Petworth, Sussex West.
Ian Sharp Antiques Ltd., Tynemouth, Tyne and Wear.
Andrew Dando, Bradford-on-Avon, Wilts.
Rene Nicholls Antiques, Malmesbury, Wilts.
Heirloom & Howard Limited, West Yatton, Wilts.
Bygones by the Cathedral, Worcester, Worcs.
The Crested China Co, Driffield, Yorks. East.
Antiques at Forge Cottage, Gargrave, Yorks. North.
Bryan Bowden, Harrogate, Yorks. North.
Muir Hewitt Art Deco Originals, Batley, Yorks. West.
David Wolfenden Antiques, Antrim, Co. Antrim,
    Northern Ireland.
Dunluce Antiques, Bushmills, Co. Antrim, Northern
    Ireland.
Peter Francis Antiques, Saintfield, Co. Down, Northern
    Ireland.
Duncan & Reid Books & Antiques, Edinburgh,
    Scotland.
Young Antiques, Edinburgh, Scotland.
Tim Wright Antiques, Glasgow, Scotland.
Nolton Antiques, Bridgend, Wales.
Islwyn Watkins, Knighton, Wales.
Passers Buy (Marie Evans), Llangollen, Wales.
Frost Antiques & Pine, Monmouth, Wales.
Magpie Antiques, Swansea, Wales.

Prints - see Maps & Prints

Rugs - see Carpets & Rugs

Russian & Soviet Art
Soviet Carpet & Art Galleries, London, NW2.
Iconastas, London, SW1.
Jeremy Ltd, London, SW1.
Mark Ransom Ltd, London, SW1.
The Andipa Gallery, London, SW3.
Antoine Cheneviere Fine Arts, London, W1.
Wartski Ltd, London, W1.
Temple Gallery, London, W11.
The Mark Gallery, London, W2.

Scientific Instruments
Finchley Fine Art Galleries, London, N12.
Trevor Philip & Sons Ltd, London, SW1.
Langford's Marine Antiques, London, SW19.
Humbleyard Fine Art, London, W11.
Johnny Von Pflugh Antiques, London, W11.
Gillian Gould at Ocean Leisure, London, WC2.
Christopher Sykes Antiques, Woburn, Beds.
Mostly Boxes, Windsor, Berks.
Mike Read Antique Sciences, St. Ives, Cornwall.
Branksome Antiques, Branksome, Dorset.
The Nautical Antiques Centre, Weymouth, Dorset.
The Chart House, Shenfield, Essex.
Chris Grimes Militaria, Bristol, Glos.
The Barometer Shop Ltd, Leominster, Herefs.
Michael Sim, Chislehurst, Kent.
Robin Fowler (Period Clocks), Aylesby, Lincs.
Patrick Marney, Diss, Norfolk.
Mayflower Antiques, Long Melford, Suffolk.
Roy Arnold Books, Needham Market, Suffolk.
Odin Antiques, Brighton, Sussex East.
Parvis Sigaroudinia, Lisburn, Co. Antrim, Northern
    Ireland.

Sculpture
Mike Weedon, London, N1.
Duncan R. Miller Fine Arts, London, NW3.
Gallery Kaleidoscope incorporating Scope Antiques,
    London, NW6.
Robert E. Hirschhorn, London, SE5.
Robert Bowman, London, SW1.
Nicholas Gifford-Mead, London, SW1.
Hazlitt, Gooden and Fox Ltd, London, SW1.
MacConnal-Mason Gallery, London, SW1.
The Mall Galleries, London, SW1.
Duncan R. Miller Fine Arts, London, SW1.
Whitford Fine Art, London, SW1.
Jonathan Clark & Co, London, SW10.
New Grafton Gallery, London, SW13.
Ted Few, London, SW17.

Joanna Booth, London, SW3.
Agnew's, London, W1.
Adrian Alan Ltd, London, W1.
Victor Arwas Gallery - Editions Graphiques Gallery
    Ltd, London, W1.
Browse and Darby Ltd, London, W1.
Eskenazi Ltd, London, W1.
The Fine Art Society plc, London, W1.
Daniel Katz Ltd, London, W1.
Messum's, London, W1.
The Sladmore Gallery of Sculpture, London, W1.
Stoppenbach & Delestre Ltd, London, W1.
Cur· Antiques, London, W11.
Hickmet Fine Arts, London, W11.
Hirst Antiques, London, W11.
Piano Nobile Fine Paintings, London, W11.
Richard Philp, London, W6.
Once Upon A Time, Truro, Cornwall.
G.W Ford & Son Ltd., Bakewell, Derbys.
Michael Wood Fine Art, Plymouth, Devon.
James Fine Art, Cheltenham, Glos.
Arthur Seager Antiques, Stow-on-the-Wold, Glos.
Geoffrey Stead, Todenham, Glos.
Quatrefoil, Fordingbridge, Hants.
Robert Perera Fine Art, Lymington, Hants.
Lacewing Fine Art Gallery, Winchester, Hants.
Wolseley Fine Arts Ltd, Hereford, Herefs.
Francis Iles, Rochester, Kent.
Jonathan Greenwall Antiques, Sandgate, Kent.
The Forge Antiques & Collectibles, Stamford, Lincs.
Pearse Lukies, Aylsham, Norfolk.
Hatfield Hines Gallery, Holt, Norfolk.
James Brett, Norwich, Norfolk.
The Barry Keene Gallery, Henley-on-Thames, Oxon.
Mary Cruz, Bath, Somerset.
David Bridgwater, Bath, Somerset.
Thompson's Gallery, Aldeburgh, Suffolk.
Edward Bigden Fine Art Ltd., Debenham, Suffolk.
Nicholas Bowlby, Poundgate, Sussex East.
Patrick and Gillian Morley Antiques, Warwick, Warks.
Louis Stanton, Mere, Wilts.
Calton Gallery, Edinburgh, Scotland.
The Roger Billcliffe Fine Art, Glasgow, Scotland.
Mainhill Gallery, Jedburgh, Scotland.
Intaglio, Chepstow, Wales.
Simon Wingett Fine Art, Erbistock, Wales.

Shipping Goods & Period Furniture for the Trade
Keith Skeel Antiques & Eccentricities, London, N1.
Regent Antiques, London, N4.
The Waterloo Trading Co., London, N4.
Madeline Crispin Antiques, London, NW1.
Tower Bridge Antiques, London, SE1.
Tavistock Antiques Ltd, St. Neots, Cambs.
Antique Exporters of Chester, Chester, Cheshire.
Michael Allcroft Antiques, Disley, Cheshire.

Manchester Antique Company, Stockport, Cheshire.
Fagins Antiques, Exeter, Devon.
Etcetera Antiques, Seaton, Devon.
Sandy's Antiques, Bournemouth, Dorset.
White Roding Antiques, White Roding, Essex.
The Barn, Petersfield, Hants.
West Lancs. Antique Exports, Burscough, Lancs.
P.J. Brown Antiques, Haslingden, Lancs.
G. G. Antique Wholesalers Ltd, Middleton Village,
    Lancs.
Tyson's Antiques Ltd, Morecambe, Lancs.
R.J. O'Brien and Son Antiques Ltd, Oldham, Lancs.
John Robinson Antiques, Wigan, Lancs.
Trade Antiques, Alford, Lincs.
A.L. Thompson, Antique Trader, Bourne, Lincs.
C. and K.E. Dring, Lincoln, Lincs.
Swainbanks Ltd, Liverpool, Merseyside.
Molloy's Furnishers Ltd, Southport, Merseyside.
Antiques Warehouse (Uxbridge), Uxbridge, Middx.
Pearse Lukies, Aylsham, Norfolk.
Bryan Perkins Antiques, Gt. Cransley., Northants.
T. Baker, Langford, Notts.
Red Lodge Antiques, Screveton, Notts.
Mitre House Antiques, Ludlow, Shrops.
M.G.R. Exports, Bruton, Somerset.
J.C. Giddings, Wiveliscombe, Somerset.
Goodbreys, Framlingham, Suffolk.
A. Abbott Antiques Ltd, Ipswich, Suffolk.
Laurence Tauber Antiques, Surbiton, Surrey.
The Old Mint House, Pevensey, Sussex East.
Monarch Antiques, St. Leonards-on-Sea, Sussex East.
Peter Smith Antiques, Sunderland, Tyne and Wear.
Martin Taylor Antiques, Wolverhampton, West Mids.
North Wilts Exporters, Brinkworth, Wilts.
Pillars Antiques, Lyneham, Wilts.
Cross Hayes Antiques, Malmesbury, Wilts.
Alan Ramsey Antiques, Stokesley, Yorks. North.
Philip Turnor Antiques, Rotherham, Yorks. South.
Dronfield Antiques, Sheffield, Yorks. South.
Georgian Antiques, Edinburgh, Scotland.
QS Antiques and Cabinetmakers, Kilmarnock,
    Scotland.
Narducci Antiques, Largs, Scotland.
Narducci Antiques, Saltcoats, Scotland.

Silver & Jewellery
George Rankin Coin Co. Ltd, London, E2.
Jonathan Harris (Jewellery) Ltd, London, EC1.
Searle and Co Ltd, London, EC3.
John Laurie (Antiques) Ltd, London, N1.
J.H. Bourdon-Smith Ltd, London, SW1.
Harvey & Gore, London, SW1.
Mary Cooke Antiques Ltd, London, SW14.
James Hardy and Co, London, SW3.
M.P. Levene Ltd, London, SW7.
Armour-Winston Ltd, London, W1.

Central Gallery (Portobello), London, W11.
H. and W. Deutsch Antiques, London, W8.
Koopman Rare Art, London, WC2.
Styles Silver, Hungerford, Berks.
Berkshire Antiques Co Ltd, Windsor, Berks.
Trinity St. Jewellers, Cambridge, Cambs.
Cameo Antiques, Chester, Cheshire.
D.J. Massey and Son, Macclesfield, Cheshire.
Romiley Antiques & Jewellery, Romiley, Cheshire.
Imperial Antiques, Stockport, Cheshire.
Little Jem's, Penzance, Cornwall.
Saint Nicholas Galleries Ltd. (Antiques and Jewellery), Carlisle, Cumbria.
Mark Parkhouse Antiques and Jewellery, Barnstaple, Devon.
David J. Thorn, Budleigh Salterton, Devon.
Ivor Doble Ltd, Exeter, Devon.
Otter Antiques, Honiton, Devon.
Extence Antiques, Teignmouth, Devon.
G.B. Mussenden and Son Antiques, Jewellery and Silver, Bournemouth, Dorset.
Battens Jewellers and Batten & Case Clock Repairs, Bridport, Dorset.
Greystoke Antiques, Sherborne, Dorset.
Georgian Gems Antique Jewellers, Swanage, Dorset.
Heirlooms Antique Jewellers and Silversmiths, Wareham, Dorset.
Robin Finnegan (Jeweller), Darlington, Durham.
E. J. Markham & Son Ltd, Colchester, Essex.
J. Streamer Antiques, Leigh-on-Sea, Essex.
Hedingham Antiques, Sible Hedingham, Essex.
Whichcraft Jewellery, Writtle, Essex.
Peter and Penny Proudfoot, Berkeley, Glos.
Caledonian Antiques, Bristol, Glos.
Greens of Cheltenham Ltd, Cheltenham, Glos.
Walter Bull and Son (Cirencester) Ltd, Cirencester, Glos.
Howards of Moreton, Moreton-in-Marsh, Glos.
A.W. Porter and Son, Hartley Wintney, Hants.
Barry Papworth Jewellers, Lymington, Hants.
Flagstaff Antiques, Cowes, Isle of Wight.
Palace Street Jewellers, Canterbury, Kent.
Owlets, Hythe, Kent.
Gem Antiques, Maidstone, Kent.
Kaizen International Ltd, Rochester, Kent.
Gem Antiques, Sevenoaks, Kent.
Chapel Place Antiques, Tunbridge Wells, Kent.
The Coin and Jewellery Shop, Accrington, Lancs.
Cathedral Jewellers, Ashton-under-Lyne, Lancs.
Ancient and Modern, Blackburn, Lancs.
Brittons - Watches and Antiques, Clitheroe, Lancs.
Leigh Jewellery, Leigh, Lancs.
St. James Antiques, Manchester, Lancs.
Charles Howell Jeweller, Oldham, Lancs.
Keystone Antiques, Coalville, Leics.
Corry's Antiques, Leicester, Leics.

Loughborough Antiques, Loughborough, Leics.
Stanley Hunt Jewellers Ltd, Gainsborough, Lincs.
Rowletts of Lincoln, Lincoln, Lincs.
Marcus Wilkinson, Sleaford, Lincs.
Dawson of Stamford Ltd, Stamford, Lincs.
C. Rosenberg, Heswall, Merseyside.
Weldons Jewellery and Antiques, Southport, Merseyside.
Bond Street Antiques, Cromer, Norfolk.
Folkes Antiques and Jewellers, Great Yarmouth, Norfolk.
Howkins Jewellers, Great Yarmouth, Norfolk.
Tim Clayton Jewellery Ltd, King's Lynn, Norfolk.
Albrow & Sons Family Jewellers, Norwich, Norfolk.
Parriss Jewellers, Sheringham, Norfolk.
Michael Jones Jeweller, Northampton, Northants.
M B G Antiques, Fine Art & Jewellery, Newark, Notts.
D.D. and A. Ingle, Nottingham, Notts.
Melville Kemp Ltd, Nottingham, Notts.
Stanley Hunt Jewellers, Retford, Notts.
Reginald Davis Ltd, Oxford, Oxon.
MGJ Jewellers Ltd., Wallingford, Oxon.
English Heritage, Bridgnorth, Shrops.
E.P. Mallory and Son Ltd, Bath, Somerset.
Castle Antiques, Burnham-on-Sea, Somerset.
M.G. Welch Jeweller, Taunton, Somerset.
A. Abbott Antiques Ltd, Ipswich, Suffolk.
The Jewel Box, Antique Jewellery & Silver, Dorking, Surrey.
Cry for the Moon, Guildford, Surrey.
Glydon & Guess Ltd, Kingston-upon-Thames, Surrey.
Horton, Richmond, Surrey.
S. Warrender and Co, Sutton, Surrey.
Church House Antiques, Weybridge, Surrey.
Paul Goble Jewellers, Brighton, Sussex East.
W. Bruford Jewellers, Eastbourne, Sussex East.
Trade Wind, Rottingdean, Sussex East.
Peter Hancock Antiques, Chichester, Sussex West.
Rathbone Law, Chichester, Sussex West.
Nicholas Shaw Antiques, Petworth, Sussex West.
A.C. Silver, Jesmond, Tyne and Wear.
Davidsons the Jewellers Ltd, Newcastle-upon-Tyne, Tyne and Wear.
Howards Jewellers, Stratford-upon-Avon, Warks.
George Pragnell Ltd, Stratford-upon-Avon, Warks.
Russell Lane Antiques, Warwick, Warks.
R. Collyer, Birmingham, West Mids.
Cross Keys Jewellers, Devizes, Wilts.
Magpie Jewellers and Antiques and Magpie Arms & Armour, Evesham, Worcs.
B.B.M. Coins., Kidderminster, Worcs.
Bygones by the Cathedral, Worcester, Worcs.
Guest & Philips, Beverley, Yorks. East.
Guest & Phillips, Driffield, Yorks. East.
Ogden Harrogate Ltd, Harrogate, Yorks. North.
Castle Gate Antiques, Helmsley, Yorks. North.

Mary Milnthorpe and Daughters Antique Shop, Settle, Yorks. North.

Barbara Cattle, York, Yorks. North.

Jack Shaw and Co, Ilkley, Yorks. West.

Aladdin's Cave, Leeds, Yorks. West.

A. & R. Ritchie, St. Helier, Jersey, Channel Islands.

Robert's Antiques, St. Helier, Jersey, Channel Islands.

N. St. J. Paint & Sons Ltd, St Peter Port, Guernsey, Channel Islands.

Ray & Scott Ltd, St Sampson, Guernsey, Channel Islands.

Dunluce Antiques, Bushmills, Co. Antrim, Northern Ireland.

Brian R. Bolt Antiques, Portballintrae, Co. Antrim, Northern Ireland.

Cookstown Antiques, Cookstown, Co. Tyrone, Northern Ireland.

McCalls (Aberdeen), Aberdeen, Scotland.

Treasures of Ballater & Rowan Antiques, Ballater, Scotland.

Joseph Bonnar, Jewellers, Edinburgh, Scotland.

Royal Mile Curios, Edinburgh, Scotland.

Cathedral Antiques, Fortrose, Scotland.

A.D. Hamilton and Co, Glasgow, Scotland.

Kilmacolm Antiques Ltd, Kilmacolm, Scotland.

Hardie Antiques, Perth, Scotland.

Henderson, Perth, Scotland.

Abbey Antiques, Stirling, Scotland.

Hazel of Brecon & Silvertime, Brecon, Wales.

Sporting Items & Associated Memorabilia

Holland & Holland, London, W1.

Below Stairs of Hungerford, Hungerford, Berks.

David Bedale, Mobberley, Cheshire.

Dolphin Antiques, Beer, Devon.

John Burton Natural Craft Taxidermy, Ebrington, Glos.

Hamilton Billiards & Games Co., Knebworth, Herts.

Halstead's Antiques, Bromley, Kent.

Books Etc., Cromer, Norfolk.

Manfred Schotten Antiques, Burford, Oxon.

Billiard Room Antiques, Chilcompton, Somerset.

Academy Billiard Company, West Byfleet, Surrey.

Burman Antiques, Stratford-upon-Avon, Warks.

Sir William Bentley Billiards (Antique Billiard Table Specialist Company), Marten, Wilts.

Grant Books, Droitwich, Worcs.

Dunkeld Antiques, Dunkeld, Scotland.

The David Brown (St. Andrews) Gallery, St. Andrews, Scotland.

Sporting Paintings & Prints

Swan Fine Art, London, N1.

Ackermann & Johnson, London, SW1.

Frost & Reed Ltd (Est. 1808), London, SW1.

The Tryon Galleries, London, SW1.

Old Church Galleries, London, SW3.

Richard Green, London, W1.

Holland & Holland, London, W1.

Grosvenor Prints, London, WC2.

Green and Pleasant, Tetbury, Glos.

Coltsfoot Gallery, Leominster, Herefs.

Marrin's Bookshop, Folkestone, Kent.

Sally Mitchell's Gallery, Tuxford, Notts.

Julian Armytage, Crewkerne, Somerset.

Julia Holmes Antique Maps and Prints, South Harting, Sussex West.

Anthony Woodd Gallery Ltd, Edinburgh, Scotland.

Stamps

Argyll Etkin Gallery, London, SW1.

Michael Coins, London, W8.

Spink & Son Ltd, London, WC1.

Stanley Gibbons, London, WC2.

Collector's Corner, Truro, Cornwall.

Penrith Coin and Stamp Centre, Penrith, Cumbria.

Northgate Antique & Collectables Centre, Bridgnorth, Shrops.

Bath Stamp and Coin Shop, Bath, Somerset.

Collectors' Corner, Carshalton, Surrey.

Corbitt Stamps Ltd, Newcastle-upon-Tyne, Tyne & Wear.

Magpie Jewellers and Antiques and Magpie Arms & Armour, Evesham, Worcs.

B.B.M. Coins., Kidderminster, Worcs.

Antiques & Collectors Centre, Scarborough, Yorks. North.

J. Smith, York, Yorks. North.

The Collectors' Centre, St Peter Port, Guernsey, Channel Islands.

Edinburgh Coin Shop, Edinburgh, Scotland.

Tapestries, Textiles & Needlework

Meg Andrews, London, N1.

Annie's Vintage Costume & Textiles, London, N1.

Alexander Juran and Co, London, N4.

Joseph Lavian, London, N4.

Anno Domini Antiques, London, SW1.

S. Franses Ltd, London, SW1.

Joss Graham Oriental Textiles, London, SW1.

Keshishian, London, SW1.

Peta Smyth - Antique Textiles, London, SW1.

The Dining Room Shop, London, SW13.

Tobias and The Angel, London, SW13.

Joanna Booth, London, SW3.

Orientalist, London, SW3.

Robert Stephenson, London, SW3.

Lunn Antiques Ltd, London, SW6.

John Eskenazi Ltd, London, W1.

C. John (Rare Rugs) Ltd, London, W1.

Partridge Fine Art Ltd, London, W1.

Pelham, London, W1.

Sampson & Horne, London, W1.

Linda Wrigglesworth Ltd, London, W1.
A. Zadah, London, W1.
Sheila Cook Textiles, London, W11.
Rezai Persian Carpets, London, W11.
Virginia, London, W11.
Storm Fine Arts Ltd, Great Shelford, Cambs.
Pirouette, Exeter, Devon.
The Honiton Lace Shop, Weston, Devon.
Robson's Antiques, Barnard Castle, Durham.
Cocoa, Cheltenham, Glos.
Anthony Hazledine, Fairford, Glos.
Huntington Antiques Ltd, Stow-on-the-Wold, Glos.
Teagowns & Textiles, Leominster, Herefs.
Past Caring Vintage Clothing, Holt, Norfolk.
Country and Eastern Ltd., Norwich, Norfolk.
Witney Antiques, Witney, Oxon.
Antique Textiles & Lighting, Bath, Somerset.
Avon Antiques, Bradford-on-Avon, Wilts.
Penny Farthing Antiques, North Cave, Yorks. East.
London House Oriental Rugs and Carpets, Boston
    Spa, Yorks. West.
Echoes, Todmorden, Yorks. West.
Hand in Hand, Coldstream, Scotland.

Taxidermy
Get Stuffed, London, N1.
Below Stairs of Hungerford, Hungerford, Berks.
John Burton Natural Craft Taxidermy, Ebrington, Glos.
Heads 'n' Tails, Wiveliscombe, Somerset.
The Enchanted Aviary, Bury St. Edmunds, Suffolk.
London Taxidermy, East Molesey, Surrey.

Tools including Needlework & Sewing
Woodville Antiques, Hamstreet, Kent.
Norton Antiques, Twyford, Norfolk.
20th Century Fashion, Clare, Suffolk.
Roy Arnold Books, Needham Market, Suffolk.

Toys- see Dolls & Toys

Trade Dealers - see Shipping Goods & Furniture for the Trade

Treen
Robert Young Antiques, London, SW11.
Halcyon Days, London, W1.
Phoenix Antiques, Fordham, Cambs.
A.P. and M.A. Haylett, Outwell, Cambs.
G.W Ford & Son Ltd., Bakewell, Derbys.
Baggott Church Street Ltd, Stow-on-the-Wold, Glos.
Prichard Antiques, Winchcombe, Glos.
Millers of Chelsea Antiques Ltd, Ringwood, Hants.
Moxhams Antiques, Bradford-on-Avon, Wilts.
Stephen Cook Antiques, Broadway, Worcs.
Michael Green Pine & Country Antiques, Harrogate,
    Yorks. North.

Brian R. Bolt Antiques, Portballintrae, Co. Antrim,
    Northern Ireland.
Islwyn Watkins, Knighton, Wales.

Vintage Cars - see Cars & Carriages

Watercolours
Gladwell & Co., London, EC4.
Finchley Fine Art Galleries, London, N12.
Lauri Stewart - Fine Art, London, N2.
Gallery Kaleidoscope incorporating Scope Antiques,
    London, NW6.
Ackermann & Johnson, London, SW1.
John Adams Fine Art Ltd, London, SW1.
Chris Beetles Ltd, London, SW1.
Miles Wynn Cato, London, SW1.
Douwes Fine Art Ltd, London, SW1.
Frost & Reed Ltd (Est. 1808), London, SW1.
Martyn Gregory, London, SW1.
Old Maps and Prints, London, SW1.
Paisnel Gallery, London, SW1.
Bill Thomson - Albany Gallery, London, SW1.
Waterman Fine Art Ltd, London, SW1.
Hollywood Road Gallery, London, SW10.
Park Walk Gallery, London, SW10.
Regent House Gallery, London, SW11.
John Spink Fine Watercolours, London, SW13.
20th Century Gallery, London, SW6.
Campbells of London, London, SW7.
Agnew's, London, W1.
Victor Arwas Gallery - Editions Graphiques Gallery
    Ltd, London, W1.
Andrew Clayton-Payne Ltd, London, W1.
Connaught Brown plc, London, W1.
The Fine Art Society plc, London, W1.
Maas Gallery, London, W1.
Mallett and Son (Antiques) Ltd, London, W1.
Mallett Fine Art, London, W1.
John Mitchell and Son, London, W1.
Waterhouse & Dodd, London, W1.
Crawley and Asquith Ltd, London, W10.
Charles Daggett Gallery, London, W11.
Justin F. Skrebowski Prints, London, W11.
Richard Nagy Ltd, London, W2.
Abbott & Holder Ltd, London, WC1.
Graham Gallery, Burghfield Common, Berks.
J. Manley Restoration, Windsor, Berks.
Windmill Fine Art, High Wycombe, Bucks.
Angela Hone Watercolours, Marlow, Bucks.
Cambridge Fine Art Ltd, Cambridge, Cambs.
Storm Fine Arts Ltd, Great Shelford, Cambs.
Baron Fine Art, Chester, Cheshire.
Lion Gallery and Bookshop, Knutsford, Cheshire.
Foundry Gallery, Hayle, Cornwall.
Tony Sanders Penzance Gallery and Antiques,
    Penzance, Cornwall.

Leigh Haworth Ltd., Newbiggin-on-Lune, Cumbria.
Medina Gallery, Barnstaple, Devon.
J. Collins & Son, Bideford, Devon.
Cooper Gallery, Bideford, Devon.
Mill Gallery, Ermington, Devon.
Skeaping Gallery, Lydford, Devon.
Devonshire Fine Art, Modbury, Devon.
Michael Wood Fine Art, Plymouth, Devon.
Hampshire Gallery, Bournemouth, Dorset.
The Swan Gallery, Sherborne, Dorset.
T.B. and R. Jordan (Fine Paintings), Stockton-on-Tees, Durham.
Brandler Galleries, Brentwood, Essex.
S. Bond and Son, Colchester, Essex.
Totteridge Gallery, Earls Colne, Essex.
Cleeve Picture Framing, Bishops Cleeve, Glos.
Alexander Gallery, Bristol, Glos.
The Loquens Gallery, Cheltenham, Glos.
School House Antiques, Chipping Campden, Glos.
The Fosse Gallery, Stow-on-the-Wold, Glos.
Laurence Oxley Ltd, Alresford, Hants.
J. Morton Lee, Hayling Island, Hants.
The Petersfield Bookshop, Petersfield, Hants.
Bell Fine Art, Winchester, Hants.
Lacewing Fine Art Gallery, Winchester, Hants.
Wolseley Fine Arts Ltd, Hereford, Herefs.
Coltsfoot Gallery, Leominster, Herefs.
The Shanklin Gallery, Shanklin, Isle of Wight.
Gallery Cranbrook, Cranbrook, Kent.
Francis Iles, Rochester, Kent.
Sundridge Gallery, Sundridge, Kent.
Redleaf Gallery, Tunbridge Wells, Kent.
Apollo Antique Galleries, Westerham, Kent.
Fulda Gallery Ltd, Manchester, Lancs.
P. Stanworth (Fine Arts), Market Bosworth, Leics.
Coughton Galleries Ltd, Market Harborough, Leics.
Graftons of Market Harborough, Market Harborough, Leics.
Crome Gallery and Frame Shop, Norwich, Norfolk.
The Westcliffe Gallery, Sheringham, Norfolk.
Norton Antiques, Twyford, Norfolk.
Castle Ashby Gallery, Castle Ashby, Northants.
Brian Sinfield Gallery Ltd, Burford, Oxon.
The Barry Keene Gallery, Henley-on-Thames, Oxon.
Marc Oxley Fine Art, Uppingham, Rutland.
Callaghan Fine Paintings, Shrewsbury, Shrops.
Adam Gallery Ltd, Bath, Somerset.
Heritage Fine Art, South Petherton, Somerset.
The Sadler Street Gallery, Wells, Somerset.
England's Gallery, Leek, Staffs.
Thompson's Gallery, Aldeburgh, Suffolk.
J. and J. Baker, Lavenham, Suffolk.
Peasenhall Art and Antiques Gallery, Peasenhall, Suffolk.
Glencorse Antiques, Kingston-upon-Thames, Surrey.
Bourne Gallery Ltd, Reigate, Surrey.

Roland Goslett Gallery, Richmond, Surrey.
Sage Antiques and Interiors, Ripley, Surrey.
John Day of Eastbourne Fine Art, Eastbourne, Sussex East.
Nicholas Bowlby, Poundgate, Sussex East.
The Canon Gallery, Chichester, Sussex West.
Wilsons Antiques, Worthing, Sussex West.
John Nicholson Fine Art, Jesmond, Tyen & Wear.
Arden Gallery, Henley-in-Arden, Warks.
Oldswinford Gallery, Stourbridge, West Mids.
Driffold Gallery, Sutton Coldfield, West Mids.
Richard Hagen Gallery, Broadway, Worcs.
Haynes Fine Art of Broadway, Broadway, Worcs.
The Highway Gallery, Upton-upon-Severn, Worcs.
James H. Starkey Galleries, Beverley, Yorks. East.
W. Greenwood (Fine Art), Burneston, Yorks. North.
McTague of Harrogate, Harrogate, Yorks. North.
E. Stacy-Marks Limited, Helmsley, Yorks. North.
Kirkgate Fine Art & Conservation, Thirsk, Yorks. North.
Coulter Galleries, York, Yorks. North.
Robin Taylor Fine Arts, Wakefield, Yorks. West.
Beverley J. Pyke - Fine British Watercolours, St Anne's, Alderney, Channel Islands.
Atelier Ltd, Grouville, Jersey, Channel Islands.
Falle Fine Art Limited, St. Helier, Jersey, Channel Islands.
The Bell Gallery, Randalston, Co. Antrim, Northern Ireland.
Phyllis Arnold Gallery Antiques, Donaghadee, Co. Down, Northern Ireland.
The Rendezvous Gallery, Aberdeen, Scotland.
The McEwan Gallery, Ballater, Scotland.
Calton Gallery, Edinburgh, Scotland.
Anthony Woodd Gallery Ltd, Edinburgh, Scotland.
The Roger Billcliffe Fine Art, Glasgow, Scotland.
Inchmartine Fine Art, Inchture, Scotland.
Mainhill Gallery, Jedburgh, Scotland.
Kirk Ports Gallery, North Berwick, Scotland.
St. Andrews Fine Art, St. Andrews, Scotland.
David Windsor Gallery, Bangor, Wales.
Michael Webb Fine Art, Bodorgan, Wales.
Simon Wingett Fine Art, Erbistock, Wales.
Rowles Fine Art, Welshpool, Wales.

Wine Related Items
Alastair Dickenson Ltd, London, SW1.
Christopher Sykes Antiques, Woburn, Beds.
Neil Willcox & Mark Nightingale, Penryn, Cornwall.
Robin Butler, Shalford, Essex.
Steppes Hill Farm Antiques, Stockbury, Kent.
Trade Wind, Rottingdean, Sussex East.
Andrew Jennings Antiques, Melksham, Wilts.

Dealers' Index

In order to facilitate reference both the names of individuals and their business name are indexed separately. Thus A E Jones and C Smith of High Street Antiques will be indexed under:

Jones, A E, Town, County.
Smith, C, Town, County.
High Street Antiques, Town, County.

THE TIMELINE SERIES

Every book in *The Timeline Series* offers a concise, striking visual chronology of its subject, whether this is the evolution of a single painter's style or the changing face of an entire movement in art, fashion or design. Despite first appearances, these are not like other books - each title pulls out to become an innovative two-sided guide. On the front, the *Timeline* shows you sixteen key images in chronological order - for example, excerpts from the crucial works of a particular artist, or details from evolving stages of an era in design. At a glance, you see a clear visual path through the development of the subject. On the back you will find all the detail - entire reproductions of the pieces discussed, succinct explorations of their context, meaning and history written by experts, biographies of the artists, and more. *The Timeline Series* offers a fresh, simple visual reference that is ideal for art-lovers, casual visitors to museums and art galleries, and students - anyone who wants to see clearly how artistic styles evolve and change over time.

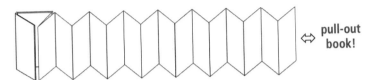

⇔ **pull-out book!**

The Timeline Book of Rembrandt

Rembrandt Harmenszoon van Rijn (1606-1669) is amongst the greatest painters and engravers of all time. He was undoubtedly the major exponent of the Dutch Golden Age in art, and explored all genres of painting, from the group portrait - which he radically reinvented with *The Night Watch* - to biblical themes, to his constant engagement with self-portraiture, to landscape. Rembrandt's career is distinguished by his forceful personality, extraordinary technical ability, unceasing experimentation and vast visual knowledge, ranging from primitive Flemish painters to the Italian Renaissance. In a life marked by glory, misery, relationships contrary to bourgeois morality and numerous bereavements, Rembrandt always strove to represent reality and nature through isolating its innermost truth, in a search often opposed to artistic convention and the decorum of contemporary society.

158 x 112 mm. 36 pp   32 col. **£5.95 Hardback**

The Timeline Book of Titian

Tiziano Vecellio ('Titian') (c.1488-1576) was among the earliest artists to leave a profound mark in the history of painting, with influences that resonate in artists from Velázquez to Cézanne. The leading painter of the High Renaissance period in Venice, his oeuvre ranges from monumental works such as the immense Frari altarpiece, to the elegiac treatment of mythological themes, to the intimate, psychological field of portraiture. Titian began in the style of Giorgione and Giovanni Bellini, before developing his own chromatic classicism until the "mannerist crisis" of the 1520s an 1530s, after which his work incorporated a more sculptural quality. His extremely productive and long life brought international fame and exceptional friendships (such as those with celebrated writers Ariosto and Aretino), long journeys, and homage from powerful rulers: he was made count by the Emperor Charles V. Throughout, Titian pursued the sense and physicality of colour; ultimately, old and virtually blind, he was painting with his fingers, in the knowledge that his end was near just as he was beginning to understand the true nature of painting.

158 x 112 mm. 36 pp   32 col. **£5.95 Hardback**

The Timeline Book of Turner

Joseph Mallord William Turner (1775-1851), 'the painter of light', was the most important English painter of the age of Romanticism. He merged his observation of natural phenomena with a particular attention to the atmospheric and an extraordinary, transformative visionary talent. After portrayals of the English countryside in the topographical tradition, such as *Frosty Morning* (1813, London, Tate Britain), experiences such as his Grand Tour of Italy, where he much admired the light and scenery of the landscape, led Turner to paint canvasses in which light is rendered with dense impastos, as in *Snow Storm - Steam-Boat off a Harbour's Mouth* (1842, London, Tate Britain), and the celebrated *Rain, Steam, and Speed - The Great Western Railway* (1844, London, National Gallery) - an expressive treatment of a strongly contemporary theme.

158 x 112 mm. 36 pp   32 col. **£5.95 Hardback**

Au Temps Perdu, Bristol, Glos.
Aucott, Barry, Hemswell Cliff, Lincs.
Auction Atrium, Kensington Church
  Street Antiques Centre, London W8.
Auger, Ferrous, London, SW8.
Auldearn Antiques, Auldearn, Scotland.
Aura Antiques, Masham, Yorks. North.
Aurea Carter, London, SW6.
Aurum Antiques, Grays Antique
  Markets, London W1.
Austin, J., London, WC1.
Austin/Desmond Fine Art, London,
  WC1.
Austin-Fell, A.J. and C.R., Holt,
  Norfolk.
Austin-Kaye, A.M., Chester, Cheshire.
Austwick, Paul, Sowerby Bridge, Yorks.
  West.
Avon Antiques, Bradford-on-Avon,
  Wilts.
Avonbridge Antiques and Collectors'
  Market, The, Salisbury, Wilts.
Axia Art Consultants Ltd, London,
  W11.

B

B & B Antiques, Stickney, Lincs.
B & T Engraving, Grays Antique
  Markets, London W1.
B&T Antiques, London, W11.
B.B.M. Coins., Kidderminster, Worcs.
B.C. Metalcrafts, London, NW9.
B.R.M. Coins, Knutsford, Cheshire.
Back 2 Wood, Appledore, Kent.
Bacou, Guillaume and Louise, London,
  E1.
Badcock, Stuart, Top Banana Antiques
  Mall, Tetbury, Glos. 1.
Baddiel, Colin, Grays Antique Markets,
  London W1.
Baddow Antique Centre, Great Baddow,
  Essex.
Badland, Bradford, Yorks. West.
Baggins Book Bazaar - The Largest
  Secondhand Bookshop in England,
  Rochester, Kent.
Baggott Church Street Ltd, Stow-on-
  the-Wold, Glos.
Baggott, D.J. and C.M., Stow-on-
  Wold, Glos.
Baggott, D.J. and C.M., Stow-on-
  Wold, Glos.
Baggott, Duncan J., Stow-on-the-Wold,
  Glos.
Baggott, Lucy and Henry, Stow-on-the-
  Wold, Glos.
Bagham Barn Antiques, Chilham, Kent.
Bags of Glamour, Grays Antique
  Markets, London W1.
Bail, A., Ash Vale, Surrey.
Baile de Laperriere, H., Calne, Wilts.
Bailey, M. and S., Ross-on-Wye, Herefs.
Bailey, Ray, The Swan at Tetsworth,
  Oxon.
Bailey, Tim, Top Banana Antiques Mall,

Tetbury, Glos. 1.
Bailey, Tony, Top Banana Antiques Mall,
  Tetbury, Glos. 1.
Baileys Home & Garden, Ross-on-Wye,
  Herefs.
Bailiffgate Antique Pine, Alnwick,
  Northumbs.
Baillie, Anthea, Windsor, Berks.
Bairsto, Peter, Tetbury, Glos.
Baker Antiques, G., Horncastle, Lincs.
Baker Asian Art, Gregg, London, W8.
Baker, B.A.J., Lavenham, Suffolk.
Baker, J. and J., Lavenham, Suffolk.
Baker, Keith, Woking, Surrey.
Baker, Sandie and Chris, Sandwich,
  Kent.
Baker, T., Langford, Notts.
Bakers of Maybury Ltd, Woking, Surrey.
Bakewell Antiques and Works of Art,
  Bakewell, Derbys.
Bakhtar Art, Grays Antique Markets,
  London W1.
Bakhtiyar Gallery, The, Stockbridge,
  Hants.
Baldock, David, Birmingham, West
  Mids.
Baldry, J., Great Yarmouth, Norfolk.
Baldwin & Sons Ltd, A.H., London,
  WC2.
Baldwin, Edward, London, WC2.
Baldwin, L., Nottingham, Notts.
Baldwin, M. and M., Cleobury
  Mortimer, Shrops.
Baldwin, R.E. and P.J., Scarborough,
  Yorks. North.
Baldwin, R.J.S., London, SW3.
Baldwin, V.F.S. and J.F., Alcester, Warks.
Bale, Craig, Bath, Somerset.
Bale, Vicki, Ditton Priors, Shrops.
Ball and Claw Antiques, Tetbury, Glos.
Ball, Jim, Tudor House, Stow-on-the-
  Wold, Glos.
Ball, John M., Marlesford, Suffolk.
Balloo Moon, Greyabbey Village, Co.
  Down, Northern Ireland.
Bampton Gallery, Bampton, Devon.
Bananarama, Top Banana Antiques
  Mall, Tetbury, Glos. 1.
Banbury Fayre, London, N1.
Bangerter, Iris, Grays Antique Markets,
  London W1.
Bangs Ltd, Christopher, London, SW6.
Bangs, Christopher, London, SW6.
Bank Gallery Antiques, Chester,
  Cheshire.
Bank House Gallery, The, Norwich,
  Norfolk.
Banks Antiques, Simon, Finedon,
  Northants.
Bannister FRGS, David, Cheltenham,
  Glos.
Bannister, Kate, Tudor House, Stow-on-
  the-Wold, Glos.
Barakat Gallery, London, W1.
Barbagallo, Sebastiano, London, SW6.

Barbagallo, Sebastiano, London, W11.
Barber, Sara, Long Melford, Suffolk.
Barbican Bookshop, York, Yorks. North.
Barclay Antiques, Headington, Oxon.
Barclay Samson Ltd, London, SW6.
Barclay, C., Headington, Oxon.
Barclay, Richard, London, SW6.
Bardawil, Eddy, London, W8.
Barfoot, Craig, East Hagbourne, Oxon.
Barham Antiques, London, W11.
Barham, M.J., London, W11.
Barham, R.P., London, W11.
Barker, Brian, Swanage, Dorset.
Barker, Janet, Treharris, Wales.
Barker, Peter, Dunsfold, Surrey.
Barkham Antique Centre, Barkham, Berks.
Barkway, Caroline, Red House Antiques
  Centre, York, Yorks. North.
Barmouth Court Antiques Centre,
  Sheffield, Yorks. South.
Barn Antiques Centre, Long Marston,
  Warks.
Barn Antiques, Barnstaple, Devon.
Barn Antiques, Nantwich, Cheshire.
Barn Full of Brass Beds, A, Conisholme,
  Lincs.
Barn, The, Petersfield, Hants.
Barnes Antiques & Interiors, Jane,
  Honiton, Devon.
Barnes Antiques, R.A., Rogers Antiques
  Gallery.
Barnes, J.A.C. and S.J. , Honiton,
  Devon.
Barnes, Mandy, Jubilee Hall Antiques
  Centre, Lechlade, Glos.
Barnes, R.A., Bicester, Oxon.
Barnes, Robin, The Swan at Tetsworth,
  Oxon.
Barnet Bygones, Barnet, Herts.
Barnett, R .K., Almshouses Arcade,
  Chichester, Sussex West.
Barnett, Viv, Chichester, Sussex West.
Barnstaple Antique & Collectors'
  Centre, Barnstaple, Devon.
Barnt Green Antiques, Barnt Green,
  Worcs.
Barometer Shop Ltd, The, Leominster,
  Herefs.
Barometer World Ltd, Merton, Devon.
Baron Art, Holt, Norfolk.
Baron Fine Art, Chester, Cheshire.
Baron Interiors, Chris, London, SW2.
Baron, Anthony R., Holt, Norfolk.
Baron, S. and R., Chester, Cheshire.
Barr, S.M and R.W., Westerham, Kent.
Barrance, John, Sawbridgeworth, Herts.
Barrance, Sue, The Swan at Tetsworth,
  Oxon.
Barratt, Mike , Warrington, Cheshire.
Barrett, Mark and Iryna, Coggeshall,
  Essex.
Barrett, P., Weymouth, Dorset.
Barrett, S.M., Seaford, Sussex East.
Barrie, K., London, NW6.
Barrington, David, Brasted, Kent.

Brown Ltd, I. and J.L. , Hereford, Herefs.

Brown Ltd, I. and J.L., London, SW6.

Brown, A., London, W1.

Brown, D.R., St. Andrews, Scotland.

Brown, Gay, London, NW1.

Brown, Gordon and Anne, Glasgow, Scotland.

Brown, J., Cleadon, Tyne & Wear.

Brown, P., Burford, Oxon.

Brown, Paul, Tringford., Herts.

Brown, Philip, Stow-on-the-Wold, Glos.

Brown, Richard, Pateley Bridge, Yorks. North.

Brown, Sharon & Jack, Lyndhurst, Hants.

Brown, Sue, Grays Antique Markets, London W1.

Brown, T.D., Edinburgh, Scotland.

Brown, Tom and Alice, Launceston, Cornwall.

Brownrigg @ Home, Petworth, Sussex West.

Browns' of West Wycombe, High Wycombe, Bucks.

Browse and Darby Ltd, London, W1.

Bruce, Diana, Jedburgh, Scotland.

Bruce, F., Strathblane, Scotland.

Bruce, H., London, WC1.

Bruce, J., Aberdeen, Scotland.

Bruce, J., Bideford, Devon.

Bruce, W.F., Lewes, Sussex East.

Bruford & Heming Ltd, London, W1.

Bruford Jewellers, W., Eastbourne, Sussex East.

Brunning, Martin and Jean, Redbourn, Herts.

Bruno Antiques, Hastings Antique Centre, St. Leonards-on-Sea, E. Sussex.

Brunsveld, S., Lymm, Cheshire.

Brunswick Antiques, Penrith, Cumbria.

Brunswick Gallery, Ribchester, Lancs.

Brunt, Iain, Leeds, Yorks. West.

Bruschweiler (Antiques) Ltd, F.G., Rayleigh, Essex.

Bryan, Ian, London Silver Vaults, London WC2.

Bryan, Tina, Wymondham, Leics.

Bryant, E.H., Epsom, Surrey.

Bryant, Frances, Sherborne, Dorset.

Bryars Ltd, Tim, London, WC2.

Brynin, Peter, Brighton, Sussex East.

Bryn-y-grog Antiques Emporium, Wrexham, Wales.

Buchan, Ian and Rhoda, Hailsham, Sussex East.

Buchinger, Teresa, Antiquarius, London SW3.

Buck Antiques, Christopher, Sandgate, Kent.

Buck House Antiques, Beaconsfield, Bucks.

Buck, Christopher and Jane, Sandgate, Kent.

Buck, W.F.A., Stockbury, Kent.

Buckler, Robin and Sue, Thornton-le-Dale, Yorks. North.

Buckley, W., Stoke-on-Trent, Staffs.

Buffalohouse Pottery, Leighton Buzzard, Beds.

Bulka, Lynn, London Silver Vaults, London WC2.

Bull and Son (Cirencester) Ltd, Walter, Cirencester, Glos.

Bull, Audrey, Carmarthen, Wales.

Bull, Audrey, Tenby, Wales.

Bull, Jonathan and Jane, Carmarthen, Wales.

Bull, Kenneth and Elliot, London, W1.

Bullock, Gabrielle Doherty, Worcester, Worcs.

Bullock, Gabrielle, Worcester, Worcs.

Bumbles, Ashtead, Surrey.

Bumpstead Antiques & Interiors, Steeple Bumpstead, Essex.

Bumpstead Arts & Antiques, Steeple Bumpstead, Essex.

Bunn, R.J. and E.R., Evesham, Worcs.

Bunting Antiques, Peter, Bakewell, Derbys.

Burbidge Antiques, M., The Antiques Complex, Exeter, Devon.

Burden Ltd, Clive A., Rickmansworth, Herts.

Burden, Philip D., Rickmansworth, Herts.

Burdett, Raymond, Bournemouth, Dorset.

Burfield, P., Ventnor, Isle of Wight.

Burford Antique Centre, Burford, Oxon.

Burgate Antique Centre, Canterbury, Kent.

Burgess - Horologist, Derek J., Branksome, Dorset.

Burgess Farm Antiques, Winchester, Hants.

Burgess, Lee, Ginnel Antiques Centre, The, Harrogate, Yorks North.

Burgess, Lee, Red House Antiques Centre, York, Yorks. North.

Burlington Paintings Ltd, London, W1.

Burman Antiques, Stratford-upon-Avon, Warks.

Burman Holtom, J. and J., Stratford-upon-Avon, Warks.

Burman, C. & L., London, W1.

Burne (Antique Glass) Ltd, W.G.T., London, SW20.

Burne, G. and A.T., London, SW20.

Burnell, F., London, NW9.

Burness, Victor, Rogers Antiques Gallery.

Burnett, CMBHI, C.A., Northleach, Glos.

Burnett, David and Sally, Ryde, Isle of Wight.

Burnham Antiques Emporium, Burnham, Bucks.

Burning Embers, Aberdeen, Scotland.

Burns, G.H., Stamford, Lincs.

Burr, Ursula, Top Banana Antiques Mall, Tetbury, Glos. 3 and 4.

Burrell, V.S., Abinger Hammer, Surrey.

Burroughs, Hilary, Farnham, Surrey.

Burrows, David E., Osgathorpe, Leics.

Burrows, Paul, Solihull, West Mids.

Bursill, Paul, Aberdeen, Scotland.

Burslem Antiques & Collectables, Stoke-on-Trent, Staffs.

Burton Antique Clocks, Ian, Auchterarder, Scotland.

Burton Antiques, Burton-upon-Trent, Staffs.

Burton Natural Craft Taxidermy, John, Ebrington, Glos.

Burton, D., Christchurch, Dorset.

Burton, J., Dorchester, Dorset.

Bush and Partners, A.E. , Attleborough, Norfolk.

Bush, Anthony, Redbourn, Herts.

Bushe Developments UK Ltd, London, N1.

Bushell, C., Honiton, Devon.

Bushwood Antiques, Redbourn, Herts.

Butcher, F.L. and N.E., Sherborne, Dorset.

Butchoff Antiques, London, W8.

Butchoff, Ian, London, W8.

Butler and Wilson, London, SW3.

Butler FSA, Roderick, Honiton, Devon.

Butler, Adrian, Hadlow Down, Sussex East.

Butler, Clifford, Top Banana Antiques Mall, Tetbury, Glos. 2.

Butler, Kelly, Leek, Staffs.

Butler, Robin, Shalford, Essex.

Butler, Roderick, Honiton, Devon.

Butler, Valentine, Honiton, Devon.

Butt Antiques, Anthony, Baldock, Herts.

Butterworth, Brian, Knutsford, Cheshire.

Butterworth, John, Potterspury, Northants.

Butterworth, John, Potterspury, Northants.

Buttigieg, Joyce M., London, SE25.

Button Queen Ltd., The, London, W1.

Button, K., Bungay, Suffolk.

By George! Antiques Centre, St. Albans, Herts.

Byatte, Ann, Stoke-on-Trent, Staffs.

Bygones by the Cathedral, Worcester, Worcs.

Bygones of Worcester, Worcester, Worcs.

Bygones Reclamation, Canterbury, Kent.

Bygones, Burford, Oxon.

Bygones, Red House Antiques Centre, York, Yorks. North.

Byles Antiques and Optimum Brasses., Robert, Bampton, Devon.

Byles, Robert and Rachel, Bampton, Devon.

Byrne, A., Londonderry, Co. Londonderry, Northern Ireland.

C

C.A.R.S. (Classic Automobilia & Regalia Specialists), Brighton, Sussex East.
Cabello, John, Plymouth, Devon.
Caedmon House, Whitby, Yorks. North.
Caen Antiques, Braunton, Devon.
Caffarella, Vincenzo, Alfies Antique Market, London NW8.
Cain, Liz, Washford, Somerset.
Caira Mandaglio, London, W11.
Cairncross and Sons, Filey, Yorks. North.
Cairncross, G., Filey, Yorks. North.
Cairns, John and Tina, Moira, Co. Armagh, Northern Ireland.
Caistor Antiques, Caistor, Lincs.
Caldwell, Carmel, Ampthill, Beds.
Cale, Kathryn, Windsor, Berks.
Caledonian Antiques, Bristol, Glos.
Calgie, John, Jubilee Hall Antiques Centre, Lechlade, Glos.
Callaghan Fine Paintings, Shrewsbury, Shrops.
Callaghan, Daniel, Shrewsbury, Shrops.
Calleja, L., Ledbury, Herefs.
Calne Antiques, Calne, Wilts.
Calton Gallery, Edinburgh, Scotland.
Calverley Antiques, Tunbridge Wells, Kent.
Cambridge Fine Art Ltd, Cambridge, Cambs.
Camden Passage Antiques Market and Pierrepont Arcade Antiques Centre, London, N1.
Cameo Antiques, Chester, Cheshire.
Cameron, Jasmin, Antiquarius, London SW3.
Cameron, Margaret, Old Bank Antiques Centre, Bath, Somerset.
Cameron, Sheila, Alfies Antique Market, London NW8.
Camilla's Bookshop, Eastbourne, Sussex East.
Campbell & Sons, A. K., Kirkcaldy, Scotland.
Campbell Fine Art, L. Christie, Rait Village Antiques Centre, Scotland.
Campbell, Andrew, Jesmond, Tyne and Wear.
Campbell, S., Colchester, Essex.
Campbell, S., Stirling, Scotland.
Campbell, William, Alfies Antique Market, London NW8.
Campbells of London, London, SW7.
Campion, R.J., London, SW6.
Candle Lane Books, Shrewsbury, Shrops.
Candlin, Z., London, N1.
Candlin, Z., London, SW3.
Cannell Antiques, M.D., Raveningham, Norfolk.
Cannon Antiques, Elizabeth, Colchester, Essex.
Canon Gallery, The, Chichester, Sussex West.

Canterbury Antiques, Canterbury, Kent.
Canterbury Bookshop, The, Canterbury, Kent.
Caplin, Victor, Alfies Antique Market, London NW8.
Capon, Patric, Bromley, Kent.
Cardiff Antiques Centre, Cardiff, Wales.
Cardiff Reclamation, Cardiff, Wales.
Cardingmill Antiques, Church Stretton, Shrops.
Carlisle Antiques Centre, Carlisle, Cumbria.
Carlton Antiques Ltd., Saltaire, Yorks. West.
Carlton Antiques, Great Malvern, Worcs.
Carlton Clocks, Amersham, Bucks.
Carlton-Sims, Patricia, Horncastle, Lincs.
Carlton-Smith, John and Michelle, London, SW1.
Carlton-Smith, John, London, SW1.
Carnegie Paintings & Clocks, Plymouth, Devon.
Carnegie, Chris, Plymouth, Devon.
Carningli Centre, The, Newport, Wales.
Carpenter Musical Instruments, John, Swansea, Wales.
Carpenter, John and Caroline, Swansea, Wales.
Carpenter, Rosemary, Truro, Cornwall.
Carpets, Richard Morant and David Black, London, W2.
Carr Antiques, Harold J., Washington, Tyne and Wear.
Carrasco, Marylise, London, SW1.
Carrington House, Llanrwst, Wales.
Carrol, Philip, Gargrave, Yorks. North.
Carroll Antiques, John, Belfast, Co. Antrim, Northern Ireland.
Carruthers, C.J., Carlisle, Cumbria.
Carruthers, J., St. Andrews, Scotland.
Carruthers, L., Buxton, Derbys.
Carshalton Antique Galleries, Carshalton, Surrey.
Cartalia.com Ltd., Kensington Church Street Antiques Centre, London W8.
Carter, D., London, W11.
Carter, Mark, Eastleach, Glos.
Cartmell, T., Tring, Herts.
CASA, London, SE15.
Case, G., Bridport, Dorset.
Casque and Gauntlet Militaria, Farnham, Surrey.
Cassidy, M., Warminster, Wilts.
Cassidy's Antiques, Warminster, Wilts.
Castaside, Alfies Antique Market, London NW8.
Castle Antiques Centre, Westerham, Kent.
Castle Antiques Ltd, Deddington, Oxon.
Castle Antiques, Edinburgh, Scotland.
Castle Antiques, Nottingham, Notts.
Castle Ashby Gallery, Castle Ashby, Northants.

Castle Bookshop, Colchester, Essex.
Castle Close Antiques, Dornoch, Scotland.
Castle Galleries, Salisbury, Wilts.
Castle Gate Antiques Centre, Newark, Notts.
Castle Gate Antiques, Helmsley, Yorks. North.
Castle Hill Books, Kington, Herefs.
Castle Reclamation, Martock, Somerset.
Caswell, Patricia, Talbot Walk Antique Centre, Ripley, Surrey.
Cathedral Antiques, Fortrose, Scotland.
Cathedral Jewellers, Ashton-under-Lyne, Lancs.
Catkins Jewellery and Antiques, Ginnel Antiques Centre, The, Harrogate, Yorks North.
Cato, Lennnox, The Edenbridge Galleries, Edenbridge.
Cato, Lennox and Susan, Edenbridge, Kent.
Cato, Lennox and Susan, Edenbridge, Kent.
Cato, Lennox, Edenbridge, Kent.
Cato, Miles Wynn, London, SW1.
Cato, Miles Wynn, Tywyn, Wales.
Cattle, Barbara, York, Yorks. North.
Caudwell, Doreen, Antiques at Heritage, Woodstock, Oxon.
Caulfield-Kerney, Fred, The Swan at Tetsworth, Oxon.
Causer Fine Art & Interiors, Martin, Norwich, Norfolk.
Cavanagh, D., Edinburgh, Scotland.
Cave and Sons Ltd, R.G., Ludlow, Shrops.
Cave, M.C., R.G., J.R. and T.G., Ludlow, Shrops.
Cave, Richard, London, W1.
Cavendish Antiques & Collectors Centre, York, Yorks. North.
Cavendish Antiques & Interiors, Cavendish, Suffolk.
Cavendish Antiques, Rupert, London, SW6.
Cavendish Fine Arts, London, SW1.
Cavendish, Rupert, London, SW6.
Cavet, Christian, London, W11.
Cavey & Associates, Chris, Grays Antique Markets, London W1.
Cawarden Brick Co Ltd, Rugeley, Staffs.
Cawson, Peter, St. Leonards-on-Sea, Sussex East.
Cayley, John, London, SW15.
Cedar Antiques Limited, Hartley Wintney, Hants.
Cekay, Grays Antique Markets, London W1.
Cellar Antiques, Hawes, Yorks. North.
Central Gallery (Portobello), London, W11.
Ceres Antiques, Ceres, Scotland.
CG's Curiosity Shop, Cockermouth, Cumbria.

Davis Ltd, Reginald, Oxford, Oxon.
Davis, Andrew and Glynis, Kew Green, Surrey.
Davis, Andrew, Kew Green, Surrey.
Davis, Mark, Ashburton, Devon.
Davis, Peter, Old Bank Antiques Centre, Bath, Somerset.
Davison, Andrew, Bridlington, Yorks. East.
Davison, Diane, Bridlington, Yorks. East.
Dawes, Philip, Durham House Antiques Centre, Stow-on-the-Wold, Glos.
Dawson of Stamford Ltd, Stamford, Lincs.
Dawson, J., Stamford, Lincs.
Day & Faber, London, W1.
Day Antiques, Tetbury, Glos.
Day of Eastbourne Fine Art, John, Eastbourne, Sussex East.
Day, Gillian and Geoff, Hertford Heath, Herts.
Day, Gillian, Rowlands Castle, Hants.
Day, Lester, St. Ives, Cambs.
Day, M., London, W1.
Day, P., Truro, Cornwall.
Day, Richard, London, W1.
Days of Grace, Budleigh Salterton, Devon.
de Albuquerque Antiques, Wallingford, Oxon.
de Albuquerque, Jane, The Swan at Tetsworth, Oxon.
De Danann Antique Centre, Dorchester, Dorset.
de Giles, Gabrielle, Sandgate, Kent.
De la Rue Antiques, W., St Peter Port, Guernsey, Channel Islands.
de Lemos, Antonio, St. Helier, Jersey, Channel Islands.
De Martini, Massimo, London, W1.
de Rin, V., London, SW3.
de Rouffignac, Colin, Standish, Lancs.
Dean, Barry, Weybridge, Surrey.
Dearden, Martin, East Pennard, Somerset.
Debden Antiques, Debden, Essex.
Debenham Antiques Ltd., Debenham, Suffolk.
Decodream, Coulsdon, Surrey.
Decorative Antiques, Bishop's Castle, Shrops.
Decorator Source, The, Tetbury, Glos.
Decoratum, Alfies Antique Market, London NW8.
Deddington Antiques Centre, Deddington, Oxon.
Dee, W & B, Top Banana Antiques Mall, Tetbury, Glos. 1.
Deerstalker Antiques, Whitchurch, Bucks.
Deja Vu Antiques, Leigh-on-Sea, Essex.
Delaforge, Rita, London, W11.
Delawood Antiques, Hunstanton, Norfolk.

Delehar, London, W11.
Delf, J., London, N1.
Dellar, P., Potter Heigham, Norfolk.
Della-Ragione, Gino, London, WC2.
Delolio, Janet and Adrian, Caerwys, Wales.
Delomosne and Son Ltd, North Wraxall, Wilts.
Demetzy Books, Witney, Oxon.
Denham Antiques, Heather, Petworth, Sussex West.
Dennett Coins, Clive, Norwich, Norfolk.
Dennett, C.E., North Cave, Yorks. East.
Denning, Sally, Wincanton, Somerset.
Dennis, J., Leicester, Leics.
Dennis, P.S. and S.M., Winchcombe, Glos.
Dennler Antiques & Interiors, Guy, Tiverton, Devon.
Dennys, Nicholas, London, SW7.
Denton Antiques, London, W8.
Denton, M.T. and E.R., London, W8.
Denton, M.T., E.R., and A.C. , London, W8.
Derbyshire Clocks, Glossop, Derbys.
Derham, R., Earsham, Norfolk.
Derval, The Edenbridge Galleries, Edenbridge.
Derwentside Antiques, Belper, Derbys.
Design Gallery 1850-1950, The, Westerham, Kent.
Desler Designs, Carol, The Swan at Tetsworth, Oxon.
Desmond, M, Antiquarius, London SW3.
Deutsch Antiques, H. and W., London, W8.
Deva Antiques, Hartley Wintney, Hants.
Devonshire Antiques, Grays Antique Markets, London W1.
Devonshire Fine Art, Modbury, Devon.
Devoy, Jean, Tattenhall, Cheshire.
Dew, Diane Elizabeth, Rogers Antiques Gallery.
Dew, Roderick, Eastbourne, Sussex East.
Dewart, Glen, Antiquarius, London SW3.
Dewdney, R., Dorking, Surrey.
D'Eyncourt, Chertsey, Surrey.
Diamond, Harry, Guildford, Surrey.
Dick, Jonathan, Horsham, Sussex West.
Dickens Curios, Frinton-on-Sea, Essex.
Dickenson Ltd, Alastair, London, SW1.
Dickenson, Alastair, London, SW1.
Dickinson Ltd, Simon C., London, SW1.
Dickinson, Simon, London, SW1.
Dickinson's Antiques Ltd, Gargrave, Yorks. North.
Dickson and Lesley Rendall Antiques, Robert, London, SW3.
Didier Antiques, Kensington Church Street Antiques Centre, London W8.
Dimech, Alfies Antique Market, London NW8.

Dimmer, I.M. and N.C.S., Cheltenham, Glos.
Ding, Jacqueline, The Swan at Tetsworth, Oxon.
Dining Room Shop, The, London, SW13.
Diss Antiques & Interiors, Diss, Norfolk.
Ditchburn-Bosch, Ursula, Pittenweem, Scotland.
Dix, S., Hastings, Sussex East.
Dixon Ltd, C.J. and A.J., Bridlington, Yorks. East.
Dixon, Charles, London, SW18.
Dixon, Christopher, Bridlington, Yorks. East.
Dixon, Helen, Alfreton, Derbys.
Dixon, N., Blakeney, Glos.
Dixon, Peter, London, W11.
Dix-Sept, Framlingham, Suffolk.
Dobbing, Pete and Elaine, West Burton, Yorks. North.
Doble Ltd, Ivor, Exeter, Devon.
Doble, I., Exeter, Devon.
Dodd, J., London, W1.
Dodge & Son, Sherborne, Dorset.
Dodge, S., Sherborne, Dorset.
Dodington Antiques, Whitchurch, Shrops.
Dodo, Alfies Antique Market, London NW8.
Doggett, F.C., Somerton, Somerset.
Doghouse (Antiques), The, Walsall, West Mids.
Dolan, Ken, Beer, Devon.
Dolby, D., Shenton, Leics.
Doll's House, The, Northleach, Glos.
Dolly Land, London, N21.
Dolly Mixtures, Birmingham, West Mids.
Dolphin Antiques, Beer, Devon.
Dolphin Quay Antique Centre, Emsworth, Hants.
Domani Antique & Contemporary, Exeter, Devon.
Dome Antiques (Exports) Ltd, London, N7.
Donay Traditional Games & Pastimes, Haywards Heath, Sussex West.
Donnachie, R.W., West Byfleet, Surrey.
Donnelly Antique Clocks, Adrian, Shrewsbury, Shrops.
Dorchester Antiques, Dorchester-on-Thames, Oxon.
Dorking Desk Shop, The, Dorking, Surrey.
Dorking House Antiques, Dorking, Surrey.
Dorney, G., Birmingham, West Mids.
Dorothy and Philip Lipman, Tudor House, Stow-on-the-Wold, Glos.
Dorrington, Maura, Talbot Walk Antique Centre, Ripley, Surrey.
Dorset Coin Company, Parkstone, Dorset.

Embden, K.B., London, WC2.

Emburey, G.D., Dorking, Surrey.

Emery and Jean Guillou, Roger, Top Banana Antiques Mall, Tetbury, Glos. 2.

Emery, Vicki, Petworth, Sussex West.

Empire Exchange, Manchester, Lancs.

Emporium Antique Centre, The, Lewes, Sussex East.

Enchanted Aviary, The, Bury St. Edmunds, Suffolk.

Engine 'n' Tender, London, SE25.

England, F.J. and S.J., Leek, Staffs.

England's Gallery, Leek, Staffs.

English and Continental Antiques, Eye, Suffolk.

English Country Antiques, Uffculme, Devon.

English Heritage, Bridgnorth, Shrops.

English Rose Antiques, Coggeshall, Essex.

English, Toby and Chris, Wallingford, Oxon.

English, Toby, Wallingford, Oxon.

Enterprise Collectors Market, Eastbourne, Sussex East.

Eprile, R., Edinburgh, Scotland.

Erwin, Marie, Greyabbey Village, Co. Down, Northern Ireland.

Eskdale Antiques, Sleights, Yorks. North.

Eskenazi Ltd, John, London, W1.

Eskenazi Ltd, D.M., London, W1.

Eskenazi, J.E., London, W1.

Esme, The Mall Antiques Arcade, London N1.

Esprit du Jardin, Wingham, Kent.

Essence of Time, The, Lichfield, Staffs.

Essex Antiques, Richard, Langford, Somerset.

Essex, B.R. and C.L., Langford, Somerset.

Essie Carpets, London, W1.

Etcetera Antiques, Seaton, Devon.

Etheridge, John W., Debenham, Suffolk.

Etherington, D., Henley-on-Thames, Oxon.

Eton Antique Bookshop, Windsor, Berks.

Eton Antiques Partnership, Windsor, Berks.

Europa House Antiques, London, SE1.

European Fine Arts and Antiques, Preston, Lancs.

Evans Emporium, Honiton, Devon.

Evans, Ann, Valley, Wales.

Evans, Bob, Honiton, Devon.

Evans, Clive, Wootton Wawen, Warks.

Evans, G., Farnham, Surrey.

Evans, H.S., Bristol, Glos.

Evans, Jeff and John, Cardiff, Wales.

Evans, M., Llangollen, Wales.

Evans, Mark, Darlington, Durham.

Evans, Mark, London, W1.

Evans, T.J., London, W11.

Evens, Anita, Criccieth, Wales.

Eversley Barn Antiques, Eversley, Hants.

Every Cloud, Talbot Walk Antique Centre, Ripley, Surrey.

Evison, Richard, Alfreton, Derbys.

Evonne Antiques, Grays Antique Markets, London W1.

Exall, Christina and Dennis, Tenterden, Kent.

Exeter Rare Books, Exeter, Devon.

Exeter Traders in Collectables Ltd, Exeter, Devon.

Exeter's Antique Centre on the Quay, Exeter, Devon.

Exning Antiques & Interiors, Exning, Suffolk.

Extence Antique Clocks, Leigh, Honiton, Devon.

Extence Antiques, Teignmouth, Devon.

Extence, T.E. and L.E., Teignmouth, Devon.

Eyles, Adrian, Gargrave, Yorks. North.

Ezhar, Top Banana Antiques Mall, Tetbury, Glos. 1.

Ezhar, Top Banana Antiques Mall, Tetbury, Glos. 3 and 4.

F

Faber, James, London, W1.

Facade, The, London, NW1.

Fagins Antiques, Exeter, Devon.

Fair Finds, Rait Village Antiques Centre, Scotland.

Fairbanks Pens, David, Westcliff-on-Sea, Essex.

Fairclough, G. and I., Kendal, Cumbria.

Fairclough, G., Kendal, Cumbria.

Fairfax Fireplaces and General Antiques, Harriet, Langley Burrell, Wilts.

Fairhurst Gallery, The, Norwich, Norfolk.

Faisal's Antiques, Grays Antique Markets, London W1.

Fakenham Antique Centre, Fakenham, Norfolk.

Falle Fine Art Limited, St. Helier, Jersey, Channel Islands.

Falle, John, St. Helier, Jersey, Channel Islands.

Falstaff Antiques, Rolvenden, Kent.

Fanny's Antiques, Reading, Berks.

Fanthorpe, Terry, Rogers Antiques Gallery.

Faques Gallery, Brighton, Sussex East.

Farahar and Sophie DuprÈ - Rare Books, Autographs and Manuscripts, Clive, Calne, Wilts.

Farmhouse Antiques, Stoke Ferry, Norfolk.

Farnham, Paul, Piccadilly Antiques, Batheaston, Somerset.

Farnsworth, S. and V., Moreton-in-Marsh, Glos.

Farouz, Pierre, Walsall, West Mids.

Farrell, G., London, W1.

Farrell, R.J., Burnham-on-Crouch, Essex.

Farrelly Antiques Ltd, Paul, The Swan at Tetsworth, Oxon.

Farriers Antiques, St Nicholas at Wade, Birchington, Kent.

Fars, D.J., Salisbury, Wilts.

Farthing, Ann, Swindon, Wilts.

Farthingale Centre, The, Hartley Wintney, Hants.

Farthings of Exmoor, Lynton, Devon.

Farthings of Rottingdean, Rottingdean, Sussex E.

Fauconberges, Beccles, Suffolk.

Fawcett, L., London, W11.

Fawkes, Keith, London, NW3.

FCR Gallery Ltd, London, W8.

Fecker, Marc, London, W1.

Feldman Ltd, R., London Silver Vaults, London WC2.

Fell, Anthony, Holt, Norfolk.

Fellner, Sandra, Grays Antique Markets, London W1.

Fentum, C., Henley-on-Thames, Oxon.

Fenwick and Fenwick Antiques, Broadway, Worcs.

Fenwick, George and Jane, Broadway, Worcs.

Fenwick, Ian and Christina, Arundel, Sussex West.

Ferder, S. and S., Lymington, Hants.

Ferdinando, Steven, Queen Camel, Somerset.

Ferguson Fine Art, Antiquarius, London SW3.

Ferguson, Alan, Edinburgh, Scotland.

Ferguson, H., Woodbridge, Suffolk.

Ferguson, James, London, SW18.

Ferguson, Lesley, Tetbury, Glos.

Ferguson, Mrs. R., Woodbridge, Suffolk.

Fergusson, James, Chichester, Sussex West.

Fernlea Antiques SGDS, Manchester, Lancs.

Ferry, Harvey, Huntercombe, Oxon.

Few, Ted, London, SW17.

Field Staff Antiques, Rochester, Kent.

Field, Jim, Rochester, Kent.

Fieldings Antiques, Haslingden, Lancs.

Fifteenth Century Bookshop, The, Lewes, Sussex East.

Fileman, David R., Steyning, Sussex West.

Fileman, David, Sandra, John, Adam, Daniel and Rachael, Steyning, Sussex West.

Finch Lighting, Hector, London, SW6.

Finch Norfolk, Simon, Holt, Norfolk.

Finch Rare Books, Simon, London, W1.

Finch, H., London, SW6.

Finchingfield Antiques Centre, Finchingfield, Essex.

Finchley Fine Art Galleries, London, N12.

Fine Art Society plc, The, London, W1.

Green, Jeremy, Chichester, Sussex West.
Green, Laurence, Manchester, Lancs.
Green, M.A., Weston, Herts.
Green, Nicholas and Christopher, Towcester, Northants.
Green, P., Romiley, Cheshire.
Green, R., Queniborough, Leics.
Green, Richard, London, W1.
Green, Robert, Rogers Antiques Gallery.
Green, Ron, Towcester, Northants.
Green, T. and A., Lamb Arcade, Wallingford, Oxon.
Green, Ted & Yvonne, Rogers Antiques Gallery.
Green, Vivian and Roger, Aldermaston, Berks.
Greenaway, C. and P., London, W1.
Greengrass Antiques, Chobham, Surrey.
Greengrass, D., Chobham, Surrey.
Greenman, Sam, London, N12.
Greens of Cheltenham Ltd, Cheltenham, Glos.
Greenstein, Saul, Grays Antique Markets, London W1.
Greenwall Antiques, Jonathan, Sandgate, Kent.
Greenway Antiques, Colin, Witney, Oxon.
Greenwich Antiques Market, London, SE10.
Greenwood (Fine Art), W., Burneston, Yorks. North.
Greenwood, Emilia, Ginnel Antiques Centre, The, Harrogate, Yorks North.
Greer, Robin, London, SW6.
Gregory, Bottley and Lloyd, London, SW6.
Gregory, George, Bath, Somerset.
Gregory, H. and C., London, W11.
Gregory, Henry, London, W11.
Gregory, Martyn, London, SW1.
Gregory, Michael, Chale, Isle of Wight.
Gregory, Michael, London, SW1.
Gregory, N., Wendover, Bucks.
Gresham Books, Crewkerne, Somerset.
Grey, Michael, Jubilee Hall Antiques Centre, Lechlade, Glos.
Grey-Harris and Co, Bristol, Glos.
Greysmith, Brenda, Ashburton, Devon.
Greystoke Antiques, Sherborne, Dorset.
Grice Antiques, Alan, Ormskirk, Lancs.
Griffin Antiques Ltd, Simon, London, W1.
Griffin Antiques, Angel Arcade, London N1.
Griffin, Emma and Nick, Leighton Buzzard, Beds.
Griffin, S.J., London, W1.
Griffith, J.J., Canterbury, Kent.
Griffiths Antiques, David, London, N1.
Griffiths Antiques, Miles, Clitheroe, Lancs.
Griffiths, J., Bath, Somerset.
Griffiths, Neville, Woolpit, Suffolk.
Griffiths, P., Narberth, Wales.

Griffiths, Richard, Tetbury, Glos.
Griffiths, W. and B., Burscough, Lancs.
Grimes House Antiques & Fine Art, Moreton-in-Marsh, Glos.
Grimes Militaria, Chris, Bristol, Glos.
Grimes, Chris and Hazel, Bristol, Glos.
Grindley, Nick, Uppingham, Rutland.
Gripper, Robert, Ascott-under-Wychwood, Oxon.
Grosvenor House Interiors, Beaconsfield, Bucks.
Grosvenor Prints, London, WC2.
Groth, Hakan, London, SW6.
Grothier, Robert, The Furniture Cave, London SW10.
Grove Antiques Centre Ltd, The, Honiton, Devon.
Grove Rare Books, Bolton Abbey, Yorks. North.
Grover, D.R., Chichester, Sussex West.
Groves, Elfyn and Elaine, Woburn, Beds.
Groves, Steven and Caroline, Melbury Osmond, Dorset.
Guest & Gray, Grays Antique Markets, London W1.
Guest & Philips, Beverley, Yorks. East.
Guest & Phillips, Driffield, Yorks. East.
Guest, Karen and Philip, Beverley, Yorks. East.
Guinevere Antiques, London, SW6.
Gulesserian, Alice, Grays Antique Markets, London W1.
Gullane Antiques, Gullane, Scotland.
Gumbrell, K., Hastings Antique Centre, St. Leonards-on-Sea, E. Sussex.
Gunst, Gaby, Tenterden, Kent.
Guth, Stephen, The Swan at Tetsworth, Oxon.
Guthrie, Chris, Honiton, Devon.
Gutlin Clocks and Antiques, London, SW6.
Gwilliam, D.L., Bruton, Somerset.
Gwilliam, Edred A.F., Cricklade, Wilts.
Gwilliams, Ray, Weybridge, Surrey.
Gwynfair Antiques, Holyhead, Wales.
Gwyrdd, Top Banana Antiques Mall, Tetbury, Glos. 2.

H
H. Antiques, Top Banana Antiques Mall, Tetbury, Glos. 3 and 4.
H.L Brown group of jewellers, York, Yorks. North.
H.L.B. Antiques, Bournemouth, Dorset.
Haas, Otto, London, NW3.
Habibi Oriental Antiques, Grays Antique Markets, London W1.
Hacker, Peter F., Harrogate, Yorks. North.
Hackett, Gregory, London, N1.
Hackler's Jewellers, Preston, Lancs.
Hadfield (Hon. FBHI), G.K. and J.V., Great Salkeld, Cumbria.
Hadfield, G.K., Great Salkeld, Cumbria.

Hadfield-Tilly, N.R., Great Salkeld, Cumbria.
Hadley Bookseller, Peter J., Harwich, Essex.
Hadlow Down Antiques, Hadlow Down, Sussex East.
Hagen Gallery, Richard, Broadway, Worcs.
Hague, C., Bristol, Glos.
Hakemi, Farah, London, W8.
Hakeney Antiques, David, Beverley, Yorks. East.
Halcyon Days, London, W1.
Haldane, J., Finningham, Suffolk.
Hale, Barbara, Top Banana Antiques Mall, Tetbury, Glos. 2.
Hale, Barbara, Top Banana Antiques Mall, Tetbury, Glos. 3 and 4.
Halewood & Sons, Preston, Lancs.
Halewood, M., Preston, Lancs.
Haley, S., Halifax, Yorks. West.
Haliden Oriental Rug Shop, Bath, Somerset.
Hall Ltd, Douglas, Brighton, Sussex East.
Hall, A., Bournemouth, Dorset.
Hall, Anthony C., Twickenham, Middx.
Hall, Christopher, Alfies Antique Market, London NW8.
Hall, D.D.J., Great Malvern, Worcs.
Hall, L.M., Great Malvern, Worcs.
Hall, Liza, Nutley, Sussex East.
Hall, N, Bath, Somerset.
Hall, Robert, London, W9.
Hall-Bakker Decorative Arts, Antiques at Heritage, Woodstock, Oxon.
Haller, B. J., Deddington, Oxon.
Hallesy, H., Swansea, Wales.
Hallett, R.A. and L. P., Llanidloes, Wales.
Halliday, James, Taunton, Somerset.
Hallidays (Fine Antiques) Ltd, Dorchester-on-Thames, Oxon.
Halliday's, Taunton, Somerset.
Hallmark Antiques, Grays Antique Markets, London W1.
Hallmark Jewellers, Brighton, Sussex East.
Hall's Bookshop, Tunbridge Wells, Kent.
Halsall Hall Antiques, Southport Antiques Centre, Southport, Merseyside.
Halstead, Roger G., Bromley, Kent.
Halstead's Antiques, Bromley, Kent.
Hamblin, J. and M. A., Yeovil, Somerset.
Hamblin, John, Yeovil, Somerset.
Hamilton and Co, A.D., Glasgow, Scotland.
Hamilton Antiques, Burnham Market, Norfolk.
Hamilton Billiards & Games Co., Knebworth, Herts.
Hamilton Ltd, Ross, London, SW1.
Hamilton, Hugh, Knebworth, Herts.
Hamilton, M. & J., London Silver

Lewis, Laura, Peel, Isle of Man.
Lewis, Leo and Mrs J. L., Bruton, Somerset.
Lewis, M. and D., London, W11.
Lewis, Michael, Yoxford, Suffolk.
Lewis, N., Hampton, Middx.
Lewis, Pauline and Robert, Halesworth, Suffolk.
Lewis, Sally, Rogers Antiques Gallery.
Lewis, Stuart D., Leigh-on-Sea, Essex.
Leyburn Antiques Centre, Leyburn, Yorks. North.
Leyland, D.J. and C.J., Woodhall Spa, Lincs.
Liberty, London, W1.
Lickley, R., Carmarthen, Wales.
Lieberman, Rachel, The Mall Antiques Arcade, London N1.
Light, P. B., Stamford, Lincs.
Light, Robert, Moreton-in-Marsh, Glos.
Lightbown, Richard, London, SW6.
Lightbown, Richard, Manningford Bruce, Wilts.
Lightfoot, Peter, Warwick, Warks.
Lillistone, C., Ipswich, Suffolk.
Limelight Movie Art, London, SW3.
Limited Editions, Mobberley, Cheshire.
Linden and Co. (Antiques) Ltd, London Silver Vaults, London WC2.
Linden, H.M. and S. C., London Silver Vaults, London WC2.
Lindfield Galleries, Lindfield, Sussex West.
Lindsay, Bruce, London, SW1.
Lindsey Antiques, North Berwick, Scotland.
Lindsey Court Architectural, Market Rason, Lincs.
Lindsey, Alan, North Berwick, Scotland.
Lindsey, E.A., Gullane, Scotland.
Lindsey, Stephen Alan, North Berwick, Scotland.
Lindsey, Stephen, North Berwick, Scotland.
Lines, Derek and Jill, Wychbold, Worcs.
Linford, Jean, Red House Antiques Centre, York, Yorks. North.
Ling, Susan, The Swan at Tetsworth, Oxon.
Lion Gallery and Bookshop, Knutsford, Cheshire.
Lion, Witch and Lampshade, Blakeney, Glos.
Lipitch Ltd, Michael, London, W1K.
Lipitch Ltd, Peter, London, SW3.
Lipka & Son Arcade, B., London, W11.
Lis, Jan, London, SW5.
Lister, Martin and Shelagh, The Swan at Tetsworth, Oxon.
Litt Antiques, David, Ampthill, Beds.
Litt, David and Helen, Ampthill, Beds.
Little Furniture Shop, A, Shrewsbury, Shrops.
Little Gallery, The, Pittenweem, Scotland.

Little Jem's, Penzance, Cornwall.
Little Nells, Durham House Antiques Centre, Stow-on-the-Wold, Glos.
Little River Oriental Antiques, Antiquarius, London SW3.
Littlebury Antiques - Littlebury Restorations Ltd , Saffron Walden, Essex.
Livesley, W.H., Macclesfield, Cheshire.
Livett, Peter and Mrs Joy, Ardingly, Sussex West.
Livingston, Rosemary, The Swan at Tetsworth, Oxon.
Livingstone, Neil, Dundee, Scotland.
Llanishen Antiques, Cardiff, Wales.
Llewellyn, F., London, SE10.
Lloyd Antiques, Robin, Ross-on-Wye, Herefs.
Lloyd, A., London, W1.
Lloyd, Andrew, Bath, Somerset.
Lloyd, M.R., Sandgate, Kent.
Lloyd, Sally, Woburn, Beds.
Lloyd, Tim, Lechlade, Glos.
Lo, Monty, Grays Antique Markets, London W1.
Lochhead, Stuart, London, W1.
Lodge, John C., Salisbury, Wilts.
Loes, Harry, London, EC1.
Logan Antiques, Mo, Ashburton, Devon.
Logan, Martin & Mo, Ashburton, Devon.
Lomax, E, Ribchester, Lancs.
Lombard Antiques, Honiton, Devon.
London Antique Gallery, London, W8.
London Cigarette Card Co. Ltd, The, Somerton, Somerset.
London House Antique Centre, Moreton-in-Marsh, Glos.
London House Antiques, Shipston-on-Stour, Warks.
London House Oriental Rugs and Carpets, Boston Spa, Yorks. West.
London House Oriental Rugs at Geoffrey Benton & Son, York, Yorks North.
London Silver Vaults, The, London, WC2.
London Taxidermy, East Molesey, Surrey.
London, Sue, Stow-on-the-Wold, Glos.
Lonesome Pine Antiques, Burnley, Lancs.
Long Melford Antiques Centre, Long Melford, Suffolk.
Long Street Antiques, Tetbury, Glos.
Long, J.W.H., Aberford, Yorks. West.
Long, Michael D., Leicester, Leics.
Long, Stephen, London, SW10.
Longmire Ltd (Three Royal Warrants), London, SW1.
Longmore, Michael, Grays Antique Markets, London W1.
Lonsdale, Barry, Ely, Cambs.
Looking Glass of Bath, Bath, Somerset.
Loomes, Brian and Joy , Pateley Bridge,

Yorks. North.
Loomes, Brian, Pateley Bridge, Yorks. North.
Loquens Gallery, The, Cheltenham, Glos.
Loquens, Stephen and Mrs Jean, Cheltenham, Glos.
Loraine Antiques, Gordon, Rait Village Antiques Centre, Scotland.
Loraine, Liane and Gordon, Rait Village Antiques Centre, Scotland.
Lord Antiques, Alan, Hythe, Kent.
Lord, Frank H., London, W1.
Lord, R.G. and M., Hythe, Kent.
Lorford, Toby, Tetbury, Glos.
Lorfords Antiques, Tetbury, Glos.
Lorie, Elisabeth, Kensington Church Street Antiques Centre, London W8.
Loska, John, Brighton, Sussex East.
Loughborough Antiques, Loughborough, Leics.
Louisa Francis & S.L. Walker, Brasted, Kent.
Love Lane Antiques, Nantwich, Cheshire.
Love, David, Harrogate, Yorks. North.
Love, R.M. and M.A., Worsley, Lancs.
Loveday at the Furniture Vault, David, London, N1.
Loveday, David, The Furniture Cave, London SW10.
Loveday, Mike, Top Banana Antiques Mall, Tetbury, Glos. 1.
Loveday, Mike, Top Banana Antiques Mall, Tetbury, Glos. 3 and 4.
Lovegrove Fine Art, Julian, Chilham, Kent.
Lovegrove, Julian, Chilham, Kent.
Lovejoy Antiques, Conwy, Wales.
Loveland, H., Talbot Walk Antique Centre, Ripley, Surrey.
Lovell, C.A., Watford, Herts.
Lovelock, Sarah, Warwick, Warks.
Lovett, Michael J., Northampton, Northants.
Low Antiques, Michael, Forres, Scotland.
Low, Gary, Melksham, Wilts.
Lowe & Sons, Chester, Cheshire.
Lowe of Loughborough, Loughborough, Leics.
Lower, Graham and Penny, Flimwell, Sussex East.
Lower, Graham, Flimwell, Sussex East.
Lower, R.R., London, W8.
Lucas, C., London, N16.
Lucas, N. and C., Amersham, Bucks.
Lucas, Peter, Penistone, Yorks. South.
Luck, R.J., Hastings, Sussex East.
Luck, S.L., West Malling, Kent.
Luck, Steve, Wallingford, Oxon.
Luckenbooth, The, Rait Village Antiques Centre, Scotland.
Luckhurst Antiques, J., Sandgate, Kent.
Lugley Antiques & Interiors, Newport,

Markham & Son Ltd, E. J. , Colchester, Essex.

Markies, Jeroen, Forest Row, Sussex E.

Marks Antiques, London, W1.

Marks Jewellers and Antique Dealers, Oldham, Lancs.

Marks Ltd, Barrie, London, N2.

Marks, Anthony, London, W1.

Marks, Michael, Grays Antique Markets, London W1.

Marlborough Fine Art (London) Ltd, London, W1.

Marlborough Parade Antique Centre, The, Marlborough, Wilts.

Marlborough Rare Books Ltd, London, W1.

Marles, O. , Sutton Valence, Kent.

Marles, O., Maidstone, Kent.

Marney, Patrick, Diss, Norfolk.

Marnier Antiques, Edward, East Knoyle, Somerset.

Marno, Felicity, London, W8.

Marpole, A., Burwell, Cambs.

Marr Antiques, Iain, Beauly, Scotland.

Marr, I. and A., Beauly, Scotland.

Marrin, Patrick, Folkestone, Kent.

Marrin's Bookshop, Folkestone, Kent.

Marriott, Ann, Chipping Norton, Oxon.

Marriott, T.I., Beaconsfield, Bucks.

Marryat, Richmond, Surrey.

Marsh Antique Clocks Ltd, G.E., Winchester, Hants.

Marshall Gallery, London, W14.

Marshall Phillips, London, W4.

Marshall, Alan, Kirton, Lincs.

Marshall, D.A. and J., London, W14.

Marshall, Isabel, Ramsey, Isle of Man.

Marshall, P., Carhampton, Somerset.

Marshall, Phyllis M. and Simon, Burford, Oxon.

Marshall, S., Norwich, Norfolk.

Marshall, Trevor, Wells, Somerset.

Marshall's Antiques Warehouse, Kevin, Hull, Yorks. East.

Marshalls of Wells, Wells, Somerset.

Martin & Son, Peter J., Windsor, Berks.

Martin (Coins) Ltd, C.J., London, N14.

Martin and Co. Ltd, Cheltenham, Glos.

Martin Antiques, Robin, London, W11.

Martin, A., Sandgate, Kent.

Martin, A., Sandgate, Kent.

Martin, Carol, Talbot Walk Antique Centre, Ripley, Surrey.

Martin, George Perez, Petworth, Sussex West.

Martin, Paul, London, W11.

Martin, Pauline, St Nicholas at Wade, Birchington, Kent.

Martin, Peter J., Windsor, Berks.

Martin, R. and S., Risby, Suffolk.

Martinez Antiques, J., Edinburgh, Scotland.

Martinez, Jacquie, Edinburgh, Scotland.

Martinez, Joe, Edinburgh, Scotland.

Martin-Taylor Antiques, David, London,

W11.

Martin-Zakheim, Christopher, London, SW1.

Martire, Francesca, Alfies Antique Market, London NW8.

Martlesham Antiques, Martlesham, Suffolk.

Martyn, Dee, Tunbridge Wells, Kent.

Mary Wise & Grosvenor Antiques, Kensington Church Street Antiques Centre, London W8.

Mascaro, R., Plymouth, Devon.

Masham, Douglas, Rotherfield, Sussex East.

Maskill, Heather, Shrewsbury, Shrops.

Mason, Bill and Sue, Great Shelford, Cambs.

Mason, Harry, Brighton, Sussex East.

Mason, Jeremy, London, SW1.

Mason, Nicola, Tunbridge Wells, Kent.

Mason, R.A., Bournemouth, Dorset.

Massey and Son, D.J., Macclesfield, Cheshire.

Massey, Allison, Grays Antique Markets, London W1.

Massingham Antiques, Roy, Brasted, Kent.

Masters, John, Westerham, Kent.

Matcham, Trevor, Old Bank Antiques Centre, Bath, Somerset.

Mathaf Gallery Ltd, London, SW1.

Matheou, M., Tetbury, Glos.

Mathias, R., St. Albans, Herts.

Matlock Antiques and Collectables Centre, Matlock, Derbys.

Matthews, Bill, Top Banana Antiques Mall, Tetbury, Glos. 3 and 4.

Matthiesen Fine Art Ltd., London, SW1.

Maud's Attic, Ipswich, Suffolk.

Mauleverer, Boroughbridge, Yorks. North.

Maurice, Alison, Hythe, Kent.

Maxfield House Antiques, Warminster, Wilts.

Maxtone Graham, R.M., Hythe, Kent.

Maxwell, Margaret, Innerleithen, Scotland.

May Antiques, Greta, Tonbridge, Kent.

May, Desmond and Ann, Brambridge, Hants.

Mayes, R.K., Ginnel Antiques Centre, The, Harrogate, Yorks North.

Mayfair Carpet Gallery Ltd, London, SE1.

Mayfair Gallery Ltd, London, W1.

Mayflower Antiques, Long Melford, Suffolk.

Mayhew, Andy, Evesham, Worcs.

Maynard Antiques, Mark, London, SW6.

Mays, Maggie, Buxton, Derbys.

Mazaheri-Asadi, Masoud, Stockbridge, Hants.

Mazar Antiques, Grays Antique Markets, London W1.

McAvoy, Mike, Ludlow, Shrops.

McBain Antique Exports, The Antiques Complex, Exeter, Devon.

McBains Antiques, Exeter, Devon., Exeter, Devon.

McCall, B., Aberdeen, Scotland.

McCalls (Aberdeen), Aberdeen, Scotland.

McCalls Limited, Aberdeen, Scotland.

McCann, A.D., Holyhead, Wales.

McCarthy, Owen, Ross-on-Wye, Herefs.

McCarthy, T.P. and C.A., Liss, Hants.

McCartney, Graham, The Swan at Tetsworth, Oxon.

McClaren, J., Gosport, Hants.

McConnell Fine Books, Deal, Kent.

McConnell, Audrey, Durham House Antiques Centre, Stow-on-the-Wold, Glos.

McConnell, Nick, Deal, Kent.

McCormick, P., Knaresborough, Yorks. North.

McCreddie, B.S., Ludlow, Shrops.

McCulloch Antiques, John, Felixstowe, Suffolk.

McDonald Antiques, Joy, London, SW13.

McDonald, Angela, London, SW13.

McDonald, Fiona, London, SW6.

McDonald-Hobley, Noele, Antiquarius, London SW3.

McEwan Gallery, The, Ballater, Scotland.

McEwan, D., P. and R., Ballater, Scotland.

McGonigle, Joseph, Glasgow, Scotland.

McGowan, P., Shenton, Leics.

McGregor, Veronica, Halstead, Essex.

McGregor, Veronica, Sudbury, Suffolk.

McHale, Tom and Mary, Chichester, Sussex West.

McHugo, M., Stourbridge, West Mids.

McKechnie, George, Brighton, Sussex East.

McKeivor, J., Chilcompton, Somerset.

McKenna and Co, London, SW3.

McKenna, C. and M., London, SW3.

McKenzie, J.W., Ewell, Surrey.

McKinley, D., Wiveliscombe, Somerset.

McKinnon, Fiona, London, WC2.

McKoys Fine Art, Robert, Alfies Antique Market, London NW8.

McLaughlin, A.J. and Mrs B., Manchester, Lancs.

McLaughlin, Ronan, Ballymena, Co. Antrim, Northern Ireland.

McLeod, David and Patricia, Knutsford, Cheshire.

McLoughlin, Alan, Truro, Cornwall.

McMonagle, David, Newcastle-upon-Tyne, Tyne and Wear.

McMullan & Son, D., Manchester, Lancs.

McNaughton's Bookshop, Edinburgh, Scotland.

McPherson Antiques, R. and G.,

Guernsey, Channel Islands.
Ray Rare and Out of Print Books, Janette, York, Yorks. North.
Ray, M.T., Nottingham, Notts.
Rayment Antiques, Derek and Tina, Barton, Cheshire.
Rayment, D.J. and K.M., Barton, Cheshire.
Rayment, D.M., Petworth, Sussex West.
Raynalds Mansion, Much Wenlock, Shrops.
Rayner Art, Simon, Jubilee Hall Antiques Centre, Lechlade, Glos.
Rayner, Barry, Tenterden, Kent.
Rayson, Gill, Henley-in-Arden, Warks.
Rb Gallery, Ginnel Antiques Centre, The, Harrogate, Yorks North.
RBR Grp, Grays Antique Markets, London W1.
Rea, C.J., Sleights, Yorks. North.
Read - Period Furniture, Alan, Horncastle, Lincs.
Read Antique Sciences, Mike, St. Ives, Cornwall.
Read Antiques, John, Martlesham, Suffolk.
Read, Bonnita, Woodford Green, Essex.
Read, James, Bruton, Somerset.
Reason, Peter, Hungerford, Berks.
Recollect Dolls Hospital, Burgess Hill, Sussex West.
Recollections Antiques Ltd, London, NW3.
Recollections, Poynton, Cheshire.
Record Detector, London, E4.
Red Goblet Ltd, Petersfield, Hants.
Red House Antiques Centre, The, York, Yorks. North.
Red Lane Antiques, Durham House Antiques Centre, Stow-on-the-Wold, Glos.
Red Lane Antiques, Jubilee Hall Antiques Centre, Lechlade, Glos.
Red Lion Antiques Arcade, The, London, W11.
Red Lodge Antiques, Screveton, Notts.
Red Shop, The, Wolverhampton, West Mids.
Redford Antiques & Interiors, Robert, Altrincham, Cheshire.
Redford, S. and R., Altrincham, Cheshire.
Redleaf Gallery, Tunbridge Wells, Kent.
Redmile, Anthony, The Furniture Cave, London SW10.
Redruth Indoor Market, Redruth, Cornwall.
Reed, Anthony, Bath, Somerset.
Reed, Marilyn, Topsham, Devon.
Reed, Martyn K., Cheam, Surrey.
Rees, Suzy, Tunbridge Wells, Kent.
Reeve, Andrew, Windsor, Berks.
Reeve, Anthony, Milton Common, Oxon.
Reeve, J.C. and D.J., Warwick, Warks.
Reeve, James, Warwick, Warks.

Reeves, P., St. Helen Auckland, Durham.
Reeves, P.W. and L., Gomshall, Surrey.
Reeves, Paul, London, W8.
Reeves, V., Canterbury, Kent.
Reference Works Ltd., Swanage, Dorset.
Regal Watches, Grays Antique Markets, London W1.
Regan, David M., Southport, Merseyside.
Regency Antique Trading Ltd., Stourbridge, West Mids.
Regent Antiques, London, N4.
Regent House Gallery, London, SW11.
Reid, Colin and Debbie, Sandiacre, Notts.
Reid, Susie, Edinburgh, Scotland.
Reid-Davies, Alison and Graeme, Berkhamsted, Herts.
Reilly, Antiquarius, London SW3.
Reilly, J., London, W1.
Reily Cousins, E.M. and S.A., Dorchester-on-Thames, Oxon.
Reindeer Antiques Centre, The, Potterspury, Northants.
Reindeer Antiques Ltd, London, W8.
Reindeer Antiques Ltd, Potterspury, Northants.
Relf Antiques, Ian, Tunbridge Wells, Kent.
Relics, Stalham, Norfolk.
Remington, Reg and Philip, Truro, Cornwall.
Renaissance, Solihull, West Mids.
Renato, Alfies Antique Market, London NW8.
Rendezvous Gallery, The, Aberdeen, Scotland.
Renney Antiques, Corbridge, Northumbs.
Retro, Stourbridge, West Mids.
Rex Antiques, Chagford, Devon.
Reynolds Antiques, C., Oakham, Rutland.
Reynolds Antiques, P., The Antiques Complex, Exeter, Devon.
Reynolds, C.H. and D.M., Pickering, Yorks. North.
Reynolds, Julia, Warwick, Warks.
Reynolds, Rosemary, Warminster, Wilts.
Reynor, Kevin, Cromer, Norfolk.
Rezai Persian Carpets, London, W11.
Rezai, A., London, W11.
Rhodes, Isobel, Woodbridge, Suffolk.
Rhodes, J., London, SW6.
Rhudle Mill, Kilmichael Glassary, Scotland.
Rich & Michael Rich, Steven, London, W1.
Richards and Sons, David, London, W1.
Richards, Jane, Heanor, Derbys.
Richards, L., London, W11.
Richards, M. and E., London, W1.
Richardson Antiques, Lindsey, Durham House Antiques Centre, Stow-on-the-Wold, Glos.

Richardson, Lindsey, Jubilee Hall Antiques Centre, Lechlade, Glos.
Richardson, Tim, Flaxton, Yorks. North.
Richardson, Tina, Bovey Tracey, Devon.
Richmond, Marion and Robin, Wigtown, Scotland.
Ricketts, Robert, Dunster, Somerset.
Rideal, Elizabeth, Waverton, Cheshire.
Rider, D.I., Pewsey, Wilts.
Ridgeway Antiques, Westcliff-on-Sea, Essex.
Ridgeway, D.A. and J.A., Bridgnorth, Shrops.
Ridler, P.W., Pershore, Worcs.
Right Angle, Brackley, Northants.
Riley, J. and M., Chichester, Sussex West.
Riley-Smith, Crispian, Kirkby Malham, Yorks. North.
Ringles Cross Antiques, Uckfield, Sussex East.
Risby Barn, The, Risby, Suffolk.
Ritchie, A. & R., St. Helier, Jersey, Channel Islands.
Ritchie, J., Weymouth, Dorset.
Ritchie, V., Kendal, Cumbria.
Riverside Antiques Centre, Sawbridgeworth, Herts.
Rivett Antiques and Bygones, Sue, Fakenham, Norfolk.
Rix, H., London, SW11.
Roadside Antiques, Greystoke, Cumbria.
Robb, Helen, Onchan, Isle of Man.
Robbs, R.J., Wisbech, Cambs.
Robert Bush at, Tower Bridge Antiques, London, SE1.
Robert, Cheney Antiques & EK Antiques, Finedon, Northants.
Roberts Antiques, Derek, Tonbridge, Kent.
Robert's Antiques, St. Helier, Jersey, Channel Islands.
Roberts, A.H., Bletchingley, Surrey.
Roberts, Dave, Great Malvern, Worcs.
Roberts, Derek and Valerie, The Edenbridge Galleries, Edenbridge.
Roberts, Doris, Lostwithiel, Cornwall.
Roberts, I., Cardiff, Wales.
Roberts, I.W. and I.E., Bolton, Lancs.
Roberts, Martyn, Bristol, Glos.
Roberts, Steve and Helen, Llandudno Junction, Wales.
Roberts, T., Bletchingley, Surrey.
Roberts, T.J., Uppingham, Rutland.
Roberts, Tim and Cathy, Ringstead, Norfolk.
Robertson Antiques, Leon, The Antiques Complex, Exeter, Devon.
Robertson, John, Reigate, Surrey.
Robertson, P.W., Hinckley, Leics.
Robertson, Scott, Edinburgh, Scotland.
Robin Antiques, Rogers Antiques Gallery.
Robinson Antiques, John, Wigan, Lancs.
Robinson, C.A., Aberford, Yorks. West.

House Antiques Centre, Stow-on-the-Wold, Glos.
Tarporley Antique Centre, Tarporley, Cheshire.
Tarrant Antiques, Lorraine, Ringwood, Hants.
Tartan Antiques, The Swan at Tetsworth, Oxon.
Tatham-Losh (Top Banana Antiques Mall), Julian, Cheltenham, Glos.
Tatham-Losh Ltd, Julian, Cheltenham, Glos.
Tatham-Losh, Julian, Tetbury, Glos.
Tatham-Losh, Julian, Tetbury, Glos.
Tatham-Losh, Julian, Tetbury, Glos.
Tattum, Christina, The Mall Antiques Arcade, London N1.
Tauber Antiques, Laurence, Surbiton, Surrey.
Taunton Antiques Market - Silver Street, Taunton, Somerset.
Tavistock Antiques Ltd, St. Neots, Cambs.
Tayler, Caroline, Freshwater, Isle of Wight.
Taylor Antiques, Martin, Wolverhampton, West Mids.
Taylor Fine Arts, Robin, Wakefield, Yorks. West.
Taylor Gallery Ltd, The, London, SW7.
Taylor, Andrew, Top Banana Antiques Mall, Tetbury, Glos. 1.
Taylor, Brian, Kelling, Norfolk.
Taylor, D., Driffield, Yorks. East.
Taylor, Jason, Ashton-under-Lyne, Lancs.
Taylor, Jeremy, London, SW7.
Taylor, M.C., Bournemouth, Dorset.
Taylor, Mark, Bournemouth, Dorset.
Taylor, Robin and Julie, Wakefield, Yorks. West.
Taylor, Seth, London, SW11.
Taylor, Stanley, Durham House Antiques Centre, Stow-on-the-Wold, Glos.
Taylor-Smith Antiques, Westerham, Kent.
Taylor-Smith Books, Westerham, Kent.
Taylor-Smith, Ashton, Westerham, Kent.
Tea & Antiques, Felixstowe, Suffolk.
Teagowns & Textiles, Leominster, Herefs.
Tebbs, J.J., Conisholme, Lincs.
Teger Trading, London, N4.
Telephone Lines, Cheltenham, Glos.
Temperley Fine and Antiquarian Books, David, Birmingham, West Mids.
Temperley, D. and R.A., Birmingham, West Mids.
Temple Gallery, London, W11.
Temple, K., Raughton Head, Cumbria.
Temple, R.C.C., London, W11.
Templeman, Bob, Abernyte, Scotland.
Templeman, Lynda, Rait Village

Antiques Centre, Scotland.
Templeman, Lynda, Rait Village Antiques Centre, Scotland.
Templeman, Robert, Doune, Scotland.
Tenterden Antiques and Silver Vaults, Tenterden, Kent.
Terry, Pamela, Rogers Antiques Gallery.
Tessier, The Swan at Tetsworth, Oxon.
Tessiers Ltd, London, W1.
Tetbury Old Books, Tetbury, Glos.
Tetlow, Robert, Debden, Essex.
Tew, T., London, N2.
Tewkesbury Antiques & Collectables Centre, Tewkesbury, Glos.
Thakeham Furniture Ltd, Petworth, Sussex West.
Thames Oriental Rug Co, Henley-on-Thames, Oxon.
Thatcher, K., Londonderry, Co. Londonderry, Northern Ireland.
The Antique Consignment Company Ltd., Southport Antiques Centre, Southport, Merseyside.
The Antique Enamel Co., London, W1.
The Bothy, East Molesey, Surrey.
The Cavern Antique & Collectors Centre, Oldham, Lancs.
The Chase Antiques Barn, Wettenhall, Cheshire.
The Clock Shop, Beaumaris, Wales.
The Curio Centre Ltd, Telford, Shrops.
The General Store & Hidden Treasures, Ringstead, Norfolk.
The Girl Can't Help It, Alfies Antique Market, London NW8.
The Heart of Hatton Garden, London, EC1.
The Looking Glass, Bourton-on-the-Water, Glos.
The Old House Gallery, Oakham, Rutland.
The Red Teapot Arcade, London, W11.
Theatre Antiques Centre, The, Framlingham, Suffolk.
Themes and Variations, London, W11.
Theobald, D., Cambridge, Cambs.
Thesaurus (Jersey) Ltd, St. Helier, Jersey, Channel Islands.
Thirkill Antiques, Leyburn, Yorks. North.
Thirteen, Alfies Antique Market, London NW8.
Thistle & Rose, Rait Village Antiques Centre, Scotland.
Thistle Antiques, Aberdeen, Scotland.
Thistlethwaite, E., Settle, Yorks. North.
Thomas, H.R. & T., Bladon, Oxon.
Thomas, N., Talbot Walk Antique Centre, Ripley, Surrey.
Thomas, Rena, Norton, Durham.
Thompson, A.L., Bourne, Lincs.
Thompson, Antique Trader, A.L., Bourne, Lincs.
Thompson, B., London, N1.
Thompson, Bruce, Norwich, Norfolk.

Thompson, J. and S., Aldeburgh, Suffolk.
Thompson, J.J., Easingwold, Yorks. North.
Thompson, N.D.A. and E.K., Honiton, Devon.
Thompson, N.F., Buxton, Derbys.
Thompson, S., Arundel, Sussex West.
Thompson's Gallery, Aldeburgh, Suffolk.
Thomson - Albany Gallery, Bill, London, SW1.
Thomson, David, Ripon, Yorks. North.
Thomson, Ian, Bakewell, Derbys.
Thomson, R.N., St. Helier, Jersey, Channel Islands.
Thomson, R.N., St. Helier, Jersey, Channel Islands.
Thomson, W.B., London, SW1.
Thomson's, St. Helier, Jersey, Channel Islands.
Thorburn, Susan, North Walsham, Norfolk.
Thorn, David J., Budleigh Salterton, Devon.
Thornbury, M.W. and C.S., Brinkworth, Wilts.
Thornhill Galleries, London, SW18.
Thornhill, J., Shrewsbury, Shrops.
Thornley, G. and E.M., Helmsley, Yorks. North.
Thornton Architectural Antiques Ltd, Andy, Halifax, Yorks. West.
Thornton, R.H. and R.J., Harrogate, Yorks. North.
Thornton, Wayne, London, W1.
Thorntons of Harrogate, Harrogate, Yorks. North.
Thorpe, Bob and Sue, Canterbury, Kent.
Thorpe, Miwa, Antiquarius, London SW3.
Thredder, Phil, Ross-on-Wye, Herefs.
Thrie Estaits, The, Edinburgh, Scotland.
Throckmorton, Isabel, Market Harborough, Leics.
Through the Looking Glass Ltd, London, W8.
Thrower, D. and V., Petworth, Sussex West.
Thrower, D. and V., Wisborough, Sussex West.
Thuillier, William, London, W1.
Thurlow, Kate, London, SW1.
Thurstans, C.M. and D., Stillington, Yorks. North.
Thwaites Fine Stringed Instruments, Watford, Herts.
Ticciati, Giovanna, Petworth, Sussex W.
Tickety Boo Antiques, Rait Village Antiques Centre, Scotland.
Tiffin, Sylvia, Penrith, Cumbria.
Tiffins Antiques, Emsworth, Hants.
Tildesley, B. and J., Thirsk, Yorks. North.
Till, Michael J., London, N1.
Tilleke, David, Redbourn, Herts.
Tilley, A.G.J. and A.A.J.C., Sheffield, Yorks. South.

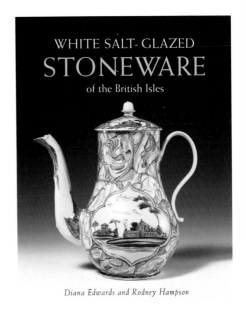

PLEASE USE THIS FORM FOR A NEW OR SUBSTANTIALLY ALTERED ENTRY

Please complete and return this form; there is no charge

NAME OF SHOP ....

ADDRESS OF SHOP ....

....

full address including county and postal code

Name (or names) and initials of proprietor(s) ....

(Mr/Mrs/Miss/or title)

Previous trading address (if applicable) ....

State whether 'Trade Only' (Yes or No) ....

BADA (Yes or No) .... LAPADA (Yes or No) ....

Year Established .... Resident on premises (Yes or No) ....

OPENING   (One entry, e.g. '9.30-5.30' if open all day or part day
HOURS: Two entries, e.g. '9.30-1.00, 2.00-5.30' if closed for lunch)

Please put 'CLOSED' and 'BY APPT.' where applicable

	Morning	Afternoon
Sunday	....	....
Monday	....	....
Tuesday	....	....
Wednesday	....	....
Thursday	....	....
Friday	....	....
Saturday	....	....

SIZE OF SHOWROOM: Small (up to 600 sq. ft.) ....

Medium (600 to 1,500 sq. ft.) ....

Large (over 1,500 sq. ft.) ....

HOW TO GET TO YOUR SHOP (BUSINESS)
Brief helpful details from the nearest well-known road:

....

....

....

....

OF WHAT DOES YOUR STOCK CHIEFLY CONSIST?

(A) Please list in order of importance	(B) Approximate period or date of stock	(C) Indication of price range of stock eg £50-£100 or £5-£25
1. (Principal stock)		
2.		
3.		

IS PARKING *OUTSIDE* YOUR SHOP (BUSINESS) Easy (Yes or No)

TELEPHONE NUMBER Business ....

Home ....

(only if customers can ring for appointments outside business hours)

V.A.T. scheme operated – Standard/Special/Both ....

SERVICES OFFERED:

Valuations (Yes or No) ....

Restorations (Yes or No) ....

Type of work ....

Buying specific items at auction for a commission (Yes or No) ....

Type of item ....

FAIRS:
At which fairs (if any) do you normally exhibit? ....

....

....

CERTIFICATION:
The information given above is accurate and you may publish it in the Guide.
I understand that this entry is entirely free.

Signed .... Date ....

Unmistakably

FRANKLIN

Our door-to-door weekly service throughout Europe is well known and very reliable.

Visit our offices in three prime European locations.

Container and Airfreight Services Worldwide.

 Alan Franklin Transport Ltd